Micro-Economic
Policy

Micro-Economic Policy

Keith Hartley

and

Clem Tisdell

JOHN WILEY & SONS

Chichester · New York · Brisbane · Toronto

Copyright © 1981 by John Wiley & Sons Ltd.

British Library Cataloguing in Publication Data:

Hartley, K.
  Micro-Economic policy.
  1. Microeconomics
  I. Title   II. Tisdell, C.
  338.5   HB171.5   80–42311

  ISBN 0 471 28026 7   (Cloth)
  ISBN 0 471 28027 5   (Paper)

Phototypeset by Dobbie Typesetting Service, Plymouth, Devon, England.
Printed in the United States of America.

To
Winifred and Mariel

Contents

viii

PART D FACTOR MARKETS AND POLICY

PART E THE PUBLIC SECTOR

Preface

Students tend to find micro-economics one of the more difficult parts of the subject: they regard it as abstract, unrealistic, and remote from 'real-world' problems. This was our starting point. We believe that micro-economics as the study of choice is *the* foundation of the subject and that economists have an obligation to show students how micro-economic theory can be used and applied.

Applied micro-economics embraces empirical work and policy issues, and our emphasis is on the latter. This book avoids the presentation of micro-economic theory in a 'vacuum'. It shows students how micro-economics can be applied to major issues of public policy. In the process, it is hoped to improve the understanding of both micro-economic *theory and policy*.

Micro-economics consists of price theory and welfare economics, embracing theories of consumer and firm behaviour, the operation of product and factor markets, the role of the state, and the 'desirability' of policy changes. We have tried to show the policy relevance of each of the major components of micro-economic theory. However, the emphasis is on general principles of micro-economic policy, rather than on providing a detailed account of any one nation's actual policies. Indeed, the different nationalities and backgrounds of the authors has contributed to the development of a text suitable for an international audience. The book is written for students interested in the application of micro-economics to policy issues in capitalist-type economies. Throughout, the emphasis is on analysis rather than description.

The book is designed for late first year and second year higher education students who have a basic knowledge of micro-economic theory. The aim is to learn through applications in a policy context. While nations will differ in the extent and form of state intervention within product and factor markets, the examples chosen are typical of the policy issues confronting many governments. Hence, our emphasis is on the *principles* of micro-economic policy; the objective is to provide students with a general 'tool-kit' which can be applied to any specific micro-policy problem.

In addition to applying *standard* theory, we have introduced students to some of the more recent developments in the subject. These include the economics of politics, bureaucracies, and public choice; the Austrian school of subjectivism; search behaviour among consumers and workers; the economics of population; managerial theories of the firm, multi-nationals, labour-managed firms, advertising, and regulation; employment contracts, human capital, and screening; energy and pollution; time–cost trade-offs, de-

xiv

industrialization, and public sector micro-economics, including defence, alliances, nuclear weapons choices, and the economics of conscription versus an all-volunteer force.

The book is divided into five parts. Part A considers how economists approach micro-policy issues and why governments need micro-economic policies, either as a means of contributing to society's welfare or to obtain votes. Part B is concerned with applications of demand, supply, and competitive market analysis. Imperfect markets, including models of firm behaviour, monopoly, and oligopoly are analysed in Part C. Factor markets in the form of labour, trade unions, and human capital markets are discussed in Part D, which concludes with a chapter on energy. Given the book's emphasis on public policy, it seemed appropriate to conclude with an analysis of the public sector (Part E). To assist students, each chapter has suggestions for further reading and there are questions for review and discussion.

Readers might be curious to know how the authors, located in Australia and England, could possibly have written a joint textbook. The enterprise was greatly facilitated by Clem Tisdell's visit to the United Kingdom when he spent the Autumn Term of 1979 located at the Institute of Social and Economic Research (ISER), the University of York. This allowed both authors to work together in planning, discussing, and writing each chapter, either in outline or in first draft form. Each author was responsible for specific chapters and parts, but both commented and agreed on each other's chapters. We are indebted to Professor Jack Wiseman, ISER, for providing office accommodation, facilities, and an attractive research environment. John Hutton, Research Fellow at ISER, kindly read and commented on the manuscript. Others who have offered specific comments, contributions, and assistance, sometimes unknowingly, included Celia Bird, Michael Coombs, Tony Culyer, Douglas Dosser, Ted Lynk, Cecil Margolis, Alan Maynard, John Nash, Bernard O'Brien, Alan Peacock, Robin Shannon, and Alan Williams. Colleagues and students at the Universities of York and Newcastle, Australia, have always been willing teachers and listeners. Barbara Dodds, Elizabeth Williams, Wendy Amos-Binks, and Margaret Johnson had the unenviable task of typing their way through our handwriting. Finally, our families have been the victims of scarcity resulting from our writing. Our thanks to Winifred and Mariel for their patience, and to our children Adam, Lucy, Cecilia, together with Ann-Marie and Christopher.

January, 1981

KEITH HARTLEY
CLEM TISDELL

PART A

The Methodology of Micro-Economic Policy

CHAPTER 1

How Do Economists Approach Micro-Economic Policy?

1.1 INTRODUCTION: MICRO- VERSUS MACRO-ECONOMICS

For many years after the Second World War, in most capitalist economies macro-economics tended to dominate public policy. This is not to imply that micro-economic policies were totally neglected. Typical examples included agricultural price support schemes, monopoly policy, regional development, rent control, and tariffs. Nevertheless, Keynesian macro-economics had emerged and it appeared to be a well-established and agreed part of economic theory. It had obvious appeals to economists interested in manipulating the system and to policy-makers seeking to avoid a repetition of the large-scale unemployment of the 1930s. Macro-economics was attractive for two reasons. First, it seemed to be relatively simple, enabling the economy to be described with a few straightforward equations. Second, it gave policy-makers the opportunity of controlling the economy through the management of aggregate demand. But, in the 1970s macro-economics became more controversial. Governments in capitalist economies were confronted with greater policy problems, particularly 'stagflation' associated with high and rising rates of both unemployment and inflation. Economists became more worried about describing complex economies with a few simple equations, especially since the relationships ignored the underlying behaviour of economic agents. For example, where does the individual firm trying to maximize profits, sales, or utility 'fit' into macro-economics? Nor does it follow that government actions to regulate aggregate demand will be motivated solely by a concern for society's welfare. Votes might not be irrelevant to democratic governments. In other words, questions were being asked about the micro-foundations of macro-economics. At the same time, governments have increasingly intervened at the micro-economic level. Subsidies have been used for regional developments and for the support of 'lame duck' and 'key' firms and industries. In some cases, the subsidies have been designed to preserve jobs, especially among large employers who would otherwise go out of business, with major multiplier effects. Elsewhere, subsidies might be used to promote the development of high technology industries such as aerospace, electronics, and nuclear power. Governments have also intervened to change industrial structure through mergers and the nationalization of private firms and industries. Large firms, obtaining scale economies in research and production, are often believed to be 'essential' to compete in world markets. An alternative view believes that 'small is beautiful'. These are all examples of state intervention concerned with the *supply* side of the economy compared with the traditional Keynesian emphasis on aggregate demand management.

Increasingly, governments have recognized the potential contribution of micro-economics to 'solving' some of the major policy problems. Policies to control inflation involve the regulation of banks and the money supply or, more directly, prices and incomes controls on firms and trade unions. Either way, governments need to understand the banks and the market environment in which they operate; they need to know what motivates firms and unions and what determines their product prices and wage bids, respectively. They also need to know how firms (including banks) might respond to state regulation and controls and whether the results are in the 'public interest'. In this context, consumers cannot be ignored, since private and publicly-owned firms aim to supply goods and services in response to the demands of private buyers and voters. Governments might wish to formulate policies to protect consumers from dangerous products and monopolies. The state might also aim to ensure that everyone is protected from hardship and income deficiency due to circumstances beyond their control. Thus, social policy will provide assistance in cash and kind to those in 'need', such as the poor, unemployed, and chronically ill. Micro-economics can contribute through enquiring whether theory offers any 'guidelines' for social policy and what might be the implications of alternative measures such as minimum wage legislation, equal pay, rent control, and 'free' health care. Finally, micro-economics can be used to analyse new and topical issues which emerge unexpectedly and which governments might not be able to ignore. The oil crisis of the 1970s is a good example, where governments were obliged to revise and rethink their energy policies. What is the appropriate response for an economy which depends upon imported oil? Micro-economics shows how taxes and subsidies can be used to influence the price of existing substitutes, such as coal and gas, as well as affecting the direction of search for new energy sources. Economists can also help to clarify some of the issues, pointing out potential conflicts in policies and the inter-temporal and generational nature of using limited stocks of energy resources (see Chapter 13). These examples, and many others, form the subject matter of this book.

This chapter introduces some of the general concepts and methodology which are used throughout the book. Initially, the scope of micro-economics is outlined, emphasizing that it is the study of choice. Controversy always exists and a framework is presented for identifying the sources of disagreement. Disputes often arise over policy objectives, the choice between alternative theories, and the selection of the 'best' policy measure. In reviewing these issues, it is difficult to avoid asking what it is that makes you believe some statements and not others.

1.2   THE SCOPE OF MICRO-ECONOMICS

Micro-economics is the study of scarcity and choice. It focuses on individual and group decision-making in parts or sectors of the economy which are more conveniently described as markets. A market is any arrangement whereby individuals undertake voluntary exchange, the basic premise being that there are gains from voluntary transactions and trading. However, capitalist economies are characterized by a large number of *interdependent* markets. For example, the demand for oil depends not only on its price but also on the prices of coal, gas, electricity, cars, and on the prices of more distant substitutes such as refrigerators and television sets, as well as on the prices of factor inputs which will determine available incomes. The interdependence between markets forms the subject area of general equilibrium (cf. macro-economics). This explores whether there exists a set of relative prices which will simultaneously clear *all* markets in an economy, with the result that each market will be in equilibrium. A perfectly competitive economy results in a general equilibrium. Having accepted interdependence, does it mean that we can only proceed by recognizing that an economy is complex, that interdependencies exist and are essential to understanding, and that we cannot avoid the fact that everything depends upon everything else? This is certainly a realistic approach which recognizes that economies are complex systems—a feature which policy-makers cannot ignore.

There is an alternative approach which seeks to simplify the complexities of general equilibrium. At the same time, this alternative *partial equilibrium* approach incorporates just enough variables to obtain sufficiently accurate answers. Partial equilibrium concentrates on equilibrium in a single market, with demand and supply analysis used as a *starting point* for explaining market behaviour and performance. An equilibrium or unchanged situation occurs when the plans of buyers and suppliers in a market are identical. Demand and supply analysis enables a complex issue to be simplified while providing explanations and predictions which have proved to be consistent with the facts. One technique for simplification incorporates a *ceteris paribus* assumption: 'other things' being equal or everything else in the economy is assumed to remain unchanged. As a result, demand and supply analysis provides a simple model for classifying and understanding price and output changes in markets. Its predictions are qualitative, relating to directions of change and not magnitudes. For example, a rise in the price of cars is usually expected to result in a fall in the quantity demand but, without data on demand curves, it is not possible to state by *how much* quantity demanded will decline. However, Austrian economists (e.g. Hayek, Kirzner) are critical of the standard obsession with equilibrium, particularly general equilibrium and perfect competition. They believe that an emphasis on market equilibrium results in a failure to understand the actual market processes through which resources are transferred from lower- to higher-valued activities during *continuous* market disequilibrium. Actual markets are characterized by ignorance and continuous change.

Ignorance creates opportunities for profits and it is the task of an entrepreneur to discover the opportunities for 'making money' before anyone else. Entrepreneurs will formulate plans on the basis of expectations about future prices and events and these are matters on which individuals have different views and subjective evaluations. Market experience as reflected in shortages, surpluses, profits, and losses will reveal the correctness of different plans. Those who guess correctly will survive and those who make mistakes will pay. However, both the Austrian and neo-classical approaches to micro-economics incorporate a major role for choice.

The study of choice

Since resources are scarce, choices cannot be avoided. Any economy, whether capitalist or socialist, has to solve a number of basic problems (choices). It has to decide:

(1) What to produce—e.g. cars, television sets, schools, hospitals, or weapons?
(2) How to produce goods and services—e.g. should coal, oil, or nuclear power be used to generate electricity?
(3) Who receives the goods and services which are produced? This is a distributional problem. Should everyone receive the same incomes or should some receive more than others—if so, how are the lucky ones chosen?
(4) Who will choose? For many activities, society might agree to leave individuals to their own devices (private individualistic choices). But there will be some activities where democratic societies will agree to accept collective or *public choices*, with decision-making delegated to governments. In these circumstances, society has to determine the rules and institutions for reaching collective choices or ranking alternatives and the 'desirability' of the outcomes. Such issues are considered in Chapters 2, 3, and 15.

Western economists are fond of using the competitive market model and such a model provides one economic system which 'solves' the choice problems outlined above. In a competitive system firms respond to consumer preferences, and this determines *what* is produced. The question of *how* to produce will be solved by profit-seeking firms aiming to combine factors so as to produce efficiently. Total output or income will be *distributed* on the basis of resource endowment and the relative scarcity of different factors of production. In such an economy, individuals are assumed to be the 'best' or only judges of their welfare. But economists are not only interested in how an economic system works; they are also concerned with how well it works. Does it give results which are 'socially desirable' or are there some faults and can such failures be 'corrected' through government intervention? This is obviously a recurring theme throughout the book and some general criteria are presented in Chapter 2.

Economic agents, behaviour, and coordinating mechanisms

Despite the complexities of markets, micro-economics simplifies analysis by concentrating on a few major elements in any economic system. These consist of decision-makers, their behaviour, and the coordinating mechanisms. A classification system is shown in Table 1.1. Broadly, economic agents consist of individuals and groups as represented by decision-making households, firms, and governments. To explain the behaviour of these economic agents, we have to know what motivates them. What are they trying to achieve? For private enterprise economies, it is usually assumed that firms and households are motivated by self-interest, guided by the price mechanism. Firms are often assumed to be profit-maximizers, although there are alternative models of behaviour as outlined in Chapter 7. Households are both consumers and workers. As consumers they are assumed to be utility-maximizers (Chapter 5). As workers, they aim to maximize income or net advantages. Individual workers in their labour market and human capital context are analysed in Chapters 10 and 11, while their group or union behaviour is considered in Chapter 12. Finally, governments are assumed to be passive agencies, maximizing something called 'social welfare'; in a democracy, however, they might be vote-maximizers. Of course, the behaviour of all economic agents will be subject to *constraints*. Thus, income, resources, information, knowledge, and the law all act as constraints. For example, laws affect economic behaviour and economic behaviour generates the need for laws (e.g. enforcement of contracts).

Table 1.1   Agents, Behaviour, and Coordination.

Decision-makers	Activities	Aims	Relevant theory	Possible coordinating mechanisms
Households	(a) Demand goods (b) Supply factors	Utility Income	Consumer choice	Prices
			Distribution theory	Voting Barter
Firms	(a) Demand factors (b) Supply goods	Profits	Theory of the firm and market structures	Dictatorship
				Force
Governments	(a) Demand factors (b) Supply goods	Social welfare; votes	Public sector economics Public choice Welfare economics	Persuasion Planning

Decision-makers are only part of an economic system. Firms and households, for instance, are involved in buying and selling. Households demand goods and supply factors, while firms demand factors and supply products. Since the various agents are making separate decisions, some mechanism is required to bring them together. Prices are one possible coordinating and allocative mechanism. Others include voting procedures as determined by the constitution; barter and bargaining; central planning and dictatorship; customs, gifts, inheritance, chance, and persuasion; together with allocation by force, fraud, deceit, and bribery. Many of these allocative mechanisms are present in any economy. Consider the arrangements for allocating resources in your household! Regardless of the method, the necessity for some allocative mechanism reflects scarcity. Resources, including time, are scarce and have many alternative uses and users. By choosing one thing, you are sacrificing the satisfaction or utility which could have been obtained from alternative courses of action. Work involves the sacrifices of off-the-job leisure; space exploration requires a 'sacrifice' of schools, hospitals, roads, and cars which could have been produced with the resources. This is what the concept of opportunity cost is all about: it focuses on the subjective evaluation of alternatives. And in considering alternatives, choices cannot be avoided. This is a simple proposition, but it is amazing the number of times that governments believe that their plans will not involve any sacrifices (e.g. election manifestoes).

1.3 CONTROVERSY AND THE METHODOLOGY OF MICRO-ECONOMIC POLICY

Micro-economics abounds with controversy, although this is not apparent from a reading of the standard textbooks. This perhaps is one of the reasons why students often appear to have greater difficulty in understanding the relevance of micro-economics to real world problems. In this context, macro-economics appears to be much more relevant and useful, especially since everyone has the opportunity of acting as Chancellor of the Exchequer or Treasury Minister! Yet most departments of government are organized on a micro-economic basis, handling parts of an economy. Usually there are separate departments responsible for sectors such as agriculture, consumer affairs, defence, education, energy, health, industry, labour, and transport. All these departments provide massive opportunities for applying micro-economics.

Think of the controversies involving micro-economics. There are continuous debates about the proper role of government and market versus state solutions (see Chapters 4, 14, and 15). For example, is there a need for a national transport policy to 'coordinate' road, rail, air, and sea transport? Why can the price mechanism not solve the 'problem'? Disputes occur about monopoly, oligopoly, and competition, and the 'best' structure for an industry (Chapters 6 to 9). Consumers are not neglected, with controversy about whether they should be protected from dangerous drugs, unsafe cars, and unhealthy food (Chapter 5). A concern with poverty and income distribution raises questions as to whether labour should receive a wage based on its productivity and whether improvements can be achieved through state action in the form of rent control, minimum wages, and equal pay (Chapters 4, 10, and 11). A government concerned with income distribution and efficiency cannot ignore trade unions. Does economic theory offer any guidelines for a public policy towards unions and professional associations (Chapter 12)? Economists will differ in their answers to these and other policy issues. Why? Disputes arise because economists and politicians will differ about the objectives of micro-economic policy, the relevance of alternative theories or explanations, and the choice of appropriate solutions. These sources of dispute provide a general framework for analysing any micro-economic policy issue. Disagreement is not, however, unique to economists. Doctors might disagree about a patient's symptoms, illness, and appropriate treatment. Scientists disagree about the use of nuclear weapons while the record of designers of aircraft, high-rise flats, and bridges provides plenty of evidence of their theories being refuted! Even laboratory experiments are not conclusive. After a major aircraft crash due to the loss of a wing, the manufacturer claimed that its laboratory fatigue tests had shown no evidence of cracks on the wing spar: wreckage from the crashed aircraft provided the evidence which laboratory tests had failed to identify!

Methodology

The methodology of economic policy involves a three-stage approach to policy issues:

(1) The objectives of micro-economic policy have to be identified. What is a government trying to achieve (i.e. its objective or subjective function)?
(2) The relevant theory has to be identified. Which part or parts of micro-economic theory 'best' explains the problems confronting policy-makers?
(3) A policy solution has to be chosen from a range of alternatives. Once again, governments cannot avoid choices: they have to choose between different objectives, competing theories, and alternative policy solutions.

Policy objectives

Micro-economic targets can be regarded as the foundations of macro-economic policy objectives. As such, they embrace product and factor markets and are concerned with employment, prices, balance of payments, growth, and income distribution objectives. At the micro-level, employment targets involve the location decisions of firms, labour mobility, restrictive labour practices, and the effects of wage increases. Price targets cannot ignore the determinants of prices, the relationship between factor and product prices, and the effects of monopolies on pricing behaviour. Balance of payments objectives lead to questions about why nations trade, the gains from trade, the operation of the foreign exchange market, and the reasons why firms export.

10

A government aiming to raise the growth rate will need to know which factors of production, market structures, and industries contribute to growth. Finally, distribution of income and wealth targets cannot ignore the determinants of wages and profits, the relevance and effects of private and state ownership of the means of production, and the likely impact of policy solutions, such as profit controls. Each of these objectives requires an understanding of basic causal factors. Why do firms change employment, prices, exports, imports, investment, wages, and profits? Conflicts are also likely between objectives. For example, growth might result in the substitution of capital for labour and hence job loss; policies designed to protect consumers from unsafe products might adversely affect innovation; while wage controls might lead to industrial disputes and distort the allocation of labour. At this point, theory is required to identify the causes of conflicts.

Micro-economic theory

A theory consists of a set of definitions and assumptions from which it is possible to make logical deductions about behaviour. There is, however, controversy as to whether a theory should be accepted or rejected on the basis of the 'realism' of its assumptions or its explanatory power and predictive accuracy. This debate is associated with Friedman (1953) who argued that theories should be tested by predictions only and not by assumptions. Indeed, he maintains that by design, assumptions are abstractions and simplifications of reality: the more unrealistic an assumption becomes, the more likely it will increase the general explanatory power of a theory. But what is meant by a 'realistic assumption'? Would we accept a theory which predicted accurately but which was based on an assumption which was not consistent with the facts? Two responses are possible. First, the advocates of more realistic assumptions can incorporate these into alternative theories, compare their predictions, and test to identify which is most accurate. Second, a less-extreme view might recognize the need for testing, but insist upon using all opportunities for empirical verification, including the testing of assumptions. Nevertheless, problems remain. If theories are to be tested, what constitutes a satisfactory test of a theory? Are interview-questionnaires and sample surveys appropriate techniques or are statistical-econometric methods superior?

Economists have a great deal of enthusiasm for econometric techniques. They are quantitative and seem to provide convincing tests of hypotheses, especially since other relevant variables can be included and held constant in the estimation process. But much depends upon the reliability of econometric techniques. Often different econometric studies of a common problem reach conflicting conclusions. They might all be equally acceptable using standard statistical criteria, such as 'goodness of fit' (R^2), significant coefficients, and Durbin–Watson statistics. As a result, advocates of alternative positions obtain empirical support for their views. Furthermore, how many economists, econometricians, and research assistants carefully check and re-check for data errors before accepting and publishing what appear to be 'very good results'? Mistakes and errors in data processing can have drastic implications for empirical results, possibly causing changes in the goodness of fit (R^2), in the significance of coefficients, and in their signs! Nor can we ignore the role of 'playometrics' or 'one-upmanship' whereby professional prestige attaches to technical sophistication for its own sake: it provides an opportunity to demonstrate intellectual aerobatics. Equally disturbing is the fact that many econometric studies simply report significant results without any indication of the number of equations actually estimated. Austrian economists are even more critical of econometrics. They regard empirical testing as superfluous since they start from a true axiom (called the 'category of action' or choice) and all other propositions deduced from it must be true. Moreover, since choices are subjective: they exist in the minds of the choosers, which makes life difficult for empiricists! Furthermore, Austrian economists maintain that since there are no constants in economic life (markets are characterized by uncertainty and disequilibrium), there is no point in quantification.

What is the contribution of theory to micro-economic policy? Theory serves three functions:

(1) It can explain the *causes* of policy problems. For example, if governments are concerned about prices and wages in, say, the car industry, theory can be used to explain the determinants of these variables.
(2) It can predict the likely consequences of government policy. For instance, it can tell us how firms and workers are likely to respond to price, profit, and wage controls. In some instances, unexpected outcomes can be identified. Thus, a government restriction on the amount of advertising which firms can undertake is likely to result in an expansion of other (less efficient) selling methods, such as the use of more sales staff or mailing campaigns. In other words, policy-makers need to recognize that markets are highly flexible, with firms continuously searching for new profit opportunities and searching to overcome state regulatory constraints. The response of banks and financial markets to government regulation is a good example of such flexibility.
(3) It can offer 'guidelines' for public policy. Here, economists often approach policy problems by asking whether economic theory provides any rules or guidelines for a public policy towards, say, consumer protection, energy, monopolies, or subsidies for 'lame ducks'. This, of course, involves issues of normative as distinct from positive economics. But if there is a category of positive welfare economics, is this distinction always so clear-cut? For example, if the statement that more is bought at a lower price than at a higher price is accepted as part of positive economics, does the same status apply to the proposition that monopoly results in a lower level of economic welfare than competition (where monopoly, competition, and welfare are clearly defined)?

The choice of policy solutions

Having used theory to explain the causes of a problem or to offer policy guidelines, it is then possible to deduce and construct policy solutions. Usually, a set of alternative solutions will be indicated. For example, an excess demand problem, such as a local shortage of skilled manpower, could be removed by acting upon supply, demand, or wages. The balance of payments can be improved through exchange rates (fixed or floating), tariffs and quotas, a domestic deflation, or subsidies to domestic firms. An optimum allocation of resources can be achieved with private competitive markets or socialism. Once again, governments must choose. They have to choose between conflicting policy objectives, competing theoretical explanations, and a variety of policy solutions.

One approach to policy choices, developed by Tinbergen, focuses on targets and instruments. Recognizing the existence of conflicts between objectives, it suggests that policy-makers require at least as many instruments as there are objectives. For instance, a state agency might support mergers and industrial re-structuring for balance of payments objectives, but an additional policy instrument is required for controlling any resulting monopoly and its consequences. Similarly, if wage controls are used for price stability objectives, some other instrument such as legislation will be required for industrial relations objectives and a further measure, such as subsidies, will have to be used for improving the allocation of labour. This is a technocrat's approach, where policy-makers are assumed to have a clearly specified objective function and use policies, like a set of levers, to achieve targets. However, this approach ignores the political, bargaining, and institutional framework within which decisions and choices are made. How is a government's objective function formulated? Presumably, it is the outcome of bargaining between groups and actors such as a President, a Prime Minister, a Cabinet, departmental heads, and bureaucrats. Within this framework, individuals and departmental representatives will have only limited information and knowledge. They will tend to seek coalitions of 'like-minded' interest groups and their choice of objectives and instruments will be constrained by the political market place (e.g. the constitution and voting rules). In such a bargaining environment, governments might be 'satisficers' rather than maximizers. After all, objective functions are not acquired without costs. As a 'satisficer', a set of targets will be selected which satisfy different interest groups, such as the Treasury, together with the Departments of Agriculture, Defence, Education, Health, Industry, and Labour. The targets are likely to be revised downwards if they cannot be achieved at reasonable cost (including potential vote losses).

1.4 CONCLUSION

This chapter has outlined some of the general concepts and examples which form the material for this book. Many of the points will recur in subsequent sections. The main features of micro-economics have been reviewed, although a summary treatment cannot do justice to the immense richness and fascination of the subject. It has many applications, some of them unusual and unexpected, such as the family, marriage, suicide, political parties, bureaucracies, crime, and police protection. Even churches are not immune and useful insights into their behaviour can be obtained by analysing them as non-profit firms combining resources of land, buildings, priests, and lay-people to produce a variety of outputs which straddle an individual's life-cycle (e.g. births, marriage, sickness, death, and the care of souls). Further examples and ideas can be obtained from the suggested readings and questions which can be found at the end of each chapter.

Consideration has also been given to methodology. Why do we believe some statements and not others? Do you believe because you have seen it with your own eyes, directly, in a book or on television? Do you accept something because it is consistent with your other beliefs, you are unable to think of any convincing objection, and it comes from a teacher? And if you require supporting evidence, would you accept an exchange of personal experiences, casual empiricism, or would you insist upon controlled experiments? Imagine that you are a member of the jury in a court of law: what would determine the way you would vote in a murder trial?

Finally, micro-economics is of continuing relevance to policy-makers. Labour mobility, regional unemployment, relative wages, house prices, education, health and poverty, together with monopoly, competition, micro-electronics, and industrial performance in 'key' industries are only a few examples. The major issue of capitalism versus socialism is ever-present. Critics of capitalism claim that it results in pollution, destroys the environment, benefits monopolies, creates massive inequalities of income, and exploits the working classes. However, none of this 'proves' that socialism is 'superior'. Admittedly, capitalism and private markets might fail to work 'properly' and this might provide an economic justification for state intervention. But here, analysts distinguish the *technical issues*, involving the causes of market failure, from the *policy issues*, concerned with the choice of the most appropriate policy solutions. Why do governments intervene at the micro-level and what determines their selection of policies? This question will be considered in Chapters 2 and 3. The rest of the book follows the general format of any standard micro-economic theory textbook. Policy applications involving markets, consumers, and supply are covered in Part B. The behaviour of private firms and policy towards imperfect markets occupy Part C. Factor markets and policy towards labour, human capital, trade unions, and energy are considered in Part D. In view of the book's emphasis on policy, Part E considers some of the micro-economics of the public sector.

READING AND REFERENCES

Dolan, E. (Ed) (1976). *The Foundations of Modern Austrian Economics*, Sheed and Ward, Kansas City.

Friedman, M. (1953). The methodology of positive economics, in *Essays in Positive Economics*, University of Chicago Press, Chicago.

Kirzner, I. (1973). *Competition and Entrepreneurship*, University of Chicago Press, Chicago.

Loasby, B. J. (1976). *Choice, Complexity and Ignorance*, Cambridge University Press, Cambridge.

Robbins, L. (1935). *An Essay on the Nature and Significance of Economic Science*, 2nd ed., Macmillan, London.

Rowley, C., and Peacock, A. T. (1975). *Welfare Economics*, Martin Robertson, London.

Stewart, I. M. T. (1979). *Reasoning and Method in Economics*, McGraw-Hill, London.

Tinbergen, J. (1952). *On the Theory of Economic Policy*, North-Holland, Amsterdam.

QUESTIONS FOR REVIEW AND DISCUSSION

1. Are *actual* socialist economies different from *actual* capitalist economies? Explain. Which do you regard as preferable and why?
2. Is predictive accuracy the best criterion for choosing between alternative theories? Give examples from micro-economics, specifying how you would test your examples. Do you believe that econometric techniques are superior to questionnaire methods? Explain.
3. How are resources allocated in (a) your household, (b) your school, college, or university? Do you regard the results as satisfactory? Explain.
4. What is the Austrian approach to micro-economics? What would persuade you to accept or reject it? What are the micro-economic policy implications of the Austrian approach?
5. Which parts of micro-economics have the greatest relevance to public policy? Explain your choice.

CHAPTER 2

Why Do Governments Need Micro-Economic Policies?

2.1 INTRODUCTION: AN OVERVIEW

This chapter provides an overview of micro-economic policy questions and the role of micro-economics in policy-making. It is pointed out that micro-economic policy advice may either be of an idealistic or technical nature and both types of policy advice may be relevant to the basic economic problem of reducing scarcity. But there are difficulties in deciding on what constitutes a reduction in scarcity. Two criteria for resolving these difficulties, Pareto's criterion and the Kaldor–Hicks criterion, are outlined and their limitations discussed. This leads to a consideration of the requirements which must be met by the operations of an economy if it is to minimize scarcity, namely achieve a Paretian ideal allocation of resources.

The requirements are first outlined for a Robinson Crusoe economy and this is also used to show how specific government policies can prevent the attainment of the Paretian ideal, i.e. add to scarcity. The Paretian requirements for minimizing scarcity are then considered for a normal economy. It is claimed, and further details are given, that Paretian optimality requires

(1) Economic efficiency in production,
(2) Economic efficiency in consumption, and
(3) An optimal conformance between production of different commodities and the desires of individuals for these commodities.

From a policy point of view, Paretian optimality might be achieved either by the operation of perfectly competitive markets or by direct commands as in a collectivist economy. But both means are shown to be imperfect for this purpose.

An Edgeworth–Bowley box is introduced to demonstrate that there are *several* Paretian ideal allocations of resources. The Paretian ideal allocation varies with the distribution of income or ownership of resources. The greatest stumbling block to determining *the* socially ideal allocation of resources is the problem of deciding on *the* ideal distribution of income. The Edgeworth–Bowley box is also used to illustrate the benefits of free trade or exchange and the possible costs of different types of government interference in free trade. This, however, is not to suggest that government interference in free trade

15

cannot be justified on Paretian and on Kaldor–Hicks grounds in certain circumstances, e.g. where traders are ill-informed.

Various micro-economic policies and possible reasons for introducing them are reviewed according to whether they are designed

(1) to strengthen the operation of market forces, e.g. measures to increase the mobility of resources,
(2) to modify or supplant market forces, e.g. policies to correct for environmental spillovers and to establish or control monopolies, or
(3) to ensure public supply or a socially optimal supply of goods that are not marketable, i.e. public goods such as defence.

These apparently 'opposed' policies may be effective in different circumstances in reducing scarcity. One of the functions of a micro-economist is to specify these circumstances.

It would, however, be a folly to believe that all government policies are based upon idealism. In most cases actual policies are the outcome of political rivalry between groups in society, involve compromise, and may indeed not satisfy the ideals of any group, let alone the ideals of an economist. In tendering policy advice one has to accept that there are social and economic constraints on the implementation of policies and these limit the type of economic policies that can be introduced. Imperfections in political and bureaucratic mechanisms of resource allocation restrict the type of policies that can be *effectively* implemented, just as there are market imperfections which cannot be eliminated by any practical means. As is stressed in this book, we need in considering and in giving policy advice to take into account imperfections in all of these areas. Economists in the past have tended to concentrate on market perfection and imperfection and to neglect the other mechanisms of resource allocation.

2.2 NATURE OF MICRO-ECONOMICS AND POLICY

Micro-economics is concerned with the universal problem of scarcity. Micro-economists have used their tools of analysis to suggest various measures to reduce scarcity or shift its impact and to predict the effects of such policies as wage, price, and income controls, employment effects of wage increases, and causes of the relative competitiveness of industries both in domestic and world markets. Given the central importance of relative scarcity (i.e. that more commodities or valued possibilities are desired than can be produced or provided, given the available limited resources of the world) most governments need to assess the relevance of alternative micro-economic policies and choose between the alternatives.

Micro-economic studies concentrate on the individual parts of the economy and the interdependence of these components in the working of the economy. Micro-economics deal with the decisions of individual actors such as firms, workers, consumers, and investors and in more recent studies with family decisions, political decisions, and the behaviour of non-profit organizations such as schools, hospitals, and charitable organizations, and the way in which these shape the pattern of industries and the allocation of resources through the aims and objectives of agents and the external market environment. One set of micro-economic theories explores the consequences, for example, of utility maximization by consumers and by voters, of profit maximization by firms, and of vote maximization by political parties.

Questions raised by scarcity

Because resources are scarce, two important questions arise. One is a positive question: how *are* resources allocated between alternative possibilities? The other is a normative question: how *should* resources be allocated between alternative possibilities? Micro-economists have had a great deal to say about both questions. Each question poses further questions such as how are and how should resources be allocated between individuals (both those alive now and those expected to be born in the future), between different productive units such as firms, between regions, between the production of different products, and between their current consumption and their conservation for the future? Resource allocation and micro-economic issues are involved in such diverse policy matters as how best to conserve non-renewable resources such as oil, the desirability of government subsidies or aid for production or employment in depressed regions, the desirability of protecting selected products or industries from foreign competition or giving them government assistance, the effect of death duties, the best means to provide relief to the needy and poor, and the influence of unemployment benefits or dole payments on the willingness of the unemployed to seek work.

Mechanisms for deciding the use of resources

The social customs and mechanisms in any country or region influence the decisions of its inhabitants about the use of its resources. In societies such as our own the price mechanism plays a considerable role in determining the allocation of resources. Each individual is free to acquire private property (resources) for productive purposes and each is free, within limits, to pursue his own self-interest in trading in resources and in using those resources which he owns. The resulting pattern of resource use may be very different to that which occurs when resources are centrally allocated by a planning body in conformity with its priorities.

Government interference and micro-economic policy

However, we must not exaggerate the extent to which private decisions determine the use of resources in our society. Governmental interference in the use of resources is widespread in our economy. The public sector is not only a large purchaser and supplier of commodities but it interferes to a considerable extent with the private sector. Typical types of interference are as follows: in foreign trade, restrictions on imports, such as tariffs and quotas on imported goods, are common; there is legislation to protect consumers, some of which specifies that products should meet certain minimum standards; various restrictive trade practices such as collective business agreements to maintain prices are banned; subsidies are given to particular regions to encourage new industries or support declining ones; some services are made available free to consumers or are heavily subsidized such as education and medical attention; social services such as unemployment benefits and invalid pensions are provided by the government; some industries obtain subsidies for their production or other incentives; and minimum levels of wages must be paid by industries. There is a considerable amount of interference by government in the private sector of the economy and the type of interference which occurs is influenced by political factors and mechanisms. These types of interference raise micro-economic policy questions. What are the costs and benefits associated with each of the above types of intervention? Is it possible to obtain the desired economic change at lower cost by using a different policy? Economists need to consider such questions. An improved knowledge of the consequences of alternative policies may sway policy-makers to adopt policies that are more likely to achieve their objectives. The proponents of policies may be wrong in assessing the effects of their policies: remote consequences may be ignored and they may be mistaken about the immediate consequences of their policies. Micro-economic knowledge can help resolve such important issues but we must consider the role of micro-economics in policy and of a policy adviser more carefully.

2.3   AIMS OR OBJECTIVES OF MICRO-ECONOMIC POLICY AND THE ROLE OF AN ECONOMIC ADVISER

An economist may involve himself in micro-economic policy advice because he wishes to foster policies in support of his own ideals or he may be employed by politicians or policy-makers to provide advice on how best they can achieve their aims—aims which may not parallel that of the economist. These alternatives might be described as:

(1) An idealistic or utopian approach based upon general philosophical considerations. Pareto's approach, to be discussed below, is of this type because Pareto wished to support the ideals underlying his theory by policy suggestions.
(2) A 'technical' approach in which the aims of the policy are specified by some individual or group of individuals, e.g. a group of politicians. In this approach, the policy adviser does not question the aims (unless these are internally inconsistent) of the individual or group hiring him but devises policies to achieve their objectives if this is possible. Privately, of course, he may or may not have the same aims as those by whom he is employed.

Both possibilities involve normative and positive economics, but in the first case the norms are supplied by the economist whereas in the latter case they are supplied by the employer. Positive economics is involved in both cases since it is necessary to know what micro-economic relationships in fact exist to identify the policies which best meet certain aims.

Reduction in scarcity as an ideal and means of achieving this reduction

One *idealistic approach* to micro-economic policy (one to which the majority of economists currently subscribe and one accepted by many policy-makers) begins from the proposition that the main aim of micro-economic policy is to reduce scarcity and/or more fairly share its burden, e.g. by altering the distribution of income. Measures to reduce scarcity or shift its burden include those designed to:

(1) improve economic efficiency in the use of resources,
(2) maintain full employment (an aim which can be seen as a part of the problem of maintaining economic efficiency; see Chapter 10),
(3) foster a desirable pattern of economic growth, and
(4) improve the distribution of income.

Many economic policies affect scarcity. Listing these under the above four headings, they include policies affecting *economic efficiency in the allocation of resources*, such as:
   freedom of trade and production and openings for trade and production;
   the payment of subsidies on the production of particular goods or on production in particular regions;
   limitations on international trade such as those resulting from tariffs on imported commodities or quotas on the quantity to be imported of particular commodities;
   measures to protect consumers such as restrictions on maximum prices and constraints on acceptable qualities of goods to be traded
those affecting *employment*, such as:
   wages, prices, and profit policies;
   subsidies for employment in depressed regions;
   measures to increase the mobility of workers such as the payment of relocation subsidies to the unemployed;
   schemes to provide more information about job opportunities to the unemployed and to employers seeking employees
those influencing *economic growth*, such as:
   schemes to influence the adoption of superior techniques of productiveness;
   measures to encourage the development of new techniques and products through subsidies for research and development expenditure;
   education policies to encourage individuals to be innovative and to make it easier for them to adjust to a changing world

those altering the *distribution of income*, such as
  social welfare benefits
  taxation
  aid to less developed countries

Most of these specific policies have implications for all the main influences on scarcity. Freedom of trade, for instance, not only affects the efficient allocation of resources but also has consequences for employment, influences economic growth, and alters the distribution of income.

Difficulties in deciding what constitutes a reduction in scarcity

But even if we accept that it is ideal for micro-economic policy advisers to suggest policies to minimize or reduce scarcity, it is difficult to decide what constitutes a reduction in scarcity. This is especially so when an economic reform makes some individuals better off and others worse off, since inter-personal comparisons of welfare need to be made to decide whether the reform increases social welfare. There have been two main responses to this problem by economists — that by Pareto and that by Hicks and Kaldor.

Pareto's criterion

Pareto's response is to concentrate on the *necessary* conditions for minimizing scarcity. The only policies which minimize scarcity are those for which it is impossible to make any individual better off (in his own estimation) without making another worse off (in his own estimation). These are the only ideal policies and it is seen as the task of the economist to identify these policies. Given this criterion, no policy can be ideal from the point of view of minimizing scarcity if it is possible by altering it to make someone better off without making another worse off.

Pareto was of the view that as far as reform is concerned any economic change preferred by at least one individual and not less preferred by any to the *status quo* can be regarded as increasing the efficiency of the economy in satisfying wants. It reduces scarcity and is desirable in his view. In practice, however, there are likely to be few policies which make at least one individual better off in his (the individual's) estimation without making any other individual worse off. Furthermore, if policies must conform to this Paretian criterion, it is clear that they will differ depending upon the initial *status quo*. Policies of this kind tend to be constrained by the *status quo*. For example, the initial distribution of the ownership of resources limits the range of policies available.

The Kaldor–Hicks criterion

Kaldor and Hicks suggested a criterion which allows more scope than the Paretian criterion. They suggest that an economic change is desirable if the gainers from the change can more than compensate the losers, i.e. if a *potential* Pareto improvement is possible. But this brings one face to face with the income distribution question. If compensation is not in fact paid to the losers, is the distribution of income worsened and, if so, is the deterioration sufficient to offset the benefits otherwise of the change? But for the moment let us concentrate on Pareto's criterion and its policy implications and return to the Kaldor-Hicks criterion later.

The nature of the Paretian ideal

In practice, and as already mentioned, policy recommendations based upon Pareto's criterion have usually been ones aimed at achieving *maximum* economic efficiency, a situation where it is impossible to make any individual better off without making another worse off. These recommendations have been concerned with the ideal, an ideal which it is necessary to fulfil no matter what is the distribution of income, if scarcity is to be minimized. The economic relationships which *need* to be satisfied to meet the ideal hold whether the economy is a socialist one, a capitalist one, or one organized along other lines.

Conditions to be satisfied for a Paretian ideal

Given that the economic world (preferences for commodities and production relationships) has *a particular set of characteristics*, economists have shown that the allocation of resources must satisfy certain conditions in order to yield a Paretian optimum. For instance, under the *normally* assumed circumstances (which require certain convexity conditions to be satisfied by the production and consumption relationships) the composition of output of products should be such that the rate at which they can be technically transformed (in production) into one another is equal to the rate at which consumers are willing (given their tastes) to substitute one for the other.

Paretian ideal production and consumption in a Robinson Crusoe economy

The necessity of this condition is easily illustrated for a Robinson Crusoe economy in which the appropriate convexity conditions are satisfied by production and consumption relationships. As will be shown, even this simple model can be used to illustrate policy problems in real economies and the model brings out the importance of both individual preferences and technical production possibilities in the scarcity problem.

Given Robinson Crusoe's resources and the amount of effort that he wishes to put into productive activity, assume that the curve ABC in Figure 2.1 represents his production possibility frontier. Given his technical knowledge, his limited resources prevent him from producing a combination of products to the right of this curve which is his scarcity constraint. Robinson Crusoe's choice problem is to maximize his utility or preferences for consuming wine and bread subject to his limited production possibilities. To specify his best

22

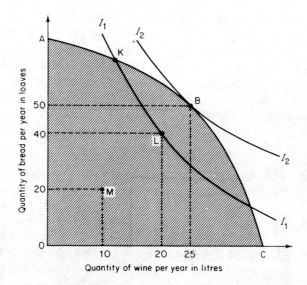

Figure 2.1   Given Crusoe's production possibilities as represented by the hatched area and his wants or desires as represented by his indifference curves, it is optimal for Crusoe to produce and consume the amount of bread and wine represented by combination B. Point B is on his production possibility frontier and conforms to the best possible extent with his preferences.

choice let us represent his tastes or preferences for bread and wine by a set of indifference curves. The indifference curves marked I_1I_1 and I_2I_2, for example, help indicate Robinson Crusoe's tastes or preferences for bread and wine. Any combination along an indifference curve is just as much desired as any other on the same curve. Combinations on higher indifference curves are preferred to those on lower curves. Therefore, given the economic situation shown in Figure 2.1, it is optimal for Robinson Crusoe to produce the quantity of bread and wine corresponding to point B. At point B the (marginal) rate of technical substitution between bread and wine equals Crusoe's (marginal) rate of indifferent substitution between these. Any other attainable production combination is on a lower indifference curve than B. For example, the production possibility at point K is on a lower indifference curve than B and therefore is less preferred than B. Similarly production possibility combinations below the production possibility frontier such as at point L do not satisfy Crusoe's wants to the greatest extent possible. Crusoe may, for example, produce a production combination below the frontier because he does not use the best techniques of production available to him.

Policies preventing the attainment of a Paretian ideal in a Crusoe economy

Let us use this Crusoe example to identify policies which can prevent the attainment of a Paretian optimum. Suppose that Robinson Crusoe is discovered by a neighbouring kingdom, and his land annexed, but he is left on his island alone except for occasional visits by the king's authorities to see that the king's laws are being obeyed. The king is opposed to the drinking of wine and believes that it is immoral for Crusoe to consume 25 litres annually. He decrees that Crusoe is not to produce and consume more than 12 litres of wine annually. By rationing Crusoe's supply of wine, the king moves him in terms of Figure 2.1 from position B to K. Crusoe is made worse off in his own estimation, i.e. made poorer by this policy. Similarly, in real world economies, when governments restrict the production of particular commodities by quotas, taxes, or other means, they are liable to reduce economic welfare.

The king, however, may feel that from an administrative point of view the best way to limit Crusoe's consumption of wine is to restrict his production possibilities. The main reason for Crusoe's large production of wine may be his discovery of an effective grape press. Seeing this the king might order the destruction of the press and forbid the building of a new one with the aim in mind not only of limiting Crusoe's wine consumption, but also of reducing the risk of the spread of knowledge of the invention to other parts of his kingdom where it is unknown. The king may fear that the spread of this knowledge would raise wine consumption, generally, and increase leisure time, so making it harder for him to maintain law and order. However, the effect as far as Crusoe is concerned is to restrict his production possibilities to a level below his production possibility frontier and he may reach a new constrained optimum at a position such as point M. As a result of this policy, Crusoe now enjoys 20 loaves of bread and 10 litres of wine per year and is much worse off than before he was regulated. In real economies, measures to restrict the introduction of new techniques (such as sometimes favoured by particular industries or unions) can keep scarcity greater than it need be and all may suffer in the end.

Or to give another example, suppose that the king decides that grapes can only be grown on that part of the island which is relatively least suitable for their production. He sees that this will also restrict the amount of wine available to Crusoe. This policy also results in Crusoe's optimal available position becoming one like M, i.e. one within the interior of his production possibility boundary. Crusoe is made poorer as a result of this policy. In real economies, the community can similarly be made poorer by policies which encourage production of commodities in relatively less productive regions by subsidizing such production or by taxing or placing limitations upon the production of commodities in areas which relatively suit their production. This occurs, for instance, in some regional policies and in some agricultural policies.

It ought to be noted that the king in this hypothetical example does not share Pareto's ideal. For one thing he believes either that the individual is not the best judge of his own self-interest or that the preferences of individuals, at least in some respects or to some extent, are unimportant. An economist, however, can point out to him some of the costs of his policies.

Conditions for Pareto optimality in normal economy

In a normal economy involving many producers and consumers, the conditions which must be satisfied to ensure Pareto optimality (a resource allocation for which it is impossible to make some individual better off without making another worse off) are more complex. However, the basic conditions to be satisfied are:

(1) *Economic efficiency in production.* It must be impossible, given available techniques, to increase the production of any valued commodity without reducing that of another by altering the allocation or use of resources. This implies that production must be on the production possibility frontier of an economy.

(2) *Economic efficiency in consumption.* Commodities must be allocated between consumers in a way which makes it impossible by re-allocating commodities to increase the satisfaction of any consumer (place him or her on a higher indifference curve) without reducing that of another.

(3) There must be *an optimal conformance* between the quantities supplied of different commodities and the desires of individuals for the various commodities. The composition of production must be such that it is impossible by altering its composition (by increasing the supply of one commodity at the expense of another) to make any individual better off without making another individual worse off. In the Crusoe case, point B in Figure 2.1 represents a composition of production which optimally conforms with desires.

While the above Robinson Crusoe model illustrates some of the conditions which need to be satisfied in an economy if it is to achieve maximum efficiency in production and an optimal conformance between production and the desires of individuals for the different commodities which can be produced, it does not illustrate economic efficiency in the exchange and consumption of commodities. However, the model to be introduced shortly, based on the Edgeworth–Bowley box, does. It illustrates how trading of commodities internationally or nationally can increase economic welfare, i.e. in this case bring about a Paretian improvement, and how restrictions on trade, such as tariffs on imports or rationing, can have the opposite effect. Furthermore, the model lends emphasis to the point that the Paretian criterion is unable to prescribe an optimal distribution of income. But before outlining the Edgeworth–Bowley box model, it should be pointed out that economists have focused their attention on two broad means for achieving Pareto optimality.

Alternative means of attaining Paretian optimality — markets and direct controls

Under suitable conditions, a Paretian optimal allocation of resources can be achieved by:

(1) the operation of perfectly competitive markets (for instance in a private enterprise economy) or
(2) direct controls or commands (for example in a collectivist economy) designed to allocate resources to achieve a Paretian optimal position by ensuring that the required production and consumption conditions are satisfied.

The Paretian optimality of either economic system (given the assumed theoretical sufficiency of knowledge on the part of the economic decision-makers) can be shown by mathematical means. These theoretical considerations have sometimes led economists to recommend that actual policy efforts should be made by the government to foster perfectly competitive markets or that governments in centrally directed economies should strive to direct their economies towards a Paretian optimum since there are no real obstacles to achieving the optimum by direction. But in both instances the suggested policies are based upon theoretical assumptions which are unlikely to be satisfied in practice. For one thing, perfectly competitive markets are not likely to occur because information is imperfect. Perfect central direction of the economy is also likely to be impossible because knowledge is imperfect.

Even if it is granted that perfect competition can occur in practice, it results in a Paretian optimum only if production and consumption relationships satisfy a range of assumptions. Given the absence of externalities, the absence of significant ranges of increasing returns to scale in production, and the fact that all goods are private goods, perfect competition can lead the economy to a Paretian optimum. However, in practice market failures do occur, and the ideal of attaining a Paretian optimum by the operation of perfectly competitive markets cannot be achieved. Market failures, which will be explored later, may call for government intervention in the economy and micro-economic policy advice is needed in this regard.

Paretian optimality in exchange and the income distribution problem illustrated by the Edgeworth–Bowley box

There is a further problem with the Paretian criterion. It gives the policy-maker no guide to the ideal distribution of income. Different allocations of resources are Paretian ideal depending upon the distribution of income or rights of individuals to resources. This can be illustrated by means of an Edgeworth–Bowley box, shown in Figure 2.2. This diagram will also be used to illustrate the advantages of trade and the drawbacks of policies restricting trade.

Imagine that there are two individuals, A and B, and that two commodities, petrol and potatoes, are available to them. The total number of potatoes and number of gallons of petrol available to both in any year is fixed. Any other two commodities can of course be taken as an example or one may wish to consider petrol a surrogate for travel and potatoes a surrogate for food. The

26

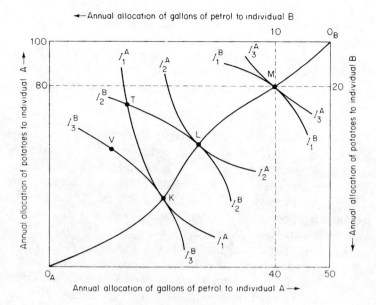

Figure 2.2 An Edgeworth–Bowley box. It shows that a number of different allocations of resources can be Paretian optimal. In this case any allocation of resources along the contract curve $O_A KLMO_B$ is Pareto optimal.

question is how to allocate the total available quantity of these commodities between the two individuals so as to achieve Paretian optimality.

The optimal allocation depends on the preferences of the individuals for petrol compared to potatoes, which can be shown in an Edgeworth–Bowley box like that in Figure 2.2. The height of this box represents the total number of potatoes available in a year and its width indicates the total number of gallons of petrol available in a year. The indifference curves marked $I_1^A I_1^A$, $I_2^A I_2^A$ and $I_3^A I_3^A$, indicate individual A's preferences for potatoes and petrol. The allocations to individual A are measured away from the origin O_A. The allocation of petrol and potatoes to individual B are measured away from the origin O_B and the indifference curves $I_1^B I_1^B$, $I_2^B I_2^B$, and $I_3^B I_3^B$ represent individual B's preferences.

An allocation of petrol and potatoes corresponding to point M (this allocates 40 gallons of petrol and 80 potatoes to individual A and 10 gallons of petrol and 20 potatoes to individual B) is Pareto optimal. Any movement away from this allocation, once it is achieved, places at least one individual on a lower indifference curve. Similarly, the allocation at point K is Pareto optimal. Indeed any allocation of petrol and potatoes corresponding to a point of tangency of the individuals' indifference curves is Pareto optimal. All the points along the (contract) curve $O_A KLMO_B$ are points of tangency between the individuals' indifference curves and represent Paretian optimal allocations.

While it is clear that there are allocations on the contract curve preferred to those not on it (for instance any allocation on KL is preferred to the allocation at point T), the Paretian criterion gives us no way of ranking the social desirability of different allocations along the contract curve. Indeed, the Paretian criterion is unable to rank social changes in which one party is made better off and another worse off. Just as the relative social desirability of K and L cannot be compared, neither can that of V and T be compared by using the Paretian criterion.

The need for a social welfare function and its non-uniqueness

It is impossible to select the ideal economic allocation of resources in the absence of a social welfare or ordering function of the alternative possible distributions of wealth or income, for there is no way of choosing between allocations which make some better off and others worse off. However, there is no agreement about how much a social welfare function can be scientifically obtained and whether or not there ought to be one such function. Hence for the economic adviser or technician, the relevant social welfare function is specified by the party or parties hiring his services and reflects their value judgements. While the relevant social welfare function may vary from individual to individual, between politicians and political parties, most such functions might be expected to satisfy Pareto's criterion, i.e. a change making at least one individual better off (in his own estimation) without making any other worse off is a social improvement. If this criterion is satisfied by the social welfare function then, as will be shown, this implies that the social optimum lies upon the utility possibility frontier of the economy, and in turn this implies the necessity of Paretian efficiency in production and exchange, and an optimal conformance between production and consumption. This can be illustrated from Figure 2.2.

Let the hatched area in Figure 2.3 represent the utility possibilities for individuals A and B given the opportunities and preferences shown in Figure 2.2. Points on the utility possibility frontier, DEH, are in one-to-one correspondence with those along the contract curve in Figure 2.2. Thus point E on the utility possibility frontier may correspond to point (allocation) L on the contract curve, and vice versa.

The optimal allocation of resources can be determined using the utility possibility set and the relevant social welfare function. For example, suppose that the relevant social welfare function reflects a very strong desire for equality of income so that the social welfare indifference curves corresponding to it are like the right-angled ones marked W_1W_1, W_2W_2, and W_3W_3 in Figure 2.3. In this case the highest attainable level of social welfare occurs at point E when both individuals are judged to obtain equal utility. In turn position E corresponds to L on the contract curve in Figure 2.2 and implies that the allocation of commodities must be the one corresponding to L if this social optimum is to be achieved.

28

Or to take another example, suppose that the relevant social welfare function reflects favouritism for individual B in the distribution of income. The social welfare indifference curves corresponding to it might be like the straight-line indifference curves $W_1'W_1'$, $W_2'W_2'$, and $W_3'W_3'$ in Figure 2.3. In this case the social optimum occurs on the utility possibility frontier at point F and in turn this implies an allocation of commodities on the contract curve, such as that at point K in Figure 2.2.

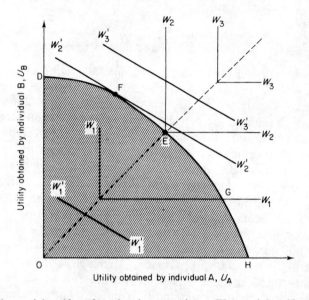

Figure 2.3 The social welfare function is not unique. The social welfare indifference curves corresponding to two possible social welfare functions are shown. One social welfare function implies that the optimum occurs at point E on the utility possibility frontier and the other implies that it occurs at point F. In both instances, Pareto's necessary conditions for a social optimum must be satisfied.

As can be seen, the two different social welfare functions imply different optimal allocations of resources. One implies the allocation at L in Figure 2.2 and the other implies an allocation such as K. Nevertheless, in both cases the *necessary* conditions for a Paretian optimum are satisfied. Indeed, these conditions must always be satisfied for a social optimum if the social decision-maker believes that any change which makes at least one individual better off without making any other worse off is a social improvement. In these circumstances, satisfaction of the Paretian conditions is *necessary but not sufficient* for a social optimum. The mere fact that these conditions are satisfied does not ensure maximization of social welfare as can be seen from Figure 2.3. The Paretian conditions are satisfied if G on the utility possibility frontier is reached, but for neither of the social welfare functions represented in Figure 2.3 is G a social optimum.

Policy implications from the Edgeworth–Bowley box: trade restrictions

At this stage it is worth while drawing some further policy implications from the Edgeworth–Bowley box introduced in Figure 2.2. The model introduced there can be used to illustrate how free trade can result in a Paretian optimum and how policies restricting trade can prevent the attainment of a Paretian optimum or rule out an otherwise possible Paretian improvement.

To avoid cluttering Figure 2.2 let us redraw and modify it as in Figure 2.4.

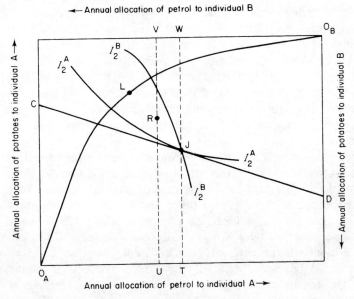

Figure 2.4   Policies restricting or limiting trade or exchange can prevent the attainment of a Paretian optimum. This is so if the allocation of commodities correspond to point J, for example, and trade is only allowed at an exchange rate indicated by CD.

In Figure 2.4 the contract curve is shown as $O_A LO_B$ and the Paretian optimal conditions for allocation are only satisfied along this curve. Trade can be mutually beneficial if the individuals have an initial allocation of petrol and potatoes away from the contract curve such as the allocation at point J. In this case, if individual A exchanges petrol with individual B for potatoes, the parties can move to position L where both are better off than before trade. If both parties are well informed about the characteristics of the commodities, free trade can only make both parties better off.

But suppose that the government decides that the distribution of goods corresponding to J is fair since it is an equal distribution and forbids trade in the goods. This prevents the parties from obtaining a Paretian optimum. For instance, they are prevented from moving from J to a position such as L and both are worse off than they could be through trade. The government's solution fails to take account of the fact that individual B has a relatively greater preference for petrol than individual A.

Again, although exchange may not be forbidden it might only be allowed at an exchange rate which makes trade unprofitable to the parties or rules out the attainment of an optimum. For instance, assume that trade is only permitted at the exchange rate indicated by the price line CD. Then no trade will occur since individual A receives too few potatoes in exchange for petrol. All permissible trading opportunities along CD are such that they would make one party worse off and hence no trade will occur. The restriction on the exchange rate results in parties remaining at J and foregoing a possible Paretian improvement such as would occur if they were not prevented by policy from moving to position L. In the real world, a government could achieve this distortion of price ratios by imposing a tax on the exchange of petrol (a tax payable in the example by potatoes). An excise or sales tax could have this effect. Or again A might be the resident of a foreign country and B a national, in which case the government can distort the price ratio by placing a tariff (tax) on the import of petrol. All such restrictions on trade can prevent a Paretian optimum from being achieved or rule out an otherwise possible Paretian improvement.

Another possibility is that the government uses quotas to restrict trade or exchange. Suppose that the government restricts individual A to exchanging a maximum of UT of petrol or, in the case of imports, limits individual B to importing this much petrol. If no other restrictions apply, trade will occur. After trade, parties will achieve an allocation along UV between the two indifference curves through point J. For instance, the new allocation may be at point R. While both are better off than at J, point R is off the contract curve and both could be made better off by further trade if it happened to be allowed. Quotas imposed by the government or by agreements between suppliers limiting domestic supplies or limiting imports are likely to prevent the attainment of a Paretian optimum and stand in the way of a Paretian improvement.

The Kaldor–Hicks criterion again

In practice it is difficult to find policies which ensure a Paretian improvement. Most policies, while benefiting some individuals, are detrimental to the interests of others. However, much of cost–benefit analysis skirts around this problem by adopting the Kaldor–Hicks criterion. This criterion regards any social change as an improvement if gainers from the change can compensate the losers (*irrespective of whether they do*) and be better off than before the change. It is sometimes argued that the application of this criterion is justified because when all policies are considered the gains and losses to individuals tend to cancel out. However, they are not certain to cancel out. Consequently, the rider is sometimes added that a social change satisfying the Kaldor–Hicks criterion is a social improvement provided that it is judged not to worsen the distribution of income (see Chapters 11 and 15).

The importance of non-economic variables in policy-making

The above idealistic changes are judged purely by reference to economic variables. But economic changes can alter social and political relationships in society. For instance, if economies of scale are important it may be possible to achieve a Kaldor–Hicks improvement by merging firms and fostering the growth of a few large firms in the economy. But by virtue of their increased size, these firms may be able to wield greater political influence, and indeed they could become sufficiently powerful to restrict the liberty of others. Economists such as Rowley and Peacock (1975) argue that such possibilities need to be taken into account before recommending an economic reform. Again measures designed to move an economy towards Paretian optimality may have unwanted sociological effects. While mobility of labour may be judged to be necessary for economic efficiency, great mobility may interfere with the cohesiveness of groups and families, and create psychological stress. Just how much weight should be put upon these non-economic effects is a moot point, but in an ideal solution they need ultimately to be taken into account.

It needs to be pointed out that there are some theories of welfare not in the main economics stream which assert that welfare depends upon the difference between material wealth and other characteristics attained or attainable and those aspired to. Welfare falls if aspirations move too far ahead of that which can be realized or obtained. Marcuse and Scitovsky suggest, for example, that welfare may not actually rise in developed economies with material wealth because advertising by companies pushes aspiration levels well above what can be achieved and increases dissatisfaction. This point of view will be discussed in Chapter 5.

Policy advice at a technical rather than an idealistic level

There is another level at which micro-economic policy advice may be valuable. It may be useful at the *technical* level. For instance, would a tariff on imports be effective in increasing the local production of a particular commodity? What level of tariff is needed to increase local production by 10 per cent.? Is there an alternative means of achieving this 10 per cent. increase in production? What are the alternative means? Advice at this level is concerned with positive relationships between economic variables.

Again it is a matter for positive economics to determine whether economic aims or objectives can be met and whether there are conflicts. Aims as formulated may be internally inconsistent or economic constraints may make it impossible to achieve all aims simultaneously. For instance, it may be impossible to minimize the degree of inequality of income and maximize the

32

level of production of commodities simultaneously. This would be so if the relationship between production and income inequality happened to be like that shown in Figure 2.5.

In this case the level of output is assumed to be a function of the degree of inequality of income. This could occur if the inequality arises out of rewards for effort which provide incentives to individuals to raise production. On the other hand, it might be argued that in some cases the causation runs the other way. Less income inequality may occur at higher levels of production because there is less involuntary unemployment when production is high and there may be a greater demand for labour relative to other factors. But no matter which way the causation flows, or whether a more sophisticated theory is needed to take account of the relationships, one cannot simultaneously maximize production and minimize income inequality if the relationship is as in Figure 2.5. There is, however, a need for empirical work to estimate the relationship between production and income inequality.

Many other examples of unrealistic objectives can be given. A policy aimed at maximizing economic growth and guaranteeing employment to individuals no matter where they reside or wish to reside would be unrealistic and/or costly. The last-mentioned objective conflicts with the first. It is an important task of an economic policy adviser to specify the possible trade-offs. For instance, there is usually a trade-off between regional assistance and economic growth. Other examples of necessary trade-off will be given throughout this text.

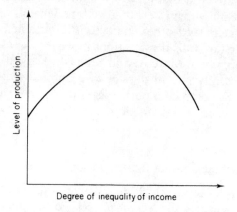

Figure 2.5   It may be impossible to minimize the degree of inequality of income and simultaneously maximize the level of production. This would be so if the relationship between the inequality of income and level of production happened to be as shown.

2.4   GENERAL MICRO-ECONOMIC POLICIES FOR ATTAINING OBJECTIVES

Micro-economic policies appear to fall into three broad categories:

(1) those policies designed to strengthen the operation of market forces,

(2) measures intended to modify or supplant the operation of market forces, and

(3) policies adopted in circumstances where market forces are incapable of operating.

Policies to strengthen the operation of market forces

Micro-economic policies designed to strengthen the operation of market forces in allocating resources are often predicated on the view that perfect competition is socially optimal. Consequently measures may be taken to foster perfectly competitive conditions. Such measures may be designed to improve the flow of information to participants in the economy and to facilitate the mobility of resources such as labour. Legislation may be passed to outlaw restrictive trade practices and collusion between businesses may be banned in order to encourage greater competition. In some instances, the operation of market forces may be strengthened by altering property rights. The operation of market forces may be strengthened by converting common property resources (available to individuals in common and without restriction) to private property. Thus, for instance, the enclosure of common grazing land and its assignment as private property strengthens market forces because individuals' returns from the land depend upon their own effort and are not interfered with by the efforts of others. However, in the case of some natural resources which are common property, such as fish and whales on the high seas, these cannot be made private property and their conservation requires international agreement.

Not all policies aimed at strengthening the operation of market forces are motivated by the view that perfect competition is socially ideal. Special interests sometimes support such policies in order to gain from them. At other times they may be supported because it is believed that some degree of competition (but not a perfect degree) is socially optimal and that actual competition should not diverge too much from the perfectly competitive ideal. Supporters of this view may also couple it with the opinion that private control of resources is preferable to public control because private individuals and organizations are likely to be better informed about future economic wants and costs than public organizations.

However, even when commodities can be marketed, markets may fail to work perfectly enough for them to ensure a social optimum. They may fail because of imperfect knowledge on the part of market participants, because of spillovers in production or consumption, because some traders have market power, or because of constraints on the behaviour of firms when decreasing average costs of production occur. Furthermore, some commodities cannot be marketed at all. Market failure occurs in both these cases and failure of this type will be illustrated below. But it does not follow that these failures will be eliminated under public control of markets. Public or civil servants, for instance, are likely to have imperfect knowledge.

Policies to control or modify market forces

Where markets works, but work imperfectly, the government may adopt policies to modify, control, or supplant the operation of markets in order to achieve a Kaldor–Hicks type of gain. Gains of this type may be realized:

(1) when individuals or groups of traders in a market have market power, as is the case of a monopoly or monopsony and exercise it, or
(2) when important externalities or spillovers occur.

Consider the externality case.

Control of externalities or spillovers

When an economic activity by one party harms or benefits another and no compensation is paid to the damaged party or payment is made by the beneficiary for this, an externality or spillover occurs. Thus a factory which emits air pollutants and damages the health and property of nearby residents without compensating them for these damages is creating a harmful or unfavourable externality or spillover. Actual examples include the emission of fluorides from aluminium plants, of lead in vapour from lead refineries, and of sulphur dioxide and corrosive gases from factories and power generating plants burning high sulphur coal. Or the spillover may take the form of water pollution with biological and chemical wastes from industry being dumped into waterways or be in the form of noise pollution. Activities involving spillovers are unlikely to be conducted on a socially optimal scale and in a socially optimal manner if these activities are determined by market forces. A Kalodor–Hicks gain can usually be obtained as a result of government intervention in such cases. For instance, consider the case illustrated in Figure 2.6. Suppose that steel is produced by a perfectly competitive industry and that it costs each firm £5 to produce a ton of steel. The private supply curve of steel (reflecting the costs borne by the producer) is the horizontal line marked SS in Figure 2.6. Given that the market demand for steel is as indicated by the curve marked DD, the market equilibrium supply of steel is 15 million tons annually. However, suppose that each ton of steel produced causes £5 worth of damage to individuals (in terms of increased ill-health, damage to the fabric of their residences, deterioration in their gardens and the freshness of their air) for which they are paid no compensation by producers. This spillover may occur because the steel industry is using high sulphur coal to smelt its steel. The marginal spillover cost of steel is £5 and the social marginal cost of producing steel is £10, i.e. equal to its costs to producers plus spillover costs, and is indicated by the horizontal line marked TT in Figure 2.6. Clearly, a Kaldor–Hicks gain can be made by reducing the annual output of steel from 15 million tons to 10 million tons, i.e. to the level where the marginal *social* costs of producing steel equals the demand for it. The community gains by the

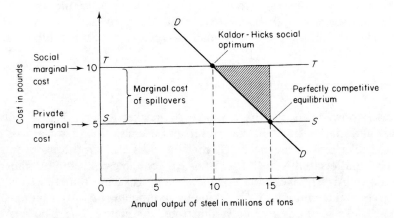

Figure 2.6 Market failure can occur as a result of unfavourable externalities or spillovers. The area of the hatched triangle indicates the extent of the social loss occurring under perfectly competitive conditions given an unfavourable spillover of £5 per ton of steel produced.

difference between the fall in total social costs (£10 × 5m. = £50 million) and the value placed on the lost output by consumers (£5 × 5m. + £5 × 2.5m. = £37.5 million). The net benefit of reducing the production of steel to 10 million tons annually is £12.5 million and is indicated by the hatched triangle in Figure 2.6. A Kaldor–Hicks social optimum occurs for the output for which the social marginal cost of producing steel equals the demand for it, i.e. the level of output for which the benefits and costs to society of steel production are equal at the margin.

There are a number of different measures which a government can take to ensure that externalities are taken into account in resource allocation. In the case of unfavourable spillovers the government can impose suitable taxes and in the case of favourable externalities pay a suitable subsidy on production. A suitable tax is one sufficient to equate private marginal costs of production with social marginal costs. In the example given in Figure 2.6, the imposition of a tax of £5 per ton of steel produced would ensure the production of 10 million tons of steel annually, a socially optimal amount, because it results in the after-tax marginal costs borne by producers being equal to social marginal cost. There are also other policy means available to the government such as quotas on production that can be used to achieve the same level of production. In other circumstances, policies might be introduced to ban harmful activities or change property rights and allow courts to determine compensation for victims of spillovers. Micro-economic policy-makers must consider the benefits and limitations of alternative policies to deal with spillovers. Is it preferable to impose a tax on output rather than a quota? Is it more efficient to tax emissions of pollutants rather than the output of the product? These issues will be discussed later

36

in the text. But observe from the above simple example that it is as a rule not socially optimal to reduce pollution to zero. At the socially optimal level of output pollution remains — spillovers are not eliminated.

Control of market or monopoly power

Market power can also be a source of market failure. When individual traders in a market have market power and exercise this, a social loss in the Kador-Hicks sense may occur. It may be possible for the government to 'perfect' markets in this case, for instance by banning collusion by traders and by outlawing restrictive trade practices, or by ensuring that there are many producers of a commodity by breaking up monopolies. A situation in which a Kaldor-Hicks gain is possible is illustrated in Figure 2.7. The curve *DD*

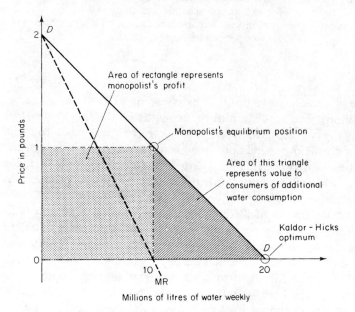

Figure 2.7   When market or monopoly power is exercised, the government may be able to intervene in the market to bring about a Kaldor-Hicks gain. A monopoly leads to a Kaldor-Hicks loss as represented by the hatched triangle.

represents the weekly demand for water in an area. Suppose that the supply of water for this area is provided by a stream and that the supplies naturally available from this stream are well in excess of 20 million litres weekly, the quantity demanded of water when it is freely available. Since the costs of supplying water are assumed to be zero and since its available supply exceeds demand, a social optimum is achieved when water is a free good. But suppose that the stream, the sole source of water supply in the area, falls into the hands of a single owner intent on maximizing his profit. A non-discriminating monopolist is able to maximize his profit by charging a price of £1 per litre for water. This restricts the consumption of water from 20 million litres weekly to 10 million litres weekly. A supply of 10 million litres maximizes the monopolist's profit since his marginal cost of supply is zero, and therefore marginal revenue equals marginal cost when marginal revenue equals zero. (At that level of supply, the price elasticity of demand is unity.) As a result of his restriction of supply, the monopolist makes £10 million in profit weekly. However, a return to the consumption of 20 million litres of water weekly (at a zero price) would result in a Kaldor–Hicks improvement. After paying the monopolist £10 million, as compensation for profit foregone and as a bribe to act benevolently, consumers would be better off than in the restricted situation by an amount equivalent to the area of the hatched triangle in Figure 2.7. This represents the additional consumers surplus to be obtained from the extra water consumption and is equal to £5 million weekly in this case.

The government may adopt a number of different policies to deal with the monopoly. It may place the ownership of different parts of the stream in many different hands thus promoting competition, it may regulate the maximum price of water, or it may itself take over the ownership of the resource and make it freely available. While all these measures could be equally efficient in this example, this is not always so. Micro-economic policy-makers need to consider the benefits and limitations of the alternative policies. Difficulty arises in particular when the cost per unit of supplying a commodity declines with the volume of its supply and per-unit costs of production of a commodity are minimized when one or a few firms supply the whole market. A natural monopoly is said to exist in this case.

In this case, a Kaldor–Hicks loss may result from government policies designed to ensure that a large number of suppliers produce the commodity. Profit-maximizing monopoly, even though not socially optimal, may be better than a situation involving many suppliers in this case. Nevertheless a Kaldor–Hicks gain may be made by the government supplying the monopolized commodity or regulating its conditions of supply such as its price so as to ensure in either case that the price of the product equals its marginal cost of supply. Yet it may be impossible to obtain a Kaldor–Hicks gain *by strengthening market forces* if per-unit costs or production decline substantially with the volume of production. At least, this may be so unless *X*-inefficiency (higher production costs due to, say, poor management or shirking) rises dramatically as the number of suppliers of a product falls. These and related issues will be discussed in the chapter dealing with monopoly.

Non-marketability — the case of pure public goods

As mentioned, in some circumstances markets are unable to operate at all to supply commodities. This is so when it is impossible or impractical to make the availability of a commodity to individuals conditional upon their payment for the commodity. In particular a commodity cannot be marketed when its supply ensures its availability to all, none of whom can be excluded from using it and none of whom experience decreased satisfaction from jointly consuming the good. Such goods are called pure public goods. In other words, in the case of pure public goods *exclusion* is impossible and there is *non-rivalry* in the consumption of the goods. There are few but important examples of *pure* public goods. Some examples might be:

(1) The destruction of mosquito larvae in swamps or of other pests having considerable mobility and range (e.g. locusts)
(2) Flood mitigation
(3) The provision of defence and military alliances (e.g. NATO)
(4) The retention of wilderness areas so as to keep options (the option of visiting such areas) available to potential users
(5) The reduction or elimination of disease 'reservoirs', such as the elimination of smallpox and reduction in sources of other communicable diseases as is being achieved by the World Health Organization and other public bodies
(6) Advertising of a generic commodity on behalf of a whole industry such as the advertising of citrus in the United States on behalf of citrus growers and of wool by the International Wool Secretariat on behalf of various countries exporting wool
(7) The supply of basic knowledge or principles for use in basic science
(8) The provision of public regulations or laws which benefit all
(9) Measures to prevent the entry of exotic diseases into a country such as quarantine measures on the entry of live animals into the United Kingdom and Australia designed to prevent, for example, the introduction of rabies
(10) Reduction in international pollution such as measures to reduce radiation, measures to limit damage to the ozone layer caused by supersonic transport, or measures to slow down the greenhouse effect on the atmosphere, i.e. the supposed tendency for industrial activity and the burning of carbon fuels to raise the temperature of the atmosphere

Unless collective or government action is taken to supply it, a smaller quantity of a pure public good is likely to be supplied than is socially optimal. This can be illustrated by the following example.

Take the case of a military alliance. Suppose that two countries in a region are jointly threatened by an attack from an outside power. They are able to buy protection or deterrent power by military expenditure. The marginal cost (incremental cost) of obtaining protection or security in the region is indicated by the curve marked MC in Figure 2.8. Suppose that each fall of 0.1 in the probability of being attacked is valued by each nation at £10 million. Hence, both nations together (each benefits jointly) value each fall of 0.1 in the probability of attack by £20 million and their combined marginal valuation of protection is as indicated by the line marked ΣMV. It is collectively optimal to raise the degree of security by 0.2, i.e. to increase the likelihood of not being attacked from 0.5 to 0.7. At this level, the marginal cost of increasing security equals the combined marginal value of doing so.

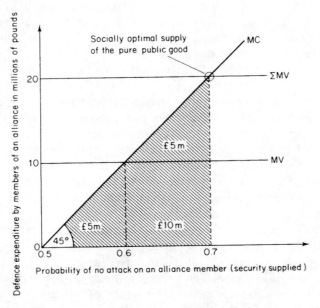

Figure 2.8 Collective or government action is usually required to ensure a socially optimal supply of a pure public good. For example, in the case of a military alliance between countries (such as NATO) it is necessary to have binding agreements on levels of defence expenditure by individual members. Otherwise some members may try to free-ride.

The alliance, however, faces the problem of ensuring that each nation contributes £10 million to defence preparations. If one nation believes that the other member of the alliance will spend £5 million on defence (choosing security level 0.6 where MC = MV), it gains by not undertaking defence spending. In this case, the marginal cost to the nation uncommitted to defence expenditure of increasing security by 0.1—i.e. of increasing the likelihood of not being attacked from 0.6 to 0.7—is £15 million (the area of the square plus the triangle indicated in Figure 2.8 for the range 0.6 to 0.7) and exceeds its incremental gain (£10 million). Consequently, one nation may free-ride and not contribute to military expenditure in its region. Or if both nations believe that the other will spend on defence, neither may undertake military expenditure. In either case the amount of security provided in the region is less than socially optimal. Collective coordinated action in which both nations share the military expenditure of £20 million is needed. This then raises the question of how the burden should be shared, e.g. on the basis of ability to pay, through progressive or proportional income taxes.

Merit goods and income redistribution as a rationale for government interference in markets

Not all government action to supply goods is intended to provide pure public goods. Some such action is for the purpose of supplying or encouraging the supply of merit goods, i.e. goods which the government believes deserve or merit greater consumption than in fact occurs. In this case the government acts to impose the preferences of one group in society upon others. Three different circumstances are worthwhile distinguishing. These are:

(1) The philanthropic case where a group desires to subsidize from its own pocket the consumption by others of *particular* goods, such as housing and medical services for the poor or education. In this case there is an earmarked or tied subsidy or assistance for the purchase of particular goods rather than a cash payment which can be spent at the recipient's discretion. The government may facilitate the transfer of this subsidy from the philanthropic group, e.g. by supplying tied foreign aid or giving subsidies for particular charities.
(2) The selfish case in which an interest group represents a product for which it has a high preference as a merit good and seeks a subsidy from the community as a whole. But it has to offset the benefits it receives against the cost to it of lobbying. The particular group may thereby benefit at the expense of the whole community. Examples of policies of this kind might include subsidies for the arts and for cultural activities, for some types of scientific research, for the development of advanced technology such as space technology or technology for nuclear fusion.
(3) The altruistic case in which individuals are believed not to be aware of their own best interests. Interference is intended to alter their behaviour, for instance their consumption of goods, so that the pattern of consumption by individuals accords more closely with others' perceptions of their best interests. Examples include measures to deter individuals from smoking cigarettes, policies to restrict the availability of various drugs, and campaigns to encourage individuals to eat foods that reduce the risk of heart and other diseases.

Governments also interfere in the operation of markets to alter the distribution of income, even though economists sometimes argue that this is an inefficient method of altering the distribution of income. Concession rates for pensioners on public transport provides an example of this although they are of no benefit to non-travelling pensioners. So too does minimum wage legislation even though this may reduce the employment of those it is intended to help. Micro-economic policies of this type need to be assessed to see whether or not they have undesirable side-effects and whether or not the aims of the policies can be attained more efficiently.

2.5   THE IDEAL AND THE POLITICALLY ATTAINABLE

The aim of much literature on micro-economic policy is to state necessary conditions and formulate policies to attain a socially ideal or optimal allocation of resources. This, for instance, is the guiding goal of Paretian welfare economics. But in the actual world these conditions and policies may be of limited relevance because of constraints (political, institutional, and otherwise) which prevent the ideal conditions being put into effect. Thus the important policy issue arises of what is the best policy given the existence of constraints which rule out a Paretian ideal solution.

Second best policies

This matter has recently been considered by economists under the title of *second best* policies. It has been shown that when it is impossible to satisfy some of the conditions for a Paretian optimum that it is usually not optimal to adopt policies which ensure that the remaining Paretian conditions are satisfied. Thus if there is a section of the economy in which perfect competition can be fostered such as the agricultural sector and Paretian conditions satisfied there, the existence of imperfect competition in another sector such as the manufacturing sector may make it socially undesirable to foster perfect competition in the agricultural sector. Because imperfect competition prevents Paretian optimality conditions being satisfied in the manufacturing sector and assuming that the policy-maker cannot change this situation, it is unlikely to be optimal to foster perfect competition in the agricultural sector (unless the links between the two sectors are weak). Second best optimal policies and conditions must be worked out from first principles in these cases, taking into account the institutional or political constraints which exist, and these conditions are *all* likely to differ from the 'first' best conditions (those in the absence of political or institutional constraints).

The stress of economic theory on equilibria

Traditional economic theory has also been criticized on the grounds that it takes inadequate account of time. Because it concentrates on equilibria and alternative possible equilibria (i.e. comparative statics) traditional theory pays little attention to the time-paths and uncertainties of economic change and disequilibria. While this criticism seems justified, equilibria and alternative equilibria are important in dynamic models (those taking explicit account of time) and hence comparative state models are a first step to these complex models which an economic policy adviser may have to construct to analyse a particular economic problem, e.g. to provide advice on floating exchange rates compared to fixed ones.

42

Realistic advice and idealistic policy advice

In conclusion, and as will become clearer from the chapter on economics and politics, economic policy advisers are likely to be called upon to give governments advice which takes account of political and institutional constraints, constraints which may be stated by politicians. Micro-economic principles and optimality conditions need further development in this area. Micro-economic policy advisers must be aware of the need to modify existing theories and develop new ones to reflect the particular policy problem under consideration. At the same time there is a role for idealistic theories which ignore short-term political and institutional constraints, since these can become a basis for long-term political and institutional reform. In both cases existing micro-economic theory contains tools likely to assist in the shaping of new theories and the modification of existing ones to fit particular complex policy problems, for instance questions about the social optimality of choosing nuclear power stations rather than conventional power stations using coal or oil.

READING AND REFERENCES

Collard, D. (1972). *Prices, Markets and Welfare*, Parts 1 and 2, Faber, London.
George, K. D., and Shorey, J. (1978). *The Allocation of Resources*, Chap. 2, Allen and Unwin, London.
Gwartney, J. D. (1977). *Microeconomics*, Part 1 and Chaps 18 and 19, Academic Press, London.
Hartley, K. (1977). *Problems of Economic Policy*, Chaps 1 and 2, Allen and Unwin, London.
Holesovsky, V. (1977). *Economic Systems*, Chap. 8, McGraw-Hill, New York.
Lipsey, R. G. (1979). *An Introduction to Positive Economics*, Chaps 1, 4, 30, and 31, Weidenfeld and Nicolson, London.
Rowley, C., and Peacock, A. (1975). *Welfare Economics*, Chaps 1 and 2, Martin Robertson, London.
Tisdell, C. (1972). *Microeconomics*, Chaps 3, 13, and 14, Wiley, Sydney.

QUESTIONS FOR REVIEW AND DISCUSSION

1. Why are there difficulties in deciding what constitutes a reduction in scarcity? Outline Pareto's criterion and the Kaldor–Hicks criterion and consider the limitations of both as a means of choosing policies to reduce scarcity.
2. Distinguish between an idealistic approach and a technical approach to policy-making. Can these approaches coincide? Are both approaches needed? To what extent do both rely on positive economics?
3. List according to their prime influence on scarcity (via economic efficiency, employment, economic growth, and the distribution of income) micro-economic-type policies affecting scarcity. Show that some of these policies have a multiple effect, e.g. affect income distribution primarily but also influence economic efficiency.
4. Explain using the Robinson Crusoe model the economic conditions that must be satisfied for Paretian optimality. The Pol Pot regime in Cambodia has been accused of destroying means of production such as hoes and implements owned by peasants. Discuss the difference between its possible ideals and those of Pareto.

5. Using an Edgeworth–Bowley box show how free trade leads to mutual gains by traders. Is it possible for this gain not to occur in certain circumstances? Illustrate using this box types of government interference in trade which can prevent the attainment of a Paretian optimum.

6. 'The Paretian ideal allocation of resources including products varies with the distribution of income or ownership of resources.' Illustrate by using an Edgeworth–Bowley box.

7. What is meant by saying that satisfaction of the Paretian conditions is necessary but not sufficient for a social optimum? Use social welfare indifference curves to illustrate your answer.

8. Show why a Kaldor–Hicks gain *might be made* as a result of government intervention in each of the following cases:
   (a) Where unfavourable environmental spillovers occur in production
   (b) A monopoly exists
   (c) A product is a public good
   Illustrate your answer.

9. Is there a role for idealistic economic theories? To what extent (and in what ways) should policy or economic policy advice take account of the politically and bureaucratically attainable?

CHAPTER 3

Do Votes Determine Policies?

3.1 INTRODUCTION

In Western economies, governments perform many activities ranging from
the management of aggregate demand, incomes, and prices to the direct
provision of goods and services such as defence, police, education, and roads.
Economists often try to explain and justify the extent of government activities
in terms of market failure. In this context, a concern with the 'public interest'
or maximizing community welfare might require governments to intervene to
reduce monopoly power in product and factor markets, to provide public
goods, and to correct externalities (see Chapter 2). Ideally, governments
should undertake activities in which they have a comparative advantage. For
example, even in private enterprise economies, governments are required to
create 'law and order' for the enforcement of contracts enabling mutually
advantageous trade and exchange in private markets. But it is not obvious that
the market failure analysis satisfactorily explains the whole range of any
government's activities at the federal, central, state, or local levels. Why, for
example, do governments often supply goods and services which could be
provided by private firms (e.g. refuse collection; transport, R & D establishments)? While there might be a case for state *finance* of some socially desirable
activities (which?), it does not necessarily require government supply. Nor can
it be assumed that government services will be operated by public spirited
officials, devoid of self-interest, responding to the public will and dedicated to
the achievement of the public interest. Indeed, it is paradoxical that
economists were willing to apply the self-interest utility-maximizing postulate
to private markets, but seemed to assume that individual behaviour somehow
changed in public office! Developments in the economics of politics and
bureaucracies provide an alternative explanation of the extent and form of
state intervention in Western economies. How are behaviour, and ultimately
choices and decisions, affected by the political market place?

The economics of politics is an example of the application of standard
micro-economics to the political market place and the problem of collective
choice. In this model, policies are the result of a process involving a search for
votes by political parties, further influenced by the budget aims of bureaucracies
supported by interest groups with a monetary involvement in the outcomes.

44

This analysis concludes that governments can *fail*. It is especially relevant since the political mechanism is often advocated as an alternative to markets as an allocative device (e.g. mixed economies, socialism). In addition, the public sector influences and affects the operation of private markets (e.g. procurement policy, regulation: see Chapters 8 and 14). Thus, we need to know how the public sector works and the efficiency of its operations.

3.2   A TAXONOMY

The political market place can be analysed like any other market. It contains buyers and sellers undertaking mutually advantageous exchange within the constraints determined by the constitution. And even the constitutional constraints can be changed through, for example, the electoral process or dictatorial edict. In democracies, the market is one where political contracts are negotiated and revised. Voting can be regarded as a contract and the political market can be analysed in terms of the contractual process, its specification, and associated commitments. For any analysis, we need to know:

(1) the agents in the market place,
(2) the objectives of the agents, and
(3) the market structure in which the agents operate.

The agents

Political markets contain voters, parties, bureaucracies, and interest groups. Voters, like consumers, demand goods, services, and policies from the governing party and they supply factors of production directly (e.g. public sector employment) or indirectly via taxation. Political parties can be regarded as firms: each party is a potential supplier. The winning party in an election becomes the actual supplier and its plans are implemented by the bureaucracies responsible for such products as defence, education, and roads. As a result, the governing party demands factors of production from households and supplies goods and services. Policies might, however, be influenced by interest groups of producers and consumers. Examples include employers and professional associations, trade unions, high unemployment areas, low profit industries, large government contractors, the education, farming, health, old age pensions, and road lobbies, as well as environmental groups and consumer protection movements. Nor are interest groups confined to national entities. International organizations, such as the EEC, IMF, NATO, and the UN, can be elements in the domestic political market place.

The objectives of agents

Any analysis of behaviour requires a specification of the objective function of the relevant decision-makers. Like consumers, voters are assumed to maximize the expected satisfaction or utility to be obtained from alternative policies, taking into account their prices through direct charges and taxation. In principle, voter preferences are determined by the same influences which affect consumer tastes and preferences in the theory of demand (see Chapter 5). Citizens will vote for the party which they believe will provide them with a higher utility from government activity. But voters are subject to knowledge and information constraints. They have to acquire information which involves search costs, and they have a limited capacity to store knowledge. This provides an opportunity for producers and other interest groups to influence policy. Producer groups, for example, can use their specialist knowledge to provide detailed and persuasive information, showing political parties that their activities are in the 'national interest' and make a 'socially desirable' contribution to jobs, advanced technology, and the balance of payments (and hence votes). Questions also arise as to why individuals vote (where voting is voluntary). After all, the direct benefits of voting are relatively small in that one vote is unlikely to affect the outcome and the costs are not trivial. Information has to be acquired about alternative candidates and a visit is required to the polls. Presumably, individuals vote because its costs are relatively small, especially if voters do not acquire much information about the candidates or if a visit to the polls is combined with other activities; or the perceived benefits of voting could make it worth while (e.g. voting might be enjoyable; see also Chapter 5).

Political parties offer policies in exchange for votes; hence, it is often assumed that parties are vote-maximizers. Politicians are assumed to be self-interested, using policies to achieve the rewards and satisfactions of office, rather than seeking office to implement preconceived policies. Of course, vote-maximization is a simplifying assumption which can be modified to reflect different constitutions, collective decision rules, and the costs of attracting voters. Parties might aim to maximize the number of elected representatives or a majority of seats. Similarly, in a winner-takes-all election, each candidate might plan to obtain 51 per cent. of the votes or simply more votes than his greatest rival, always assuming that a candidate knows the number of votes for his rivals! Expressed more generally, it is assumed that the governing party will be seeking re-election and the opposition will be striving for office. Clearly, at an election, competing parties have to choose how to allocate their available resources and candidates between different constituencies where the probabilities of success range from almost zero to 100 per cent. The larger parties might gain scale economies in, for example, advertising, fund-raising, and the employment of specialist research and information staffs. Even so, parties are likely to find it too costly (and not worth while) to aim for 100 per cent. of the votes! Similarly, a party might regard it as worth while to contest a seat where it has little chance of winning. The marginal cost might be relatively low and there are possible benefits in continuing to demonstrate a national presence and in using such constituencies as a training ground for new candidates.

Once elected, the policies of the governing party are implemented through the bureaucracy. However, a government can find that it is costly to achieve compliance with its objectives. How can a President, a Prime Minister, a Cabinet, or a Secretary of State ensure that their wishes are actually implemented? Problems arise because bureaucrats are experts on the possibilities of varying output, as well as on the opportunities for factor substitution. Although some of these substitution possibilities can result in perverse outcomes for a government (assuming that they have a clear idea of their policy objectives), they might be too costly for any individual Minister to monitor, police, and eliminate completely. In this way, bureaucracies can affect the quantity and efficiency of public sector output. Government bureaucracies are defined as non-profit organizations in the public sector and they embrace ministries, departments, and other state agencies (including international organizations such as the IMF). Only recently have economists developed economic models of bureau behaviour which offer testable propositions. A starting point was the assumption that bureaucrats are budget-maximizers. Such an objective enables bureaucrats to satisfy their preferences for salary, power, patronage, public regulation, and the perquisites of office. This behavioural assumption can relate to either the absolute or relative size of the bureau (i.e. the bureau's budget relative to the government's total budget). Further modifications have been based on a more general utility function in which bureaucrats exhibit a preference for staff *inputs* and organizational slack, as well as output. In total, the economic models suggest that bureaucrats have incentives and opportunities for satisfying their own preferences rather than the voters. They will obviously favour bureaucratic solutions in the belief that all such solutions are 'good' and more are desirable, regardless of cost. Examples include support for the public regulation of private industry, for administrative procedures to control inflation, for economic planning, and for redistribution in kind rather than cash. Predictably, bureaucrats will oppose 'hiving-off' their activities to the private sector. However, the situation is complicated by the fact that government employees are voters and thereby constitute a substantial interest group.

Interest or pressure groups try to influence government policy in their favour. For example, producer groups might try to 'buy' monopoly rights by 'purchasing' protection from competition. They lobby for tariffs and import controls, or the regulation of prices and restrictions on the entry of 'unreliable' firms offering 'inferior and unsafe' products (e.g. drugs). Producers are the beneficiaries rather than consumers (cf. air fares). Effectively, there is trade and exchange between governments and interest groups (a negotiations democracy?). In this situation, governments can be regarded as supplying favourable legislation to groups which outbid their rivals. A group will be willing to pay a 'price' which reflects the expected value of the protective legislation to its members. Payment may take the form of cash contributions to the governing party, votes, bribes, or the supply of persuasive information, including advertisements and specialist consultancy reports, as well as payments-in-kind through the provision of campaign speakers and accommodation for political meetings. Information is especially important in explaining the role of interest groups. Vote-sensitive politicians have to be well informed of public opinion. Where voter preferences are diverse and uncertain, politicians are likely to incur substantial costs in collecting information. In comparison, interest groups are well informed in their specialist areas, so providing a low cost source of expertise to vote-conscious politicians. This is most attractive if the group has a large membership. Moreover, legislation promising benefits to an interest group is likely to attract the support of group members. But if interest groups appear so influential, why are there not more of them? Presumably, the number and size of groups is partly explained by the costs of forming and maintaining them. If these costs were reduced, more groups would be formed. Costs are incurred in establishing the organization to obtain collective goods, such as favourable legislation. There are costs of identifying potential group members, communicating between them, bargaining about the distribution of benefits, as well as the outlays for staffing and policing the group. Free-riding is a major problem, particularly for large groups. Since the benefits of government policies are available to all (public goods; see Chapter 2), no individual has an inducement to be a member of a specialist group—in which case, groups would not exist! This has led Olson (1965) to conclude that unless the group is small or there is coercion or some incentive to make individuals act in their common interest, then self-interested individuals will not act to achieve their common or group interests. Certainly it cannot be concluded that *groups* will be self-interested simply because *individuals* are self-interested. A lobbying organization, a trade union, a professional association, or any other body working in the interests of a large group of firms, or workers in an industry, would receive no assistance from self-interested individuals in the industry. But if this is the case, how do we explain the existence of large groups (e.g. trade unions, doctors)? According to Olson, large and powerful lobbying groups are usually the *by-products* of organizations which obtain their support and income either through coercion or by offering private (i.e. non-collective) benefits to individual members. For example, there might be legal requirements that practising lawyers must be members of the appropriate bar association (cf. a closed shop). Others professional bodies such as doctors, accountants, and architects have the authority to govern themselves by specifying minimum standards and qualifications for practitioners, as well as the power to discipline members who fail to maintain the requisite ethical standards. Membership of a professional body might also provide valuable private benefits through access to insurance on favourable terms, professional support in the event of negligence and malpractice suits, and the provision of technical journals and conferences. Thus, both coercion and inducements are used to maintain large organizations which can then act as a lobby and pressure group.

Market structure

Finally, analysis of the political market requires consideration of the market structure in which each agent operates. Both political and economic factors will influence structure. A nation's constitution will determine its voting and collective choice rules and, within such constraints, the costs of transactions will further affect market structure (see Chapter 7). An assessment of structure involves consideration of:

(1) The number of voters and political parties in the market (i.e. buyers and sellers). Are there large or small numbers?
(2) The size distribution of voters and parties in the market. Is any party or voter large in relation to the size of the market?
(3) Entry conditions. Can new voters and parties enter the market or are there entry barriers? If there are entry restrictions, why do they exist and what form do they take? For example, only registered citizens over the age of, say, 18 might be allowed to vote. There might also be barriers to the entry of new political parties through, say, legal restrictions on access to television.
(4) The form of competition in the market. Do political parties compete in price or in non-price forms? Changes in taxation and direct charging are the major price variables. Other forms of competition and product differentiation include public expenditure, subsidies, and policies to improve or replace the operation of private markets (see Chapter 2).

A structural analysis enables markets to be classified according to their degree of competition or the lack of it. Questions then arise about the performance of the political market place and the extent to which it results in a Pareto optimum. How do political markets compare with private markets and competition?

3.3 THE PERFORMANCE OF POLITICAL MARKETS

Political markets can be compared with the perfectly competitive model. Like firms, parties offer policies to voters in exchange for votes. If political markets were perfectly competitive, parties would compete and eliminate abnormal political 'profits', where these take the form of discretionary behaviour reflected in the pursuit of supplier interests rather than those of the voter. Thus, with large numbers of relatively small voters and political parties and no entry restrictions, the political market would result in a competitive solution (Pareto optimal), with parties responding to the wishes of voters. But, just as private markets can 'fail', so too can political markets. Various imperfections exist in the political process which affect adversely the extent to which the system fully and accurately satisfies voter preferences. Some of these imperfections are also points of contrast with private competitive markets and they include:

(1) Competition in democratic political markets is infrequent and discontinuous. Usually, voters make a binding decision resulting in the election of government for a fixed term of office. In other words, voters cannot re-contract daily.
(2) Competition in the political market is of the 'all-or-nothing' type. The majority party obtains the *entire* market, whereas in private markets buyers who are in a minority might still be able to purchase from their preferred firm.
(3) The nature of contracts in political markets. Voters cannot 'bind' politicians to an agreed, and clearly specified, set of policies; hence elected representatives have discretion. They can choose when to implement their election promises, they can rank policies, and they can select people who might never be subject to direct electoral representation (e.g. judges, bishops, defence chiefs). Moreover, the actual revelation of voter preferences can be affected (distorted) by the electoral system. Votes are often for a package of policies rather than specific issues. A voter might prefer a left wing view of distribution but a right wing view of individual freedom. Which should he choose and what does his choice reflect about his true preference ordering? Further opportunities for discretionary behaviour arise because a majority voting system can fail to establish a clear, unambiguous ordering of society's preferences or its social welfare function (see Chapter 11, Table 11.2).
(4) The supply side is imperfect. In some democracies, there are only two or three effective parties so that political competition is imperfect. Significantly, in private markets, the presence of duopoly or oligopoly would be regarded as a source of market failure. Also, once elected, the governing party becomes a monopoly supplier for its term of office.

In assessing the political process, a major methodological difficulty arises in that *actual* political markets are compared with *ideal* competitive solutions in private markets. This has led to the criticism that comparisons are being made between muddle and model when it would be more appropriate and accurate to compare *actual* institutional arrangements (i.e. imperfect political processes and imperfect private markets). Constitutions can, of course, differ to provide varying opportunities for the political process to reflect and satisfy voter preferences. For example, alternative voting rules are possible, such as unanimity, proportional representation, or majority voting; there could be general and primary elections, or referenda, together with opportunities for voting at federal or central as well as state and local elections. Economists can contribute in this area by analysing the implications of different voting rules. Consider the unanimity rule. It seems particularly attractive for Pareto optimal solutions. A society which has a public sector and tax policy which is Pareto optimal will be unable to alter such a policy if a change requires unanimous support. With a Pareto optimal solution, any change must make at least one person worse off, so that one citizen will vote against the change, hence preventing it. Similarly, any public policy which receives unanimous support must result in an actual Pareto improvement. But a unanimity rule is likely to result in the *status quo*: policy is unlikely to change. In contrast, majority voting allows policy changes which are *potential* Pareto improvements. A change which makes three individuals better by £50 each and one worse off by £3, would have a majority in its favour, and the potential gainers would be able to overcompensate the potential loser. But this is not always the outcome. Majority rules can accept policy changes in which the potential gainers could not overcompensate the losers. In such a case, the potential losers might then find it worth while to bribe the potential gainers to vote against the change!

Political markets also generate other devices allowing voters to register their preferences and so overcome any apparent deficiencies in the community's voting rules. The possibilities including log-rolling, political participation, interest groups, private provision, and mobility. Log-rolling is a vote-trading arrangement whereby individuals exchange their less urgent for their more urgent desires. Legislator A might offer to support B's favourite policy in return for similar support from B when A's preferred policy is being considered. In this way, the intensity of preferences can be registered and there are opportunities for mutually advantageous trade and exchange. This raises the possibility of introducing more specific and complete contractual arrangements into the political market place. Attractive though such contracts might seem (cf. private markets where you agree to pay a firm £x for painting your house at a specific time and an agreed quality), they are likely to be extremely costly to write, execute, and enforce.

Where citizens are dissatisfied with the existing parties, they could respond by increased political participation. This might involve starting a new party or trying to change the position of an existing party, depending on the relative costs of the alternatives. Or interest groups might enable individuals to achieve gains which would be too costly to obtain through the voting mechanism. Or individuals might respond to government deficiencies by seeking the private provision of goods and services, and the formation of voluntary clubs (e.g. swimming, tennis, golf). In the last resort, people can always move to a different locality or country, or they can organize a revolution.

Further understanding of political markets can be acquired by analysing the behaviour of parties and bureaucracies. What are the predictions of the economists' models of politics and bureaucracies? Are these predictions consistent with the facts?

3.4 ECONOMIC MODELS OF POLITICS

A major contribution was Anthony Downs' *An Economic Theory of Democracy* (1957). It assumes that voters are utility-maximizers and that political parties are vote-maximizers. Voters will compare the present value of the expected satisfaction from the re-election of the present government with that which might be obtained if the rival parties were in office. Citizens will vote for the party which they believe will provide them with the highest utility. Voters might reach their decisions about *future* performance by considering a government's *past* record in relation to its original promises and the beliefs about how well the opposition would have performed in the same period.

In seeking votes required for office, vote-maximizing political parties have the task of identifying the preferences of citizens. The median voter theorem provides a starting point for the analysis of party behaviour. Assume a decision is required on a single major issue and that opinion can be represented on a political spectrum ranging from left to right (socialist to conservative). Each voter has single-peaked preferences, such that he votes for the candidate closest to this preferred position. Voters are assumed to be normally distributed across the political spectrum, as shown in Figure 3.1. With two parties and majority voting, both parties will adopt the policy favoured by the median voter. In other words, two-party competition and majority voting satisfies voters in the middle or the centre rather than voters at either extreme of the political spectrum. The problem for political parties is to identify the

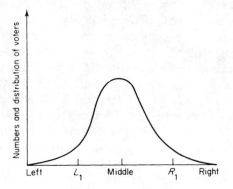

Figure 3.1 Consensus politics. Vote-maximizing parties, seeking office, will not locate at the extremes of the political spectrum, say L_1 and R_1. Each can gain more votes by moving towards the centre. Just like oligopolists, parties will tend to cluster towards the centre of almost any distribution of demand (see Chapter 9, Figure 9.7). Marginal cost functions could be imposed on the diagram, showing the costs which each party has to incur to acquire extra votes and reach the centre.

exact location of the middle of the distribution! For economists, there are also questions concerning the *determinants* of the distribution of voters across the political spectrum and the long-run stability of the distribution. Alternative distributions are possible. For example, the mass of voters might be almost equally divided between each of the political extremes; or voters might be fairly evenly distributed across the whole political spectrum, so resulting in a multi-party system. But are such distributions determined by economic factors in the form of information and transactions costs for voters and parties, or by history, or by such sociological factors as the 'balance of class forces'?

The predictions of the models, examples, and evidence

The economics of politics models give a number of predictions which are relevant in explaining micro-economic policy:

(1) In a two-party democracy, both parties agree on any issues favoured by a majority of voters. Consensus politics tends to emerge, with both parties offering similar and vague policies.
(2) Where the median voter is decisive, redistribution will be towards the *middle* of the income distribution.
(3) The voters who are best informed on any policy issue are those whose income is directly affected by it (i.e. the income-earners in the area likely to affected by policy changes). Such voters are likely to be less informed on policies that affect them as consumers. As a result, the policies of democratic governments tend to favour producers more than consumers.

In two-party systems, there are numerous examples of consensus politics. Parties might adopt similar policies towards discrimination in the labour market, minimum wage legislation, and training, as well as towards rent control, support for domestic defence industries and monopolies, mergers, and restrictive practices policy. However, parties will try to differentiate their policies; otherwise they would be identical and non-rival (they behave like dupolies in, say, the soap powder business). A socialist party will tend to favour more public ownership and state solutions, while conservatives will prefer *laissez faire*. Neither party will move to the extremes of the political spectrum, namely complete socialism or unbridled free enterprise: such extremes are prevented by the potential losses of moderate voters. Nor is the evidence on this hypothesis restricted to casual empiricism. A study of the UK Conservative and Labour Parties in the elections between 1924 and 1966 concluded that both parties had tended to move nearer to each other and that a process of convergence had taken place over time (Robertson, 1976).

Alternative predictions about income distribution have been formulated from different models. Altruists and normative theories of redistribution usually suggest that redistribution ought to be from the rich to the poor (see Chapter 11). Alternatively, Marxists and socialists would allege that redistribution is from the poor to the rich and others in 'power'. But the economics of politics predicts that the median voter is in power, so that redistribution is towards the *middle* of the income distribution. The median voter hypothesis on redistribution has also achieved empirical support when tested against the altruistic and socialist hypotheses (Mueller, 1979).

A distinctive feature of the Downs model is its prediction that government policies will be pro-producer and anti-consumer (cf. Chapter 2). This prediction emerges because of substantial transactions and information costs in political markets. Given that information is costly to acquire and that there are gains from specialization and division of labour, people are best informed in the area of their speciality, namely their producing or income-earning activity. Producer groups embrace firms and unions. In addition:

(1) They can afford the substantial investments in information to influence government policy. Producer groups have to show governments that they are more knowledgeable than the best-informed voters. To be influential, interest groups have to be specialists in their preferred policy area, whereas voters are generalists. Specialization demands expert knowledge and information which can be costly to acquire. Since producer groups are already knowledgeable about their area, the costs to them of acquiring information can be relatively low; there might be scale economies in the collection and distribution of information and, in the case of firms and trade unions, some of the information costs can be charged to the enterprise. Moreover, with only small numbers, the costs of creating a group and avoiding the 'free-rider' problem can be more readily, and cheaply, solved.

(2) They find it worth while to invest in information. The potential returns from purchasing information to influence policy are sufficiently large to make costly investments worth while. Income-earners are most likely to gain directly and significantly from influencing policy in their favour. Since voters usually earn their income in one activity (i.e. a firm, a union, and in one locality) but spend in many, the area of earning or producing is much more vital to them than their spending or consuming activities (Downs, 1957).

It might seem surprising that vote-sensitive governments ignore large numbers of consumers and are influenced by small numbers of producers. Vote-maximizing governments will be concerned about the income and utility of voters only insofar as these affect votes. If a government knows that a citizen's income is affected by its policies, and the citizen is aware of this, then the government will carefully assess the effect of its policies on the voter. The less a citizen knows about policy options and their effects on his income and utility, the more likely he will be ignored by a government, hence increasing the governing party's opportunities for discretionary behaviour. Certainly there are numerous examples of policies which favour producers rather than consumers. Tariffs and import controls favour domestic firms and create domestic jobs, while the consumer pays in the form of higher prices (see Chapter 4, Figure 4.16). Similar results occur with policies supporting agricultural prices (e.g. the EEC's Common Agricultural Policy), influencing the location of industry, subsidizing lame duck firms, favouring domestic firms in allocating government contracts, and supporting prestige high technology projects, such as Concorde. Governments might also be ambiguous and inconsistent in their treatment of monopolies and mergers. They might adopt an anti-monopoly and pro-competition policy and then fail to implement it. Or vague elements (e.g. an undefined 'public interest') might be introduced into the legislation and the task of interpretation might be given to an independent agency, with further opportunities for discretionary behaviour. But if such policies are detrimental to consumers (and there are numerous examples in this book), why are they adopted? Why do consumers not protect themselves by forming an interest group to influence government policy in their favour? The answer is that such groups are costly to form. There are large numbers of consumers which have to be located, and negotiations and bargaining are required to share the burdens and benefits over the group. Without a group, an individual consumer will find it costly to acquire information on the price effects of agricultural support schemes, monopolies, regional policy, and tariffs; and any resulting benefits to an *individual* consumer are likely to be small although large numbers of free-riders will *each* derive relatively small gains. The result is that governments will tend to *oversupply* special interest legislation favouring *producer* groups.

Political business cycles

Once elected, the governing party becomes a monopoly supplier of goods and services. As such, it has the opportunity to use its policies to directly influence voter preferences. It can, for example, offer subsidies to major firms (producer groups) in marginal constituencies or introduce import controls for low-profit industries concentrated in such constituencies. The government can also use aggregate demand policies to increase its chances of re-election. To increase its popularity, it can embark on expansionary policies prior to an election. Such use of aggregate demand management as a potential vote-winner raises the possibility of politically created business cycles. Indeed, the management of aggregate demand and 'stop–go' policies might appear attractive to vote-sensitive politicians, since a government can be seen to be involved in 'controlling' the economy. But much depends on the success of such demand management, its relationship to voter preferences, and the memory of voters.

The political business cycle assumes that voters are myopic and focus on the current election period, tending to forget the past. Following an election victory, the government will aim to control inflation by deflating the economy, so raising unemployment. This will occur in the politically safe period after an election victory. Such a policy might be presented and interpreted as an investment in the future to 'squeeze inflation out of the system and create permanent jobs' (inflation–unemployment trade-off). Over the government's term of office unemployment is steadily reduced, and if voters are myopic they will assess the government on its performance at the time of the election (e.g. during the current election year). *After the election*, there is a significant increase in inflation and the cycle is repeated. In these circumstances, traditional Keynesian fiscal policy seemed especially appropriate. Budget deficits allow politicians to spend their way out of a recession without raising taxes or charges; hence their attraction as potential vote-winners. In contrast, budget surpluses to combat inflation require reduced spending and/or higher taxes: both are unattractive to voters and there is also opposition from bureaucrats who dislike their budgets being cut. Consequently, government manipulation of the economy for votes results in a preference for budget deficits, increased public expenditure, and inflationary pressures.

Voters are often criticized for being myopic. But the political business cycle model also suggests that politicians can be short-sighted. The public sector can be as myopic or even more so than individuals, with adverse consequences for efficiency in resource allocation. After all, private markets are often condemned for 'failing' to take a long view! Nor is it necessarily valid to assume that voters have limited memories and that they do not learn from experience. For example, after repeated experience of the political business cycle, voters might learn of a subsequent deflation following an election victory and so favour a rival party offering a better, and apparently costless, solution (e.g. an 'ideal' incomes policy). However, the acceptability of the political business cycle model also depends on its empirical validity. Evidence from the United Kingdom, the United States, and West Germany shows that a government's popularity is affected by economic variables, namely unemployment, inflation, and real income, and that there is support for a political–economic cycle in these countries. The equations for testing the model are of the general form:

$$P = P(U,p,y,R)$$

where

P = a measure of the governing party's popularity (e.g. percentage lead over its main rival)

U = national unemployment rate

p = inflation rate

y = growth of real disposable income

R = other relevant variables (e.g. expected time to the next election, depreciation of the government's lead over its term of office)

The evidence indicates that increases in both unemployment and inflation adversely affect a government's popularity (a negative relationship), while higher real income has a favourable effect (a positive relationship). But such results are not beyond criticism. It is far from clear whether the equations represent demand or supply side variables, equilibria or disequilibria in political markets. Moreover, if a governing party knows the effect of economic variables on its popularity, why does it lose elections? Modern Austrian economists would not be surprised at election defeats since the school maintains that there are no constant relations in economics, so that no measurement is possible. Finally, the political business cycle model contains only *macro*-economic influences and neglects the micro-economic foundations. If a government pursues an expansionary policy to increase its popularity prior to an election, are the micro-economic effects of higher aggregate demand completely irrelevant? For example, public expenditure can be increased through alternative public works programmes favouring defence, hospitals, roads, or schools, each with different industrial and regional implications; or state-owned industries could be required to increase investment; or more subsidies could be offered to clearly identifiable groups, such as large firms in marginal constituencies or training programmes for unemployed school-leavers. Nor does the model consider the role of bureaucrats in determining government policies.

3.5 ECONOMIC MODELS OF BUREAUCRACY

Bureaucracies are public sector non-profit organizations which are responsible for advising federal, central, state, and local governments on the extent and form of micro-economic policy, including any opportunities for new initiatives. Their responsibilities range from the provision of public goods, such as defence, to purchasing goods and services from the private sector; they are involved in regulating private firms and industries, collecting taxes, and administering redistribution policies. Further examples dominate the remainder of this book! But how do such non-profit organizations behave and do they perform efficiently?

Bureaucracies supply information, goods, and services to the governing political party and, ultimately to the community. They are usually monopoly suppliers, protected from possible public and private sector rivals through a governing party's allocation of property rights and restrictions on new entrants. Normally, each government department tends to specialize (e.g. education, employment, highways, housing, transport), there being no competition or rivalry between different parts of the *public* sector for the provision of specific services. This applies both within and between cities, within and between state or local governments, as well as between local and federal or central administrations. For example, within a city, the municipal passenger transport and fire departments are not generally invited to bid for the refuse collection service, and vice versa. Similarly, the housing repairs and highways maintenance departments are not normally rivals for government building contracts. Nor are private firms invited to tender for some of the traditional functions of government (e.g. careers advice and job search, schooling, refuse collection, fire services). The absence of competition and rivalry means that bureaucrats have opportunities for discretionary behaviour. They are interest groups of experts and specialists and, in the absence of alternative sources of information and comparative cost data, the government as buyer and sponsor might not be sufficiently well informed to question a bureau's budget requests. Not surprisingly, bureaucrats are often supporters of increased 'coordination, rationalization, and centralization' within the public sector, so creating larger departments: such reorganization is reputed to eliminate the alleged 'duplication and wastes' of competition! The outcome is bilateral monopoly with bureaus acting as monopolists and the governing party as a monopsonist, purchasing desired levels of service in return for an agreed budget. There are, however, limitations on the extent to which the wishes of the governing party will be implemented. Such limitations mean that bureaucrats have opportunities to further their own ends.

Opportunities for discretionary behaviour arise in large organizations in non-competitive markets and where objectives and end-outputs are vague and ill-defined. Large organizations encounter difficulties of coordination, so resulting in control loss. In such organizations, both ministers and senior bureaucrats will find it costly to achieve complete compliance with their wishes. Each level in an hierarchy increases the chances that an order will be changed, either deliberately or accidentally. Consider an organization with four hierarchical levels and all subordinates executing 80 per cent. of their orders: at the fourth level, only about 40 per cent. of a minister's orders will be effective. Orders might be misunderstood, incapable of being executed, or subordinates might be unwilling to cooperate. In these circumstances, opportunities arise for bureaucrats to deliberately distort or hoard information to further their own ends. Various measures can be used to reduce such distortions, including independent audits and the appointment of external advisers. Or, incentives might be offered for the release of valuable information: new ideas could be rewarded with prizes, promotion, or attendance at international conferences. While control loss arises in all large organizations, both public and private, the opportunities for discretion are reinforced in non-competitive markets. As monopolists, bureaucrats can pursue self-interest, with implications for economic decisions and policy outcomes. The situation is reinforced by the bureaucrat's employment contract which is often incompletely specified and lacking in efficiency incentives, so giving further opportunities for exercising discretion. Of course, it might be claimed that large organizations, monopolies, and incompletely-specified employment contracts also exist in *private* markets. If so, there are opportunities for improving performance in both sectors. However, in the private sector, there are consumers, rival firms, a more clearly defined output, a take-over mechanism, the risking of private funds and employment contracts which provide monetary rewards for increased efficiency: all these act as 'policing' mechanisms. Such controls are absent in the political market place. Voters might not be able to express their views on a specific issue, such as a state support for Concorde or similar projects. Nor is it a simple task for a politician at the ministerial or city council level to challenge a bureaucracy's information, advice, and budget requests. All of which raises questions about the behaviour of bureaucracies.

Predictions, examples, and evidence

A starting point is Niskanen's (1971) model in which bureaucrats as utility-maximizers have every incentive to maximize their budgets. Larger budgets enable bureaucrats to satisfy their preferences for salary, perquisites of office, public regulation, job opportunities, power, and patronage. The model assumes that bureaucrats can operate as perfect price discriminating monopolists, extracting the available consumer surplus from the purchasing government (bilateral monopoly). Effectively, a bureau offers a total output in exchange for a budget, an example of which is shown in Figure 3.2. A department will offer an output which provides the largest possible budget consistent with covering total costs. Output will exceed the social optimum (Q_c), hence the prediction that bureaus 'overproduce', giving too large an output. On this basis, it is likely that industries and services supported by monopoly ministries and state agencies will be too large. Figure 3.2 also compares public and private monopolies, showing that the latter will produce at Q_m, giving 'too little' output, but the private profit-maximizing monopolist results in smaller welfare losses than a budget-maximizing bureaucracy.

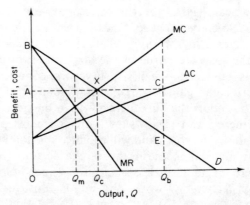

Figure 3.2 A budget-maximizing bureaucracy. The community's demand for the government service (the demand function of the median voter) is represented by D, with MR as marginal revenue and marginal and average costs as MC and AC, respectively. A budget-maximizing bureaucrat will produce at Q_b where the largest possible budget is obtained, subject to the constraint that total revenue equals total cost. At Q_b the budget is OACQ$_b$ which equals OBEQ$_b$. Consumer surplus of ABX at Q_c is used to increase output to Q_b (ABX = XCE). For comparative purposes, the competitive output or social optimum is Q_c and the output for the private profit-maximizing monopolist is Q_m. The welfare losses at Q_m are smaller than at Q_b.

Budget maximization can affect the behaviour of bureaucracies. In aiming to raise their budgets, departments have every incentive to overestimate or exaggerate the demand for their preferred policies and to underestimate the costs of policies and projects. This can affect the ways in which bureaucrats present information to politicians. Bureaus can stress the social benefits of a project in the form of jobs, high technology, and its contribution to the balance of payments. In the defence field, where they have a monopoly of information, the armed forces and the defence department can exaggerate the threat from a potential enemy and point to the numbers of its troops, tanks, aircraft, ships, and nuclear warheads. Bureaus can formulate programmes which will be supported by producer groups likely to benefit from contracts and they can suggest policies which are potential vote-winners for a government. Departments can also hire independent consultants to provide further expertise supporting their case. After all, the case for a new public expenditure programme can be enhanced if it has the approval of reputable, independent consultants which have assessed the scheme using all the latest cost–benefit, statistical, econometric, and survey techniques of appraisal. Possible vote losses from any increased taxation and inflation required to finance greater public expenditure will be widely diffused among the electorate, so that the adverse effects are likely to be quite small.

While bureaucracies and interest groups are usually enthusiastic about social benefits, they are understandably silent on the reliability of a project's cost estimates and on any external costs. A ministry might deliberately underestimate the costs of a project in order to 'buy into' a new programme. Cost estimates which are 'too low' can lead a government to buy 'too much' of a project which appears to be a relatively cheap. Once started, public sector projects are difficult to stop. Agents in the political market place have an interest in continuation and the costs are borne by the taxpayer. Projects create interest groups of architects, engineers, scientists, surveyors, contractors, and unions, each with relative income gains from the continuation of the work. Such groups are likely to support the bureaucracy with a budgetary involvement in the project. Bureaucrats can easily show vote-conscious politicians that a project is in the 'national interest' and will produce substantial social benefits. Such behaviour is not unknown in the public sector. Examples of cost estimates which were substantially less than actual expenditures have occurred with weapons, high technology work, and major construction programmes (see cost escalation in Chapter 14). Although cost escalation occurs on private commercial projects, it raises different issues for efficiency. Market-based organizations are less likely to persist with unproductive or obsolete projects since the necessary support will be removed by the market. Budget-conscious departments will also be reluctant to recognize and estimate any external costs. Examples include noise from new airports and new, state-financed, jet engines, as well as the pollution and environmental effects from the establishment of coalfields, off-shore oil drilling, and the possible hazards and risks associated with nuclear power stations. It is in a department's interest to ignore or underestimate such social costs. Thus, to raise their budgets, bureaucracies have an incentive to underestimate costs and exaggerate demands. In the process, they can also justify their preferred output by creating an impression of allocative efficiency, as shown in Figure 3.3

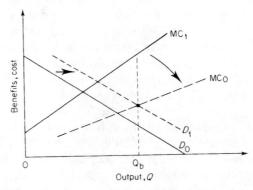

Figure 3.3 Bureaucracy behaviour. Assume that Q_b is the budget-maximizing output; see Figure 3.2. Bureaus can create an impression of allocative efficiency by overestimating demand—D_1 instead of D_0—and underestimating costs—MC_0 instead of MC_1.

The model has numerous applications. Examples from the fire service, state high technology programmes, and city building projects are sufficient to illustrate its potential and show how it can be combined with the economics of politics. Many fire services are bureaucracies operated by city, regional, or state authorities. In bargaining about budgets, fire departments will aim to supply protection to meet all possible contingencies. They will insist that an 'adequate' cover requires the purchase of the latest sophisticated equipment, ignoring its costs and the probability of its use. A fire officer's employment contract provides no inducements to respond to economic incentives: he does not share in any savings. Indeed, any savings might accrue to rival departments or even to the Treasury. Thus, the system creates incentives to *spend*. In the circumstances, there is every incentive to provide cover to meet the worst-possible contingency or catastrophe. Also, callers requesting the fire service are judged incapable of assessing the extent of any fire. Consequently, the service insists that the minimum response to any emergency requires, say, two vehicles. Think of the cases where most of the local fire brigade turns out to extinguish a small cooker fire! In addition en route to any emergency, the fire service creates sufficient externalities (noise) to remind the local community of its existence and 'performance'. Finally, in bargaining with politicians for its budget, the fire department can always use its ultimate 'weapon' and point to the possible political (i.e. vote) consequences of any loss of life due to 'inadequate' fire protection following budget cuts. The result is likely to be expensive solutions providing 'too much' fire protection (i.e. overinsurance).

High technology projects are particularly attractive to bureaucrats and interest groups of scientists, engineers, and technologists interested in expanding the frontiers of knowledge at the taxpayer's expense. Examples include state involvement in computers, micro-electronics, nuclear power stations, and space satellites. Median preference voters are likely to be uncertain about the benefits and costs of government support for advanced technology: they will be attracted by its potential benefits, but wary of the likely costs and possibilities of failure. In the circumstances, vote-sensitive politicians are likely to be influenced by those who are best informed, namely interest groups of experts. Such groups, which are likely to benefit from a ministry's increased spending, will have every incentive to support the bureaucracy's exaggerated claims of major social benefits. References will be made to the need to keep a nation in the forefront of technology, to the valuable (but difficult to quantify) fall-out for the rest of the economy, to the provision of the next generation of jobs, to the possibility of a new technological revolution, and the need to avoid 'undue' dependence on foreign technology. Vote-conscious politicians might be attracted by such alleged benefits, especially if state support for new technology appears to offer a means of 'solving' a nation's economic problems. Where such projects have to be undertaken in collaboration with other nations (e.g. European space satellites; see Chapter 14), bureaucrats further benefit from the opportunities for international travel and its associated amenities. Thus, the high technology example shows the possible range of beneficiaries in the political market place. Domestic industry, scientists, and jobs will be favoured. Politicians will expect to gain votes through the allocation of government funds to clearly identifiable groups. Bureaucrats benefit from a larger budget, the discretionary power in allocating contracts, and the need for monitoring and policing the work to ensure that the 'best value for money is obtained' and the public interest is protected. Rarely is it asked whether the resources used in government-supported high technology work would make a greater contribution to employment, balance of payments, and technology objectives and, ultimately, to human satisfaction, if they were used elsewhere in the economy.

Further insights into how bureaucrats obtain a larger budget can be obtained by examining the information which they present to the governing party. Consider the case for a new city-financed building, such as an arts, conference, or sports centre. Or take the case which might be used to persuade a city to bid for the Olympic Games. It can be argued that the project is 'vital' to prevent a city 'sliding down the league table' and that we must 'go ahead and subsidize the scheme because our rivals have done so'. References will be made to social benefits in the form of extra local spending from the new project which, together with existing business, will give a 'substantial' total benefit: note the potential confusion between *marginal* and *total* benefits. It will, of course, be argued that the social benefits are difficult to quantify, but nonetheless are believed to be substantial! On the cost side, estimates might not be presented on a consistent price basis with, say, 1978 expenditures simply added to 1982 outlays. This, plus the omission of interest charges, the neglect of life-cycle, and external costs (e.g. noise, pollution), understates the true opportunity cost of a project. Further 'pressure' can be placed on city decision-makers if the scheme is presented with a 'keenly competitive price' determined by selective tendering, providing a 'unique and final opportunity' to proceed. And, after all, if the project does not 'go ahead', all the previous expenditure will be 'wasted'. Indeed, completion for its own sake sometimes becomes a point of honour. It is not unknown for city politicians and officials to argue that, having embarked on a scheme and having been fully committed to it for some time, it is the city's view that it must be carried through to its conclusion, despite the heavily inflated costs.

While these arguments *appear* persuasive, they are often emotional, lacking in economic analysis and devoid of empirical support. For example, use of the word 'vital' invites questions of vital to whom, and is it vital regardless of cost? The 'rivals are subsidizing' argument is dubious since if they wish to offer free gifts, a local community could respond by accepting them and specializing elsewhere. Indeed, in appraising any scheme, the likely costs and benefits of alternative projects have to be considered, including a 'do nothing' option (e.g. why not 'slide down the league table'?). Nor is the 'substantial benefits' argument convincing in the absence of evidence showing that the benefits are greater than could be obtained from alternative uses of the resources. At its most general, the benefits argument simply suggests that *any* new local project will have multiplier effects. By itself, this is not a convincing case for choosing an arts centre rather than, say, new houses, schools, or roads. Moreover, it is possible that the difficulties of quantifying social benefits might reflect the fact that there is nothing to be measured! As for costs, references to a 'keenly competitive price' are misleading for decision-making if the project design has not been 'frozen' and a firm fixed-price contract cannot be awarded. Indeed, examples have arisen where two to three years after the start of a major building project, city officials have declared that its cost estimates will become more reliable as the contract proceeds towards completion! Arguments about cancellation are also confusing, since previous expenditures are 'sunk' costs where the sacrifices have already been incurred. Nor is cancellation necessarily 'wasteful'; it may be cheaper than continuing with the project, and past expenditures can provide benefits in the form of valuable information and knowledge.

While the Niskanen (1971) model is persuasive at the level of casual empiricism, there are limitations. Its prediction that the public sector will be 'too large' is difficult to subject to direct empirical test. The model also assumes that bureaucracies are technically efficient. Modifications have been introduced to allow bureaucrats to maximize a utility function containing both output and a preference for discretionary expenditures (i.e. the pursuit of other goals, such as on-the-job leisure; see Chapters 7 and 15). Such modifications result in the prediction that bureaucracies are both technically and allocatively inefficient. There are studies showing that for airlines, fire services, and refuse collection, private firms are lower-cost suppliers than public agencies—hence the suggestion that there is considerable X-inefficiency or slack in the public sector. The addition of X-inefficiency to the model also results in further examples of behaviour which are intuitively attractive. Paperwork has been introduced into the analysis. Paperwork is a characteristic of bureaucracies, both in their internal organization and in their dealings with the private sector. Understandably, private industry is critical of the numerous demands it receives to complete official forms, a process which can be costly. But paperwork is attractive to utility-maximizing bureaucrats when negotiating with politicians for a larger budget. Paperwork is an output indicator which can be used to inflate a bureau's costs in a way which the government sponsor cannot easily check. And the harder it is to measure a bureaucracy's output, the easier it will be to deceive the sponsor. Once a bureau has obtained its budget, it can shift some of the costs of paperwork onto private firms. And bureaucrats can 'consume' the cost 'savings', namely the difference between the original *estimate* of total costs at the budget-bargaining stage and the new 'lower' costs after a budget has been allocated. A simplified example is shown in Figure 3.4. There are, however, limits on a bureaucracy's ability to shift some of its costs onto private industry. Firms will eventually respond by lobbying politicians and pressing for less bureaucracy and for the work to be 'hived-off' to the more efficient private sector.

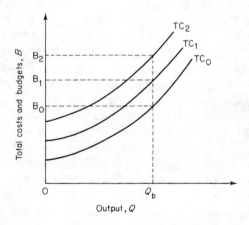

Figure 3.4 Bureaucratic behaviour and costs. For simplicity, assume that the government requires an output of Q_b from the bureaucracy and that it will pay the total costs of producing the output. The true minimum total cost curve is represented by TC_1, resulting in a budget of OB_1. However, the bureau will try to persuade the government that TC_2 is the appropriate cost curve; if successful, the bureau will receive a budget of OB_2. The difference between B_2 and B_1 represents the bureaucrats' discretionary expenditures. Once a budget of OB_2 has been received, the bureaucracy can increase its discretionary expenditures by shifting some of its costs (e.g. paperwork, tax collection) onto private industry. As a result of such shifting, the bureau's new total cost curve might be TC_0, so raising its discretionary expenditures to B_2B_0.

3.6 CONCLUSION: VOTES, POLICY, AND METHODOLOGY

This chapter posed the question: do votes determine policies? The economic models of politics and bureaucracies suggests that voters are one element in a policy model. Others include government and rival political parties, bureaucracies, and interest groups. These elements can be summarized in a general form, although a more detailed specification is required:

$$E = E(V,G,r,b,i,Z)$$

where E = economic policy (e.g. measured by expenditure either in total or by programme)
V = votes
G = governing party
r = rival political parties
b = bureaucracies
i = interest groups
Z = other influences (e.g. in the case of education, the age distribution of the population is a relevant variable)

If votes determine policies, questions have also to be asked about the determinants of votes. A starting point is the theory of consumer demand. Applied to voters, standard consumer theory would provide an explanation in terms of prices, incomes, and tastes. The result is a voting model of the general form:

$$V = V(P_g,P_p,y,U,\dot{p},R)$$

where V = votes (e.g. the choice between rival parties)
P_g = price of government goods and services
P_p = price of private goods and services
y = income of the voter
U = unemployment rate in each voter's constituency
$\dot{p}$ = inflation rate in each constituency
R = other relevant influences (e.g. the costs of search and the cost of voting)

The economics of politics and bureaucracies are attractive in that they seem to describe real world events. But description plus casual empiricism are insufficient for the acceptance of a theory. Much more work is required in clarifying concepts, such as producer groups. Is a producer group a large firm located in a high unemployment area or a firm in a marginal constituency? Do governments actually favour such groups? More fundamentally, are there alternative explanations of policy? If so, it is necessary to identify differences in the predictions offered by alternative models and assess their relative empirical validity. Marxists, for example, would explain policy in terms of the 'struggle of class forces' and the need for public expenditure and subsidies to lame duck firms to maintain capitalism. Applied to a nation's military spending Marxists would assert that defence expenditure is necessary for the maintenance of capitalism as a viable international system. In contrast, standard economic theory would start with the concept of a public good and analyse defence spending as an optimization problem. Defence output in the form of 'protection' is then maximized subject to constraints of resources, efficiency, technology, and information. Alternatively, the economics of politics and bureaucracies would explain military spending in terms of the vote-maximizing behaviour of governments and politicians, and utility-maximizing actions of bureaucracies supported by producer groups in the form of weapons firms (i.e. the military–industrial complex). Advocates of other explanations of military power might, of course, claim that 'class forces' underlie the economics of politics model. Analysts have the task of identifying alternative predictions from these various 'explanations'. Otherwise, 'explanation' becomes a matter of choice between deities: Chicago, Moscow, Peking, Mecca, or Rome?

In summary, the economics of politics has resulted in economists including political and bureaucratic variables in their models. It provides an explanation of the extent and form of state intervention, including the size and growth of the public sector in Western economies. The analysis is obviously applicable to the whole range of micro-economic policies (e.g. see the remaining chapters in this book). A general conclusion is that government solutions can also 'fail'. But if both private markets and governments can fail, what is left?

READING AND REFERENCES

Arrow, K. J. (1951). *Social Choice and Individual Values*, Wiley, New York.

Bennett, J. T., and Johnson, M. H. (1979). Paperwork and bureaucracy, *Economic Inquiry*, July, XVII, pp 435–451.

Breton, A. (1974). *The Economic Theory of Representative Government*, Aldine, Chicago.

Buchanan, J. M., and Tullock, G. (1962). *The Calculus of Consent*, University of Michigan Press, Ann Arbor.

Buchanan, J. M., et al. (1978). *The Consequences of Mr Keynes*, IEA, Hobart Paper 78, London.

Buchanan, J. M., et al., (1978). *The Economics of Politics*, IEA, Readings 18, London.

Doel, H. van den (1979). *Democracy and Welfare Economics*, Cambridge University Press, London.

Downs, A. (1957). *An Economic Theory of Democracy*, Harper and Row, New York.

Downs, A. (1967). *Inside Bureaucracy*, Little, Brown, Boston.

Frey, B. S., and Schneider, F. (1978). A politico-economic model of the U.K., *Economic Journal*, June **1978**, 243–253.

Hartley, K., and McLean, P. (1978). Military expenditure and capitalism; a comment, *Cambridge Journal of Economics*, 2 (also Reply by R. Smith),pp 287–292.

Hartley, K., and Peacock, A. (1978). Combined defence and international economic co-operation, *World Economy*, 1, June; pp 327–339.

Mueller, D. C. (1979). *Public Choice*, Cambridge Surveys of Economic Literature, Cambridge University Press.

Niskanen, W. A., Jr. (1971). *Bureaucracy and Representative Government*, Aldine-Atherton, Chicago.

Niskanen, W. A., Jr. (1973). *Bureaucracy: Servant or Master?*, Institute of Economic Affairs, Hobart Paperback 5, London.

Olson, M., Jr. (1965). *The Logic of Collective Action*, Harvard University Press, Cambridge, Mass.

Robertson, A. (1976). *A Theory of Party Competition*, Wiley, Chichester.

Tullock, G. (1976). *The Vote Motive*, Institute of Economic Affairs, Hobart Paperback 9, London.

QUESTIONS FOR REVIEW AND DISCUSSION

1. Why do people vote?
2. Which economic model(s) best explains the extent and form of state intervention in your country?
3. Construct an economic model to explain the behaviour of any producer interest group with which you are familiar.
4. Carefully explain how you would test any economic model of government bureaucracy.
5. The critics of government bureaucracy often:
   (a) ignore bureaucracies in large corporations and
   (b) compare actual bureaucracies with perfect markets (i.e. muddle with model). Evaluate these two criticisms. What is your response to them?
6. Would a perfectly competitive solution in the political market place be socially desirable?
7. What determines the distribution of voters across the political spectrum?
8. Does the evidence on political business cycles confuse correlation with causation?
9. Can the economic theories of politics and bureaucracies be used to explain the creation and continued existence of the International Air Transport Association (IATA)?
10. Does the economics of politics provide a satisfactory explanation of
    (a) government subsidy policy or
    (b) government defence expenditure?

PART B

Demand, Supply, Markets, and Policy

CHAPTER 4

Competitive Markets and Price Regulation

4.1 INTRODUCTION

Spillovers or externalities can result in a social (Kaldor–Hicks) welfare loss, even under perfectly competitive conditions, and as pointed out in Chapter 2 may call for government intervention in markets. But actual government intervention in competitive markets is not limited to correcting their operations to allow for externalities. There is considerable government interference in competitive markets even when externalities do not occur. *The purpose of this chapter is to consider how and why governments interfere in competitive markets when externalities are absent and the effects that such intervention has.* Government policies to maintain, to limit, or to stabilize product or factor prices, and government regulation of prices in international markets are examined.

But before considering these specific aspects it is worth while to digress and clarify the meaning of different types of market competition since this chapter concentrates on government intervention in perfectly competitive and purely competitive markets, intervention which in the absence of externalities is liable to result in a Kaldor–Hicks social welfare loss.

Defining the state of competition in an industry and in markets generally is not as straightforward as it may appear at first sight. It is likely to depend on the ease of entry of new firms into the industry, the number of producers in the industry, and the ease with which other products can be substituted for those of the industry. An industry tends to be more competitive the easier is entry into it, the larger are the number of producers in the industry, and the more nearly other products substitute for those of the industry.

Defining competition

Two broad approaches to defining the state of competition in an industry are discernible in the economics literature. One approach defines competition in an industry by reference to its *structure* and the other defines it by reference to the *performance* of the industry. The traditional approach is the structural one. The state of competition in an industry is defined by the number of producers in an industry, conditions of entry into the industry, the degree or absence of collusion between market participants, and the degree to which their products are identical or differentiated. Thus a *purely competitive industry* is one in which there are many sellers and buyers (so many that the supplies or purchases of any individual do not influence the price of the commodity), commodities are homogeneous, and therefore perfect substitutes and entry and exit in the long run is easy. Markets for fish and vegetables are usually of this type. In a *perfectly competitive market* these characteristics are satisfied but in addition traders in the market have perfect knowledge of the relevant economic variables. At the other end of the competition spectrum is pure *monopoly*. This is characterized by a single seller of a product with no close substitutes and the absence of possible entry by other firms. Posts and telecommunications in many countries are a state monopoly. *Oligopoly* is a market situation in which there are few sellers. The supply of motor cars and of man-made fibres is oligopolistic. A *monopsony* is said to exist when there is a single buyer of a commodity and an *oligopsony* arises when there are few buyers of a commodity. Each of these circumstances has implications or likely implications for the degree of competition in an industry. In this Chapter we shall concentrate on purely competitive and perfectly competitive markets, but other market structures will be considered in later chapters.

Stock characteristics of perfect competition and of monopoly

However, it is useful now to summarize the 'stock' characteristics of perfect competition and monopoly and compare these as in Table 4.1. Assuming that market participants have perfect knowledge, the structural characteristics stated in the top part of the table given rise to the performance characteristics mentioned in the lower part of the table. In assessing markets some economists and lawyers have concentrated on the structural characteristics of industries but others have been more concerned about the performance characteristics of markets.

Performance definitions of competition compared to structural characteristics

Performance definitions of competition pay little attention to market structure but concentrate on the question of whether the performance of an industry is similar to that which might be expected under pure competition. If there is little divergence between the price charged for a product and the marginal cost of producing it, an industry might be regarded as workably competitive by this approach if its long-term profits are not excessive, if technological progress and innovation occurs at a socially desirable rate, and if avoidable waste and inefficiency does not occur in the running of businesses in the industry. Given this approach it is feasible for an industry which is structurally oligopolistic to be workably competitive. If it is shown that an industry is workably competitive (despite its structure) this is sometimes used to argue that the market situation is socially acceptable. (See Figure 4.1.)

Table 4.1 'Stock' characteristics of perfect competition and monopoly.

Characteristics	Perfect competition	Monopoly
Structural		
Number of firms	Large	One
Size of firms	Small relative to industry output	Sufficiently large to produce all of industry output
Entry	Free (in long run)	Barriers to entry
Product	Homogeneous	Homogeneous — lack of close substitutes
Performance		
Pricing and resource allocation	Price equals marginal cost — therefore allocation of resources is Pareto optimal	Price exceeds marginal cost — therefore allocation of resources is not Pareto optimal
Profit	Normal (average) in the long run	Above normal in the long run
Organizational slack or X-inefficiency	Absent	May be present
Diffusion of technology	Rapid	Rate of adoption uncertain
Rate of technical progress and innovation	Uncertain	Uncertain

There are possibly no markets in practice which are perfectly competitive and few which are purely competitive. The degree of perfection of knowledge and mobility of resources required for the operation of perfect competition is so great that it can only be approached. But the perfectly competitive model provides an ideal or a benchmark as a basis for welfare judgements and comparison. The model is useful in a similar way to Euclidean geometry. Both refer to limiting cases but both have applications to the actual world because the degree of approximation is sufficiently close for many purposes.

Freely operating purely competitive markets are not common. Many are regulated by governmental policies. Although the most common purely competitive markets are those for agricultural products, many agricultural markets are regulated by governments. For example, milk prices and entry into milk production and supply is regulated by the government in the United Kingdom, Australia, and many other countries whereas trading in fish and fresh vegetables and on the stock exchange is not as a rule regulated. Money, capital, and foreign exchange markets have been or are controlled. Resource markets such as those for unskilled, semi-skilled, and even skilled labour are usually regulated. In many countries minimum rates of pay, salary, and/or conditions for particular types of work are specified by wage-regulating bodies or tribunals such as Wages Councils in the United Kingdom and the Australian Arbitration and Conciliation Commission in Australia. Similarly, restrictions are placed upon the purposes for which land can be used, especially in urban

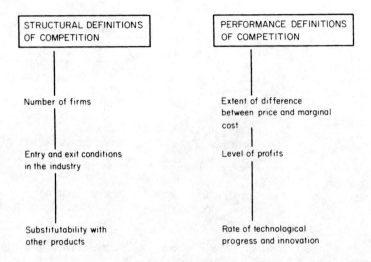

Figure 4.1 Some of the different factors taken into account in structural and performance definitions of competition.

areas. In the United Kingdom there is rent control in the housing market, and UK prices and income policies have 'controlled' factor incomes. In Australia, the Prices Justification Tribunal has interfered to control price increases for products produced by large companies.

4.2 WHY DOES THE STATE REGULATE COMPETITIVE MARKETS?

The amount of state regulation of competitive markets is considerable. Why is there so much intervention? This may be explained by idealistic considerations and the economics of politics. One idealistic reason for intervention, as mentioned in Chapter 2, is to allow for externalities or spillovers. But the government may also intervene in markets to 'improve' the distribution of income, e.g. by subsidizing meals for schoolchildren or medical care, or to foster the supply of merit goods. Its aim may be to increase the support of, or *votes* for, the party in power and/or may be in response to demands from particular political *pressure groups*. While state intervention in markets may be based on idealistic social welfare considerations, this intervention is sometimes (or may be often) based upon political realities of a non-idealistic nature, can add to scarcity, and, despite intentions to the contrary, may injure those whom it is designed to assist. Let us consider in more detail some of the reasons why governments interfere in competitive markets.

Information failure (due to externalities or spillovers)

As mentioned in Chapter 2, externalities or spillovers such as those caused by polluting economic activities may give a government scope to intervene and bring about a Kaldor–Hicks improvement. Externalities in the supply of information may provide another reason for government interference with markets. Less information may be collected and disseminated by individuals than is collectively of value. Individual search for information may be much more risky than collective search and an individual may not be able to sell all information which he collects or spreads at its full value to others. For instance, suppose that there is a piece of information or knowledge worth £10 each to 100 individuals but that it costs £12 to collect or discover it. Once one individual discovers the information all can share it at no extra cost. Collectively the information is worth £1,000 and far exceeds its cost of discovery of £12. But the information may not be salable, for instance, because once one individual discovers it and acts on it all become aware of the information. In the absence of government intervention, the information is unlikely to be collected because any collector loses £2. The government may solve this problem by subsidizing the collection and provision of information (for instance, it may subsidize basic research) or by making the information the property of the discoverer in appropriate cases so that it becomes salable as are certain inventions, for example, under patent law.

Pressures from producers for government enforcement of cartel-like arrangements

Producers in most competitive markets stand to gain if they can jointly restrict their supplies to a market. By doing this, as a rule they raise the price of their product and profits above their competitive levels. Existing producers in an industry also stand to gain if they can restrict the entry of new competitors into their industry. But in industries where the number of producers is large and entry barriers are few, producers face many difficulties in jointly restricting their supplies and jointly raising barriers to entry to their industry. Difficulties (such as organizers providing benefits to free-riders) arise in forming associations of producers and in ensuring that individual producers do in fact restrict their supplies to the market. Moreover, the more successful is any association or cartel in raising profits in its industry the greater is the incentive for new firms to enter the industry, expand supplies, and push profits down again. A cartel once formed is threatened by its own members and from potential entrants to the industry, and the threat is greater the more successful it is in raising prices. Where the number of suppliers in the market is large, suppliers therefore may lobby the government to help police cartel-type rules for the industry.

The conflict between the individual interest of suppliers and their collective interest in limiting supplies to a market is illustrated in Figure 4.2, where for simplicity the short-run situation is taken in which entry into the industry is not possible. Crude oil supplies are taken as the example in this case but agricultural markets for milk, wheat, eggs, and similar products provide other possible illustrations, as does the supply of airline seats and taxis. Let DD in

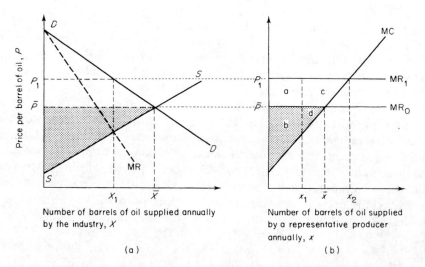

Figure 4.2   Illustration of the incentive for individual suppliers to break an agreement to limit supplies even though restriction is in their collective interest. For this example, the higher the agreed price in a cartel such as OPEC the greater is the incentive of individual suppliers to undercut the price and/or exceed their supply quotas.

Figure 4.2(a) represent the market demand curve for crude oil and the broken line MR represent the marginal (additional) revenue obtained by the industry from selling oil. Given the industry supply curve SS, market equilibrium *under competitive conditions* would be established at a price of $\bar{P}$ per barrel and for an annual supply of $\bar{X}$. Assuming that curve SS represents marginal costs in the industry, the profit obtained by all members collectively in the industry is represented by the dotted triangle in Figure 4.2(a). The corresponding profit for a representative supplier is as indicated by the dotted triangle in Figure 4.2(b), it being assumed that the curve marked MC is the supplier's marginal cost curve.

Suppose that suppliers of crude oil agree to restrict their suppliers of oil and reduce the annual supply of oil by the industry from the market equilibrium one of $\bar{X}$ to X_1. In the absence of the entry of new oil producers into the industry, the price of oil rises to P_1 per barrel and the profitability of oil production increases. But as can be seen from Figure 4.2(b), each individual producer faces a dilemma. Suppose that the agreed production quota or limit for the producer considered in Figure 4.2(b) is x_1. If all abide by their agreement collectively to restrict production to X_1, the profit of the producer considered in Figure 4.2(b) is equal to the area of the rectangle surrounding a plus the area of the quadrilateral surrounding b. His profits are higher than in the absence of agreement, i.e. exceed the area of the dotted triangle. But he has a strong incentive to break the agreement and not restrict his production. If he expands his production to x_2 and others keep to the agreement he increases his profit by the area of the triangle consisting of parts c and d. Indeed, no matter whether others in the industry keep or break the agreement, e.g. supply $\overline{X}$, the individual supplier has an incentive to produce more than x_1 and thereby increase his profit. But if all producers act in this way, collective output will not be limited, all will fail to make gains, and the cartel will be ineffective. On the other hand if all suppliers feel morally obliged to honour the agreement (a result by no means assured) profits in the industry are raised and this may encourage new firms to enter the industry. Such entry (together with the increased use and development of substitutes such as coal and nuclear fuel instead of oil) will reduce the profitability of action by existing suppliers to limit production and is likely to lead to the breakdown of the cartel.

Thus an oil cartel such as OPEC is under constant threat of collapse. To the extent that it raises the market price of crude above its equilibrium level, individual members have an incentive to accept a slightly lower price, non-OPEC suppliers such as the United Kingdom expand supplies at the cartel price, and the search for new oil reserves and substitutes for oil increases in non-OPEC countries. While short-term gains may be made by the cartel, its profitability and viability may diminish with the passage of time.

Because an industry consisting of a large number of suppliers faces considerable difficulty, i.e. costs in enforcing cartel-type arrangements among its members and in restricting entry of new suppliers to its industry, it is likely to seek government regulation if it aims to restrict competition or modify market behaviour. It may, for instance, aim to raise or maintain incomes of suppliers already in the industry either by limiting the number of new entrants to the industry or by restricting the supplies of existing producers. The government may restrict entry, for example, by requiring all producers to be licensed, issuing licences to existing producers but not to new firms or only to new firms in special circumstances. Production of suppliers may be limited by specifying maximum quantities to be sold or by limiting the use of productive resources in the activity. For instance, in order to limit sugar production, the maximum area to be used by each grower for growing sugar beet or cane may be restricted or each poultry farmer's allowable number of hens may be restricted in order to limit egg production, as is done, for instance, in some Australian states. In the airline industry, national governments tend to restrict supply by licensing the routes available to international aircraft operators. In many cities, taxis have to be licensed and the number is restricted.

Stabilization of incomes and prices in an industry

Another purpose of governmental regulation of a competitive industry is sometimes to stabilize incomes or prices in the industry. In particular the prices of primary products tend to be very unstable, and governments sometimes intervene to stabilize these. In Australia, for instance, the government attempts to reduce fluctuations in the prices paid to farmers for wool and for wheat. One means of reducing price fluctuations is by the use of buffer stocks. During periods of low demand or those in which price would otherwise be lower than average the government or its agency buys the commodity whose price is to be stabilized and stockpiles it. It thereby pushes the market price of the commodity up. During periods of high demand or those in which price would otherwise be higher than average, the agency releases supplies to the market from its stockpile thereby keeping the price closer to its average level. It has recently been suggested that the United Nations should operate international buffer stock schemes in order to stabilize the prices of primary products being traded by less-developed countries. But as will be discussed later, such schemes may fail to stabilize incomes. They can also be a ploy or a 'cover-up' to increase the incomes of producers.

Pressure from participants on the competitive side of a market to regulate prices on its non-competitive side

Occasionally competitive sellers or buyers in a market are faced by buyers or sellers, respectively, with market power. Consequently, competitive market participants may seek government control of the prices paid by buyers or those charged by sellers having market power. If the competitive side of the market is successful in obtaining government regulation of prices, the distribution of income moves in their favour and the allocation of resources *may be* improved in the Kaldor–Hicks sense.

If there are many sellers selling to a single buyer (a monopsonist) his purchases are likely to influence the price of a traded commodity. By reducing his quantity of purchases, the monopsonist may lower the price of the commodity to his advantage. The government by setting a suitable minimum price for the commodity can ensure that sellers receive a higher price than otherwise and sell a greater quantity than otherwise. Similarly, if many buyers face a single seller (a monopolist) the government may be able to improve the economic position of buyers by setting an appropriate maximum price for sales of the product. In the United States, for instance, the government sets maximum prices for gas, electricity, and telephone services which are supplied by private monopolies.

Having pointed out some of the reasons why the state regulates competitive markets let us now consider some specific examples of regulation of competitive product, factor, and international markets. In doing so, we shall consider why there is regulation in specific cases and its effects, including possible undesirable side-effects.

4.3 PRICE REGULATION IN PRODUCT MARKETS: SOME EXAMPLES

The prices of some products are regulated by governments 'to improve' the distribution of income or to aid 'disadvantaged' groups. When this takes the form of a maximum allowable price less than the equilibrium one, demand exceeds supply at the price and shortages occur. Price is not allowed to carry out the function of allocating supplies to potential buyers and other methods of matching demand and supply are necessary or come into play, such as the issue of rationing cards or coupons by the government, the establishment of priorities for different types of buyers by the government, or the decisions about priorities may be left to sellers and they may, for instance, adopt a first-come-first-served philosophy and/or impose purchasing limits on their customers. Blackmarkets (illegal trading in the regulated commodity) at prices higher than the equilibrium one are also likely to spring up.

Maximum prices — rent control

While price controls for basic commodities were common during and for a number of years after the Second World War, they are now less common. Nevertheless, governments in many non-communist countries have placed controls in recent years on price and wage increases in an attempt to control the rate of inflation. Furthermore, particular prices such as housing rent in the United Kingdom and in some Australian states, and rates of interest to be charged by banks or finance companies continue to be regulated, as is the price of bread in some Australian states. In communist (socialist) countries prices of most commodities are regulated, and maximum prices are sometimes less than those necessary to ration out supplies exactly.

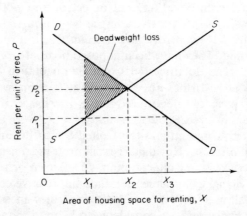

Figure 4.3   Excess demand results from decreeing a maximum price for a commodity less than its equilibrium price. Means other than price alone are then used to allocate supplies to buyers. In the above case, a rent ceiling of P_1 results in the demand for housing space for renting, exceeding the available supply by $X_3 - X_1$. The deadweight or Kaldor–Hicks loss of rent control is shown by the hatched triangle.

The example shown in Figure 4.3 illustrates the problem. Suppose that the decreed maximum rent (price) for housing space is less than the market equilibrium rent. In Figure 4.3 the market equilibrium rent is P_2, but suppose that a maximum rent of P_1 is decreed. The available space for renting falls from X_2 to X_1 and the quantity of space demanded for renting rises from X_2 to X_3. The gap between the quantity of space available at P_1 and that demanded (the excess demand) is $X_3 - X_1$. The problem, then, is how to allocate the quantity available to the individuals demanding it since price is not permitted to perform this function. As pointed out above ration coupons and ad hoc methods may be used for this purpose. In the latter case it is not certain that the 'disadvantaged' will be favoured. Furthermore, there are often legal ways to circumvent the spirit of the law. For instance, the practice is growing in Britain of letting houses with 'furnishings' and the rental of furnishings is adjusted upwards to allow for the shortfall on house rent which is regulated.

The purpose of setting a maximum price for a commodity may be to bring the commodity within reach or more easily within reach of families with lower incomes. But at the lower price they may find it more difficult to obtain supplies (because total supply falls, as did housing space for renting in the above example) and it can be argued that there are more effective means of dealing with poverty such as by cash payments. However, we cannot conclude that price controls with rationing by government are never a socially and politically acceptable solution. This depends on the relevant social welfare function. But all methods of rationing are not equally efficient in satisfying wants. Methods which do not allow trading of ration quotas or coupons by those initially allocated these are not efficient. This is clear, for example, from Figure 2.4 (an Edgeworth–Bowley box) where if individuals A and B are allocated coupons for an equal amount of petrol and potatoes but are not permitted to trade, this is inferior to trading as was discussed.

In some countries price controls have been imposed in recent years with an 'unusual' aim in mind. They have been imposed in an effort to stem *inflation*. In Australia, the Prices Justification Commission played a role in limiting price increases by large firms. For instance, such firms were not permitted automatically to pass on negotiated wage increases if these exceeded government guidelines. Freezes of prices and incomes were also attempted for a time in the United Kingdom and the United States during the 1970s in an attempt to control inflation. One danger from prolonged general price control is that the pattern of resource allocation may be frozen or restricted so that it does not adjust to changing consumer demands and relative costs of production.

Prices are not allowed to perform rationing roles in some special cases because the goods concerned are considered to be merit goods. The nature of these goods was discussed in Chapter 2 but essentially they are goods which the government believes merit greater consumption than would occur as a result of free choice. It may also be believed that the consumption of the goods yields favourable externalities.

Subsidized or free university education

University education provides an obvious example. In the United Kingdom and Australia, there are no fees for (national) students studying university courses and the costs of running universities are largely met by the government. Not only is university education publicly financed but it is publicly supplied.

In a short-run situation, the market for university education may be like that shown in Figure 4.4. The curve SS indicates the total available number of university places and DD indicates the demand for university places by those having reasonable prospects of success. If prices (fees) were used as an allocative mechanism, the equilibrium fee would be £500 per year and 0.5 million students would attend university. But suppose that fees are abolished. At old entrance standards, 1 million students wish to undertake studies at university but only 0.5 million places are available. Demand is excessive and some mechanism instead of price is needed to choose university entrants. Universities are likely to demand higher educational qualifications for entry and this is equivalent to pushing the demand curve (of the qualified) back to D_1D_1 and restoring short-term equilibrium. Individuals with lower qualifications but ability and willingness to pay who would have entered are now excluded.

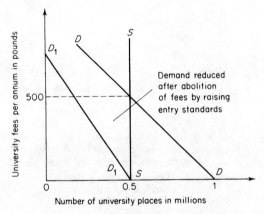

Figure 4.4   A case of price regulation — the abolition of university fees. In this case, the abolition of fees results in an excess demand for university places and criteria for entry such as a degree of academic excellence may need to be adjusted upwards so as to ration out available places.

Those with higher qualifications but unable to pay fees or with low willingness to do so may now enter. The scheme might be justified by the belief that it makes for greater equality of opportunity based upon ability. But it ought to be observed that the scheme has redistributional effects. For instance, university students are financed by the rest of the community and most university students may come from higher income families. An alternative means of providing opportunities is through scholarships or loans for educational purposes. In the long run, given the circumstance shown in Figure 4.4 and where DD is the demand curve of those with a reasonable chance of success, there is likely to be pressure on the government to provide more university places by expanding universities.

82

Subsidized or free health services

It is quite common for price not to be permitted to allocate health services. This may be because the electorate believes that health is a merit good and that there is a social obligation to assist the sick, that subsidized health services help to insure individuals against the risk of a major illness or accident, and that favourable externalities may be obtained from a healthier population. In the United Kingdom the National Health Service ensures that most health services are free. In Australia a system of compulsory health insurance operated in the past for some years.

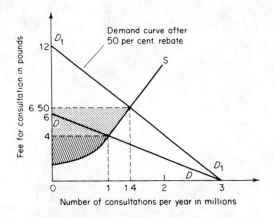

Figure 4.5 Effect of medical insurance on doctors' incomes and in increasing consultations. Medical insurance raises the demand for doctors' services and increases their income. In the above case, the increase in doctors' incomes after the introduction of medical insurance is shown by the dotted area and the annual number of consultations rises from 1 to 1.4 million.

Basically all were insured under the Australian scheme and a part of any health expense was refunded to the patient. The effect of such a scheme can be illustrated by Figure 4.5, where *DD* represents the demand for medical consultations and *SS* the supply of consultations in the absence of compulsory insurance. The equilibrium price per consultation is £4 and the equilibrium number of consultations is 1 million annually. The profit received by medical practitioners is indicated by the hatched area. Suppose that compulsory insurance is introduced and that a 50 per cent. rebate is paid to patients for each consultation. This means, for instance, that a patient who is charged £12 by the doctor for a consultation receives a rebate of £6 and so only pays £6 for the consultation. The equilibrium number of consultations rises to 1.4 million annually and the fee per consultation increases to £6.50. The profits received by doctors rise by the dotted area and doctors are among the beneficiaries of the scheme. In fact, it would be surprising if they did not support this type of regulation.

The effects of free health services as in the United Kingdom are analysed rather differently. Patients are not charged for consultations and thus payments to medical practitioners, for example, are divorced from charges to patients. Figure 4.6 can be used to illustrate this type of situation, where *DD* represents the demand for medical consultations in the absence of government interference and *SS* is the supply curve. The equilibrium number of consultations is 10 million annually and the equilibrium fee is £5 per visit. Suppose now that patients are not charged for consultations. The demand for medical consultations in these circumstances is then 20 million annually. The available supply will depend upon the amount which the government pays to doctors for consultations. If it pays doctors £8 per consultation the number of consultations offered equals the total demanded (20 million) and the profits of doctors rise by an amount equivalent to the dotted area. But if the government uses its bargaining strength to fix payments to doctors at less than £8 per consultation, supply falls short of demand. For example, if it sets its payment to doctors at £5 per consultation available consultations fall short of consultations demanded by 10 million annually. In this situation some method (other than price) is needed to determine the patients to be seen by doctors. For instance, time available for consultations by doctors may be rationed by patients queueing and waiting. In consequence some patients (those for whom time is valuable) may make private arrangements (outside the health scheme) with doctors to pay fees to ensure speedy attention.

While government payments to doctors under a national health scheme may be such as to raise their incomes, their incomes are not certain to rise. The government may use its bargaining power to reduce doctors' incomes and

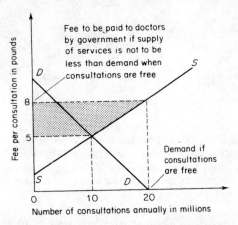

Figure 4.6 Illustration of a scheme of 'free' medical consultations. A scheme such as the National Health Service in the United Kingdom results in an increased demand for consultations. Unless the fee paid by the government to doctors for each consultation is appropriately increased (to £8 in the above case) demand for medical services exceeds their supply. In the absence of sufficient government recompense to doctors, queuing (which imposes a cost on those waiting) may be used to ration the limited supply of medical services.

84

consequently the available quantity and quality of medical services may fall. Further, such schemes may make for greater uniformity of incomes between doctors. The effects of subsidized or free hospital services and pharmaceuticals can be analysed in a similar way to the above, but in some cases allowance should be made for oligopoly or monopoly, for instance, in the supply of drugs.

Stabilization of income and prices—buffer stocks and stabilization funds for agricultural products

Governments sometimes interfere in markets in an attempt to stabilize incomes or prices. This is most frequently done for agricultural products. The United Nations as a part of its proposals for the *Second Development Decade* has been considering buffer stock schemes for stabilizing prices of primary products exported by developing countries.

There are a number of different means of stabilizing prices, but stabilization of prices need not stabilize the incomes of suppliers of products. Indeed, in some circumstances price stabilization destabilizes the incomes of suppliers.

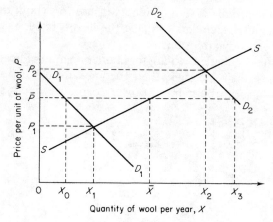

Figure 4.7   Illustration of the buffer stock method of stabilizing the price of a commodity. This example shows how the method can be used to stabilize the price of wool at $\bar{P}$ when the demand curve for wool fluctuates between D_1 and D_2. Buffer stock schemes have been used to help stabilize wool prices and the prices of some other primary products such as tin, and to stabilize foreign currency exchange rates.

Figure 4.7 can be used to illustrate the buffer stock method of stabilizing the price of a commodity. Assume, for example, that the commodity is wool (an intermediate product), that SS is its supply curve, and that the demand for wool is as indicated by D_1D_1 for half the time and D_2D_2 for the remainder of the time. In the absence of government intervention the equilibrium price of wool then fluctuates between P_1 and P_2 and the equilibrium quantity supplied varies between X_1 and X_2. Now suppose that the government intervenes and requires all wool to be sold to the government or its agents and sets the price for purchases and sales of wool at $\bar{P}$ per unit. During periods of low demand (i.e. when the demand curve is D_1D_1) government purchases of wool, $\bar{X}$, exceeds its sales X_0 and the government adds $\bar{X} - X_0$ to its stocks. During periods of high demand (i.e. when the demand curve is D_2D_2) sales of wool by the government, X_3, exceed its purchases $\bar{X}$ by $X_3 - \bar{X}$ and the government must draw on stocks to cover the deficit. In this example, quantities added to stocks during periods of low demand equal those drawn during periods of high demand and price is stabilized at the average of its otherwise fluctuating values. But if the average demand for the product alters unpredictably, a buffer stock scheme is likely to fail. In the case where the average level of demand for the product falls unpredictably, stocks purchased by the government under a buffer stock scheme rise excessively and in effect the scheme may subsidize overproduction in relation to the level of demand for the commodity.

The price received by a producer of a commodity may alternatively be stabilized by means of a *stabilization fund*. This may be achieved by the government purchasing all of the commodity as before at $\bar{P}$ and, if the previous circumstances apply, selling the supplies to purchasers at market clearing prices. In the example shown in Figure 4.8 this involves the sale of wool to buyers at P_3 in periods of high demand and at P_0 in periods of low demand. Consequently the government holds no stocks of wool. However, in periods of high demand the government's receipts from wool sales exceed its spending on purchases of wool by $(P_3 - \bar{P})\bar{X}$ whereas in periods of low demand its payments for wool exceed its receipts from the sale of wool by $(\bar{P} - P_0)\bar{X}$.

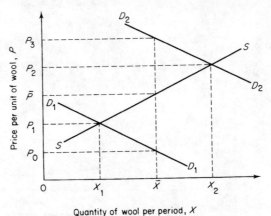

Quantity of wool per period, X

Figure 4.8   An illustration of the use of a stabilization fund to stabilize the price paid to suppliers of a commodity. This method has been used in New Zealand to help stabilize the price paid to wool growers for wool. In the above case the method stabilizes the price paid to growers at $\bar{P}$ but increases the range of fluctuation in price for buyers from $P_2 - P_1$ to $P_3 - P_0$. In contrast, the buffer stock method (Figure 4.7) stabilizes the price to both buyers and sellers but increases supply fluctuations.

86

Thus excess funds obtained in periods of high demand can be used to offset the deficit of funds in periods of low demand. In this case, excess receipts and excess payments exactly offset each other in different periods. Excess receipts obtained in periods of high demand are held in a stabilization fund and this fund is drawn on to meet deficient receipts in periods of low demand. No stocks are held by the government under this method of stabilization, but this method faces similar problems to buffer stock schemes as far as the prediction of long-term alteration in demand is concerned.

It is sometimes believed (erroneously) that the stabilization of a product's price will also stabilize the incomes of its producers. But a price stabilization scheme may fail to stabilize receipts or incomes of suppliers. This is illustrated by the example in Figure 4.9, where DD is the demand curve per period for the commodity under consideration. This curve forms a rectangular hyperbola (the demand curve is of unitary elasticity throughout) and consequently total revenue (price times quantity) is the same irrespective of the price of the product. Thus if the supply function fluctuates between S_1 and S_2 because of seasonal conditions, for example, total receipts (gross incomes) remain unaltered even though the price varies between P_1 and P_2. Suppose that S_1 occurs for half of the time and S_2 for the remainder and the government adopts either a buffer stock scheme or a stabilization fund method to stabilize the price paid to suppliers at a level of $\bar{P}$. The effect is to destabilize the receipts of suppliers. The receipts obtained by suppliers when supplies are low ($\bar{P}X_1$) are much lower than when supplies are bountiful ($\bar{P}X_2$). The effect of price stabilization in this case is to increase the variability of the incomes of suppliers.

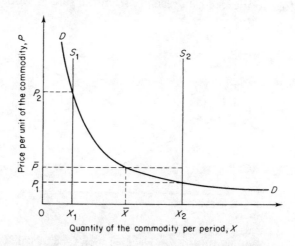

Figure 4.9   A case in which price stabilization destabilizes the income of suppliers. It is sometimes erroneously believed that farm incomes can be stabilized by stabilizing the prices of farm products. In this example, stabilization of the price of the commodity at $\bar{P}$ changes a perfectly stable income to a fluctuating one.

Common Market Agricultural Policy (CAP) and the support of farm incomes

Governments in industrialized countries frequently interfere in agricultural markets in an attempt to maintain or raise farm incomes. They may do so to 'improve' the distribution of income or to gain votes from the rural sector of the economy. But policies designed to maintain agricultural prices above their equilibrium levels are not identical in their effects. It is therefore interesting to compare British agricultural policy for maintaining farm incomes prior to its joining the EEC and its policy after joining and adopting the Common Agricultural Policy of the EEC. In both cases, policy is designed to maintain the price paid to the farmer, but in the pre-EEC situation this was financed by taxpayers whereas in the post-EEC situation this is financed to a considerable extent by consumers of agricultural products. Some effects of the alternative policies can be seen from the following *caricatures*.

Pre-EEC situation: Suppose, as illustrated in Figure 4.10, that the price of an agricultural product is to be maintained above equilibrium at a price level of P_2 but that supplies are to be sold at the market clearing price of P_1. The deficiency in receipts compared to payments to farmers, $(P_2 - P_1)X_2$, is met by the UK government from general taxes. For simplicity, assume that the agricultural product is entirely home-produced. This policy results in a dead-weight loss indicated by the hatched triangle in Figure 4.10 and redistributes income in favour of producers of the agricultural product in question. The hatched triangle (deadweight loss) indicates that even if farmers were to receive the same level of subsidized income, consumers could be made better off by a reduction in the production of the agricultural product X to $\bar{X}$. This is because the marginal value of commodities foregone (indicated by the supply curve of X which equals the marginal cost of production of X) exceeds the extra value of X to consumers (as indicated by the demand curve for X) when production is expanded beyond $\bar{X}$. The taxation effects of the policy on distribution are uncertain. But insofar as staple agricultural products are subsidized, the demand for which is relatively income-inelastic, the policy relatively redistributes real income in favour of those consumers on lower incomes, even if taxation is proportional to income. If taxation is progressive, this policy further favours those on lower incomes because they contribute proportionately less to farm subsidies through taxation than higher income-earners.

Post-EEC situation: In the post-EEC situation, agricultural products are sold to consumers at the supported price payable to farmers. Surplus production is stored and is sold, wherever an opportunity arises, at extremely low prices to buyers outside the EEC such as the USSR. Any deficiency in receipts compared to payments to farmers is met from taxation. The operation of the policy can be illustrated from Figure 4.11 which portrays the same market situation as in Figure 4.10 for the United Kingdom. At the support price P_2, X_1 of the agricultural product is sold to consumers and thus $X_2 - X_1$ has to be

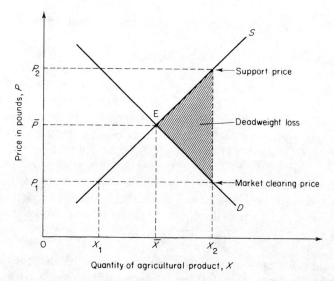

Figure 4.10   Illustration of the Kaldor–Hicks welfare (deadweight) loss associated with the United Kingdom's pre-EEC agricultural price policy. In this hypothetical case the loss is equivalent to the area of the hatched triangle. In this case the government's supported price to farmers is P_2, X_2 of the agricultural product is supplied, and this is cleared to consumers at a price P_1. The deficiency in receipts from consumers compared to payments to farmers is $(P_2 - P_1) X_2$ and is met from general taxation.

stored unless it is sold outside the EEC. For simplicity assume that the surplus can be sold to the USSR at a price of P_0 per unit. Thus a subsidy payment of $P_2 - P_0 (X_2 - X_1)$ to farmers must be met from taxation.

The transfer by taxation may be, but need not be, less than in the pre-EEC situation. Furthermore, in the post-EEC situation the deadweight loss of the policy is as indicated by the hatched area in Figure 4.11 which far exceeds that in the pre-EEC situation, i.e. the hatched triangle in Figure 4.10. While income is redistributed in favour of the agricultural producers of the commodity, as before, there is no real redistribution in favour of consumers of the agricultural product. Indeed, assuming that demand for the agricultural product is income inelastic, income is relatively redistributed away from those on lower incomes, because the prices of basic agricultural products to them are forced above their equilibrium levels. Thus it might be argued that the post-EEC situation for the United Kingdom involves greater inefficiency in the composition of production and, in the view of many, a worsened distribution of real income.

4.4   PRICE REGULATION IN FACTOR MARKETS: SOME EXAMPLES

Regulation of prices of the factors or production is not uncommon and the resources of labour and capital appear to be more often the subject of such

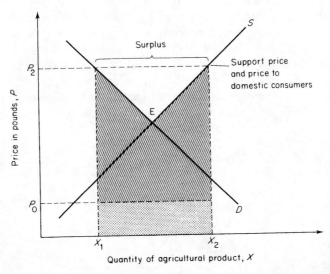

Figure 4.11 Hypothetical application of CAP (Common Agricultural Policy) to a UK agricultural product. The product price is still maintained at P_2 for farmers but supplies are not cleared. Consumers pay P_2 (the same price as that received by farmers) and stocks are stored to be sold outside the EEC as the opportunity arises. The deadweight loss of this policy is greater than prior to CAP and it has a very regressive impact on income distribution. In this example the post-EEC deadweight loss, as indicated by the hatched area, exceeds the pre-EEC loss, indicated by the hatched area in Figure 4.10.

regulation than land. However, this does not imply that there are no regulations affecting the market for land. In fact there are many regulations, for instance the zoning of the use of land in urban areas, affecting the price of land.

Minimum wage rates

Minimum wage rates are set by regulatory bodies in some countries. When the minimum wage rate for a particular type of labour *is less than* the equilibrium wage rate and perfect competition occurs, the price control has no effect on the level of employment of this type of labour and wages obtained. But if there is some ignorance among labourers, the regulation could reduce the likelihood of a labourer receiving a wage well below the equilibrium rate. In the example shown in Figure 4.12 a minimum wage rate of w_1 (since it is less than the equilibrium wage rate) does not affect the amount of employment of women.

But the minimum wage rate may be set by a wage-regulating authority at a level in excess of the equilibrium rate in an effort on income distributional grounds to assist those who would normally earn lower pay, or strong trade union may be able to negotiate an above-equilibrium award in the industry with the same aim in mind and the possible additional aim of increasing the

90

total wage bill. *If* there is monopsony, oligopsony, or collusion between hirers of labour this policy *can* be effective in achieving its objectives and in raising total employment of the group concerned. But if the hiring side of the labour market is competitive the policy has the adverse side-effect of reducing employment in the industry or among the group 'protected' by such wages. As for the total wage bill, this will fall if wage rates are at levels on the elastic (upper) portion of the demand curve for labour and will only go up if wages are in the region of the inelastic (lower) portion of the demand curve.

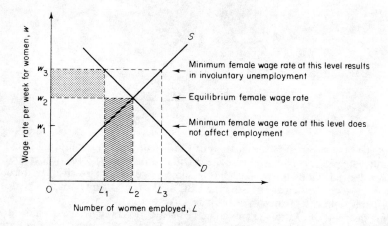

Figure 4.12   A minimum wage rate in excess of the equilibrium wage rate leads to involuntary unemployment if markets are competitive. In this case a minimum wage rate of w_3 for women results in the involuntary unemployment of $L_3 - L_1$ women and in fewer women (L_1) being employed than in the absence of intervention (L_2).

These effects can be illustrated by means of Figure 4.12 which considers the employment of women. The argument might apply where the rule of equal pay for women would result in a wage rate for women above the equilibrium rate for the employment of women. In the example shown in Figure 4.12 the fixing of a minimum weekly wage rate for women of w_3 (i.e. a wage rate in excess of the equilibrium level) leads to a fall in the employment of women in comparison to the unregulated position. This fall is equal to $L_2 - L_1$. If employment is an important consideration, the regulation may be regarded as injurious to the interests of women. Also at the minimum wage rate of w_3 involuntary unemployment occurs among women in the sense that more women wish to work, L_3, than can find employment, L_1. At a wage rate of w_3 the difference between the number of women seeking work and those able to find work is $L_3 - L_1$. Furthermore, in this case the regulation reduces the total wage bill paid to women because the loss shown by the hatched area exceeds the gain as shown by the flecked area, since wage rates are on an elastic part of the demand curve for the employment of women (see also Chapter 10, Figure 10.3).

Regulated rates of interest, dividends, and profits

The rate of interest on loans are often controlled by governments. In many countries the government specifies a lower than normal maximum rate of interest for loans for particular purposes. In some countries loans for the purchase of new or first homes are at a maximum rate below the normal and loans for rural investment are available at reduced rates. Interference of this type may stem from income redistribution considerations (e.g. the desire to assist families to purchase a first home) and from political considerations such as the desire to win votes in rural seats. The effect of such regulations is likely to reduce the supply of funds for the purposes in question and make it necessary to ration the available supply by some means other than price.

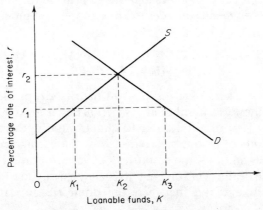

Figure 4.13 Controls on the maximum rate of interest lead to a shortage of available funds if the maximum rate is less than the equilibrium one. In this case, a ceiling on the rate of interest of r_1 results in an excess demand for funds of $K_3 - K_1$ and in less loanable funds being supplied than in a free market.

This is illustrated in Figure 4.13. Given the supply and demand curves indicated there, the equilibrium rate of interest is r_2 and the equilibrium quantity of loanable funds supplied and demanded is K_2. Suppose that the maximum rate of interest on funds is set at r_1, i.e. at a level below the equilibrium rate. The effect is to reduce the available quantity of loanable funds to K_1 and increase the demand for funds to K_3. Consequently, the demand for funds exceeds the supply of funds by $K_3 - K_1$. Thus, for instance, first-time house buyers whom it is intended to assist by such policies may find that less funds are available to them and there is keener competition for available funds. Some means other than the rate of interest must be used to distribute the relatively limited funds. In these circumstances, the government may provide lending institutions with guidelines or priorities to be followed in their lending. For instance, borrowers may be expected to find a higher proportion of a house's price from their own savings, loans may not be available on established houses, etc. Consequently, funds will not be allocated in the most efficient manner if this is determined by willingness to pay, and income distribution effects can be the opposite to those intended. The wealthier members of the community (especially if collateral and deposits are a consideration) may be favoured in the queue for funds.

In a competitive world, controls on the maximum level of dividends payable can reduce the amount of funds supplied by investors to companies and reduce capital formation, but the position is complex. If high dividends are a consequence of unappropriated rents (low royalties being paid to the government, for example, for the use of minerals), controls on dividends up to a point may not reduce the available supply of risk capital. The complexity of the situation is clear from the fact that less-developed countries tend to treat foreign direct investment in different ways. Some limit the remission of profits and dividends to parent companies and others provide for tax concessions and in effect subsidize dividends in order to attract foreign capital.

4.5   PRICE REGULATION IN INTERNATIONAL MARKETS: SOME EXAMPLES

International markets for goods, for factors of production, and for currencies are subject to a number of restrictions. In many countries, imported goods are subject to tariffs (taxes) or to quotas limiting their quantity. International movements of labour are restricted by the immigration requirements of many countries and in some countries outward migration is limited. Most countries regulate dealings in foreign currencies, usually in order to maintain a more stable exchange rate between the domestic currency and foreign currencies.

Fixed exchange rates

Consider the regulation of foreign exchange markets using Figure 4.14 for illustrative purposes. This figure shows the exchange market for pounds sterling and a foreign currency, say US dollars, where *DD* indicates the demand for dollars by those wishing to exchange pounds sterling for dollars and *SS* indicates the supply of dollars by those wishing to obtain pounds sterling in return for dollars. The demand for US dollars reflects the foreign demand for US exports (these have to be paid for in dollars) and the demands of foreigners wishing to invest in the United States. The supply of US dollars depends upon the demand of Americans for imports and their desire to invest abroad. The equilibrium rate of exchange in this case is 50p to the dollar. At this rate of exchange the balance of payments of the United Kingdom and the United States is in equilibrium. But suppose that the UK government controls the exchange of pounds sterling for dollars and fixes an exchange rate of 40p to the dollar. (One of the reasons for regulating or fixing the exchange rate may be to reduce the uncertainty of firms and individuals engaging in international

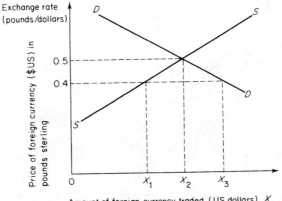

Figure 4.14 A foreign exchange market in which equilibrium occurs when the US dollar costs 50p. Suppose, however, that the Bank of England fixes the exchange rate at 40p to the dollar. The pound is then overvalued in relation to the dollar and the demand for dollars for foreign exchange purposes exceeds their supply by X_3 - X_1. Some mechanism (such as priorities for different purposes for which foreign exchange is required) is needed to ration out the reduced supply of dollars.

trade. For instance, if a UK exporter is to be paid by a US importer at an agreed dollar price on delivery of the exports, the UK exporter runs the risk if the exchange rate is floating that the value of the pound will appreciate so that he receives a lower payment after converting his dollar receipts in pounds than originally expected.) At this exchange rate of 40p to the dollar, the demand for dollars exceeds their supply by X_3 - X_1. The limited supply of dollars (to be exchanged for sterling) may be rationed and a blackmarket may arise in the exchange of dollars. In some less-developed countries the regulation of exchange rates is accompanied by rationing of available foreign currencies, foreign exchange blackmarkets, and illegal entry of foreign currency.

Countries which attempt to maintain a fixed exchange rate or a relatively fixed exchange rate frequently make use of a buffer stock type of approach to maintain exchange price stability. This approach can be illustrated by the example given in Figure 4.15. Suppose that fluctuations in the exchange rate between pounds sterling and US dollars are due to variations in the demand for dollars and for half of the time the demand is as indicated by D_1D_1 and for the remainder of the time as indicated by D_2D_2. In the absence of regulation the exchange rate fluctuates between P_1 and P_3. Suppose now that the UK government sets the exchange rate at P_2 and the central bank (the Bank of England) or its agents are in charge of all foreign currency transactions involving sterling. The central bank adds X_2 - X_0 dollars to its reserves when demand is D_1D_1 and draws an equal amount from reserves, X_4 - X_2, when demand is high. It is therefore possible for the central bank to use its reserves, provided that low and high levels of demand occur in suitable sequence, to

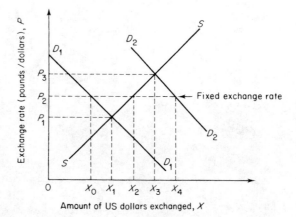

Figure 4.15 Stabilization of the exchange rate by the use of (buffer stock) reserves of foreign currency. In this case a buffer stock system enables the exchange rate to be stabilized at the fixed exchange rate of P_2. In the absence of intervention the exchange rate fluctuates between P_1 and P_3.

stabilize the exchange rate. But there is no guarantee that the sequence of demand variations will be satisfactory in practice. Furthermore, levels of demand and supply curves may alter unpredictably and make stabilization difficult to achieve because reserves are insufficient to maintain the rate at which the exchange rate is pegged. This can lead to periodic crises of confidence and speculation about the exchange rate, thus creating considerable uncertainty if a change in the pegged rate of exchange appears imminent. It has been suggested that this type of uncertainty might be more damaging to trade than that which occurs when exchange rates are flexible because then exchange rates may be continually adjusted by small amounts.

Most governments operated fixed or pegged exchange rates from 1944 to the early 1970s under the Bretton Woods system. But now managed flexible exchange rates are the rule for most countries. Exchange rates are managed only to the extent that central banks intervene to smooth out what appear to be very short-term gyrations in the rates of exchange. Otherwise rates are free to find their own level as a result of the operation of market forces.

Tariffs and quotas on imports

Consider now the effects of restrictions on imports of goods by means of tariffs or quotas. These may be imposed by the government in an attempt to maintain domestic employment, to improve the profitability of the operations of domestic producers, and to raise revenue for the government's use. Take yarn as an example and suppose that the domestic demand for yarn is as indicated by $D_H D_H$ in Figure 4.16 and that the domestic supply is as indicated by $S_H S_H$. In the absence of international trade, the domestic price of yarn and the equilibrium quantity traded correspond to E_3, assuming that the market for yarn is perfectly competitive. But suppose that yarn can be imported at a price of P_1 per unit and that the supply from abroad is perfectly elastic as indicated by S_F. Under free-trade conditions the price of yarn in the domestic economy falls to P_1, X_1 of yarn is produced at home, and $X_4 - X_1$ is imported. Suppose now that the domestic government imposes a tariff of $P_2 - P_1$ upon each unit of yarn imported in order to protect local yarn producers and increase employment in yarn production. This tariff alters the equilibrium trading conditions in the domestic market from E_1 to E_2. Imports of yarn fall from $X_4 - X_1$ to $X_3 - X_2$, domestic production rises by $X_2 - X_1$, and employment in yarn production increases. The profits of firms producing yarn in the domestic economy rise by the equivalent of the hatched area in Figure 4.16 and the government raises $(P_2 - P_1)(X_3 - X_2)$ in revenue from the tariff. Consumers are worse off as a result of the tariff. The price of yarn is raised and the consumption of yarn falls. But domestic producers of yarn (capital and labour) benefit because protection from imports results in greater profits, employment, and possibly wages for them. Domestic firms producing yarn

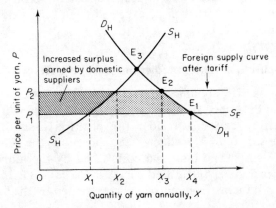

Figure 4.16 An example of the effect of a tariff on imports, assuming perfect competition in the domestic industry. The tariff raises the price of yarn in the domestic market, expands local production, reduces imports, and increases the surplus earned by domestic suppliers. In contrast, as discussed below, domestic production may fall when a tariff or import quota is imposed if the domestic industry is *imperfectly* competitive. In the above case, imports fall after imposition of the tariff by $(X_2 - X_1) + (X_4 - X_3)$, local production rises by $X_2 - X_1$, and the surplus of domestic suppliers rises by the hatched area. But if this gain in producers surplus is offset against the loss in consumers surplus, the net social loss (in the Kaldor–Hicks sense) from the imposition of the tariff amounts to the flecked area.

may therefore lobby for protection. They are likely to be supported by yarn labour unions in this lobbying since the tariff results in greater employment of yarn workers and could raise the wage obtained by them. Interested parties, however, will need to weigh the costs of lobbying against its expected benefits to them.

Nevertheless, it should be noted that the loss in consumers surplus as a result of imposition of the tariff (equal to the hatched plus the flecked area in Figure 4.16) exceeds the gain in the surplus of domestic producers (the hatched area) by the flecked area. This means that consumers could more than bribe producers not to press for the tariff and be better off without it. But such bribes cannot be organized because there are large numbers of consumers and each one has an incentive to free-ride. Indeed, most consumers may fail to perceive that the tariff exists and that they are damaged by it. Each consumer might lose only a small amount of consumers surplus (for example £1 annually) so it may not pay an individual (given that search is not costless) to search for the determinants of the price of yarn even though, if there are 50 million consumers, the total loss in consumers surplus is £50 million annually.

The above are the usual effects of a tariff in competitive markets. In markets in which competition is *imperfect* a tariff can lead to a reduction in local production and employment rather than a rise as in the competitive case because producers take advantage of their enhanced monopoly position to restrict supplies. Nevertheless, in this case, as the result of the imposition of a tariff, the profits and prices of local producers of the protected product are still likely to rise and imports can be expected to fall if foreign supply is not perfectly inelastic.

Imperfect competition modifies predictions about the effects of tariffs

Let us be more specific about the type of modifications that must be made to predictions about the effects of tariffs when imperfect competition rather than perfect competition exists. Consider the position assuming a *domestic* monopoly in the supply of a product X. Suppose that the demand, marginal revenue, average costs, and marginal costs faced by the monopolists are as shown by the appropriately identified curves in Figure 4.17. In this figure the supply curve of product X from abroad is represented by the horizontal curve marked S_F.

The domestic monopolist clearly needs a minimum tariff on imports of X of $T_1 = P_1 - P_F$ if he is to survive. At this level of tariff the price of X is P_1 and the monopolist supplies X_1 to the domestic market and $X_3 - X_1$ is imported because the demand curve faced by the monopolist after the tariff is P_1BD. If a higher tariff is granted but is still less than $T_2 = P_2 - P_F$ (where P_2 corresponds to the intersection point of the monopolists marginal cost of production curve and the domestic demand curve for X), the monopolist's output and employment rises. But if a still higher tariff is imposed, the monopolist takes advantage of his protection from imports to raise his profit by reducing his output and employment and increasing the scarcity of his product. He finds that this policy increases his profit and thus, in this region, a higher rate of tariff reduces output and employment in producing X. This pattern holds until the tariff becomes high enough to enable the monopolist to charge the maximum monopoly price P_M without fear of competition from imports.

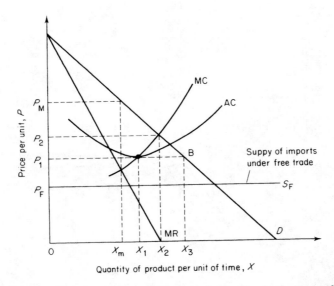

Figure 4.17 A diagram to illustrate the impact on the behaviour of a domestic monopolist of tariffs on the import of competitive products. Depending upon the circumstances discussed above the tariff can lead either to an increase or a decrease in the monopolist's level of output whereas under perfect competition an increase in the tariff on a product can normally be expected to result in an increase in its domestic production.

Should the tariff exceed this level, $T_M = P_M - P_F$, the monopolist will not decrease his output and employment further but leaves these unchanged.

The relationship between output and employment, the level of imports, and the profits earned by the domestic monopolist are indicated in Figure 4.18. This shows that both the domestic monopolist and the workers (or their union) in industry X have a common interest (as in the perfectly competitive case) in raising the tariff to level T_2, but (unlike the perfectly competitive case) a higher rate of tariff (one between T_2 and T_M) is damaging to the interest of workers in X in terms of their level of employment and possibly level of wages, even though it improves the level of profit earned by the monopolist. Workers in a particular industry do not always benefit from protection of that industry by a tariff and employment can sometimes be increased by lowering tariffs.

Import quotas

An import quota can be used to achieve a similar effect to a tariff. In the competitive example shown in Figure 4.16 a quota limiting the annual import of yarn to $X_3 - X_2$ units would result in the equilibrium trading conditions being achieved which correspond to E_2. The supply curve of yarn for the domestic economy after the imposition of the quota is equal to S_H plus the import quota at prices equal to or above P_1. At prices below P_1 no yarn is

98

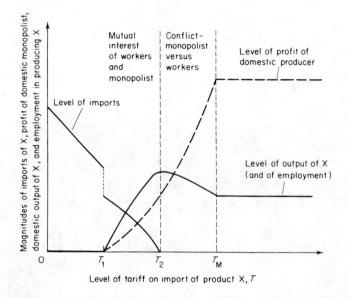

Figure 4.18 Relationship between various magnitudes and the level of a tariff on a product, assuming that domestic supply of the product is in the hands of a monopoly. Specifically, assuming the monopoly-type situation shown in Figure 4.17, general relationships for the following are shown as a function of the level of tariff imposed on the imports of X: the level of imports of X, the profit of the domestic monopolist, the quantity of output of X produced by the monopolist, and the level of employment in the production of X.

imported and the supply curve from domestic production alone applies. In contrast to a tariff, however, import quotas yield no revenue to the government unless they are auctioned to importers. In the absence of auctioning some method of rationing quotas among importers is needed. Those lucky enough to obtain a quota obtain a windfall gain. Together importers benefit in the above example by increased profit of $(P_2 - P_1)$ $(X_3 - X_2)$ if quotas are not auctioned. Income is therefore not only redistributed in favour of domestic producers of yarn but also in favour of merchants importing yarn.

4.6 CONCLUDING COMMENTS

Regulation of competitive markets (product, factor, and international markets) is widespread. Competitive markets are regulated for a variety of reasons and by diverse means. But policy-makers do not always obtain the results that they aim for through regulation and their policies can give rise to undesirable (and in some cases unforeseen) side-effects, such as those pointed out in this chapter. The chapter also underlines the point that it is necessary to pay considerable attention to political self-interest as a factor influencing the extent and type of regulation of competitive industry.

READING AND REFERENCES

Gwartney, J. D. (1977). *Microeconomics*, Chap. 3, Academic Press, London.
Hartley, K. (1977). *Problems of Economic Policy*, Chap. 8, Allen and Unwin, London.
Lipsey, R. G. (1979). *An Introduction to Positive Economics*, Chap. 10, Weidenfeld and Nicholson, London.
Mansfield, E. (1979). *Microeconomics*, Chap. 2, Norton, London.
Tisdell, C. A. (1974). *Economics of Markets*, Chaps 3 and 4, Wiley, Sydney.
Turvey, R. (1971). *Demand and Supply*, Allen and Unwin, London.

QUESTIONS FOR REVIEW AND DISCUSSION

1. Outline two broad approaches to defining the state of competition in an industry. Distinguish between monopoly and perfect competition in terms of stock characteristics.
2. 'It seems surprising that there should be so much state regulation of competitive markets considering that perfectly competitive markets allocate resources efficiently.' Discuss and give general reasons why the state has intervened in competitive markets and general ways in which it has intervened.
3. 'It has been reported that some members of OPEC (e.g. Libya) have recently exceeded their production quotas and the price of oil has only been maintained by Saudi Arabia (the largest producer) lowering its supplies. But Saudi Arabia will not continue to accommodate renegade members of the cartel in this way and is expected to raise its supplies.' Illustrate the type of difficulties which such a cartel faces both from members of the cartel and from external sources.
4. Rent controls can result in a deadweight social loss and may not help those they are intended to help. Explain and discuss.
5. Discuss the case for and against 'free' (no fees) university education and health services. Using supply and demand analysis and assuming that the government finances university education and health services, show how demand for these services could well exceed their supply and consider the difficulties that then arise in allocating the limited supply between consumers.
6. Outline two methods for stabilizing the price paid to suppliers of a commodity. Do these methods have different implications for the stability of prices and supplies to consumers? Can there be a conflict between price and income stabilization?
7. In comparison to pre-EEC agricultural price policies, the United Kingdom is suffering a greater welfare (Kaldor–Hicks) loss from post-EEC agricultural price policies. Explain and discuss.
8. 'Minimum wage rates and ceilings on the rate of interest may fail to assist those they are intended to help.' Illustrate but also consider cases in which these policies might assist, for instance where information is imperfect or monopsony exists.
9. 'A fixed international exchange rate may be maintained by a type of buffer stock scheme.' Explain and indicate circumstances in which the scheme will fail.
10. Consider the effects on domestic supplies, profits, imports, and prices of a commodity of the imposition of a tariff on imports, assuming that the domestic industry is perfectly competitive in structure. Show that a Kaldor–Hicks loss occurs. What effect may the tariff have on other industries? Repeat this increase for an import quota. Does a quota differ in its effects from a tariff?

11. 'When a domestic industry is imperfectly competitive some of the general economic effects of a tariff (or of an import quota) are the same as under perfectly competitive conditions but other general effects differ.' Explain.

CHAPTER 5

Consumers and Policy

5.1 INTRODUCTION AND OVERVIEW

Consumer demand plays an important normative and positive role in policy-making. As pointed out in Chapters 2 and 3, it is important in determining the welfare gains from economic activity (e.g. for a Paretian optimum there should be an optimal conformance between what consumers want and the composition of production) and, indeed, economists since Adam Smith have tended to stress the point that consumption is the end-purpose of all production. Economic systems are often judged by how well they meet the demands of consumers.

But demand relationships are important *positive* components of many policy decisions. If a tax or import tariff, for instance, is to be imposed on a particular commodity the government will need to know the demand function for that commodity (and the supply function) if it wishes to predict the effect of the tax on the quantity consumed of the commodity and aims to estimate its tax revenue. A large firm which hopes to influence the sales of its products needs to be familiar with the factors determining this demand. A government which engages in 'international resource diplomacy' or adopts policies for the conservation of resources needs to take account of demand relationships.

Both positive and normative aspects of demand theory are considered in this chapter. The main positive areas covered are the testing and predictive accuracy of demand theories and elasticities of demand with policy applications. The normative parts of the chapter deal with consumer welfare and sovereignty in terms of traditional and new theories and with market failure, for instance, as a result of imperfect information on the part of the consumer and the need or otherwise for consumer protection.

5.2 PREDICTIVE ACCURACY AND TESTING
OF DEMAND THEORY

Traditionally economic theory has stressed the influence of prices and incomes on the demand for commodities. In so doing, economists have not denied that other influences such as social interdependence, tastes, advertising, and ignorance can be of importance but have felt the study of these other forces might more appropriately be undertaken by other academic disciplines such as psychology and sociology. But carried to extremes, such rigid demarcations are of limited value when policies are being formulated.

Development of demand theory

The introduction of the concept of demand curves, implanted in the mainstream of economic thought by Marshall (1890) in the nineteenth century, helped to specify the relationship between the quantity demanded of a commodity and its price with considerable accuracy and improved the predictive potential of economic theory. One main principle emerged: the quantity demanded of a commodity usually increases as its price is lowered, other things held constant. In other words, the demand curve for a commodity is normally downward sloping when expressed as a function of the price of the commodity. Marshall assumed that *consumers maximize their utility* in purchasing commodities with their limited incomes and argued that consumers obtain *diminishing marginal utility* if they increase their consumption of any commodity, and it is basically diminishing marginal utility which is the prime cause of downward sloping demand curves. In the twentieth century Hicks, using indifference curve analysis, increased the precision of this theory, following in the wake of advances by a number of theoreticians. The use of indifference curves strengthened the basic theory since they made it unnecessary to assume cardinal (measurable) utility as in the Marshallian case. The Hicksian theory of demand still concentrates on the influence of price on the quantity demanded of a commodity but the effect of a price change is divided into two parts: an income effect and a substitution effect.

The income effect, which was ignored in Marshall's analysis, occurs because a fall in the price of a commodity increases the real income of the consumer and the substitution effect arises because a fall in the price of a commodity reduces its price relative to the price of other commodities. The substitution effect always increases (other than in exceptional circumstances when it is zero) the quantity demanded of a commodity whose price has fallen, all other things constant. This effect always tends to make for a downward sloping demand curve. The income effect may reinforce the substitution effect so ensuring a downward sloping demand curve. It does so (and this is considered to be the *normal* case) if the consumption of the commodity rises with income, other factors constant. On the other hand, if the consumption of the commodity falls with increased income (if the commodity is *inferior*), the income effect operates against the substitution effect (the income effect tends to reduce the quantity demanded of the commodity subject to the decrease in price), but *only in exceptional cases* is it likely to more than counteract the substitution effect and result in a demand curve which is upward sloping over at least a part of its range. When this exceptional case occurs the good is said to be a Giffen good. Possibly potatoes and sausages are two such goods (Hicks, 1946; Lipsey, 1979; Tisdell, 1972).

Indifference curves, substitution, and income effects: a policy application

Consider a possible application of Hicks' theory to population policy. A government wishes to stimulate population growth and to do so intends to pay parents a subsidy which rises with the number of their children. Will this subsidy lead to families of greater size? This can be analysed using Figure 5.1. The indifference curves in Figure 5.1 (indicated in the usual way) represent the preferences of a couple for income for themselves and for numbers of children.

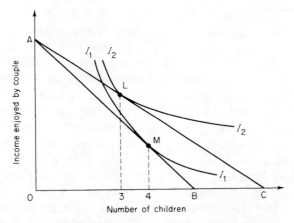

Figure 5.1   The payment of a bonus to parents rising with the number of their children may reduce rather than increase the size of families. In this case the negative income effect of the subsidy more than offsets the substitution effect.

But children are not costless. For simplicity assume that the price line or trade-off between the income enjoyed by the couple and the number of their children is linear. Let us suppose that given their income possibilities it is AB. Then the optimal number of children for this couple is 4 and they achieve equilibrium at position M.

Now consider the effect of a government subsidy on the number of children which swings the price line around to AC. The couple reach a new equilibrium at position L and their optimal number of children falls to 3. The subsidy therefore reduces population growth, if this couple is typical, rather than increases it as hoped. Children are 'inferior goods', fewer are wanted as income rises, and the income effect more than counteracts the substitution effect.

On the other hand, the income effect of the subsidy may reinforce the substitution effect. Independent evidence might indicate that in the country concerned the number of children in families tends to rise with the income of households. If this is so, Hicks's theory predicts that the subsidy will be effective in raising the size of the family. In this case the income effect and the substitution effect operate in the same direction and reinforce one another.

If evidence suggests that family size falls with income, further information will be needed to predict the effect of the family allowance or subsidy. Only if the negative income effect is large enough, relative to the substitution effect, will family size fall rather than increase after the introduction of a subsidy based on the number of children. Hicks' approach pinpoints the information needed for greater accuracy in prediction, i.e. the required evidence on the magnitudes of the income effect and the substitution effect.

Limitations of Hicksian theory, social effects on demand, imperfect knowledge

But even Hicks' advanced theory does not account for a number of influences on demand which need to be taken into account for predictive purposes in different circumstances. Social influences such as the bandwagon effect, snob effect, and Veblen effect are not taken into account. When the bandwagon effect applies to a commodity, the quantity of the commodity purchased by each consumer rises, other things equal, as more of it is purchased by others. The opposite is the case for the snob effect. The possibility also cannot be ignored that the price paid for a commodity is sometimes of social significance. The price paid may act as a signal to others, for instance the price paid for perfume. When the apparent price paid impresses others and the purchaser deems this consequence to be important the Veblen effect is said to operate, and this effect may cause a demand curve to slope upwards over a range. In some circumstances, as pointed out by Gabor (1977), consumers take the price of a product as an indicator of its quality, i.e. in a world of imperfect information consumers use price as a signal of higher quality.

Lancaster — characteristics and demand

Lancaster believes that traditional demand theory by concentrating on the demand for commodities per se has less predictive ability than can be achieved by considering the demand for commodities in terms of the characteristics inherent in them. He has developed a theory based upon the demand for characteristics or attributes in commodities. While his theory is not without limitations (the availability of a characteristic is assumed to be *proportional* to the quantity of a product and relevant characteristics can be difficult to identify) it can be used to predict the likely demand for new products combining known characteristics. For instance, an attempt has been made to use it to predict the demand for characteristics in new cars such as fuel economy, roominess, and power, and thus the overall demand for cars containing these characteristics in different degrees.

Price only one of the factors influencing demand

In all the above-mentioned theories the price of a commodity is considered to be an important determinant of the demand for it. Is its significance over-stressed? Are economists ignoring other variables of predictive importance? Some available evidence suggests that this is so, especially as far as new products are concerned. J. Udell (1964), for instance, found in a survey of 200 American firms that a half did not consider pricing as one of the five most important decision variables influencing their marketing success. For individual firms, factors such as advertising and promotion, presentation of product, novelty of product, location of outlets, and reputation of the firm may be more important determinants of demand than the price of its product.

A firm may be restricted by the nature of market competition in the amount of profitable use it can make of price to influence the demand for its product. In particular, in oligopolistic markets (markets having few sellers) firms may be restricted to charging the established or conventional price for a product because any lower price is matched or more than matched by competitors. This assumption underlies the 'kinked' demand approach to analysing oligopolistic markets (see Chapter 9). Such firms may concentrate on other avenues for competition such as advertising and product differentiation.

The range of variables which can influence the demand for a product are wide and depend upon the time-period for which demand is to be estimated and on the product involved. One or more of these variables, other than price, may need to be incorporated specifically in the demand model. Variables such as the size of the population and its ethnic and age composition, the level and distribution of income in the community, available leisure time, the available range of commodities and their prices, the degree of unemployment and inflation, expectations about prices, new products, and supplies, and replacement patterns of durable goods may need to be taken into account. Developments in the technology of consumption can, for instance, greatly alter a wide range of demands for products as has the introduction of the motor car. No simple mechanical demand model ('off the hook') is adequate for predicting demand for all commodities. Models have to be modified or constructed to meet the situation in hand. Failure to do this may result in misleading predictions with dire policy consequences. Nevertheless standard demand models do introduce important variables and illustrate pitfalls in estimating and predicting demand which occur in other models. Consider these pitfalls.

Estimation of demand curves — time-series method

Demand curves may be estimated by using data from time-series, cross-sectional data, or information obtained from experience or interviews. Consider the case where the demand for a product is believed to depend principally on its price. Suppose that a series of past market prices and quantities sold of the product are available. In special circumstances, this series identifies a demand curve for the product, or in other circumstances, identifies a supply curve for the product or may identify neither a supply nor a demand curve. A demand curve for the product is identified when:

106

(1) the only price subject to variation is the price of the product,
(2) other determinants of demand are constant,
(3) the supply curve alone is subject to variation, and
(4) the observed prices and quantities traded of the product are equilibrium prices.

For instance, suppose that the following prices and quantities of sale of the product are observed for the years indicated:

Year	Price in pounds	Quantity sold in millions
1980	1	4
1981	3	2
1982	2	3
1983	4	1

and the conditions just mentioned apply. This identifies the demand curve marked *DD* in Figure 5.2 and the observed price and quantities are located at the intersection points of the demand curve and the (hypothetical) supply curves, appropriately labelled and represented by the broken lines in Figure 5.2.

But price and traded quantity observations for a period may fail to identify a demand curve. If the conditions mentioned above apply and the demand curve for the product is subject to variation and the supply curve is stationary, price–quantity observations identify the supply curve for the product. The

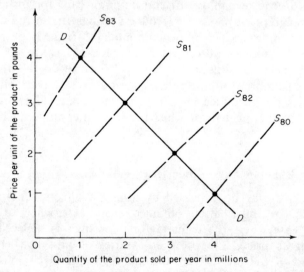

Figure 5.2 The observed prices and quantities sold during a four-year period, shown by the solid dots, identify a demand curve in this case. The supply curve is shifting and the demand curve is stationary.

reader may wish to illustrate this in the same way as was done for a demand curve in Figure 5.2, remembering that the observations (as a rule in this case) fall along a positively sloped curve. On the other hand, if the price and quantity observations are disequilibrium ones, or if both the supply curve and demand curve for the product are subject to shifts, the observations may identify neither a demand curve nor a supply curve for the product. The latter case is illustrated in Figure 5.3. The same price–quantity observations apply in Figure 5.3 as in Figure 5.2, but the supply and the demand curves for the product, as appropriately labelled, shift in each of the years in which observations are made. The line LL linking the price–quantity observations in this case does not identify a supply nor a demand curve.

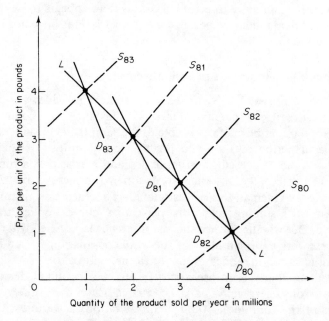

Figure 5.3   The observed prices and quantities sold during a four-year period, shown by the solid dots, fail to identify either a demand or a supply curve in this case. Both the supply curve and the demand curve are shifting.

The identification problem is not limited to demand models stressing price as a determinant of demand. It can also, for instance, arise in models emphasizing advertising expenditure as an important determinant of demand. For instance, if a company's supply of funds for advertising is a fixed proportion of its sales receipts, the time-series of the value of its past sales and its levels of advertising expenditure may identify this supply curve, rather than consumers' expenditure on the company's product as a function of the company's level of advertising expenditure.

Other methods for estimating demand — cross-sectional data

Cross-sectional data provides another possible means for estimating demand curves. If there are regional variations in the price of the product, purchases per head in the different regions may be used as data to estimate demand for the product as a function of its price. However, systematic differences between regions can make the results misleading. For instance, suppose that the data *indicates* that the demand per head for a product is $p = 10 - 0.2x$ where p represents its price and x indicates the quantity demanded. If the lowest prices for the product occur in regions where individuals also have the lowest income, the cross-sectional data will reflect the influence of both income and prices on demand. The actual demand curve might be more responsive to price variations than appears to be the case from the estimated demand curve because income variations have not been allowed for in the estimates.

Experimentation and surveys to estimate demand

Experimentation with a sample of consumers provides another possible means of estimating a demand curve. For instance, the commodity under consideration might be made available to the sample of consumers at different prices over a period of time and the varying quantities of their purchases recorded and the data used to estimate demand per head as a function of the price of the commodity. In other words a new product can be trial-marketed and a per-capita demand curve estimated. The further step might then be considered of assuming that this per-capita curve applies to the whole population. But whether or not the last inference is justified will depend upon how representative the sample is of the whole population and on how well the experimental situation replicates that of the actual world.

Another possibility is to use a survey method to obtain demand data. A sample of consumers may be asked to indicate their likely quantity of purchases of the commodity (under consideration) at various prices and the data used to estimate the market demand curve. This method runs foul of the same difficulties as the last method and in addition there is the problem of whether respondents are reliable and truthful. The situations posed are hypothetical and therefore anticipated reactions by respondents could be unreliable. Furthermore, respondents may deliberately understate their demand at high prices in order to induce price-setters to charge lower prices. Bias in responses is a problem.

Alternative models of demand — replacement and product cycle models

Many other models for predicting demand exist. These include replacement models and product cycle models. Replacement models are relevant for durable consumer goods such as cars and refrigerators and take the expected economic life of such products into account. Product cycle models are based

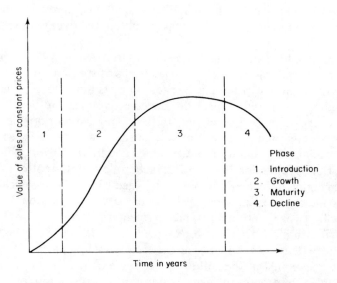

Figure 5.4 Typical product cycle patterns of sales for a successful new product. The quantity sold of the product can be expected to follow a similar pattern.

upon typical patterns of market penetration by new products. A typical pattern for sales for a successful new product is like that shown in Figure 5.4. There is an initial introduction stage followed by a fast growth stage if the product is successful, a mature phase in which maximum market penetration is achieved, and then a decline in sales as new products replace the old. The elongated S-shape of the product cycle may reflect the following:

(1) *Learning* curves. Individuals may need a number of exposures or trials of a product before they learn about or accept its superiority and individual learning curves tend to be of an S-shape.
(2) *Diffusion* of knowledge takes time and some patterns of diffusion give rise to this logistic-type curve.
(3) The distribution of innovators and laggards. The propensity to try the novel (or take risk) may be normally distributed and this can give rise to a logistic curve of this type.

Thus the typical product cycle pattern appears to reflect the fact that we live in a world of imperfect information in which *learning and search* take time and are of great importance.

The problem for a company marketing a new product is to estimate the precise form of its product cycle if it adopts this representation of demand, which incidentally is a rather crude one because it does not take account of specific influences on demand such as price. The degree of prediction using this method may, however, be improved by segmenting the population of potential purchasers into groups of similar individuals, predicting the product cycle for each group and combining these to obtain the overall time-pattern of sales.

The product cycle relationship has been used by Vernon (1966) to predict the flow of international trade and changing patterns of specialization of countries in the production of new products. Vernon suggests that new products tend to be first produced and sold in large developed economies and then production spreads to other developed countries. In the stage of a world-wide decline in demand, production tends to become concentrated in less-developed countries with little production remaining in developed countries. Rayon and cellulosic man-made fibre production has, for instance, followed this pattern. For those countries engaging in technology policy designed to modify technical progress in domestic industry, the product cycle model raises the question of when is it likely to be best for a nation's producers to enter the product cycle of a new product. Will a nation benefit most by being a leader in technology, a close follower, or a laggard? Further micro-economic knowledge is needed to answer this question. But the following are some of the factors which would need to be taken into account. The first entrant obtains a monopoly but this could be temporary and it could be costly to establish the market. Learning may be costly in terms of mistakes. A later entrant may be able to learn from the mistakes of others but could miss the market because early entrants are established and have raised market entry barriers. This has led one group of economists to speculate that a nation (or a firm) is likely to gain most from producing a new product as an *early follower* rather than a leader. But the issue is complex and a complete consideration of it requires specific attention to be given to consumer welfare.

5.3   CONSUMER WELFARE. HOW IS IT TO BE TAKEN INTO ACCOUNT?

Consumers, since the time of Adam Smith, have been given a central role in the theory of economic welfare. Indeed, many economists have come to judge economic systems by how well they serve the needs of consumers. Systems in which consumers are sovereign (systems responsive to the expressed needs of consumers) are the most desirable ones in the opinion of many economists. For example, as pointed out in Chapter 2, if a Paretian optimum is to occur it is necessary for there to be an optimal conformance between production and the desires of consumers for different commodities, i.e. for the rate of product transformation to be made equal to the rate of indifferent substitution. Furthermore, economic policy advice often hinges on the extent to which alternative policies increase consumer welfare, for instance as measured by rises in consumer surpluses.

The mainstream of economic theory makes a number of fundamental assumptions about consumer welfare as far as consumer sovereignty and non-satiation are concerned. Not surprisingly these assumptions have been subjected to challenge in recent years.

Criticism of traditional views of consumer welfare

Consumer sovereignty: The view that an economic system should respond to the wishes of consumers has been challenged by some socialist writers on the basis that individuals are not always the best judge of their own self-interest. Other writers such as Galbraith (1967) go so far as to maintain that in corporate economies consumers' preferences are manipulated through advertising and promotion by corporations so that consumers' preferences no longer reflect their basic desires. Again our preferences may not be independently determined but may in part be shaped by our social setting. Furthermore, the consumer-orientated view of man is claimed to be too narrow and the welfare of man should be judged in relation to all of his roles, including his role as a worker and as a political and group participant in society generally.

Non-satiation and dependence of welfare on quantity of commodities consumed: Established economic theory maintains that consumers cannot be satiated by commodities as a whole. In other words, greater quantities of *some* commodities always raise the welfare of a consumer, even though the consumer may be satiated by other commodities. An implication of this is that if a narrow view is taken (in which possible environmental trade-offs are ignored) consumers prefer more income to less. Furthermore, it justifies the preoccupation of economists with policies to reduce scarcity by increasing the supply of available commodities.

A variety of objections have been raised. Some writers claim, in contradiction of the traditional view, that consumers can be readily satiated in affluent economies. This is so notwithstanding the fact that most consumers are observed to desire higher incomes and levels of consumption in such societies. These desires are 'false'. They are fostered by corporate advertising, foisted on individuals, and mask their own self-interest. For example, individuals may be encouraged to desire more and richer food with subsequent deleterious effects on their health and fitness — effects contrary to their own self-interest. This raises the question of whether consumers should be protected by public policy and whether or not they can be protected. These matters are discussed later in this chapter.

It has also been emphasized by critics that traditional demand theory concentrates on marketed commodities (or at least marketable ones) and stresses the importance of personal income for welfare, thereby neglecting the importance of non-marketable goods such as public goods. Consequently in traditional economic theory, for example, the importance of non-traded commodities of an environmental kind (such as the provision of clean air, parks) tends to be ignored.

Does consumer welfare depend on aspiration levels?
An unorthodox application of indifference curves

Doubts have been expressed about the proposition that consumer welfare depends solely on the quantity of commodities enjoyed by the consumers.

112

It has been claimed, for instance, that welfare depends upon the *expected* level of consumption (or the level aspired to) and the actual level. The relationship may takes various forms. But it may be most common for consumer utility to rise with actual income and with the excess of actual income over that aspired to:

$$U = f(Y, Y - A) \qquad (\frac{\partial U}{\partial Y} > 0, \frac{\partial U}{\partial (Y - A)} > 0)$$

where U represents the utility obtained by a consumer, Y is his actual income, and A is the level of income aspired to.

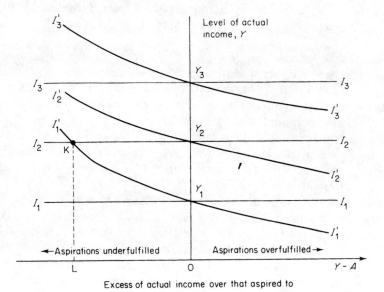

Figure 5.5   The horizontal indifference curves correspond to a situation in which a consumer's level of utility is independent of his aspirations about income whereas the downward sloping set corresponds to one in which utility is not independent of such aspirations. In the latter case, if aspirations rise and actual income remains constant, utility falls.

Figure 5.5 illustrates two possibilities using indifference curves. The set of horizontal indifference curves corresponds to the traditional view — utility depends only on the level of income. Utility is independent of aspirations in the traditional model. The downward sloping set of indifference curves, on the other hand, corresponds to a situation in which both actual income and aspirations about income are important determinants of utility. This set of curves indicates that at any income level, a consumers's utility is higher the lower is the level of income aspired to by him, i.e. the greater is $Y - A$. Utility can be influenced by manipulating actual income or the level of income aspired to. It is possible that, as income falls, the slope for such trade-off may be reduced and the indifference curves in Figure 5.5 may tend towards horizontal ones. This model illustrates how traditional concepts, in this case indifference curves, can be used to construct new or modified theories.

Policy implications of aspiration–welfare theory — the theses of Marcuse and Scitovsky

It should be noted that if aspirations are an important determinant of welfare, this opens up new policy possibilities. The government can influence welfare by influencing aspirations. The possibility should also not be overlooked that aspirations may affect the level of effort and production of individuals. Policy in some communist countries is designed to influence production through variations in aspirations or targets. But governments in these countries have to face the possibility that if targets are set too high in relation to what is possible, this may breed intense dissatisfaction and result in less production than if targets had been more realistic.

One of the points of view of Marcuse (1964) can be interpreted in terms of Figure 5.5. Marcuse claims that under corporate capitalism levels of consumption aspired to by consumers outrun those that are possible. This is because of advertising pressure by corporations designed to raise their sales. As a result dissatisfaction is manufactured among consumers (and workers) and this may become sufficiently extreme to result in violence such as that which occurred in France in the 1970s. Certainly, if the downward sloping indifference curves shown in Figure 5.5 apply, inflated aspirations would reduce consumer utility. Suppose that the consumer's actual income is OY_2 but that he is persuaded to aspire to consumption requiring an income of $OY_2 + OL$. If his aspirations accorded with his income, he would be placed on indifference curve $I_2'I_2'$ but given the higher aspirations his combined outlook places him at position K on the lower indifference curve $I_1'I_1'$. If one accepts *this point of view* there is a case for limiting the amount of advertising. But all advertising does not have the same effect. Some is informative and there is also a possibility that it yields utility in other ways which are discussed later in this chapter.

Scitovsky (1976) feels that dissatisfaction among consumers in affluent societies stems from different causes. He agrees that income and utility are not positively related but suggests that dissatisfaction may occur for those materially well off (e.g. the middle-aged couple with 'everything') because of lack of variety, challenge, uncertainty, and change.

Determinants of welfare are more complex and wide ranging than those taken into account in traditional consumer theory. While for some problems traditional theory may capture the most important influences on welfare, for other problems aspiration theories suggest it is inadequate. Policy-makers need a range of welfare theories in their tool-kit.

Consumers surplus—a practical tool for piecemeal policies?

If a policy-maker is concerned with a range of options or alternatives limited to a small part of the economy, he may be able to compare the effects of the alternatives on consumer welfare by using consumers surplus. Consumers surplus takes account of the willingness of the consumer to pay for a commodity. More precisely, consumers surplus is the difference between the maximum amount a consumer would have been willing to pay for the quantity purchased of a commodity and the amount actually paid by him, and can be approximated by the appropriate area under the demand curve.

For example, suppose that a decision has been made to establish a national park in a region but that a choice has to be made between two sites or areas of equal opportunity cost. The decision between the two sites is to be made solely on the relative value to recreational users of the area. If the demand curves for visits to the alternative sites can be determined, these may be used to estimate the value of potential users of the alternative sites. The demand curve for visits to site A might be as shown on the left-hand side of Figure 5.6 and that for visits to site B might be as shown on the right-hand side. If entry to the park is free, a greater number of visits (2 million per year) will be made to site B than to site A where there will be 1 million visits per year. But the value placed by visitors on site A as indicated by consumers surplus is much higher for site A than for site B. The hatched area under the demand curve for visits to site A is much greater than the hatched area under the demand curve for visits to site B. This indicates that the appropriate choice is site A rather than site B.

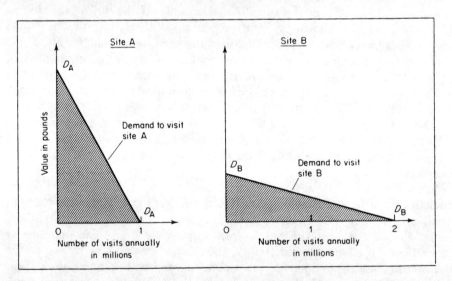

Figure 5.6 An application of the concept of consumers surplus to social choice. If a choice has to be made between two sites for a national park, admission to which is free, site A is more highly valued by consumers than site B, even though site B would be more frequently visited than site A.

Consumers surplus has many other policy applications. Suppose that a faster intercity train is under consideration but involves higher overheads than the existing service. Furthermore, suppose that if the faster service is introduced that it will completely replace the slower one. In order to decide whether the new service is likely to be justified, railway authorities may compare the additional consumers surplus generated by the faster service with the increased overheads incurred in introducing it. If the increased surplus is in excess of the extra overheads, it may be decided to go ahead with the conversion. To take a simple example, suppose that the marginal cost of operating the alternative services is the same and constant, as indicated by curve MC in Figure 5.7. In this Figure, D_1D_1 indicates the demand for the existing service and D_2D_2 shows the demand for the new service. Assuming marginal cost pricing, the increased consumers surplus generated by the new service is as represented by the hatched area. If this hatched area exceeds the extra overhead costs of the faster rail service, this would favour the replacement of the slower service by the faster one.

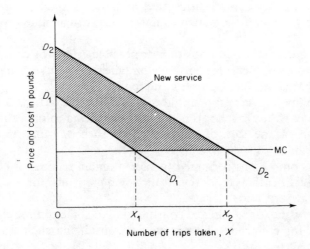

Figure 5.7 The extra consumers surplus generated by a faster train service is indicated by the hatched area. If this exceeds the extra cost of overheads of the faster service, the introduction of the new service as a replacement for the slow service may be justified.

However, the use of consumers surplus in policy-making is not without limitations. More advanced analysis indicates that a number of different conceptions of consumers surplus are possible. It also should be pointed out that consumers surplus is based upon prevailing or projected demands which reflect the existing or projected income distribution and tastes. If these are regarded as unacceptable, recommendations based upon consumers surplus will also be unacceptable.

116

5.4 MARKET FAILURE, IMPERFECTIONS, AND CONSUMER PROTECTION

In orthodox demand theory, as for instance presented by Hicks, consumers are so well informed that they always dispose of their income in the best possible way from their point of view. They are never disappointed about the bundle of commodities they purchased and could not be made better off by another available set. But in practice consumers do not have such perfect knowledge about the prices of commodities and their characteristics.

Examples of consumer protection policies

Because of this imperfection of knowledge, most countries have introduced policies to protect consumers. Policies take a number of forms. These include:

(1) The fixing of maximum prices, especially maximum interest rates, in some instances with the idea in mind of protecting individuals from 'over-charging'. Some of the effects of these policies were discussed in Chapter 4.
(2) Requirements that commodities meet minimum standards prescribed by the government, e.g. food such as milk, meat; drugs, motor vehicles, for instance.
(3) Requirements that the composition or possible effects of commodities be disclosed to consumers, for instance on labels or in advertising, as in the case of tobacco products, poisons and foods.
(4) Education by the government about the possible effects of different commodities either in schools or through the media to the general public.
(5) Prohibition of the sale of various goods such as guns and drugs of different kinds.
(6) Restrictions on persons permitted to supply certain services or commodities such as qualifications and registration requirements for medical prac-titioners, lawyers, and teachers.
(7) Compulsory and/or subsidized consumption of some commodities such as education for children. The motive for subsidizing such a *merit good* might be paternalism.
(8) Requirements about honesty in advertising and in claims for products, for instance about the weight of goods.
(9) In some countries, there is also a period of time in which a consumer can renounce an agreement to purchase a commodity, for instance if the buyer has been subjected to sales pressure by a door-to-door salesman.

Are the above restrictions on freedom of choice justified? They might be if the consumer is not the best judge of his own self-interest or if these measures sufficiently and economically reduce the consumer's cost of searching for an optimum choice. Schemes for consumer protection are as a rule not costless and need to be subjected to cost–benefit analysis. Sometimes on closer analysis they are found to be means to protect special producer groups rather than consumers. Let us consider ways in which consumer may be damaged or may benefit from consumer protection policies.

Costs of consumer protection—quality restrictions

If consumers are reasonably well informed minimum quality standards may reduce the welfare of consumers and increase the rent of those firms and resource-owners in a position to supply higher quality products at a profit. Take the simplest case in which consumers alone are damaged. Let us suppose that there is a continuum of qualities of a product, that the cost per unit of production of each quality is constant in relation to the quantity produced of that quality, but the cost per unit of production is higher for production of better quality goods. The cost per unit of production as a function of quality might rise in the way indicated in Figure 5.8, and the distribution of sales of the various qualities of the product, assuming that each quality is sold at its cost of production, might be as shown in Figure 5.9.

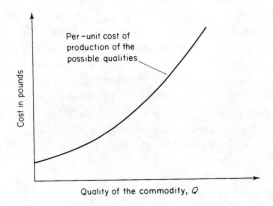

Figure 5.8   Per-unit costs of production of each quality is constant but per-unit costs are higher for the production of better quality goods in this example.

Suppose that in order to 'protect' consumers against products of shoddy quality that the government passes a regulation banning the sale of commodities of a quality less than Q_2 (Figure 5.9). If consumers are reasonably well informed, consumers purchasing commodities of lower quality than Q_2 are damaged by the government regulation. Take the case of a consumer who would normally buy only quality Q_1 of the commodity and allocates a fixed budget to purchasing the commodity. Suppose, further, that if the consumer is denied quality Q_1 that it is optimal for him to spend his earmarked budget on the lowest available quality of the product, Q_2. Figure 5.10 can be used to illustrate the effect on the consumer of not allowing the sale of a quality less

118

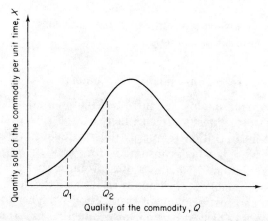

Figure 5.9 Distribution of quantity sold of various qualities of the commodity, assuming that each quality is sold at its per-unit cost of production.

than Q_2. The budget line LM indicates the quantities of the commodity with quality Q_1 and Q_2 which the consumer can purchase from his earmarked budget for the commodity. In the absence of protection the consumer reaches equilibrium at point M and purchases only quality Q_1 of the commodity and reaches the indifference curve I_2I_2. But if the consumer is protected by the minimum approved quality being Q_2, the consumer reaches a new equilibrium at point L and is placed on a lower indifference curve, I_1I_1. The quality regulation, far from assisting the consumer, reduces his welfare.

In some instances, however, consumer protection protects particular producer groups—the producers of 'better quality' products. It is, for

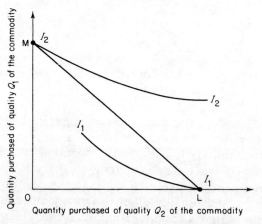

Figure 5.10 Protection of the consumer from a low-quality product reduces his welfare in this case. If quality Q_1 is banned, the consumer is shifted from equilibrium M to L in this case.

example, not unknown for domestic producers to claim that imports of competing products are of inferior quality and to try to have these imports restricted ostensibly to protect domestic consumers. In reality, however, their prime motive is often their own protection and domestic consumers may not be benefited.

Benefits from consumer protection given search costs

Nevertheless, consumers can benefit from some forms of protection. Measures to ensure honesty or accuracy in the labelling and description of commodities often confer, as will be shown below, a net benefit on consumers. Uncertainty about characteristics, weights, qualities, and so on, of commodities offered for sale can reduce consumer welfare. Policies to protect exclusive rights to trade-marks may be justified on this basis and regular checks on weights (scales) and measures and on specified weights and claims about products by public authorities may be justified. It may be more economical for the government to assume this policing function than for each buyer to try to protect his own self-interest by checking for himself. Individual checking or search involves duplication of effort by many individuals and the government may be able to achieve economies of scale in protecting consumers.

How much is it worth to a buyer to have the characteristics or quality of the commodity he is purchasing accurately specified? Naturally this will vary from commodity to commodity, but the value of increased accuracy will not be unlimited. Take a particular example. Suppose that a consumer is planning to purchase a particular quantity of a commodity X, which he believes is most likely of quality Q_2. If it is of quality Q_2 the value to him of the purchase is £100, but in his view there is only a 0.5 probability of its quality being Q_2. There is a 0.25 probability of the quality being Q_1, in which case the value of the purchase is £40, and also a 0.25 probability of the quality being Q_3, in which case the consumer values the purchase at £110. Thus, given the degree of uncertainty that exists, the expected value of purchase is

$$E(V) = 0.5 \times £100 + 0.25 \times £40 + 0.25 \times £110 = £87.50$$

Thus if the quality of the product could be accurately identified as Q_2 on average the consumer would be prepared to pay £100 – £87.50 = £12.50 for this or would value the information by this much.

Presumably the consumer could carry out a test or pay for a test to be made to determine the quality of product with accuracy. But this test might cost him more than £12.50, in which case it would not be worth while. On the other hand, the supplier might find it more economical to determine accurately the quality of the product. He will be producing many batches and may obtain economies of scale in testing and measurement. But the consumer needs to be reasonably sure that the supplier's claims are reliable. This *a consumer may learn* from experience. However, this can be costly to the buyer for a reliable producer may not be found at first. Furthermore, new suppliers are disadvantaged even if they are honest because they have to prove themselves before buyers purchase their products in quantity. This restricts competition by favouring established firms. On the other hand, if a public authority actively takes measures to ensure that claims made by suppliers are accurate this is an advantage to buyers and to new honest suppliers. Yet we must not be too hasty in accepting the social desirability of detailed and accurate descriptions of goods. There are limits to the extent to which it is socially worth while and economical to describe goods offered for sale accurately. An increase in detailed description of goods should, if a Kaldor–Hicks loss is to be avoided, be carried to the point where the expected marginal value of this greater information to consumers is equal to the extra cost to suppliers. To proceed beyond this amount of information is to impose a Kaldor–Hicks loss on society. Nevertheless, it is clear that public policies requiring honesty and accuracy in description and trading of goods *can* (but need not) confer a net social benefit, and public rather than private enforcement of the appropriate regulations may be socially optimal.

To illustrate the last point, consider a dishonest supplier who indicates that the quality of his product in the above example is Q_2 when in fact it is Q_1. The unwary purchaser in the above example suffers an effective loss of £60. His remedy is legal action against the supplier. But this can be uncertain and even if he succeeds (and receives £60 in compensation) the actual proceedings will take time and he may, after allowing for this time, be out of pocket by, say, £80. Therefore, he may not take action on this petty claim and the supplier goes on cheating others and creating uncertainty in his trade. The *social* value of arresting the cheat's behaviour may well be considerably in excess of the cost to an individual of attempting to stop it because of the externalities involved. A case for public action may exist because of collective or group benefits.

An interesting example of public protection of traders is in relation to the currency. The government itself takes considerable trouble to guard against counterfeiting of the currency. At an earlier time when coins contained precious metals the practice of clipping coins was banned and coins were produced with rolled (milled edges) as a protection to traders. This considerably reduced transaction costs—i.e. the need for individuals to test coins given in exchange on every occasion in which they were involved in exchange. Government action conferred a net social benefit.

It might be held that consumer associations are adequate to protect the consumer. They provide information for a joining fee. However, they are limited in the information they are able to provide (they give information for a sample) and the costs of their checking the qualities or characteristics of products rather than suppliers can be higher. There is also the possibility of their information being passed on to non-members, in which case non-members obtain a free-ride and the activities of the consumer association may be more restricted than is socially optimal.

New products can create special problems for consumer protection since all their effects may not be known at their time of development. In the case of new drugs or pesticides, for example, governments may require considerable testing of these before they are released for sale to the public. The benefits foregone by delaying the introduction of a possibly superior drug must be weighed against the risk of its having unforseen ill effects. Should the consumer be allowed to choose between the risks? Is paternalistic intervention justified? If the individual is given all the known facts is it not reasonable for him to decide on his own risks? Paternalists might argue that some individuals cannot understand all the facts or that individuals should be restrained from being 'foolhardy', but a liberal would not be likely to adopt this view. On the other hand, if unfavourable externalities are likely to be imposed on others (e.g. the individual may become dependent on others (invalided) or his or her children may suffer deformities) a liberal would consider that there may be a case for government intervention.

One problem encountered in government protection against new products is that in fact superior products may not be developed because of the uncertainty of government approval or the products may be excluded from the market for a socially excessive time. For instance, policies to delay the introduction of new drugs until side-effects are thoroughly explored do provide a benefit by reducing the risk of the introduction of drugs with crippling side-effects, but on the other hand they also slow down the introduction of drugs with no such effects and this imposes a cost in terms of prolonged suffering and deaths which might have been avoided by speedier use of the drug. Both benefits and *costs* must be weighed up.

Digression on search by consumers

The above analysis recognizes that consumers do not have perfect knowledge but search and learn. Search may take many forms, but as the drug case just mentioned indicates these can involve great risks when consumers learn by doing or by trying, and the effects of such trials may not be fully reversible.

Search and the gathering of information is not costless and this must be taken into account in optimizing any welfare function. In general, it is only economic to pursue these activities up to the point where their marginal expected benefit is equal to their marginal cost. This means as a rule that it is most economic to terminate search and information-gathering before perfect knowledge is attained. If economic gain is to be maximized it is usually rational not to seek perfect knowledge.

The above optimal search rule has many implications. It helps to explain:

(1) Why different suppliers can charge somewhat varying prices for the same product and all obtain sales as pointed out by Stigler (1961).
(2) Why richer individuals tend to be more ignorant of the prices of food items

than those on lower incomes, as found by Gabor (1966). (The cost of search or keeping track of this information in terms of *alternatives fore-gone* may be greater for the rich and the marginal utility of extra real income obtained as a result of attention to relative prices is possibly smaller for the rich than the poor.)

(3) Why consumers expend great search effort when purchasing durable items involving a large outlay such as a house or car as shown by Katona (1960). The expected benefits from search and the initial degree of ignorance can be expected to be high in such cases and so the optimal search level is high, other things equal.

But even if individuals do undertake an optimal amount of search and information-gathering, from their point of view this does not mean that this activity is optimally organized from a social point of view. Economies of scale may be achieved by government searching and testing and per-unit costs could indeed be declining with the volume of these activities, producing a tendency to natural monopoly, as discussed in Chapter 8. While a private firm (or a consumer association) could sell these services there is likely to be market failure because the information gathered cannot be perfectly marketed. Some consumers are likely to gain access to the information (public good) without paying for it, for instance by having it passed on by others who have purchased it. A private market may undersupply information about commodities. Again, if externalities or spillovers from the consumption of products are important this could call for government intervention. For instance, if the consumption of a product is likely to affect future generations adversely intervention could be called for (see Chapter 10).

Externalities and intervention in consumption

Various types of externalities may provide a basis for government inter-vention in consumption. In nearly all countries there are restrictions on the amount of noise which can be emitted by automobiles, for example, and on the allowable emissions of carbon monoxide from cars. In the absence of regulations on noise, automobile purchasers would be inclined to purchase noisier vehicles if this reduced their private cost.

Figure 5.11 illustrates the type of policy decision that may have to be made between the saving of fuel and the toleration of pollution, and is an example of energy policy problems such as those to be discussed in Chapter 13. The curve passing through ABC represents the trade-off between fuel used in cars and the pollution caused by them. In the absence of controls on pollution, individuals economize on fuel and cause pollution corresponding, say, to A. But suppose that the social welfare trade-off between pollution and fuel used is as represented by the indifference curves W_0W_0, W_1W_1, and W_2W_2. Since greater pollution and greater use of fuel can be regarded as yielding disutility, that is as 'bads', welfare increases as the quantities of both are lowered. Thus

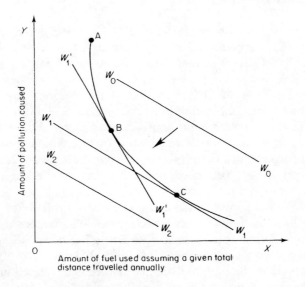

Figure 5.11 Because of externalities excessive pollution from cars may occur in the absence of government control. But if the cost of less pollution is greater fuel consumption this must be taken into account in a social decision. If the value of fuel rises relative to the value of a clean environment, it may be optimal to allow greater pollution to save fuels. In the case shown, the social optimum shifts from C to B as the relative value of fuel rises.

greater social welfare corresponds to lower social indifference curves rather than to higher ones as in the normal case. The socially optimal (pollution, fuel consumption) combination is at C and policies need to be introduced by the government to guide consumers to this position. But what would be the effect of a rise in the value of fuel? If the value of fuel rises *relative* to the value of environmental quality, government policy needs to be modified to permit more pollution to save fuel. If the indifference curves tilt so that $W_1' W_1'$ becomes a relevant one, the new optimum corresponds to position B. Given the steep rise in oil prices that has occurred a number of governments have had to consider whether or not to modify their controls on emissions from motor cars.

Economists have recognized that some wants of consumers cannot be catered for through the market system but can only be met through the political system because exclusion from supplies is impossible. These goods, *pure public goods*, include items like defence and some environmental factors. As mentioned in Chapter 2, public goods may not be supplied or may be supplied in smaller quantities than is socially optimal unless collective action is taken. Their supply is affected by market failure and government action is needed to direct their supply and level of consumption.

Advertising and consumer welfare

While some of the possible effects of advertising have already been mentioned in this chapter and more detailed discussion occurs in later chapters, especially Chapter 9, there are some aspects which are worth briefly noting now. Advertising has been a matter for controversy among economists. The controversial views of Galbraith and Marcuse about advertising have already been mentioned. Occasionally social reformers claim that advertising wastes resources and misleads and confuses consumers. What should be the policy of the government towards advertising? A case would seem to exist for government enforcement of honesty in advertising on the same ground (and to the same extent) as that suggested above for accuracy in specifications of commodities. But even if advertising is accurate, resources used in advertising may be wasted from a Kaldor–Hicks social point of view. Take an oligopolistic market for instance. A supplier may try to increase his market share by raising his expenditure on advertising only to find that other oligopolists follow suit and market shares remain unchanged. If the overall demand for the product is inelastic, producers in the oligopolistic market become trapped in a high-cost advertising campaign in which no one benefits (except advertising agents). It is not clear what the government should do, if anything, to reduce the waste. The government might act as an arbitrator for the parties in the hope that they will agree to cut their advertising expenditure by common consent. In New South Wales the government performed a similar role in overseeing a reduction in the number of retail outlets for petrol which under competitive pressure were judged to have become 'excessive in number'. As predicted by the monopolistically competitive market model (discussed in Chapters 6 and 7) long-term entry of new petrol stations had apparently resulted in all or most having excess capacity.

In imperfect markets, advertising can be important in creating barriers to the entry of new firms. Thus it can result in reduced competition. Consequently, prices may be kept higher than otherwise to the detriment of consumers. This matter is discussed in detail in Section 8.3. The psychological associations fostered by much advertising is more important than the overt message communicated. This, for instance, is reasonably clear in the case of cigarette smoking. The appeal of advertisements for cigarettes is so great that in most countries such advertising must carry a health warning and is not permitted on television. The danger exists that such 'psychological' advertising will cause a consumer to act against his own self-interest, but it need not do this and associations can be valued. Advertised associations, for instance in the case of perfumes, could easily increase the perceived value of the product to the consumer and be 'beneficial'. While some advertising is valued by consumers and is socially valuable because it is informative, some non-informative advertising is socially valued because its images are valued. Furthermore, there could be occasions on which the means justifies the ends, risky though such an approach to policy is. In order to induce consumers to try a superior new product, it may be necessary to catch the consumer's attention by other than informative means.

Thus, the welfare effects of advertising are complex and varied. A dogmatic government policy towards advertising would appear difficult to justify since advertising can take a variety of forms and serve different purposes. But this is not an invitation to non-intervention. Public interference can be justified in instances such as those discussed above.

Political power of consumers

Political rather than market power has become of increased importance in the allocation of resources and the functioning of economies. Writers such as Downs (1957) argue that the political power of consumers is small compared to that of producers. The gains to any individual consumer from political action is likely to be small compared to the possible gain by a producer and on a cost–benefit analysis the consumer is not likely to take political action. Indeed he may even fail to notice that his interest is damaged. For instance, suppose that protection of a domestically produced product is under consideration and that a company stands to benefit by a £1 million annual increase in profit if the protection is approved. Consumers are disadvantaged by £1 each per year and if there are 20 million of them their combined loss is £20 million annually. The company standing to gain can spend a considerable sum to ensure introduction of the protection and still benefit. On the other hand, no individual consumer is likely to find it worth while to oppose the scheme politically since the cost of his opposition is likely to exceed his possible benefit. Indeed, a consumer may not even find it worth while to find out (search involves costs) the extent to which he is disadvantaged, since it may cost more than £1 to do so; therefore consumers rationally remain ignorant.

While collectively consumers have an incentive to oppose the introduction of protection, they may have to be organized into a political pressure group to do this effectively. But this is not easily achieved for each consumer has an incentive to free-ride: to enjoy the benefits of political action without contributing to its cost. The benefit from political action (reversal of the protection decision) is of the nature of a pure public good. No consumer can be excluded from the benefit of reversal because he failed to contribute to the political campaign for reversal and this is why free-riding is a problem. Again transaction costs and risks are involved in trying to form consumer political pressure groups. These costs may fall heavily or disproportionately on those trying to seed or form such groups, so that in net it is unprofitable for any individual or small group of individuals to foster the formation of a pressure group.

Despite this, associations of some consumers have been formed and legislation has been passed that helps to protect consumers. This includes legislation against restrictive practices and against monopolization. But whether or not the main political force behind such measures has been consumers or competitive businessmen adversely affected in their own business by the restrictive trade practices of other businessmen, remains an open question.

5.5   ELASTICITIES OF DEMAND AND POLICY

The above discussion concentrated on normative policy matters. It is worth while balancing the discussion by considering some positive policy applications of simple demand elasticity concepts. Let us briefly consider policy applications of own-price elasticities, income elasticities, and cross elasticities to such matters as sales taxes, pollution taxes, controls on the export of resources such as uranium, government planning of an economy's infrastructure, public policy on the regulation of monopoly, and decision-making about urban transport systems. Applications of each of the concepts are outlined in turn.

Own-price elasticities of demand — policy applications to sales tax and to pollution control

Using own-price elasticities of demand let us consider the impact on government revenue of a sales tax on a commodity. The revenue obtained by the government is greater, the smaller is (varies inversely with) the own-price elasticity of the commodity on which the tax is levied, i.e. the more inelastic is the own-price elasticity of demand for the commodity, other things equal. This can be illustrated by the example shown in Figure 5.12, where SS represents the supply curve of the commodity on which the government is considering the imposition of a sales tax (or excise tax) of T per unit of sales. The problem is to estimate the tax revenue which will be obtained by the government. If the demand curve is completely inelastic as indicated by D_1D_1 the government's tax revenue will be TX_3, for the market will reach a new equilibrium at (X_3,P_3) because the after-tax supply curve is $SS + T$. But if demand is more elastic, the equilibrium quantity demanded falls. If the demand curve is D_2D_2, for instance, the equilibrium quantity traded after imposition of the tax falls to X_2 and government tax revenue is therefore less. It is even less if the demand curve is perfectly elastic, as shown by D_3D_3 in Figure 5.12. Thus the more elastic the demand, the smaller is the government revenue. It may be no coincidence that commodities such as cigarettes and alcohol for which demand is relatively inelastic are also often subject to high government sales taxes. Note that the more inelastic is the demand curve the greater is the increase in equilibrium price resulting from the imposition of the tax and therefore the greater is the incidence of the tax on consumers. The incidence of a sales tax on consumers varies inversely with the elasticity of demand for the commodity on which it is imposed.

The effects of a pollution tax levied on production can also be considered in terms of Figure 5.12. Suppose that SS represents the private marginal cost of supply of the commodity and $S + T$ represents its social marginal cost of supply. To bring the private marginal social cost of supply into line with the

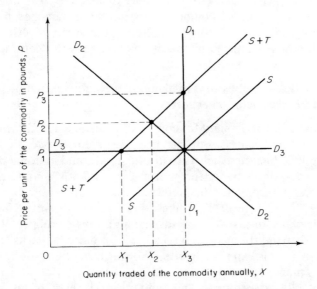

Figure 5.12 The more inelastic is the demand for a commodity, the greater is the revenue obtained by the government from a sales tax on the commodity. The figure is also used to illustrate the point that the more elastic the demand curve, the more effective is a pollution tax on production in reducing pollution, assuming a given normal supply curve.

social marginal cost, the government may decide to impose a pollution tax of T on each unit of the commodity produced. Do the polluters (producers) pay the tax? What effect does the tax have on the amount of pollution? The answer to these questions, assuming a given normal supply curve, depends upon the elasticity of demand for the commodity. If the demand for the commodity is perfectly inelastic as shown by D_1D_1, the level of production of the commodity is unaffected by the pollution tax and the price of the product rises by whole per-unit amount of the tax. On the other hand, if the demand for the commodity is perfectly elastic as shown by D_3D_3, the full burden of the pollution tax falls on producers, production of the commodity falls from X_3 to X_1, and therefore there is a considerable reduction in pollution. If the demand curve has an elasticity between these extremes, the burden of the pollution tax partially falls on producers and partially on consumers and there is some reduction in pollution. The burden of the tax on producers and the reduction in pollution is greater, the more elastic is demand for the commodity.

The slogan is sometimes heard that the polluter (meaning the producer) should pay. But as we have seen if a pollution tax is levied on a polluter's production this may be passed on to consumers. However, it can be claimed that consumers are just as responsible for the pollution as the actual producer if they demand products whose production necessarily causes pollution, and that both consumers and producers should be forced to take the social consequences of their choices into account. Incidentally, the above analysis leaves the question open of compensation for those damaged by pollution. Should the revenue obtained from the pollution tax by the government be used to compensate those damaged by the production activities causing pollution?

Income elasticities — applications to planning the supply of public facilities and to agreements on exports

Income elasticities of demand for commodities can be useful for planning by government and by business. For instance, they are useful to the government in planning public facilities such as roads, hospitals, and national parks. If the income elasticity of demand for motor cars is known and the expected percentage rises in income can be predicted, this provides an estimate of likely car numbers in the future. This likely number in turn may influence the government's plans for providing roads and highways. Similarly, if the income elasticities of demand for medical services and for national parks are known to be high and income is expected to rise, allowance can be made for this in the government's plans to provide such facilities.

While not all governments participate in international commodity agreements, a number do so for energy supplies. The Australian government, for instance, participates in agreements on the export of Australian uranium, and one of its considerations is the price offered in long-term contracts for the supply of uranium. In negotiations during the early part of the 1970s, the Australian government held out for a greater price than that offered by buyers in the belief that increased oil prices would greatly increase the demand for uranium for electricity generation. But later in the 1970s it was found that world incomes had not grown as fast as anticipated, and as the demand for electricity was *income elastic*, the demand for electricity did not expand as rapidly as predicted. The Australian government was therefore prepared to enter into contracts for the supply of uranium at lower prices than those originally hoped for. Thus in negotiations about the supply of energy resources, knowledge about appropriate income elasticities can be of value.

Cross elasticities of demand — applications to public regulation of monopolies and to urban transport policies

The cross elasticity of demand between two commodities indicates the extent to which they are substitutes or complements. If the cross elasticities are *negative*, the products are *complements*, and if they are *positive*, the products are *substitutes*. Thus in the case illustrated in Figure 5.13 commodity A is a substitute for commodity B if the demand curve for A as a function of the price of B has a positive slope like D_1D_1 and a complement if it has a negative slope like D_2D_2.

Cross elasticities of demand have applications to a variety of public policies. In considering whether public action ought to be taken to deal with a private

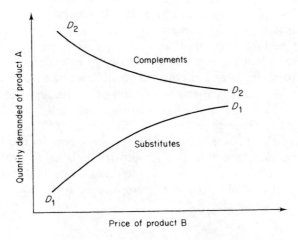

Figure 5.13   The cross elasticities of demand for substitutes are positive and for complements are negative.

monopoly, the extent to which other products are substitutes for the monopolist's product needs to be taken into account. The mere fact that a firm is a single seller (monopolist) in a market does not confer on it monopoly power. If the degree of substitutability of the monopolist's product for other products is high, the monopolist has little market power and little may be gained by attempting to control his monopoly. Intense competition from substitutes may restrain the monopolist from raising the price of his product to any extent above the marginal cost of its production.

   Cross elasticities are also relevant to some urban transport policies. Suppose that roads in a city are congested by private cars and the government operates buses and electric trains in the city. The government is considering subsidizing its bus and rail services so that low bus and rail fares can be charged to encourage private motorists to use these facilities rather than their own cars. The success of the policy will depend upon the degree of substitutability between private and public transport. Evidence indicates that the cross elasticity of demand between public and private transport is low but positive. Thus lower fares on public transport may do little to relieve traffic congestion in the city.

5.6   CONCLUSION

   This discussion has illustrated that micro-economics can be usefully applied to a variety of normative and positive policy decisions involving consumers. While standard analysis can sometimes be used for this purpose, in most instances standard analysis must be modified and extended to deal with the particular problem under consideration. But even when extension of the analysis is necessary, standard analysis frequently supplies useful concepts and tools for this purpose, as for instance was illustrated by the application of indifference curves in those theories regarding aspirations as an important component of welfare. By simplifying and organizing our view of the world in terms of general concepts, micro-economic theory enables us to better comprehend the complex effects and alternative possibilities of economic policies and thereby (given our limited capacities and abilities to understand and deal with the world) can and does help us in problem-solving. But it would be stupid of us to believe that the best conceptions (however defined) and tools have already been developed or that the existing ones are best for dealing with every micro-economic problem. While using and recognizing the value of current micro-economic tools in policy, we need to remain rationally sceptical and be on the lookout for more satisfactory perceptions, about which we may also remain rationally sceptical.

READING AND REFERENCES

Gabor, A. (1977). *Pricing: Principles and Practices*, Heinemann, London.

Galbraith, J. K. (1967). *The New Industrial State*, Hamish Hamilton, London.

Hey, J. (1979). *Uncertainty in Microeconomics*, Martin and Robertson, Oxford.

Hicks, J. R. (1946). *Value and Capital*, Preface and Chaps 1 and 2, Clarendon Press, Oxford.

Katona, G. (1960). *The Powerful Consumer*, McGraw-Hill, New York.

Lipsey, R. G. (1979). *An Introduction to Positive Economics*, Chaps 7, 9, and 13 to 15, Weidenfeld and Nicolson, London.

Mansfield, E. (1979). *Microeconomics*, Chaps 3 to 5, Norton, New York.

Marcuse, H. (1964). *One Dimensional Man*, Routledge and Kegan Paul, London.

Marshall, A. (1890). *Principles of Economics*, 1st ed., Macmillan, London.

Scitovsky, T. (1976). *The Joyless Economy*, Oxford University Press, Oxford.

Stigler, G. J. (1961). The economics of information, *Journal of Political Economy*, **69**, June, 213–225.

Tisdell, C. A. (1972). *Microeconomics*, Chap. 6 and A.6, Wiley, Sidney.

Tisdell, C. A. (1974). *Economics of Markets*, Chap. 5, Wiley, Sydney.

Udell, J. (1964). The role of price in competitive strategy, *Journal of Marketing*, **28**, 44–48.

Vernon, R. (1966). International investment and international trade in the product cycle, *Quarterly Journal of Economics*, **80**, May, 190–207.

QUESTIONS FOR REVIEW AND DISCUSSION

1. How does Hicks' theory of demand (which relies on indifference curves) differ from Marshall's? What are the main limitations of Hicks' theory?
2. Suppose that in an effort to stem the rate of population increase a government is considering imposing a tax on parents which is to rise with the number of their children. Using indifference curves and distinguishing between income and substitution effects, illustrate circumstances in which the tax leads to larger families and others in which it leads to families of reduced size.
3. What factors other than price may influence purchases of a product?

4. Outline four general means that can be used to estimate demand curves and give limitations of each.
5. 'Time-series data may identify a supply curve rather than a demand curve or neither curve.' Explain and illustrate.
6. Why might the product cycle curve of market sales or market penetration of a new product have a logistic form? To what extent is this curve a consequence of ignorance on the part of consumers?
7. Discuss the following views:
   (a) Consumers *should not* be sovereign and *are not* sovereign in the market system.
   (b) A consumers utility does not continually rise with the level of his optimal consumption of commodities but may also depend on his aspirations.
8. Television stations frequently rate different television programmes in terms of *the relative number* of viewers. When consumers surplus is considered, there is a serious limitation in this evaluation method. What is the limitation? Illustrate by means of a diagram.
9. Try to draw a diagram to illustrate how the optimal level of search effort might be determined. You will need a marginal expected benefit curve as a function of the level of search effort and a marginal cost curve as a function of such effort. Explain how shifts in these curves may alter the optimal level of search effort.
10. 'While consumer protection can benefit consumers it can also damage consumers.' Discuss and explain.
11. 'Spillovers or externalities from consumption may call for government interference in choice by consumers.' Discuss.
12. Taking account of the views of Marcuse and Galbraith as well as *other* views, show how advertising can lead to a social loss. Explain carefully what you mean by a social loss. Also outline circumstances and types of advertising that could be socially beneficial.
13. 'Consumers are a weak political pressure group.' Explain.
14. Outline one policy application of each of the following:
    (a) the own-price elasticity of demand for a product,
    (b) income elasticities of demand, and
    (c) cross elasticities of demand.

CHAPTER 6

Costs, Supply, and Policy

6.1 INTRODUCTION AND OVERVIEW

Every national policy decision or choice requires a consideration of costs, usually in terms of opportunity costs. Opportunity costs are measured by the value of alternatives foregone as a result of choosing one possibility rather than alternative possibilities. The relevant cost of choosing one alternative from a set of possible choices is the value of the best alternative foregone. It is the purpose of this chapter to explain and illustrate policy applications of the concept of opportunity costs, to consider other cost concepts such as sunk costs, which are important for policy purposes, and to examine cost and supply relationships typically experienced by firms and industries and consider their implications for micro-economic policy.

The discussion deals first with the concept of opportunity costs and then illustrates how (social) opportunity costs are automatically taken into account by firms in a perfectly competitive market system and can yield a Paretian optimum. But perfectly competitive markets can fail and as a result a divergence occurs of marginal social opportunity costs from the marginal private opportunity costs experienced by individual decision-makers (e.g. firms), for instance as a result of spillovers, as illustrated in Chapter 2. This may call for government intervention in the operations of the economy. But as will be pointed out, governments and government bureaucrats may fail to take proper social account of marginal social opportunity costs and this may be in their *own* bureaucratic self-interest in trying to maximize their budgets and power over resources. When government intervention is contemplated on the grounds of market failure, it is necessary to weigh carefully the social costs of likely *government failure* against the social costs of *market failure*.

As is illustrated below, proper account is often not taken of sunk costs or historical expenses in decision-making. They ought to be regarded as *bygones* and should not affect current decisions (except, of course, one should learn from mistakes). Bureaucrats and other policy-makers sometimes make strategic use of sunk costs in order to increase the size of their budgets. On projects of doubtful economic worth they may try to sink as much money (resources) into them as possible and as early as possible so that future funding then only becomes dependent upon the *added* net benefits to be achieved by bringing the project to completion.

Policies for accelerating the replacement of machinery (modernization schemes) are criticized on the grounds that they may fail to take account of opportunity costs and it is emphasized that traditional economic theory does not take account of X-inefficiency as an element influencing the cost levels achieved by firms and bureaucracies. X-inefficiency can be an important influence on costs when management has discretion not to maximize profit for instance, because shareholders are divorced from control over their company.

Finally, the form of per-unit cost curves of production and supply curves are considered and it is suggested that the U-shaped per-unit cost curve may not be typical of several industries. Applications of the various forms to government policies to eliminate excess capacity in industries and to policies to promote merger by firms are explored. Learning by experience, a neglected element in traditional theories of costs, but one which can be important, is taken into account and is shown to be relevant, for instance, to policies to encourage infant industries. Without a sound knowledge of cost concepts and relationships policy-making and the evaluation of policies is perilous.

6.2 COSTS AS AN OPERATIONAL CONCEPT

The opportunity costs of choosing one alternative rather than another are the opportunities foregone. All economic choices involve an opportunity cost because they result in valued alternatives being foregone by decision-makers. Indeed an economic problem and the subject of economics only exist because choice about the use of resources is not costless. Pleaders for greater public provision of particular goods, such as defence, health, and roads (including bureaucrats in the civil service who have a personal interest in expansion of their activities), frequently fail to point out the costs of their proposals in terms of other economic possibilities foregone, such as foregone leisure time, private goods, or public goods such as education.

Perfect competition, opportunity costs, and the duality theorem

In a market system, opportunity costs are taken into account by economic agents following their own self-interest and, in the absence of market failure, the process results in a Paretian optimal level of economic welfare if perfect competition exists. Assuming a given amount of resources, the production possibility frontier represents the necessary trade-off in production of commodities. If we take a particular company producing tapes and records and employing a particular amount of resources, its production possibility set might be like the hatched area OABC in Figure 6.1. The opportunity cost of producing more tapes is the number of records foregone, but from the company's point of view (assuming that it is a profit-maximizer) opportunities foregone are valued in terms of profit foregone.

Because of its given employment of resources (and in the last instant this employment must always be given) and thus its fixed outlay for them, the

134

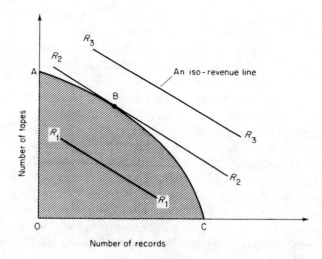

Figure 6.1   At point B the production (marginal) opportunity cost of producing tapes rather than records equals the relative value placed upon records and tapes by consumers. Under perfect competition, a firm will produce combination B.

company maximizes its profit by maximizing its revenue subject to its production possibility constraint. The company's profit-maximizing production of records and tapes can be seen from Figure 6.1. Its revenue possibilities can be represented by a series of iso-revenue (equal revenue) curves like those marked R_1R_1, R_2R_2, and R_3R_3 in Figure 6.1. The curves of iso-revenue identified by subscripts of higher number correspond to higher levels of total revenue—for movements in a NE direction in Figure 6.1 total revenue rises. The iso-revenue curves are straight lines because their slope depends on the relative prices of tapes and records and these prices are constant for firms operating under perfect competition. In this case, the profit-maximizing output of records and tapes corresponds to point B. At this point, the slope of the firm's product transformation curve, i.e. the rate of product transformation (representing marginal production trade-offs), *equals* the slope of an iso-revenue line, i.e. the relative prices of tapes and records (representing the firm's marginal revenue or marginal profit trade-offs). Marginal profit and marginal revenue are equal in this case because at the last instant all costs are given or fixed: the assumption of the Austrian school of economics holds.

In a perfectly competitive market system in equilibrium, the production combination at point B is also optimal from the point of view of consumers, for at this point the rate at which consumers are *willing* to substitute the commodities in consumption (as indicated by the slopes of their indifference curves) equals the rate at which they have to substitute them in the production process. At point B rates of indifferent substitution equal the rate of product transformation of tapes and records, a necessary condition for a Paretian welfare optimum. This *equality is brought about because all consumers face the same set of trading prices as producers. Price parity* is satisfied. As shown, producers equate their rate of product transformation to these relative prices in order to maximize profit. In order to maximize utility subject to their income constraint consumers must equate their ratio of indifferent substitution to this *same* set of relative prices. Hence, the self-interest of all parties leads to rates of product transformation and rates of indifferent substitution being equalized. Given the distribution of income, the perfectly competitive system ensures that there is no alternative allocation of resources (opportunities foregone) that is more highly valued by consumers. Thus this example has illustrated the *duality theorem*—the theorem that perfect competition automatically results in a Paretian optimum.

But perfectly competitive systems do not exist in reality and externalities may result in a divergence of private and social opportunity costs, as pointed out in Chapter 2. Markets may fail to take adequate account of social opportunity costs. But so too can governments. This may be emphasized by considering some examples.

Opportunity costs and government and bureaucratic failure

Take the case of a government able to allocate a limited budget between public provision of health services or income transfers for the poor. Both may be considered very worthy causes, but the amount that can be provided of each is restricted by the limited government budget. The trade-off frontier for the alternatives may be like ACF in Figure 6.2. This frontier indicates that as more funds are allocated for public medical services, the incremental increase in these services declines or an increase in public health services becomes relatively more costly in terms of the *amount* of income support which has to be foregone to provide these. Health services may be relatively inelastic in supply and become more so as the amount supplied increases.

Suppose that the government's *aim is to achieve a particular level of 'healthiness' in the community* and that public provision of health services and income support are strategies contributing to healthiness. Combinations of income support and public health provision along Q_1Q_1 might meet this standard, where Q_1Q_1 is *an isoquant* showing the inputs of public health services and income support required to produce a given level of healthiness in the community and its shape indicates that *substitutability* between the inputs is possible. Other insoquants defining the production possibilities such as Q_2Q_2 and Q_3Q_3 exist. The higher ones correspond to higher levels of healthiness. Assuming that the whole budget is to be allocated, the *required standard* is met either by the allocation at D or B, but in the absence of further information there is no basis for choosing between these alternatives on the basis of the above criterion. The Health Department, however, is likely to favour position B and the Social Security Department position D, since in the former case the

136

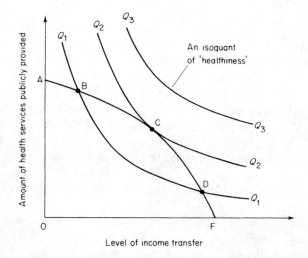

Figure 6.2   Required trade-off between income transfers and quantity of public health services (given a limited budget) as indicated by curve ACF. Health services, like other commodities, are not costless in terms of alternatives foregone.

Health Department is larger and in the latter case the Social Security Department is larger than it would otherwise be.

If the government wished *to maximize* the healthiness of the community (rather than achieve the satisfactory level or standard indicated by Q_1Q_1) the allocation at position C in Figure 6.2 would be optimal relative to its allocative possibilities. But it is possible that the Health Department would not support the allocation at C because although this allocation maximizes healthiness it results in fewer health services being provided, than, say, would be needed at B. Bureaucrats in the Health Department may wish to maximize their power over resources by maximizing their budget or supply of services. This department may be in a position to muster enough votes in the Cabinet to ensure the choice of B rather than C.

But should opportunities foregone be evaluated by the government merely on the basis of their effect on healthiness? Income transfer itself may have some value placed on it by the government apart from its effects on health. The relative value of this income redistribution consideration needs to be taken into account. Consequently considering the government's alternatives and given its new preference function in which a weight is placed both on income redistribution and on healthiness, its optimal choice is likely to be on the trade-off frontier to the right of position C. Hence, once trade-offs and values relevant to the problem are *fully* considered, the government's welfare function supports some reduction in the attainable health of the community for the sake of greater income support. In this model, income support has a price when carried beyond C in terms of foregone health (for instance a movement from C to D means a shift from isoquant Q_2Q_2 to isoquant Q_1Q_1 and hence a lowering of healthiness) but up to C there is no such cost even though public health services are foregone (for instance a movement from B to C means a shift from isoquant Q_1Q_1 to isoquant Q_2Q_2, so raising healthiness and at the same time increasing income transfers). A choice of B under political pressure from the Health Department would mean that *some* healthiness *and some* income transfers are 'needlessly' foregone.

Science policy example — care in evaluating opportunity costs

The importance of carefully considering required trade-offs or opportunity costs can be illustrated by another hypothetical example from science policy. Suppose that a nation is using a given amount of resources on scientific effort to produce ideas at home and to import ideas from abroad. The allocation of scientific resources for home production and import of ideas can be varied and consequently changes the number of ideas imported and the number produced domestically. The production possibility set of ideas (given the quantity of resources used for scientific effort) might be as indicated by the hatched area OABCD in Figure 6.3. The shape of this set indicates that along the boundary AB the import of ideas complements home production of ideas and along the boundary DC home production of ideas complements the import of ideas. In the first instance, the import of ideas stimulates local inventiveness and in the

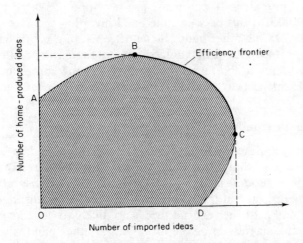

Figure 6.3   While the production of many commodities is strictly competitive, that of others can be complementary up to a point, as in the above case. Unless production possibility frontiers are adequately explored serious policy errors can be made. For instance, a policy which aimed to maximize the number of ideas produced at home by concentrating all resources on home production of ideas and allocating no resources to the transfer of ideas from abroad would lead to production at point A and fail in its objective.

latter case local inventiveness (minimum skill or knowledge about science) facilitates the import of ideas. From this relationship it is clear that the extremely nationalistic goal of maximizing the output of home-produced ideas will not be achieved if the concentration of resources on home production of ideas is too restrictive of the import of ideas, for then the number of ideas may fall along AB of the boundary of the production possibility set. Provided that more ideas are more highly valued than less, the only efficient allocations of scientific resources are those corresponding to the boundary of the production possibility frontier between B and C. This is the efficient set or frontier. The optimal choice in this set depends upon the relative valuation placed upon home-produced and imported ideas (see Chapter 14).

Sunk costs and opportunity costs

Sometimes opportunity costs are not correctly evaluated because sunk costs are not ignored in decision-making. Sunk costs are historical outlays which cannot be recovered. They are bygones. Thus if I purchase a piece of machinery for £1,000 and it costs £500 to install it, the historical cost of this equipment is £1,500. If after it is installed the best price (net) that can be obtained for it is £100 (maybe for scrap), the *sunk* cost is £1,400 and its opportunity cost after installation is £100. Prior to purchase, however, its opportunity cost (profit disregarded) is £1,500. Historical and sunk costs are irrelevant to decisions about the future *operation* of the machine. Thus if the net operating profit per year from the machine turns out to be £8 per year and the best rate of interest is 10 per cent., profit can be increased by selling the machine for £100 if it has been installed and investing the £100 at the going rate of interest. On the other hand, if the net operating profit happens to be £15 annually, profit would be maximized by continuing to operate the machine rather than by selling it and investing the money at the going rate of interest. Historical and sunk costs in no way affect the optimal use decision.

Sunk costs and the economics of bureaucracy and politics

While this may appear clear, the principle is not always taken into account. Sometimes it is argued that the mere fact that so much has already been outlaid on a project is a good reason for it to continue, otherwise all the earlier investment may be lost. But this or much of this past expenditure may already be a sunk cost and if further expenditure is not likely to be recovered this will merely add to the magnitude of the loss. On the other hand, the fact that a large amount of costs is already sunk is not a reason for discontinuing a project. If a positive return can be obtained from further expenditures on the project after allowing for their opportunity costs and for the realizable value of resources already committed (for instance the scrap value of equipment), it is profitable to continue the project even though sunk costs are considerable. Hence the longer that cancellation of a project is delayed the more worth while it is to complete the project. Thus the more specifically resources are already committed to a project and therefore the less the scope for using them elsewhere, the lower is their recoverable cost and, other things equal, the greater the likelihood of continuation of a project being optimal once it has commenced. If, furthermore, the flexibility of committed resources tends to become less as a project develops, the probability that it will be optimal to complete the project increases. So for a bureaucrat interested in the completion of a project, it is optimal for him to delay its review as long as possible and commit resources as inflexibly as possible to the project as quickly as possible. Consequently bureaucrats to increase their own budgets may promote and carry through projects which have high opportunity costs.

Anglo-French cooperation in the development of the Concorde supersonic transport illustrates the importance of opportunity costs. Both countries fully committed themselves to this development and no arrangements were made for considering the research by stages and considering its termination at each stage, even though it had become clear to both parties prior to completion of the project that all costs would be sunk and a loss would be made on further expenditure. It appears even at the prototype stage that it would have been more profitable to have terminated the project rather than to have built a number of aircraft for commercial use. The project is expected to have cost Britain and France together £1,700 million (1975 prices) and the actual aircraft purchased by British Airways and Air France are reported to be making an operating loss. The only reason for completing the project might have been the matter of national prestige. But even national prestige involves an opportunity cost. Alternative means may have given more prestige for the same cost or the same prestige at a lower cost. Trade-offs need to be considered.

Plant modernization or replacement policies failing to take account of social opportunity costs

The importance of opportunity costs and of disregarding sunk costs can be seen from another policy context. Policies to subsidize or encourage the replacement of old machines may result in economic waste as illustrated in Figure 6.4. Suppose that all existing machines or plants in an industry are one period (e.g. decade) old and incorporate or embody the techniques of the early period and have no alternative use except in the industry concerned (and no scrap value). If the marginal cost of operating these plants up to full capacity is constant, the opportunity cost of operating them is their total *variable* cost of operation. Suppose that a new technique is discovered and embodied in plants that can be purchased in the current period t. Average *total* cost of operation of the new plants incorporating the new technique are lower than for new plants incorporating the old technique. So if any new plants are to be installed it is more profitable to install those incorporating the new technique. If DD represents demand in period t and X_{t-1} is the output accounted for by old plants working at full capacity and having a marginal cost of operation MC_{t-1}

140

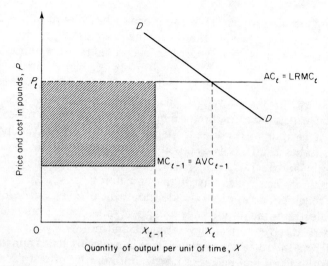

Figure 6.4 Policies to encourage rapid modernization of an industry by replacing plants embodying old techniques with those embodying new techniques can fail to take account of opportunity costs and add to scarcity. In this example, the deadweight cost of replacing existing plants producing X_{t-1} by modern ones is represented by the hatched area.

and if AC_t represents the average costs of production with new plants embodying the new technique (equals the *long-run* marginal costs of introducing new plants since long-run average cost is constant), it is *optimal to install* sufficient modern plants to supply $X_t - X_{t-1}$ of the product. At this level of supply, long-run marginal costs are equal to the value of the last unit of output supplied. It is *not socially optimal to replace* the existing plants. To do so would add to the total costs of producing X by the equivalent of the hatched area. This is so since the opportunity cost of new expenditures is at best equal to itself whereas the only opportunity costs involved in operating existing machines are total *variable* costs. Policies such as tax concessions and subsidies for the replacement of old plants or machinery incorporating old-fashioned techniques *can* add to scarcity rather than reduce it. Technological efficiency and economic efficiency are quite different.

Importance of marginal costs in policy-making

In considering costs, economists tend to emphasize the importance of marginal costs of production (the additional cost of producing an extra unit of output of a commodity) as an important cost consideration to be taken into account in profit maximization. Indeed, profit maximization by a firm requires that its level of production be such that its marginal cost of production equals its marginal revenue from selling its output. Furthermore, marginal costs represent opportunity costs at the margin of a firm's operations.

An advantage claimed for the marginalist approach to optimization is that it economizes on the amount of information needed to determine an optimum. While the output necessary to maximize profit could in theory be found by enumerating the profit corresponding to every output possibility, this can be time-consuming and could be costly to the firm if it tried to determine its complete profit function by trial. Mathematically, the marginalist search for a maximum of profit considers only variations of profit in the neighbourhood of critical values, namely those quantities of output for which marginal cost equals marginal revenue. One problem, however, is that an actual firm may not know the relevant mathematical functions. But this is not necessary in practice because in many situations a firm can proceed by trial-and-error to an optimum. A firm can observe the marginal change in its revenue and in its costs by experimentally altering output and use this information to guide it to its optimum without its having to enumerate *all* possibilities. It can engage in optimal search procedures relying on marginalist principles.

Nevertheless, as discussed in depth in Chapter 7, economists such as Hall and Hitch (1939) have expressed doubts about whether actual firms do use marginalism to determine an optimum. Their empirical study indicates that firms engage in full cost pricing, i.e. base their price for products on average costs of production at normal capacity plus a profit mark-up. Some writers have argued from this that firms are not profit-maximizers and that prices are determined on the basis of costs rather than demand. It has been pointed out by Machlup (1967), for instance, that in some circumstances the above approach is consistent with profit maximization. Recent econometric evidence, however, tends to support the traditional view that both demand and costs are important long-term determinants of prices, even though prices appear to be relatively stable or inflexible in the short-term.

Neglect of marginalism in policy decisions — preference of bureaucrats and erroneous use of cost–benefit analysis

Serious error can be made in optimization problems if marginal opportunities are not explored and major alternatives are not taken into account. This can be illustrated by a research and development (R & D) problem involving a trade-off between cost and time. Assume that a decision has been made to launch a R & D project to provide a technical breakthrough in a particular field, e.g. a method for safe disposal of nuclear wastes, landing a man on Mars, building a new SST airliner, setting up a space shuttle. The cost of achieving this break-through is likely to be greater the more quickly the breakthrough is desired, so that the cost function for a breakthrough is like that shown in Figure 6.5 by the curve marked CC. To determine the optimal expenditure on R & D in relation to the delay factor, the (discounted) benefit of a breakthrough after any span of time must be considered. The curve marked BB in Figure 6.5 might, for instance, be the total benefit in this case. While this benefit might rise with delay at first, it is shown to fall eventually. It might eventually fall as a result of a rise in likelihood that others (other nations, other firms) will make the breakthrough. The benefits and costs represented by *BB* and *CC* are assumed to be appropriately discounted to the start of the project.

The optimal time in which to aim for a breakthrough is t_m assuming that net benefits are to be maximized, and this implies an optimal discounted expenditure on research of E_1. For the breakthrough time t_m, the marginal benefits of waiting equal the marginal costs of waiting. At this point, the marginal reduction in research costs as a result of delay is equal to the marginal fall in benefits caused by this delay, as indicated by the equal slopes of the tangents to the total cost and total benefit curves at t_m.

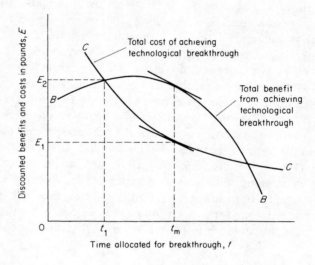

Figure 6.5 The optimal breakthrough time for this research project is t_m, being the span for which the marginal savings in cost of delay equals the marginal fall in benefits as a result of delay. Although benefits exceed cost after t_1, speedier breakthrough than at t_m is not optimal.

However, bureaucrats desiring to maximize their expenditure and their control of resources may argue for speedier development, for instance for development within a time-span of t_1 with an expenditure of E_2. Indeed, they might even employ cost–benefit analysts to reinforce their wishes. The cost–benefit analyst can show that the discounted benefits of the project equals the discounted cost at t_1 and that if the rate of interest represents the alternative use of the investment the project is worth while, proceeding with at an expenditure level of E_2. But as already pointed out this leaves out of consideration those time/cost/benefit trade-off possibilities which can raise net benefits even further, such as those in the neighbourhood of t_m.

X-inefficiency as an element in costs

The per-unit cost curves normally used in economic analysis represent the minimum attainable costs of producing the alternative levels of output. The average cost curve normally used in economic analysis therefore is the lower boundary of attainable average costs given the known techniques of production. This is represented in Figure 6.6 by the curve marked SAC.

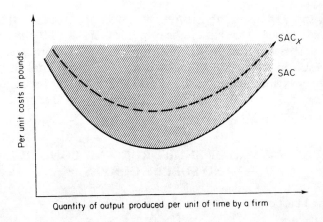

Figure 6.6 The curve SAC represents the type of short-run average cost curve normally used in economic analysis and indicates that costs are minimized at each level of output. Per-unit costs may in fact fall in the hatched area due to X-inefficiency.

Actual average cost, however, may lie above this in the hatched area. This may occur because management fails to use the available cost-minimizing technique or because management and employees fail to make the effort and take the *necessary* action to minimize cost. Production involves effort and the need for decisions to be made by a range of employees, all of whom have some discretion in the production decision process. There is room for variation in the conscientiousness and ability with which employees fulfil their roles because their actions cannot be completely regulated and *contracts* cannot be exactly specified and fully enforced with profit. Thus due to this factor variations occur in per-unit costs between firms and countries using exactly the same techniques of production and producing the same levels of output.

Liebenstein describes inefficiency (other than technological inefficiency) resulting in per-unit costs in excess of the attainable minimum (for each level of output) as X-inefficiency. Even though the firm uses the best technique, X-inefficiency can cause its actual short-run average cost curve to be like the broken line marked SAC_X in Figure 6.6. Because contracts cannot completely specify and determine the behaviour of individuals employed by a company, there is scope for variation in their conscientiousness, for attention to detail, and for organizational slack. As Leibenstein (1966) puts it:

> . . . for a variety of reasons people and organisations normally work neither as hard nor as effectively as they could. In situations where competitive pressure is light, many people will trade the disutility of greater effort, of search, and the control of other people's activities for the utility of feeling less pressure and of better interpersonal relations.

Individuals enjoy some on-job leisure. One effect of this can be that inputs are not combined efficiently so that on the cost side it can be difficult to disentangle allocation inefficiency and X-inefficiency. It is also true that organizational slack can result in technological inefficiency. Organizational slack can cause both allocative and technological inefficiency. If a certain degree of organizational slack is the social norm X-inefficiency need not even disappear in a purely competitive economic system.

6.3   THE NATURE OF SHORT-RUN AND LONG-RUN COST AND SUPPLY CURVES

The U-shaped cost curve

Economists have assumed that typically firms have U-shaped average cost of production curves. While this relationship might be typical in agriculture, it appears to be less common for manufacturing industry. The assumed typical (Marshallian) average cost relationships are illustrated in Figure 6.7. This figure shows a selection of three short-run average cost curves marked SAC_1, SAC_2, and SAC_3 and a corresponding long-run average cost curve marked LRAC which is the envelope (lower boundary) of all the possible short-run average cost curves. The minimum efficient scale of plant or optimum size of firm (that minimizing per-unit costs of production) corresponds to an output of $\bar{X}$ and has the short-run average costs represented by SAC_2.

Under perfectly competitive market conditions and in the long run firms are forced to adopt the scale of plant which minimizes the long-run average cost of production, otherwise they make a loss and fail to survive. Under perfect competition and in the long run the price of the product produced by a firm becomes equal to its minimum long-run average costs of production. Because of contractual arrangements profit is a residual for the firm. If in the short term a firm earns above normal profit this is because entry of new firms is impeded. To the extent that a firm's source of short-term above normal profit is its access to superior factors of production (such as superior management) which in the short-term are not paid their long-term rent, competition from other firms in the long run for these factors will force up their prices until no firm has a cost advantage in this regard. Under perfect competition and in the long run all firms operate a minimum efficient scale plant at minimum cost,

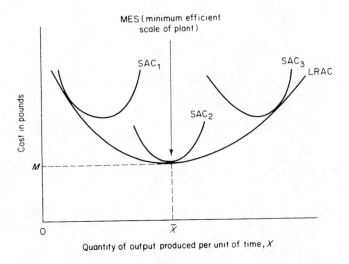

Figure 6.7 Economists have assumed that typically short-run and long-run average cost curves for production are U-shaped like those shown. In the above case the minimum efficient scale of plant is that corresponding to SAC_2.

but, as will be discussed later, this need not occur under imperfect competition.

Doubts about U-shaped short-run cost curves — the reversed-L alternative

In recent years economists such as J. Johnston (1960) have claimed that the short-run per-unit costs of firms are better characterized by the cost curves shown in Figure 6.8 than by U-shaped ones. This cost relationship implies that the firm's short-run supply curve is of a reversed-L shape rather than positively sloped as is normally assumed. The firm's average variable cost is constant and equal to its marginal cost until its production utilizes the full capacity of existing plant. To increase production beyond this full capacity level is virtually impossible or prohibitively expensive, given the existing plant. Average total cost is represented in Figure 6.8 by the downward sloping curve marked ATC.

In this reversed-L model, firms may be in short-term equilibrium when they have excess capacity and their average total cost is falling. The demand for the output of the industry may, for instance, have fallen from D_1D_1 to D_2D_2 as indicated in Figure 6.9, in which the industry supply curve is shown as SS. The lower branch of this curve is equal to average variable cost, OB. In this case, total excess capacity equivalent to $X_F - X_2$ develops. Political pressure may be put on the government by firms and unions in the industry to grant a subsidy on sales. Firms may point to excess capacity and point out that their per-unit costs will be lowered if this capacity is utilized, and trade unions may point to the employment raising impact of the subsidy. Suppose that a subsidy of AB is

146

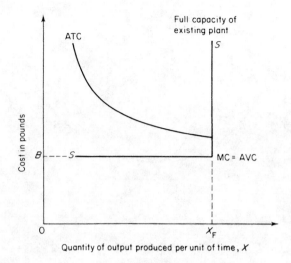

Figure 6.8   The supply curve of a manufacturing firm may be characterized by a reversed-L supply curve like that marked SS. Its average variable cost of production is constant and equal to its marginal cost up to its full capacity level of output, X_F.

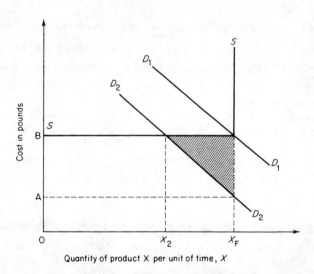

Figure 6.9   If the short-run supply curve of a manufacturing industry supplying product X is as indicated by SS and demand is D_2D_2, excess capacity occurs in the industry. Although a subsidy on supplies designed to achieve full capacity lowers average total costs (the subsidy excluded), it results in a deadweight economic loss, represented by the hatched triangle.

granted. It can be shown that it will result in a Kaldor–Hicks deadweight loss, indicated by the hatched area in Figure 6.9. This loss occurs because D_2D_2 represents the value to consumers of additional production of X and short-run marginal cost (represented by OB because average variable costs are constant) indicates the marginal value to consumers of resources (used in producing X) if employed in producing alternative products. Although the *total per-unit* costs of production will fall if output expands to full capacity, given the demand curve D_2D_2 in Figure 6.9 and the fact that the marginal cost represents the opportunity cost of resources, a policy designed to assist production to full capacity adds to scarcity. If demand has permanently fallen to D_2D_2, then *in the long run* it is optimal to reduce the number of plants in the industry and eliminate excess capacity by doing so.

Optimal industry structure and long-run average costs — empirical evidence on economies of scale

The nature of long-run cost curves are particularly important for economic efficiency when there is only room on economic efficiency grounds for a few firms or plants in an industry. If long-run average cost declines with production, it is possible for an industry consisting of a few firms to reach an equilibrium in which all firms are operating below minimum efficient scale and hence production of the industry is achieved at greater per-unit cost than would be the case if that production were shared by fewer firms. Economies of scale in the production of some manufacturing products are such that the whole output of an industry can be most economically supplied by one or a few plants, i.e. by a monopoly or an oligopoly. One or a few plants operating at minimum efficient scale may be able to satisfy the whole demand for the product of an industry. This is illustrated in Table 6.1 which sets out the (maximum) number of plants needed to supply UK output at minimum per-unit cost. The table also gives the increase in costs which would occur if UK minimum efficient scale output happened to be equally shared by twice the number of plants needed to minimize cost. As indicated, four plants or less would minimize the costs of producing the UK output of some manufactured goods, for instance chemicals, cars, diesel engines, and dyes.

Doubts about U-shaped long-run average cost curves

Note that Table 6.1 gives the *maximum* number of plants consistent with minimizing the cost of UK output. A smaller number of plants could also minimize unit costs of production. This is because in manufacturing industry the long-run average cost curve as suggested by Bain may have a horizontal minimum segment like AB in Figure 6.10 and then turn up like $LRAC_1$ or even remain horizontal like $LRAC_2$. Only in the case where the long-run average cost curve is U-shaped is the number of plants needed to minimize the cost of producing an industry's output uniquely determined. Both Bain (1972) and

Table 6.1 Maximum number of plants needed in the United Kingdom to produce the UK output of selected products at lowest per-unit costs and the percentage rise in cost resulting from a doubling of the number of plants.

Product	Maximum number of plants needed to produce UK output at minimum cost	Percentage rise in costs as a result of doubling the number of plants in the previous column if output is equally divided
Turbo-generators	1[a]	5[b]
Aircraft	1[a]	20[b]
Electronics (radar, computers)	1[a]	8–10[b]
Machine tools	1[a]	5[b]
Dyes	1	22
Refrigerators, washing machines	2	8
Electric motors	2	15
Diesel engines	2	4
Cars	2–3	6
Chemicals	3–4	9
Steel	3–12	5–10
Cement	9–14	9
Oil refining	10	5
Bicycles	12	Small
Bread	100–200	15
Bricks	200	25
Footwear	500	2

[a]A single plant would not reach minimum efficient scale.
[b]Approximation based upon percentage increase in unit costs at 50% MES (minimum efficient scale) compared with unit costs at MES.
Sources: Pratten (1971) and Cmnd 7198 (1978).

Pratten (1971) found no evidence to support the contention that U-shaped long-run average cost curves are the general rule in manufacturing industry. Indeed, their empirical evidence suggests that it is more likely that long-run average costs continually decline with output and approach a constant limit or become constant. There is no strong evidence to indicate that they typically turn up after a point. Consequently, as suggested by Joan Robinson (1933), it is typically the size of the market and other factors which limit the size of the firm and/or its rate of growth.

An equilibrium excessive number of plants or firms in an industry

In practice the number of plants in manufacturing industries often exceed the number needed to minimize the cost of producing the output of these industries. An excessive number of plants from this point of view (not the only point of view because liberals such as Rowley and Peacock (1975) would be prepared to forego possible economic gain to guard against the possible

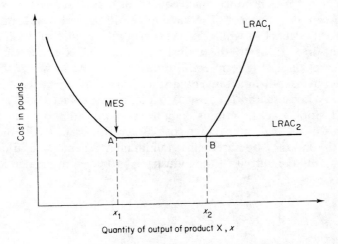

Figure 6.10 Long-run average costs for a manufacturing plant may typically have a horizontal segment such as AB and not be U-shaped with a unique minimum. In the above case, the minimum efficient scale corresponds to an output of x_1.

political power of big business and monopolies) may occur because adjustment to long-term equilibrium can take a considerable amount of time or the state of competition in an industry may permit an excessive number of plants to exist in the long run. In a monopolistically competitive industry, as is pointed out in the next chapter, firms may operate in long-run equilibrium at less than minimum efficient scale and with excess capacity. While unit costs (and prices) exceed minimum unit costs in this case, it is possible that consumers are prepared to pay higher prices for greater variety. However, there are competitive circumstances in which consumers clearly lose as a result of an excessive number of plants and a Kaldor–Hicks gain can be made by reducing the number of plants.

Consider the following example. Assume that all firms in an industry and all entrants have the same long-run average cost curves and that the industry produces a homogeneous (that is non-differentiated) product. Furthermore, suppose that demand is equally divided among suppliers (since consumers are indifferent about suppliers), all of whom charge the same price. Each firm regards its demand curve as $1/n$th that for the industry when n represents the number of firms in the industry. Thus if the industry demand curve is

$$p = a - bX$$

where p is the price of the product and X is the quantity demanded, each individual firm considers its demand curve to be

$$p = a - \frac{b}{n} X$$

and *sets a price* for its product which equates its marginal revenue $(a - \frac{1}{2}b/nX)$ to its long-run marginal cost. The same price will be set by all firms. If above normal profit occurs this will induce entry (in the absence of significant entry barriers) of new firms to the industry. Entry will continue (in the large numbers case) until long-term equilibrium is achieved in which the demand curve faced by each firm is tangential to its long-run average cost curve as in Figure 6.11. Because the (imagined) demand curve faced by each firm is downward sloping, each attains long-term equilibrium on the downward sloping part of its long-run average cost curve. Consequently, in the long-run plants in the industry operate below minimum efficient scale, a deadweight loss occurs, and the output of the industry is produced at greater cost than is necessary.

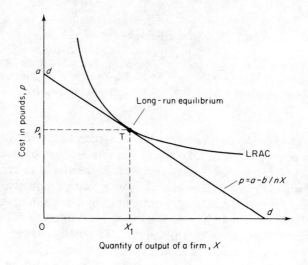

Figure 6.11   As a result of entry, the demand curve faced by a firm rotates on a point *a* until it is tangential to the long-run average cost curve as shown at point T. Even in an industry producing a homogeneous product firms may come into equilibrium at a point such as T. They operate at less than MES and a social loss occurs.

Let us specifically identify the deadweight loss that occurs as a result of the duplication of firms or plants in a decreasing cost industry. Take the above model and assume for simplicity that in long-term equilibrium there are two firms in the industry just able to earn normal profit. Thus if in Figure 6.12 *DD* represents the market demand curve for the industry's product, *dd* (half-way between *DD* and the *Y* axis) is the hypothetical demand curve faced by each firm. Each firm is in equilibrium at a point such as T so each produces X_1 of the product and $2X_1 = X_2$ is supplied to the market and is sold at a price of p_1.

Given the cost and demand conditions in the industry, the Paretian optimal level of supply for the industry is X_4, the level of supply for which long-run marginal cost equals demand, and can only be achieved if one firm alone supplies the market and supplies this amount. The deadweight loss due to duplication consists of two components, or the Kaldor–Hicks gain of shifting from a situation in which both firms produce X_1 to one in which one only supplies the market and produces X_4 consists of two components. The total Kaldor–Hicks gain is as follows:

(1) $(p_1 - G_1)X_2 = (p_1 - G_1)2X_1$, the total cost saving as a result of X_2 being produced by one firm rather than production being equally shared, *plus*
(2) the hatched area in Figure 6.12, which is the difference between the additional value of extra production and its marginal cost.

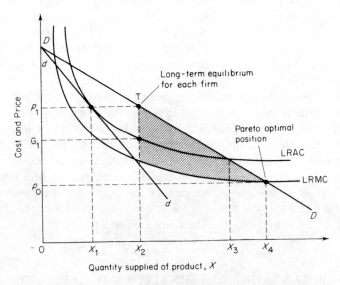

Figure 6.12   Long-term equilibrium in the large group decreasing cost case occurs at a point like T where all firms just earn normal profit. As explained in the text, duplication of firms under decreasing cost conditions can lead to large Kaldor–Hicks welfare losses.

As can be seen, a substantial deadweight loss may occur as a result of duplication. It might, of course, be held that marginal cost pricing is not practical in the decreasing cost case because the monopolist would make a loss. But even if the monopolist were to adopt average cost pricing, i.e. charge a price equating long-run average cost and demand, the deadweight loss of duplication would still be substantial. It would be equal to the cost saving indicated in (1) above *plus* the hatched area described in (2) *less* the area of the hatched triangular-type figure bounded by LRMC between X_3 and X_4.

The previous argument that Kaldor–Hicks losses arise from duplication of plants or firms if costs are decreasing also applies in the kinked demand curve oligopolistic case in which rivals match any cut in price below the 'customary' level which equates their long-run marginal cost and marginal revenue (based upon their proportional share of industry demand) but do not follow any increase in price above this level. A Kaldor–Hicks loss occurs in this 'small' group case and Figure 6.12 can be easily modified to show this.

The possibility of firms operating in an industry at less than minimum efficient scale, even in the long term, raises the question of whether or not it may be desirable for a government to foster mergers in an industry. In Japan and within Europe mergers have been fostered by governments, e.g. in the man-made fibre industry, to improve the international competitiveness of the domestic industry. In the United Kingdom, the government has used its purchasing policy to foster mergers by suppliers of airframes, engines, and helicopters. Depending upon the circumstances, mergers may enable greater plant economies to be obtained because the number of plants can be reduced, multi-plant economies may be reaped, and greater distribution and selling economies and financial economies may be obtained. Mergers may also reduce risks and increase the market power of the firms merging. It is possible, however, for X-inefficiency to increase under the protective umbrella of greater market power and the rate of technical progress may taper off. Empirical evidence indicates that even though it may be possible for merged firms to earn greater profit by taking advantage of economies of scale, such economies do not appear to be realized, at least in the medium and short term. Most studies indicate that the profitability of companies tends to fall after a merger, even though merged companies may grow at an increased rate, and there is little evidence to suggest economies of scale are the main reasons for mergers. Managerial considerations such as the desire for increased security, market power, and growth may play a larger role in merger decisions. The significance of these motives for the theory of the firm will be discussed in Chapter 7.

6.4   LEARNING, EXTERNALITIES, AND POLICY

Evidence on the importance of learning by doing

On the whole traditional economic analysis has neglected learning and experience as an influence on supply. Especially in new and complex manufacturing it has been observed that productivity improves with practice and experience. Arrow (1962) has called this 'learning by doing'. Significant studies of this phenomenon in the aircraft industry have been completed by Hartley (1965) in the United Kingdom and by Alchian (1950) in the United States. Both economists find that labour productivity in building airframes rises with the *cumulative* number built. In fact Hartley's evidence is that an '80 per cent learning curve' applies. As the (cumulative) total output of airframes is doubled, direct labour input per aircraft declines by 20 per cent. Consequently, direct labour used in producing aircraft varies in the way indicated by curve AL in Figure 6.13. Curve AL shows direct labour used *per* aircraft as a

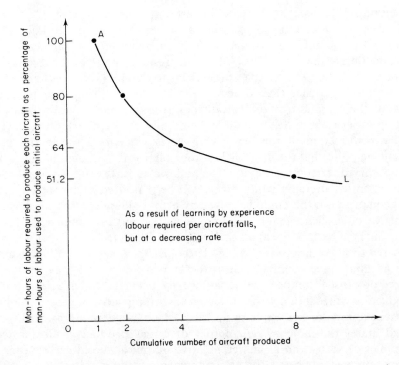

Figure 6.13 Labour required to produce each aircraft declines with experience or learning as the cumulative number of aircraft produced rises. As a result of a *doubling* of cumulative aircraft production, labour requirements may typically fall to *80 per cent.* of their original level per aircraft, as indicated above.

percentage of labour required to produce the first aircraft. The curve declines at a decreasing rate as cumulative aircraft output rises (learning becomes of less significance) and approaches a limit.

Similar results have since been obtained for shipbuilding, the production of radar equipment, and the manufacture of metal products. As pointed out by Baloff (1966), these improvements in productivity may not be due solely to increased manual skill, but can also reflect an improvement in managerial and engineering skills with experience. Furthermore, beyond some limit to cumulative output, no further increases in productivity can be expected since learning and experience has reached its limit.

Policy implications of learning by doing

Learning by doing has a number of policy implications. As a result of learning by experience, a firm's unit costs of producing any level of output may fall with its cumulative output to date, at least until its cumulative output reaches some limit. In other words, a firm's static average cost curve as a function of its current output may *shift* down (nearer to the *X* axis showing current output levels) with increases in past output or experience.

If this is so, a country introducing a new manufacturing technique from abroad or the manufacture of a new product may find that it can keep its costs of production at the lowest level by initially restricting use of the techniques to one or a few firms. This enables these firms to obtain a larger volume of sales and greater experience than otherwise, so rapidly lowering their production costs. As the demand for home production rises and once initial entrants have built up experience, other firms may be permitted to embark on production. So the introduction of the new technique is sequenced. Japan has used a sequencing policy but the drawback of the policy is that it gives initial entrants a temporary domestic monopoly. The policy also leaves the government with the problem of deciding which firms will be permitted to be early entrants, though in principle this could be solved by firms bidding for this privilege.

The learning phenomenon also implies that countries commencing production using new technology at an early stage are likely to be at a cost advantage compared to latecomers, even though latecomers have no natural disadvantage. Thus an innovative country such as the United States with a large domestic market obtains a competitive advantage by being a leader in the use and introduction of technology. Apart from the learning advantage, it also obtains early economies of scale (Vernon, 1966). In a large economy such as the United States the large *current* output of a new product yields substantial economies of scale, *and* a high cumulative output achieved early means that the per-unit cost curve as a function of current output is shifted down quickly and would be much lower than that for a country embarking on production of the new product at a later stage. Late entrants (countries or firms) can be placed at a severe cost disadvantage because of their lack of learning experience.

The learning effect has been suggested as a reason for temporarily protecting infant industries in countries not in the forefront of technological advance. The protection may enable local firms in a technologically lagging country to learn and build up experience by supplying a protected market. This may eventually allow firms to lower their unit cost below that of competitors if the country in question has a comparative natural advantage in supplying the temporarily protected product. Protection is then no longer necessary. The problem from a policy point of view, however, is that it is not always possible to tell whether an infant industry will become viable and how long this is likely to take.

External economies as a source of falling per-unit costs and as reason for market failure

A firm may experience economies from its own expansion or from the growth of its whole industry (or complementary industries). If a firm experiences economies from expanding its own output its unit costs fall and *internal economies* are said to be present. If its unit costs fall, other things equal, as a result of the expansion of the whole industry *external economies* are said to occur. If the opposite effects are present, internal diseconomies and external diseconomies are respectively said to occur. Mathematically suppose that a firm's average cost of production, AC, are a function of its own output, x, and that of the whole industry, X:AC $= f(x,X)$. If $\partial f/\partial x < 0$, internal economies occur. If $\partial f/\partial X < 0$, external economies are present. A reversal of these inequalities implies internal diseconomies and external diseconomies, respectively.

If external economies can be reaped from the expansion of the whole industry, this may, but need not, result in the failure of markets to attain a social optimum. Markets adjust by localized private reactions (by each firm maximizing its own profit and each consumer his own utility) and in certain cases these reactions reinforce external economies so that a social optimum does eventuate as a result of participants following their own blind interest. But this does not always happen. To illustrate this take an extreme case.

Suppose that the productivity of a resource depends solely upon the number of units of the resource present in a region or area. Let Y represent the total quantity of the product produced by the resources. Assume that the production function of the resources in area 1 is as represented by OBC in Figure 6.14 and the production function in area 2 is as indicated by OBD.

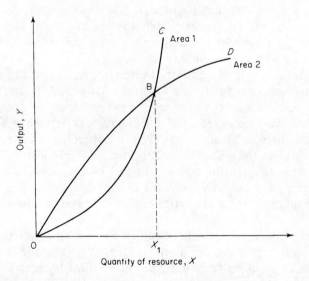

Figure 6.14 The average productivity of resource X is highest in area 2 when its quantity is less than X_1 but greater in area 1 when it exceeds X_1. Initially all of the resource may locate in area 2 and there may be no self-correcting mechanism to alter this location once X expands beyond X_1.

Each unit of X receives a return equal to its average productivity. Now if X increases from zero its average productivity will initially be highest in area 2 and development is likely to take place there. However, if the quantity of resource X increases beyond X_1 it is optimal to locate all of X in area 1. But since units of X may be under the control of many individuals (and the production function in area 2 may not be known with certainty) there is no simple mechanism to encourage a shift of resources from area 2 to area 1 once the quantity of X exceeds X_1, and as the quantity of X increases this resource may still continue to concentrate in area 1. In a manner similar to this industries may continue to grow in regions where they initially developed, even though this is no longer the most productive location. Similarly, existing cities or towns (which are to a large extent productive units) may continue to attract individuals and other resources and expand even though this is no longer the most productive location for the resources. In some countries this has influenced regional policy. Governments have established new cities by intervention, have given subsidies to firms locating away from major cities, or have taxed those firms at higher rates locating in major cities.

Spillovers and the divergence of social and private marginal costs

Another possible cause of market failures are spillovers or externalities in the production of commodities. These cause the marginal social costs of supplying commodities to diverge from the private marginal costs of supplying commodities. From a policy point of view it is important to consider what is the best means to ensure that such externalities are taken into account by producers. In this regard let us compare a tax on the emission of pollutants from an industry with a quota on these emissions.

Imagine that the marginal spillover or external cost imposed by the emission of a pollutant from an industry is a function of the total level of emission by the industry. Spillovers of the industry have a global rather than a localized impact. Let the curve marked ABC in Figure 6.15 represent the marginal spillover costs imposed by emissions from a particular industry and let the curve DBF represent the marginal cost to firms in the industry of controlling the level of emissions. In the absence of any control, the industry emits a quantity E_2 of a pollutant. However, the socially optimal level of pollution is E_1, where the marginal costs of controlling emissions equals the marginal costs of spillovers.

The level of emission of E_1 could be achieved by the government imposing at tax of T on each unit of the pollutant emitted. Weighing the tax against the marginal cost of reducing emissions, producers find it profitable to reduce their collective emission of the pollutant by $E_2 - E_1$. The uniform tax also ensures that the reduction in emissions is distributed between producers in a way which minimizes the costs of the reduction in pollution achieved.

Each firm reduces its level of emission of pollutants until the marginal cost of its abatement equals the tax rate on emissions. Because the tax rate on emissions is the *same* for all firms, their profit-maximizing behaviour results in each firm abating its pollution until the marginal costs of abatement are equal for all. Thus a necessary condition for minimizing the costs of pollution abatement in the industry is satisfied, namely that each firm reduce its level of pollution until the marginal cost of abatement is equal for all. Firms with lower marginal costs of abatement will reduce their pollution levels by more than those with high marginal costs.

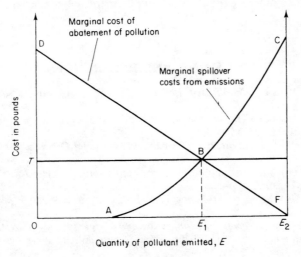

Figure 6.15 The socially optimal level of pollution is that for which the marginal spillover cost of emissions equals the marginal cost of abatement. This occurs for a quantity of emissions of E_1 and can be achieved as a result of a per-unit tax of T on emissions.

If a tax on emissions is used, the government does not have to impose special restrictions on firms as far as pollution is concerned, since, given the global pollution, firms automatically share the burden of reducing pollution between them in an efficient (cost-minimizing) way. In comparison, if quotas are used to restrict pollution and if the marginal cost of pollution abatement varies between firms, quotas or limits on emission have to be determined by the government for each firm. To allocate quotas in a way which minimizes the cost of abating pollution, the government needs a considerable amount of information. It needs to know each firm's marginal cost of pollution abatement. To collect this information can be difficult and costly. Incidentally, the taxation approach to controlling pollution can be regarded as a pricing approach. Firms are required to pay a price (in this case a uniform tax) for polluting and the optimal price (tax) is set to equate the marginal social value of pollution abatement with the marginal cost of abatement.

6.5 CONCLUSION

The discussion has shown how important it is to evaluate costs correctly in taking them into account in policy-making and that while marginal opportunity costs may be automatically and optimally (from a Paretian social viewpoint) taken into account in the market system, this does not always happen because of market failures, such as spillovers. On the other hand, government interference does not automatically correct for these failures. Indeed, as shown, it can be in the self-interest of politicians and bureaucrats to foster misperceptions of costs in order to increase their power and their influence over resources.

READING AND REFERENCES

Alchian, A. (1950). *Reliability of Progress Curves in Airframe Production*, Rand, RM-260-1.

Arrow, K. J. (1962). The economic implications of learning-by-doing, *Review of Economic Studies*, **29**, 155–173.

Bain, J. S. (1972). *Essays on Price Theory and Industrial Organization*, Little, Brown, Boston.

Baloff, H. (1966). The learning curve: some controversial issues, *Journal of Industrial Economics*, **14**, June, 275–282.

Boswell, J. (1976). *Social and Business Enterprises*, Chaps 3, 4 and 5, Allen and Unwin, London.

Cmnd. 7198 (1978). *A Review of Monopolies and Mergers Policy*. HMSO, London.

Hall, R. L. and Hitch, C. J. (1939). Price theory and business behaviour, *Oxford Economic Papers*, **49**, May, 12–45.

Hartley, K. (1965). The learning curve and its application to the aircraft industry, *Journal of Industrial Economics*, **13**, 122–128.

Johnston, J. (1960). *Statistical Cost Analysis*, Wiley.

Leibenstein, H. (1966). Allocative efficiency vs. X-efficiency, *American Economic Review*, **56**, June, 394.

Lipsey, R. G. (1979). *An Introduction to Positive Economics*, Chap. 17, Weidenfeld and Nicolson, London.

Machlup, F. (1967). Theories of the firm: marginalist, managerial, behavioural, *American Economic Review*, **57**, 1–33.

Pratten, C. F. (1971). *Economies of Scale in Manufacturing Industry*, Cambridge University Press.

Robinson, Joan (1933). *The Economics of Imperfect Competition*, Macmillan, London.

Rowley, C. K. and Peacock, A. T. (1975). *Welfare Economics: A Liberal Restatement*, Martin Robertson, London.

Tisdell, C. A. (1972). *Microeconomics: Theory of Economic Allocation*, Chaps 3, 7, 13, 14, 18, and 19, Wiley, Sydney.

Turvey, R. (1971). *Demand and Supply*, Chap. 4, Allen and Unwin, London.

QUESTIONS FOR REVIEW AND DISCUSSION

1. 'The duality theorem depends upon the price parity principle and economic agents seeking their self-gain (i.e. firms maximizing profits and consumers their utilities). The theorem shows that under perfect competition social opportunity costs are properly (in Pareto's sense) taken into account in the market system.' Explain and discuss.

2. Indicate at least two reasons why decisions by politicians or bureaucrats may fail to take proper account of social (or group) opportunity costs. Illustrate your answer with actual or hypothetical cases.

3. What are sunk costs? Why in terms of opportunity costs are they irrelevant for current and future decisions? Explain why a bureaucrat who is interested in seeing a project fully funded and brought to completion may aim for the greatest possible level of sunk costs in the project as quickly as possible.

4. 'Policies designed to subsidize the replacement of manufacturing plants or machinery (modernization programmes) may fail to pay attention to opportunity costs and may not be socially optimal.' Explain and discuss.

5. Explain how marginal cost concepts can reduce the costs involved in the decision-making process. Are marginalist concepts important in decision-making by firms?

6. 'Cost–benefit analysis which fails to take full account of opportunity cost trade-offs in time may be favoured by bureaucrats and politicians.' Explain and discuss.

7. Some economists doubt whether U-shaped short-run and U-shaped long-run average cost curves are typical in manufacturing (and tertiary) industries. What alternatives have been suggested? What policy implications may the alternative long-run average cost curves have for the optimal number of firms in an industry?

8. 'An excessive (from a Kaldor–Hicks viewpoint) *equilibrium* number of firms in a decreasing cost industry is possible. Markets do not always have an in-built mechanism that ensures a socially optimal number of firms.' Illustrate and discuss.

9. On what factors does learning by doing depend and how does it affect input requirements as the cumulative level of production rises? What factors may help to explain the cost advantage of the United States in producing some new products? Distinguish between economies of scale and economies due to learning.

10. 'The learning phenomenon may mean that it is socially optimal to sequence the production of a new product or technique between firms in a country when it is introduced from abroad. But there are also difficulties in pursuing such a policy.' Discuss.

11. Distinguish between external economies for a firm and internal economies. Using these concepts explain why there may be no in-built mechanism in the economy to ensure optimal-sized cities. What types of policies have been introduced to deal with this problem? What are the dangers associated with such interventionist policies?

12. 'If spillovers exist marginal social costs are likely to diverge from marginal private costs, but a tax such as a pollution tax can be used to bring these costs into equality and create *a* social optimum. At this social optimum, a spillover may continue to exist. The tax approach to control is more efficient than allocating spillover quotas to polluters.' Discuss carefully.

PART C

Imperfect Markets

CHAPTER 7

The Behaviour of Firms

7.1 INTRODUCTION

The firm is one of the foundations of micro-economics. It acts as both a buyer and seller. Firms buy factors of production and combine them to produce goods and services. They can be privately or publicly owned, large or small in size, operating in different market structures. This does not mean that economic models of the firm are restricted to private firms in agriculture, manufacturing, and services plus state-owned industries providing goods and services for sale to consumers. Other private and state organizations can be analysed as firms. Examples include banks, charities, churches, cooperatives, political parties, and trade unions, together with government bureaucracies, state agencies, hospitals, schools, military bases, museums, prisons, sports centres, and universities. Some of these will be non-profit organizations. Economists need to know whether the market environment, the form of ownership, and the incentives facing the managers of an organization affect the behaviour and performance of firms.

To economists, firms are represented by a set of cost and revenue schedules and an objective function. This analytical framework is used to explain the behaviour of firms as reflected in their demands for labour, capital, and technology and their decisions about prices, outputs, and product quality. Such decisions also determine the size of firms. Traditionally, economists have analysed firms as profit-maximizers, but modern theories allow the pursuit of other aims such as sales, growth, and staff, or even 'satisfactory' performance. It is often believed that in private markets, departures from profit maximization are only possible under imperfect competition. This chapter provides a link between the previous sections which analysed competitive markets under profit-maximizing assumptions and the following parts which consider product market imperfections, factor inputs in the form of labour and energy, as well as the micro-economics of the public sector (e.g. bureaucracies). The analysis will be largely confined to private firms. Once again, the aim is to provide a framework which can be used to analyse a multitude of policy issues.

Consider the sheer extent of government policies towards private firms. There are taxes and subsidies on both factor inputs and outputs. For example, governments subsidize capital (physical and human investments), labour, research and development, and the subsidies might be restricted to one firm, an industry, or to all firms located in a certain region. How will firms respond to such subsidies? Similarly, a concern with inflation requires an understanding of the determinants of prices at the firm and industry level, and the likely effects of cost increases (e.g. wages). Worries about the balance of payments require a knowledge of the determinants of a firm's export performance and whether, for example, a buoyant home market is 'good' for overseas sales. There is also a need to predict how firms will respond to a government-promoted expansion of demand. Will they increase output and take on more labour, so helping the achievement of employment targets? Also, governments often intervene in specific markets through re-structuring and regulatory policies. In such circumstances, it is necessary to know whether mergers and regulation will affect firm behaviour and, if so, what might be the likely results for prices, output, employment, profits, technical progress, and efficiency. Sometimes policy measures which seem attractive can produce unexpected and undesirable outcomes. For instance, a policy to control advertising might lead firms to search for alternative, less efficient, and equally undesirable substitutes (e.g. more salesmen). Thus, models are required to explain and predict firm behaviour. Governments need to know how firms will respond to policy measures. In particular, policies which are introduced on the assumption that firms are profit-maximizers might be ineffective if enterprises pursue other goals.

Clearly, it is necessary to know the circumstances under which firms might pursue other objectives and the likely effects on their behaviour and performance. This chapter starts by outlining some of the central ideas in the development of theories of the firm. An explanation is required for the existence of firms, after which alternative objectives will be considered, together with their policy implications.

7.2 THE DEVELOPMENT OF THEORIES OF THE FIRM

This is not a text on the history of economic thought. Nevertheless, the development of ideas provides a fascinating study in methodology. In this respect, theories of firm behaviour can be most usefully presented in an historical context. Why, at any moment in time, is a particular theory rejected and a set of new ideas accepted? Does the history of economic thought show that theories of the firm have been rejected because of 'unrealistic' assumptions or because of a failure to offer accurate predictions? How, in fact, were our theories tested in the past? Today, there are sophisticated econometric techniques which can be applied through computers. In the past—before the Second World War—economists had to use graphs and plotted observations over time, always assuming that data were available. Official statistics were not as well developed or were non-existent. Or, tests were based on simple observations of the 'casual empiricism' type. Alternatively, in the 1930s, questionnaire and interview techniques were a popular method used by the

Oxford group of business economists. They simply asked businessmen what they were doing, how they behaved, and why.

When questions are asked as to why some theories are accepted and others are rejected, more general issues are raised about technical progress in ideas and the nature of the knowledge market. The point to be stressed here is that very little is known about the production function for economic knowledge and scientific progress. Economists frequently analyse industrial structure, conduct, and performance; they analyse industrial R & D, invention, innovation, and technical progress in firms and industries. While they are fond of asking these questions about the economy, they are more reluctant to apply the same analytical framework to their own knowledge market. How scientists operate in seeking to establish knowledge is largely shielded from analytical and empirical study. The history of economic thought can make a major contribution to understanding technical progress in the knowledge market. Were new models of the firm developed by individual economists working alone or were they part of a larger research term studying common problems? Were there rivals working in similar areas and how far were the new ideas developed through private correspondence, seminars, and publications? In other words, economists can be regarded as firms, working as one-man or multi-person research teams in different market environments (see Chapters 8 and 9).

The next task is to trace the development of ideas on the firm and this will be presented in the form of a story, linking some of the ideas of the key actors, such as Marshall, Chamberlin, Robinson, and Coase on the theory side; and Berle and Means, together with Hall and Hitch, on the empirical side. Inevitably the approach is superficial, the aim being to select a few key names which need to be known and which help to clarify developments in this field.

Marshall and the representative firm

Marshall introduced the representative firm and the biological life-cycle. He drew an analogy between the trees in the forest and the birth, growth, and inevitable decline of the typical business firm. Marshall's (1890) trees of the forest analogy went like this:

> . . . the young trees of the forest . . . struggle upwards through the shade of their older rivals. Many succumb on the way and a few only survive; those become stronger every year; they get a larger share of light and air with every increase of their height and at last they tower above their neighbours and seem as though they would grow for ever. But they do not; sooner or later age tells on them all; the taller ones gradually lose vitality; and one after another they give place to others which have on their side, the vigour of youth.

This biological life-cycle approach resembles a model of the growth and decline of firms, incorporating change and dynamics rather than a static equilibrium. Using this model, Marshall replaced the idea of long-run equilibrium and the marginal firm with the concept of a representative firm. This is *neither* a new entrant nor a well-established firm, but it is a firm with average access to internal and external economies. For Marshall, equilibrium in an industry is where the representative firms earns normal profits. He defined a representative firm as 'in a sense, an average firm; it has had a fairly long life, and fair success, which is managed with normal ability and which has normal access to internal and external economies'.

There are obvious difficulties in giving any operational meaning to the concept of the representative firm. What, for example, is a 'fairly long' life and 'fair' success? However, two developments were emerging in this period:

(1) There was the growth of the joint-stock company and limited liability, which raised the possibility of a permanent business firm which could outlive, and have a separate existence from, its entrepreneurial founder and owner. Marshall recognized this, so that by 1910, he had modified his trees in the forest analogy: 'As with the growth of trees, so it *was* with the growth of businesses, before the great recent development of vast joint-stock companies which often stagnate but do not readily die.'
(2) Economists were becoming more troubled by the existence of increasing returns to scale. How was it possible to reconcile increasing returns with competitive equilibrium? Here it should be remembered that the standard Marshallian view was that the theory of competition, together with the theory of monopoly, completed the economist's 'box of tools' for analysing the structure of modern industry. And in the competitive model, it was decreasing returns to scale which limited the size of firms: demand formed no limit to size, since it was perfectly elastic at the ruling price.

This brings us to the inter-war period, and the years of high theory in micro-economics. It was not solely a period of revolution in macro-economics; Chamberlin and Joan Robinson provided a 1930s revolution in micro-economics.

Chamberlin and Robinson: theory in the 1930s

Chamberlin's book *The Theory of Monopolistic Competition* and Joan Robinson's *The Economics of Imperfect Competition* were both published in 1933. Mention must also be made of Sraffa (1926) who contributed to the development of ideas which suggested that with increasing returns to scale and many firms competing against each other, the size of firm would be limited by downward sloping demand curves. Chamberlin and Robinson were the pioneers of the marginal approach to the theory of the firm and the notion that profit maximization requires the equality of marginal cost and marginal revenue. Chamberlin, in particular, introduced product differentiation and brand loyalties in markets consisting of large numbers of firms, with free entry and each firm faced with a downward sloping demand curve. In other words, there could be competition without horizontal demand curves and there could be downward sloping demand curves without monopoly. The result was monopolistic competition, with possible examples being garages, shops, and taxi-cabs. One of the implications of Chamberlin's model was his tangency solution. This predicted firms with excess capacity in the short run and unexploited economies of scale (see Chapter 6 and Figures 6.11 and 6.12). Thus, there would be too many firms in the industry, each of less than optimal size. Policy-makers often use these features as an argument for re-structuring an industry through state-supported mergers.

Evidence in the 1930s

The 1930s was also important for empirical work. In 1932, there was the pioneering work of Berle and Means which found US evidence of the divorce or separation between ownership and control in the large firm. It was argued that control had passed into the hands of the salaried management (e.g. the Managerial Revolution). With managerial control the possibility arises that managers might pursue their own objectives which could differ from the profit-maximizing concern of the shareholders.

Against this background, there was a major attack on profit maximization by two Oxford economists, Hall and Hitch (1939). As a result of talking to businessmen, Hall and Hitch argued that firms do not attempt to maximize profits. For example, they have no idea of marginal cost, marginal revenue, and the elasticity of demand. Instead, prices are based on the *full cost* principle. With this principle, prices are determined by estimating average direct costs (constant over a large output range) plus an allowance for overheads and a profit margin (see Chapter 7, Figure 7.7).

Change since 1945

Criticisms of profit maximization have led to the development of alternative objective functions. Managerial theories of the firm consider the implications of maximizing sales (Baumol, 1959), growth (Marris, 1964), or a more general utility function (Williamson, 1964). Such models operate within the constrained maximization framework. An alternative approach has been developed by the organization-behavioural theorists (Cyert and March, 1963; Simon, 1966). On this view, firm behaviour cannot be separated from its internal organization. Firms are coalitions of different interest groups, including shareholders, workers, unions, and managers of various departments (e.g. production, finance, sales). Information is not freely available and each group is likely to pursue different and conflicting policy objectives, with the result that firms will 'satisfice' rather than maximize. Objectives are specified as targets or aspiration levels: they are likely to be revised upwards if easily achieved and downwards if they are difficult to attain. Further theoretical developments have attempted to model the behaviour of labour-managed firms or worker cooperatives in which labour hires capital (Meade, 1972; Vanek, 1975).

Critics have also concentrated on the market environment within which firms operate and the static, partial equilibrium approach. The analysis of monopolistic competition and the tangency solution have also been criticized. For example, what is the meaning of an *industry's* demand curve for different products (e.g. motor cars); indeed, what is an industry in this model? What prevents firms forming a cartel to produce the industry's output in a smaller number of plants exploiting scale economies and earning abnormal profits? There is also the fundamental methodological issue of whether the monopolistic competition model yields alternative predictions from the theories of competition and monopoly. Chicago economists have argued that if models are judged by predictions rather than assumptions, then perfect competition plus some monopoly when required performs as well as, or better than, monopolistic competition. Other economists claim that monopolistically competitive situations are more appropriately analysed as oligopoly markets. For example, three garages in a road form an oligopoly in the relevant local market. But, as will be shown, economic models of oligopoly are far from satisfactory.

Achievements and problems

Any survey must consider what has been achieved and what are the remaining unsolved problems. A comparison between Marshall and a modern textbook shows technical sophistication. Partly as a result of the efforts of Chamberlin and Robinson, economic models of the firm are now presented both geometrically and mathematically. Marginalism and calculus are used to present a clear, unambiguous model of the firm pursuing a variety of objectives. Economists can use this 'tool-kit' to analyse firm behaviour in different industrial situations (e.g. car, chemicals, footwear, and textile firms). Even so, are economists missing something?

An obvious deficiency is the general lack of empirical work on firm behaviour and the predictive accuracy of alternative models. Often this reflects the impossibility of obtaining sufficiently comprehensive and accurate data for individual firms. In addition, economists might be missing something by concentrating upon equilibrium. Models of the firm are usually static, equilibrium constructs. But real firms operate in a dynamic world of uncertainty. Markets are always changing and the future is uncertain. In these circumstances, firms are likely to be in permanent disequilibrium, always adapting to, and adjusting to, change. This emphasis on firm behaviour under uncertainty and doubts about the traditional emphasis on the firm in equilibrium has been reflected in *subjectivism*, associated with some Austrian economists (e.g. Hayek; Mises). This school focuses on the behaviour of individuals and groups in a world of uncertainty — in a world where individuals and firms do not have perfect information and knowledge and markets are not in long-run equilibrium. There is a further problem which is basic to this subject area and which was raised by Coase (1937). How can economists explain the existence of firms?

7.3 WHY DO FIRMS EXIST?

Transaction costs are a central part of any answer. Even in markets, transactions and exchange are not costless. Firms economize on transaction costs, where these include the costs of search, acquiring information, negotiating, bargaining, and reaching contractual agreements. Paradoxically, in capitalist economies, firms can be viewed as islands of central planning where market exchanges are eliminated and replaced with an entrepreneur who monitors and directs production. Within a firm, workers are directed by rules and orders, not by wages. But why are prices, markets, and exchange used for transactions between firms and with consumers, but not for transactions *within* firms? There are two reasons:

(1) Teamwork is more productive: there are gains from specialization, including economies of scale.
(2) Firms economize on transactions with the suppliers of resources, particularly labour.

The advantages of teamwork can be seen by envisaging its absence. Consider the possibility of independent individuals each specializing in a specific task, then selling their output to another individual producer who undertakes a further part of the job, and so on, to a final individual who sells the finished product. As an example, think of car assembly. One individual could manufacture part of the car and then sell the part to another individual who would add a further part towards the assembly of the car. On this basis, a long assembly line under one roof would not be required and the separate activities in car production could be done individually and coordinated through prices. Firms achieve this 'coordination' without the price mechanism. Why?

One reason is that teamwork is more productive. In many activities, a larger output can be obtained from a team than from separate outputs produced by independent individuals. A team allows beneficial specialization of tasks, with individuals as painters, electricians, assemblers, clerks, and managers. The possibility of managerial economies for large-scale outputs has led some organizationalists to claim that with appropriate management techniques no firm is too large to manage. They point to examples such as the Catholic Church and the size of armies in the Second World War. On this view, factors other than management limit the size of firms, for otherwise an economy would consist of only one firm. However, costs cannot be ignored. While teamwork is often more productive, it also has to be worth while. The larger team output compared with separate individual production has to exceed the costs of organizing and disciplining members of the team. With teams, problems arise because there can be shirking and 'free-riding'. In contrast, independent production means that an individual who produces less bears all of the costs of extra leisure. In a team, the costs of an individual's preference for more on-the-job leisure are not borne by the worker alone: some are shifted onto the group and the share of costs borne by the 'free-rider' is likely to be smaller with a large group. One solution to shirking and 'free-riding' is to hire a monitor to discipline the team. Sports teams use managers and coaches; factories hire managers, foremen, and supervisors; while schools have head-masters. But who monitors the monitor? One possibility is to make the monitor the residual claimant, receiving what is left after paying the team members their contractually agreed price. In this way, the monitor bears the risks. Traditionally, in capitalist firms, capital hires labour, but in worker cooperatives the risk-bearing roles are reversed and labour hires capital.

The contractual arrangements for sharing the residual affect behaviour and performance within the firm. Such matters cannot be ignored by policy-makers. Where all the workers share in the residual, as in labour-managed enterprises, there are greater incentives for the monitor to shirk. It has been suggested that, in such circumstances, the losses from greater shirking by the monitor will exceed the benefits of less shirking by a large number of residual-sharing workers. In capitalist enterprises, much depends on the type of firm. With an owner-managed unit, a single person receives all the profits and there is no sharing. Alternatively, self-policing through profit-sharing might be used in small teams such as partnerships. Companies or corporations appear to be similar to large labour-managed firms in that shirking and free-riding is likely where profits are shared among a large number of shareholders and liability is limited. However, rather than incur the costs of trying to control and improve management decisions, a dissenting shareholder can readily 'escape' by selling his shares. As a result, managerial shirking in companies with large numbers of shareholders will be policed by competition from new groups of potential managers, either from outside the firm (take-over) or from within the enter-prise. In contrast, in non-profit enterprises such as charities, mutual associa-tions, and state-owned enterprises, including hospitals and schools, there are no shareholders with private property rights in the activity. As a result, any potential profits are 'consumed' within the enterprise in such forms as luxury offices, on-the-job fringe benefits, and expense accounts.

This explanation for the existence of firms relies upon teamwork being worth while with a monitor, or his appointed agent, acting as a 'dictator'. It is the monitor who hires, fires, promotes, and allocates labour within the firm. In other words, within the firm there is an hierarchy in which workers and managers can be regarded not as antagonistic, but as complementary, members of the team. Everyone willingly agrees to accept the decisions of a monitor. As a result, a firm resembles a command economy in which coordination is achieved not by prices but by issuing orders and commands to workers. However, the hierarchy is a voluntarily agreed and mutually advantageous contractual relationship. The transaction advantages and costs of this contractual relationship need to be explained.

For simplicity, let us return to our imaginary world of no firms, with production undertaken by separate individuals. In principle, it would be possible to combine the resources owned by many different persons through a *multilateral contract* between the individuals. Such a contract would specify for each individual the type and quantity of resources to be supplied to the productive process, the time of supply, and the price of the transaction. But such a complex contract would be costly to negotiate and costly to enforce. Firms reduce these transaction costs. They obtain the advantages of team production with the much lower cost method of a *bilateral contract*. Each individual does not have to deal separately with every other agent in the productive process; instead each individual deals only with a single entity, the firm. The firm substitutes a single incomplete contract—an *employment agreement*—for many complete contracts. In this way, it economizes on the costs of negotiating separate contracts. And the employment agreement is usually expressed in general terms, which allows the firm to adapt and adjust to changing market conditions.

Various forms of contractual relationships exist between workers and firms both within and between enterprises. These might offer a wage for a clearly specified task, a salary contract providing a fixed income for an agreed period, a profit-sharing arrangement, or an apprenticeship which provides training in return for a given length of service. *Employment contracts are a crucial determinant of firm behaviour and performance in both the private and public sectors* (see Chapters 10 and 15). The firm has to devise and negotiate contracts which police factor productivity and offer incentives and rewards for achieving organizational goals. The actual form of the employment contract, and the costs of policing and enforcing it, will determine the opportunities for discretionary behaviour and on-the-job leisure, as reflected in X-inefficiency. Problems arise because no top manager, particularly in a large organization, has the knowledge and the time to monitor everyone. Self-interested individuals will seek opportunities for hoarding and distorting information to their benefit. Firms will respond by searching for contracts and internal organizational arrangements which will reduce opportunities for discretionary behaviour and result in the pursuit of the organization's goals. Internal monitoring devices and incentives include payment by results, promotion, supervision, and fringe benefits. Personnel departments can provide information on workers and managers: they can search for, and screen, new recruits and ascertain their motivation through, say, the use of references, certificates, and selection tests. However, internal monitoring is costly. In competitive markets, pressure from rivals will provide external policing. Interestingly, some large firms try to simulate external competitive policing through changes in their form of organization, although there might be trade-offs through the effects on scale economies. Large companies can be organized as unitary or multi-divisional firms. The unitary form (U-form) company is organized by function such as development, production, finance, marketing, and sales. Since divisional heads will aim to maximize their own function, there is a greater probability that goals other than maximum profits will be pursued. The multi-divisional form (M-form) consists of a set of semi-autonomous operating divisions organized, say, on a product basis. This form promotes competition in product markets and creates an internal capital market with each division bidding for scarce funds. On this basis, Williamson (1975) has suggested that the M-form favours goal pursuit and least-cost behaviour more nearly associated with profit maximization than does the U-form. There is support for this hypothesis, with the M-form showing superior profit performance.

The argument can be summarized. The standard analysis assumes that firms can be represented by a set of revenue and efficient cost schedules in which a manager has the simple task of maximizing profits. In this form, some of the interesting problems, insights, and aspects of firm behaviour are assumed away. Internal organization is ignored. Firms lack perfect information and knowledge about the motivation of their workers and the profit-maximizing combinations of factors. They respond with an employment contract for the efficient organization of team production. In executing and enforcing this contract, the firm becomes a privately-owned information market with specialist knowledge on the productivity of its owned and hired factors of production. In the circumstances, it has been argued that transactions and transaction costs rather than technology determine the choice of organizational form for exchange. The shift of transactions from market exchange to hierarchy is largely explained by economies in transactions costs. Having explained the existence of firms, attention must now be given to alternative models of behaviour and their policy implications.

7.4 ALTERNATIVE MODELS OF FIRM BEHAVIOUR

Three developments led to a reappraisal of the traditional profit-maximizing postulate. First, evidence seemed to show that firms did not maximize profits: the theory appeared to be based on unrealistic assumptions about marginal cost and revenue. Second, the separation of ownership and control was believed to allow managers opportunities for pursuing their own goals rather than those of the shareholders. Third, discretionary behaviour and the pursuit of managerial goals was believed to be more likely in imperfect markets. The result was the development of models in which firms maximize sales, or growth, or a utility function containing such variables as staff, managerial emoluments, and organizational slack. Such managerial theories and profit maximization can be regarded as a general class of utility-maximizing models, where there are differences in the variables which enter the utility function. With profit maximization, profits are the only element in the entrepreneur's utility functions: this can be represented by a set of horizontal indifference curves, as shown in Figure 7.1(a). In contrast, the inclusion of other variables besides profit can be represented by more conventional downward sloping indifference curves, as shown in Figure 7.1(b), where X represents some other variable (e.g. managerial emoluments). Where other elements only enter the decision-maker's utility function (as in non-profit organizations), the result is a set of vertical indifference curves, as shown in Figure 7.1(c).

Separation of ownership and control

In addition to its possible implications for firm behaviour, this particular issue involves questions about the distribution of economic and political power within capitalist economies. Have managers and the technostructure replaced the traditional capitalist class and, if so, how might this affect an economy's performance? Moreover, if governments wish to raise their economy's growth rate, would it be desirable to support growth-maximizing firms? If so, under what conditions are such firms likely to emerge?

Without some qualifying conditions, the mere fact that ownership and control are separated does not necessarily mean that managers fail to maximize profits. Much depends on the costs and form of the employment contract negotiated between top managers and shareholders. Presumably, the argument about the separation of ownership and control means that a manager's departures from the interests of shareholders are less likely to be discerned and 'policed'. This argument is not wholly convincing. If some managers are pursuing their own ends, then rivals are always likely to emerge either from within or outside the firm. Indeed, the internal organization of firms can be regarded as a private competitive market in labour and capital as individuals and groups compete for top jobs and scarce funds. Also, if managers exercise discretionary behaviour which is attractive to others, there is likely to be competition for such jobs, so that wages will reflect the *net* advantages of the work (see Chapter 10). Similarly, if shareholders are aware of some of the opportunities for managerial slack and shirking, then they will make corresponding adjustments to monetary contracts. On this view, widely dispersed shareholding does not necessarily imply lower wealth for shareholders compared with firms where ownership is less dispersed (Alchian, 1977).

The role of market structure

General opinion suggests that a firm's objective function will depend upon *market structure*. Under competition, profit maximization is required for survival, whereas imperfect markets allow the pursuit of other objectives. However, which is the relevant market: for goods or factors? Even where product market competition is absent, competition in capital markets will ensure that profit-maximizers find it profitable to take over companies which are pursuing other aims. Competition in capital markets will allocate monopoly rights to those who can use them most profitably. Thus, governments concerned with efficiency in resource allocation might find it

174

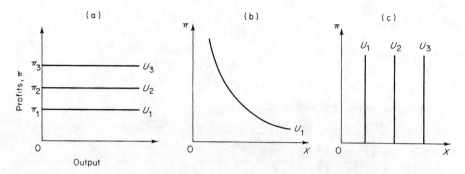

Figure 7.1 Utility-maximizing firms. Indifference curves are shown by U_1, U_2, U_3 where utility U_2 exceeds U_1, and so on. A higher level of satisfaction or utility is preferred. In diagrams (b) and (c), X can represent any other non-profit variable in the utility function, e.g. size, growth, staff.

useful to concentrate their policies on the proper functioning of *capital markets*. It is, however, possible that monopoly firms might be unwilling to maximize profits through fear of government intervention to regulate 'excessive' rates of return! Nor is it necessarily the case that competitive firms must be profit-maximizers. If entrepreneurs prefer 'independence' they might be prepared to pay for it by accepting a rate of return which is below the competitive level (e.g. self-employed businessmen and shopkeepers): hence, general utility maximization could be possible under competitive conditions. Such a conclusion is also consistent with a subjectivist interpretation of firm behaviour and choices.

Subjectivists regard equilibrium as a special case in the analysis of dynamic markets which are characterized by disequilibrium and continuous entrepreneurial adjustment to constant change. Within such dynamic markets, firms operate under uncertainty where costs are never fully measurable by anyone other than the individual incurring the costs. Faced with uncertainty and limited knowledge of the available options, individuals will have different views and valuations about the alternatives open to them. Errors are likely and markets exist to compare subjective evaluations and correct errors. Such an interpretation has major implications for both theory and public policy. Subjectivists maintain that costs are subjective rather than objectively measurable outlays: they exist in the mind of the decision-maker or chooser, so that they cannot be measured by anyone else, including economists and econometricians. It is accepted that in full, timeless, certain, general equilibrium, subjective costs can be represented by money outlays, but subjectivists claim, convincingly, that the real world is never in such an equilibrium. Their analysis of choice as non-predictable decisions requires the abandonment of much of standard equilibrium economics with its mathematical rigour and predictability of outcomes (see below and Wiseman, 1980). The policy implications of this approach are equally devastating. It is argued that empirical work and economic policy based on conventional models assuming certainty and full equilibrium may well be wrong in many cases. For example, if costs are subjective, what is the meaning of a government instructing the managers of state-owned enterprises to make price equal to marginal cost? Whose interpretation of marginal cost is being used? This is most pertinent since under state or public ownership the costs of any choice are less fully thrust upon the decision-maker than under private ownership (Alchian, 1977).

Profit maximization and other models

The alternative models of firm behaviour raise a fundamental methodological issue and one which is relevant to policy formulation. Should economists choose between the alternatives on the basis of the realism of assumptions or their predictive accuracy? Consider the alternatives which result in determinate outcomes. Sales maximization associated with Baumol (1959) was believed to be typical in oligopoly markets. Firms maximize sales revenue subject to a minimum profit constraint. Larger sales might give managers satisfaction from greater size and its associated prestige and security; their salaries might also be related to sales performance rather than profits. An example is shown in Figure 7.2 where the sales-maximizer's price–output decisions can be compared with a profit-maximizer. It can be seen that, *ceteris paribus*, sales maximization results in a lower price and a larger output than under profit maximization. Obviously, the minimum profit constraint is crucial to sales maximization. It is defined as the amount which just satisfies shareholders. But what determines this minimum acceptable level? With competitive product and capital markets, this amount would coincide with the maximum profit position.

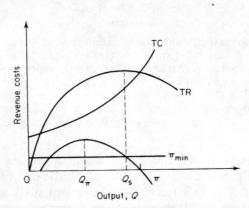

Figure 7.2 Sales maximization. A sales-maximizer will aim to obtain the maximum total revenue (TR), subject to the minimum profit constraint (π_{min}). Actual profit possibilities are shown by π which represents the difference between total revenue and total cost (TC). In this example, the sales-maximizing output is Q_s (it could be less with a greater minimum profit constraint). A profit-maximizer produces output Q_π.

176

An alternative model, due to Marris (1964), assumes that firms are growth-maximizers subject to the desire to avoid being taken over. In this model, firms have a valuation ration which is the ratio of the stock market value of the enterprise to its accounting or book-value. The relationship between the valuation ratio and the growth rate is shown by the valuation curve which reflects the relationship between growth and profitability and the present value of shareholders' dividends (profits) and capital gains (growth). After a point, increased growth will reduce the valuation ratio. As this ratio falls (substantially below 1.0), the stock market valuation becomes less than the book-value of the firm's assets and a take-over becomes more likely. In other words, this model incorporates a role for the capital market as a mechanism for 'policing' firm behaviour. An example is shown in Figure 7.3 where the firm maximizes a utility function showing that satisfaction depends on growth and the valuation ratio, subject to the constraints of the valuation curve and the desire to avoid a take-over. In this model, managers desire the power, prestige, status, and possibly salary associated with growth (g). They also derive utility from their company's standing in the stock market and the

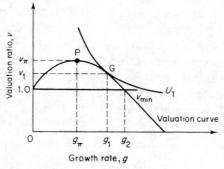

Figure 7.3   Growth maximization. The valuation curve shows the relationship between the valuation ratio (v) and the growth rate (growth of assets, g). Utility depends on v and g and the growth-maximizer is an equilibrium at G, compared with the shareholders' or profit-maximizing equilibrium at P (which maximizes the present stock market value of the company). An alternative position is shown where growth only is maximized, subject to a minimum valuation ratio located at 1.0; this corresponds to vertical indifference curves and results in growth rate g_2.

security from take-over (v). Shareholders will prefer the maximum market value (position P) and, in a growth context, this is interpreted as the profit-maximizing solution since it maximizes the present stock market value of the company. In contrast, utility-maximizing managers will aim at a higher growth rate and a correspondingly lower valuation ratio (position G). Since this model depends upon the threat of take-over, some insights into its empirical validity can be obtained by considering the role of the stock market as a disciplinary and policing mechanism. Evidence shows that, at least for large firms, the stock market does not compel such enterprises to maximize profits in order to reduce their chances of being taken over. Capital market discipline appears to be weak, which might provide tentative support for non-profit-maximizing models of firm behaviour. This is reinforced by evidence which shows that mergers are often associated with a *decline* in profitability. As for the growth maximizing model, it seems that the valuation ratio is not a 'good' discriminator between acquired firms and companies not taken over. However, evidence on the apparent inefficiency of the capital market has to be treated with some caution. The evidence is *ex post*, whereas firm behaviour is based on *ex ante* subjective assessments which are in the minds of decision-makers and which are likely to differ from actual results. Moreover, information is not freely available and it is costly to search the capital market for all potential candidates for take-over; hence transactors might discriminate between take-over candidates on the basis of less costly and subjective criteria. Such an interpretation would be acceptable to subjectivists, although it creates problems for empirical work and policy-makers! For example, if it is believed that the facts about the capital market support state intervention to promote mergers and re-structuring for greater efficiency, what 'improved' decision-making criteria will be used by the government, especially in dynamic situations characterized by ignorance and uncertainty?

A more general utility-maximizing model of firm behaviour has been constructed by Williamson (1964). In this model, managers have a preference for expenditures on staff, managerial emoluments, and discretionary investment expenditures, subject to the need for reported profits to be at some minimum 'acceptable' level. This is a formal expression of the satisfaction and prestige which managers obtain from the number of staff under their control, luxury offices, company cars, expense accounts, and other fringe benefits. In the general utility-maximizing case, managers have discretion and this will result in higher staff expenditures and greater managerial slack than for a profit-maximizer. Two examples are shown in Figure 7.4. In the staff model, the firm maximizes a utility function containing both profits and staff expenditures. Predictably, utility maximization results in a larger staff and smaller profits (position A) compared with profit maximization (position P), as shown in Figure 7.4(a). Another variant assumes that the firm derives satisfaction from profits and managerial emoluments. These are discretionary additions to salary and other expenditures or 'corporate personal consumption', which are not required for profit maximization. Firms will be constrained by a budget line linking the extremes of maximum profits or diverting all profits to spending on managerial emoluments. With satisfaction derived from both profits and managerial emoluments, firms will obviously prefer more discretionary expenditures than a profit-maximizer, as shown by positions B and P, respectively, in Figure 7.4(b).

Do the different models yield alternative predictions?

As outlined above, there are a variety of different models of firm behaviour. How do we choose between them? For example, observations of actual product prices cannot be used to distinguish between the different models. The fact that a car is priced at £x does not confirm that firms are profit-maximizers or anything else. In these circumstances, economists use a comparative statics methodology. This considers the price–output responses of different types of firms to changes in demand and taxation. Various types of taxation are analysed, namely a profits tax, a lump sum tax (or any increases in fixed costs), and a sales tax which will shift marginal cost upwards. The aim is to use different taxes to change average and marginal, fixed and variable costs and to predict the effects on the firm's prices and output. To illustrate both the methodology and its policy relevance, consider a government which is contemplating raising the demand for an industry's products. This could be achieved through government procurement policy or, indirectly, through a general expansion of aggregate demand or through changes in the price and

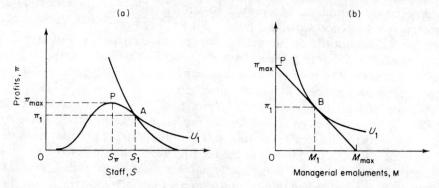

Figure 7.4 Utility maximization. Diagram (a) shows the staff model where $U = U(\pi, S)$ and the 'hump'-shaped curve is a profit frontier showing the profit levels associated with different staff expenditures. Profit maximization occurs at P and utility is maximized at A, with a larger staff. Diagram (b) shows the managerial emoluments model where $U = U(\pi, M)$; the preferred combination is position B compared with the profit-maximizing solution at P. In this diagram, actual profits equal maximum profits minus actual managerial emolument (for example $\pi_1 = \pi_{max} - M_1$). A profits tax results in a downward shift of the budget line, pivoting around M_{max} (which is unaffected by the profits tax).

availability of consumer credit for 'selected' goods (e.g. hire purchase arrangements for cars). Alternatively, a government might be considering subjecting an industry to a profits tax or a lump sum tax or an increase in tax rates. How might firms with different objectives react to such policy changes?

Demand and taxation policy

Three models will be compared, namely profits, sales, and utility maximization. For simplicity, the comparisons will be restricted to the *output* response of firms to the policy changes. The results of the exercise are summarized in

Table 7.1, where the output responses have been derived by making the appropriate shifts in the demand and cost schedules facing each type of firm. The taxes can be considered either as the introduction of a new tax or an increase in rates, the lump sum tax being equivalent to a rise in fixed costs. For an increase in demand, all three models give the same qualitative predictions, i.e. an expansion of output, and if employment depends on output, there will be an associated increase in jobs. However, the firms have different output responses to higher taxation. Profit-maximizers will not change output in response to higher profits and lump sum taxes (at least in the short run). Both sales- and utility-maximizers reduce output in response to the introduction of, or increase in, a lump sum tax. However, this only distinguishes between profit maximization and the other models. Alternative predictions for each type emerge in response to a profits tax. Sales-maximizers will reduce output and

Table 7.1   Comparative statics: output responses of firms

Model	Increase in demand	Increase in lump sum tax	Increase in profits tax rate
Profit maximization	+	0	0
Sales maximization	+	—	—
Utility maximization	+	—	+ (?)

utility-maximizers are likely to raise it. In the utility-maximizing model, a profits tax probably raises expenditure on managerial emoluments and leads to a greater preference for staff: if so, the increased staff will be associated with a higher output (output and staff are positively associated). Of course, in empirical work, it might not be possible to obtain the required data to hold constant other relevant variables affecting changes in output (e.g. home and export demand; changes in technology and costs). Nor might there be many examples of the required tax changes.

7.5   POLICY APPLICATIONS

Models of firm behaviour can contribute to policy formulation in two ways. First, they can help to explain the facts which might be matters of concern to governments. Second, they can be used to predict the likely implications of alternative policy measures, so helping governments to select their preferred option. This section will illustrate both these contributions by examining two sets of policy problems, namely the export performance of firms and subsidies. Exports have been chosen because of the frequent concern of governments with balance of payments targets. A model is required to explain why firms export and whether, for example, a high pressure of demand in the home market is 'good' or 'bad' for exports. Subsidy policy is an extensive area and emphasis will be given to the employment effects of labour subsidies and the reactions of firms to recessions and regulation. Of course, governments might be reluctant to subsidize private firms. They might prefer to support the formation of worker cooperatives. If so, a model is required to explain and predict the behaviour of labour-managed firms. Nationalized industries are discussed in Chapter 15.

Exports and the pressure of domestic demand

Governments often claim that in order to increase exports to achieve their balance of payments targets, home demand has to be reduced to free resources for an expansion of overseas sales. Broadly, this hypothesis asserts that, in the short run and with a fixed exchange rate, exports are affected by domestic demand, with a high pressure of demand in the economy adversely affecting its export performance. It is argued that a deflation of domestic demand will have both 'push and pull' effects on the export performance of firms and industries. A deflation will release goods and resources from supplying the home market, so allowing firms to increase their exports: they will be 'pushed' into overseas markets. Also, if a deflation means that firms can no longer sell their products in the home market, they will be encouraged to search for foreign markets (the 'pull' effect). At this point, it is necessary to ask what contribution theory can make to identifying the circumstances under which a domestic deflation will improve exports; and, are there any exceptions? Clearly, a model of firm behaviour is required which incorporates both home and overseas markets.

Consider a profit-maximizing firm producing a single product as a monopolist in the home market and faced with a competitive world market. Effectively, the firm acts as a price-maker or searcher at home and a price-taker abroad. For a profit-maximizer, home and export markets simply represent possible opportunities for profits. The short-run price–output decisions of this firm and the allocation of its total output between the two markets can be analysed in the same way as a discriminating monopoly. An example is shown in Figure 7.5. A profit-maximizer will produce an output of Oq_t, with Oq_d domestic sales and the rest for export (Figure 7.5a). The home market price of the product will exceed its export price. Similarly, profits per unit of domestic output will exceed the unit profitability of exports. Now, if a deflation of domestic demand in the economy leads to a decrease in the firm's home market demand, the result will be a rise in output exported. In other words, this simple model predicts an inverse relationship between a firm's exports and the pressure of home demand (Figure 7.5b).

The model can be modified to allow the firm to act as a price-maker in both home and overseas markets (i.e. downward sloping demand curves in each market). For such a profit-maximizing firm, the predicted short-run effect on exports of a change in domestic demand will depend upon its cost conditions. Depending on whether the firm is subject to increasing, decreasing, or constant marginal costs, different short-run relationships can be predicted between exports and the pressure of domestic demand. Increasing marginal

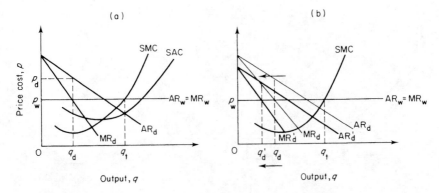

Figure 7.5 Exports and domestic demand. Average and marginal revenue and short-run cost schedules are shown by AR, MR, SAC, and SMC; subscripts d and w refer to domestic and world markets, respectively. With two markets, profit maximization requires equality between MC and the *combined* MR curve. Initially in diagram (a), total output is q_t with $q_d q_t$ for export. A domestic deflation leaves *total* output unaffected (diagram b), but domestic sales fall and hence exports rise. Shifts in the firm's domestic demand curve will be associated with variations in its domestic prices, but export prices will remain unchanged.

costs are required for an inverse relationship between a firm's exports and home demand. Other cost conditions give different predictions, as shown in Figure 7.6. Decreasing marginal costs result in a positive relationship: a reduction in a firm's home market sales will be associated with a fall in exports and such a relationship is often claimed to be characteristic of volume producers, such as motor car manufacturers (Figure 7.6a). With constant marginal costs, a change in the firm's domestic demand conditions will have no effect on its exports (Figure 7.6b).

The fact that the profit-maximizing model has predicted all the possible short-run relationships between exports and domestic demand might be regarded as sufficient for analytical purposes. Critics of profit maximization have suggested that benefits other than profits might be obtained from exporting. Firms sometimes claim that exports provide benefits in the form of prestige, security through market diversification, and the possibility of expansion which might be impossible to achieve at home. It is not at all obvious that these alleged benefits are inconsistent with profit maximization and consistent with some other aim (which?). However, some critics have proposed the full-cost principle as an alternative explanation of business behaviour. As such, the principle is really an explanation of pricing which implies that firms might be pursuing objectives other than maximum profits, but it fails to specify these objectives. Basically, it is a supply-side or cost hypothesis of pricing in which product prices depend on average variable costs plus a costing margin which includes an allowance for overheads and a profit mark-up. An example is shown in Figure 7.7, where the firm is working at

182

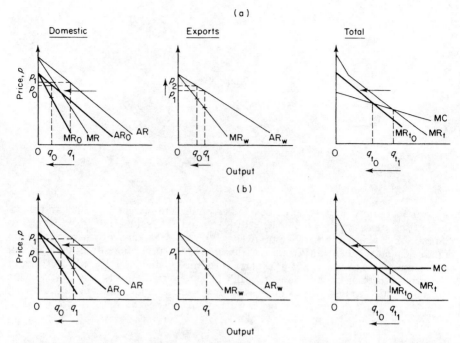

Figure 7.6 Exports and different cost conditions. The discriminating monopolist is a price-maker in both home and export markets. The *total* market shows the combined marginal revenue curves before and after a deflation. Decreasing costs are shown in diagram (a), with a deflation reducing exports. Constant marginal costs are shown in diagram (b), where exports are unaffected by a deflation.

capacity, supplying both home and export markets. Consider the effect on exports of an increase in home demand. With strict full-cost pricing, the immediate result is excess demand at the ruling price, as reflected in order books, lengthening delivery dates, and waiting times. The initial effect on exports will depend on the firm's criteria for determining priorities in a queuing situation. For example, overseas sales are likely to be adversely affected if domestic firms lengthen the delivery dates for their exports at a faster rate than their foreign competitors. Subjectivists, however, would be especially critical of the full-cost pricing principle simply because it is based on measured (realized) outlays which in disequilibrium cannot be accurate representations of opportunity costs.

Analysis shows that predictions about the short-run relationship between exports and domestic demand are related to the firm's objectives, together with its market and cost conditions. In fact, a decrease in the home demand for a firm's products can be associated with an increase, or a reduction or no change in overseas sales. Predictions can be obtained on domestic and export prices, queueing, and the relative profitability of home and overseas sales. Empirical work at the firm and industry level in the United Kingdom has shown a diversity of experience in the relationship between exports and domestic demand not only between industries but also between different overseas markets for the same industry. Such a finding makes life difficult for policy-makers! Moreover, a substantial amount of interview-questionnaire evidence now exists showing that product prices are determined on the basis of estimated costs modified for market conditions (e.g. competition, market research, prices of existing products): such findings refute the simple supply-side version of the full-cost hypothesis (Cooper, Hartley, and Harvey, 1970).

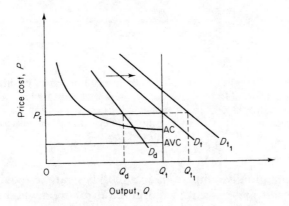

Figure 7.7   Full-cost pricing. The full-cost price is P_f estimated on the basis of average cost (including average variable cost) plus a profit mark-up. Capacity ouput is Q_t. Assume that initially the total demand D_t for the product results in the firm being able to sell the whole of its output at P_f. With given costs, prices will be the same in both home and export markets, with Q_d sold at home and the rest for export. An increase in domestic demand will shift the total demand curve to D_{t_1}, creating excess demand of $Q_{t_1} - Q_t$ at the ruling price.

Subsidy policy

Governments often subsidize labour to achieve employment targets, either at the regional or national level. Models of firm behaviour can be used to predict the employment effects of a labour subsidy. An example for a profit-maximizing firm is shown in Figure 7.8. A labour or job subsidy results in both substitution and scale effects. The substitution effect leads to the substitution of labour for capital. Also, if the subsidy reduces the firm's marginal costs, prices will fall and output rises, so that there is a scale effect. If both labour and capital are normal factors, the scale effect will reinforce the substitution effect and further increase employment.

Job subsidies appear attractive since they have an immediate impact and they seem to 'save' on state unemployment payments. But appearances are no substitute for analysis and evidence. Labour subsidies are likely to have 'displacement effects' in that employment preservation in subsidized firms is purchased at a cost of jobs lost in non-subsidized enterprises. Also, when

184

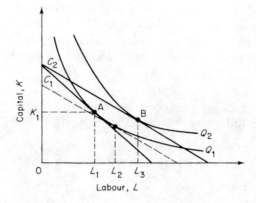

Figure 7.8   Job subsidies. The firm is initially in equilibrium at position A where the isocost line C_1 is tangential to the isoquant Q_1. A labour subsidy leads to a new isocost line at C_2, a higher output Q_2, and a new equilibrium at position B. The substitution effect raises employment from L_1 to L_2; the scale effect further increases employment from L_2 to L_3.

assessing the quantitiative impact of job subsidies care is required to ensure that the number of jobs 'saved' in subsidized firms are *net* additions, directly attributable to subsidies rather than other influences. Nor are subsidies necessarily conducive to efficient performance: they might be used to finance existing or even higher levels of organizational slack (*X*-inefficiency). Consider a firm receiving a lump sum subsidy. A utility maximizer, enjoying profits and managerial emoluments, would use the subsidy to increase both these preferred 'goods'. However, the government might respond by imposing profit controls on the recipients of subsidies (e.g. to prevent extra profits being earned at the taxpayer's expense). As a result, the firm is likely to 'consume' even more managerial perks, as shown in Figure 7.9 (see Chapter 14, Figure 14.1). Subsidized firms subject to profit controls could also have a reduced incentive to resist wage increases. Indeed, the existence of state subsidies might induce firms to become subsidy maximizers, seeking revenue from governments and bureaucrats rather than private consumers!

Utility maximization and recessions

The inefficiency aspect of subsidies suggests an alternative policy option. Governments sometimes claim that a recession is required to 'shock' firms into improved efficiency, so reducing organizational 'slack'. Such a policy might be appropriate for utility-maximizers and satisficers, and where governments aim to raise technical efficiency. For example, faced with a dramatic decline in demand, utility-maximizers are likely to make drastic reductions in their staff compared with profit-maximizers, as shown in Figure 7.10. Thus, the

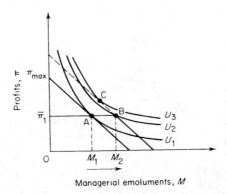

Figure 7.9 Utility-maximizers and subsidies. The firm is initially in equilibrium at position A. It now receives a lump sum subsidy but is unable to increase its profits above π_1. The result is a 'corner solution' at position B where the firm consumes more managerial perks, M_2, than with its preferred position at C.

managerial discretion model predicts substantial adjustments in staff during adversity. There is some empirical support for this hypothesis. In addition, studies show that firms respond to adversity by reducing such discretionary expenditures as company cars, chauffeurs, and office spending.

Worker cooperatives

Rather than subsidize private capitalists, governments might prefer to support worker cooperatives or labour-managed firms. It is believed that worker control will remove the conflict between labour and capital (e.g. industrial disputes, strikes, restrictive labour practices), and raise the productivity of individual workers and managers. What is likely to happen if workers hired capital instead of capitalists hiring labour? Some answers are provided by economic models of labour-managed enterprises.

In a model associated with Meade (1972), a worker cooperative or labour-managed firm (LMF) is assumed to maximize the net earnings or income per worker. Capital and other inputs would be hired and the cooperative would sell its products at market prices. Risks would be borne by labour, with surpluses and losses distributed between the workers according to an agreed sharing system (e.g. equality or sharing based on skills). As a result of a change in ownership, incentives are likely to differ between LMFs and profit-maximizing firms (PMFs) in capitalist economies. It is believed that in worker cooperatives, the sense of participation in decision-making may be greater. Self-policing is also expected, since any extra profits due to improved productivity will accrue to the workers as owners. Yugoslavia is the classic example of a self-managed economy, but other instances occur in capitalist

186

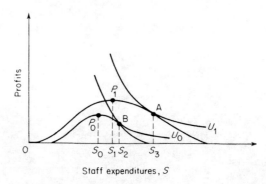

Figure 7.10 Utility maximization and adversity. A utility-maximizer will respond to adversity by making the adjustment from position A to B and the profit-maximizer adjusts from P_1 to P_0.

systems, particularly with professional groups such as accountants, doctors, lawyers, and orchestras. A model of the LMF in long-run equilibrium is shown in Figure 7.11. The LMF is assumed to be a price-taker, aiming to maximize average net earnings. In a perfectly competitive economy, both LMFs and PMFs will, in the long run, result in an efficient (Pareto optimal) allocation of resources. Both will employ the same quantity of labour, *ceteris paribus*. The PMF will equate the marginal value product of labour with the ruling wage which will be the same as that paid by the cooperative. However, while the final outcome is identical, the short-run adjustment process differs. In competitive markets, a rise in products prices will cause PMFs to *increase* output and employment. But in the short run, a LMF will respond by *reducing* employment and output, so as to continue maximizing average net earnings. Such a short-run response by a LMF might not be the reaction desired by a government committed to raising employment. Of course, in the long run, new and existing PMFs will compete away any abnormal profits and labour will be attracted to high-wage sectors. Similarly, in a self-managed economy, above-average earnings will lead to the formation of new worker cooperatives in the high-earnings industries.

The model of the LMF is not without its critics. Conflicts might arise in determining the rules for sharing surpluses and losses between labour of different skills. Similarly, the cooperative will have to determine rules for admitting new workers and the property rights of leavers. There might also be difficulties and costs of internal 'policing', especially in large LMFs where individual preferences for income and leisure will differ and where there are opportunities for 'shirking and free-riding'. Moreover, models of the LMF might not be appropriate where policy-makers wish to expand the opportunities for industrial democracy without changing ownership. Within Europe, for example, there is substantial support for some form of worker representation on the boards of directors of private firms. It is argued that industry's future

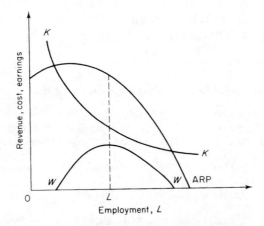

Figure 7.11 A labour-managed firm. The diagram shows a LMF in long-run competitive equilibrium. The average revenue product of labour is ARP. Capital is the only other factor, and its fixed rental results in a capital cost per worker represented by a rectangular hyperbola, *KK*. Average net earnings are the difference between the ARP curve and *KK*, represented by the curve *WW*. Average net earnings are maximized at employment *L*. Of course, if the LMF is maximizing a utility function containing both earnings and employment, it will employ more than *L* workers.

ability to adjust to change will depend upon the approval and support of its workforce and that those affected by decisions must be involved in the decision-making process (e.g. closures, new machinery, redundancy). Clearly, this is a subject area where there are opportunities for further analytical and empirical work. What are the likely implications of different forms of industrial democracy for firm behaviour and performance? Will industrial democracy raise or lower productivity and have adverse or favourable effects on investment and inflation?

7.6 CONCLUSION

This chapter has explained why firms exist and has outlined alternative models of behaviour. For policy purposes, one of the fundamental issues concerns the appropriateness of alternative theories of the firm. Consideration has been given to the relationship between objectives, on the one hand, and ownership and market structures, on the other. For example, will a change from public to private ownership, together with greater competition, improve economic efficiency? Some models, such as satisficing, seem to provide accurate descriptions. The firm is viewed as a coalition of different interest groups, with entrepreneurs making 'side payments' for the cooperation of the various groups. But is descriptive accuracy the 'best' or only criterion for choosing between alternative theories? Another criterion would be alternative predictions and their empirical validity. Here, it is interesting to note that there are a number of circumstances where alternative models result in similar qualitative predictions. In this situation, policy advisers might find that the basic profit-maximizing postulate continues to provide an adequate *starting point* for analysis.

READING AND REFERENCES

Alchian, A. (1977). *Economic Forces At Work*, Liberty Press, Indianapolis.

Baumol, W. J. (1959). *Business Behavior, Value and Growth*, Macmillan, New York.

Berle, A. A., and Means, G. C. (1932). *The Modern Corporation and Private Property*, Harcourt Brace, New York.

Chamberlin, E. H. (1933). *The Theory of Monopolistic Competition*, Harvard University Press, Cambridge, Mass.

Coase, R. H. (1937). The Nature of the Firm, *Economica*, November, vol 4, pp 386–405.

Cooper, R., Hartley, K., and Harvey, C. (1970). *Export Performance and the Pressure of Demand*, Allen and Unwin, London.

Cyert, R. M., and March, J. G. (1963). *A Behavioral Theory of the Firm*, Prentice-Hall, Englewood Cliffs, N.J.

Devine, P. J., *et al.* (1979). *An Introduction to Industrial Economics*, Allen and Unwin, London.

King, J. (Ed.) (1980). *Readings in Labour Economics*, Part 2, Oxford University Press.

Marris, R. (1964). *The Economic Theory of Managerial Capitalism*, Macmillan, London.

Marshall, A. (1890). *Principles of Economics*, 8th ed., pp 315–318, Macmillan, London, 1920.

Meade, J. (1972). The theory of labour-managed firms and of profit-sharing, *Economic Journal*, **82**, March 1972 (Supplement).

Robinson, J. (1933). *The Economics of Imperfect Competition*, Macmillan, London.

Simon, H. A. (1966). Theories of Decision-Making in Economics and Behavioural Science in *Surveys of Economic Theory*, vol. III Royal Economic Society, Macmillan, London.

Sraffa, P. (1926). The Laws of Returns Under Competitive Conditions, *Economic Journal*, December, vol 36, pp 535–550.

Tisdell, C. A. (1972). *Microeconomics*, Wiley, Sydney.

Tisdell, C. A. (1974). *Economics of Markets*, Wiley, Sydney.

Wildsmith, J. R. (1973). *Managerial Theories of the Firm*, Martin Robertson, London.

Williamson, O. E. (1964). *The Economics of Discretionary Behavior: Managerial Objectives in a Theory of the Firm*, Prentice-Hall, Englewood Cliffs, N.J.

Williamson, O. E. (1975). *Markets and Hierarchies: Analysis and Anti-Trust Implications*, Free Press, New York.

Wiseman, J. (1980). Costs and decisions, in *Contemporary Economic Analysis* (Eds D. Currie and W. Peters), Vol. 2, Croom Helm, London.

Vanek, J. (Ed.) (1975). *Self-Management: Economic Liberation of Man*, Penguin, Harmondsworth.

QUESTIONS FOR REVIEW AND DISCUSSION

1. Why do firms exist? What are the policy implications of your analysis?
2. Does the full-cost pricing principle explain the behaviour of firms in
   (a) the motor car industry,

(b) commercial banking, and
(c) the distributive trades?
3. Predict the effects of a domestic deflation on a firm's export performance. How would you test your predictions?
4. Do employment contracts explain the behaviour and performance of firms in the public and private sectors? What are the implications of your analysis for state subsidies to private firms?
5. Are costs subjective or objective? What are the policy implications of these alternative interpretations?
6. What is the policy relevance of firms pursuing non-profit objectives? Explain and give examples.
7. What would be the effect on a nation's manufacturing industry if all firms became workers' cooperatives? Does a knowledge of welfare economics enable you to determine whether such firms are 'desirable'?
8. Critically evaluate the theoretical and empirical basis of X-inefficiency. What are the public policy implications of your conclusions?
9. 'Changes in the internal organisation of firms have mitigated capital market failures by transferring functions traditionally imputed to the capital market to the firm instead' (Williamson, 1975). Evaluate this statement showing the implications of your analysis for empirical work on the efficiency of the capital market and for public policy.
10. Which theory of the firm is your preferred choice? Why? What are the policy implications of your choice?

CHAPTER 8

Monopoly—Regulation and Control

8.1 INTRODUCTION AND OVERVIEW

As was illustrated in Chapter 2, monopoly in a market can result in an economy not achieving a Paretian optimum. A Kaldor–Hicks loss occurs because in order to maximize profit a monopolist raises the price of his product above its marginal cost of production. He fosters scarcity of the monopolized good. Consequently consumers are left in a position where the value to them of using extra resources to produce the monopolized product exceeds the value of these resources to them when used to produce alternative products. The *opportunity cost* of producing more of the monopolized product as far as consumers are concerned is the value of alternative products (foregone) which might have been produced by the resources allocated to production of the monopolized product. As illustrated in Chapter 6, if externalities are absent, these opportunity costs are automatically and optimally taken into account under perfect competition. But this does not occur under monopoly. It would be a fluke even under propitious second best conditions for a monopoly to result in a Paretian optimum or a Paretian optimum in an institutionally constrained economic system. But as we shall see in this chapter, monopoly *may be* superior to perfect competition in *dynamically* reducing scarcity.

Just as perfect competition is an ideal or abstract type so is monopoly. The difficulties of defining monopoly and measuring monopoly power and the pitfalls of various measures are discussed in this chapter. The traditional profit-maximizing model of monopoly, assuming the *absence of entry*, is outlined and the consequences of a monopolist's behaviour for consumers' surplus is explored. The extent of losses in consumers' surplus as a result of monopoly compared to the alternative of perfect competition is shown in a static setting to depend on the inelasticity of the demand for the monopolized product and on the inelasticity of marginal cost. This leads on to a discussion of the relative benefits of monopoly and perfect competition in a dynamic setting involving technological change and to a consideration of 'X-inefficiency' under monopoly and the possible social costs of this compared to 'allocative' inefficiency. The possibility is then allowed of non-profit-maximizing behaviour on the part of a monopolist (discussed in Chapter 7), and some of the effects and welfare consequences of this are explored.

Entry conditions are extremely important in determining whether and for how long a monopoly lasts and these conditions influence the behaviour of 'incumbent' monopolists. Consequently, in any discussion of monopoly behaviour it is important to take potential entry into account. In this chapter, account is taken of *barriers to entry* such as absolute cost barriers (for instance raised by patenting and learning differences), legal barriers, and economies of scale such as may stem from technology or advertising and marketing.

After models of monopoly behaviour have been outlined and explored, the discussion logically turns to consider government regulation of monopolies, government action to prevent the formation of monopolies, and the seemingly inconsistent policy of public encouragement of the formation of monopolies, for instance by fostering mergers of firms. Issues discussed include the following. Are public monopolies the answer to problems and difficulties of regulating or preventing private monopolies? What patterns of behaviour can be expected from bureaucrats managing public monopolies and how are politicians likely to influence the behaviour of such enterprises? Is there a separation of ownership and control or management of public enterprises and what consequences does this have? Is government failure to be expected and how does it compare with market failure?

The last portion of the chapter draws together empirical evidence on some of the effects of monopoly. It looks at empirical evidence on the size of the deadweight loss due to monopoly, the influence of monopoly on pollution, and the state of the environment, monopoly, and dynamic change (amount of research and development, patenting, and invention), and advertising.

8.2   THE NATURE OF MONOPOLY

Monopoly as an ideal type

Monopoly is a market situation in which there is just a single seller of a commodity. It is traditionally regarded as the polar opposite of perfect competition. The *traditional* relationship of different types of competition in the selling of commodities is represented roughly by the spectrum shown in Figure 8.1. However, a number of assumptions such as impossibility of entry of competitors have to be made to ensure that a monopoly situation is in fact the polar opposite of perfect competition.

Just as few markets are perfectly competitive, there are few absolute monopolies in the sense that the seller does not have to take account of actual competition from other commodities or the threat of potential entrants to his industry via new technology. Nevertheless, this does not mean that predictions based on the 'ideal' type are valueless. Some markets approach the ideal type sufficiently closely for the predictions of the monopoly model to apply. Indeed, some members of the Chicago School and Lipsey (1979) claim that models of perfect competition and monopoly are adequate for most predictions about market operations.

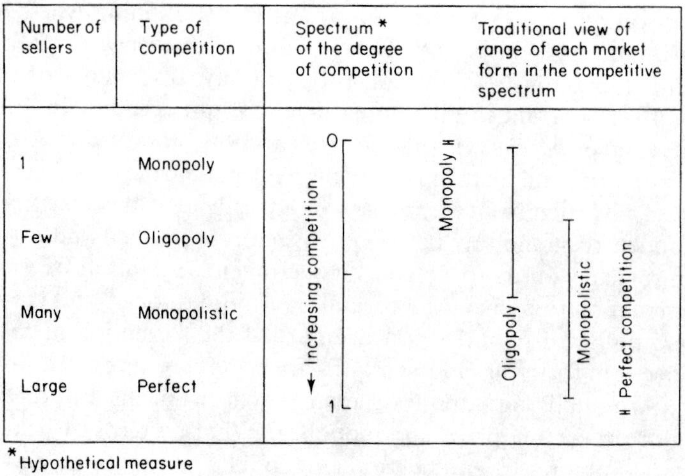

192

Number of sellers	Type of competition	Spectrum * of the degree of competition	Traditional view of range of each market form in the competitive spectrum
1	Monopoly		Monopoly =
Few	Oligopoly	Increasing competition (0 → 1)	Oligopoly
Many	Monopolistic		Monopolistic
Large	Perfect		= Perfect competition

*Hypothetical measure

Figure 8.1 A characterization of the traditional spectrum of types of competition in the selling of the commodities. Notice that there is some overlap between oligopoly and monopolistic competition in terms of the degree of market competition.

Examples of monopolies

Examples of monopolies include:

(1) Postal and telephone services in most countries are monopolized. Although these monopolies have governmental protection in most cases, they receive some competition from courier services.
(2) Developers of new drugs often obtain a monopoly for a limited period of time in the supply of these drugs as a result of patent protection.
(3) Caprolactum, an essential ingredient in the supply of some synthetic fibres, is supplied by a sole producer in the United Kingdom — ICI.
(4) Stevedoring and wharf labourers in the United Kingdom, Australia, and several other countries operate closed shops, thus giving their union a monopoly in the supply of such labour.
(5) Government bureaucracies such as those operating railways, providing water and sewerage services, and some health services have a monopoly or near-monopoly in their supply.

The market power of a monopolist

The economic consequences of a monopoly in a market depends (1) on the market power of the monopolist and (2) on his market behaviour, i.e. the extent to which he exercises his power, and this is likely to depend upon his objective function. The mere fact that a firm is the sole seller of a product does not mean that it has or significantly has monopoly or market power, i.e. the ability to raise its price profitably above the marginal cost of production of the product. As will be recalled, under perfect competition price equals the marginal cost of production of a commodity and a firm has no ability to sell at a higher price—it is a price-taker. The power of a monopolist to raise the price of a product above his marginal cost of production (or more generally to raise the price of a commodity above its supply price—the minimum price needed to call forth a particular level of supply) depends upon

(1) the inelasticity of demand for the commodity which in turn depends upon such factors as the availability and closeness of substitutes for the commodity and
(2) the ease with which new suppliers can enter the industry, i.e. the costs or barriers to their entry.

In contemplating the possible public control of a monopoly consideration needs to be given to both of these elements. If the demand for a monopolist's product is very elastic and if entry of new firms or suppliers (for example, from abroad) is easy, the case for public regulation of a monopoly may be weak because the monopolist has little scope to raise his price effectively above his marginal cost of production and is threatened if lower-cost sources of supply emerge.

Measuring monopoly power

Various measures of monopoly power have been suggested. These include:

(1) *The Lerner index.* The Lerner index measures the degree of monopoly power by the extent to which the price of a product diverges from its marginal cost of production in relation to its price. The Lerner index is obtained from the formula

$$L = \frac{P - MC}{P}$$

where P is the price of the product and MC represents its marginal cost of production. Under perfect competition $P = MC$ and so $L = 0$. But under monopoly $P > MC$ and so $L > 0$. As will be discussed, an excess of price over marginal cost is liable to result in a misallocation of resources. Under monopoly conditions the Lerner index will be greater the more inelastic is the demand for a monopolist's product and the less is the threat of entry.

From a practical point of view there are a number of difficulties involved in using the Lerner index as a measure of monopoly power. Marginal costs are not always known and are not always easy to estimate. Also one must consider whether or not the index is to be based upon monopoly power exercised or upon potential power. If the monopolist is a profit-maximizer these will not differ, but if the monopolist charges less than his profit-maximizing price the index based upon his actual price will be less than that based upon his potential. Furthermore, it is necessary to consider the time-period involved. A firm may have great monopoly power in the short-term, for instance, but little in the long-term because new substitutes may be developed by rivals and buyers or consumers have a greater ability to economize and to switch to substitutes in the long-term compared to the short term. For these reasons the Marshallian long-run demand curve can be expected to be more elastic than a short-period one and so the Lerner index is lower in the long-run.

(2) *Excess returns as a measure of monopoly power.* Under perfect competition firms (at least in the long-run) only earn a normal or average return on capital invested, but under monopoly above normal or average returns may persist, even in the long-run. Some economists have therefore used the level of returns or profit as an indicator of monopoly power. Harberger (1954), for instance, does this in his study of monopoly. However, monopolists may not choose to maximize their profit (they may, for example, try to maximize revenue) and this limits the value of the level of returns as a measure of monopoly power. Again in applying this measure consideration needs to be given to the *time-period* for which returns can be maintained. Can they be maintained for one year, five years, or ten years above the levels which would prevail under perfect competition? Even perfectly competitive firms can earn abnormal profit in the short-run if demand for their product suddenly increases. This is because it takes time to adjust supplies and for new firms to enter the industry.

(3) *Concentration ratios or market share as a measure of monopoly power.* A relatively crude measure of monopoly power is the size of a firm's share of its market. The larger this share the greater is its presumed market power.

General effects of monopoly

In general the effect of a monopoly depends upon the monopolist's market power and his behaviour. Market power is a necessary but not sufficient condition for monopoly to result in a misallocation of resources because a monopolist may choose not to exploit his monopoly power, as, for instance, illustrated below in discussing Figure 8.6.

There are four main possible effects of monopoly to consider. These are:

(1) Its impact on the *allocation of resources*. If a monopolist has market power and exercises it to raise the price of his product above its marginal cost of production, resources are misallocated. Resources are misallocated in the sense that the value consumers place on extra production of the commodity (as indicated by the price they are willing to pay) exceeds the additional cost of producing an extra amount of the commodity.

Consequently, as pointed out in Chapter 2, a deadweight social loss occurs. Such a loss is likely (but not certain), even in second best conditions, even though the policies for correcting it may not at first be obvious.

(2) Its influence on the *distribution of income*. A monopolist by exercising his monopoly power may earn above average profit and so redistribute income in his favour. He obtains his abnormal profit by creating an artificial scarcity.

(3) The difference monopoly makes to *economic growth* compared to alternative market forms. As we shall see, there is a difference of opinion among economists on whether monopoly promotes or retards economic growth in comparison to alternative market forms.

(4) The likely *political interference* of a monopolist compared to participants in a more competitive market environment. A monopolist, other things equal, is likely to have a greater incentive to lobby on behalf of his industry than would a supplier in a more competitive industry because the monopolist appropriates all the benefits to suppliers in the industry from 'assistance' to the industry, whereas in a competitive industry a supplier must share the gains with other suppliers. Thus a monopolist is likely, for instance, to find it more profitable to mount a campaign for tariff protection for his industry from imports than would a supplier in a more competitive industry. Again a monopolist is more likely to find it profitable to keep himself better informed (than a large number of competitors) about any factor affecting his industry, including political measures which may affect it, and to take action to alter the course of events if this is in his interest.

In order to assess the possible economic impact of monopoly and of policies to control it, it is necessary for us to consider the behaviour of monopolists.

8.3 BEHAVIOUR OF MONOPOLISTS AND CONSEQUENCES— NO ENTRY TRADITIONAL PROFIT-MAXIMIZING MODEL

Economists traditionally have assumed that monopolists, like other firms, maximize their profit. Let us outline some implications of this assumption, assuming that no entry is possible into the industry being considered. We shall then discuss some alternative behavioural possibilities.

Deadweight loss from monopoly

In order to maximize his profit a monopolist must equate his marginal cost of production to his marginal revenue from his sales of the product. In the absence of price discrimination this results in a price for the product which exceeds the marginal cost of its production and, as explained in Chapter 2, leads to a deadweight (Kaldor–Hicks) social loss. In the constant average cost case shown in Figure 8.2 where the curves are identified by obvious abbreviations, the deadweight social loss amounts to the area of the triangle marked *d*. The

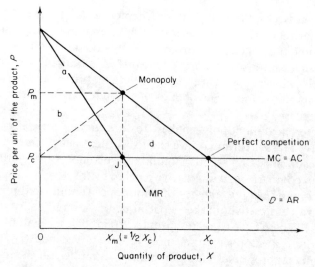

Figure 8.2 Consumers surplus under monopoly amounts in this case to the area of triangle *a* whereas under perfect competition it amounts to the combined area of triangles *a*, *b*, *c*, and *d*, *four times as much as under monopoly*.

question arises of why this is not 'captured' if all *could* be made better off as a result of an alteration in the policy of the monopolist from producing a quantity which equates marginal revenue and marginal cost to one equating average revenue or market demand and marginal cost. The problem basically seems to be one of how consumers can be organized to pay the monopolist a bribe to alter his behaviour. Costs would be involved in organizing the bribe and some consumers may try to free-ride. Transaction costs of considerable magnitude provide barriers to the formation of politically effective consumer groups.

Extent of loss of consumers surplus from monopoly

Figure 8.2 enables us to make some predictions about the extent to which consumers may suffer as a result of a traditional monopoly. Assuming that perfect competition is a possible alternative to monopoly, and that in this alternative situation the demand curve D is the same for the industry and that the competitive supply curve for the industry is equivalent to MC, equilibrium quantity and price under perfect competition are X_c and P_c, respectively, and consumers surplus is equivalent to the combined areas of triangles *a*, *b*, *c*, and *d*. Under monopoly, supply is X_m (equals half that under perfect competition) and price is P_m so that consumers surplus is equal to the area of the triangle marked *a*. Since the four triangles *a*, *b*, *c*, and *d* can be shown to be congruent, monopoly in this linear constant cost case reduces consumers surplus to a *quarter* of that under perfect competition.

Loss in consumers surplus as a result of monopoly depends on inelasticity of the marginal cost curve

If the marginal cost curve is upward sloping through point J, the loss in consumers surplus as a result of monopoly is less. Indeed, in the extreme case where this cost curve is vertical there is no loss and no difference between the two market forms in their effect. *The more inelastic is supply the smaller the loss in consumers surplus as a result of monopoly* and also the smaller the deadweight loss. (The reader may wish to draw two or three alternative supply curves through point J and consider their comparative effects.)

Loss in consumers surplus as a result of monopoly depends on inelasticity of demand

As a rule the magnitude of the loss in consumers surplus and of the dead-weight loss resulting from monopoly is greater (when compared to perfect competition) the more inelastic is the demand for the monopolized product. This can be illustrated from Figure 8.3.

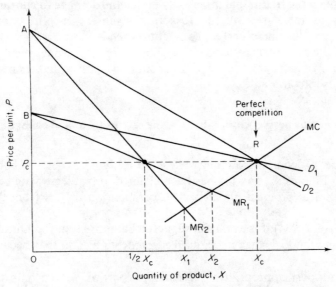

Figure 8.3   When the demand curve is more inelastic (D_2 compared to D_1) the loss in consumers surplus as a result of monopoly is greater. Thus if MC is the supply curve, output falls by $X_c - X_2$ if D_1 applies and by $X_c - X_1$ if D_2 applies and monopoly occurs. The loss in consumers surplus is greater in the last case.

In this example, two demand curves D_1 and D_2 are shown. Assuming that industry equilibrium under perfect competition corresponds to point R, D_2 is relatively more inelastic than D_1 in this equilibrium. A greater loss in consumers surplus occurs if D_2 rather than D_1 is the case and the competitive supply curve (equals marginal cost for the monopolist) is not perfectly inelastic. Consider first the simple case in which the competitive supply curve (equals marginal cost) is constant and passes through P_cR. On the basis of the argument just considered above, the loss in consumers surplus as a result of monopoly is ¾ area of $\triangle BP_cR$ when D_1 is the case and ¾ area of $\triangle AP_cR$ when D_2 is the case, and is clearly much larger in the more inelastic case, i.e. for the last-mentioned one. The deadweight loss is equal to one-quarter of the area of these triangles. In this particular case, output by the monopolist is the same in the inelastic and elastic case. But if marginal cost is increasing (but not vertical) as indicated by the curve MC in Figure 8.3, the reduction in supplies by the monopolist compared to the quantity supplied under perfect competition is greater the more inelastic is demand. Also, of course, as before the rise in price is greater the more inelastic is demand. In Figure 8.3, supplies fall by only $X_c - X_2$ if the more elastic demand curve D_1 applies, but fall by $X_c - X_1$ if the more inelastic curve D_2 applies. Consequently, since $D_2 > D_1$ in this range, the *loss in consumers surplus is considerably higher when demand is more inelastic. Thus consumers are likely to suffer a greater loss the more inelastic is the demand for the commodity which is monopolized.*

Hence given the traditional monopoly model the damage to consumers from monopoly as measured by the loss in consumers surplus compared to consumers surplus under perfect competition tends to be greater (1) the more inelastic is the marginal cost curve and (2) the more inelastic is the demand for the product. In assessing the effect of monopoly, policy-makers need to take both aspects into account.

Monopoly versus perfect competition if the rate of technical change is different

The type of comparison between monopoly and perfect competition outlined in Figures 8.2 and 8.3 has been claimed to be illegitimate because the rate of technical progress under perfect competition differs from that under monopoly.

Schumpeter (1954), for example, suggests that more rapid technical progress occurs under monopoly than under perfect competition. This may occur because:

(1) A monopolist appropriates a greater proportion of the return from an invention in his industry than does a company sharing a market with competitors who may imitate the invention or discovery without payment or full payment to the inventor. By virtue of his dominant market position a monopolist retains his effective property right in any of his inventions. This makes it more profitable for a monopolist to invent and innovate than for a competitive firm.
(2) A monopolist earns excess profit which provides him with funds for investment and he may use these in fostering technical progress.

(3) Innovation may be less risky for a monopolist, for instance because he would find it more profitable to purchase or obtain more information about the market prospects of a potential innovation than would one firm among many in the same market.

(4) It may also be true, as Schumpeter believed, that a monopoly is not safe from long-term competition. Competition may come from new products and new sources of supply and the business of a monopolist may only survive if he is technically progressive.

On the other hand, some economists argue that technical progress is likely to be slower under monopoly because competitive pressures are weak.

Even if technical progress is more rapid under monopoly than under perfect competition this does not ensure that consumers are able to buy the products involved at a lower price under monopoly. For price to be actually less under monopoly than would occur under perfect competition with less technical progress, the monopoly must result in a substantial reduction in per-unit costs of production. This can be seen from Figure 8.4.

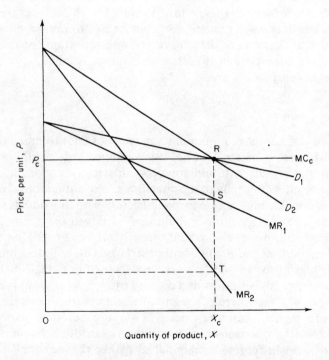

Figure 8.4 Greater technical progress under monopoly compared to perfect competition does not guarantee consumers a lower price for a product than under perfect competition. If the demand curve happened to be D_1, per-unit costs would need to fall below S for the monopoly price to be less than the perfectly competitive price P_c.

Suppose that the curve identified by D_1 represents the demand curve for the product of the industry and that MC_c represents the supply curve under perfect competition. Under perfect competition, the equilibrium quantity supplied is X_c and the equilibrium price is P_c. If monopoly is to result in a higher output than X_c and a lower price than P_c it must introduce techniques which lower per-unit costs of production by more than RS. Any smaller reduction in per-unit costs of production will not benefit purchasers of product X. Faster technical progress under monopoly is not sufficient to ensure gains to the purchasers of the monopolized product.

The more inelastic is the demand for a product the greater must be the production in per-unit costs of production achieved by a monopolist, if consumers are to enjoy a lower price for the product than under perfect competition. This can also be seen from Figure 8.4. The demand curve D_2 is more inelastic than D_1 relative to position R, the perfectly competitive equilibrium. But if D_2 applies per-unit costs must fall under monopoly by more than RT if the price of X is to be lower under monopoly. The more inelastic is the demand for a product the greater must be the comparative rate of technical progress under monopoly to ensure that prices are lower than they would have been under perfect competition. Conversely, the more elastic is demand, the smaller needs to be the relatively faster rate of technical progress under monopoly to ensure a price reduction in comparison to perfect competition. Thus the degree of elasticity of demand can be one important consideration in deciding whether monopoly in a particular instance is advantageous or disadvantageous to consumers.

X-inefficiency again

As discussed in Chapter 6, monopolists may choose not to maximize profit and be X-inefficient in the sense of not using resources efficiently to produce whatever output is produced at minimum cost. Instead of making an effort to minimize cost by attending fully to the direction and coordination of employed resources a monopolist may decide to avoid friction with individuals within his firm and 'take it easy'. Given this in-built inefficiency in the operation of the business he may still, however, maximize profit *subject to it*. Thus although costs are not minimized and profit cannot therefore be absolutely maximized, profit may be maximized *subject* to a certain degree of in-built X-inefficiency. Consumers suffer by higher prices as a consequence of the in-built inefficiency and it can be argued that there is a waste of resources insofar as the costs of production are higher than they need be—more resources are used in supplying output than is necessary. For instance, in the example shown in Figure 8.5, MC_E might represent marginal cost when the monopolist operates so as to minimize cost and MC_I might be his marginal cost given his in-built degree of X-inefficiency. As a result of this 'in-built' inefficiency the price of the product is P_I rather than P_E and output is X_I rather than X_E. Due to the presence of the X-inefficiency there is a loss in consumers surplus represented by the marbled area. Furthermore, X-inefficiency wastes resources in the sense that it adds the equivalent of the hatched rectangle to the cost of producing X_I, i.e. adds to the per-unit cost of production.

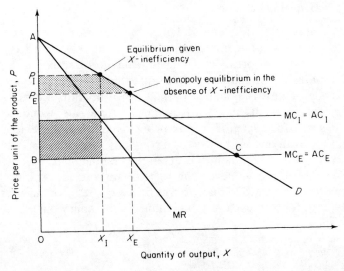

Figure 8.5 X-inefficiency may occur under monopoly. It results in a loss of consumers surplus and 'a waste' of resources, in the sense that the per-unit costs of producing output are higher than under competitive conditions where X-inefficiency is more likely to be absent or less. In the above case the Kaldor–Hicks loss due to X-inefficiency (MC_I > MC_E) consists of the loss in consumers surplus shown by the marbled area plus excess costs shown by the hatched area.

The loss of consumers surplus as a result of X-inefficiency is greater the more inelastic is the demand for the product relative, for instance, to the perfectly competitive equilibrium, position C. (You may wish to draw a steeper demand curve through this point and observe the effect on the marbled area.) But note also that in the constant cost case the loss in consumers surplus due to X-inefficiency is much smaller than that due to the restrictive allocative impact of monopoly on supply. As shown above, the restrictive (allocative) impact of monopoly (its raising of price above marginal cost) leads to a loss of three-quarters of consumers surplus compared to that under perfect competition, i.e. to a loss of ¾ area of $\triangle ABC$. The additional *loss due to X-inefficiency*, the marbled area, is less and indeed cannot exceed the area of $\triangle AP_EL$, that is ¼ area of $\triangle ABC$. The X-inefficiency loss of consumers surplus becomes relatively more important, however, if marginal cost is increasing. Nevertheless, a priori, it does not appear to be as great as might have been imagined at first sight. We shall discuss this again when Harberger's (1954) findings are considered.

It might also be recalled, as discussed in Chapter 6, that increased X-inefficiency may offset potential gains from the merger of firms. Even though economies of scale may be possible, the potential of these for reducing per-unit costs may be more than offset by greater X-inefficiency.

Non-profit-maximizing behaviour

While the presence of X-inefficiency implies non-profit-maximizing behaviour on the part of a monopolist, at least in relation to the internal control of the firm, non-profit-mazimizing behaviour can be more pervasive for the monopolist may not strive to maximize his profit in selling to buyers. The occurrence of and the scope for non-profit-maximizing behaviour by firms has already been discussed in Chapter 7. As a rule, a monopolist has considerable scope for engaging in non-profit-maximizing behaviour because he lacks market rivals and in the case of a company there may be failure of the capital market. He may, for example, act in the manner suggested by Baumol, i.e. try to maximize the value of the sales of his product subject to some satisfactory rate of return. He may do this because sales give business prestige and he may wish for a 'quiet life', one unhurried by angry buyers. Behaviour

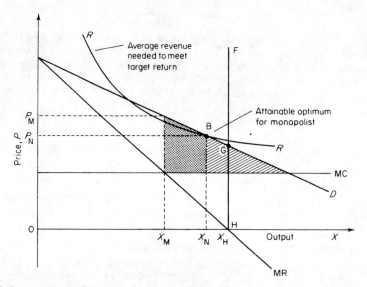

Figure 8.6 A monopolist may aim to maximize his value of sales subject to a target rate of return. On average this results in less restriction of output than if profit maximization is his aim. It also results in a smaller deadweight loss than otherwise. In the above case, the deadweight loss is shown by the hatched triangle. Note that total revenue reaches a maximum when the quantity of the monopolist's sales is X_H (MR = 0 for X_H). If RR only cuts the demand curve above or at G, the monopolist's optimum output corresponds to the lower intersection point (B in the above cas) and is constrained by the profit target. However if RR cuts the demand curve below G the monopolist's optimum output is constrained to X_H by his sales revenue aim.

of this type is likely to lead to greater supplies by the monopolist and to a smaller deadweight loss than otherwise. This can be illustrated by Figure 8.6.

In Figure 8.6 demand and cost curves facing a monopolist are indicated in the usual way and MR is the marginal revenue corresponding to the market demand curve D. The line RR indicates the minimum level of average revenue needed to achieve the target return of the monopolist. It is assumed that subject to his meeting his target rate of return, the monopolist aims to maximize his revenue. In this case, he produces X_N and sells it at P_N compared to X_M sold at P_M if he maximizes profit. The deadweight social loss amounts to the hatched area and is much smaller than would be the case for profit maximization. In the profit-maximizing case, the deadweight loss amounts to the hatched area plus the dotted one. A sales-maximizing monopolist may therefore not distort the allocation of resources as much as a profit-maximizing one. On the other hand, he could spend a socially excessive amount on advertising his product. This will be discussed later.

8.4 MONOPOLY BEHAVIOUR TAKING POTENTIAL ENTRY INTO ACCOUNT

A monopolist may alter his market behaviour or strategy if he is faced by the threat of entry of a competitor even though the monopolist continues to try to maximize his profit. He may try to raise barriers to the entry of competitors and lower his prices to deter potential entrants. Barriers to new entrants may be:

(1) legal ones, i.e. restrictions to entry embodied in statutes;
(2) absolute per-unit cost disadvantages which may occur because the monopolist controls the least-cost technology, for instance through patent protection, or obtains resources such as minerals or energy from the government or its agencies at a privileged low price;
(3) stemming from economies of scale in production and/or distribution; and
(4) arising from large advertising and promotion campaigns of branded products of the monopolist.

The effect of the threat of entry on a monopolist's pricing behaviour depends not only on the height of barriers to entry but also on the expected behaviour by his rivals after entry. A variety of different types of behaviour are possible after entry. An entry or entrants may allow the established firm to be the price-leader if the established firm has the lowest per-unit costs, or if there are many entrants the market may tend towards a perfectly competitive one after entry. Another possibility which has been given much attention in recent economic literature is that the established firm will continue after entry to supply and sell the same quantity of supply as before entry. The remainder of market demand after entry is supplied by entrants. This is known as the Sylos postulate.

Effect of absolute barriers

The effect of absolute barriers to entry, if the Sylos postulate applies, can be seen from Figure 8.7. Let D represent the demand curve for product X and the line marked MC_E represent the marginal cost and average cost of production experienced by the established firm. In the absence of any threat of entry, the established monopolist would find it profitable to produce X_M of the product and sell it at P_M. But suppose that a potential rival has per-unit costs as indicated by MC_R. The potential rival finds it profitable to enter the market if the established firm supplies less than X_R to the market. Thus taking this entry element into consideration, the marginal revenue curve of the established firm consists of the heavy lines shown in Figure 8.7. Since the marginal cost of the established firm passes through the discontinuous part of this modified marginal revenue curve, the most profitable policy of the established firm is to supply X_R to the market at a price of P_R, the entry-forestalling price. *Unless* the entry-forestalling price exceeds that which maximizes profit in the absence of possible entry (P_M in this case) the most profitable policy for the established firm is to charge the entry-forestalling price and supply all demands at this price.

But if the entry-forestalling price P_R exceeds the absolute monopoly profit-maximizing price of P_M, then the established firm maximizes its profit by charging P_M, i.e. a price less than P_R. Note also that until $P_R > P_M$ the entry-

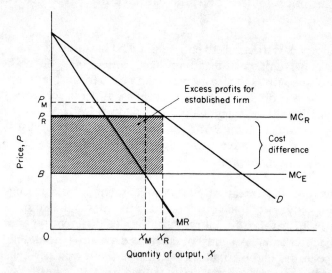

Figure 8.7   Because of the risk of entry, a monopolist may find it most profitable to charge an entry forestalling price, a price lower than otherwise. The greater the per-unit cost disadvantage of his potential rival, the higher is the most profitable price for the established firm to charge likely to be and the greater its profit. Given the cost difference shown by $MC_R - MC_E$, the established firm can charge P_R without inducing entry and makes abnormal profits, indicated by the hatched area.

forestalling price and the profit-maximizing price of the established firm is greater the higher is the per-unit costs of production of the potential rival. Furthermore, if $P_R < P_M$, the excess profits of the profit-maximizing established firm, as indicated in Figure 8.7 by the hatched rectangle, is higher the greater is the per-unit cost disadvantage of the potential entrant.

Rapidly increasing economies of scale as a barrier

Apart from differences in the per-unit costs experienced by established firms and the expected per-unit costs of entrants (absolute cost difference), economies of scale can form entry barriers. These barriers depend not only on the size required for the minimum efficient scale of operation but also on the rapidity with which average costs fall with the firm's volume of production. The steeper (i.e. the faster the rate of decline of) the average cost curve of production, the greater other things equal (including MES) can be the price charged by established firms without provoking entry. Also this price tends to be higher the larger is the minimum efficient scale.

The last-mentioned effect can be illustrated by a simple example. Assume that the scale of operations of a firm is unique and results in per-unit costs of production of position B and a level of output of $\bar{x}$, as illustrated in Figure 8.8. The larger is $\bar{x}$ the greater can be the price charged by established firms without provoking entry if the Sylos postulate applies. If $\bar{x} = \bar{x}_1$ established firms can charge up to P_1 for product X without triggering entry if the market demand curve is as indicated by curve D in Figure 8.8. But if the required scale is greater, say $\bar{x} = \bar{x}_2$, an even higher price, P_2, can be charged without enticing entry.

Figure 8.9 illustrates the impact of a more rapid fall in per-unit costs with scale. The curve C_2C_2 represents per-unit costs for the *same* minimum efficient scale as C_1C_1. The minimum efficient scale occurs in both instances for an output of $\bar{x}$. Per-unit costs fall more rapidly in the first case and in this case of rapidly increasing economies of scale established firms can charge up to P_2 without encouraging entry. If costs fall more slowly with scale as indicated by C_1C_1 established firms cannot charge more than P_1 without provoking entry. Rapidly increasing economies of scale may therefore enable established firms to charge higher prices than otherwise without provoking entry.

Advertising expenditure can be one source of substantial economies of scale with volume of sales. Many types of advertising require a large fixed outlay and this implies a rapid decline in per-unit selling costs with volume of sales. Thus a firm trying to enter an industry in which advertising expenditure by established firms is considerable (such as in soaps and detergents, and cigarettes) may find this advertising a major barrier; the barrier may protect established firms and enable them to charge a higher price than otherwise without initiating entry. One reason why established firms may maintain high levels of expenditure on advertising and promotion may not always be to compete with one another but to deter potential entrants.

206

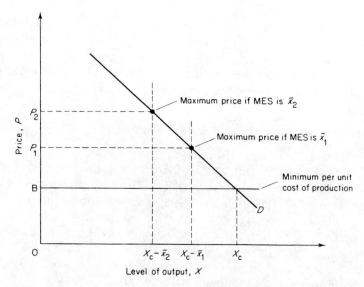

Figure 8.8   The maximum price which an established firm(s) can charge without provoking entry tends to be greater the larger is the minimum efficient scale of operations. This maximum price is P_1 if the (unique) MES is $\bar{x}_1$. At P_1 it is just profitable for a new firm to enter, add $\bar{x}_1$ to industry output, and so lower the price of the product to OB. At the larger scale $\bar{x}_2$, it is only just profitable to enter and add $\bar{x}_2$ to industry supply if $P = P_2$. Note that X_c corresponds to the output of a perfectly competitive industry in the absence of scale barriers.

Policy discussion on entry

A government may be in a position to reduce the market power of a monopolist by making entry or potential entry of new firms or new sources of supply easier in some instances. For example, imports of commodities which may compete with a monopolist's product may be permitted to enter at a lower tariff, and where restrictive legislation such as licensing laws limit possible entry of competitors these may be relaxed. Sometimes, however, governments by interfering in monopoly-like market situations add to restrictions on entry rather than reduce these since the regulatory body established for an industry tends to become a captive client of established firms. The economics of politics and bureaucracy suggests that established firms in an industry may be the major pressure group affecting the behaviour of the regulatory body if it is set up for an industry. Therefore, there is a risk that the regulatory body will act to restrict entry rather than encourage it.

8.5   PUBLIC ACTION TO REGULATE MONOPOLIES

Public action to regulate the activities of or restrict the formation of monopolies may be based upon one or more of the following factors previously mentioned:

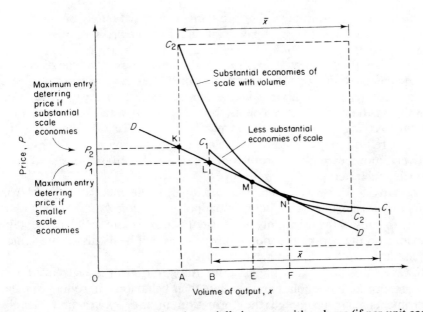

Figure 8.9   If economies of scale substantially increase with volume (if per-unit costs of production fall rapidly with volume) established firms may be able to charge higher prices than otherwise without provoking entry. Thus for C_2C_2 the maximum entry deterring price P_2 exceeds that for C_1C_1, P_1. For instance, if C_2C_2 applies and price is P_2, a new entrant would just find it profitable to enter and add AF to the quantity of the product supplied by the industry. If C_1C_1 applies and price is just equal to P_1 a new entrant would just find it profitable to enter and add BE to the quantity of the product supplied by the industry. P_2 and P_1 are located by 'sliding' the per-unit costs of each plant to the left until tangency is achieved with the industry demand curve at N and M respectively. Each of these prices then corresponds to the intersection point with the demand curve of the vertical from the left-hand end-points of the respective cost curves. K corresponds to the intersection point for C_2C_2 and L that for C_1C_1.

(1) *The allocative loss* caused by monopoly as a result of a monopolist raising the price of his product above its marginal cost of production.
(2) *The redistributive effect* from the monopolist earning above normal profit.
(3) *Possible dynamic inefficiency* of monopoly because it *may* impede technical progress.
(4) The *possible X-inefficiency* in the management of the business.
(5) The likely *political power of a monopolist*.

Public action to prevent the formation of monopolies can take a number of forms. Apart from adopting measures to encourage entry of competitors or competing supplies, governments may forbid large companies to acquire competing firms or forbid merger where this would be likely to lead to monopoly or one firm obtaining a monopoly-like position in the market. There is provision for this type of government action in legislation in the United States, the United Kingdom and Australia. Legal tests for monopoly are often crude. For instance, they are sometimes based purely on the market share held by a single firm and pay scant regard to the presence of substitutes or the degree of substitutability as measured by cross elasticities.

Where a monopoly already exists the government may intervene directly to regulate the maximum price that the monopolist can charge as, for instance, is the case for telephone services in the United States. There the regulatory commissions tend to adjust maximum prices to ensure a fair (or normal) rate of return on the capital invested in public utilities. To the extent that the allowable returns may be slightly above normal, this encourages utilities to use relatively more capital in production than would minimize the cost of producing their output.

Alternatively the government may nationalize the industry or otherwise ensure that it is operated as a public monopoly. It may feel that this will make it easier to control the monopoly and easier to ensure more socially acceptable behaviour on the part of the monopolist. But as will be discussed in the next section these results are by no means assured.

However, it is not always the case that the government is eager to prevent the formation of monopolies and regulate their behaviour. In some instances, governments have promoted the formation of monopolies and business mergers. Arguments that have been used to support this policy include:

(1) It is necessary to increase economic efficiency because firms obtain a fall in per-unit costs of operation by expanding their size. A natural monopoly exists.
(2) It improves dynamic efficiency by speeding up technical progress and investment.
(3) It is necessary if the domestic industry is to compete in international trade and investment and maximize its gains from international trade and direct investment overseas.
(4) It improves the coordination of the economy compared with that which would be achieved by private enterprise and makes government planning more effective by reducing uncertainty about the operation of the economy.

As mentioned in Chapter 6, studies of the effects of business mergers in the United Kingdom indicate that there is no acceptable evidence to indicate that business mergers do in fact result in a lowering of per-unit costs of production. Furthermore, technical progress can slow down as a result of monopoly. Advantages may be obtained from international trade but possibly at the expense of overseas buyers and domestic consumers because of the use of restrictive practices. The use of restrictive practices in international trade can result in *all* being made worse off in the Kaldor–Hicks sense. Nevertheless, particular nations (some of the developed countries) with industrialists having considerable monopoly power through the development of advanced technology could gain on balance from the encouragement of domestic monopolies when international trade is taken into account.

209

8.6 PUBLIC MONOPOLIES

Difficulties in regulating private monopolies

Public regulation of private monopolies involves several difficulties. For instance, a public body regulating the maximum price to be charged by a monopolist may be unable to determine the price which will equate the demand for the monopolist's product with his marginal cost of production. The actual marginal cost and demand curve indicated in Figure 8.10 may be unknown to the authority and it may not be able to obtain information to eliminate its ignorance. If it knew these curves the optimal maximum price would be P_R, which would induce the monopolist to produce X_R of the product. This regulated price would be optimal from a Kaldor–Hicks point of view in the absence of externalities and second best considerations. As a result of the regulation the monopolist's marginal revenue curve would be discontinuous, as indicated by the solid lines, which means that the monopolist supplies X_R of the product rather than X_M.

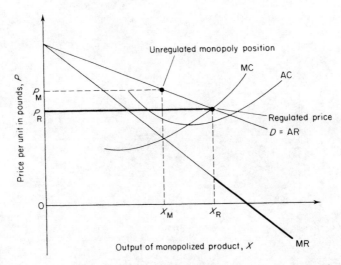

Figure 8.10   A case in which price to be charged by a monopolist is regulated so as to equate marginal cost and demand. Because of ignorance on the part of the regulating body, marginal cost pricing may not always be practical. Given the regulated price P_R the monopolist's effective demand curve is the one indicated by the heavy lines.

It might be thought that the regulatory authority could discover the optimal regulated price level by trial-and-error. A myopic profit-maximizing monopolist would fail to supply all demands for his product if the regulated price happened to be set below P_R, the value for which marginal cost equals demand. The problem might then appear to be one of the authority raising the ceiling price until all demands are *just* met. But a monopolist would not need

210

to be very clever to thwart this approach. It would pay the monopolist to maintain an artificial scarcity until the authority raises the regulated price to P_M. By the way, this problem creates a difficulty for the operation of Lange and Taylor's (1938) model of competitive socialism because a state enterprise with monopoly power may operate in a similar way to a private monopolist.

There is the further difficulty that marginal cost pricing is not always compatible with the continued existence of a firm. When average costs of production decline with the volume of production, marginal cost pricing causes a firm to make a loss and the firm will go out of existence unless it obtains a grant to cover this loss. The firm makes a loss in these circumstances because when average costs are falling marginal cost is below average cost. For instance, in the case illustrated in Figure 8.11 if the regulated price is set at P_R and *if* the firm produces X_R it makes the loss shown by the hatched area and it would need a lump sum grant of this amount to remain in existence. The danger in the government underwriting the loss of the firm, however, is that this may encourage the firm to become inefficient since it has some assurance that its losses will be covered.

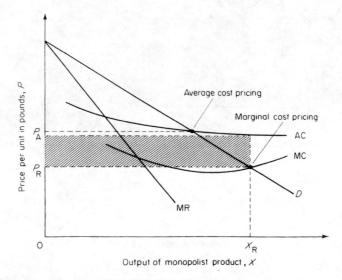

Figure 8.11 Marginal cost pricing leads to a loss for the monopolist if average cost falls with the volume of output. In the above instance if price is regulated to P_R and X_R is supplied (so equating marginal cost and demand) the loss shown by the hatched area is incurred by the monopolist.

To avoid the necessity of paying the monopolist a subsidy, the government may determine a ceiling price which would result in the monopolist supplying an output equating his average cost of production with demand. In the case shown in Figure 8.11, this is a price of P_A. However, the regulating authority may have insufficient information about costs and demand to determine this price accurately. This may provide managers of regulated industries with an incentive to inflate their costs, for instance by following policies for their own personal gain in the expectation that the regulation price will be altered to cover the inflated levels of cost. The policy may also encourage X-inefficiency. Revenue-maximizers, for instance, may aim for a *regulated price* which ensures the level of sales for which marginal revenue equals zero. They may engineer this by inflating their per-unit costs to the level of this *desired* regulated price. Of course, this also applies to managers of public entrprises.

To counteract this tendency Demsetz (1968) has suggested that the right to operate monopolies be put up for public bidding at regular intervals. Interested firms or members of the public would tender a price at which they would be willing to supply the monopolized product. The lowest price tendered would be accepted.

Public ownership as a means of overcoming difficulties of regulating private monopolies

While public ownership of monopolies may appear to be a way of overcoming the information problems involved in controlling private monopolies, it is not necessarily a solution. Public enterprises have their own identity; their managers foster the interests of these enterprises as they see them and may make information available selectively to the public and other branches of government. The information problem is not overcome though it could be reduced in some instances. The annual reports which public enterprises make to Parliament contain selected and insufficient information to enable a careful and detailed assessment of their performance to be made. Indeed, there are a few instances in Australia where such enterprises are not required to report to Parliament regularly.

Members of the general public frequently do not find it worthwhile to bring pressure upon public enterprises through the political process to improve their economic efficiency. The gain of any individual agitator is likely to be small in relation to the cost of the effort to him, since other individuals who also stand to gain may free-ride on his efforts. Politicians of the government may also (especially if they are members of the board of the public enterprise or a minister at least nominally responsible for the public enterprise) be sympathetic to the public enterprise's own managerial position. Opposition politicians may be critical from time to time of performance but are likely to be hampered by a lack of information about the public enterprise. Thus the political forces regulating a public enterprise in the general interest may be weak. This may encourage allocative and X-inefficiency by public enterprises and members of the management of public enterprises may be tempted to follow policies based upon their own (possibly narrow) perceptions and interests. Perfection (for instance marginal cost pricing in the absence of second best problems) is not guaranteed by public operation of enterprises since the political process does not appear to make for the presence of powerful watchdogs.

Because of the difficulty faced by Parliament in keeping itself informed about public enterprises and the role that they are performing, it has been suggested that when a public enterprise is formed it should be stipulated that it will go out of existence in a specified number of years unless it can justify its continued existence to Parliament before that time. This has been called the sunset principle by US politicians and is indicative of the problem of regulating public enterprises.

Aspects of bureaucracy and public enterprise

Public bureaucrats (members of the civil or public service) have a considerable amount of power and discretion which they may use to foster their own ambitions. It has been suggested that they may aim to maximize their budgets. They may regard these as an index of their power over resources. In doing this they are likely to be assisted by appropriate pressure groups in the society. For instance, a Department or Ministry of Agriculture will be supported by associations of farmers in moves to gain funds which assist farmers and a Department of Industry or Manufacturing may be assisted by groups of manufacturers and a symbiotic relationship may grow up between the two. The economics of politics suggests that in this process producer groups will be more strongly represented than consumer groups.

As far as public enterprises are concerned the 'empire-building' tendency of bureaucrats may reveal itself in a number of different ways. One possibility is to *maximize sales receipts* and spend an amount equal to these receipts. As mentioned earlier, a public enterprise may adjust its average costs upwards to the *price level* needed to maximize its total revenue, if the enterprise is only expected by the government to earn a normal return. Or an attempt may be made to maximize the *volume* of sales and, subject to this, to maximize revenue. The empire-building preferences of public enterprises may be reflected in a preference for average cost pricing in increasing cost cases compared to marginal cost pricing and in attempts to charge a zero or very low price for supplies at the margin. One might expect generally a preference for two-part tariffs on the part of public enterprises interested in maximizing the volume of their sales, the second part of the tariff being zero or below marginal cost so as to expand the volume of sales.

An example of this latter approach is the method of charging for reticulated water supplies in many areas. Often this takes the form of a flat or fixed charge or rates based upon property values with a zero marginal charge for the amount of water used. The public water authority then tries to obtain sufficient funds to undertake investment to meet all demands at this zero marginal price. But as can be seen from Figure 8.12 this approach results in a deadweight social loss. If the demand for water is as represented by curve D_1 the Kaldor-Hicks social loss amounts to the dotted area plus the hatched area. The social loss is smaller if demand is more inelastic. For instance, if the demand curve is as indicated by D_2, the Kaldor–Hicks loss only amounts to the hatched area. If the demand curve is D_1, the marginal price for water is P_1, which equates the marginal cost of supplying it with the demand for it. In regions where demand for water is more elastic there may be a stronger case for marginal cost pricing than in areas where demand is very inelastic. In many areas of Australia and the United States where a large proportion of water is used outside the home on gardens, demand tends to be elastic, whereas it may be more inelastic in Britain since a higher proportion of water is used within the home. This means that there could be a stronger case for marginal cost pricing of household water in Australia and the United States than in Britain.

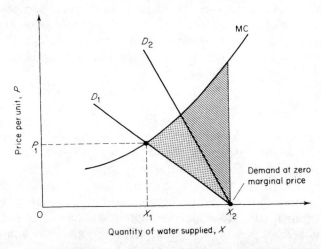

Figure 8.12 'Empire-building' tendencies of managers of public enterprises may lead them to favour zero marginal pricing as in the water industry. This results in a Kaldor–Hicks social loss, the extent of the loss being greater the more elastic is demand. Above this loss equals the hatched plus the dotted area when the demand curve is D_1 and the hatched area if the demand curve is D_2.

The behaviour of public enterprises can vary considerably, and much more study of them is needed taking into account political considerations. It cannot be assumed that the establishment of a public enterprise will result in an ideal solution to a monopoly problem because government involves complex organizational and interaction problems. Government failure is to be expected (see Chapter 15).

8.7 FURTHER ASPECTS OF MONOPOLY

Empirical evidence about the extent of monopoly losses

Primitive attempts have been made to measure deadweight losses due to monopoly. Harberger's (1954) study is the earliest and best known one. Harberger concluded (on the basis of data on the US manufacturing industry for 1924–1928) that the annual *actual* total deadweight or Kaldor–Hicks loss from monopoly in the United States amounted to about one-tenth of 1 per cent. of its GDP. His estimate of this allocative loss is based upon the special assumptions of constant long-run average costs of production and a unitary elasticity of demand for products.

This estimated loss is lower than many economists may have expected. But the low relative loss could reflect the unwillingness of monopolists to exploit their monopoly power fully and their restriction of price levels to deter potential entrants. The result does not prove that there is no need to be concerned about monopoly. Monopoly power may be exploited in particular instances and can result in a considerable Kaldor–Hicks loss, as pointed out in Section 8.3.

Again it needs to be remembered that the allocative loss *as measured by Harberger* is only part of the possible social loss from monopoly. For instance, monopoly *may* result in greater X-inefficiency and slower technical progress than, say, under conditions of oligopoly.

Pollution and monopoly

It has been suggested that the behavoiur of monopolists to restrict supplies in order to increase their profit may be a blessing in disguise if the production of the monopolized products causes unfavourable externalities or spillovers. Under unregulated perfect competition production will tend to be excessive from a social point of view if such externalities occur. But monopoly need not result in an optimal correction and the monopolist has no incentive to use socially optimal techniques of production, i.e. techniques which minimize the cost of production when all spillovers are taken into account.

It has been pointed out that a monopolist may be able to internalize externalities which would otherwise exist between producers if there happened to be several producers in an industry. He would therefore take these externalities into account in organizing the production of the industry.

From a political point of view, it needs to be remembered that it may be more difficult for environmentalists to countervail against a monopolist than against a large number of producers operating the same industry. The monopolist is likely to find it more profitable to engage in political action which will benefit him, including counteracting pressures of environmentalists, than would a large number of producers who face a free-rider problem and must meet the costs of collectively organizing themselves for political action.

Research and development, patenting and innovation

Evidence about the effect of monopoly on the rate of technical progress is inconclusive although Schumpeter has suggested on theoretical grounds that monopoly and big business might speed up technical progress.

Little direct evidence is available about the impact of monopoly on the level of research and development expenditure and its effect on the volume of inventive output. While the major proportion of industrial R & D expenditure in developed countries is accounted for by a few large firms, research intensities (the proportion of R & D expenditure to sales, for instance) tend to rise as the size of the firm increases and *then fall off* at very large sizes according to the findings of Mansfield (1979) and of Scherer (1965). But of course one should not only take the input to R & D effort into account but also the value of inventive output. On the basis of his study of the chemical, steel, and petroleum industries in the United States, Mansfield concluded that the inventive output per dollar of R & D expenditure seems to be lower for the largest firms in these industries than for medium-sized firms.

Mansfield's result is not inconsistent with Freeman's (1974) finding that large firms (those with more than 1000 employees) are responsible for most innovations and that the proportionate share of medium and large firms (200 and over employees) is in excess of their proportionate share of employment and output. But firms can of course be large without monopolizing an industry.

It should be noted that the patent system provides an interesting example of the creation of monopolies by government intervention. On the payment of a fee to the government, an inventor is granted exclusive property rights in his invention for a specified period of time. Various arguments have been put in favour of such a grant. For instance, it has been suggested that the monopoly profit which may be obtained through a patent may provide inventors with greater incentive to invent and innovate, thus speeding up technical progress. The question to be considered, then, is whether the allocative and other losses from granting a temporary monopoly are less than the benefits obtained from speedier technical progress, for example, in the form of lower prices and the speedier introduction of products with new qualities.

Advertising and monopoly

In assessing the welfare effects of monopoly one may also wish to take account of its effects on the level of advertising. Kaldor (1940–41) and Telser (1964) have suggested that monopoly can lead to a socially excessive level of advertising. However, as Tisdell (1972) has pointed out a monopolist may from a social viewpoint undersupply advertising in some circumstances because he only appropriates a *part* of the marginal social gain from informative advertising.

Dorfman and Steiner (1954) have theorized that, other things equal, advertising intensities are likely to be higher the more inelastic is the demand for a product. Thus, other things equal, advertising intensities could be higher when monopolies are present than when they are absent. But as will be seen in the next chapter the evidence on this is inconclusive.

216

8.8 CONCLUSION

To assess the social consequences of monopoly merely in terms of its static allocative effects may be misleading. One needs as a rule to take account also of its dynamic consequences, for instance its influence on the rate of technological change and its implications for the distribution of income and for the working of the political system. One needs to be sanguine about idealistic public attempts to regulate private monopolies and to establish state monopolies to guard against the shortcomings of private monopolies. In both cases, government and bureaucratic organizational failures (some of which cannot be eliminated because men have *limited abilities*, for instance, to collect and to process information) may mean that idealistic policies cannot be fulfilled. Such policies may be based upon an unrealistic view of the world and of the political organizational process. But this is not an argument for despair and inaction. There may well be circumstances in which public intervention is justified even after 'the warts' of the political and bureaucratic process are taken into account. But it would be foolish to neglect the warts or pretend that they do not exist.

READING AND REFERENCES

Demsetz, H. (1968), Why Regulate Utilities?, *Journal of Law and Economics*, **XI**, April, 55–65.

Devine, P. J., Lee, N., Jones, R. M., and Tyson, W. J. (1979). *An Introduction to Industrial Economics*, Chaps 2, 5, and 10, Allen and Unwin, London.

Dorfman, R. and Steiner, P. O. (1954), Optimal advertising and optimal quality, *American Economic Review*, **44**, 826–836.

Freeman, C. (1974), *The Economics of Industrial Innovation*, Penguin, London.

Harberger, A. C. (1954). Monopoly and resource allocation, *Proceedings of the American Economic Association*, **1954**, 77–87.

Hartley, K. (1977). *Problems of Economic Policy* Chaps 9, 10, and 11, Allen and Unwin, London.

Kaldor, N. (1940–41). Economic aspects of advertising, *Review of Economic Studies*, **18**, 1–27.

Lange, O. (1938). On the Economic Theory of Socialism; and Taylor, F. M. (1938). The Guidance of Production in a Socialist State, in Lippincot, B. (ed.), *On the Economic Theory of Socialism*, University of Minnesota Press, Minneapolis, pp 41–142.

Lipsey, R. G. (1979). *An Introduction to Positive Economics*, Chaps 20 to 23, Weidenfeld and Nicolson, London.

Mansfield, E. (1979). *Microeconomics*, Chap. 10, Norton, London.

Scherer, F. (1965). Firm size, market structure, opportunity and the output of patented inventions, *American Economic Review*, **55**, Dec., 1110–1120.

Schumpeter, J. A. (1954), *Capitalism, Socialism and Democracy*, Allen and Unwin, London.

Telser, L. G. (1964). Advertising and competition, *Journal of Political Economy*, **72**, 537–562.

Tisdell, C. A. (1972). *Microeconomics: The Theory of Economic Allocation*, Chaps 9, 19, 21 and 22, Wiley, Sydney.

Wiseman, J. (1978). The political economy of nationalised industry, in *The Economics of Politics*, pp 72–92, Institute of Economics Affairs, London.

QUESTIONS FOR REVIEW AND DISCUSSION

1. Outline three measures of monopoly power and carefully state the limitations of each. How could cross price elasticities be an important consideration in deciding whether a monopolist has monopoly power? What other considerations are important in deciding whether monopoly power exists?
2. 'Market power is a necessary but not sufficient condition for monopoly to result in a misallocation of resources.' Explain. In what sense might monopoly result in a misallocation of resources? What other general social effects might a monopoly have?
3. 'Profit-maximizing behaviour by a monopolist results in a loss of consumers surplus compared to that under perfect competition.' Explain. How great may this loss be? On what factors does the size of the loss depend? What implications might this have for deciding whether or not government interference with a monopoly is desirable?
4. 'While monopoly may lead to a greater rate of technical progress and innovation than perfect competition this does not ensure lower prices than under conditions of perfect competition.' Discuss.
5. What is X-inefficiency? Show that the Kaldor–Hicks loss from X-inefficiency under monopoly consists of two components. Is this loss likely to exceed that due to 'allocative' inefficiency?
6. Does non-profit-maximizing behaviour by a monopolist *necessarily* result in a smaller deadweight loss than profit-maximizing behaviour? Illustrate your answer.
7. 'The effect of the threat of entry on a monopolist's pricing behaviour depends on the expected behaviour by his rivals after entry.' Explain. What is the Sylos postulate? Do you believe that it is realistic?
8. 'The effect of the threat of entry on a monopolist's pricing behaviour depends on the height of barriers to entry.' Explain and illustrate for absolute cost barriers and barriers created by economies of scale.
9. The policies of governments in relation to monopoly are *seemingly* inconsistent. On the one hand there are policies to regulate monopolies and prevent their formation and on the other hand policies exist to encourage the formation of monopolies. Why do these different policies exist and to what extent are they inconsistent?
10. Suppose that a government wishes to regulate the behaviour of a private monopoly so that its production is brought into line with that required for a Pareto optimum. What policies could it adopt? What would be the main obstacles to the government achieving its objective?
11. 'A government is more likely to be able to achieve economic efficiency and a Paretian optimum through a public monopoly than by attempting to regulate a private monopoly.' Discuss.
12. What objectives may public bureaucrats have? How might these objectives influence the pricing behaviour of public enterprises? How can they result in a Kaldor–Hicks social loss?
13. Harberger found that the deadweight social loss due to monopoly in the United States was low. How low? Explain generally how he obtained his results and critically discuss the policy implications claimed for them.
14. Draw a diagram to show that where an unfavourable externality arises from the production of a commodity that monopoly *may* result in a Kaldor–Hicks

improvement compared to perfect competition. Must such an improvement occur or is a deterioration possible as a result of monopoly? What difference might a consideration of the economics of politics make to the 'rosy view' about monopolists and the environment?

15. 'Evidence about the effect of monopoly on the rate of technical progress is inconclusive as is that about the impact of monopoly on advertising.' Explain and discuss, taking account of the possible welfare effects of both of these activities.

CHAPTER 9

Oligopoly and Policy-Making

9.1 INTRODUCTION

Oligopoly is a typical market form in present-day industrial economies. It describes a market situation in which there are few sellers of a commodity or closely competitive commodities. Each seller usually holds a sizeable share of the market. The commodities oligopolized, in the hands of few sellers, may be homogeneous or differentiated. A characteristic of oligopolistic markets is that sellers recognize that their individual decisions about marketing their commodities such as changes in prices charged or in their level of advertising effort not only influence their own volume of sales but also sales of their competitors. Consequently competitors (rivals) may react by altering their marketing programme in response to a market change by an oligopolistic competitor. Thus expected variations in the marketing behaviour of rivals needs to be taken into account by an oligopolist contemplating a change in his market behaviour.

The presence of oligopoly is likely to depend on the definition or size of the market. At the international level one can expect more competitors than at a national level, and more at a national level than at a regional level. For instance, while textile fibre production in the United States is in the hands of about 10 producers, in the non-communist world there are about 30 independent producers. Steel production is oligopolistic or monopolized in many countries but supplies are more competitive internationally.

The range of important products oligopolized either within larger national or community markets is considerable. Most high technology products such as advanced computerized equipment and jet airliner production (on a world-wide scale) are controlled in their supply by oligopolists. Supplies of alumina and aluminium, refined copper, steel, petroleum products, cars, tractors, trucks, typewriters, cigarettes, detergents—to give a few examples—are oligopolized. Within national markets banking is sometimes, as in Australia, in the hands of an oligopoly. Frequently firms operating in oligopolistic industries are limited liability public companies in which ownership and management are separated. These institutional arrangements (as discussed in Chapter 7) may alter the behaviour of firms and this may be especially important in oligopolistic industries.

220

This chapter discusses some of the difficulties involved in modelling oligopolistic behaviour, some of the policy implications of the models, and the possible effect of oligopoly on the volume of advertising and its likely influence on the rate of technical progress. In the last section organizational and institutional arrangements such as those discussed by Galbraith and associated with the emergence of large oligopolistic firms are considered. Do we in fact have a dual economy with one part of it organized by small firms and markets and another part controlled by oligopolies and monopolies in which planning rather than market forces is the dominant feature? If so, what policy implications does this have?

9.2 MODELLING OLIGOPOLISTIC BEHAVIOUR

Modelling of oligopolistic behaviour is difficult. This is because the reactions of oligopolistic competitors can be so varied. Nevertheless, several models are available to assist in the understanding of typical oligopolistic markets. Kinked demand curve models, price leadership models, and cartel models have all proven to be of value for understanding the operation of oligopolistic markets and these will be outlined here. All of these models indicate ways in which oligopolists cope with the uncertainty arising from their close interdependence. There may be a strong desire on the part of the management of oligopoly to reduce uncertainty in their market environment and this may help to explain why the following models appear to be of so much value in understanding the operation of oligopolistic markets.

Kinked demand curve model

It has been observed, for instance by Markham (1951) and by Sweezy (1939) and by Hall and Hitch (1939), that prices of commodities sold in oligopolistic markets tend to be 'sticky'. They remain stationary for significant time-intervals and alter by jumps so that when price levels are graphed against time they tend to form a stepped function. One possible explanation of this is based upon the theory that an oligopolist may face a kinked demand curve for his commodity.

The kink arises because of the possible reaction of market rivals to the marketing behaviour of an oligopolist. If we restrict our attention to pricing as the relevant marketing variable, an oligopolist may face a demand curve for his product like the kinked one marked d in Figure 9.1. The kink occurs at a conventional or acceptable price P_A for the commodity. It is an acceptable price in the sense that if the oligopolist charges this price or a higher one his rivals do not alter their marketing arrangements, for instance they do not alter their prices. But if the oligopolist under consideration should happen to charge a price less than the conventional one, P_A (general circumstances in the industry not having altered), rivals do react in an attempt to retain their share of the market. For instance, they may lower their prices to match those of the oligopolist or lower them by a greater amount so sparking off a 'price-cutting' war. If it is assumed that rivals react by matching an oligopolist's price-cut below the conventional price, the oligopolist's demand curve below P_A may look like the lower end of curve d in Figure 9.1. The lower portion is steeper than the upper portion of the demand curve for the oligopolist's product because matching behaviour by rivals only occurs when the oligopolist lowers his price below P_A.

Because of the kink in the demand curve for an oligopolist's product, the associated marginal revenue curve is discontinuous, as indicated by the two heavy lines in Figure 9.1, and the discontinuity occurs directly below the kink in the demand curve. If the oligopolist's marginal cost of production or of supply passes through the gap in these marginal revenue curves, his profit-maximizing strategy is to charge the acceptable or conventional price P_A and meet all demands at this price. In the case illustrated all demands can be met by supplying x_1 of the product. On the other hand, if an oligopolist's marginal cost of supply should pass through the upper branch of the marginal revenue curve he would maximize his profit by charging a price higher than the conventional one; should it pass through the lower branch, he *may* make the greatest profit by charging less than the conventional price. But in the latter case, he may face the risk of a price war.

In the kinked demand curve case, there is a high probability that the firm's optimal pricing strategy for maximizing its profit is similar to that for

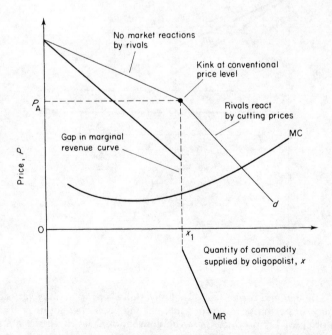

Figure 9.1   A kinked demand curve for an oligopolist's product and associated discontinuous marginal revenue curves. This can arise from the market responses of rivals.

222

maximizing its value of sales. Sales maximization and profit maximization can result in the same price and supply level for an oligopolist faced by a kinked demand curve. This is so if the conventional price maximizes the firm's profit and if the branches of its marginal revenue curve do not intersect the X-axis, and so MR is negative for $x \geq x_1$. In the example given in Figure 9.1, the price P_A and the supply x_1 maximizes both the firm's profit and the value of its sales.

If the kinked demand curve applies, *substantial variation can occur in the demand for a firm's product or in its cost of production and the firm does not find it profitable to alter* the *price* of its product from the conventional level. This is illustrated in Figure 9.2. If the demand curve d_1 and corresponding marginal revenue curve MR_1 applies, a rise in the firm's marginal cost of supply from MC_1 to MC_2 leaves its profit-maximizing price unaltered at P_A. Similarly, a rise in the demand for the firm's product which shifts its demand curve to d_2 and its marginal revenue to MR_2, leaves its profit-maximizing price unchanged at P_A because the marginal cost curves continue to pass through the gap in the marginal revenue curves.

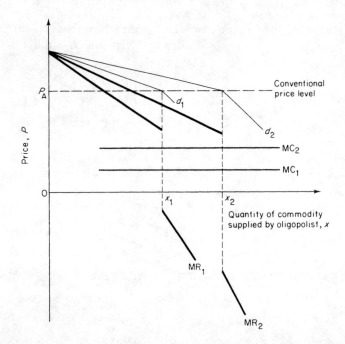

Figure 9.2 The demand for an individual oligopolist's product may vary considerably, and so too may his per-unit costs of production, and yet it may not be profitable for him to alter the price of his product from the conventional level. In the above case, the conventional price P_A maximizes profit even if there is an alteration in the demand curve from d_1 to d_2 or a change in marginal costs from MC_1 to MC_2.

This model provides one possible explanation of why oligopolists may maintain stable conventional prices even though their *individual* costs or demand conditions change appreciably. On the other hand, an alteration in the cost or demand conditions facing *all* oligopolists in a market is liable to lead to a change in the conventional or acceptable price levels. The kinked demand curve model, the characteristics of which do *not* require overt *collusion* between oligopolists, has two other important implications:

(1) Wage increases or improvements of conditions of work need not result in reduced employment, especially if the increases apply to one or a few firms. Although marginal cost may rise, the MC curve may continue to pass through the gap in the MR curve.

(2) There is *no price competition* between oligopolists so market competition must take other forms. Non-price competition is likely to be important in an oligopolistic market and occurs via advertising, product presentation, quality variations, product variety, and other means.

The theory begs the question, however, of how conventional or acceptable price levels are determined and altered. They may be set by a price-leader, there may be customary rules for altering established prices such as upward variation to pass on all general cost rises, manufacturers or wholesalers may 'recommend' prices to retailers, or there may be some consultation between firms as to their intentions when general cost rises occur so that a consensus emerges. New acceptable prices may fall in a range, for instance a 20 to 30 per cent. price rise might be acceptable as a result of a 25 per cent. rise in general costs but a 10 per cent. rise might not be acceptable because it implies 'chiseling'. Any firm increasing its price by such a small amount and persisting in such behaviour might expect retaliatory action from its rivals. This is a matter which would benefit from further study. With the rapid rates of inflation of recent years, price changes even in oligopolistic industries have become more frequent and it is doubtful whether oligopolies have acted as dampeners on the rate of inflation. It may also be interesting to note that an OECD study of the likely effects of pollution taxes on firms in oligopolistic industries in Italy concluded that it expected most of these costs to be passed on to consumers in the form of higher prices for the products concerned.

Price leadership models

As suggested above, the conventional price in a kinked demand curve situation may be set by a price-leader. However, there is not a single form of price leadership but a range of forms. The barometric and dominant firm models of price leadership are of particular interest.

In the *barometric case* one firm or supplier, not necessarily the lowest cost or largest producer, acts as the barometer for the whole industry and alters its price when conditions alter in the whole industry. The leader is recognized as having a 'good feel' for industry conditions and its leadership may be reinforced by past behaviour in the industry. Bethlehem Steel is reputed to be the price-leader in the US steel industry but US Steel is the largest producer. Bethlehem's lead is traditionally followed by other steel producers. It has been claimed that the international wheat market is dominated by an oligopoly consisting of the United States, Canada, and Australia. In international trading of wheat (which is controlled by governments) Canada acts as the price-leader although the United States is the dominant supplier. In order to maintain its position as price-leader, Canada must pay regard in setting its price to the policy objectives of the other two suppliers.

In the *dominant firm case*, a firm may be the price-leader because it is financially stronger than the others in the oligopolistic markets or has lower per-unit costs of production. The predictions of this model are relatively precise if the following conditions are satisfied: other firms charge the same price as the price-leader, the leader aims to maximize profit and aims to satisfy that part of market demand which would not be met by rivals. This is illustrated by Figure 9.3. Assuming a homogeneous product, let the curve marked D be the market demand for the product and let S_F represent the supply of followers at alternative prices set by the leader. The difference between D and S_F gives

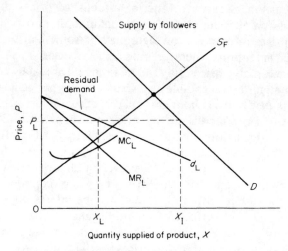

Figure 9.3   Price leadership by a dominant firm aiming to maximize its profit. In the case shown, the price-leader sets the market price at P_L and supplies X_L of market demand.

the demand for the leader's supply and is shown by the curve marked d_L. The marginal revenue curve corresponding to d_L is indicated by MR_L. If the leader aims to maximize his profit and MC_L is his marginal cost of production, the most profitable price from his viewpoint will be P_L. Other firms follow this lead. The leader supplies X_L of the product to the market and the remainder of demand, $X_I - X_L$, is met by followers.

This model implies (other things equal) that the price-leader adjusts the price charged by him upwards if his marginal costs of production rise or if the demand for his supplies increase. This may happen if the market demand for the product expands or if the costs of inputs rise generally. There is no reason to expect the price-leader to be hesitant about passing on inflationary cost rises. Indeed, he may adjust price in anticipation of future inflationary cost rises if he restricts price alterations to discrete intervals, and this could speed up the rate of inflation.

Cartel models

The possibility of cartels (associations of suppliers) forming and aiming to maximize their joint profit or increase their profit by a common policy, for instance of each restricting supply, was discussed in Chapter 2.

If a cartel happens to agree on a policy of maximizing the joint profit of its members, it is relatively easy in principle to determine its optimal pricing and supply policy. The cartel should adopt the same policy as a multi-plant monopolist. Total quantity supplied of the commodity and its price should be adjusted so that marginal revenue in the market and marginal cost in the industry are equal and production should be allocated between plants or firms so that the marginal costs of production of all operating plants are equal.

However, it is not certain that cartel members will agree to policies to maximize the joint profit of members because of conflicts between members about sharing the joint profit. A firm may resist the allocation of a small production quota even though the firm has high per-unit costs of production and this allocation would maximize collective profit. The firm may succeed by political means in the cartel organization in obtaining a higher quota at the expense of collective profit. Political in-fighting over the share of collective profits is likely to rule out a pure monopoly-type solution. This problem, however, is reduced if the companies involved merge, although it is not certain to be eliminated if units within the company have separate identities.

Cartel arrangements are permitted within the Common Market in particular circumstances. For instance, EEC man-made fibre manufacturers formed a cartel-like arrangement during the late 1970s to reduce capacity in the industry and similar 'rationalization' has been allowed in Japan.

Two well-known international cartels are OPEC (Organization of Petroleum Exporting Countries) and IATA (International Air Transport Association). OPEC consists of a group of major oil-exporting countries which place an export tax on oil and meet regularly to decide a common policy on the level of oil export taxes and supplies with the aim in mind of maintaining or increasing the monopoly profits of exporting countries. Multi-national companies supplying oil from OPEC countries must charge a price to buyers at least sufficient to cover the oil export tax plus their costs of production. Aldeman (1972) has claimed that multi-national companies are essential to the success of the scheme because in their absence 'chiselling' and secret discounts would be more common and this would undermine the cartel. As pointed out in an earlier chapter, cartels are under constant threat from within and from without and OPEC is no exception. Individual members can profit from marginally undercutting others in price but if all do this the cartel fails. Similarly, new entrants to the industry are encouraged by increased profits, and non-cartel members in oil such as the United Kingdom may have no incentive to limit supplies. Particular consideration will be given to OPEC in Chapter 13 which deals with energy.

In the case of IATA, its aim has been to determine common international air fares on principal routes and it has been aided in this policy by governments, many of which own international airlines. But IATA has had to face both internal and external threats. Some of its members have offered 'extras' such as lower than normal hotel rates, low internal air fares, finance for tours at lower than normal interest rates, or car hire to win business. An external threat has also been posed by some charter operators and by non-IATA operators such as Laker with his sky-train.

Other models of oligopolistic behaviour

Other models of oligopolistic behaviour include those by Cournot (1838), Bertrand (1883), von Stackelberg (1952), and those stemming from the 'theory of games'. Cournot's model is an interaction model of the follower–follower type. In the duopoly case, each duopolist adjusts his output to maximize his profit on the assumption that his rival's output of the last period is unaltered. Both do this until an equilibrium is reached. A problem of the model is that neither duopolist learns that in fact the assumption of unchanged output by the rival does not hold except in equilibrium. The Bertrand model is similar to the Cournot model. In this model duopolists alter prices charged by them rather than their supplies.

Von Stackelberg's model covers a broader range of possible behaviour than either Cournot's or Bertrand's. Apart from follower–follower types of situation, it examines leader–follower types. Leader–follower types assume that one oligopolist or duopolist is the leader and that others follow. In deciding on the best policy from his point of view the leader takes account of the reactions of other suppliers to his policies. But if more than one firm tries to lead, the von Stackelberg model gives no solution.

In some such instances, the theory of games is able to predict an outcome even though it too is limited in its powers of prediction. The theory has been widely considered as a means for modelling situations of economic and social conflict and behaviour following the publication by J. von Neumann and O. Morgenstern of *Theory of Games and Economic Behaviour* (1944). Predictions of the theory appear strongest for situations of pure conflict which are often modelled by *two-person zero-sum games*. Two-person zero-sum games involve two parties or players and the gain of any party from the game equals the loss of the other so that *gains* of all players *add to zero*. But most oligopolistic situations are not zero sum, i.e. the gain of one party or set of parties is not equal to the loss of the other but may be at the expense of 'non-players' such as consumers. This has limited the applicability of game models as predictors of oligopolistic behaviour. However, applications of the theory to advertising and to product differentiation are considered below.

Oligopolistic competition through variables other than price and non-profit maximization

Micro-economic texts tend to stress the importance of price as a variable in competition between firms. This may be because price is an important variable or could be because price is a variable which can readily be taken into account in building economic models. Model-building is highly regarded by most economists and this could influence the choice of variables. A study by J. G. Udell (1964) indicates that price may not be as an important variable in marketing as is sometimes thought. He found from a survey of 200 American firms that half did not consider price as among the first five most important decision variables influencing their market success. But even if price is not an important variable, managers need to take account of *price* and non-price variables as *alternative* possible methods of competing with rival firms, and models based upon price as a variable may throw light upon behaviour associated with other variables. Advertising expenditure, for instance, is one means of competing. But in an oligopolistic industry a firm increasing its advertising intensity needs to have regard to the effects of this on its rivals. If its intensity of advertising increases beyond a customary or acceptable level, rivals may react by increasing their advertising intensity to a similar extent and a *kinked demand* relationship occurs.

Oligopolists are frequently suppliers of a range of products and apart from competing by means of price may compete by means of:

(1) variations in the terms of credit;
(2) advertising, promotion, and presentation of products, such as packaging;
(3) the variety and range of products supplied and available such as in the case of supermarkets;
(4) services provided such as after-sales service on durable products, assistance if problems arise in the use of the product, and widespread availability of such services; and
(5) through the development and supply of new products or improvements in existing products as a result of R & D effort and search by the companies concerned.

Some of these competitive means such as advertising and R & D effort are discussed later in this chapter. Studies of the marketing strategies of oligopolistic suppliers of synthetic fibres show that suppliers use all of the above means to compete with one another (Tisdell and McDonald, 1979).

Most of the oligopolistic models mentioned above assume that the aim of the firm is to maximize its profits. As discussed in Chapter 7 firms need not have this objective, for instance because of the separation of ownership and management. To the extent that non-profit maximization is important the above theories are restricted in application.

9.3 ADVERTISING AND OLIGOPOLY

One criticism sometimes made about oligopoly is that it results in a socially excessive level of advertising. But the critics do not always provide a clear guide to their criterion for a social optimum. It is true that *in some* circumstances oligopoly results in a socially excessive level of advertising in the Kaldor–Hicks sense but it does not do so in all cases. In some cases informative advertising may be inadequate under oligopoly in the sense that a Kaldor–Hicks gain might be made by increasing its level. These aspects will be discussed presently.

Advertising intensity and market structure

Empirical evidence suggests that advertising intensities (the ratio of advertising expenditure to the value of sales) tend to be highest in oligopolistic industries, lower under monopoly, and least under competitive conditions. Sutton (1974) found that the relationship between advertising intensity and concentration ratios tended to be of the inverted U-shape shown in Figure 9.4. This relationship indicates that advertising intensities reach a maximum of around 2.9 per cent. for a concentration ratio of about 64 per cent., fall to zero at 19 per cent. or smaller concentrations, and to about 1 per cent. under

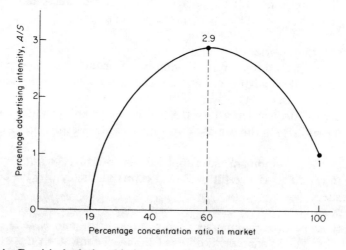

Figure 9.4 Empirical relationship between advertising intensity and market concentration suggested by Sutton.

complete monopoly. But these results are based upon a narrow sample of UK consumer goods and the model does not appear to apply to producer industries.

Advertising intensities could be higher under oligopoly than under alternative market forms for a number of reasons:

(1) Price competition may not be prevalent (as suggested by the kinked demand curve) under oligopoly and advertising may provide an alternative means of competition.
(2) More new products and products of a complicated type *may* be introduced by oligopolists than by suppliers in other types of markets so that a greater amount of informative and 'awareness'-type advertising may be required.
(3) Oligopolists may be prone to a competitive advertising trap (to be discussed below) which locks all of them into high levels of advertising expenditure.
(4) The greater the concentration of supplies in the industry the greater may be the incentive of the dominant firms to engage in advertising designed to deter entry.

An advertising trap and applications of theory of games

Consider the possibility of oligopolists becoming trapped into high advertising intensities. This could occur if each either (1) aims to maximize its profit or (2) attempts to maximize its market share. The trap is easily illustrated by means of a non-zero-sum game matrix.

Take the profit maximization case first. For simplicity assume duopolists with two available strategies each, namely to employ low advertising intensities (L) or high intensities (H). The available strategies of each are shown in the following matrix. The profits of the firms depend upon the strategies jointly employed by them and the hypothetical figures in the body of the matrix shown for each strategy, the profit received by firm 2 and firm 1, respectively. Thus if firm 2 adopts a low advertising intensity and firm 1 a high intensity the profit for firm 2 is 6 units and for firm 1 is 12 units, as shown by the entry (6, 12) on Table 9.1.

Table 9.1   If each firm tries to maximize its own profit each will choose a high intensity of advertising. Consequently, the profit of each will be lower than if both had adopted a low advertising strategy.

		Strategies of firm 1 $\rightarrow$	
		L_1	H_1
Strategies	L_2	(10,10)	(6,12)
of firm 2 $\downarrow$	H_2	(12,6)	(8,8) ← Stable equilibrium

230

It can be seen from the matrix that whatever strategy is adopted by firm 2, firm 1 makes the most profit by adopting strategy H. Similarly, it can be seen that whatever strategy firm 1 adopts firm 2 makes the most profit by adopting strategy H. In order to maximize its profit each is liable to choose H, a high advertising intensity, and this choice forms a stable equilibrium. Both firms become trapped in this equilibrium as in the well-known prisoner's dilemma problem of game theory. Each could earn greater profit if they jointly switched to a low advertising intensity but they would need to cooperate and to trust one another for this agreement 'to work'.

Duopolists or oligopolists concerned primarily with market share can also become trapped into high levels of advertising expenditure benefiting none of them. This can be illustrated by means of a *zero-sum* game such as that shown in the matrix below (Table 9.2). As before, assume the existence of oligopoly and that each firm has two alternative strategies, a high intensity (H) and a low intensity (L). The body of the matrix shows the market share (proportion) obtained by firm 1 when the indicated joint strategies are adopted. For instance, if firm 1 adopts a high intensity of advertising (H_1) and firm 2 a low intensity (L_2), firm 1 obtains 0.8 of the market. This market share may also be regarded as having been lost by firm 2. Whatever share firm 1 gains firm 2 loses, and vice versa. Hence the zero-sum nature of the situation.

Table 9.2   If duopolists aim to maximize their market share a two-person zero-sum game emerges, the outcome of which is likely to be a high intensity of advertising by both firms. In the above case, strategies H_1 and H_2 are the solution of the game.

		Strategies of firm 1 →		
		L_1	H_1	Row max
Strategies of firm 2 ↓	L_2	0.5	0.8	0.8
	H_2	0.2	0.5	0.5* ← Minmax (loss)
	Col min	0.2	0.5*	

Maxmin (gain)

Stable equilibrium

If both firms wish to maximize their market share they are in conflict. Assuming both to be rational and well informed, each would be wise to suppose that the other will try to minimize the gain of the opponent. Thus firm 1 would be wise to assume that firm 2 will attempt to minimize firm 1's share of the market. Therefore, firm 1 (to do the best it can in the circumstances) should adopt the strategy which maximizes the minimum gain associated with each of its available strategies. Its minimum gain associated with L_1 is 0.2 and with H_1 is 0.5. Hence, its maximin choice is H_1. Similarly, firm 2 will try to minimize its maximum loss. This occurs when it chooses H_2. Thus both firms are led to adopt strategies of high intensity advertising and their choice forms a stable equilibrium. However, note that their market shares are no different to those which would have eventuated if *each* had adopted a low intensity of advertising. They have become trapped into a high level of advertising by their own competitiveness and this is a very stable outcome.

Benefits and costs to buyers of advertising

Such competitive advertising behaviour need not benefit consumers or buyers. They may know the qualities of the advertised product well and may gain no image satisfaction or social benefit from the advertising. The sole impact of the advertising may merely be on the way that comparatively fixed aggregate sales of a relatively homogeneous product is shared between firms. The advertising primarily keeps buyers 'evenly' aware of all sources of supply. In these circumstances, a Kaldor–Hicks gain could be made by firms reducing the intensity of their advertising. Possibly at times in the past competitive advertising of petrol has fitted this case.

However, we need to consider generally the type of benefits that advertising activity may have for buyers or consumers. It is also interesting to speculate about the effect of advertising expenditure on price levels.

Advertising may reduce the cost to a buyer of searching for or obtaining information about products. It can be less costly for sellers to provide information in this way than for buyers to seek required products by advertising or similar means. In supplying information by advertisement sellers may tend to undersupply it from a social point of view. Profit-maximizers will disseminate information until their marginal profitability from this activity is zero. But at this level of dissemination the marginal value to buyers or consumers of information may still remain positive. Hence from a social point of view greater dissemination of information would be socially worth while. This does not occur because sellers cannot appropriate all the gains from *additional* information. This problem is illustrated in Figure 9.5. The curve indicated by MPS is the marginal profitability to sellers of providing information and that indicated by MSV is the marginal social value of disseminating information which equals MPS plus the marginal value of information to buyers (MVB). Sellers disseminate Q_1 of information but a social optimum would be achieved by supplying Q_2 of information. Although consumers gain from the provision of information by sellers, gains are not maximized by the policy of sellers. There is underprovision of information from a social point of view.

A number of aspects of advertising are difficult to evaluate but nevertheless warrant mention. In some cases messages are forced on individuals (as joint consumption) and to some and in some instances the messages are considered to be repulsive and an intrusion. On the other hand, these messages may be highly valued in some cases and may provide a product with an image which is valued by the buyer. Advertising can also increase demand for products, the consumption of which is detrimental to the seeming interests of buyers. For

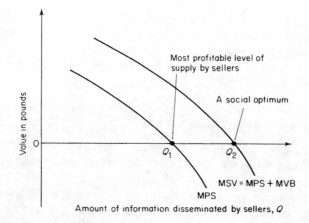

Figure 9.5   While sellers may play a useful social role in providing information through advertising their supply is likely to be less than socially optimal since they do not appropriate all marginal gains.

instance, could cigarette smoking and the taking of drugs be encouraged by cigarette and drug advertisements?

The effect of advertising on price levels can vary and is not known with certainty. When advertising expands demand and marginal cost is rising it is likely to result in a rise in price, but if marginal cost is falling it may lead to a fall in the price of the advertised product. However, even in the last case it is necessary to be cautious for if monopolistic large-group competition prevails advertising may result in higher prices, even if per-unit costs are decreasing. This is illustrated in Figure 9.6. There the costs of a representative monopolistically competitive firm are shown. The curve indicated by AOC is its average operating costs and its average total cost curve includes average operating costs plus average advertising costs. In the absence of advertising in the industry, the firm might come into a long-term tangency equilibrium at a point such as C. But if advertising is a practice common to all firms, the firm reaches a long-term equilibrium at a point such as B (where its average total cost curve is tangential to its demand curve after advertising) and only makes normal profit. The price of the product in equilibrium B is higher than in case C and in both instances price exceeds marginal cost. However, it cannot be concluded, *ipso facto*, that consumers are worse off as a result of the advertising even though it is possible for them to be worse off.

Public policies and advertising

Despite ambiguities about the impact of advertising, public policies have been adopted and suggested to influence it. For instance, in many countries the advertising of cigarettes and tobacco products is restricted. Advertisements

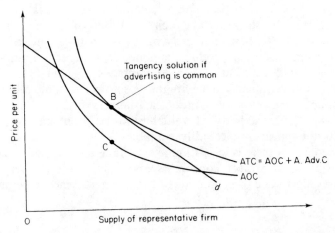

Figure 9.6 Under conditions of monopolistic large-group competition advertising may result in a higher price for the advertised product. In the case shown the equilibrium of the representative firm may be reached at point B rather than at C.

must carry a health warning and are not permitted by means of some media such as television. The rationale for the interference is that individuals may be influenced to smoke, especially the young, against their long-term health interests and the habit may become addictive. The judgement is made that if advertising is free at least some individuals will be unable to choose in their best long-term interest. Their choice may also have external repercussions in the long-term, for instance if they become sick and dependent on others. Nevertheless, there are dangers in restricting the flow of information to individuals in their own long-term interest. It is not always clear that others are better judges and most of us value the right to be wrong.

Sometimes types of advertising are banned on the grounds that they cause 'environmental pollution', unfavourable externalities. In some cities such as Canberra in Australia neon and billboard advertising is restricted. Programmes of the BBC and the Australian Broadcasting Commission carry no advertising—a feature appealing to many viewers and listeners.

Restrictions on advertising often have a displacement effect. For instance, as a result of the restriction on television advertising cigarette companies have increased their relative expenditure using other media. Furthermore, by increased sponsorship of televised sporting fixtures they have continued to have indirect access to television coverage.

The intensity of advertising varies considerably between industries and according to Sutton's (1974) study is least in industries consisting of many firms with little concentration of market power. It is possible that as a result of this distribution of advertising, awareness by individuals of the value of products supplied in competitive markets is not as great as for those supplied by oligopolies, and this may mean that consumers do not make the type of choices they would make if they had a 'balanced' view of available products. Their choice may be slanted too much in favour of products supplied by oligopolists. If this is so, one remedy might be to take collective action to increase information about products supplied in competitive markets as the International Wool Secretariat has attempted for wool. Indeed, Kaldor suggests that a government agency might be set up to supply all information about products. However, this has clear dangers because bureaucrats are imperfect and the availability of valuable information may be stifled. No perfect solution appears to be readily available.

In many countries there is legislation against false and misleading advertising. This is designed to protect consumers and may indirectly benefit honest competitive sellers. The pros and cons of such interference were discussed in Chapter 5.

9.4 PRODUCT DIFFERENTIATION

What is the likely effect of oligopoly on the available variety and differentiation of products? The American economist Harold Hotelling (1929) has suggested that oligopolistic firms tend to minimize product differentiation, locate together, and supply similar products. Their similar products are designed to satisfy buyers with *median* tastes.

Principle of minimum product differentiation

This principle holds if products can be differentiated by a single characteristic, lambda (λ) say, for the degree of whiteness or degree of sweetness; if consumers purchase the product having the characteristic closest to their preferred degree of the characteristic; if each firm finds it profitable to supply the product only in one degree of the characteristic but can supply any of the degrees at the same per-unit cost; and if aggregate demand is relatively fixed. This can be illustrated by an example for a duopoly.

Let the degree of the characteristic, λ, present in the products of the duopolists be measured on a scale from zero to one and assume that the relative frequency with which each of the possible degrees of the characteristics are most preferred by buyers forms a rectangular distribution as in Figure 9.7. The median buyer prefers a product containing 0.5 of λ. Thus both duopolists will supply a product containing 0.5 of λ. No product differentiation occurs and each duopolist obtains 50 per cent. of the market. If any duopolist were to diverge from $\lambda = 0.5$ he would run the risk of obtaining less than 50 per cent. of the market. For instance, given the distribution in Figure 9.7, if one chose $\lambda = 0.8$, the other duopolist if he supplied a product of $\lambda = 0.5$ would obtain 65 per cent. of the market. He obtains all customers preferring $\lambda \leq 0.5$ plus all preferring $0.5 \leq \lambda \leq 0.65$, given that customers purchase the product of nearest available quality. On the other hand, if the rival supplied a product of

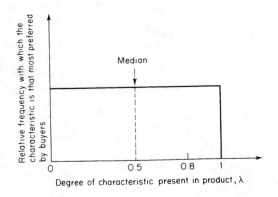

Figure 9.7   Given Hotelling's assumptions and the above distribution, duopolists will supply identical products containing a characteristic in the degree most preferred by the median buyer, namely $\lambda = 0.5$ in this case.

$\lambda = 0.79$ he would gain 79 per cent. of the market, i.e. the custom of all buyers preferring a quality of $\lambda < 0.8$.

It could be argued that consumers' tastes would be most adequately satisfied if one duopolist supplied a product of $\lambda = 0.25$ and the other a product of $\lambda = 0.75$. In that case, each would still obtain 50 per cent. of the market. But this is not a stable solution because one firm can obtain a greater share of the market by moving closer towards the type of product produced by his rival.

Minimum product differentiation illustrated by a zero-sum game

The theory of two-person zero-sum games is possibly the most satisfactory means by which to see that the median outcome is the most likely solution. It forms a stable equilibrium which is a maxmin gain solution in terms of game theory. In matrix form, 'the game' involving the duopolists may be represented in the way shown in Table 9.3. λ_1 represents the choice of degrees of the characteristic available to firm 1 and λ_2 represents the choices available to firm 2. Their market shares depend upon their joint choices. Entries in the matrix show the share of the market obtained by firm 1. Some of the diagonal entries are shown. All diagonal entries (for both diagonals) would be 0.5, indicating that for these joint strategies the duopolists would share the market equally. Minimum gains by firm 1 approach the figures shown at the foot of the matrix. For $\lambda_1 < 0.5$, these figures are given by λ_1 and for $\lambda_1 > 0.5$ are given by $1 - \lambda_1$. The maxmin gain for firm 1 occurs for $\lambda_1 = 0.5$. The *maxmin gain* is the maximum of possible minimum gains. Similarly the minmax loss for firm 2 occurs for $\lambda_2 = 0.5$. The *minmax loss* is the minimum of possible maximum losses. Hence both duopolists reach a *stable equilibrium* by producing a product with a characteristic of $\lambda = 0.5$, catering for the median preference. For this choice, the maxmin gain of firm 1 equals the minmax loss for firm 2.

Table 9.3   A zero-sum game can be used to illustrate Hotelling's suggestion that duopolists will cater for the median preference of buyers and produce an identical product. In the above case a stable equilibrium or solution to the game only occurs when both suppliers produce an identical product with the same degree of the characteristic, $\lambda = 0.5$, catering for the median preference. Entries in the table show the gain in market share by firm 1 (equals loss in market share by firm 2).

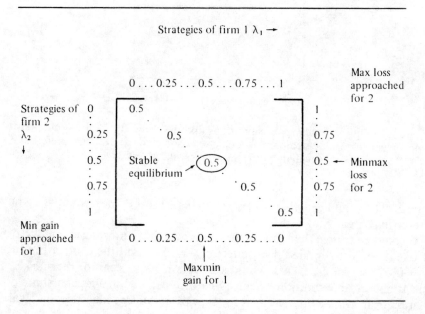

If either unilaterally alters its choice of strategy it will be worse off than otherwise.

The minimum gain approached by firm 1 is shown in Figure 9.8 as a function of λ_1 by the solid lines, and reaches a maximum for $\lambda_1 = 0.5$. The maximum loss approached by firm 2 is shown in Figure 9.8 as a function of λ_2 by the broken lines, and reaches a minimum for $\lambda_2 = 0.5$. These results confirm the earlier insights that a stable solution occurs when both firms produce a product with characteristic $\lambda = 0.5$ to satisfy the median preference.

Applications of Hotelling's principle

Hotelling suggested that his theory might have an application outside economics. He considered that it might help to explain why the election platforms of major parties tend to be similar and aimed at the voter with the median preference on major issues (see Chapter 3).

Hotelling's theory has been used to help justify public supply or supplementary supply of broadcasting and television by public enterprises such as the BBC and the Australian Broadcasting Commission. It has been suggested that commercial stations and channels will supply relatively undifferentiated programmes aimed at the median listener or viewer and that the interests of

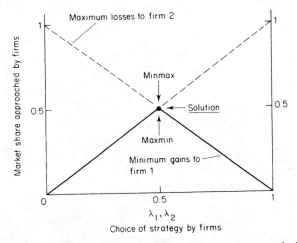

Figure 9.8 Diagrammatic illustration of a zero-sum game solution employing minimum product differentiation by duopolists. As Hotelling points out, it may also help to explain the similarity of party platforms in a two-party political system.

better educated individuals will be neglected. Government supply or supplementary supply, it is claimed, adds to the available variety of programmes.

Qualifications to Hotelling's principle

One must be careful about pressing Hotelling's hypothesis too far. The assumptions needed for the theory to hold do not always apply. Consumers may not buy or may buy in lower quantities if a product is not supplied with the degree of the characteristic most preferred by them and the per-unit cost of production of suppliers can be different. The last difference in itself makes for variety because producers with a high cost per unit need to differentiate their products from those with low costs in order to survive. If a low-cost producer has transport selling costs which rise as he attempts to sell to buyers further away from his location or to buyers seeking a product with a characteristic further away from his, the high-cost producer may be able to survive by catering for demands on the fringe. This is illustrated in Figure 9.9. Suppose that a low-cost producer locates at λ^* and has per-unit production costs of λ^*B. When transport or selling costs are added to this, the low-cost producer's per-unit total cost of reaching buyers at the different locations is shown by the curve ABC. A high-cost producer with per-unit production costs, say, of λ^0E could not survive by locating near λ^*. But assuming the location of the low-cost producer fixed and the overall per-unit costs of the high-cost producer to be as shown by FEC, the high-cost producer could survive by locating at λ^0 and thus supplying a product well differentiated from that of his rival. In countries with high per-unit costs of production but having non-median tastes, local

238

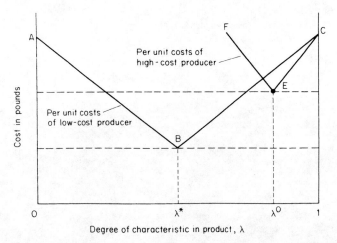

Figure 9.9   In order to survive, the high-cost producer may have to differentiate his product sufficiently from that of the low-cost producer. If the low-cost producer above chooses λ^* the high-cost producer can maximize his market share by choosing to supply λ^0 i.e. a well-differentiated product.

producers may survive in competition with low-cost imports catering for world-wide median tastes by producing a differentiated product aimed at local tastes.

The available evidence is insufficient to conclude that, in general, oligopoly leads to a lowering in the degree of product differentiation. Indeed it has been argued by some by reference to the monopolistic competition model that oligopoly in some markets results in excessive variety from a social point of view. Furthermore, governments both in the United Kingdom and in Australia have in the past put pressure on car manufacturers, for example, to reduce their variety of models and frequency of model changes with a view to lowering car costs and prices. In turn this has resulted in increased consumer demand for imported vehicles as a result of search by consumers for differentiation. Marris (1964) in his theory of managerial capitalism suggests that oligopolistic management-dominated firms have considerable incentives to promote a variety of products. Marris argues that oligopolistic firms are typically multi-product suppliers, that their management places a high value on the growth of the firm, and that this growth may be fostered by developing and adding a greater variety of products to the firm's range. Thus the question of the general effect of oligopoly on product differentiation and the optimal degree of product differentiation is not as yet settled.

9.5   TECHNICAL PROGRESS

The likely general impact of oligopoly on the rate of technical progress is uncertain. In part this is because the rate of technical progress has several dimensions and is therefore difficult to measure unambiguously. Factors which need to be taken into account when considering the rate of technical progress include:

(1) levels of research and development effort and expenditure;
(2) the level of inventive output and the value of this output;
(3) the rapidity of innovation (commercial application of inventions); and
(4) the rate of diffusion and application of new techniques.

Superior performance by a market structure or market form in one of these dimensions may be offset or more than offset by an inferior performance in another of these dimensions.

Parker (1974, pp. 62–78) has expressed the view that technical progress is likely to be faster under oligopolistic conditions than for any other market form. This is because sufficient competition exists between firms in an oligopoly (compared to monopoly) to spur them on to develop and apply new techniques, but competition is not as intense as under perfect competition. Such intense competition may slow technical progress since cost-reducing techniques and successful innovations may be rapidly copied by rivals (property rights are not available or cannot be protected), thus leaving little profit for inventors and innovators. Furthermore, perfectly competitive firms have no *excess* profit in the long run for investment in research and development and to cushion them against the risks of research and development and innovation. More attention may also be given to research and development under oligopoly since, as discussed earlier in this chapter, non-price competition tends to be more important in oligopolistic markets than price competition. If one accepts Parker's hypothesis, the index of the rate of technical progress as a function of the intensity of competition in a market would tend to be of an inverted U-shape. It is possible that R & D intensities and aggregate inventive output may be higher and the rate of innovation faster under oligopolistic market conditions than under alternative market forms.

Empirical evidence about the effect of the nature of the competition on technical progress is slight. However, private research intensities do tend to be lower in industries consisting of many small competitive firms such as in agriculture. But much research and development of relevance to agriculture, for instance for tractors and pesticides, is done by secondary industry which sells producer goods to farmers. Research intensities tend to be high in markets which are typically oligopolistic such as aircraft supply, electronics, chemicals, pharmaceuticals, and transport equipment. But it is not clear that oligopoly is the cause of such high intensities. The industries may be ones which give a high return on R & D effort and the high intensities might be observed even if monopoly existed in these industries. In the United States and in the United Kingdom these high research intensities are also heavily influenced by government contracts for defence research and development and defence equipment.

Much more evidence is available about the likely impact of the size of a firm on technical progress. Galbraith (1957) claims in *American Capitalism* that modern industry consisting of *large firms* is an almost perfect instrument for bringing about technical change. But the available evidence does not support the view that the bigger a firm in an industry the greater is its rate of technical progress.

Both Scherer (1965) and Mansfield (1979) found in their study of American industry that R & D intensities of the largest firms in the oligopolistic industries studied tended to be lower than for medium- to large-sized firms. The evidence suggests that within an industry R & D intensities may bear an inverted-U relationship to the firm-size variable. Mansfield also found that average productivity of research and development (inventive output) rises with firm size and then declines for firms very large in size. While larger firms may speed up innovation if large amounts of capital are required for an innovation, many innovations are within the financial capacity of small to medium firms. However, it is possibly *in this area of innovation* that *larger firms tend to have an advantage over smaller ones* as originally suggested by Schumpeter (1954). Nevertheless, it is clear that very large firms are not the perfect instruments for technical progress in *all* industries and the extent to which they are socially optimal or the best socially feasible instrument for technical progress in any industry is unclear.

Can technical change be too rapid?

Even economists can be easily lulled into believing that a faster rate of technical progress is desirable. This is not only because technical progress has brought clear advantages to mankind since the Stone Age but because we live in a society in which there are strong pressure groups favouring greater technical progress and publicizing support for it. If a Galbraithian outlook on modern society (to be discussed in Section 9.6) is accepted, technocrats in big companies (engineers, scientists, managers directing them) desire high rates of technical progress to support the growth of their companies and for self-fulfilment (utility maximization), and these technocrats dominate modern society, greatly influencing government bureaucrats, the government, and even universities and academic endeavours. Business managers and scientists, including academic scientific pressure groups and government bureaucrats, cooperate in pressing for greater scientific and technical change. In these circumstances, the costs of technical change may not be taken into consideration or adequately considered.

Technical change can as a rule only be purchased at a cost. For instance, greater expenditure on research and development effort is likely to be at the expense of other alternatives such as improved hospitals, schools, and roads. The marginal sacrifice needs to be taken into account but of course is difficult to evaluate since the results of research and development are so uncertain.

The rate of innovation and replacement of techniques can also be too rapid from a social point of view. For instance, it was pointed out in the discussion relating to Figure 6.4 that government schemes to subsidize acceleration of the replacement of machinery may lead to a social loss. Barzel (1968) has put forward the view that innovation may be more rapid under oligopoly than is socially desirable. Environmentalists have also expressed concern about the types of technical changes that have occurred in modern societies and many believe that insufficient attention has been given to the environmental spillovers associated with the use of new technologies such as in the commercial use of nuclear power.

Public policies in support of technical change

Governments in industrial economies interfere in many ways to influence technical change. In several OECD countries subsidies, grants and low interest loans are available to industrial firms to encourage industrial research and development and innovation. Governments themselves conduct a considerable amount of research of general value to industry and in many countries agricultural research is largely financed by government and conducted in government laboratories. Industrial research in the big science fields such as nuclear energy is given considerable support by the governments of the major industrial countries, as of course is research and development for defence purposes.

Why should government support and subsidize research and development? The following are *some* of the arguments that have been advanced in favour of such subsidies:

(1) Individuals and organizations engaging in research and development and in innovation do not appropriate all the marginal net benefits of their activities and there is therefore a tendency for research and development to be undersupplied from a social point of view. All marginal net gains may not be appropriated by inventors and developers, for instance, because others may quickly imitate a successful invention or improve on it without rewarding the inventor for his contribution or rewarding him fully. This is so despite the existence of the patent system. Patents do not protect all discoveries (e.g. discoveries of scientific principles), it can be costly to a patentee to enforce his patent rights, and it may be possible to use patented information to 'out-invent' the patented invention.

(2) Research and development activities and innovation are risky and un-certain in their rewards. Risk-averse individuals and corporations may therefore, as pointed out by Arrow (1962) undersupply these activities from a Kaldor–Hicks standpoint. But of course it is difficult to measure the risks involved.

(3) Capital markets are not perfect and lenders may be risk-averse (in the sense that for the same mean rate of return the investment with the lower variance of rate of return is preferred) so that the problem mentioned in (2) is reinforced.

There are other possible bases for interference. A useful summary and critique of these and the above arguments is given by Pavitt (1976). While the case for the government to subsidize or support *basic* research seems strong on efficiency grounds, government interference further along the development chain brings greater dangers. This is especially so when the opinions of public bureaucracies are substituted for the predictions and risk-taking of private firms. Eads and Nelson (1971) have argued that government support for the development of specific civilian products such as SST or nuclear energy plants is liable to be misguided and divorced from market considerations. There is the further danger in public funding of research and development that large firms may have a disproportionate effect on and share in the allocation of public funds in support of research and development, for Downs' theory suggests that they are more likely to find it worth while (profitable) to lobby politicians and bureaucrats than small firms or consumers.

9.6 INSTITUTIONAL ASPECTS OF OLIGOPOLY AND OF INDUSTRIAL SOCIETIES

The danger always exists in discussing economic problems in detail that we may fail to see the woods for the trees. Institutional arrangements within society as a whole affect its micro-economic operation and as these arrangements evolve or alter with the passage of time the functioning of the economic system may alter. For instance, the increased importance of the limited liability company, of non-agricultural sectors, and of management separated from ownership implies that our economy may operate in a quite different manner to that of the nineteenth century and that the economic theories developed in that period may be less applicable to this century. This view has been pressed by Galbraith, Marris, and others.

A Galbraithian overview of present capitalistic industrial societies

The elements in Galbraith's (1967) overview of present-day industrial economies are to be found in the writings of several economists but Galbraith has done more than most to make these views known to a wide audience and present them in the context of the whole society. The following are the main features of the Galbraithian overview:

(1) Sellers (firms) in the economy belong to a *dual system*. One sector of the dual system consists of small competitive firms dominated by the operation of markets. The other sector consists of large oligopolistic or monopoly-like firms not dominated by markets but in a position to control or manipulate markets, input prices, and government policies. This is the industrial planning sector and in the United States consists of the 500 or so largest companies in the manufacturing sector.

(2) Technocrats (the managerial, scientific, and technical class) are the

dominant group in present-day society and are the decision-making force in the industrial planning sector. The American economist, Veblen (1924), predicted this trend in society.

(3) Shareholders have no or little effective power over management, as observed earlier by Berle and Means. Thus, management has considerable scope to pursue its own objectives.

(4) Technocrats in the private planning sector have strong links with government and the government bureaucracy. Movement and contact between government and private bureaucracies is frequent. But, more importantly, on the basis of the theory of Downs, larger firms find it more profitable to lobby than smaller ones. The industrial planning sector is likely to have much more political influence and involvement than the competitive market sector.

(5) Technocrats have a high desire for the growth of their corporations and use their power to inflate demand for goods produced by the planning sector. They concentrate on developing new products and markets and on advertising and promotion, and this fosters overconsumption of products supplied by the planning sector. Elements of this view are to be found both in the writings of Marris and of Marcuse.

The Galbraithian view is a caricature but we cannot dismiss it because of this. It is important to try to test and where necessary qualify the hypotheses involved. There are limits to the extent to which technocrats can manipulate demand, but what are these limits? Large companies sometimes fail in their bids to market new products and make considerable losses. For instance, Ford failed in its attempt several years ago to market the Edsel successfully, and Chrysler has made large losses. Large companies are not as 'powerful' as appears to be claimed. As pointed out earlier, the very largest firms in industries do not appear to put as much effort into technical progress as Galbraith suggests. How great is the political influence of technocrats, say, compared to pressure groups of farmers?

Given his view of economy Galbraith believes that it is an idle dream to aim for a completely competitive market system. Rather he believes that a more realistic and effective aim is to encourage monopoly and countervailing groups in what would otherwise be competitive markets, to foster unionism and socialization of some sectors of the economy, to subsidize the market sector, and to introduce price controls to push up prices in the market sector. A case *might* be made out for such policies on second best grounds and *feasible* income redistribution grounds. Although Galbraith recommends greater government interference in the market sector as a means of improving the operation of the economy, he does not closely examine the prospects for this and the likely effects of his proposals. It might be observed that to a considerable extent the proposals of Galbraith are already in operation. For instance, agricultural prices are widely maintained by government interference. This suggests that there are powerful political forces in society besides technocrats.

Furthermore, unionism is widespread in the United Kingdom and Australia and integrated into the social system.

Multi-national firms

Multi-national companies epitomize the rise of and importance of large industrial corporations. In Galbraith's terms they are involved in the international use and administration of resources, often by non-market means. Such companies are *common in high technology oligopolistic industries* and frequently these are industries with substantial barriers to entry and economies of scale.

They provide a means for the expansion of companies into new markets and the international transfer of technology by non-market methods. It has been claimed that multi-national companies have grown in importance because they are an efficient means for companies to appropriate gains from new technology developed by them (Parker, 1974, p. 206). An alternative for the companies concerned would be to license their technology to local firms overseas. But local companies may not have sufficient management expertise or, if they do, could eventually improve on the technology to the detriment of the licensor, and the growth of the licensee could make it more difficult for the licensor to enter the market concerned at a later stage.

Multi-national corporations are also likely to increase the international flow of commercial information (between their branches), for instance information about market possiblities. Since information is a valuable resource, these flows may be an added benefit for multi-national companies.

Of course there is no economic reason why companies should find it most profitable to stop their economic operations at national borders. Diversification and horizontal and vertical integration extending beyond national borders can yield economies and increase the profitability of a company's operation. National borders are artificial constructions.

The benefits received by host countries from the presence of multi-national companies can vary from little or no benefit to a substantial one. Where a multi-national company is mining in a host country using imported management and skilled labour and has sufficient political influence to pay low royalties and export the mineral, the host may receive little benefit. But in other cases where the development of local skills and management expertise are stimulated by the presence of a multi-national corporation, the host country might obtain much greater benefit.

The assessment of multi-national companies is complicated since assessments are liable to be tinged with feelings of nationalism and doubts about where the national loyalties, if any, of such corporations lie. Do these corporations pose a challenge to the state and to nationalism? If so, is this a bad thing? It has been claimed that *some* multi-national companies have interfered with the sovereignty and political independence of some of the smaller developing countries and have supported coups, for instance, in some

Latin American states, e.g. ITT in Chile. This is a matter for concern if it is true.

9.7 CONCLUSION

A wide range of issues remain unresolved about the effects of multi-national companies and the effect and nature of the operation of oligopolistic industry. The evidence, however, indicates that no single available theory fits all cases and that blanket hypotheses are unlikely to apply to all cases. This needs to be kept in mind when framing public policies because one needs to be cautious about interference when one is uncertain of its effects.

Most theories of oligopolistic behaviour point to the importance of non-price competition and of administered and non-market mechanisms in the modern industrial state and international economy. This is true both of the kinked demand curve, Galbraith's theory, and theories linked with it. But no matter how large the firm and how important administrative rather than market mechanisms are in determining the firm's internal use or allocation of resources, at some stage it has to buy resources in markets and it must sell its product in markets. Its survival depends on a market test and its power to manipulate the test is limited. But even if the power of oligopolists is limited, final assessment of the oligopolistic form must take account of the extent to which firms can and do manipulate markets and political decisions. Problems such as those mentioned in Chapter 5 cannot be dismissed without serious debate and study, just as the Galbraithian theory cannot be uncritically accepted. *Rational skepticism* is required and we need to adjust our probabilities about what is true by collecting and sifting more evidence.

READING AND REFERENCES

Adelman, M. A. (1972), *The World Petroleum Market*, Johns Hopkins University Press, Baltimore.

Arrow, K. J. (1962). Economic Welfare and the Allocation of Resources for Invention, in D. Lamberton (ed.) (1971), *The Economics of Information and Knowledge*, Penguin, London.

Barzel, Y. (1968). Optimal timing of innovations. *Review of Economics and Statistics*, **50**, 348–355.

Bertrand, J. (1883). Theorie Mathématique de la Richesse Sociale, *Journal des Savants*, Paris, 499–508.

Brems, H. (1968). *Quantitative Economic Theory*, Chap. 22, Wiley, New York.

Cournot, A. (1838). *Researches into the Mathematical Principles of the Theory of Wealth*, Macmillan, New York.

Eads, G. and Nelson, R. (1971). Government support of advanced civilian technology, *Public Policy*, **1971**, 405–427.

Galbraith, J. K. (1957). *American Capitalism*, Hamish Hamilton, London.

Galbraith, J. K. (1967). *The New Industrial State*, Hamish Hamilton, London.

Gwartney, J. D. (1979). *Microeconomics*, Chaps 10 and 11, Academic Press, London.

Hibdon, J. E. (1969). *Price and Welfare Theory*, Chaps 12 and 13, McGraw-Hill, New York.

Hotelling, H. (1929). Stability in competition, *Economic Journal*, **39**, 41–57.

Lipsey, R. G. (1979). *An Introduction to Positive Economics*, Chap. 23, Weidenfeld and Nicolson, London.

Mansfield, E. (1979). *Microeconomics*, Chap. 12, Norton, New York.

Markham, J. W. (1951), The Nature and Significance of Price Leadership, *American Economic Review*, **41**, 891–905.

von Neumann, J. and Morgenstern, O. (1944). *Theory of Games and Economic Behaviour*, Princeton University Press, Princeton.

Parker, J. E. S. (1974). *The Economics of Innovation*, Longman, London.

Pavitt, K. (1976). Government support for industrial research and development in France, theory and practice, *Minerva*, **1976**, 331–354.

Stackleberg, H. von (1952). *The Theory of the Market Economy*, Hodge.

Sutton, C. J. (1974). Advertising, concentration and competition, *Economic Journal*, **1974**, 56–59.

Sweezy, P. (1939), Demand Under Conditions of Oligopoly, *Journal of Political Economy*, **47**, 568–573.

Tisdell, C. A. (1972). *Microeconomics: Theory of Economic Allocation*, Chap. 9 and Appendix to Chap. 9, Wiley, Sydney.

Tisdell, C. A. and McDonald, P. W. (1979). *Economics of Fibre Markets*, Chap. 2, Pergamon Press, Oxford.

Veblen, T. (1924). *The Theory of the Leisure Class*, Allen and Unwin, London.

QUESTIONS FOR REVIEW AND DISCUSSION

1. What is oligopoly? Is it common in particular sectors of the economy? Why is it important for an oligopolist to take account of the behaviour of his rivals? Do you believe that many stereotypes patterns of oligopolistic behaviour evolve as means of reducing uncertainty between rivals?

2. Does the kinked demand curve help to explain price rigidities and price stability in oligopolistic markets?

3 .'A government which wished to control prices in an oligopolistic market where price leadership occurs would only need to control the prices charged by the price leader.' Discuss and consider the limitations of this view.

4. The continued effective operation of a cartel is usually under a twin threat. What are these threats? Take an actual cartel and give some evidence of the threats.

5. Give the broad outlines of some models of oligopolistic markets apart from the kinked demand curve, price leadership, and cartel models. Why is there such a variety of models?

6. What forms does non-price competition by oligopolists take? How important is it in oligopolistic markets in comparison to price competition?

7. Compare likely advertising intensities under oligopoly with those under other forms. What are the likely effects of differences in advertising intensities between markets?

8. 'Oligopolists can become caught in an advertising trap and this can result in a Kaldor–Hicks loss in social welfare.' Explain.

9. What factors would you want to take into account in assessing the social benefits and costs of advertising by oligopolists?

10. Outline public policies (actual or proposed) to control advertising and the supply of information. What is the rationale behind such policies? What dangers may they pose?

11. Outline the principle of minimum product differentiation and give a simple proof of it in terms of game theory. What limitations and applications does it have?

12. The general effect of oligopoly on product differentiation is not as yet settled.

Why? Are there competing theories? Do you believe that the government should interfere in some industries to reduce the variety of very similar products offered for sale?

13. 'It is common to speak about the rate of technical progress as though it is easily measured. But the rate of technical progress has several dimensions, not easily combined in a single index.' Explain.

14. Outline Parker's hypothesis (and his reasons for holding it) that the rate of technical progress is likely to be higher under oligopoly than any other market form. Would you want to qualify the hypothesis?

15. Critically discuss Galbraith's view that large firms are almost the perfect instrument for bringing about technical progress.

16. Why do governments subsidize research and development? Is this socially desirable? Is it necessarily socially desirable to accelerate or maximize technological change?

17. Outline Galbraith's perspective on current capitalist industrial economies. Do you believe that his view is realistic?

18. Why do multi-national firms exist and what functions do they perform? How might their presence be beneficial to host countries and how could their presence impose costs on host countries?

PART D

Factor Markets and Policy

CHAPTER 10

Labour Markets

10.1 INTRODUCTION: THE SCOPE OF MANPOWER POLICY

Manpower policy embraces all aspects of government policy towards labour as a factor of production and the operation of the market for labour. While the list of potential policy issues is extensive, they can be classified around the broad demand, supply, and relative wage variables in the market. Examples include state involvement in relative pay, particularly between the public and private sectors, as well as information provision and policies towards the unemployed, training and re-training, mobility, and regional development. Governments might also make provision for special groups, such as the disabled, school-leavers, the long-term unemployed, the elderly, women, and immigrants. Such policies often reflect a concern with both economic and social objectives. Indeed, labour markets are often regarded as 'different' since they involve transactions in people and their services. People are both consumers and workers, and the income obtained from work will clearly affect their consumption levels. Not surprisingly, governments aiming to reduce poverty have frequently intervened to raise the wages of the low paid through, for example, legislation on minimum wages and equal pay. Such policies can have perverse effects and they raise basic questions about the function of labour markets.

This chapter will outline the economic arguments which might justify government intervention in the labour market and the likely effects of inter-vention. Consideration will be given to the characteristics of labour markets, the behaviour of individuals in the market, and the predictive power of economic models. Emphasis will be placed on whether governments need a public policy towards the labour market and, if so, the possible form of such a policy. Specific examples to be considered will include job search, unemploy-ment, and legislation on discrimination. Governments are also major employers. Military conscription or the draft will be taken as an example of labour demand by the public sector. However, this chapter will not provide a detailed account of human capital theory and unions. The analysis of training and mobility as human investments and their implications for social policy will be presented in Chapter 11. Similarly, the appraisal of trade unions and their effects on relative wages and efficiency is given in Chapter 12.

10.2 THE FUNCTIONS AND ACHIEVEMENTS OF LABOUR MARKETS

In capitalist economies, labour markets aim to allow mutually advantageous trade and exchange between willing buyers and sellers of labour. In this context, the buyers consist of private and public sector firms, as well as non-profit organizations which employ labour, such as the armed forces, charities, churches, government bureaucracies, hospitals and schools. By bringing together buyers and sellers, labour markets contribute to the production of goods and services to satisfy consumer preferences, as well as providing incomes to workers. In fact, labour markets are a fascinating study of the complexity of allocative choices. Think of what they do. They provide a bewildering variety of jobs and relative incomes, for men and women, young and old, full- and part-time, both self-employed and employees. These jobs will require different skills and be located in different regions, in the private and public sectors, and in agriculture, mining, construction, manufacturing, and service industries. Even in a static world, this would be a complex allocative task for any central planner: change makes life even more difficult! Labour markets have to adjust to technical progress, new suppliers, and changing consumer preferences (see Chapter 15). New firms emerge requiring labour, and existing enterprises substitute machinery for workers. Examples include computers, jet airliners, and micro-electronics. Households have not escaped technical change with servants and full-time housewives being replaced by machinery such as central heating, canned food, freezers, cookers, and dish-washers. Change requires new skills, sometimes in different locations. Labour markets adapt to these changes through, for example, firms re-training their workers in new skills and through the movement of employers and labour between regions (and nations).

The end-results of labour markets are expressed in observed outcomes which provide answers to a set of questions about pay and employment. What determines relative earnings and why are successful popstars, soccer players, and cricketers paid much more than nurses? Why do accountants, judges, lawyers, and university teachers generally receive more than workers involved in dirty, dangerous, and disagreeable manual jobs, such as coal-mining, refuse collection, and deep-sea fishing? Why are men usually paid more than women, whites more than blacks? There are also questions about employment. What determines employment and unemployment, and what is full employment? Can workers price themselves into, as well as out of, jobs? But the fact that actual labour markets seem to answer these questions does not mean that the outcomes are 'socially desirable'. A clear destinction is required between positive economics which aims to explain facts and normative issues concerned with the desirability of the outcomes. Some criteria are required for assessing performance.

Performance criteria

As a starting point, Paretian welfare economics would assess the performance of labour markets in terms of their conformity with the competitive model. In such markets, labour would receive the value of its marginal product. Converting these performance indicators into operational concepts would lead governments to assess labour markets in terms of their efficiency as clearing mechanisms. In particular, labour markets can be judged by criteria relating to unemployment and their adaptability to change. Inevitably, they will also be judged by the 'appropriateness' of their relative pay structures. Governments might dislike an income distribution based on marginal productivity and determined by market forces. Thus, distributional issues cannot be avoided. Why, for example, should nurses be paid less than successful popstars? Should not the drivers of trains and buses be highly paid since they are 'responsible' for the safety of large numbers of people? And in the public sector, how is it possible to measure the marginal productivity of firemen, policemen, and army tank commanders in peace-time? Critics of market solutions sometimes suggest that public sector pay should be determined on the basis of comparability. But what is the comparable reference group for an army tank commander and who determines the degree of comparability? What if tank commanders disagree with the results? In other words, economists can contribute to the formation of manpower policy by predicting the effects of alternative pay structures and their relative conformity to the Pareto criterion. They can point to the shortages and surpluses which are likely to emerge if governments interfere with market-determined wage rates. And they can provide explanations of differences in relative pay. Such contributions do not require complex economic models. The competitive model provides an analytical basis for understanding behaviour and results in the labour market, but a preference for such an approach requires some justification (see Chapters 2 and 4).

Some procedural clarifications

The characteristics of a competitive market for labour provide a basis for examining some of the more significant possible imperfections in the way such manpower markets actually operate. However, we do not begin from an exposition of these characteristics in the belief that a perfectly competitive market is likely to be created in our lifetime! The labour market has a number of unusual features not least that the persons (labour force) offering services in it are also the community whose interests the market exists to serve. There is, for example, always a potential (though not a necessary) conflict between labour market policies concerned with economic efficiency, and particular views of the broader aims of social policy. Rather, the exposition provides a 'benchmark', or 'ideal type'. It facilitates an examination of the nature and practical significance of labour market imperfections, thereby identifying the potential opportunities for state intervention to correct market failures. Such an approach is also relevant for subsequent chapters since it outlines the market environment within which policies towards training, mobility, and trade unions must be formulated and implemented.

10.3 THE COMPETITIVE LABOUR MARKET

A competitive labour market contains many buyers and sellers, each acting as a price-taker and possessing information on prices throughout the system, with free entry and exit from the market. In such a market, a firm's demand for labour will depend on the wage rate and the productivity of additional units of labour (marginal productivity). The supply of labour will depend on the wage rate, workers' preferences between income and leisure, the view taken of the non-pecuniary aspects of particular jobs, and the available job opportunities. In a competitive economy with full employment, wages and salaries in various markets will be determined by demand and supply, and prices will be the mechanism for allocating scarce labour between alternative uses. The model predicts that an increase in the demand for labour in an occupation, industry, or area will result in a relative rise in wage rates. Workers will be attracted to the relatively high wage activity, which is also the sector in which output, and hence their contribution to output, has come to be more highly valued. Similarly, a decrease in the demand for labour will result in a relative decline in real wage rates in that sector and a consequent reduction in labour employed. However, the downward adjustment in wage rates will offset some of the quantity reductions which would otherwise be required. Thus, in a competitive market, if other things remain constant, wage changes between activities will reflect changes in relative scarcities and so indicate the need for re-allocation of labour. The adjustment will take the form of labour moving from lower to higher paid occupations until the allocation required by market forces is achieved. As a result, in a system where prices allocate manpower and other resources between uses, prices (including wages) and outputs of products will always be changing in directions that respond to consumer preferences. Such adjustments will eliminate any 'shortages' or 'surpluses' generated by changes in consumer tastes or in the technical conditions of production. In other words, variations in relative wages will 'clear' the labour market, so removing vacancies and unemployment.

Why do wages differ?

In competitive markets differences in wage rates between occupations reflect the relative scarcity of various types of labour. Wage rates will differ because of variations in the monetary and non-monetary advantages of jobs, differences in the ability of labour, costs of training, and the geographical mobility of workers (see Chapter 11). Clearly, some sources of differences in relative wage rates will exist even in an economy not subject to change. People differ in ability, aptitudes, and commitment to learning, and different skills and abilities are differentially scarce and hence would be differentially rewarded. Also, jobs differ in their security, cleanliness, and safety, and workers may attach value to such job attributes. To the extent that they do so, relative wages will reflect differences in these *non-monetary attributes*, even in an unchanging economy. Office jobs are relatively safe and pleasant compared with coal-mining, steeplejacks, and trawling.

Other differences in relative wage rates at any time will result from changes in the patterns of labour demand in the economy, as explained above. In a competitive system, the response of labour to changes in market requirements will depend partly upon the time taken for the system to record and disseminate information about relative scarcities. Once the market signals its changing requirements for manpower, the degree of response of labour to a change in wage rates will depend on the costs of geographical and occupational mobility. Here, much depends not only on the costs of mobility and training but also on the extent to which individuals are able to obtain funds for worthwhile human investments (see Chapter 11). A competitive labour market requires that adjustments should be able to take place with reasonable freedom, unhindered either by cost and financing barriers or by other barriers to the entry of labour into particular occupations.

The nature of these obstacles to entry is complex. Apart from the simple cost obstacles, it has been argued that the labour market comprises a set of *non-competing groups*, the different markets being separated from one another by economic barriers, social prejudice, and snobbery. Within each market, the wage-adjustment processes described above would operate, but not between the non-competing groups. The emphasis in this formulation has traditionally been upon the relation between social·distinctions and entry barriers. However, there seems no reason to take so narrow a view: all barriers to entry not related to production requirements constitute market imperfections. Barriers related to sex, colour, or religion, for example, are as much policy-relevant obstacles to the satisfactory operation of the market as are training and other obligations imposed by trade unions with the purpose of restricting the supply of skilled labour rather than of ensuring competence. Such entry barriers are a further source of differences in relative pay.

The implications for public policy

The description of the ideal labour market provides guidance for policy-makers. If reality is to approach the competitive model, then governments will need to give attention to:

(1) The number and size distribution of buyers and sellers.
(2) Entry conditions, both those imposed by trade unions and professional associations, and those which arise from the unwanted activities of other non-competing groups.

(3) The conditions of geographical and occupational mobility (training and re-training) and the adaptability of the system to technological change.

(4) The relation between detailed micro-economic policies and the need to provide an appropriate macro-economic context. In particular, it will be necessary to adopt policies to deal with techological and cyclical unemployment.

(5) The efficiency with which the system collects and transmits information.

This lengthy shopping list underlines the fact that labour market policy must necessarily be considered as an entity. As an illustration, take the frequent concern of governments with shortages of skilled manpower and their belief that more training is the only policy solution. The competitive model provides a useful framework for analysing the problem. A permanent shortage of skilled labour suggests excess demand at the ruling wage rate, with wages either failing to adjust upwards or repeatedly settling below the market-clearing price (see Chapter 4 and Figure 4.3). Skill shortages can emerge for many reasons, related to such factors as entry conditions, training, mobility, information provision, and government pay policies, together with difficulties in raising funds for human investments. For example, monopoly unions can change the structure of relative wages, especially between skilled and unskilled tasks. Not surprisingly, any narrowing of wage differentials reduces the incentive of individuals to undertake training and bear some of its costs. Unions can further contribute to skill shortages through entry restrictions for particular trades and lengthy apprenticeships. As a result, it is not surprising that supply responds only slowly and inadequately to changes in demand. Thus, if an efficiently operating labour market is required in which shortages will be absent, policy-makers need to consider the market as a whole and not simply one aspect of manpower, such as training. However, objection to the competitive model as a potential or approximate description of reality in any capitalist economy may be based upon the observations that barriers to entry exist, that some workers are immobile, and that the market is hampered by inadequate information. It may also be claimed that other policy objectives should, and do, override the objectives that can be served by a competitive market. These objections cannot be ignored.

Entry barriers and immobility

Critics of the competitive model point to the fact that most wage rates in capitalist economies are negotiated not between individual workers and their individual employers but between trade unions and employers' associations. Also, workers are believed to be immobile, either inherently because they attach a high value to their present location or because they are unable to finance geographical movement or the acquisition of a new skill. Finally, it is said, workers normally have very poor information about current earnings from different jobs—much less about potential future changes. If valid, these considerations seem sufficient to demand government intervention in the labour market, since they imply that the competitive pressures which are required for the allocation of labour between alternative uses are at least partly absent. But how important are these imperfections in practice?

There is, in fact, a substantial amount of evidence which is consistent with the predictions of the competitive model. In many capitalist economies, the net geographical movement of population is in the direction predicted by the theory: namely from regions of little opportunity, where long-run earnings are relatively low, to areas of higher wages, more job opportunities, and relatively low unemployment rates. In other words, movement is towards areas where there are expectations of higher lifetime earnings for the household. However, some critics have concluded that what appears to be a response to opportunities to increase earnings could be equally consistent with the attraction of employment possibilities and other non-wage factors. Such a conclusion is somewhat misleading since only when other things are held constant does the orthodox model explain geographical and occupational mobility in terms of variations in relative wage rates. When this is not so, movement is explained by differences in net advantages. Indeed, the model emphasizes that it is total net advantages and not merely wages which determine the occupational choices of workers and that relative wages only determine job choice in a framework in which other job properties are unchanged. There are obvious difficulties in obtaining evidence about these (expected) non-wage differences. Since they are not marketed, information must be sought about the subjective estimates of the workers who move between jobs—and, ideally, of workers who might have moved but did not! Elsewhere, instances of *apparently* irrational behaviour in decisions concerning occupations and skills become consistent with rationality once it is recognized that systematic job search and consideration of alternatives is not a costless process.

In total, there is some evidence to support the view that labour markets operate in the general direction that the competitive model would predict, albeit imperfectly. This is not to claim that the model is incapable of modification and that there are no alternative explanations of labour market behaviour. Some of the modern developments concerning search, households, uncertainty, and internal labour markets will be outlined below, while subsequent chapters will introduce human capital and trade unions into the analysis. Nonetheless, if governments wish to achieve an optimum allocation of resources, there are opportunities for state intervention to remove or 'correct' identifiable labour market imperfections. Possibilities include anti-monopoly policies, unilateral tariff reductions to increase competitive pressures, measures to improve labour mobility and information flows, together with policies to prevent trade unions from restricting the entry of qualified persons to any occupation. Critics, however, might claim that there are other, more important, policy objectives relating to labour markets.

The importance of other policy objectives

One argument for displacing the market can be dealt with quickly. This is the argument that the labour market generates an 'undesirable' distribution of income, which justifies state intervention in wage determination. To right wing economists, this proposition rests on a misunderstanding of the function of markets. They are seen as mechanisms for allocating limited resources between many users and providing signals about relative scarcities. Interference with this allocative process might be based upon the fact that the wrong signals are being given because of market imperfections, which the intervention is designed to remove. On this view, correction of the distribution of income generated by the labour market is a matter for the tax system, which need not affect the functioning of specific labour markets and which can be related to incomes and responsibilities rather than to occupations.

A more substantial set of problems concerns policy towards full employment and economic growth. The discussion so far has proceeded on the assumption that there would be no overall demand deficiency which generated unemployment, much less simultaneous conditions of inflation and rising unemployment. Nor has account been taken of the fact that economic growth with technological change may raise average incomes, but does so at the price of an obligation to accept skill obsolescence and the need for job change, with the implied possibilities of workers needing to undertake re-training and/or experiencing unemployment. These are important and complex issues which cannot be ignored. There is, of course, scope for debate about the role of the state in unemployment policy. Insofar as different occupations carry a different risk of unemployment (and high-risk occupations are frequently highly paid), there would seem to be sound reasons for requiring workers to insure themselves against unemployment at premiums that reflect such differential risks (perhaps by relating the premiums to past work experience?) If this were all, state involvement could be limited to legislation making unemployment insurance compulsory. But there are other considerations. First, macro-economic policy is a matter for the state, so that private insurers would be taking not only risks related to technological change (which might well be insurable in the aggregate) but also risks related to the government's management of the economy. These are not only difficult for the private insurer to deal with: they also support an argument of principle, that the state should bear at least part of the costs of unemployment as state policy is a major influence upon its size and character. Further, as mentioned above, the labour force is the *raison d'etre* of the productive process as well as a part of it. If the labour market works in a fashion that produces what are thought to be conditions of unreasonable hardship for particular families, then the community will want to redistribute income towards those concerned. On this basis, whether unemployment insurance is provided by the state or by compulsory private arrangements, the state would carry a continuing residual obligation to provide for income deficiency due to unemployment (see Chapter 11).

To complete this unavoidably inadequate summary, there is the question of job change in a dynamic economy. Left to themselves, labour markets appear to operate imperfectly in this area because workers cannot provide adequate security for loans to facilitate job change. The essential similarity in this respect between *geographical* and *occupational* mobility (requiring finance for training) will be apparent. Additionally, however, it must be recognized that state-supported policies to facilitate labour mobility may be a necessary precondition for acceptance by the community of dynamic change and its concomitant skill obsolescence. There is, of course, room for argument as to how far the state should intervene to influence the growth process, but there can be little doubt of the practical importance of the insecurity generated for workers by dynamic change. The policy options include redundancy pay as compensation for job loss, together with state assistance towards mobility, re-training, and job search. Mention of job search raises questions about the performance of labour markets in providing and transmitting information.

10.4 THE ECONOMICS OF INFORMATION

The competitive model assumes perfect information. But actual labour markets are not like agricultural commodities and stock exchanges where prices are clearly recorded. Labour is heterogeneous. People differ in their motivation and commitment to work, their abilities and skills, as well as in their tastes and preferences, and hence in their supply prices. Jobs also differ in their stability of employment, opportunities for overtime, training, and promotion, together with general working conditions, all of which are reflected in the wage offered by employers. Given such diversity of workers and jobs, both buyers and sellers in the labour market have to search in order to obtain the 'best' terms. In other words, search provides information on the terms of trade in the labour market.

Information is not costless: resources with other valued uses have to be employed to obtain it. This fact alone casts some doubts upon the frequent assertion that 'labour is not a commodity' and consequently there should only be free or non-profit-making employment information services. In reply, it might be accepted that labour is not *only* a commodity, in that workers are also a major part of the community. Nevertheless, the community has as great an interest in the efficient use of labour resources, and hence in the efficient operation of the labour market, as it has in the efficient use of any other factor of production. If the provision of information involves costs, then, within the context of the competitive labour market model, it will be provided only if the anticipated benefits from having it justify the costs to be incurred. Workers will be willing to continue to 'buy' more information until its extra benefit is expected to be less valuable than the incremental cost of purchase. Thus, the model can be developed to incorporate a market in information. Trainees, for example, will require information on the costs of different training methods and the expected market value of the resulting skills. The 'information market' would be a complex one, since information can be acquired in a diversity of fashions. For example, learning by experience, by obtaining information based on the experience of friends, or by reading advertisements in the newspapers and trade journals are all methods of searching the labour market. Such methods are not costless and frequently involve substantial time-costs, and the least-cost solution for the individual worker (or firm) might be to use none of them, but rather to purchase information from a specialist job agency. In other words, a competitive market will be characterized by a variety of information channels, including specialist agencies offering to sell information at a price.

Information, job search, and labour market decisions

The fact that information is not costless provides a basis for further understanding of behaviour in the labour market. Indeed, it is possible to combine information and job search with the ideas of human capital, the concept of the firm used by Coase, and internal labour markets. And the analysis can be presented in the *household* context rather than that of the individual worker.

Consider the background against which individuals make labour market decisions. An individual might be aiming to maximize the present value of his expected lifetime earnings or expected utility over the life-cycle, where utility allows the inclusion of net advantages into the analysis. This is a standard optimization problem with the individual maximizing subject to a set of constraints in the form of available resources, the efficiency of resource use (which will depend on technical progress), a limited amount of information, and uncertainty (no one can accurately predict the future). On the constraints side, the individual as a worker makes decisions in a household context. As a young worker, it will be his parent's household; with age, his own household. In other words, both the labour market and lifetime behaviour of the individual takes place in a household setting. There are a number of features of households which can affect labour market behaviour:

(1) Households possess a stock of monetary and physical assets in such forms as current and expected savings, goods, and services. These form a wealth constraint for the household which will usually exceed that available to an individual. This is often reflected in families acting as a 'cushion' and providing a source of internal funds and collateral for loans. Such funds might be a source of income during strikes, unemployment, job search, and training.

(2) Households possess a stock of human capital (see Chapter 11). In fact, the household can be regarded as an information agency. It has human capital in the form of information and knowledge about job opportunities and skills.

(3) Households supply factor services, but an individual's offer decisions

might be affected by the supply behaviour of other members of the household. For example, if a married man loses his job, his wife might go out to work, or if a man has a job, his wife might not work—all of which affects participation or activity rates in an economy. These rates are measured by expressing the employed and registered unemployed as a percentage of the population of working age.

(4) Households not only supply factor services but also produce goods and services (e.g. housewives' services). Indeed, households add to the stock of factors (children). In this interpretation, a household is a firm. Using the Coase framework, the household is another island of central planning in a market system, and the existence and extent of the household is explained in terms of an organization for minimizing transactions costs. For example, married men do not have to re-contract every time they want a meal!

Within the household framework, individual workers make a continuous set of labour market decisions. For example, workers have to search for and to choose a job, some of which might require industrial training. They have to choose whether to stay in the job or to change it (to quit). A change of job involves a search for other work and the search can take place either on or off the job. Or the choice might not be theirs and they might lose a job (redundancy and unemployment), in which case they have to search for another job. Searching for another job might require further investments in moving to a new location or acquiring a new skill. All these labour market decisions will be related to the worker's views about expected wage rates and incomes. At varying points in his working life, he might change his views about incomes in different jobs, and these views will determine his minimum offer price or his reservation wage. The offer price is also likely to change as the worker learns from experience, and household experience can be substituted for individual experience.

The labour market decisions outlined above form the *economics of job search*. This is a standard search process. Information is limited and costly to acquire and both workers and employers must search to find jobs and to fill vacancies. The analysis can be developed further by interpreting human capital theory in terms of information and knowledge embodied in human beings. On this basis, labour market decisions reflect a search process as workers and firms invest in acquiring additional information and knowledge about rates of exchange in the labour market, and in further reducing imperfections in knowledge by acquiring marketable skills. For example, in making career choices, individuals invest in themselves by acquiring information about different jobs. They also invest in themselves through education and training which represent 'knowledge-improving' investments. However, labour market decisions are made in a world of uncertainty. How do economic agents respond and adapt to uncertainty?

Uncertainty

Much depends on an individual's preferences and attitudes towards risks. Is he risk-average or a gambler? Nonetheless, a worker can respond to uncertainty in various ways:

(1) Savings can be acquired.
(2) A general skill can be obtained which has value to a large number of employers.
(3) Individuals can locate in areas of excess labour demand.
(4) A person can join a trade union which might attempt to establish and to protect a worker's 'property rights' in his job and in his skills.
(5) A group of workers in the community could persuade vote-conscious governments to introduce legislation establishing a workers' property rights in his job. Examples include legislation on employment protection, industrial democracy, and redundancy payments.

Search is not confined to workers. Firms are also searching the labour market. They are searching for labour with minimum productivity requirements in relation to the agreed wage; or they are searching for manpower with specific characteristics, such as degrees; or they are searching for labour with characteristics which increase the probability that the worker will stay with the firm, so allowing it to recoup some of its investment in search, hiring, and possibly training the worker. For firms, a major uncertainty arises because labour is mobile. Unlike a machine, individuals can choose to leave a firm. How do firms respond to this uncertainty (i.e. labour mobility)? Various methods are used:

(1) Screening processes can be used to select labour which is more likely to be immobile.
(2) Fringe benefits can be 'tied' to the company and these might reduce mobility. Examples include company sports and health facilities, as well as cheap meals.
(3) Fringe benefits can also be 'tied' to the length of service. Examples include paid holidays and occupational pensions.
(4) Employment contracts. A firm's uncertainty about a new worker's ability motivation, and potential mobility might be reflected in the form of the employment contract. Typically, these vary and might take the form of sequential spot contracts or an authority relationship or provisions for incentive pay, training, and pension rights. Some contracts require an individual to stay with the firm for a specified period, with premature departure involving repayment of part of the employer's hiring and training costs.
(5) Firms can create internal labour markets. For example, firms might restrict entry to lower level jobs, obtain experience of the worker and

promote from within on the basis of seniority. This policy provides both information on new entrants and 'ties' the interests of the worker to the firm in a continuing way, so increasing the firm's willingness to invest in training. If rivals operate a seniority system, a voluntary 'quit' might involve a worker in substantial promotion costs.

Internal labour markets

An internal labour market forms a non-competing group. It is a 'closed' labour market which is confined to the establishment, firm, or industry, where there are a clear set of rules about entry, exit, and movement within the internal labour market. In other words, the internal organization of a firm — its internal labour market — is an administered system with rules about wages and the allocation of labour. Internal labour markets contrast with the classical open, unstructured markets where there is no attachment between the worker and the employer other than the wage: workers do not have a claim on any job and employers do not have a hold over any man. Thus, internal labour markets can be regarded as a method of obtaining a return on a firm's investment in its workers (e.g. search, hiring, screening, supervising, and training). As such, they can be interpreted as a form of employment contract, in which case, there are clear interrelationships between human investments, employment contracts, and internal labour markets. Indeed, internal labour markets might be an efficient solution for firms searching for information about the productivity of their manpower, while providing incentives and rewards for pursuing organizational goals and, at the same time, trying to obtain a return from investments in their workers. References to efficiency also raise questions about the possibilities of failure in information markets.

Should governments intervene in information markets?

The efficient operation of the labour market partly depends upon the transmission of information about relative scarcities in the economy. If, for example, labour is unaware of income and employment prospects in different jobs, this will impair the extent to which workers will respond by acquiring new skills and moving from the declining to the expanding regions and sectors of the economy. In the circumstances, both workers and firms in private enterprise economies find it worth while to invest in the acquisition of market information. The result is an extensive private sector information market embracing specialist job agencies, advertisements, certificates, licences, correspondence, phone calls, and informal contacts. Such methods can involve substantial money and time costs. Despite the willingness to pay for information, private competitive markets are not likely to provide as much of the commodity as consumers require. Some kinds of information are so general in character that it may be difficult to establish property rights in them with the consequent possibility of underprovision if information is left to be supplied by private markets. It is also a frequent characteristic of such information that it can be supplied to more people at very low additional cost, so that private provision might produce conditions of technical monopoly. Thus, state intervention in information markets can be rationalized on grounds of its public good characteristics and technical monopoly. There is a further general argument for government intervention. Through its macro-economic policies, the state creates the context within which a competitive labour market might operate. This involves the state in the 'information business'. Information is required about its own plans, and about its inferences from those plans for the *general* development of the labour market. Any such information has to be hedged by qualifications, since state agencies have no special access to knowledge about the future. A major value of this type of information is that it can also be assessed by others. At the same time, the state's macro-economic policy role might be argued to support some subsidization of information provision beyond the amounts individuals would want to pay for. This could be justified if the cost of the resultant information is less than the benefits in increased community output obtained by shortening the periods spent in unemployment or the lags in adjusting to changes in labour demand.

The existence of market failure does not, however, indicate the most appropriate policy solution. Various alternatives are possible, including the state subsidization of private information agencies, the state provision of grants and loans to individuals for investment in job search, as well as the public ownership or regulation of technical monopolies. Clearly, there will be differences of opinion about the appropriateness of private and state *finance* and state *provision* of information. Advocates of market solutions will claim that in a competitive labour market there is no reason or principle why workers should not pay for job information, but there must be access to funds for worthwhile investments. Such funds might take the form of loans or equities related to the marketability of the job information (see Chapter 11). Critics of market solutions might prefer state provision of information through a government employment agency offering its services to workers at zero price. Such an option could reflect a general community preference for public ownership of technical monopolies. Budget-maximizing bureaucracies are unlikely to oppose this policy! In addition, some state finance and provision of information could be justified because much labour market information is generated within government. Where there is a public social security system, it is likely that for certain kinds of information the state is potentially the lowest-cost organization for its collection and distribution. Finally, state finance and provision of job information is often defended in terms of 'helping the unemployed'. Similar arguments have been used for public policies towards training, re-training, and mobility. Inevitably, distributional issues cannot be avoided. Economists can contribute to policy formulation by seeking clarification of government objectives, identifying potential conflicts, and outlining the implications of alternative solutions. In view of its importance to labour market policy some consideration has to be given to unemployment.

10.5 UNEMPLOYMENT

Unemployment is obviously a cause for concern. Usually, the policy problem embraces their numbers and percentages, as expressed in the recorded unemployment statistics, its duration, and regional distribution, as well as its impact on particular groups, such as school-leavers, immigrants, and older workers. Unemployment also means lost output, it affects government expenditure and revenue, and it has social impacts. Moreover, there are dynamic effects. For example, while unemployment tends to cause some workers to withdraw from the labour force, the experience of unsuccessful job search might mean that the discouraged work effect 'spills over' into future years and future generations. Nor can unemployment be ignored by vote-sensitive governments (see Chapter 3). Clearly, the subject embraces both macro- and micro-economics, with the latter providing the material for this section. For simplicity, three policy issues will be assessed, relating to the reliability of unemployment statistics, the micro-economic causes of unemployment, and the likely effects of unemployment pay and labour market legislation.

Are the official unemployment statistics reliable indicators of the state of the labour market?

Any answer to this question depends upon what ought to be measured. Theory provides a conceptual framework for an answer. The 'new' micro-economics approach suggests that there is a natural rate of unemployment reflecting labour adjustments and imperfections. This view resembles that of the classical economists where full employment occurs at the market-clearing real wage rate. In equilibrium, any unemployment is *voluntary*, reflecting a worker's preferred income–leisure position. The modern micro-economics also recognizes that in equilibrium there is likely to be some unemployment due to job search, movement between jobs, and labour market imperfections. Indeed, in this model, the existence of information costs means that unemployment, vacancies, and flexible prices can co-exist, even where competitive markets are in equilibrium. Such outcomes make life exceptionally difficult for governments trying to interpret the unemployment statistics as a guide to policy formulation!

Official unemployment figures are often used as an indicator of the state of demand and supply in the labour market. Usually, they are a record of those who actually register as unemployed with the state's manpower agency. The total might consist of those who are wholly and temporarily unemployed, as well as those who cannot find jobs or will not work at what they perceive as the ruling wages. But some of these groups might be voluntarily unemployed or using unemployment for job search (e.g. some unemployed could be self-employed in job search). Other people might not be registered with the state's employment agency, even though they are willing to work and searching for a job. Between countries, differences in definition, coverage, and accuracy make international comparisons difficult, if not misleading.

Proposals have been made for more accurate economic indicators of the state of the labour market. Some economists have argued that particular groups should be excluded from the official unemployment statistics. Examples might include school-leavers, those frictionally and structurally unemployed, the voluntarily unemployed, and the unemployables. But what is the economic logic of excluding a specific group and how would the various categories be identified and measured? Alternative suggestions have been made for a more comprehensive measure of labour slack in an economy. Such a measure might embrace unemployment and activity rates, international migration, labour hoarding, and hours worked per annum. Interesting though these proposals might be, they are often aimed at providing *macro*-economic indicators. Life at the micro-level is much more difficult. At this level, the more accurate official statistics often relate to unemployment in *regional* labour markets. Industry and occupational data can be less reliable indicators of surpluses and shortages. The former are usually based on an individual's previous industrial employer, even though the worker might be mobile between industries and possess skills which are transferable. Similarly, occupational data require a classification system based on skill categories and market groups which are separated by gaps in the chain of substitutes. Training policy, for example, cannot be divorced from data on current and forecast occupational unemployment rates. Policy-makers need to know whether the statistics provide an accurate indication of persistent skill shortages. They also require information on the education and training content of the skills which are in excess demand, together with the opportunities for substitution. In other words, without reliable micro-economic data on the state of labour markets and their efficiency it is difficult for governments to formulate policy solutions. But there is a prior requirement for understanding the causes of unemployment.

Search unemployment

There is no shortage of micro-economic hypotheses to explain the apparent failure of labour markets to clear. Why does excess supply not lead to aggressive wage cutting by both buyers and sellers? Wage stickiness might be due to worker resistance to wage reductions, particularly where there are trade unions. Or firms might be reluctant to cut wages if they feel that there would be costs in the form of antagonizing the remaining employees, so adversely affecting productivity, as well as making it costlier to recruit labour when sales improve. Or there could be widespread notions of fairness, together with social pressures and legislation which might prevent redundant workers from undercutting employed labour. Alternatively, unemployment even in competitive markets might be explained by information costs. In this model, workers might prefer search unemployment rather than accept a pay cut to retain a job.

Consider a situation where there is a decrease in the demand for a firm's product. Employers might respond by requiring a wage cut for labour to continue in employment. However, where knowledge of market opportunities is limited and costly to acquire, a worker might sensibly believe that a better offer could be obtained with some search. And if searching is more efficiently undertaken off-the-job, it might be worth while for a worker to refuse a wage cut, choose unemployment, and search the labour market. Choosing unemployment as a means of searching for a job is not costless. Current consumption is sacrificed in return for expected future benefits which would make search unemployment worth while. Benefits take the form of a better paid job or one with greater non-monetary advantages. A simple model determining the average duration of search unemployment is shown in Figure 10.1. Workers lack perfect information and knowledge, so the longer they search for a job, the better the wage offers they discover. However, the longer they search, the more they are likely to revise downwards their reservation wage or supply price. As a result, the equilibrium period of search is determined where the reservation wage and wage offer curves intersect.

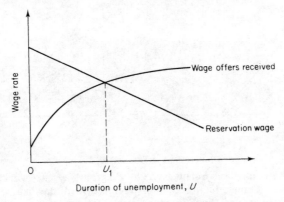

Figure 10.1   Search unemployment. Searching leads to the discovery of better wage offers. The wage offers curve represents the average of offers in general. At the same time, longer search leads workers to revise downwards their reservation wage (i.e. supply or offer price). The equilibrium period of search unemployment occurs where the curves intersect, at U_1, i.e. where at the margin the benefits of search are just equal to its costs. It is, of course, possible that after a point the wage offer received declines with the duration of unemployment (e.g. skills lose value if they are not used).

Effects of state unemployment pay

A government concerned with both economic and social objectives will be interested in discovering whether state unemployment pay contributes to a *rise* in unemployment. After all, unemployment payments are likely to reduce the

268

costs of both unemployment and job search. The hypothesis can be derived from an income–leisure model and an example is shown in Figure 10.2. State unemployment pay results in a parallel shift in a worker's budget line and, if leisure is a normal good, more will be preferred, as shown in Figure 10.2(a). However, in testing for a relationship between unemployment and unemployment benefits, allowance has to be made for the effects of 'other influences'. Theory suggests an alternative hypothesis, namely that as people become richer they will demand more leisure which is then reflected in voluntary unemployment! An example is shown in Figure 10.2(b) where a higher wage rate leads to income and substitution effects, resulting in the choice of more leisure and income. In other words, in testing for any disincentive effects of state unemployment pay, allowance has to be made for the impact of rising living standards on observed unemployment. The evidence suggests that state unemployment pay has disincentive effects; but there are doubts about its precise magnitude with some studies estimating a relatively small impact on the level of unemployment. This is not the only example of a policy measure which results in conflicts between objectives. Other examples have occurred with labour market legislation, some of which has had unemployment effects.

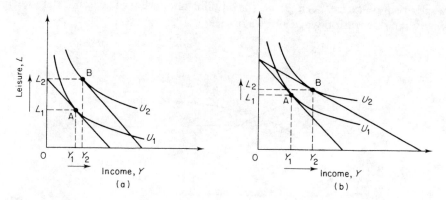

Figure 10.2 State unemployment pay. In diagram (a) the worker is initially in equilibrium at A. The introduction of state unemployment pay can be represented by a parallel shift in the budget line (income effect). The new equilibrium is at B. This example shows a corner solution, with the worker consuming the maximum available leisure, i.e. all his available time is allocated to leisure. In diagram (b), following a rise in the wage rate, the worker moves from an initial equilibrium at A to a new preferred combination at B (reflecting both income and substitution effects). Thus, with rising real incomes, people will demand more leisure, which is then observed as higher unemployment.

10.6 LABOUR MARKET LEGISLATION

Labour markets are often characterized by differences in pay between men and women, whites and blacks, nationals and immigrants. They are also markets in which workers might not have any rights of protection against unfair dismissal and where they might be subject to unhealthy and dangerous jobs. Understandably, vote-sensitive governments and budget-conscious bureaucrats believe that such characteristics are socially undesirable and can be eliminated through legislation and the establishment of state regulatory agencies. Examples include legislation on equal pay and minimum wages, as well as laws against discrimination on grounds of race and sex. Legislation has also been used to establish a worker's property rights in a job through laws relating to employment protection, contracts of employment, and health and safety at work. In each case, it is always a source of surprise to governments that legislation and attempts to administer markets through laws result in unexpected and undesirable side-effects and outcomes which differ from the original intentions. And yet, as shown throughout this book, micro-economics can predict some of these effects.

Differences in pay and employment opportunities are often related to race, religion, and sex. Such differences are not necessarily an accurate indicator of labour market discrimination. Differences in pay between men and women, between nationals and immigrants, Catholics and Protestants, or whites and blacks might be due to differences in relative scarcities related to variations in productivity, motivation, education, and training, as well as hours of work and the non-monetary aspects of jobs. However, differential access to education and training together with occupational and union entry barriers based on race, religion, or sex can create non-competing groups. As a result, the exclusion of minorities and women from particular occupations means that they 'crowd into' unrestricted occupations so reducing relative wages in these jobs. In addition to such general explanations, specialist economic models of discrimination have been developed. These explain labour market discrimination in terms of imperfect information and prejudice by firms, workers, or consumers. In searching for labour, firms will lack perfect information, so that they will develop 'rules of thumb' to screen applicants for jobs. Experience might lead employers to conclude that, on *average*, blacks, women, and minorities are less productive than whites and men. Such a conclusion will result in a firm discriminating against individual minorities and women who are more productive than their group average. Prejudice is a further explanation of discrimination. Employers might dislike particular groups and refuse to hire them, even at the expense of lost profits. For example, where there are no productivity differences between blacks and whites, or Catholics and Protestants, an employer's utility function might contain a preference for whites and Protestants. In this situation, the employer's *discrimination coefficient* will determine how much cheaper blacks and Catholics will have to be before they are hired. But prejudice need not be restricted to firms. Employees might prefer not to work with minorities or women. Similarly, consumers might prefer particular types of labour, such discrimination being likely to arise in service industries (e.g. accountants, restaurants, hairdressing).

These explanations have been criticized. In particular, in the long run, competitive forces are likely to eliminate some types of discrimination. For example, non-discriminating firms will have lower labour costs so that they would outcompete discriminating firms, driving them out of business. Or the higher profits earned by non-discriminating firms would induce rivals to copy. Modern radical economists prefer alternative explanations of discrimination. They attribute the subordinate status of women in the labour market to the needs of capitalism and its institutions. According to the radical view, the nuclear family and the drive for male supremacy within the household have forced women into the specialized roles of child-rearing and family maintenance within a capitalist system designed primarily for the participation and benefit of men. Such views provide extensive opportunities for critical appraisal! Terms and concepts have to be defined, testable hypotheses have to be constructed, and some effort is required to deduce the critics' view of the 'ideal' world where these 'problems' would somehow be eliminated. Nor can empirical evidence be ignored. Where international data are available, this shows that, on average, women earn less than men in both capitalist and socialist economies. Can legislation solve the problem?

Consider the case of legislation on equal pay for men and women doing the same jobs. The effects of the legislation are similar to those for minimum wage laws and can be predicted using demand and supply analysis (see Chapter 4). If the legislation is effective in raising wage rates above their market-clearing level, there will be a decline in female employment and the creation of unemployment. Profit-maximizing firms will respond to equal pay by replacing women with men and machines. Thus, equal pay will raise the wage rates of those women who remain employed. But the legislation leads to perverse results. Some of those who are supposed to benefit find themselves without jobs and there will be an increase in the demand for *male* substitutes! An example is shown in Figure 10.3. However, both the monopsony and shock effect cases provide possible exceptions to the unemployment impact of equal pay laws (see Chapter 12, Figure 12.7). Indeed, in defence of equal pay legislation, some economists have argued that monopsony is more likely to apply to women, especially married women who tend to be immobile. There is a further possibility. Workers might break the law rather than accept the unemployment consequences of legal solutions. In other words, illegally low wages might be preferred to unemployment and no wages.

Economists can also analyse the effects of laws relating to employment protection, contracts of employment, unfair dismissal, and redundancy payments. Effectively, such laws establish or extend workers' property rights in their jobs. They make it more expensive for firms to employ and to dismiss labour. Inevitably, firms will adopt various responses to the legislation. Capital will be substituted for labour; there will be a greater use of subcontractors, overtime, and temporary employment contracts; employers will be more selective in recruiting labour; and marginal firms in competitive export markets, where rivals might not be subject to such legislation, might have to close. As a result, the legislation will favour those who have jobs.

Similar results arise with health and safety at work legislation. The costs of conforming to the legislation might lead to the elimination of marginal firms. Not surprisingly, workers and trade unions might oppose such laws, preferring unhealthy and dangerous work to healthy and safe unemployment. A further aspect of labour market legislation is often neglected by economists and this concerns the arrangements by which governments recruit labour for their armed forces.

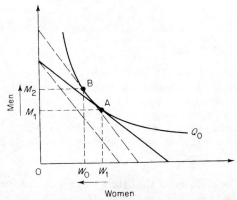

Figure 10.3 The substitution effects of equal pay. Consider a simplified production function with men and women as factor inputs. Prior to equal pay legislation, the firm is in equilibrium at A, producing output Q_0 (isoquant). The introduction of equal pay causes an inward shift in the isocost line and a change in relative factor prices. If the firm continues to produce Q_0, there will be a substitution effect, leading to a new equilibrium at B and the employment of more men. The analysis can be complicated by considering men and women as perfect substitutes or used in fixed-factor proportions.

10.7 MILITARY MANPOWER

The recruitment of manpower for a nation's defence services is an example of public sector demand for labour where the government is a monopsonist (see Chapter 15). Governments have to choose between conscription (the draft or national service) and volunteer forces, or a mix of both. Conscription appears to be an attractive solution. A government simply passes a law requiring all young people to serve in the armed forces for a minimum period. Manpower is obtained cheaply at a price dictated by the government, with corresponding budgetary savings in achieving a given size of defence force. This is illustrated in Figure 10.4 where conscripts receive a wage considerably below their supply price. Conscription has also been advocated as a solution to a nation's unemployment problem. National service replaces unemployment, 'saves' state unemployment pay, and provides beneficial training, experience, and discipline to young people. Such arguments require serious appraisal. What are the economic arguments against conscription and in favour of an all-volunteer force?

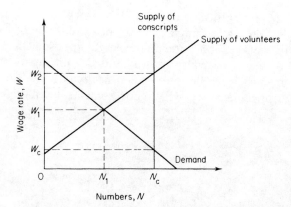

Figure 10.4 Conscription. An all-volunteer force of N_1 could be obtained at a wage rate of W_1. A conscript force of N_c could be obtained at a wage of W_c compared with W_2 if it were obtained on a voluntary basis. The difference W_2W_c shows the extent to which conscripts are underpaid, i.e. a budgetary saving of $W_2W_c \times ON_c$, although the state could choose to pay an even lower wage to the inelastic supply of conscripts.

The first point to be stressed is that the budget outlays for a conscript force are not an accurate indicator of economic efficiency in resource use. They are not a true indicator of opportunity costs in the form of the foregone alternatives or society's valuation of the alternative uses of the conscript labour. For example, a trained doctor who is highly valued by the civilian economy would have to serve as a relatively cheap conscript where his military wage would not indicate the community's valuation of his services. Since manpower is relatively cheap, military commanders are encouraged to substitute labour for capital (weapons) and adopt labour-intensive force structures. They will also have to maintain a substantial training industry determined by the requirements of conscription. Thus, conscription is inefficient as well as being involuntary servitude or coercion. Where exemptions operate, it also has potential for inequity. For instance, rich children can avoid or delay conscription by undertaking higher education and lengthy training which might qualify for exemption. The employment and training argument for conscription is similarly suspect. It is not sufficient to argue that unemployed labour has no alternative-use value and hence conscription would be costless (nothing is sacrificed). In such circumstances, *any* use of unemployed labour would be costless, including painting old people's homes, restoring derelict land, or working in a factory. Also, it must be remembered that conscription will not be restricted to the unemployed and will involve employed labour with its inevitable sacrifices. Finally, conscription is not the only nor necessarily the most efficient solution to unemployment. Other options include aggregate demand policies together with further education and training programmes as well as mobility measures. Indeed, if the argument is that conscription would provide training to unemployed youths, the economic question is whether the armed forces or civilian training industries are more efficient trainers in supplying skills which have value in *civilian* labour markets. Moreover, to use conscription as a *short-run* employment creator leads to questions about the proper objectives of defence policy. Is it concerned with protection and security, or employment creation?

Economic analysis predicts that the abolition of conscription and its replacement with an all-volunteer force will raise the relative cost of military manpower. This will encourage substitutions between capital (weapons) and labour as well as between skilled and unskilled, men and women, military personnel and civilians, and regulars and reserves. An example of the effects on manpower and weapons is shown in Figure 10.5. An all-volunteer force also allows the military to obtain a worthwhile return on their training investments. Conscription is a relatively costly method of training manpower to cope with the increasingly complex and rising skill requirements of modern weapons. The more efficient solution requires highly skilled, experienced, and hence long-service regulars, able to use effectively and to maintain modern weapons, so providing the forces with a return on their substantial and rising training investments. This means that armed services cannot ignore the relative efficiency of alternative employment contracts (e.g. length of service) as a means of obtaining a return on their human investment. Different types of contract involve individuals sacrificing the 'rights' to their labour services and a related transfer of 'claims' to an employer in exchange for agreed payment and conditions of work. Clearly, an all-volunteer force relies upon voluntary exchange rather than the slavery-type contracts associated with conscription. But all employment contracts, even conscription, involve transaction costs in the form of search, negotiation, bargaining, hiring, training, and retaining labour, as well as providing incentives and rewards, and arrangements for monitoring and policing performance. Predictably, the military favours hierarchical and fixed-term employment contracts, which seem to be an attractive method of meeting uncertainty. They are, however, incomplete contracts frequently lacking any economic incentives. For example, do military commanders have any inducements to substitute capital for labour as manpower becomes relatively more expensive? Or does the form of the employment contract and the costs of enforcing it allow and encourage individuals at all levels to be opportunistic, to hoard or distort information, and generally to pursue discretionary behaviour?

10.8   CONCLUSION

This chapter has shown how the competitive model can be used to explain labour market behaviour. The analysis was developed to include households, information costs, search, employment contracts, and internal labour markets. Explanations have been offered for differences in relative pay, unemployment, and discrimination. Policy solutions involving information provision, unemployment pay, and labour market legislation have been

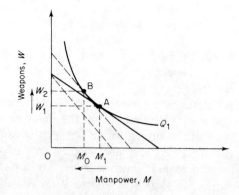

Figure 10.5 Manpower and weapons. With conscription, the least-cost combination of manpower and weapons to produce defence output Q_1 is shown at A. An all-volunteer force will raise the relative price of manpower, leading to an inward pivot of the isocost line (for a given expenditure). If defence output is to remain unchanged at Q_1, the new equilibrium will be at B, where there has been a substitution of weapons for manpower, together with increased defence expenditure.

assessed. It is not claimed that the treatment has been comprehensive. In particular, developments in human capital theory have to be considered, as well as the labour market impact of trade unions. These are the subject of the following chapters.

READING AND REFERENCES

Addison, J. T., and Siebert, W. S. (1979). *The Market for Labor: An Analytical Treatment*, Goodyear, Santa Monica, Calif.

Alchian, A. (1977). *Economic Forces at Work*, Liberty Press, Indianapolis.

Fisher, M. R. (1971). *The Economic Analysis of Labour*, Weidenfeld and Nicolson, London.

Fulop, C. (1971). *Markets for Employment*, Institute of Economic Affairs, London.

Hartley, K. (1977). *Problems of Economic Policy*, Chaps 12 and 13, Allen and Unwin, London.

Hauser, M., and Burrows, P. (1969). *The Economics of Unemployment Insurance*, Allen and Unwin, London.

Hey, J. (1979). *Uncertainty in Economics*, Martin Robertson, Oxford.

King, J. E. (Ed.) (1980). *Readings in Labour Economics*, Parts 2, 4, and 5, Oxford University Press, Oxford.

OECD (1965). *Wages and Labour Mobility*, Paris.

Oliver, J. M. (1979). *Law and Economics*, Chaps 4 to 6, Allen and Unwin, London.

Phelps-Brown, H. (1977). *The Inequality of Pay*, Oxford University Press, Oxford.

Tisdell, C. (1972). *Microeconomics*, Wiley, Sydney.

Tisdell, C. (1974). *The Economics of Markets*, Wiley, Sydney.

Worswick, G. D. N. (Ed.) (1976). *The Concept and Measurement of Involuntary Unemployment*, Allen and Unwin, London.

QUESTIONS FOR REVIEW AND DISCUSSION

1. What are labour markets for — economic or social functions?
2. Is the competitive model of the labour market capable of being tested and refuted? Explain and specify your empirical tests.
3. Why does relative pay differ? Are such differences socially desirable? What are the policy implications of your analysis?
4. What is the proper role of the state in unemployment insurance?
5. 'Labour is not a commodity.' Do you agree? Explain and identify the policy implications of your conclusion.
6. What are internal labour markets? Should they be banned?
7. Should governments provide labour market information at zero price through state-owned job agencies? Explain in relation to alternative policy options.
8. Does the search model provide a satisfactory explanation of unemployment in any market with which you are familiar?
9. Is military conscription (draft) an efficient solution to unemployment?
10. What are the implications of the theory of second best for public policy towards the labour market?

CHAPTER 11

Human Capital and Social Policy

11.1 INTRODUCTION: THE SCOPE OF HUMAN CAPITAL THEORY

The economics of human resources offers explanations of individual and group (household) behaviour over the life-cycle. It provides a common analytical framework for apparently diverse issues such as:

(1) Labour market behaviour, as reflected in job choice, training and re-training, wage determination, and age–earnings profiles, as well as job search and mobility (both domestically and internationally — brain drain), together with fringe benefits and employment contracts.
(2) Compulsory schooling and voluntary education, as well as health care and retirement.
(3) Income distribution and poverty.
(4) Family decisions, including marriage (a search process) and the choice of the number of children.
(5) Technical progress. Research and development leading to innovation involves the creation and dissemination (or the protection via patents) of the valuable information and knowledge which is initially embodied in human beings (e.g. scientists).

The common characteristic of these activities is that they involve human beings in an investment decision and the associated creation of human capital. They apply the standard economic theory of investment and capital where investment decisions are a sacrifice of present consumption in return for an expected higher income in the future. For example, individuals who continue with formal education beyond the minimum compulsory level or who undertake additional training after entering a job (e.g. apprenticeship) are effectively making an investment decision and bearing present costs in the *expectation* that they will acquire a productivity-raising investment which will improve their future income stream. Similarly, job search and mobility can be analysed as investment decisions, with individuals investing in themselves. This 'non-separability' of human capital is one of its distinguishing charac-teristics. With human capital, the property rights in the investment reside in, and cannot be separated from, the individual. As a result, problems arise in financing human investments since society usually rejects particular employment contracts (e.g. slavery) as contrary to the public interest. Policy-makers have to decide whether private markets will underinvest in human beings so resulting in 'too little' education and training and hence skill shortages, together with insufficient mobility and information.

11.2 HUMAN CAPITAL, THE LIFE-CYCLE, AND SOCIAL POLICY

The extensive nature of human resource studies is reflected in the range of potential economic and social policies. An indication of the scope of the subject and its corresponding policy implications is shown in Table 11.1 which outlines the simplified life-cycle behaviour of an individual.

Table 11.1 shows some of the human investment decisions over the life-cycle from birth through compulsory schooling to the labour market, and, ultimately, retirement. Government social and economic policies can be related to the life-cycle, and may take the form of payments-in-kind, subsidies, or cash. Thus, health policies offering 'free' or subsidized hospital care and access to doctors are available to all age groups. Income-deficiency payments provide cash for the poor, large families, the unemployed, the disabled, and the widowed. Emphasis might be placed upon special groups with payments in cash and kind for children (e.g. child cash benefits and 'free' schooling), and state pensions for the retired. Payments-in-kind can also take the form of state-provided and financed education, training and re-training courses, and information services (via state employment offices), all of which are available to actual or potential workers and are financed through the general tax system. Other policies might aim to control 'key' prices, especially so-called 'necessities' such as bread and housing, or minimum prices might be imposed as in the case of minimum wage legislation and equal pay within labour markets. Such an extensive range of policies, especially those with social objectives, requires some explanation. Why do governments have such policies and which is the most appropriate form of policy?

Does economic analysis offer any guidelines for social policy?

Government social policies often reflect distribution of income targets and the pursuit of a more desirable distribution. While Paretian welfare economies offers no criterion for the best distribution, it can identify a class of optimal or efficient distributions. It has been developed to suggest the desirability of individual decisions and the possibility that institutions to promote voluntary exchange will undertake some redistribution (Pareto-efficient redistribution). In other words, individuals can derive satisfaction from their income *and* other people's. Examples include voluntary transfers through private charities and special appeals for funds to help victims of natural disasters (e.g. flood, famine, earthquakes, explosions). Furthermore, it has been shown that under certain conditions, progressive income taxes can result in Pareto-optimal re-distribution (Hochman and Rodgers, 1969).

278

Table 11.1 The life-cycle behaviour of an individual.

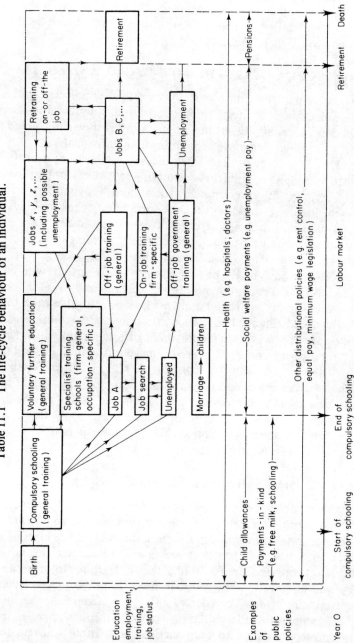

The compensation principle can also be applied to social policy. For example, technical change makes some education, information, training, and worker skills obsolete but, unlike old machinery, individuals cannot be scrapped. In this situation, society might agree that for economic growth to be worth while, the potential gainers should be able to overcompensate the potential losers. However, policy-makers have to define and identify the potential losers from a change and estimate the magnitude of their loss. The compensation principle suggests that the losers will be those who experience a reduction in utility. Unemployment from job loss due to new technology is a sufficient, but not a necessary, condition for inclusion in the losers' category; other losers who retain their jobs but experience utility losses are more difficult to identify operationally! Moreover, the compensation principle undertakes interpersonal comparisons of gains and losses in utility, using money as a measuring rod.

An alternative approach to social choice and policy has been provided by Rawls' (1973) concept of a just distribution. With this approach, individuals start from a hypothetical 'veil of ignorance' as to their initial position in society. The result is a social contract in which the primary goods of liberty, income, and other sources of self-respect in society are distributed equally, except where inequality is to the benefit of the least-advantaged individuals and groups. Thus, to treat everyone equally (equality of opportunity) requires that society should favour those with fewer native assets and those born into the less-favourable social positions. For example, resources in education might be allocated to improve the long-term prospects of the least favoured, such as the less intelligent. On the Rawls criterion, no one would gain from basic inequalities in the social system except on terms which improve the situation of the less fortunate. According to Rawls (1973, p. 347), if governments and the law '. . . keep markets competitive, resources fully employed, property and wealth widely distributed over time, and . . . maintain the appropriate social minimum, then if there is equality of opportunity underwritten by education for all, the resulting distribution will be just.' Social policy involving the state's obligation to protect individuals and groups over the life-cycle has a major role in such a society. However, the Rawlsian system requires a clear definition of the worst-off or least fortunate in society. These are unlikely to be restricted to the poor and might embrace the mentally and physically ill and handicapped. Moreover, once it is remembered that *actual* constitutions exist, problems can arise in implementing the Rawls principles, or any others. Society might be allowed to express its preferences on the acceptability of alternative social systems, assuming that they can be clearly defined. Majority voting does not always provide an unambiguous outcome, as shown in Table 11.2.

Consider a majority voting system, with three voters, confronted with three alternative social systems, say Rawls (X), the Pareto criterion (Y), and the compensation principle (Z). Table 11.2 shows that a majority prefers X to Y and Y to Z. A government might reasonably conclude that X is preferred to Z,

Table 11.2   Voting and social choices: the paradox of voting.

Voters	Rank in order of preference		
	First Choice	Second Choice	Third Choice
Mr 1	X	Y	Z
Mrs 2	Y	Z	X
Ms 3	Z	X	Y

but this would be incorrect. A majority prefers Z to X, which illustrates the difficulties of using a majority voting system to rank social choices. Of course, it might be argued that this outcome would not arise if the government's preferences were dominant or dictatorial. Further problems arise once it is recognized that social policies will be formed and implemented in the political market place. What 'rules' should be given to politicians and bureaucrats to achieve Rawls' just distribution, or any other? Take the simplest problem of a fair division: society has to divide a given cake between a set number of people. If a fair division is an equal one, the appropriate rule would be to require the person dividing the cake to take the last piece. In this case, the cake would be divided equally since this would give the cutter the largest possible share. But how is such a simple rule applied to a complex set of social institutions administered by politicians and bureaucrats who might be self-interested rather than impartial? Indeed, in the Downs model, social policies are explained by the vote-maximizing behaviour of politicians, advised by budget-conscious bureaucracies. These might be further influenced by interest groups of consumers and producers seeking preferential treatment (e.g. tax exemption for house-buyers, subsidies to regions). In the political market place, democratic governments are likely to redistribute income towards the median voter and hence towards the middle of the income distribution.

Which is the most appropriate form of policy?

Once a government has decided upon its income distribution objectives, it has to choose between alternative policy instruments to achieve its targets. The broad options include cash payments, subsidies (to products or factors), or payments-in-kind, involving private or public supply. Much depends upon the government's belief about the desirability of individual decisions and its general preference for market-improving or market-displacing policies. Right wing politicians will favour market-improving measures which allow consumers and workers opportunities for individual choice. Examples include negative income taxes, cash bounties, and education vouchers. Left wing politicians often favour public ownership and sometimes believe that individuals are not the best judges of their welfare. They will favour state schools, training centres and hospitals, free milk, rent control, and publicly owned housing. The effects of these alternative policies on consumer satisfaction and the quantities purchased are shown in Figure 11.1.

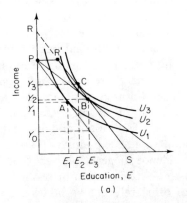
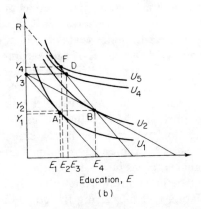

Figure 11.1 Alternative social policies. Governments might wish to increase the consumption of education. The analysis could be applied to other 'socially desirable' commodities such as health, housing, or training. The diagrams show the effects on utility and amounts purchased of cash transfers (C and F), price subsidies (B), payments-in-kind and vouchers (C and D).

Governments might regard education as a 'socially desirable' commodity and wish to increase its consumption. Prior to any policy action, the individual is initially in equilibrium at A in Figure 11.1. If the government subsidized the price of education, the consumer would move to a new equilibrium at B in Figure 11.1(a): he will be at a higher level of satisfaction or utility, namely U_2, purchasing more education, E_3, now that it is relatively cheaper. Alternatively, the state could offer the individual a lump sum cash payment equivalent to the price subsidy of Y_2Y_0. Cash payments are equivalent to income effects, and for a normal good the consumer will move to a new equilibrium at C on the budget line RS in Figure 11.1(a): utility is higher than with a price subsidy, but less education is purchased and more is spent on other goods. Or the government could offer education vouchers. The voucher is a tied gift and, if it is non-tradeable, it results in a new budget line PR'S. In Figure 11.1(a) both a voucher and cash payments give the same results, with equilibrium at C. Figure 11.1(b) shows a different case with a voucher and cash payments resulting in equilibria at D and F, respectively. Thus, if policy aims to maximize consumer satisfaction, then for a given state expenditure cash payments are preferable; but if society wishes to encourage education, price subsidies are superior.

11.3 INCOME DISTRIBUTION AND HUMAN CAPITAL THEORY

Before public policies can be formulated to improve income distribution, the causes of inequality have to be identified. Human capital theory is closely related to the study of income distribution, with earnings differentials and inequality explained by individual differences in human investments. For example, the human capital model predicts a concave age–earnings profile and simple examples are shown in Figure 11.2. These show that individuals who undertake additional years of education and/or training increase their lifetime earnings. In fact, a set of age–earnings profiles can be envisaged, reflecting the separate impact of different amounts of schooling, training, and learning, each of which can occur at various points during the life-cycle. As a result, more educated and highly skilled workers will earn more than the less educated and unskilled. Thus, human capital in the form of different amounts of education and training might explain earnings differentials and inequality. Indeed, US studies have claimed that human capital explains two-thirds of annual earnings inequality, although other evidence suggests a lower contribution, perhaps around one-third. Such estimates encounter major problems in isolating and measuring the contribution of other relevant variables such as ability, age, sex, family background, and labour market imperfections. Nor must it be assumed that formal education is the only human capital input and hence *the* explanation of inequality. Figure 11.2 shows that industrial training cannot be ignored.

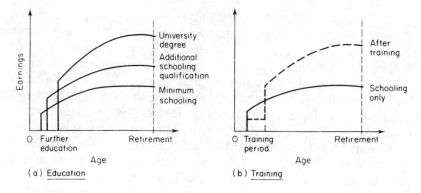

Figure 11.2 Age–earnings profiles. Diagram (a) shows that additional years of education beyond minimum schooling increases lifetime earnings. Three cases are shown: no qualifications (minimum schooling), an additional schooling qualification (e.g. certificate), and a university degree. Diagram (b) shows that individuals who undertake training after a certain number of years of schooling will receive a lower income during their apprenticeship, but a higher income with the acquisition of a skill.

Education and training: Are they different?

Education and training are concerned with human investments. Both involve the acquisition of marketable skills which raise the present value of an individual's expected earnings. Skills are acquired in a variety of institutions. Compulsory schooling provides basic skills of reading, writing, and numeracy which are marketable throughout the economy. Thereafter, individuals can acquire further skills by continuing with formal education or by undertaking industrial or occupational training. Nor is skill acquisition confined to the younger age range. It can continue over an individual's life-cycle, although training investments will decline towards retirement since there is a shorter period for obtaining a return on the requisite human investment. The training of a typist illustrates the diversity of training arrangements. Typing skills can be acquired through self-teaching, or during compulsory schooling, or by full-time attendance at a private fee-paying college, or on-the-job, or through post-employment day release, or through evening classes in a public or private institution, or through state-sponsored re-training schemes for, say, the unemployed or married women re-entering the labour market. In other words, industry and education establishments in the public and private sectors are involved in industrial training and re-training, so there is little to be gained from a refusal to recognize that these different institutions all contribute to skill acquisition.

11.4 TRAINING MARKETS: HOW ARE SKILLS OBTAINED?

Training is obtained in markets which are both varied and extensive. Training markets contain large numbers of buyers and sellers embracing a variety of courses, certificates, training methods, and institutions in both the public and private sectors of the economy. In this form, the training market is the set of institutional and organizational arrangements for the purchase and sale of marketable skills through training, re-training, and information acquisition over an individual's life-cycle.

The diversity of training supply arrangements reflects the varied demands of buyers, who consist of private individuals, firms, and governments. Individuals have different preferences for training over their life-cycle, as well as differences in their willingness to acquire skills through the use of work time or the sacrifice of leisure (consumption time). Firms also have varied demands for training, sometimes buying specialist training, including 'crash' courses from outside establishments or training workers within the plant. Governments behave in a similar way for their employees (e.g. civil service, armed forces), training them within the work-situation and sending them, for example, on day-release courses. Governments also affect training through intervention in the market for skill-acquisition (e.g. by subsidy policy) and through direct provision (state training centres).

On the supply side, the training industry consists of private commercial establishments concerned with the profitability of training and public sector non-profit enterprises. In each sector, skills are acquired either in *specialist training enterprises* or in *existing productive units*. Various training methods are used. There is training undertaken in the work-situation, through day release, evening classes, correspondence, and sandwich courses, as well as through full-time further education. These training methods can be classified as learning-by-doing ('sitting-with-Nellie'), on- and off-the-job training. For many occupations the different methods offer alternative means of acquiring the necessary skills, so that there are possibilities of substitution. The combination of training methods used in practice to acquire a particular skill will depend on the preferences of trainees, occupational requirements, and the relative costs to those providing and acquiring the training. Often, the costs of training are shared in varying proportions between trainees, firms, and the state.

In some nations, both private fee-paying and subsidized state training schools exist. Typically, public sector education and training courses are subsidized so that fees are less than costs or are made available at zero price and might also attract an earmarked grant (e.g. university students) or a weekly training allowance. In these circumstances, questions arise about the continued existence of a substantial and specialist fee-based private training industry. A plausible explanation is that the public sector is 'failing' to fully and accurately satisfy the preferences of trainees, so that the private sector continues to exist as a viable entity in response to worth while market opportunities. In other words, the private sector is responding to market opportunities which are not being satisfied by the public sector. For example, the state education and training sector might limit the entry of potential trainees through various non-price rationing schemes (examination grades as an entry requirement for universities) or through a preference for specific age groups, such as the 16–21 range. Or others might be deterred because courses are offered only on a full-time basis for a period determined by the institution when some individuals might prefer to acquire skills more quickly (crash courses) or on a part-time basis, using their leisure rather than work time and over a period chosen by the individual. And, of course, the public sector might be slow to respond to both changing skill requirements and new training methods. The result might be a viable private training industry, with fee-paying schools offering, say, language, secretarial, and computing courses as well as courses in art, music, dancing, and driving.

The time taken to acquire a skill varies according to the training methods and the occupation. Skills such as those of a waitress can be acquired in a relatively short time, usually measured in hours or a few days, whereas a craftsman might require a five-year apprenticeship beginning at 16. The training required for teachers, doctors, and lawyers is measured in years. The successful completion of some training is recognized by the award of a certificate: Ordinary and Higher National Certificates, diplomas, and university degrees. Where such certificates are treated as evidence of competence or are necessary for entry into particular labour markets, they enhance the earnings expectations of their owners. This distinguishes the markets for human and physical capital. With human capital, it is not possible to market the capital resource independently of its owner: skills can be marketed but not transferred. For this reason, certificates of skill proficiency (e.g. degrees) are different from share certificates. Certificates of skill proficiency cannot be used to pass property in the skill to others, since transfer of the certificate does not transfer possession of the skill. An explanation is required of the human investment process. For simplicity, the analysis will concentrate on industrial training but the model can be extended to embrace other human investments such as further education, labour mobility, and job search.

The costs of training: How are training costs defined?

Training as an investment involves present costs. Three sets of economic agents can be distinguished, namely individuals, firms, and the state, and each might be involved in training costs. Each will invest in training and re-training so long as it is *expected* to be worth while, and views on the expected benefits will depend upon labour market information on past, current, and future relative scarcities.

For the individual, training costs are defined as all the direct money outlays incurred in skill-acquisition, such as tuition fees, the purchase of books, materials, and equipment, and any extra maintenance costs directly attributable to training. In addition, costs include a major element which is frequently ignored, namely opportunity costs in the form of any *foregone earnings* which an individual incurs during the training process—i.e. the difference between the trainee wage and earnings in the next-best alternative occupation. Of course, firms rather than individuals might bear the costs of training and such costs would include the employment of training staff, buildings, and equipment, any 'lost' output due to training, and the extent to which a trainee's wage exceeds the individual's current marginal productivity. Alternatively, the state might bear some or all the costs of training through, for example, 'free' or subsidized provision of education and training (e.g. in universities, business schools, state skill centres). What are the likely benefits of training for these different agents?

Effectively, the returns to training investments accrue to individuals in the form of higher future income. Or, more generally, individuals benefit through the present value of the expected lifetime monetary and non-monetary gains from the sale of the acquired skill. Firms might benefit through the contribution to greater profits, and the community gains from any net social benefits such as greater output and 'education for citizenship.' However, competitive markets do not *guarantee* a skilled worker a higher income simply because he possesses a skill. The existence of pay differentials between skilled and unskilled workers depends on the relative scarcities of the different types of labour.

General and specific training: Who pays for training?

In the typist-training example given above, the costs of training are variously distributed. Individuals bear some or all of the cost (including sacrificed leisure) for 'self-teaching' and attendance at fee-paying schools and evening classes. On-the-job training costs might be borne by employers, whereas the costs of day release might be shifted to the trainee and the state, with the state bearing the costs of full-time training in government training units.

What determines the distribution of training costs between individuals, firms, and the state? Here, the distinguishing feature of human capital is relevant. Although human investments are in principle similar to investment in physical capital, there is one major difference. In non-slave societies and in the abence of slavery-type contracts, the 'capital' resulting from training and skill-acquisition remains with the individual regardless of the source of finance. *The property rights in training investments (and other human investments) are vested in the individual worker, so that human capital and workers cannot be separated.* This has major implications for the distribution of training costs between individuals and firms and requires a distinction between two limiting cases, namely general and specific training.

General training provides a set of transferable skills which have value to a large number of firms in the economy. Specific skills are non-transferable and have value to only one firm, namely the initial training enterprise. Compulsory schooling with its provision of general competence in verbal and written skills is an example of general training. Examples of *completely* specific skills are hard to come by: they might include astronauts, military missile operatives, British Rail engine drivers, Concorde pilots, and the basic induction course which most firms provide to introduce new workers to their management and organization procedures. Clearly, many skills contain a mixture of both general and specific elements. For example, secretaries have a skill which is of value to a large number of employers, but each firm is likely to have a specific 'house-style'. Similarly, specific training usually contains a general element in the form of improved written and verbal skills and mathematical competence, some of which might contribute to 'education for citizenship' (with the state willing to bear some of the costs of such 'education').

The distinction between general and specific skills explains the distribution of training costs between workers and firms. In competitive markets, the costs of general training will usually be borne by workers, even in those cases where firms *provide* such training. Consider a firm which pays for the general training of its workers. To obtain a return on such training investments, it has to pay its newly-skilled workers a wage less than their (current) marginal product. But rival firms who have not borne the costs of training will be willing to pay a market wage reflecting the productivity of the newly-trained worker. Thus, if the training firm does not pay the market wage, it will lose its newly-skilled workers to rivals, but if it pays the competitive wage it will fail to obtain a return on its training investments, which will therefore prove to be unprofitable. So, either way, the firm which pays for general training will suffer a loss.

In contrast, the costs of specific training will be borne by the firms. Such training has no value to rivals, so that the firm can pay a wage less than the marginal productivity of the newly-trained labour. Similarly, without guaranteed job security, individuals have no incentive to bear such training costs, since the skills concerned cannot be marketed elsewhere. However, since labour is free to move, firms have an incentive to pay specifically-trained workers a wage greater than their next-best alternative in order to reduce the probability of labour turnover and so ensure that the firm captures a return on its specific human investments. The implications for age–earnings profiles are shown in Figure 11.3.

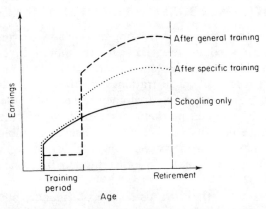

Figure 11.3   Earnings and skills. This is a simple example with only one training period and no further training investments during the life-cycle. Generally-trained workers bear the costs of training; hence their wage is below that paid to workers with schooling only. Firms also finance specific training. The profile reflects the hypothesis that, *ceteris paribus*, specific trained workers earn less after training than those more generally-skilled.

While the model is usually presented in terms of general and specific or transferable and non-transferable skills, the causal factor in the distribution of training costs is *labour mobility*. Predictably, firms attempt to protect any training investments through a variety of devices, some of which convert firm-general into firm-specific skills, so increasing a firm's willingness to finance what appears to be general training. The options available to firms include employment contracts, non-transferable company pensions, company houses, cars, sports, welfare and health facilities, subsidized meals, sick pay, holidays, and salaries — all related to length of service, as well as internal labour markets offering promotion through seniority. A local monopsony might also explain a firm's finance of general, as well as specific, training.

Slavery, the armed forces, footballers, and entertainers provide examples of efforts to establish ownership, or property rights, in individuals, so increasing a firm's willingness to invest in general training. But even slave societies find it costly to guarantee the productivity of labour inputs. Elsewhere, contracts might be limited or too costly to enforce. Football players are bought and sold for transfer fees, although movement to another industry means the loss of the club's asset. There are no transfer fees if a leading international footballer becomes a monk! Apprenticeships are probably the best-known example of the use of contractual arrangements to increase a firm's willingness to invest in general training. During training, the apprentice's productivity is likely to be less than the firm's training costs; once trained, the requirement to complete a specified period of apprenticeship enables the firm to recover its training investments by ensuring that the wage is less than the worker's productivity.

11.5 FINANCE FOR HUMAN INVESTMENTS: CAN INDIVIDUALS BORROW FOR HUMAN INVESTMENTS?

Firms will be willing to invest in training so long as it is expected to be worth while, taking into account the riskiness of human investments (labour mobility) and the costs of 'tying' labour to the training firm. Individuals will undertake a similar assessment of training, but they are likely to encounter a major restriction on the extent to which they can invest in themselves, namely the limitations of the capital market. Individuals have to incur present costs for expected future benefits but, in the absence of suitable collateral (e.g. assets, insurance policies, property) or savings, how can they obtain funds for worthwhile training investments (or other human investments, such as job search or mobility)?

The capital market is the obvious source of finance, but problems arise because the potential trainee is unable to pledge the proposed investment as collateral (it cannot be marketed independently of himself) and expected future earnings are not a sufficiently attractive prospect to potential lenders. The market for *physical* capital is different since the purchaser of a new machine or a car can pledge the asset as collateral for the loan. *Thus, the capital market could be a possible source of failure for human investments, the failure being more likely for worker-financed (general) training than for firm-financed (specific) training.* In effect, capital market imperfections mean that workers might be unable to finance worthwhile training because the courts are likely to regard long-term slavery-type contracts as involuntary servitude; hence there are restrictions on individuals pledging future earnings as security for a loan. Perhaps the legal constraints on labour contracts should be classed *not* as a capital market imperfection (the market would really be failing if it ignored such legal constraints) but rather as a legal constraint on the property and exchange rights of individuals in their own skills. The result is likely to be under-investment in human capital. An example is shown in Figure 11.4.

A given skill, S_1, can be obtained with various combinations of cost (C) and time (T) inputs. A shorter training period requires greater resources and cheaper training implies a longer time-scale. A variety of isoskill functions exist, each corresponding to different skill levels (S_1, S_2, . . ., S_n). Economic agents, namely trainees, firms or the state, have to choose the optimal combination of skills, time, and costs. The solution requires the ordering of these variables in terms of their expected market values to the investing agent. For simplicity, the analysis will concentrate on trainees, although it can be applied to any economic agent. For each skill, there will be an income or

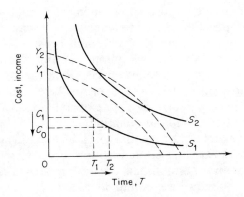

Figure 11.4 Capital markets and training. Owing to capital market imperfections, individuals might not be able to finance their optimal training expenditures. As a result, skill S_1 might continue to be optimal, but the individual will have to substitute time for cost and select a longer training period which he can afford.

returns function showing the various present values of the expected lifetime incomes from the skill at different points in time over the individual's life-cycle. With a given discount rate, it is assumed that the expected value of the skill will decline over a person's life-cycle, tending to zero with retirement or death or obsolescence of the skill. In Figure 11.4, the present value functions Y_1 and Y_2 correspond to skill levels S_1 and S_2, respectively: $Y_2 > Y_1$ and $S_2 > S_1$ where S is measured in quality units (e.g. certification). An income-maximizing trainee will aim to maximize the difference between the expected skill value and training costs ($Y - C$). In Figure 11.4, the optimal solution is to select skill S_1 with an optimal training period of T_1 at a cost of C_1. However, imperfections in the human capital market might restrict the extent to which individuals can raise funds for worthwhile training investments. If C_0 is the maximum training expenditure which an individual can finance, skill S_1 might continue to be optimal, but the individual will substitute time for cost and select a longer training period. The resort to time-intensive training methods ($T_2 > T_1$) is likely to be reflected in the use of a person's consumption time through attendance at, say, evening classes. If the capital market constraint is sufficiently great, the trainee might be obliged to select a lower level of skill, with implications for income distribution. In the circumstances, questions arise about the approximate magnitude of the underinvestment in human capital and the most appropriate policy solution from alternatives such as state-guaranteed loan or equity finance to individuals, subsidies to firms, and legislative changes to permit individuals to trade the property in themselves as voluntary contracts of slavery.

Private capital markets might attempt a partial solution to the human investment problem through the use of voluntary contracts in which individuals would obtain funds for training and in return agree to repay willing lenders from future earnings. Labour mobility is a major obstacle to such a solution since it raises the transactions costs of enforcing such contracts. Transactions costs would not disappear with a state loans scheme administered through a state manpower bank. In comparing state and private financing solutions, much depends on the costs of administration, policing, and enforcement for a voluntary contracts system. It has been argued that the state has a technical monopoly in this area since, if loan repayments were combined with income tax collection, the marginal costs of a state-operated loans scheme would be less than private solutions. Without quantitative evidence, this is by no means obvious. The state might have a potential cost advantage in administration and enforcement but, in the absence of competition, bureaucracies are unlikely to be X-efficient. Moreover, established public bureaucracies might lack the banking expertise required to assess individual loan applications, so that any scheme for a state manpower bank would require substantial 'set-up' costs, and it is unlikely to have the experience and comparative advantage of existing specialist financial institutions (e.g. banks). Also, if a substantial private market in human investment finance were to develop, specialist debt-collection agencies are likely to emerge in an effort to minimize transactions costs. Once again there are no costless solutions.

11.6 THE PREDICTIONS OF HUMAN CAPITAL THEORY: WHAT ARE ITS IMPLICATIONS FOR TRAINING POLICY?

State intervention might be required whenever training markets are not working 'properly'. Market failure can arise because of monopolies, human capital financing problems, restrictive practices, and entry barriers (e.g. apprenticeships, professions). Or externalities might lead markets to provide 'too much' of some types of training and skills and 'too little' of others. For example, there might be 'too much' on-the-job specific training and 'too little' off-the-job general training; or too few engineers and scientists and too many economists. Policy could attempt to correct the situation by subsidizing 'desirable' training methods and skills. An example is shown in Figure 11.5. Governments might believe that firms are underinvesting in off-the-job (general) training. In Figure 11.5 the firm's initial equilibrium is at A, where a combination of ON_1 on-the-job and OF_1 off-the-job training results in a given output of trained labour, Q_0. If the firm now receives a subsidy for off-the-job training, there will be a shift in the isocost line and new equilibrium at B. The movement to B comprises a substitution effect of F_1F_2 and a scale effect of F_2F_3, the net result being an expansion in off-the-job training and a larger output of trained labour.

Although private markets can fail, it has to be remembered that state solutions can also fail. Politicians are likely to be influenced by interest groups of trainers and educators who generally believe that all training is 'good' and more is 'desirable', regardless of cost. Bureaucrats might also be concerned with raising their budgets by exaggerating the demand for training and under-estimating its costs. This is most likely where specialist state agencies are established and given discretion in the formulation and operation of training policy, including the power to raise revenue by imposing taxes or levies on industry. The result could be a training policy which ignores consumer interests and which has potential for substantial inefficiency.

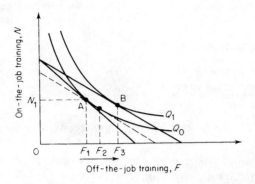

Figure 11.5 Training methods and subsidies. Each isoquant shows the varying combinations of on- and off-the-job training (substitutes) which can be used to produce given quantities of trained or skilled labour (where $Q_1 > Q_0$). The subsidy to off-the-job training results in a movement from A to B. The substitution effect F_1F_2 leads to the substitution of off-the-job for on-the-job training methods. If both training methods are normal factors, the scale effect will reinforce the substitution effect and further increase off-the-job training from F_2 to F_3.

When applied to industrial training, human capital theory provides answers to a number of policy-relevant issues:

(1) Who pays for training? The costs of specific training will be borne by firms whereas general training will be worker or state financed. Table 11.3 shows different training methods and institutions classified by their general or specific content. However, the fact that human capital is embodied in individuals who retain the relevant property rights during their lifetime (non-transferable at death, although information can be transferred) is central to an understanding of the special character of the human invest- ment market. *It is the fact that individuals are potentially mobile, rather than the general or specific content of training, which determines the distribution of training costs between individuals, firms, and the state.* In other words, the general and specific skills theorem is really a proposition about labour mobility and about the costs of establishing (voluntary) property rights in human beings: the lower the labour turnover, the greater will be a firm's willingness to pay for training and hence the more all training resembles specific training (i.e. training is treated *as if* it were specific).

(2) How can firms avoid training costs? Firms can reduce or avoid training costs through various devices:

Table 11.3 A classification of training methods. Some skills can be general to a firm but specific to an industry or an economy (e.g. linguists, lawyers), while other skills might be marketable in many nations (e.g. doctors).

General training	Specific training
Off-the-job training	Sitting-with-Nellie training
Schooling	On-the-job training within the plant
Further education	
Industrial training	
Economy-wide training	
State-owned training centres	

(a) Training costs can be shifted to workers (general training) or to major suppliers.

(b) Firms can substitute capital for labour—either at an existing technology or through a new technology.

(c) Firms can recruit skilled labour.

A firm's choice will depend partly on the relative costs of the alternatives, including any costs of transactions and search. For example, option (a) might involve bargaining, whereas (c) involves search costs which might rise, depending on the number of skilled workers demanded and the state of the labour market.

(3) Are skill shortages due to poaching? Policy-makers often believe that poaching is a major cause of skill shortages. It is claimed that firms frequently poach skilled manpower from elsewhere rather than training for themselves, so that private markets underprovide training in general skills. But this interpretation of poaching assumes, incorrectly, that all training costs are borne by firms. Human capital theory shows that general or transferable skills will tend to be worker-financed, while specific or non-transferable training will be firm-financed. If poaching applies to specific skills and the training firm offers its specific trained labour a wage rate higher than the next-best alternative, how do rivals poach? Indeed, why do they poach since specific skills have no value to rival firms? If, as policy implies, poaching refers to general skills, doubts arise about the nature and extent of any loss which *firms* experience from the 'theft' (is it labour mobility?) of skilled labour. At the same time, underinvestment in transferable skills can arise if individuals are unable to finance worthwhile training investments. But this suggests the need for a policy emphasis on the provision of finance for individual trainees!

(4) What is the effect of training on earnings and income inequality? The human capital model predicts a concave age–earnings profile, reflecting the impact of schooling, general and specific training, and learning (experience). With learning-by-doing, individuals become more efficient the more frequently they perform a task, and this applies to both general and specific skills (see Figure 6.13). Learning has a number of implications

for human capital theory. First, while training is expected to result in a higher future income, the income effects might be raised further and continuously (but at a decreasing rate) due to subsequent learning-by-experience. Where wages reflect marginal productivity (e.g. incentive payments) the income benefits of learning tend to accrue to labour: this is likely with general skills. Second, learning means that the value of skills can *appreciate* with use since each application of the skill increases a worker's *stock* of knowledge. Third, learning shows that interruptions to production (including product changes or modifications) require workers to re-learn, and this has implications for the effects of unemployment on the market value of skills. For example, training policy which aims at short-run employment creation during the training process, regardless of the subsequent market value of the skills, is likely to have perverse results and be inefficient. If a newly-skilled worker cannot obtain employment, he is likely to 'forget' quite quickly, with possible 'frustrated expectations' and adverse effects on both attitudes to work and the future value of government training schemes.

(5) What are the implications for the education and training industry? The model predicts that the demand for post-compulsory schooling and for different types and methods of industrial training and work experience will be responsive to:

(a) the direct and indirect costs of each of these activities;

(b) expected variations in the earnings differentials associated with extra amounts of schooling and training; and

(c) whether individuals can borrow for education and training investments. Most lending institutions require collateral for a loan but human investments cannot be separated from individuals. In the absence of suitable collateral, workers might not be able to finance worthwhile training investments. In other words, inequalities in the distribution of non-human wealth (collateral) will affect worker access to capital markets.

(6) What is the relationship between training and unemployment? In a downturn, firms will tend to 'lay-off' untrained or even generally-trained workers (no training costs borne by firm), while workers with specific training are less likely to be laid-off (fixed or sunk employment costs, with labour as a quasi-fixed factor). The theory of labour as a quasi-fixed factor postulates that a profit-maximizing firm's sunk employment costs will be recouped through rents, represented by the difference between marginal revenue product and the wage rate. Figure 11.6 shows that the greater a firm's sunk employment costs, the smaller the reduction in employment for a decline in product demand.

11.7 CONCLUSION:
HAS HUMAN CAPITAL THEORY BEEN SUCCESSFUL?

In recent years, there have been major criticisms of human capital theory. Much of the research and empirical work has concentrated on education

294

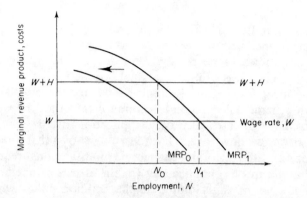

Figure 11.6 Labour as a quasi-fixed factor where W is the wage rate; H represents fixed employment costs (sunk costs) such as search, hiring, and training costs; MRP is the marginal revenue product. With sunk employment costs, the initial equilibrium is where $MRP_1 = W + H$ (= marginal labour costs, MLC); without fixed employment costs, equilibrium is where $MRP = W$ (= MLC). Consider an unexpected downturn in demand to MRP_0. Sunk costs are now irrelevant for short-run decisions; hence the firm with H costs will continue to employ N_0 ($MRP_0 = W$). But where the wage rate is the only labour cost (e.g. unskilled; generally-trained workers) the firm will reduce employment from N_1 to N_0.

(mostly in the United States), with relatively little on training. Criticisms have been made of the failure to develop a theory of occupational choice, incorporating search behaviour (role of information). Moreover, is it really valid to maintain that human investment differs from physical capital investment? For example, although machines cannot walk, they can be bought and sold (cf. labour mobility and turnover) or even stolen (cf. poaching). Nor are a machine's performance certificates 'guaranteed' independently of labour cooperation. So caution is required in attempting to distinguish human investment from other kinds of capital investment. The essential difference lies in non-separability of human capital and the consequent problems of raising finance for education, training, and other human investments.

At the policy level, some critics have concluded that education and training programmes have 'failed'. For example, it is asserted that the characteristics which economists had associated with productivity (schooling and training) appear to have had little effect on the employment prospects of large numbers of urban employees: unemployment, poverty, and income inequality are still with us. Admittedly, we need to know much more about the success or failure of education and training policies and probably some of the initial claims for these policies were overstated: some studies used inadequate control groups and considered too short a post-training period. But the major criticism of human capital theory has come from the advocates of the *screening hypothesis*.

The screening hypothesis asserts that education serves mainly as a screening, or certification device. At the time of hiring, employers are uncertain about the potential employees' productivity, so education certificates and qualifications might be used as an *initial* screening device, with individuals selected on the basis of 'trainability' (rather than existing skill levels). If so, the observed correlation between earnings and length of schooling might conceal a more fundamental correlation between schooling and the attributes that characterize 'trainability' (i.e. education certifies a worker's trainability). Thus, with the screening hypothesis, education simply provides a selection device for employers. In which case, is education the most efficient selection mechanism we can devise? The screening hypothesis implies waste in the system. For example, is a university degree required to signal to a potential employer that the holder of the degree possesses the personal characteristics to be a successful airline hostess? Part of the answer depends on whether education is state or privately financed. Subsidies make higher education worth while to students, so that labour is less available to employers at the school leaving stage. Otherwise, if education as a screening device is inefficient, the private sector might be expected to step in with superior alternatives.

Methodologically, the screening hypothesis is difficult to distinguish from the human capital model of schooling. Screening by educational qualifications means that such qualifications become worthwhile investments. Nor is it obvious whether, and how, the screening hypothesis applies to industrial training. Moreover, it is not too difficult to 'reconcile' the screening and human capital approaches by regarding education, training, and other human investments as part of the economics of information and knowledge. Education and training are concerned with buying and selling information and knowledge (skills, some of which are associated with 'performance' certificates) and with the market value of information embodied in economic agents. For public policy purposes, the relevant question is whether information markets are working 'properly'.

READING AND REFERENCES

Becker, G. S. (1964). *Human Capital*, NBER, New York.

Blaug, M. (Ed.) (1968). *The Economics of Education*, Vol. 1, Penguin, London.

Blaug, M. (1970). *An Introduction to the Economics of Education*, Allen Lane, London.

Culyer, A. J. (1980). *The Political Economy of Social Policy*, Martin Robertson, London.

Hartley, K. (1977). Training and retraining for industry, in *Fiscal Policy and Labour Supply*, Institute for Fiscal Studies, Conference Series 4, London.

Hartley, K. (1974). Industrial training and public policy, in *Economic Policies and Social Goals* (Ed. A. J. Culyer), Martin Robertson, London.

Hockman, H. M., and Rodgers, J. D. (1969). Pareto-optimal redistribution, *American Economic Review*, 59, pp. 542–57.

Lamberton, D. J. (Ed.) (1971). *Economics of Information and Knowledge*, Penguin, London (e.g. Boulding, Stigler, Arrow, Demsetz).

Maynard, A. K. M. (1975). *Experiment with Choice in Education*, Institute of Economic Affairs, Hobart Paper 64, London.

Peacock, A. T. and Wiseman, J. (1964). *Education for Democrats*, Institute of Economic Affairs, Hobart Paper 25, London.

296

Rawls, J. (1973). Distributive justice, in *Economic Justice* (Ed. E. S. Phelps), Penguin, London.

QUESTIONS FOR REVIEW AND DISCUSSION

1. 'The test of whether a resource is an economic resource or a free resource is price: economic resources command a non-zero price, but free resources do not' (Mansfield). True or false? What are the implications of your answer for social policy?
2. What are the policy implications of a life-cycle approach to individual and group behaviour?
3. Does economic analysis offer any guidelines for social policy? Give examples.
4. What is a 'just distribution'? Has it any policy relevance?
5. Which do you regard as preferable: cash payments, subsidies (specify), or payments-in-kind? Explain your choice and illustrate with examples from (a) housing, (b) unemployment, and (c) poverty.
6. Are education and training different? Who pays for (a) education and (b) training? Are the financial arrangements for education and training equitable?
7. Does the capital market 'fail' to invest in human beings?
8. Do private enterprise economies 'overinvest' in on-the-job training and provide 'too little' off-the-job training?
9. Are student grants a product of imperfections in the human capital market? Would student loans or equities be preferable?
10. Are skill shortages due to poaching?

CHAPTER 12

Trade Unions

12.1 INTRODUCTION: WHAT IS THE PROBLEM?

Unions always arouse controversy. Critics point to union bargaining power, restrictive labour practices, overmanning, closed shops, strikes, and picketing. Supporters stress their contribution to mitigating some of the less desirable aspects of free markets, such as monopsony, long hours of work, and dangerous working conditions (i.e. countervailing power). Marxists view wage levels as the outcome of a constant struggle between workers and capitalists (who are these groups?), with workers aiming to raise wages above the subsistence level and reduce the 'surplus value' accruing to capitalists. In fact, unions raise a set of micro-economic and public policy issues embracing efficiency in resource allocation and income distribution. Examples are:

(1) The effects of unions on economic and technical efficiency. The popular belief is that unions adversely affect productivity and efficiency through restrictive practices, featherbedding, 'make-work', and barriers to labour mobility. Otherwise, if unions favourably affected productivity, there would be more instances of firms supporting the unionization of their workers.
(2) Unions viewed as monopolists, with monopoly power enabling them to set wages above the competitive level. The hypothesis is that unions influence relative wages in favour of their members. This raises the empirical question of the magnitude of any wage differential compared with similar non-union labour.
(3) The sources of a union's monopoly power. Unions adopt various methods to control the supply of labour. These include:
    (a) Entry restrictions in the form of lengthy apprenticeships, licences, and professional qualifications (e.g. doctors, lawyers).
    (b) Closed shops, where only union members are employed.
    (c) Strikes, which indicate the ability of a union to withdraw labour and to prevent labour being offered at terms less than the union wage rate (i.e. to prevent undercutting or chiselling).
    (d) Lobbying governments to secure 'favourable or protective' legislation (e.g. closed shops, licences).

297

(4) The policy implications of monopoly unions and restrictive labour practices. There are at least two issues. First, whether governments should treat monopoly unions and restrictive labour practices in the same way as they deal with monopolies, mergers, and restrictive agreements in *product* markets. Or is labour in some sense 'different'? Are the differences due to labour being voters in the political market? Second, questions arise about the appropriate role of the law in relation to trade union behaviour. Emphasis is often placed on industrial relations and collective bargaining and the law relating to the enforcement of contracts, the right to strike, picketing, and closed shops. Some governments use the law as an instrument for 'improving' industrial relations through, for example, the imposition of compulsory arbitration, strike ballots, and a 'cooling-off' period before a strike. Legislation might also prevent strikes in certain 'essential' services, such as the armed forces, gas supply, and the police. Presumably, constraints on strike action will be reflected in the net advantages and disadvantages of a job and hence in relative wages. In total, the law affects the use of coercion by unions and the 'balance of power' between labour and capital in private enterprise economies.

The development of any public policy towards trade unions has to start from an understanding of their behaviour. Explanations are required of their existence and objectives. The sources of any monopoly power have to be identified and predictions are required about union behaviour in a bargaining context, including any constraints on their actions. Also, theory can offer a greater understanding of the efficiency implications of restrictive labour practices. Furthermore, these issues are relevant to anti-inflationary policy, particularly since the supporters of cost-push models completely ignore the micro-economic foundations of union behaviour.

12.2 WHY DO UNIONS EXIST?

Trade unions and professional associations (e.g. accountants, doctors, lawyers, solicitors) consists of groups of individual workers which can be compared with cartels in product markets. They can be viewed from a variety of perspectives, namely as clubs, information agencies, hedging devices, or organizations aiming to raise labour's share in the national product. It might be thought that individuals join a group or club because they expect membership to be worth while. In return for a membership fee, the union as a club offers a set of 'products', from information and legal services to collective agreements on wages and conditions of employment. But many of the club's products are collective goods, available to all workers, regardless of union membership. In that case, individuals have every incentive not to join a union, thereby 'free-riding' (see Chapter 3).

Public goods and free-riding: the case for coercion

Olson (1965) has argued that insofar as unions obtain any benefits, these are usually public goods. Any higher wages and improved conditions of employment negotiated by a union or professional body are available to everyone, including non-members. If so, self-interested individuals will not willingly and voluntarily contribute to the costs of a union since they will receive the benefits regardless of membership! Olson claims that large modern unions avoid collapse and remain in existence, mainly through compulsion and coercion. This takes such forms as closed shops or compulsory membership as a condition of employment, together with private courts, picketing, violence, blacking, and 'sending people to Coventry'. In addition, unions offer private benefits to members including insurance and welfare benefits, legal aid, assistance with job search, job protection, negotiation of seniority rights, grievance procedures, and redundancy pay. For an individual, the relevant questions are the valuations which are placed on these private benefits and whether they could be obtained more efficiently in other ways. Nevertheless, Olson believes that compulsory membership and coercion are the major explanation for the continued existence of large unions.

The fact that unions provide collective benefits has sometimes been used to justify the closed shop as an acceptable form of coercion in a market economy. Like a firm, a union can be regarded as an organization for reducing transactions costs in situations where there are benefits to be obtained from exchange involving large numbers—i.e. where the potential gains to exchange can be captured only with the agreement of a large number of workers. In these circumstances, union leaders claim that 'those who benefit should pay' and that coercion is required to obtain the available collective benefits and prevent 'free-riding'. This is not a completely convincing economic argument for the closed shop. There seems to be no technical or economic reason why unions could not negotiate employment contracts on behalf of their members, leaving others to reach individual bargains with their employers. In other words, exclusion is possible, but it would involve different transactions costs. Also, if a union failed to attract sufficient members, there would be an adverse effects on its monopoly power and hence its ability to obtain any collective benefits. Nor is it sufficient to claim that closed shops are justified because they are a legal requirement: the law can always be changed! However, legal support for the closed shop might be explained by the economics of politics. Vote-sensitive governments are likely to be influenced by unions combining to form a major interest group. Such groups will also oppose changes in legislation which would adversely affect their market power. Opposition might take the form of national strikes, increased militancy in wage negotiations, withdrawal from government agencies, demonstrations, and the lobbying of politicians, together with newspaper and television advertisements presenting the union case. A classic example was the trade union opposition to the UK Conservative Government's 1971 Industrial Relations Act.

Unions: information and hedging

The analysis of unions as clubs is not unrelated to the view that they act as information agencies and hedging devices. Both information and hedging might be some of the goods provided by the club. As information agencies, unions can supply data to their members on the terms of trade in the labour market. Obviously, members will be interested in relative wage rates and the non-monetary aspects of various jobs, including the performance of rival unions. A union can also act as the workers' auditor of management, conveying information to employers about production methods and labour productivity, as well as monitoring and enforcing employment contracts. As information agencies, unions might have a market-improving function. Private competitive markets are likely to underprovide information, due to its public good aspects and the costs (difficulties) of establishing property rights in the commodity. Unions might correct some of this market failure by supplying additional information to club members. This aspect of behaviour has been further developed, with the suggestion that a union is a forum through which estimates of expected wage and price inflation are formulated and assessed. In this way, members can express their beliefs and expectations about future events, the result being a group judgement (cf. futures markets). Moreover, as agencies for formulating inflationary expectations, it has been suggested that unions and collective bargains are a technique for promoting monetary equilibrium under inflationary conditions.

Information and expectations are also related to uncertainty. In this context, a union can be regarded as a hedging device through which workers can respond to uncertainty. Given that no one can accurately predict the future, workers can respond in various ways. They can acquire a general skill or move to an area of excess labour demand. Or they can attempt to establish and protect the property rights in their job by joining a union. Nevertheless, information and hedging are not the generally accepted reasons for the existence of unions. Traditional explanations stressed the contribution of unions to raising wages. Once again, these are one of the collective goods available to club members.

Unions: wages and labour's share

The standard view is that unions aim to raise labour's share in the national product and to achieve this at the expense of profits. This argument involves three stands. First, has labour's share increased? Second, do unions explain any increased share? Third, has any increased labour share been at the expense of profits? There are, of course, limits on the extent to which unions might successfully 'squeeze' profits in a capitalist economy. Firms can respond to higher wages by substituting capital for labour or raising product prices and, ultimately, capital requires a minimum return to induce it to remain in an activity. Neo-classical theory explains factor shares in terms of quantities employed and their relative prices or marginal productivities. In competitive markets, an increase in the relative price of labour will lead to its substitution by a relatively cheaper factor. Labour's share will depend upon the responsiveness of employment to the increase in relative wages, as determined by the elasticity of substitution (σ). If this elasticity is less than unity, factor substitution will be difficult and, following a rise in wage rates, labour's share will increase. The general relationship between wage rates, labour income, and total product is shown in Figure 12.1.

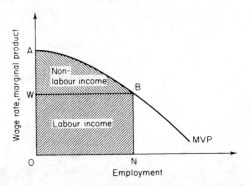

Figure 12.1   Labour's share. In a perfectly competitive economy in long-run equilibrium, wages will equal the value of the aggregate marginal physical product (MVP). The total value of output produced is the area OABN. Labour's income is OWBN and the income accruing to other factors is WAB (i.e. profit and other property incomes). Labour's share of the total product is OWBN/OABN. Readers are left to examine the short- and long-run effects on labour's share of an increase in wage rates with different slopes of the MVP curve.

Traditionally, economists were impressed by the apparent historical constancy of the share of *wages* in national income. An explanation was provided by the Cobb-Douglas production function (1928):

$$Q = AK^\alpha L^\beta$$

where Q is output, A refers to the state of technical knowledge, K measures the stock of physical capital, L is labour input, while α and β are constants representing the shares of capital and labour, respectively.

In this model, the elasticity of substitution is unity, which implies constant factor shares. In addition, with constant returns to scale, the sum of the marginal products exactly equals the total product (i.e. the 'adding-up' problem is solved). Such a result is compatible with a perfectly competitive equilibrium so long as firms are operating at the minimum point of a U-shaped long-run average cost curve. Using this approach, labour's share was estimated at between 60 and 75 per cent. of national income and this seemed to 'fit the facts' in a number of countries, such as Australia, the United

302

Kingdom and the United States. If, as the model suggests, the shares of labour and capital are constant, it implies that trade unions are unable to influence labour's aggregate share. However, the Cobb-Douglas production function has been subject to both analytical and empirical criticisms. Doubts have been expressed about the concept of the aggregate production function for the whole economy and generalizations based on empirical results from manufacturing. There are difficulties of measuring and valuing the total stock of physical capital. Critics point to the limiting assumptions of a perfectly competitive equilibrium, constant returns to scale, and a unit elasticity of substitution. Further problems arise in measuring technical progress and adjusting for *human* capital inputs. In addition, since the mid-1960s, new evidence has emerged. This shows that in most Western nations labour's share of the national product has actually been increasing for some time. Such estimates include both wages and *salaries* in determining the share of pay. Also, the rising share occurs regardless of whether or not the imputed earnings of the self-employed are included in the definition of labour's share. Evidence for the United Kingdom is shown in Table 12.1. It can be seen that over the long-run, labour's share in the United Kingdom has risen from 47 per cent. for 1910–1914 (it was 45 per cent. in the 1860s) to some 70 per cent. in the 1970s. Simple arithmetic shows that for any nation a rising labour share must be accompanied by a fall in the share accruing to other non-labour groups (i.e. property income). However, this does not necessarily mean that labour's rising share has been achieved at the expense of the corporate *profits* component of national income. Other non-labour groups could have experienced a decline (e.g. the self-employed and rent). This might be acceptable to trade unionists, especially if their objective is more widely interpreted as raising labour's share at the expense of property incomes in general. But do unions explain labour's rising share?

Why has labour's share increased?

Various explanations have been offered for labour's rising share, with unions forming only one of a number of explanatory variables. Part of the increase could reflect measurement biases. Structural changes in an economy might involve a shift towards labour-intensive sectors such as services and government, with the latter appearing to be especially labour intensive due to the difficulties of valuing government capital assets (e.g. roads, military bases, and weapons). Studies show that, even after adjusting for these measurement problems, labour's share has increased substantially. Alternative theories of distribution have also emerged to explain the facts: these include a production function approach, macro-economic theories, monopoly firms, and bargaining models.

A generalized production function approach to factor shares concentrates on the roles of technical progress, relative factor prices, and the elasticity of substitution. Over the long-run, technical progress has been substantial,

Table 12.1   Labour's share, United Kingdom.

Years	Labour (wages and salaries)	Income from self-employment	Rent	Corporate profits	Net property income from abroad
	Income shares as percentage of GNP				
1910–14	47.3	16.2	11.0	17.1	8.4
1921–24	58.5	17.2	6.8	13.0	4.5
1925–29	58.1	16.1	7.5	12.5	5.8
1935–38	58.9	13.2	8.8	15.0	4.1
1946–49	65.3	12.3	4.0	16.8	1.7
1955–59	67.0	9.2	4.5	18.0	1.3
1964–68	67.6	8.0	6.4	16.8	1.2
1976	71.3	9.3	7.0	15.4	1.1

Source: Burkitt and Bowers (1979, p. 61). Reproduced by permission of Macmillan, London and Basingstoke.

Notes:
(a) Due to the residual error of national income accounting, the 1976 data sum to more than 100.
(b) Some of the years were selected to show the possible impact of major wars.

causing major shifts in production functions and affecting both physical and human capital. Technical progress in the capital goods industries could have contributed to a fall in the relative price of new capital goods. Also, it is possible that past innovation has depleted the opportunities for *further* labour-saving, relative to capital-saving, technical progress. If so, the resulting capital-saving innovation will lead to a smaller proportion of capital in the input mix and a corresponding rise in labour's share. At the same time, the rising share for labour has been accompanied by an observed increase in real wages and an associated fall in the relative price of capital. This suggests an elasticity of substitution of less than unity. Unions *might* have entered this process through any possible effects in raising relative wage rates and, also, through restricting the possibilities for factor substitution. Alternatively, some of the increase in labour's share might reflect greater inputs of human capital.

Some critics of the production function approach have formulated a macro-economic model of distribution (e.g. Kaldor, 1955–56). Such models show the contribution of aggregate demand and the different savings propensities of capitalists and workers. It is assumed that the propensity to save out of profits is greater than the savings propensity of wage-earners. In this model, total savings out of a given income form the adjustment mechanism. If planned investment exceeds intended savings, then the required increase in total savings will be achieved by raising profits relative to pay. For example, firms will eventually respond to excess aggregate demand with higher prices and profit margins, so increasing the profits share in national income and hence raising actual savings to the required level. Trade unions appear to have no direct influence in this macro-economic model of distribution. Moreover, the model might be more appropriate as an explanation of cyclical, rather than long-run, variations in income distribution. Its lack of any micro-economic basis is a further cause for concern.

Other models of distribution are micro-economic and stress the contribution of monopoly firms and bargaining power. With profit-maximizing monopoly firms, it has been hypothesized that the share of pay will vary inversely with the degree of monopoly power (Kalecki, 1954). Monopoly firms can set prices to earn abnormal profits, so that the share of profits is likely to be higher as the amount of competition in an industry declines. After reviewing the international evidence, one economist concluded that 'the general drop in the share of profits between 1914 and the 1920s does not seem to have been accompanied by the heightened competition to which monopolistic pricing theory would attribute it' (Phelps-Brown, 1968, p. 28). Once again, this model has no direct role for unions. In contrast, bargaining theories of distribution recognize that both parties to a wage bargain have the ability to dictate the terms of exchange. Unions have, of course, attempted to acquire bargaining power through becoming monopoly suppliers of labour. Superficially, the international evidence seems impressive, with the long-run historical growth of unions and of militancy which seems to have coincided with labour's rising share. But correlation must not be confused with causation. Indeed, the reverse causation is plausible with higher wage rates resulting in increased union membership. And satisfactory tests of the *quantitative* effects of unions on labour's share require the specification of a model which incorporates other relevant explanatory variables. Some of these other influences have been outlined above, such as technical progress and relative factor prices. Additional explanatory variables might include the effects of major wars (see Table 12.1), international competition, and extensions in the role of the state, particularly in the adoption of full-employment policies. In total, the available evidence on the effects of unions ranges from zero to some impact on distributive shares. A sample of verdicts is:

(1) 'No union influence on labour's share can be detected' (Rees, 1973, p. 220).
(2) For five major nations and over the long-run, 'rises in pay have not squeezed profits' (Phelps-Brown, 1968, p. 17).
(3) 'The increase in the labour share could equally have been due to inflation, to state intervention or to increased trade union pressure' (King, 1972, p. 54).
(4) 'From the complex of influences affecting income distribution union activity does not appear to have been decisive, though it was significant in the UK under certain conditions at certain times' (Burkitt and Bowers, 1979, p. 72).

Finally, in assessing the evidence, a distinction might be made between the long- and short-run impact of unions on factor shares. For example, in the United Kingdom there was a substantial fall in the share of profits of manufacturing companies from 21 per cent. of output in 1968 to under 4 per cent. in 1976. Some economists (Bacon and Eltis, 1979) have explained this in terms of workers resisting further cuts in personal consumption. It is argued that between 1961 and 1969, market sector workers financed the growth of the non-market sector (e.g. public sector; see Chapter 15) from their personal consumption. By 1969, workers' consumption was squeezable no more and they responded to extra taxes by successfully squeezing the share of profits. Apparently, this was achieved through negotiating prices and incomes policies with governments which were unfavourable to profits; through the introduction of new legislation which reinforced property rights (e.g. employment protection); and through strengthening the influence of the militants in the trade union movement. The possibility that unions influence governments through their effects on labour market legislation and prices and incomes policies can also be related to the economics of politics. Tentative hypotheses have been developed suggesting that, *ceteris paribus* money wage rates grow faster under left-wing governments.

In addition to the possible contribution of unions to increasing labour's share, there is a further possibility. Unions might have obtained higher wages at the expense of unorganized labour, as well as at the expense of consumers and those who lose their jobs.

Unions: relative wages and unorganized labour

Monopoly unions might be expected to raise the wages of their members but such increases might be at the expense of unorganized labour, so resulting in a redistribution between different labour groups. The predicted effects of a union on relative wages and the allocation of labour are shown in Figure 12.2. If wages rise in the union sector, employment falls and the labour released causes wages to fall in the unorganized industries. Once unions have fully exploited their monopoly power, the wage differential is likely to be a once-and-for-all effect. The resulting misallocation of labour and welfare losses as represented by lost output are shown by the shaded area in Figure 12.2.

Evidence from UK and US studies confirm the existence of a union–non-union differential, but there are disagreements about the precise magnitude. A set of British studies gave a median wage differential in the region of 25 per cent., although estimates ranged from zero to almost 50 per cent. Similarly, a sample of American studies gave a median differential of 15 per cent., with a range from 0 to 5 per cent. to as high as 55 to 70 per cent. Estimation difficulties abound. The direction of causation might be from higher wages to greater unionization, rather than the opposite. Similarly, variables other than trade unions can result in higher wage rates. Examples include differences in labour quality (e.g. skills, motivation, males–females) and in the non-monetary aspects of different jobs, as well as any increased demand for labour. Failure

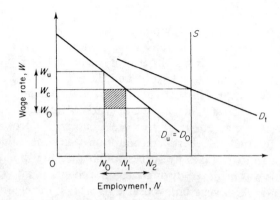

Figure 12.2 Union wage differentials. Consider an economy with a fixed supply of homogeneous labour, S. The demand curves for the union and unorganized sectors are identical and represented by $D_u = D_0$ (union and unorganized, respectively), giving a total demand curve of D_t. Initially, there is a competitive equilibrium with wage rate W_c, each sector employing N_1. Assume a union is formed which raises wages to W_u; employment in the union sector falls to N_0. If labour markets clear, supply in the unorganized sector will increase and wages will fall to W_0; employment in this sector rises to N_2. In this simplified model, the area under each demand curve up to the employment level represents the total product of each sector and the reduction in total output is shown by the shaded area, i.e. about one-half of the wage differential multiplied by the employment change.

to incorporate these other influences in empirical work might lead to 'overestimates' of the wage effects of trade unions. More fundamental problems concern the 'counter-factual': what would happen to wage rates in the absence of unions? Without unions, pay would differ from the income accruing to unorganized labour simple because unions affect non-union wages by spillover effects (see Figure 12.2). Thus, while the evidence suggests that wage rates are higher where the labour force is covered by a collective bargain compared with a completely 'uncovered' industry, some caution is required before accepting the precise quantitative estimates. A further qualification is required. Much of the above analysis of the existence of unions assumed implicitly that they aim to raise wages. Is this a satisfactory specification of their objectives? If not, what are they trying to maximize?

12.3 THE OBJECTIVES OF UNIONS AND PROFESSIONAL ASSOCIATIONS

As with firms, various objective functions are plausible. Unions might be trying to maximize wage rates, or employment or membership (i.e. growth and size of union), or the wage bill. Or they might be maximizing a general utility function containing both monetary and non-monetary aspects of employment. Such a generalized preference function might consist of wages, jobs, hours of work, fringe benefits, together with hiring, firing, training, and promotion procedures, as well as agreements on working practices and discipline. Alternatively, unions might be satisficers, aiming at target levels of wage rates, membership, and union funds. Some of these objectives are not easy to interpret. For example, it is sometimes suggested that unions act like profit-maximizing monopoly firms. An example is shown in Figure 12.3 where, acting like a profit-maximizing firm, the union raises wage rates above the competitive level. But what is the meaning of the shaded area in Figure 12.3? The surplus could be distributed to the union, or to its members, or shared between both parties. It could be appropriated by the union in the form of membership fees, so that the union acquires funds, or it might be distributed as windfall gains to members.

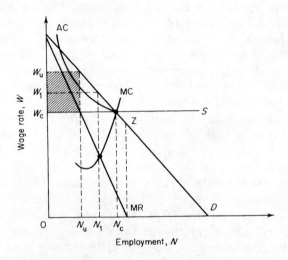

Figure 12.3 A profit-maximizing union. Initially, the market is competitive, with W_c and N_c representing the equilibrium wage rate and employment. Assume that labour is unionized (costlessly) so that S now represents the supply curve of union labour to one firm. The marginal revenue curve (MR) shows the effect on the total wage bill of variations in wage rates. Acting like a profit-maximizing monopolist, the union would equate MR and the supply price of labour (= marginal labour cost), setting the wage at W_u. But if monopolization involves costs, the appropriate average and marginal cost curves for a monopoly union might be AC and MC. If so, the new equilibrium combination is W_1N_1. In contrast, point Z maximizes the wage bill.

Similar analysis is required of alternative objective functions. A desire to maximize the wage bill would involve setting employment where marginal revenue is zero, corresponding to point Z in Figure 12.3. Whether the resulting wage rate is above or below the competitive level will depend on the elasticity of labour demand at the competitive position. Clearly, if this objective involves setting a wage below the competitive non-union level, the union is unlikely to survive! Difficulties also arise where a union adopts a simple objective such as maximizing wage rates. With this objective, the logical implication is to continue raising wage rates until the union has only one member. Such behaviour would be costly to police, since the union would have to prevent increasing numbers of unemployed members from 'undercutting'. Nor is it clear how, with falling employment, the union would retain its monopoly power. Indeed, once voting, political, and bureaucratic elements are incorporated into the analysis, it is unlikely that such a simple objective would be pursued.

The internal organization of unions

Trade unions usually consist of elected officials operating in a political market place determined by the union's constitution. The voting arrangements, together with the period of tenure and the employment contract for union leaders, will influence their motivation and behaviour. For example, where skilled and unskilled workers are members of the same union but the latter form the majority, then the median voter model predicts that union policy will favour the unskilled. However, where union officials are elected for life, they have greater opportunities for discretionary behaviour and the pursuit of 'goods' which enter more directly into their utility functions. Examples might include salary, luxury offices, expense accounts, union cars, secretarial staff, on-the-job leisure, and the prestige from negotiating with governments (e.g. political honours). Even in this situation, there are constraints on the independent, discretionary behaviour of union officials. Members can express their preferences through lobbying or forming opposition groups within the union, or they can resort to unofficial action (e.g. unofficial strikes). As a result, a utility function might emerge (how? whose?) reflecting a concern with, say, employment as well as wage rates; an example is shown in Figure 12.4. But simple propositions about unions raising wage rates require an examination of the sources of their monopoly power.

12.4   UNIONS AS MONOPOLIES

Theory would define a monopoly union as a single seller of labour with no close subsitutes (see Figure 12.3). Since these are the characteristics which define a monopoly union, it has to be presumed that they can be readily identified and observed in actual labour markets. Consider the definition in more detail, beginning with the concept of a single seller. Are single sellers prevalent in actual labour markets?

Once it is recognized that there is a multiplicity of union types, the concept of a single seller is by no means straightforward. Nor is the identification of the relevant labour market. For example, in the United Kingdom there are few industrial unions which are the sole suppliers of labour to one industry. Elsewhere, there are professional associations and craft unions which attempt to regulate the supply of certain categories of skilled labour; there are white

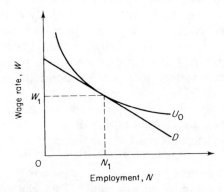

Figure 12.4 A utility-maximizing union. A union is faced with a downward-sloping labour demand function, D. Higher wage rates result in lower employment. If it has a utility function, $U = U(W,N)$, its utility-maximizing combination will be W_1N_1.

collar unions; and there are general unions which recruit all workers, particularly semi-skilled and unskilled. But the general union tends to resemble a conglomerate firm which is large in absolute or aggregate terms. If this is the case, there are worries about using *aggregate* unionization as an indicator of monopoly power in an *individual* labour market.

Questions also arise about the process through which any monopoly union emerges. After all, if individual workers have different preferences, there would appear to be opportunities for a competitive number of unions in a market. Paretians might regard large numbers and diversity as 'socially desirable', but from the viewpoint of an individual union, competition and competitive wages are unattractive! They are likely to respond with inter-union agreements to avoid competition (e.g. no poaching agreements). Mergers between unions are a further possibility and will occur so long as each party regards a merger as worth while and mutually beneficial. Such developments might even be supported by governments. Politicians and bureaucrats might believe that a merger movement will reduce transactions costs or the costs of 'doing business' with the unions (e.g. negotiations on industrial relations legislation, the welfare state, and prices and incomes policies). A reduction in the number of recognized bargainers might also contribute to the desire for a 'quiet life and on-the-job leisure' by governing politicians and bureaucrats.

Monopoly power also depends upon the possibilities of substitution which face unions. Here, there are extensive possibilities, all of which create problems for unions seeking to establish and maintain their monopoly position:

(1) Non-union labour might be substituted for union labour.
(2) Capital can be substituted for labour.
(3) Technical progress can result in labour-saving innovations as well as

extending the possibilities for replacing skilled with unskilled labour. An emphasis on de-skilling might result in the extinction of a single-skill craft union whose skills become obsolescent. Examples include locomotive firemen and Glenn Miller-type dance bands whose music is replaced by that provided by pop groups with electronic aids.

(4) Firms can substitute foreign locations for domestic locations (e.g. direct investment overseas).

(5) Consumers can buy close substitute products, either from domestic or foreign sources of supply. As a result, there is a higher probability that unionized firms will become bankrupt in the short- or long-run.

To maintain their monopoly power, trade unions and professional associations respond to these substitution possibilities. They can introduce restrictions on factor substitution. Examples include the use of firemen on diesel locomotives, minimum manning requirements on new machinery (e.g. for 'safety'), a minimum period of training, apprenticeships, requirements for nationality, certification, and professional qualifications, as well as the introduction of a closed shop. In other words, to maintain its monopoly, a union can try to raise the costs to the firm of factor substitution (i.e. it can try to make it relatively costly to replace union labour). In addition, unions can support tariff protection and import controls, restrictions on overseas investment, state subsidies for domestic industries, together with public ownership. Furthermore, the union movement as a *whole* can form a major interest group to influence vote-sensitive governments. For example, as a collective body, the union movement can lobby for legislation which establishes and protects a worker's property rights in his job (e.g. legislation on closed shops, employment protection, and redundancy pay). Unions can also support the extension of the public sector. After all, public sector output is often difficult to measure (e.g. health, safety, defence) and activities are not subject to competition from rival firms. Bureaucrats and managers of state industries do not have any income incentives to resist union demands. And the costs of public sector wage increases can always be distributed among large numbers of taxpayers, where specific labour outlays form only a small component of public expenditure (see Chapters 3 and 15). Given that unions have monopoly power, how are they likely to behave in a bargaining situation?

12.5 UNION BARGAINING AND CONSTRAINTS

Typically, unions bargain in a bilateral monopoly situation where a firm as a sole buyer faces a union as a single seller of labour services. Often, bargains occur at the national level and embrace employer and union representatives. Economic models of wage bargaining under bilateral monopoly usually give indeterminate outcomes (see Chapter 2 on the Edgeworth box and Chapter 9 on game theory). An example is shown in Figure 12.5, where the union wage demand exceeds the employer's offer. The result is collective bargaining, with the outcome depending on such factors as bargaining skill, learning-by-experience, bluff, game strategy, and the expected costs and benefits of strikes and lockouts. As a result, wages appear to be determined by bargaining factors rather than market forces.

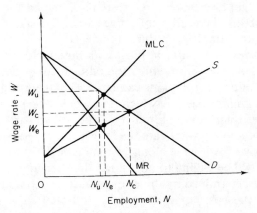

Figure 12.5 A bargaining model. Labour demand and supply curves are represented by D and S, respectively, and the competitive equilibrium is W_cN_c. A profit-maximizing union will equate marginal revenue (MR) and marginal cost as represented by the union's labour supply curve, S; it will aim to sell N_u at W_u. If the employer's group is a monopsony it will equate marginal labour cost (MLC) with marginal revenue product, requiring N_e labour at a wage rate of W_e. Thus, the union wants W_u and the employer's offer is W_e.

Strikes

In a bilateral monopoly bargaining situation, each party has to assess the expected costs and benefits of agreeing or disagreeing. Strikes and the threat of strikes are the major elements in a union's bargaining power. In principle, a union will strike if it is expected to be worth while, i.e. if the present value of the expected gain over the contract period exceeds the expected costs. Gains will take the form of a higher wage rate or the monetary equivalent of improved job conditions, while the costs will consist of the income losses associated with a stoppage. Some of these income losses might be reduced if strikers or their relatives can obtain state welfare payments, or support from union funds, or if other members of the household (e.g. wives) enter the job market. Strikes are, of course, designed to impose costs on employers through lost profits, liquidity problems, and a loss of consumer goodwill.

When bargaining, both unions and employers have to guess the other's aims, valuations, and sticking points (i.e. their preference functions). Although information emerges during the bargaining process, some of the signals and messages can be deliberately distorted as each party struggles for an advantage. Threats of strikes and lockouts are obvious tactics. However, it

312

is significant that in the real world collective agreements predominate. In other words, *determinate* outcomes are typical. In such circumstances, some economic models suggest that strikes are *mistakes*. Strikes can occur through accidents and miscalculations, where one or other party is overoptimistic and incorrectly assesses the other's preference function and sticking points. Some strike activity might also be required to remind management of the effectiveness of union threats. Typically, collective bargaining starts with a union claim which exceeds the employer's initial offer (see Figure 12.5). Collective bargaining involves each party adjusting its initial bid until an agreement is reached. Consider a model in which the adjustment process depends on the expected length of a strike. Unions can be viewed as having a resistance curve showing the minimum wage rate which they would accept rather than undergo a strike of a given duration. This curve slopes downwards, indicating that a union will accept a lower wage rate the longer the expected length of a strike. Similarly, employers will have a concession curve reflecting the highest wage rate which they will be willing to pay rather than accept a strike. The shape of the curve will be determined by the costs of agreeing to a union wage demand compared with the costs of resistance as reflected in a strike. The firm's concession curve slopes upwards, showing that the employer will be willing to pay higher wages in order to prevent increasingly lengthy strikes. An example is presented in Figure 12.6. Interestingly, using simplifying assumptions, one economic model (Hieser, 1970) has estimated that a determinate outcome of the bargaining process will be achieved at a wage rate corresponding to an elasticity of labour demand of minus 5/3!

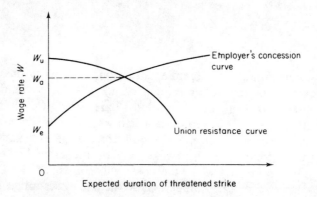

Figure 12.6 Bargaining and strikes. The Hicks model is based on union resistance and employer concession curves dependent upon the expected length of a strike. The employer's initial offer is W_e and the union's first claim is W_u (see Figure 12.5). Skillful bargaining results in a wage W_a, which is greater than the employer's initial offer but less than the union's first claim.

Empirical work on strikes has to start with an appropriate definition of strike activity. Possible measures include the number of stoppages, the number of workers involved, or the number of working days lost, each within the year, with appropriate adjustments for total employment (e.g. number of stoppages a year per 100,000 workers employed). Much of the resulting empirical work is ad hoc. Equations are estimated containing a variety of plausible economic explanatory variables, such as unemployment, profits, and plant size, together with money and real wages as well as inflation rates. Some of the results suggest that unemployment has a negative effect and increasing plant size a positive impact on strike records. But strikes are not the only option for unions. They can 'work to rule', ban overtime, 'go slow', and resist new working procedures. Such behaviour has implications for public policy towards strikes. Where strikes are made less attractive, unions can respond by substituting other forms of action and behaviour. Such responses are also likely where employers attempt to protect themselves through the creation of private strike insurance schemes.

The employment effects of union wage increases

Are there any limits on the ability of monopoly unions to raise wage rates? Labour demand curves are a major constraint since higher wage rates for some members will be achieved at the expense of lost jobs for others. The magnitude of any adverse employment effects resulting from a higher wage will depend upon the elasticity of demand for union labour. As originally developed by Marshall (1890), this elasticity is determined by four conditions:

(1) the elasticity of demand for the product (i.e. the good being produced),
(2) the importance of union labour in production costs,
(3) the ease of substituting other factors of production, including non-union labour, for union workers (i.e. the elasticity of substitution), and
(4) the elasticity of supply of the cooperating factors of production.

In general, the greater is each of these four conditions, the larger will be the elasticity of demand for union labour. As a result, the greater will be the adverse employment effect of a union wage increase. It follows that union power to raise wage rates *without major job losses* requires an inelastic product demand plus labour forming a relatively small part of total production costs, together with difficulties in substituting other factors for union labour and an inelastic supply of cooperating factors. Such conditions are also likely to explain the growth of unions, since they indicate the potential benefits from collective action (but the costs of organizing should not be neglected). Airline pilots, doctors, lawyers, teachers, and maintenance workers in capital-intensive industries are examples of groups where conditions are potentially favourable to union power. In the case of certain essential public services, where demand is inelastic, the state might constrain union power through 'no strike' legislation. Examples might include the armed forces in wartime, police, and gas workers. Elsewhere, unions can attempt to create these favourable conditions. For instance, in an oil crisis, miners in a state-owned coal industry can increase their bargaining power in a strike through picketing and so prevent supplies reaching coal-fired electricity generating stations. Also, they can obtain the support of dockers in 'blacking' coal imports. In this way, a miner's union can impose substantial costs not only on coal consumers but also on the rest of the community (e.g. via disruption of national electricity supplies to firms and households). However, such action might only result in short-run gains. Nuclear power might eventually replace coal as a source of electricity (see Chapter 13). Governments can also respond through stockpiling coal at electricity stations and changing the law on picketing.

Where the elasticity conditions favour a union or professional association the resulting wage increase will represent a *windfall gain* for those who retain their jobs. But the higher wage rate will attract other workers and new entrants to the labour force. Entry restrictions will exist. As a result, queues will develop of workers willing to pay the costs of entry, whether in money or time. Bribes and lobbying costs might be required to secure preferential treatment in the market. Eventually, the costs of entry will be 'bid up' until the successful entrant secures no higher return than could be obtained elsewhere. In other words, the higher income in the union-restricted occupation is required to compensate for the entry costs. This does, of course, add a further qualification to the interpretation of the observed wage differential between union and non-union labour. It also means that once a person is successful in entering the restricted occupation, he will support the union and its existing practices for life: otherwise he will earn less than normal profits on his investment in securing entry (see Chapter 11).

Are there any exceptions to the adverse employment effects of a union wage increase?

In addition to the conditions outlined above, there are three further cases where higher union wages do not necessarily result in job losses. These are associated with imperfect markets and embrace the 'shock effect', monopsony, and oligopoly (see Chapter 10 on minimum wage laws).

The shock effect depends upon the existence of organizational slack or X-inefficiency in firms. Inefficiency is likely to arise in imperfect markets where there are no competitive or environmental influences forcing firms to minimize costs. In this situation, it is argued that a union wage increase might *shock* the firm into greater efficiency, with no job losses. Such possibilities are not unlimited and will be exhausted once a firm reaches its efficient production function. At the policy level, government prices and incomes policies can have a shock effect. Where slack exists, a state prices and pay board might approve union wage increases but prevent firms from raising prices.

In monopsony markets, there exists a range over which wages might be increased without any adverse employment effects. An example is shown in Figure 12.7: a union ensures that labour is only sold at a uniform wage where marginal and average labour costs are identical. In practice, the opportunities for such wage increases depend on the existence and extent of monopsony in labour markets. Possibilities are airline pilots, teachers, and nurses where there exist state-owned airlines and state-run education and health services, respectively. Other examples include one-company towns, professional sport, astronauts, and military manpower. Such examples are by no means universal. In Western economies, labour markets are characterized by alternative employers and by mobility, so that the monopsony case can be exaggerated.

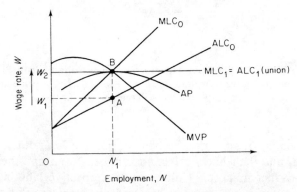

Figure 12.7 Unions and monopsony. A profit-maximizing monopsonist will equate marginal labour cost with marginal value product (for simplicity, assume a competitive product market). Employment will be N_1 and the wage paid W_1. Monopsony profit is shown by W_1ABW_2. If labour is now unionized, wages can rise to W_2 and employment remains unchanged. Effectively the union insists that all labour be sold at a uniform wage, so ending the difference between marginal and average labour cost.

Finally, oligopoly markets provide further opportunities for union wage increases without job losses. The kinky demand model results in a range of indeterminacy in an oligopolist's price–output decisions (see Chapter 9). Over this limited range, it is possible for an oligopolist's marginal cost curve to shift upwards (e.g. due to union wage increases), without any effect on price and output. An example is shown in Figure 12.8. However, while oligopoly is often believed to be a typical market form, their price–output behaviour will depend upon the objective function. Even if the kinky demand model is accepted, unions are unlikely to have sufficient knowledge to enable an accurate estimation of the magnitude of the range of indeterminacy.

12.6 UNIONS: RESTRICTIVE LABOUR PRACTICES AND EFFICIENCY

The popular view is that unions impose restrictive labour practices which adversely affect productivity and result in allocative and technical inefficiencies. Governments wishing to achieve an optimal allocation of resources have to be

316

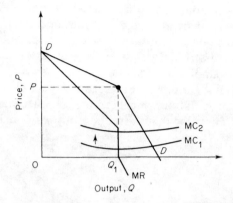

Figure 12.8 Unions and oligopoly. A profit-maximizing oligopolist will produce Q_1. If a union wage increase raises marginal costs from MC_1 to MC_2, price and output, and hence employment, will remain unchanged.

aware of the extent of such practices in an economy, the union rationale for their existence, and their likely effect on firm behaviour and the operation of labour and product markets. Union-created restrictive labour practices are often extensive, ranging from entry requirements to rules relating to working conditions and, ultimately, dismissal. They affect the hiring, utilization, and dismissal of labour, as well as its mobility. Well-known examples are lengthy apprenticeships, certification requirements, closed shops, demarcation, featherbedding or make-work, together with seniority and redundancy rules. Explanations for the existence of unions and professional associations have already been provided, including the contribution of such practices to maintaining monopoly power. But what are the likely effects of such practices on firm behaviour and labour markets? Two examples will be analysed, namely featherbedding and the effects of unions on labour supply.

The economics of featherbedding

   Featherbedding can be defined as a labour working rule which causes a firm to hire or retain more labour of a certain type than it would otherwise at the ruling wage rate. Unions often introduce featherbedding rules in response to the threat of a decline in employment resulting from, say, technical progress or a decrease in demand. Firemen in diesel locomotives are a classic example; others occur in printing and dockwork. Consider the simple case where a union secures a wage increase and the firm wants to respond by reducing employment, as shown in Figure 12.9. Assume that the union insists that employment remains unchanged. A profit-maximizing firm will be prevented from achieving a tangency position. As a result, the firm will incur higher costs to achieve a given output and this will be represented by an upward shift in its

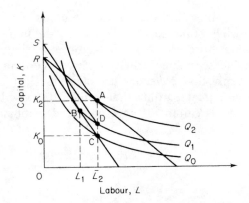

Figure 12.9   Featherbedding. The diagram shows isoquants and isocost lines. Initially, a profit-maximizing firm is in equilibrium at A. When wage rates rise, the firm's long-run equilibrium will adjust from A to B and employment will decline from L_2 to L_1 with the new output at Q_1. The union insists that employment remains at L_2. If the firm's expenditure is unchanged, it will locate at C, with K_0 capital and output falling to Q_0 (corner solution). To produce Q_1, the firm has to raise its expenditure (by RS), locating at point D, which is not a tangency position.

average cost curve. In addition, the increased wage rates will raise marginal costs, so leading to higher prices. Such restrictive labour practices are an obvious source of X-inefficiency. They are likely to be prevalent in monopoly industries and in markets which are protected from foreign competition, including the public sector (see Chapter 15). Furthermore, the economics of politics suggests that in public enterprises and firms receiving state assistance, there could be government and bureaucratic complicity in featherbedding. It might be too costly for politicians and bureaucrats to 'attack' overmanning, particularly in high-unemployment areas. Costs will be incurred in the form of lost votes, less leisure, and smaller budgets for the affected bureaucracy. Even so, governments with an interest in the efficiency of resource allocation cannot ignore the extent and magnitude of featherbedding in an economy. Unfortunately, few quantitative economic studies are available. One historical estimate concluded that unionization adversely affected productivity in the UK coal industry (Pencavel, 1977). A totally unionized coalfield produced some 20 per cent. less output than a completely non-unionized field. It was also suggested that in the mid 1970s, output losses due to unionism in the rest of the UK economy were likely to be greater!

Union restrictions on labour supply

Unions can also affect the labour supply of their members through imposing constraints on hours worked. This can affect the utility levels of workers. Two examples are presented in Figure 12.10. In case (a), individuals are not allowed

318

to work more than a specific number of hours, so effectively imposing an income limit. Case (b) shows a situation where a union requires a reduction in hours worked following an increase in wage rates: the individual is unable to respond by supplying more effort. Both examples in Figure 12.10 result in workers being unable to achieve their preferred combinations. Unionists would, of course, reply that *collective* action results in the attainment of a higher budget line and greater utility than could otherwise be obtained, even though some individuals cannot achieve preferred combinations of income and leisure.

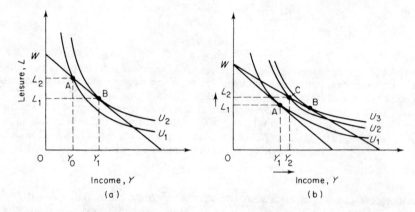

Figure 12.10 Unions and hours worked. In diagram (a) the union prevents an individual from working more than WL_2 hours. Thus, he is constrained to position A when his preferred position is B, i.e. at A he has to accept lower income, more leisure, and hence lower utility (U_1) compared with B. In diagram (b) the individual is initially in equilibrium at A. Assume a union achieves a wage increase and requires a reduction in hours worked to WL_2. Thus, the individual moves to position C which results in higher utility, but his preferred position is B.

12.7   CONCLUSION: IS THERE A NEED FOR GOVERNMENT INTERVENTION?

Nations differ in their policies towards trade unions. At one extreme there is a preference for a comprehensive legal framework governing collective bargaining, strikes, picketing, and closed shops. An alternative is a system of voluntary collective bargaining with the state supporting reforms through publicity and persuasion. Instead of examining specific solutions, this section will show how the methodology of economic policy can be used to appraise any government policy towards trade unions. The policy problem has to be defined, its causes identified, and a solution chosen from a set of alternatives.

The market failure paradigm suggests that governments aiming at optimum resource allocation will intervene wherever there are substantial imperfections or externalities. Monopoly and oligopoly unions, restrictive labour practices, and mergers between unions are obvious examples of imperfections. Similarly, significant externalities can arise through strikes and picketing, particularly where the actions involve firms, workers, and consumers not directly involved in a dispute. Explanations of such union behaviour and its predicted effects have been outlined in this chapter. Such understanding is obviously central to the formulation of any public policy. If a government wishes to improve the operation of labour markets it needs to intervene to correct these failures. Union-created imperfections can be removed through some form of discretionary or non-discretionary anti-monopoly policy which could also embrace union mergers and restrictive labour practices. Externalities can be internalized through legislative changes making it unlawful for unions to use secondary picketing, blacking, and sympathy strikes to inflict damages upon parties who have nothing to do with a dispute. Such policies are, in fact, often used in *product* markets. For example, state regulatory agencies frequently criticize monopoly and oligopoly firms for excessive profits, entry barriers, restrictive agreements, inefficiency, and a failure to innovate. Applying similar competitive criteria to unions and professional associations would require consideration of the rate of return on union membership, entry conditions, featherbedding, and other restrictive labour practices as well as a union's contribution to technical progress. However, in some instances, particularly with professional associations, it will be claimed that a restrictive agreement is required to protect the public against injury, damage, dishonesty, and incompetence. Examples include accountants, doctors, lawyers, solicitors, and teachers. Such arguments require critical appraisal. Are consumers rather than suppliers not the best judges of what is in their own interests? Also, some economic models of regulation suggest that the beneficiaries are likely to be suppliers rather than consumers. Regulation protects an established group from competition from so-called 'quacks, cowboys, and inferior suppliers offering services for gain and reward'. But are professional groups not motivated by gain and reward? There are also worries about competition within an established profession. Some groups restrict advertising so making it difficult for consumers (who are supposed to benefit?) to obtain information on alternative suppliers. Further restrictions on competition occur through the fixing of standard fees, the failure to publicize charges, and resistance to new ideas and technical change. Claims are sometimes made that professional groups employ non-professionals to undertake their work, often without supervision. Examples might include conveyancing work for houses, the preparation of accounts, and the treatment of sick patients (e.g. doctors' receptionists make judgements about the urgency of telephone calls for attention and appointments; see Chapters 5 and 8).

Why might a government be unwilling to subject trade unions and professional associations to the type of anti-monopoly policy it operates in product markets? There are at least three interrelated possibilities. *First*, governments are usually concerned with distributional objectives and not solely allocative efficiency. Unions might be seen as agencies for achieving a desirable redistribution of income between labour and other groups. This objective is likely to differ between right- and left-wing governments. It also raises questions about the role of taxation as a redistributive instrument. *Second*, policy-makers might regard unions as second-best constraints, so that the standard rules for a Pareto optimum are no longer appropriate. With this argument, difficulties arise in determining whether current policy is achieving a second- or nth-best solution. Questions also arise about the nature of the union constraint. If the constraint is policy-created and supported, it implies a preferred outcome. An unwillingness to change policy raises questions about the aims of the government, and leads to a third possibility. *Third*, policy might be explained by the economics of the political market place. Unions as a whole represent a major interest group with substantial votes. They are also attractive to politicians and bureaucrats because of the opportunities they seem to offer for negotiating vote-winning anti-inflationary pay policies and a 'quiet life'. But if a vote-sensitive government accepts unions as a policy-created constraint, are there any options for state intervention?

One possibility would be to implement an active pro-competition policy in *product markets*. Competition could be used as a policing mechanism to induce management and employees to reduce X-inefficiency (complete elimination might be too costly). Further opportunities exist for the use of indirect policies. Labour market measures, designed to improve resource re-allocation, might contribute to the acceptance of change, particularly if they reduced the costs imposed on workers. Examples include state income-deficiency payments and training and mobility policies. Alternatively, the state could 'buy out' restrictive labour practices. Such a policy might be rationalized in terms of the compensation principle (see Chapter 2). A related possibility would give state subsidies to firms to guarantee job security, the belief being that this would eliminate restrictive practices. But in the case of restrictive labour practices, why is state intervention required? Why can firms not buy out restrictions through, for example, productivity bargaining? Moreover, these policies focus on restrictive practices which form only one dimension of the trade union 'problem'.

Governments are also concerned with the environment for collective bargaining and the procedures for solving industrial disputes, particularly strikes. Legal solutions are sometimes advocated. These involve the enforcement of contracts and compensation for damages due to breach of contract, including damages arising from secondary picketing and sympathetic strikes. Problems arise where such solutions are introduced into a system of voluntary collective bargaining. Unions view legal changes as an attack on their traditional powers. In addition, difficulties arise in determining the responsibility for a strike and its consequences; whether any damages and fines should be paid by the union or individual officials; and whether breaches of the law constitute criminal acts with the possibility of imprisonment. Given such problems, industrial democracy solutions have been proposed. These can take various forms, including worker directors, supervisory boards, joint consultation, and labour-managed firms (see Chapter 7). The supporters of industrial democracy believe that it will reduce industrial conflict and raise productivity by removing restrictive labour practices. Critics claim that it will have adverse effects on private investment as investors will require a higher return to compensate for the perceived greater risks. There are also fears of adverse effects on labour-saving technical progress and great inflationary pressure in labour markets (due to greater union bargaining power). Clearly, there are opportunities for micro-economists to examine the causal relationships in these competing hypotheses and to determine their empirical validity.

READING AND REFERENCES

Addison, J. T., and Siebert, W. S. (1979). *The Market for Labor: An Analytical Treatment*, Goodyear, Santa Monica, Calif.

Bacon, R., and Eltis, W. (1979). Britain's economic problem: an interchange, *Economic Journal*, June, 402–415.

Burkitt, B., and Bowers, D. (1979). *Trade Unions and the Economy*, Macmillan, London.

British Journal of Industrial Relations, (1979). London, **XV**, July.

Cobb, C. W. and Douglas, P. H. (1928). A theory of production, *American Economic Review*, **8**, March, 139–165.

Donovan, Lord. (1968). *Report of the Royal Commission on Trade Unions and Employers' Associations, 1967–1968*, Cmnd 3623, HMSO, London.

Hieser, R. O. (1970). Wage determination with bilateral monopoly in the labour market, in King, J. E., ed. (1980). *Readings in Labour Economics*, Oxford University Press, Oxford.

Institute of Economic Afairs (1978). *Trade Unions: Public Goods or Public Bads?*, IEA, Readings 17, London.

Kaldor, N. (955–56). Alternative theories of distribution, *Review of Economic Studies*, **23**, 94–100.

Kalecki, M. (1954). *The Theory of Economic Dynamics*, Allen and Unwin, London.

King, J. E. (1972). *Labour Economics*, Macmillan, London.

King, J. E. (Ed.) (1980). *Readings in Labour Economics*, Oxford University Press, Oxford.

McCarthy, W. E. J. (Ed.) (1972). *Trade Unions*, Penguin, London.

Pencavel, J. (1977). The distributional and efficiency effects of trade unions in Britain, *British Journal of Industrial Relations, July, pp. 137–156.*

Phelps-Brown, E. H. (1968). *Pay and Profits*, Manchester University Press, Manchester.

Rees, A. (1973). *The Economics of Work and Pay*, Harper, New York.

Smith, C. T. B., *et al.*, (1978). *Strikes in Britain*, Department of Employment, Manpower Paper 15, London.

QUESTIONS FOR REVIEW AND DISCUSSION

1. Why do unions and professional associations exist? Should public policy treat unions and professional groups differently?
2. Which models of trade union and firm behaviour 'best' explain any recent strike with which you are familiar? Does the same model(s) explain why collective agreements emerge without strikes?
3. Predict the effect of the formation of a trade union on a firm's pricing,

employment, and investment behaviour. Explain how you would test the predictions of your model.

4. What are the sources of union monopoly power? Does your analysis suggest that public policy should treat union monopolies differently from private monopolies in product markets? Do professional associations merit special treatment?

5. Does labour deserve 100 per cent. of the national product?

6. Are trade unions and professional associations utility-maximizers? Explain.

7. (a) Have unions and professional associations raised the wages of their members?
   (b) If so, how and at whose expense?

8. (a) Are closed shops in the 'public interest'?
   (b) Are licensing and certification desirable for some professional groups? Explain why and which groups, if any.

9. How many monopoly unions can you name? Carefully explain the economic criteria used in your selection and identify the sources of each union's monopoly power.

10. Are restrictive labour practices and strikes 'undesirable'? Is state intervention required to solve these problems? Why?

CHAPTER 13

Energy and Resource Markets

13.1 INTRODUCTION

Importance of energy resources

Energy, obtained and obtainable from a diversity of sources, is important both in production and in consumption. The high standard of living enjoyed in most industrial countries is made possible by a huge use of energy resources. Many of these resources (such as oil, coal, and natural gas) are not renewable. Without depleting these non-renewable resources, we could not at present maintain our high standard of living. But this raises many queries. To what extent are we justified in depleting resources which could be left for future generations? Do markets ensure an optimal rate of depletion of non-renewable resources? Is government interference in the use of energy resources desirable and has the interference that has occurred helped solve problems raised by the energy crisis? These are a few of the questions that are considered in this chapter.

Energy is obtained and is obtainable from many sources, some of which are listed in Table 13.1. Those in the renewable list all depend indirectly on energy from the sun. These sources can become exhausted, for example, if species are harvested to extinction and of course they are limited in supply. Reserves of many of these sources of energy such as timber have been seriously depleted, but of course in the industrial world little timber is now used for energy purposes. This was not always the case.

Table 13.1 Some sources of energy supply.

Renewable	Non-renewable	Flow
Timber and plants	Oil	Solar
Alcohol from sugar-cane, grain, etc.	Coal	Wind and waves
Methane from animal waste products	Natural gas	Hydro
Dung and straw	Oil shale	Tidal
Animal fats and oils	Tar sands	
	Uranium	
	Geothermal	

While the sources of energy supplies for human use have changed greatly over the centuries, even in the short-term substantial changes have occurred. Since 1950, the proportion of the world's energy supplies derived from coal has fallen considerably while that obtained from oil and natural gas rose substantially, as shown in Table 13.2. But total energy consumed rose by more than fourfold in the 23-year period from 1950 to 1973, so total consumption of coal also expanded. The switch to oil and natural gas was a reflection of their relatively low price in comparison to coal and their less polluting effect in many cases. But in 1973 oil prices increased more than fourfold (from $2.59 per barrel in January 1973 to $11.65 in January 1974) and have since remained relatively high. This has stimulated the demand for coal, especially for electricity generation. We can expect the price mechanism to encourage this substitution of coal for oil in the long-term. Possibly the future pattern of use of energy sources will be a rising proportion of demand met from coal, then uranium, and then solar energy and flow resources.

Table 13.2 United Nations estimates of world energy consumption and energy sources, 1950–1973.

	1950	1960	1970	1973
Total (10^{15} Btu)	76.8	124.0	214.5	250.4
Coal (%)	56	44	31	29
Oil (%)	29	36	45	49
Natural gas (%)	9	14	18	19
Other (%)	6	6	6	3

Why should energy resources be different?

While energy supplies affect our current standard of living so too does food and shelter. Furthermore, while some energy resources are not renewable they are not unique in this respect. For instance, copper and lead deposits are not renewable although recycling of copper and lead is possible. On the other hand, some energy resources are flow resources such as solar energy and this is a possible basis for optimism in the very long-term.

A characteristic of energy supplies is that they are usually in the hands of oligopolies, large firms, and governments. For example, this is true in many countries for oil and gas, coal and uranium, and electricity. But this is not unique to energy supplies. Oligopoly occurs, for instance, in copper, bauxite, and alumina supplies and is present in several manufacturing and service industries.

It is not clear that energy resources are unique from an economic point of view. Many of the problems raised in this study of energy resources also arise for other non-renewable resources.

Markets for energy resources

The presence of imperfect competition due to the existence of oligopoly, cartels, and government interventions in energy markets has just been mentioned. To what extent is the present energy crisis a result of market failure and of government intervention in energy supply and use? Markets may fail to allocate resources efficiently because of the presence of imperfect competition, externalities including public 'bads', and uncertainty. Governments may also fail as a result of such factors as short-term political pressures, the inefficiency of bureaucracy, and the imperfection of knowledge on the part of bureaucrats. To some extent we may be faced with a choice between imperfect alternatives in a world of uncertainty.

Market or government failure may occur at any of the marketing stages for energy resources. It can occur at the primary resource stage, at an intermediate stage, or in the final markets for energy supplies; and each of these possibilities will be considered in this chapter. Table 13.3 indicates these stages and some of the associated activities.

Table 13.3   Broad overview of stages in energy supply and use and associated activities.

Stage	Associated activities
Primary	Exploration, mining, transport of raw material
Secondary or intermediate	Processing of raw material, refining, grading and transport of processed raw material, conversion to electricity, petrol, etc.
Final stage	Use by firms and producers outside the energy industry of processed energy supplies for productive activity; use by consumers of processed energy supplies such as petrol and electricity for consumption: e.g. consumption for transport, provision of heat, cooling, and lighting, and operation of labour-saving devices around the home

13.2   THE RATE OF EXPLOITATION OR DEPLETION OF ENERGY RESOURCES

A simple model of depletion of stocks or reserves

In considering how to allocate the use of a resource over time, one must place a value on its use in different time-periods. As a rule the value is taken into account by discounting future receipts and expenses. From the point of view of the firm the same annual profit a number of years off is worth less or is of smaller value than the same current profit. For instance, even ignoring inflation, £99 in a year's time is worth less than £99 now because one has the option of investing £99 now and obtaining the capital *plus* interest at the end of the year. If the interest rate is 10 per cent., one obtains £108.90 at the end of the year compared to £99. Alternatively, if a 10 per cent. interest rate applies the *present value* of £99 payable in one year's time is £90 since this is the amount which would need to be invested to yield £99 in one year's time. The present value of a sum payable in the future will be smaller (the amount of discount to be applied to the sum is larger) (1) the higher is the interest rate and (2) the further into the future is the time when the sum is payable.

A profit-maximizing firm may be expected to adopt the production and marketing plan which *maximizes the present value* of its operations if capital markets are perfect. The adoption of such a plan would mean that it could by using the capital market have more profit or suprlus in every period than by adopting any other strategy. Consider a simple case of the exploitation of a non-renewable resource and suppose that it is being mined by a perfectly competitive firm using inputs that are in *fixed* availability in each time-period. Such a firm would maximize its present discounted value or profitability if it maximized the present value of its total revenue. This is so because the fixed availability assumption about inputs implies that marginal costs equal zero. Assuming that plans extend for two periods and that one product (X) is produced (for instance coal), a perfectly competitive firm maximizes its current value by adopting the plan which maximizes present discounted revenue:

$$\pi = p_1 x_1 + \hat{p}_2 x_2$$

subject to its production function

$$f(x_1, x_2) = 0$$

where p_1 represents the price of X, say coal, in period 1
$\hat{p}_2$ represents the discounted price of X in period 2
x_1 is the output and supply of X in period 1
x_2 is the output and supply of X in period 2
The discounted price, $\hat{p}_2$, is given by the formula

$$\hat{p}_2 = \frac{p_2}{1 + r}$$

where p_2 is the price of coal in period 2 and r is the rate of interest. Note that $\hat{p}_2$ is larger the higher is p_2 (the price of X in the second period) and the lower is the rate of interest.

The operation of this model can be illustrated by means of Figure 13.1. The production function there is shown by the curve BCDE. Suppose that the relative discounted prices for X are such that the discounted isorevenue curves are as represented by the sample marked 1, 2, 3. The perfectly competitive firm's optimal strategy is then to supply levels of output in each of the periods corresponding to position D. But suppose that either (1) the price of X rises in period 2, or (2) its price falls in period 1, or (3) the rate of interest falls so that the line marked 2* is typical of the new discounted isorevenue curves. Then position C corresponds to the optimal output in each of the periods; this involves a greater output in period 2 than in period 1 and therefore greater conservation of resources in period 1.

Other things equal, a rise in the relative value of resources in period 2 compared to period 1 (i.e. a rise in the ratio p_2/p_1) leads to greater conservation of resources in period 1. Markets are responsive to changing relative values as reflected in prices at different time-periods. Also, other things equal, a rise (fall) in the rate of interest reduces conservation (increases conservation). A rise in the rate of interest reduces $\hat{p}_2$ and the firm's desire to speed up the availability of funds since they can now earn a higher return (rate of interest) by investing available funds in alternatives.

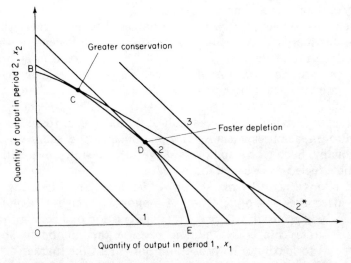

Figure 13.1 A rise in the future relative to the present price of a resource or a lowering in the rate of interest results in greater conservation of the resource.

Market failure

The above model indicates the type of effects that the price mechanism is likely to have on the depletion of a non-renewable resource under conditions of perfect competition. Although this model is a useful benchmark it fails to mirror reality in a number of respects.

The model takes insufficient account of the importance of uncertainty, for instance about future prices and interest rates. Assuming risk aversion and uncertainty about future prices the speed of depletion of resources is liable to increase with uncertainty about future prices because future certainty equivalent prices are lowered. Hence a competitive market may result in an over-rapid rate of depletion of resources from a theoretical Kaldor–Hicks standpoint since firms base their decisions on certainly equivalent prices.

There are also problems in deciding on the appropriate rate of interest to use for discounting since a range of rates exist in reality. Firms may be expected to

328

apply rates of interest prevailing in the private sector which may be higher than in the public sector. It has been argued by some economists that private market or opportunity cost rates of interest are undesirably high from a social point of view. The rate of social time preference (the rate of interest reflecting social preferences) should be lower. Indeed, two famous economists, Ramsey (1928) and Pigou (1932), have argued that the rate of social time preference should be zero. Argument on this subject is complex but is usefully summarized by Howe (1979). The implication, however, is clear. Competitive markets result in a faster rate of depletion of non-renewable resources than is socially desirable. In terms of Figure 13.1 they result in operation at point D rather than at a point like C, assuming that the discounted isorevenue curve, 2*, is based upon a socially optimal rate of time preference.

The speed of depletion of energy resources may be socially excessive if unfavourable marginal externalities exist and if these depend on the rate of mining or the use of the energy resources. Thus radiation in an area or the ability of an area to absorb harmful side-effects from mining may depend upon the rate at which mining proceeds. As will be discussed later, there may also be global spillovers to consider such as the possible greenhouse effect of the build-up of carbon dioxide as a result of the burning of fossil fuels, fall-out from hydrogen bomb explosions, and oil spillages and slicks which spread internationally. Such global spillovers suggest that a slow-down in the utilization of some fuels may be called for.

Imperfections caused by market power in the selling of energy resources may also affect their rate of depletion. A monopoly, such as that attempted by OPEC, can be expected to reduce the rate of depletion of an energy resource in comparison to a competitive market because the monopoly holds back supplies so as to maximize its profit and not 'spoil' the market. It has even been said that 'a monopolist is a conservationist's best friend'. However, monopoly would only result in a socially optimal rate of conservation by chance.

The possible impact of monopoly on the rate of depletion of a resource in comparison to perfect competition can be illustrated by Figure 13.2. For simplicity two periods are assumed and mining of the resource is assumed to be costless. The curve marked D_1 represents the demand for the mineral, X, in period 1 and MR_1 is the corresponding marginal revenue curve. The curve marked D_2^* is the discounted demand curve in period 2 and MR_2^* is the corresponding marginal revenue curve. Utilization rates for three possibilities need to be considered:

(1) Available supplies of the mineral X_S exceed $X_{1C} + X_{2C}$, the combined quantities which would be supplied under perfect competition if supplies are not limited. In this case, the mineral is free under perfect competition, X_{1C} is supplied in period 1 and X_{2C} in period 2, and the carryover is $X_S -(X_{1C} + X_{2C})$. Under monopoly, profits are maximized by equating MR_1 and MR_2^*, and in this case X_{1M} of the mineral is supplied in period 1

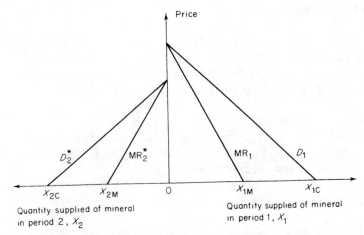

Figure 13.2 If available supplies of a mineral exceed $X_{1M} + X_{2M}$ (the maximum supply by a monopolist not to spoil his market) the monopolist will conserve more of the mineral than a perfectly competitive industry.

and X_{2M} in period 2. A smaller quantity is supplied in each period and there is a greater carryover at the end of the planning interval.

(2) Available supplies X_S fall in the range $X_{1M} + X_{2M} < X_S \leq X_{1C} + X_{2C}$. There is no carryover of stocks at the end of the planning period under perfect competition but there is a carryover under monopoly. Monopoly results in greater conservation.

(3) If available supplies are $X_S \leq X_{1M} + X_{2M}$ there is no carryover of the mineral at the end of the planning period either under monopoly or under perfect competition.

However, the mere fact that monopoly is likely to result in greater conservation does not imply that it is socially optimal. In the above case remaining stocks of the mineral may, for instance, have no value at the end of the planning period and the effect of the monopoly could merely be to reduce welfare by its restrictive policies. If mining or use of the mineral happened to have unfavourable externalities it would be a 'fluke' if a monopolist optimally corrected for these because his actions are directed towards his own private benefit, not social benefit, and there is no mechanism to make the two coincide.

The effect of oligopolies on the rate of depletion of a non-renewable resource is uncertain. Where a cartel is formed the impact would be similar to that for a monopoly. However, if the Galbraithian view is accepted oligopolies could stimulate a socially excessive rate of depletion by encouraging present consumption by their manipulation of demand through advertising and other means. On the other hand, oligopolies could undertake considerable research and development designed to develop alternative energy resources.

Market reaction to depletion

The above simple models, while highlighting some aspects of market performance, fail to take account of other aspects. As the depletion of an energy resource, say oil, proceeds a number of market reactions might be expected assuming that the price of oil rises:

(1) Exploration effort may increase.
(2) Marginal oil reserves may be used or called into production.
(3) Substitution of other sources of energy or other factors of production or elements for oil may be encouraged.
(4) Research and development efforts to save oil and to find substitutes for it are likely to be encouraged.

In relation to substitution possibilities it might be noted that while other fuels or electricity may be substituted for oil, other factors such as labour and capital may also be substituted. In the home, for instance, greater attention may be given to insulation to save on heating expenses and warmer clothing may be worn.

Studies suggest that the price mechanism plays an important role in determining the direction of research and development, invention, and innovation (Schmookler, 1966; Ruttan, 1977). The price mechanism induces innovation to reduce constraints imposed by resources in short supply. But will free markets act sufficiently well in this respect as far as energy constraints are concerned or is government intervention (as is now occurring on a wide scale) desirable?

Government intervention in the exploitation of energy resources

One aspect of market failure is not mentioned above and can be important in the case of oil and natural gas, for instance. It occurs when such resources are common property, i.e. shared in common by a number of firms. If a number of firms are drawing oil or natural gas from a common pool, they can be expected to deplete it at a faster rate than is socially optimal. No firm has an incentive to conserve the resource because any of the resource conserved by it may be taken by other firms. In such circumstances, there is a case for the government to give exclusive property rights for each pool to one firm, putting different pools in the hands of different firms if necessary to prevent the emergence of an overall monopoly.

A common-property problem can also arise in exploration for minerals. Until these are discovered and a mining claim is lodged, all may search for these in common. In consequence too great a quantity of exploratory resources and exploring firms from an economic efficiency viewpoint may crowd into the most promising areas. In the case of oil and natural gas this problem has been reduced in the United Kingdom and Australia by the government releasing blocks of country for oil exploration. Each block is allocated to a single firm for exploration and development purposes.

But it would be naïve to believe that government does, or can, efficiently correct by its own interference for market failure in the exploitation of non-renewable resources. Governments are imperfect because their information is imperfect and they are subject to the imperfect operations of political pressure groups. In democratic systems with elections at regular intervals parties may be tempted to take a short-term view and adopt policies designed to obtain votes or political funds in the short-term. Depending upon the particular case this can result in a faster rate of exploitation of energy resources (such as would occur if petrol or oil production happened to be subsidized to keep the price to the consumer down) than is desirable from a Kaldor–Hicks viewpoint or a slower one (such as might occur in a marginal seat in which the conservationist lobby is strong in that electorate).

As mentioned earlier the effect of a subsidy on oil production can be expected to be depletion of supplies at a faster rate. This is true *a fortiori* if there is a risk that the subsidy may be lowered or eliminated in the future. A subsidy on exploration for oil, coal, etc., may also be expected to speed up depletion of the world's reserves (known plus unknown) because the discoveries are likely to include some reserves which can be mined at low cost. It might be held that a subsidy could be justified to compensate for the risk factor in exploration but in the case of very large oil companies the risk in relation to their size may be small. Also it needs to be kept in mind that exploration uses resources and that it is only justified from a social point of view in any period up to the level where the social marginal value of it equals its marginal cost. The alternatives for using resources must be kept in mind.

Governments frequently only give mining rights to particular firms in an area for a specified relatively short period of time, e.g. 15 years. Since there is some uncertainty about whether the company's mining lease will be renewed at the end of the period, this tends to speed up the rate of depletion.

Again, the royalties paid to the government by mining companies may not accurately reflect the economic rent of their site and reserves. Where this occurs in a country selling the mineral at world prices, mining companies may obtain part of the rent. This acts as a subsidy to exploration and if there is a risk that the industry might be nationalized in the long-term or less favourably treated in terms of royalty charges leads to a faster rate of depletion.

This problem of unappropriated rents might be reduced by a bidding system for mining rights, if buyers are competitive. But if monopsony, oligopsony, or collusion in buying exists, bidding systems do not provide a means for the state to extract all the economic rent from its mineral reserves. This and associated problems have led some countries (e.g. Papua-New Guinea) to consider the imposition of a natural resources tax. In effect all or a proportion of the profit of the company mining a mineral in excess of that necessary to give it a normal or specified return on capital is taken by the government. But this scheme is by no means perfect. Several possible effects are:

(1) Escalation of costs and increase in X-inefficiency by the firm to reduce its surplus profit.
(2) 'Sweetheart agreements' with unions to give high wages to employees in the mine.
(3) A possible lowering of the profitability of exploration and therefore less exploration.
(4) Arranged increased costs by multi-national mining companies through *transfer payments* between international branches of the company. For instance, machinery or 'know-how' may be purchased from an overseas branch of the company at an inflated price and indirectly profit may be transferred from a high tax country to one with a low tax rate by this method.

Thus it can be seen that measures may be taken by mining companies to circumvent natural resource taxes, and some of these may result in a misallocation of resources. The problem of extracting economic rent, however, remains an important income distribution question, especially as far as mining in less-developed countries is concerned.

Where a government itself is mining an energy resource, e.g. as is done by the British Coal Board, it might be anticipated that 'adequate' account will take of externalities or spillovers in mining decisions. But this by no means holds. Public enterprises have a limited charter, and may interpret their role narrowly. For instance, a coal board might see as its principle function the supply of coal and members might be more inclined to judge their performance by the quantity of coal supplied and sold than by an evaluation of the social value of their activities. Thus a coal board left to its own devices may take inadequate account of environmental spillovers and external checks may need to be put on its activities to ensure that spillovers are taken into account.

Another area in which government intervention may influence the use of non-renewable resources is through assistance to and contributions to research and development designed to influence the availability and use of energy resources. While, as mentioned earlier, the price mechanism can be expected to induce innovation and R & D in areas of resource shortage, it is, for reasons mentioned in Chapter 9, not a perfect mechanism. A case would seem to exist for government intervention, particularly in assisting basic research because of the externalities involved. However, at the same time the dangers of using a political mechanism for allocation should not be overlooked.

Until recently much of the world's research expenditure on energy was concentrated on nuclear research with government assistance. Some of this research was related to defence. The concentration still exists but more funds are now being used in other areas such as coal and solar research. The allocation may to some extent reflect the interests of large companies and scientists rather than areas of greatest social benefit. Large industrial countries have engaged in competitive duplication of nuclear energy research for commercial use. *Possibly* this has resulted in a waste of resources (in the sense that the same findings could have been obtained using less resources) even though it is recognized that duplication of research activities need not be wasteful (Tisdell, 1981).

13.3   THE CHOICE OF AN ENERGY SOURCE

Substitutability of energy resources

Short-term substitutability of energy resources tends to be very low since most machinery and capital is designed to operate utilizing a particular form of energy. In the production of electricity, power stations are designed to operate using a particular fuel (coal, oil, nuclear) and little or no substitution may be possible. However, in the long-term (possibly 10 to 15 years from the planning stage) the type of station built and the fuel to be used can be altered and substitution in the very long-term is comparatively easy.

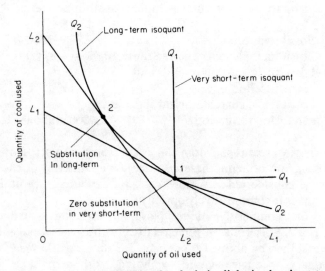

Figure 13.3   Substitution possibilities for fuels is slight in the short-term but may be considerable in the long-term.

Figure 13.3 indicates hypothetical substitution possibilities between oil and coal in the production of electricity in the very short-term and in the long-term. In the very short-term, substitution is impossible as indicated by isoquant Q_1Q_1 and a change in relative prices would leave the relative use of oil and coal unaltered at 1. But in the long-run isoquants may be like Q_2Q_2, indicating that substitution is possible. In the long-term and assuming that the same amount of electricity is to be generated, a rise in the relative price of oil reduces its use. A rise in the price of oil relative to coal (which alters the isocost lines so that

L_2L_2 rather than L_1L_1 becomes tangential to Q_2Q_2) results in a shift in the use of energy resources from point 1 to point 2 in Figure 13.3. Given that a rise in the relative price of oil has occurred since 1973 and that this relativity can be expected to be maintained, long-term substitution of coal and nuclear power for oil can be expected in electricity production. Long-term substitution for oil can also be expected to occur in other areas of use, for example, in home heating.

Scarcity and long-term subsitution possibilities — an optimistic view

In contrast to the predictions of the Club of Rome, there is a view, expressed for example by Nordhaus (1974), that the gravity of the energy crisis is greatly exaggerated. While oil deposits are dwindling, large deposits of coal and other fossil fuels exist, and nuclear power has the potential to supply extremely great quantities of energy. On the basis of 1970 figures Nordhaus estimated the following world resource–consumption ratios (in years) for energy. These give the number of years that *known* energy resources (reserves) are expected to last if they are drawn on to maintain current annual consumption levels:

1. Fossil fuels only   500 +
2. Fossil fuels plus current nuclear technology   8,000 +
3. Fossil fuels, current nuclear and
   breeder technology   1 million +
4. Fossil fuels, current nuclear, breeder,
   and fusion technology   53,000 million +

These figures may suggest that Doomsday is still some way off. However, the cost of recovering and utilizing these resources, even in terms of energy input alone, could rise considerably as more marginal resources are utilized. But even here Nordhaus is comparatively optimistic.

On the basis of a competitive model, Nordhaus estimates that final energy products will rise 2.2 per cent. in price relative to the general price level over the next 50 years, then by about 1.3 per cent. for the next 100 years, and then become stationary as nuclear-based technology ultimately takes over the supply. Steep but not insuperable price rises in energy products can be expected until around the end of the next century. Whether or not this will constitute a serious drag on consumption and the standard of living will depend on the level of technological change and productivity increase. If a 2.5 per cent. growth rate in productivity could be maintained, energy prices would tend to fall relative to average incomes. Rates of this order have been attained in some past decades but can they be maintained? It is clear that rising energy prices *could* place a drag on consumption and the standard of living over the next 50 years, unless some unexpected breakthrough in energy technology occurs.

The course and consequences of energy price changes are difficult to predict for such long periods but it is clear that prices will depend on (1) advances in energy and other technologies (a supply factor), (2) demand as influenced by population and income increases and technological change, and (3) discoveries of new energy deposits. If the price of energy does rise, as is likely, this need not lead to a fall in the standard of living because technological progress, for example, may be sufficiently rapid in non-energy producing industries.

Externalities or spillovers

In deciding on the use of an energy source it is important from a social point of view to take associated externalities and spillovers into account. As discussed in earlier chapters, individuals and private companies are unlikely to take spillovers into account in their decision-making. It is even doubtful whether public enterprises and individual government departments can be expected to take into account all of the spillovers involved in their decision-making. A department responsible for mining or a coal board may take a narrow view of its responsibilities (a view which is likely to differ from that of the government department responsible for the environment, for instance) and may not take account of loss of amenity and spillovers resulting from its decision. For instance, the British Coal Board's plans to commence large-scale open-cut mining of low grade coal in Leicestershire *may* not pay due regard to the loss in scenic amenity in the area. This action would be consistent with the first part of the thesis that budget-maximizing agencies usually (1) underestimate costs and (2) overestimate demand. From a social point of view it is necessary to find a way to value scenic amenity and take it into account. It is still possible that after cost–benefit analysis of this type the mining may be a socially optimal choice or a modification of plans may be called for.

In considering spillovers from the use of energy resources it is useful to distinguish between local spillovers and global spillovers. Local spillovers are externalities confined to a limited area or region while global spillovers have an impact on the whole globe.

Local spillovers from the use of fossil fuels include rises in carbon monoxide levels and the occurrence of chemical smog from car exhausts; increases in sulphur oxide and nitrogen oxide levels and the occurrence of acidic rains as a result of the use of higher sulphur coal or oil; and increases in particulate matter due to the burning of coal, the emission of heat wastes into water, and the atmosphere as at power stations. The use of nuclear fuels involves risks of local radiation and the occurrence of large heat losses.

On a global scale, several possible externalities exist. It has been suggested that the burning of *fossil* fuels is having a 'greenhouse effect' on the globe. It is causing a rise in carbon dioxide levels and this combined with heat losses from the use of fuels and other factors may be causing the temperature of the Earth's atmosphere to rise. The consequence could be a premature melting of the polar ice caps and a marked rise in the level of the seas with flooding of a considerable amount of the world's land mass. It has been predicted

(Nordhaus, 1974) that at current levels of activity that it is unlikely but not impossible for the 'greenhouse effect' to trigger melting of the ice caps. Within 50 years we could come uncomfortably close to carbon dioxide levels which might trigger the melting of the caps. However, there may be no problem if we are on a long-term swing towards another Ice Age (as has been suggested by some scientists)—the greenhouse effect might be beneficial in helping to slow it down! The net effect still remains uncertain.

In the case of nuclear fuels the possibility of increasing radiation levels on a world scale is an unfavourable global spillover, as are heat losses. Nuclear energy is globally hazardous in that considerable damage on a world-wide scale could result from a major accident. The safe storage of used nuclear fuels and wastes poses a great problem because of the potential damages which can be caused by the wastes and the extremely long periods for which they remain a danger. While technology may be developed to reduce this danger and/or ways may be found of using the wastes productively, this is one of the greatest present hazards involved in the use of nuclear energy. But the risk needs to be seen in perspective.

Both fossil fuels and nuclear fuels have unfavourable externalities and risks and it is not clear immediately which poses the smallest danger. Attempts have been made to quantify the health impacts of the alternative sources of energy when used to generate electricity. Lave (1972) found that the cost of mine accidents, mine chronic diseases, and quantifiable effects on the health of the public of coal usages are 16 to 220 times higher for coal than for the use of uranium to generate the same amount of electricity, judging by experience to date. This has led Howe (1979) to conclude that: 'There seems little doubt that the day-to-day noncatastrophic impacts of coal-fired electric generation are more damaging than those of nuclear.' Conceivably, however, a major nuclear accident could change this picture for it is based on past experience. There is a further problem, as has been pointed out, that both fuels *could* have catastrophic global effects when used on a large scale (the greenhouse effect and the radiation hazard). But the available evidence does not clearly point towards coal as having lower environmental costs than uranium as a fuel.

13.4 MARKET IMPERFECTIONS IN ENERGY SUPPLIES AND THE QUESTION OF SELF-SUFFICIENCY IN SUPPLIES

Cartels, oligopsony, and oligopoly in the oil industry

Since 1973, OPEC (Organisation of Oil Exporting Countries) has dominated discussion of oil supplies. This cartel of 13 members was founded in 1960 and controls three-quarters of the non-communist world's oil exports. However, it was not until 1973 that it obtained substantial rises in the price of oil as a result of agreement between the countries concerned.

At the present time the agreed price of Saudi Arabian light oil forms the base price on which other members of the cartel are supposed to set their price, adjusting this price by a factor to reflect the difference in the quality of their own oil. But cartel members are reported to find it difficult to agree on a common price structure and there are reports of 'chisseling' by some OPEC members, e.g. Libya. Saudi Arabia, the largest oil producer is reported to be less willing to take a very short-term view and has expanded its supplies of oil and moderated the rate of price increase. It may be less willing to take a short-term view because it fears other OPEC countries are gaining at its expense and it may recognize that current policies are speeding up substitution of other fuels for oil. In general, the types of theoretical difficulties for cartels mentioned in Chapters 2 and 9 are evident. How the cartel would react to a sudden decrease in the demand for oil is difficult to judge but it is possible that this could reduce cooperation between members.

As one countervailing strategy to OPEC, 20 countries, all of which (except Norway and the United Kingdom) are net importers now or in the foreseeable future, have formed IEA (International Energy Agency) to adopt a cooperative approach, especially to the oil position. They have agreed to set country-by-country ceilings on their oil imports and for monitoring of the extent to which individual countries abide by the agreement. But one major importer, France, remains outside IEA and, as in the case of a cartel, a cooperative monopsonistic arrangement runs the risk that individual members will decide to follow their own self-interest to the detriment of the association as a whole.

Since 1973 the share in the world's oil trade of the seven major world oil companies (British Petroleum, Exxon, Gulf, Mobil, Royal Dutch/Shell, Standard Oil of California, and Texaco) which have in the past dominated world oil exploration, production, and distribution has declined significantly. In 1973 these companies controlled over 60 per cent. of the non-communist world oil trade either through long-term contracts or equity participation, but by 1979 this share had fallen to around 40 per cent. This fall has occurred because a number of OPEC countries have nationalized their oil industries, there has been an increase in government-to-government sales, and more oil is being sold on the spot market and to smaller companies. But the seven major oligopolists remain important and in several cases where government-to-government deals have been made one or more of these companies have been appointed agents of the importing country. The present market is far from perfect and this imperfection has possibly been increased by government-to-government dealings and a tendency towards bilateral monopoly involving OPEC countries on the one hand and IEA countries on the other.

Trade union power

The bargaining power of trade unions within industries supplying energy needs can be considerable. The final products of such industries, e.g. electricity, petroleum, and coal, are as a rule in relatively inelastic short-term demand and the industries are usually capital-intensive rather than labour-intensive. In oil refineries, for example, little labour is used in relation to capital and if plants are closed down the chemical processes take a considerable period to re-start. A strike is likely to be relatively more costly to the oil company than the strikers. Therefore, oil companies may be prepared to concede improvements in working conditions easily.

It has been suggested that this has happened, for instance, in Australia in the past. Oil companies have been criticized by the government for making sweetheart agreements. They have been criticized by the government as undermining attempts to moderate wage-push inflation. Wage increases in the oil industry may stimulate demands for higher wages in other sectors as workers and other trade unions try to maintain their relative wage rate (see Chapter 12).

Strikes in important energy sectors can have significant political repercussions as the British coal strike of the winter of 1973–1974 demonstrated. Following this strike and the attempt of the government to moderate the wage claims of miners, the Conservative Government (Heath) lost office.

Self-sufficiency and the export of energy resources

The industrialized countries of the non-communist world are on the whole heavily dependent upon the import of energy resources, principally from less-developed areas. The United Kingdom is fortunate in being one of the few industrialized countries at present which are not heavily dependent on imports of energy resources. Although it does import uranium and coal, the United Kingdom is exporting oil and supplies most of its own coal.

The energy crisis, international political instability, and the uncertainty of available imports have prompted importers of energy resources to consider means of reducing dependence on imports of energy resources. But greater self-sufficiency or reduced dependence on imports is not costless to the country concerned and the benefits to be obtained from any policy in this area need to be weighed against the costs.

Policy arising from concern about energy imports may be directed:

(1) towards increasing domestic self-sufficiency or
(2) towards reducing the risks inherent in importing energy resources.

Imports of energy sources may be lowered by reducing domestic demand for energy (or demand for energy imports) or by increasing the supply of energy from domestic sources. But neither policy can be expected to be costless to the importing country. For instance, a tariff on energy imports may lower imports of energy sources to some extent but at the same time lower domestic real incomes and reduce exports dependent upon the import of energy materials. An acceleration in the supply of energy resources from domestic sources, for instance by subsidizing home supplies, is also likely to reduce domestic incomes. The marginal cost (value of alternatives foregone) of *accelerating* home supplies can be expected to exceed the price or cost to the economy of imports and so this substitution leads to a fall in the domestic standard of living. In other words, there is a loss in gains from trade which would normally stem from international specialization of production in accordance with comparative advantage. Furthermore, while the accelerated use of local reserves of energy resources may reduce dependence on imports in the short-term this may imply greater dependence in the long-term as local reserves are depleted. However, from a political point of view and considering the sacrifices involved, it may still be worth while for a nation to subsidize the development of some supplies from domestic sources. For instance, from South Africa's point of view it may have been politically worth while for it to produce petroleum from coal even though the cost of this petroleum was higher than the cost of imported petroleum. Of course, a role remains for economists in such cases, namely to advise on the economic costs of pursuing political goals and the least-cost means of achieving these goals (see Chapter 14).

Risks associated with energy imports may also be reduced in other ways. These include:

(1) Diversification of countries of origin of supplies.
(2) Diversification of types of energy sources imported.
(3) Holding of stocks of imported energy sources.
(4) Diplomatic action, especially in country-to-country agreements.
(5) Military action to ensure security of supply routes and the independence of supplying countries.

Each of these possible actions involves an economic cost which needs to be weighed against its expected benefits. The holding of stocks of energy resources, for instance, involve storage cost. The storage costs for coal and oil may be such that it is only economic to cushion against uncertainty in supply of these in the short-term. On the other hand, it could be economic to store uranium (since its volume is small in relation to energy potential) to provide long-term security of energy supplies.

Exporters of energy resources also have policy problems and dilemmas. Some of these problems have already been discussed in relation to OPEC, which aims to increase the profits of its members from oil exports by monopoly-like action and at the same time conserve oil reserves.

Exporters of non-renewable resources need to consider how much of these to export currently and how much to conserve. Greater exports now mean less availability of the non-renewable resources for future generations in the country. How much weight is to be placed on the possible demands of future generations? Are their interests best served by conservation and limiting exports of non-renewable resources? In the last respect it needs to be observed that they need not be. Current exports *may* stimulate investment and research and innovation in the exporting country and may lead to means of using alternative resources so that the position of future generations is better than it would have been otherwise. But of course this need not happen. Greater current income could be used on current consumption. There is also another possibility to consider. A resource which is valuable now may become valueless or of little value in the long-term. In the long-term fusion technology, for instance, could result in uranium supplies having a low value. While uranium prices might rise during the next 30 years they could then slump as nuclear fuel is processed and reused and fusion technology is introduced.

The presence of multi-national companies in the exploitation of known energy resources may alter depletion patterns. One would expect faster rates of depletion (and greater levels of export) by multi-nationals in countries in which multi-nationals are more uncertain about their future. For instance, this might be so if they expect nationalization or the occurrence of political upheavals. These expectations may be held in relation to several developing countries. By contrast, slower rates of depletion and development of energy resources in more stable countries (the developed countries?) may occur. Even under competitive conditions (multi-nationals or not) higher rates of interest (and uncertainty in LDCs) may mean that in a market system non-renewable resources are depleted at a faster rate in LDCs than in developed countries (see Figure 13.1 and discussion). But exploration needs also to be taken into account in weighing up this problem. Less exploration is likely to occur if rates of interest are high and the future is uncertain, so LDCs might be left with a higher ratio of undiscovered resources (which of course are 'conserved' for the future) than developed countries.

13.5 GOVERNMENT INTERVENTION IN THE FINAL USE OF ENERGY SUPPLIES

Government intervention has had a variety of effects on the final use of energy resources. In some cases it has encouraged greater use of these resources; in other cases it has reduced their use or encouraged substitution between energy resources.

Policies tending to encourage use of energy or resulting in socially excessive use of energy resources

Countries or states with energy resources sometimes attempt to attract foreign investment by providing energy resources at a discount to foreign firms. For instance, New South Wales has attempted to attract aluminium refineries by providing special discounts on electricity to such refineries. One of the major inputs is subsidized and this apart from encouraging the use of a greater amount of energy is also likely to favour the installation of electricity-intensive technologies. The least-cost input mix from a social point of view is unlikely to be used. Some of the oil-producing countries have done likewise to attract direct foreign investment.

It is possible that the prices of some energy resources do not reflect their full social costs. Prices may not reflect spillovers associated with their use. A Pigovian tax, it could be argued, varying with the externalities generated by different fuels should be imposed upon their use. In many countries no such taxes are imposed and this tends to encourage a socially excessive level of use of fuels.

Public enterprises supplying energy such as electricity or gas do not aim to reduce the demand for their products. On the contrary, they advertise to encourage greater demand for their products and encourage the purchase of equipment designed to use their products. In this respect their behaviour seems to be little different to that of private enterprises. Public enterprises selling electricity or gas frequently have a multi-part tariff or pricing structure. It has been suggested that they may price the marginal units of energy purchased (in their declining scale of charges based on volume purchased) below the marginal cost of production in order to stimulate demand. As mentioned in Chapter 8, bureaucrats may place a high weight upon the quantity of sales achieved by their organization.

In some countries, including the United States, the government has moderated the rate of petrol price increases by placing ceilings on petrol prices. The principal aim has been to moderate the rate of inflation. The effect in the past has been to stimulate demand for petrol and limit supply so that demand exceeds supply. In the absence of government rationing, supplies have been allocated by ad hoc means such as petrol queues and weekend closing.

Measures intended to reduce energy use

Some fiscal measures have been adopted which reduce the use of oil. In many countries, petrol or sales taxes are imposed and car registration fees rise with the weight of the vehicle. The latter policy, however, is intended to relate the charge to road wear caused rather than to reduce petrol consumption. It is an inefficient policy for reducing petrol consumption.

In some countries governments have not been prepared to rely solely on fiscal measures. Mandatory restrictions have been imposed. The United States has set minimum fuel economy standards for new cars being manufactured. The standard rises each year and by 1985 will be 27.5 miles/gal. Markets are not being left to determine choice. Is there some type of market failure in this case? The real problem may stem from the fact that the United States controls the price of petrol so that it is lower than the world price. The market is not free to perform its guiding role in the economy.

In a number of countries maximum speed limits on roads have been lowered in the expectation that this will reduce the use of fuel and greater information has been made available by governments to encourage fuel savings by individuals.

Some other non-market policies that have been adopted by individual countries to reduce energy use include:

(1) Changed housing standards (set by local government bodies) aimed at reducing energy loss.

(2) Subsidies on home insulation as in the United Kingdom.
(3) Car pooling (organized by local government authorities).
(4) Greater provision for low-energy transport, e.g. bicycle paths.
(5) In some instances, encouragement to use public transport through provision of more services and subsidized fares.
(6) Subsidies and tax concessions to businesses to reduce energy use.

Policy measures encouraging substitution of fuels

A number of the policies mentioned above could effect substitution. For instance, policies taxing petrol consumption could encourage the sale of electrically powered cars. But some policies appear to be directly aimed at substitution. In the United States and in Germany, tax deductions are available for the installation of solar energy units. New Zealand gives interest-free loans for the installation of solar equipment and Sweden provides grants and loans. The rationale behind such schemes varies but may reflect the following considerations:

(1) There are few spillovers from using solar energy compared to alternative forms of energy. However, against this must be offset the spillovers caused in manufacturing solar equipment using conventional energy sources.
(2) Use of solar energy helps conserve non-renewable energy sources which are being used at a socially excessive rate. However, against this must be set the energy requirements (using conventional sources) for producing solar equipment.
(3) The subsidy stimulates demand and enables learning-by-doing to take place and this may be advantageous to a country in terms of exports of solar energy equipment if it obtains a technology and learning lead.

But can the subsidy for the installation of solar equipment be too high from a social point of view? This is possible because the production, installation, and maintenance of solar equipment is not costless in terms of opportunities foregone. After allowance is made for *social* opportunity costs, there will be circumstances in which non-solar energy equipment is socially optimal.

A considerable rise has occurred in government subsidies for and direct involvement in energy research. Much of this research is aimed at developing substitutes for conventional energy sources. While externalities, risk, and social-time discount considerations provide a case for government intervention in supporting research and development, there are, as mentioned earlier, dangers in the political and bureaucratic allocation of such funds. The allocation may be influenced by the relative political power of different pressure groups (and if the theory of Downs is correct, big businesses may form dominant pressure groups) and the motivation of bureaucrats to maximize budgets. The heavy allocation of the R & D budgets of major industrial countries to nuclear energy research *may* reflect such factors.

13.6 CONCLUSION

Markets do not work perfectly in allocating energy resources and in stimulating the use of such resources and research and development. But it would be a folly to believe that government intervention will correct for these imperfections and lead to a perfect state. Government intervention *can* and sometimes does worsen the problem from a social viewpoint. Government is not in the hands of idealists but is a result of interactions between different groups seeking their own self-interest as a rule. A socially ideal outcome is not to be expected. Thus we appear to be faced with a dilemma. We have imperfect markets and imperfect governments. Does it imply that we can say nothing about the choice? No, but it implies that economists must give more attention to the effects of actual political and bureaucratic mechanisms. Given a particular political or bureaucratic mechanism it may be possible to decide that a non-market solution is socially superior (e.g. in the Kaldor–Hicks sense) to a market solution (or vice versa) even though both are imperfect. It may also be possible to suggest reforms in the political and bureaucratic system which might result in a social improvement (e.g. in the Kaldor–Hicks sense) without resulting in perfection. Thus economists are changing the focus of their enquiries.

READING AND REFERENCES

Howe, C. W. (1979). *Natural Resource Economics*, Chaps 1, 5, 7, 8, and 9, Wiley, New York.

Lave, L. B. (1972). Air pollution damage, in Kneese, A., and Bower, B., eds, *Environmental Quality Analysis*, Johns Hopkins Press, Baltimore.

Mansfield, E. (1979). *Microeconomics*, Chap. 18, Norton, London.

Nordhaus, W. D. (1974). Resources as a constraint on growth, *American Economic Review Papers and Proceedings*, **1974**, 22–26.

Pigou, A. C. (1932). *The Economics of Welfare*, Macmillan, London.

Ramsey, F. P. (1928). A mathematical theory of savings, *Economic Journal*, **38**, 543–559.

Ruttan, V., *et al.* (1977). *Induced Innovation in Agriculture*, Fifth World Congress, International Economic Association, Tokyo, August 1977.

Schmookler, J. (1966). *Invention and Innovation*, Harvard University Press, Cambridge, Mass.

Solow, R. M. (1974). The economics of resources or the resources of economics, *American Economic Review Papers and Proceedings*, **1974**, 1–14.

Tisdell, C. A. (1972). *Microeconomics: Theory of Economic Allocation*, Chap. 16, Wiley, Sydney.

Tisdell, C. A. (1981). *Science and Technology Policy: Priorities of Governments*, Chapman and Hall, London.

Wilson, C. L. (1977). *Energy: Global Prospects 1985–2000* (Report of the Workshop on Alternative Energy Strategies), Part 1, McGraw-Hill, New York.

QUESTIONS FOR REVIEW AND DISCUSSION

1. 'Energy is obtained and is obtainable from a diversity of sources.' Explain. What are the main sources of energy at present and how and why has their relative use altered with the passage of time?

2. Do energy resources have special qualities which make them different from other resources from an economic point of view?

3. 'A profit-maximizing firm may be expected to adopt the production and marketing plan which *maximizes the present value* of its operations.' Explain.

4. Show how in a perfectly competitive market system greater conservation of a resource results from a rise in the future price of a resource relative to its present price.

5. Why might the market system fail to conserve a socially optimal amount of a resource? Do you accept the proposition that a monopolist is a conservationist's best friend?

6. How might an economic system relying on the market mechanism react to the depletion of or reduction in reserves of a non-renewable resource such as oil?

7. 'While there may be a social or economic case for government intervention in the exploitation of energy resources, it would be naïve to believe that the government does or can efficiently correct for market failure.' Discuss.

8. What is a natural resource tax? What are the likely economic advantages and disadvantages of such a tax?

9. 'The price mechanism is more likely to induce greater substitution of energy resources in the long run than in the short run.' Explain. Do you accept Nordhaus' view about the likely future supply of energy resources?

10. What difference might externalities or spillovers make to the optimal social choice of an energy source? Take, for example, the choice of coal or nuclear power as an energy source.

11. What types of market imperfection arise in the oil industry? What types of uncertainty occur as a result of these imperfections?

12. What measures can a country take to reduce the risks involved in its import of energy supplies? What are the economic costs of such measures?

13. What types of economic policy decisions may be faced by the governments of countries exporting energy resources?

14. What effect might multi-national companies have on the world-wide pattern of depletion of non-renewable resources? Why?

15. 'Government policies on the use of energy resources are inconsistent. Some policies stimulate socially excessive use of energy resources, others encourage reduced energy consumption, and still others favour the substitution of fuels.' Outline these policies and the reasons for them.

16. Do you believe that subsidies for the installation of solar equipment and for home insulation could be justified on economic grounds?

PART E

The Public Sector

CHAPTER 14

The Contract State

14.1 INTRODUCTION: CONTROVERSY AND THE CHOICE SET

Government procurement policy embraces the public sector purchase of goods and services from private firms. It involves governments in a set of choices about what to buy, who to buy it from, and how. In other words, decisions are required on the type of goods and services to be purchased, the choice of contractor, and the form of contract. Uncertainty increases the problem of choice. Questions arise about the most appropriate market, institutional and contractual arrangements for coping with uncertainty.

At one extreme, uncertainty is absent and the competitive model is applicable. The government as a buyer knows what it wants; the products exist and are being bought and sold in something resembling a competitive market (e.g. office furniture, buildings, houses, vehicles). In such circumstances, the state simply acts as a competitive buyer, specifies its requirements, and invites competitive tenders. The lowest bid is selected and a fixed-price contract is awarded. At the other extreme, governments are not always certain about the type of product which they wish to buy, as with high technology goods (e.g. weapons, electronics, Concorde, nuclear power, and telecommunications). Moreover, within the domestic market, there might be relatively few potential suppliers and no other buyers (e.g. defence, UK Post Office). In this case, uncertainty occurs in a bilateral monopoly bargaining situation where both buyer and seller have opportunities for exercising bargaining power and discretionary behaviour in a non-competitive or imperfect market. The buyer might have to choose a contractor and select a contract for a project which does not exist and which might involve a substantial jump in technology or the 'state of the art'. For example, a modern combat aircraft might take 8 to 10 years to develop and will remain in service for a further 20 years, so that the buyer has to anticipate a variety of technical developments as well as economic and political changes among both allies and likely enemies over a 30-year time horizon. Such advanced technology projects are often associated with cost escalation and overruns, time slippages, and major modifications, leading to allegations of contractor inefficiency, especially where the work is undertaken on a cost-based contract with no incentive provisions. Sometimes projects are cancelled, giving rise to further allegations of 'waste and incompetence' by

347

both the buyer and the contractor. Protection of something called the 'public interest' is a recurring theme. One interpretation requires the negotiation of 'fair and reasonable' prices on non-competitive government contracts and the achievement of 'good value for money'. A wider interpretation of the 'public interest' starts from the magnitude of government expenditure and the range of goods and services acquired from the private sector and raises issues of power, control, and democracy involved in the partnership between the state and industry. Further complications arise because the objectives of procurement policy frequently embrace 'ends' additional to the actual acquisition of goods and services. Considerations of the 'national interest' might be used to justify government purchase from a higher-cost domestic supplier. The 'need to protect' a nation's technology, its jobs, the balance of payments, or its 'strategic and key' industries are some of the 'ends' which typically are purchased by the state.

Government procurement policy is a controversial subject area, relatively unexplored by economists. It can be analysed with the methodology of economic policy. There are questions about the scope and objectives of procurement policy, the relevant analytical framework, and the appropriateness of alternative competitive and contractual policies.

14.2 THE SCOPE OF PROCUREMENT POLICY: SOME DIFFICULTIES OF DEFINITION

The extensive nature of government contracting policies creates problems of definition. Broadly, procurement policy consists of the allocation of various types of government contracts for the purchase of consumption and investment goods from private sector firms both domestically and overseas. Government or the public sector includes central or federal government departments, state and local authorities, publicly-owned firms and industries, and other state agencies. Through these organizations the output purchased by the public sector can range from such standard items as food, furniture, cars, housing, general building (e.g. schools, hospitals, factories), and civil engineering (roads, bridges, harbours, sewerage) to more complex products like airliners, communications systems, computers, drugs, motorways, nuclear power stations, space satellites, and weapons. Services purchased might include design and technical advice, consultancy, management, research, and training. In this way, the scope and extent of procurement policy is defined by the existing organization and range of goods and services bought by the public sector from private firms.

Where a government is a monopsonist, its procurement decisions can determine technical progress through the type of product demanded, as well as employment, the size of an industry, its structure (i.e. size of firms and mergers), entry, and exit; and, through regulation, it can directly affect prices, profits, and efficiency. In these circumstances, procurement embraces other policy objectives which cannot be ignored in assessing the purchased 'product'.

Similar difficulties of definition and scope arise in relation to government subsidy policy. Using a production function approach, subsidies can be classified into those for output and for factor inputs of labour, capital, and research and development (technical progress). Constraints usually exist such that subsidies might be limited to certain regions (e.g. high unemployment areas), a specific sector of the economy (e.g. manufacturing rather than services), to one industry (e.g. shipbuilding), or to an individual firm. Similarly, factor subsidies can be constrained to 'approved' investments (e.g. plant and machinery), to specified research and development work (e.g. Concorde), to 'approved' training methods and skills, as well as to clearly identified groups such as the unemployed, school-leavers, older workers, and 'approved' worker cooperatives. Time constraints might be imposed (e.g. a temporary employment subsidy) and the subsidies can be in cash, or kind, or earmarked. Examples include federal or central government cash grants to state or local authorities, free factory space in high unemployment localities, and grants designated for training unskilled, unemployed workers. Inevitably, questions arise about the economic logic of subsidy policy, especially its relationship to the Paretian model, as well as its internal consistency. *Who*, for example, is maximizing *what* for the benefit of *whom*? Nevertheless, subsidies to private firms enable governments to achieve desired objectives. As such, subsidy policy and the role of public money in the private sector can be included in a wider interpretation of procurement policy. Other forms of state intervention which affect procurement policy include preferential purchasing, tariffs, and import quotas. For example, government purchasing departments might give preferential treatment to firms in high unemployment areas. Alternatively, a highly-localized industry which is declining because of import competition might receive tariff protection (see Chapter 4, Figure 4.16).

The extensive nature of government procurement has usually been reflected in a state's organizational and regulatory arrangements. Changes often occur in the number and size distribution of government departments, with new entrants and exits. Such changes can result from:

(1) The growth of the public sector. Examples include more state ownership or the desire of vote-sensitive governments to be seen to be searching for solutions to a nation's economic problems. For instance, an energy or technology problem might lead to the creation of a new government department.
(2) A desire to rationalize departments, to centralize public sector purchasing, and to introduce more accountable management units. For example, specialist procurement agencies might be created for defence, for the purchase of all government stationery requirements, and for the acquisition of buildings, equipment, and transport for public clients.

Government procurement also raises issues of regulation and public accountability. With non-competitive contracts, government departments might be required to negotiate 'fair and reasonable' prices. Specialist regulatory agencies might be established for monitoring and policing non-competitive contracts. Such bodies might have the powers to investigate and re-negotiate contracts where profits are found to be 'excessive'. However, some models of regulation suggest that this arrangement might benefit industry rather than society! Public accountability might also be reinforced by specialist constitutional committees with the specific function of assessing each government department's expenditure plans and their outcomes.

14.3   POLICY OBJECTIVES: WHAT ARE THE AIMS OF GOVERNMENT PROCUREMENT POLICY?

The immediate aim of procurement policy is to secure the 'best value for money spent', which is usually interpreted as the 'most suitable goods at the most satisfactory price'. Where a government wishes to buy an existing product, a 'satisfactory' price can be obtained through competitive tendering. Price criteria are used for the choice of contractor and a firm fixed-price contract is allocated to the lowest bidder. Provided the market is competitive, the process is impersonal and requires no arbitrary judgement about what is 'reasonable'. However, there is a view on contractor selection which maintains that competition is a useful, but not necessarily essential, means to the end of achieving value for money. Policy-makers often prefer selective to open competition. Critics claim that open competition raises the costs of abortive tendering for an industry and increases the risks of contractor bankruptcy. Selective competition is believed to avoid these alleged disadvantages by restricting tendering to a limited number of firms (possibly 5 to 10 firms) from an approved list and of known reliability. The underlying economic models for these alternative views are clearly a matter for critical appraisal. What assumptions are being made about firm behaviour? Is it assumed that firms are profit-, sales-, or utility-maximizers, or satisficers, and what are the price–output and efficiency implications of different behaviour? And central to the arguments about open versus selective competition must be whether the various hypotheses are consistent with the facts.

Discretionary behaviour by governments and bureaucrats becomes possible with non-competitive contracts and where non-price criteria (quality, delivery, etc.) are major elements in value for money. With non-competitive contracts, the aim of policy is to pay 'fair and reasonable' prices. These are usually prices based on either actual or estimated costs plus a 'reasonable' profit rate defined by the state's profit formula. Of course, even where there is 'equality of information' and post-costing there can be no presumption that in an imperfect market a contractor's cost levels will be X-efficient. Moreover, so long as a 'fair and reasonable' price is negotiated, a concern with 'value for money, suitable goods, and satisfactory prices' provides opportunities for governments to satisfy wider policy targets. The most 'suitable goods' might be domestic rather than foreign, or supplied by a lame duck firm in a high unemployment region, or provided by a firm which observes the government's pay guidelines or its anti-discrimination and equal pay legislation. Contracts can also be used to encourage mergers and so re-structure industries. In the circumstances, import saving, domestic technology, jobs, and price stability might be part of the 'product' being bought; they are often elements in a government's objective function.

In some instances, the arguments used to justify state support of an industry reveal the underlying policy aims and provide an indication of the valuations being placed upon chosen objectives. For example, an industry might be supported because it is claimed to be a high-skill, high-value-added sector which makes an important contribution to the balance of payments and which, without state support, would decline, so leading to substantial job losses. Such arguments for state supprot tend to be presented in emotional terms, using catastrophe language and gross numbers which ignore completely the alternative-use value of resources. Indeed, using these arguments are there any firms and industries which would *not* qualify for state support? The relevant question is whether the resources used in the industry would make a greater contribution to employment, technology, the balance of payments, and, ultimately, human satisfaction, if they were used elsewhere in the economy. Moreover, once wider policy 'ends', such as jobs and technology, become part of the procurement choice and the purchased 'product', they accentuate the problems of public accountability. Choices and decisions are always subjective and in the absence of a clearly specified objective function, how is it possible to evaluate the *efficiency* of government procurement? There might also be a potential conflict between 'value for money' and the requirements of public accountability. Public accountability might inhibit innovation and lead to a preoccupation with the lowest tender price and lower priority to completion on time. The system of incentives for civil servants and their general attitude towards risk could be a causal factor. Critics sometimes claim that civil servants tend to be judged by failure and this inevitably conditions their approach to work, leading to delays in decision-making and the blurring of responsibility.

14.4 THEORY AND PROCUREMENT POLICY: THE CONCEPTUAL FRAMEWORK

Explanations of government procurement behaviour require the construction of the underlying policy model. This can be deduced from the standard criticisms of procurement policy, a government's perception of the policy problem, and its choice of the preferred solution. Usually, public procurement authorities are concerned with reducing escalation in cost, time, and quality while preventing excessive prices and profits, and providing contractors with efficiency incentives. Such features are most prevalent with uncertainty and non-competitive contracts. For example, uncertainty affects both buyers and sellers. It might take the form of unexpected technical problems, modifications, and changing requirements, all of which contribute to escalation in development and production costs and delays in delivery. On the supply side, it is recognized that in non-competitive markets, firms might not be X-efficient: hence, criticisms are made if incentive contracts are not used in such markets or if contractors are reluctant to risk private funds, and if the buyer fails to enforce penalty clauses in contracts (e.g. for delays or poor performance).

The criticisms of contracting and the various recommendations for 'solving' the problems can be used to deduce a government's optimal purchasing policy. Where some form of competitive tendering is possible, there is usually a presumption that competitive pressures together with fixed-price contracts provide the appropriate efficiency incentives and policing arrangements for 'fair and reasonable' prices. With non-competitive work, where prices have to be negotiated, there is often a preference for clearly-specified contracts with constraints on the buyer's financial liability, together with regular progress reports to the sponsoring department and to society's elected representatives. To stimulate efficiency in imperfect markets, there might be a general dislike of cost-plus contracts and a preference for incentive and fixed-price arrangements, with prices determined at the start of the work and the contractor subject to regulatory review (e.g. a review board for post-costing and re-negotiation of government contracts).

The underlying policy model contains a mixture of positive and normative propositions offering extensive opportunities for critical evaluation. There are propositions about 'fair' prices (what is 'fair'?) and the deisrability of avoiding escalation (regardless of costs?). Potential conflicts are likely between some of the procurement objectives, such as reducing escalation in both cost and time, as well as regulating profits without adversely affecting efficiency. Various economic models can be used to analyse procurement policy. The market structure–conduct–performance paradigm can be used to assess the allocative efficiency of different market structures, ranging from competitive tendering to non-competitive situations. A concern with broader policy aims such as jobs, technical 'fall-out', and the balance of payments suggests externalities and the use of market failure analysis. Alternatively, governments might not be social welfare-maximizers, in which case the economics of politics and bureaucracies might provide more accurate explanations of procurement policy. In this context, vote-maximizing governments are likely to favour producer interest groups (e.g. major contractors) while bureaucracies aiming to maximize budgets have every incentive to underestimate the costs of policies and overestimate their alleged benefits. Indeed, bureaucracies and politicians might enjoy the 'discretionary power' associated with the allocation of non-competitive contracts; this might explain the attractions of a selective tendering policy and the official opposition to a truly competitive solution.

Further analytical difficulties arise in formulating policy rules for improving *ex ante* decision-making under uncertainty. There are alternative methods of coping with uncertainty and economists are interested in identifying the costs and benefits of the various options. Information and knowledge is not costless and it can be purchased at different points in the life-cycle of a project, ranging from the initial design and development stage to the construction of a prototype and, ultimately, a production decision. Advanced technology projects are the classic example of public sector choice under uncertainty (e.g. modern weapons, nuclear power stations, micro-electronics). They can be bought 'off the drawing board', with only paper or design competition and the successful bidder receiving a contract for development and production work. This is believed to reduce the costs of competition but, at the same time, there are higher risks of technical failure as well as the removal of competitive pressure from the successful contractor. Alternatively, competition could be continued beyond the design stage through, say, the government purchase of relatively cheap competing prototypes. In this way, a government might postpone its final choice until it has more information on the actual performance of competing designs. An example was the US experiment with a 'fly-before-you-buy' policy which was used to choose between competing prototype combat aircraft. However, such a policy is frequently rejected because it is believed to lead to delays and to involve higher development costs through competitive 'duplication'. But the critics implicitly compare an actual competitive procurement policy with an ideal (but never achieved) project, ordered off-the-drawing board, which never encounters any technical problems, cost escalation, or delays! The general point remains. In buying advanced technology projects, a government has to choose the point in the development cycle at which competition should cease and selection occur. And economists can make a contribution by showing that alternative policies involve different costs and benefits and, where possible, offering evidence on orders of magnitude.

Economists can also contribute to the evaluation of procurement policy by analysing its positive economics content. There are hypotheses about firm behaviour in imperfect markets and the expected reaction of enterprises to different contractual incentives and regulatory constraints. However, firms in imperfect and regulated markets have opportunities to pursue non-profit objectives, so that procurement and regulatory policy formulated on the assumption of profit-maximizing behaviour under competition might not produce the expected outcomes. An example is shown in Figure 14.1 where a utility-maximizing contractor is subject to a state-determined limit on profits. As a result, the firm has an incentive to substitute staff or other discretionary expenditures for profits.

Economic models also provide a framework for analysing the causes of escalation in costs, time, and quality which are common sources of concern in public procurement. It is not unknown for public projects to cost more than their original estimates, to be considerably delayed, and to be 'gold plated', built to unnecessarily high standards, and lavishly equipped. Nor is such escalation unique to defence and government-financed high technology projects. There are examples of cost escalation in civil as well as defence sectors, in central or federal and local or state government, in construction as

354

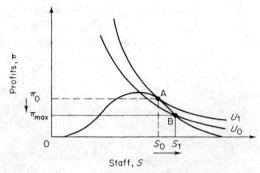

Figure 14.1   Profit regulation and firm behaviour. Utility depends on profits and staff expenditures S (e.g. number of secretaries). In the absence of profit restrictions, utility is maximized at point A. The introduction of a government profit constraint will restrict the firm to B, where utility is lower and increased staff expenditures are substituted for profits.

well as research and development, and in private industry. Cost escalation can be defined as the relationship between the original cost estimate on a specific development, construction, or production task and the actual outlays, expressed in constant prices. If, say, actual expenditure is twice the initial estimate, the escalation factor is 2.0. Some UK examples of cost escalation are shown in Table 14.1. Escalation, slippages, or overruns also apply to time-scales and the output of a project.

Table 14.1   Examples of cost escalation.

Project	Cost escalation (constant prices)
Concorde	4.7
London Court conversions	2.1–3.22
UK military aircraft and missiles	2.7
Liverpool Teaching Hospital	1.9
UK private commercial projects (i.e. chemicals, computers, electronics, engineering, and textiles)	1.05–1.5

The causes of escalation can be shown using a 'trade-off' between costs and the time required to develop or construct a given type of project. For example, the development of a new supersonic airliner, a moon landing, or the exploitation of a new oil-field can be achieved with varying combinations of cost and time inputs. Faster development is costlier, and an example of the trade-off is shown in Figure 14.2. Consider a public project such as a new sports complex, conference centre, opera house, or an advanced combat aircraft. Initially, the construction or development of a project involves a set of *plans* about its performance, cost, and time-scale, between which there are

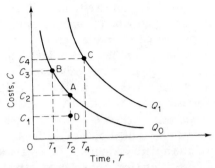

Figure 14.2 The causes of cost escalation. Different levels of quality or performance are represented by Q_0 and Q_1, with Q_1 reflecting a higher quality or performance (e.g. a faster aircraft) than Q_0. The model shows that the planned quality of a project depends on inputs of costs and time or duration (cf. Figure 11.4); it is also assumed that the technology is given and that Q_0 and Q_1 are efficient frontiers.

possibilities of substitution. Figure 14.2 provides an analytical framework which explains escalation in terms of urgency, modifications, and unforeseen technical problems, together with contractor optimism and performance.

In Figure 14.2, a given quality or performance Q_0 might be initially estimated to cost C_2, requiring T_2 years to complete (position A). Actual costs can exceed estimates if a project is required earlier than planned. Urgency can lead to 'crash' programmes with more resources being required if the project (Q_0) is needed earlier at, say, T_1 (position B). Furthermore, urgency might cause inefficiency in a government's procurement agency, so further contributing to escalation. There could be 'hasty' decision-making, 'inadequate' project specification, and relatively 'poor' government financial control and estimation. Escalation can also be caused by unexpected project changes with modifications, alterations, or improvements resulting in Q_1 being purchased at cost C_4 and time T_4 (position C). Or a project might encounter unforeseen technical problems, especially if it involves a 'jump' in technical knowledge and hence substantial uncertainty; for example Q_0 in Figure 14.2 might be a band rather than a well-defined single line. This is a likely source of cost escalation if contractors and the bureaucracy tend to respond to uncertainty by submitting a minimum or most-optimistic cost estimate rather than a central point estimate from a range of feasible outcomes. Indeed, consideration has to be given to contractor behaviour as a possible source of escalation. With a given quality Q_0, escalation might be due to the deliberate underestimation of costs, say, C_1 instead of C_2 for duration T_2 (position D). Such behaviour might reflect the efforts of an income-maximizing contractor to 'buy into' an attractive new programme by offering optimistic cost, time, and quality estimates, thereby establishing a temporary monopoly. In competitive markets with firm fixed-price contracts, this optimism, especially in costs, would result in losses and possibly bankruptcy. But in non-competitive markets with cost-based contracts, a firm's optimism will be financed by the purchasing government, so that the penalties for underestimation might be absent. The situation could be reinforced by any budget-maximizing aim of bureaucracies sponsoring the project, supported by interest groups of scientists, architects, and planners with a preference for new technology and new designs: they would have an incentive to underestimate costs. Once a contractor has been selected, then cost-based contracts are unlikely to deter modifications, ambitious technical proposals, or X-inefficiency. As a result, firms might behave as though the *actual* (*ex post*) time–cost relationship is positive, which will be reflected in both cost *and* time slippages, with extra time being costlier. Clearly, this analysis of the micro-economics of escalation raises questions about the extent of competition for public procurement and the type of contract which finances overruns.

14.5 POLICY INSTRUMENTS: PERFORMANCE AND RESULTS

Once the government has determined the optimal point in a product's life-cycle at which to terminate competition and select a project, there remains the choice of both contractor and contract type. The former involves a choice between competitive tender and negotiation; the latter requires a choice between cost-reimbursement and fixed-price contracts, or some intermediate incentive arrangement.

The choice of contractor

The application of the competitive model to tendering requires open competition with large numbers of bidders, the absence of entry restrictions, and a clear product specification so that seller rivalry and buyer choice can be restricted to the price domain. In this model, the buyer simply has to select the lowest bidder and award a fixed-price contract. Discretionary behaviour, including favouritism and corruption, is less likely. Departures from the model arise where non-price criteria, such as technical characteristics, quality, delivery, and 'wider policy aims', enter into the buyer's choice set.

Public authorities often prefer selective to open competition. Since open competition is likely to result in lower prices, some explanation is required for the general opposition to this method. One possibility is that public buyers regard open competition as 'too costly': it involves substantial transactions costs for the buyer and it is believed to raise the costs of tendering for industry. Consider the transactions costs involved in organizing an open competition and acting as a competitive buyer. The public agency will have to search for the 'best buy', which will be the lowest price, assuming there is a clearly-defined product. Search is not costless and it will require the public buyer to specify a product or at least outline a broad requirement, so that contractors can submit meaningful bids. Lower prices might be obtained by approaching more firms, but searching will cease when its expected savings through lower prices equals the costs of obtaining the extra information (i.e. optimal search). The details of the competition have to be advertised, printed, and distributed to potential bidders and enquiries have to be handled. When submitted, each bid has to be carefully assessed and checked, a selection procedure is required, and the bidders have to be informed of the outcome. Selective competition is believed to reduce some of these search and transactions costs since only a limited number of firms from an approved list and of known reliability are invited to tender. Also, since contracts are often imperfect and cannot be completely specified, the use of 'reputable' firms might minimize the procurement agency's transactions costs. The successful contractor is the lowest bidder from the group of invited firms. Not only does this appear to reduce buyer search costs but it is believed to avoid the 'wasteful duplication' of estimating and tendering resources. Usually, only a few firms on the approved list will be invited to bid for a contract, the aim being to ensure that in the long-run all firms on the list have an opportunity to tender.

The supporters of selective competition claim that it is the simplest way of demonstrating that regard has been paid to the public interest. But simplest to whom — society, taxpayers, or the bureaucracy acting as the government's agent — and whose interpretation of the public interest is being used? What are the price implications and resource costs of selective, compared with open, competition? What about new entrants, X-inefficiency, and the probability of collusion? Select lists might remain unchanged, so that there is neither new entry nor exit. It is also likely that the criteria required for entry onto an approved list will reflect a *bureaucrat's* preference for avoiding and minimizing risks: hence governments as buyers are unlikely to be presented with information on the price implications of alternative risks associated with different contractors, including innovators. Nor can it be assumed that firms will be cost-minimizers when only a small group of approved enterprises are invited to tender and the buyer determines the invitation list. Indeed, selective competition resembles oligopoly with entry restrictions. It shows how governments can determine the extent of the market, so that any market failure is policy-created and policy-preferred. However, there are no costless solutions. The choice is between open competition with lower prices and a belief of a greater risk of bankruptcy, or selective tendering which is believed to reduce the risks of default, but at a higher price. In each case evidence is required on the probability of bankruptcy and the magnitude of price differences. But open and selective competition are not the only methods for contractor selection. Non-competitive and negotiated contracts are common. Negotiation occurs if a monopoly exists or if competition is 'inappropriate' (e.g. emergency repairs of damaged sewers). Or policy-makers might exclude competition by allocating more profitable production contracts to the firm which has undertaken the less-profitable development work. Once again, this is not the only solution. Development and production could be separated, with contracts for each stage allocated on a competitive basis and research and development rewarded at market rates. However, if development and production work were undertaken by different contractors, there would be problems of establishing and protecting property rights in new ideas and the associated costs of transferring technology.

Contractor selection also involves wider choice issues which are often highlighted with the purchase of defence equipment and advanced technology items such as airliners, computers, micro-electronics, nuclear power stations, and space satellites. For developed nations with an established manufacturing base, the choice set can be illustrated by considering two limiting policy options. At one extreme, a nation could adopt the nationalist or complete independence solution and purchase all its military and high-technology equipment domestically. This would involve sacrificing the gains from international specialization and trade. At the other extreme, a nation could 'shop around', acting as a competitive buyer, and purchase its weapons and technology from the lowest-cost suppliers within the world market. For many countries, this would probably mean buying more abroad, especially from the United States, with the attendant worries of 'undue' dependence on one nation and the fear of an American monopoly of the world's high-technology goods. Opposition to such a policy would also arise from domestic interest groups of national producers and trade unions, supported by bureaucrats with a preference for domestic suppliers, and vote-sensitive governments might believe that there are more votes in allocating contracts to national rather than foreign firms located overseas. Between these extremes, there are various intermediate policies. A nation could undertake the licensed manufacture or co-production of foreign equipment. This is likely to be costlier than purchasing 'off-the-shelf' from the established supplier. But there are alleged benefits through domestic jobs, the saving of both foreign exchange and research and development resources, together with access to new technology. Alternatively, a country could participate in a joint project with other nations. European examples have occurred with aircraft, missiles, and space satellites, including the Anglo-French Concorde, the French–German–UK–Dutch–Spanish participation in the Airbus and the UK–German–Italian Tornado combat aircraft. Joint projects involve two or more nations sharing the R & D costs of a project and combining their production orders. In this way, a nation can retain a domestic industry while being involved in high-technology work which would be 'too costly' to undertake alone.

Cost functions can illustrate the costs of alternative government procurement options, so allowing policy-makers to compare expenditures with expected benefits. Figure 14.3 shows a simplified example which can be developed to incorporate more realistic assumptions and complications. Development and production cost curves are shown separately, each based initially on X-efficient behaviour. For simplicity, it is assumed that prices depend on unit costs and that a government wishes to purchase 100 units of a given product, say an aircraft or a computer. Research and development is a fixed item which is required independently of the number to be manufactured. If a nation prefers to be independent, it cannot avoid incurring all the required

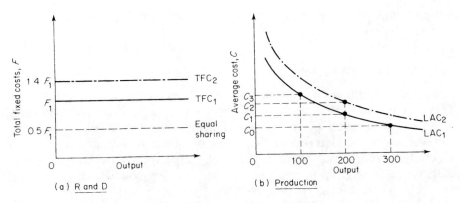

Figure 14.3 The costs of alternative policies. Research and development costs are shown as TFC in diagram (a). Unit production costs are shown by long-run average cost curves, LAC, in diagram (b). Initially costs are based on TFC_1 and LAC_1, but, with inefficiencies, the relevant cost curves could be TFC_2 and LAC_2, or even higher cost curves. For example, comparing a national venture with a joint project, the latter might lead to savings in unit production costs of $C_3 - C_2$, instead of $C_3 - C_1$ in the ideal case.

R & D costs, namely F_1 in Figure 14.3(a). For 100 units, the average manufacturing costs are C_3, as in Figure 14.3(b). Alternatively, two nations each requiring 100 units could combine to share equally the R & D costs, so halving each nation's development bill $(0.5F_1)$. Compared with an independent solution, a doubling of output for a joint project should also reduce unit production costs to C_1 (see the learning curve in Figure 6.13). In contrast, a direct buy 'off the shelf' from a foreign manufacturer already producing, say, 200 units of the item will result in average production costs of C_0. Licensed production of 100 units will involve manufacturing costs of at least C_3. With this option and a direct buy from abroad, there could be an additional negotiated contribution (royalty) towards the innovator's development expenditures. For licensed manufacture, this must be less than F_1 in Figure 14.3(a), otherwise independence is cheaper. But these are only simplified examples, based on the assumption of given and efficient cost functions. For example, international joint projects might result in higher development and production costs, compared with a one-nation venture. Higher R & D costs might be caused by duplication, especially if each partner government attempts to establish and protect its property rights in advanced technology. In other words, national and equity constraints might prevent the selection of the least-cost suppliers. Some studies have suggested that total R & D costs on joint projects might be equal to the squre root of the number of nations involved: hence for two countries the actual fixed outlays could be $1.4F_1$ in Figure 14.3(a). On production, joint projects can lead to higher costs, reflecting increased coordination and transport, together with duplicate final assembly lines. Thus, the collaborative premium shown by LAC_2 might mean average manufacturing costs of C_2 for the joint output, so that there are some savings compared with a national venture but less than in the ideal case.

Contract types: Fixed prices

With the selection of a contractor there remains the choice of contract type. There are two limiting cases, namely firm fixed-price and cost-plus contracts, with various intermediate types. Governments frequently favour fixed prices and these can be determined by open or selective competition, or by negotiation. *Firm* fixed prices are generally used for contracts of relatively short duration (e.g. up to two years), such as building and civil engineering projects. Where the work is long-term, fixed-price contracts can contain clauses allowing for variations in the prices of labour and materials. In this context, though, there are no obvious market failures preventing firms from bearing risks and estimating likely inflation rates over the period of the contract, whatever the length. Someone in the economy either in the private or the public sector has to bear risks and the process is not costless.

Generally, fixed-price contracts are used where the work required can be clearly specified and the uncertainties are removed (e.g. production as opposed to R & D work). The aim is to place the contractor at risk and provide the maximum efficiency incentives, both of which require the price to be agreed *before* the work begins. If the contractor beats a competitively-determined fixed price, he retains the whole of any extra profits or, in the opposite case, bears all the losses. However, problems arise with non-competitive fixed-price contracts, especially where a government is a monopsonist and negotiates with a single supplier. Since competition is absent, the market cannot be used to determine prices, to provide competitive pressures for efficiency, and to 'regulate' profits through entry and exit. Instead, in non-competitive situations, prices and profits have to be negotiated. Government buying agents are concerned with minimizing the taxpayers' liability, so they aim to negotiate 'fair and reasonable' prices. For non-competitive fixed-price contracts, these are prices based on *estimated* costs plus a state-determined profit margin. Such contracts assume that firms are profit-maximizers and that governments can *estimate* X-efficient costs (see Figure 14.1). The state's profit rules for non-competitive contracts might be based on a target rate of return on capital or costs, designed to provide contractors with a return equal to the average earned by the whole of manufacturing industry. Higher profit rates might be awarded for risk work and for contractor performance and there can be upper and lower limits on the profitability of non-competitive government contracts. Indeed, regulatory agencies might be created to police and monitor the returns on such contracts and to re-negotiate any cases of 'excessive' profits. But how do 'excessive' profits arise?

Fixed-price contracts specify the price to be paid for an agreed quantity and quality of product, together with delivery dates. A typical non-competitive fixed-price contract is shown as follows:

$$P_f = E_0 + \pi_g \tag{14.1}$$

where E_0 = total *estimated* outlays or expenditures for the required output. This total comprises direct labour, materials and bought-out parts (variable costs) and fixed outlays or overheads (fixed costs). Direct labour costs might be estimated using a labour learning curve (Figure 6.13) and an agreed wage rate. Fixed outlays might be recovered by applying an overhead recovery rate to estimated direct labour costs.

π_g = the government-determined profit margin, calculated as a rate of return ($r\%$) on capital employed (rK) or costs (rC)

With fixed-price contracts, profits will exceed the government-determined margins whenever a firm's actual costs are *below* the original estimates. For example, if costs are estimated to be £100 million and the state allows a profit margin of 10 per cent. on costs, the firm will receive a lump sum payment of £110 million on completion of the work. An example is shown in Figure 14.4. If actual costs are, say, £90 million, its realized profits will be £20 million, which represents a return of some 22 per cent. on cost.

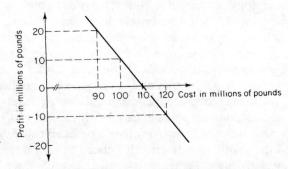

Figure 14.4 Profits and fixed-price contracts. Estimated costs are £100m., on which the state allows a profit or fee of £10m. If the final cost is £110m., the profit received is zero and further cost increases result in losses.

Firms can reduce actual costs below the estimated level through two sources. *First*, they can raise efficiency. *Second*, there might be errors in the government's cost estimates, so that the negotiated price is not based on x-efficient behaviour. As a result, the actual profits earned on fixed-price contracts will be 'excessive' in the sense of exceeding the state-determined profit rates. Equation (14.2) shows the determinants of a firm's actual profits on fixed-price work:

$$\pi = \pi_g + s(E_0 - A_0) \tag{14.2}$$

where π = actual profits received by the contractor

π_g = profit sum negotiated and agreed by the government and the firm

s = the rate at which any difference between E_0 and A_0 will be shared between the firm and the government

E_0 = estimated outlays

A_0 = actual expenditures

With fixed-price contracts where $s = 1$, so that the firm retains the whole of any difference between estimated and actual outlays, $\pi > \pi_g$ when $E_0 > A_0$. This provides a basis for determining excessive profits, especially if $E_0 > A_0$, not as a result of increased efficiency but due to inaccuracies in the state's cost estimates. Such inaccuracies can result from the estimating techniques used by the government, differences in the information available to both parties, and their behaviour in the bargaining process (cf. wage bargaining, Chapter 12). With non-competitive fixed-price contracts, a firm wishing to increase its profits above the state-determined level has every incentive to maximize its estimated, and minimize its actual, outlays.

Cost-plus contracts

Advanced technology projects confront state procurement authorities with the classic problem of choice under uncertainty. They have to determine the optimal distribution of risks between the buyer and the contractor. In these circumstances, some form of cost-reimbursement contract is usually adopted with the state bearing most, if not all, of the risks. Under a cost-plus a percentage profit contract (e.g. research and development for military aircraft or space systems), the firm recovers all its actual outlays regardless of their level, plus a government-determined percentage profit. Such contracts are believed to offer little or no efficiency incentives: they have been called 'blank cheque' contracts. Since the profit sum is directly related to costs, the contractor is almost encouraged to incur higher costs and to search for perfection! An example is shown in Figure 14.5.

It is likely that cost-plus pricing in non-competitive markets provides contractors with the financial framework for cost escalation and labour hoarding. Economists can contribute to policy by formulating these propositions into testable hypotheses. Cost escalation has already been analysed (Figure 14.2). The labour-hoarding hypothesis provides a further example of the problems in applied economics. Hypotheses have to be specified clearly and related to an established theoretical framework so that appropriate empirical tests can be undertaken. For example, in weapons markets, it is believed that defence contractors follow a labour-retention policy financed by cost-based government contracts. These beliefs arise from the frequent observation that the cancellation of weapons contracts leads to employment reductions, but usually by much less than the numbers involved on the project (see Figure 11.6). Thus, the central hypothesis is that cost-plus defence contracts result in excess employment which is reflected in a sluggish employment response to

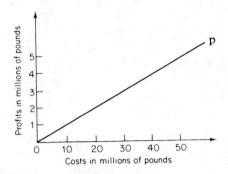

Figure 14.5 Profits and cost-plus a percentage profit contracts. With this form of cost-plus contract, profits (π) depend directly on the percentage profit rate (p) to be applied to costs (C), that is $\pi = pC$. In this example, $p = 10$ per cent. (0.1), so that an increase in costs from £20m. to £50m. raises profits or the fee from £2m. to £5m.

cancellations and a relatively labour-intensive reaction to an increase in sales. In other words, it is predicted that employment behaviour in weapons markets will differ from that in a normal commercial environment. Empirical tests of this hypothesis require a model which identifies the major determinants of employment. The standard approach starts from a production function (e.g. Cobb-Douglas) and derives an employment model as shown in equation (14.3). In this model, employment is determined by output, technology, and capital:

$$L = f(Q,A,K)$$ 14.3

where L = employment
   Q = output
   A = state of technology
   K = capital stock

The labour-hoarding hypothesis can be tested by estimating the relationship between employment and output, *ceteris paribus*. For cancellations and down-turns, the resulting elasticity of employment with respect to variations in output is predicted to be lower for defence contractors compared with civilian enterprises. In other words, the hypothesis can be tested by estimating employment elasticities for defence industries compared with other industries not dependent on government defence contracts. But empirical work is not without its analytical and statistical problems. There could be alternative explanations of sluggish employment behaviour by defence contractors. For example, the announced redundancy figures associated with the cancellations of weapons might be deliberate exaggerations, reflecting an attempt by producer interests supported by budget-conscious bureaucracies to influence the decisions of vote-maximizing governments. Also, data might not be available and there are difficulties in obtaining accurate and reliable indicators of technology and the capital stock (see Figure 11.6).

Not surprisingly, criticisms of cost-plus a percentage profit contracts has led to the introduction of incentive contracting for government R & D work. A simple form is the cost-plus a fixed fee, where the fee is based on *estimated* costs. While the firm recovers all of its allowable costs, its fixed fee remains constant regardless of actual expenditures. An example is shown in Figure 14.6(a).

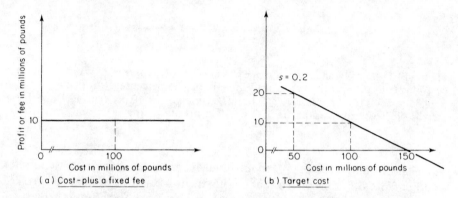

Figure 14.6   Incentive contracts. In both cases, costs are estimated at £100m. With a cost-plus a fixed fee, the firm receives a fee of £10m. based on estimated costs, and this fee remains constant regardless of actual costs ($s = 0$; see equation 14.2). With a target cost contract and a sharing ratio of 80:20 ($s = 0.2$), the firm's profits will be £20m. if its actual costs are £50m., while losses are incurred when actual costs exceed £150m. Additional constraints can be introduced into target cost contracts, such as a maximum and/or minimum fee.

Alternatively, a target cost contract might be negotiated. This is based on estimates and consists of an agreed target cost, a profit rate based on the target, and a sharing ratio whereby cost savings or losses are shared in a specified proportion between the government and the contractor. For example, the target cost could be £100 million, the target fee £10 million, and the sharing ratio 80:20. If the actual cost equals the target, the firm receives the target fee of £10 million. If actual costs exceed the target, the firm bears 20 per cent. of the extra cost, with adverse effects on its fee; and vice versa where actual costs are below target. An example is shown in Figure 14.6(b). Of course, with a target cost contract and a bilateral monopoly bargaining situation, a contractor has an incentive to bargain for the maximum possible target cost and for a favourable sharing ratio. As a result, a firm's observed performance on an incentive contract might reflect its relative success in the bargaining process!

14.6   CONCLUSION

Government procurement raises an array of analytical, empirical, and policy issues to which micro-economics can contribute. It embraces the study of government and firm behaviour in various market and bargaining situations and the choice of the most appropriate contractual arrangements for coping with uncertainty. However, there remains a fundamental issue. Why do governments 'contract-out' rather than undertaking the work themselves and is there 'too much or too little' contracting-out? For example, are there any economic arguments for undertaking research and development in state-owned establishments rather than in the private sector? And if research and development were government supplied, how would society ensure that such units satisfied consumer preferences rather than the desires of scientists, technologists, bureaucrats, and other interest groups? Such questions require a study of the public sector.

READING AND REFERENCES

Harman, A. (1970). *A Methodology for Cost Factor Comparisons*, Rand, RM 6269, Santa Monica, Calif.

Hartley, K. (1977). *Problems of Economic Policy*, Chap. 11, Allen and Unwin, London.

Hartley, K., and Cubitt, J. (1976–77). Cost escalation in the UK, in *The Civil Service*, Expenditure Committee, HC 535-III, Appendix 44, HMSO, London.

Peck, M., and Scherer, F. (1962). *The Weapons Acquisition Process*, Harvard University Press, Cambridge, Mass.

Turpin, C. (1972). *Government Contracts*, Penguin, London.

QUESTIONS FOR REVIEW AND DISCUSSION

1. What should be the objectives of government procurement policy?
2. What are the 'best' contractual, organizational, and institutional arrangements for government procurement of high-technology items?
3. Which models of firm, bureaucratic, and government behaviour 'best' explain cost escalation on government projects? Is cost escalation undesirable?
4. Should a nation purchase all its defence equipment from domestic firms? Evaluate in relation to alternative policies.
5. How would you define 'excessive' profits on government contracts? How are firms likely to respond to state controls on profits?

CHAPTER 15

What is the Optimum Size
of the Public Sector?

15.1 INTRODUCTION: SOME POLICY ISSUES

People have different views on the 'proper' role of government. Such views are reflected in alternative economic systems, ranging from the extremes of capitalism and socialism and embracing intermediate cases such as mixed economies and workers' control. Alternative economic systems differ in their use of market prices and government planning as 'coordination' mechanisms and also in the extent of private and state ownership of the means of production and the resulting opportunities for individual freedom. Different systems can be assessed in terms of various economic criteria, such as allocative efficiency, equity, and growth. Ultimately, choices between the alternatives depend on values and these will determine the role of the state. Libertarians believe that government is 'too big' and that 'government is best that governs least': they prefer to expand private markets and opportunities for individual freedom and choice. Socialists believe that in market economies the state serves the interests of the capitalist class and they are opposed to the monopolies, exploitation of workers, and the massive inequalities in income and wealth associated with private ownership of the means of production. This chapter will show how micro-economics can be used to analyse some of the issues associated with controversies about the proper role of government and the resulting size of the public sector in market economies. Since many of the specific issues have been analysed in each of the previous chapters in this book, the analysis will focus on whether the public sector is 'too large'. A starting point is to consider whether economic theory offers any policy guidelines. It will be shown that economic models of politics and bureaucracies offer predictions about the size and efficiency of the public sector. Consideration will also be given to the 'de-industrialization' hypothesis and to possible solutions to reduce size and improve efficiency in the public sector.

15.2 DOES ECONOMIC THEORY OFFER ANY GUIDELINES?

Governments are often involved in policies towards the agricultural, manufacturing, and service sectors, as well as towards regions and high technology. Paretian welfare economics suggests that an optimal economic and industrial structure can be left to market forces in the form of domestic and foreign consumer preferences, and the competitiveness of domestic and foreign firms. In this way, properly working competitive markets will determine the optimal allocation of resources between agriculture, manufacturing, and services and between regions, as well as the optimum size of both firms and the manufacturing sector. However, private markets might fail to work 'properly'. Some goods and services desired by society might not be provided by private markets or might be underprovided. Examples include public goods such as national defence, basic research and development, law and order, and arrangements for regulating and administering the operation of markets such as state agencies for competition, anti-pollution, and health policies (see Chapter 2). Such sources of market failure provide an economic justification for state intervention in market economies. In principle, the optimum size of the public sector is achieved when, at the margin, the expected benefits and costs of additional state intervention are equal. But there are alternative *forms* of state intervention, each with their different costs and benefits. For example, private monopolies might be controlled by reducing tariffs, by de-mergers, by regulating prices and profits, or by state ownership. Similarly, even if the arguments for *state finance* of some activities were accepted (which activities and why?), there remain extensive possibilities for the *private provision* of services which are often publicly-provided. Examples might include government training centres and export departments, weapons firms, road and air transport, public utilities, education, health and city services, such as refuse collection and house building (see Chapter 14). In principle, activities such as defence, law, and protection could also be contracted-out to private suppliers, namely mercenaries and private protection and law enforcement agencies. The fact that such functions are normally government-supplied often reflects 'wider considerations', such as a concern with democracy, the distribution of power within society, and its potential for abuse and the possibilities of corruption. Where public provision is accepted, should it be supplied by national, regional, state, city, or local governments? People might prefer smaller authorities with local autonomy and be willing to pay a premium where this involved sacrificing any scale economies which would be available to larger units. Inevitably, in assessing alternative forms of state intervention, problems arise in identifying and valuing costs and benefits. In particular, whose valuations are to be used in any decision? Nor does Pareto optimality necessarily require private ownership; given certain conditions, it can be achieved under perfect socialism (cf. perfect competition). Nevertheless, the existence of market failure does not imply that the existing public sector in any market economy is of optimal size. Interesting questions also arise in selecting the most appropriate indicators for measuring the size of the public sector. Should we use government expenditure or employment, absolute amounts, or proportions of totals, and how are state assets to be valued?

The benefits and costs of state intervention

In the Paretian model, state intervention is expected to result in net benefits through the achievement of an optimal allocation of resources. Allocative improvements arise from the removal of significant imperfections in factor and product markets, from the provision of public or collective goods in amounts which would not otherwise be provided, and through 'correcting' externalities. Examples which have already been discussed include consumer protection and energy policies (Chapters 5 and 13). But state intervention is not costless. Direct costs arise from the creation of a bureaucracy which is required to produce public sector output, including regulatory activities. For this purpose, resources have to be bid away from alternative uses in the private sector. Either the bureaucracy is financed through general taxation or through direct charging for its services. There are also possible indirect, unexpected, and sometimes perverse effects from state intervention and these have to be included in any cost–benefit calculus. For example, in an apparent effort to protect patients and improve safety, many governments have imposed restrictions (e.g. licences) on the introduction of new drugs developed by private industry (see Chapter 5). This involves direct costs in the form of the staff and resources used in the state's regulatory agency, as well as the costs imposed upon private industry in conforming to the regulatory requirements. Governments might require specific tests to be undertaken and passed satisfactorily before a new drug can be tested on humans in a clinical situation, followed by additional tests and satisfactory performance before a product licence is awarded. As a result, it will take longer to develop and market new drugs, with fewer being marketed, so that some patients are likely to suffer! Economists can contribute to policy formulation by quantifying some of the direct and indirect costs of regulation, leaving society to decide upon the desirable amount. We need to know how many people and resources are involved in regulation; how much longer it takes to develop a new drug and the magnitude of the extra development costs; and whether regulation has had any observable effects on patient safety.

Taxation, incentives, and the Laffer curve

Part of the debate about the costs and benefits of government activity and the optimum size of the public sector involves taxation and its effects on incentives. It has been argued that a large public sector requires correspondingly high taxation. As a result, there are reputed to be adverse effects on incentives to enterprise and effort, with corresponding implications for an economy's competitiveness and its growth rate. Thus, some governments have claimed that incentives must be improved by allowing people to keep more of what they earn.

Theory shows that incentives can operate through their effects on the labour supply. Lower income taxes are equivalent to an increase in wage rates and the effect on the supply of effort will depend on the relative strengths of the income and substitution effects (see Chapter 10). For the incentive argument to work, the substitution effect has to be dominant. However, theory offers no a priori predictions about the relative strengths of the income and substitution effects. Thus, the relationship between income taxes and effort has to be resolved through empirical testing. One possible approach involves the estimation of a Laffer curve for an economy.

A Laffer curve shows the relationship between tax rates and tax revenue, with the latter being zero at the extreme tax rates of 100 per cent. and zero. Between these two extremes, there is assumed to be some point of maximum tax revenue, as shown in the Laffer curve in quadrant I of Figure 15.1. A trade-off between GDP and the tax rate is shown in quadrant III. As tax rates rise (e.g. for distributional objectives), the operation of net disincentive effects is likely to result in a fall in GDP. A similar trade-off between GDP and tax revenue is outlined in quadrant IV. Higher tax revenue requires higher tax rates, with adverse effects on GDP. Of course policy-makers interested in incentive effects require evidence on the precise shapes and slopes of the various schedules shown in Figure 15.1.

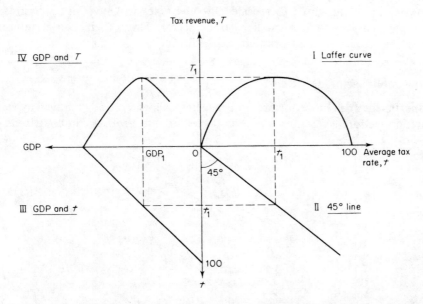

Figure 15.1   The Laffer curve analysis. This is illustrative only and assumes other things are constant (e.g. economic growth can shift the schedules). A simplified (smooth) Laffer curve is shown in quadrant I. Tax revenue is maximized (T_1) at an average tax rate of t_1. Quadrant III shows the relationship between GDP and average tax rates, with t_1 associated with GDP_1. Quadrant IV shows the relationship between GDP and tax revenue, with T_1 associated with GDP_1. The peak in the schedule in quadrant IV shows that points to the right of GDP_1 are inefficient; the same revenue could be raised with a higher GDP. The actual shape of the various schedules might be much more complex.

The displacement effect and the size of the public sector

Arguments about taxation and its incentive effects also involve the size of the public sector. Taxation can act as a constraint on government expenditure. In a model developed by Peacock and Wiseman (1967), government and bureaucrats prefer to spend more money, but voters do not like to pay higher taxes, and vote-sensitive politicians cannot ignore voter preferences. In normal times, public expenditure would show a gradual upward trend, reflecting the higher tax revenue from rising real incomes and a constant tax rate. During periods of crisis and social upheavals, such as wars, public expenditure would rise much more rapidly, with an associated increase in the levels of taxation. Electorates will accept higher taxation during a crisis. The resulting upward displacement in public expenditure and in the size of the public sector is called the 'displacement effect'. Following the crisis, public expenditure and taxation do not fall to their original levels; voters are likely to become more tolerant of the higher taxation. An example of the displacement effect is shown in Figure 15.2.

Some of the policy issues about the size of the public sector are now clearer. Taxation and public expenditure are related elements in the controversy. Displacement effects result in a larger public sector. In contrast, policies to improve incentives through reduced income taxes will involve reductions in public expenditure and a smaller public sector. How, then, can economists assess the efficiency of government expenditure?

Is the public sector inefficient?

Inefficiency can be defined to embrace both allocative and technical aspects. Paretian welfare economics suggests that state intervention can contribute to

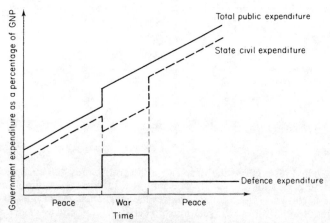

Figure 15.2 A permanent displacement effect. The trend in government expenditure during the war continues into the post-war years. In this example, there are upward shifts in both defence and state civil expenditures.

the achievement of an optimum allocation of resources and such an outcome would *not* be inefficient. But actual public sectors do not operate in a Paretian world where all the marginal conditions for an optimum are satisfied. Certainly, the market failure paradigm does not explain the whole range of activities undertaken by modern governments, both nationally and locally. Instead, the public sector in market economies operates in the political market where there is potential for government failure: hence, some functions of government are more likely to be explained by the economics of politics and bureaucracies (see Chapter 3). This provides an analytical framework for assessing the claims often made by right-wing politicians that the public sector is 'too large'. Usually, these claims embrace budgets, outputs, and factor inputs.

Consider a government which wishes to reduce public expenditure and enforce cash limits on spending departments, while improving efficiency and reducing waste (it might be too costly to eliminate waste completely). At the same time, the government could be committed to reducing public sector manpower, with an associated desire to change the labour mix by economizing on the numbers of central government civil servants, reducing local government manpower, and restricting the numbers of managers and administrators in its state health and education services. Such a government will soon discover that it is costly to achieve compliance with its objectives. How can a Cabinet and individual Ministers, with limited knowledge and time, ensure that their wishes are actually implemented? If it is costly to achieve compliance, there will be an optimal amount of non-compliance or control loss and the possibility of perverse outcomes. Problems arise because bureaucrats are experts on public sector production functions. They are experts on the opportunities for varying output and for factor substitution in response to budgetary cuts. Take, as an example, behaviour in state-owned hospitals where the government might be trying to 'economize' through imposing 'cash limits' on spending. How might such cash limits affect the purchase of, say, new high-technology medical equipment?

Every year, doctors and specialist groups will submit bids for new capital equipment, such as scanners, X-ray equipment, or a new computerized cardiac arrest unit. Usually, there will be excess demand. Assume that it is Dr D's turn in the 'queue' and that he is allowed to acquire new X-ray equipment on condition that he finances its running costs from his annual recurrent budget, which is subject to cash limits. Motivation and behaviour within this framework has three significant features:

(1) No administrator has the competence to question the doctor's professional judgement on the need for the equipment. Nor can specialist supplies officers question whether a cheaper item might be as effective. The usual story is that a doctor colleague in a nearby hospital has recently acquired some Japanese equipment with all the latest technical aids and gadgets, and his friend wants the same or even better!

(2) A doctor's employment contract provides no inducements to respond to economic incentives: he does not share in any savings and economies. Indeed, any savings might accrue to rival departments within the hospital or to the local hospital authority or even to the central government treasury. Moreover, a failure to spend an allotted budget or a refusal to bid for an allocation might incur the opprobrium of staff within the doctor's unit, as well as from colleagues in other spending departments. Thus, the system creates incentives to spend.

(3) Doctors can respond to cash limits on spending by using their specialist knowledge and discretion to reduce output in *their preferred areas*. An obvious strategy is to reduce output in those areas which will increase a doctor's chances of obtaining a larger budget in the future. For example, he could lengthen the queue for X-rays by making short-run economies in cooperating labour inputs (e.g. clerical staff might be reduced, so increasing the waiting time for an X-ray!)

Such examples of behaviour are not unique to state-owned hospitals: they are likely to occur in other parts of the public sector. An immediate requirement for any analysis is a model which offers explanations and testable predictions about the behaviour of public bureaucracies. And the model has to address itself to the issues which often dominate debates about the size of the public sector. Does theory predict that the public sector will be 'too large' and will be characterized by waste and inefficiency? Can the models be developed to include manpower as well as showing the response of bureaus to budget cuts?

15.3 ECONOMIC MODELS OF BUREAUCRACY AND THE SIZE OF THE PUBLIC SECTOR

The economics of politics would explain the size of the public sector as a response of vote-maximizing governments to the preferences of the median voter. At the same time, the model recognizes that the voters who are best informed on a policy issue are those whose incomes are directly affected by it, with democratic governments responding to such interest groups. In the public sector, this means government employees or bureaucrats. The Niskanen model predicts that budget-maximizing bureaucrats will 'overproduce', the result being allocative inefficiency in the public sector (see Chapter 3). This model can be developed to include x-inefficiency, budgets, and manpower, as shown in Figures 15.3 and 15.4.

Figure 15.3 incorporates manpower into the Niskanen model of bureaucrats as budget-maximizers (see Figure 3.2). Four sectors are shown, namely output, total budgets, manpower, and real wages. Initially, bureaucrats are assumed to be X-efficient. Quadrant I shows the bureau's output (Q_b) exceeding the social optimum (Q_c), and the implications for total budgets and total costs are shown directly in quadrant II. The manpower implications of the bureau's output can be derived from the bureaucracy's X-efficient production function relating

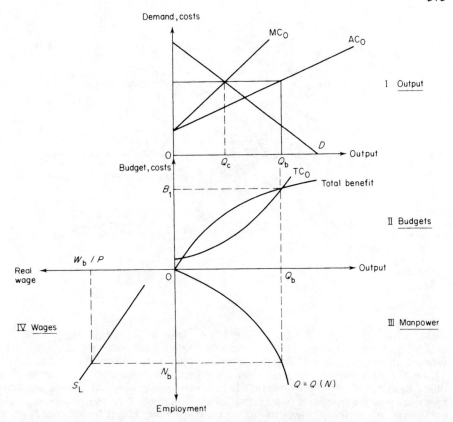

Figure 15.3   Budget maximization and manpower. Quadrant I is identical to Figure 3.2 with Q_b as the bureau's output and Q_c as the competitive output. Quadrant II shows total budgets and total costs directly, with the bureau maximizing its budget subject to the constraint that total revenue (budget) equals total costs (Q_b). It should be emphasized that the total benefit schedule assumes perfect price discrimination, with bureaus extracting the available consumer surplus. The employment implications of budget maximization are shown in quadrant III (N_b), and the resulting real wage is derived in quadrant IV (W_b/P).

output and employment, as shown in quadrant III. The real wage required to attract and retain a bureaucracy labour force of N_b is shown by the labour supply function in quadrant IV (W_b/P). One further implication of the model is relevant to the public sector debate. It is often claimed that many state activities are justified by decreasing costs (see Chapter 8). However, this might be the result of bureaucrats trying to estimate the governments' demand curve for the bureau's output. A downward-sloping demand curve would mean that a bureau would offer a larger output at a lower unit price (at least up to Q_c in Figure 15.3), even though the true underlying costs were constant or increasing! Nevertheless, in debates about 'inefficiency and waste' in the

374

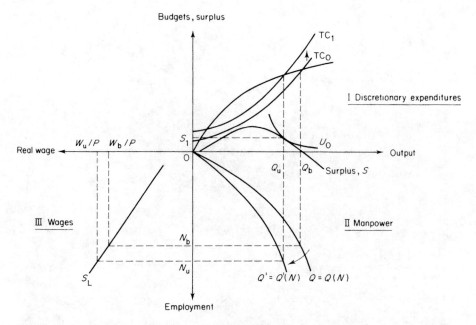

Figure 15.4   Utility maximization. Panel I is the same as panel II in Figure 15.3. For simplicity, the diagram of demand and marginal-average cost schedules has been omitted. In panel I, Q_b is the output of Niskanen budget-maximizing bureaucracy, with TC_0 as the minimum cost of production. A bureau which maximizes a more general utility function ($U = U(Q,S)$ where S is surplus) — will produce at Q_u and consume inefficiency in the form of a higher cost schedule, namely TC_1. If it is assumed that bureaucrats prefer to use their surplus on staff, the result might be a higher level of employment N_u, where $N_u > N_b$ as shown in panel II. Strictly, this implies a utility function $U = U(Q,L)$ where L is labour input. The real wage implications of N_u are shown in panel III.   ·

public sector, the model in Figure 15.3 is limited to allocative inefficiency.

In the Niskanen model, budget maximization is equivalent to maximizing output subject to the budget constraint: bureaus do not derive any satisfaction from discretionary expenditures. Figure 15.4 modifies the model to incorporate discretionary expenditures, technical inefficiency, and a preference for staff inputs. Panel I in Figure 15.4 assumes that bureaus are utility-maximizers, where utility depends on both output and discretionary expenditures (U_0). Also, panel I shows the surplus curve which represents discretionary expenditures or a fiscal residual. This is the difference between the total budget for a bureau and its *minimum* costs of production. A utility-maximizing bureaucrat with a preference for output and surplus will choose the combination Q_uS_1. The surplus provides bureaucrats with opportunities for discretionary expenditures on salary, promotions, new offices, additional staff, on-the-job leisure, and payments to consultants and interest groups supporting the bureau. As a result, bureaus will be technically inefficient and costs will rise above the minimum level (from TC_0 to TC_1). In other words, output Q_u involves 'waste' in the sense of X-inefficiency. Next, let it be assumed that the bureau has a preference for staff. In this case, discretionary expenditures will be used to buy labour inputs. An examples is shown in panel II of Figure 15.4, where the bureaucracy chooses an inefficient production function resulting in the employment level N_u. The implications for real wages are shown in panel III.

The analytical framework outlined in Figure 15.4 suggests that the public sector will be 'too large' as well as technically inefficient and will contain 'too many' civil servants. Ultimately, of course, the acceptability of such a model of behaviour and performance depends on its explanatory power and predictive accuracy. There remain extensive opportunities for empirical testing and, in the absence of satisfactory tests, the model has some tentative support from casual empiricism. For example, an official study of local government in the United Kingdom reported criticisms of local authorities for overstaffing and operational inefficiency, especially in direct labour organizations; for the proliferation of departments and chief officer posts, and the upgrading of posts and internal promotion following local government reorganization; for unnecessarily high standards in building and equipment; for defective incentive bonus schemes; and for a spate of new town halls (Layfield, 1976).

The effects of budget cuts

Will cuts in a bureaucracy's budget improve efficiency, reduce waste, and release manpower? The model in Figure 15.4 predicts that a budget cut is likely to reduce output, with a possible move towards the social optimum! After all, the government and the bureaucracy will be operating in a bilateral monopoly bargaining situation with the former lacking expert and independent information on the bureau's efficient production function. What is the likely behaviour of the production function in such a situation, and especially in an environment of budget cuts? Civil servants and officials might respond to a cut by labour hoarding. They might try to protect jobs by shifting the bureaucracy's production function and offering only token manpower savings. After all, in the absence of alternative suppliers and cost-comparisons, bureaucrats can shift a department's production function at their discretion and in their favour. An example is shown in Figure 15.5. Such behaviour seems to have arisen in the United Kingdom following the general decline in student numbers for teacher training. In the education faculty of one polytechnic, the average lecturer teacher-hours per week dropped from 16 in 1977 to 8 in 1978, and total annual teaching hours were more than halved: staff were reduced from 50.7 to 47.1. It might, of course, be argued that productivity increases in the public sector are low relative to the private sector and that this is a source of rising relative costs of government-supplied services. But is low productivity an inherent characteristic of the technology involved in state-supplied services or does it reflect the behavioural framework within which bureaucrats operate?

These alternative hypotheses could be easily tested by allowing extensive experiments in competitive bidding for some of the functions traditionally undertaken by national, state, city, and local governments.

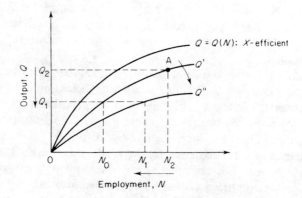

Figure 15.5 Labour hoarding. A utility-maximizing bureaucrat is initially in equilibrium at point A with output–employment $Q_2 N_2$, as derived in Figure 15.4. A budget cut results in a reduction in output from Q_2 to Q_1, but, if the bureaucracy can shift its production function to Q'', employment will fall to N_1 rather than N_0.

15.4 IMPROVING EFFICIENCY WITHIN THE PUBLIC SECTOR

Various proposals have been made to improve both the technical and allocative efficiency of the public sector. New management techniques have been suggested to assist governments in resource allocation and to improve rational analysis in policy-making. The number and variety of so-called 'rational' techniques is ever expanding and includes cost–benefit analysis, evaluation research, impact assessment, futures research, and social indicator research. Cost–benefit analysis involves the monetary valuation for society of all the expected costs and benefits (including externalities) of a policy or project in relation to the alternative choices. The aim is to select the policy or project which is most worth while to society. A related technique is evaluation research which aims at assessing the performance of government programmes. What are the policy objectives? How can they be measured? Were the objectives achieved, and at what cost? Planning Programming Budgeting Systems (PPBS) are a good example of this approach. Other variants include Management by Objectives (MBO) and Zero-Based Budgeting which, through annual evaluations of programmes, aims to eliminate or reduce activities which have become 'dubious'. Environmental and social impact assessments were a response to the alleged deficiencies of cost–benefit analysis and the apparent neglect of non-economic criteria in judging the worth of a project. Environmental analysis assesses all the direct and indirect environmental effects of an activity such as air pollution, the disposal of nuclear waste, or earth moving — e.g. the effects on present and future vegetation growth, fresh water, farming, forestry, fishing, and tourism. Similarly, social impact assessment identifies the effects of policies, including new technology, on all dimensions of living conditions including demographic, social, and economic aspects. Futures research tries to provide governments with some picture of the future in terms of both what might happen and what will happen. Finally, social indicators research provides measures of socio-economic well-being or welfare. Examples range from crime rates to efforts at measuring the 'quality of life'.

All these rational techniques have a number of common problems:

(1) Confusion often arises between allocative and technical efficiency and effectiveness. A programme might be effective in achieving its objectives, but at what cost? Similarly, technical efficiency is a necessary, but not a sufficient, condition for allocative efficiency (see Chapter 2).
(2) Typically, policy decisions are not made by one individual but are the outcome of a search and bargaining process involving a variety of individuals and groups. Some fascinating problems arise in identifying the various agents in public sector decision-making and in modelling their behaviour (i.e. what are the various groups trying to maximize?).
(3) Since policy-making is about politics, particularly distributional equity, value judgements cannot be avoided. The task is to identify what, and whose, value judgements are part of the allegedly 'rational policy analysis'.
(4) There is a preference for quantification and a tendency to ignore qualitative data. One view maintains that 'if it cannot be measured, ignore it'. Alternatively, it seems reasonable to require the analyst to specify and list those aspects of any policy evaluation which are regarded as relevant, but which cannot be quantified.
(5) There is a real danger that 'rational techniques' in policy analysis will be used to support, serve, and reinforce the budget-maximizing aims of bureaucracies. And, in the last resort, administrators can refuse to cooperate where it is not in their personal interests to have programmes examined in great depth. Efforts to measure a bureaucracy's performance lead to the inevitable response that output cannot be measured, that there is no truth in numbers, that our activities are 'priceless', and that vulgar notions of cost–benefit analysis do not apply to us!

Some of these points require elaboration and illustration. This is best undertaken by considering the application of one of the 'new' management techniques to a major government spending department and its allocative choices. The technique to be assessed is Programme Budgeting, or PPBS, as applied to defence. It shows how micro-economics provides a framework for evaluating defence spending as one of the classic public goods. In particular, what is the contribution of a budgetary system to determining whether a nation spends 'too much' or 'too little' on defence and whether given expenditures are technically efficient? Can the budgetary system be used by politicians and society to assess the efficiency with which the Defence Department or Ministry and the Armed Forces use scarce resources?

Defence, efficiency, and budgets

A government aiming to maximize social welfare will allocate scarce resources between military and civil goods in an effort to make society 'better off'. Ideally, resources are allocated to defence until the additional expected benefits of the expenditure are equal to its extra costs, where costs are the sacrifices of public and private civil goods and services (schools, hospitals, roads, houses, cars, and television sets). In addition to choosing the optimum size of the military budget, governments are also involved in further choices about the allocation of a budget between manpower and weapons, nuclear and conventional forces, and between land, sea, and air forces. Moreover, choices are made under uncertainty. Assumptions have to be made about the behaviour of potential enemies, technical progress in new weapons, and the future growth rate of the economy.

Scarcity and efficiency in the allocation and use of resources is central to economics. In this sense, defence choices are not unique. Defence involves the converson of inputs into outputs, this production process being determined by the military production function. Indeed, the military sector can be regarded as an industry or group of firms seeking to combine most efficiently the inputs of capital, labour, land, and enterpreneurship to maximize defence 'output'. In this context, the aim of defence policy or output is usually expressed in such terms as peace, security, protection, the probability of survival, and the saving of human lives. As an industry, the armed forces consist of a large number of units and bases (firms), each with a commanding officer who acts as an entrepreneur or manager combining various weapons and manpower to produce a variety of defence products (e.g. air defence; protection of shipping; deterrence). But defence differs from other private industries, such as cars and chemicals, in one resource-relevant way. For defence, there are no private markets to establish the price of the industry's output and to show society's valuation of the activity; nor are there rival suppliers of defence forces within an economy and profitability cannot be used to assess the efficiency with which a Defence Department and its military commanders use scarce resources. Indeed, defence is usually regarded as the classic example of a pure public good (see Chapter 2). This creates problems in determining the optimum size of the military budget. Democratic societies find it difficult to express a judgement on the value of protecting human lives when individual voters are unable to express a preference for different amounts of defence (i.e. limitations of the voting system), where there are incentives to 'free-ride' under a defence umbrella and where difficulties arise in any government trying to aggregate individual preferences into society's welfare function. Predictably, various pragmatic criteria have been used to determine a nation's optimum defence expenditure. These include a nation's involvement in wars, its commitments, the state of international tension, and the behaviour of potential enemies, as well its economic performance and membership of alliances. And yet, defence is a major user of society's limited resources, so that it is important to examine the means available for monitoring and improving efficiency in this area of decision-making. Do traditional methods of budgeting provide an information framework for assessing defence choices?

An example of a traditional input budget is shown in Table 15.1. This table is based on the traditional form of the Defence Budget as it used to be presented annually in the United Kingdom. It only showed annual expenditures by each Service for the items specified. Being restricted to a one-year period means that traditional budgets do not show the total systems or life-cycle costs of current defence decisions. Admittedly, some of the information is useful for assessing choices and efficiency in resource-use. Information is given on pay, research, and development and the production of new weapons for each Service. The remaining budget headings are not very helpful, unless decision-makers are worried about the size of the army's food and

Table 15.1   Input budgets

	Ministry of Defence expenditures (£m.)				
	Army	Navy	Air Force	Central	Total (£m.)
1. Pay of:					
(a) Service personnel					
(b) Reserve Forces					
(c) Civilians					
2. Movements					
3. Supplies:					
(a) Petrol, oil					
(b) Food					
(c) Fuel and light					
(d) Miscellaneous					
4. Research and production:					
(a) R & D					
(b) Production					
5. Works, buildings, land					
6. Miscellaneous services, etc.					
Totals					

lighting bill! In other words, input budgets do not provide information on outputs and the objectives of defence policy; nor on the relationship between life-cycle inputs and specific outputs; nor on the possibilities for, and implications of, substitution between various inputs in relation to defence outputs. For example, it does not help policy-makers in deciding whether more resources should be allocated to nuclear or conventional forces, to land, sea, or air forces, and what the implications might be for defence output. How can efficiency in resource-use be assessed and improved when traditional input budgets do not show the products of the defence industry and their costs of production? Programme or output budgeting provides a framework for assessing information and questioning the aims of a government department and its use of resources.

Programme budgeting in defence

Programme budgeting or PPBS emphasizes objectives, outputs, and total resource costs. It seeks answers to four questions:

(1) What are the objectives of the Defence Department and is it possible to formulate a set of programmes which can be related to these objectives?
(2) What are the current and expected life-cycle resource costs of each programme?
(3) What are the results or outputs of each programme?
(4) Are there alternative methods of achieving each programme and what are the costs and outputs of each alternative (i.e. cost-effectiveness studies)?

An example of a programme budget as used for UK defence expenditure is shown in Table 15.2. Compared with traditional budgets, it shows some of the outputs of the defence industry, their costs of production, and the possibilities for substitution. For example, in 1980–1981 the cost of BAOR was similar to the total budget for the Navy's Combat Forces. Similarly, the existing nuclear deterrent was relatively cheap and was less than the expenditure on reserves or air defence. Moreover, if the United Kingdom decided that it was spending 'too much' on defence, the information in Table 15.2 shows some of the options available to policy-makers. A search for savings of over £1,000 million (1980 prices) would be equivalent to the abolition of BAOR, or the cancellation of most of the R & D programme, or the end of training.

Expenditure figures are, however, only inputs and any appraisal of efficiency in the defence sector cannot ignore outputs or the combat effectiveness of the armed forces. Here, however, published data tend to be measures of intermediate, rather than final, output. Numbers of ships, regiments, and aircraft squadrons are misleading in the absence of data on the average age of weapons and their operational availability at any moment. The number of service personnel are similarly misleading if their training and skill levels (productivity) are ignored. In other words, published data fail to provide any indications of final outputs as reflected in deterrence, protection, damage limitation, and, ultimately, the chances of survival in different conflict situations.

The micro-economics of strategic nuclear weapons choices

Programme budgeting simply provides decision-makers with the type of information required by any well-run organization. Once this is recognized, it can be applied to situations not usually analysed by economists. An example concerns the UK's nuclear weapons policy and whether to replace its existing

Table 15.2   A programme budget for UK defence, 1980–1981

Programme	Cost (£m.)	Output
1. Nuclear Strategic Forces	165	4 Polaris submarines
2. Navy Combat Forces:	1,461	132 vessels
e.g. cruisers, destroyers, frigates	(635)	(49 vessels)
submarines	(253)	(23 vessels)
3. European Ground Forces:	1,746	95,200 regular troops
e.g. British Army of the Rhine (BAOR)	(1,227)	(55,000 regular troops)
Home Forces	(492)	(37,100 regular troops)
4. Other Army Combat Forces	105	14,900 regular troops: e.g. Hong Kong; Mediterranean
5. Air Force General Purpose Forces:	1,865	68 squadrons
e.g. strike, attack, reconnaissance	(620)	(20 squadrons)
air defence	(199)	(9 aircraft squadrons plus 8 missile squadrons)
6. Reserve formations	213	263,500 reserves
7. Research and development:	1,479	
e.g. military aircraft	(509)	e.g. Tornado; Nimrod
guided weapons, electronics	(414)	e.g. radar; improved Sky Flash
8. Training	975	e.g. military academies; training units
9. Repair facilities in the United Kingdom	705	e.g. 5 Royal dockyards; Royal Ordnance factories
10. War and contingency stocks	224	
11. Other support functions	1,820	e.g. Whitehall, pensions
Total expenditure:	10,785	
(a) Forces pay and pensions	2,804 (26%)	316,900 regular service personnel
(b) Civilian pay	1,618 (15%)	255,500 civilian staff
(c) Equipment	4,422 (41%)	Land, sea, and air systems, including spares
(d) Buildings	1,941 (18%)	
	10,785 (100%)	

The major UK defence programmes are shown. For some programmes, examples are given of the main items of expenditures and resulting outputs. In the United Kingdom, this is called a functional costing system and a ten-year planning period is used. Note, however, that the choice of major programmes is a peculiar mix of outputs and inputs, arranged partly by individual Service, partly by geography, and partly by weapons. Only programmes 1 to 6 relate to combat activities; the remainder are support functions.

independent strategic nuclear deterrent force of Polaris submarines. Sensible public choice on a new nuclear deterrent requires information on the costs and benefits of alternative policies, as shown in Table 15.3. The main weapons options are Trident or cruise missiles launched from land, sea or air; or extending the life of Polaris; or expenditure on conventional forces. Further choices exist between developing each weapon system in the United Kingdom, buying off-the-shelf from the United States (or France), manufacturing under licence in the United Kingdom, or developing in collaboration with Europe or the United States.

Table 15.3 shows the type of information which is required on each option. On the cost side, the Trident system was initially expected to involve a capital cost of £5,000 million (1980 prices), plus payments-in-kind. Some of the cruise missile options seem relatively cheap methods of maintaining an independent deterrent (i.e. are more cost-effective). Alternatively, the £5,000 million for Trident would buy a substantial quantity of conventional equipment, say 36 nuclear-powered fleet submarines or some 500 Tornado aircraft, or finance BAOR for about 4 years. Much, of course, depends on the reliability of cost estimates for new weapons: cost escalation factors of 2.0 are typical on advanced technology weapons (see Chapter 14). Moreover, the critical question concerns the relative contribution of the options to the UK's defence output. What will be the extra contribution of nuclear weapons to the safety and protection of the United Kingdom compared with spending a similar amount on conventional forces? How many soldiers can be replaced by, say, Trident without adversely affecting defence? In addition, the expected lifetime economic benefits of each option will enter the choice set. Consideration will be given to their jobs, balance of payments, and technology contributions. But the exact nature and magnitude of such benefits has to be specified more clearly. For example, any jobs benefits could be shown by total numbers (how many?), the type of job (e.g. skilled), and its location. Advanced technology benefits require estimates of numbers, type, and their value to the national economy. Difficulties of measurement should not discourage a search for quantification. Often measurement problems indicate that there is nothing to measure!

Some limitations of programme budgets

Programme budgeting is no more than a useful technique for stimulating clearer thinking about the aims, costs, and performance of a government department. It generates the type of information which is required for efficiency in government decision-making—be it defence, education, health, roads, or transport. But individuals are still required to make decisions about the optimum size of a budget. Indeed, the information published in programme budgets reflects the outcome of past decisions in the political market. In this situation, programme budgeting might be used to support and serve the budget-maximizing aims of a department. Even the emphasis of programme budgets on alternative costs and outputs might not show a Ministry's marginal cost function but, instead, its estimate of the government's demand schedule for the activity. Moreover, in defence, civil servants and military commanders are not motivated by the desire for profits; nor are they

Table 15.3   Nuclear weapons choices.

Policy options	Costs to the United Kingdom	Defence output	Economic benefits to the United Kingdom: jobs, balance of payments, technology, others (specify)
1. Trident			
(a) Off-the-shelf buy from the United States			
(b) US missiles; UK submarines	£5,000m. capital cost *plus* UK assistance in defence of US bases (at £5m. per annum)	4 submarines, which guarantees one on-station continuously, each carrying 16 missiles	
2. Cruise missiles			
(a) Submarine-launched:			
US missiles	£1,668m.		
UK missiles	£2,834m.		
(b) Land-based:		Assuming that 12 targets must be attacked	
US missiles	£246m.		
UK missiles	£911m.		
(c) Air-launched:			
US missiles	£894m.		
UK missiles	£2,555m.		
3. Extend life of Polaris			
4. European collaborative venture			
5. Conventional forces	£5,000m.	*Examples:* 500 Tornado aircraft or 60 destroyers	

All costs are in 1980 prices. The cruise missile data are broad estimates for both missiles and launcher costs required to strike 12 targets (i.e. assuming losses due to enemy action); two options are shown, namely a purchase of missiles from the United States and a UK development and manufacture of cruise missiles, which is costlier due to the lack of technology and the shorter production runs (Memorandum by IISS, in Expenditure Committee's *Future of UK's Nuclear Weapons Policy*, HC 348, HMSO, London, 1979, p.92). It must be stressed that the table is illustrative only and can be expanded to include other weapons and wider policy aims.

subject to competitive pressures from rivals. This non-competitive situation is reinforced where programme budgeting is used to support organizational reforms leading to the creation of a larger, more centralized department (e.g. elimination of 'duplication'), the result being an increase in the monopoly power of the Defence Ministry. In this type of institutional environment, individuals are most unlikely to minimize costs unless there are strong pressures for them to do so. Thus, it is likely that the expenditure figures used in a Defence Ministry's programme budget will reflect X-inefficient solutions. It appears that '. . . better analysis and information are not a general solution to the problems of bureaucracy. The superior performance of market institutions is not due to their use of more or better analysis. The primary differences in the performance of different organizations are due, rather, to differences in their structure and in the incentives of their managers' (Niskanen, 1971). In which case, how can society control bureaucracies and their propensity to spend?

15.5 METHODS OF CONTROLLING BUREAUCRACIES

Ideally, a starting point is the need to specify a clear, unambiguous objective function for government activities, reflecting community preferences and minimizing opportunities for discretionary behaviour. If such an objective function could be specified(!), governments would have to ensure compliance. Governments can try to achieve their objectives through hiring, firing, and promoting senior personnel; through bargaining about budgets and offering funds for preferred policies; through organizational changes to promote competition and rivalry; through introducing new information and budgetary systems; and by appointing independent outside experts to provide alternative sources of advice. Some solutions are not always successful. Organizational changes to promote competition between bureaus, say between the army, navy, and air force, might result in collusion rather than rivalry. Departments experiencing budget cuts might respond with 'savings' based on reductions in long-term spending plans ('fairy gold'); by threatening to cancel projects located in high unemployment areas and marginal constituencies ('sore thumbs'); and by offering 'token-paper' savings, while protecting their 'prestige' projects (e.g. those which offer satisfaction to civil servants rather than consumers).

Ultimately, the behaviour of bureaucrats and the efficiency with which they provide services will be determined by the prevailing form of the employment contract. For example, in the armed forces does the employment contract provide inducements and rewards for military personnel to respond to economic incentives and substitute weapons for manpower as labour becomes relatively more expensive? Alternatively, are military employment contracts incomplete and extremely difficult and costly to monitor, so allowing individuals and groups at all levels opportunities for hoarding and distorting information and pursuing discretionary behaviour, the result being substantial organizational slack? The same questions can be applied throughout the public sector, to civil servants, city officials, doctors, and teachers. If, however, modified public sector employment contracts (i.e. more completely specified, with more economic incentives) are rejected as 'impossible' (why?), there is an alternative solution. Governments can sell or 'hive-off' state activities to the private sector, they can abolish legislative barriers to new entrants, and private firms can be invited to compete for contracts to supply state services. The possibility of private sector solutions leads to the debate about de-industrialization.

15.6 THE PUBLIC SECTOR AND DE-INDUSTRIALIZATION

One version of the de-industrialization hypothesis maintains that the public sector and government spending preempts resources, both of capital and labour, forcing a contraction in manufacturing industry. The result is 'too few' producers to the detriment of industry's, and hence the economy's, investment and export performance. Higher government spending might 'crowd out' private expenditure. If the 'crowding-out' occurs in private sector investment, particularly in manufacturing, then it is possible that the size of the public sector as reflected in state spending will adversely affect manufacturing investment. Indeed, Bacon and Eltis (1978) have developed a model in which a growing shift of resources from the production of goods and services which can be marketed at home and overseas to the provision of unmarketed public services will adversely affect an economy's growth rate, reduce investment, and weaken its balance of payments, as well as accentuating both inflation and 'obstructive' trade union behaviour. The distinction between market and non-market sectors is not necessarily the same as that between private and public sectors. Profitable nationalized industries market their entire output, but they are in the public sector. However, if nationalized industries make losses, while houses and other public services are supplied at prices below costs, they are part of the non-market sector which draws on the market sector for its consumption and investment requirements. In this form, the de-industrialization hypothesis has been offered as an explanation of the UK's economic performance in the 1960s and 1970s. If valid, it suggests that improved economic performance can be achieved through a public policy which expands the market sector by cutting public spending, including subsidies to both nationalized and private industries.

The public sector version of the de-industrialization hypothesis has been extensively criticized, both analytically and empirically. To its advocates, the main problem appears to be the relative decline in a nation's manufacturing industry. But this might be due to 'other causes', such as a long-run decline in both price and non-price competitiveness. Similarly, a relatively poor investment record in manufacturing might reflect a lack of demand rather than the supply of funds. Critics have also suggested that the public sector might have been expanded to achieve full employment, in which case labour and resources would not have been attracted from manufacturing. Moreover, if the public sector is 'too large', what is its optimum size? And what are the implications of a smaller public sector? For example, which items of government expenditure are to be reduced? Are these items being provided inefficiently or is there no demand for them, and, if no demand exists, why were they ever provided? This raises questions about how society expresses its relative valuations of government services. An analytical framework is required to clarify some of these issues.

Part of the controversy can be represented as a debate about the shape of an economy's production possibility frontier and its actual position in relation to both the boundary and society's welfare function. An example is shown in Figure 15.6. The production possibility frontier has ranges showing a positive relationship between public sector and manufacturing output. This reflects the possibility that, up to a point, increases in government production might favourably affect manufacturing output. Also, the largest manufacturing output is unlikely to be associated with a zero-sized public sector (and vice versa). For an economy located within its boundary (e.g. point S), an expansion of the public sector can be achieved without any sacrifice of manufacturing goods (and vice versa). Society's preferred combination of public sector and manufacturing goods is located at position T in Figure 15.6. In this sense, the combination shown at R results in a public sector which is 'too large'. However, some explanation is required of why a society might be located at R, a point which is neglected by the existing public sector versions of the de-industrialization hypothesis. One explanation is provided by the

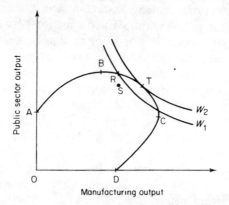

Figure 15.6 The public sector and manufacturing. The production possibility boundary is represented by ABCD and society's preference functions by W_1 and W_2, with $W_2 > W_1$. Over the ranges AB and DC there is a positive relationship between output in the public sector and manufacturing. The range BC shows the more conventional trade-off between the two outputs. The postulated frontier also shows that the maximum manufacturing output is associated with a positive-sized public sector. The shape of ABCD can be determined by empirical testing. Position T is society's preferred combination, located on the highest welfare function. Point R, associated with a larger public sector than at T, gives lower welfare. Point S is located within the frontier.

economics of politics and bureaucracies, and particularly by the models of bureaucracy developed in this chapter. Such models also highlighted some of the problems likely to be encountered in controlling bureaucracies and cutting the size of the public sector. But if society prefers a smaller public sector and more manufacturing goods, does this mean that the state requires an industrial policy?

Do governments need an industrial policy?

Answers to this question can be approached with the standard methodology of economic policy which seeks to identify the policy problem, its causes, and the range of alternative solutions. What is de-industrialization, why does it occur, and what can be done about it? Policy-makers often view the problem as de-industrialization or the relative decline of industry, especially the manufacturing sector, and the need to reverse this decline. For example, the European Economic Community has recognized that it will have to adapt to a new international division of labour in which labour-intensive, and to an increasing degree capital-intensive, industries have developed in the rest of the world and are now major competitors. Usually, the official policy view is that the health of manufacturing is of vital importance to national economic performance and that manufacturing has failed to respond adequately to changes in the pattern of world demand and suffers from structural rigidities, some of which are reflected in bottlenecks.

At the outset, any analyst requires a clear, unambiguous statement of the policy problem. If, as alleged, industry has not responded 'adequately', what would be an 'adequate' response and why has it failed to respond 'adequately'? If 'structural rigidities' are the answer, what are they, where do they exist, and why? Structural rigidities are supposed to be reflected in 'bottlenecks', although the term is rarely defined. If it means excess demand at the ruling price or wage, what is preventing relative prices from adjusting upwards and clearing markets? Imperfections are a possible cause. In which case, it is necessary to know whether the imperfections are policy-created through, for example, state restrictions on prices and incomes. There are more fundamental worries about bottlenecks. The illusion that bottlenecks can be removed completely resembles the *nirvana* approach to economic policy, where scarcity no longer exists and costs can be ignored. Nor is it possible to neglect uncertainty. Policy-makers cannot predict accurately the future: today's bottlenecks might be tomorrow's surpluses! Uncertainty will always exist about future changes in demand and supply in both domestic and world markets. Consumers' preferences are not static with, for example, cars replacing motor cycles and television being substituted for newspapers as well as for 'live' cinema, theatres, and sports performances. Supply-side changes are caused by new entrants, lower-cost sources of supply, and technical progress (e.g. computers, micro-electronics, nuclear power). In other words, the comparative advantages and disadvantages of a nation's industries are not fixed forever. But if a government's industrial policy involves 'picking the winners', it cannot avoid choices under uncertainty Which are likely to be the new growth sectors and job creators over the next ten or twenty years? To economists the issue involves the choice of the most appropriate institutional and policy arrangements for coping with, and responding to, uncertainty. Private markets with governments correcting any major failures are one possibility. It is argued that among large numbers of firms, with different views about the future and risking their funds, some are more likely to guess the future more accurately, and there are always opportunities for new entrants and exits. An alternative solution would be a single, centralized government decision-making body. But a single body could have a great chance of being wrong! Also, the economics of politics and bureaucracies suggests that decision-making by such a body will be strongly influenced by interest groups of bureaucrats and producers. In this situation, firms might be induced to seek revenue from governments rather than private consumers. If the central body is 'wrong', the impersonal committee can be blamed and the taxpayer finances the costs of failure.

Why is there an industrial problem?

Once the policy problem has been clearly specified, its causes have to be identified. Compared with other countries, the relatively poor performance of a nation's manufacturing industry might be due to government policy and to significant failures in factor and product markets. The hypothesis that the public sector has preempted resources to the detriment of industry's investment and export performance has already been outlined. Factor markets, embracing capital and labour, might also be sources of relatively poor industrial performance. It is often alleged that private capital markets 'fail' to give priority to the 'needs' of industry, allocating funds to housing and 'speculative ventures'. Sometimes, such views reflect a potential misunderstanding about the operation of private capital markets. If capital markets fail to allocate funds (at the ruling prices) to high-risk projects of the Concorde-type, this might be evidence that the market is, in fact, working properly and believes that there are more profitable alternative users of its funds. This is not to claim that all private capital markets are 'counsels of perfection'. Instead, it suggests that convincing evidence of market failure has first to be identified, after which consideration can be given to the causes of any failure.

Labour markets can also be a cause of relatively poor industrial performance. Shortages of skilled labour and relatively low labour productivity might reflect 'inadequate' consultation, overmanning, restrictive practices, industrial disputes, 'poor' management, and immobility. Once again, there is a danger of emphasis being given to *effects* rather than *causes*. What would be adequate consultation and why do restrictive practices and strikes occur? Why is management poor? Is it, and what is the evidence? It might be that a lack of competition in product markets allows firms to be relatively inefficient, pursuing aims other than maximum profits. Whatever the explanations of poor industrial performance, questions arise as to what contribution, if any, public policy can make to solving these problems.

One view maintains that left to themselves private markets will fail to improve a nation's economic performance. Supporters of Myrdal's (1957) model of a cumulative and circular chain of causation maintain that once a nation starts to decline, it will continue to contract and experience a vicious downward spiral. Difficulties arise in determining whether a nation is following a Myrdal downward spiral or whether equilibrium economics is relevant and the economy is experiencing the resource re-allocations resulting from changing demands and comparative advantages in world markets. The model can be further criticized.

A concern with de-industrialization usually leads to a policy emphasis on manufacturing. This is reputed to be the dynamic sector of the economy, with the greatest potential for productivity growth through technical progress and increasing returns to scale. In other words, the underlying growth model postulates that a nation's growth rate depends on the growth of its manufacturing sector. However, a policy emphasis on production tends to neglect services and other non-manufacturing activities (e.g. agriculture, mining, oil, and gas). Also, it might be that some of the beliefs about the relative lack of technical progress in non-manufacturing activities reflects the difficulties of measuring productivity and output in these sectors. But if governments require an industrial policy, what form should it take?

Some policy options

A distinction can be made between the technical issues concerned with the causes of market failure and the policy issues involving the choice of the most appropriate solution. Controversy usually arises over the form of industrial policy. Left-wing governments favour extending public ownership and greater state intervention aimed at re-structuring industry through mergers and using subsidies to support lame ducks. Right-wing governments prefer market solutions, with a smaller public sector, lower personal taxation to increase incentives, and competition policy for removing imperfections and improving efficiency in product, capital, and labour markets. Such solutions involve some state intervention through, for example, regulatory agencies for identifying market imperfections and subsequently enforcing and policing competition policy. Both sets of views reflect an increased emphasis on micro-economic policies, including the efficiency of supply, compared with the more traditional approach whereby economic policy was dominated by macro-economics and the management of aggregate demand. However, the greater emphasis on micro-economic 'solutions' requires some criteria for the selection of specific markets and industries for policy action. For example, market-type solutions require competition to be defined as an operational concept.

390

An alternative approach involves the selection of 'key' industries.

One policy designed to reverse de-industrialization aims to remove obstacles to the growth of some of a nation's 'key' industries. Economic analysis offers no guidelines for identifying a 'key' industry. Indeed, general equilibrium models stress the interdependency of product and factor markets within an economy. Nevertheless, policy-makers have used various criteria to define 'key' industries. They can be defined in terms of size, such as employment, output, or export performance. Or, they might be industries whose performance is 'important' to the rest of the economy (e.g. components suppliers), or industries which, on the basis of past performance, are likely to be successful. Or, they might be sectors which are expected to provide the next generation of new highly-paid jobs which will be required by those who are displaced by productivity increases. Of course, the criteria for selecting 'key' industries will emerge in the political market and will be influenced by vote-sensitive governments, budget-conscious bureaucrats, and income-maximizing producer groups.

Even if policy can identify the 'winners' and 'losers', as well as those with potential for success, what should be done, particularly in a world of uncertainty? Should the already progressive and growing industries be stimulated and supported? But these might be at their peak. Or should help be given to industries which are lagging behind? But these are already declining sectors where state support might be costly in terms of opportunities foregone. Moreover, if the capital market is working properly, doubts arise about some of the proposals for assisting firms and industries which show potential for success. Nevertheless, where state assistance is required, choices have to be made between aid in cash or kind. Financial assistance requires further choices between loans and subsidies (to firms or investment or labour?).

Subsidy policy

Economic theory suggests that if a nation wishes to achieve an optimum allocation of resources, there are two criteria for subsidies. First, subsidies are required whenever marginal cost pricing is applied in a decreasing cost activity. An example is shown in Figure 15.7, where a subsidy is necessary to cover the losses associated with marginal cost pricing (assuming no price discrimination). Second, subsidies are required whenever there are substantial social benefits such that private firms left to themselves would provide less than is socially desirable. This argument is often used to justify many activities which governments claim to undertake in the 'national interest'. Thus, subsidies might be rationalized on the grounds of jobs, regional employment, defence, high technology, the balance of payments, and the 'shortcomings' of the capital market (see Chapter 3). Many of these alleged benefits require critical evaluation, concentrating upon their analytical and empirical basis. Rarely is attention given to whether the resources would yield greater social benefits if they were used elsewhere in the economy.

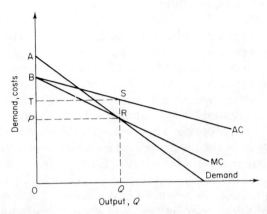

Figure 15.7 Marginal cost pricing and subsidies. Decreasing average and marginal costs are shown by AC and MC, respectively. Marginal cost pricing is based on the intersection of the demand and MC schedules, at position R. As a result, there are losses of PRST. The welfare maximum at R is represented by the net surplus ARB. At R, the potential gainers could overcompensate private firms for sacrificing profit maximization and operating at R.

Increasingly, governments in developed nations, such as the EEC, are stressing the 'need' to subsidize high-technology industries. It is believed that the future competitiveness of European industry will depend on its ability to 'mobilize new technologies', especially in 'key' R & D industries such as aerospace, computers, electronics, nuclear power, and telecommunications. Research and development is regarded as a 'key' element in innovation and it is characterized by high risk, long-term rather than immediate returns, and technical 'spillovers' to the rest of the economy. Such arguments for state support have some analytical basis. Competitive markets will tend to underinvest in research. This market failure can arise because of the risks and uncertainties of research, the costs of establishing complete property rights in marketable ideas, and increasing returns in the use of information (i.e. both externalities and decreasing marginal costs). Critics of such market failure analysis have shown that a free enterprise economy is likely to result in the 'correct' or optimal adjustment to risk and uncertainty once it is recognized that such adjustments are not costless. Nor is the issue of property rights unique since the 'theft' of all information cannot be eliminated at reasonable cost; and this applies to any valuable asset. Even if the market failure analysis is accepted, it does not necessarily constitute a case for state support of a specific industry, such as aerospace or micro-electronics. Governments cannot avoid choices about the allocation of scarce resources between alternative research activities and institutions in the public and private sectors, and between manufacturing and the rest of the economy.

392

Public ownership (nationalization)

Once the case for state subsidies has been accepted, a further policy choice is required between private or public ownership. Distributional judgements obviously enter into such a choice. After all, it might be thought that if society is financing a private firm, it would be equitable to share in any resulting wealth-creation. Also, with private firms, there might be substantial transactions costs in negotiating and monitoring subsidies. Nationalization is not, however, the only policy option. There are alternatives, such as the creation of worker cooperatives or the state requiring an equity in private firms receiving subsidies. Each alternative will involve different costs and benefits. For instance, private firms in competitive markets might be technically more efficient than enterprises in a nationalized industry, but governments might believe that subsidies to state-owned units are less costly to administer and monitor and that such enterprises can be compelled to conform to economic planning targets and wider policy objectives (e.g. job-preservation and hence votes).

There are other general arguments for state ownership. These are:

(1) The desire to plan and control the 'commanding heights' of the economy (e.g. steel?).
(2) The control of private monopoly power, including the technical monopoly case.
(3) To enable *social* costs and benefits to be incorporated into decision-making.
(4) To preserve defence industries and promote high technology (e.g. aerospace).
(5) To improve industrial relations and extend worker participation and industrial democracy.

As emphasized throughout this book, there are alternative solutions to policy problems. An economy can be controlled through macro-economic policy rather than via the so-called 'commanding heights' (wherever those might be!). Private monopolies might be controlled through price or profit regulation or through lower tariffs, without creating a *public* monopoly. Similarly, social costs and benefits can be incorporated through tax-subsidy policy or through changes in legislation to re-define property rights. Questions also arise about the extent to which nationalized industries have been successful in improving industrial relations, extending industrial democracy and allowing for social costs and benefits. Furthermore, state ownership creates a set of problems. Objectives have to be specified, pricing and investment rules are required, and performance has to be assessed and monitored.

Pricing and investment rules are related and cannot be divorced from the objectives of state enterprises. A concern with optimum resource allocation requires prices equal to long-run marginal cost which will also be a point on a short-run marginal cost curve. Such a pricing 'rule' is not without its difficulties.

Marginal cost has to be defined and measured, and will differ between the short- and long-run. Lumpiness could mean that the extra cost of another passenger on an empty aeroplane is almost zero; for a full aircraft, the marginal cost is the price of another plane (similarly for a bus, train, bridge, or tunnel). Further problems with marginal cost pricing arise because of technical inefficiency, distributional considerations, externalities, and second best solutions:

(1) Where state industries are monopolies, there are no alternative cost yard-sticks nor competitive pressures against which governments and society can assess true marginal opportunity costs. In such a market structure, there are substantial opportunities for discretionary behaviour and organizational slack.
(2) Increasing or decreasing costs result in surpluses or losses, respectively (see Figures 15.7 and 15.8). Each has distributional implications between society and consumers of the state enterprise's output.
(3) External economies and diseconomies cannot be ignored in assessing the marginal benefits and costs of a nationalized industry's output. State-owned coal-mines which deposit waste in beautiful countryside and on holiday beaches are minimizing the enterprise's costs and not society's!
(4) Since the conditions required for an optimum allocation are unlikely to be achieved throughout the economy, the second-best pricing rule for a public enterprise is likely to involve a departure from strict marginal cost pricing. In the case of substitute products, if prices elsewhere exceed marginal costs, then, the appropriate rule might be for price to exceed marginal cost in the state enterprise.

Alternative pricing rules exist. Public enterprises could be instructed to act a as profit-maximizers or they could be required to 'break even', charging a price equal to average cost. Alternatively, they could act as sales revenue-maximizers or adopt zero pricing. Each alternative has different price, output, employment, investment, and financial implications. An example is shown in Figure 15.8. Under increasing costs, marginal cost pricing leads to surpluses, while the break-even rule results in a lower price and greater output (cf. decreasing costs), and zero pricing gives the maximum consumer surplus, but at considerable cost. Given such predictions, governments can choose the pricing solution which best achieves their policy objectives.

15.7 CONCLUSION

This chapter has surveyed and analysed some of the elements which are central to any debate about the optimum size of the public sector. Questions arise about the 'proper' role of government. Trade-offs have been identified, such as the Laffer curve and de-industrialization. Bureaucratic behaviour has been shown to be a major explanation of the size of the public sector and of

394

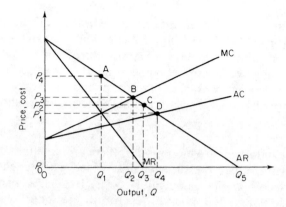

Figure 15.8 Alternative pricing rules. The price–output predictions of alternative pricing rules are shown under increasing costs. Point A shows the profit-maximizing combination with no price discrimination, B is the marginal cost pricing outcome, C is the sales revenue-maximizing position, D is where price equals AC and Q_5 is the zero-price position. A similar analysis can be applied to the cases of constant and decreasing costs (see Figure 15.7), but there will be different relative price implications for the marginal cost and break-even rules.

possible inefficiency, waste, and labour-hoarding. Recognition of the micro-economics of bureaucracies also leads to a more general proposition, namely that bureaucrats (and everyone else) show an infinite capacity for ingenuity and adaptation. People can adjust and play any games, ranging from PPBS to cash limits and marginal cost pricing. They will search for opportunities to pursue self-interest and exercise discretion, and, in the process, they will respond to constraints and their absence. The solution appears simple. Bureaucracies have to be confronted with fixed budgets, output constraints, and a more completely-specified employment contract with fewer opportunities for discretionary behaviour; and they require incentives to provide governments and society with information on efficient trade-offs. Such are the economics of utopia!

READING AND REFERENCES

Bacon, R., and Eltis, W. (1978). *Britain's Economic Problem: Too Few Producers*, Macmillan, London.

Blackaby, F. (Ed.). (1979). *De-Industrialisation*, Heinemann, London.

Brown, C. V., and Jackson, P. (1978). *Public Sector Economics*, Martin Robertson, London.

Carley, M. (1980). *Rational Techniques in Policy Analysis*, Heinemann, London.

Edwards, F. R., and Stevens, B. J. (1978). The provision of municipal sanitation services by private firms, *Journal of Industrial Economics*, December, **XXVII**, pp. 133–147.

Hartley, K. (1981). UK defence: a case study of spending cuts, in *Big Government in Hard Times* (Eds M. Wright and C. Hood), Martin Robertson, London.

Layfield, F. (1976). *Local Government Finance*, Cmnd 6453, HMSO, London.

Myrdal, G. (1957). *Economic Theory and Underdeveloped Regions*, Duckworth, London.

Niskanen, W. (1971). *Bureaucracy and Representative Government*, p.212, Aldine Atherton, Chicago.

Orzechowski, W. (1977). Economic models of bureaucracy: survey, extensions and evidence, in *Budgets and Bureaucrats: The Sources of Government Growth* (Ed. T. E. Borcherding), Duke University Press, North Carolina.

Peacock, A., and Wiseman, J. (1967). *The Growth of Public expenditure in the UK*, Allen and Unwin, London.

Tisdell, C. A. (1981). *Science and Technology Policy: Priorities of Governments*, Chapman and Hall, London.

Williams, A. (1972). Cost-benefit analysis: bastard science? and/or insidious poison in the body politik?, *Journal of Public Economics*, **1**, 199–225.

QUESTIONS FOR REVIEW AND DISCUSSION

1. What is the proper role of government?
2. How would you identify a market failure?
3. Is the public sector inefficient? How would you test such a proposition?
4. Predict the response of a bureaucracy to a 20 per cent. cut in its budget. Illustrate your answer with examples from central, state, or local government.
5. Can programme budgeting improve efficiency in the public sector? Explain how such an improvement would occur.
6. Critically evaluate the analytical and empirical basis of the argument that lower income taxes will strengthen incentives.
7. Do economic models of politics and bureaucracy predict a displacement effect?
8. Construct a programme budget for either tourism or the Catholic Church. Explain your choice of programmes and evaluate their contribution to improving efficiency.
9. Evaluate the behavioural and efficiency implications of alternative forms of employment contract for civil servants. Which is your preferred solution?
10. Examine the analytical and empirical basis of the de-industrialization hypothesis. What are its implications for the size of the public sector?

Author Index

398

Subject Index

Advertising 107, 111, 205, 228–234
  and consumer welfare 124–125
  and game theory 229–238
  and monopoly 215
  and oligopoly 228–238
  and policy 232–234
  costs and benefits of 231–232
Agricultural markets 73–74, 77–78, 84–88, 144
Agricultural policy 87–88, 212
Aircraft 152–153 (*see also* Concorde)
Air France 152–153
Airlines 225–226
Allocative efficiency (*see also* Resource allocation)
  and bureaucracy 60–61, 63
  and government 45, 368
  and monopoly 194–195
  and unions 297–298, 315–321
  examples of 19
  Paretian 15, 173, 377
Allocative mechanisms 8
Altruism 40
Arrow impossibility theorem (see Paradox of Voting)
Arts subsidies 40
Aspiration–welfare theory 111–113
Assumptions
  and Paretian optimum 25
  and realism 10, 164, 172, 175
  testing of 10
Austrian economics 5, 11, 56, 134, 168

Balance of payments 9, 60, 164, 385
Bank of England 93
Bargaining 310–315, 362, 375
BBC 233, 236
Bilateral monopoly 58–59, 310–312, 375
Blackmarkets 79, 93
Brand loyalty 167

Bretton Woods 94
British Airways 139
British Coal Board 332, 335
Budget deficits 56
Budget maximization 47, 59–64, 136, 372–376
Budgets and efficiency 378–380
Buffer stocks 77, 84–88
Bureaucracy 45, 47
  and factor substitution 47, 371
  and sunk costs 138–139
  control of 384–385
  economic models of 57–64, 372–376
  output measure 64, 371
Bureaucrats
  incentives 61
  objectives 47, 58, 63, 139, 141–142, 212–213, 372–376
Business cycles 55–57

Capitalism 170, 173, 242–244, 366
  and socialism 13, 65, 297
  and women 270
Capital markets 176, 326, 388 (*see also* Human capital)
Cartels 75–77, 225–226, 298, 336–337
Cash limits 371–372
Ceteris paribus 5, 363
Choice 5, 6–7
  private individualistic 6
  public or collective 6, 347–348, 367
Churches 13, 163
Closed shops 297, 299
Club of Rome 334
Coal 324
  conservation of 327–328
  mining rights 331–333
Cobb-Douglas 301–302, 363
Coercion 48, 299

401

404

408

410

Ninth Edition

City Politics

The Political Economy of Urban America

Dennis R. Judd

University of Illinois at Chicago

Todd Swanstrom

University of Missouri, St. Louis

Routledge
Taylor & Francis Group

LONDON AND NEW YORK

First published 2015, 2012, 2010 by Pearson Education, Inc.

Published 2016 by Routledge
2 Park Square, Milton Park, Abingdon, Oxon OX14 4RN
711 Third Avenue, New York, NY 10017, USA

Routledge is an imprint of the Taylor & Francis Group, an informa business

ISBN: 9780205996391 (pbk)

Cover Designer: Suzanne Behnke

Library of Congress Cataloging-in-Publication Data
Judd, Dennis R.
    City politics : the political economy of urban America/Dennis R. Judd, University of Illinois at Chicago—Ninth edition.
        pages cm
    Includes index.
    ISBN 978-0-205-99639-1—ISBN 0-205-99639-6
    1. Municipal government—United States.   2. Urban policy—United States.
    3. United States—Economic policy.   4. Sociology, Urban—United States.
    I. Title.
    JS331.J78 2015
    320.8'50973--dc23
                                                                    2014008983

BRIEF CONTENTS

CONTENTS

v

PREFACE

The first edition of *City Politics* was published in 1979, and since that time the book has undergone changes as profound as the subject matter with which it deals. To keep it current and relevant, we have always taken care to describe significant new developments both in the "real world" and in the literature of the field; in this ninth edition, for example, we include material on the recent debates over immigration policy, voting rights, the continued fiscal problems that cities face, and the urban impacts of inequality. In making these changes, we have included enough citations so that students will be able to conduct further research of their own.

Over the years, *City Politics* has been used in college courses at all levels, from community colleges to graduate courses in research universities. *City Politics* has reached across disciplines, too; it has found its way into courses in urban politics, urban sociology, urban planning, urban geography, and urban history. We have relied upon three elements to make it relevant to such a broad audience: a strong and original thematic structure with a blending of the vast secondary literature with primary sources and recent scholarly materials, new data, and our own original research. To make the complex scholarship of the field as accessible and interesting as possible, we build the book around an admittedly sweeping narrative. As far as possible, each chapter picks the story up where the previous one left off, so that the reader can come to appreciate that urban politics in America is constantly evolving; in a sense, past and present are always intermingled.

Three threads compose the narrative structure of the book. From the nation's founding, a devotion to the present, the private marketplace and a tradition of democratic governance have acted as the twin pillars of American culture. All through the nation's history, cities have been forced to strike a balance between the goal of achieving local economic prosperity and the task of negotiating among the many contending groups making up the local polity. An enduring tension between these two goals is the mainspring that drives urban politics in America, and it is also at the center of the narrative that ties the chapters of this book together.

The governmental fragmentation of urban regions provides a third dynamic element that has been evolving for more than a century. A complete account of American urban politics must focus upon the internal dynamics of individual cities *and* also upon the relationships among the governmental units making up urban regions. Today, America's urban regions are fragmented into a patchwork of separate municipalities and other governmental units. With the rise of privatized gated communities in recent decades, this fragmentation has become even more complicated. In several chapters of this edition of *City Politics*, we trace the many consequences that flow from this way of organizing political authority in the modern metropolis.

We divide the book into three parts. Part I is composed of five chapters that trace the history of urban America in the first long century from the nation's founding in 1789 through the Great Depression of the 1930s. This "long century" spans a period of time in which the cities of the expanding nation competed fiercely for a place in the nation's rapidly evolving economic system. At the same time, cities were constantly trying to cope with the social tensions and disruptions caused by wave after wave of immigration and a constant movement from farm to city. These tensions played out in a struggle between an upper- and middle-class electorate and working-class newcomers. The New Deal of the 1930s brought the immigrants and the cities they lived within into the orbit of national politics for the first time in the nation's history, with consequences that reverberated for decades.

In Part II, we trace the arc of twentieth-century urban politics. Over a period of only a few decades, the old industrial cities went into a steep decline, the suburbs prospered, and a regional shift redistributed population away from the industrial belt to other parts of the country. For a long time, urbanization had been driven by the development of an industrial economy centered in a few great cities. But the decline of industrial jobs and the rise of a service economy profoundly restructured the nation's politics and settlement patterns; as a result, by the mid-twentieth century the older central cities were plunged into a social and economic crisis of unprecedented proportions. In the years after World War II, millions of southern blacks poured into northern cities, a process that incited a protracted period of social unrest and racial animosity that fundamentally reshaped the politics of the nation and of its urban regions. Affluent whites fled the cities, carving out suburban enclaves in an attempt to escape the problems of the metropolis. The imperative of governance—the need to find ways of brokering among the contending racial, ethnic, and other interests making up the urban polity—became crucially important.

Part III of the text focuses on the urban politics produced by the deindustrialization and globalization processes of the 1980s and beyond. The emergence of a globalized economy is one of its defining features. Older central cities and entire urban regions that had slipped into decline began to reverse their fortunes by becoming major players in the post-industrial economy. At the same time, the fragmentation within metropolitan regions has taken on a new dimension because cities fiercely compete for a share of metropolitan economic growth. Today, central cities and their urban regions are more prosperous, but at the same time more fragmented than ever, and one consequence is that social and economic inequalities are being reproduced on the urban landscape in a patchwork pattern that separates urban residents.

These developments can best be appreciated by putting them into historical context. As in the past, urban politics continues to revolve around the two imperatives of economic growth and the task of governance. As in the nation's first century, cities are engaged in a fierce competition for new investment. The great tide of immigration that took off in the nineteenth century shaped the politics of cities for well more than a century. The intense period of immigration that began in the 1970s has yet to run its course, and it, too, will reverberate through all levels of the American political system for a long time to come. Any account of urban politics in the present era will be greatly enriched if we recognize that we are a nation of immigrants, and always have been. The several new features incorporated into this ninth edition include:

- A comprehensive discussion of the bitter debates over immigration policy
- An expanded discussion of the controversies over voting rights
- New material on the fiscal crisis that still faces many cities
- An expanded and updated discussion of minorities and urban governance
- An updated discussion of recent trends in inequality
- Incorporation throughout the text of recent data from the U.S. Census Bureau

Dennis R. Judd would like to thank Sam Bassett and Anahit Tadevosyan for their valuable research assistance and intellectual companionship. We also wish to thank Melissa Mashburn, our editor at Longman, for helping to keep the book on track.

Dennis R. Judd
Todd Swanstrom

CHAPTER 1

City Politics in America: An Introduction

Three Themes

The political dynamics of America's cities and urban regions have remained remarkably similar over time. From the nation's founding to the present, a devotion to the private marketplace and a tradition of democratic governance have been the pivotal values defining American culture. Finding a balance between these two imperatives has never been easy; indeed, the tension between the two is the mainspring that energizes nearly all important political struggles that occur at the local level. The *politics of growth* becomes obvious when conflicts break out over public expenditures for such things as airport construction, convention centers, and sports stadiums. Projects like these are invariably promoted with the claim that they will bring prosperity to everyone in the urban community, but such representations do not lay to rest important concerns about whether these are the best or the most effective uses of public resources. The fact that there is conflict at all lays bare a second imperative: the *politics of governance*. Public officials and policymakers must find ways to arbitrate among the many contending groups and interests that demand a voice in local government. The complex social, ethnic, and racial divisions that exist within America's cities have always made governance a difficult challenge. A third dynamic has evolved in step with the rise of the modern metropolis over the past century: the *politics of metropolitan fragmentation*. During that period, America's urban regions have become increasingly fragmented into a patchwork of separate municipalities. One of the consequences of the extreme fragmentation of political authority within metropolitan regions is that it helps perpetuate residential segregation, and makes it nearly impossible to devise regional solutions to important policy issues such as urban sprawl.

The growth imperative is so deeply embedded in the politics of American cities that, at times, it seems to overwhelm all other issues. Urban residents have a huge stake in the continued vitality of the place where they live; it is where they have invested their energies and capital; it is the source of their incomes, jobs, and their sense of personal identity and community. Because of the deep attachments that many people form for their local community, its continued vitality is always a high priority. Throughout American history, "place loyalty" has driven civic leaders to devote substantial public authority and resources to the goal of promoting local economic growth and prosperity. In the nineteenth century, for instance, cities fought hard to secure connections to the emerging national railroad system by providing huge subsidies to railroad corporations. Today, the details are different, but the logic is the same: since the 1970s, cities have competed fiercely for a share of the growing market in tourism and entertainment, the "industry without a smokestack." To do so, they have spent huge amounts of public money for such things as convention centers, sports stadiums, cultural institutions, and entertainment districts. These kinds of activities, all devoted to the goal of promoting local economic growth, are so central to what cities do that it would be impossible to understand urban politics without taking them into account.

The imperative of governance arises from the social, racial, and ethnic differences that have always characterized American society. America is a nation of immigrants, and for most of the nation's history, anxiety about the newcomers has been a mainstay of local and, for that matter, national politics. Attempts to curb immigration can be traced back to the 1830s, when the Irish began coming to American shores in large numbers. Episodes of anti-immigrant reaction have flared up from time to time ever since, especially during times of economic stress. Ethnic and racial conflicts have been such a constant feature of American politics that they have long shaped national electoral and partisan alignments. This has been as true in recent decades as at any time in the past. At the metropolitan level, bitter divisions have often pitted central cities against suburbs, and one suburb against the next.

The extreme fragmentation of America's metropolitan areas has its origins in the process of suburbanization that began unfolding in the late nineteenth century. For a long time, the term "urban" referred to the great cities of the industrial era, their diverse mix of ethnic groups and social classes, and their commanding national presence as centers of technology and economic production. The second "urban" century was very different. Increasingly, the cities of the industrial era became surrounded by rings of independent political jurisdictions – what came to be called suburbs. Beginning as early as the 1920s, the great industrial cities centers went into a long slide even while the suburbs around them prospered. Ultimately, an urban geography emerged that was composed of a multitude of separate jurisdictions ranging from white and wealthy to poor and minority, and everything in between. Recently the central cities have begun to attract affluent (and especially younger) residents and the suburbs have become more representative of American society as a whole. Even so, a complicated mosaic of governments and even privatized gated communities continue to be important features in the daily life of urban residents: where people live greatly influences with whom they come into contact with, their tax burdens and level of municipal services, and even their political outlook. Within metropolitan areas there is not one urban community, but many.

The three strands that compose city politics in America—the imperative of economic growth, the challenge of governance, and the rise of the fragmented metropolis—can be woven into a narrative that allows us to understand the forces that have shaped American urban politics, both in the past and in our own time. Reading a letter to the editor of the local newspaper protesting a city's tax subsidy for a new stadium (a clash of values typical of the politics of growth); walking down a busy city street among people of every color and national background (which serves as a reminder of the diversity that makes governance a challenging task); entering a suburban gated community (and thus falling under the purview of a privatized governing association, still another of the many governing units that make up the metropolis): all of these experiences remind us that there are consistent patterns and recurring issues that shape the political dynamics of urban politics in America.

The Politics of Growth

Local communities cannot be preserved without a measure of economic vitality, and this is why growth and prosperity have always been among the most important priorities for urban residents and their civic leaders. Founded originally as centers of trade and commerce, the nation's cities and towns came into being as places where people could make money and find personal opportunity. From the very beginning, European settlement in North America involved schemes of town promotion. The first colony, Jamestown, founded in 1607, was the risky venture of a group of English entrepreneurs who organized themselves into a joint stock company. Shares sold in London for about $62 in gold. If the colony was successful, investors hoped to make a profit, and of course the colonists themselves had gambled their very lives on the success of the experiment. Likewise, three centuries later, when a flood of people began spilling beyond the eastern seaboard into the frontier of the new nation, they founded towns and cities as a way of making a personal bet on the future prospects of a particular place. The communities that grew up prospered if they succeeded in becoming the trading hub for a region and an export platform for agricultural and finished goods moving into the national economic system. For this reason, the nineteenth-century movement across the continent placed towns at the leading edge of territorial expansion:

> America was settled as a long, thin line of urban places, scattering outward and westward from the Atlantic seaboard. The popular imagination has it that farmers came first and villages later. The historian's truth is that villages and towns came first, pulling farmers along to settle the land around and between urban settlements.[1]

Each town was its own capitalist system in miniature, held together by the activities of entrepreneurs in search of profit and personal advancement. The restless pursuit of new opportunities encouraged the formation of what urban historian Sam Bass Warner has called a national "culture of privatism," which stressed individual efforts and aspirations over collective or public purposes: "[The] local politics of American cities have depended for their actors, and for a good deal of their subject matter, on the changing focus of men's private economic activities."[2] The leading philosophy of the day promoted the idea that by pursuing their own individual interests, people were also contributing to the welfare of the community.

On the frontier, the founders of cities and the entrepreneurs who made their money in them recognized that in order to ensure their mutual success, they would have to take steps to promote their city and region. Local boosters promoted their city's real or imagined advantages—a harbor or strategic location on a river, for example, or proximity to rich farming and mining areas. They also boasted about local culture: music societies, libraries, and universities. And they went further than boasting; they used the powers of city government to promote local growth. Municipalities were corporations that could be used to help finance a variety of local undertakings, from subscriptions in railroad stock to improvements in harbors and docks. There was broad support for such undertakings because citizens shared in the perception that local economic vitality was absolutely necessary to advance the well-being of the urban community and everyone in it.

Today, support for measures to promote the local economy continues to be bound up with people's attachments to place and community. Without jobs and incomes, people simply cannot stay in the place that gives life to family, neighborhood, and local identity. The environmental and social effects of the oil spill in the Gulf of Mexico in the spring and summer of 2010 illustrate this point. As the disaster unfolded, it seemed certain that thousands of jobs would be lost in a long arc stretching from southern Louisiana to the Florida coast. At the time, tourism was expected to drop by half on Florida's Gulf Coast, costing the state at least 200,000 jobs.[3] In Louisiana, fishing, shellfish, and other industries seemed to be on the verge of being wiped out. When people talked about the disaster to news reporters, they spoke not only of the loss of livelihood, but also, with great emotion, about its effect on family values and community traditions—about the loss of a "way of life."

No matter how calamitous, the oil spill was not likely to make coastal communities disappear overnight, no matter how hard it may have been to recover (fortunately, the long-term consequences of the spill were not as severe as many feared). People identify with the community within which they live, and they are often reluctant to move even in the face of genuine hardship. The resilience of community was illustrated in the 1970s and 1980s when massive losses of businesses and jobs hit the industrial heartland of the Midwest and Northeast. The rapid deindustrialization of a vast region threatened the existence of entire communities. The Pittsburgh, Pennsylvania, region experienced a 44 percent loss in manufacturing jobs from 1979 to 1988, three-quarters of them related to steel. Unemployment levels reached as high as 20 percent, not only in Pittsburgh, but also in Detroit and several other cities of the industrial belt.[4] Some people fled for more prosperous areas of the Sunbelt, but a great many of them elected to stay. Rather than giving up, in city after city public leaders took measures to rebuild their economies; indeed, in most places the cause of local renewal took on the character of a permanent crusade. Communities of the Gulf Coast reacted in a similar way. People resisted leaving; instead, they put their efforts into regenerating their local economies and strengthening their communities because they were not willing to abandon the traditions and cultures that brought meaning to their lives.

It might seem that the intimate connection between material well-being and community identity would leave little room for disagreement over the premise that cities must do everything they can do all the time to promote local prosperity. But this commitment does not always translate into support for every politician and developer's bright idea or ambitious proposal. Disputes break out because policies to promote growth cannot benefit everyone equally; they are not always sensible or plausible; and there are always winners and losers. For renters and low-income residents, the gentrification of their neighborhood may bring higher rents and home values that ultimately force them to move. Growth in the downtown corporate and financial sectors may create some high-paying jobs for educated professionals but leave many central-city residents with low-paying jobs or on the unemployment rolls. A downtown that encroaches on nearby neighborhoods may benefit the businesses located in the new office towers but may also compromise the quality of life for nearby residents. People who do not care about sports may resent helping to pay for a new football stadium. Different perspectives such as these explain why there is frequent disagreement about how to promote growth, even though everyone believes that local prosperity is a good thing.

The use of eminent domain by local governments illustrates the kinds of disputes that can divide communities. All across the nation, cities have aggressively used their power to take private property for "higher uses" to make way for big-box stores, malls, condominium projects, sports stadiums, and a great many other initiatives. For most of the nation's history, local governments have possessed the authority to take property without the owners' consent if it serves a legitimate public purpose.[5] Public officials have liberally interpreted this power as a useful tool for economic development, but homeowners and small businesses who find their property condemned so that it can be sold to a big developer look at it with a skeptical eye. On December 20, 2000, a group of homeowners led by Sussette Kelo filed a suit challenging a decision by the city of New London, Connecticut, to cede its eminent domain authority to a private corporation that wanted to raze their homes. Things came to a head on June 23, 2005, when the U.S. Supreme Court upheld lower court rulings in favor of the development corporation. The Court's decision ignited a firestorm of protest that swept the nation. In response to the public furor, by the fall of 2006, state legislatures in 30 states had enacted legislation to restrict the use of eminent domain, and hundreds of towns and cities had done likewise. In the fall elections of 2006, voters in 12 states passed referendums prohibiting the taking of property for private development if it did not serve a clear public purpose.[6]

The lesson from the *Kelo v. New London* case is that despite the fact that almost everyone embraces the goal of local economic growth, sometimes the policies to promote it clash with other values, such as individual property rights, the health of a neighborhood, or a preference for less governmental intrusion. Everyone may seem to share the same interest in promoting the well-being of the urban community, but they frequently disagree over how to make that happen.

The Politics of Governance

International migration is transforming societies around the globe, and the United States is no exception. More immigrants came to the United States in the 1990s than in any previous decade in the nation's history, and the flow has continued into the twenty-first century. The social and political effects of large-scale population movements are often on display in big global cities such as Miami, New York, Chicago, and San Francisco, and in many smaller places as well. For this reason, in the global era, as in the past, city politics often pivots around issues of racial and ethnic identity and feelings of community solidarity at least as much as around issues of economic development.

Until the mid-nineteenth century, when colonial-era values still prevailed, men of wealth and high social standing made most of the decisions for the urban community. In the cities, "leadership fell to those who exercised economic leadership. All leadership, political, social, economic, tended to collect in the same set of hands."[7] Business owners, professionals, and aristocrats ran municipal affairs without challenge. The members of this social and political elite shared a mistrust of what Thomas Jefferson called "mobocracy," a word he used to signify his opposition to rule by popular majority. Governance was remarkably informal. Local notables served on committees formed to build public wharves, organize town watches, and build and maintain public streets, and even the most essential services, such as crime control and fire prevention, generally relied on the voluntary efforts of citizens. Such a casual governmental structure fit the pace of life and the social intimacy of small communities.

By the industrial era of the 1850s, cities were growing at breakneck speed, and they were also becoming socially stratified and ethnically complex. Waves of immigrants were crowding into densely packed neighborhoods. They came from an astonishing variety of national cultures, from England, Ireland, Germany, the Scandinavian countries, and later from Italy and a broad swath of eastern European countries. From time to time, ethnic tensions rose to a fever pitch, and tipped over into violence time and again. In the industrial cities, the colonial-era style of politics could not survive the change, and in time, a new generation of urban leaders came onto the scene. They came from the immigrant precincts and entered politics by mobilizing the vote of the urban electorate. Their rise to power set off decades of conflict between wealthy and middle-class elites and the immigrants and their leaders, a story we tell in Chapters 3 and 4.

In the twentieth century, large movements of people continued to flood into the cities, but the ethnic and racial composition of these urban migrations changed dramatically. The immigrant flood tide ended in the early 1920s, when Congress enacted legislation that nearly brought foreign immigration to a halt. By then, however, a massive internal population movement was already picking up speed. In the first three decades of the twentieth century and again in the years following World War II, millions of African Americans fled the hostile culture of the South for jobs and opportunity in the industrial cities. They were joined by successive waves of destitute whites fleeing the unemployment and poverty of Appalachia and other depressed areas, and by Mexicans crossing the border to escape violence and poverty in their own country. These streams of migration virtually guaranteed that twentieth-century urban America would be riddled with violent racial conflict. One consequence of the rising tensions in the cities is that millions of white families left their inner-city neighborhoods and fled to the suburbs. A social and racial chasm soon separated cities from suburbs, and echoes of that period continue to reverberate to this day.

A vivid example of the continuing racial divide was on display in New Orleans in the late summer of 2005. When the storm surge from Hurricane Katrina breached the dikes surrounding New Orleans on August 29, 2005, 80 percent of the city was flooded and nearly 100,000 people were left to deal with the consequences. Wrenching images of human suffering filled television news programs: 25,000 people trying to live under impossible conditions in the Superdome, 20,000 more in the Convention Center, residents fleeing across bridges and overpasses and desperately waving from rooftops. More than 1.5 million people were displaced, 60,000 homes were destroyed, and 1,300 people died.[8] African American neighborhoods located on the lowest and least desirable parts of the city bore the brunt of the destruction. The racial segregation that made this possible is a legacy of New Orleans' past, and despite the civil rights advances that protect the rights of minorities to live where they choose to, it is a pattern that has not disappeared—in New Orleans or anywhere else.

In the meantime, bitter conflicts have, once again, broken out over foreign immigration. The massive flows of immigrants in recent decades have made cities culturally and socially dynamic places, but they have also meant that ethnic identity has continued to fuel conflict in national and city politics. The passage of Senate Bill 1070 by the Arizona Senate on April 23, 2010, provoked a furious reaction across the country. The Arizona law authorized police officers to detain anyone stopped for "any lawful purpose" if they suspected the person of being in the country illegally. The legislation brought an outcry of opposition from many quarters, including calls for boycotts of Arizona products and travel. President Obama decried the legislation, indicating that his administration would protect the civil rights of all U.S. citizens if they were subjected to state laws on the basis of their race or ethnicity.[9] In cities with substantial Hispanic populations, protests broke out against the Arizona law. The Los Angeles and Chicago city councils passed resolutions supporting an Arizona boycott, and other cities considered doing the same. On the opposite end of the political spectrum, the controversy energized Republicans and conservatives. Almost everywhere, the immigration controversy exposed a deep national division that continues today.

The racial and ethnic complexity of metropolitan areas guarantees that the art of arbitrating among the contending groups making up the local political system will be hard to master. In the multiethnic metropolis of the global era, effective governance takes on real urgency. Governmental authority springs from the obligation of public institutions to make decisions that are binding upon all members of society. To retain the legitimacy to govern in a democratic system, the government must seem sufficiently responsive to a large enough proportion of the electorate, and at the same time there must be opportunities for the political losers to seek redress. The ethnic and racial complexity of cities makes this a daunting challenge.

The Fragmented Metropolis

Any account of city politics over the twentieth century must be located, in some part, within an often-rehearsed narrative that traces the decline of the central cities and rise of the suburbs, a period brought to a halt only recently by the unexpected revival of core cities. The process of suburbanization created the modern American metropolis, which is made up of a multitude of political jurisdictions large and small, wealthy, middle class, and poor. For decades, the basic urban pattern involved an extreme racial segregation, with most blacks living in central cities, and most whites—especially the affluent ones—living in the suburbs. More recently, the geography of the American metropolis can be more accurately described as a mosaic, with ethnic and racial groups scattered across the urban landscape. Despite the significant changes, however, suburban jurisdictions still differ sharply from one another, and the gap between the richest and the poorest is as great as ever. The fracturing of politics creates a dynamic in which central cities and suburbs compete with one another across many dimensions.

Today's metropolitan regions are typically fragmented into hundreds of governmental jurisdictions. By 2002, there were 87,900 governments in the United States. In addition to the federal government and the governments of the 50 states, there were 38,971 local governments: 3,034 county and 35,937 sub-county governments, including 19,431 municipalities and 16,506 townships. The remainder, comprising over one-half of the total, is composed of special-purpose local governments, including 13,522 school districts and 35,356 special districts,[10] each of them established at some point in time to take on particular tasks, such as the running of toll bridges or the building of sewer systems, or the financing of new suburban developments. In addition, special authorities by the hundreds have been created to finance and manage such things as convention centers, sports stadiums, entertainment districts, and waterfront developments. Every year more are added to the list.[11]

The consequences of metropolitan fragmentation are too numerous to fully describe. Perhaps the most basic is that people tend to identify themselves with a local place rather than as regional citizens. Except when their team wins the Super Bowl or the World Series, most people have no connection to anything as abstract as a metropolitan community. This tendency is encouraged by the fact that political fragmentation and the local identity that comes with it serves some practical ends, and is especially advantageous for affluent suburban residents. Within all metropolitan regions, a vigorous competition takes place among jurisdictions for people and businesses capable of helping the local tax base. The winners in this metropolitan sweepstakes see the public revenues go up, which allows them to finance a higher level of services and more public amenities even if tax rates go down. This system of incentives prompts every local government to adopt policies that benefit their own citizens at the expense of neighboring communities. Cities fight hard to outbid one another for big-box stores, retailers, and malls. They typically retain consultants to help them negotiate deals with developers, which may include a combination of eminent domain for land acquisition, land improvements and public services, tax abatements, and even direct payments. If successful, these efforts bring in tax revenues that support schools, police and fire departments, and other services and amenities, and they leave less for everyone else.

Another reason urban residents tend to identify with their local community (the "home team") is that by keeping government close to home, they are able to make critical decisions about taxes, services, land use, and other important public policies. Historically, residents of suburbs have been especially concerned about maintaining the "character" of their communities, and frequently this concern has been expressed as a desire to exclude people based on race, ethnicity, and social class. In the history of urban America, strategies of exclusion have been aimed at a remarkable array of different groups. In the twentieth century, the desire to maintain racial segregation prompted suburban jurisdictions to enact policies meant to protect their communities from change. More recently, privatized, gated communities have become important means for accomplishing the same goal. These residential developments, which are often defended by gates, walls, and other physical barriers, are governed by homeowners associations that assess fees for maintenance, services, and amenities; in this way, the residents are able to separate themselves from surrounding neighborhoods and even from the municipalities that surround them. Affluent homeowners manage to achieve a remarkable degree of separation from the less well-off, and by doing so they have changed the contours of local politics almost as much as the suburbs did a generation ago.

The proliferation of condominium developments and gated communities has had a paradoxical effect. On the one hand, they have made it possible for people to live in extreme isolation from one another even when they are close by. On the other hand, they have facilitated a patchwork pattern of urban residence that breaks down the large-scale pattern of racial and ethnic segregation that once divided inner-city "slum" from affluent suburb. It is difficult, however, to tell if these spatial patterns make all that much difference to anyone except middle-class and affluent urban residents. A prominent urban scholar, Peter Marcuse, has proposed that a retreat into geographic isolation and fortification erodes a shared sense of community and citizenship.[12] This is, perhaps, the inevitable consequence of the fragmented metropolis no matter what geographic form it may take.

The Challenge of the Global Era

Successive waves of immigration from all over the world have created the fragmented and multiethnic metropolis of the twenty-first century. Spatial fragmentation interacts with racial and ethnic diversity in complex ways. In cities closely connected to the global economy, symbols of corporate power, personal wealth, and luxury consumption stand in stark contrast to neighborhoods exhibiting high rates of poverty, violence, and physical dereliction. Frequently, shocking levels of inequality are visible on the same block, a fact driven home when office workers walk by homeless people or stop to eat at an expensive restaurant staffed by minimum-wage employees. Highly paid professionals working in the global economy drive up the price of downtown real estate to stratospheric levels and lead the gentrification of nearby neighborhoods, leaving run-down areas behind. Gentrification and renewal have helped revive the fortunes of central cities, but these processes have also had the effect of fragmenting the urban landscape.

Likewise, metropolitan areas are fractured by a geography that reflects the inequalities and demographic processes of the twenty-first century. Political fragmentation facilitates a pattern of segregation that sorts people out according to racial and ethnic identity and social class differences. A historical analysis would suggest that there is nothing new about this. All through the twentieth century, the white middle class escaped the cities by moving to the suburbs. Now, however, the city–suburban divide inherited from the past is breaking up into a much more complicated metropolitan pattern. Ethnic and racial groups are widely distributed throughout metropolitan areas. The 2000 census revealed that more than half of all Latinos, almost 40 percent of blacks, and 55 percent of Asians lived in suburbs, and in many urban regions, the proportions were much higher.[13] Many more suburbs than before are ethnically diverse. The problem is that ethnic and racial diversity of this sort does not add up to a more coherent metropolitan community. Achieving effective governance in such a circumstance remains as one of the unfinished challenges of this century.

Endnotes

1. Lawrence J. R. Herson and John M. Bolland, *The Urban Web: Politics, Policy, and Theory* (Chicago: Nelson-Hall, 1990), p. 43.
2. Sam Bass Warner Jr., *The Private City: Philadelphia in Three Periods of Its Growth* (Philadelphia, PA: University of Pennsylvania Press, 1968), p. 4.
3. Douglas Hanks, "Oil Spill Disaster Could Cost Florida 200,000 Jobs," *Miami Herald* (June 9, 2010), www.miamiherald.com/2010/06/09/167269/oil-disaster.
4. Dennis Judd and Michael Parkinson, "Urban Leadership and Regeneration," in *Leadership and Urban Regeneration: Cities in North America and Europe*, ed. Dennis Judd and Michael Parkinson (Thousand Oaks, CA: Sage Publications, 1989), pp. 13–30.
5. For a history and full discussion, see Wikipedia, http://en.wikipedia.org/wiki/Eminent_domain.
6. See Institute of Justice, www.ij.org/private_property/connecticut/index; William Yardley, "Anger Drives Property Rights Measures," *New York Times* (October 8, 2006), www.nytimes.com.
7. Herson and Bolland, *The Urban Web*, p. 46.
8. Louise Comfort, "Cities at Risk: Hurricane Katrina and the Drowning of New Orleans," *Urban Affairs Review* 41 (March 2006): 501–506.

9. Peter Baker, "Obama and Calderón Decry Ariz. Immigration Law," *New York Times* (May 19, 2010), http://www.nytimes.com/2010/05/20/world/americas/20prexy. html.

10. U.S. Bureau of the Census, *2002 Census of Governments* (July 2002), http://ftp2. census.gov/govs/cog/2002COGprelim_report.pdf.

11. Nancy Burns, *The Formation of American Local Governments: Private Values in Public Institutions* (New York: Oxford University Press, 1994).

12. Peter Marcuse, "The 'War on Terrorism' and Life in Cities After September 11, 2001," in *Cities, War, and Terrorism: Towards an Urban Geopolitics,* ed. Stephen Graham (New York: Blackwell, 2005), pp. 274–275.

13. John Logan, "The New Ethnic Enclaves," in *Melting Pot Suburbs: A Census 2000 Study of Suburban Diversity,* ed. William H. Frey (Washington, D.C.: Center for Urban and Metropolitan Policy, Brookings Institution Press, June 2001), p. 2.

PART I

The Origins of American Urban Politics: The First Century

CHAPTER 2

The Enduring Legacy

National Development and the Cities

When the U.S. Constitution was ratified in 1789, the cities of the new nation were perched on the edge of a ragged coastline of a vast, mostly unexplored continent. Only five of these cities—Boston, New York, Philadelphia, Baltimore, and Charleston—had reached a population of 10,000 people. In the decades to follow, the social and economic development of the nation depended as much on the growth of its cities as on the expansion into the continental interior. A little more than a century later, 40 percent of Americans lived in towns and cities, and the nation's economy had become more industrial than agricultural. The symbols and the reality of the industrial age—belching smokestacks, wave after wave of foreign immigrants, social disorder, and racial and ethnic strife—all were concentrated in the cities. Although most Americans were recently descended from immigrants themselves, many of them soon developed a fear and distrust of cities and the people who lived within them. The antiurban attitudes formed in this turbulent century became a defining feature of American culture that has endured right up to the present day.

The industrial economy required a constantly growing supply of cheap and plentiful labor. A flood of foreign immigration began to surge into the country in the 1840s, and it did not ebb until Congress passed legislation to curb it, in 1921 and 1924. Most of the immigrants settled in crowded urban neighborhoods close to the factories. Social and cultural differences divided the newcomers from the people who had arrived earlier, and sometimes the tensions escalated into violence. The new immigrants—poor, often illiterate, unfamiliar with the language and customs of their new country, and unaccustomed to city life—struggled to cope with miserable conditions in overcrowded slums. Those who had come to America at an earlier time generally viewed those who came later as culturally and morally inferior. The mixture of runaway urban growth, the industrial revolution, and the successive waves of immigration guaranteed that the nineteenth-century urban experience would be tumultuous.

This history is relevant because the same dynamics still energize urban politics today. Through all of the nineteenth century and in the first years of the twentieth century, waves of foreign immigration provoked anxiety and conflict, and often this became expressed in a rejection of the city and of the distinctive

14

urban culture it nurtured.[1] Similarly, massive demographic movements have brought turmoil over the last half century or more. In the years after World War II, at the same time that millions of southern blacks poured into the cities of the North, millions of white families fled to the suburbs. One consequence of these historic movements was that those living in the suburbs came to think of the cities they had left behind almost as enemy territory. More recently, a wave of foreign immigration has set off a clash of cultures and fueled political conflict in both national and local politics. In some states and cities, the anxiety about the newcomers has been expressed in legislation intended to make it impossible to rent housing or provide jobs to illegal immigrants, and to reduce social spending and require English-only instruction in the schools. Understanding that these kinds of conflicts have a long history in urban America helps to put today's political controversies into a useful context.

OUTTAKE

City Building has Always Required Public Efforts

In the nineteenth century, the intense competition among cities ignited a "struggle for primacy and power" in which "like imperial states, cities carved out extensive dependencies, extended their influence over the economic and political life of the hinterland, and fought with contending places over strategic trade routes." In the American West, local boosters sometimes faced a daunting challenge in promoting their towns because many of them were, in fact, hard, isolated places in which to live. Promoters bragged about any positive feature, and just as frequently they invented fanciful tales because they had a lot at stake: "Questioning a place's promise affected not just those doing the questioning but also all who had put stock, mental and material, in the place." Everyone living in a place, from town councils to realtors and chambers of commerce, was vigilant in discouraging any negative information from leaking out. Instead, local boosters made the smallest places seem like centers of high culture and the most desolate deserts sound like fertile land waiting for the plow.

But town promoters did not rely upon marketing alone. After midcentury, when a national railroad network began to emerge, it became clear that in order to prosper or even survive, cities would have to find a way to connect to it. To do so, civic boosters aggressively employed the power and resources of local government. To induce railroad companies to make connections to their city, they raised private subscriptions to buy railroad stock, paid for local stations and offloading facilities, gave away free land, and sometimes offered direct cash subsidies. The railroads raised much of their capital for building new rail lines by striking good bargains with cities, and ultimately secured more public subsidies from cities than from state governments or from Congress. The competition for rail connections became so frenzied that railroad companies were building new lines just to obtain subsidies from local governments. When a lot of these lines failed to generate enough freight and passengers to make them pay, hundreds of rail companies went belly up, leaving towns and cities with big debts but nothing to show for them, and no way to pay.

There are striking parallels with the intense inter-urban competition that goes on today. In recent decades, huge public resources have again been devoted to the cause of boosting local economic vitality. As in the nineteenth century, civic boosters are fired with the conviction that their own prospects and the fate of their cities hangs in the balance. Since the 1970s, cities have engaged in a virtual arms race to revitalize waterfronts and build stadiums, convention centers, malls, and entertainment centers. Cities compete to host events like auto races, music festivals, and special museum exhibits. All of this activity is inspired by the idea that cities must replace the smokestacks of an earlier era with an economy revolving based on services as well as tourism, entertainment, and culture.

People who support such efforts make the argument that public expenditures benefit everyone because they form the basis of a healthy local economy. Obviously not everyone agrees. Heated debates regularly erupt over questions about what should be built, who should pay for it, and who really cashes in. Many people have a nagging suspicion that taxpayers foot the bill while well-connected developers and the business elite reap the rewards. When the controversies of the 1870s are compared to those of today, one can get a feeling of déjà vu all over again.

Source: The two quotations are from Richard C. Wade, *The Urban Frontier: Pioneer Life in Early Pittsburgh, Cincinnati, Lexington, Louisville, and St. Louis* (Chicago: University of Chicago Press, 1959), p. 103; David M. Wrobel, *Promised Lands: Promotion, Memory, and the Creation of the American West* (Lawrence: University Press of Kansas, 2002), p. 71.

A Century of Urban Growth

In the industrial age, cities grew at a frantic pace that had no historical precedent. In 1800, London was the only city in the world to approach a population of 1 million people, and Paris, with a population of 547,000, ranked second among the cities of continental European.[2] At the time, just over 60,000 people lived in New York, which made it more than one-third larger than the second, Philadelphia, with its 41,000 people, and more than twice the size of the next in line, Baltimore. Astonishingly, only 100 years later, 11 cities had topped the million-person mark, including London at 6,586,000, Paris at 2,714,000,[3] New York at 3,437,000, and Chicago at 1,698,575. Over the span of the same century, the percentage of the population living in towns[4] and cities in England and Wales increased from 25 to 77. Never before had cities grown so big or so fast, and never before had such a high proportion of the population lived in cities. The urban historian Eric Lampard has noted that, "the period c. A.D. 1750–1850 [is] one of the crucial disjunctions in the history of human society. Whatever constraints had hitherto checked or moderated the growth and re-distribution of population were suddenly relaxed."[5] Commenting on the growth of cities in 1895, the *Atlantic Monthly* pointed out that, "The great fact in . . . social development . . . at the close of the nineteenth century is the tendency all over the world to concentrate in great cities. This tendency is seen everywhere."[6]

The American experience paralleled these developments. In most of the decades between the first national census of 1790 to the census of 1920, the urban population (defined by the Census Bureau as people living in cities and towns of 2,500 or more) grew more than twice as fast as the U.S. population as a whole. The only significant exception to this trend showed up between 1810 and 1820, when homesteaders and farmers streamed across the Appalachian Mountains to settle the Old Northwest (now western Pennsylvania, Ohio, and Indiana). Soon, however, even the expanding frontier could not absorb enough people to keep up with the rate of growth in the cities. Urban change on this scale was an entirely new and often shocking experience. As late as 1840, a full half century after the nation's founding, only one American in ten was officially classified in the census as "urban." In the two decades leading up to the Civil War, however, cities began growing at an astonishing rate. Foreign immigrants began pouring into the industrial cities in search of jobs in the factories; and a steady migration from farm to city picked up speed for the same reason. As late as 1840, only 11 percent of the American population lived in cities and towns, but by 1860, the Census Bureau officially classified 20 percent of the American population as urban, and this proportion doubled to almost 40 percent by century's end (see Figure 2.1). Twenty years later, the national census revealed that more than half of all Americans—51 percent—lived in cities or towns. In much less than a century, the United States had gone from a mostly rural to one that was rapidly becoming more urban.

Because they were important centers of finance and trade, right from the beginning the cities perched on the eastern seaboard benefited from national development even when it was occurring on the distant frontier. New York maintained its supremacy as a financial and commercial hub, and its status as the nation's premier city was ensured in 1825, the year the Erie Canal was completed. The canal linked the city directly to the Great Lakes, which placed it at the end of a giant funnel that gathered the resources of a vast hinterland into New York harbor, where they could be placed into a worldwide trading system. After the Civil War, New York consolidated its position when it became a great manufacturing city. Jostling throngs of immigrants passed through the port of New York, and many of them decided to go no further. From just 369,000 people in 1840, the city's population exploded to over 3.4 million by 1900—a shocking 10-fold increase in only 60 years! By 1920, when its population reached 5.6 million, New York had firmly consolidated its position as a leading global center of finance, trade, and manufacturing.

Yet, despite its incredible growth, New York's share of the nation's urban population fell steadily throughout the century. This is because thousands of new towns and cities sprang up as the nation expanded westward, and these places often grew much faster even than New York—although, it must be

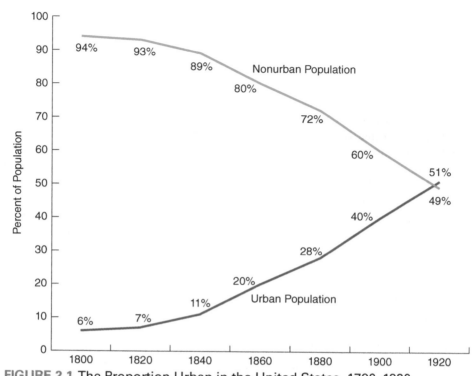

FIGURE 2.1 The Proportion Urban in the United States, 1790–1920

Sources: U.S. Department of Commerce, Bureau of the Census, *Historical Statistics of the United States, Colonial Times to 1970*, pt. 1, Bicentennial ed. (Washington, DC: U.S. Government Printing Office, 1975), p. 8; U.S. Department of Commerce, Bureau of the Census, *1970 Census of Population*, vol. 1, *Characteristics of the Population*, pt. 1 (Washington, DC: U.S. Government Printing Office, 1973), p. 42.

emphasized, none of them were destined to challenge its supremacy. In 1800, 18 percent of the nation's urban population lived in New York City, but by the century's end, this proportion had fallen to 7 percent.[7] New York City remained the largest by far, but over time other cities assumed prominent places in an increasingly integrated national and international urban network. The data in Table 2.1 help tell this story. New York grew from a city of 137,388 in 1820 to a multi-million-person metropolis a century later, but over the same period other cities were also bursting at the seams. Philadelphia had a population of 64,000 in 1820, topped 565,000 by 1860, and grew to a city of more than 1.8 million by 1920. Boston increased its population from 43,000 in 1820 to nearly 178,000 in 1860, and to almost 750,000 by 1920. Meanwhile, a great many places, large and small, experienced a similar transformation.

Cities in the continental interior grew at almost unbelievable rates, often morphing from small frontier towns to busy urban centers in only a few years. St. Louis, the old French settlement where Lewis and Clark outfitted their expedition in 1805, exploded from a town of only 16,000 people in 1840 to a city 10 times that size by 1860, and reached 772,000 by 1920. But Chicago's growth was perhaps most startling of all. In the 20 years from 1840 to 1860, it

TABLE 2.1 Population and Rate of Growth in Five Large Cities, 1820–1920[a]

	New York City[b]	Percentage Increase	Chicago	Percentage Increase	Philadelphia	Percentage Increase	St. Louis	Percentage Increase	Boston	Percentage Increase	Percentage Increase In U.S. Population
1820	137,388		—		63,802		4,598		43,298		
1830	220,471	60%	—		80,462	26%	5,847	27%	61,392	42%	33%
1840	369,305	67	4,470		93,665	16	16,469	182	93,383	52	33
1850	660,803	79	29,963	570%	121,376	30	77,860	373	136,881	47	36
1860	1,183,148	79	112,172	274	565,529	366	160,773	107	177,840	30	36
1870	1,546,293	31	298,977	167	674,022	19	310,864	93	250,526	41	27
1880	2,061,191	33	503,185	68	847,170	26	350,522	13	362,839	45	26
1890	2,507,474	22	1,099,850	119	1,046,964	24	451,770	29	448,477	24	26
1900	3,437,202	37	1,698,575	54	1,293,697	24	575,000	27	560,892	25	21
1910	4,766,883	39	2,185,283	29	1,549,008	20	687,029	20	670,585	20	21
1920	5,620,048	18	2,701,705	24	1,823,779	18	772,897	13	748,060	12	15

[a]These five cities were ranked as the five largest in the 1910 census.
[b]Using the consolidated borough boundaries of 1898.

Sources: Glen E. Holt, personal files; U.S. Department of Commerce, Bureau of the Census, *The Growth of Metropolitan Districts in the United States: 1900–1940*, by Warren S. Thompson (Washington, DC: U.S. Government Printing Office, 1947); Blake McKelvey, *American Urbanization: A Comparative History* (Glenview, IL: Scott Foresman, 1973), pp. 24, 37, 73.

was transformed from a swampy frontier village of 4,500 to a city of more than 112,000. And the people just kept on coming. Chicago quickly left St. Louis in the dust, and by 1920 its population had soared to 2.7 million people, putting it second only to New York.

Places such as St. Louis and New Orleans (on the Mississippi River), Chicago (at the foot of Lake Michigan), and Cincinnati (on the Ohio River) had begun as major trading centers, transferring goods through the Great Lakes or the inland river system to the eastern seaboard cities or directly to Europe. After the Civil War, they quickly emerged as leading industrial centers. Smaller cities and towns prospered by finding a specialized niche in this emerging urban hierarchy. At the top of the pyramid, the largest cities became industrial powerhouses and asserted commanding reach over vast hinterlands. Second-tier cities developed more specialized economies and generally served as transfer points to the larger urban centers. The bottom of the hierarchy was composed of the multitude of small towns that shipped agricultural and extractive resources gathered from mines, forests, and farms to feed the warehouses and factories located in the big urban centers, which then placed the raw materials into international commerce or used them to produce manufactured goods.

Inter-Urban Rivalries

Individual cities did not prosper by relying upon happenstance and chance. Town promotion became a way of life for local boosters, who competed for the settlers and investors who swept across the continent. The fortunes of cities were only partially determined by locational advantages—what might be called "place luck." Transportation connections—turnpikes, canals, and, later, railroads—were also crucial in determining a city's destiny. Links to the national transportation network could instantly secure a city's future by expanding its reach into the hinterland surrounding it and by tying it into national and international trade networks. Because such connections were so important to a city's prospects, promoters freely used the fiscal resources and powers of local governments to secure them. In the early century, canal building reached a fever pitch, but within a few years the railroads provided better links to other cities and to broader markets. Cities scrambled to offer subsidies to railroad corporations in the form of free land and terminal facilities and stock purchases. The logic was simple: Rising real estate values were expected to provide more than enough additional revenues to pay off the debts. These hopes did not always pan out, but any city that failed to make the effort to secure good rail links would surely die on the vine.

The battle for rail connections was fought with white-hot intensity. Before the railroads, it was possible to transport corn by wagon only 125 miles, and wheat only 250 miles, before the cost made them unmarketable.[8] Beyond that distance, agricultural land was almost worthless for anything except subsistence farming because there was no way of getting crops to market. The cost and inconvenience of hauling goods on horse-drawn wooden wagons guaranteed that settlements without access to water transportation would never amount to much. In the first decade of the nineteenth century, a ton of goods could be shipped all the way from Europe for the same amount it cost to haul it 9 miles over roads.[9] Inland cities without waterfronts could not conceivably compete with port and river cities as centers of trade. All that changed with the coming of the railroads. The emerging rail network opened up huge areas of farmland to commercial agriculture, which not only allowed the countryside to fill in but also resulted in soaring land values and population growth for the cities able to secure a connection. Local promoters were anxious to shape patterns of trade and economic development in their favor because they were keenly aware that they were involved in a competition in which some cities would prosper, but others would die on the vine.

The building of the Erie Canal demonstrated how cities might gain a measure of control over their own destinies. In 1817, the New York State legislature authorized money for the construction of a 364-mile waterway to connect the Hudson River to Lake Erie. When the canal opened in 1825, it became possible to ship huge volumes of agricultural and extractive goods from the continental interior through the Great Lakes to Buffalo, down the canal, and on to the port at New York, where they could be distributed along the eastern seaboard, used in factories, or shipped to Europe. Many producers and shippers abandoned the long, circuitous, and hazardous journey down the Ohio, Missouri, and Mississippi rivers to the port at New Orleans. New York's direct connection to the heartland via the canal quickly vaulted it past other eastern seaboard cities in population and volume of trade. By 1860, 62 percent of the nation's foreign trade passed through New York's harbor.[10]

The lesson was not lost on city boosters elsewhere. Civic leaders lobbied their state capitals for financial assistance to build canals. Pennsylvania, Maryland, Virginia, North Carolina, and South Carolina financed expensive canal projects designed to cut through the Appalachians. More than 3,000 miles of canals were dug between 1824 and 1840, most of them operated by state governments.[11] About 30 percent of the costs were raised through private sources, but public financing was essential for such ambitious undertakings.[12]

Canal building was so expensive, the engineering so complicated, and the natural barriers often so formidable that most cities could not hope to build them unless state legislatures helped out. Natural topographic barriers left many places out of the competition altogether. But the railroad era ignited an interurban competition that almost any city might join. Until the railroads, water was the singularly critical ingredient determining a city's fate; canals were just a means of trying to make up for what nature had not endowed. In the first decades of the nineteenth century, for the river towns such as St. Louis, Pittsburgh, Cincinnati, and New Orleans, the steamboat had been "an enchanter's wand transforming an almost raw countryside of scattered farms and towns into a settled region of cultivated landscapes and burgeoning cities."[13] In the 1850s, the enchanter's wand was passed to the railroads. The rail lines became rivers of commerce, capable of carrying huge volumes at amazing speeds over long distances. The railroads guaranteed that America's frontier would eventually vanish and a network of cities, towns, and villages would spread over the continent.

In 1840, only 2,800 miles of track had been laid, most of it in the urban East. No connection reached even as far west as Pittsburgh. The early steam locomotives were hazardous and unreliable contraptions, blowing up with a regularity that provoked opposition to their use in urban areas. Lacking the capital to take on bigger projects, railway companies built short lines. Because each company devised its own gauge (width between the rails), at the end of each line goods had to be unloaded from one company's cars and put onto cars that fit the next company's rails. Even with these limitations, however, the early rail system was vastly superior to the only alternative: horse-drawn wooden wagons.

Rail lines were built at astonishing speed, and by the 1880s the adoption of standard gauge sizes made the system much more efficient. In 1857, the newly consolidated Pennsylvania Railroad first connected Pittsburgh to Chicago. Three years later, 11 trunk lines ended in Chicago and 20 branch and feeder lines passed through it, making the city the nation's largest rail center terminus. By 1869 and with much fanfare, the symbolic Golden Spike was pounded in at Promontory Point, Utah. It completed the first cross-continental route by joining the Union Pacific line originating on the East Coast to the Central Pacific line starting in San Francisco. Within a few years, the outline of the modern rail system was almost complete, a spider's web with strands reaching into every section of the country. In just the half century between 1850 and 1900, the network expanded from 9,021 miles of track to 258,784 miles.[14]

More miles of track were laid more quickly than in any other nation in the world. This explosive growth could be traced to the massive public subsidies pumped into railroad building. Until the 1890s, most private corporations lacked the ability to raise the capital that would later become routine for them. Subsidies from governments at all levels helped make the railroads "America's first big business."[15] In the Pacific Railways Acts of 1862 and 1864, the federal government gave huge swaths of land to the railroad corporations, which they could use for rail construction and to raise capital. But some involvement by the states was critical because the federal government considered transportation to be mostly a state responsibility. Treasury Secretary Albert Gallatin's 1808 plan for a federal system of turnpike and harbor improvements had failed to gain congressional approval because of regional rivalries.[16] Following President Andrew Jackson's veto of a federal turnpike bill in 1830, transportation became viewed more as a state than a federal responsibility.

The states responded by feverishly subsidizing canal and railroad construction, but their eagerness to assume risk was also tempered by experience. The Panic of 1837 bankrupted scores of canal companies and some of the early steam railroad lines, which caused private investors and the states alike to lose their investments. Taxpayers and politicians were up in arms, and "revulsion against internal improvements" swept the country.[17] In the 1840s, many states wrote prohibitions against loaning money or buying stock in private corporations. Facing new restrictions at the state level, railroad promoters shifted their efforts to cities, which raced to outbid one another for railroad stock.

The anarchic competition for rail connections imposed many costs, including overbuilding and redundancies that resulted in bond defaults and bankruptcies. Up to 1861, 25 to 30 percent of all direct investment in railroad building was supplied by state and local governments. The cities were the biggest spenders; they contributed an estimated $300 million in direct subsidies; the states spent $229 million and the federal government $65 million.[18] In addition, the federal government and the states offered generous land grants, which the railroad companies quickly converted to cash by selling the land to settlers. In the post–Civil War period, the railroads accumulated so much property that they sent agents to the Scandinavian countries, Germany, and elsewhere to recruit immigrants to buy and settle it. Partly because the railroad companies recruited heavily there (and also because of hardships in their homeland), one-sixth of all Swedish citizens left for the United States in the last half of the nineteenth century, many of them settling in a broad swath of territory paralleling rail routes from the Great Lakes through the Dakotas and Montana.

Railroad owners became adept at playing cities against one another in an attempt to secure lucrative subsidies. By the 1850s, cities along the eastern seaboard were floating bond issues so they could invest in railroad stock, clear rights-of-way, and build terminal facilities—actions intended to ensure rail connections. The competition quickly spread west. In the 1860s, the business leaders of Kansas City, Kansas, sold bond issues to private investors, gave the proceeds to a railroad company, and persuaded Congress to approve a federal land grant to the company. As a result of its success in this venture, Kansas City prospered while its nearby rival Leavenworth stagnated (today, Leavenworth is known mainly for its federal prison).[19] Denver's board of trade raised $280,000 to finance a 100-mile spur line to obtain access to the intercontinental track that ran through Cheyenne, Wyoming.[20] Some of Denver's businesses had already moved to Cheyenne in the expectation that its position astride the intercontinental line would make it the premier city of the Rocky Mountain West. Their ambitions were frustrated when rail lines from all directions began to converge on Denver, thus securing its status as the dominant city of the Rocky Mountain region. The results of this long-ago battle are still obvious: today, Cheyenne's image is tied mostly to its annual rodeo, the Cheyenne Frontier Days.

No city benefited from railroad building as dramatically as did Chicago, whose phenomenal growth was founded on its access to agricultural and extractive products gathered from a vast region. Corn and grain, cattle and hogs, and iron ore and coal poured into Chicago through the Great Lakes and over the rails. The city became a center for steelmaking; the manufacture of agricultural implements, tools, and machines; slaughtering and meatpacking; and trade. By the mid-1870s, Chicago eclipsed St. Louis as the Midwest's premier city, a feat accomplished partly through the success of its local business community in securing rail links. Chicago built its first railroad in 1852 and then helped finance feeder lines into the city. The city also invested in grain elevators, warehouses, switching yards, and stockyards. By contrast, for too long St. Louis's business community held fast to the faith that the Mississippi River steamboats would continue to be the key to the city's prosperity. By the time St. Louis began seeking rail connections, Chicago's lead was overwhelming. Although Chicago also enjoyed a considerable advantage because it was located on the Great Lakes and was right next door to the most fertile farming regions of the Midwest, its aggressive leadership reinforced its favorable location.

For many years, the question of whether cities should go into debt to secure rail connections was beyond public dispute. Urban voters enthusiastically supported the issuance of city bonds to finance railroad subsidy schemes. As long as everyone's attention was riveted on external threats to the local economy, nearly everyone supported the idea that everything possible should be done to attract rail connections. Local promoters were encouraged to think that virtually any scheme that benefited them personally was also in the public's interest: "Developmental policy was almost wholly a product of consensus-building among groups of merchant elites to support particular canal, turnpike, rail and other projects in response to merchant elites in nearby communities."[21] From 1866 to 1873, the legislatures of 29 states granted over 800 authorizations for aid by local governments to railroad projects.[22] A study of governmental aid to railroads in New York found that no community ever voted against subscribing to railroad stock.[23] The votes were usually so lopsided as to be a foregone conclusion.[24]

The fight for rail connections improved the fortunes of many a city, but the overheated competition brought disaster to some. Railroad promoters played one town against another in search of better subsidies. The inter-urban competition grew often so fierce that many cities bid up the subsidies beyond what was economically rational. City governments incurred huge debts on a hope and a promise. In New York State, 50 towns bypassed by a major rail line joined in a $5.7 million stock subscription to the New York and Oswego Railroad. Zigzagging across the state to link the towns, the company went bankrupt shortly after completing the line in 1873 because the areas it served had too few people and products to sustain a viable business. Most of the investments made by the towns were wiped out, with taxpayers left holding the bag.[25]

Promoters exaggerated the positive effects expected of public subsidies, predicting rapid town growth, rising real estate values, and overflowing municipal treasuries. Profits on railroad stocks, they often promised, would eliminate the need for local taxes altogether. For most cities, however, "the direct effect on government finances was on the whole unfavorable."[26] Too many cities bought stock that went bust, or the new lines brought far less prosperity than promised. Cities that had heavily invested in speculative railroad ventures regularly found themselves dragged into fiscal crisis. Some cities defaulted on their debts in the 1860s, but it was merely a harbinger of things to come. The three-year depression that began in 1873 was precipitated, more than anything else, by the overbuilding of railroads and the overvaluing of railroad stock and local real estate. Hundreds of towns and cities were forced into default. In 1873, an astounding $100 million to $150 million of municipal debt was involved in railroad bond defaults—one-fifth of all the municipal debt in the nation.[27]

Municipal defaults on railroad bonds and revelations of political corruption associated with railroad building affected politics at all levels. Citizens rebelled against paying back eastern financiers for bonds that had become worthless. In some cases, the lines had not even been built. When federal marshals came to towns to collect the debts, they were sometimes run off by shotgun-wielding mobs. Cries of debt repudiation filled the air, and some cities and states won court battles to forgive their debts.[28] From 1864 to 1888, the most common type of case before the U.S. Supreme Court involved railroad bonds.[29] Many states adopted restrictions on local debt and limited the aid that could be given to private corporations.[30] Financial and political abuses by railroad barons fueled a populist rebellion against big business that shook the national political system.[31]

Industrialization and Community

At the time of the nation's founding and for several decades after, the politics of American cities were controlled primarily by an aristocratic and merchant elite. Such a system could not survive the urban growth and the economic and technological changes wrought by industrialization. In only a few years, cities changed from relatively compact communities held together by personal relationships and shared community norms to sprawling industrial cities characterized by social stratification and segregation, constant population change, and social and political conflict. By degrees, the governing class inherited from an earlier era lost its grip on local political systems. Increasingly, urban politics became a battleground revolving around social class and ethnic identity.

Before the emergence of the industrial city, trading cities sprang up along navigable waterways and harbors. The economy of the merchant cities was intimately tied to trade and commerce: the importation and distribution of European goods; the regulation of docks and farmers' markets; the financing and insuring of ships and goods; the printing of accounting ledgers, handbills, and newspapers. Educated aristocrats, importers, bankers, wholesalers, and shopkeepers were numbered among a city's most prominent citizens. A notch down in the social order were the craft workers, artisans, and individual entrepreneurs—shoemakers, hatters, bakers, carpenters, blacksmiths, potters, butchers, wheelwrights, saddle and harness makers, and shipwrights. At the bottom were sailors, domestic workers, servants, and the unskilled workers who moved goods from docks to warehouses. Social differences were clearly marked and widely accepted; overall, in colonial New England the inequality in wealth was about the same as in the slaveholding South.[32] At the time of the Revolution, about three out of four white persons in Pennsylvania, Maryland, and Virginia had come to America as indentured servants, until they paid their debts they were not free to join the paid labor force.[33]

The lifeblood of the mercantile cities (called the "city of merchants" by historians) flowed along the waterfront. Wharves and docks, warehouses, clerks' offices, banks, newspapers and printing establishments, taverns and breweries, and private homes all clustered close to the riverfront or harbor. This compact "walking city" was bounded by the distance the inhabitants could walk within an hour or two. Typically, the area of urban settlement spread about 2 miles from the center, but most people lived in densely packed neighborhoods stretching only a few blocks from the water. The small size of the merchant cities moderated the effects of inequality by fostering "a sense of community identification similar to that of traditional societies."[34] Most goods were produced in small shops by skilled artisans who employed one or two apprentices, and these often lived on the premises. Workers clustered together in shanties or back alleys within a short distance of the comfortable homes of wealthy merchants.

In his study of colonial Philadelphia, the historian Sam Bass Warner found that people of different occupations lived apart, but it was a proximate segregation: "It was the unity of everyday life, from tavern, to street, to workplace, to housing which held the town together in the eighteenth century."[35] Class conflict was moderated by this intimate geography as well as by a sense that everyone's welfare depended on the commercial success of the city. The merchant class was expected to run the city's affairs, and it did. With few exceptions, wealthy aristocrats and merchants presided over the public affairs of the city, and they encountered little opposition.[36] Consistent with their view that the scope of local government ought to be limited, they spent little on public services. In 1810, for instance, New York City spent only $1 per capita on all governmental functions put together.[37]

Casual and consensual governance of this sort began to disappear by the second half of the nineteenth century. In 1850, not much more than 10 percent of all workers in America were engaged in manufacturing, and they produced less than 20 percent of the nation's economic output. Only two decades later, however, industrial production exceeded the commercial and agricultural sectors in value added to the economy, and by the turn of the century, manufacturing accounted for more economic value than both sectors combined.[38] Industrialization moved economic production from small shops and homes into factories. Before the Civil War, manufacturing establishments rarely employed more than 50 workers, and even in large cities they ranged between 8 and 20 workers. In 1832, for example, the average-sized manufacturing establishment in Boston employed 8.5 workers.[39] But in the years following the Civil War, manufacturing firms grew quickly in size. In agricultural implements and machinery, the number of employees per establishment increased from 7.5 in 1860 to 79 in 1910. In malt liquor breweries, the number of workers increased from 5 to 39, and in iron and steel establishments, from 54 to 426.[40]

The transformation of small businesses into big corporations spawned a class of industrial magnates who flaunted their wealth by building mansions and estates, throwing lavish parties, and constructing monuments to themselves.[41] Capital became increasingly concentrated in large firms. Limited-risk corporations,[42] were relatively rare before the Civil War, produced 60 percent of value in manufacturing by the turn of the century.[43] (Such corporations raise capital by selling stocks to investors, who risk their investment but not their personal assets if the company fails.) Twelve firms were valued at over $10 million in 1896, but by 1903, 50 firms valued at more than $50 million.[44] Several giant corporations formed between 1896 and 1905, including U.S. Steel, International Harvester, General Electric, and American Telephone and Telegraph, became models of the modern corporate form of the twentieth century.

As the workplace became increasingly impersonal, hierarchical, and rigid, relationships between employers and workers became distant and even hostile. As machine-tooled, standardized parts replaced handcrafted goods, the number of unskilled workers multiplied. Standardized production had begun as early as 1798, when Eli Whitney designed a musket with interchangeable parts. Over time, standardized components made it possible to make a variety of goods rapidly and cheaply. Such products as clocks, sewing machines, and farm machinery, which had once been assembled by craft workers, were now made in big factories. The huge military orders placed during the Civil War prompted the mass production of shoes and clothing. Factory methods of production required specialized, repetitive work and a rigid distinction between management and workers and work became regimented and closely monitored.

Class differences sharply separated urban neighborhoods. While immigrant working-class tenement slums crowded close to the downtown business districts or in bottomlands near the docks and factories, middle-class neighborhoods tended to be located away from the teeming crowd. The wealthy claimed exclusive areas, often located on hills, where the air was fresher and the residents commanded pleasing views (almost everywhere, "the heights" came to signify high social standing). Wealthy people began to spend their weekends and holidays on bucolic suburban estates.

A series of transportation improvements allowed people to commute farther from their place of work. When the omnibuses were introduced to the streets of New York City in 1828, they represented a minor revolution in urban transportation. The way people commuted to work had changed little for hundreds of years. The wealthy owned or rented carriages; everyone else walked or, rarely, rode a horse. The omnibus made it possible for larger numbers of people to ride, in effect, in an enlarged version of the carriage. From the 1830s until the Civil War, dozens of omnibuses careened down the streets of the industrial cities. Basically, an enlarged version of the long-distance stagecoach, the omnibus was pulled by a team of two to four horses and typically carried up to a dozen people. Omnibuses were crowded and uncomfortable, cold in the winter, hot in the summer, and slow, barely moving faster than a person could walk. The coaches swayed and lurched over cobblestones and rutted unpaved streets.[45] A newspaper of the time complained that "during certain periods of the day or evening and always during inclement weather, passengers are packed in these vehicles, without regard to comfort or even decency."[46]

Despite the discomforts, commuters who could afford the fares—merchants, traders, lawyers, artisans, managers, junior partners—crowded into these crude conveyances. The advantages were many. The omnibus ran on a fixed schedule and route, and it picked up and dropped off passengers at frequent intervals. The fixed fare, typically a nickel, was a small fraction of the cost of renting a hackney coach. The omnibus was thus more convenient and less expensive than any alternative mode of traveling except walking. By encouraging in some urban residents the "riding habit,"[47] the omnibus marked the beginning of the end of the walking city. Almost immediately, the American city began fragmenting into distinct neighborhoods and enclaves.

Steam railroad lines, which made their first appearance in Boston in the 1830s, made it possible for a select few commuters to live at some distance away, but there were a few drawbacks. Steam engines were suited for constant speed rather than for frequent stops and starts, they were expensive to build and operate, and they were fearfully loud and prone to blowing up. They did not, therefore, compete with omnibuses on crowded urban streets but instead facilitated a commute by a privileged few to smaller towns and villages some miles away from the urban center. The 40- to 75-cent fares were out of reach for all but the wealthy (the average laborer made about $1 a day; sometimes skilled workers made as much as $2 a day).[48] Even so, by 1848, one-fifth of Boston's businessmen commuted daily by rail.[49]

In the 1850s, horse-drawn streetcars replaced omnibuses on main thoroughfares. Because they were pulled on rails rather than over potholed streets, the horsecars carried twice as many passengers and traveled almost twice as fast as an omnibus. Horsecars were cheaper, too, and their affordable cost "contributed to the development of the world's first integrated transportation systems."[50] In the larger cities, the lines radiated from the center like spokes on a wheel. Because horsecars could travel 6 to 8 miles in an hour, middle-class residential settlements began to spread that far and more from the city center. (The rule of thumb, then as now, was that most people were willing to commute up to an hour, but not much more.) In addition, the horsecar lines sometimes extended well beyond built-up areas, serving hospitals, parks, cemeteries, and independent villages.[51] Wherever they reached, land speculators and builders bought up property in the expectation that development would follow and real estate values would rise.

In 1888, Frank Julian Sprague revolutionized urban transit when he installed the first electric streetcar system in Richmond, Virginia.[52] The motive force driving the electric streetcar came from a wheeled carriage that moved atop an overhead cable. This device trolled along the wires, pulling the car as it went. The "troller" gave the trolley car its name.[53] Trolley cars had so many advantages over horsecars that despite the expense of installing overhead wires, traction companies and cities rushed to install them. In 1890, 60 percent of the nation's streetcars were still pulled by horses, but 12 years later the figure was less than 1 percent.[54] Trolleys traveled almost twice as fast as horsecars. Areas 6 to 8 miles from the city center could now be reached in half an hour, making it possible for people to live 10 miles or more from work. And electric streetcars were infinitely cleaner than the horsecars they replaced. City residents had always complained about "an atmosphere heavy with the odors of death and decay and animal filth and steaming nastiness."[55] The trolley removed thousands of horses, together with their daily tons of manure, from the streets.

The horse-drawn streetcars and the electric trolleys (and a few decades later, the automobile) facilitated, each in its turn, an increasing segregation of settlement and land use. Until the 1870s, crowded financial and retailing districts were located close by and even mixed in with warehouses and factories.[56] In the last third of the nineteenth century, however, well-defined downtown shopping and financial districts sprang up. Middle-class people developed a new shopping habit. They rode the streetcars downtown to buy goods in the new generation of chain and department stores, which were able to grow larger because more people could get to them. The first chain retail company, the Great Atlantic and Pacific Tea Company, was organized in 1864, and A&P stores soon expanded to other cities. Frank W. Woolworth opened his five-and-dime store in Lancaster, Pennsylvania, in 1879, and by the 1880s Woolworth's became a familiar marquee in downtown areas.[57] The middle-class habit of shopping in downtown stores for major purchases persisted right up until the end of the 1950s, by which time the streetcar system had been dismantled in most cities.[58]

The development of social and ethnic segregation among neighborhoods, cities, and suburbs eroded the sense that everyone lived cooperatively in a mutually beneficial urban community. If the term "community" once evoked images of a diverse assortment of people rubbing shoulders in their daily lives, it gradually came to refer to the patterns of interaction among people living within homogeneous neighborhoods. The poor began to inhabit distinct enclaves, as did the middle class and the wealthy. The intimate sense of community that gave the merchant cities their distinctive character became a thing of the past, little more than a nostalgic remembrance.

The Immigrant Tide

The final blow to the social structure and politics of the preindustrial city was delivered by the flood tide of immigration that swept over the cities in the latter half of the nineteenth century. The industrial economy depended on a constantly expanding pool of cheap labor. Millions of foreign immigrants were pushed out of their homelands by war, civil unrest, and hardship, and pulled to American shores by opportunity. They worked on the railroads, in meatpacking, in steelmaking, in coal and lead mining, and in factories of every kind. Simultaneously, an unprecedented migration from farm to city was set in motion. Between 1830 and 1896, developments in farm machinery cut in half the average time and labor required to produce agricultural crops. In the four decades after the Civic War, the time required to harvest wheat was cut by 95 percent and labor costs for farming fell by one-fifth.[59] The new machinery drove up the capital investment required to start and run a farm and it required fewer hands than before. The millions of farm laborers and young people who could no longer find work streamed into the industrial cities in search of jobs and opportunity.

In the century between 1820 and 1919, 33.5 million foreign immigrants came to America. The Irish and then the Germans set off the first big surge.

A famine that swept Ireland in the mid-1840s pushed desperate families to make the wrenching decision to leave their homeland (forever after, an unrequited yearning has been the most common theme running through Irish music). Irish peasants subsisted primarily on potatoes and vegetables grown on tiny rocky plots of ground and in strips of soil along the roads, the only usable land not claimed by their English landlords. When a potato blight swept through Europe in the 1840s, its effects were more devastating in Ireland than elsewhere. Between 1845 and the mid-1850s, up to one-fourth of Ireland's peasants starved to death. Many of the survivors streamed into Liverpool and bought or bartered passage on ships heading for America.

In the same decade, years of civil war pushed a flood of German immigrants to America. The data displayed in Table 2.2 reveal that, all through the 1840s and 1850s the Irish and Germans kept coming. In this period, these two groups accounted for made up more than 70 percent of all new arrivals. Immigrants from the American "motherland," England, made up less than 14 percent of the flow, with an assortment of different nationalities making up the rest. America would never be the same.

After the depression of 1873–1876 the numbers of immigrants surged to levels never before experienced in the nation's history. In the decade of the 1970s, 2.7 million foreign immigrants came to America, and this number doubled, to 5.2 million in the 1880s. The depression of 1893–1896 slowed the flow for a brief time, but the number of arrivals in the first decade of the twentieth century soared to the highest level in American history, to over 8 million people, with an additional 6.5 million pouring in between 1910 and 1920. These astonishing numbers were driven by people coming from countries not much represented in the American population up to that point. Irish and Germans kept coming, but by the 1880s they accounted for just 40 percent of the immigrant flow, and after the turn of the century their numbers plummeted, to 8 percent of the total. Immigration from the United Kingdom continued to fall decade by decade. Italians, Greeks, immigrants from several eastern European nations (Bohemians, Czechs, Slavs, Lithuanians, Poles), and Jews made up the difference. In the 1890s, Jews from Russia and Austria–Hungary, together with Catholics from Italy, accounted for 42 percent of arrivals, and their numbers swelled to more than 60 percent in each of the two decades from 1900 to 1920. Between 1900 and 1920, 14.5 million immigrants entered the country.[60] These numbers would surely have increased still more if Congress had not enacted restrictive immigration laws in 1921 and 1924.

Wherever they were headed, the Statue of Liberty gave them their first view of America, making it the most enduring symbol of America's immigrant history. Sixty percent of all European immigrants between 1820 and 1919 passed through New York harbor. Between the turn of the century and World War I, two-thirds of all the immigrants entering the United States were processed through New York's Ellis Island (which was closed in 1954). Almost three-fourths of the new arrivals, 24 million in all, settled in the cities. By 1870, remarkably, more than half the population of at least 20 American cities were foreign-born or children of parents who had immigrated. In some cities

TABLE 2.2 Decennial Immigration to the United States, 1820–1919

	1820–1829	1830–1839	1840–1849	1850–1859	1860–1869	1870–1879	1880–1889	1890–1899	1900–1909	1910–1919
Total in millions	0.1	0.5	1.4	2.7	2.1	2.7	5.2	3.7	8.2	6.3
Percentage of total from:										
Ireland	40.20%	31.70%	46.00%	36.90%	24.40%	15.40%	12.80%	11.00%	4.20%	2.60%
Germany	4.5	23.2	27	34.8	35.2	27.4	27.5	15.7	4	2.7
United Kingdom	19.5	13.8	15.3	13.5	14.9	21.1	15.5	8.9	5.7	5.8
Scandinavia	0.2	0.4	0.9	0.9	5.5	7.6	12.7	10.5	5.9	3.8
Canada	1.8	2.2	2.4	2.2	4.9	11.8	9.4	0.1	1.5	11.2
Russia					0.2	1.3	3.5	12.2	18.3	17.4
Austria–Hungary					0.2	2.2	6	14.5	24.4	18.2
Italy					0.5	1.7	5.1	16.3	23.5	19.4

Sources: From N. Carpenter, "Immigrants and Their Children," *U.S. Bureau of the Census Monograph*, no. 7 (Washington, DC: U.S. Government Printing Office, 1927), pp. 324–325.

TABLE 2.3 Proportion of Immigrant Population in Cities of 500,000 or more, 1870 and 1910

		Percentage Foreign-Born	Percentage Foreign-Born or Native-Born with at Least One Foreign Parent[a]
New York	1870	44%	80%
	1910	40	79
Chicago	1870	48	87
	1910	36	78
Philadelphia	1870	28	51
	1910	25	57
St. Louis	1870	36	65
	1910	18	54
Boston	1870	35	63
	1910	36	74
Cleveland	1870	42	75
	1910	35	75
Baltimore	1870	21	38
	1910	14	38
Pittsburgh	1870	32	58
	1910	26	62
Mean for all eight cities (each counted equally)	1870	40	72
	1910	32	72

[a]Native-born with foreign parents is unavailable in the 1870 census. The figures for 1870 are estimated by adding 80 percent to the number of foreign-born. In all cases, this should yield a safely conservative estimate.

Sources: U.S. Department of the Interior, Superintendent of Census, The Ninth Census (June 1, 1870), vol. 1, Population and Social Statistics (Washington, DC: U.S. Government Printing Office, 1872), p. 386; U.S. Department of Commerce, Bureau of the Census, Thirteenth Census of the United States Taken in the Year 1910, vol. 1, Population 1910 (Washington, DC: U.S. Government Printing Office, 1913), p. 178.

the proportion reached much higher levels. As shown by the data in Table 2.3, by 1870, first- and second-generation immigrants accounted for at least 72 percent of the populations of eight cities of more than 500,000 people. Eighty percent of New York City's population was made up of first- and second-generation immigrants, and in Chicago an astounding 87 percent of the population was composed of the foreign-born and their American-born children.

And they kept on coming. Despite a huge and continuing migration from rural areas to the cities in the latter years of the nineteenth century, by 1910 the proportion of first- and second-generation immigrants in most cities was about the same as it had been 40 years before. In 1920, more than 80 percent of the Italians, Irish, Russian, and Polish newcomers were urban, as were 75 percent of the immigrants from the United Kingdom.[61] By the census of 1920, just before Congress passed restrictive legislation, 58 percent of the population of American cities of more than 100,000 people was first- or second-generation immigrant.[62]

Although clustered disproportionately in a few northeastern and midwestern industrial centers, immigrants spread out to all the cities that could offer industrial jobs. Large numbers also fanned out to the growing cities of the continental interior, went on to mining camps, or joined railroad construction gangs. About one-third of the arriving Germans settled outside towns and cities altogether. A smaller proportion of Scandinavians moved to cities than any other nationality group because many of them were enticed by agents sent to the Scandinavian countries by railroad corporations, which were trying to find buyers for some of millions of acres of land the companies had secured through government land grants. Enough Scandinavians settled in rural areas in Wisconsin, Minnesota, the Dakotas, and throughout the Midwest that only 55 percent were classified as urban in the census of 1920.

As soon as they arrived, immigrants encountered hostility and sometimes violence. A special enmity was reserved for the Irish because they were raggedly poor and Catholic. Irish workers could rarely read or claim a skilled occupation. Most of them took menial, temporary, low-paying jobs—moving goods on the waterfront, building streets and roads, and working in slaughterhouses and packinghouses. Because of their poverty and their religion and their peasant origins, they became etched in the public mind as dangerous, alcoholic, criminal, and dirty. Anti-Catholic and anti-Irish riots broke out on a regular basis. Irish churches, taverns, and neighborhoods were attacked by mobs whipped up by a rhetoric that spoke of "an invasion of venomous reptiles . . . , long-haired, wild-eyed, bad-smelling, atheistic, reckless foreign wretches."[63] Protestant Yankees were in a position to hire, promote, and fire. Even as late as the 1920s, want ads in Boston frequently added "Protestant" as a qualification for employment.[64] The Irish clustered on the lowest rungs of the social and economic ladder well into the twentieth century.

The Germans encountered far less antipathy because many were wealthy or from middle-class backgrounds. Unlike the Irish, they were escaping war and political turmoil, not poverty and starvation. They brought with them music and literary societies and a commitment to formal education. Although the Germans nominally faced a greater language barrier than did the Irish, the widely used Gaelic and the Irish brogue sounded just as foreign to American ears as did the German language.

The opportunities available to the different ethnic groups varied in relationship to the level of animosity directed toward them. In late-nineteenth-century Boston, "a pecking order favored some groups over others."[65] The Irish and

Italians competed for the lowest wages and lowest-skill jobs. Only the few blacks who lived in cities occupied a lower social position. German and recent British immigrants were generally able to enter middle-class occupations right away, and those who possessed an exceptional education or a special skill might achieve success very quickly. Russian and eastern European Jews, who came in the 1890s and later, placed emphasis on formal education and business. Although anti-Semitism kept them out of corporations and larger business enterprises, they succeeded in carving out a distinct economic niche as job brokers, middlemen, and shopkeepers.

Most of the immigrants crowded into densely packed neighborhoods near the waterfront and factories. In the 1840s and 1850s, real estate speculators and landlords shoehorned them into deteriorated houses, attics and basements, and unused warehouses and factories. Housing was so scarce and rents so high that a lot of property-owning families made money by renting extra space in their own living quarters.[66] Narrow three- and four-story buildings divided into tiny spaces sprang up in alleyways and on back lots. On vacant lots and behind and between buildings, immigrants crowded into sheds and shanties.

The first tenement districts began to spread in New York City as early as the 1850s, and made their appearance in other cities soon after. As middle-class families left the city center, it became cost-efficient to raze older structures and replace them with buildings designed to crowd as many people as possible into the available space. The tenement—the name given to any low-cost multiple-family rental building—became a universal symbol of the American urban slum, and by the twentieth century, multistory buildings of any kind came to represent city living. At the same time, the freestanding house evolved into a cultural expression of suburban living. The most notorious tenement structure was the dumbbell—so named because two 28-inch-wide air shafts provided the only light and air to the interior rooms. Based on an award-winning 1879 design, the dumbbell maximized economic return at the expense of ventilation and sanitation. Tenants on the upper floors would pitch their garbage down the shafts, where it was left to rot. On each floor, tenants shared one or two public toilets and a sink, and these were always located next to ventilation shafts, with their foul and fetid air. By 1893, 70 percent of the population of New York City lived in tenements, most of them dumbbells.[67]

Despite the problems caused by overcrowding, the concentration of the immigrant groups into densely packed enclaves was crucially important in easing their assimilation into urban life. Within these densely packed wards, a variety of religious and social institutions sprang up to nurture ethnic traditions and a sense of solidarity and shared identity. The immigrant neighborhoods also facilitated the rise of a style of politics based on ethnic solidarity that began to bring immigrants in the American political system. By the 1880s, urban party machines began to emerge based on the relationship forged between ethnic voters and a new breed of politicians skilled at mobilizing their followers. In Chapter 3 we describe this historic development.

The Capacity to Govern

As the industrial cities grew, the capacity of local governments to respond to the needs of their residents came into question. For many urban dwellers, in the latter half of the nineteenth century the conditions of life ranged from squalid to barely tolerable. Epidemics periodically swept through, sometimes killing several hundred people in a summer. Streets turned to seas of mud in winter and to dust bowls in summer, and in every season they were littered with refuse and piles of steaming horse manure. A Swedish novelist commented that Chicago in 1850 (when it still had only 30,000 people) was "one of the most miserable and ugly cities," where people had come "to trade, to make money, and not to live."[68]

The residents of the cities complained about the conditions of daily life, but no one was sure what municipal governments should do about the situation. In the American political tradition, there was an abiding suspicion of government; most people seemed more concerned about its potential dangers than about the ways in which it might be put to positive use. This suspicion was reinforced by a deeply rooted culture of privatism—the idea that progress comes through individual rather than through collective endeavors. Although urban leaders were able to persuade their fellow citizens that local government should support schemes promoting the local economy, it was much more difficult to talk them into taxing themselves to support the services that might improve the local quality of life.

Even in the large cities full-time, paid, uniformed police forces were rare until the mid-nineteenth century. The law was generally enforced by part-time or volunteer night watches and constables. Volunteer fire gangs answered the fire alarm. Individual property owners swept the streets and collected refuse. Even as population growth made city life increasingly unpleasant, city residents were reluctant to acknowledge that municipal government might do better than the community's own efforts. Against this background, it is a puzzling fact that, municipal governments vastly increased their responsibilities in the latter half of the nineteenth century. In New York City, for instance, per capita city expenditures increased from $6.53 in 1850 to $27.3 in 1900.[69] During this half century, cities spent more money and employed more people than either the state governments or the national government. When governmental spending was cataloged for the first time in the federal census of governments in 1902, local governments accounted for half of all governmental expenditures in the United States.[70]

Despite a national culture that preferred minimal government, over the course of a century municipal responsibilities vastly increased. Three major reasons can be offered to explain this unexpected outcome. First, new services were provided in cases when urban residents of all classes felt threatened by imminent catastrophe or crisis. Second, local boosters assumed the lead in organizing public services when the absence or inadequacy of these services threatened the economic vitality of the city. And third, by the late nineteenth century, a growing middle class became intolerant of urban conditions that had previously been considered unpleasant, but normal or inevitable.

In the colonial period and for many years after, urban services were minimal. Essential as they were to the basic health of urban citizens, for instance, water systems were chronically inadequate. In the early nineteenth century, most city residents got their water from wells, and these were often contaminated by waste. As a result, outbreaks of contagious diseases occurred with disturbing regularity. In the summer of 1793, 10 percent of Philadelphia's population died from yellow fever.[71] The city's economy came to a standstill, and a third of the population and virtually all wealthy families fled for the summer months. Outbreaks of yellow fever or cholera occurred in Philadelphia, Baltimore, and New Haven (Connecticut) in 1793; in New York City, Baltimore, and Norfolk (Virginia) in 1795; and in Newburyport (Massachusetts), Boston, and Charleston (South Carolina) the next year.[72] Nearly a dozen cities were hit in 1797; three-fourths of Philadelphia's population fled and 4,000 people died (which amounted to about 7 percent of the population).[73]

Such catastrophes prompted cities to invest in waterworks, drain swamps, and to regulate the keeping of animals and the dumping of refuse. Philadelphia was goaded by its epidemics to construct the first municipal waterworks in the nation's history. Begun in 1799 and operational in some parts of the city by 1801, it piped water from the upper Schuylkill River. Over time, Philadelphia's system was constantly improved by the merchant elites who ran the Watering Committee. By the 1840s, however, these elites began to withdraw from political activities, partly because competition for political office from a new generation of public leaders had become more intense. Without their guiding hand on the committee, the water supply system became less and less adequate.[74] Only with great reluctance did the city government assume the responsibilities an increasingly inept Watering Committee.

Despite the manifest need, municipal services tended to lag behind need because they were generally provided only in response to a crisis: "municipal authorities, loath to increase taxes, usually shouldered new responsibilities only at the prod of grim necessity."[75] Devastating outbreaks of yellow fever, typhoid, and cholera periodically made their rounds, especially in the cities such as New Orleans and Memphis that lagged furthest behind in providing uncontaminated water supplies. Several urban water systems were built in the 1850s, and by the Civil War 70 towns were served by waterworks. For the most part these were privately owned and operated by the 80 private companies that had sprung up for this purpose.[76] The systems were partial and primitive. Except in the wealthy neighborhoods where water was piped into homes, most people had to fetch the water from street hydrants and hand pumps. As late as 1860, only about one-tenth of Boston's residents had access to a bathtub, and only 5 percent of the homes had indoor water closets.[77]

Urban water supplies were generally polluted by human and animal waste. In most cities, sewage was collected in huge community cesspools, which had to be dug out frequently. Even when sewer pipes carried waste away from the city, the main result was merely to send the polluted water downstream.

Serious typhoid epidemics broke out in the cities along the Merrimac River in Massachusetts in the 1880s because residents were drinking water that carried the sewage of cities located upstream. Because of Boston's habit of dumping wastes directly into its harbor, by 1877 Boston Harbor had become "one vast cesspool."[78] Until the 1920s, crowded residential districts were dotted with outdoor privies, and water, bearing a burden of horse manure and other refuse, flowed in open gutters along the streets. The sources of contamination were so numerous that only those cities that piped their water from watersheds far away from urban settlement were able to avoid a contaminated water supply.

Ultimately, the water supply problem could be solved only through the development of adequate technology. Even Philadelphia's relatively sophisticated system delivered its water with only the heaviest silt filtered out.[79] Pumps frequently failed; in the winter, pipes froze. People found dirt, insects, and even small fish gushing from the taps. During the first decade of the twentieth century, when modern filtration techniques were developed, death rates in New York, Boston, Philadelphia, and New Orleans fell by one-fifth.[80]

Epidemics prompted cities to build sewers to carry the waste away from heavily populated neighborhoods. In 1823, Boston began installing the nation's first sanitary sewers. Other large cities followed suit, but slowly. By 1857, New York City, which by then had a population of nearly a million people, had a system of sewers under only one-fourth of its streets, and most of these were storm water rather than sanitary sewers.[81] Taxpayers resisted the high cost of laying underground pipes and installing costly pumps. Although most of the big cities had constructed sewers by the 1870s, these were usually paid for by the property owners who subscribed, leaving vast areas—always the neighborhoods inhabited by the poor—without service.

A perceived crisis of a different sort forced cities to begin financing and organizing professional police forces. As cities grew in size and complexity, rising levels of violence, crime, and disorder threatened to disrupt the lives of every urban resident. The unceasing influx of immigrants provoked ethnic conflict, pushed up crime rates, and broke apart the bonds of community. In the 1830s and 1840s, rioting directed against Irish immigrants and free blacks broke out regularly in Philadelphia. In frontier cities, the connection between rapid population growth and social instability was painfully obvious. A constant stream of river men, wagon drivers, and traders moved into and out of bustling cities like San Francisco, St. Louis, and New Orleans. Saloons proliferated; gambling and prostitution flourished. During the gold rush years of the 1850s, violent crime became such a fact of everyday life in San Francisco that merchants funded vigilante committees to keep order. Before long, however, the vigilantes organized their own crime rings and became almost as dangerous as the criminals they were supposed to catch.[82]

In 1845, Boston became the first city in the United States to provide uniforms for its officers. The same year, when its population numbered more than 400,000, New York finally replaced its rag-tag army of part-time police with a full-time force. Even then, though, the police continued to go about their jobs in street clothes, completely untrained and without supervision.[83] Eight years later, the city's police finally received uniforms and some modest training. Until the late 1830s, Philadelphia relied on a mix of part-time posses, militia, and night watches, and none of them wore uniforms.[84]

New York's police forces were in constant turmoil for many years. There was resistance to the idea of creating a professional police force because the two political parties that contended for power in the city regarded the police as an important source of patronage jobs. Following the 1857 mayoral election, the new mayor fired everyone on the force and installed officers who were loyal to him. The former officers refused to quit their jobs, and so for several months the city was patrolled by two competing police forces. In June of that year, a full-scale riot broke out between the two groups.[85] Similar confusion repeated itself in 1868, when the newly elected Democratic governor removed all of the city's police commissioners because they were Republicans. The commissioners refused to vacate their offices. Finally, the state legislature resolved the dispute by assuming the authority to appoint them.

Episodes like this illustrate why it took so long for the cities to build modern, fully professionalized police forces. Many people feared that, as a quasi-military organization, the police might be used by one political faction against another. This fear was well founded. Police departments were deeply affected by ethnic and racial prejudices, and also by political loyalties. Such problems persist right up to the present day. A presidential commission investigating the urban riots of the 1960s found that police conduct was the most common provocation causing the rioting.[86] In the nineteenth century and still today, police officers are granted a great deal of discretion, and often enough they do not apply the law dispassionately.

If it seems that an atmosphere of crisis was necessary to goad governing elites into organizing and financing municipal services, this fact still begs an important question: What provoked a sense that there was a crisis? Objective conditions, however dire, may be adjusted to, considered normal, or appear to be beyond anyone's control. The answer to the question is that political leaders held ambitious aspirations for their cities and for themselves. Chronic problems such as crime, poor sanitation, and impassable streets not only diminished the quality of life for urban residents but these problems also threatened local economic vitality. Faced with this reality, civic elites and business leaders preferred to support public services rather than allow their city to slip into decline.

Once provided, urban services became institutionalized; they quickly seemed normal and routine; there could be no going back to a time when they were not available. This was especially true for services such as water systems and fire departments that required the construction of permanent infrastructure and investment in expensive equipment. In this way, the responsibilities of city governments grew inexorably, step by step. In the early nineteenth century, when confronted with a problem, the cities' aristocratic and merchant class would typically organize a committee to decide what to do. Over time, such informal arrangements gave way to services provided by full-time paid employees. Again, the evolution of Philadelphia's waterworks is instructive. At first, the Watering Committee raised money through private donations and individual subscriptions to the water service. Prominent merchants led the committee until 1837.[87] But over the next few decades, the system expanded until it provided water to all citizens, and it became necessary to impose taxes to support it.

Milwaukee's volunteer fire department gave way to paid professionals in the 1850s when new steam pumps proved too complicated for volunteers to maintain and operate.[88] In the same decade, public works employees began to maintain the streets when it became too difficult to find volunteers for the task. Trained employees were hired to run the sewer system when the city council provided funds to expand it to cover most of the city. When the Milwaukee city council required vaccinations for smallpox, local health services became too complex for volunteers. In this way, the day-to-day administration of municipal services was gradually put in the hands of paid employees. "Politics became a full-time business and professionals moved in to make careers of public office."[89]

In the last third of the nineteenth century, a growing middle class began to demand improved water and sewer systems,[90] and by the 1890s popular pressure was mobilized to demand better services of all kinds. From the 1850s to the 1870s, assistance to railroads had been the largest single cause of municipal debt. In striking contrast, during the last 30 years of the century, the cities went into debt mainly to finance the expansion of new services and to build infrastructure.[91] Because of rising standards of public health, new technologies, even when very expensive, were quickly adopted. The construction of integrated sewerage systems provides an instructive example. Systems of separate sanitary and storm sewers were not completed in most cities until very late in the nineteenth century. Laying sewer pipe was a huge public works project for any city. Nevertheless, the number of miles of sewer pipe increased fourfold from 1890 to 1909.[92]

By the turn of the century, American cities, in general, provided more and better services than did their European counterparts, with more miles of sewer and water mains, more miles of paved streets, more street lamps, better mass transportation, and more fire departments with better equipment.[93] Urban residents in the United States used more than twice as much water per capita as did their counterparts in England and many times more than city dwellers in Germany,[94] probably because flush toilets and bathtubs were far more widespread in American cities.[95] The cities also vastly expanded public health efforts. Using the new science of bacteriology, health inspectors examined children in schools, checked buildings for ventilation and faulty plumbing, and inspected food and milk.[96] Such public health measures, when combined with the completion of integrated sewer systems and installation of new water filtration technology, dramatically reduced typhoid mortality rates.[97] Overall death rates fell sharply in the big cities, by 20 percent or more in New York, Chicago, Cleveland, Buffalo, and other cities in the 1890s,[98] and just as sharply again after the turn of the twentieth century.[99]

The late nineteenth century was the golden age for American city building. The massive investment in physical infrastructure placed city governments at the cutting edge of technology, resulting in such engineering marvels as the

Brooklyn Bridge and New York's Croton aqueduct system, with its thousands of miles of pipes and reservoirs. The Parks Movement and the City Beautiful Movement, both supported by urban elites and the middle class, swept the nation, resulting in urban amenities such as parks, ponds, formal gardens, bandstands, ball fields, broad tree-lined avenues, and ornate public buildings. Urban residents came to expect a level of municipal services that would have been inconceivable in an earlier time. The squalor of the nineteenth-century industrial city began to yield to the relative safety, cleanliness, and health of the twentieth-century metropolis.

Municipal services have continued to evolve over the past century. Cities today provide a remarkable array of services. They build and maintain a public infrastructure—roads, bridges, sewer lines, sewage treatment plants, water mains, parks, zoos, hospitals, and sometimes even universities. They provide police and fire protection. They collect garbage (or pay someone who does). They run public health services that inspect restaurants, vaccinate children, and test for the HIV (AIDS) virus. Through city zoning ordinances, they influence the location of homes, factories, office buildings, restaurants, and parking lots. Through local building codes, they regulate such matters as plumbing, wiring, building materials, the height of structures, and architectural styles. Cities poison rats and sometimes try to scare away pigeons. These public undertakings, and many more, are essential to the safety and well-being of people living in urban environments. Without them, urban life would quickly become not only dangerous but intolerable.

The Limited Powers of Cities

The ability of American cities to adapt to changing circumstances is a remarkable story, all the more so because they were mostly left on their own to devise solutions to the problems that faced them. The national government was distant and indifferent: only in the twentieth century would the federal government establish any relationship to the cities. State legislatures were alternately hostile and indifferent. For the most part, the legislatures—made up as they were by part-time politicians who met for a few weeks or months every other year— paid little attention. More than anything else, rural legislators wanted to keep urban politicians and the constituencies that supported them from intruding into their domain. The independence of cities led Alexis de Tocqueville, in his classic work *Democracy in America* (1835), to emphasize that local governments in the United States were sovereign. He compared them to independent nations: "Municipal independence is . . . a natural consequence of the principle of the sovereignty of the people in the United States: all the American republics recognize it more or less."[100] But his assessment was not quite accurate. The autonomy of cities owed more to an attitude of indifference to how they governed themselves than to their legal status. Although state legislatures clearly possessed the legal authority to control the cities within their boundaries in almost every detail, they exercised that right only sometimes, although when they did they could be unpredictable and capricious. Cities might seem to be independent, but this was true only because state legislatures generally lacked the time and interest to notice what they were up to.

Advocates for the right of cities to govern themselves without outside interference pleaded their cause in articles, books, and court rulings.[101] Mostly it was to no avail; the courts consistently upheld the powers of the states to define the powers and obligations of local governments. In 1819, in the *Dartmouth College* case, the U.S. Supreme Court held that cities were created by the states and their charters could therefore be amended or rescinded at will. (By contrast, private corporations were protected from interference by the constitutional provision against "impairing the obligation of contract."[102]) A second definitive case was handed down in 1868, when the chief justice of the Iowa Supreme Court, John F. Dillon, declared that states could rightfully exert total control over their cities, with no restrictions whatsoever:

> Municipal corporations owe their origin to, and derive their powers and rights wholly from, the legislature. It breathes into them the breath of life without which they cannot exist. As it creates so it may destroy. . . . Unless there is some constitutional limitation on the right, the legislature might, by a single act, if we can suppose it capable of so great a folly and so great a wrong, sweep from existence all of the municipal corporations of the state, and the corporations could not prevent it. . . . They are, so to phrase it, the mere tenants at will of the legislature.[103]

Judge Dillon was motivated by the fact that cities had been active in providing subsidies to railroads, and he reasoned that if they could help private corporations so directly, they could regulate them as well. Dillon's missionary zeal was also fired by a conviction that dangerous riffraff governed the cities: "men the best fitted by their intelligence, business experience, capacity and moral character, for local governors and counselors are not always, it is feared—it might be added, are not generally—chosen."[104] His solution was that state governments and courts, like stern parents, should closely supervise their cities and strictly limit their privileges. In 1872, Dillon published his *Treatise on the Law of Municipal Corporations*. Originally 800 pages long, by the time the fifth edition was published in 1911, it had grown to five thick volumes.[105] By then, Dillon's work had become the bible on municipal law. By 1924, William Munro, the author of a leading textbook, *The Government of American Cities*, wrote that Dillon's rule was "so well recognized that it is not nowadays open to question."[106]

Motivated by a similar distrust of cities—or, rather, of immigrant voters—state legislators took steps to ensure that no matter how fast and big cities might grow, their representatives to the statehouse would never be able to gain a majority of seats in state legislatures. Most rural legislators would probably have agreed with the delegate to the New York State constitutional convention of 1894 who said, "the average citizen in the rural district is superior in intelligence, superior in morality, superior in self-government to the average citizen of the great cities."[107] This attitude reflected a long-standing animosity to cities and everything urban. Decades earlier, Maine's constitutional convention of 1819 had established a ceiling on the number of representatives who could serve towns in the state legislature. In 1845, the Louisiana legislature limited New Orleans to 12.5 percent of the state's senators and 10 percent of the state's assemblymen. (The population of New Orleans accounted for 20 percent of the state's total.[108]) By the end of the century, every state had ensured that no matter how large its cities became, representatives from rural legislative districts would continue to hold a commanding voting majority in state legislatures.

By then, more people lived in the cities of some states than outside them. If their influence in state legislatures had grown in step with their populations, cities would have been able to secure state financial support for the expansion of city services. In fact, however, cities received practically no help at all. If urban voters had managed to exert more influence in state politics and in state governments, they also could have asserted a political voice in national affairs. Rural elites firmly controlled the state party caucuses that nominated governors, members of Congress, senators, and presidents, and therefore ethnic minorities and other urban voters had no effective means of influencing governmental policies at the state or national levels. The underrepresentation of the cities resulted in indifference to their problems in state legislatures, governors' offices, Congress, and the White House. Traffic congestion, slum housing, orphaned children, contagious diseases, poverty—none of these problems interested rural and small-town legislators or the members of Congress and presidents beholden to state party leaders who answered to rural constituents.

Underrepresentation of cities throughout the federal system exerted profound and long-lasting consequences, for it allowed governmental leaders at all levels to wash their hands of the devastating effects of industrialization and urbanization. In the late nineteenth century, powerful populist movements pushed for the recognition of the right of labor unions to organize. In the first 20 years of the twentieth century, reformers lobbied state legislatures to adopt universal health insurance, workers' compensation, and relief programs for widows, children, and the elderly. A groundswell of opposition to child labor swept the country; nevertheless, the federal government did not adopt child labor legislation until 1916; even then it was struck down by the Supreme Court two years later.[109] These and other reforms that would have benefited cities and their residents were delayed until the New Deal of the 1930s. Many other policies, such as federal aid to education, health care for the aged and poor (Medicare and Medicaid), federal aid to the cities, and a variety of social programs, would surely have been adopted long before the 1960s if the cities had been represented in state and national politics in proportion to their share of the national population.

The federal courts finally moved against legislative malapportionment in the 1960s, more than 40 years after the 1920 census showed that a majority of Americans lived in urban places. In *Baker v. Carr* (1962), a group of Knoxville residents challenged the fact that the Tennessee legislature had not been reapportioned since 1901.[110] Their lawyers argued that citizens living in urban areas were being deprived of "equal protection of the law," as guaranteed by the

Fourteenth Amendment to the U.S. Constitution. The important court decision that decided this case, as well as others, came on June 15, 1964, when the U.S. Supreme Court, in *Reynolds v. Sims*, ruled that state legislative apportionments must follow a "one man, one vote" principle.[111] Within a few years, for the first time in the nation's history, state legislative and congressional districts were apportioned to give city residents equal representation.

By the time the courts imposed the one-man, one-vote remedy, it was too late to be much of much consequence. By the 1960s the older industrial cities were rapidly losing population, and the suburbs Sunbelt were booming. This demographic transformation brought about a historical shift in the balance of national power. If cities had gained equal representation in state legislatures and in Congress decades earlier, urban voters might have been able to secure from the federal government as well as from many states funding for such local priorities as mass transit, public housing, urban revitalization, and public health programs. But the American political system had been biased against the urban electorate for a reason: the people who lived in the cities of America had long been regarded as "strangers in the land."[112] In light of such deeply rooted attitudes, the fact that American cities responded to their problems as well as they did must be regarded as a remarkable success.

Endnotes

1. Robert A. Beauregard, *Voices of Decline: The Postwar Fate of U.S. Cities* (New York: Blackwell, 1993).
2. London proper had 957,000, but the greater London area had 1,117,000 people.
3. Brian R. Mitchell, *European Historical Statistics, 1750–1970* (New York: Columbia University Press, 1975), p. 76.
4. Defined as settlements with a population of at least 5,000.
5. Eric Lampard, "Historical Aspects of Urbanization," in *The Study of Urbanization,* ed. Philip M. Hauser and Leo F. Schnore (New York: Wiley, 1965), p. 523.
6. "The Inevitability of City Growth," reprinted from *Atlantic Monthly,* April 1985, in *City Life, 1865–1900: Views of Urban America,* ed. Ann Cook, Marilyn Gittell, and Herb Mack (New York: Praeger, 1973), p. 17.
7. Eric H. Monkkonen, *America Becomes Urban: The Development of U.S. Cities and Towns, 1780–1980* (Berkeley: University of California Press, 1988), p. 78.
8. D. Philip Locklin, *Economics of Transportation,* 7th ed. (Homewood, IL: Irwin, 1972).
9. Allan R. Pred, *The Spatial Dynamics of Urban–Industrial Growth, 1800–1914* (Cambridge, MA: MIT Press, 1966), p. 103.
10. David M. Gordon, "Class Struggle and the Stages of American Urban Development," in *The Rise of the Sunbelt Cities,* ed. David C. Perry and Alfred J. Watkins (Beverly Hills, CA: Sage, 1977), p. 64.
11. George Rogers Taylor, *The Transportation Revolution, 1815–1860* (New York: Holt, Rinehart & Winston, 1951), p. 52.
12. Carter Goodrich, *Government Promotion of American Canals and Railroads, 1800–1890* (New York: Columbia University Press, 1960), pp. 266–267.
13. Richard C. Wade, *The Urban Frontier: Pioneer Life in Early Pittsburgh, Cincinnati, Lexington, Louisville, and St. Louis* (Chicago: University of Chicago Press, 1959), p. 70.

14. U.S. Department of Commerce, *Historical Statistics of the United States, Colonial Times to 1970*, pt. 2, (Washington, DC: U.S. Government Printing Office, 1975), pp. 728, 731.
15. Alfred D. Chandler, *The Railroads: The Nation's First Big Business* (New York: Harcourt Brace Jovanovich, 1965).
16. Paul Kantor, *The Dependent City Revisited: The Political Economy of Urban Development and Social Policy* (Boulder, CO: Westview, 1995), p. 24.
17. Carter Goodrich, "The Revulsion against Internal Improvements," *Journal of Economic History* 10, no. 2 (November 1950): 145–169.
18. David Chalmers, *Neither Socialism nor Monopoly* (Philadelphia: Lippincott, 1976), p. 4.
19. Blake McKelvey, *American Urbanization: A Comparative History* (Glenview, IL: Scott Foresman, 1973), pp. 25–26.
20. Ibid.
21. Paul Kantor with Stephen David, *The Dependent City: The Changing Political Economy of Urban America* (Glenview, IL: Scott Foresman, 1987), pp. 499–500.
22. Goodrich, *Government Promotion*, p. 241. Goodrich estimates that until 1860, local governments provided 29 percent of total public subsidies (p. 268). The proportion of local contributions increased significantly after the Civil War. In his study of New York from 1826 to 1875, Harry Pierce concludes that three-quarters of the subsidy came from local governments and one-quarter from the state. See Harry H. Pierce, *The Railroads of New York: A Study of Government Aid, 1826–1875* (Cambridge, MA: Harvard University Press, 1953).
23. Ibid.
24. In 1849, for example, the voters of Cleveland approved a $100,000 subscription to stock in the Cleveland and Pittsburgh Railroad by a vote of 1,157 to 27. Despite the enthusiasm of the voters, the stock never paid any dividends and eventually sold at far below par. Charles C. Williamson, *The Finances of Cleveland* (New York: Columbia University Press, 1907), pp. 218–220.
25. Goodrich, *Government Promotion*, p. 42.
26. Ibid., p. 272. One study gave the following figures for New York: "Only 52 of the 297 municipalities that bought stock in a railroad disposed of their securities at par or better, 162 held stock with no market value" (Pierce, *The Railroads of New York*), p. 273.
27. A. M. Hillhouse, *Municipal Bonds: A Century of Experience* (Upper Saddle River, NJ: Prentice Hall, 1936), p. 39.
28. Goodrich, *Government Promotion*, pp. 268–271. Repudiation goes beyond default, which is simply a failure to pay the debt on time. Repudiation declares an unwillingness to ever repay the debt.
29. Alberta M. Sbragia, *Debt Wish: Entrepreneurial Cities, U.S. Federalism and Economic Development* (Pittsburgh: University of Pittsburgh Press, 1996), p. 91.
30. Goodrich, "Revulsion against Internal Improvements"; see also Sbragia, *Debt Wish*, Chapter 5.
31. Lawrence Goodwyn, *The Populist Movement* (New York: Oxford University Press, 1978).
32. Edwin J. Perkins, *The Economy of Colonial America* (New York: Columbia University Press, 1980), p. 157.
33. Philip Foner, *History of the Labor Movement in the United States* (New York: International, 1975), pp. 13–18.
34. Howard P. Chudacoff, *The Evolution of American Urban Society* (Upper Saddle River, NJ: Prentice Hall, 1975), p. 26.

35. Sam Bass Warner Jr., *The Private City: Philadelphia in Three Periods of Its Growth* (Philadelphia: University of Pennsylvania Press, 1968), p. 21.

36. Kantor, *The Dependent City,* p. 22.

37. Ibid., p. 33.

38. Pred, *The Spatial Dynamics,* p. 16.

39. Ibid., p. 170.

40. Ibid., pp. 68–69.

41. The skyscraper boom on Fifth Avenue between 1900 and 1915 was largely fueled by the desire of rich individuals to outdo one another in pretentious architecture. See Seymour I. Toll, *Zoned American* (New York: Grossman, 1969), Chapter 2.

42. Chartered by the states, limited-risk corporations allowed the selling of shares to investors whose liability in case of corporate failure was limited to their direct investment. In partnerships, the partners were liable for all debts incurred by the company, and these could easily exceed the partners' own assets. The corporate form of business organization thus made it easier to raise capital, for investors risked less than in other forms of business investment.

43. U.S. Department of the Interior, Census Office, *Census Reports of 1900,* vol. 7, *Manufacturers,* pt. 1: "United States by Industries" (Washington, D.C.: U.S. Government Printing Office, 1902), pp. 503–509.

44. William Miller, "American Historians and the Business Elite," *Journal of Economic History* 9 (1949): 184–208.

45. Kenneth Jackson, *Crabgrass Frontier: The Suburbanization of the United States* (New York: Oxford University Press, 1985), p. 35.

46. George Rogers Taylor, "Building an Intra-Urban Transportation System," in *The Urbanization of America: An Historical Anthology,* ed. Allen M. Wakstein (Boston, MA: Houghton Mifflin, 1970), p. 137.

47. Glen E. Holt, "The Changing Perception of Urban Pathology: An Essay on the Development of Mass Transit in the United States," in *Cities in American History,* ed. Kenneth T. Jackson and Stanley K. Schultz (New York: Knopf, 1972), p. 327.

48. Taylor, "Building an Intra-Urban Transportation System," p. 139.

49. C. G. Kennedy, "Commuter Services in the Boston Area, 1835–1860," *Business History Review* 26 (1962): 277–287.

50. Jackson, *Crabgrass Frontier,* p. 41.

51. David Ward, *Cities and Immigrants: A Geography of Change in Nineteenth-Century America* (New York: Oxford University Press, 1971), p. 4.

52. Jackson, *Crabgrass Frontier,* p. 108.

53. Ibid.

54. Gary A. Tobin, "Suburbanization and the Development of Motor Transportation: Transportation and Technology and the Suburbanization Process," in *The Changing Face of the Suburbs,* ed. Barry Schwartz (Chicago: University of Chicago Press, 1975), p. 99.

55. "The Smell of Cincinnati," *Enquirer* (Richmond, VA), November 15, 1874, in *City Life,* ed. Cook, Gittell, and Mack, p. 143.

56. Ward, *Cities and Immigrants,* Chapter 3.

57. Blake McKelvey, *The Urbanization of America, 1860–1915* (New Brunswick, NJ: Rutgers University Press, 1963), p. 54.

58. For an excellent history of America's downtowns, see Robert M. Fogelson, *Downtown: Its Rise and Fall, 1880–1950* (New Haven, CT: Yale University Press, 2001).

59. Samuel P. Hays, *The Response to Industrialism, 1885–1914* (Chicago: University of Chicago Press, 1957), p. 14.

60. Thomas Monroe Pitkin, *Keepers of the Gate: A History of Ellis Island* (New York: New York University Press, 1975), p. ix.
61. Ward, *Cities and Immigrants,* p. 56.
62. Ibid., p. 52.
63. John Higham, *Strangers in the Land: Patterns of American Nativism, 1860–1925* (New Brunswick, NJ: Rutgers University Press, 1955), pp. 54–55.
64. Stephen Thernstrom, *The Other Bostonians: Poverty and Progress in the American Metropolis, 1880–1970* (Cambridge, MA: Harvard University Press, 1973), p. 160.
65. Ibid.
66. Charles N. Glaab and A. Theodore Brown, *A History of Urban America* (New York: Macmillan, 1967), p. 160.
67. Gwendolyn Wright, *Building the American Dream: A Social History of Housing in America* (Cambridge, MA: MIT Press, 1983), p. 123. Dumbbell waiters are rope-pulley devices used to move small items up and down a shaft in multistory buildings.
68. Glaab and Brown, *A History of Urban America,* p. 86.
69. Ibid., p. 180.
70. Terrence J. MacDonald and Sally K. Ward, eds., *The Politics of Urban Fiscal Policy* (Beverly Hills, CA: Sage, 1984), p. 14.
71. Nelson M. Blake, *Water for the Cities: A History of the Urban Water Supply Problem in the United States* (Syracuse, NY: Syracuse University Press, 1956), p. 6.
72. Ibid., pp. 102–103.
73. Ibid., p. 6.
74. Warner, *The Private City,* pp. 107–109.
75. Arthur N. Schlesinger, "A Panoramic View: The City in American Life," in *The City in American Life,* ed. Paul Kramer and Fredrick L. Holborn (New York: Capricorn Books, 1970), p. 23.
76. McKelvey, *The Urbanization of America,* p. 13.
77. Edgar W. Martin, *The Standard of Living in 1860* (Chicago: University of Chicago Press, 1942), pp. 44–47, 89–112.
78. McKelvey, *The Urbanization of America,* p. 90.
79. Ibid., p. 13.
80. Ibid., p. 90.
81. McKelvey, *American Urbanization,* p. 44.
82. Fred M. Wirt, *Power in the City* (Berkeley: University of California Press, 1974), p. 110.
83. James F. Richardson, "To Control the City: The New York Police in Historical Perspective," in *Cities in American History,* ed. Jackson and Schultz, pp. 272–289.
84. Warner, *The Private City,* Chapter 7.
85. Richardson, "To Control the City," p. 278.
86. *Report of the National Advisory Commission on Civil Disorders* (New York: Bantam Books, 1968).
87. Warner, *The Private City.*
88. Bayrd Still, *Milwaukee: The History of a City* (Madison: State Historical Society of Wisconsin, 1984), Chapter 10.
89. Warner, *The Private City,* p. 86.
90. Sbragia, *Debt Wish,* p. 76.
91. Ibid.
92. Ibid.
93. Jon Teaford, *The Unheralded Triumph: City Government in America, 1870–1900* (Baltimore: Johns Hopkins University Press, 1984), Chapter 8.

94. Ibid., p. 222.
95. Ibid., p. 221.
96. Ibid., p. 247.
97. Stanley K. Schultz, *Constructing Urban Culture: American Cities and City Planning, 1800–1920* (Philadelphia: Temple University Press, 1989), p. 174.
98. Ibid., p. 246.
99. McKelvey, *The Urbanization of America,* p. 90.
100. Alexis de Tocqueville, *Democracy in America,* vol. 1 (New York: Shocken Books, 1961), p. 60.
101. For citations, see Gerald Frug, "The City as a Legal Concept," *Harvard Law Review* 93, no. 6 (April 1980): 1113–1117.
102. See *Dartmouth College v. Woodward,* 4 Wheat. 518 (1819).
103. *City of Clinton v. Cedar Rapids and Missouri River Railroad Co.,* 24 Iowa 455–475 (1868).
104. Schultz, *Constructing Urban Culture,* p. 73.
105. Ibid., p. 69.
106. William Munro, *The Government of the American Cities,* 3rd ed. (New York: Macmillan, 1924), p. 53.
107. Mark I. Gelfand, *A Nation of Cities: The Federal Government and Urban America, 1933–1965* (New York: Oxford University Press, 1975), p. 11.
108. Ibid.
109. *Hammer v. Dagenhart et al.,* 247 U.S. 251 (1918).
110. *Baker v. Carr,* 369 U.S. 189 (1962).
111. *Reynolds v. Sims,* 377 U.S. 533 (1964). "One man, one vote" was the term used in the Court's decision.
112. Higham, *Strangers in the Land.*

CHAPTER 3

Party Machines and the Immigrants

Machines and Machine-Style Politics

The image of the rotund, cigar-smoking machine politician handing out buckets of coal to poor widows and cutting deals in smoke-filled rooms in the back of taverns holds a sacred place in the lore of American politics. What continues to make it fascinating is its colorful, larger-than-life aspect: the politician who is passionate, free-wheeling, and generous to his loyal constituents, but also self-serving, venal, and corrupt. The television series *The Sopranos* or Francis Ford Coppola's film *The Godfather* may come to mind because they serve as reminders that machine politicians and the Mafia shared a general style. The occasions when machine politicians crossed the line into thuggish violence are generally exceptions, but not enough for comfort. Recall, for example, *The Untouchables* television series and movie, based on the heyday of the Chicago machine of the 1920s and 1930s, when politicians, judges, and police officers were bought off by Al Capone and speakeasy owners, and FBI agent Elliott Ness arrived on the scene to take on not only Capone, but an entire system of criminal and political corruption. There have been instances when information fed by machine members to criminal gangs has been used to kill informants, and even cases when investigative reporters have been killed.[1] But lurid episodes such as this give an inaccurate impression of how most machines operated. The day-to-day business of maintaining a machine was ordinary and prosaic.

The impressions from the era of machine politics are still very much alive, but they are misleading in key respects. It is true that the machines thrived on corruption, some spectacularly so. But it is also true that machine politicians provided a path by which ethnic voters could gain a measure of access to a political system that had excluded them. Looked at in this way, the machines were, in effect, mechanisms that facilitated the assimilation of immigrants into American culture. Over time, the machines declined, and they pretty much disappeared by the second half of the twentieth century. Even so, they helped shape the contemporary American city, and their legacy still lives on.

Some degree of machine-style politics—a style that relies on material incentives to nurture loyalty—is present in every political system. Silver-haired, country-club "suits" who help their favored developers obtain zoning variances for a suburban mall are acting as much like machine politicians as a ward boss who provides assistance to a constituent dealing with a rat inspector who wants to close down a restaurant or apartment building. In politics, material incentives come in many forms: a patronage job, a government contract, a zoning variance, a fixed parking ticket, an expedited business license, and more. In all political systems, claims to lofty ideals are often little more than fig leaves covering naked self-interest. For this reason, something more than a style of politics based around material rewards is necessary if we are to accurately employ the term "machine."[2] Specifically, the urban machines were organizations held together by a combination of ethnic identity and partisan loyalty. They were also, to varying degrees, hierarchical and disciplined, often controlled by a single leader, a "boss," or a tightly organized clique that shared power. They were democratic in the sense that they expended great energy to mobilize voters, but they also preserved a high degree of independence from outside influences through an internal system of command, coordination, and control.

Machines prospered for a time because of the social and political circumstances of the industrial age, which nurtured tightly knit ethnic communities sharply divided from the rest of society. Many of America's big industrial cities were once governed by party machines. Between 1870 and 1945, 17 of the nation's 30 cities with populations of more than half a million people were governed through boss rule and a disciplined, hierarchical party organization at some point.[3] In most of these cities, a factional machine-style politics operated for some time before the actual machines emerged. With only rare exceptions, the classic machines flowered in the last years of the nineteenth century and the first two or three decades of the twentieth century, after which those that still remained went into to decline. Boss rule peaked sometime in the 1920s. In 1932, the year Democratic candidate Franklin D. Roosevelt won the presidency, 10 of America's 30 biggest cities were ruled by machine bosses. Today, the machine is pretty much extinct. The death of Chicago boss Richard J. Daley in 1976 marked the end of the era of the classic party machines, which relied on patronage and the distribution of material incentives to keep their organizations intact.[4]

Despite the demise of these storied organizations, any serious discussion of American urban politics must take them into account because the political struggles of that time still reverberate at all levels of the political system. Early in the twentieth century, the machines became the object of a sustained campaign to clean up politics and reduce the influence of immigrant voters. The reforms adopted to end machine rule undeniably reduced corruption, but they also changed the rules of the game to the disadvantage of people at the lower end of the social spectrum. Even today, conflicts regularly break out involving the question of whether it should be easy or hard for people to register to vote. Battles over the rules that govern participation in the political system are bitterly fought because political outcomes reflect the composition of the electorate and the mix of interest groups that try to exert influence. These skirmishes go back more than a century, and they continue to the present day because so much is at stake.

OUTTAKE

Machines Had Two Sides

The careers of two machine politicians, James and Tom Pendergast of Kansas City, Missouri, illustrate both the positive and the negative sides of machine politics.

In 1876, James Pendergast, an Irishman with a short, thick neck and massive arms and shoulders, moved to Kansas City. Just 20 years old and with only a few dollars in his pocket, he rented a room in the West Bottoms ward, an industrial section on the floodplain of the Missouri River. The residents of West Bottoms worked in the meat packinghouses, machine shops, railroad yards, factories, and warehouses of the area. Blacks, Irish, Germans, and rural migrants lived in crowded four- and five-story tenements and tiny shanties. Overlooking this squalid area of dirt streets and open sewers was Quality Hill, where the wealthy elite lived. Pendergast held jobs in the packinghouses and in an iron foundry until 1881, when he used racetrack winnings to buy a hotel and a saloon.

He named the saloon Climax, the name of the lucky long-shot horse that gave him his start. The Climax Saloon became a social center of the First Ward, which put Pendergast in a position to meet the people of the ward. His generosity made him many friends. On payday, he cashed payroll checks and settled credit agreements; he posted bonds for men who had been arrested for gambling. His business flourished: "Men learned that he had an interest in humanity outside of business and that he could be trusted, and they returned the favor by patronizing his saloon and

giving him their confidence." In this way, Pendergast's politics and his everyday life became one and the same. He soon found himself being promoted for an alderman's seat, which he won in 1892.

The same year, Pendergast opened another saloon in the Second Ward, located in the city's North End. In that saloon he employed 22 men to run gambling tables, and in his West Bottoms ward he continued to employ a large gambling staff. Gambling was run on a large scale in Kansas City. Opening his own operations in the North End enabled Pendergast to forge close relationships with the politicians of that ward, and he soon became as influential in the Second Ward as he was in the First. He was able to secure police protection for gambling and liquor operations by paying off police officers and manipulating the choice of a police chief in 1895.

Pendergast could have run for mayor, but he preferred to exert his influence behind the scenes. By 1900 he was so powerful that he was able to select his preferred candidate for City Hall personally. In return, the grateful mayor gave Pendergast control over hundreds of patronage jobs and appointed Pendergast's brother, Tom, to the position of superintendent of streets. More than 200 men were employed by the streets department, which placed orders for gravel and cement with suppliers and contractors loyal to the machine. James Pendergast also gained control over positions in the fire department and was named the city's deputy license inspector, an important job because saloons and other business establishments needed licenses to operate. As the final step in consolidating his political authority, by 1902 he had personally selected 123 of the 173 patrolmen on the police force. Although he never ran for mayor, he was Kansas City's most powerful politician.

Like all the urban machines, Pendergast's organization was sustained by web of mutually beneficial relationships. Machine bosses distributed material rewards and expected loyalty in return. Some of them made this implicit bargain explicit, but the most effective ones never had to. A politician could get a lot of mileage out of only a modest amount of help; the word spread. James Pendergast expressed the principle in this way: "I've been called a boss. All there is to it is having friends, doing things for people, and then later on they'll do things for you." The First Ward voters reliably elected him by at least a 3-to-1 margin, and without discernible fraud. It never occurred to him that he would need to steal an election.

Jim Pendergast's style contrasted starkly with his brother Tom's. Tom, who inherited the Kansas City Democratic organization after James died, resorted to a mixture of fraud and coercion to maintain discipline and win elections. In the summer of 1914, Tom Pendergast's organization "used money, repeat voters, and toughs to produce North Side majorities" to gain approval of a proposed railway franchise. Machine workers distributed liquor and money in black and Italian neighborhoods. They "paid men to vote under assumed names; and election judges who questioned some of those dragged off the streets and out of flop houses to vote were intimidated and abused, both verbally and physically." On election day in 1934, four persons were killed by thugs. Two years later, an attempted assassination and massive fraud at polling places led to an investigation that eventually resulted in 259 convictions for election fraud and criminal behavior.

Jim Pendergast succeeded in politics because he went out of his way to ascertain the needs of his constituents. By building a powerful political organization, he was able to provide them with jobs and other prized benefits. When his brother Tom took over, corruption and intimidation became the order of the day because he had not nurtured any real connection to his electoral constituency. The story of the two Pendergasts highlights a question often asked about the classic party machines: Were they vehicles for democracy or were they inherently flawed by the concentration of power they facilitated?

Source: Lyle W. Dorsett, *The Pendergast Machine* (New York: Oxford University Press, 1968). Quotations are from pp. 14, 26, 59, 60.

The Origins of Machine Politics

The rise of the urban party machines was made possible by two factors: the emergence of a mass electorate and industrialization.[5] When the Constitution was ratified in 1789, only about 5 percent of adult white males were eligible to vote, and it took decades for the political systems of American cities to become fully democratic. Property qualifications for voting began to be eased after 1776, and by 1850 virtually all free white males were eligible to vote in city elections.[6] Until the 1820s, most mayors were appointed by governors or city councils. Beginning with Boston and St. Louis in 1822, charter revisions gradually transformed the office into a popularly elected post, and by 1840 this practice had become almost universal.[7] In the presidential election of 1840, 80 percent of adult white males went to the polls, the highest rate in any major democracy.[8] The spread of universal male suffrage coincided with the explosive growth of cities. From the 1830s to the 1920s, more than 30 million immigrants came to the United States, most of them pouring into the cities. As soon as they were citizens, if they were male, they could vote. A new breed of enterprising politician learned to profit from this circumstance.

In most of the industrial cities, a "friends and neighbors" or "local followings" style of politics evolved that fit perfectly with the decentralized nature of local governmental structures. Aldermen were elected from wards, and because these electoral units tended to be small, politicians were able to enter politics as a natural consequence of their personal connections. No one benefited from this arrangement more than pub owners. Saloons were central to the day-to-day life of working-class neighborhoods. Pub owners were considered reliable sources of information and advice. The density of pubs in immigrant neighborhoods was astonishing. In 1915, for example, there was a saloon for every 515 residents in New York, but the ratio was even greater in Chicago, which had a saloon for every 335 of its inhabitants.[9] In most cities there was at least one pub for every 50 males.[10] In late-nineteenth-century Chicago, half the city's total population entered a saloon every day.[11] Many machine politicians got their start as pub owners. Of New York City's 24 aldermen in 1890, 11 were pub owners. Pub owners made up a third of Milwaukee's city council members in 1902 and a third of Detroit's aldermen at the turn of the century.[12]

Party machines managed to combine two seemingly incompatible qualities: the absence of formal rules, and a disciplined organization. Machine politicians were not "hired" into party organizations, and they did not have a formal job description. Their ability to deliver votes and their skill at forging alliances with other politicians determined their standing within the organization. Normally, a machine politician started at the bottom and worked his way up. Precinct captains, who were responsible for getting out the vote in the smallest and most basic political unit of the city, knew each voter personally, often as a friend and neighbor. To secure a following at this level, a politician had to be known not only as a person involved in politics but as someone who participated in local community life. Politicians climbed the political ladder only if they demonstrated they could reliably deliver the vote. If they did, the next rung they reached for was alderman.

Most machine politicians came from backgrounds that offended silk-stocking elements. Schooled in rough-and-tumble political competition, they generally were men of incredible energy, quick temper, and rough manners. At the least, they loved what they were doing; they felt no alienation from their job. Politics was everything the machine politicians knew and did—it was their social life, their profession, their first love. They pursued political power, not high social standing.[13] George Washington Plunkitt, a member of the Tammany Hall organization in New York, advised against what he called the "dangers of the dress suit in politics." "Live like your neighbors," Plunkitt admonished aspiring politicians, "even if you have the means to live better. Make the poorest man in your district feel that he is your equal, or even a bit superior to you."[14]

Disciplined political organizations emerged when skillful leaders succeeded in persuading enough of their fellow politicians that everyone would benefit if they cooperated. When enough of them came together, a military-style hierarchy emerged, with those lower in the organization waiting for their chance to move up. This structure was once described by Frank Hague, the Jersey City boss, to columnist Joseph Alsop, who wrote, "He [Hague] was talking in the dining room of one of the local hotels. He took the squares on the tablecloth to illustrate precincts and wards, tracing them out with his finger, and he explained the feudal system of American politics, whereby the precinct captain is governed by a ward lieutenant, the lieutenant by a ward leader, and each ward leader by the boss."[15]

As shown in Figure 3.1, precincts and precinct captains constituted the foundation of the typical machine organization. The average precinct had 400 to 600 voters, and precinct captains were expected to know them by name. Thirty to 40 precincts were generally included within a ward. The captains of the precincts were chosen by and worked for the ward's alderman. The alderman served

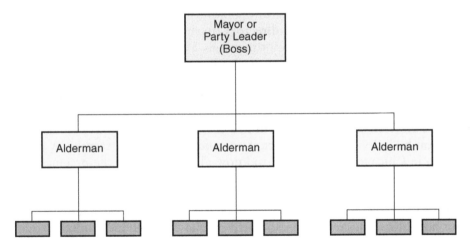

Precinct Captains

FIGURE 3.1 The Organization of Machine Politics.

The organization of local political machines, or parties, parallels the formal structures of government but is also separate from them. Like the mayor, the party leader or boss controls the entire city, or perhaps county. The alderman represents a ward in the city council or on the board of aldermen. The alderman may or may not serve as ward leader of the party. Each ward consists of many precincts or election districts. Precinct captains are responsible for delivering the vote in their precinct.

In principle, power flows from the bottom up: Precinct captains elect the ward leaders, and the ward leaders elect the party boss. But in fact, power flows from the top.

as the chair of the ward's party committee, unless he selected a committeeman to supervise the precinct captains on his behalf. Finally, the aldermen reported to the machine boss, who was usually but not always the mayor.

The hierarchical structure of the machine held together because everyone gained by cooperating in what was, in essence, a "system of organized bribery."[16] Bosses and individual aldermen had at their disposal patronage jobs in police, fire, sanitation, and streets departments—and occasionally even in private industry. Construction projects, such as levee construction or road building, could give a boss control over hundreds of permanent and temporary jobs. Precinct captains usually held low-level jobs arranged through the machine, perhaps serving as supervisors on street crews. Ward committeemen were rewarded with higher-paying administrative posts in the city government. Aldermen and other elected officials often owned lucrative insurance companies, ran their own construction firms, or owned saloons. The most menial jobs were passed along to some of the loyal voters who turned out faithfully on election day.

An understanding of the patronage ladder can be gained by examining one of the last machines to exist in any American city, the one run by Richard J. Daley, mayor of Chicago from 1953 until his death in 1976. In the early 1970s, the Cook County Central Committee (which contains Chicago) had about 30,000 positions available for distribution. Most of these jobs were unskilled; 8,000 were available through Chicago's departments and commissions, including street cleaners, park supervisors, and the like.[17] The jobs ranged from $3,600-a-year elevator operators and $6,000-a-year stenographers to $25,000-a-year department directors (in the early 1970s, a skilled factory worker in a union plant made approximately $9,000 per year). Individual ward committeemen controlled as many as 2,000 jobs. (Richard J. Daley had begun his career as committeeman of his ward.) There were (and still are) 50 wards in the city of Chicago, with an average of 500 to 600 patronage jobs available in each of them in the 1970s.[18]

The election-day result determined the number of jobs available for distribution by individual precinct captains and ward committeemen. A precinct captain in Chicago was expected to know all the voters in the precinct and to be known by them. "When a man is given a precinct, it is his to cover, and it is up to him to produce for the party. If he cannot produce for the party, he cannot expect to be rewarded by the party. 'Let's put it this way,' [one alderman said] 'if your boss has a salesman who can't deliver, who can't sell his product, wouldn't he put in someone else who can?'"[19]

Alderman Vito Marzullo was a member of the Chicago organization. Every week he scheduled a formal audience with his constituents. Flanked on each side by a precinct captain, he heard their complaints:

A precinct captain ushered in a black husband and wife. "We got a letter here from the city," the man said. "They want to charge us twenty dollars for rodent control in our building." "Give me the letter, I'll look into it," Marzullo replied. The captain spoke up. "Your daughter didn't vote on November fifth. Look into it. The alderman is running again in February. Any help we can get, we can use."[20]

In the course of hearing his constituents, Marzullo exclaimed, "Some of those liberal independents in the city council, they can't get a dog out of a dog pound with a ten-dollar bill. Who's next?" Marzullo then arranged to have a traffic ticket fixed, agreed to recommend someone for a job at an electric company, refused to donate money to the Illinois Right to Life Committee ("Nothing doing . . . . I don't want to get into any of those controversies. People for it and people against it."), agreed to try to find a job for an unemployed truck driver, and gave $50 to a welfare mother. Responding to several more requests, he offered to "see what I can do."[21]

During the Richard J. Daley years, the Chicago machine was structured like a political pyramid. Committeemen and the aldermen directed the captains of the precincts within their wards; they, in turn, reported to the Cook County Central Committee. Although most of the city machines that operated a half-century before were similarly organized, some were directed from the top with an iron hand, as in Daley's Chicago; others were little more than loose confederations of politicians jealous of their own turf. However tightly run the individual machines were, they all revealed the same qualities: They were rooted in neighborhoods, and a combination of material incentives and ethnic and community attachments held them together.

Being close to constituents did not necessarily mean the machines can be regarded as a model of democracy at work. Although all machines provided something to their supporters, most of them also engaged in election fraud. Because so many opportunities were available, few machine politicians could resist the temptations offered by bribes and backroom deals. But as an answer to the impression that machines were nothing but cesspools of corruption, some historians and social scientists called attention to some of their positive achievements. They have offered three main arguments in defense of the machines: That they (1) centralized power and "got the job done," (2) served as vehicles of upward mobility for immigrants, and (3) helped assimilate the immigrants into American life. In the next three sections, we examine these claims.

Did Machines "Get the Job Done"?

It has generally been assumed that political machines evolved in the late nineteenth century to fill a vacuum left by the absence of effective local governments. City governments were often inept and inefficient because they relied on a chaotic division of responsibilities among a multitude of separate officials, boards, and departments. The mayor generally wielded little authority. The city council or board of aldermen typically controlled the budget and made most of the important decisions. Day-to-day administrative responsibilities were generally assumed by committees whose members were appointed by the city council, or sometimes by some combination of the mayor, state legislature, governor, or other state or local official. At election time, a long list of names on the ballot made it impossible for voters to know anything about the candidates. Edward Sait wrote in 1933 that "when the people or particular groups among them demanded positive action, no one had adequate authority to act. The machine provided an antidote."[22] In other words, he was saying, machines were necessary if anything was to get done.

If it is true that machines arose mainly to fill a void left by disorganized and inefficient government, then we would expect to find that machines prospered best in cities where governments were the most politically and administratively fragmented. The problem with this idea is that by the time most machines came into being, reformers devoted to the cause of streamlining municipal governance had already achieved their goal of concentrating more power in the hands of mayors and a cadre of full-time civil service administrators.[23] The municipal reformers had imagined that these changes would make officeholders more accountable to the electorate, and that informed voters would elect a "better class" of refined and educated leaders to office. They were sorely disappointed with the results. As it turned out, it was easier to build disciplined machine organizations where local government had been streamlined and centralized than where it remained fragmented and chaotic. Jersey City, New Jersey supplies an instructive example. In 1913, reformers there persuaded the voters to fuse legislative and executive functions into one five-member commission. When the machine mayor, Frank Hague, gained control of the city commission, he was able to accomplish something he had tried many times before: consolidate his power over a faction-ridden Democratic Party and become the uncontested boss of Jersey City.[24]

Control of municipal government was a prize worth pursuing. Between 1870 and 1900, municipal workforces grew even faster than urban populations,[25] and local governments spent more money than either the federal government or the state governments.[26] Cities ran up debts at a feverish pace to finance water systems, lay sewers lines, pave streets, build parks and public buildings, deepen harbors, and improve public health.[27] Even cities with fractious and divided politics, such as Los Angeles, made huge investments in infrastructure.[28] The political support for urban infrastructure and services was sufficiently strong that city budgets and workforces were bound to expand, regardless of how a city was run.[29] A study of cities from 1890 to 1940 found no difference between machine and nonmachine cities in the overall level of public expenditures.[30]

Corruption could make the price of "getting the job done" astonishingly high. Probably the most notoriously corrupt machine in American history was led by William Marcy "Boss" Tweed, who ran the infamous Tweed Ring in New York City from 1868 to 1871. In three years, Tweed took $30 million to $100 million of public funds for himself and his cronies. Under his regime, the machine's traditional take of 10 percent on construction contracts ratcheted upward. A courthouse project originally estimated to cost $250,000 ended up costing taxpayers $14 million. At least 90 percent of this cost overrun went to pay payoffs, bribes, and fake contracts.[31] Tweed's rule has been called the politics of "rapacious individualism" because everyone in the machine seemed to be after personal wealth. Ultimately, the availability of so many spoils undermined the discipline of his organization. Because Tweed was not able to count on the loyalty of his fellow politicians, he was forced to buy it directly, and therefore his authority was fragile and short-lived.[32] In 1869 and 1870, the city's debt increased from $36 million to $97 million. By 1871, when Tweed was arrested, the city was bankrupt.

Machine bosses realized that the artful distribution of spoils was the key to holding their organizations together. The rapid growth of city services guaranteed there would be plenty of largesse to spread around. Mayors and city councils negotiated lucrative multiyear contracts for streetcar operations and utility services (such as electricity, gas, and telephone). Cities issued tavern and liquor licenses and regulated gambling and prostitution (or had the option of looking the other way when they were illegal). They engaged in a continuous stream of public works projects, including the building of roads, bridges, public buildings, sewer and water systems, streetlights, and parks. There was money to be made on both ends of these transactions.

The operations of Abraham Reuf's regime, which ruled San Francisco just after the turn of the century, provide some insight into the wealth of opportunities available to people who entered politics.[33] Reuf was an attorney who never held public office, but his law practice gave him access to those who did. In October 1901 his handpicked candidate took over the mayor's office, and within days Reuf spread the word that the city's laws against prostitution would be strictly enforced. He advised the brothel owners that it would be wise to have an attorney—specifically himself—who could effectively represent their interests. The owners quickly got the point and agreed to pay him a fourth of their business profits, half of which Reuf split with the mayor. This arrangement allowed the brothels to continue operating without fear of prosecution. Reuf also provided his professional "advice" to saloon owners that it would be wise to pay premium prices for a low-quality whiskey supplied by one of Reuf's legal clients. In return, the saloon owners were protected from police raids.

San Francisco invested huge resources in municipal services, and businesses competed for the contracts. A lot of money was at stake. The mayor, the city council, or a utilities commission could, in a single stroke of a pen, enrich a business owner by awarding a contract to build trolley lines, install streetlights, supply gas, or install telephones. The temptation to make decisions secretly in smoke-filled rooms was overwhelming. The chair of the public utilities committee of the San Francisco Board of Supervisors reminded a group of business leaders in January 1906:

> It must be borne in mind that without the city fathers there can be no public service corporations. The street cars cannot run, lights cannot be furnished, telephones cannot exist. And all the public service corporations want to understand that we, the city fathers, enjoy the best of health and that we are not in business for our health. The question at this banquet board is: "How much money is in it for us?"[34]

There seemed to be plenty of money for everyone. When two telephone companies submitted competing bids to supply service to the citizens of San Francisco, Reuf collected a $1,200 monthly "attorney's fee" from one company while secretly accepting a $125,000 bribe from the other. Reuf persuaded the board of supervisors to award the contract to the company that paid the biggest bribe. Keeping $63,000 for himself, he used a loyalty test to distribute the remainder of the $125,000 to the individual supervisors: $6,000 each to those who had taken no independent bribes (showing they were not trying to compete with Reuf), $3,500 to those voting correctly despite bribes to do the opposite, and nothing at all to those who did not cooperate.

Reuf's tenure as the power behind the mayor's throne ended when he was indicted and tried for corruption. Ironically, his downfall was precipitated by too much success. After seeing how lucrative local politics could be, more and more of the politicians around him struck out on their own in search of profit and opportunity, and before long the feeding frenzy attracted attention and the jackals began to turn on one another.

Reuf's behavior was more reckless than usual, but in almost all cities, machine leaders forged alliances with illicit business owners. The relationship benefited both sides in the partnership: The businesses were free to operate without having to worry about the law, and the politicians could count on a steady flow of favors and bribes. One of the reasons that machines flourished so much in the 1920s is that the national prohibition of liquor sales opened unprecedented opportunities for selling police protection to speakeasies and bootleggers. Prohibition facilitated a cooperative arrangement between machines and organized crime not only in Chicago, where the collusion was especially notorious, but all over the country, in big cities and small. In many cases, the level of flagrant corruption and rising levels of violence brought a reaction that brought the machines down for good.

Machines took bribes from legitimate enterprises, too. The machines governed the cities during a period of explosive growth in population, services, and construction. Even if local politicians tried to be honest, business tycoons eager to expand their empires were eager to spread their money around to get what they wanted. They found it convenient to work with politicians who could make decisions expeditiously behind the scenes. Big businesses paid bigger bribes than anyone else, and this put them in a position to negotiate monopoly contracts on favorable terms. The franchises typically were granted for periods of 50 to 100 years, and some specified no terminal dates at all.[35] In the 1880s and 1890s, national financial syndicates made millions of dollars by gaining control of street railway franchises. In 1890, there were 39 street railway companies in Philadelphia, 19 in New York City, 24 in Pittsburgh, 19 in St. Louis, and 16 in San Francisco.[36] There was simply not enough business for all of them, and by the turn of the century only one or two major street railway companies operated in most cities.

In light of the numerous opportunities for personal enrichment, it may seem surprising that a number of machine leaders refused to cash in to enrich themselves. The extent and style of corruption varied considerably from one city to the next. In the 1930s, Boss George Cox was credited with bringing "positive and moderate reform government to Cincinnati."[37] In the years when Richard J. Daley was boss (1955–1976), Chicago was known as "the city that works" because the mayor saw to it that services were delivered effectively. Daley was popular with voters both because they felt he was responsible for getting things done, and because there was never any evidence that he took money for himself.[38] For all of his life he and his family lived in a modest bungalow in an old Irish neighborhood close to the stockyards.

Were Machines Vehicles of Upward Mobility?

A leading sociologist once proposed that the machines succeeded partly because they provided "alternative channels of social mobility for those otherwise excluded from the more conventional avenues of 'advancement.'"[39] In the nineteenth century, many employers refused to hire the Irish; "Irish need not apply" was printed on many an employment notice. For the ethnics who found public employment, local politics was "like a rope dangling down the formidable slope of the socioeconomic system" that poor immigrants could grab to pull themselves up.[40]

Ample evidence supports the thesis that the urban machines aided the upward mobility of their immigrant supporters. Although it is not exactly a typical story, politics was a key element in the rise of the Kennedy clan from poverty to wealth and national power. President John F. Kennedy's grandfather on his mother's side, John "Honey Fitz" Fitzgerald, rose from a ward heeler running errands for an alderman to the office of mayor of Boston. Kennedy's grandfather on his father's side was a respected ward politician and saloon-keeper whose contacts helped the early career of the president's millionaire father, Joseph P. Kennedy, who made a fortune in bootleg liquor.[41]

Despite the many stories describing how boys from poor immigrant families rose through the ranks of local machines, the evidence supporting the idea that the machines enhanced the upward mobility of immigrants is mixed. It is important to realize that these tales are colorful partly because they are exceptional, and in any case they apply to the Irish more than to any other immigrant group. In most cities Irish politicians mastered the art of machine politics before anyone else, and they incorporated other ethnic groups into their coalitions only if it was absolutely necessary for winning elections. Later-arriving immigrants generally found it hard to get a toehold into the political system. In New York City, for example, the machine organization called *Tammany Hall* was run by and for the Irish. Although Jews and Italians represented 43 percent of New York's population by 1920, in the same year only 15 percent of the city's aldermen and assemblymen were Jewish and only 3 percent were Italian.[42]

Most of the big-city machines were dominated by Irish politicians from the beginning, and they stayed that way.[43] Between 1900 and 1930, the machines in New York City, Jersey City, and Albany, New York, added nearly 100,000 municipal jobs. Close to two-thirds of these jobs went to Irish constituents, even though the Irish accounted for only about one-third of the population in these cities. The Irish were especially vigilant about maintaining iron-fisted control over police forces. As late as 1970, for instance, 65 percent of police officers in Albany were of still of Irish descent, even though no more than 25 percent of the city's population could trace their ancestry to Ireland.[44]

Eventually, some skilled politicians managed to challenge the control wielded by Irish machine bosses by appealing to the groups that had been left out. Fiorello LaGuardia, elected mayor of New York City in 1933, smashed the Tammany organization, which had dominated the city's politics for almost a century. LaGuardia was a master at ethnic politics, perhaps because "half Jewish and half Italian, married first to a Catholic and then to a Lutheran of German descent, himself a Mason and an Episcopalian, he was practically a balanced ticket all by himself."[45] This rich ethnic heritage helped him to assemble an electoral coalition composed of disgruntled Jews, Italians, and other excluded groups. Likewise, in the 1920s Anton Cermak became mayor of Chicago by building "a house of all peoples."[46] By reaching out to Italians, Jews, Czechs, and Poles, Cermak won the 1931 mayoral election with 65 percent of the vote, and once in office he solidified his authority by adeptly distributing patronage, recruiting candidates for machine positions, and fighting against Prohibition, which almost all ethnics opposed. La Guardia and Cermak's success revealed that any political organization built on an overly narrow base was vulnerable to challenge.

It perhaps goes without saying that blacks were excluded from most of the urban machines. Chicago became a notable exception because in the 1920s the city's machine leaders recognized that they could reliably secure the vote in the segregated South Side wards simply by creating "submachines" run by black politicians who were subordinate in every way to the white machine organization.[47] William Dawson, a member of Congress from 1942 until his death in 1970, ran a submachine in Chicago's South Side ghetto, but white politicians kept him carefully in check. Dawson reliably delivered huge pluralities for machine candidates from the black wards, but black voters received relatively little in return.[48] Throughout Chicago's history, weak and inexperienced black politicians who accepted a devil's bargain were recruited into the machine: In exchange for a measure of freedom to pursue their own ambitions, they delivered the vote and kept a militant black leadership from emerging.[49] The legacy of such practices was still apparent in the Richard J. Daley years. Although blacks made up 40 percent of Chicago's population in 1970, they held only 20 percent of the government jobs in the city, and most of those jobs were the least desirable.[50] A study of a typical ward in Chicago found that the machine consistently over-rewarded middle-class voters at the expense of loyal working-class voters, with blacks getting the least of all.[51]

Disaffected African American voters finally challenged the Chicago machine organization in the 1980s. In 1983 a charismatic black politician, Harold Washington, assembled a coalition of poor people, blacks, Hispanics, and white liberals to defeat the machine's mayoral candidate.[52] His victory set off a prolonged racial tug-of-war in the city council between his supporters and the Old-Guard members of the machine, but when Washington died in his office of a heart attack on November 15, 1987, the new groups he had brought into politics continued to exert a voice. In 1989, Richard M. Daley, the son of Richard J., won the mayor's race by successfully reassembling the remnants of his father's organization, forging alliances with African American and Latino politicians, and establishing a close relationship with the downtown business establishment. He was elected to office five times because he understood the principle that to govern effectively, he needed to build a broad base of support.

Machine leaders had believed it made perfect sense to keep their coalitions only as big as necessary.[53] The more groups making up the alliance, the greater the interethnic squabbles over the distribution of patronage and the thinner the distribution of rewards. As a consequence, "once minimal winning coalitions had been constructed, the machines had little incentive to naturalize, register, and mobilize the votes of later ethnic arrivals."[54] For entrenched machines, expanding the electoral base past the minimum number of voters needed for winning elections just complicated things. The art was to strike a balance to ensure that a coalition that was just large enough, and sometimes they miscalculated.

The machines distributed benefits that were of great value to their supporters. According to Jessica Trounstine, in the early years of the twentieth century, "public jobs frequently paid better wages than private employment," and access to public jobs allowed the Irish and sometimes other groups to escape the discrimination they faced in the private marketplace.[55] The problem was that the number of public jobs was pitifully small compared to the jobs available in the private economy. In 1900, Tammany's vaunted patronage army made up 5 percent of New York City's workforce. It is true that from 1900 to 1920 local governments grew so fast that public employment accounted for 20 percent of all urban job growth,[56] but for most people, including the immigrants, private industry rather than patronage provided the best opportunities for upward mobility.

Although for decades the Irish laid claim to a disproportionate share of the jobs provided by municipal government, it took a long time for them to catch up to the gains made by some other ethnic groups. Scandinavians, both Germans, and Jews, for example, participated relatively little in machine politics, and yet they joined the American middle class faster than the Irish did. The Irish did not achieve economic parity with these groups until the 1960s and 1970s. Despite this mixed record, however, the benefits supplied by the machines to their loyal supporters were better than nothing, and for the individuals who received them they were precious indeed. On the whole, immigrant voters got back about as much as they could have expected for what they could give in return.

Did the Machines Help Immigrants Assimilate?

Without doubt, the urban party machines helped to assimilate millions of impoverished immigrants into a culture that was fearful of and hostile to almost every newly arriving ethnic group. Machine politicians nurtured a sense of community and belonging in the immigrant wards. They sponsored picnics, patriotic gatherings (such as Fourth of July celebrations), baseball teams, choirs, and youth clubs. The local party organization was an important community institution, and one of the main alternatives to the pubs: the Democratic Club was a place where men played cards and checkers or just talked.[57]

With the material resources at their disposal already devoted to their core constituency, machine politicians learned to satisfy immigrants who arrived later with largely symbolic benefits. In New York City, Tammany leader "Big Tim" Sullivan, an Irishman, ruled the Lower East Side even though as early as 1910 it was 85 percent Jewish and Italian. He retained the loyalty of his constituents through a mixture of favors and artful gestures:

> He and his Irish lieutenants distributed coal, food, and rent money to needy Jews and Italians on the Lower East Side. Tammany's police department opened up station houses as temporary shelters for the homeless. Sullivan expedited business licenses for ethnic shopkeepers and pushcart peddlers. He shamelessly "recognized" the new immigrants with symbolic gestures and donned a yarmulke to solicit Jewish votes. Sullivan solicited Italian votes by sponsoring legislation to make Columbus Day a holiday.[58]

Many immigrants felt like outsiders in the dominant Protestant and middle-class culture of the United States. One of the secrets of the machines' appeal was that they tolerated the immigrants' "strange" practices and defended them from the dominant culture.[59] This was an important benefit that machine politicians could deliver at little cost. Although working-class communities in American cities were not economically independent, they were, to a remarkable degree, socially independent. Immigrants built their own churches, mutual aid societies, and clubs for drinking and gambling. Machine politicians supported such activities because they were handy venues for campaigning and political organizing.[60]

Machine politicians appealed to and were supported by immigrant voters, in part, because they represented the possibility of success in this strange new country. Almost all machine politicians came from lower-class immigrant origins. One study of 20 bosses found that 15 were first- or second-generation immigrants; 13 had never finished grammar school; and most had gone into politics at a young age, serving as messengers or detail boys at rallies and meetings.[61] Machine leaders, therefore, became symbols of success. Immigrants may not have read the Horatio Alger stories, but in machine bosses they could see men who had risen out of poverty. Aspiring politicians often accepted this interpretation of themselves, too; they viewed themselves as examples of what could be done with hard work and a little luck along the way. These real-world examples of upward mobility were sources of pride and hope for the masses of immigrants who lived and worked under incredibly difficult conditions. However, symbol exceeded substance, especially for later-arriving southern and eastern European immigrants. Irish politicians would shrewdly pick a handful of men from other immigrant groups and place them in lesser positions on the ballot to demonstrate their generosity. Meanwhile, the bread-and-butter patronage stayed home.

The immigrants paid a high price for assimilation on these terms. Machines rarely attempted to address the collective needs of their constituents. Instead, the immigrant voters were encouraged to "cast their ballots on the basis of ethnicity rather than policy considerations."[62] The immigrants gave their support not as an act of consciousness about group goals but because it was easy to do and plausible alternatives were few. The vote was a minimal commitment for the immigrant but a sufficient one for the machine. Constituents could hardly expect miracles in return.

The operating principles and structures of the urban machines encouraged the politicians who ran them to steer clear of ideological battles. To deal with their constituents' requests effectively, machine politicians had to learn the art of manipulating power within the framework of a political and economic order that they did not control. A premium was placed on simple pragmatism, the ability to pull strings to get things done. Idealism was scorned. If a constituent came to complain about a building inspector, the politician's job was to make things nice with the inspector. Changing the building code was irrelevant and even counterproductive because it might reduce the need for the politician's services and would offend local property owners as well.

Machines were hostile to political movements that tried to reform the system because such movements threatened their control of the immigrant vote. Until the 1930s, most machines vigorously opposed labor unions. In the first years of the twentieth century, Irish machine politicians ordered the police to attack labor organizers in Lawrence, Massachusetts, and in New York City.[63] In Pittsburgh's 1919 steel strike, the machine likewise ordered police to harass strikers.[64] After Franklin D. Roosevelt's landslide victory in the presidential election of 1932, some of the big-city machines forged alliances with the moderate trade unions, but the relationship was never easy to maintain. The machines expected the unions to respect their turf by keeping out of local politics and focusing mainly on state and national politics and on labor–business relations.

On balance, it may be argued that the machines stunted the immigrants' potential as a political force. Working-class immigrants desperately needed reforms such as widows' pensions, better working conditions, laws regulating hours and wages (especially for women and children), and workers' compensation. On occasion, machine politicians supported these reforms as well as the regulation of utilities, the legal recognition of labor unions, and the regulation of insurance companies.[65] But the selective and often halfhearted support for a few reform measures did not exactly transform machine politicians into crusading reformers. Machine politicians were willing to declare their support for reform legislation at the state level if it made them look good, but they never became active advocates for progressive causes. Machine politicians could be quite capricious, for immediate political circumstances always took precedence over principle.

Machine politicians rarely considered how things could be changed. They often referred to reformers as "goody-goodies" or "goo-goos" who, they thought, were in politics for a few thrills. ("Goo-goo" was derived from "good government," often the reformers' rallying cry.) Much of their disdain was rooted in the social differences between themselves and middle- and upper-class reformers. As a result, they had an excessive respect for the pragmatic fix.

The Social Reform Alternative

Defenders of the machines have argued that there were few alternatives to their pragmatic style of politics, that in the face of the vast economic and political resources held by corporations and wealthy elites, machine politicians milked the system on behalf of their constituents as effectively as they could. From this way of thinking, criticizing machine politicians for what they failed to do is an exercise in wishful thinking about what might have been.

The view that the machines accomplished as much as they could for their constituents fails to take into account the full range of opportunities available to them. The Progressive Era got its name because a generation of reformers were intent on improving the quality of life for immigrants and workers. They campaigned for support from both working-class immigrants and middle-class voters, but at every turn they encountered resistance both from machine politicians and members of the business community.[66] The examples of mayors who went in a different direction show, however, that it was possible to overcome such opposition. Mayors Tom L. Johnson of Cleveland, Ohio (1901–1909), Samuel "Golden Rule" Jones of Toledo, Ohio (1897–1903), and Brand Whitlock of Toledo (1906–1913) all won election by fighting against high streetcar and utility rates and for fair taxation and better social services. Their campaigns became models for like-minded reformers across the country. Reform-oriented mayors in Jersey City, Philadelphia, and Cincinnati attempted to increase municipal revenue by raising taxes on businesses and wealthy property owners and by renegotiating streetcar and utility franchises. But machine bosses bitterly fought reform in these cities, just as they had a few years earlier when similar efforts were mounted in Cleveland and Toledo.[67]

The career of Hazen S. Pingree, who served as Detroit's mayor from 1890 to 1898, shows there were enormous possibilities for accomplishing reforms that would benefit ordinary people. Born in Maine to a poor farmer and itinerant cobbler, Pingree's background did not suggest he would one day become a political reformer. After fighting in the Civil War, Pingree moved to Detroit, where he worked as a leather cutter in a shoe factory. After a few years, he and a partner pooled their savings to purchase the outdated factory. By modernizing the machinery and producing a new line of shoes that fit current fashions, Pingree managed to become independently wealthy. He was picked as the Republican candidate for mayor in 1889, mostly because he was the only member of the exclusive Michigan Club who could be persuaded by its members to run. The business leaders who controlled Republican politics trusted him, as a member of the club, to advocate the usual program of low taxes and a minimal array of municipal services. In any case, few of them imagined he would win, and they had grown accustomed to working with the reliably cooperative Irish-dominated Democratic machine.

To their deep disappointment, Pingree was not a typical business candidate. He campaigned in the ethnic wards, and even kicked off his campaign by drinking whiskey in an Irish saloon. Pingree was a big hit with German and Polish voters, who had long been ignored by the Irish politicians. He called attention to the endemic corruption of the machine and advocated an eight-hour work-day for city employees. His willingness to seek the ethnic vote was the foundation on which he built his subsequent political success.

Pingree's programs, and the strategies he used to implement them, reveal how much might have been accomplished in other American cities. When Pingree took over city hall, Detroit had one of the worst street systems in the nation. Many of the streets were made of wooden blocks, which caught fire in the summer and sank into the mire in the winter. The few paved streets were pocked with ruts and potholes. Pingree quickly realized that collusion between paving contractors and machine politicians was at the heart of the street problem. He launched an aggressive campaign against this arrangement, appealing to his business supporters by pointing out that the prosperity of the city depended on good streets. His insistent efforts led the city council to adopt strict paving specifications; as a result, by 1895 Detroit had one of the best street systems in the United States.

It was not long before Pingree understood that the local business establishment was responsible for many of Detroit's problems. He challenged the high fare charged for a ferry ride across the Detroit River to Belle Isle Park. The company dropped its rate from 10 cents to 5 cents after the mayor threatened to revoke its franchise or put into operation a municipal ferry service. Pingree also found that private companies had located along the Detroit River waterfront, often on municipal property, which choked off public access to water and recreation. He took action to open up waterfront areas for public use.

Pingree's fight with the Detroit City Railway Company turned him into a true social reformer willing to use public authority to curb private power to benefit the city's residents. At a time when streetcar companies in other cities were converting from horses to electric power, Detroit's company refused to make the change. In April 1891 the company's employees went on strike, presenting a perfect opportunity for Pingree to begin a battle for modernization and lower fares. The three-day strike culminated in a riot in which workers and citizens tore up the tracks, stoned the streetcars, and drove off the horses. Pingree ignored the company's request to call in the state militia and instead took the position that privately owned public services were "the chief source of corruption in city governments."[68] Pingree's stance precipitated a protracted, bitter fight to regulate the streetcars. This conflict vaulted him to national prominence.

Many business leaders had supported the strike, believing the street railway was so badly run that it was hurting local business. The business community was mainly interested in more reliable service, but Pingree went further and pressed for lower fares and municipal ownership. Such a position ran afoul of business leaders when the company passed into the hands of an eastern business mogul. The new owner's first action was to pack the company's board of directors with prominent businessmen from Detroit. The company then demanded that the city negotiate a more favorable franchise. Pingree countered with a lawsuit meant to terminate the existing company in favor of municipal ownership. At that point, the company bought Pingree's own attorney away from him and proceeded to offer bribes to city council members, including a $75,000 bribe to Pingree himself. The Preston National Bank dropped Pingree from its board of directors; he lost his family pew in the Baptist church; and he and his friends were shunned in public. The lesson Pingree learned from all this was that business supported reform only on its own terms. And he also began to form his own analysis about what was wrong with America's cities.

In 1891, Pingree began attacking the tax privileges of the city's corporations. The railroad, he observed, owned more than one-fifth of the property value in the city but paid no taxes at all because of the tax-free status granted to it by the state legislature. Shipping companies, docks and warehouses, and other businesses escaped local taxation by claiming that their principal places of business existed outside the city. The city's biggest employer, the Michigan-Peninsula Car Company, paid only nominal taxes. Although he was not successful in equalizing the tax burden, Pingree was able to modify some of its worst features, especially the practice of assessing, for tax purposes, real estate owned by wealthy people at rates far below its value. Pingree earned the special enmity of the city's elite by successfully campaigning for a personal property tax on home furnishings, art objects, and other luxury items.

On April 1, 1895, Detroit began operating a municipal electric plant to supply power for its streetlights. This ended a five-year running battle between Pingree and the private lighting company. Pingree's main argument against the private control of electricity was that it cost too much. Pingree gathered voluminous information to show that Detroit's service was more expensive and less reliable than service in other cities. Despite the merits of his case he would have lost, but a scandal tipped the scales in his favor. In April 1892, Pingree walked into a city council meeting waving a roll of bills and dramatically accused the Detroit Electric Light and Power Company of bribing council members. The mayor had been sure to pack the room with his working-class supporters. With Pingree's followers whipped into a dangerous mood, the council members hastily capitulated.

Pingree used similar tactics in his fights with the gas and telephone interests. To force the Detroit Gas Company to lower its natural gas rates, he initiated a campaign to inform the public about the high price of Detroit's gas. When his attempt to force lower prices stalled in the courts, he persuaded the public works board to deny permits to excavate streets for the purpose of laying gas lines. When the gas company attempted to dig anyway, Pingree saw to it that the owners were arrested. "Possession is a great point," argued Pingree. "Let them get their gas systems connected and then they could float their $8,000,000 of stock in New York City and become too powerful for the city to control. Detroit would be helpless in the hands of corporations as never before in her history."[69]

The battle raged on, with Pingree next encouraging users not to pay their gas bills. As public resistance against the Detroit Gas Company mounted, investors' confidence in the company plummeted, precipitating a plunge in the company's stock values. Even after Southern Pacific Railroad magnate Samuel Huntington became the company's principal investor, stock prices continued to fall, and Huntington negotiated an agreement to lower the price of gas from $1.50 per cubic foot to $0.80.

In his fourth term, Pingree took on the Bell Telephone Company. Again, the issue was high prices and inadequate service. This time he helped organize a competing phone company that charged less than half of Bell's rate, and in only a few months the newly formed Detroit Telephone Company was serving twice as many customers as Bell. In response, Bell Telephone initiated a rate war and began to improve its equipment and service. By 1900, when Michigan Bell bought out Detroit Telephone, Detroit had the lowest telephone rates and the most extensive residential use among large American cities.

No other mayor in America accomplished such a broad program of social reform. In his last two terms, Pingree traveled around the country making speeches and gathering ideas about what to do next. He wrote prolifically. He inspired reformers all over the country, and his national prominence helped him bring more reform to his own city. After winning four terms as the mayor of Detroit, Pingree went on to serve two terms as the governor of Michigan, where he continued to fight for reform.

Hazen Pingree recognized the necessity of building a broad-based coalition of support. He so assiduously courted ethnic voters that by his fourth term he had even won the dependable Irish away from the Democratic machine. In effect, he pieced together his own machine, filling patronage jobs with his own supporters and firing his opponents. However, "he absolutely refused to tolerate dishonesty or theft."[70] Unlike Detroit's machine politicians, who regularly exploited ethnic hostilities to win votes in their wards, Pingree tried to unify working-class Poles, Germans, Irish, and the middle class. In short, he was aware that to accomplish reform it was necessary to "recruit a coalition of power sufficient for his purpose."[71] A great many political machines had likewise constructed powerful electoral coalitions, but the politicians who built them were more interested in furthering their own careers than in making the economic and political system more just.

Ethnic Politics in Today's Cities

Cities are once again magnets for millions of immigrants, and as a consequence, struggles over racial and ethnic political participation have become highly charged. Despite their shortcomings, the machines showed respect for the newcomers and distributed highly valued resources. Considered in this light, an intriguing question arises: What strategies can the more recent immigrant groups employ to gain a voice in local political systems? Would recent immigrants and ethnic and racial minorities benefit if they were able to build political machines much like those that existed a century ago? The historical record indicates that the answer is "not much." And in any case, the rules of the game that regulate political processes have changed so much that such a strategy would be impractical.

The urban machines brokered a deal with both poor immigrants and economic elites, and each of these groups gave up something and got something in return. Business elites ceded control over local governments to working-class ethnic politicians who controlled armies of patronage workers, supported in part by income from bribes paid by businesses and corporations. In return, machine politicians essentially promised to leave business alone. In effect, the two sides struck a bargain by recognizing a sharp separation between the market and the public sphere. This compromise was important in managing the tension between capitalism, with its attendant inequalities, and popular democracy.[72]

On the whole this turned out to be a bad bargain for the machines' ethnic supporters. Rather than passing out favors and low-paying jobs, machine politicians could have emulated Hazen Pingree by attacking the practices that inflated the cost of urban services and infrastructure. They could have gone farther, too, and forged alliances with labor unions to pursue programs designed to modify dangerous working conditions, long hours, child labor, and low pay. Instead, they discouraged immigrants from organizing around their common interests.

There is reason to believe that today's urban residents can expect even less even if well-oiled machine organizations came into power. The machines prospered in rapidly growing industrial cities that required massive expenditures on roads, bridges, sewers, streetcar systems, schools, and parks.[73] The resulting government jobs, contracts, and franchises were traded for the political support necessary to sustain the party organizations. By contrast, in today's cities it would be extremely difficult to assemble the patronage and other material rewards necessary to build and maintain disciplined organizations. City services are now administered through civil service bureaucracies, and merit employment systems have been put in place so patronage can no longer be regularly delivered on the basis of personal or political relationships. Federal prosecutors would quickly sniff out patronage and vote-buying arrangements, which were outlawed long ago.

The last of the old-style machines, presided over by Chicago's Mayor Richard J. Daley, died along with him in 1976. From April 1989 to April 2011 his son, Richard M. Daley, assembled a disciplined political organization, and in a few respects it resembled his father's. The "rubber stamp" city council almost always endorsed his proposals; even on controversial issues, few aldermen dared to vote no.[74] Even so, the political style and policy priorities of the younger Daley were utterly different from his father's. The elder Daley ran campaigns primarily through aldermen and precinct captains; for his son, the most effective techniques involved direct mail and television ads crafted by the best political consultants that money could buy. To pay for media campaigns, new sources of money were tapped. In his father's day, machine workers provided critical financial support for the machine. By contrast, the contributions for Richard M.'s campaigns came primarily from the sectors making up the new global economy—lawyers, bankers, insurance agencies, and the conventions, tourism, and entertainment industry. For the 1999 mayoral campaign, the financial services industry contributed roughly 10 percent of the cost of the campaign and the legal community produced 5.5 percent. The tourism, entertainment, and hospitality industry, which had given very few dollars to previous mayors, emerged as a significant supporter for Daley, accounting for

4 percent of his campaign contributions in 1999. The owner of the Chicago Blackhawks hockey team threw in $10,000, and another $10,000 came from a livery firm from Frankfort, Illinois (which sponsors carriage rides in tourist areas of the city). The union representing hotel employees gave Daley's campaign $30,000. By contrast, government officials produced less than 2 percent of Daley's financial support.[75]

The second Daley maintained his authority by distributing a new kind of white-collar "pinstripe" patronage to lawyers, brokers, financial consultants, advertising and public relations firms, and lobbyists. The big volumes of money required for mayor's campaigns went more to media advertising than to grass-roots campaigning. Media-centered campaigns have replaced door-to-door and face-to-face campaigns at all levels of the American political system. The election of media mogul Michael Bloomberg as mayor of New York City in 2002 suggests that media-based politics has become common in the larger cities of the United States. National issues such as abortion rights, gay rights, and social welfare spending have also become important in local politics almost everywhere.[76] Because voters care about many national issues, it is difficult to imagine how an old-style party machine oriented to ethnic voters or to a politics of immediate material rewards would again emerge in any city.

Richard M. Daley ran a tight-knit political organization in the five terms he served as mayor, but whether it should be called a "new machine" or not is subject to debate.[77] Even though it clearly had some of the elements of the classic machines, it operated in a very different fashion. As a way of securing support among a new generation of ethnic voters, City Hall distributed as many jobs as possible to pro-Daley groups, but changing circumstances made the job difficult and even hazardous. The problem with the long-standing practice of fixing job applications for favored applicants was revealed late in 2005, when federal prosecutors began looking into the city's hiring practices. On July 6, 2006, the former director of the mayor's Office of Intergovernmental Affairs and three other former employees of the mayor's office were convicted in federal court of doctoring job applications, which violated a 1969 court decree forbidding the city from making patronage appointments. (The so-called Shakman decree carried the name of Michael Shakman, a Chicago lawyer who had filed suit against the city to stop patronage hiring.) Although Mayor Daley denied any knowledge of the practices, the corruption investigation threatened to spread out of control when the convicted employees and others fearing they might be prosecuted began talking to investigators. Federal prosecutors and the FBI promised that more was to come. Some people thought at the time it might even bring the mayor down.[78] By the end of 2007, two of the mayor's aides were serving terms in federal prison, and the investigation was still going on in 2010. The string of highly publicized cases kept Chicago's special style of politics in the news, and the presidential campaign of 2008 brought it to a national audience. But the truth is that long era of the classic party machine ended when the father, Richard J. Daley, died of a heart attack in his office in 1976. With his death, the last remnants of a colorful era slipped into the past.

Endnotes

1. Jessica Trounstine, "Challenging the Machine-Reform Dichotomy," in *The City in American Political Development*, ed. Richardson Dilworth (New York: Routledge, 2009), pp. 77–97.
2. Raymond Wolfinger, "Why Political Machines Have Not Withered Away and Other Revisionist Thoughts," in *Readings in Urban Politics: Past, Present, and Future*, ed. Harlan Hahn and Charles H. Levine (New York: Longman, 1984), p. 79. Wolfinger makes the distinction that we draw here between machine politics and a centralized machine. See also Roger W. Lotchin, "Power and Policy: American City Politics between the Two World Wars," in *Ethnics, Machines, and the American Urban Future*, ed. Scott Greer (Cambridge, MA: Schenkman, 1981), p. 9.
3. M. Craig Brown and Charles N. Halaby, "Machine Politics in America, 1870–1945," *Journal of Interdisciplinary History* 17, no. 3 (Winter 1987): 598. To qualify as a dominant political machine, a machine-style party had to control both the executive and the legislative branches of the city for an uninterrupted series of three elections.
4. One of the last classic machines, the O'Connell machine in Albany, New York, lost its grip in the 1980s. See Swanstrom and Ward, "Albany's O'Connell Organization: The Survival of an Entrenched Machine," paper delivered at the American Political Science Association Convention (Chicago, September 1987). In Chicago, Richard M. Daley, the son of Richard J., still presides over a disciplined machine, but it relies on well-funded media campaigns and a high level of amenities and services, rather than on patronage and spoils, for its support. For a comprehensive history of machine politics in Chicago, see Dick Simpson, *Rogues, Rebels, and Rubber Stamps: The Politics of the Chicago City Council, 1863 to the Present* (Boulder, CO: Westview Press, 2001).
5. Amy Bridges, *A City in the Republic* (Cambridge, UK: Cambridge University Press, 1984), p. 8.
6. Donald S. Lutz, *Popular Consent and Popular Control: Whig Political Theory in the Early State Constitutions* (Baton Rouge, LA: Louisiana State University Press, 1980), p. 105; Advisory Commission on Intergovernmental Relations, *Citizen Participation in the American Federal System* (Washington, DC: U.S. Government Printing Office, 1979), p. 41.
7. William Bennett Munro, *Municipal Government and Administration* (New York: Macmillan, 1923), p. 94.
8. William N. Chambers, "Party Development and the American Mainstream," in *The American Party System: Stages of Political Development,* 2nd ed., ed. William Nisbet Chambers and Walter Dean Burnham (New York: Oxford University Press, 1975), p. 12.
9. Jon M. Kingsdale, "The 'Poor Man's Club': Social Functions of the Urban Working-Class Saloon," in *The Making of Urban America*, ed. Raymond A. Mohl (Wilmington, DE: Scholarly Resources, 1988), p. 123.
10. Ibid.
11. Ibid.
12. Ibid., p. 130.
13. "He [the boss] does not seek social honor; the 'professional' is despised in 'respectable society.' He seeks power alone, power as a source of money, but also power for power's sake." Max Weber, "Politics as a Vocation," in *From Max Weber: Essays in Sociology*, ed. H. H. Gerth and C. Wright Mills (New York: Oxford University Press, 1946), p. 109.

14. William L. Riordan, *Plunkitt of Tammany Hall* (New York: Dutton, 1963), p. 50.
15. Quoted in Dayton McKean, *The Boss* (Boston: Houghton Mifflin, 1940), p. 132.
16. Edward C. Banfield and James Q. Wilson, *City Politics* (New York: Vintage Books, 1963), p. 125.
17. Milton Rakove, *Don't Make No Waves . . . Don't Back No Losers: An Insider's Analysis of the Daley Machine* (Bloomington, IN: Indiana University Press, 1975). The following material on Daley's machine is drawn from Rakove.
18. Ibid., pp. 114–115.
19. Ibid., p. 115.
20. Ibid., p. 120.
21. Ibid., p. 122.
22. Edward McChesney Sait, "Political Machines," in *Encyclopedia of the Social Sciences*, ed. Edwin R. A. Seligman (New York: Macmillan, 1933), p. 658. See also Robert M. Merton, *Social Theory and Social Structure* (New York: Free Press, 1949), pp. 126–127. For decades, Merton's functional analysis of political machines was widely accepted, but it has been seriously challenged in recent years. See Steven P. Erie, *Rainbow's End: Irish-Americans and the Dilemmas of Urban Machine Politics, 1840–1985* (Berkeley: University of California Press, 1988); Alan DiGaetano, "The Rise and Development of Urban Political Machines," *Urban Affairs Quarterly* 24, no. 2 (December 1988): 247, Table 3; M. Craig Brown and Charles N. Halaby, "Functional Sociology, Urban History, and the Urban Political Machine: The Outlines and Foundations of Machine Politics, 1870–1945," Unpublished conference paper (Albany: Department of Sociology, State University of New York at Albany, n.d.).
23. A. DiGaetano, "The Rise and Development of Urban Political Machines," pp. 257–262. See also M. Craig Brown and Charles N. Halaby, "Bosses, Reform, and the Socioeconomic Bases of Urban Expenditure, 1890–1940," in *The Politics of Urban Fiscal Policy*, ed. Terrence S. McDonald and Sally K. Ward (Beverly Hills, CA: Sage), p. 90.
24. DiGaetano, "The Rise and Development of Urban Political Machines," p. 261. Urban politics is often portrayed as a morality play in which reformers are pitted against machine politicians. In fact, machines often used reforms to consolidate their power and put reformers on the ballot in order to legitimate their rule. On the other side, reformers often created their own type of political machines. For a critique of the dichotomy between bosses and reformers, see David P. Thelen, "Urban Politics: Beyond Bosses and Reformers," *Reviews in American History* 7 (September 1979): 406–412. For an example of a reformer who created a new type of political machine, see Robert Caro's masterful biography of Robert Moses, *The Power Broker: Robert Moses and the Fall of New York* (New York: Vintage Books, 1974).
25. DiGaetano, "The Rise and Development of Urban Political Machines," p. 247, Table 3. For more information on the expansion of city governments in the late nineteenth century, see Jon C. Teaford, *The Unheralded Triumph: City Government in America, 1870–1900* (Baltimore: Johns Hopkins University Press, 1984); Eric H. Monkkonen, *America Becomes Urban: The Development of U.S. Cities and Towns, 1780–1980* (Berkeley: University of California Press, 1988).
26. Terrence J. McDonald and Sally K. Ward, eds., *The Politics of Urban Fiscal Policy* (Beverly Hills, CA: Sage, 1984), Introduction, p. 14.
27. Ibid.
28. Lotchin, "Power and Policy," p. 11.

29. Stanley K. Schultz, *Constructing Urban Culture: American Cities and City Planning, 1800–1920* (Philadelphia: Temple University Press, 1989).

30. Brown and Halaby, "Bosses, Reform, and the Socioeconomic Bases of Urban Expenditure, 1890–1940," p. 87. Interestingly, the authors found that machine cities, after reform—such as the establishment of a city manager form of government—spent more than other cities (p. 89).

31. Many sources of information are available on the Tweed Ring. The two books used here are Alexander Callow Jr., *The Tweed Ring* (New York: Oxford University Press, 1966), and Seymour J. Mandelbaum, *Boss Tweed's New York* (New York: Wiley, 1965). For a provocative, yet ultimately unpersuasive, defense of Tweed, see Leo Hershkowitz, *Tweed's New York: Another Look* (Garden City, NY: Anchor Books, 1977).

32. Martin Shefter, "The Emergence of the Political Machine: An Alternative View," in *Theoretical Perspectives on Urban Politics,* ed. Willis D. Hawley et al. (Upper Saddle River, NJ: Prentice Hall, 1976), p. 21.

33. The information presented here on Abraham Reuf's machine is taken from Walter Bean, *Boss Reuf's San Francisco* (Berkeley: University of California Press, 1952; reprinted 1972). Only direct quotations from Bean are cited by page in subsequent notes.

34. Ibid., pp. 93–94.

35. Paul Kantor, with Stephen David, *The Dependent City: The Changing Political Economy of Urban America* (Glenview, IL: Scott Foresman, 1988), p. 104.

36. Ernest S. Griffith, *A History of American City Government: The Conspicuous Failure, 1870–1900* (New York: Praeger, 1974), p. 183.

37. Zane Miller, *The Urbanization of Modern America: A Brief History* (New York: Harcourt Brace Jovanovich, 1973), p. 121.

38. Ester R. Fuchs and Robert Y. Shapiro, "Government Performance as a Basis for Machine Support," *Urban Affairs Quarterly* 18, no. 4 (June 1983): 537–550.

39. Merton, *Social Theory and Social Structure,* p. 130.

40. Robert A. Dahl, *Who Governs? Democracy and Power in an American City* (New Haven, CT: Yale University Press, 1961), p. 34.

41. See Doris Kearns Goodwin, *The Fitzgeralds and the Kennedys: An American Saga* (New York: Simon & Schuster, 1987).

42. Martin Shefter, "Political Incorporation and the Extrusion of the Left: Party Politics and Social Forces in New York City," in *Studies in American Political Development,* vol. 1, ed. Karen Orren and Stephen Skowronek (New Haven, CT: Yale University Press, 1986), p. 55.

43. Erie, *Rainbow's End,* p. 69.

44. Terry Nichols Clark, "The Irish Ethic and the Spirit of Patronage," *Ethnicity* 2 (1975): 341–342.

45. Caro, *The Power Broker,* p. 354.

46. John Allswang, *A House for All Peoples* (Lexington, KY: University Press of Kentucky, 1971).

47. For a useful review of the relationships between African Americans and political machines, see Hanes Walton Jr., *Black Politics: A Theoretical and Structural Analysis* (Philadelphia: Lippincott, 1972), Chapter 4.

48. William J. Grimshaw, *Bitter Fruit: Black Politics and the Chicago Machine, 1931–1991* (Chicago: University of Chicago Press, 1992).

49. Ibid.

50. Erie, *Rainbow's End,* p. 165.

51. Thomas M. Guterbock, *Machine Politics in Transition: Party and Community in Chicago* (Chicago: University of Chicago Press, 1980).

52. See Paul Kleppner, *Chicago Divided: The Making of a Black Mayor* (DeKalb: Northern Illinois University Press, 1985).

53. Michael Johnston, "Patrons and Clients, Jobs and Machines: A Case Study of the Uses of Patronage," *American Political Science Review* 73, no. 2 (June 1979): 385–398.

54. Erie, *Rainbow's End*, p. 218.

55. Jessica Trounstine, *Political Monopolies in American Cities: The Rise and Fall of Bosses and Reformers* (University of Chicago Press, 2008), p. 11.

56. Ibid., pp. 48, 242.

57. For a discussion of the role of political clubs in the evolution of Tammany Hall, see Shefter, "The Emergence of the Political Machine," p. 35.

58. Erie, *Rainbow's End*, pp. 102–103.

59. Kenneth D. Wald argues that ethnics supported machines not so much in response to socioeconomic disadvantage but out of an awareness of their social marginality and in the belief that machines would defend them from external pressures; see his "The Electoral Base of Political Machines: A Deviant Case Analysis," *Urban Affairs Quarterly* 16, no. 1 (September 1980): 3–29.

60. It would be misleading to say that such practices simply reflected the desires of poor immigrants. Irish family life was disrupted by the easy availability of illicit entertainment. Catholic priests and a significant proportion of the immigrant population opposed vice activities.

61. Harold Zink, *City Bosses in the United States* (Durham, NC: Duke University Press, 1930).

62. Wolfinger, "Why Political Machines Have Not Withered Away," p. 70.

63. Allan Rosenbaum, "Machine Politics: Class Interest and the Urban Poor," paper delivered at the annual meeting of the American Political Science Association (September 4–8, 1973), pp. 25–26.

64. Ibid., p. 26.

65. John D. Buenker, *Urban Liberalism and Progressive Reform* (New York: Scribner, 1973). Joseph J. Huthmacher also provides evidence of machine legislators' support for reform; see his "Urban Liberalism and the Age of Reform," *Mississippi Valley Historical Review* 44 (September 1962): 231–241.

66. For the distinction between social and structural reformers, see Melvin G. Holli, *Reform in Detroit: Hazen S. Pingree and Urban Politics* (New York: Oxford University Press, 1969), Chapter 8. We discuss the social reformers in this chapter; in Chapter 4 we discuss the structural reformers.

67. Martin J. Schiesl, *The Politics of Efficiency: Municipal Administration and Reform in America, 1880–1920* (Berkeley: University of California Press, 1977), pp. 80ff.

68. Quoted in Holli, *Reform in Detroit*, p. 42.

69. Ibid., p. 92.

70. Ibid., p. 195.

71. Peter Marris and Martin Rein, *Dilemmas of Social Reform* (New York: Atherton Press, 1967), p. 7.

72. Kantor, *The Dependent City*, pp. 117–118. Machine politicians appealed to voters on the basis of where they lived (their ethnic identification), not on the basis of where they worked (their class identification). Thus machine politics reflected the "city trenches" that have divided the American political landscape into community politics and workplace politics and blunted political action by the working class.

See Ira Katznelson, *City Trenches: Urban Politics and the Patterning of Class in the United States* (New York: Pantheon, 1981).

73. See James C. Scott, "Corruption, Machine Politics, and Political Change," *American Political Science Review* 63 (December 1969): 1142–1158; Clarence N. Stone, Robert K. Whelan, and William J. Murin, *Urban Policy and Politics in a Bureaucratic Age*, 2nd ed. (Upper Saddle River, NJ: Prentice Hall, 1986), Chapter 7.

74. Simpson, *Rogues, Rebels, and Rubber Stamps*, p. 280.

75. Ibid., pp. 280–290.

76. Elaine Sharp, ed., *Culture Wars and Urban Politics* (Lawrence: University Press of Kansas, 1999).

77. Larry Bennett, "The Mayor among His Peers: Interpreting Richard M. Daley," unpublished paper (June 2008).

78. Rudolph Bush and Dan Mihalopoulos, "Daley Jobs Chief Guilty"; Dan Mihalopoulos and Charles Sheehan, "Jurors Kept Focus on Case"; Gary Washburn, "Daley's Plans for Re-election Turn Murky"; and John Chase, "Things Are Not Over, FBI Boss Here Says," *Chicago Tribune* (July 7, 2006), pp. 1, 6.

CHAPTER 4

The Reform Crusades

The Reformers' Aims

In 1902, George Washington Plunkitt, a veteran of New York's legendary Tammany Hall machine organization, pontificated that reformers "were mornin' glories—looked lovely in the mornin' and withered up in a short time, while the regular machines went on flourishin' forever, like fine old oaks."[1] At the time Plunkitt delivered that pearl of homegrown wisdom, he had a valid point, but just barely. Even as he spoke, reform movements were springing up in cities all across the country. The reformers aimed to dismantle the party organizations that thrived on immigrant votes, but these movements tended to be short lived, exactly as Plunkitt observed. Reformers were often successful in persuading state legislatures to enact some reforms intended to undermine the machines; for example, some states took the administration of services out of the hands of boards of aldermen and city councils and put them under the control of professional administrators. But despite such measures, they found it hard to destroy the basic foundation of machine politics. This was not easy to do because machine politicians had a close and often personal relationship with their constituents. Their firm grip on the reins of municipal government gave them the power to decide such matters as hiring for public jobs, streetcar and utility franchises, construction contracts, and the provision of city services. Plenty of patronage and money, the lifeblood of machine politics, were bound up in these decisions.

In the estimation of the reformers, the cities were at the mercy of criminals who plundered the public purse for personal gain, but their efforts to change this state of affairs were often frustrated. Although reformers in Cleveland, New York, Chicago, and other cities sometimes succeeded at throwing machine politicians out of office and getting some of them prosecuted in the courts for corruption, the offending politicians were easily replaced by men cut from the same cloth. Commenting on this fact of life, Englishman James Bryce expressed the view that "the government of cities is the one conspicuous failure of the United States."[2] Reformers shared his opinion. Writing in 1909, the author of a textbook on municipal government made this assessment:

> The privilege seeker has pervaded our political life. For his own profit he has willfully befouled the sources of political power. Politics, which should offer a career inspiring to the noblest thoughts and calling for the most patriotic efforts of which man is capable, he has . . . transformed into a series of sordid transactions between those who buy and those who sell governmental action.[3]

Concerns about political corruption were closely connected to a rising fear of foreign immigrants. The reaction against the "Great Unwashed" had been building for a long time. As early as 1851, an article in the *Massachusetts Teacher* asked,

> The constantly increasing influx of foreigners . . . continues to be a cause of serious alarm to the most intelligent of our people. What will be the ultimate effect of this vast and unexampled immigration . . . ? Will it, like the muddy Missouri, as it pours its waters into the clear Mississippi and contaminates the whole united mass, spread ignorance and vice, crime and disease, through our native population?[4]

The earlier generations of immigrants were scandalized by lurid newspaper accounts of prostitution, gambling, and public drunkenness in the immigrant wards. Religious moralists secured state and local laws abolishing prostitution, gambling, and Sunday liquor sales. To teach immigrant children middle-class versions of dress, speech, manners, and discipline, reformers passed laws requiring school attendance and raised the upper age limit for mandatory schooling. Truant officers were hired to search for wayward youth.

The vicious reaction against immigrants aggravated the racial, class, and religious tensions that had divided America for almost a century. Immigrants were compared to the Goths and Vandals who invaded the Roman Empire in the second century A.D. In his book *Our Country*, the Reverend Josiah Strong accused them of defiling the Sabbath, spreading illiteracy and crime, and corrupting American culture and morals. Gathered into the cities, he said, immigrants provided "a very paradise for demagogues" who ruled by manipulating the "appetites and prejudices" of the rabble.[5]

The spatial segregation that separated neighborhoods provided fuel for the fears and prejudices of the more privileged members of society. By the turn of the century, all large cities contained sprawling, overcrowded immigrant ghettos near the waterfronts and factories, with middle- and upper-class neighborhoods located farther from the urban center. Jobs, though, were concentrated in downtown districts, and affluent city residents could hardly escape seeing, on their way to work and to shop, the rundown tenements, dirty streets, and littered alleys where the immigrants lived.

The fight to reform the urban political system was mounted by an alliance that brought together wealthy industrialists and other members of the upper class, well-educated members of the middle class, and middle-class voters. Andrew Carnegie and John D. Rockefeller initially financed the New York City Bureau of Municipal Research, founded in 1906. The U.S. Chamber of Commerce provided office space and paid the executive secretary of the City Managers Association for several years. Civic clubs and voters' leagues generally contained names from elite social directories, and the professionals involved in reform tended to be the most prestigious members of their professions. They succeeded in selling their message to growing numbers of middle-class voters. Between 1870 and 1910, the number of clerical workers, salespersons, government employees, technicians, and salaried professionals multiplied 7.5 times,

OUTTAKE

Municipal Reform Was Aimed at the Immigrants

The municipal reforms of the early nineteenth century were designed to undercut the electoral influence of working-class and immigrant voters. Virtually all machine politicians came from working-class, immigrant origins. Most machine bosses, like their followers, had little formal education; typically they had started out in politics by carrying messages and working on Election Day. Reformers were at the other end of the social spectrum. Most of the prominent reformers of the Progressive Era were upper-class people, and many, in fact, were wealthy industrialists, with names like McCormick, du Pont, Pinchot, Morgenthau, and Dodge. Most of them had a college education in a day when this fact marked a very select social stratum.

Machine politicians, ethnic voters, and working-class groups usually opposed reform because they correctly perceived that these were designed to make it more difficult for working-class candidates to win public office. In the big cities where they exerted a commanding electoral presence, immigrant voters were generally successful in opposing key features of the reform agenda, but elsewhere the reformers managed to reduce the political influence of those they called the Great Unwashed. The reformers' aims were laid bare in the 1938 municipal elections in Jackson, Michigan. The local chamber of commerce persuaded voters to approve a charter that replaced wards with an at-large election system. Working-class and immigrant candidates now had to compete for votes outside their own neighborhoods; no longer could they win a council seat simply by winning enough votes in their own wards. The slate of candidates sponsored by the chamber of commerce swept into office. The new mayor and the council members celebrated with a reception in the Masonic hall, which excluded Catholics from membership, and once in power, they dismissed most of the city's Roman Catholic employees.

Sources: George Mowry, The Era of Theodore Roosevelt, 1900–1912 (New York: Harper & Row, 1958); James Weinstein, The Corporate Ideal in the Liberal State, 1900–1918 (Boston: Beacon Press, 1968).

from 756,000 to 5,609,000.[6] The growing middle class constituted a formidable political force, and with their support the reformers accomplished most of their major aims within a couple of decades. The way Americans elect their leaders, hire public employees, and administer public services still reflects the politics of the reform era.

The Fertile Environment for Reform

In the first decades of the twentieth century a reform impulse swept the nation, energized in equal measure by concerns about corruption at all levels of government and the enormous power wielded by corporate moguls. Several developments ushered in the period known as the Progressive Era. Ostentatious displays of wealth contrasted starkly with grinding poverty in city and countryside. Newspapers, magazines, and books created a keen awareness about these conditions among upper-class and educated middle-class readers. By the turn of the century, falling paper prices and technical advances in rapid printing made it possible to produce high-quality mass-circulation newspapers and magazines. During the 1890s, newspaper circulation doubled and then tripled. A multitude of new periodicals appeared. All that was required to develop a mass audience was a way to popularize the press. Muckraking was such a technique. Crusading journalists investigated and reported "inside stories" exposing organized vice and the corruption of the urban machines. They also wrote sensational accounts about pervasive corruption in the national government, big business, the stock market, and the drug and meatpacking industries.

Beginning with its September 1902 issue, *McClure's* magazine printed a series of seven articles by Lincoln Steffens that told lurid stories of municipal corruption in the nation's big cities. In October, *McClure's* carried an article by Ida Tarbell exposing corporate corruption and profiteering by John D. Rockefeller's Standard Oil Company. Colorful stories of this kind attracted a large readership because they fed an insatiable appetite for shocking accounts of wrongdoing in business and government. Over the next few years, *Munsey's, Everybody's, Success, Collier's, Saturday Evening Post, Ladies' Home Journal, Hampton's, Pearson's, Cosmopolitan*, and dozens of daily newspapers published stories that contributed to a popular feeling that America's political, economic, and social institutions had become corrupt. Big business was accused of producing unsafe and shoddy goods, fixing prices, and crushing competition. There were exposés of fraudulent practices in banking; heartrending accounts of women and children working at long, tedious, and dangerous jobs in factories and sweatshops; and stories about urban poverty, prostitution, white slavery, and business–government collusion to protect vice.

An outpouring of books played on the same themes. In 1904, Steffens gathered his *McClure's* articles together into a best-selling volume, *The Shame of the Cities*. Other popular titles included *The Greatest Trust in the World*, an exposé of price-fixing and collusion in the steel industry; *The Story of Life Insurance*; and *The Treason of the Senate*, which detailed systematic bribery of U.S. senators. Several novelists entered the field. In his novel *An American Tragedy*, Theodore Dreiser described the corrupting influence of greed on a self-made small-town boy. Dreiser's *Sister Carrie* and David Graham Phillip's *Susan Lenox* vividly portrayed how the impersonal forces of urban life victimized young women. In *The Financier*, Dreiser's story revolved around the ruthless drive for power and wealth, using the Chicago streetcar magnate Charles Yerkes as his model.

The literature produced by the muckrakers—an epithet applied to them in 1906 by President Theodore Roosevelt, referring to a character in John Bunyan's 1645 book *Pilgrim's Progress* who was too busy raking muck to look up and see the stars—was influential in building popular interest in reform. Although the details of reform were often dull and unexciting to the average citizen, the muckrakers' stories gave a feeling of drama and urgency to the cause of reform.

No work was more influential than Upton Sinclair's *The Jungle*, a classic work still assigned in college courses. Sinclair tells a riveting story of a Lithuanian immigrant's fight to survive in a corrupt and chaotic Chicago. Beaten down by destitution and poverty, eventually his wife becomes a prostitute, his children die, and he becomes a socialist revolutionary. Sinclair's nauseating accounts of the conditions in Chicago's meatpacking industry (the rats, feces, chopped fingers, and spoiled meat swept into sausage vats) catalyzed a national crusade that prompted Congress to establish the U.S. Food and Drug Administration in 1905.

The political backlash created by the muckrakers catalyzed the formation of organizations dedicated to the goals of regulating business practices, improving working conditions, imposing standards on the professions, and reforming government. Business leaders organized the National Civic Federation in 1900. By advocating workers' compensation and other modest social insurance schemes, the founders of the federation hoped to undermine more militant demands proposed by union organizers.[7] The National Child Labor Committee was organized in 1904 to fight for child labor legislation. In 1910, the National Housing Association brought together housing reform groups from many cities to campaign for building codes. Numerous public officials' associations and municipal research bureaus came into existence specifically to promote municipal reform: the National Association of Port Authorities, the Municipal Finance Officers Association, the American Association of Park Superintendents, the Conference of City Managers, and the National Short Ballot Association.

Although flagrant corruption energized campaigns to "throw the rascals out" in a few cities in the 1870s and 1880s, the issues tended to be local and the remedies specific to an immediate circumstance. But in the 1890s, the reform cause was transformed into a national crusade. Citizens' groups sprang up all across the country to lobby for improved public services and honesty in government. The problems faced by the reformers varied little from one city to the next. Like-minded reformers from different cities soon began to exchange advice and information about their efforts. It did not take long before these informal networks became transformed into national organizations.

In 1894, delegates to the First Annual Conference for Good City Government met in Philadelphia to establish the first national municipal reform organization, the National Municipal League. The delegates to the conference were united in the belief that machine politicians and their immigrant constituents had corrupted democratic institutions in the cities. But they disagreed about the measures that should be taken to change this situation. "We are not unlike patients assembled in a hospital," one of the participants put it, "examining together and describing to each other our sore places."[8] After the formation of the National Municipal League, the nationalization of reform proceeded quickly. Within two years, 180 local chapters were affiliated with the league, and, by the turn of the century member organizations had sprung up all across the country. In their annual meetings, reformers got a chance to compare notes, and by the time they met in November 1899, the members of the National Municipal League were able to reach agreement on a model municipal charter they could use as a blueprint for "good government."

As a strategy for undermining the close relationship between politicians and their immigrant constituents, the Municipal League's model charter recommended that electoral wards be abolished; instead, each city council member would be elected "at-large," that is, by all the voters of the city. It recommended the abolition of the party label on election ballots, on the premise that uneducated voters cast their ballots for a symbol, but not a name. The charter urged reformers to fight for civil service appointment procedures so that party officials would not be able to use public jobs for patronage. The league also said that local elections should be held in different years than national and state elections, so that the national political parties would find it more difficult to influence local affairs.[9]

The reformers wanted to kick the rascals out, but they also wanted to make local government more efficient and accountable to the tastes and preferences of middle-class voters. The model charter drawn up by the league urged reformers to give the mayor the power to appoint top administrators and to veto legislation. The assumption behind this reform—called "strong mayor government"—was that with authority centralized in the hands of the mayor, voters would be able to hold the mayor accountable for the city's overall governance, and the spoils system presided over by city councils would be disrupted. As they saw it, the main problem was the style of politics in which city council members or aldermen cut deals behind the scenes. Finally, the league urged city reformers to seek home rule, which would give cities, and their voters, broad powers to control their own affairs without meddling from state legislatures.

Through all these reforms, the municipal reformers intended to place the affairs of the city into the hands of educated upper- and middle-class voters and, increasingly, in a cadre of professionally trained and credentialed administrators. Within a few decades, the municipal reform movement managed to build a bureaucratic mode of governance that generations of Americans have often complained about.

The Campaigns Against Machine Rule

The intense enmity shared by the reformers toward the urban machines and their immigrant constituents motivated them to cast about for a variety of remedies for the ills they observed. Some reformers went so far as to question the wisdom of universal suffrage, claiming the immigrants were too ignorant and illiterate to vote intelligently. The Tilden Commission, appointed by the New York legislature to investigate the Tweed Ring scandals in New York City, recommended in 1878 that suffrage be restricted to those who owned property.[10] The commission's report was reprinted in an 1899 issue of *Municipal Affairs*, the National Municipal League's magazine, and many reformers read it approvingly. Andrew D. White, the first president of Cornell University, summed up the case for disenfranchising the immigrants in an 1890 issue of *Forum*:

> A city is a corporation; . . . as a city it has nothing whatever to do with general political interests. . . . The questions in a city are not political questions. . . .
> The work of a city being the creation and control of the city property, it should

logically be managed as a piece of property by those who have created it, who have a title to it, or a real substantial part in it, . . . [and not by] a crowd of illiterate peasants, freshly raked in from the Irish bogs, or Bohemian mines, or Italian robber nests.[11]

However attractive the idea of attaching property qualifications to the vote might have been, such a drastic remedy was simply impractical. To wage a campaign on this issue would certainly have provoked a negative reaction, even from some of the groups that supported reform. From the constitutional period until the Jacksonian reforms of the 1820s and 1830s, most states had restricted the vote to owners of property. The abolition of these restrictions had been celebrated as a triumph for popular democracy. Virtually everyone understood that the time had passed when the ownership of property could be required as a condition for voting, but a few reformers tried to do it anyway. The 1912 charter of Phoenix, in the new state of Arizona, restricted voting in municipal elections to taxpayers, but the state courts invalidated the restriction as unconstitutional.[12] Even before Phoenix's attempt to restrict the vote, it was clear that the reformers would have to find less direct and more creative methods to reduce the influence of the riffraff and rabble.

Few reformers seriously questioned the idea that immigrants should participate in the democratic system. They were convinced the real problem with elections was that they were run by machine politicians who took advantage of their immigrant constituents, and they were not entirely wrong. Municipal elections were notoriously chaotic and corrupt, conducted, as they were, in the absence of well-established rules and regulations. Because the political parties were considered private organizations, their nominating procedures were not regulated at all. To select candidates for public office, political parties held nominating conventions and ward caucuses according to their own changeable and unwritten rules, often on short notice and at locations known only to insiders. It was not unusual for caucuses to be held in the back rooms of saloons owned by ward bosses. According to one scholar,

> This was the period of massive voting frauds. In the elections of 1868 and 1872, 8 percent more people voted in New York state than were registered. In 1910, when the New York City vote was challenged and recounted, half of the votes were found to be fraudulent. In New Jersey, the stuffing of ballot boxes was so common that the state legislature replaced the wooden boxes with glass ballot jars. In Pennsylvania and Michigan, gangs of thugs moved from polling place to polling place beating up the opposition and voting at will. Fictitious and repeat voters, false counting, and stuffed ballot boxes were such regular features of city elections that voting statistics from this period are suspect.[13]

A Philadelphia politician once boasted that the signers of the Declaration of Independence were machine loyalists: "'These men,' he said, 'the fathers of American liberty, voted down here once. And,' he added with a sly grin, 'they vote here yet.'"[14]

Machine workers sometimes completed the ballot for voters or accompanied them into the voting booth. "Farmer Jones," a member of the Chicago machine in the 1890s, revealed to an inquiring reformer how he guaranteed voter loyalty:

> [The reformer asked,] "When you got the polling stations in your hands, what did you do?"
>
> "Voted our men, of course."
>
> "And the negroes, how did they vote?"
>
> "They voted as they ought to have voted. They had to."
>
> ". . . how could you compel those people to vote against their will?"
>
> "They understood, and besides," said he, "there was not a man voted in that booth that I did not know how he voted before he put the paper in the judges' hands."[15]

On the chance that other methods were not sufficiently reliable, some machines directly paid for the vote. The 1896 election in the First Ward of Chicago provides a good example:

> The bars were open all night and the brothels were jammed. By ten o'clock the next morning, though, the saloons were shut down, not in concession to the reformers, but because many of the bartenders and owners were needed to staff the First Ward field organization. The Bath, Hinky Dink and their aides ran busily from polling place to polling place, silver bulging in their pockets into which they dug frequently and deeply. The effort was not in vain, and the outcome was gratifying.[16]

Not trusting in fraud alone, machine politicians sometimes resorted to intimidation and violence. In his 1898 campaign for alderman, the Chicago ward boss John Powers threatened voters and told business owners they would lose their business licenses unless they supported him.[17] "Hinky Dink" Kenna and "Bathhouse John" Coughlin of Chicago's First Ward defended their loyal constituents but routinely harassed opponents. In the bootleg era of the 1920s, organized crime and machine politics became closely coupled in Chicago. Gangland hits were visited on meddling politicians who stood outside the inner circle of men controlling and protecting illegal liquor, speakeasies, prostitution, and gambling.

Flagrant election-day corruption energized those who opposed such abuses. Ed Crump, the boss of Memphis, Tennessee, won his first mayoral election in 1909 by watching the polls himself. He personally stopped the use of marked ballots by a machine organization he was opposing, in one case by hitting a voter in the face.[18] In Pittsburgh's state and city elections of 1933, the Democrats and Republicans—both rightly fearing fraud by the other party—mobilized opposing armies of poll watchers. The state police were called in to keep the peace, and lawyers and judges stood by to provide quick court action.[19]

In the late 1890s, reformers introduced several measures intended to reduce election fraud. The key reforms included:

- *Voter registration and literacy requirements.* These requirements reduced repeat voting and stopped the practice of importing voters for an election. By 1920 almost all states had imposed registration laws.

- *Australian ballot.* This was a ballot that could be marked only by the voter, and it was cast in secret. Before the Australian ballot was introduced in the 1880s, the parties printed the ballots and often marked and placed them in a ballot box in front of observers. The ballots were even handed to voters already marked. Use of the Australian ballot became universal after the turn of the century.
- *Nonpartisan elections.* Reformers fought hard to remove party labels of any kind from municipal, election ballots. Where they succeeded, voters had only one clue as to how they should vote: the printed name of the individual candidate.

Although these reforms brought a measure of order and honesty to urban elections, they also had the effect of reducing voting participation by immigrants and less educated voters. Where there were no precinct captains and party workers to help voters register or look over a sample ballot, large numbers of voters were effectively disenfranchised. Twenty-five percent of the white males of voting age in the United States in 1900 were first-generation immigrants, and two-thirds of them had come from non-English-speaking countries. In the industrial cities, typically more than two-thirds of the voters were foreign-born immigrants. Illiterate voters often asked for help in reading and filling out the ballot, or requested one that was already completed. When they showed up at the polling place, no one questioned their right to cast a vote. After reforms were adopted, they were required to register in writing, often months before an election. And when they went to the polling station they now faced an election judge, a voting booth, and a printed ballot they could not read. Machine politicians were often able to get around the problems of the secret ballot by controlling the polling places, but these actions exposed them to the possibility of criminal prosecution.

By 1905, voter registration laws had been placed on the books in most of the states.[20] In the next few years, states and localities set up election boards, made it illegal to vote more than once, and tried to define the legitimate uses of campaign funds. Although enforcement was uneven, especially in the cities—the machines continued to control prosecutors and the courts in many places—the existence of new laws provided the basis for investigations and prosecutions when the middle- and upper-class public became disturbed about corruption.

Once electoral reforms were put in place, municipal reformers focused their attention on the machine organizations. It was obvious that machine politicians derived their strength from ethnic neighborhoods and that the machines relied upon the ability of uneducated voters to easily identify a party label printed on the ballot. By voting a straight party ticket, the voter did not have to read the candidates' names. To make it harder for the voters to support machine candidates in this way, the reformers fought hard for two reforms—nonpartisan ballots and at-large elections.

Reformers argued that party labels encouraged blind loyalty to a political organization. They wanted a more "rational" informed voter who possessed the ability to "accumulate and carry in his head the brief list of personal preferences and do without the guidance of party names and symbols on the ballot."[21] The reformers asserted it was the responsibility of citizens to educate themselves and to vote for the best candidates strictly on their merits, not on the basis of party loyalty or ethnic solidarity. Brand Whitlock, the famous reform mayor of Toledo, Ohio, observed,

> It seems almost incredible now that men's minds were ever so clouded, strange that they did not earlier discover how absurd was a system which, in order to enable them the more readily to subjugate themselves, actually printed little woodcuts of birds—roosters and eagles—at the heads of the tickets, so that they might be more easily and readily recognize their masters and deliver their suffrages over to them.[22]

Just as the reformers intended, the nonpartisan ballot made it harder for immigrants to vote as a bloc. Reading their alderman's printed name could be hard for illiterate voters. Recognizing the party symbol on the ballot was infinitely easier than reading the names of candidates.

The reformers also believed that nonpartisan elections would change the types of candidates seeking public office. The party organization supplied campaign money and workers and freed working-class candidates from the necessity of holding a normal job, which would have denied them time to participate in politics. Few politicians in the cities could have started or stayed in politics without the resources supplied by a party organization. Local parties pooled resources and built cooperative relationships among politicians; without them, people of wealth and social standing tended to hold an overwhelming advantage. This result was, in fact, the objective of the nonpartisanship crusade—to make politics once again a calling appropriate to the educated and cultured classes.[23]

The proposal to replace wards with at-large elections was designed to break the link between neighborhoods and machine politicians. Andrew White complained that "wards largely controlled by thieves and robbers can send thieves and robbers" into public office, and "the vote of a single tenement house, managed by a professional politician, will neutralize the vote of an entire street of well-to-do citizens."[24] The remedy was to require every candidate for the city council to campaign for support from voters wherever they lived in the city; rarely, in such a system, could one neighborhood or ethnic group produce enough votes to carry an election. Gone would be the politics of trade-offs, logrolling, and compromise among legislators representing their own wards:

> For decades the election of councils by wards had superimposed a network of search for parochial favors, of units devoted to partisan spoils, and of catering to ethnic groups that time and again had either defeated comprehensive city programs or loaded them with irrelevant spoils and ill-conceived ward projects. The ward and precinct were the heart of machine control, and the councils so elected were usually also infested with corruption, however acceptable the councilors may have been to the voters of their wards.[25]

Wards potentially gave even relatively small ethnic and racial groups some leverage. Lithuanian voters, for example, might be able to send a Lithuanian alderman to the city council, even if they constituted a tiny proportion of a city's total population. Wards multiplied the points of access through which groups and individuals could influence public officials. At-large elections had an opposite effect. If the city is one big electoral district, candidates representing ethnic and racial groups clustered in specific neighborhoods are handicapped; in order to be elected, they are forced to broaden their appeal to groups distributed over many neighborhoods. Because campaigns covering a city are costly and time consuming, wealthier candidates have a built-in advantage. In such a system, personal wealth and social status become the ingredients of political success.

Civil service hiring systems constituted the last big plank in the reform platform. Civil service rules were crucial because they stopped the machines from rewarding loyal supporters with patronage jobs; instead, written and oral civil service examinations would become the sole basis for hiring municipal employees, and a system of tenure and seniority would make employees safe from political firings. Reformers thought of civil service as the silver bullet because without patronage, they expected the machines to quickly wither away.

The package of reform proposals generally were rejected in the industrial cities where ethnics made up a large proportion of the electorate. In smaller places, even when the machine threat did not seem plausible, reformers were often successful in making the sale. A melodramatic rhetoric of corruption and venality turned the machines into a scary bogeyman hiding just around the corner, ready to pounce at the first opportunity.[26] Such stories could just as well be, and often were, imported from cities hundreds of miles away. The reformers' job was made all the more easier because the residents of small urban places tended to share their view that local government should do little else but provide essential public services such as water, sewage disposal, streets, and perhaps libraries.

The electoral rules installed in the era of reform are much in evidence in contemporary cities. Before 1910, nonpartisan elections were almost unknown, but by 1929 they were utilized in 57 percent of the cities with populations of more than 30,000.[27] By the 1960s, a large number of states required their cities to use nonpartisan elections; these included Minnesota, California, Alaska, and most of the western states. In 10 more states, nonpartisan ballots were used in 90 percent or more of the cities (the exceptions usually being cities above a specified size). In the West, 94 percent of cities used nonpartisan elections. The eastern seaboard is the only region of the country where more cities use partisan than nonpartisan elections. The big cities managed to buck the trend: Among those with more than 500,000 people, 85 percent still print party labels on the ballot.

Reformed electoral systems were designed to reduce the influence of working-class ethnic voters, and plenty of evidence indicates that they accomplished their intended purpose. In the first years of the twentieth century, working-class candidates, some of them socialists, were elected to city offices in dozens of cities.[28] The spread of at-large elections made it much harder for candidates of this stripe to win. In Dayton, Ohio, socialists elected two aldermen and three assessors from working-class wards in the 1909 elections. This shocking outcome motivated local elites to mount a furious campaign to install an at-large system. By the 1913 election it was in place. In that year's election, the socialists received 35 percent of the popular vote and, in 1917, 44 percent, but because all candidates were elected at-large, in neither year were the socialists able to elect a single candidate. Similarly, in 1911 Pittsburgh adopted at-large elections, with the result that upper-class business leaders and professionals pushed lower- and middle-class groups out of their places on the city council and the school board.[29]

St. Louis provides a graphic example of these two electoral systems at work. The members of the city's board of aldermen compete for office through partisan elections in each of the city's 28 wards (see Figure 4.1). In a city that was 41 percent African American in 1970, race had become a hotly

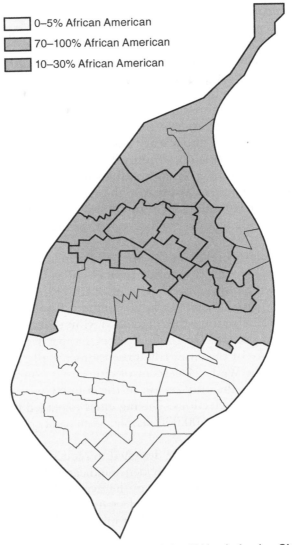

FIGURE 4.1 Racial Composition of Municipal Wards in the City of St. Louis, 1977.

contested terrain. Because of St. Louis's ward system, 10 blacks won seats on the city's board of aldermen in the 1977 municipal elections (and 11 by 2000). All of them represented predominantly African American wards located in the northern half of the city. By contrast, all of the 18 wards with a majority of white voters elected white aldermen. (As in many cities, *alderman* is an official term in the St. Louis city charter and does not refer exclusively to males.)

These results differed sharply from the outcome of the St. Louis school board elections because all the candidates were required to compete in at-large contests. In 1977, at a time when 70 percent of the public school enrollment was African American, not a single black candidate made it onto the school board. All five of the seats on the ballot went to white middle-class candidates because few white voters would support an African American candidate. The ward system ensured that African Americans would be represented in the city's legislative body, but the rules governing school board elections produced a different outcome.

Over time, virtually all cities in the southwestern United States adopted some combination of nonpartisan and at-large elections. Partly as a result, a style of politics evolved in that region that was tilted heavily in favor of business elites. "Frugality, efficiency, and professionalism in public administration" have always been the themes guiding the governance of southwestern cities, but a multitude of governmental units have been willing to take on a great many responsibilities to promote local development.[30] For decades, legions of bureaucrats and professionals have found employment in special districts and authorities devoted to developing land, providing water, dredging harbors, supplying electricity, and lobbying the federal government so that business could grow.[31] Until the 1960s, candidates for public office tended to be selected by business associations. As a result, the cities of the Southwest produced a distinctive type of machine politics, though of course its participants did not give it that label. Voters tended to turn out for elections at a much lower rate than in the industrial cities of the North.[32] This state of affairs began to change in the 1960s only when civil rights and neighborhood groups mobilized in several Sunbelt cities to challenge the tightly knit regimes that had long been dominated by business interests.

"Efficiency and Economy" in Municipal Affairs

In the earliest years of the movement for municipal reform, "efficiency and economy" became code words for good government. When Theodore Roosevelt addressed the delegates to the First Annual Conference for Good City Government in 1894, he urged them to go beyond their moral outrage at the way things were being run to find ways of streamlining and improving government: "There are two gospels I always want to preach to reformers. . . . The first is the gospel of morality; the next is the gospel of efficiency. . . . I don't think I have to tell you to be upright, but I do think I have to tell you to be practical and efficient."[33] In truth, it is doubtful the reformers needed such advice. Municipal reformers were hard at work searching for guideposts marking the way to good governance. If they succeeded at kicking the rascals out, they needed to know what to do with their inheritance.

The extreme disorganization of city governments gave the reformers a big target to aim at. All through the nineteenth century, cities had tended to add new responsibilities and services piecemeal, one small step at a time. By late century, every city was governed by a multitude of independent boards and commissions administering municipal services. Organization charts had never been drawn up, making it impossible to make sense of how any individual city was run. This state of affairs seemed like a perfect recipe for chaos and corruption. Typically, a city was governed by a city council, with each of the aldermen representing a ward. Reformers claimed that this system produced a political culture of log-rolling and vote-trading. Aldermen also got in the habit of filling the multitude of committees, boards, and commissions with their political cronies, who also took bribes when the opportunity arose. What was to be done? The reformers agreed that the best solution was to replace ward-based with at-large elections. The idea was that individuals with the personal resources to run city-wide campaigns would tend to win, and that therefore a better of class of person would end up occupying the mayor's office. This assumption was often, but not always, borne out. Campaigns covering an entire city were expensive, and in the late nineteenth century candidates for mayor paid most of their own campaign costs.[34] As a result, mayors generally came from prominent, even upper-class, backgrounds. Working-class ethnic candidates came to the office mainly in cities with a disciplined party organization with a broad and diverse base.

To enhance the authority of mayors and administrators, state legislatures regularly intervened to take budgetary and supervisory authority from elected councils and to give these powers to mayors or to full-time boards and commissions whose members were appointed by the mayor. In 1891, the Indiana legislature gave the Indianapolis comptroller the authority to draft the budget; the council retained the authority to lower, but could not increase, appropriations. New charters granted the mayors of Cleveland and Indianapolis the right to remove executive officials, a feature that was also adopted in charters approved in other states: New Orleans in 1896 and Baltimore in 1898.[35] In 1892, New York's legislature mandated a Board of Estimate and Apportionment, modeled on New York City's, for all cities over 50,000 in population. In the 1870s and 1880s, state legislative committees assumed financial or administrative control of the police departments of Detroit, Baltimore, Boston, St. Louis, Kansas City, and New York.

Reformers became accustomed to lobbying legislatures to enact legislation that would favor the reform cause. When they intervened in this way, legislatures became, in effect, referees among the contending interests that were trying to control local politics. Even if they had wanted to, state legislatures could not have been completely insulated from the political battles occurring in the cities. Local governments provided key public services, and representatives to state legislatures answered to local constituents; as a consequence, local and state affairs were closely entwined: "The ordinary work of state politics was local affairs, and an ordinary branch of local government was the state legislature."[36] Most legislators were not inclined to interfere actively in issues arising from local governments outside their legislative districts, and rules governing the apportionment of legislative districts limited the number of legislators coming from big cities. Research has shown that "virtually all bills affecting big cities were introduced by representatives from those cities."[37] Nonlocal representatives "routinely deferred to local governments."[38] Therefore, the important question became: Who, if anyone, spoke for local governments?

Ordinarily, the legislators who represented the biggest cities came from the more privileged sectors of society, and this occurred even where machines governed.[39] They were business leaders, bankers, lawyers, and other men of professional and social standing. The men of wealth and social prestige refused to run in the ethnic wards against immigrant saloonkeepers and party loyalists, but they possessed the personal resources to compete and win in state legislative districts. In addition, members of many of the boards and commissions of city government were appointed by governors, legislative committees, and mayors, and thus they were "protected from popular control, insulated from the undue influence of the city's aldermen, and dominated by those perched proudly on the top rung of the urban social ladder."[40]

By these means, reformers achieved some check on the ward-based city councils, but they were looking for a more comprehensive approach that might transform the governance of the city from top to bottom. To accomplish this, they thought, they needed to agree on a coherent theory of governance to guide their efforts. By the late 1890s, such a theory began to take shape, built around the premise that a singular "public interest" could be defined that benefited all citizens equally and objectively. The reformers rallied around four sacred principles of reform: (1) *low taxes*: there must be strict budgetary controls to ensure taxes would be kept as low as possible and public services delivered at the lowest possible cost; (2) *no politics*: the day-to-day administration of city government should be strictly separated from "politics"; (3) *administrative expertise*: experts with training, experience, and ability should run city services; and (4) *efficiency*: government should be run like a business, with cost efficiency being the ultimate touchstone for good government. This last plank in the "good government" platform was derived from the principles guiding the scientific management movement that swept the country during the Progressive Era. As businesses became ever larger, accountants, engineers, and corporate managers were busily inventing the structure of the modern corporation. What emerged was a quasi-military model of hierarchical administrative control.

In 1911, Frederick Winslow Taylor became a household name with the publication of his book *The Principles of Scientific Management*.[41] Taylor's life work was devoted to the application of military discipline and hierarchy to the workplace, factory, and even daily life. He urged employers to study the movements of individual workers to discover how work tasks could be organized to achieve maximum output with a minimum expenditure of each worker's time and energy. Taylor promised that the application of his efficiency principles would bring progress, prosperity, and happiness to society and material wealth to all. By making management into a science, Taylor said, it would be possible to achieve harmony and cooperation between owners and workers because both had the same interest in maximizing output. There was even a spiritual side; principles of efficiency would allow each worker to develop "his greatest efficiency and prosperity."[42] The essence of the Taylor catechism was that "In the past, the man has been first; in the future the system must be first."[43] Taylor and his disciples spread an urgent message: "Soldiering" (slow work) and inefficiency should be stamped out at home as well as at work. Popular magazines featured articles on efficient housework—describing, for instance, how a homemaker could sequence her daily chores and arrange appliances and furniture to minimize wasted movement while doing household work. By playing upon a universal desire for prosperity and social harmony, the efficiency movement quickly achieved the status of a secular religion; the scientific management movement swept across the country.

To its disciples, scientific management seemed to promise a bloodless revolution, a solution to hostile employer–worker relations, disastrous economic panics, and poverty and want. Efficiency societies sprang up in cities all over the country, and efficiency experts were in great demand as speakers.[44] Taylor's followers invaded the factories to spread the gospel of efficiency. Efficiency and scientific management—"business methods"—also became the model for municipal reform. The advantages of applying efficiency principles to the workings of government seemed obvious: "The rising prestige of technicians in industry and the increasing demand for new public works and municipal services strengthened the desire for more technical efficiency in local government."[45]

In 1912, Henry Brueré, the first director of the privately funded New York Bureau of Municipal Research, published a book applying efficiency principles to municipal management.[46] Brueré argued that much of the mismanagement in New York City "formerly attributed to official corruption and to popular indifference was really due to official and popular ignorance of . . . orderly and scientific procedures."[47] What these procedures amounted to were elaborate accounting and reporting devices designed to codify the responsibilities of city officials, the actions taken by them to carry out their duties, the costs of equipment and personnel, and other details. Brueré invented a scoring system whereby the efficiency of cities could be rated and compared, and with the performance of a city reduced to a number. Cities were to be rated on the basis of such items as: "Is a record kept of all city property?" "How often are the treasurer's books audited?" "Twenty questions on the protection of milk supply." "Is the location of houses of prostitution known and recorded?"[48] In all, Brueré and his aides used a list of 1,300 standardized questions to rate cities from the "worst governed" to the "best."

In 1913, Brueré was given the opportunity to make New York City efficient. In November of that year, one of Brueré's closest confidants, John Purroy Mitchell, was elected New York's mayor. Mitchell appointed Brueré to the office of city chamberlain (the mayor's policy adviser). Brueré immediately launched an attack on Tammany Hall's patronage system and managed to push through the first fully fledged civil service system in the nation. Brueré assigned the task of designing the details of the civil service system to Robert Moses, a young staff member at the New York Bureau of Municipal Research. Moses carried out his assignment with the enthusiasm of a Taylorite fanatic. He proposed a system in which every municipal employee would be closely and constantly monitored at work by efficiency experts trained to rate each worker's efficiency by applying an elaborate mathematical formula. The responsibilities of employees were codified and "given a precise mathematical grade. These grades would . . . be used as a basis for salary increase and promotion."[49] To implement his system, Moses instructed his assistants to draw up rating forms, which he then distributed to supervisors. The idea was that each day, the supervisors would hand a scorecard containing a mathematical score to every employee. City workers would be paid, promoted, or fired on the basis of their performance.

Such a system, if implemented fully, would have fallen of its own weight. There was no way to ensure objective ratings. The amount of time required to rate employees would have resulted in a truly enormous civil service administrative staff. Instead of spending the prodigious amounts of money required to hire hundreds of specially trained supervisors, Moses tried to rely on existing city employees. The 50,000 city employees steadfastly refused to use the reporting forms, objecting that the system was hopelessly time consuming and unwieldy, and arbitrary and capricious to boot.

The elaborate system established during Mitchell's mayoral tenure illuminates the values, assumptions, and foibles of the reformers. As Taylor had put it, "The natural laziness in men is serious, but by far the greatest evil from which both workmen and employers are suffering is the systematic soldiering which is almost universal."[50] Reformers were taking on the formidable task of remaking human beings. Such an ambition could only be based on a fundamental distrust of people as they were. An essential human element was lacking. Mayor Mitchell, while trying to reorganize city departments and implement civil service procedures, tried to reduce all "unnecessary" programs and expenditures. He instituted cutbacks in school expenditures, asked teachers to work without salaries in the summers, tried to close down special schools for persons with mental disabilities, and reduced park and recreational expenditures.[51]

New York's civil service proposals were too draconian even for most reformers, but some of the abstract principles made sense. Streamlined administration and better-trained city workers clearly could save money and improve services. Cities across the country adopted civil service systems but omitted New York City's impossibly complicated reporting system. In addition to the cities, the federal government and the states soon entered the field. President William Howard Taft appointed a Commission on Economy and Efficiency, and President Woodrow Wilson later created the Bureau of Efficiency. Between 1911 and 1917, 16 states established efficiency commissions. These commissions generally recommended streamlining budgeting procedures, centralizing more power in the governor's office, consolidating state agencies, and establishing civil service systems.[52]

The Business Model

The principles of scientific management suggested that municipal government should be modeled as closely as possible on the business corporation. Reformers pointed out that the municipal governments inherited from the past were terribly cumbersome and dysfunctional. A history of reform written by scholars sympathetic with this view described the problem in these terms: "The reformers, who tried to get good men into office, found . . . that, even if they elected a mayor or council, they were intolerably handicapped by the existing systems of municipal government. [Due to] the principles of separation of powers and of checks and balances . . . there was no single elective official or governing body that could be held responsible for effecting reform."[53] Reformers claimed that the "weak mayor" form of government that existed in most cities dispersed authority among too many politicians—elected aldermen plus the legions of appointed members of boards and commissions. Trying to make sense of it all, they employed organizational charts like the one shown in Figure 4.2. In this "weak mayor" organizational chart, the mayor presides over meetings of the city council, but the council presides over the departments that provide city services. The question being asked was simple: who could the voters blame if they were dissatisfied with the way the city was being run?

It was supposed that businesses operated efficiently because there was a clear separation between policymaking, which was located in a board of directors, and the tasks of day-to-day administration, which was left in the hands of professional executive officers and their employees. Applied to cities, this model would leave policymaking to elected officials, who represented their constituents, just as a board of directors in a business answered to stockholders. The policies they enacted, however, were to be implemented by professional administrators schooled in the principles of cost accounting and personnel management.

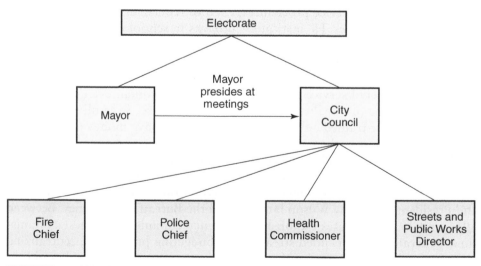

FIGURE 4.2 Weak Mayor Government.

The business model required an executive with sufficient authority to run the company. Applying this insight to city government, advocates of reform lobbied for city charters that would reduce the number of elected officials and create a "strong mayor" with authority to appoint most city officials and veto legislation. In 1899, the National Municipal League published a model city charter that contained charts much like the one displayed in Figure 4.3. In this scheme, the mayor presides at the top of a hierarchical chain of command with clear lines of authority and accountability. A city council of five to nine members, each elected at-large, replaces the boards of aldermen that were typical of the time. Reformers thought that with this arrangement in place, voters would be able to clearly understand who was in charge of the affairs of the city, and thus hold them accountable for how well they did their jobs.

Now that the reformers felt confident they knew what to do if they won control of the cities, they launched a crusade for "home rule." They asked state legislatures to grant the cities the authority to set their own tax rates, regulate their internal affairs, and decide how and where to provide services. In this way, the cities would be free to realize the full potential offered by their new and efficient governmental structures. At its state constitutional convention in 1875, Missouri became the first state to write a general home rule charter for its cities, although the legislature retained control of St. Louis's police budget. The state still retained ultimate legal power, but Missouri's cities would not have to seek approval for their every action, as long as they stayed within their broad charter authority. Cities were now permitted to hire new sanitation workers and firefighters, for example, or build a new street without consulting with members of the legislature. The general charter spelled out the range of services to be provided, but not such details as salary levels, the location of firehouses and streets, and the number of city employees. The home rule movement, pushed hard by

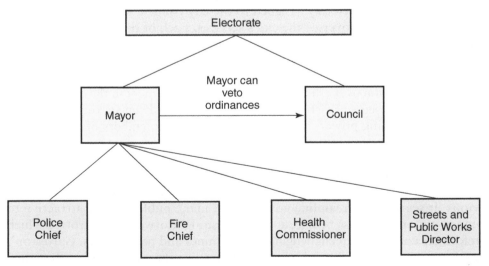

FIGURE 4.3 Strong Mayor Government.

the National Municipal League and other organizations, quickly spread across the country. By 1925, 14 states had granted home rule to their cities, and today virtually all cities are governed by "home rule" charters.

Commission and Manager Government

Galveston, Texas, established the first municipal government derived explicitly from the model of the business corporation. In 1894, Galveston's business and professional leaders organized a campaign to elect business leaders to the most significant positions in the city government. The following year, a coalition of city council members and business leaders secured a charter amendment from the Texas legislature that abolished wards and created at-large elections. To the reformers' great disappointment, however, this new election procedure did not result in the sweeping changes its sponsors had hoped for. Over the next few years, a few businessmen were elected to the city council, but on important matters they were regularly outvoted.[54]

A natural disaster provided the pretext for business and corporate leaders to assert themselves decisively. On September 8, 1900, hurricane-driven waves breached the seawall protecting Galveston, and the inrushing sea washed over the town, killing 6,000 of the town's 37,000 residents. Half of the property in the city was destroyed. In an effort to rebuild the city, business leaders organized the Deepwater Committee and set out to gain control of local government. The members of the committee argued that if "a municipality is largely a business corporation,"[55] then it follows that it should be run like one, with the voters acting in the role of stockholders and a board of directors—an elected commission—responsible to them. Guided by this principle, the Deepwater Committee drafted an outline of a commission form of government and asked the state legislature to approve it. Their proposal was promptly enacted.

The Galveston Plan created a five-member commission that exercised the legislative powers previously assigned to the city council, as well as the administrative authority to oversee the city's services. Each of the commissioners assumed responsibility for a department of government. Such a concentration of authority seemed entirely appropriate, and even necessary, in the context of the emergency that followed the hurricane. Initially, the commission was even granted jurisdiction over criminal and civil law enforcement in the city, although a state court subsequently struck down this authority. Even so, the commission exercised sweeping powers. Headed by five leading members of the business community, Galveston initiated a vigorous rebuilding program, and, in the process, the city reduced its debts and restored and improved public services.

The notable success of Galveston's experiment in commission government gained national attention. The new idea spread like wildfire. Its appeal was obvious: It seemed to streamline government, make public service attractive to upper- and middle-class people, and offer a straightforward plan around which reformers could rally in challenging the machines and party bosses. Galveston's performance so impressed business leaders in other Texas cities that they pressed the Texas legislature to allow them to follow Galveston's example and install commission government. By 1907, seven major cities in the state had imitated Galveston's charter, including Houston, Dallas, and Fort Worth.

In 1908, voters in Des Moines, Iowa, gave the commission concept a shot in the arm by placing it within an entire package of reform. In addition to a five-member commission, Des Moines adopted the initiative, referendum, and recall; nonpartisan and at-large elections; and a civil service system. This package, which reformers labeled the Des Moines Plan, caught on rapidly. The Plan was adopted by 23 cities in different parts of the nation in 1909 and by 66 cities in 1910.[56] By September 1915, at least 465 cities were governed by a commission, and by 1920 about 20 percent of all cities with populations of more than 5,000 had adopted the model.[57] During these years, a few states made commission government compulsory for their cities, and in most states it became an option for cities that wanted to adopt it.

Reformers promoted the Des Moines Plan as a cure for every ill, sure to bring less taxation, more efficient public services, and a "better class of men" to government. In city after city, it was promoted as a means of making government more businesslike. Accordingly, chambers of commerce and other organized business groups became the strongest backers. The Commercial Club succeeded in pushing through Des Moines's new charter in 1907, although, interestingly, the first commissioners voted into office represented a working-class slate—much to the dismay of the charter's sponsors.[58] In Pennsylvania, the Pittsburgh Chamber of Commerce organized a statewide convention of business organizations to persuade the state legislature to require cities above a minimum size to adopt commission government. The coalition of bankers, merchants, and manufacturers secured the legislation in 1913.[59]

Despite its appeal, commission government had some problems. To its critics, its worst feature was that it did not fit the business model faithfully enough. A commission was not truly like a board of directors because commissioners engaged in both policymaking and administration. Because each of the commissioners headed a separate administrative department, they often refused to cooperate. Sometimes they built personal empires by handing out jobs and contracts, thereby acting a lot like the machine politicians they had replaced. It was hard for the mayor to prevent such practices because each of the commissioners was a "first among equals." This defect was the chief complaint of the secretary of the National Short Ballot Association, Richard S. Childs. Noting that commission government was "an accident, not a plan" (referring to the Galveston emergency that brought it into being), he addressed the problem of having five coequal executives: "The theory that the commission as a whole controlled its members in their departmental activities became neglected—the commission could not discipline a recalcitrant member."[60] Childs noted that commissioners typically ignored one another ("You attend to your department and quit criticizing mine") or exchanged favors and support ("I'll vote for your appropriation if you'll vote for mine").[61] This was not the model of efficiency that reformers like Childs had in mind.

The crusaders for reform responded to these criticisms by putting forward a new idea: place administrative authority into the hands of a professional manager specifically trained for the job. As elected officials, the mayor and the council would continue to make policy decisions, but the city manager would be responsible for the day-to-day operations of government. "The reform leaders realized that technical ability could not be expected of elected officials, and they hoped that a strong mayor could appoint trained technicians and administrators as department heads."[62] In this way, the reformers hoped, the city manager would bring to local government administrative expertise and accountability.[63]

This time, the reformers intended to get the business model right. In 1913, the National Municipal League issued a report (written by Childs) recommending that commission government be abandoned in favor of the city manager plan. Only six years later, in 1919, the league amended its model charter to recommend that cities adopt the city manager form of government. In only a few years the city manager plan replaced the commission model, and by the 1920s, the commission form was regarded as a failed experiment.

Between 1908 and 1912, several Midwestern cities hired city managers. The idea caught on in earnest when Dayton, Ohio, changed its city charter. As in Galveston, a natural disaster served as the catalyst. In 1913, John H. Patterson, president of the National Cash Register Company, persuaded the Dayton Chamber of Commerce to draft a new city charter. The chamber established the Bureau of Municipal Research to promote the idea, and the Committee of One Hundred, a group funded by the business community, sponsored a slate of candidates. By organizing a campaign ward by ward, the business slate put several Republican candidates on the city council, but they were still outnumbered by politicians representing the local Democratic machine. It appeared that charter reform had failed to accomplish its purpose. Two months later, however, the Miami River flooded the town, and the municipal government was slow to organize emergency services. Patterson turned his factory into a shelter for flood victims, and virtually overnight he became the town's leading citizen. Business leaders pressed the state governor to put Patterson in charge of an effort to draw up a new city charter. A few months later, the committee headed by Patterson recommended the city manager model, and the voters soon registered their approval.[64]

The results were spectacular. The new government improved public services, retired most of the city debt, instituted new budget-making procedures, enforced a uniform eight-hour day for city employees, and established civil service. Because of its widely advertised success the Dayton Plan, with its city manager system, quickly became the nation's most popular "good reform" reform model. Although rarely instituted in the big industrial cities, it became the most common form of government in smaller cities around the country. In the five years before 1918, some 87 cities adopted manager charters, and 153 did so between 1918 and 1923. During the next five years, 84 more cities were added to the list.[65]

The city manager plan became popular because it appeared to be the best expression of the reformers' desire to find an objective, nonpolitical, efficient way to run local government. Almost all arguments for reform were founded upon analogies to business organizations. The *Dallas News* promoted the manager plan in 1930 by asking, "Why not run Dallas itself on a business schedule by business methods under businessmen? . . . The city manager plan is after all only a business management plan. The city manager is the executive of a corporation under a board of directors. Dallas is the corporation. It is as simple as that. Vote for it."[66]

Despite the references to the business model, it was hard to hide the fact that the city manager plan was designed not only to bring efficient government, but also to ensure the election of a different class of people who would insulate government from the influence of the Great Unwashed. A few participants in the reform crusades recognized the issue this raised about democratic processes. A delegate to the 1913 meeting of the League of Kansas Municipalities, after listening to his colleagues orate about the necessity of treating the city as a business, protested that "a city is more than a business corporation" and "good health is more important than a low tax rate."[67] However, the vast social chasm dividing municipal reformers from the rest of the urban populace made such sentiments anathema to most reformers.

Reformers made ambitious claims about the benefits to be realized by adopting businesslike models of government. Without doubt some of their promises were overblown. Studies have shown that the adoption of city manager government had little, if any, effect on the level of city expenditures.[68] Machine and reform cities taxed at about the same rate and spent similar amounts on key public services. The major difference between them was that they distributed services and other valuable governmental benefits to different constituencies. Reform governments tended to neglect lower-income neighborhoods so that they could reward their supporters in more affluent parts of the city. They built libraries, increased services to homeowners (such as free refuse collection), and zoned land to maximize new housing developments. Above all, they promoted policies that benefited downtown businesses and corporations. Bureaucratic rules made it easy to control the distribution of rewards, as well. In the 1980s, for instance, citizens in the city of New Haven found that, "acquiring delivery of some services like tree pruning or waste disposal required attaining a series of permits from offices open at irregular, infrequent times."[69]

Bureaucratic systems often make things difficult for workers who do not have flexible hours and for people not skilled at filling in forms and following formal rules. Wouldn't it be a lot easier if a person could just tell their local alderman what they need? As convenient as that might seem, there are disadvantages for that system, too. Political appointees tend to be less professional, insiders get better treatment than anyone else, and some level of petty corruption is more or less inevitable. Whatever its frustrations, government by bureaucracy is generally less biased than any system based on political favors.[70]

Did Reform Kill the Machines?

Admirers of the reform crusades always assumed the party machines died out because the reformers succeeded in cleaning up local politics. A large number of machines had short lives of only a decade or so before they went into slow decline or the politicians that ran them suddenly lost their grip. Between 1909 and

1918, machines fell apart in Dayton, Ohio; Detroit and Grand Rapids, Michigan; Los Angeles; Portland, Oregon; Milwaukee; Minneapolis; San Francisco; and Seattle. In each case, some variety of reform was adopted and civil service systems changed hiring rules.[71] Most of the machines that survived this era died by the mid-1950s, if not before, including New York's Tammany Hall. By World War II, it would have been impossible to find a city left completely untouched by reform. Voter registration was universal and civil service hiring was nearly so; at-large, nonpartisan elections were used in most cities. Even in the big industrial cities where reform was generally less successful, election rules underwent some degree of change. Boston, New Orleans, and Pittsburgh had switched to at-large elections; Memphis and Detroit had adopted both at-large and nonpartisan elections. Denver, New Orleans, Philadelphia, Cleveland, and Pittsburgh also became nonpartisan before World War II.[72]

There can be little doubt that these reforms made a difference, but it is also clear that they did not "cause" the big-city machines to collapse. The scholarly evidence confirms the observation that "The adoption of structural reform was not sufficient to eliminate or preclude the appearance of machine politics."[73] Machines were often adept at adjusting to the new rules of the game. In 15 cities, machines actually benefitted from strong mayor and city manager systems.[74] The reformers accomplished their goal of making someone accountable to voters, but the voters did not always respond as the reformers hoped. After Cleveland adopted the city manager plan in the 1920s, the machine put a party hack into the post.[75] Richard J. Daley built his powerful machine in Chicago, beginning with his election in 1955, despite the fact that the city's elections were nonpartisan and the vast majority of its employees were civil servants.

In most cases, the machines died because they were unable to adapt to the population and economic transformations that were changing the cities. Over time the immigrant base began to shrink. Irish immigration dropped sharply after the turn of the century; the bulk of new immigrants came from Italy and Eastern Europe. The Irish had been the mainstay groups for most machines, and, as their numbers declined, machines found their support gradually eroding. If they were to continue to exist at all, machines would have to adapt to the times. In New York City, Fiorello LaGuardia put together a coalition of Italian and Jewish voters to defeat Tammany Hall's candidate in 1933, and in the process he built his own, more inclusive version of machine politics. In Chicago, Anton Cermak transformed the machine by bringing Italians, Jews, Czechs, and Poles into its orbit. James Michael Curley, Boston's longtime boss, lasted longer than most other bosses, probably because the Irish were such a dominant force in the city, but he was finally defeated for reelection in 1949.[76] When he was elected mayor in 1955, Richard J. Daley was able to keep the Chicago machine from fracturing by adding middle-class white voters and the downtown business elite to its traditional base in the ethnic neighborhoods, and by rebuilding ties to African American politicians who could deliver the vote in the sprawling black-belt neighborhoods of south and west Chicago.

The second decisive blow to the machines occurred when their immigrant supporters began moving up the economic ladder. As immigrants joined the ranks of the middle class, the petty favors and patronage offered by the machines carried less weight, both in material and symbolic terms, than they had in an earlier era. After World War II, immigrants and the children of immigrants joined the mass movement to the suburbs. Precinct captains saw their neighbors moving out of the city, and sometimes they moved, too. Machines were not generally successful in reaching out to the new generation of immigrants, poor whites, and blacks who streamed into the cities during and after World War II.[77]

The Reform Legacy

Although the municipal reform movement has long since passed, the reforms adopted in that era still reverberate throughout the American political system. Rules governing elections and representation continue to be battlegrounds because they involve disputes over the role of government in determining who will reap the benefits of public policy.[78] Conflicts over the "rules of the game" were rekindled in the 1960s and in the decades to follow because of clear evidence that racial and ethnic minorities were consistently underrepresented at all levels of the American political system. The Voting Rights Act of 1965 was enacted as a way of incorporating blacks into the national political system. Federal registrars were sent into jurisdictions to register blacks, and in some cases, Hispanics and Native Americans. At the local level, lawsuits were filed in the federal courts challenging the electoral rules inherited from the Progressive Era. Groups such as the National Association for the Advancement of Colored People (NAACP) and the United Latin American Citizens sought to invalidate at-large electoral systems, claiming that they violated the Fourteenth Amendment guarantee of equal protection of the laws. They also asked the courts to review the boundaries of state legislative and congressional districts because, they claimed, many of them had been expressly drawn to place hurdles in the way of minority participation. The courts sometimes upheld challenges to at-large elections but issued inconsistent rulings on the constitutionality of legislative boundaries drawn to dilute minority representation (a practice known as racial gerrymandering).[79] The intensity of the battles fought in and out of the courts serves as a reminder that the rules of governing participation in the political system are as crucial today as they were during the reform crusades 100 years ago.

Research has consistently shown that at-large elections reduce the influence of racial and ethnic minorities.[80] In response to the accumulating evidence and over the strenuous objections of the Reagan administration, in 1982 Congress amended the 1965 Voting Rights Act to make it easier for minorities to challenge local election practices. Congress passed the amendments, contained in Section 2 of the new act, in reaction to a 1980 U.S. Supreme Court decision that had required litigants to demonstrate an *intent* to discriminate before an election rule could be declared invalid.[81] In Section 2, Congress specified that challenges to local election rules could meet a much easier standard than before: They would be considered illegal if they merely had the *effect* of underrepresenting minorities in elected positions.

On June 30, 1986, the Supreme Court handed down a landmark decision, *Thornburg v. Gingles*, interpreting the 1982 amendments.[82] This case came to the Court after the U.S. Justice Department brought suit against the state of North Carolina, arguing that several multimember state legislative districts in North Carolina violated the voting rights of blacks because in those districts white candidates invariably won all seats.[83] The Court ordered North Carolina to create single-member districts and laid down standards for deciding when at-large and multimember district systems would be considered suspect: (1) when litigants could show it would be possible to create at least one single-member electoral district that would give a minority group an electoral majority; (2) when it could also be demonstrated that the minority group seeking more representation was politically cohesive; and (3) when it could be shown that whites had previously voted as a bloc to prevent minority candidates from being elected.[84]

At-large district systems have since been successfully challenged throughout the United States. In 1986, after finding that at-large elections made it impossible for African American candidates to win, a federal court ordered several Alabama counties to institute single-member districts for electing county commissioners.[85] In a 1987 lawsuit filed against the city of Springfield, Illinois, a federal judge ordered the city to expand the number of its electoral districts from five to ten. Because only 10.8 percent of the city's population was African American, the expansion to 10 districts was necessary if any one of them was to contain a majority of black voters.[86] (Interestingly, a different federal judge did not require this solution in a similar suit filed against the Springfield Park District.[87]) In the same year, the city of Danville, Illinois, expanded its city council to 14 members elected from seven wards after a federal judge threw out its previous system in which a three-member commission and a mayor were all elected at-large.[88]

The numerous court decisions arising from the 1982 amendments to the Voting Rights Act produced an extraordinary amount of confusion about local election rules. All through the 1980s and into the 1990s, court decisions called into question the electoral systems of hundreds of cities, counties, townships, and special districts. To preempt court action, some local governments voluntarily redrew district and ward boundaries to facilitate minority representation. Frequently, this required devising districts with tortuously meandering boundaries.[89] The attempt to redraw boundaries, however, is not a solution available to every city. It may, in fact, be available only to those whose minority populations live in highly segregated circumstances rather than in several distinct but unconnected neighborhoods, because in segregated cities it is easier to draw boundaries that seem coherent. In a series of decisions beginning in 1993, the U.S. Supreme Court invalidated congressional district boundaries that did not meet standards of "compactness, contiguity, and respect for political subdivisions."[90]

Although the courts seemed to be enforcing the compactness standard for a time, it did not necessarily signal an end to all redistricting meant to achieve representation for particular racial or ethnic groups.[91] The Court's standard could be met simply by increasing the number of legislative districts; smaller districts to ensure that even small minority neighborhoods could exercise influence in some of them. For several years, it was unclear whether there was some upper limit to the number of districts a local government might have to draw to achieve the equitable representation of minorities. By 1987, however, it seemed likely (despite the city of Springfield case) that, under normal circumstances, the number of districts already existing would be left alone.[92]

The courts took up more technical considerations as well. For example, in drawing legislative boundaries was it sufficient to count the entire minority population, or only the voting-age minority population? Most courts decided that a majority voting-age population was required.[93] Could two or more minority groups be combined so that the two together constituted the majority of voters in a district? Only, the courts said, if it could be shown that the groups were politically cohesive—and research makes it clear, for example, that blacks and Latinos do not generally vote similarly.[94]

In 1991, the issue of minority representation was placed at the forefront of the political infighting over congressional reapportionment required as a result of the decennial census of 1990. Because state legislatures approve the boundaries for congressional districts, party control at the state level was crucial. In 1990, there were 37 blacks and Latinos in Congress. In 1992, as a result of redistricting, 19 additional blacks and Latinos were elected to Congress. In many states, it was Republicans, working with the Congressional Black Caucus, who promoted the formation of districts safe for minority candidates. This move not only increased the number of minority representatives in Congress, but also the number of districts where a Republican candidate was competitive.[95] Complicated gamesmanship of this sort became a standard feature of legislative apportioning.

In June 1991, the Supreme Court ruled that judicial elections in Louisiana and Texas violated the 1982 Voting Rights Act because at-large election districts diluted the electoral strength of minorities. A flurry of lawsuits followed that challenged election procedures for state and local judges. Traditionally, nearly all state and local judges have been elected at-large—that is, multiple positions are filled in each electoral district. This perhaps explains why, as of 1985, only 3.8 percent of judges in state courts were African American and only 1.2 percent were Latino.[96]

The court decisions brought a revolution in local electoral practices. In 1981, 66.5 percent of cities used at-large electoral systems. By 1986, in a space of only five years, the proportion had fallen to 60.4 percent.[97] This very significant change can be traced to research demonstrating that changing from at-large to district elections did, as anticipated, improve the representation of blacks and Latinos.[98] Cities almost everywhere came under pressure to institute a ward system or to redraw existing ward and district boundaries. In 1991, for example, African American leaders in St. Louis threatened to go to court to force a redrawing of the boundaries of the city's 28 wards. At the time, 11 of the 28 aldermen were African American, but a new ward map would have made it mathematically possible to give half of the wards a majority of African American voters.[99]

Court cases in the 1990s seemed to signal that except in extreme circumstances the courts wanted to get out of the business of telling state and local governments how to draw their electoral districts. In an interesting twist, the courts also indicated that electoral districts that were gerrymandered to excessively increase or decrease minority representation now would be treated as suspect. In *Shaw v. Reno* (1993), the U.S. Supreme Court ruled that a very oddly shaped district in North Carolina made up almost entirely of blacks was illegally gerrymandered, calling such districts "political apartheid." Speaking for the majority, Sandra Day O'Connor wrote, "When a district obviously is created solely to effectuate the perceived common interests of one racial group, elected officials are more likely to believe that their primary obligation is to represent only the members of that group, rather than the constituency as a whole."[100] The Court left the door open for modest attempts to take race into account in redistricting by declaring that race could not be the "predominant factor" in drawing district boundaries, and in 1996 it declared that each case would be decided on its own merits and that minority districting might be permissible if the boundaries were sufficiently compact and coherent.[101] These rulings had the effect of discouraging the drawing of tortuous boundaries but otherwise did not change the status quo significantly. Over the subsequent years, courts have been very reluctant to take on such issues.

After the municipal reforms of the Progressive Era, it took more than half a century for questions about representation and local democracy to resurface as a contentious political issue. The years since the Voting Rights Act of 1965 may be properly regarded, therefore, as the first reform period since the Progressive Era to be aimed specifically at local electoral politics. It should be emphasized that the recent reform movement was mobilized as a result of the civil rights era of the 1960s, which asked fundamental questions about the fairness of the electoral systems put in place decades before. The new era of reform has increased representation for African Americans and for Latinos; their new-found influence has brought important changes in public policies.[102]

The Battles Continue

Bitter conflicts over the rules of the game still go on, although the main battleground has shifted from electoral districts to voter registration rules. Especially since the razor-thin and controversial presidential election decision in 2000, Republicans and Democrats have become locked in a protracted struggle over voter registration requirements. Both parties have a lot at stake. As in the Progressive Era, strict voter registration rules tend to reduce participation for minorities, the poor, and others who find it more difficult to negotiate the bureaucratic labyrinth. The outcome of the presidential election of 2000 was decided before Election Day in the state of Florida, when the Republican secretary of state invalidated the registration of more than 70,000 black voters because of technical problems with their applications, such as a misspelled name or failure to change address. Several hundred were invalidated mistakenly because their names matched those on a list of convicted felons. These actions proved to be decisive; ultimately, the election was determined by a little more than 500 voters.

Both parties took the lesson to heart. Democrats redoubled efforts to make it easier to register and to mobilize voter registration drives. The Republican Party fought such reforms in a state-by-state skirmish. When immigration became a contentious national issue, their attempts to impose stricter rules of registration began to bear fruit. In 2008, a major battle erupted over whether states should impose proof of citizenship as a condition of registration, and a photo ID as a condition to vote. Previously, in most of the 25 states that required a form of identification at the polls, identification could come in several forms, including utility bills, pay checks, driver's licenses, or student or military IDs. The wave of new laws were proposed that would require passports, birth certificates, or naturalization papers as a condition of voting. Democrats charged that these proposals were thinly veiled attempts to discourage low-income and minority voters from coming to the polls; Republicans countered by asserting they were merely measures to reduce voting fraud.[103]

It is hazardous to take any of these claims at face value. It is clear that conflicts over voter participation reflect the political interests of the antagonists, a point driven home by controversies over the registration of college students in the period leading up to the 2008 presidential election. In September 2008, a local elections registrar in Virginia (a Republican) announced that Virginia Tech students who registered to vote in Blacksburg might lose scholarships or become subject to Virginia state taxes if they listed their campus as their voting address. His announcement clearly contradicted a U.S. Supreme Court decision granting students the right to vote where they go to school, but it nevertheless provoked confusion on the Virginia Tech campus. As it turns out, the Virginia case was not an exception. Eleven states discourage student voting by refusing to treat P.O. boxes and dormitories as legitimate mailing addresses for determining a permanent residency. Others have specified that out-of-state driver's licenses cannot be used to vote. All of these cases virtually invite election officials to throw out votes in close elections, as occurred in Florida in 2000.[104]

In the two years following the 2010 elections, 180 new voting restrictions were introduced in 41 states, and Republican state legislators have continued to support new voting restrictions. In January 2013, the Virginia Senate passed a redistricting map designed to reduce Democratic representation by at least eight seats. The map was defeated in the House but set a tone on voting rights for the legislative session.[105] The first three months of 2013 saw 55 new voting restrictions proposed in 30 states. At the end of March 2013, Republican lawmakers unveiled a new idea to cut the early-voting window in half, thereby eliminating same-day voter registration and Sunday voting. Critics argue that Republican policymakers are determined to place obstacles between voters and the ballot box as a way of reducing voting participation by minorities.[106]

Republicans in North Carolina were particularly active in proposing voter restrictions in 2013. Senate Bill 721 proposed reducing early voting to six days, eliminating same-day voter registration, and imposing a five-year delay on the eligibility of persons with a past felony conviction to vote and new voter ID restrictions.[107] Florida had already taken the lead in denying ex-felons voting rights, After taking office in 2011, Governor Rick Scott eliminated the automatic restoration of voting rights for nonviolent ex-offenders. The African American population in Florida stood at 16.5 percent in 2010, but black inmates made up 31.5 percent of the state prison population. Citing such statistics, activists asserted that Florida's rules had the effect (and probably the intent), of suppressing the minority vote. Howard Simon, the executive director of ACLU Florida stated, "this is one of the few government programs that has worked precisely as it was designed, namely to try to suppress the vote of as many African Americans as possible. It was designed that way in 1868, and it continues to have that effect in 2013."[108]

In 2013, the Commonwealth Institute estimated that 869,000 registered voters in Virginia would lack the new forms of identification required by new voter ID bills. Whereas in the 2012 election, voters in Virginia were able to vote by showing a form of ID from a variety of sources such as a utility bill or a concealed handgun permit, the new law restricted acceptable ID to a drivers license, passport, state-issued ID card, a student photo ID or an employee photo ID.[109] Studies have shown that restrictions like these reduce voting turnout for young people and minority voters.[110] A report by political scientists at the University of Chicago and Washington University found that, "17.3 percent of black youth and 8.1 percent of Latino youth said their lack of adequate ID kept them from voting, compared with just 4.7 percent of white youth."[111] Even in states with no voter ID laws, 65.5 percent of black youth were asked to show ID at the polls, compared to 42.8 percent of white youth.[112]

In 2012, Viviette Applewhite, a white 93-year-old female and former hotel housekeeper in Philadelphia, had her pocketbook stolen in a supermarket, thereby losing her only form of identification, her Social Security card. When she was not allowed to vote in the presidential election she initiated a lawsuit against the state of Pennsylvania. In her view "They're trying to stop black people from voting so Obama will not get re-elected."[113]

Students have also been affected by the proposed restrictions. In North Carolina, Senate Bill 666, which was introduced in 2013, proposed a tax penalty for parents whose children registered to vote at a college address by stipulating that they would not be able to claim that child as a dependent for state income tax purposes. Bill 667 proposed that student voters who changed their voting registration would be required to register their new address within 60 days and pay local property taxes.

While advocates of restrictions like these asserted that the laws are designed to ensure the integrity of elections by preventing voter fraud, opponents point to the fact that nearly every state legislature that had passed voter ID laws was Republican-run, and that the constituencies which were most affected are new requirements tended to vote Democratic.[114] Whatever side one takes in such controversies, it is clear that voting rules are not (and cannot be) neutral, and that they can determine the outcome of elections. The National Conference of State Legislatures estimated that more than 15 states could have stricter ID requirements heading into the 2016 presidential elections.[115]

How can it be, more than a century after voter registration and polling rules were first enacted, that issues of political participation continue to be so divisive? The era of municipal reform suggests the answer. Reform is always motivated by political goals and purposes, however noble the stated principles may seem. In politics, the rules governing participation matter more than almost anything else because they determine who will govern, and therefore who will benefit. Accordingly, they will always be the object of conflict and contention.

Endnotes

1. William L. Riordon, *Plunkitt of Tammany Hall* (New York: Dutton, 1963), p. 17.
2. James Bryce, *The American Commonwealth*, 3rd ed., vol. 1 (New York: Macmillan, 1924), p. 642.
3. H. E. Deming, *The Government of American Cities: A Program of Democracy* (London and New York: Putnam, 1909), p. 194.
4. Quoted in Michael B. Katz, *School Reform: Past and Present* (Boston: Little, Brown, 1971).
5. Josiah Strong, in *Our Country*, ed. Jurgen Herbst (Cambridge, MA: Belknap Press, Harvard University Press, 1963; first published in 1886), p. 55.
6. Samuel P. Hays, *The Response to Industrialism, 1885–1914* (Chicago: University of Chicago Press, 1957), p. 73.
7. James Weinstein, *The Corporate Ideal in the Liberal State, 1900–1918* (Boston: Beacon Press, 1968).
8. Melvin G. Holli, "Urban Reform in the Progressive Era," in *The Progressive Era*, ed. Louis L. Gould (Syracuse, NY: Syracuse University Press, 1974), p. 137.
9. Frank Mann Stewart, *A Half Century of Municipal Reform: The History of the National Municipal League* (Berkeley: University of California Press, 1950), Chapter 1.
10. Samuel Haber, *Efficiency and Uplift: Scientific Management in the Progressive Era, 1890–1920* (Chicago: University of Chicago Press, 1964), p. 99.
11. Andrew D. White, "City Affairs Are Not Political," originally titled "The Government of American Cities," *Forum* (December, 1890), pp. 213–216; reprinted in Dennis Judd and Paul Kantor, eds., *The Politics of Urban America*, 2nd ed. (New York: Addison Wesley Longman, 2002).
12. Amy Bridges, "Winning the West to Municipal Reform," *Urban Affairs Quarterly* 27, no. 4 (June 1992): 511.
13. Arthur T. Hadley, *The Empty Polling Booth* (Upper Saddle River, NJ: Prentice Hall, 1978), p. 61.
14. Alexander B. Callow Jr., ed., *The City Boss in America* (New York: Oxford University Press, 1976), p. 158.
15. William T. Stead, *If Christ Came to Chicago* (Chicago: Laird and Lee, 1894), pp. 56–57.
16. Lloyd Wendt and Herman Kogan, *Bosses in Lusty Chicago* (Bloomington: Indiana University Press, 1967), p. 169.
17. Allan F. Davis, *Spearheads for Reform* (New York: Oxford University Press, 1967), pp. 156–162.
18. William D. Miller, *Mr. Crump of Memphis* (Baton Rouge: Louisiana State University Press, 1964), p. 74.
19. Bruce M. Stave, *The New Deal and the Last Hurrah: Pittsburgh Machine Politics* (Pittsburgh: University of Pittsburgh Press, 1970), p. 77.
20. Ernest S. Griffith, *A History of American City Government: The Conspicuous Failure, 1870–1900* (New York: Praeger, 1974), p. 71.

21. Richard S. Childs, *Civic Victories: The Story of an Unfinished Revolution* (New York: Harper and Brothers, 1952), p. 299. In this passage, Childs was referring to the short ballot reform in conjunction with nonpartisanship. The short ballot reformers advocated fewer elected officials so voters would not be confused and elected officials would be held accountable to voters.
22. Edward C. Banfield, ed., *Urban Government: A Reader in Administration and Politics* (New York: Free Press, 1969), p. 275. Selection from Brand Whitlock, *Forty Years of It*, preface by Allen White (New York and London: Appleton, 1925; first published in 1914).
23. Haber, *Efficiency and Uplift*, pp. 99–101.
24. White, "City Affairs Are Not Political," pp. 213–216.
25. Griffith, *A History of American City Government*, p. 130.
26. Amy Bridges, *Morning Glories: Municipal Reform in the Southwest* (Princeton, NJ: Princeton University Press, 1997), Chapter 8.
27. Willis D. Hawley, *Nonpartisan Elections and the Case for Party Politics* (New York: Wiley, 1973), p. 14. Subsequent information on the use of nonpartisan elections is from Hawley, pp. 15–18.
28. Weinstein, *The Corporate Ideal*, p. 109. Subsequent information on the Dayton election is from Weinstein.
29. Samuel P. Hays, "The Politics of Reform in Municipal Government in the Progressive Era," in *Social Change and Urban Politics: Readings*, ed. Daniel N. Gordon (Englewood Cliffs, NJ: Prentice Hall, 1973), pp. 107–127.
30. Bridges, *Morning Glories*, p. 146.
31. Ibid., Chapter 7.
32. Ibid., pp. 144–145.
33. Quoted in Holli, "Urban Reform in the Progressive Era," p. 144.
34. Ibid., p. 47.
35. Ibid., p. 45.
36. Nancy Burns and Gerald Gamm, "Creatures of the State: State Politics and Local Government 1871–1921," *Urban Affairs Review* 33, no. 1 (September 1997): 90.
37. Ibid., p. 86.
38. Scott Allard, Nancy Burns, and Gerald Gamm, "Representing Urban Interests: The Local Politics of State Legislatures," *Studies in American Political Development* 12 (Fall 1998): 294; see also Nancy Burns, Laura Evans, Gerald Gamm, and Corrine McGonnaughy, "The Local Politics of State Legislatures," paper delivered at the annual meeting of the Midwest Political Science Association (April 25, 2002).
39. Allard, Burns, and Gamm, "Representing Urban Interests," p. 68.
40. Ibid., p. 76.
41. Frederick Winslow Taylor, *The Principles of Scientific Management* (New York: Harper and Brothers, 1919; first published in 1911).
42. Ibid., p. 140.
43. Ibid., p. 7.
44. Haber, *Efficiency and Uplift*, p. 56.
45. Harold A. Stone, Don K. Price, Kathryn H. Stone, *City Manager Government in the United States: A Review After Twenty-Five Years* (Chicago: Public Administration Service, 1940), p. 5.
46. Henry Brueré, *The New City Government: A Discussion of Municipal Administration Based on a Survey of Ten Commission-Governed Cities* (Upper Saddle River, NJ: Prentice Hall, 1912).
47. Ibid., p. v.

48. Ibid., pp. 27–29.
49. Robert A. Caro, *The Power Broker: Robert Moses and the Fall of New York* (New York: Oxford University Press, 1969), p. 75.
50. Taylor, *The Principles of Scientific Management*, p. 20.
51. Melvin B. Holli, *Reform in Detroit: Hazen S. Pingree and Urban Politics* (New York: Oxford University Press, 1969), p. 167.
52. Haber, *Efficiency and Uplift*, p. 115.
53. Stone, Price, and Stone, *City Manager Government*, p. 4.
54. Martin J. Schiesl, *The Politics of Municipal Reform: Municipal Administration and Reform in America, 1880–1920* (Berkeley: University of California Press, 1977), pp. 134–135.
55. Quoted in Weinstein, *The Corporate Ideal*, p. 96.
56. Clinton R. Woodruff, ed., *City Government by Commission* (Upper Saddle River, NJ: Prentice Hall, 1911), pp. 293–294.
57. Childs, *Civic Victories*, p. 138.
58. Hays, "The Politics of Reform," p. 116.
59. Weinstein, *The Corporate Ideal*, p. 99.
60. Childs, *Civic Victories*, p. 137.
61. Ibid.
62. Stone, Price, and Stone, *City Manager Government*, p. 5.
63. Griffith, *A History of American City Government*, p. 167.
64. Ibid., p. 166; Schiesl, *The Politics of Municipal Reform*, pp. 175–176.
65. Weinstein, *The Corporate Ideal*, pp. 115–116.
66. Quoted in Stone, Price, and Stone, *City Manager Government*, p. 27.
67. Quoted in Weinstein, *The Corporate Ideal*, pp. 106, 107.
68. Anirudh V. S. Ruhil, "Structural Change and Fiscal Flows: A Framework for Analyzing the Effects Of Urban Events," *Urban Affairs Review* 38, no. 3 (January 2003): 396–416.
69. Jessica Trounstine, *Political Monopolies in American Cities: The Rise and Fall of Bosses and Reformers* (Chicago: University of Chicago Press, 2008), pp. 162–163.
70. Ibid., p. 163.
71. Alan DiGaetano, "Urban Political Reform: Did It Kill the Machine?" *Journal of Urban History* 18, no. 1 (November 1991): 37–67.
72. Ibid.
73. Ibid.
74. Ibid.
75. Ibid., p. 67.
76. Ibid.
77. Steven P. Erie, *Rainbow's End: Irish-Americans and the Dilemmas of Urban Machine Politics, 1840–1985* (Berkeley: University of California Press, 1988).
78. Karen M. Kaufmann, *The Urban Voter: Group Conflict and Mayoral Voting Behavior in American Cities* (Ann Arbor: University of Michigan Press), p. 19.
79. Jay M. Shafritz, *The Dorsey Dictionary of American Government and Politics* (Homewood, IL: Dorsey Press, 1988), pp. 244–246. A legislative district is considered gerrymandered when it is drawn with tortuously meandering boundaries as a means of advancing the interests of a party or group. The term comes from a district drawn in Massachusetts in 1811 and signed into law by Governor Elbridge Gerry.
80. Robert L. Lineberry and Edmond P. Fowler, "Reformism and Public Policies in American Cities," *American Political Science Review* 61 (September 1967): 701–716; Chandler Davidson and George Korbel, "At-Large Elections and Minority Group

Representation: A Re-examination of Historical and Contemporary Evidence," *Journal of Politics* 43 (November 1981): 982–1005; Jerry L. Polinard, Robert D. Wrinkle, and Thomàs Longoria Jr., "The Impact of District Elections on the Mexican American Community: The Electoral Perspective," *Social Science Quarterly* 71, no. 3 (September 1991): 608–614; Richard L. Engstrom and Michael D. McDonald, "The Effect of At-Large versus District Elections on Racial Representation in U.S. Municipalities," in *Electoral Laws and Their Political Consequences*, ed. Bernard Grofman and Arend Liphart (New York: Agathon, 1986), pp. 203–225; W. E. Lyons and Malcolm E. Jewell, "Minority Representation and the Drawing of City Council Districts," *Urban Affairs Quarterly* 23 (1988): 432–447; Delbert Taebel, "Minority Representation on City Councils: The Impact of Structure on Blacks and Hispanics," *Social Science Quarterly* 59 (1982): 729–736; Jeffrey S. Zax, "Election Methods, Black and Hispanic City Council Membership," *Social Science Quarterly* 71 (1990): 339–355.

81. *City of Mobile v. Bolden*, 446 U.S. 55 (1980).

82. *Thornburg v. Gingles*, 106 S. Ct. 2752 (1986).

83. A multimember legislative district is just like an at-large system that covers an entire city. All candidates for city council seats must run in the same district; by contrast, in a ward system, a single alderman or council member represents each ward.

84. C. Robert Heath, "*Thornburg v. Gingles:* The Unresolved Issues," *National Civic Review* 79, no. 1 (January–February 1990): 50–71.

85. *Dillard v. Crenshaw County*, 649 F.Supp. at 289 (C.O. Ala. 1986).

86. *McNeal v. Springfield*, 658 F.Supp. at 1015, 1022 (C.D. Ill. 1987).

87. *McNeal v. Springfield Park District*, 851 F.2d at 937 (7th Cir. 1988).

88. *Derrickson v. City of Danville*, 87–2007 (C.D. Ill. 1987).

89. Joseph F. Zimmerman, "Alternative Local Electoral Systems," *National Civic Review* 79, no. 1 (January–February 1990): 23–36.

90. The quotation is from *Shaw v. Reno* 509 U.S. 630 (1993), commonly known as Shaw I. Other cases are *Miller v. Johnson*, 63 U.S.L.W. 4726 (1995); *Shaw v. Hunt*, 64 U.S.L.W. 4437 (known as Shaw II); *King v. Illinois Board of Elections*, 65 U.S.L.W. 3353 (1996); and *Abrams v. Johnson*, 65 U.S.L.W. 4478.

91. Carmen Cirincione, Thomas Darling, and Timothy O'Rourke, "Does the Supreme Court Have It Right?" paper delivered at the 1997 annual meeting of the American Political Science Association, Washington, DC (August 28–31, 1997).

92. Heath, "*Thornburg v. Gingles*," pp. 51–53.

93. Ibid., pp. 54–55.

94. Ibid., pp. 55–59; Charles S. Bullock III, "Symbolics or Substance: A Critique of the At-Large Election Controversy," *State and Local Government Review* 21, no. 3 (Fall 1989): 91–99.

95. Edward Blum and Roger Clegg, "The GOP's 2002 Racial Redistricting Dilemma," *Weekly Standard* (October 17, 1992).

96. Scott Armstrong, "Minorities Seek More Clout on the Bench," *Christian Science Monitor* (October 1, 1991), pp. 1–2.

97. International City Management Association, "Municipal Election Processes: The Impact on Minority Representation," *Baseline Data Report* 19, no. 6 (November–December 1987): 3–4.

98. Ibid., pp. 6–9; Polinard, Wrinkle, and Longoria, "The Impact of District Elections," pp. 608–614.

99. Tim O'Neil, "Blacks Want Half of City's Wards in Redistricting," *St. Louis Post-Dispatch* (June 8, 1991), p. 3A.

100. *Shaw v. Reno*, 92 357 (1993). In 1996 the Court rejected a somewhat redrawn 12th congressional district in North Carolina yet again.
101. *Miller v. Johnson*, 515 U.S. 900 (94 631), 1995; *Bush v. Vera*, 571 U.S. 900 (94 805), 1996.
102. Stephen Ansolabehere, Alan Gerber, and James Snyder, "Equal Votes, Equal Money: Court-Order Redistricting and Public Expenditures in the American States," *American Political Science Review* 96, no. 4 (December 2002): 767–777.
103. Ian Urbina, "Voter ID Battle Shifts to Proof of Citizenship," *New York Times* (May 12, 2008), www.nytimes.com/2008/05/12/us/politics/12vote.html.
104. Nikki Schwab, "Confusing Voter Registration Laws Could Affect Presidential Election," *U.S. News and World Report* (September 24, 2008), www.usnews.com/articles/campaign-2008/09/2008/09/24.
105. Ari Berman, "New Voter Suppression Efforts Prove the Voting Rights Act is Still Needed," *The Nation* (March 28, 2013), http://www.thenation.com/blog/173562/new-voter-suppression-efforts-prove-voting-rights-act-still-needed#.
106. Steve Benen, "Three Months, 30 States, 55 New Voting Restrictions, "*MSNBC: The Maddow Blog* (March 29, 2013), http://maddowblog.msnbc.com/_news/2013/03/29/17518283-three-months-30-states-55-new-voting-restrictions?lite.
107. Chris Kromm, "Art Pope-Backed Lawmaker Leads Push for New Voting Restrictions In NC," *The Institute for Southern Studies: Facing South* (April 3, 2013) http://www.southernstudies.org/2013/04/art-pope-backed-lawmaker-leads-push-for-new-voting-restrictions-in-nc.html.
108. Bill Kaczor, "Florida Leads in Denying Ex-Felons Voting Rights," *The Associated Press* (April 14, 2013), http://www.tallahassee.com/viewart/20130414/POLITICSPOLICY/304140029/Florida-leads-in-denying-ex-felons-voting-rights.
109. Berman, "New Voter Suppression Efforts Prove the Voting Rights Act is Still Needed."
110. Benen, "Three Months, 30 States, 55 New Voting Restrictions."
111. Berman, "New Voter Suppression Efforts Prove the Voting Rights Act is Still Needed."
112. Emily Schultheis, "Study Finds Voter ID Laws Hurt Young Minorities," *POLITICO* (March 12, 2013), http://www.politico.com/story/2013/03/study-finds-voter-id-laws-hurt-young-minorities-88773.html.
113. Ethan Bronner, "Legal Battles Erupt Over Tough Voter ID Laws," *The New York Times* (July 19, 2012).
114. Ibid.
115. Kathy Steinmetz, "A License to Vote? GOP Lawmakers Push Voter IDs," *TIME Magazine: Swampland* (April 4, 2013), http://swampland.time.com/2013/04/04/a-license-to-vote-gop-lawmakers-push-voter-ids/.

CHAPTER 5

Urban Voters and the Rise of a National Democratic Majority

City and Nation in the Twentieth Century

From today's perspective, it may be hard to imagine a time when there was political support for programs to help the cities. Today, voters living in central cities account for only about 10 percent of the national vote during presidential elections, and neither political party has much incentive to promote programs for such a small part of their base. Attention to the problems of the cities emerged at a time when the calculation was different. Voters living the industrial belt stretching from New England and through the Midwest and in some cities beyond were important to Democratic candidate Franklin D. Roosevelt's landslide victory in the presidential election of 1932, and for decades after, they continued to play a decisive role in determining the national balance of power between the two parties. The nation's 11 largest cities accounted for 27 percent of the popular vote in 1932 and a commanding majority in several of the industrial states with the largest numbers of electoral college votes.[1] For the first time in the nation's history, in the 1930s the politicians representing urban voters began to wield influence in national politics. Their loyalty to the Democratic Party fundamentally shaped American politics until the election of Republican Ronald Reagan in 1980.

Modern American liberalism, as expressed in the New Deal programs of the 1930s and the Great Society programs of the 1960s (these terms were borrowed from the campaign slogans of Presidents Roosevelt and Lyndon Baines Johnson), can be traced to the mobilization of the urban electorate during the years of the Great Depression. The alliance that became the foundation for the Democratic Party's ascendancy was made up of two wings, the urban North and the "solid South." Urban voters in northern cities voted Democratic because they benefited from the outpouring of programs enacted during the New Deal years. Legislation proposed by Roosevelt and supported by the big Democratic majorities in Congress granted powers to regulate the economy and to assist citizens in times of need. Urban working-class people were helped by labor legislation such as Section 7a of the National Industrial Recovery Act and the

110

OUTTAKE

Urban Ethnics Became a Mainstay of the Democratic Party

It is often supposed, mistakenly, that voters in the central cities have always voted Democratic. But until the New Deal years, about half of the party machines that ruled the cities were Republican. The Democratic machines did little to deliver votes to the national ticket, either, because their leaders had little connection to the national or even to the state party organizations. At the state level, party organizations were dominated by rural, not city, politicians. Machine politicians had gotten into politics through their precincts and wards, and they specialized in a politics of ethnicity and trade-offs, not abstract principles. The machines were strictly local organizations, a product of the segregation of ethnic voters from the rest of American society.

When ethnic politicians from the cities ended up in the state legislature, they found that they received little pay and even less respect. It was often a kiss of political death to be sent away to small upstate or downstate towns like Albany, New York, or Springfield, Illinois, away from friends, family, community, and constituents. When New York City's machine organization, Tammany Hall, sent Al Smith to the state legislature at the age of 30, he had scarcely been outside lower Manhattan. He felt as if he were exiled, sent away to a foreign country:

> Al Smith went to Albany unprepared to be legislator—or even to sleep away from home. . . . [O]vercome by the intricacies of the legislative process, he sat day

after day in the high-ceilinged chamber in silence.

> As he sat there staring down at the desk, a page boy would deposit another pile of bills on it. The wording was difficult enough for the expert. It might have been designed to mock a man whose schooling had ended in the eighth grade, who had never liked to read even the simple books of childhood, who, he had once said, had in his entire life read only one book cover to cover: *The Life of John L. Sullivan.**

Before Al Smith, who was later elected governor of New York and nominated as the Democratic presidential candidate in 1928, Tammany politicians had never prospered in Albany.

Personal loyalties and their pocket books motivated urban ethnic voters. When precinct captains took them to the polls, they voted for the local party organization, not for a cause. What in their background would excite them about complicated national issues such as tariff policy or child labor legislation? The upshot was that even when a powerful machine dominated a city, the party bosses and their loyal constituents mostly ignored gubernatorial and presidential elections.

All this changed quickly in the 1930s, when urban ethnic and labor union workers became important to the New Deal coalition.

Source: Robert A. Caro, *The Power Broker: Robert Moses and the Fall of New York* (New York: Knopf, 1974), pp. 118–119.

*John L. Sullivan was a famous boxing champion.

Wagner Labor Act, which established workers' compensation for death or injury, safety and workplace regulations, and the right of workers to organize unions. As a result, union members became reliable Democratic voters. The African American electorate also became important to the northern wing of the party. Even in the 1930s, decades before civil rights legislation became politically viable, the Roosevelt administration took steps to ensure that blacks received some appointments to federal posts and a share of the benefits from job and relief programs. Although southern voters would eventually become estranged from the party, until the civil rights legislation of the 1960s they stayed in the fold because a lot of the New Deal legislation benefited them too, and the bitterness of the Civil War and reconstruction years had not yet faded enough to allow them to make the leap to the Republican Party. The odd coalition between urban voters in the North and the one-party Democratic South was forged as an alliance of convenience that began to break apart in the 1960s, when racial animosities drove a wedge between inner-city blacks, white working and suburban voters, and southern conservatives. When the New Deal coalition dissolved for good in the 1980s, the cities' influence in national politics vanished.

A New Political Consciousness

In 1912 a Harvard political scientist wrote, "before many years have passed, the urban population of the United States will have gained numerical mastery."[2] He based this prediction on a simple calculation of demographic trends.[3] In the 30 years from 1890 to 1920, more than 18 million immigrants poured into America's cities. These immigrants came mainly from Italy, Poland, Russia, Greece, and Eastern Europe. They were overwhelmingly Roman Catholic and Jewish. They made up the preponderance of the workforces in the iron and steel, meatpacking, mining, and textile industries. Few spoke English when they arrived, and many were illiterate even in their native languages.

The ever-present nineteenth-century nervousness about the "strangers in the land" escalated into a national phobia in the next century. The viciousness of the campaigns launched against immigrants gradually made them aware that they had a stake in national, and not only local, politics. Immigrant voters had been brought into politics by the urban party machines, but these were strictly local organizations that stayed away from big political issues. But they could scarcely remain neutral when the cultural values and customs they and their constituents held dear came under attack.

The campaigns for prohibition were aimed squarely at immigrants and their cultural values. Proposed to the states by Congress in 1917 and ratified in 1919, the Eighteenth Amendment prohibited the sale and distribution of alcoholic beverages. Small-town Methodists and Baptists—joined in their crusade by upper- and middle-class Protestants in the cities and in the privileged suburbs—claimed that if the immigrants were forced to abstain from alcohol it would reduce poverty, improve workers' efficiency and family life, and end immorality and crime. Prohibition became the most compelling political issue of the first two decades of the century because it gave middle-class Protestants and rural voters a practical way to express their hostility toward the foreign immigrants crowded into the industrial cities:

> [Drinking] was associated with the saloonkeepers who ran the city machines and who used the votes of the whiskey-loving immigrant . . . with the German brewers and their "disloyal" compatriots who drank beer and ale. . . . The cities, which resisted the idea that "thou shalt not" was the fundamental precept of living, were always hostile to prohibition. The prohibitionists, in turn, regarded the city as their chief enemy, and prohibitionism and a pervasive antiurbanism went hand-in-hand.[4]

To the members of the Protestant middle class, the sins of liquor were indistinguishable from what they saw as the depraved cultural customs of Catholic immigrants. Southern and western newspapers reflexively connected crime, national origin, and liquor. When it was not legitimate to attack foreigners directly, it was easy to attack them indirectly through the surrogate liquor issue, allowing "prohibition partisans to talk about morality when in reality they were worried about cultural dominance and political supremacy."[5]

Prohibition and religion were intimately connected. To most Protestant Americans, the Roman Catholic Church represented evil incarnate. It signified ostentatious authority—the robes, the ceremony, and the architecture of Catholic churches seemed like an affront to the simplicity and informality of small-town life. Like the right-wing groups of the 1950s obsessed by the idea that an international communist conspiracy was poised to subvert the American political system, religious fundamentalists of the early twentieth century were convinced that the Roman Catholic Church was dedicated to the goal of world-wide domination.

By exploiting such fears, the Ku Klux Klan attracted millions of followers. Revived in Atlanta in 1915, for a few years the Klan enjoyed spectacular growth in both the North and the South. Klan membership skyrocketed in California, Oregon, Indiana, Illinois, Ohio, Oklahoma, Texas, Arkansas, and throughout the South. In 1924, at its peak, 40 percent of the Klan's membership resided in Ohio, Indiana, and Illinois. Half of its membership was located in cities of more than 50,000, with chapters of hundreds of members in such cities as Chicago, Detroit, Indianapolis, Pittsburgh, Baltimore, and Buffalo.[6] The Klan remained as a powerful political force until at least the mid-1920s. It helped elect a member of the Senate; governors in Georgia, Alabama, Oregon, and California; and 75 members of the House of Representatives.

Although the Klan found its most enthusiastic support among less educated fundamentalist Christians, its message also reached a broader audience. In 1916, Madison Grant, curator of New York City's Museum of National History, published *The Passing of the Great Race*, in which he worried that Aryans might someday be overwhelmed by dark-skinned races. His book was elevated to the status of a scientific work, along with Lothrop Stoddard's *The Rising Tide of Color against the White World-Supremacy* (1921).

Congress responded to the rising xenophobia with the Emergency Quota Act of 1921 and the National Origins Act of 1924. Both laws drew support from intellectuals, labor leaders, rural people from all sections of the country, and anxious middle-class voters. The Emergency Quota Act reaffirmed the total exclusion of Chinese, which had been legislated by Congress in 1882, and established a national origins quota of 3 percent of the population of other nationality groups as recorded in the 1910 census. The law succeeded in cutting immigration from 805,228 in 1920 to 309,556 in 1921–1922.[7] Three years later, the National Origins Act reduced the origins quota to 2 percent and established the 1890 census as the new baseline. The effect of the legislation was to drastically reduce immigration by ethnic groups that had come to the United States primarily since 1890. Italian immigration was reduced by 90 percent; British and Irish immigration, by contrast, declined by just 19 percent.[8] The overall immigrant flow fell sharply, from 357,803 in 1923–1924 to 164,667 in 1924–1925.

In floor debates on the two immigration bills, members of Congress reviled the foreign-born of the cities in language that could have been lifted from Ku Klux Klan pamphlets. This furious assault taught immigrant voters that national politics affected them, and in the 1920s they began to express their new understanding. Before long, it became apparent they "were not going to support candidates who wanted them to stop drinking, Protestantize their schools, or tell them as often as possible that they were inferior."[9] Opposition to prohibition was the one political issue that unified Catholic immigrants, regardless of national origin.

Earlier, when the State of Illinois began enforcing restrictive drinking laws in 1906, ethnic immigrants had launched protests and launched efforts "to endorse political candidates and lobby city and state governments to protect the free sale and consumption of liquor."[10] Over the next three decades, the number of naturalized immigrants registered to vote rose sharply, and they turned out at very high rates for local elections.[11] They were clearly becoming a political force to be reckoned with, and one of the causes that could motivate them was Prohibition. Anton Cermak, the future mayor of Chicago, began his political career in the 1920s by becoming one of the leaders of the campaign for repeal.[12] Al Smith, the Democrats' nominee for president in 1928, gained support among immigrant voters because he opposed Prohibition and he was, as an Irish Catholic, one of them. In effect, Prohibition taught immigrants that politics was not only local, but also national.

The Changing Political Balance

Before the 1930s, neither the Republicans nor the Democrats paid much attention to the cities. The Republicans, the triumphant party of Abraham Lincoln, emerged from the Civil War as the dominant party controlling Congress and the presidency. Between 1860 and 1928, the Republicans won 14 of 18 presidential contests and controlled both houses of Congress more than half of the time. Because the party's main base of support was made up of financial, industrial, and commercial interests, it opposed taxes on business, enacted high tariffs on foreign imports, encouraged private exploitation (mineral, grazing, homesteading) of federal lands in the West, and used federal troops to quell strikes. At the same time, the Republicans gained support from middle- and working-class voters in the North because the party presided during a long-term economic expansion tied closely to frontier development and industrial production.

For several decades after the Civil War, the Democratic Party tried to hold together an uneasy alliance made up of Southerners and an assortment of groups opposed to economic domination by east-coast "big money." The party's presidential candidates appealed for support from urban workers, but a lot of other interests jostled for attention too. The chronic problem for the Democrats' coalition was its fragility. The issues that held it together arose from the abiding enmity of Southerners to the party of Lincoln, the insecurities of small farmers about credit and prices, and the tensions between business and industrial workers, but aside from their resentments, these groups had little if anything in common. The party did better during the periodic downturns but lost ground when the economy improved.

The fragile nature of this alliance was revealed at the 1924 Democratic Convention, held in Madison Square Garden in New York City. The Democrats treated the first radio audience of a national convention to a futile 16-day, 103-ballot marathon that listed 19 candidates on the first ballot and 17 on the 100th. The galleries booed the speeches of Southerners and Westerners, especially when William Jennings Bryan, a three-time failed candidate for president, asked the convention to reject a proposed resolution condemning the Ku Klux Klan by name. The motion to condemn the Klan brought forth such heated oratory that police were brought onto the convention floor in case a riot broke out. Delegates shouted at and cursed one another. When the final vote on the resolution was taken, it lost by one vote, 542 3/20 to 541 3/20. Demands for a recount were drowned out when the band struck up "Marching through Georgia," which incited the southern delegates to paroxysms of rage. After 16 days, the convention finally nominated a presidential candidate, John W. Davis, who almost nobody wanted and few of the delegates even knew.[13]

The crowds and the din of New York City confused and frightened the delegates from the towns and farms of the South and West. They found New Yorkers unfriendly and rude, and the city seemed all too easy to get lost in. Delegates who "wandered downtown to Fourteenth Street to gawk at Tammany Hall with its ancient Indian above the door reacted as if they expected to see an ogre come popping out. Almost all delegates were dismayed by the New York traffic, the noise and hustle."[14] Their antagonism toward the city was reaffirmed every day the convention dragged on through the stifling July heat. Small-town reporters filled their hometown newspapers with vivid accounts of the horrors of the city.[15]

Only four years later the Democrats named Al Smith, the four-term governor of New York, as their presidential candidate. The convention was held in Houston, Texas, the first time either of the parties had met in the South since the Civil War. The nomination laid bare bitter divisions. Smith represented everything that was anathema to the city haters. He was the first Roman Catholic nominated for the presidency and an ardent opponent of Prohibition and the Ku Klux Klan. He was a self-made member of the nation's most notorious machine, Tammany Hall. He said "foist" instead of "first" and wore a brown derby, which only accentuated his bulbous nose and ruddy complexion. Smith proudly reminisced about his past: swimming in the East River and working at the Fulton Fish Market as an errand boy. Considering these fractious conflicts, how could he have been nominated? Once he was nominated, why did the party not simply break apart?

Southern and aggrieved farmers had little choice but to stay within the fold because they had come to share, however crudely, a class interest. The party had become—mostly by default because the Republicans took an uncompromising probusiness stand—the "little man's" party. Those who opposed Republican policies could never hope to have a voice in national politics unless they cooperated with one another. Despite their differences, most of the delegates to the 1928 convention wanted to avoid a repeat of the Madison Square Garden debacle. Few delegates thought Smith could win, but no other candidate was available who was capable of bridging the divisions in the fractious party. As the four-term governor of New York, he had gained national prominence as a progressive leader who had created state parks and beaches, sponsored workers' safety legislation, and financed public improvements throughout the state. He had reorganized state government, making New York the model for progressives who believed in efficiency principles. Admired by progressives for his record as governor and supported by Democratic organizations and their ethnic supporters, his nomination could be denied by rural delegates, but only at the cost of another fiasco like 1924—multiple ballots and a guaranteed loss for the presidential nominee. There was even reason to believe Smith might have a chance. In his victorious gubernatorial run in 1924, he had received 100,000 more votes than the losing Democratic presidential ticket in New York.

In 1928, the Democrats gave the nomination to Al Smith. He lost several southern and border states and won only 41 percent of the national vote, but his candidacy marked the beginning of the party's increasing reliance on the urban electorate. Both in 1920 and 1924, the 12 largest cities in the United States had, taken together, given a decisive majority to the Republicans. Now the tables were turned, and the Democrats gained ground. As later elections were to prove, this marked the beginning of a long-term trend in which voters in the cities cast most of their ballots for Democrats.[16]

For the Roman Catholic ethnics in the cities, Smith's campaign educated them about the national issues of Prohibition, ethnicity, and religion. Smith campaigned with his brown derby and his theme song, "The Sidewalks of New York." Protestants shuddered at the idea of a Catholic in the White House. His stand on Prohibition made drink the leading issue of the campaign. Blue-blood upper-class Protestants found him beneath them. The campaign highlighted the issues of race, religion, culture, and social class so clearly that never again would the urban ethnics be unmindful of their stake in the national political system.

The election of 1928 brought a Democratic electoral plurality to the industrial cities where immigrant voters lived. In 1920, the Republican presidential ticket carried the 12 largest cities by more than 1.5 million votes, and in 1924 the ticket did almost as well. But in 1928, with Al Smith as the Democratic candidate, the Republican margin in the cities shrank to a narrow 210,000 votes. In the 1932 election, the Democrats beat the Republicans in the big cities for the first time, and decisively, by almost 1.8 million votes.[17] Franklin Delano Roosevelt's landslide demonstrated that the Democrats now had a firm lock on the urban electorate. Since then, the old industrial cities have normally voted heavily Democratic, and this fact proved to be especially decisive in the outcomes of two presidential elections. In 1948 Harry S. Truman barely won the national popular vote, but he carried the cities by nearly 1.5 million votes. Urban voters again provided the crucial difference in the 1960 election, when they put John F. Kennedy over the top.

The Depression and the Cities

The Great Depression came as a shock to Americans and to their public leaders. Especially for the rapidly growing middle class, the 1920s had been a decade of prosperity and optimism. Business leaders and politicians promoted the idea that sustained economic growth was virtually limitless. A strong undertow of poverty ran below the surface in the immigrant slums and on farms alike, but for the growing middle class an air of prosperity prevailed. It was an age that extolled mass consumption and complacency. For a time, the discontents of the industrial age seemed long past.

October 24, 1929, is the symbolic beginning of the Great Depression. On that day—Black Thursday—disorder, panic, and confusion reigned on the New York Stock Exchange. Stock prices virtually collapsed. For several months prices had sagged, then rallied, then sagged again, with each trough lower than the previous one and each peak less convincing. When the bottom fell out, "the Market . . . degenerated into a wild, mad scramble to sell, . . . the Market . . . surrendered to blind, relentless fear."[18] In one morning, 11 well-known speculators committed suicide. From Wall Street the economic catastrophe rippled outward, with consequences that fundamentally reshaped American politics.

Over the next three years, the nation sank ever deeper into economic stagnation. In the spring of 1929, the unemployment rate stood at 3.2 percent. Within a few months, the number of unemployed exceeded 4 million, representing 8.7 percent of the labor force.[19] By 1932, 24 percent of all workers—more than 12 million in all—could not find jobs. In the depths of the Depression, during the spring of 1933, the number of unemployed reached 13 million workers, fully one-fourth of the labor force.[20]

The Depression dragged on for a decade. Unemployment levels remained above 20 percent in both 1934 and 1935 and dropped below 15 percent only in 1937. Most of those who managed to find work made less than before. From 1929 to 1933, the average income of workers fell by 42.5 percent.[21] Weekly wages dropped from an average of $28 in 1929 to $17 by 1934, and workers faced the constant threat of layoffs. Many jobs were reduced from full-time to part-time status, and employers cut wages and hours to meet payrolls. For example, the payroll of the nation's largest steel company, U.S. Steel, was cut in half from 1929 to 1933, and in 1933 the company had no full-time workers at all.[22] Steel mills operated at only 12 percent of capacity by 1932.[23]

The basic structure of the capitalist system seemed irreparably damaged. In the three years following the stock market collapse, national income fell by 44.5 percent. By the summer of 1932, stocks had fallen 83 percent below their value in September 1929.[24] By the end of 1932, 5,096 commercial banks had failed. Farm income declined from $7 billion in 1929 to $2.5 billion in 1932.[25] For many farmers whose incomes had been sharply dropping throughout the 1920s, the Depression came as a final blow.

The statistics of disaster painted a portrait of human suffering. Between 1 million and 2 million men rode the rails and gathered in hobo jungles or camped in thickets and railroad cars. Others lived in "Hoovervilles," clusters of cardboard, scrap wood, and scrap metal shacks in empty lots and city parks. Those who had been chronically poor in the 1920s were now hungry and destitute. They stood in bread lines, ate from garbage cans, or went begging from door to door. One-quarter of all homeowners lost their homes in 1932, and more than 1,000 mortgages a day were foreclosed in the first half of 1933.[26] By March 1933, when Franklin D. Roosevelt was inaugurated as president, 9 million savings accounts had been lost.[27]

Never before had the nation faced an economic catastrophe of this magnitude, nor was there a tradition of federal government assistance for the unemployed and destitute.[28] However, unemployment and poverty were certainly not new. In the period from 1897 to 1926, unemployment levels in four major industries fluctuated around the 10 percent level,[29] and poverty was a chronic condition of industrialization and immigration. What made the Great Depression unique were its depth, persistence, and broad reach. In earlier depressions, including the panics of the 1870s and 1890s, production and employment declined much less severely, and recovery began within a year or two.[30] The Great Depression of the 1930s lasted for over a decade, it touched all classes, and people at all income levels felt its effects. The measure of the crisis of the 1930s was not just unemployment and poverty but also the breakdown of economic institutions.

No one knew how to respond. President Herbert Hoover firmly resisted intervention by the federal government and instead launched two national drives to encourage private relief. Late in 1930 he appointed the President's Emergency Committee for Employment. Its main charge was to encourage state and local committees to expedite public construction and coordinate public and private funding for relief efforts. In August 1931 he formed the President's Organization on Unemployment Relief, whose job was to help organize private unemployment committees in states and communities.

Despite Hoover's stubborn opposition to federal assistance, two programs were funded during his administration. First, the Federal Home Loan Bank Act supplied capital advances to a small number of mortgage institutions so they could forbear rather than foreclose on mortgages in default. This program saved a few banks. Second, the Emergency Relief and Construction Act extended $300 million in loans to state and local governments so they could continue to provide relief to indigent people.

Hoover was hardly alone in opposing aggressive federal action. Until 1932 most governors took a "we'll do it ourselves" attitude toward solving unemployment and its associated problems.[31] Two governors refused to work with the President's Organization on Unemployment Relief, even though federal funds were not involved.[32] The officials of financially strapped local governments were also skeptical of federal aid. In July 1931 the socialist mayor of Milwaukee wrote to the mayors of the largest 100 cities, asking them to come to a conference to discuss a joint request for a national relief program. He got no response at all from many of the major cities, and several mayors criticized the idea, arguing that federal aid would constitute "an invasion of community rights."[33]

In the 1932 campaign, the Democrats accused Hoover of doing too much rather than too little. Their nominee, Roosevelt, promised to balance the budget while accusing Hoover of having presided over "the greatest spending administration in peace times in all our history."[34] It was apparent that the weight of the past lay heavily on both political parties. Against a cultural tradition that extolled individualism and free enterprise, there was great reluctance to expand the powers of government—especially the federal government—to meet the crisis. Nevertheless, when Roosevelt was inaugurated on March 4, 1933, he set in motion a concentrated period of reform that vastly increased the powers of the federal government in areas of business regulation, farm policy, and social insurance. Why did Roosevelt break so thoroughly from the American tradition of limited national government?

The new president's change of heart was motivated by the overwhelming sense of crisis that ushered him into the White House. Between his election in November and his inauguration in March, the nation passed through the worst months of the depression.[35] The economy teetered on the brink of utter collapse. In February 1933, some of the nation's biggest banks failed. "People stood in long queues with satchels and paper bags to take gold and currency away from the banks to store in mattresses and old shoe boxes. It seemed safer to put one's life's savings in the attic than to trust the financial institutions in the country."[36] Roosevelt wondered if anything would be left to salvage by the time he assumed office. By Inauguration Day, 38 states had closed their banks, and on that day the governors of New York and Illinois closed the nation's biggest banks.[37] The New York Stock Exchange stopped trading. The Kansas City and Chicago Boards of Trade closed their doors. "In the once-busy grain pits of Chicago, in the canyons of Wall Street, all was silent."[38]

It was also one of the harshest winters on record. In desperation, people overran relief offices and rioted at bank closings. Relief marchers invaded state legislative chambers. Farmers tried to stop foreclosure proceedings and blockaded roads. Amid marches, riots, arrests, and jailings, many people feared there might be a revolution against the capitalist system. The demands for some kind of response became almost impossible to resist.

In its first 100 days, Roosevelt's administration presented Congress with a flood of legislative proposals.[39] On March 9, Roosevelt signed the Emergency Banking Act. The act extended financial assistance to bankers so they could reopen their doors and gave the government authority to reorganize banks and control bank credit policies. It received a unanimous vote from a panicked Congress, sight unseen. A flurry of legislation followed: the Civilian Conservation Corps (March 31), the Agricultural Adjustment Act and the Federal Emergency Relief Act (May 12), the Tennessee Valley Authority (May 18), the Federal "Truth in Securities" Act (May 27), the Home Owners' Loan Act (June 13), the National Industrial Recovery Act (June 16), and more than a score of other bills.

Most of the legislative onslaught was designed to stimulate, regulate, and stabilize the most important economic institutions of the economy. But the benefits filtered down. After the Emergency Banking Act was passed, depositors gained enough confidence to put their money back into the banks. After passage of the National Housing Act (signed into law in 1934), homebuyers were able to secure long-term mortgages from banks, whose loans were guaranteed by the federal government. Foreclosures on farms and homes fell sharply when the government, through the Farm Credit Administration and Home Owners' Loan Corporation, agreed to buy up defaulted mortgages. New Deal programs affected millions of lives by salvaging savings, houses, and farms. Nevertheless, the New Deal's attempts to reform the economy were designed more to bring stability to financial institutions than to fight poverty and destitution. Home lending and farm credit programs primarily helped the nation's important economic institutions and secondarily aided the heavily mortgaged middle class.

The other side of the New Deal included its public works and relief programs. Between 1933 and 1937, the federal government administered public works programs for several million people and supplied direct relief to millions more. The earliest of the public works programs was the Civilian Conservation Corps (CCC). Overall, the CCC employed more than 2.5 million boys and young men. In 1935 alone, 500,000 men were living in CCC camps. They planted trees, built dams, fought fires, stocked fish, built lookout towers, dug ditches and canals, strung telephone lines, and built and improved bridges, roads, and trails. Their contribution to conservation was enormous; the CCC was responsible for more than half of all the forest planted in the United States up to the 1960s.[40]

The Civil Works Administration (CWA) was much larger and broader in scope. Established in November 1933, it employed 4.1 million by the third week of January 1934, and within a few months it employed almost a third of the unemployed labor force.[41] Although the CWA lasted for less than a year—Roosevelt ended it in the spring of 1934 because he thought it was too costly—it enabled many families to survive the bitter winter of 1934. The CWA was "immensely popular—with merchants, with local officials, and with workers," and its demise was resisted in Congress.[42] The Public Works Administration (PWA) enjoyed a longer run, and its impact was more lasting. In six years, from

1933 to 1939, the PWA built 70 percent of the new school buildings in the nation and 35 percent of the hospitals and public health facilities.[43]

The Federal Emergency Relief Act (FERA), which Roosevelt signed into law on May 12, 1933, was never as popular as public works legislation because it undercut the cherished principles of work and independence by making relief money directly available to the destitute. Roosevelt himself viewed the Federal Emergency Relief Administration with distaste, thinking it would sap the moral strength of the poor. Roosevelt constantly sought ways to cut its budget, but the destitution and the civil disorder that prevailed in Roosevelt's first term made the program necessary. In the winter of 1934, 20 million people received FERA funds.[44]

The FERA was treated as an embarrassing necessity. The government's response was understood to be an emergency measure, comparable to helping victims of catastrophes such as floods, earthquakes, and tornadoes. Congressional debate on the FERA received little coverage by the media. When the act was passed on May 9, 1933, the *New York Times* only mentioned it on page 3 in a column listing legislation passed by Congress. The day after President Roosevelt put his signature to it, it made page 21 of the *Times* but only in reference to the appointment of the administrator. In a culture that extolled individualism, competition, and hard work, people were uncomfortable with the idea of relief.

Roosevelt frequently expressed doubts about relief and public works programs. He preferred economic recovery to government spending, but his response to the economic emergency vastly broadened the electoral base of the Democratic Party. Public works and relief created a loyal following among middle- and working-class people who benefited. By the 1936 election, and for decades thereafter, voting in small towns split between the Republicans on the wealthier side of the tracks and the working class and poor on the other. The most reliable new Democratic following, however, could be found in the cities. Urban ethnics, especially if they were union members, learned to vote Democratic. The New Deal programs also broke African American voters away from the Republican Party. Before the 1936 election, a prominent black publisher counseled, "My friends, go turn Lincoln's picture to the wall. That debt has been paid in full."[45] In that election, blacks gave Roosevelt 75 percent of their votes, and they have voted heavily for the Democrats ever since.

The Great Depression fundamentally altered the group composition of the party system in the United States. In addition to its traditional base in the South, the Democratic Party now claimed solid support among workers, blacks, and the poor in the northern cities, where large numbers of the working class and the poor were concentrated. The party's electoral coalition broadened sufficiently to ensure that Democratic candidates would be competitive in presidential contests and that Democrats would hold majorities in Congress in most years. In 1936, the Gallup poll found that 59 percent of farmers favored Roosevelt (Agricultural Adjustment Act, Farm Credit Administration, Farm Mortgage Corporation, abolition of the gold standard); 61 percent of white-collar workers (bank regulation, Federal Housing Administration, savings deposit insurance); 80 percent of organized labor (government recognition of collective bargaining, unemployment insurance, work relief); and 68 percent of people under age 25 (Civilian Conservation Corps, National Youth Administration). Among lower-income groups, 76 percent favored Roosevelt, compared with 60 percent of the middle class.[46] By contrast, upper-income groups identified overwhelmingly with the Republican Party, and they do so to this day.

Cities Gain a Voice

The Great Depression marked a turning point in American politics. To secure the votes of urban ethnics, Democratic candidates reliably supported the New Deal's initiatives. The voice of the cities in national politics was also amplified in these years by another development: the forging of a direct relationship between the federal government and the cities. Three elements stand out as key factors in this development: (1) a fiscal and social crisis in the cities, (2) indifference by the states, and (3) the forging of an alliance among city officials for the purpose of securing a federal response to their problems.

Even before Roosevelt took office, the cities had exhausted their resources. In the 1920s they had borrowed heavily to finance public improvements and capital construction. They were already deep in debt when the onset of the depression confronted them with rising unemployment and poverty. Local officials could not avoid seeing the misery and want on their streets. Faced with a manifest emergency, they provided relief funds as rapidly as they could, but it was not enough. Municipal governments simply lacked the financial resources to cope with the emergency.

Cities entered the depression after they had already financed a multitude of new public improvement programs. In the 1920s cities had built roads to accommodate the millions of automobiles flooding onto the streets. The auto imposed heavy new costs on local governments. Cities invested in traffic signals, police cars, garbage trucks, school buses, snowplows, roads, and bus and airline terminals. In response to demands from the rapidly expanding middle class, cities increased spending for education, built new school buildings and public libraries, and invested heavily in improving parks and recreational facilities.

Local governments made heavier investments in these areas than either the state or the federal governments. During the 1920s counties and municipalities spent 55 to 60 percent of all public funds in the nation, and their total debts mounted to $9 billion.[47] From 1923 to 1927, while the states increased expenditures by 43 percent, spending by the largest 145 cities rose by 79 percent, and cities of 100,000 or more increased their budgets by 82 percent.[48] In the latter cities expenditures for work relief and welfare shot up by 391 percent from 1923 to 1932; during the same period, states increased their relief and welfare budgets by only 63 percent. In the last year of the Hoover administration, the 13 cities with populations above 100,000 spent $53 million more than all the states combined for public welfare. Over the decade of the 1920s federal grants actually declined from 2 to 1.3 percent of all public expenditures.[49]

The 13 biggest cities incurred 50 percent more debt in the 1920s, and many of them were hard pressed, even early in the Depression, to pay for government services and public improvements.[50]

The Great Depression placed unprecedented responsibilities on city officials at the very time that fiscal resources were drying up. Cities were unable to generate enough tax revenues to keep pace with their additional responsibilities. Two-thirds of the revenue for city budgets came from property taxes. Falling property values brought a 20 percent decline in property tax revenues from 1929 to 1933.[51] At the same time, the rate of tax delinquency increased from 10 to 26 percent in cities of over 50,000 in population.[52] Between 1931 and 1933, tax losses resulted in a reduction in the budgets of the largest 13 cities from $1.8 to $1.6 billion.[53] State-imposed debt limitations did not allow cities to borrow for day-to-day services. In principle, cities were allowed to borrow for capital improvements, but this option soon evaporated as well. By 1932, because of their high debt loads, cities found it impossible to sell long-term bond issues to investors. In 1932 and 1933, many states and municipalities, including Mississippi, Montana, Buffalo, Philadelphia, Cleveland, and Toledo, were unable to market any bond issues at all.[54] Temporary loans with high interest rates replaced long-term notes.

When the cities financed public works programs to help the unemployed, their budgets quickly ran dry. Municipal governments lacked sufficient resources to treat the depression's symptoms, yet many mayors saw this as their principal mission. Detroit's experience revealed the impossibility of the task. In the fall of 1930, Frank Murphy won a surprise victory in a special mayoral election on a campaign promising unemployment relief.[55] His efforts to provide relief by expanding public jobs and welfare in Detroit attracted national attention. He appointed an unemployment committee, operated an employment bureau, sponsored public works projects, raised private donations for poor relief, and consulted with private firms about rehiring workers. Detroit did more than any other city for its unemployed, but its compassion was costly. With over 40,000 families receiving relief and one-third of the workforce out of work, it was spending $2 million a month for relief in 1931, far more than second-place Boston.[56]

The burden soon brought financial ruin to the city, and by the spring of 1931, Detroit faced municipal bankruptcy. To avoid default on its debts and payroll, Murphy curtailed the city's health and recreational services and slashed the fire and police department budgets. Only an emergency bank loan allowed Murphy to meet the June 1931 payroll, but even this measure was not enough. Under pressure from the New York banks that held most of Detroit's bonds, Murphy was forced to cut relief expenditures in half during 1932. Thousands of families were dropped from the relief rolls as it became painfully obvious that Detroit could not single-handedly solve the local problems caused by a national economic calamity.

The mayors of other cities were learning the same lesson. Finally, their sense of desperation galvanized them to take action. In the spring of 1932, Murphy issued invitations to the mayors of the major cities to attend a conference. In

June, representatives from 29 cities met in Detroit with a single purpose in mind. Murphy stated the cities' case succinctly: "We have done everything humanly possible to do, and it has not been enough. The hour is at hand for the federal government to cooperate."[57] New York City's mayor likewise pleaded for assistance:

> The municipal government is the maternal, the intimate side of government; the side with heart. The Federal Government doesn't have to wander through darkened hallways of our hospitals, to witness the pain and suffering there. It doesn't have to stand in the bread lines, but the time has come when it must face the facts and its responsibility.
>
> We of the cities have diagnosed and thus far met the problem; but we have come to the end of our resources. It is now up to the Federal Government to assume its share. We can't cure conditions by ourselves.[58]

The mayors' demands for federal assistance represented a turning point in federal–local relations. Historically, there had been no direct relationship between cities and the federal government. Many local officials felt it was illegitimate to ask the federal government for help, and others feared any aid, thinking it might cause their cities to lose their independence. Only a few months before, most of the mayors had declined to attend a similar mayors' conference suggested by the mayor of Milwaukee.[59] Desperation finally made them reconsider.

The situation was made worse by the fact that state governments refused to respond to the cities' plight. While municipal governments' expenditures on jobs and relief skyrocketed, the states sharply cut back; "As tax revenues dwindled and unemployment increased, economy in government became a magic word."[60] Beginning in 1932, several states slashed their budgets: Arizona by 35 percent; Texas, Illinois, Vermont by 25 percent; South Carolina by 33 percent. As state tax revenues declined, public works and construction programs were curtailed. In 1928 the states had spent $1.35 billion for public works projects, mainly in the form of road building, but this amount was reduced to $630 million by 1932 and to $290 million for the first eight months of 1933.[61] On average, per capita spending for highways and education fell only slightly from 1927 to 1932,[62] but some states made drastic cuts. Tennessee, for example, failed to provide funds for its rural schools for much of 1931.[63] State educational institutions, especially universities, were hard hit. During 1933, education budgets had dropped by 40 percent in Maryland, 53 percent in Wyoming, and more than 30 percent in several other states.[64] All of these cutbacks reduced public payroll and thus aggravated the unemployment crisis.

Relief spending by the states went up in the early years of the depression, from $1.00 per capita in 1927 to $3.50 four years later.[65] But the amount of welfare provided by the states was small and failed to come close to what was needed even in those few states willing to increase their effort. From mid-1931 to the end of 1932, welfare spending by the states increased from $500,000 to $100 million, but almost all of the money was provided by a few states, principally New York, New Jersey, and Pennsylvania. When the New Deal began, only eight states provided any money at all for relief.[66]

Local officials petitioned the states for help, as the depression wore on their pleas sounded increasingly desperate.[67] Except for the very few states that provided relief payments to the unemployed, no response was forthcoming. State governments were slow to respond to the needs of their cities because rural representatives controlled their legislatures. In state after state, legislative districts were drawn up to ensure that rural counties would outvote cities in the state legislative chambers. In Georgia, each county was represented equally in the legislature, regardless of its population.[68] Likewise, Louisiana granted each parish at least one representative in the state senate and house. Rhode Island applied this standard to every town.[69] Without exception, all the states made sure that representatives from rural areas would continue to hold legislative majorities, no matter how much a state's population might become concentrated in the cities.

There were important political stakes in this pattern of underrepresentation. If cities were allowed to gain majorities in legislatures simply because of their growing populations, political alignments and party structures would fundamentally change. Incumbent rural legislators would be unseated, and it is likely that a shift in legislative power would have favored more generous policies for the cities. The persistent underrepresentation of urban areas resulted in indifference to urban problems. Traffic congestion, slums, inadequate park space, and smoke pollution did not interest rural and small-town legislators. Governors, too, tended to be insensitive to urban issues; indeed, they were remarkably indifferent to the social calamity unfolding all around them. Governors' and legislators' national conferences ignored the depression. At the 1930 governors' conference in Salt Lake City, for example, the major topics of discussion included such topics as the essentials of a model state constitution, the need for constitutional revisions, constitutional versus legislative home rule for cities, and the extent of legislative control of city governments.[70] Likewise, the 1931 conference studiously avoided any mention of the economic crisis. In the face of such indifference, the cities had nowhere to go but to the federal government.

There was a danger that the special plight of the cities would disappear from view because the gathering disaster of the Great Depression affected the entire nation. Conditions in many rural areas were even worse than in the cities. Grinding poverty was pervasive in the Appalachian region and throughout the South; families lived in one-room hovels, children walked around with bellies distended by malnutrition, and some parents could not afford to clothe their children to send them to school. A drought from the Midwest to the Rockies turned much of the Plains into a vast dust bowl; in the winter of 1934, New England's snow turned red from the huge billowing clouds of dust blowing from Texas, Kansas, and Oklahoma. Families left the ravaged land by the thousands. The experiences of those heading for California provided the grist for John Steinbeck's moving novel *The Grapes of Wrath*.

Roosevelt and his advisers instinctively distrusted city politics and urban culture. Roosevelt's first public works program, the CCC, was inspired by his feeling that the moral character of unemployed youth in the cities would be improved by living in the country.[71] Roosevelt felt "small love for the city."[72]

One of the president's closest advisers confessed that "since my graduate school days, I have always been able to excite myself more about the wrongs of farmers than those of urban workers."[73] In its first two years, the New Deal accomplished a comprehensive farm policy of guaranteed price supports, crop allotments to reduce supplies and increase prices, and federally guaranteed mortgages. By contrast, in 1937 it produced its first specifically urban program. The Public Housing Act (also called the Wagner-Steagall Public Housing Act after the names of its legislative sponsors) provided slum clearance and public housing on a very limited scale.

Despite the indifference they initially encountered, city officials managed to forge close relationships with politicians and administrators in Washington, D.C. The New Deal's first relief and recovery programs were administered through the states, but federal programs were later enacted that put local officials in charge. Federal officials administered the three largest public works programs—the PWA, CWA, and the Works Progress Administration—in cooperation with both state and local officials. The Federal Emergency Relief funds were channeled through the states, but local relief agencies actually administered the funds. In several cities, such as New York, Pittsburgh, and Kansas City, local Democratic machines found that the new federal resources allowed them to rebuild their strength.[74] Local officials found themselves testifying to congressional committees about programs that affected the cities. By 1934 a southern mayor observed, "Mayors are a familiar sight in Washington these days. Whether we like it or not, the destinies of our cities are clearly tied in with national politics."[75]

The Urban Programs of the New Deal

The first hint of any national concern about the problems of urban America came in 1892, when Congress appropriated $20,000 to investigate slum conditions in cities with more than 200,000 people.[76] In the report that followed, the commissioner of labor informed Congress that all of the nation's big cities contained block after block of rundown tenement districts that packed immigrants together into often unsafe and unsanitary conditions. The commissioner made much of the fact that these areas had a higher incidence of arrests and saloons than anywhere else in the country. In effect, the report amounted to a moral condemnation of city life.

Federal assistance for the construction of urban housing can be traced to the entry of the United States into World War I. In 1918, Congress authorized direct federal loans to local realty companies.[77] At a cost of $69.3 million, 8 hotels, 19 dormitories, 1,100 apartment units, and approximately 9,000 houses were constructed to house wartime shipyard workers in 27 cities and towns.[78] Later the same year, Congress approved the nation's first public housing program, designed to accommodate defense plant workers who needed housing near wartime factories. The U.S. Housing Corporation was created to manage the program. In the brief three months of the program's existence, the Housing Corporation built 6,000 single-family dwellings, plus accommodations for

7,200 single men, on 140 project sites scattered around the country.[79] As soon as the war was over, all of these federally owned housing units were sold to private owners, and in this way the government removed itself from the housing business.

The first significant federal intervention into housing came during the Great Depression. Even during the prosperous 1920s, the nation's cities contained rundown business districts and residential slums. As the depression wore on, the situation deteriorated; landlords and owners invested little or no money in repairs and renovation, and the construction of new housing slowed to a crawl. The solutions to the problems of housing and slums lay beyond the financial capacity of local governments. The slums that had long plagued the nation's cities slowly became defined as a national and not only local problem, and urban officials and business elites who were concerned about the condition of their business and residential districts looked to the national government for help.

In 1932, the last year of Herbert Hoover's presidency, Congress created the Reconstruction Finance Corporation (RFC) and authorized it to extend loans to private developers for the construction of low-income housing in slum areas.[80] Only two projects were actually ever undertaken, with over 98 percent of the money spent in three slum blocks of Manhattan to construct Knickerbocker Village, with its 1,573 apartments.[81] This program had two purposes. On the one hand, it was supposed to help revive the construction industry; on the other hand, it was supposed to increase the supply of low-income housing in New York. In the case of Knickerbocker Village, the first goal won out. Eighty-two percent of the slum families who initially moved into the apartments were soon forced to move back to the slums they had left because of the escalating rents charged by the owners.[82]

Franklin D. Roosevelt implemented a long list of national programs designed to stimulate the economy and bring the depression to an end. One of the first of these, the National Industrial Recovery Act of 1933, included a minor provision authorizing "construction, reconstruction, alteration, or repair, under public regulation or control, of low-rent housing and slum clearance projects."[83] The Housing Division of the PWA was charged with administering this provision. At first, the PWA tried to entice private developers into constructing low-income housing by offering them low-interest federal loans. This strategy reflected one of the major purposes of the program, which was "to deal with the unemployment situation by giving employment to workers . . . [and] to demonstrate to private builders the practicability of large-scale community planning."[84] But contractors and home builders did not find low-interest loans sufficiently attractive, and only seven projects ever met specifications and were approved. As a result, the PWA decided to bypass the housing industry altogether and finance and construct its own federally owned housing. The U.S. Emergency Housing Corporation was established for this purpose in 1933, and it asserted the right to use eminent domain to force the owners of slum property to sell so that the land could be prepared for construction.

Federal administrators ran into a problem when court decisions in Kentucky and Michigan declared that the federal government could not use eminent domain if it usurped the authority of state and local governments.[85] In response, they tried another tack. The Emergency Housing Corporation decided to make low-income housing grants to local public housing authorities. States could legally charter local authorities, and previous court cases made it clear that the states could use eminent domain to accomplish a variety of public purposes. With the offer of federal money dangled before them, city officials lobbied their state legislatures to allow them to create local housing authorities to receive the funds. By the end of the PWA public housing program in 1937, 29 states had passed enabling legislation allowing local governments to operate local public housing authorities, and 46 local housing agencies had already come into existence.[86] These authorities built almost 22,000 public low-income housing units in 37 cities.[87]

For all the effort to get the PWA program off the ground, the eventual results were mixed, at best. More low-income units were torn down through slum clearance than were ever built. Local public housing authorities were closely tied to the housing industry in their communities, and as a result a substantial proportion of PWA funds was used not to build housing, but to help politically connected owners sell their properties at inflated prices.[88] These properties were then slated for clearance, even though there were no plans to replace the housing units that were to be razed. In all these respects, the PWA experience provided a warning for the future: Program goals were easily subverted if local communities were allowed to make all of the important decisions.

The PWA experience became the administrative model for future housing programs. It was accepted that if federal grants were made available for public housing in the future, local public housing agencies would become the recipients of the funds and federal agencies would not try to build public housing units themselves. When the Public Housing Act of 1937 replaced the PWA program, it was based on the principle that housing programs would be implemented through federal grants-in-aid to local housing authorities. Under the legislation, public housing would be built and administered by local agencies, not by the federal government, and real estate agents and contractors would handle land sales and construction. Its stated purposes were:

> To provide financial assistance to the states and political subdivisions thereof for the elimination of unsafe and unsanitary housing conditions, for the eradication of slums, for the provision of decent, safe, and sanitary dwellings for families of low-income and for the reduction of unemployment and the stimulation of business activity, to create a United States Housing Authority, and for other purposes.[89]

The Public Housing Act of 1937 was "designed to serve the needs of low-income families who otherwise would be unable to afford decent, safe, and sanitary dwellings."[90] Because real estate agents, builders, and banks could not make much profit by constructing public housing projects, they steadfastly opposed the program. As far as they were concerned, government-owned housing competed with the private real estate market, and its only redeeming virtue was that public housing provided jobs in the construction industry. But this benefit failed to outweigh the unpopularity of providing housing subsidies to the bottom third of the population. As explained by the president of the National Association of Real Estate Boards, the housing industry's philosophy was that low-income housing should become available through a filter-down process:

> Housing should remain a matter of private enterprise and private ownership. It is contrary to the genius of the American people and the ideals they have established that government become landlord to its citizens. There is a sound logic in the continuance of the practice under which those who have the initiative and the will to save acquire better living facilities and yield their former quarters at modest rents to the group below.[91]

To make sure middle-class families could not opt out of the private housing market by moving into public housing, the legislation contained specific limitations on the costs and quality of rental units and a restriction that occupancy be strictly limited to low-income families. A requirement was also added that the number of new housing units constructed could not exceed the number of slum dwellings torn down.[92]

The 1937 act authorized the U.S. Housing Administration (USHA) to extend low-interest loans to local public housing agencies. The loans could cover up to 100 percent of the cost of financing slum clearance and building low-income housing units. The USHA was also authorized to make grants and annual subsidies to local housing agencies for the operation and maintenance of housing units after they were built. The USHA and its successor agencies, the Federal Public Housing Authority (1942–1946) and the Public Housing Administration (1946–the present), completed a total of 169,451 low-income public housing units under the authority of the 1937 housing act.[93]

World War II was the third national emergency (the others were World War I and the Great Depression) recognized by Congress as requiring the production of publicly built and financed housing. In addition to 50,000 housing units built during the war through the 1937 housing act authorizations, 2 million more units were provided through temporary and emergency programs to house workers who streamed into cities to take jobs in defense industry plants. Around a million of these were privately built with federal financial assistance, and another million were completed under programs that left ownership in the hands of the federal government.[94] As soon as the war ended, these government-owned units were sold on the private market.

The New Deal Legacy

The New Deal transformed American politics. The Great Depression persuaded local officials that it was legitimate to seek federal assistance. To help them do so, they formed an enduring urban lobby organized specifically to represent cities in the federal system. Through the United States Conference of Mayors (USCM), formed in 1932, mayors met annually to discuss their mutual problems. The USCM financed a permanent office in Washington to lobby for urban programs. Together with the International City Management Association (now the International City and County Management Association), the National Municipal League, the American Municipal League, and other organizations representing local public officials, cities developed the capacity to lobby federal administrators, Congress, and the White House.

The nation's first urban programs reflected the political pressures that local officials were able to bring to bear on Washington. Through the 1937 Housing Act, the federal government undertook slum clearance and built public housing. In the late 1930s, federal policymakers expressed a concern about urban problems. In 1937 the National Resources Committee, composed of federal administrators and experts appointed by the president, published a pamphlet titled *Our Cities: Their Role in the National Economy*.[95] The report asserted that slums and urban blight threatened a hoped-for economic recovery and recommended federal action to improve the economic performance of cities. Four years later the National Resources Planning Board issued a report, *Action for Cities: A Guide for Community Planning*, which recommended that cities devise local plans to combat blight and the federal government provide assistance for this purpose.[96] In 1944, a federally assisted highways bill was enacted; unlike highway legislation passed in the 1930s, this time the cities got their fair share of construction money. Five years later, in 1949, Congress passed a massive program to build public housing and clear slums in the inner cities.

Between 1953 and 1961, when a Republican president, Dwight Eisenhower, occupied the White House, urban interests were able to push through only one significant new program, the Interstate Highway Act of 1956, an accomplishment made possible because Republicans wanted it too. From 1959 to 1961, President Eisenhower even eliminated public housing requests from the federal budget. But in the wake of the election of John F. Kennedy in 1960, the urban lobby again found a receptive environment, and it did not take long for it to seize the moment. The New Deal experience had convinced city officials they had a right to argue for their interests in Washington, and they were already organized for the task. For years to come, Democrats in the White House and Congress would ignore the concerns of groups representing the cities, and the urban voters they spoke for, at their peril.

Endnotes

1. Samuel J. Eldersveld, "The Influence of Metropolitan Party Pluralities in Presidential Elections since 1920: A Study of Twelve Key Cities," *American Political Science Review* 43, no. 6 (December 1949): 1200.
2. W. B. Munro, *The Government of American Cities* (New York: Macmillan, 1913), p. 27.
3. In the first significant suburban movement of the twentieth century, which lasted from the late 1890s to about 1914 (the outbreak of World War I), the rate of growth in the suburbs exceeded the rate of growth in many central cities, but the total population gains in those cities were much larger than the population gains in suburbs.

Growth rates can be deceptive when expressed as percentage increases on a small original population base.

4. William E. Leuchtenburg, *The Perils of Prosperity, 1914–1932* (Chicago: University of Chicago Press, 1958), pp. 213–214.
5. Robert K. Murray, *The 103rd Ballot: Democrats and the Disaster in Madison Square Garden* (New York: Harper & Row, 1976), p. 9.
6. Kenneth T. Jackson, *The Ku Klux Klan in the City, 1915–1930* (New York: Oxford University Press, 1967).
7. Murray, *The 103rd Ballot*, p. 7.
8. Ibid.
9. Kenneth Finegold, *Experts and Politicians: Reform Challenges to Machine Politics in New York, Cleveland, and Chicago* (Princeton, NJ: Princeton University Press, 1995), p. 174.
10. Jessica Trounstine, *Political Monopolies in American Cities: The Rise and Fall of Bosses and Reformers* (Chicago: University of Chicago Press, 2008), p. 87.
11. Ibid., p. 98.
12. Ibid, p. 87.
13. Murray, *The 103rd Ballot*.
14. Murray, *The 103rd Ballot*, p. 103.
15. For good accounts of the 1924 convention, see Murray, *The 103rd Ballot*; Edmund A. Moore, *A Catholic Runs for President: The Campaign of 1928* (New York: Ronald Press, 1956); and Arthur M. Schlesinger Jr., *The Crisis of the Old Order, 1919–1933* (Boston: Houghton Mifflin, 1956).
16. John D. Hicks, *Republican Ascendancy, 1921–1933* (New York: Harper, 1960), p. 212.
17. Samuel Lubell, *The Future of American Politics*, 3rd revised ed. (New York: Harper & Row, 1965).
18. John Kenneth Galbraith, *The Great Crash, 1929*, revised ed. (Boston: Houghton Mifflin, 1979; first published in 1961), p. 99.
19. Lester V. Chandler, *America's Greatest Depression, 1929–1941* (New York: Harper-Collins, 1970), p. 5.
20. Ibid.
21. Ibid., p. 35.
22. William E. Leuchtenburg, *Franklin D. Roosevelt and the New Deal, 1932–1940* (New York: Harper & Row, 1963), p. 19.
23. Ibid., p. 1.
24. Chandler, *America's Greatest Depression*, p. 19.
25. Ibid., p. 57.
26. Arthur M. Schlesinger Jr., *The Coming of the New Deal* (Boston: Houghton Mifflin, 1957), p. 3.
27. Leuchtenburg, *Franklin D. Roosevelt*, p. 18.
28. Most relief was given by local public and private agencies. Although many states had programs for relief to designated categories of people—dependent children, people who are blind or disabled—few of these were actually funded.
29. Arthur E. Burns and Edward A. Williams, *Federal Work, Security, and Relief Programs* (New York: Da Capo Press, 1971), pp. 1–2; first published as *Research Monograph 24* (Washington, DC: Works Progress Administration, Division of Social Research, 1941).
30. James T. Patterson, *The New Deal and the States: Federalism in Transition* (Princeton, NJ: Princeton University Press, 1969), p. 30.

31. Ibid., p. 15.

32. Ibid.

33. Mark I. Gelfand, *A Nation of Cities: The Federal Government and Urban America, 1933–1965,* Urban Life in America Series (New York: Oxford University Press, 1975), p. 35.

34. Leuchtenburg, *Franklin D. Roosevelt,* p. 11.

35. Inauguration Day was changed to January by the Twentieth Amendment to the Constitution, ratified in 1933.

36. Leuchtenburg, *Franklin D. Roosevelt,* p. 39.

37. Ibid.

38. Ibid., p. 40.

39. For a thorough account of New Deal programs, see Burns and Williams, *Federal Work.*

40. Leuchtenburg, *Franklin D. Roosevelt,* p. 174.

41. Burns and Williams, *Federal Work,* pp. 29–36.

42. Leuchtenburg, *Franklin D. Roosevelt,* pp. 122–123.

43. Ibid., p. 133.

44. Josephine Chapin Brown, *Public Relief, 1929–1939* (New York: Holt, Rinehart & Winston, 1940), p. 249.

45. Quoted in William E. Binkley, *American Political Parties: Their Natural History* (New York: Knopf, 1943), p. 284.

46. Ibid., pp. 380–381.

47. Patterson, *The New Deal and the States,* p. 26.

48. Calculated from James A. Maxwell, *Federal Grants and the Business Cycle* (New York: National Bureau of Economic Research, 1952), p. 23, Table 7.

49. Ibid.

50. Gelfand, *A Nation of Cities,* p. 49.

51. U.S. Department of Commerce, Bureau of the Census, *Historical Statistics on State and Local Government Revenues, 1902–1953* (Washington, DC: U.S. Government Printing Office, 1955), p. 12.

52. Maxwell, *Federal Grants and the Business Cycle,* p. 27, Table 11.

53. Ibid., p. 24, Table 8.

54. Ibid., p. 29.

55. Gelfand, *A Nation of Cities,* p. 31.

56. Ibid., p. 32.

57. Ibid., p. 36.

58. Ibid.

59. Ibid., p. 34.

60. Patterson, *The New Deal and the States,* p. 39.

61. Ibid., p. 40.

62. Ibid.

63. Ibid., p. 44.

64. Ibid., p. 47.

65. Ibid., p. 40.

66. Brown, *Public Relief,* pp. 72–96.

67. George C. S. Benson, *The New Centralization: A Study in Intergovernmental Relationships in the United States* (New York: Holt, Rinehart & Winston, 1941), pp. 104–105.

68. Robert G. Dixon Jr., *Democratic Representation: Reapportionment in Law and Politics* (New York: Oxford University Press, 1968), p. 174.

69. Ibid., pp. 71–75, 80, 86–87.
70. Patterson, *The New Deal and the States*, p. 45.
71. Leuchtenburg, *Franklin D. Roosevelt*, p. 52.
72. Ibid., p. 136.
73. Guy Rexford Tugwell, quoted in ibid., p. 35.
74. Finegold, *Experts and Politicians*, p. 12; Bruce M. Stave, *The New Deal and the Last Hurrah: Pittsburgh Machine Politics* (Pittsburgh: University of Pittsburgh Press, 1970); Lyle W. Dorsett, *Franklin D. Roosevelt and the City Bosses* (Port Washington, NY: Kennikat, 1977); Dorsett, *The Pendergast Machine* (New York: Oxford University Press, 1968).
75. Quoted in Gelfand, *A Nation of Cities*, p. 66.
76. Public Law 65–102, 65th Cong. (1918); refer to Congressional Quarterly Service, *Housing a Nation* (Washington, DC: author), p. 166; Edith Elmer Wood, *Recent Trends in American Housing* (New York: Macmillan, 1931), p. 79.
77. Congressional Quarterly Service, *Housing a Nation*, pp. xiii.
78. Joint Resolution 52–22, 52d Cong. (1892); refer also to U.S. Congress, House, *Your Congress and American Housing—The Actions of Congress on Housing*, 82d Cong., 2d sess., 1952, H. Doc. 82-532, p. 1.
79. Public Laws 65–149 and 65–164, 65th Cong. (1918); refer also to Twentieth Century Fund, *Housing for Defense* (New York: Twentieth Century Fund, 1940), pp. 156–157; Congressional Quarterly Service, *Housing a Nation*, p. 18.
80. Refer to the Emergency Relief and Reconstruction Act, Public Law 72–302, 72d Cong. (1932).
81. The only other loan made under this authorization was $155,000 for rural housing in Ford County, Kansas.
82. Edwin L. Scanton, "Public Housing Trends in New York City" (Ph.D. dissertation, Graduate School of Banking, Rutgers University, 1952), p. 5.
83. Public Law 73–67, 72d Cong. (1933).
84. From a statement by Harold L. Ickes, Secretary of Interior and Public Works Administrator, quoted in Bert Swanson, "The Public Policy of Urban Renewal: Its Goals, Trends, and Conditions in New York City," paper delivered at the American Political Science Association Meeting (New York, September 1963), p. 10.
85. *U.S. v. Certain Lands in City of Louisville, Jefferson County, Ky., et al.*, 78 F.2d 64 (1935); *U.S. v. Certain Lands in City of Detroit et al.*, 12 F. Supp. 345 (1935).
86. Refer to Glen H. Boyer, *Housing: A Factual Analysis* (New York: Macmillan, 1958), p. 247.
87. Richard D. Bingham, *Public Housing and Urban Renewal: An Analysis of Federal-Local Relations*, Praeger Special Studies in U.S. Economics, Social, and Political Issues (New York: Praeger, 1975), p. 30.
88. Nathaniel S. Keith, *Politics and the Housing Crisis since 1930* (New York: Universe Books, 1973), p. 29.
89. Public Law 75–412, 75th Cong. (1937). Also found in U.S. Congress, House Committee on Banking and Currency, *Basic Laws and Authorizations on Urban Housing*, 91st Cong., 1st sess., 1969, p. 225.
90. Roscoe Martin, "The Expended Partnership," in *The New Urban Politics: Cities and the Federal Government*, ed. Douglas Fox (Pacific Palisades, CA: Goodyear, 1972), p. 51.
91. Keith, *Politics and the Housing Crisis*, p. 33.
92. The restriction limiting participation to low-income families, seen from a comparative perspective, is a root cause of the failure of public housing in America. See

Arnold J. Heidenheimer, Hugh Heclo, and Carolyn Teich Adams, *Comparative Public Policy: The Politics of Social Choice in Europe and America* (New York: St. Martin's Press, 1975), pp. 69–96.

93. Public Law 76–671, 76th Cong. (1940), relating to defense housing needs; Public Law 80–301, 80th Cong. (1946), suspended cost limitations for some low-income housing projects.

94. U.S. Housing and Home Finance Agency, *Fourteenth Annual Report* (Washington, DC: U.S. Government Printing Office, 1961), p. 380.

95. U.S. Department of the Interior, National Resources Committee, Urbanism Committee, *Our Cities: Their Role in the National Economy* (Washington, DC: U.S. Government Printing Office, 1937).

96. Philip J. Funigiello, "City Planning in World War II: The Experience of the National Resources Planning Board," *Social Science Quarterly* 53 (June 1972): 91–104.

PART II

The Urban Crisis of the Twentieth Century

CHAPTER 6

The City/Suburban Divide

A Century of Demographic Change

The twentieth-century movement of millions of people from the central cities to the suburbs constitutes one of the "great population migrations in American history."[1] The suburbs had begun drawing affluent families from the densely packed neighborhoods of the industrial cities as early as the turn of the century, and in the prosperous 1920s the suburbs began growing in earnest.[2] The suburban movement paused for a time in the years of the Great Depression and World War II, but turned into a gathering stampede as soon as postwar prosperity made it possible. The 1970 census revealed that, for the first time, more Americans lived in suburbs than in either rural areas or the central cities. And the suburbs just kept on growing. All through the 1980s and 1990s, suburban communities continued to sprawl in ever-widening arcs around the historic urban centers.

A second great story of the twentieth century involved the several successive waves of migration in the opposite direction, into the cities. From the turn of the century to the 1930s, blacks left the South and poured into the industrial cities of the North, Mexican immigrants made their way to cities of the Southwest, and the great rural-to-urban migration that had begun in the nineteenth century continued to unfold. After World War II, these restless waves of movement reached flood tide. White families living in desperate poverty fled the Appalachian coal fields and depressed areas scattered across rural areas of the country. They were joined by millions of African Americans who pulled up roots and struck out for the cities of the North. Mexicans continued to filter across the border but in larger numbers than before, and by the late century their presence had ignited an anti-immigrant backlash.

Measured in social and political turmoil, the postwar migration of 5 million African Americans out of the South was clearly the most traumatic of all these population movements.[3] In the mid-1960s, a new phrase, "the urban crisis," was coined as a way of referring to the rapidly emerging geography of extreme segregation that separated whites, who now lived primarily in the suburbs, from blacks, who were concentrated in the central cities. In the popular imagination, the phrase came to signify the collision of two powerful cultural stereotypes: "the black ghetto," on the one hand, and, on the other, the American dream of homeownership and upward mobility. These contrasting images called attention to a fundamental fact of American life: in a single generation, racial segregation had become the transcendent issue in national politics and culture, in the

North as well as in the South. Americans became accustomed to thinking in dichotomies—city/suburban, black/white, ghetto/subdivision, poor/affluent—and these habits of thought consistently cast cities in a dismal light.[4] The suburbs became identified, in the popular imagination, with tranquil subdivisions with cul-de-sacs and green expanses of lawn; at the same time, images of race, poverty, crime, and slums symbolized the inner cities. By the 1970s, stories of murder, mayhem, and drugs in urban neighborhoods became a means by which local news stations could shore up their ratings. For white Americans, crime and violence became symbols for the inner city and the people who lived there.[5]

Since the mid-1980s, the United States has been undergoing still another demographic transformation. Millions of immigrants have been making their way to the United States from countries all over the world, but for the first time in the nation's history most of them are bypassing the cities entirely and moving directly into the suburbs or beyond. This movement has been transforming both the geography and the politics of urban areas in unexpected ways. The tensions of urban society are no longer rooted mainly in differences between city and suburb. Today, the racial and ethnic groups that make up urban society are spread throughout metropolitan regions. As of 2006, the Hispanic population in the United States exceeded the African American population,[6] and by midcentury, Latinos are expected to outnumber blacks by more than two to one.[7] Already, these trends are bringing about profound social and political changes to the nation and to its urban areas.

OUTTAKE

Anti-Immigrant Passions Have Reached a Fever Pitch

Unlike any period in the past, immigrants are now moving nearly everywhere in the United States. It was once assumed, correctly, that foreign immigrants tended to concentrate into a few gateway cities, and from there spread out to older inner-city neighborhoods. In recent years, however, this pattern has changed so much that many suburbs have become as ethnically diverse as the historic cities at the metropolitan core. In the 1990s, for example, immigrants from an impressive number of countries moved to the suburbs of Long Island: Japanese, Koreans, Vietnamese, Indians, Pakistanis, and Iranians from Asia, and Guatemalans, Cubans, Haitians, and Salvadorans from the Caribbean and Latin America. Immigrants are also moving to cities of all sizes and small towns and rural areas in almost every region of the country. Some rural areas have been changed almost overnight as immigrant workers moved to be near meat packing plants, poultry operations, and agribusinesses devoted to raising livestock or processing agricultural products.

Such massive changes have spawned fear and resentment, and it is clear that the most inflamed passions have been aimed at undocumented immigrants from Mexico. Hundreds of measures have been introduced into state legislatures to curb and regulate immigration. In 2007, state legislatures considered 1,562 immigration-related measures and enacted 240 of them, a threefold increase over 2006. Among other things, these laws made it a felony for an employer to hire an illegal immigrant, even unknowingly, or for an illegal immigrant to hold a job; made it harder for illegal immigrants to get state ID papers or driver's licenses; and barred illegal immigrants from receiving unemployment insurance or other public services. Over the next two years, local governments adopted literally thousands of anti-immigrant ordinances, many of them of doubtful legality, and police departments took measures to rid their communities of illegal immigrants— and, critics charged, of all Hispanics. As a pretext for deportation, local police departments targeted Hispanic people they thought might be immigrants by arresting them for minor crimes, or detained Hispanics merely on the suspicion that they might be in the country illegally.

The hostility toward immigrants was inflamed by the economic crisis that began to unfold in 2008. By 2010, it had reached a fevered pitch not seen since the anti-immigrant hysteria that swept the country almost 100 years before. When Arizona's governor signed into law the nation's strictest anti-immigration law on April 23, 2010, it unleashed a firestorm of protest. The legislation made it a crime to fail to carry identification proving citizenship, and empowered police to arrest anyone if they had a "reasonable cause" to suspect a person was in the country illegally. While conservatives in the Republican Party praised the law, critics called for boycotts on Arizona travel, hurried to prepare legal challenges, and sponsored street protests and rallies. Opponents charged that the law would encourage racial profiling and harassment. President Obama also criticized it, saying that the legislation "threatened to undermine basic notions of fairness that we cherish as Americans. . . ." Meanwhile, a series of unintended consequences from the law's passage began to unfold. Hundreds of thousands of illegal immigrants and Hispanic citizens began an exodus that had already been taking place since 2008. The number of foreclosures and vacant homes skyrocketed. It was estimated that the impact on the housing market alone could run into hundreds of millions of dollars and that the state's economy would lose more than $26 billion if all undocumented immigrants were to leave. Nevertheless, it was unclear if economic realities could much influence the course of a controversy stirred up by such emotions.

Sources: Dan Anderson, "Times Topics: Immigration and Refuges," *New York Times* (June 9, 2008): 20, Randal C. Archibald, "Arizona Enacts Stringent Law on Immigration," *New York Times* (April 23, 2010), Seth Hoy, "Another Unintended Consequence of AZ Immigration Law: More Foreclosures and Vacant Homes," *AlterNet*, www.alternet.org/rights/147211.

Streams of Migration

Three periods of migration and foreign immigration created the crisis of segregation, race, and poverty that beset America's cities by the second half of the twentieth century.[8] The data in Table 6.1 reveal that the first wave began in the early twentieth century and crested just before the Great Depression. Between

	TABLE 6.1	**Rural-to-Urban Migrant Streams in Twentieth-Century America**			

Migrant Group	Principal Migration Period	Approximate Number of Migrants[a]	Origin	Destination
Appalachian whites	1940–1970	1,600,000	Southern Appalachian Mountains (Kentucky and West Virginia)	North-central states
Mexicans	1910–1930	700,000	Mesa Central primarily, also Mesa del Norte	Texas and southwestern states
	1940–1970	700,000	Mesa Central primarily, also Mesa del Norte	Texas and California
Blacks	1910–1930	1,250,000[b]	Mississippi delta, Atlantic black belt, coastal plain	Illinois, Ohio, Michigan, New York, and Pennsylvania
	1940–1970	5,000,000[b]	Mississippi delta, Atlantic black belt, coastal plain	Cities everywhere

[a]These figures are approximate. The data for the Mexican migration, for example, are obscured by contract labor, two-way migration, and illegal entrants.
[b]U.S. Bureau of the Census, *Historical Statistics of the United States: Colonial Times to 1970* (Washington, DC: U.S. Government Printing Office, 2002). Greenberg's original table lists 1 million blacks, 1910–1930, and 3.5 million blacks, 1940–1965.

Source: Adapted from Stanley B. Greenberg, *Politics and Poverty: Modernization and Response in Five Poor Neighborhoods* (New York: Wiley, 1974), p. 19.

1910 and 1930, some 700,000 Mexicans moved into Texas, New Mexico, Arizona, and California, and more than a million blacks left the southern states for Chicago, Detroit, Cleveland, New York City, Pittsburgh, Philadelphia, and other cities of the industrial Midwest and Northeast. The second, much bigger wave washed over the cities during World War II and did not ebb until the late 1960s. From 1940 to 1970, up to 5 million blacks and 700,000 Mexicans moved into America's inner cities. During this same period, more than a million and a half impoverished whites also left rural and small-town life, although their migration received little attention.

Between 1910 and 1926, the bloody and protracted violence of the Mexican Revolution drove Mexicans into the southwestern states. Although the revolution released millions of peasants from their feudal relationship with landholders, it left many of them without a way to make a living. Bloody confrontations between a Mexican government dedicated to land reform and landowners who resisted change drove the newly liberated peasants into Texas, Arizona, and

California. During World War II and its aftermath, employment opportunities in the southwestern states induced still more Mexicans to cross the border. By 1970, 5.5 million Mexican Americans were living in the American Southwest, accounting for more than 90 percent of all the people of Mexican descent in the United States.[9] By 2000, 17.9 million Mexican Americans were spread out in the South and throughout the western states, about 87 percent of the nation's total.[10] Hispanic immigrants from several other Latin American countries streamed into the states of the Southwest in even larger numbers in the 1980s and 1990s, pushed by political repression and poverty and pulled by the availability of jobs.

The inexorable decline of the coal industry from the 1930s to the 1960s in the southern Appalachian Mountains and the Cumberland Plateau of Virginia, West Virginia, and Kentucky forced the desperately poor families in mining communities to flee year by year by the thousands. The exodus reached such proportions after World War II that some counties in Appalachia were almost depopulated. In his moving book *Night Comes to the Cumberlands*, Harry Caudill describes the abject poverty that forced families and entire communities to pick up and leave their marginal farm plots and shabby towns. Families could trace their roots in Appalachia several generations back. Homesickness for the hills and hollows left behind became a lament often expressed in folk and bluegrass music. In the 1950s alone, a quarter of the population deserted the Cumberland Plateau, settling in cities and towns of Kentucky, Tennessee, Maryland, Virginia, and the industrial belt of the upper Midwest.[11] A steady stream of impoverished white families living in the smaller coal fields of southern Illinois, Kentucky, and Arkansas joined them. The new migrants, who were scarcely more welcome than blacks and Hispanics, were derisively called Hoosiers, Okies, and Arkies. Like the flood of African Americans and the lesser stream of Hispanics, they crowded into rundown urban neighborhoods, although unlike these groups, they had the option of moving into small towns or trailer parks located at some remove from the inner city. More than class origins or poverty, race was the great dividing line of American urban life.

The two great waves of African American migration, one before the Depression and the other in the years after World War II, were by far the largest regional population movements of the twentieth century, and they had the most enduring effects. Historians have referred to the exodus of blacks from the South between 1910 and 1930 as "the Great Migration" because it was "one of the largest and most rapid mass internal movements of people in history—perhaps the greatest not caused by the immediate threat of execution or starvation."[12] In the decade from 1910 to 1920, 450,000 blacks moved out of the South, followed by another 750,000 in the 1920s.[13] In the 20 years between 1910 and 1930, about a million blacks—one-tenth of all blacks living in the South—moved to cities in the Northeast and Midwest. In just 20 years, the black population living outside the South shot up by 134 percent, and the proportion of the nation's black population residing in the South dropped from 89 to 79 percent.[14]

Like the generations of European immigrants who preceded them, African Americans were pushed by crisis and pulled by opportunity. Poverty and unemployment in the South provided the push, jobs in the North the pull. Beginning in southern Texas in the late 1890s and sweeping eastward through Georgia by 1921, boll weevil infestations wiped out cotton crops, forcing black sharecroppers off the land. In the same period, an abrupt decline in European immigration occasioned by World War I, combined with the sudden rise of armaments industries, produced labor shortages in the industrial cities of the North.

Almost all the African Americans leaving the South settled into densely packed neighborhoods in northern cities. Only 10 percent of the nation's blacks lived in cities of 100,000 or more in 1910; this percentage increased to 16 percent in 1920 and to 24 percent by 1930.[15] The biggest cities lured most of the migrants. The proportion of blacks living in cities smaller than 100,000 declined from 1910 to 1930, but the proportion increased substantially in cities of over 100,000.[16] Thus, the Great Migration was made up of two principal components: Blacks were becoming northern, and they were becoming urban.

African Americans made up more than 2 percent of the population in only a handful of northern cities in 1910. By 1930, however, they accounted for 18 percent of the population of Gary, Indiana, and 16 percent in East St. Louis, Illinois, with its stockyards, rail yards, and heavy industry. As shown in Table 6.2, in the same two decades, black populations had grown two to three times as large in the big cities. By 1930, percentages ranged from almost 5 percent in New York City to 7 percent in Chicago and 8 percent in Cleveland, to just over 11 percent in St. Louis and Philadelphia. African Americans became concentrated in well-defined ghettos. In north Harlem in New York City, about one-third (36 percent) of the population was African American in 1920, but this proportion increased to 81 percent by the 1930 census.[17]

The North was a "promised land" that offered an escape from the violent racism of the South and the opportunity for economic advancement. Southern blacks began their trek to northern cities and states as a means of escaping

TABLE 6.2 Growth of Black Population in Several Cities, 1910–1930

City	Total Population			Percentage Increase		
	1910	1920	1930	1910–1930	1910	1930
New York	91,709	152,467	327,706	257.3%	2%	5%
Chicago	44,103	109,458	233,903	429.3	2	7
Philadelphia	84,459	134,229	219,599	160.0	5.5	11
St. Louis	43,960	69,854	93,580	112.9	6	11
Cleveland	8,448	34,451	71,889	751.0	1.5	8

Source: U.S. Bureau of the Census, Negroes in the United States, 1920–1932 (Washington, DC: U.S. Government Printing Office, 1935), p. 55.

the shackles of the southern caste system. The migration northward had already commenced when, in May 1917, the publisher of the *Chicago Defender* launched "The Great Northern Drive" to persuade blacks to move. Founded in 1905, by World War I the *Defender* already had reached a circulation of 100,000, and blacks read it avidly throughout the South. The *Defender's* editorials exhorted blacks to come north to the land of opportunity, where they could find employment and, if not equality, at least an escape from harassment and violence. Its columns of job advertisements added substance to the vision of the "promised land." At the same time, the *Defender* exposed the terrible conditions experienced by blacks living in the South. Lynchings and other forms of intimidation were regularly highlighted in lurid detail. Moving out of the South was portrayed as a way to advance the cause of racial equality for all blacks.[18]

The *Defender* was only one of many voices encouraging African Americans to abandon the South. Those who had already moved wrote letters to relatives and friends describing their new life in glowing terms. Despite job and housing discrimination in the North, they found conditions preferable to those they had left behind. Throughout the South, blacks lived under a reign of terror. From 1882 to 1930, there were 1,663 lynchings in the five states of the Cotton Belt alone—Alabama, Georgia, Louisiana, Mississippi, and South Carolina—and 1,299 blacks were legally executed.[19] In the 10 southern states, more than 2,500 blacks—an average of about one person per week—were lynched between 1880 and 1930.[20] The legal systems of the southern states were so completely rigged that the difference between lynching and legalized murder by police and the courts was not much more than a technicality. Blacks who failed to obey the racial caste system, even inadvertently, could expect immediate retribution in the form of beatings or worse. Failing to step off the sidewalk, forgetting to say "sir" or "ma'am," or looking a white person in the eye could bring a sudden and violent reaction. As a way of enforcing strict obedience, lynchings had long been a way of life throughout the southern states. Frequently these descended into orgies of depravity, the victims slowly tortured to death with blowtorches or other devices, and the mobs carrying off clothing and body parts as souvenirs.[21]

The opportunities for leaving such conditions improved in proportion to labor shortages in northern factories. After war broke out in Europe in 1914, factory owners found themselves with lucrative armaments contracts but too few workers. They sent labor agents into the South with free train tickets in hand, which could be exchanged for a labor agreement. Southern white employers and planters took steps to prevent the exodus of their cheap labor. Magazines, newspapers, and business organizations decried the movement, as in this October 5, 1916, editorial in the Memphis *Commercial Appeal*:

> The enormous demand for labor and the changing conditions brought about by the boll weevil in certain parts of the South have caused an exodus of negroes which may be serious. Great colonies of negroes have gone north to work in factories, in packing houses and on the railroads. . . .

The South needs every able-bodied negro that is now south of the line, and every negro who remains south of the line will in the end do better than he will do in the North. . . .

The negroes who are in the South should be encouraged to remain there, and those white people who are in the boll weevil territory should make every sacrifice to keep their negro labor until there can be adjustments to the new and quickly prosperous conditions that will later exist.[22]

States and communities went to great lengths to discourage migration. Jacksonville, Florida, passed an ordinance in 1916 levying heavy fines on unlicensed labor agents from the North. Macon, Georgia, made it impossible for labor agents to get licenses and then outlawed unlicensed agents. The mayor of Atlanta talked to blacks about the "dreadfully cold" northern winters.[23] In some communities, police were sent to railroad stations to harass blacks near the stations, keep them from boarding trains, or even drive them off the trains.

But the "promised land" beckoned, and despite all obstacles the exodus continued. What the new arrivals found was opportunity—but not equal opportunity—and persistent discrimination. Whenever blacks attempted to move into white neighborhoods, they were harassed or violently assaulted. In the workplace, they were the last hired and the first fired. They were kept in the most menial occupations. Job opportunities were limited not only by employers but even more so by labor unions, which generally prohibited blacks from membership. Because the North was more heavily unionized than the South, there were actually fewer opportunities in some occupations, especially for skilled laborers.[24] In both union and nonunion shops, white workers often refused to work alongside blacks. To avoid trouble, employers assigned blacks to the least desirable jobs.

African Americans found it hard to adjust to urban life. Hardly any of them had previously lived in a city. Many had never even participated directly in the cash economy. Sharecroppers had often worked under contracts with provisions that they buy only from the planters' stores and then with scrip and credit rather than cash. Some of them had never even seen U.S. currency, and they were often cheated and overcharged.

These conditions, when amplified by the intense segregation into dilapidated, overcrowded ghettos, led to astonishing levels of social pathology. The arrest rate for blacks in Detroit in 1926 was four times that for whites. Blacks constituted 31 percent of the nation's prison population in 1923, although they made up only 9 percent of the total population. The death rate in Harlem between 1923 and 1927 was 42 percent higher than in New York City as a whole, even though Harlem's population was much younger than the overall city population. Harlem's infant mortality rate was 111 per 1,000 births, compared with the city's rate of 64 per 1,000. Tuberculosis, heart disease, and other illnesses also far exceeded the rates for the city's general population.[25]

Blacks moving into northern cities were often surprised when they encountered a level of hostility, racism, and discrimination that was almost as bad as in the South. Restaurants and stores refused to serve them; banks typically refused to give them loans. Cemeteries, parks, bathing beaches, and other facilities were put off limits or divided into "white" and "colored" sections. Many dentists, doctors, and hospitals refused to treat blacks. Worse, the violence that had plagued them in the South followed them everywhere they went. On July 2, 1917, 39 blacks and 5 whites died in a race riot in East St. Louis, Illinois.[26] In the infamous "Red Summer" of 1919, race riots broke out in more than 20 cities, all of them involving attacks by white mobs on blacks. Chicago's riot of that summer started when a black teenager inadvertently swam across a strip of water separating the beach designated "For Coloreds Only" from the one reserved for whites. A crowd stoned the boy to death and then terrorized blacks throughout the city for days. From July 1, 1917, to March 1, 1921, Chicago experienced 58 racial bombings.[27] Unemployed blacks were forced out of Buffalo by city police in 1920. That same year, in perhaps the worst mass murder of blacks in U.S. history, more than 300 blacks were killed by white mobs in Tulsa, Oklahoma—an incident covered up for almost 80 years before it was brought to light.[28] Almost everywhere, blacks who attempted to move into white neighborhoods were terrorized by cross burnings, vandalism, and mob violence.

In all cities, restrictive covenants were attached to property deeds to keep African Americans from buying into white neighborhoods. Deeds with racial restrictions were filed in the office of the county clerk or the register of deeds and enforced by the courts. Chicago, with more than 11 square miles covered by restricted deeds in 1944, was typical of northern cities.[29] Neighborhood improvement associations sprung up in new subdivisions and, by legal prosecution and social persuasion, they forced homeowners to accept and abide by restrictive covenants. The result was that racial segregation in northern cities had become firmly fixed even before the second great wave of black migration, which was many times larger than the first.

Racial Conflict in The Postwar Era

Although the movement to the North slowed to a crawl in the years of the Great Depression, during World War II it picked up momentum and soon reached levels far exceeding anything that came before. As in the years of the Great Migration, factory jobs pulled blacks into northern cities, and conditions in the South provided a push. The mechanization of southern agriculture, in particular the widespread adoption of the mechanized cotton picker, threw hundreds of thousands of sharecroppers and farm laborers out of work. From Texas, Louisiana, and Arkansas, blacks streamed into cities of the West, especially in California; from the middle South, they moved to St. Louis, Chicago, Detroit, Cleveland, and other cities of the Midwest; and from Mississippi and eastward in the Deep South, they moved to Washington, D.C., New York, Boston, and other cities in the East. In 1940, 77 percent of the nation's blacks still lived in the southern states but by 1950 only 60 percent lived in the South. Over the next two decades the South's share declined to 56 percent (in 1960) and to 53 percent (in 1970).[30] Almost all the northward-bound migrants ended up in cities.

As blacks continued their trek out of the South, the pressure on the urban housing stock intensified. The African American families crowded into segregated areas expressed resentment about the invisible walls that kept them out of the more desirable areas inhabited by whites.[31] At the other end of the scale, virtually all whites felt an imperative to keep their neighborhoods segregated.[32] Realtors made sure that blacks stayed out of white areas by refusing to show them homes there, or by rejecting their business altogether. Sometimes, though, realtors made money by doing exactly the opposite. To induce white homeowners to sell their homes at bargain prices, some realtors distributed handbills or went door-to-door announcing that blacks were moving onto the block. Panicked homeowners were eager to sell out cheap, and at the other end of the process the realtor was able to charge a premium for blacks who wanted to buy homes in the "busted" neighborhood.[33]

The tactics employed by homeowners to resist the movement of blacks into their neighborhoods assumed some of the aspects of war. In the 1950s, a homeowners' movement swept through the neighborhoods of Detroit. Neighborhood associations organized meetings to urge their neighbors not to sell to blacks and to discuss strategies of resistance. At night, when they could most effectively terrorize their victims, crowds gathered in front of houses newly purchased by black families, shouting racial epithets and insults; strewing garbage on the lawn; breaking windows with stones, bricks, and bottles; tearing down fences; breaking car windshields; and, if all else failed, setting fire to the house.[34] Racial change occurred in block-by-block skirmishes, with whites making a slow retreat until panic precipitated a sudden exodus. By the mid-1960s, resistance had given way to "white flight," and white families were fleeing from the neighborhoods of central cities.

For both blacks and whites, the racial wars shattered lives and left an enduring legacy of bitterness. Whites who fled in panic sold their homes at bargain-basement prices. Blacks who had to abandon their houses in the face of intimidation often lost their investments and any hope of moving out of the slums. Many neighborhoods never recovered from the turmoil; for others, it would take decades, if it happened at all. In 2005, Detroit was a city in which 11 percent of the population was white and 82 percent was African American. The contrast to its suburbs was stark: there, African Americans comprised less than 10 percent of the population.[35]

As a result of the two streams flowing in opposite directions—blacks moving into the cities, whites fleeing to the suburbs—the demographic composition of the central cities changed almost overnight. By the mid-1960s, a yawning racial chasm separated the central cities from the suburbs. In the wake of urban riots in 1965 and 1966, a series of presidential commissions gave expression to the rising concern that the extreme segregation of urban areas had developed into a national crisis. The National Commission on Civil Disorders of 1967 (called the Kerner Commission after its chair, Illinois governor Otto B. Kerner) warned of "two nations, one black, one white—separate and unequal."[36] With this phrase, the commission was merely acknowledging a reality that anyone could easily observe. Table 6.3 shows that in 1940, blacks accounted for more than

TABLE 6.3 Percentage of Blacks in Central Cities and Suburban Rings in 12 Selected Standard Metropolitan Statistical Areas (SMSAs), 1940, 1970, and 2000[a]

	Central City			Suburban Ring		
	1940	1970	2000	1940	1970	2000
New York[b]	6%	23%	29.5%	5%	6%	10%
Los Angeles–Long Beach	6	21	12	2	7	6
Chicago	8	34	37	2	4	11
Philadelphia	13	34	45	7	7	12
Detroit	9	44	83	3	4	9
San Francisco–Oakland	5	33	12	4	9	6
Boston	3	18	28	1	2	3.5
Pittsburgh	9	27	28	4	4	5
St. Louis	13	41	52	7	8	13
Washington, D.C.	28.5	72	61	14	9	23
Cleveland	10	39	52	1	1	11
Baltimore	19	47	65	12	6	14.5
All 12 SMSAs	9	31	33.5	4	6	10

[a]Except for St. Louis, Baltimore, and Washington, D.C., figures refer to the consolidated metropolitan statistical areas (CMSAs), which are not strictly comparable to the standard metropolitan statistical areas (SMSAs) used in earlier years. For 2000, additional central cities are included for some urban areas: Oakland for San Francisco–Oakland; Bridgeport (Connecticut), Newark, Jersey City, and New Haven for New York. As of 2000, Washington, D.C., and Baltimore were considered central cities of a single metropolitan area, but they are kept separate to facilitate accurate comparisons with earlier censuses. Camden has also been deleted as a separate central city for the Philadelphia region. Calculated from U.S. Bureau of the Census, *Census of 2000*, www.census.gov.
[b]Includes data from the Nassau–Suffolk SMSA, which was deleted from the New York City SMSA in 1971. They are included to maintain comparability across time periods.

Source: Data for 1940 and 1970 adapted from Leo F. Schnore, Carolyn D. André, and Harry Sharp, "Black Suburbanization, 1930–1970," in *The Changing Face of the Suburbs*, ed. Barry Schwartz (Chicago: University of Chicago Press, 1976), p. 80. Reprinted by permission. The figures here were transposed to yield data on black percentages.

10 percent of the population in just 4 of 12 big cities; on average, the proportion was 9 percent. Only 30 years later, African Americans made up 72 percent of the population in Washington, D.C., 47 percent in Baltimore, 44 percent in Detroit, 39 percent in Cleveland, and 41 percent in St. Louis.

Although the opposing streams of movement began to slow in the 1970s, the racial gap continued to grow more extreme right up to the end of century. By the 2000 census, African Americans accounted for large majorities in several cities even while the suburbs contained relatively few African Americans. The data displayed in Table 6.3 reveal that even as late as the census of 2000, African Americans accounted for barely more than 10 percent of the suburban population (and sometimes less) in most of the leading metropolitan areas: 11 percent in Chicago's suburbs, 9 percent in Detroit's, and 5 percent in Pittsburgh's; 3.5 percent in Boston's, and 11 percent in Cleveland's. High levels of residential segregation between suburban jurisdictions shows that the racial disparities inherited from the era of the urban crisis continue to persist.

The Emergence of a New Kind of Poverty

Inevitably, the mass migration of rural blacks to the inner cities and their concentration into densely packed urban neighborhoods created intractable social problems. Blacks were not only crowded into segregated slums, but their plight was also aggravated by their high rate of poverty and the constant influx of new arrivals. A large proportion of blacks lived in areas in which almost everyone was poor. Ironically, the problem of concentrated poverty worsened at the same time that housing opportunities for middle-class blacks improved. As the African American middle class abandoned the ghetto, they left behind the families that lacked the resources to make the same move. The result was that poverty became more concentrated, even, than before. In 1970, the Census Bureau classified more than one-fourth (27 percent) of the census tracts located in the 100 largest cities as officially designated "poverty" tracts where at least 20 percent of the residents lived in households with incomes that fell below the federal government's poverty line. Two decades later the percentage of poverty tracts had reached 39 percent. [37] In 2005, the poverty rate in large cities (18.8 percent) was twice as high as in the suburbs (9.4 percent), and this ratio had not changed for decades.[38]

African Americans, Hispanics, and American Indians are far more likely to live in high-poverty neighborhoods than whites.[39] A 2011 survey study found that overall, African American and Hispanic households live in neighborhoods with more than one and a half times the national poverty rate. The differences, though, may be even more extreme than that statistic seems to suggest—for example, in 2010 African American and Hispanic households earning more than $75,000 lived in less affluent and resource-rich neighborhoods than white households earning less than $40,000.[40]

In the 1980s, the sociologist William Julius Wilson used the term *underclass* to refer to people who were concentrated in low-income areas and who were chronically out of work and out of the social mainstream.[41] The media, politicians, and social scientists quickly appropriated the term, using it to refer loosely to "a constellation of behaviors or conditions, including being poor and living in the inner city, being chronically unemployed, on welfare, homeless, residing in a single-parent family (especially with illegitimate children), having a criminal record, or using drugs (especially crack cocaine)."[42] Although this list clearly included behaviors that might be exhibited throughout society or by poor people regardless of where they lived, the term was normally used to refer to African Americans exclusively. Frequently, "underclass" was defined so broadly that it included blacks not living in poverty areas at all but who allegedly exhibited a single characteristic (such as unemployment or single parenthood) that was thought of as "underclass." In short, the underclass concept became a way of speaking about race without actually admitting that race was the topic of conversation.[43]

Because the underclass concept was widely exploited for ideological purposes and as a media stereotype, most scholars abandoned it. Wilson stopped using the term and began instead to refer to the harmful effects that result from segregating the poor together as "concentration effects."[44] Later, he used the term *the new urban poverty*, and his main focus turned to the high proportion of unemployed males in areas with high poverty rates: "poor, segregated neighborhoods in which a substantial majority of individual adults are either unemployed or have dropped out of the labor force altogether."[45] Without work, he said, a necessary structure for daily life disappeared, and the activities that replaced work—such as hanging out on the corner, engaging in petty crime, becoming involved with drugs—undermined family life. Wilson linked the persistent joblessness among African Americans to the steep decline of manufacturing jobs in the 1970s and 1980s. In the past, African Americans held a disproportionate share of blue-collar jobs, and even though their employment in the service sector rose sharply in the period of deindustrialization, full-employment wages declined by 25 to 30 percent by the mid-1990s.[46] Wilson's research was alarming because it appeared that the conditions of life in the inner-city ghettos were getting worse, with no end in sight. It was a dismal conclusion to reach fully a quarter century after the civil rights legislation and the programs of the Great Society.

A large number of studies documented the startling dimensions of the unresolved problems of inner-city poverty neighborhoods. More than two-thirds of African American families were headed by single women. By itself this would not have seemed so bad, except that in 1993 families headed by divorced women made 40 percent as much as households headed by a husband and a wife.[47] Households headed by women who had never been married made only 21 percent as much, and *two-thirds* of all children in such families lived in poverty (compared to one-tenth of children in married-couple families).[48] Since the mid-1970s, middle-class families had been able to maintain high living standards because there were typically two wage earners in the household. Increasingly, a large proportion of African American women were forced to work in low-paying and seasonal jobs. When combined with the rising unemployment levels among African American men, the pathways out of poverty seemed few indeed.

Health and health care in inner-city poverty areas continued to deteriorate after the 1970s. Families in poverty generally lacked health insurance, and so were forced into overcrowded health clinics and emergency rooms. For these reasons, in 1990 the United States had among the highest infant mortality rates in the industrialized world.[49] The overall national rate was about 10 deaths for every 1,000 live births in the late 1980s, but the rate for inner-city poverty neighborhoods approached that of developing countries. In 1988–1989, for example, the infant mortality rate in central Harlem was 23 per 1,000 births, about the same as in Malaysia.[50] In the 1980s, the drug epidemic began to devastate inner-city minority neighborhoods. The murder rate among young black males tripled between 1984 and 1991, in part because of crack cocaine and heroin use.[51] Young men in well-armed gangs fought one another to control the lucrative business. The connection between crack and violence went beyond the gangs, however. Because crack was so addictive, users resorted to robbery, burglary, car theft, and prostitution to feed their habit.

Fueled by turf wars between gangs engaged in the drug trade, violent crime soared in American cities in the late 1980s and early 1990s.[52] In 1990, New York City set a record with 2,262 murders, yet its per capita homicide rate ranked it only slightly above average for the country's 25 largest cities.[53] Violent death reached pandemic proportions among young black and Latino males in inner-city areas. Citing the fact that homicide was the leading cause of death for black males aged 15 to 24 in 1990, the federal Centers for Disease Control and Prevention (CDC) stated the casualty rate was approaching that of war. According to a study in the *New England Journal of Medicine*, young men in Harlem, primarily because of high homicide rates, were less likely to survive to the age of 40 than their counterparts in Bangladesh.[54] A late-1980s survey of schoolchildren in Chicago found that an astonishing 24 percent of them had personally witnessed a murder.[55]

Despite the fact that overall crime rates fell after 1990, there continued to be a high level of random violent crime in low-income minority areas. Gang warfare had become a fact of life in low-income minority communities, and innocent bystanders frequently got caught up in street-level violence. This trend has continued in recent years. For instance, although 2009 was the safest year in New York in more than four decades, in the first 11 weeks of 2010, the city-wide murder rate increased 22.8 percent over the same period as in 2009, and most of this occurred in a few high-poverty areas.

The problems in the urban ghetto in the late twentieth century bred a national obsession with crime and violence. In 1990, approximately 20 percent of front-page news stories and local news broadcasts focused on violent crime.[56] A 10:00 P.M. newscast typically contained live footage of reporter standing at a crime scene in front of a minicam, the talking head soon giving way to a video collage of a bloodstained street or sidewalk, shocked spectators, and perhaps grief-stricken friends and relatives. The discourse about the inner cities became "our . . . national morality play," a performance made up of sensationalized and exaggerated narratives of good and evil, the "good" in the suburbs, and the "evil" in the cities.[57]

In the 1990s, the stark divide between cities and suburbs began to melt away, and thus the main defining characteristic of the postwar urban crisis began to disappear. At the national level, other issues—terrorism, economic crisis, immigration, and the environment—have largely displaced concern about the cities and their problems. As suburbs have become more diverse they have also become more "urban," and the revitalization of the central cities has restored a sense that they are vital and interesting places. These momentous developments tend to obscure the fact that many of the social problems associated with the urban crisis persist. Blacks still remain more highly segregated than any other racial or ethnic group in American society, and poverty and violence remain as intractable problems in poor neighborhoods. The urban crisis took a long time to develop, and its effects will echo for a long time to come.

The Suburban Exodus

To understand how the urban crisis of the twentieth century emerged so quickly, it is not sufficient to focus solely on the segregation of African Americans into inner-city neighborhoods. The mass exodus of the white population is the other side of the coin. Wealthy people began leaving the cities in the nineteenth century, but only in small numbers. Hardly anyone noticed because the industrial cities were prosperous and crowded. In the twentieth century, urban America underwent a historic sea change when the movement to suburbs accelerated at the same time that the industrial cities began to lose their economic vitality. The denouement to this process came in the years after World War II, when white families of all social classes began to desert the cities en masse.

The movement to the suburbs came in four great bursts, each fueled by some combination of middle-class prosperity, transportation innovations, a desire for a larger house and a higher standard of living—and a growing rejection of the city. Although a few suburbs began to form as early as the mid-nineteenth century, when railroads made it possible for a few affluent urban dwellers to escape the teeming masses in the densely packed cities, the first burst of suburban development began later in the century, with the building of a streetcar network. A second surge, which came in the 1920s, was energized by middle-class prosperity, the adoption of the automobile, and the building of paved roads. But the two suburban movements that truly altered the geography of urban America and redefined its national politics have come over the past half century or so: first, in the 1950s and 1960s, with the flight of middle- and working-class white families from the city, and second, the movement of minorities and immigrants not only to the cities, but throughout metropolitan areas. As we shall see, these successive periods of suburban growth changed the contours of American urban politics in their own distinctive ways.

The Romantic Suburban Ideal: 1815–1918

The first faint hint of a city/suburban split became evident quite early in the nation's history. The desire to escape from the maddening crowd can be traced not only to the conditions in the industrial cities but also to a deeply ingrained hostility to urban life that dates to the nation's founding. Historians have often noted Thomas Jefferson's suspicion that cities undermined the democratic impulse. According to Jefferson, "The mobs of great cities add just so much to the support of pure government, as sores do to the strength of the human body."[58]

In the 1830s and 1840s, the disdain for urban life was reinforced by the literature of the Romantic Movement, whose writers admired nature and abhorred cities, technology, and modernism.

A series of nineteenth-century transportation innovations allowed an increasing number of city dwellers to leave the crowded streets of the historic city center. In 1814, Robert Fulton began operating a steam ferry service between Manhattan and Brooklyn, thus making Brooklyn the nation's first commuter suburb.[59] A few years later, a select class of wealthy people rode in luxury cars pulled by steam locomotives to mansioned districts a few miles from the built-up city, but for most of them these residences served as weekend and country homes. In the years after the Civil War, rail improved connections enabled wealthy families to live in pristine isolation from the problems of industrial society. Some railroads lost money on day-to-day operations, but that did not prevent railroad entrepreneurs from amassing fabulous fortunes through suburban land speculation.[60] Llewellyn Park, located 13 miles outside the boundary of New York City, was founded in 1853 by a wealthy entrepreneur who thought that placing people in a natural setting would revive religious and moral values. Lake Forest, founded in 1857 as a railroad suburb a few miles north of Chicago, was designed around a picturesque village square surrounded by tree-shaded lanes winding among the hills and bluffs along Lake Michigan. After the Civil War, more suburbs modeled on the picturesque landscaping ideal of the Romantic Movement made their appearance: "gracefully-curved lines, generous spaces, and the absence of sharp corners, the idea being to suggest and imply leisure, contemplativeness and happy tranquility."[61] Even today, most of the suburbs built on this model retain their exclusive character: In contrast to the grid-patterned streets of cities, these suburbs look like "scattered buildings in a park," the homes integrated with nature, with no hint of the grimy factories on which this suburban wealth was based.[62]

The image of the suburb as a romantic idyll reflected a growing disenchantment with urban life. At the turn of the century, a back-to-nature movement, built on a romanticized version of nature and rural environments, swept the country. Boy Scouts, Campfire Girls, Woodcraft Indians, and several other organizations sought to expose children to the healthy influence of nature study. Children's literature was filled with stories of adventure in "natural" settings. Adults, too, were thought to be purified and rejuvenated by visits to the countryside. Bird-watching and nature photography became major pastimes. Tourism to national parks boomed, especially after the turn of the century, when automobiles became available to the middle classes.

Although the suburban ideal was intimately linked with a yearning for an idealized version of nature, suburban residents had no intention of giving up the amenities and advantages of the cities they had left behind. Instead, they attempted a fusion of both worlds—the urban and the rural—in the suburbs. Magazines and newspapers of the day were filled with articles on the advantages of suburban life as an amalgam of city conveniences and rural charm. In 1902, one magazine writer claimed that suburban living could "offer the best of chances for individualism and social cooperation."[63] The next year, *Cosmopolitan* carried an article hailing the "new era" of suburban living:

> The woeful inadequacy of facilities of communication and transportation which formerly rendered every suburbanite a martyr to his faith have, in great measure, been remedied; and moreover, residents in the environs have now reached the happy point where they consider as necessities the innumerable modern conveniences of the city house which were little short of luxuries in the suburban residence of yesterday.[64]

The turn of the century brought a flood of advertisements describing suburban living as a dreamland landscape of springs, orchards, and forests, where the inhabitants enjoyed bathing, fishing, and shooting, all while living in houses with the modern conveniences of hot water, gas lighting, and telephones.[65] One ad promised "A Country Home with All City Comforts," while another talked of crops of oats and hay, orchards, trees and shrubbery, fruit trees, and other accompaniments of the rural environment.[66] The lush ads featured drawings and photographs of wide expanses of lawn, trees, and meticulously tended gardens.

When horse-drawn streetcars began to run on city streets in the 1850s, the opportunity to escape the noise and anarchy of the industrial city filtered down the social ladder; now professionals and small businessmen were able to commute up to 3 miles from the downtown precincts. Cities still remained quite compact, but all that changed with the coming of the electric trolley in the 1890s. By tripling the distance of a practical commute, the trolley increased the amount of land available for residential use by an incredible 900 percent. American's urban areas began to spread inexorably outward.

By the 1890s, the electric streetcar had quickened the pace of suburban development, and it did not take long for a more affordable version of the suburban dream to emerge. A new generation of suburbs sprang up along the boundaries of the older cities, such places as University City, Missouri, just outside St. Louis, and Oak Park, 8 miles west of Chicago. These suburbs preserved the basic idea of the romantic ideal even while incorporating physical elements of the city, with grid street patterns, houses planted in rows along a sidewalk, and yards in the back. The quickened pace of suburban development was tied to an intellectual and sentimental reaction against the city. Academic writers promoted the idea that "our great cities, as those who have studied them have learned, are full of junk, much of it human."[67] A Boston University professor called city life "a self-chosen enslavement" and indicated that "the psychological causes of urban drift are socially most sinister."[68] Already, it was possible to discern a presentiment of the attitudes that would later be directed at African Americans in the post–World War II era. Cities were thought to nurture every conceivable sort of evil, as evidenced by such titles of sociological research as *The Social Evil in Chicago; Five Hundred Criminal Careers; The City Where Crime Is Play; Family Disorganization; Sex, Freedom and Social Control*; and *The Ghetto*.[69] Cities had few defenders and a host of critics.

The Automobile Suburbs: 1918–1945

For awhile, it seemed that suburban development posed no threat to the vitality of the industrial city. In hindsight, though, it is clear that this state of affairs could not last. The data in Table 6.4 can be read as a narrative revealing that even before the automobile became popular, the suburbs around several big cities were growing fast enough to suggest that suburban growth might eventually pose a problem. Between 1900 and 1910, New York City's population increased by 39 percent, but in the same decade its suburbs grew even faster, by 61 percent. Meanwhile, the number of people living in Chicago's suburbs skyrocketed, growing by 88 percent in the first decade of the century. Meanwhile, St. Louis's suburbs grew at an even faster pace of 91 percent. As more and more people took to the streetcars and the early automobile, the trend accelerated. A new kind of urban form began to emerge, too. Los Angeles, which began to grow in the era of the automobile, began to spread out even before the city was fully formed.

TABLE 6.4 Metropolitan Area Population, 1900–1940 (Increases in Population Expressed as Percentage Growth and Number of People Added)

	1900–1910		1910–1920		1920–1930		1930–1940	
Districts	Central City	Outside Central City	Central City	Outside Central City	Central City	Outside Central City	Central City	Outside Central City
Boston	20%	23%	9%	21%	4%	21%	−1%	3%
Chicago	29	88	23	79	25	74	0.6	10
Cleveland	46	46.5	40	140	12	126	−1	13
Los Angeles	206	553	81	108	115	158	−3	30
New York City[a]	39	61	18	35	23	67	8	18
St. Louis	19	91	12.5	26	7	71	−1	16
Mean for all metro districts (nation)	34	38	25	32	21	47	4	14

[a]Includes growth of population in New York City proper and in satellite areas of New York State. New Jersey population is excluded.

Source: U.S. Bureau of the Census, *The Growth of Metropolitan Districts in the United States, 1900–1940*, by Warren S. Thompson (Washington, DC: U.S. Government Printing Office, 1947), especially Table 2.

Still, the day when suburban growth might be regarded as a problem was some way off. The cities were madhouses of activity, and on their borders a few people lived their quieter lives. Between 1900 and 1920, for instance, New York City grew by 2.2 million people; over the same period, the suburbs beyond the city limits increased by 190,000. This meant that the suburbs had more than doubled in 20 years, but this hardly mattered when considered in the larger context: in 1920, New York City's population was 5.6 million people, making the suburban population of 379,000 seem awfully small.

The same could be said for all of the big cities. Almost everything was concentrated close to downtown. Industrial and manufacturing facilities remained near the water and rail transportation facilities located at or near the historic center. Between 1904 and 1914, St. Louis lost some industry to its suburbs (its share of industrial employment fell from 95 to 90 percent of the area's manufacturing establishments), as did Baltimore (96 to 93 percent) and Philadelphia (91 to 87 percent), but these cities were the exception rather than the rule.[70] The industrial cities overwhelmingly dominated the economies of their urban regions. Men left the suburbs in the morning to commute to their jobs downtown, and at night they returned home. Suburban residents went downtown to shop for cars, appliances, and practically everything else. Railroad and streetcar suburbs prospered, but the people who lived in them were still dependent on downtown jobs and downtown businesses. Downtown streets were constantly jammed with traffic.

Though it took a few decades for the process to unfold, ultimately the automobile utterly transformed the urban landscape. When it first made its appearance, the car was mainly an expensive toy for the rich. Henry Ford made it affordable in 1908 when he introduced the Model T, a car for the masses that was reliable and easy to operate. After he introduced the moving assembly line in 1913, Ford managed to reduce the cost of a Model T each year, from $950 in 1910 to $290 by 1924. Car ownership skyrocketed. American car production increased from 63,000 automobiles in 1908 to 550,000 by 1914. After World War I, car production reached new highs, rising from 2.27 million automobiles in 1922 to 4.45 million in 1929.[71] The construction of adequate roads lagged seriously behind car ownership, but this problem was eventually solved when the driving public successfully pressed for more state and federal funding.

The automobile allowed an increasing number of middle-class Americans to make the move to the suburbs. The streetcar suburbs had sprung up along the rail tracks, leaving big patches of undeveloped land in between. The car made it possible to fill in the gaps. Vast new tracts of land were opened to land speculation and suburban development, and the upper-middle class invested much of its newfound money in suburban real estate. Total national wealth doubled in the 10 years from 1912 to 1922, and from 1915 to 1925 average hourly wages climbed from 32 to 70 cents.[72] Residential land followed suit by doubling in value during the 1920s.[73]

These circumstances conspired to push suburban development to unprecedented levels. In the 1920s, the cities of Boston, St. Louis, and Cleveland grew more slowly than ever in their history, but their suburbs boomed, both in total population and rates of growth. The truck and the automobile began to change well-established economic patterns as well. The proportion of factory employment in the cities of more than 100,000 residents declined between 1920 and 1930, and this trend was likely to continue because the new assembly-line production techniques required a lot of land rather than vertical buildings, and this land was most easily found in the suburbs. Still, it would take decades for the process of decentralization to fully work itself out. The volume of downtown office space tripled in the 1920s, and employment continued to soar in most central cities.[74] For the old industrial cities the day of reckoning was still a ways off.

The Great Depression of the 1930s signaled the twilight of the city-building era. As the data in Table 6.4 reveal, Boston, Los Angeles, St. Louis, and Cleveland all lost population in the 1930s; so did Philadelphia, Kansas City, and the New Jersey cities—Elizabeth, Paterson, Jersey City, and Newark (the latter cities are not shown in the table). San Francisco, which had added 27 percent to its population in the 1920s, suddenly stopped growing. Small manufacturing cities of New England and the Midwest slid into decline—Akron and Youngstown, Ohio; Albany, Schenectady, and Troy, New York; Joplin, Missouri; and New Bedford, Massachusetts.

The Great Depression hit the suburbs hard, too, because now most upper-middle- and middle-class people lacked the means to buy a new home. Some suburban development still occurred, but it was slow and uncertain. The rate of growth in New York's suburbs fell from 67 percent in the 1920s to only 18 percent in the 1930s. In the same decade, Chicago's suburban expansion slowed from 74 percent in the 1920s to 10 percent in the 1930s; Cleveland's dropped from 74 to 13 percent and Los Angeles's from 158 to 30 percent. All through the 1930s, the effects of the Great Depression stubbornly lingered. With the coming of World War II, materials needed for housing construction were commandeered for the war effort. Suburban growth came to a standstill.

The Bedroom Suburbs: 1946–1970s

The slowdown in housing construction during depression and war would have caused a serious housing shortage all by itself, but the postwar baby boom made the situation worse. After falling to a low point in the years of the Great Depression, the birth rate began to rise in 1943 and climbed rapidly in the postwar years, when 16 million GIs returned to civilian life.[75] By 1947, 6 million families were doubling up with relatives or friends because they could not find a home of their own.[76] The housing industry geared up to meet the demand, pushing single-family housing starts from only 114,000 in 1944 to 1,692,000 by 1950.[77] Virtually all of this new construction occurred in the suburbs.

Utilizing mass-production methods and sophisticated marketing techniques, big construction companies began to dominate the industry. Big firms accounted for only 5 percent of all houses built in 1938, but increased their share of the market to 24 percent by 1949, and a decade later they produced 64 percent of all new homes.[78] The preferred method was to buy tracts of land on the outskirts of cities and to create entire new subdivisions by bulldozing everything to an even surface and constructing houses quickly using standardized production techniques. The emergence of cookie-cutter residential developments stimulated a boom in suburban construction. In the 10 years between 1940 and 1950, the suburbs experienced a 36 percent gain; in the same decade, the core cities they surrounded grew by only 14 percent. In fact, however, postwar suburban growth had occurred much faster than these statistics suggest because no subdivisions at all were built until 1946, when wartime restrictions on building materials finally ended. After the war, the pent-up demand for housing ignited a virtual gold rush to new suburban subdivisions. In earlier decades, suburban development had been mainly an upper- and middle-class phenomenon, but now it filtered down to embrace working-class families, too. Federally insured home loans, cheap energy, and new, efficient building technologies made it less expensive to build a new house in the suburbs than to rehabilitate a home or rent an apartment in the city. The nation's homeownership rate increased from 44 percent in 1940 to 63 percent by 1970.[79]

The suburban boom accelerated during the prosperous years of the 1950s. Virtually all the cities that had prospered in the industrial era were losing population, some at a dramatic pace. Cities all through the industrial belt stretching from New England through the Great Lake states were hemorrhaging population. Between 1950 and 1960, Boston's population shrunk by 13 percent; by comparison, the population losses in that decade were 12.5 percent in St. Louis and 4 percent in Cleveland. From there, things got quickly worse. In the 1960s, St. Louis lost 17 percent of its population, 17 percent in the 1970s, and an extraordinary 27 percent in the following decade. In 1950, before it started its long slide, 857,000 people resided within the city, but by century's end only 335,000 people were left.[80]

In the 40 years from 1950 to 1990 virtually all of the old industrial cities hemorrhaged population. Even after the 1970s, when the first hints that things might turn around began to appear in some places, some cities continued their long slide. The downtowns and neighborhoods of most of the industrial cities were clearly on the rebound by the end of the century, but even so many of them continued to lose population, though at a slower rate than before. Between the 2000 census and 2003, Cleveland, Baltimore, Flint (Michigan), Detroit, and Cincinnati all shrank by 3.5 percent or more, an experience shared by 30 other older cities.

Table 6.5 shows that as the central cities continued to shrink, their share of metropolitan population rapidly declined. Already by 1940 only 29 percent of the people in metropolitan Boston resided in the city, a reflection of the fact that suburbanization there had begun earlier than in most places. Before the war Chicago still had 70 percent of its region's population, compared to 64 percent for Cleveland and New York and 57 percent for St. Louis. Even in metropolitan Los Angeles, which had begun sprawling in the early years of the century, more than half of the population still lived within the city limits. But the postwar suburban exodus changed regional geographies very quickly. When the 2000 census was conducted, just 10 percent of the population of metropolitan Boston lived within the city In the St. Louis region only 13 percent still

TABLE 6.5 Share of Metropolitan Population Living in Selected Central Cities, 1940–2000[a]

	Percentage Living in Central City			
	1940	1960	1980	2000
Boston	29.0%	21.8%	11.0%	10.1%
Chicago	70.4	51.5	37.0	31.6
Cleveland	64.1	32.1	19.5	16.2
Los Angeles	51.6	32.0	25.8	22.6
New York	64.3	50.5	37.8	37.8
St. Louis	57.0	35.0	18.8	13.4

[a]It is difficult to calculate precise figures over time of city/suburban ratio because the Census Bureau's definition of metropolitan areas has changed from time to time. Corrections have been made to minimize this problem. Although Lorain–Elyria counties were not included in the 1940 Cleveland metropolitan area, they have been added because these counties were included from 1960 and thereafter. For Boston, the four major counties are included for 1940 and 1960, which is comparable to the regional definition from 1970 to 2000.

Sources: U.S. Bureau of the Census, *Statistical Abstract of the United States* (Washington, DC: U.S. Government Printing Office, various years): 1987, pp. 29–31, Table 34; 1993, pp. 37–39, Table 42; 2003, p. 32, Table 27.

claimed the city as their home, and in the Cleveland metropolitan area, only 16 percent did so. Among older industrial cities, New York and Chicago stood out as exceptions because they still captured as high as one-third of their region's population in 2000.

The suburbs of the 1950s and 1960s were by no means all cut from the same cloth. The legacy of the past was plain to see, with middle-class housing tracts, a sprinkling of working-class blue-collar subdivisions, a few isolated areas populated by blacks, and, of course, the enclaves inhabited by the wealthy. But most of the housing tracts built in the postwar years were marketed to white middle-class families. Some suburbs were remarkably uniform, with row after endless row of houses looking as if they had been produced on the same assembly line, an impression that turned out to be close to the truth. Suburbia came to be portrayed in the popular media as a place of look-alike streets and regimented people, where bored couples with small children spent their free time watching television and picking crabgrass out of their lawns, and where the men commuted to office jobs, leaving behind lonely housewives to care for the children in culturally sterile environments. This image of suburbia was captured in three best-selling novels published during the period: *The Man in the Gray Flannel Suit* (1955), *The Crack in the Picture Window* (1956), and *The Split Level Trap* (1960). Although the cultural images of suburbia undoubtedly traded on stereotypes, they were close enough to the truth to strike a responsive chord.[81]

By the mid-twentieth century, civic elites in the central cities were thoroughly alarmed that the suburbs threatened the vitality and even viability of the urban core. It was not only that the suburbs were growing so fast. As affluent white families deserted, they were leaving behind a population made up of blacks and poor people. Increasingly, suburbanization was understood in racial terms; the phrase "white flight" started to be heard, suggesting that suburban development was motivated in part by racism, a suggestion for which there is abundant evidence.[82] The riots of the mid-1960s called attention to the fact that racial segregation on this scale might legitimately be regarded as a national problem. In 1967, when the National Commission on Civil Disorders called attention to the stark dichotomy between the cities and suburbs, the suburbs had already become far removed from the conditions that attracted the commission's concern. Increasingly, suburban residents regarded the cities as reservations for blacks, and many blacks had become completely estranged from the rest of America.[83] All of the ingredients that defined the twentieth-century urban crisis had come together into an explosive mixture.

The Rise of the Multiethnic Metropolis

By the end of the 1960s, the momentous movements that had brought millions of African Americans to northern cities had pretty much ran their course; indeed, in the decade of the 1990s 579,000 blacks returned to the South.[84] The biggest demographic change, however, involved the movement of large numbers of African Americans to the suburbs, and this occurred at exactly the same time that white flight had begun to ebb. A surge of foreign immigration added another ingredient to the mix. After the 1960s the pace of immigration steadily gained momentum, and by the last decade of the century it had reached a level not experienced for 100 years. By the new millennium, the segregation of blacks and whites was being supplanted by a new reality: the politics of urban America was becoming multiracial and multiethnic. Unlike any previous period of immigration, more immigrant groups were settling in the suburbs than in the central cities. Ethnic enclaves began springing up in a lot of unlikely places.

The number of foreign immigrants entering the country in the 1990s exceeded every other decade of the twentieth century except 1910–1920, and the movement continued until the recently, when the number of persons obtaining legal permanent residence status began a steady decline. From 2000 to 2005, the immigrant flow increased 16 percent, and the newcomers were showing up in all regions of the country. In the same five-year period, Indiana experienced a 34 percent rise, and several other states also far exceeded the national rate: South Dakota, with a 44 percent increase, compared to 32 percent in Delaware, 31 percent in Missouri, and 26 percent in New Hampshire.[85] According to census estimates, in September 2004 there were 11.6 million legal permanent residents in the United States, with 8 million of them eligible to be naturalized; in addition, more than 5 million undocumented immigrants were thought to reside within the nation's borders.[86] In 2011, 1,062,040 immigrants obtained legal permanent status, which was a slight drop from the rate in previous years.[87]

TABLE 6.6 Immigrants by Place of Origin, 1951–2000

| Year | Percentage of Total Immigration | | | | | Total Number (Thousands) |
	Europe	Asia[a]	Canada[a]	Other Western Hemisphere[b]	All Other[c]	
1951–1960	57%	6%	11%	22.5%	3%	2,515.5
1961–1970	37	13	9	39	2	3,321.7
1971–1980	18	36	3	40	3	4,493.3
1981–1990	10	38	2	47	3	7,338.1
1991–2000	14	32	1.5	48	5	9,092.9
2011	7.9	42.5	1.2	38	9	1,062.04

[a]Cambodia, China, Taiwan, Hong Kong, India, Iran, Israel, Japan, Korea, Philippines, Thailand, Vietnam, and "other Asia."
[b]Mexico, Caribbean, Central America, South America.
[c]Africa, Australia, New Zealand.

Sources: U.S. Department of Justice, Immigration and Naturalization Service, *Statistical Yearbook of the Immigration and Naturalization Service, 1989* (Washington, DC: Government Printing Office, 1990), pp. 2–5; and U.S. Bureau of the Census, *The Official Statistics, Statistical Abstract of the United States, 2003* (Washington, DC: U.S. Government Printing Office, 2004).

The rate of immigration increased decade by decade after 1950. Table 6.6 reveals that during the 1950s, 57 percent of the foreign immigrants came from Europe, 22.5 percent from the Western Hemisphere south of the United States, and 6 percent from Asia. But the composition of the immigrant stream changed dramatically over time. Immigrants from European countries fell sharply to less than 10 percent of the total number of arrivals in the 1980s before rebounding briefly to about 14 percent because of a surge from Russia and the formerly communist countries of Eastern Europe. By 2009, the number of European immigrants fell back to slightly less than 10 percent of the total immigrant flow, and has risen only slightly in the years since.[88] In the decade of the 1980s, Asian immigrants shot up from 6 percent to more than 38 percent of the total immigrant flow before settling back to 30 percent or so. The biggest surge came from the Western Hemisphere south of the United States, mostly from Mexico and Latin America. Since the turn of the century, immigrants from that region have constituted about half of all arrivals to the United States. In 2011, the leading countries of birth of new legal permanent residents were Mexico (14 percent), China (8.2 percent), and India (6.5 percent).

The laws governing immigration from the 1920s to the mid-1960s were adopted in a climate of xenophobic fear and resentment. The National Origins Immigration Act of 1924 established an annual quota that could not exceed 2 percent of the base population of foreign-born nationality groups already in the country as of 1890. This restriction accomplished its intended goal of drastically reducing immigration by all nationality groups except those from northern Europe. In debating the legislation, members of Congress made it clear that they considered Slavs, Jews, Italians, Greeks, and other people of the countries of Eastern Europe to be inferior. The new law slashed annual immigration by these nationality groups by more than 90 percent.

By the 1960s, the changing political climate made overt racist formulas of this kind unacceptable. In the Hart-Cellar Act of 1965, Congress essentially put immigrants from all countries on an equal footing and granted a high priority to family reunification. Special provisions for political refugees from socialist and communist countries increased the rate of immigration even more, and the ethnic composition of the immigrant flow changed radically. After the 1960s, between 80 and 85 percent of the immigrants entering the United States were of Hispanic or Asian origin. (As of the 2000 census, the U.S. Census Bureau used the terms *Latino* and *Hispanic* interchangeably; we follow that practice here.) People of both ethnic categories came from many nations—Hispanics from a vast area from the Caribbean to the tip of South America, Asians from the arc of countries from Japan to India.

In 1990, Congress again reformed the immigration laws, and as a result of the legislation, the number of legal immigrants allowed into the country increased by 40 percent. The law more than doubled the number of visas granted to foreigners with job skills needed in the United States, and it allowed the highest percentage of European-origin groups into the country since Hart-Cellar.[89] Immigration from Eastern Europe, Russia, and the nations that had been a part of the former Soviet Union increased sharply. By the mid-1990s, the United States was admitting more legal immigrants than all the rest of the nations of the world combined.[90]

Asians were the fastest-growing ethnic group in the 1980s, with the metropolitan areas of Los Angeles, San Francisco, and New York having the largest Asian communities. The number of people coming from Asia in the 1980s almost equaled the number from all countries of the Western Hemisphere south of the U.S. border. But in the last decade of the century Asian immigration slowed while Hispanic immigration increased.[91] In 2009, the number of persons obtaining legal permanent residence status, whose region of last residence was Asia, was 394,874 of the 1,130,818 total legal permanent residents. During the same period the number from Mexico, the Caribbean, Central and South America rose to 457,366. As a result of the rising volume of the immigrant flow and the relatively large size of Hispanic families, in 2005 Hispanics outnumbered blacks for the first time in the nation's history, a trend which has held—in 2010, blacks made up 12.6 percent of the total U.S. population, while persons of Hispanic or Latino origin constituted 16.3 percent.[92]

Hispanics arriving from the Caribbean, Latin America, Central America, and South America was made up of a complex mixture of languages, cultures, and nationalities. Significant numbers from the Caribbean were black, which thoroughly confused census categories (nearly all other Hispanics filling out the census forms fit the "white" racial category). In 2000, nearly 8 percent of blacks in the United States were foreign born, with the figure over 200 percent in New York, Florida, and New Jersey.[93] The Census Bureau found it difficult to identify ethnic categories accurately in New Mexico (where 42 percent of the population is officially classified as Hispanic) because many families are descended from residents who lived in the region generations before most American settlers arrived; as a consequence, even if they were once citizens of Mexico (before New Mexico was ceded to the United States in 1846), they cannot accurately be classified as coming from there.

Figure 6.1 reveals that the racial and ethnic composition of the immigration stream differs remarkably among the seven metropolitan areas receiving the largest numbers of immigrants in 2004. In Orange County, California, which is composed of numerous interlocking cities, Mexicans and Vietnamese are the largest immigrant groups, followed by Filipinos, Koreans, and Indians. By contrast, Cubans were the most numerous group to arrive in Miami in the same year, and nearly all the rest were from other Caribbean and Latin American countries. Mexicans easily led the list in Los Angeles and Houston, but a significant number also came from Asia and elsewhere in Latin America. The immigrant flow to the New York region was so diverse that only Dominicans accounted for more than 10 percent of the total; the other leading groups were Chinese, Jamaicans, Guyanese, Bangladeshi, Indians, and Ecuadorians. Washington, D.C., attracted a diverse mixture of Asian and Hispanic immigrants, with a significant number of

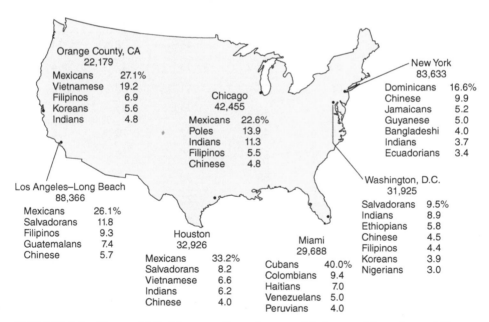

FIGURE 6.1   Seven U.S. Metropolitan Areas with Largest Immigrant Flows (One Year), Fiscal Year 2004.

Note: "Chinese" includes immigrants from mainland China only.

Source: Department of Homeland Security, www.uscis.gov/graphics/shared/statistics/yearbook/2005/ImmSupTable2fy04D.xls

Ethiopians added to the mix. In the Chicago region, Mexicans led all nationality groups, with Poles and Indians next.

In 1987, more than 93 percent of legal immigrants coming to the United States settled in urban areas, and more than half of them moved into just seven metropolitan areas. Notably, many of these immigrants bypassed the central cities and moving directly to suburbs. The statistics displayed in Table 6.7 show recent trends for the nation's 14 most diverse metropolitan areas (for areas of more than 500,000). In all of the 14 central cities listed there, minorities comprised half or more of the population when the census of 2000 was taken.

In all but four of these same urban regions, more than 40 percent resided in the suburbs. In the Washington, D.C., and Newark areas, blacks still outnumbered Hispanics, but the differences were much smaller in the New York and Chicago metropolitan regions. In the other Sunbelt urban regions shown in Table 6.7, Hispanics constituted the largest racial or ethnic group by far.

TABLE 6.7　City and Suburban Minority Shares, Year 2000 Metropolitan Areas with Populations Over 500,000 (in Percentages)

Metro Area	City	Suburban	Latino	Black	Asian
Los Angeles	69%	69%	45%	8%	14%
New York	65	32	13	12	4
Chicago	65	26	11	8.5	5
Washington, D.C.	61	40.5	8.5	22	7
Houston	68	40	23	10	5
Dallas	62	31	15	9	4
Riverside	51	53	38	7	4
Phoenix	37	30	21	3	2
Orange County	70	40	22	1	14
San Diego	50	40	27	4	6
Oakland	67	48	19	8	17
Miami	82	78.5	56	19.5	1.5
Newark	86	34	11	17	4.5
San Francisco	56	43	19	3	17

Source: Adapted from William H. Frey, *Melting Pot Suburbs: A Census 2000 Study of Suburban Diversity* (Washington, DC: Center on Urban and Metropolitan Policy, Brookings Institution Press, June 2001), p. 14.

Asians constituted less than 10 percent in all metro areas of the Sunbelt except for those clustered around Los Angeles, Orange County, Oakland, and San Francisco.

The census of 2000 showed that more than three-fourths of the nation's Hispanics lived in five states of the Southwest, plus Florida. Half of the Hispanics residing in the United States lived in California and Texas, despite the fact that all but two of the cities with the largest Hispanic populations, Chicago and New York, are located in other states (the other three leading cities are Los Angeles, Houston, and San Antonio).[94] Approximately 80 percent of the Hispanics in the southwestern states came originally from Mexico, compared to 60 percent for the United States as a whole. But in the 1990s, Mexican-origin immigrants began to spread across the nation, with the largest percentage occurring in North Carolina (479 percent increase), Arkansas (388 percent), Georgia (374 percent), Tennessee (327 percent), and Nevada (271 percent).[95] What was once mainly a regional phenomenon has become a truly national trend. In 2011, persons of Hispanic or Latino origin composed 16.7 percent of the total U.S. population, making people of Hispanic origin the nation's largest ethnic or race minority.[96] Regional variations are substantial. In New Mexico, 46.7 percent of the state's population was Hispanic in 2011, the highest of any state, and Hispanics constituted at least one-fifth of the population in California and Texas.[97]

Adverse economic conditions in Mexico and poverty and political repression in other countries pushed most of the Hispanic immigrants northward. Economic opportunity in the United States exerted the necessary pull. The minimum wage in the United States was approximately six times the prevailing wage in Mexico in 1990, which was higher than in most other Latin American countries.[98] Illegal immigration helps account for persistently low wages and low levels of education among Latinos. Undocumented aliens are willing to take (or are coerced into taking) jobs paying less than the minimum wage, and they often end up in sweatshops, meat-processing plants, or agricultural jobs working under abysmal conditions. Frequently led across the border by professional smugglers, called *coyotes* for their predatory habits, undocumented immigrants live at the margins of American society. Because they live in constant fear of detection by the United States Citizenship and Immigration Services (USCIS), a bureau of the Department of Homeland Security, they are in no position to bargain with employers.

To deal with the problem of illegal immigration, Congress enacted the Immigration Reform and Control Act (IRCA) in 1986, which established stiff penalties for employers who knowingly hired illegal aliens. At the same time, the law made it possible for illegal immigrants who had already entered the country to achieve citizenship by registering with the Immigration and Naturalization Service (INS). Within four years of the passage of the IRCA more than 2 million illegal aliens attained legal status, and the INS stepped up efforts to find employers who violated the law. One of the unintended effects of the 1986 reform is that many employers began to discriminate against anyone who looked or sounded like they came from anywhere south of the U.S. border.[99] Reflecting a growing national anxiety about illegal immigration, the successor agency to the INS, the USCIS, began to round up undocumented immigrants in spectacular, well-publicized raids. After the U.S. Senate failed to pass an immigration bill in 2006, several states adopted legislation requiring employers to check the backgrounds of employees; in addition, by 2008, 15 states had passed laws established criminal penalties for smugglers who bring immigrants into the country.[100]

The reactions against immigrants prompted towns and cities across the nation to adopt an extraordinary variety of laws that required, for example, business owners to check the identity of potential employees, property owners to check the backgrounds of renters, public buildings to post "English only" signs, and other measures. Local police departments rounded up anyone looking like immigrants for minor violations, such as, in Georgia, fishing without a license.[101] These actions, many of doubtful legality, gave police the pretext for beginning deportation orders. Arizona took this strategy a step further when the state senate passed legislation in April 2010 that empowered the police, when interacting with people on a routine basis, to question anyone suspected of being in the country illegally.[102] There was speculation that Texas might follow suit.[103]

Has the Urban Crisis Disappeared?

The twentieth-century urban crisis of city versus suburb, black versus white, is coming to an end. In the past, most immigrants settled in central cities, often moving into neighborhoods already occupied by the same ethnic group, but the recent pattern of settlement has become more complex and less predictable. In a break from historic patterns of settlement, many of immigrants are bypassing the central cities entirely and moving directly into suburbs. By 2000, 55 percent of Asians, 50 percent of Latinos, and 39 percent of blacks lived in suburbs, and the proportions were much higher in many Sunbelt metropolitan urban regions.[104] Several of the communities that minorities moved into are now ethnically diverse, which reduces the extreme polarization between central city and suburb that characterized urban areas only a few years ago.

The movement to the suburbs has had the effect of moderating the extremely rigid pattern of racial and ethnic segregation that was the defining feature of the twentieth-century urban crisis. Research shows that in the 1990s, the level of segregation declined in 272 metropolitan statistical areas (MSAs) and increased in only 19 MSAs.[105] Most of the metropolitan areas where segregation increased were located in second-tier older industrial cities in the Northeast and Midwest, which tend to be less diverse than the faster-growing metropolitan areas elsewhere. In one study, the authors found that between 1970 and 2000 all ethnic groups had become more spatially assimilated, although blacks remained more segregated than Asians or Latinos.[106] The dismal findings from earlier studies of residential segregation were distilled into a book titled *American Apartheid*,[107] but more recent census data would not necessarily justify such a title.

Recent research on urban poverty offers evidence that some other aspects of the urban crisis may be easing as well. In the 1990s the number of people living in neighborhoods of concentrated poverty—which researchers define as areas where 40 percent or more of the residents are under the poverty line—fell dramatically in the 1990s, by 24 percent, or 2.4 million people.[108] The proportion of people living in high-poverty neighborhoods fell among all racial and ethnic groups, and the sharpest declines were in cities in the Midwest and South, such as Detroit, Chicago, St. Louis, Milwaukee, Memphis, New Orleans, Houston, San Antonio, and Dallas. Researchers referred to the decline in concentrated poverty as "stunning progress."[109] It should be noted that these figures changed, little when the effects of the Great Recession were reported in the 2010 census.

There is also evidence that the social ills that gave rise to the label "the urban underclass" have become less concentrated than before. In the 1970s and 1980s, four indicators of underclass status—female-headed households, high school dropouts, male unemployment, and welfare dependence—were highly concentrated in areas of high poverty. The clustering of these social ills in a few areas fell so dramatically in the 1990s that the scholars conducting the research called the trend "nothing short of profound." The researchers drew the conclusion that "many fewer neighborhoods now resemble the depressing descriptions of the inner city that were commonplace in journalistic and scholarly accounts of previous years."[110]

Crime rates also went into a steep decline. For the nation as a whole, violent crime per 100,000 persons decreased by 29 percent from 1990 to 2000 (after an increase of 20 percent from 1987 to 1990), and the murder rate fell by 41 percent (after a 13 percent increase).[111] The drop in crime was even more dramatic in big cities than elsewhere; homicide rates, for example, fell by 75 percent in New York City from 1990 to 2003 (from more than 2,200 in 1990 to 597 in 2003).[112] Although the rate of violent crime has increased in some cities since then, overall crime rates have continued to drop, often to levels not seen in decades. In 2009, there were 1,318,398 violent crimes, a decrease of 5.3 percent from 2008, 5.2 percent from 2005, and 7.5 percent from the 2000 level.[113] The trend continues—in 2011, an estimated 1,203,564 violent crimes occurred nationwide, a decrease of 3.8 percent from 2010.[114]

Despite the accumulating evidence that things have changed in urban regions, it would be premature to conclude that the urban problems of the twentieth century—high levels of segregation, inequality and poverty, and racial and ethnic tensions—are disappearing. The urban crisis was defined by reference to the great city/suburban divide. This geographic pattern is slowly changing, and in that important sense the old urban crisis is mostly a thing of the past. But some of the problems previously associated with broad swaths of central-city ghetto neighborhoods are now cropping up all over the place. Although concentrated poverty has declined somewhat in central cities, it has not fallen in the suburbs or in rural areas.[115] Notably, in metropolitan areas with the highest rates of suburban growth, economic segregation dropped the least in the 1990s.[116]

The prospects for the central cities have improved, but the benefits from this turnaround have been selective. By many measures, downtowns and residential areas in the central cities have been on the rebound since sometime in the 1990s. Fifteen large older industrial cities—including, for example, St. Louis, Gary, Baltimore, Buffalo, Pittsburgh, Cincinnati, and Detroit—continued to lose population in the 1990s, but the rate of loss slowed. Declining population could no longer be interpreted as a reliable measure of decline. Many cities were becoming less densely populated and single and childless households were replacing larger families. In effect, the cities were exporting social problems to the suburbs by replacing poorer families with more affluent single, professionals who have led the gentrification of old neighborhoods.[117]

The inequalities between the downtown professional class and the residents of minority neighborhoods have become transparently obvious in cities tied closely to the global economy. Global cities have attracted a more diverse profile of immigrants than any other cities.[118] Jobs are the lure. The concentration of multinational businesses, financial services corporations, and the businesses connected to them draws highly educated workers from all over the globe. But the greatest demand for jobs (at least expressed in numbers) is found at the other end of the job market. Lower-status service workers are indispensable to the working of a global city—clerical workers, janitors and cashiers, nannies, cooks and busboys, maintenance and security workers, hotel maids, and a multitude of personal-service specialists from masseuses and personal shoppers to dog walkers: These kinds of jobs are taken disproportionately by immigrants and minorities. The jobs generally pay little, with the result that inequality escalates upward. New York's experience is revealing. In the late 1980s, the poorest 20 percent of the population in the New York metropolitan region accounted for 5 percent of incomes, but the top 20 percent of wage earners had a 45 percent share. By 1997, the percentage of earnings claimed by the poorest quintile had fallen to just above 2 percent, whereas the richest quintile received 56 percent of all earnings. While New York was becoming more affluent, it was also become poorer; between 1990 and 2000, the poverty rate rose from 29 to 32 percent of households.[119]

Rising inequality is occurring not only in global cities but throughout American society. In 1980, the bottom one-fifth of the population earned 4.3 percent of all earned income, but only a few years later, in 1998, the poorest fifth of wage earners accounted for just 3.6 percent. Meanwhile, from 1980 to 1998 the richest fifth increased its share from 44 to 49 percent. Perhaps even more telling, the top 5 percent of wage earners had increased its share of earnings in the same period from 16 to 21.4 percent.[120] As of 2011, the United States has a higher level of income inequality than Europe, Canada, Australia, and South Korea—a wealth gap which is increasing more rapidly than that of any other nation[121]

In 2011, the richest 1 percent of Americans took home almost 24 percent of the total national income, an increase of almost 9 percent from 1976. As a reporter for the *New York Times* wrote, ". . . you no longer need to travel to distant and dangerous countries to observe such rapacious inequality. We now have it right here a home. . . "[122] From 1980 to 2005, the richest 1 percent took away more than four-fifths of the total increase in the national income. Such a concentration of income at the top tier of earners has only occurred three times in the twentieth century: in 1915 and 1916, at the end of the Gilded Age, and again in the late 1920s prior to the stock market crash.[123]

Minorities continue to significantly lag behind in income and wealth. Indicators of economic well-being show that Hispanics, as a group, have a long way to go to catch up with the general U.S. population. The median income for Hispanic families in 2006 was 72 percent of the average earnings for non-Hispanic white families (down from 75 percent in 2001) but above the average earnings of black families, which was 61 percent of white family income.[124] While the 2010 census showed that nearly 28 percent of Americans 25 and older had bachelor's degrees, it also showed the great racial disparity in education. The rate for black Americas was 17 percent, and only 13 percent for Hispanic Americans. The lag in educational qualifications, plus a measure of discrimination, has meant that Hispanics have occupied lower rungs on the job ladder. Even though they held 12 percent of all jobs in 2000, only 6 percent of Hispanics worked in managerial or professional positions.[125] The economic crisis that began in 2008 affected Hispanics and blacks disproportionately. By March 2009 the unemployment rate for whites reached 7.3 percent, but for Hispanics it had climbed to 12.9 percent and 13.8 for blacks.[126] During the recovery, unemployment rates for whites has fallen far faster than for any either of these groups.

It is unrealistic to expect that inequality on this scale can occur without an increase in social problems. Within urban areas, extreme inequality has always been expressed in two ways: social disorder (in the form of crime, riots, and family disorganization, for instance) and residential patterns of segregation. No one knows whether the crime rates or the incidence of concentrated poverty will continue to fall. However, unless job and educational opportunities improve, it is certain that social tensions will rise. These tensions may be expressed in a different spatial geography than in the past, but some people may wonder whether this amounts to a difference that makes no difference.

Endnotes

1. Barry Checkoway, "Large Builders, Federal Housing Programs, and Postwar Suburbanization," in *Marxism and the Metropolis: New Perspectives in Political Economy*, ed. William K. Tabb and Larry Sawers (New York: Oxford University Press), p. 156.
2. Population growth on the outskirts probably exceeded population growth in the center before the 1920s. However, before 1920, annexation of suburban land by central cities obscured the statistical trend. See John D. Kasarda and George V. Redfearn, "Differential Patterns of City and Suburban Growth in the United States," *Journal of Urban History* 2, no. 1 (November 1975): 53.
3. Nicolas Lemann, *The Promised Land: The Great Migration and How It Changed America* (New York: Vintage Books, 1991), p. 6.
4. Robert A. Beauregard, *Voices of Decline: The Postwar Fate of U.S. Cities* (Cambridge, MA: Blackwell, 1993).
5. Dennis Judd, "Urban Violence and Enclave Politics: Crime as Text, Race as Subtext," in *Managing Divided Cities,* ed. Seamus Dunn (Keele, Staffordshire, UK: Ryburn Publishing, Keele University Press, 1994), pp. 160–175.

6. U.S. Bureau of the Census, *Statistical Abstract of the United States* (2005), www .census.gov/prod/2005pubs/06statab/pop.pdf.

7. Pew Research Center, *Social and Demographic Trends* (Washington, D.C., Pew Charitable Trusts, 2008).

8. A brief but excellent account of these movements may be found in Stanley B. Greenberg, *Politics and Poverty: Modernization and Response in Five Poor Neighborhoods* (New York: Wiley, 1974), pp. 15–27.

9. See ibid., pp. 15–27; and Leo Grebler, Joan W. Moore, and Ralph C. Guzman, *The Mexican-American People* (New York: Free Press, 1970), p. 113.

10. U.S. Bureau of the Census, *Statistical Abstract of the United States*.

11. Harry M. Caudill, *Night Comes to the Cumberlands* (Boston: Little, Brown, 1962).

12. Lemann, *The Promised Land*, p. 6.

13. Stewart E. Tolnay and E. M. Beck, "Rethinking the Role of Racial Violence in the Great Migration," in *Black Exodus: The Great Migration from the American South*, ed. Afrerdteen Harrison (Jackson: University Press of Mississippi, 1991), p. 20.

14. Robert B. Grant, ed., *The Black Man Comes to the City: A Documentary Account from the Great Migration to the Great Depression, 1915–1930* (Chicago: Nelson-Hall, 1972), p. 27; see pp. 16–30 for a complete set of statistics on black migration from 1890 to 1930. These data are used throughout this section.

15. Ibid., p. 22.

16. Ibid., p. 23.

17. Winfred P. Nathan, *Health Conditions in North Harlem, 1923–1927*, Social Research Series No. 2 (New York: National Tuberculosis Association, 1932), pp. 44–45, excerpted in Grant, *The Black Man Comes to the City*, pp. 59–61.

18. *Chicago Defender*, reprinted in Grant, *The Black Man Comes to the City*, pp. 31–40.

19. Tolnay and Beck, "Rethinking the Role of Racial Violence," p. 27.

20. Philip Dray, *At the Hands of Persons Unknown: The Lynching of Black America* (New York: Random House, 2002).

21. A collective amnesia has erased much of this past from America's consciousness. A recent book of photographs from the period is shocking but an effective antidote to cultural denial. See James Allen, *Without Sanctuary: Lynching Photography in America* (Sante Fe, NM: Twin Palms Publishers, 2000).

22. Memphis *Commercial Appeal* (October 5, 1916), reprinted in Grant, *The Black Man Comes to the City*, pp. 43–44.

23. *Chicago Defender* (August 12, 1916), reprinted in Grant, *The Black Man Comes to the City*, p. 45.

24. Herbert Northrup, *Organized Labor and the Negro* (New York: Kraus Reprint, 1971).

25. These statistics are from several sources excerpted in Grant, *The Black Man Comes to the City*, pp. 58–61.

26. See Elliott M. Rudwick, *Race Riot at East St. Louis, July 2, 1917* (Carbondale: Southern Illinois Press, 1964), for a discussion of this event.

27. Chicago Commission on Race Relations, *The Negro in Chicago: A Study of Race Relations and a Race Riot* (Chicago: University of Chicago Press, 1922), p. 122.

28. Tom Kenworthy, "Okla. Starts to Face up to, '21 Massacre," *USA Today* (February 18, 2000), p. 4A.

29. Grant, *The Black Man Comes to the City*, p. 71.

30. U.S. Department of Commerce, Bureau of the Census, *Census of Population 1970: General Social and Economic Characteristics* (Washington, DC: U.S. Government Printing Office, 1972), pp. 448–449, Table 3.

31. Douglas Massey and Nancy Denton, *American Apartheid: Segregation and the Making of the Underclass* (Cambridge, MA: Harvard University Press, 1993), pp. 89, 91.
32. Ibid., p. 91.
33. Rosalyn Baxandall and Elizabeth Ewen, *Picture Windows: How the Suburbs Happened* (New York: Basic Books, 2000), p. 202; Ray Suarez, *The Old Neighborhood: How We Lost in the Great Suburban Migration, 1966–1999* (New York: Free Press, 1999), pp. 40–41.
34. Quoted in ibid., pp. 252–253.
35. U.S. Bureau of the Census, *American FactFinder* (2005), http://factfinder.census.gov /home/saff/main.html?_lang=en.
36. National Advisory Commission on Civil Disorders, *Report of the National Advisory Commission on Civil Disorders* (New York: Bantam Books, 1968), p. 1.
37. John Kasarda, "Inner-City Concentrated Poverty and Neighborhood Distress: 1970 to 1990," *Housing Policy Debate* 4, no. 3 (1993): 253–302.
38. Alan Berube and Elizabeth Kneebone, *Two Steps Back. City and Suburban Poverty Trends 1999–2005* (Washington, D.C.: Brookings Institute, 2006).
39. Rolf Pendall, Elizabeth Davies, Lesley Freiman, and Rob Pitingolo, *A Lost Decade: Neighborhood Poverty and the Urban Crisis of the 2000s* (The Urban Institute, for the Joint Center on Political and Economic Studies, September 2011).
40. John R. Logan, *Separate and Unequal: The Neighborhood Gap for Blacks, Hispanics and Asians in Metropolitan America* (Brown University, July 2011).
41. Wilson, op. cit., *The Truly Disadvantaged.*
42. Michaela di Leonardo, "White Lies/Black Myths: Rape, Race, and the Black Underclass," *The Village Voice* (September 22, 1992), p. 31.
43. Norman Fainstein, "Race, Class, and Segregation: Discourses about African-Americans," *International Journal of Urban and Regional Research* 17, no. 3 (1993): 384–403.
44. Wilson, *The Truly Disadvantaged.*
45. Wilson, *When Work Disappears*, p. 19.
46. Ibid., p. 31.
47. Ibid., p. 92.
48. Ibid., p. 93.
49. Lisa W. Foderaro, "In Harlem, Children Reflect the Ravages U.N. Seeks to Relieve," *New York Times* (September 30, 1990), p. 1.
50. Walter J. Jones and James E. Johnson, "AIDS: The Urban Policymaking Challenge," *Journal of Urban Affairs* 11, no. 1 (1989): 85.
51. Joel A. Devine and James D. Wright, *The Greatest of Evils: Urban Poverty and the American Underclass* (New York: De Gruyter, 1993), p. 167.
52. Robert D. McFadden, "New York Leads Cities in Robbery Rate, But Drops in Murders," *New York Times* (August 11, 1991), p. 1.
53. See James Diego Vigil, *Barrio Gangs: Street Life and Identity in Southern California* (Austin: University of Texas Press, 1988).
54. Ronald Kotulak, "Study Finds Inner-City Kids Live with Violence," *Chicago Tribune* (September 28, 1990), p. 1.
55. Jonathan Kozol, *Rachel and Her Children: Homeless Families in America* (New York: Crown, 1988), p. 9.
56. Margaret T. Gordon and Claudette Guzan Artwick, "Urban Images in the Mass Media" (research proposal, Urban University Research Consortium, June 17, 1991), p. 2.
57. di Leonardo, "White Lies/Black Myths," p. 31.

58. Quoted in James A. Clapp, ed., *The City: A Dictionary of Quotable Thoughts on Cities and Urban Life* (New Brunswick, NJ: Center for Urban Policy Research, Rutgers University, 1984), p. 129.

59. Ibid., pp. 25–30. Robert Fishman dates the first true suburb somewhat earlier, in the 1790s in Clapham and other villages outside London; see Robert Fishman, *Bourgeois Utopias: The Rise and Fall of Suburbia* (New York: Basic Books, 1987), p. 53.

60. For accounts of railroad suburbs and land speculation, see Kenneth T. Jackson, *Crabgrass Frontier: The Suburbanization of the United States* (New York: Oxford University Press, 1985), Chapter 5; Fishman, op. cit., *Bourgeois Utopias*, Chapter 5; and Harry C. Binford, *The First Suburbs: Residential Communities on the Boston Periphery, 1815–1860* (Chicago: University of Chicago Press, 1985).

61. John W. Reps, *The Making of Urban America: A History of City Planning in the United States* (Princeton, NJ: Princeton University Press, 1965), p. 344.

62. The phrase "scattered buildings in a park" is Lewis Mumford's; see his *The City in History: Its Origins, Its Transformations, and Its Prospects* (New York: Harcourt, Brace and World, 1961), p. 489.

63. Editorial, (New York) *Independent* (February 27, 1902), p. 52.

64. Weldon Fawcett, "Suburban Life in America," *Cosmopolitan* (July 1903), p. 309.

65. Advertisement in *Country Life in America* (November 1906), p. 3.

66. Advertisement in *Country Life in America* (March 1908), p. 474.

67. Robert Park, Ernest W. Burgess, and Roderick D. McKenzie, *The City* (Chicago: University of Chicago Press, 1925), p. 109.

68. Quoted in Peter J. Schmitt, *Back to Nature: The Arcadian Myth in Urban America* (New York: Oxford University Press, 1969), p. 180; original quotation found in Ernest Groves, "The Urban Complex," *Sociological Review* 12 (Fall 1920): 74, 76.

69. A more complete list of titles can be found in Schmitt, *Back to Nature*, pp. 180–182.

70. Gary A. Tobin, "Suburbanization and the Development of Motor Transportation: Transportation Technology and the Suburbanization Process," in *The Changing Face of the Suburbs*, ed. Barry Schwartz (Chicago: University of Chicago Press, 1976), p. 100. See also U.S. Bureau of the Census, *Industrial Districts: 1905, Manufactures and Population*, Bulletin 101 (Washington, DC: U.S. Government Printing Office, 1909), pp. 9–80; and U.S. Bureau of the Census, *Census of Manufactures: 1914*, vol. 1, *Reports by States with Statistics for Principal Cities and Metropolitan Districts* (Washington, DC: U.S. Government Printing Office, 1918), pp. 564, 787, 1292.

71. These data are cited in Tobin, "Suburbanization and the Development of Motor Transportation," pp. 102, 103, and are also available in National Industrial Conference Board (NICB), *The Economic Almanac 1956: A Handbook of Useful Facts about Business, Labor and Government in the United States and Other Areas* (New York: Crowell for the Conference Board, 1956).

72. Tobin, "Suburbanization and the Development of Motor Transportation," pp. 102, 103.

73. Ibid.

74. Jackson, *Crabgrass Frontier*, pp. 174, 184.

75. The birthrate (the number of live births per 1,000 population) increased from 18.4 in 1936 to 26.6 in 1947. U.S. Bureau of the Census, *Historical Statistics of the United States, Colonial Times to 1970*, Bicentennial ed., pt. 2 (Washington, D.C.: U.S. Government Printing Office, 1975), p. 49.

76. Jackson, *Crabgrass Frontier*, p. 232.

77. Ibid., p. 233.

78. Checkoway, "Large Builders, Federal Housing Programs, and Postwar Suburbanization," pp. 155–156.

79. U.S. Bureau of the Census, *Historical Statistics of the United States, Colonial Times to 1970*, p. 646.

80. U.S. Department of Commerce, *Bureau of the Census, Census of Population, 1950*, vol. 1 (Washington, DC: U.S. Government Printing Office, 1952), p. 69, Table 17; *Census of Population, 1970*, vol. 1, *Characteristics of the Population*, pt. A, p. 180, Table 34; *Census of Population, 1980*, suppl. reports, *Standard Metropolitan Statistical Areas and Standard Consolidated Statistical Areas*, p. 2, Table B, p. 6, Table 1, and p. 49, Table 1; *State and Metropolitan Areas Data Book*, 1991, Table D; Bruce Katz and Robert Lang, ed., *Redefining Urban and Suburban America: Evidence from Census 2000* (Washington, DC: Brookings Institution Press, 2003), pp. 47–50.

81. For criticisms of the 1950s stereotype of suburbia, see Bennett M. Berger, *Working-Class Suburb: A Study of Auto Workers in Suburbia* (Berkeley: University of California Press, 1968); and Herbert J. Gans, *The Levittowners: Ways of Life and Politics in a New Suburban Community* (New York: Pantheon Books, 1967).

82. Thomas M. Guterbock, "The Push Hypothesis: Minority Presence, Crime, and Urban Deconcentration," in *The Changing Face of the Suburbs*, ed. Barry Schwartz (Chicago: University of Chicago Press, 1976), p. 26.

83. National Advisory Commission on Civil Disorders, *Report of the National Advisory Commission on Civil Disorders*, p. 1.

84. William H. Frey, "Census 2000 Shows Large Black Return to the South, Reinforcing the Region's 'White-Black' Demographic Profile," U.S. Bureau of the Census, PSC Research Report No. 02-473 (May 2001).

85. Rick Lyman, "Census Shows Growth of Immigrants," *New York Times* (August 15, 2006), www.nytimes.com.

86. Department of Homeland Security, Office of Immigration Statistics, www.uscis.gov /graphics/shared/statistics/publications/LPRest2004.pdf.

87. "2009 Yearbook of Immigration Statistics: Table 1," *U.S. Office of Immigration Statistics*; "2011 Yearbook of Immigration Statistics: Table 1," *U.S. Office of Immigration Statistics*.

88. Ibid.

89. Robert Pear, "Major Immigration Bill Is Sent to Bush," *New York Times* (October 29, 1990), p. A1; see also Stephen Castles and Mark J. Miller, *The Age of Migration: International Population Movements in the Modern World* (New York: Guilford Press, 1993), p. 249.

90. Rodman D. Griffin, "Illegal Immigration," *CQ Researcher* 2, no. 16 (1992): 364.

91. U.S. Bureau of the Census, *1990 to 1998 Annual Time Series of Population Estimates by Age, Race, Sex, and Hispanic Origin* (January 2000), http://www.census .gov/population/estimates/county/casrh_doc.txt.

92. "Quick Facts: USA," *U.S. Bureau of the Census*.

93. Frey, "Census 2000 Shows Large Black Return to the South, Reinforcing the Region's 'White-Black' Demographic Profile."

94. U.S. Census Bureau News, "Census 2000 Paints Statistical Portrait of the Nation's Hispanic Population," www.census.gov/press-release/www/releases/archives /population/00434/html.

95. Ibid.

96. "USA People QuickFacts," United States Census Bureau (2013), http://quickfacts. census.gov/qfd/states/00000.html.

97. "New Mexico People QuickFacts," United States Census Bureau (2013), http://quickfacts.census.gov/qfd/states/00000.html.

98. Alejandro Portes and Ruben Rumbaut, *Immigrant America: A Portrait* (Berkeley: University of California Press, 1990), p. 10.

99. Reported in Charles Kamasaki and Paul Yzaguirre, "Black-Hispanic Tensions: One Perspective," paper delivered at the annual meeting of the American Political Science Association (Washington, DC, August 29–September 1, 1991), p. 5. See also Castles and Miller, *The Age of Migration.*

100. Julia Preston, "Surge in Immigration Laws around the U.S.," *New York Times* (June 23, 2008), www.nytimes.com/2007/08/06/washington/06immig.html.

101. Dan Anderson, "Times Topics: Immigration and Refugees," *New York Times* (June 9, 2008), www.nytimes.com.

102. Randal C. Archibald, "Arizona Enacts Stringent Law on Immigration," *New York Times* (April 24, 2010), p. 1.

103. "The Immigration Law Fallacy" (June 16, 2010), Examiner.com (Dallas Tea Party Examiner).

104. Logan, "The New Ethnic Enclaves in America's Suburbs," a report by the Lewis Mumford Center for Comparative Urban and Regional Research (Albany, NY, 2002), p. 2; William H. Frey, *Melting Pot Suburbs: A Census 2000 Study of Suburban Diversity* (Washington, DC: Center for Urban and Metropolitan Policy, Brookings Institution Press, June 2001).

105. Edward L. Glaeser and Jacob L Vigdor, "Racial Segregation: Promising News," in *Redefining Urban & Suburban America*, ed. Katz and Lang, pp. 211–234.

106. Jeffrey M. Timberlake and John Iceland, "Change in Racial and Ethnic Residential Inequality in American Cities, 1970–2000," *City & Community* 6, no. 4 (December 2007): 335–365.

107. Massey and Denton, *American Apartheid.*

108. Paul Jargowsky, *Stunning Progress, Hidden Problems: The Dramatic Decline of Concentrated Poverty in the 1990s* (Washington, DC: Brookings Institution Press, 2004), pp. 1–2.

109. Ibid., p. 1.

110. Paul A. Jargowsky and Rebecca Yang, "The 'Underclass' Revisited: A Social Problem in Decline," *Journal of Urban Affairs* 28, no. 1 (2006): 76.

111. U.S. Bureau of the Census, *Statistical Abstract of the United States 2003,* Table 305, Crimes and Crime Rates, by Type of Offense: 1980 to 2001, p. 199.

112. Federal Bureau of Investigation, *Uniform Crime Reports.*

113. "Violent Crime in the United States, 2009," *U.S. Department of Justice.*

114. "Crime in the United States: 2011," FBI Uniform Crime Reports (2011), http://www.fbi.gov/about-us/cjis/ucr/crime-in-the-u.s/2011/crime-in-the-u.s.-2011/violent-crime/violent-crime.

115. Ibid.

116. Rebecca Yang and Paul A. Jargowsky, "Suburban Development and Economic Segregation in the 1990s," *Journal of Urban Affairs* 28, no. 3 (2006): 253–273.

117. William H. Frey and Alan Berubé, "City Families and Suburban Singles: An Emerging Household Story," in *Redefining Urban & Suburban America*, ed. Katz and Lang, p. 265.

118. Mark Abrahamson, *Global Cities* (New York: Oxford University Press, 2004), pp. 99–100.

119. Ibid., p. 101.

120. U.S. Bureau of the Census, *The Changing Shape of the Nation's Income Distribution, 1947–1998*, p. 3, Table 1 (published June 2000), http://www2.census.gov /prod2/popscan/p60-204.pdf.

121. Tami Luhby, "Global Income Inequality: Where the U.S. Ranks" *CNN Money* (November 8, 2011).

122. Nicholas Kristof, "Our Banana Republic," *The New York Times* (November 6, 2010).

123. Louis Uchitelle, "The Richest of the Rich, Proud of a New Gilded Age," *The New York Times* (July 15, 2007).

124. U.S. Bureau of the Census, *The 2009 Statistical Abstract of the United States*, Table 669, www.census.gov/compendia/statab.

125. U.S. Bureau of the Census, *Table 11, Employment Status of Civilian Population, Sex, Race, and Hispanic Origin* (2005), www.bls.gov/html.

126. Ibid., Table A-2.

CHAPTER 7

National Policy and the City/Suburban Divide

The Unintended Consequences of National Policies

By the end of World War II, there was a growing national concern about the condition of the inner cities. The neglect of basic infrastructure brought about by the Great Depression and the war could be observed in the decay of business districts, the dilapidation of older housing stock, and the tattered state of roads, bridges, parks, and urban amenities. These problems seemed all the more urgent because of overcrowding. The wartime boom had brought a crush of new residents to cities, but housing was hard to find. At first, the suburban subdivisions seemed like a welcome safety valve, but while they grew, the cities slid ever deeper into decline. This was alarming because the industrial cities had always been the engines of the American economy, and thus their fate seemed inextricably tied to the nation's well-being.

Even before the war was over, congressional leaders from both political parties began to consider ways to address the sorry state of the cities. After several years of haggling over details, in 1949 Congress approved ambitious urban renewal and public housing programs, and over the next few years these programs leveraged an astonishing amount of private investment—$35.8 billion by 1968.[1] Despite the best of intentions, however, the federal effort to help the cities failed, in considerable measure because other federal policies were, at the same time, igniting a suburban housing boom. These deep contradictions virtually guaranteed policy failure because the left hand was trying to revive the cities while the right hand was undermining that effort.

Even the federal programs designed to help the cities often had exactly the opposite effect. The massive slum clearance projects financed by the urban renewal program razed low-income housing units faster than public housing could be produced. The effect was to sharply reduce the supply of housing available to African American homebuyers and renters. All through the 1950s and 1960s, hundreds of thousands of low-income blacks were displaced, and they were forced either to play a game of musical slums or move into high-rise public housing projects that ultimately turned into architectural eyesores and vertical ghettos. Because they were denied access to the suburbs by discriminatory policies implemented by the real estate industry and federal administrators, middle-class blacks were forced into an intense competition for housing in neighborhoods already occupied by white homeowners. Meanwhile, federally insured loans made it possible for millions of white middle-class families to find new housing in the suburbs. Still another federal program financed a national system of freeways that made it easy for suburbanites to commute long distances. When considered in their entirely, the mix of federal policies that affected metropolitan development intensified racial segregation in the cities and subsidized white flight to the suburbs.

Although the federal government shifted course in the 1960s, the changes came too little and too late. Racial discrimination in the buying and selling of real estate was outlawed by the 1968 Civil Rights Act, and federal programs were enacted to make funds available to minority homeowners. But the pattern of extreme racial segregation between city and suburb was, by then, too firmly established to be easily reversed. A metropolitan pattern of rigid racial segregation was fixed in place, and the national government had helped to create it.

OUTTAKE

Highway Programs Contributed to the Decline of the Cities

It is inaccurate to use the phrase "national urban policy" when referring to the policies that have influenced urban development in the United States. There has never been a national policy for the cities. Instead, a mixed bag of uncoordinated programs has been adopted at different times and for different purposes. Although some of these programs profoundly impacted cities and urban regions, their urban effects were rarely given serious consideration, and even if they had, the political forces at work and the complexity of the governmental system in the United States would have made it virtually impossible to achieve a comprehensive and well-coordinated strategy of urban development.

Highway programs serve as an enlightening example. For decades, the federal government devoted massive resources to build a national highway system, but the powerful effects of that program on cities and urban areas were mostly ignored. Early in the twentieth century, the federal government began providing aid for state-constructed roadways as a way of connecting farmers to the national economic system and opening up rural areas for settlement. By the 1930s, federal aid had become focused on a more abstract objective of promoting the use of the automobile. The political muscle of the automobile industry expanded in step with its economic importance. The states established trust funds that relied primarily upon gasoline taxes, and federal legislation in 1934 established penalties for any state that used any auto taxes for other purposes than building and maintaining highways.

The federal role expanded enormously in 1956 when Congress declared the intention to create a

42,000-mile national system of interstate highways. As in previous years, the taxes used to finance the system were "disproportionately collected in cities and disproportionately spent outside of cities," which reflected the power of rural interests in state legislatures and the aims of the highway engineers. It also accorded with the thinking of President Eisenhower, who thought that an integrated system of highways was important to the national defense because in times of war, it would be easier to move troops and equipment. There was another consideration as well. It was widely thought that the concentration of populations and economic activity in cities made the United States vulnerable if atomic warfare broke out. An influential city planner warned that urban areas had to decentralize or face disaster, saying that "If we delay too long, we may wake up some morning and find that we haven't any country, that is, if we wake up at all that morning." The lesson to be drawn is that even when the policymakers took some notice of the urban impacts of their policies, they considered these to be secondary, if they mattered at all.

Sources: Quotations are from Owen D. Gutfreund, *20th Century Sprawl: Highways and the Reshaping of the American Landscape* (New York: Oxford University Press, 2004), p. 56; Robert M. Fogelson, *Downtown: Its Rise and Fall, 1880–1950* (New Haven, CT: Yale University Press, 2001), p. 392.

The Politics of Slum Clearance

Following World War II, a powerful and diverse coalition lobbied Congress to enact a federally funded slum clearance program. Local public officials and business leaders were alarmed by the condition of downtown business districts and nearby residential areas. Public housing administrators, labor unions, social workers, and liberal Democrats were concerned about the plight of the poor and argued that the residents of dilapidated neighborhoods had a moral right to adequate housing. Realtors, developers, financial institutions, and local business elites had entirely different reasons for favoring slum clearance. They were concerned not so much about the conditions of life in the slums as for the security of their own investments in inner-city property. Clearly, the widespread deterioration of commercial and residential areas threatened the economic vitality of the central cities. For this reason, the National Association of Real Estate Boards (NAREB) favored a federally funded program of urban renewal even though it maintained a venomous opposition to public housing programs, in large part because of the real estate industry's interest in preventing government competition with private developers and landlords.[2]

A coalition of groups important to the Democratic Party fought for the principle that public housing must be included in any urban renewal program funded by the federal government. Organized labor led the way in criticizing the real estate industry's fixation on its own bottom line. Local government officials represented by the U.S. Conference of Mayors, the National League of Cities, and the American Municipal Association lined up behind a program of urban renewal that included public housing. These groups formed an alliance powerful enough to prevent the legislation before Congress from being sabotaged by bickering over details. In the spring of 1949, Congress approved the Housing Act. Despite intense lobbying by real estate agents and their allies to throw out the public housing provision, it was kept in the final bill, but only by a razor-thin five-vote margin. The final version of the legislation was then passed by a bipartisan majority of northern Democrats, urban Republicans, and a few southern Democrats.[3]

In the 1949 Housing Act, Congress declared a national commitment to rebuild the cities, eliminate slums and blight, and provide decent housing for the nation's citizens. The preamble to the act, titled a "Declaration of National Housing Policy," offered a sweeping statement about the need for a housing program:

> The general welfare and security of the Nation and the health and living standards of its people require housing production and relating community development sufficient to remedy the serious housing shortage, eliminate substandard and other inadequate housing through the clearance of slums and blighted areas, and the realization as soon as feasible of the goal of a decent home and suitable living environment for every American family.[4]

Business interests and the housing industry got what they wanted in the bill but were forced to accept public housing in the bargain. In the end, the housing bill received the endorsement of key business, real estate, and housing interests because the legislation gave control over the urban renewal and public housing programs to local public authorities. Title I of the act empowered the Housing and Home Finance Agency (HHFA) to distribute grants-in-aid to help local urban renewal agencies absorb the cost of buying and clearing renewal sites. After this process was complete, urban renewal agencies were allowed to "write-down" the cost of the properties so they could be sold to developers at bargain prices. Because part of the "write-down" was covered by federal grants, it amounted to a direct subsidy to well-connected developers.

Tenants and slum dwellers displaced by renewal programs were supposed to be supplied with "decent, safe and sanitary dwellings." Title III of the bill, which funded low-rent public housing, authorized (but did not appropriate money for) the production of 810,000 government-subsidized housing units over a six-year period. This amounted to 10 percent of the estimated national need for new low-cost dwellings. Occupancy preferences were given for veterans and families displaced by Title I (clearance) activities. Federal administrators imposed per-room and per-unit cost limitations to prevent "extravagance and unnecessary" amenities, and imposed tenant eligibility requirements to minimize competition with the private housing market and to ensure that public housing benefited only the neediest families.

How Local Politics Shaped Urban Renewal

Local political and economic elites were far more concerned about the economic decline of central business districts (CBDs) than they were about slum residents. Business leaders and politicians were convinced that encroaching slums were responsible for the steady decline in property values and retail activity in the downtown areas. Despite the fact that the legislation seemed to favor residential development, right from the beginning local renewal agencies placed a much higher priority on commercial development than low-income housing, a practice made possible by the flexible way federal administrators interpreted the provisions of the housing act. Guidelines issued by the HHFA defined any renewal project that allocated 51 percent or more of its funds to housing as a "100 percent housing" project. In its effect and intent, this standard gave local authorities permission to emphasize commercial development over other uses despite the "predominantly residential" language contained in the original legislation.

Public housing immediately ran into trouble. In the abstract, housing for low-income people might seem worthwhile, but at the local level it ran into determined opposition. Experiences with housing legislation passed in the 1930s had already showed that it was likely there would be problems. In December 1946, when the Chicago Housing Authority (CHA) tried to move a few families of African American veterans into a public housing project built with funds from the housing act of 1937, white mobs jeered and threw stones. In August 1947, menacing mobs gathered to keep blacks from moving into a project on the city's southwest side. A contingent of police was assigned to protect the black families, and they stayed six months.[5] The CHA learned its lesson well, and backed off any further attempts to integrate housing projects.

After passage of the 1949 housing act, the Chicago experience was repeated in cities across the country. In city after city, local chapters of the NAREB organized opposition to public housing projects. In vitriolic campaigns, the opponents of subsidized housing played on fears that public housing might be used to promote racial integration. Between 1949 and the end of 1952, public housing programs were rejected by referenda in Akron, Houston, Los Angeles, and almost 40 other cities. Social and political realities at the local level made public housing a volatile issue. Local officials were acutely aware "there could hardly be many votes to be gained in championing the cause—and perhaps a great many lost."[6]

By contrast, slum clearance and economic redevelopment were programs that local political interests were happy to embrace. Seizing on redevelopment as a way to secure federal funds, in city after city, enterprising mayors managed to assemble powerful alliances to support the cause of redevelopment. Corporate executives were the most important members of the coalition, but other crucial participants were involved as well. Real estate and small business owners, metropolitan newspapers, and the construction trades unions lent their support. A prominent urban scholar, Robert Salisbury, observed that this "new convergence of power" that brought public power and private resources together turned urban renewal into an almost irresistible force capable of overwhelming all opposition.[7]

The programs financed by the Housing Act were perfect vehicles for mayors who wished to secure their personal political futures. After he was elected mayor of Chicago in 1955, Richard J. Daley forged a powerful civic coalition to launch an ambitious program to revitalize Chicago's downtown Loop and lake-front. In Boston, the candidate selected by the business-sponsored New Boston Committee defeated longtime machine boss James Michael Curley in the 1951 mayoral race, then backed the massive clearance of Boston's Italian West End and the construction of a government center. Ultimately, Boston's renewal program took 10 percent of the city's land area.[8] In 1950, St. Louis's mayor, Joseph Darst, received national publicity when his city became the nation's first to secure federal funding for urban renewal. Raymond Tucker, who replaced him in 1953, was even more aggressive in pushing clearance projects. He assembled a broad coalition that included all of the major corporations in the city—69 businesses in all—and managed to persuade them to raise $2,000,000 in private capital to help fund the local urban renewal agency. An almost identical alliance came together in New Haven, Connecticut, where the young Democrat Richard Lee won several terms by leading an ambitious renewal effort. Lee's political capital derived from his ability to marry the public resources made available through the program with the political and financial support of business leaders. Mayor Lee referred to this coalition as

> the biggest set of muscles in New Haven. . . . They're muscular because they control wealth, they're muscular because they control industries, represent banks. They're muscular because they head up labor. They're muscular because they represent the intellectual portions of the community. They're muscular because they're articulate, because they're respectable, because of their financial power, and because of the accumulation of prestige they have built up over the years as individuals in all kinds of causes.[9]

Mayors and business leaders tended to share the view that the economic fortunes of their cities depended on the health of the downtown. In the 1950s, the flight of the middle class to the suburbs was seriously undermining the economic viability of the inner cities. Because the central business district was the center of activity where the local business establishment held heavy real estate and business investments, it was only logical that businesses would try to protect their investments. The need for political visibility and campaign contributions from wealthy donors ensured that elected officials would favor downtown sites. Those areas were generally the oldest in the cities and therefore easily designated as officially "blighted" by the local urban renewal authority, the first step in a process that led to condemning and clearing property.

The members of the urban renewal coalition needed one another. Local officials coveted the investment capital and the public prestige the business community possessed. In turn, leaders in the business community realized that governmental authority was a necessary ingredient for a successful redevelopment effort. Public authority was, in the first instance, called on to apply for federal funds through an officially constituted urban renewal agency. The government's power of eminent domain, which allowed it to condemn "blighted" property for a "higher" public use, was crucial for land assembly because individual property owners could not otherwise be compelled to sell. Finally, the unique ability of local renewal agencies to secure the necessary write-down subsidies and loans from the federal government made local officials and agencies indispensable to business leaders who wanted urban redevelopment. In this way, "this strange coalition"[10] became a singularly dominant force in local politics.

Over the years, the urban renewal program "engineered a massive allocation of private and social resources" in cities all over the United States.[11] Public funds were used to make downtown areas more desirable to investors. By 1968, private institutions had committed $35.8 billion in 524 renewal projects across the nation.[12] From 1953 to 1986, when the last money left in the pipeline was finally exhausted, over $13 billion in direct federal spending had been committed to urban renewal.[13] At the same time, the huge federal expenditures authorized by the National Defense Highway Act of 1956 provided hundreds of thousands of jobs and considerable profits to construction firms building limited-access highways through urban neighborhoods.

The clearance of neighborhoods associated with urban renewal and highway building soon ignited resistance and controversy. Although business leaders talked glibly about benefiting all the residents of the city through the provision of jobs and increases in business investment, it became painfully apparent that viable and even thriving neighborhoods were often destroyed in the process. In Boston, block after block of well-kept bungalows and row houses, grocery stores, barber shops, bakeries, and taverns—all the elements making up historic, safe, thriving Italian neighborhoods in Boston's West End—were leveled. *Blight* was such an ambiguous term that it could be, and often was, applied even to healthy neighborhoods.[14]

All across the country, community protests called attention to the destruction caused by urban renewal and highway construction projects. According to one scholar, "development issues . . . dominated the neighborhoods" in the 1950s and 1960s in the four cities he studied.[15] Despite the intensity and frequency of protests, however, in the end neighborhoods won few victories. This poor record of success reflected that fact that the groups opposing renewal were small and often easily divided. The residents of neighborhoods put a priority on protecting their own turf but rarely saw any reason to expend scarce resources to help someone else. By astutely selecting renewal and redevelopment sites, urban renewal administrators found it easy to pursue a strategy of divide and conquer.

Atlanta provides an excellent example of how this kind of politics worked. Beginning in 1952, Atlanta's Metropolitan Planning Commission became concerned about the movement of blacks into neighborhoods close to the central business district. In its report of that year, *Up Ahead*, the commission maintained that "from the viewpoint of planning the wise thing is to find outlying areas to be developed for new colored housing." The commission recommended "public policies to reduce existing densities, wipe out blighted areas, improve the racial pattern of population distribution, and make the best possible use of central planned areas."[16] The actual goal, which was only thinly disguised by this rhetoric, was to move blacks into areas farther from the downtown area and to secure land near the CBD for redevelopment.

The Central Atlanta Improvement Association, an organization that represented corporate interests, energetically promoted clearance. Corporate leaders took special care to obtain the support of the Chamber of Commerce, which represented smaller businesses. The Atlanta Real Estate Board was brought on board with reassurances that renewal would help maintain segregated housing patterns and that no public housing would be built on properties cleared by urban renewal. At the same time, the corporate and public leadership gained support from leaders of the black community by promising that land would be made available for the construction of single-family, owner-occupied housing for blacks well away from the downtown. Years later, downtown Atlanta was still undergoing massive clearance and reconstruction and a huge enclosed mall called the Peachtree Center was slowly replacing the historic downtown.

The local renewal coalitions born in the 1950s used their political muscle to crush opponents. Although almost any city could be selected as a suitable example, San Francisco's single-minded pursuit of downtown renewal is especially revealing.[17] In 1953, the San Francisco Board of Supervisors approved a plan to clear several blocks adjacent to the financial district and south of Market Street. This area, with its market stalls, narrow passageways, and constant bustling activity, stood in the way of plans to remake the downtown into a collection of corporate, cultural, and tourist facilities. By the late 1950s, civic leaders had settled on a plan to clear the area for a sports arena and convention center that would be named the Yerba Buena Center. Planners envisioned that Yerba Buena would help support the city's financial district and become a magnet for further development.

This vision appealed to the scores of corporate giants located in the heart of the city, including Standard Oil of California, Southern Pacific, Transamerica Corporation, Levi Strauss, Crown Zellerbach, Del Monte, Pacific Telephone and Telegraph, Bethlehem Steel, and Pacific Gas and Electric. Among the many financial institutions located in downtown San Francisco were Bank of America, Wells Fargo, Crocker National Bank, Bank of California, Aetna Life, John Hancock, and Hartford Insurance. During the 1960s, the buildings that housed these institutions utterly changed San Francisco's skyline. Twenty-three high-rises were constructed in downtown San Francisco between 1960 and 1972.[18]

The director of the San Francisco Redevelopment Agency, M. Justin Herman, became the "chief architect, major spokesman, and operations commander" for the massive renewal project. Under his leadership, the redevelopment agency hired several hundred professionals and dozens of consultants and applied for millions of dollars in federal urban renewal subsidies. Herman regarded even the mildest criticism of his project as an attempt by parochial interests to stand in the way of progress. In 1970, he was quoted as saying, "This land is too valuable to permit poor people to park on it."[19] He was cited in a major publication in 1970 as "one of the men responsible for getting urban renewal" renamed "the federal bulldozer" and "Negro removal":

> He was absolutely confident that he was doing what the power structure wanted insofar as the poor and the minorities were concerned. That's why San Francisco has mostly luxury housing and business district projects—that's what white, middle-class planners and businessmen envision as ideal urban renewal.[20]

Federal administrators turned a blind eye to the fact that the Yerba Buena Center project was being planned with no thought of building replacement housing for the people who lived in the area. During the summer of 1969, local residents challenged the project in federal court, arguing that the 1949 Housing Act required the renewal agency to find safe and suitable housing for people displaced by clearance. The judge who heard the case concluded that the secretary of the Department of Housing and Urban Development "had not been provided with any creditable evidence at all" in regard to the redevelopment agency's plan to relocate residents.[21] Temporarily stopped in its tracks, the agency eventually agreed to increase the hotel tax in San Francisco in order to finance the construction of some low-income housing to absorb the area residents displaced by the Yerba Buena Center. Eventually a series of court battles, plus the escalating costs of building the center doomed the project, and it was never built. It was a rare and widely celebrated victory for the opponents of urban renewal.

Organized opposition at the national level emerged in the early 1960s. Liberal critics viewed urban renewal as a "federally financed gimmick to provide relatively cheap land for a miscellany of profitable, prestigious [private] enterprises."[22] Conservatives were equally appalled by the results of the program. At its inception and through its early years, business leaders and politicians expected a miraculous reversal of central-city decline. The optimism soon turned into frustration. By the late 1960s, it took an estimated four years to plan a typical clearance project and an additional six years to clear the site. Frequently, by the time it was ready for redevelopment the original plans had long been abandoned.[23] Even generous write-downs to lower the cost of acquisition often failed to entice developers. Meanwhile, blighted and slums continued to spread; indeed, it appeared that the displacement of residents only accelerated the deterioration of nearby neighborhoods.

Racial Segregation and "The Projects"

The public housing program turned out to be a cruel hoax because it promised to improve the lives of slum dwellers but instead made things worse. African Americans who moved to the cities in the great migrations of the twentieth century were crowded into rundown neighborhoods clustered near the urban core. Because much of the oldest and most dilapidated housing was located near central business districts, clearance projects displaced blacks more than anyone else. Critics coined the phrases "black removal" and "Negro clearance" as a way of referring to the fact that two-thirds of the people displaced in the first eight years of the program were black.[24] Economic and racial barriers left them no choice other than to move to another area much like the slum they had left behind: "Given the realities of the low-income housing market . . . it is likely that, for many families, relocation [meant] no more than keeping one step ahead of the bulldozer."[25] Thus a new game was added to the harsh realities of urban life—"musical slums."

Black families displaced by urban renewal clearance found their options to be few. They had the choice of either moving into public housing projects or to other slum areas, where they paid higher rents because the overall supply of low-rent housing units was rapidly dwindling. By the end of 1961, clearance projects had eliminated 126,000 housing units. The 28,000 new units that replaced them could house less than one-fifth of the 113,000 families and 36,000 individuals displaced by clearance.[26] There was a 90 percent decline in the supply of low-income housing within redevelopment areas during the first 10 years of the program's operation.[27] Only $34.8 million of the urban renewal funds—less than 1 percent—was used for relocation assistance, placing a disproportionate share of the cost of the program on the slum residents who were forced to move.[28]

Their status as displaced slum residents conferred on blacks "the dubious privilege of eligibility for public housing."[29] For potential renters, the problem was that public housing was basically designed to fail. The first and perhaps most important impediment was that eligibility was restricted to those who could not afford to rent on the private housing market. The real estate lobby would have tolerated no other policy. The insidious result was to concentrate those poor families together that, for whatever reasons, were unable to improve their circumstances. Tenants who got jobs and increased their incomes were evicted. Already, in the 1950s, the concentration of families in poverty meant that public housing projects were prone to high levels of violence and juvenile crime. Over the years, public housing tenants were increasingly made up of "broken families, dependent families, and welfare families."[30] If the families whose incomes went up had been able to stay in their apartments by paying higher rents, the rise in social pathologies might have been moderated,[31] and the rental income they paid would have helped make public housing more economically viable.

The second flaw was related to the fact that public housing projects almost always were built on sites carefully separated from more desirable parts of the city. This meant that "the projects" were surrounded by slums, and most of these areas were inhabited by blacks. From the beginning, most public housing projects were segregated by explicit policy in all but a few northern states. It is true that, nationwide, nonwhites accounted for only 38 percent of all public housing tenants in 1952, and 46 percent by 1961. Significant portions of the buildings were occupied by whites and were, for a time, considered desirable by young families headed by veterans, who received first priority.[32] However, strict racial segregation between projects was the universal norm. But by the time President John F. Kennedy signed an executive order forbidding the racial segregation of public housing projects in 1962, it could have little practical effect because by then the overwhelming majority of tenants in large cities were African American anyway; white families found it easy to find other housing, but black families did not. Thus, the public housing program had the perverse effect of reinforcing and intensifying the racial segregation that prevailed before it was adopted.

The third fatal flaw of the public housing program was that the units themselves were cheap and shoddily built. Everything about public housing served as a constant reminder to its tenants and to everyone else that this was a grudging welfare program. To save money on site preparation and construction costs, cities built clusters of high-density high-rise buildings. The African American writer James Baldwin might have been describing almost any of these projects when he referred to those in Harlem as "colorless, bleak, high and revolting."[33] Of course, big American and European cities are full of high-rises that command steep rents from affluent clientele, but such structures, especially when built cheaply, "were not suitable for poor people with big families."[34] It was difficult for parents to supervise children even when play facilities were available. Elevators were often broken and stuck, laundry rooms were many floors removed from tenants' apartments, and dark hallways and stairwells were poorly lighted even when bulbs were available.

The Cabrini-Green projects north of Chicago's Loop began as two-story brick row houses built to house war workers in World War II. All of the occupants were white. In 1958, these houses were replaced by 15 high-rise buildings, and another 8 were constructed in 1962. These 19-story rectangular monstrosities loomed over the surrounding neighborhoods. The same situation existed in New York City, where public housing typically rose to more than 20 stories. The Pruitt-Igoe project in St. Louis, built between 1954 and 1959, was composed of 2,762 apartments in 33 eleven-story buildings on a 57-acre site. By the time the last building was completed, the project was already a community scandal.[35] By 1973, it had become an international symbol for the failure of American public housing. In that year, photographs that made *Life* magazine's "The Year in Review" showed the shocking spectacle of one of the buildings imploding from hundreds of charges of carefully placed dynamite. As a monument to a policy failure, the episode could hardly have been more dramatic and fitting: Explosives experts got the opportunity to hone their demolition skills on buildings that had been completed, with awards to the architectural firm, just 15 years before.

In 1965, Congress approved rent supplement programs as an alternative to public housing construction. The idea was that if the government paid part of the rent, low-income families would be able to choose their own housing on the private market. The Housing and Urban Development Act of 1968 required that a majority of privately constructed housing units built on redevelopment sites be reserved for low- and moderate-income families.[36] These steps began a long-term trend away from governmentally constructed public housing. Public housing and urban renewal met their effective demise in the 1970s. In 1974, urban renewal was merged into the Community Development Block Grant program. During the Nixon administration public housing was allowed to wither away; dropping from 104,000 starts in 1970 to only 19,000 by 1974.[37] A few years later, public housing was essentially abandoned when the Reagan administration eliminated low-income housing built by the government in favor of programs that subsidized landlords by giving housing vouchers to prospective tenants.

National Policy and Suburban Development

In the decades after World War II, millions of white families moved from the cities to the suburbs. Suburban growth would have occurred with or without governmental policies that hurried it along. Operating on its own, the private real estate market would have supported, as it did in the past, a movement to the urban periphery. But by accelerating the pace of suburban development the federal government guaranteed that central cities would quickly empty even while the suburbs prospered. The National Housing Act of 1934 and the Serviceman's Readjustment Act of 1944 made it possible for millions of American families to purchase their first suburban home. These programs were an unalloyed blessing for the white families who poured into the suburbs, but they also had important unintended consequences.

Until the Great Depression of the 1930s, the government played little direct role in housing provision. The notable exception was that the federal and state courts enforced restrictive covenants attached to property deeds; usually, such attachments restricted the sale of homes in urban neighborhoods to whites only. Restrictive covenants exerted a huge impact on the housing market, but the role of the courts was not considered to be a matter of government policy; rather, enforcement of the covenants was considered a private contractual matter between buyer and seller that the courts were occasionally called upon to mediate.

During the Great Depression, the federal government was prompted to intervene in the nation's housing market because it constituted a significant sector of the national economy. Second only to agriculture as an employer, during the depression the housing industry experienced a sudden, devastating contraction. Before the stock market crash of October 1929, 900,000 new housing units came on the market each year, but in 1934 this number had fallen to one-tenth as many. Throughout the 1930s, housing starts lagged far behind the demand for new housing.[38] In Chicago, only 131 new housing units were constructed in all of 1933, compared with 18,837 in 1929 and 41,416 in 1926.[39] Across the nation, 63 percent of the workers in the housing industry were unemployed in 1933. Foreclosures on millions of mortgages brought hardship to homeowners and drove thousands of banks out of business. Something had to be done to keep millions of people from becoming homeless and to save the banking system.

The National Housing Act of 1934 created both the Federal Housing Administration (FHA) and the Federal Savings and Loan Insurance Corporation (FSLIC). The FHA assumed much of the risk in the housing market by insuring most of the value of home loans made by banks. The FSLIC insured individual savings accounts up to $5,000 (this level has since risen in a series of steps to more than $250,000). It was hoped that such insurance would inspire confidence by potential savers and investors, so people would be encouraged to put their savings into banks instead of in shoeboxes and under their mattresses. These savings accounts, in turn, would enable savings and loan institutions to invest more capital in the floundering housing market.

The most important provision of the housing act is Section 203, the basic home mortgage insurance program under which the bulk of FHA insurance has been written up to the present day. Fully 79 percent of all FHA-insured units from 1934 to 1975—about 9.5 million units representing a face value of more than $109 billion—came under the provisions of Section 203.[40] The act specified that 80 percent of the value of the property financed by banks would be insured through the FHA. (Later, through the Housing and Urban Development Act of 1974, this share was increased to 97 percent of the first $25,000 and

80 percent of the remaining value. Since then the formula has been changed from time to time.) Under FHA guidelines, the low risk assumed by the lending institution permits the borrower to pay a low down payment, with the remaining principal and interest spread over a period of up to 30 years.

There were many different interpretations about the main purpose of the 1934 National Housing Act. Title I of the act provided FHA insurance for loans used for "permanent repairs that add to the basic livability and usefulness of the property."[41] Social welfare liberals saw Title I as a means of eliminating substandard living conditions in the central cities by providing low-interest, low-risk loans. City officials hoped Title I would entice affluent people to stay within the city limits and remodel their homes rather than move to new homes in the suburbs. Downtown business interests had a different goal in mind: They favored it because they thought it could shore up downtown property values. Most banks, savings and loan institutions, real estate agents, and contractors had another thing in mind entirely. They regarded Section 203 as a way to finance new construction in the suburbs. In lobbying for the housing act, they had agreed to Title I only as a compromise to facilitate quick congressional action.

Despite the impression one might get from reading the 1934 legislation, over the years almost all the government's resources were devoted to promoting suburban housing development. Congress never appropriated much money to finance Title I repairs for existing property, but it provided generous support for the home insurance provisions of Section 203. Freed of most of the risk entailed in making a loan, banks were quick to liberalize loan terms.

TABLE 7.1   Relative Burden of Loan Terms, 1920s and 1960s[a]

Decade and Lender	Terms
1920s	
Savings and loan association	60 percent of house value loaned for 11 years fully amortized
Bank or insurance company	50 percent of house value loaned for 5 years unamortized (balance due at end)
1960s	
Conventional lender	75 percent of house value loaned for 20 years fully amortized
FHA	95 percent of house value loaned for 30 years fully amortized

[a]For a house equal to approximately 2.5 times the purchaser's annual salary.

Source: Table from *Shelter and Subsidies: Who Benefits from Federal Housing Policies, Studies in Social Economics* by Henry J. Aaron (Washington, DC: Brookings Institution Press, 1972), p. 77. Copyright © 1972.

Table 7.1 shows how much more difficult it was to buy a home before the passage of the FHA program. In the 1920s, banks ordinarily required down payments of 30 to 50 percent, and amortized the loan over a maximum of five years, often with a balloon payment (the remainder of the loan) due at the end. Savings and loan institutions, which amortized loans for up to 11 years, were slightly more generous. The FHA program changed all that, and in 1944, when Congress approved legislation making veterans eligible for special loan terms, loan terms for new housing became even more liberal. Under the FHA, a home-buyer could get a 30-year mortgage with only 5 percent down. The VA allowed banks to finance a mortgage with no down payment at all. The FHA and VA programs helped increase the federally insured share of the mortgage market from 15 percent in 1945 to 41 percent by 1954, and these programs provided an incentive for the banks to ease loan terms on conventional loans as well.[42] By the 1960s, the typical home loan could be obtained with a 25 percent down payment and was amortized over 30 years.

The FHA loan guarantee program fundamentally changed the home credit market. Between 1935 and 1974, more than three-fourths of the FHA-insured home mortgages financed new (as opposed to existing) housing.[43] The proportion of all homes that were owner occupied rather than rented increased from 44 percent in 1940 to 63 percent in 1970, and to 68 percent in 2002.[44] As shown in Table 7.2, more than one-third of all homes purchased in 1950 and 1955 were financed through the FHA or VA programs, and the proportion of new single-family home sales financed under these programs varied from a low of 26 percent (in 1960 and 1990) to a high of 50 percent (in 1970). In 1995, FHA/VA financed 19 percent of mortgages, and the proportion fell to 14 percent in 2002.[45] The declining reliance on FHA and VA loans in the 1990s occurred mainly because lending institutions began offering variable-rate and other creative forms of mortgage financing that made buying a home easier for almost everyone.

Virtually all of the new homes bought with FHA/VA loans were built in the suburbs. Throughout the 1940s and 1950s, the FHA displayed an overwhelming bias in favor of the suburbs; for instance, in its first 12 years it did not insure a single dwelling in Manhattan. In part, this bias reflected a widespread cultural preference for less dense, single-family neighborhoods, which were normally found in the suburbs, over the denser, multiunit neighborhoods in the cities. But the roots of the FHA policy went beyond a simple matter of architectural form or geography. The real agenda was racial. FHA administrators were convinced that neighborhoods should be racially and ethnically segregated.

FHA mortgage insurance programs relied upon the private-sector lending institutions that processed the actual loans. From the beginning, the FHA absorbed the values, policies, and goals of the real estate and banking industries.[46] The staff of the FHA was drawn from the ranks of those industries, and it was only logical that the FHA's philosophy would parallel theirs. On the surface, it might seem that the "FHA's interests went no farther than the safety of the mortgage it secured."[47] This is a bit misleading because in the minds of FHA administrators, the soundness of a neighborhood and its racial makeup could not

TABLE 7.2 Use of FHA- and VA-Insured Loans in the United States, 1950–2002

Year	Percentage of Private Housing Financed through the FHA or VA[a]
1950	35%
1955	41
1960	26
1965	30
1970	50
1980	36
1990	26
1995	19
2002	14

[a]Data from 1950, 1955, and 1960 for all private-sector housing. Data from 1965 to 2002 for newly built, private-sector, single-family homes actually built and sold within the reporting year. These new methods are not strictly comparable; the percentages for all private-sector housing will tend to be somewhat smaller than for private-sector, single-family housing built and sold within the reporting year. This bias will tend to understate FHA/VHA financing for 1950, 1955, and 1960.

Sources: U.S. Bureau of the Census, *Historical Statistics of the United States to 1970, Colonial Times to 1970*, pt. 2 (Washington, DC: U.S. Government Printing Office, 1975), pp. 369, 641 (for 1950, 1955, 1960); *Historical Statistics of the United States* (Washington, DC: U.S. Government Printing Office, various years) 2003: pp. 611–612, Tables 943–945; 2002: pp. 591–592, Tables 921–923; 1999: pp. 724–725, Tables 1201–1202; 1998: pp. 718–719, Tables 1199–1201; 1993: pp. 718–719, Tables 1221, 1224; 1989: p. 715, Tables 1262–1263; 1987: p. 706, Tables 1273–1274; 1982–1983: p. 748, Tables 1341–1342; 1973: pp. 684–685, Tables 1156–1158; 1969: pp. 697, 698, Tables 1071, 1075.

be separated. The FHA administrators took some pains to make sure that banks understood the connection. When it issued its underwriting manual to banks in 1938, one of the guidelines instructed loan officers to steer clear of changing or racially mixed areas:

> Areas surrounding a location are [to be] investigated to determine whether incompatible racial and social groups are present, for the purpose of making a prediction regarding the probability of the location being invaded by such groups. If a neighborhood is to retain stability, it is necessary that properties shall continue to be occupied by the same social and racial classes. A change in social or racial occupancy generally contributes to instability and a decline in values.[48]

A revealing glimpse into how sensitive FHA administrators were to the issue of race can be gained by reading the language of a 1933 report submitted to the agency by one of its consultants, Homer Hoyt, a well-known sociologist and demographer at the time. He offered his view that land values and the racial composition of a neighborhood were closely linked, and that it was possible to determine the desirability/undesirability of racial and ethnic groups with some precision. His list was, he said, an accurate representation of each group's "beneficial effect upon land values":

> If the entrance of a colored family into a white neighborhood causes a general exodus of the white people it is reflected in property values. Except in the case of Negroes and Mexicans, however, these racial and national barriers disappear when the individuals of the foreign nationality groups rise in the economic scale or conform to the American standards of living. . . . While the ranking may be scientifically wrong from the standpoint of inherent racial characteristics, it registers an opinion or prejudice that is reflected in land values; it is the ranking of races and nationalities with respect to their beneficial effect upon land values. Those having the most favorable effect come first in the list and those exerting the most detrimental effect appear last:
>
> 1. English, Germans, Scotch, Irish, Scandinavians
> 2. North Italians
> 3. Bohemians or Czechoslovakians
> 4. Poles
> 5. Lithuanians
> 6. Greeks
> 7. Russian Jews of lower class
> 8. South Italians
> 9. Negroes
> 10. Mexicans[49]

FHA administrators advised the developers of residential projects to draw up restrictive covenants barring sales to nonwhites before they applied for FHA-insured financing.[50] Banks were made to understand that even "a single house occupied by a black family in an urban neighborhood, even one tucked away on an inconspicuous side street, was enough for the FHA to label a predominantly white neighborhood as unfit for mortgage insurance."[51] Through such policies, the federal government required the banks to ensure that new subdivisions were strictly segregated. Thus, federal policy acted as a powerful instrument to establish the social and racial patterns that emerged in urban America in the postwar years.[52] Between 1946 and 1959, blacks purchased less than 2 percent of all of the housing financed with the assistance of federal mortgage insurance.[53] In the Miami area, only one black family received FHA backing for a home loan between 1934 and 1949, and there is "evidence that he [the man who secured the loan] was not recognized as a black" at the time the transaction took place.[54]

When the U.S. Supreme Court ruled in 1948 that racial covenants attached to property deeds could not be constitutionally enforced in courts of law, the FHA was forced to amend its official policies. In 1950, the FHA revised its underwriting manual so it no longer openly recommended racial segregation or restrictive covenants. However, it did nothing to reverse the effects of its previous policies, and took no actions to discourage real estate agents, developers, or lending institutions from discriminating against blacks. Until the passage of the Housing Act of 1968, it was still legal and customary for real estate agents and mortgage institutions to discriminate on the basis of race. Indeed, any real estate agent who broke the industry's unwritten code on this issue was liable to be barred from membership in the local real estate association and from its listings services.

Under Title VIII of the Civil Rights Act of 1968,[55] Congress outlawed racial discrimination in housing. Its provisions were sweeping, barring discrimination in rentals and sales and in the provision of information about cost and availability, advertising, purchasing, construction and repair, and real estate services and practices. The statute mandated that each of the federal regulatory agencies involved with the real estate industry take affirmative steps to enforce both the spirit and the letter of the law.[56]

The 1968 legislation opened the suburban housing market to African Americans. Between 1970 and 1980, the number of blacks who lived in suburbs grew by almost 50 percent, an increase of 1.8 million persons.[57] One in ten blacks living in the central cities in 1970 moved to the suburbs during this period, and the percentage of urban blacks living in the suburbs increased from 16 to 21 percent.[58] In the 1980s, the trend continued. By the 1990 census, about 25 percent of urban black families lived in the suburbs; about 85 percent of white families did so.

Blacks who moved to the suburbs tended to have higher incomes than those who stayed behind.[59] Suburbanization undoubtedly expanded housing choice for blacks, but those who moved to the suburbs in the 1970s and 1980s remained about as segregated from whites as they were before.[60] Blacks moved mostly into older inner-ring suburbs, where they displaced white residents, much as they had previously in central cities.[61] These older suburbs tended to have many of the same problems as central-city neighborhoods. In general, the suburbs to which blacks moved had lower tax bases, higher debts, poorer municipal services, lower socioeconomic status, and higher population densities than did suburbs that were mostly white.[62]

Most suburban whites had little contact with suburban blacks. In the mid-1980s, 86 percent of the white residents of suburbs lived in jurisdictions with a black population of less than 1 percent.[63] Even those suburbs that were statistically mixed tended to be segregated internally, and there is evidence that segregation intensified in the 1980s.[64] Why was the racial segregation characteristic of the cities being replicated in the suburbs? Research indicated that discrimination, not social class or income, tended to determine residential location.[65] Socioeconomic differences between blacks and whites accounted for less than 15 percent of the segregation among suburbs in 1980.[66] Research conducted in the St. Louis area indicated that in the 1980s, nonracial factors such as housing cost and economic factors seemed to be less important in explaining patterns of residential segregation than in any previous decade,[67] and this pattern persisted into the 1990s.[68]

Racial discrimination in housing continued even though legislation had outlawed it, in part because the enforcement provisions of the 1968 legislation were weak. Rather than being granted positive responsibilities for identifying discrimination, the Department of Housing and Urban Development (HUD) was permitted only to receive complaints initiated by individual citizens. By thus assuming a passive rather than an active enforcement role, it was easy for HUD to avoid controversy by treating each case as an isolated occurrence rather than as part of a general pattern. For citizens, the time and red tape involved in initiating a complaint was daunting, and thus all through the 1970s the volume of HUD-processed complaints remained low. Interestingly, enforcement improved somewhat under a Republican president, Ronald Reagan, when HUD took steps to publicize the remedies available under the 1968 civil rights legislation. Partially as a result, the number of complaints that HUD received rose sharply in the 1980s. Still, most citizens bypassed HUD and state and local civil rights agencies and went directly to the courts.[69] By focusing on individual remedies rather than on positive efforts to enforce compliance, the governmental role in fair housing enforcement remained small and inconsequential.

Some of the policies initiated by the federal government to eliminate housing discrimination benefited blacks, but in very limited ways. The Equal Credit Opportunity Act of 1974, the Mortgage Disclosure Act of 1975, and the Community Reinvestment Act of 1977 (CRA)[70] were intended to ensure that blacks receive equal consideration for home loans and that banks stop redlining areas where blacks lived. (*Redlining* derives its name from the red line drawn on maps to designate neighborhoods too risky for loans, regardless of the creditworthiness of the individual applicant.) Following enactment of the 1974, 1976, and 1977 legislation, banks became the targets of protests and litigation of community groups challenging redlining practices. Rather than contest a blizzard of litigation and to avoid problems with federal regulators, many banks entered into negotiations with community groups. According to one estimate, by 1991 approximately $18 billion in urban reinvestment commitments had been negotiated in more than 70 cities across the country.[71] However, just as it would be premature to conclude that all redlining stopped, it would be inaccurate to assume all individual loan applications were judged strictly on their merits. Social change rarely comes that easily or rapidly. A 1992 study by the Federal Reserve Bank of Boston found that minorities were roughly 60 percent more likely to be turned down for a mortgage, even after controlling for 38 factors affecting creditworthiness, such as credit history and total debt.[72]

The spatial configuration of today's metropolitan areas still reflects a generation of policies that encouraged suburbanization and racial segregation. These policies had tremendous effects because they altered the dynamics of housing markets decisively in favor of suburban development and racial segregation. The series of legislative remedies enacted in the 1960s and 1970s brought about a change in long-established practices, but these remedies could not be expected to work miracles. Social customs and racial attitudes still influence how social, racial, and ethnic groups become sorted out on the urban landscape.

Suburbs, Highways, and the Automobile

As we have seen, for several decades federal housing and urban renewal policies facilitated the racial and socioeconomic segregation of America's urban areas. The National Defense Highway Act of 1956 amplified the effects of these policies. The highway act financed the construction of a massive system of limited-access freeways that ensured the triumph of the automobile over urban mass transit. "Automobility" enabled Americans to implement a version of Henry Ford's solution to urban problems: "We shall solve the problems of the city by leaving the city."[73] Metropolitan highway systems made Ford's abandonment strategy practical, but mainly for affluent white families able to make the suburban move.

As its title implies, the 1956 National Defense Highway Act was justified partly on military grounds—two of its stated purposes were to aid the movement of troops and supplies and to help evacuate American cities in case of a nuclear attack. The main rationale, however, was that freeways would stimulate the economy by creating a national system of superhighways linking all of the major metropolitan areas in the nation. Within urban areas, the new expressways were expected to solve the growing problem of traffic congestion. A committee appointed by President Eisenhower asserted that suburbs were superior to cities and recommended that the new freeway system be used to decentralize American urban areas.[74] That is exactly what the new freeways did.

The 1956 legislation placed federal gasoline taxes and new excise taxes on tires and heavy vehicles into a Federal Highway Trust Fund. Congress established a grant-in-aid formula of a 90 percent federal and a 10 percent state share for construction. The federal government agreed to distribute the funds for the 42,500-mile system on the basis of need. Because costs in built-up urban areas were greater, urban areas got a lion's share of the funds.

In the years leading up to the legislation, urban planners debated with highway engineers about how a national highway system should be built. Urban planners wanted to design highway systems that would shape regional development and revitalize declining central cities. By contrast, highway engineers believed the new interstate system should be designed with one goal in mind: to move people and goods in the most efficient manner from point A to point B. This meant, in effect, that freeways would be routed directly from the suburbs to the central cities and whatever got in the way would have to go. The engineers got their way. The 1956 act was written so that the funds allocated by the federal government would be administered by state highway departments with no input from urban planners. As one historian put it, "Since federal and state road engineers controlled the program, they had few incentives to include urban renewal, social regeneration, and broader transportation objectives in the programming."[75] When highways were built through urban areas, state highway planners chose routes without reference to their effects on existing neighborhoods.

Laying wide ribbons of concrete had different effects in crowded cities than in the open countryside. As the highway builder Robert Moses said in a speech before the National Highway Users Conference in 1964, "You can draw any kind of picture you like on a clean slate . . . but when you operate in an over-built metropolis, you have to hack your way with a meat axe."[76] The meat axe approach turned out to be the main method Moses used to build his highways, displacing 250,000 people in the New York City area alone.[77] Because the highway engineers wanted to cause the least disruption to private commercial land values, highways were routed through residential areas, especially those with the cheapest housing occupied by poor people and minorities.[78] The program was justified not only as highway building but also as slum clearance. According to one estimate, the uncompensated loss to city residents who were displaced averaged 20 to 30 percent of one year's income.[79]

The methods used to ram freeways through urban areas left a damaging imprint that lingers to the present day. The highways took land off the tax rolls, destroyed intact neighborhoods, and separated downtown areas off from their waterfronts. In St. Louis, Interstate 70 erected a barrier between the Mississippi River waterfront from its downtown that made downtown revitalization difficult. By dividing the South Bronx from the rest of the city, the Cross-Bronx Expressway in New York helped turn the South Bronx into an infamous ghetto. Scholars estimate that the unsightliness of the Fitzgerald Expressway in Boston reduced surrounding property values by about $300 million.[80] In 2004, after more than 15 years of work and more than $15 billion in funding, Boston completed a massive project to tear down the expressway and replace it with an underground tunnel. The land once occupied by the freeway was turned into a park.

The meat axe approach favored by the engineers provoked "freeway revolts" all across the nation.[81] One of the first victories for opponents came in 1959 when San Franciscans successfully prevented the completion of the Embarcadero Freeway. If the protests had failed, a freeway would today run along the shores of the San Francisco Bay, making the later development of such tourist attractions as Ghirardelli Square and the Wharf almost impossible. Protests forced highway planners to become more sensitive to aesthetic and social considerations, but not before irreversible harm had been done to hundreds of urban neighborhoods and waterfronts.

By the 1980s, the price tag for building the interstate system exceeded $100 billion. While highway building received huge subsidies year in and year out, urban mass transit was starved. Unlike Europe, where gasoline taxes had always been used to help support mass transit, federal gas taxes in the United States could not be allocated for that purpose until 1975. Funding for urban mass transit gradually increased after the mid-1970s but remained small. Senator Gaylord Nelson of Wisconsin estimated that up to the 1980s, 75 percent of government expenditures for transportation in the United States in the postwar period had been spent on highways and roads, but only 1 percent was allocated to urban mass transit (most of the rest was spent for railroads and shipping).[82]

The result of these policies is that Americans depend on the automobile for urban travel more than people in any other nation. Although other advanced industrial nations such as Germany, Britain, and Japan embraced the automobile, they also maintained modern systems of mass transit as workable alternatives, despite the fact that automobile use has increased sharply in those countries. In the

United States, by contrast, between 1950 and 1977, as the volume of automobile traffic on urban roads more than tripled, urban mass transit ridership declined by over half, and it has not rebounded since. For the United States as a whole, only 4 percent of workers used public transit to commute to work in 2000—a decline from a peak of 5.4 percent in 1983.[83] In all but a handful of cities in the Northeast, notably New York City, less than 5 percent of workers use mass transit.

In the 1990s, concerns about urban air pollution and long commuting patterns emerged on the national policy agenda, in considerable part because Democrats enjoyed majorities in Congress. In 1992, Congress passed the Intermodal Surface Transportation Efficiency Act (ISTEA, commonly referred to as "ice tea").[84] The significance of ISTEA is that it took substantial authority over interstate highway funds from politically insulated state transportation departments, which had always been dominated by highway engineers, and put decisions about urban transportation systems into the hands of metropolitan planning organizations (MPOs). Governed by delegates representing municipal governments within urban regions, MPOs assumed authority over funding categories designed to reduce auto congestion and improve air quality.

The ISTEA legislation encouraged regional transportation planning by "flexing" federal highway funds, a process that allowed a portion of motor vehicle taxes to be spent on mass transit and even bicycle and pedestrian uses, if local transportation planners chose to. Between fiscal year 1992 and fiscal year 1999, $33.8 billion was available for transfer from transportation programs to transit projects, but local planners decided to transfer only 12.5 percent, or $4.2 billion, of this amount. Some states, such as New York, Massachusetts, California, and Oregon, transferred more than one-third of highway funds available to them to transit use; others transferred little or none.[85]

The precedent set for local flexibility was carried over in the 1998 Transportation Equity Act for the Twenty-first Century (TEA 21), which replaced ISTEA. Under this legislation, highway builders were required to submit studies of the air quality effects for major new federally funded projects. But despite the new efforts to encourage the funding of public transportation, as shown in Table 7.3, the proportion of commuters using automobiles rose only slightly from 1990 to 2006, and for most metropolitan areas, less than 4 percent of commuters used mass transit. Improvements in mass transit systems might improve these numbers, but even after the 1998 legislation, adequate funding for that purpose was not made available to most transit authorities. On average, state and local governments still provided 90 percent of the funds for mass transit systems.

In 2008, sharply rising gasoline prices provided incentives for people to reduce the use of their cars. As gas prices climbed to a national average of more than $4 for regular gasoline during that summer, buses, interurban trains, and light-rail systems became packed with riders. Cities such as New York and Boston, with their well-developed transit systems, showed an increase of 5 percent or more, but by far the largest increases in ridership, in the 10 to 15 percent range, occurred in urban areas that have been the most dependent on the automobile. However, in most metropolitan areas it will be difficult to significantly change transit patterns. Mass transit systems are not developed well enough to conceivably absorb

TABLE 7.3 Commuting Patterns 1990–2006, Selected Metropolitan Areas

	Percentage Public Transit 1990	Percentage Public Transit 2006
Boston	10.6%	8.9%
Chicago	13.7	10.8
Dallas	2.4	1.6
Denver	4.2	4.2
Los Angeles	4.6	4.9
New York	26.6	26.2
St. Louis	3.0	2.4
San Francisco	9.3	9.2

Note: Urban area definitions in 2006 are slightly larger than those previously used, and therefore include more low-transit ex-urban areas than before. However, this method does not change ridership statistics significantly.

Source: 1990 data, U.S. Bureau of the Census, Summary File 3, Transit Ridership Share 1990 (July 2004), www.census.gov.

more than a very small fraction of commuters, even if they run full all the time. In places like Denver, St. Louis, and any number of other cities, light-rail systems are important for transporting visitors to and from airports and for bringing fans to downtown ball games and other events, but they do not, and cannot, carry a large proportion of daily commuters. As a result of decades of investment in highway systems, urban transportation systems are well established and commuting habits are basically fixed. Any significant changes will require very costly infrastructure investments that will take years to complete.

Mass transit systems tend to be chronically underfunded. During the financial crisis of 2008–2009, several metropolitan areas reduced service on their transit systems. The irony is that fiscal problems were occurring at the same time that ridership had increased. This was because only about one-fifth of the revenues from mass transit systems come from fares; the remaining portion is raised through state and local taxes, and these were sharply declining. In early 2009, the Metropolitan Transit Authority of New York City was trying to close a $1.2 billion budget gap. In the St. Louis area, officials were temporarily closing 2,300 bus stops, a move that threatened to raise unemployment levels by stranding workers who relied on the system. Likewise, transit authorities almost everywhere were considering fare increases and service cuts.[86]

Local officials looked to the federal government with high expectations that help was on the way. The American Recovery and Reinvestment Act of 2009, signed into law by President Obama on February 17, 2009, made

$27.5 billion available for surface transportation, highways, roads, and bridges. As part of the administration's "green" initiative, about $12 billion was reserved for mass transit. Because the program was regarded mainly as a jobs initiative, federal administrators indicated that the funds had to be spent only on infrastructure projects such as new train cars, track repair, and station renovations.[87] These measures were likely to improve the quality of service, but they would do nothing for the most basic long-term problem for mass transit in the United States: a funding system that worked against investments in systems that might appreciably alter transit patterns in metropolitan areas.

The Damaging Effects of National Policies

It is a tragic irony that the urban programs initiated after World War II contributed to racial segregation and discrimination. While urban renewal clearance programs bulldozed slum housing, public housing projects segregated blacks more than ever. Meanwhile, white middle-class Americans were paid, in essence, to move to the suburbs, and expensive new freeway systems eased their commute to their jobs in the center city. For decades, millions of white middle-class families were able to secure loans guaranteed by the federal government. It allowed them to move into new suburban developments, where housing values appreciated. For white middle-class America in the postwar period, the home became the principal source of family worth and savings, money that could be invested in a child's education, in a bigger or newer house, or saved for retirement. Until the late 1940s, federal policy excluded African Americans from federal home loan programs, and it took until the late 1960s, when open-housing legislation was passed, for African American families to be able to enter the real estate market in any meaningful sense.

With or without federal programs, a high degree of residential segregation would have evolved in metropolitan areas. But if federal housing programs had not actively discouraged banks from lending to blacks, some middle-class African American homeowners would have been able to find affordable and desirable housing by buying new homes, instead of moving into neighborhoods already occupied by whites. With this dynamic in operation, the presence of blacks in a neighborhood would not have become so automatically equated, in the popular imagination, with neighborhood changes and declining property values. Equally important, if African Americans had been able to buy homes wherever they chose much sooner, they also would have been able to invest in the future. For decades, most African Americans were denied this crucial means of life savings and upward mobility.

Despite significant progress in breaking down racial barriers, family wealth remains as one of the enduring differences between black and white American families. In 1995, the median net worth (assets minus debts) for white households was $49,030, compared to $7,073 for black households—a ratio of 1 to 7.[88] The median net financial assets (cash that is immediately available) in the early 1990s was $6,999 for white families but *zero* for black families.[89] This gap, which measures the ability of families to pass on life chances from generation to generation, was created in substantial measure by governmental programs. Many of the effects of these policies may have been unintended, but they were no less powerful because of that fact.

Endnotes

1. John H. Mollenkopf, "The Post-War Politics of Urban Development," in *Marxism and the Metropolis: New Perspectives on Urban Political Economy,* ed. William K. Tabb and Larry Sawers (New York: Oxford University Press, 1978), p. 140.
2. Mark Gelfand, *A Nation of Cities: The Federal Government and Urban America, 1933–1965,* Urban Life in America Series (New York: Oxford University Press, 1975), p. 14.
3. See Nathaniel S. Keith, *Politics and the Housing Crisis since 1930* (New York: Universe Books, 1973), pp. 41–100.
4. Housing Act of 1949, Public Law 81–171, Preamble, sec. 2, 81st Cong. (1949).
5. Martin Meyerson and Edward C. Banfield, *Politics, Planning, and the Public Interest* (New York: Free Press, 1955).
6. Leonard Freedman, *Public Housing: The Politics of Poverty* (New York: Holt, Rinehart and Winston, 1969), p. 55.
7. Robert H. Salisbury, "The New Convergence of Power in Urban Politics," *Journal of Politics* 26 (November 1964): 775–797.
8. Mollenkopf, "The Post-War Politics of Urban Development," p. 138.
9. Quoted in Robert A. Dahl, *Who Governs: Democracy and Power in an American City* (New Haven, CT: Yale University Press, 1961), p. 136. For another insightful example of the use of urban renewal by political entrepreneurs, see Jewel Bellush and Murray Hausknecht, "Urban Renewal and the Reformer," in *Urban Renewal: People, Politics and Planning,* ed. Jewel Bellush and Murray Hausknecht (Garden City, NY: Doubleday, Anchor Books, 1967), pp. 189–197.
10. Gelfand, *A Nation of Cities,* p. 161.
11. Mollenkopf, "The Post-War Politics of Urban Development," p. 140.
12. Ibid., p. 138.
13. Williamson, Imbroscio, and Alperovitz, *Making a Place for Community,* p. 76.
14. Herbert J. Gans, *The Urban Villagers: Group and Class in the Life of Italian-Americans* (New York: Free Press, 1962), Chapter 13.
15. John H. Mollenkopf, "On the Causes and Consequences of Neighborhood Political Mobilization," paper delivered at the Annual Meeting of the American Political Science Association (New Orleans, September 4–8, 1973).
16. Quoted in Clarence N. Stone, *Economic Growth and Neighborhood Discontent: System Bias in the Urban Renewal Program of Atlanta* (Chapel Hill: University of North Carolina Press, 1976), pp. 48–49.
17. See Chester Hartman et al., *Yerba Buena: Land Grab and Community Resistance in San Francisco* (San Francisco: Glide, 1974). The following material on the Yerba Buena controversy draws on this excellent book. In most cases, citations are limited to quotations or specific data.
18. Ibid., p. 31.
19. Ibid., p. 19.
20. Ibid., p. 190.
21. Ibid., p. 128.
22. National Commission on Urban Problems, *Building the American City* (New York: Praeger, 1969), p. 153. This commission, appointed by the president, was established

in January 1967 and headed by former Illinois senator and longtime urban policy advocate Paul H. Douglas.

23. Ibid., pp. 164–165.
24. See Martin Anderson, *The Federal Bulldozer: A Critical Analysis of Urban Renewal, 1949–1962* (Cambridge, MA: MIT Press, 1964), p. 65; compare Rossi and Dentler, *The Politics of Urban Renewal,* p. 224.
25. Chester Hartman, "The Housing of Relocated Families," in *Urban Renewal: The Record and the Controversy,* ed. James Q. Wilson (Cambridge, MA: MIT Press, 1966), p. 322, as reprinted from *Journal of the American Institute of Planners* 30 (November 1964): 266–286.
26. Anderson, *The Federal Bulldozer,* pp. 65–66; see also Bellush and Hausknecht, "Urban Renewal and the Reformer," p. 13.
27. Anderson, *The Federal Bulldozer,* p. 65.
28. Mollenkopf, "The Post-War Politics of Urban Development," p. 140.
29. Freedman, *Public Housing,* p. 140.
30. Lawrence M. Friedman, *Government and Slum Housing: A Century of Frustration* (Chicago: Rand McNally, 1968), p. 121.
31. Freedman, *Public Housing,* p. 111.
32. Friedman, *Government and Slum Housing,* p. 123.
33. James Baldwin, *Nobody Knows My Name* (New York: Dial Press, 1961), p. 63, quoted in Freedman, *Public Housing,* p. 117.
34. Friedman, *Government and Slum Housing,* p. 121.
35. Lee Rainwater, *Behind Ghetto Walls: Black Families in a Federal Slum* (Chicago: Aldine, 1970).
36. Housing and Urban Development Act of 1968, Public Law 90–448, 90th Cong. (1968).
37. U.S. Department of Housing and Urban Development, *1974 Statistical Yearbook of the U.S. Department of Housing and Urban Development* (Washington, DC: U.S. Government Printing Office, 1976), p. 104.
38. Stephen David and Paul Peterson, eds., *Urban Politics and Public Policy: The City in Crisis* (New York: Praeger, 1973), p. 94.
39. Charles Abrams, *The Future of Housing* (New York: HarperCollins, 1946), p. 213.
40. Bureau of National Affairs, *The Housing and Development Reporter* (Washington, DC: Bureau of National Affairs, 1976).
41. Ibid.
42. Calculated from data in Congressional Quarterly Service, *Housing a Nation,* p. 6.
43. U.S. Department of Housing and Urban Development, *1974 Statistical Yearbook of the Department of Housing and Urban Development,* pp. 116–117.
44. U.S. Bureau of the Census, *Historical Statistics of the United States, Colonial Times to 1970,* pt. 1, Bicentennial ed. (Washington, DC: U.S. Government Printing Office, 1975), p. 646; for 2002 data, Danter Company, www.danter.com/statistics/homeown.htm.
45. Compiling reliable statistics on FHA/VA loans is difficult because of inconsistent data over time. The most accessible source is the *Statistical Abstract of the United States* (Washington, DC: U.S. Government Printing Office) for various years.
46. For a discussion of this phenomenon, see Murray Edelman, *The Symbolic Uses of Politics,* 7th ed. (Champaign: University of Illinois Press, 1976), pp. 44–76. We are indebted to Jeffrey Gilbert for several of the ideas contained in this section.
47. Michael Stone, "Reconstructing American Housing" (unpublished manuscript), quoted in Chester W. Hartman, *Housing and Social Policy,* Prentice Hall Series in Social Policy (Upper Saddle River, NJ: Prentice Hall, 1975), p. 30.

48. Quoted in Brian J. L. Berry, *The Open Housing Question: Race and Housing in Chicago, 1966–1976* (Cambridge, MA: Ballinger, 1979), p. 9.

49. Quoted in ibid., pp. 9, 11.

50. Luigi M. Laurenti, "Theories of Race and Property Value," in *Urban Analysis: Readings in Housing and Urban Development,* ed. Alfred N. Page and Warren R. Seyfried (Glenview, IL: Scott Foresman, 1970), p. 274.

51. Richard Moe and Carter Wilkie, *Changing Places* (New York: Henry Holt, 1997), p. 48.

52. Charles Abrams, quoted in Norman N. Bradburn, Seymour Sudman, and Galen L. Gockel, *Side by Side: Integrated Neighborhoods in America* (Chicago: Quadrangle Books, 1971), p. 104.

53. Gelfand, *A Nation of Cities,* p. 221.

54. Nathan Glazer and David McEntire, eds., *Housing and Minority Groups* (Berkeley: University of California Press, 1960), p. 140.

55. Public Law 90–284, 90th Cong. (1968), Title VIII ("Fair Housing"), sec. 805.

56. D.C. Public Interest Research Group (DCPIRG), Institute for Self-Reliance, and Institute for Policy Studies, *Redlining: Mortgage Disinvestment in the District of Columbia* (Washington, DC: Authors, 1975), p. 3.

57. U.S. Department of Housing and Urban Development, *1974 Statistical Yearbook of the Department of Housing and Urban Development,* pp. 116–117.

58. Thomas A. Clark, "The Suburbanization Process and Residential Segregation," in *Divided Neighborhoods: Changing Patterns of Racial Segregation,* ed. Gary A. Tobin (Newbury Park, CA: Sage, 1987), p. 115; Larry Long and Diane Deare, "The Suburbanization of Blacks," *American Demographics* 3 (1981), cited in Douglas S. Massey and Nancy A. Denton, "Suburbanization and Segregation in U.S. Metropolitan Areas," *American Journal of Sociology* 3 (November 1988): 592–626.

59. Kenneth T. Jackson, *Crabgrass Frontier: The Suburbanization of the United States* (New York: Oxford University Press, 1985), p. 205.

60. John R. Logan and Harvey L. Molotch, *Urban Fortunes: The Political Economy of Place* (Berkeley: University of California Press, 1987), p. 195.

61. Clark, "The Suburbanization Process and Residential Segregation," pp. 115–137.

62. Massey and Denton, "Suburbanization and Segregation in U.S. Metropolitan Areas," pp. 592–626.

63. Logan and Molotch, *Urban Fortunes,* p. 194.

64. Douglas S. Massey and Mitchell L. Eggers, "The Spatial Concentration of Affluence and Poverty during the 1970s," *Urban Affairs Quarterly* 29, no. 2 (December 1990). See also S. Roberts, "Shifts in 80's Failed to Ease Segregation," *New York Times* (July 15, 1992), pp. B1–B3.

65. John F. Kain, "Housing Market Discrimination and Black Suburbanization in the 1980's," in *Divided Neighborhoods: Changing Patterns of Racial Segregation,* ed. Gary A. Tobin (Newbury Park, CA: Sage, 1987), p. 68.

66. John Farley, *Segregated City, Segregated Suburbs: Are They the Products of Black-White Socioeconomic Differentials?* (Edwardsville: Southern Illinois University, 1983), cited in Joe T. Darden, "Choosing Neighbors and Neighborhoods: The Role of Race in Housing Preference," in *Divided Neighborhoods: Changing Patterns of Racial Segregation,* ed. Gary A. Tobin (Newbury Park, CA: Sage, 1987), p. 16.

67. John F. Farley, "Race Still Matters: The Minimal Role of Income and Housing Cost as Causes of Housing Segregation in St. Louis, 1990," *Urban Affairs Review* 31, no. 2 (November 1995): 244–254.

68. Public Policy Research Centers, University of Missouri–St. Louis, *Analysis of Impediments to Fair Housing: St. Louis County* (St. Louis: Author, 1995).

69. William E. Nelson and Michael S. Bailey, "The Weakening of State Participation in Civil Rights Enforcement," in *Public Policy across States and Communities,* ed. Dennis R. Judd (Greenwich, CT: JAI Press, 1985), p. 160.
70. Public Law 94–200, 94th Cong. (1975), Title III, and Public Law 95–128, 95th Cong. (1977), Title VIII.
71. Calvin Bradford, *Community Reinvestment Agreement Library* (Des Plaines, IL: Community Reinvestment Associates, 1992), as cited in *From Redlining to Reinvestment: Community Responses to Urban Disinvestment,* ed. Gregory D. Squires (Philadelphia: Temple University Press, 1992), p. 2.
72. Mitchell Zuckoff, "Study Shows Racial Bias in Lending," *Boston Globe* (October 9, 1992), p. B1.
73. Henry Ford, quoted in J. Allen Whitt and Glenn Yago, "Corporate Strategies and the Decline of Transit in U.S. Cities," *Urban Affairs Quarterly* 21, no. 1 (September 1985): 61.
74. Alan Lupo, Frank Colcord, and Edmund P. Fowler, *Rites of Way: The Politics of Transportation in Boston and the U.S. City* (Boston: Little, Brown, 1971), p. 184.
75. Mark Rose, *Interstate Express Highway Politics, 1941–1956* (Lawrence: Regents Press of Kansas, 1979), p. 97.
76. Quoted in Helen Leavitt, *Superhighway—Superhoax* (Garden City, NY: Doubleday, 1970), p. 53.
77. Robert A. Caro, *The Power Broker: Robert Moses and the Fall of New York* (New York: Random House, 1974), p. 19.
78. Between 1951 and 1974, for example, 89 percent of the 10,000 households displaced by public projects in Baltimore were black. See Anthony Downs, *Urban Problems and Prospects* (Chicago: Marsham, 1970), pp. 204–205.
79. Ibid., p. 223.
80. John R. Meyer and Jose A. Gomez-Ibanez, *Auto Transit and Cities* (Cambridge, MA: Harvard University Press, 1981), p. 177.
81. By 1970 there were 400 struggles under way by community groups to oppose highway construction. Harry C. Boyte, *The Backyard Revolution: Understanding the New Citizen Movement* (Philadelphia: Temple University Press, 1980), p. 11.
82. Jackson, *Crabgrass Frontier,* p. 250.
83. U.S. Federal Transportation Administration (USFTA), *Summary of Travel Trends, 1995 National Personal Transportation Survey,* December 1999; USFTA and U.S. Bureau of Transportation Statistics, *National Household Travel Survey,* 2001.
84. This account of ISTEA relies on Paul G. Lewis, "The Politics of Structure in Transportation Policy: Resuscitating Metropolitan Planning Organizations Under ISTEA," paper delivered at the Annual Meeting of the Urban Affairs Association (Toronto, Canada, April 17, 1997).
85. Pietro S. Nivola, *Laws of the Landscape: How Policies Shape Cities in Europe and America* (Washington, DC: Brookings Institution Press, 1999), p. 15.
86. Michael Cooper, "Rider Paradox: Surge in Mass, Drop in Transit," *New York Times* (February 3, 2009), www.nytimes.com/2009/02/04/us/04trans.html.
87. Ibid.
88. Melvin Oliver and Thomas Shapiro, *Black Wealth/White Wealth: A New Perspective on Racial Inequality* (New York: Routledge, 1997), pp. 85–87.
89. Ibid.

CHAPTER 8

Federal Programs and the Divisive Politics of Race

The Brief Life of Inner-City Programs

The problems of racial segregation and discrimination, poverty, and inner-city decline burst onto the nation's political agenda in the 1960s. For a brief time, urban problems became the main focus of national policy. The National Commission on Urban Problems (1958), the National Commission on Civil Disorders (1967), the President's Task Force on Suburban Problems (1967), President Nixon's Commission on Population Growth and the American Future (1972), and a host of state and city task forces decried the segregation of blacks and the poor in ghetto areas of the central cities. A great deal of hope was invested in the social and urban policies of the 1960s, but many of these programs became embroiled in political controversy and proved to be short-lived.

In the 1964 presidential race, the Democratic candidate, Lyndon Johnson, promised to build a Great Society by launching an aggressive effort to solve the pressing social problems of the time. The Democratic landslide that year gave him the legislative majority needed to implement literally hundreds of programs in only the two-year period from 1965 to 1967. By the 1968 election, spending for the Vietnam War had already begun to undermine support for the Democratic agenda, but racial divisions proved to be even more decisive. The landslide win by the Democrats in 1964 masked a development that would soon compromise the party's ability to win presidential elections. The issue of race was tearing apart the coalition the Democrats had fashioned in the 1930s. Although President Johnson won by historic margins elsewhere, he lost in the one part of the country where Democrats had never been challenged, the Deep South. The Republican standard-bearer, Barry Goldwater, received 87 percent of the popular vote in Mississippi, close to 70 percent in Alabama, and substantially more than 50 percent in Louisiana, Georgia, and South Carolina. After 1964, Republican candidates regularly carried the South for the first time since the carpetbagger governments imposed on southern states in the years after the Civil War.

Richard Nixon's victory in the 1968 election made it clear that it was impossible to separate the issue of race from the political fate of social welfare and urban programs. This had become obvious as early as the 1930s, when southern Democrats in Congress often expressed their concern that New Deal

OUTTAKE

Racial Divisions Eventually Doomed Urban Programs

The federal urban programs of the 1960s were adopted in response to civil disorders in the cities and the serious social problems highlighted by racial turmoil. The federal response fractured the Democratic Party, which relied upon urban voters from the North and reliable support in the southern and border states. The urban vote had been essential to the Democrats for decades. Time after time, overwhelming Democratic majorities in the big cities balanced out Republican pluralities in the suburbs and small towns, providing the margin of victory in key states holding large blocs of electoral votes. The Democrats would have lost the presidency in 1940, 1944, and 1948 without the big turnout in 12 big cities in the nation. The urban electorate was essential to John F. Kennedy's victory in the close election of 1960. Kennedy beat Nixon by a razor-thin 112,000 votes, a margin of less than one-tenth of 1 percent, but he carried 27 out of the 39 largest cities. In 1964, Lyndon Johnson won by an unprecedented landslide, with the cities delivering lopsided results that exceeded the national average by 10 percent or more.

The attempt to address the long-standing grievances of African Americans alienated white Southerners and white working-class voters almost everywhere. In 1968, the Republicans capitalized on resentment provoked by the successes of the civil rights movement. The Democratic presidential candidate, Hubert Humphrey, carried only one southern state, Texas. Across the South, he won just 31 percent of the vote, running behind both Republican Richard Nixon (34.5 percent) and Alabama governor and third-party candidate George Wallace (34.6 percent), who ran as an avowed segregationist. In 1968, the Nixon campaign adopted law and order as its main theme. This had also been the campaign slogan of the Republican nominee in 1964, Barry Goldwater, but he had handled it crudely and ineptly. Goldwater's television ads tried to convey an impression that America's cities were in ruins by showing scenes of blacks rioting. In the scenes meant to portray Goldwater's vision of the American past he would like to restore, blacks were shown picking cotton. The ads that Nixon aired four years later were less blatant, although they were not subtle either. One of his television spots showed scenes of urban riots, with a Nixon voice-over calling for "some honest talk about the problem of order." At least blacks were not shown in a rendition of a bucolic agricultural past.

Richard Nixon won 32 percent of the African American vote in 1960, when he lost to Kennedy, but even though his share fell to 12 percent in the 1968 election, he still beat Hubert Humphrey. One of the president's closest advisers, John Erlichman, told civil rights administrators that "blacks are not where the votes are, so why antagonize the people who can be helpful to us politically?" After the 1960s, the Republican Party mostly wrote off the African American vote. The Republican base became increasingly conservative, embracing working-class whites, a (now) solid Republican South, suburban and Sunbelt Republican voters, and the religious right. The results of the 2000 presidential election, which George W. Bush lost by 500,000 popular votes, suggested that the Republican coalition was losing some of its energy. Bush entered the White House only because the Electoral College favors small and less populated states. Nevertheless, it is clear that cities did not figure much in the overall tally. Democrats have drawn the logical conclusion that programs meant for the cities cannot get them much political mileage.

Sources: Statistics and quotations from Theodore H. White, *The Making of the President, 1960* (New York: Atheneum, 1961), p. 1201; John Mollenkopf, *The Contested City* (Princeton, NJ: Princeton University Press, 1983), p. 83; Kathleen Hall Jamieson, *Packaging the Presidency: A History and Criticism of Presidential Campaign Advertising* (New York: Oxford University Press, 1984), pp. 202–203; Joseph McGinnis, *Selling the President, 1968* (New York: Trident Press, 1969); Numan V. Barley and Hugh D. Graham, *Southern Politics and the Second Reconstruction* (Baltimore: Johns Hopkins University Press, 1975), pp. 126–127; Everett Carl Ladd Jr., "The Shifting Party Coalitions, 1932–1976," in *Emerging Coalitions in American Politics*, ed. Seymour Martin Lipset (San Francisco: Institute for Contemporary Studies, 1978), p. 98; A. James Reichley, *Conservatives in an Age of Change: The Nixon and Ford Administrations* (Washington, DC: Brookings Institution Press, 1981), pp. 145, 186.

programs might be used to upset traditional racial relationships. In the postwar years, they successfully fought to ensure that public housing would not be used to promote racial integration. As long as the programs advanced by Democratic liberals did not challenge race relations in the South, southern Democrats were willing to go along. But this tacit bargain ended with the civil rights legislation and the social programs of the 1960s.

In the public's imagination, the Great Society became identified as a constellation of programs that primarily benefited inner-city blacks. The truth is that no significant programs were aimed so narrowly. Funds for Head Start and the War on Poverty, for example, were spread broadly across the country, to urban and rural areas alike, and social programs such as Medicare and Medicaid benefited people regardless of where they lived. But impressions mattered. From 1969 to 1976, when Republican presidents Richard Nixon and Gerald Ford occupied the White House, many of the Democratic-sponsored programs came under attack, and Ronald Reagan's victory in the 1980 presidential election quickly brought an end to most urban programs. Most of the Great Society programs lasted for 20 years or less, and they never received enough resources to plausibly remedy the problems they were meant to address.

The Democrats and the Cities

When President Kennedy took office on January 20, 1961, his administration was already committed to helping the cities. Even before his campaign, Kennedy had concluded that the problem of the cities was "the great unspoken issue in the 1960 election."[1] During the campaign, the Democrats discussed doing something about the urban crisis, whereas the Republicans tried to avoid such issues. "If you ever let them campaign only on domestic issues," confided presidential nominee Richard M. Nixon to his aides, "they'll beat us."[2] President Kennedy "emerged as an eloquent spokesman for a new generation. In presidential message after message Kennedy spelled out in more detail than the Congress or the country could easily digest the most complete programs of domestic reforms in a quarter century."[3]

The Kennedy administration mapped out an ambitious agenda. Poverty, racial segregation, juvenile delinquency and crime, bad schools, and a host of other social problems were discovered in the 1960s only in the sense that they were no longer "out of sight, out of mind." They had existed for a long time and were no worse and little different by the beginning of the Kennedy administration than they had been under Presidents Roosevelt, Truman, and Eisenhower. What made them seem worse was their greater visibility. Martin Luther King Jr. understood the task of creating visibility during the civil rights demonstrations in 1963. "I saw no way," he later commented, "of dealing with things without bringing the indignation to the attention of the nation."[4]

King turned the civil rights issue into a national crisis in Birmingham, Alabama, in the summer of 1963. What started in Birmingham spread across the South and even filtered into northern cities. During the summer, there were 13,786 arrests of demonstrators in 75 cities of the 11 southern states.[5] In the 10 weeks that followed nationally publicized police attacks on demonstrators in Birmingham, the Justice Department counted 758 demonstrations across the nation. It quickly became clear that the administration could no longer avoid dealing with civil rights. The brutal treatment of civil rights demonstrators throughout the South was being televised in the living rooms of millions of American homes. By mid-June, 127 civil rights bills had been introduced in the House of Representatives. The Kennedy administration, like it or not, was being drawn into the nation's most significant and divisive internal conflict since the Civil War.

The political pressures applied by the civil rights movement were reinforced by the influence of the black electorate. As John C. Donovan observed in his book *The Politics of Poverty*, "The greatest strength of the Negro communities lies in its voting power, in its numbers, and in their strategic location."[6] In the South, the black population was geographically diffused and systematically denied the right to the vote. When they moved to northern cities, blacks gained the franchise. Their votes were concentrated in the cities of the states holding a majority of the electoral college votes—Illinois, California, Massachusetts, Ohio, Michigan, New Jersey, New York, Texas, and Pennsylvania. Kennedy targeted his campaign on these key states, and the 68 percent plurality that black voters gave him was crucial to his razor-thin victories in Illinois, Missouri, and other states. In 1956, Adlai Stevenson, the liberal Democratic candidate from Illinois, had received 61 percent of the black vote.[7] If Kennedy had not done better, he would have lost the election: "It is difficult to see how Illinois, New Jersey, Michigan, South Carolina, or Delaware (with 74 electoral votes) could have been won had the Republican Democratic split of the Negro wards and precincts remained as it was, unchanged from the Eisenhower charm of 1956."[8]

On June 11, 1963, President Kennedy overruled his advisers and announced he would propose a civil rights bill. When Kennedy was assassinated on November 22, the bill had just reached the House Rules Committee. The assassination created an emotionally charged atmosphere that the new president, Lyndon Baines Johnson, adroitly exploited. Opinion polls indicated overwhelming public support for civil rights legislation. Seizing the moment, Johnson added new provisions to the legislation and harried Congress into acting quickly. When Republicans joined with northern Democrats to move the bill out of the House Rules Committee, the bill was sent to the floor, where it passed by a vote of 290 to 130. On June 6, 1964, the Senate mustered the necessary two-thirds vote to overcome a filibuster mounted by Southerners, and the legislation passed.

The Civil Rights Act of 1964 outlawed discrimination in public accommodations, thus effectively striking down the South's Jim Crow laws that had denied blacks equal access to bus stations, restaurants, lunch counters, theaters, sports arenas, gasoline stations, motels, hotels, and lodging houses. It outlawed racial discrimination in the hiring, firing, training, and promoting of workers. It barred discrimination in the administration of federal grants. A year later, Congress passed the Voting Rights Act, which not only outlawed literacy tests and other discriminatory voting restrictions but also provided that federal registrars could replace local registrars in counties where there had been a history of discrimination against black voters.

Taking advantage of the post-assassination atmosphere, President Johnson also pressed for a program to redress economic inequalities.[9] Kennedy's advisers had persuaded him that the time had come for his administration to devise a program to attack poverty and unemployment. In June 1963, Kennedy had told Walter Heller, the chair of his Council of Economic Advisors, to appoint a task force of officials who would be responsible for proposing a program to attack poverty. Although Kennedy's commitment to a program was almost certain by the time of his assassination, it was not clear how hard he would have fought for it.

President Johnson was told about the proposed antipoverty program only two days after assuming office, but he quickly responded, "That's my kind of program. It will help people. I want you to move full speed ahead."[10] The idea of an ambitious, highly visible program appealed to Johnson's desire to be perceived as a second Roosevelt, as a president who would go down in history as the one who completed the social agenda left unfinished in the 1930s. In his first State of the Union address, on January 10, 1964, President Johnson announced he would seek a "total effort" to end poverty in the United States. Using a grandiose military analogy, he said, "This Administration here and now declares unconditional war on poverty in America, and I urge this Congress and all Americans to join me in that effort."[11] When Johnson signed the Economic Opportunity Act on August 8, he had two big legislative victories, the civil rights act and his "war on poverty," to carry into the presidential campaign.

The 1964 campaign provided the setting for a contentious national debate over the federal government's role and responsibilities. The Republican nominee, Barry Goldwater, was one of the few non-Southerners to vote against the civil rights act in the Senate. He attacked the welfare programs funded through the Social Security Act of 1935 and even questioned the immensely popular old-age insurance program established through that legislation. The Republican Party's platform warned that "individual freedom retreats under the mounting assault of expanding centralized power."[12] Lyndon Johnson, by contrast, called for a Great Society that would eliminate poverty and treat other social ills through federal action on civil rights, the cities, health care, welfare, education, and employment.

Johnson won the election by a historic landslide, receiving 61 percent of the popular vote and picking up 486 electoral college votes to Goldwater's 53. The dimensions of the landslide allowed the Democrats to ignore the fact that Goldwater had swept several southern states that Democrats had always carried. The president's coattails were long; Democrats commanded a 289-to-146 majority in the House to go along with a 67-to-33 majority in the Senate.

The Democrats' overwhelming victory set the stage for a period of legislative activism not seen since Roosevelt's fabled First Hundred Days of 1933. Between 1964 and 1966, Congress authorized 219 new programs, which included some of the most important and enduring social initiatives of the 1960s. In 1965, Congress approved Medicare for the elderly and Medicaid for welfare recipients. The Elementary and Secondary Education Act provided federal grants to schools. Food stamps, an experimental program tried during the Kennedy years, became permanent in 1966. New and expanded educational and job-training assistance was made available for individuals with mental and physical disabilities. The public housing and urban renewal programs were expanded, and a new "Model Cities" program to treat the problems of cities was initiated. In 1966, Congress also created a new cabinet-level department, the Department of Housing and Urban Development (HUD), to administer urban programs.

Figure 8.1 shows that spending on federal regional and community programs rose sharply from 1962 to 1980, but fell even more until 2005; since then, spending has increased slightly to about the level that it was in 1985, at the beginning of President Reagan's second term. In 1962, the federal government spent $3.8 billion on these programs (in constant 2008 dollars; the actual figure that year was $445 million), and $24.2 billion by 1980 (2008 dollars; $9.2 billion in actual dollars). Local governments became increasingly dependent on intergovernmental transfers from federal and state governments. In 1950, grants from states and from the federal government accounted for only 10 percent of the revenues making up local budgets, but this proportion rose to over 26 percent of municipal revenues by 1978. But then the bottom fell out, and by the end of the 1990s only 7 percent of city budgets came from intergovernmental revenues. This proportion rose slightly to 10 percent in 2008.

The explosion in federal spending was energized by the conviction that the national government should take the nation in a new direction. Not since the closing of the frontier in the 1870s had the federal government attempted so forcefully to chart a course for the nation. The Louisiana Purchase of 1803, a

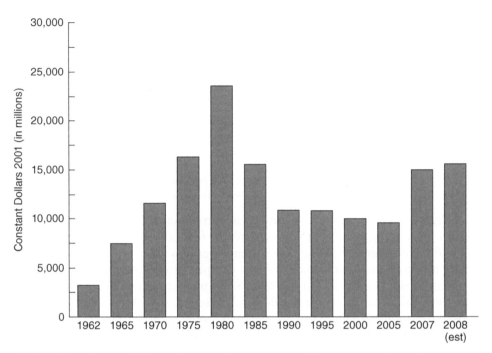

FIGURE 8.1 Federal Spending on Regional and Community Development, 1962–2008 (in 2008 Dollars)

Note: Figures exclude spending on disaster relief.

Sources: U.S. Office of Management and Budget, *Budget of the United States Government, Fiscal Year 2009, Historical Tables* (Washington, DC: U.S. Government Printing Office, 2008), pp. 62–71, Table 3.2, Function 450, Community and regional development; Federal Spending on Regional and Community Development, 1962–2002 (in 2001 Dollars).

succession of township and homestead acts, generous land grants to railroad companies, and an aggressive military policy toward the Indians supported the federal government's intention to open up the West in the nineteenth century.[13] In the 1960s, the president and Congress pursued a national agenda of comparable ambition. This time, the national government set out to eliminate poverty, erase racial discrimination, provide equal opportunity in education and jobs, and revitalize cities and communities.

The national emphasis on equality and social justice was reflected in clear terms in the case of the Civil Rights Act of 1964, when the federal government served notice that its new civil rights statutes would override state and local racial practices. The preambles to the grant programs of Kennedy's New Frontier and Johnson's Great Society articulated a variety of national goals. Consider this example, from the Manpower Development and Training Act of 1962:

> It is in the national interest that current and prospective manpower shortages be identified and that persons who can be qualified for these positions through education and training be sought out and trained, *in order that the nation may meet the staffing requirements of the struggle for freedom.*[14]

Or the Economic Opportunity Act of 1964:

The United States can achieve its full economic and social potential as a nation only if every individual has the opportunity to contribute the full extent of his capabilities and to participate in the workings of our society. *It is, therefore, the policy of the United States* to eliminate the paradox of poverty in the midst of plenty in this nation.[15]

And the Demonstration Cities and Metropolitan Development Act of 1966 (the so-called Model Cities legislation):

The Congress hereby finds and declares that *improving the quality of urban life is the most critical domestic problem facing the United States.*[16]

Imagine such statements of intention introducing hundreds of pieces of legislation, ranging from rent supplements to federal school aid to crime control, and the complexity of the new system of grants becomes readily apparent. Hardly an economic or a social problem escaped attention, and each program specified its own complicated methods of implementation. Recipient institutions were subjected to complex rules and close scrutiny. After all, it makes no sense to fund a national priority unless the money is going to be used carefully, according to prescribed guidelines and standards.[17]

The War on Poverty and Model Cities programs attracted attention because they were sold with grandiose promises about what they would accomplish. In 1964, when Lyndon Johnson proposed the War on Poverty, he announced his objective was "total victory."[18] Such a promise could not possibly be fulfilled no matter how well the program might be implemented. As it turned out, the War on Poverty became a lightning rod for controversy, as did the Model Cities program, which was funded through the Demonstration Cities and Metropolitan Development Act of 1966. Under the terms of the War on Poverty, community action agencies were instructed to operate with the "maximum feasible participation" of the poor. Likewise, Model Cities agencies were supposed to galvanize participation by local residents by giving them a role in planning. City halls and other agencies of local government were cut out of the loop. The idea was to create new institutions in the cities capable of mobilizing the energies of people outside the established power structure. An early program guide distributed by the Office of Economic Opportunity said that to qualify for funding, local antipoverty programs should involve the poor from the very first "in planning, policy-making, and operation."[19]

These programs were, in effect, a means of fomenting a revolution in local politics. According to two scholars, Frances Fox Piven and Richard A. Cloward, many of the Great Society programs were formulated to preserve and strengthen the Democratic Party's advantage in the industrialized states holding the largest blocs of Electoral College votes.[20] Frustrated that local politicians had repeatedly shown an unwillingness to mobilize the votes of inner-city blacks, federal administrators tried to work directly with organizations and leaders in black communities. The expectation was that blacks would vote Democratic in return.

A multitude of new agencies was established to receive and distribute federal dollars. Of all the community action funds the Office of Economic Opportunity spent by 1968, only 25 percent was given to public agencies. The remainder went to organizations such as universities, churches, civil rights groups, settlement houses, family services agencies, United Way programs, and newly established nonprofit groups.[21] Likewise, only 10 percent of the funds distributed through programs administered by the Department of Health, Education, and Welfare was passed through to state and local governments.[22]

A handful of programs became controversial when political activists associated with them became embroiled in highly publicized fights with mayors and local government officials. In Syracuse, San Francisco, and the state of Mississippi, local administrators of antipoverty programs led protest actions against mayors, welfare departments, and school boards, demanding the implementation of programs that responded to complaints from the black community. Although such protests were organized in only a few cities, local authorities were upset when they saw federal monies flowing into their jurisdictions to groups and organizations that regularly opposed city hall. Such organizations encouraged complaints about all sorts of things—police brutality, the hiring of teachers, welfare policies, public housing maintenance—the list could be endless.

Despite such controversies, the War on Poverty and the Model Cities programs continued to receive congressional support mainly because the funds were distributed in a large number of states and congressional districts. Politicians of both parties were able to take credit for delivering federal dollars to local constituencies. To broaden the base of support in Congress, the Johnson administration abandoned its original intention to restrict the antipoverty and Model Cities programs to a few "demonstration" projects. Instead, the federal funds were spread as thinly as thought necessary to secure annual program budgets. The deleterious effect of this strategy was that it virtually guaranteed that no program in any city could deliver on its promises.

The Republicans and the New Federalism

When Richard Nixon assumed the presidency in January 1969, it seemed likely that the Great Society programs would be dismantled. Somewhat surprisingly, however, from 1969 through 1976, when Republicans held the presidency, aid to state and local governments actually climbed, from $20 to $59 billion, staying well ahead of inflation.[23] Funding continued to rise because the Democrats controlled Congress and a powerful constellation of interest groups influential with both parties rallied to the cause. Even some Republican congressional representatives, governors, and local officials wanted the flow to continue. After a failed attempt to kill the War on Poverty in 1969, President Nixon bowed to political realities and set a middle course by trying to reform rather than eliminate urban programs.

Nixon signaled his desire to fundamentally change how federal programs were administered. He spoke of the grant programs as producing a "gathering of the reins of power in Washington," which he saw as "a radical departure from the vision of federal-state relations the nation's founders had in mind." He proposed a New Federalism, meant to restore "a rightful balance between the state capital and the national capital."[24] To reduce federal authority, Nixon wanted to take the decisions about how to spend money out of the hands of federal bureaucrats and give the authority to local governments. A revenue-sharing program was the first major initiative of the New Federalism. Revenue sharing gave local officials extraordinary latitude in deciding how to spend federal money. Because of the lack of detailed federal oversight, revenue-sharing dollars were intermingled with other monies that flowed into the treasuries of the more than 39,000 state, county, township, and municipal governments across the nation. As a consequence, they could not be traced beyond the reports filed with the Treasury Department by local officials.

Revenue-sharing monies constituted a small supplement to the tax revenues of state and local governments. In 1974, the $4.5 billion apportioned among 35,077 local governments accounted for an average of 3.1 percent of their revenues for that year.[25] Financially strapped big cities were under pressure to use revenue-sharing funds just to keep things going; as a consequence, they spent nearly all of their revenue-sharing dollars on day-to-day operations and maintenance.[26] Congressional Democrats complained that the programs ignored the needs of disadvantaged populations, but for Republicans that was the whole point. The program continued at a low level until 1986, when President Reagan killed it.

The Community Development Block Grant (CDBG) program, enacted by Congress in 1974 and signed into law by President Gerald Ford in January 1975, remains today as the only significant survivor of the major urban policies enacted in the pre-Reagan era. It has survived so long because it has been useful to so many people. For local officials, it is a source of much-needed funding. It has enjoyed broad bipartisan support because CDBG funds go to thousands of communities. Unlike for general revenue sharing, cities were required to submit an annual application for CDBG funds even though they were automatically eligible. But the process was quite painless. By the end of the program's first year, HUD Secretary Carla Hills reported that her department had reduced the average review period from two years for the programs that the Community Development Act replaced to 49 days, and that applications averaged 50 pages, compared with an average of 1,400 pages for the old urban renewal applications alone.[27]

In the first few years, a recurring issue was that communities were spending their CDBG money in violation of program guidelines. The original legislation included a requirement that cities give "maximum feasible priority" to low- and moderate-income areas.[28] Communities were often accused of ignoring this requirement, a fact documented by the Department of Housing and Urban Development.[29] That community development funds would be spent in affluent areas was hardly a surprising turn of events because local political elites exerted a controlling voice in the allocation process. In most local communities, poorer residents had little influence. As a result of this circumstance, Little Rock, Arkansas, for example, spent $150,000 of the city's block grant funds to construct a tennis court in an affluent section of town. When questioned about this use of funds, the director of the local Department of Human Resources unpersuasively claimed that "ninety-nine percent of this money is going to low and moderate income areas." But he revealingly continued, "You cannot divorce politics from that much money. We remember the needs of the people who vote because they hold us accountable. Poor people don't vote."[30]

President Carter and the Democrats' Last Hurrah

In the four years that he was in office, Democratic president Jimmy Carter attempted to give urban programs some of the attention they had received in the past, but his difficulties showed just how much the contours of national politics had changed since the 1960s. There was good reason for Carter to respond favorably to the older industrial cities. Inner-city voters had remained faithful to the Democrats for decades, and they gave Carter his margin of victory in several states in the 1976 presidential election. Accordingly, the administration tried to develop policies that would shore up support among urban voters. The president persuaded Congress to pass an amendment to the revenue-sharing program that added an "excess unemployment" factor to the distribution formula.[31] Cities with high unemployment levels received all the money. He successfully sought increases in CDBG funding and significantly amended the program in 1978 to help the big cities. Large increases were legislated for Comprehensive Employment and Training Act (CETA) programs, which gave money to local training centers and to local governments to put people to work repairing parks and public facilities. Despite these accomplishments, however, by the time Carter left office he seemed to be abandoning urban policy altogether, a process that would reach its logical conclusion under his Republican successor, Ronald Reagan.

Soon after Carter assumed office in January 1977, his administration began efforts to reward key members of his electoral base. An effort was launched to amend the Community Development Act so that more aid would flow to the older industrial cities. As it happened, the original distribution formula adopted in 1974 discriminated against the worst-off cities of the Northeast and Midwest. The older industrial cities were destined to receive a declining share of CDBG funds over time, whereas fast-growing Sunbelt cities were going to receive more.[32] This was mainly because the formula for distributing the money was partially tied to each city's total population. The older cities would lose funds over time simply because they were rapidly shrinking; by contrast, Sunbelt cities were growing.

The administration initiated efforts to persuade Congress to revise the formula to take into account population *loss* in a city.[33] As soon as the legislation was introduced, a bitter feud broke out between representatives from the Northeast and Midwest and the congressional delegations from southern and western states. Ultimately, the new formula won in a vote that divided along regional, not party, lines: Representatives from the East and Midwest voted overwhelmingly in favor, while almost all of those from the South and West voted against. Although the legislation passed the house in May 1977, the battle within Congress showed that in the future, regional divisions were likely to become fundamentally important factors in national politics.

The fight over the block grant program marked a watershed. In the Great Society years, urban programs had emphasized social purposes. By contrast, during the Carter administration, urban programs began to stress a different goal: leveraging private investments in troubled cities and neighborhoods. Because it relied upon the dynamics of the private market, it attracted support from local officials in both the North and South, regardless of their partisan affiliation. The first test of this bipartisan strategy came in 1978, when Congress approved the Urban Development Action Grants (UDAG) program. Over the years, UDAG were used to build festival malls such as Union Station in St. Louis and Harborplace in Baltimore; to expand convention centers; to repair historic buildings; to support neighborhood improvements; and to build public infrastructure (such as improved streets, new lighting, landscaping, and fountains) that might leverage private investment.

As time went on, it became apparent that the administration was retreating from any emphasis at all on social, as opposed to economic, development goals. On March 28, 1978, President Carter announced, with great fanfare, a comprehensive new urban policy that emphasized private investment. Asserting "the deterioration of urban life in the United States is one of the most complex and deeply rooted problems of our age," The president stated that "the federal government has the clear duty to lead the effort to reverse that deterioration."[34] The centerpiece of President Carter's proposal was a national development bank, which would be authorized to guarantee loans to businesses in depressed urban and rural areas; in addition, the administration wanted to offer tax credits for businesses hiring ghetto youths, a labor-intensive public works program, and more money for housing rehabilitation. The amount of additional money requested was relatively modest (about $4.4 billion), but this did not deter Carter from promising a "new Partnership involving all levels of government, the private sector and neighborhood and voluntary organizations."[35]

President Carter's ringing call for a comprehensive urban policy raised hopes in city halls, but it quickly turned into an abject political failure. The only major legislative proposal enacted into law was the Targeted Employment Tax Credit. The timing was bad for any new legislative initiative.[36] In 1978, California voters passed Proposition 13, which sharply reduced local property taxes. The gathering strength of a tax revolt across the nation helped shape a mood of fiscal conservatism in Congress and a go-slow approach in the White House.[37] Sensing a change in the political climate, Carter did an about-face in the last two years of his term, turning his attention away from urban policy toward the problems of the national economy and the cost and availability of energy. A sharp decline in manufacturing jobs and the flight of manufacturing outside the country became the leading domestic issues of the 1980 presidential campaign.

After Carter's election in 1976, Mayor Kenneth A. Gibson of Newark had spoken for many Democratic mayors when he remarked "we have every reason to believe that this is the beginning of a new relationship between the White House and the nation's mayors."[38] The new relationship, however, proved to be short-lived. Even if Carter had won the 1980 presidential race, it is doubtful any significant urban programs would have emerged in a second term.

Republicans and the End of Federal Assistance

In the campaigns of 1980 and 1984, the Republicans virtually wrote off the African American vote. Richard Wirthlin, Ronald Reagan's campaign strategist, advised before the 1980 election that the "Reagan for President 1980 campaign must convert into Reagan votes the disappointment felt by Southern white and rural voters."[39] Reagan won only 10 percent of the black vote in 1980 and slightly less in 1984. In 1984, however, three out of four southern whites supported him. The Reagan White House actively worked to undo civil rights guarantees, slashing the budgets of civil rights enforcement units and slowing or stopping enforcement.[40] The Reagan administration also set out to dismantle federal programs designed to help the cities, and over the course of eight years it largely succeeded.

President Reagan's agenda mapped out a radical new departure in federal policy. Philosophically, Reagan believed that the federal government should stop helping the cities altogether. Instead, he thought, they, and the people who lived within them, should help themselves. In a press conference held in October 1981, President Reagan suggested the residents of cities where unemployment was high should "vote with their feet" and move to more prosperous areas of the country.[41] His remark ignited an instant political controversy, but, in fact, it was consistent with the recommendations of a presidential commission appointed by his predecessor, Jimmy Carter. In a report issued only a few weeks after Reagan took office, the Presidential Commission on the National Agenda for the Eighties urged that the national government stop helping cities. The commission emphasized that federal policies should be used to promote national economic growth, but these policies should be neutral about where that growth occurred:

> It may be in the best interest of the nation to commit itself to the promotion of locationally neutral economic and social policies rather than spatially sensitive urban policies that either explicitly or inadvertently seek to preserve cities in their historical roles.[42]

Recommending that the federal government let the process of decay in some areas and growth in others take its natural course, the commission noted that cities adapt and change in response to economic and social forces. This process of adaptation, said the commission, should be facilitated, rather than altered, by governmental policy:

> Ultimately, the federal government's concern for national economic vitality should take precedence over the competition for advantage among

communities and regions.[43] To attempt to restrict or reverse the processes of change—for whatever noble intentions—is to deny the benefits that the future may hold for us as a nation.[44]

The policies subsequently pursued by the Reagan administration signaled a historic turn. For the first time since urban policy was first enacted in the 1930s, policymakers operated on the assumption that cities were valuable only if they contributed in a positive way to the national economy. Three researchers at the University of Delaware called the new policy direction "a form of Social Darwinism applied to cities."[45] Cities would survive if they could manage to regenerate their local economies. Otherwise, they would be allowed to wither away.

The Reagan administration began to slash federal urban aid, proclaiming "the private market is more efficient than federal program administrators in allocating dollars."[46] Cities were instructed to improve their ability to compete in a struggle for survival in which "state and local governments will find it is in their interests to concentrate on increasing their attractiveness to potential investors, residents, and visitors."[47] The assumption was that free enterprise would provide a bounty of jobs, incomes, and neighborhood renewal, and such local prosperity would make federal programs unnecessary. The CDBG and UDAG programs were spared deep cuts in the 1983 budget, as was revenue sharing. The administration had wanted to reduce these programs too, but the White House heard the pleas of governors and mayors, quite a few of them Republican. Local government representatives came away relieved that the budget cuts were less drastic than they had feared. Only two years later, however, the administration realized its goal of eliminating most urban programs.

Urban programs gave way to a new priority: cutting taxes. On February 18, 1981, President Reagan proposed a massive tax cut to stimulate the economy. The legislation quickly sailed through Congress, and when Reagan signed the Economic Recovery Tax Act on August 13, 1981, he proclaimed "a turnaround of almost a half a century of . . . excessive growth in government bureaucracy, government spending, government taxing."[48] In its final version, the act reduced individual tax rates by 25 percent over three years and also substantially reduced business tax liability. The revenue losses were huge. In just the first two years, $128 billion was lost to the federal treasury, and by 1987 this figure rose to more than $1 trillion.[49] In combination with massive increases in military spending, the 1981 tax cuts created huge budget deficits.

The Tax Reform Act of 1986 reduced federal revenues even further. Tax rates fell only modestly or not at all for most taxpayers, but they were cut drastically for the rich. In subsequent years, a perception that tax burdens fell unfairly on the middle class helped fuel a tax revolt. George H. W. Bush won the presidency in 1988 partly with the promise, "Read my lips: no new taxes." Within a few months, the administration slashed spending for programs for education, housing, health, and welfare. (It should be pointed out, however, that later in his term President Bush went along with a bill raising some taxes in order to reduce the accumulating federal deficit. By some accounts, this cost him his bid for a second term.)

President Reagan initiated the first reductions of consequence in grants-in-aid expenditures since the 1940s. Broad entitlement programs with middle-class recipients, such as the old-age and survivors' benefits funded through the Social Security Act of 1935, veterans' benefits, and Medicare, were affected only marginally. By contrast, deep cuts and new eligibility restrictions were imposed on public assistance programs for the poor. Medicaid, which was available through the states to welfare recipients, was subjected to tighter eligibility requirements, but Medicaid outlays soared anyway because of rising medical costs. Enrollment in Aid to Families with Dependent Children (AFDC) fell by half a million. A million people lost food stamps. It became harder to get unemployment benefits; whereas 75 percent of the unemployed received benefits during the recession of 1975, only 45 percent were able to qualify during the 1982–1983 recession.[50]

Several urban programs were also killed off by the end of Reagan's first term, including revenue sharing and federally assisted local public works. The UDAG grants were eliminated in 1986, although a trickle of money continued to flow in the administrative pipeline for several years (the total spending fell from an annual level of between $400 and $500 million for the first 10 years of the program [fiscal years 1978 to 1987] to $200 million in fiscal 1988 and dried up to a nominal $3 million by fiscal 1994).[51] Other budget cuts also affected the cities. Most subsidies for the construction of public housing were eliminated. Only 10,000 new units a year were authorized after 1983, compared with the 111,600 new or rehabilitated units authorized for 1981.[52]

Despite his opposition to urban programs of almost any kind, President Reagan moved to put his stamp on a "Republican" approach to the cities by proposing legislation meant to stimulate private investment in troubled inner-city neighborhoods. On March 7, 1983, Reagan sent his draft of the Urban Enterprise Zone Act to Congress and asserted that the legislation represented a sharp departure from past policy:

> Enterprise zones are a fresh approach for promoting economic growth in the inner cities. The old approach relied on heavy government subsidies and central planning. A prime example was the model cities program in the 1960s, which concentrated government programs, subsidies and regulations in distressed urban areas. The enterprise zone approach is to remove government barriers, bring individuals to create, produce and earn their own wages and profits.[53]

Although the president claimed that the enterprise zone legislation was a "fresh approach," it was actually built on concepts pioneered by the Carter Administration. Since at least 1974, federal policy had stressed the role of government in subsidizing private investment. In the Reagan years, the enterprise zones idea surfaced from time to time, but it was far down on the president's policy agenda. After George H. W. Bush's election to the presidency in 1988, the idea continued to receive an occasional nudge from the White House, but urban policy of any kind did not surface as a meaningful item on the president's legislative agenda until very late in his term.

dministration of George H. W. Bush was not motivated by its elec-
base or its ideology to propose any kind of urban legislation. In the 1988
presidential election, Bush used racial issues to mobilize his base. Republicans
ran an attack ad that featured a police photograph of Willie Horton, who had
raped a woman in Maryland and stabbed her fiancé while on a weekend pass
from a Massachusetts prison. The Democratic candidate, Michael Dukakis, had
been the governor of Massachusetts at the time. According to Bush's campaign
director, Lee Atwater, the fact that Willie Horton was black was the key element
explaining the ad's emotional impact.

In the 1992 election, the Bush campaign refined its racial appeals by resorting to a code language that used attacks on cities as a signifier of race and
welfare-state liberalism. In one of the opening salvos of the campaign, Vice
President Dan Quayle attacked New York City by saying, "The liberal vision of
a happy, productive and content welfare state hasn't even worked on 22 square
miles of the most valuable real estate in the world."[54] A later Quayle attack
prompted a *New York Post* headline: "City to Dan Quayle: DON'T DIS' US!"[55]
An editorial in the *New York Times* called Quayle's attacks an attempt to make
New York City "The Willie Horton of 1992."[56]

Despite the administration's rhetoric, late in his term President Bush made
some faint gestures in the direction of urban policy. The pressure to do so came
on April 29–May 3, 1992, when serious rioting broke out in Los Angeles. Measured by the number of deaths (53), injuries (2,383), property damage (over
$700 million), and the response required to reestablish order, the Los Angeles
riot was the country's worst episode of civil disorder in the twentieth century.[57]
Many people thought the riot could be used as an opportunity to call attention
to the problems of urban America. Two weeks after the riots, 150,000 people
descended on Washington for a Save Our Cities/Save Our Children rally. As
the atmosphere of crisis faded, however, urban issues got lost in election-year
politics. Democratic candidate Bill Clinton initially blamed the riots on "twelve
years of denial and neglect" by Presidents Bush and Reagan, but fearing he
might be accused of advocating new spending programs, Clinton soon muted
his criticisms.[58] On Monday, May 5, Bush's press secretary, Marlin Fitzwater,
said the Great Society's programs of the 1960s were to blame for the rioting.
Nevertheless, in an attempt to look like he was responding positively, President
Bush proposed an emergency aid package. In June, Congress passed $1.3 billion
in emergency aid that allocated $500 million for summer jobs, $382 million
for loans to businesses damaged or destroyed in the riot areas, and some flood
relief for the city of Chicago.

Through the summer and early fall of 1992, Congress worked on a larger
and more permanent urban aid bill. A version was finally approved by the
House on October 6 and the Senate on October 8. The legislation would have
created 25 urban and 25 rural enterprise zones and financed so-called weed and
seed programs that combined enhanced law enforcement with job training and
education programs. The bulk of the legislation, however, was made up of an
array of items that had nothing to do with cities, including liberalized (tax-free)
retirement accounts for upper-income people and a provision for the repeal of

luxury taxes on yachts, furs, jewels, and planes (Democrats backed this amendment as enthusiastically as Republicans). It was estimated that of the $30 billion the bill would cost over five years, about $6 billion would be used to help depressed areas in cities.[59] By the time the legislation was passed and sent to the White House for President Bush's signature, the election was over. Bush vetoed it, using the excuse that it was contaminated by pork-barrel amendments.

The CDBG program was the only major urban program to survive the Reagan/Bush years. CDBG spending fell from $4 billion in the 1981 fiscal year to $2.8 billion in fiscal 1990 before rebounding slightly in fiscal 1992, the year the Democrats reclaimed the White House. Under President Clinton, CDBG spending rose modestly to $4.6 billion by the 1996 fiscal year,[60] and to $5.1 billion by Clinton's last budget, the 2001 fiscal year (when adjusted for inflation, however, funding for the program actually stayed even). Under President George W. Bush, the level of funding fell, but the program was not eliminated entirely.[61]

Political Reality and Urban Policy

As a self-styled "new Democrat" who wanted to project an image as a friend of the "forgotten middle class," Bill Clinton could not be expected to place aid to cities or to the poor on the front burner. In the 1992 presidential election, the Clinton campaign decided to concentrate on appealing to the white suburban middle class and to assume that inner-city voters would support him anyway because they had no place else to go. Clinton's electoral strategy succeeded in making him the first Democrat to be elected to two full terms since Franklin D. Roosevelt. Clinton succeeded by winning back many of the white suburban voters who had deserted the party in 1980. Even so, he still lost the overall white vote by a 39 to 41 percent margin. He carried huge pluralities in the cities, coming out of New York City, for example, with almost a million-vote lead. His ability to capture 82 percent of the African American vote was crucial to his victory.

A compelling logic informed Clinton's suburban strategy. By the 1990 census, 48 percent of the nation's population lived in suburbs. Because they tended to turn out for elections at a relatively high rate, it seemed certain they would cast a majority of the national vote in the 1992 election.[62] In addition, large proportions of suburban voters were so-called Reagan Democrats, blue-collar and middle-class voters who had abandoned the party to vote Republican in the three previous presidential elections. They were heavily concentrated in the older suburbs in key states such as New Jersey, Michigan, and California, which could deliver the big blocs of electoral college votes coveted by every presidential candidate. To bring them back to the fold, Clinton wanted to avoid identifying himself with policies that were targeted to cities, and especially to blacks.

In developing his strategy, Clinton followed the advice of a well-known African American sociologist, William Julius Wilson, whose 1987 book, *The Truly Disadvantaged*, warned against race-specific policies. Wilson, who was a friend and adviser of the president, recommended a "hidden agenda" in which inner-city minorities might be helped "by emphasizing programs to which the more advantaged groups of all races and classes can positively relate."[63] In an interview before the election, Wilson praised Clinton's programs for targeting "all low- to moderate-income groups, not just minorities."[64]

Clinton ended up devising what two scholars called a "stealth urban policy" composed of programs that were not specifically targeted to cities but would be beneficial to them.[65] In their campaign book, *Putting People First*, Bill Clinton and Al Gore advocated policies designed to help the middle class and the disadvantaged equally. Clinton's highly successful campaign bus tours avoided the inner cities and gave the media ample opportunities to photograph the candidate against small town and rural backdrops. After winning the nomination, Clinton did attend a meeting of the United States Conference of Mayors (USCM) and lent his support to a public works initiative. Clinton stressed, however, that the principal goal was to stimulate the economy and that aiding cities would be a secondary effect.

Clinton began his presidency with the intention of rewarding the cities that had voted lopsidedly for him. To accomplish this, he put together a $19.5 billion economic stimulus bill that included $4.4 billion for public works (mostly in cities), $2.5 billion for community development grants, and $735 million for inner-city schools and jobs. Led by minority leader Bob Dole (R.-Kans.), Senate Republicans filibustered the bill, refusing to let it come up for a vote. Lacking the 60 votes necessary to end the filibuster, the Democrats were forced to back down. Eventually, all that was passed was a very modest bill not targeted at the cities at all, a $4 billion extension of unemployment benefits for the chronically unemployed.[66]

The only significant new urban initiative that the Clinton administration could claim was the Empowerment Zones/Enterprise Communities (EZ/EC) program, which was included as Title XIII of the Omnibus Budget Reconciliation Act of 1993. Republicans and even many conservatives had supported the enterprise zones idea in the Reagan and Bush years because it was based on a strategy of cutting taxes and regulations in inner cities, with the intention of stimulating investment in depressed neighborhoods. Conservatives liked it because it mirrored the Republicans' national-level policies. The Clinton administration adopted this same free-market approach. To promote investment in EZ/EC zones, tax credits were provided for employers who hired workers who lived in the zone, and businesses located within the zones became eligible for accelerated depreciation on business property and tax-exempt bond financing for new construction. Grant money was also made available to assist zone residents in obtaining education, job training, and child care so that they could work. Ultimately, 31 Empowerment Zones were created across the country, and 74 additional distressed areas (33 in rural areas) also won grants, but these were small in comparison to the full-fledged Empowerment Zones.

Empowerment Zones proved to be the only politically viable urban program left. The midterm 1994 elections dealt a near deathblow to urban policies. Led by House Speaker Newt Gingrich and his Contract with America (labeled Contract on America by detractors), the Republicans won control of both houses of Congress for the first time in 40 years. The Republicans were hostile to the little that remained of federal urban programs. Speaker Gingrich called for the elimination of the Department of Housing and Urban Development, asserting, "You could abolish HUD tomorrow morning and improve life in most of America." He was blunt about why HUD was being singled out for especially harsh treatment: Its "weak constituency," he said, "makes it a prime candidate for cuts."[67]

In a desperate attempt to stave off disaster, HUD secretary Henry Cisneros proposed to "reinvent" his department in ways pleasing to conservatives. Announced a month and a half after the 1994 election, HUD issued a *Reinvention Blueprint* calling for a consolidation of the department's programs into three flexible block grants that would be administered by cities and states. The plan also proposed converting all public housing aid to vouchers, which would allow recipients to find housing wherever private landlords would take them. Reinventing HUD became the centerpiece of Clinton's National Urban Policy Report, issued in July 1995.[68]

The decline in public housing and urban programs began well before Clinton came into office, but the fact that a Democrat was now in the White House did not change things very much. In the Reagan and Bush years, HUD experienced the largest cuts of any cabinet-level department in the federal government. HUD budget authority (what Congress authorizes it to spend) fell from 7.5 percent of the total federal budget in 1978 to 1.3 percent by 1990. During the Clinton administration, annual HUD spending recovered slightly, but this only enabled HUD to meet past commitments for housing subsidies. Four programs of special interest to city governments, General Revenue Sharing, Urban Development Action Grants, Local Public Works, and Antirecession Fiscal Assistance, were zeroed out—were eliminated entirely.

The welfare reform bill Clinton signed in August 1996 also hurt the cities. The Personal Responsibility Act of 1996 converted Aid to Families with Dependent Children into a block grant run by the states. In addition to a 64 percent decline in welfare spending from 1990 to 1998, food stamps and community services programs were sharply reduced. Three programs—child nutrition, supplemental (infant) feeding, and housing assistance—increased somewhat only because they were linked to welfare reform efforts. Medicaid costs climbed substantially (by 146 percent), but the big winner was justice assistance, which skyrocketed 1,250 percent in less than a decade. Although some of this money went to cities, the states used most of it to build prisons. Obviously, crime control trumped any other social purpose.

The Cities' Fall from Grace

Until the election of Barack Obama to the presidency in November 2008, both political parties had largely abandoned the cities. It was a matter of making a political calculus. In the case of the Republicans, party leaders had long sought to capitalize on white suburbanites' disaffection from the Democratic-sponsored civil rights and antipoverty policies of the 1960s. What is more interesting is the way the past friend of the cities, the Democratic Party, has shied away from urban issues. In 1968 the Democrats used the word *city* 23 times in the party platform adopted at their presidential nominating convention. It did not appear even once in the 1988 platform. The substitute term, *hometown America*, signaled a recognition that the suburban vote had grown in importance. In 1992 and 1996, Clinton avoided policies targeted to cities and concentrated his appeals on the suburban middle class. Notably, in the 2000 campaign, Democratic candidate Al Gore mentioned urban sprawl as a significant national issue. By the new century, urban policy no longer referred to central cities but to urban regions.

The near-invisibility of cities in national politics can be explained by a simple fact: today, central-city voters are a very small fraction of the national electorate. The central cities of the 32 largest metropolitan areas reached a high-water mark of 27 percent of the electorate in 1944, but by 1992 they accounted for just 14 percent of the national vote,[69] and 12 percent by the 2000 election. As shown in Figure 8.2, the share of their states' votes cast by their largest cities has fallen steadily for half a century in New York, Illinois, Pennsylvania, Michigan, and Massachusetts.[70] In 1952, New York City voters represented 48 percent of the statewide electorate, but by the 2000 presidential election their proportion of the statewide vote had fallen to 32 percent. Chicago claimed 41 percent of the Illinois presidential vote in 1952 but only 20 percent by 2000.

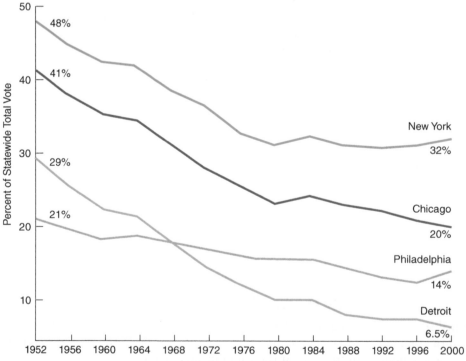

FIGURE 8.2 City Proportion of Actual State Electorate, 1952–2000

Sources: Richard Scammon, *America Votes* (various issues); U.S. Bureau of the Census, *Census of Population and Housing,* various years; and reports of actual city votes from county boards of elections (and newspapers for 1996 election). Data compiled by Richard Sauerzopf. Data from 2000 from Peter Dreier, John Mollenkopf, and Todd Swanstrom, *Place Matters,* 2nd ed. (Lawrence: University Press of Kansas, 2004), p. 282.

Cities also lost representation in the U.S. House of Representatives. Between 1963 and 1994, the number of congressional districts with a majority of the population coming from central cities fell from 94 to 84, and over the same period the number of districts with a majority of suburban voters increased from 94 to 214. In 1994, after the Republicans took control of the House, the proportion of leadership positions held by representatives from districts with a sizable proportion of central-city voters fell precipitously, from 30 to 10 percent.[71] Similar trends reduced the influence of the big cities in state governments as well.[72] The number of states with suburban electoral majorities climbed from 3 in 1980 to 14 in 1990, and increased again when seats were reapportioned as a result of the 2000 census.

It is generally assumed the suburbs now hold the key to winning national elections. Suburban votes were critical to the presidential victories of Presidents Ronald Reagan and George H. W. Bush; Reagan won huge landslides in 1980 and 1984 even though he only carried about a third of the central-city vote. In the 1988 election, suburban voters gave Bush such a comfortable cushion that he could have carried almost all of the northern industrial states without a single vote from the big cities in those states. By contrast, the central-city electorate was an important part of Bill Clinton's winning coalition in 1992 and 1996. In 1992 New York City provided Clinton with 92 percent of his nearly 1-million statewide vote margin, and Clinton lost to Bush in suburban Long Island (Nassau and Suffolk counties). In 1996, Clinton did even better in the cities, winning 67 percent of the vote in Milwaukee, 74 percent in Boston, 76 percent in St. Louis and New York, and 80 percent in Chicago.[73] In the 2000 presidential election, Al Gore won similar pluralities in the cities, but it was not enough to overcome George W. Bush's near-sweep of southern and less urban, less populated states of the Plains and the West. Gore won the national popular vote by more than 500,000 votes, but Bush was able to win the election by commanding a bare majority of votes in the Electoral College.

Even though President Clinton owed a debt to big-city voters for his two election victories, he did not make urban issues a priority. During his presidency, federal spending for the cities continued to fall. Clearly, Clinton felt he could take his urban base for granted, and he was right. This strategy did impose a potential cost on the Democrats, however, because as the federal government turned away from the cities, voter turnout in them went into a steep slide. Indeed, in the past half century, 40 percent of the loss in the proportion of votes cast in the 32 largest cities can be traced to falling turnout and not to shrinking population.[74]

The End of Urban Policy

At first blush it would appear that Barack Obama's election put the voters of central cities and their constituency groups into a more favorable position than they had enjoyed for decades. For the first time since the Carter administration, the president signaled that he might pay attention to urban problems. Only a few weeks after taking office, the Obama administration announced the appointment of Adolfo Carrion, the president of Borough of the Bronx, as its "urban czar," with the charge to coordinate the urban-related programs then on the books. That goal has not been realized. It would be a daunting job merely to identify the programs that influence cities and urban regions. An even harder task would follow. These programs are located in dozens of agencies operating under almost all of the cabinet-level departments. Even with a lot of attention and political muscle from the White House, it is not clear what "coordination" would amount to. Probably for this reason, as time passed little was heard from the urban czar, and there was no prospect that urban issues would be able to compete in a crowded political agenda any time soon.

Still, it should be noted that more than at any time in decades, programs initiated by the Obama administration significantly influenced metropolitan development and improved the fiscal condition of states and cities. The American Recovery and Reinvestment Act, which authorized the expenditure of $787 billion over a 10-year period, was critically important to states and localities. The act allocated $79 billion to provide fiscal assistance to states, an important initiative because the states were imposing deep budget cuts that threatened to make the post-2007 recession worse. In addition, the legislation authorized $144 billion for infrastructure projects, which included $32 billion for transportation projects, $10 billion for rail and mass transit, and $2 billion for airports.[75] School districts were slated to receive $41 billion in grants for construction projects and other activities. The legislation set aside money for a wide array of activities to promote clean energy and conservation. Among other initiatives, the administration also announced a $1 billion program to put 5,500 more police officers on the streets.[76]

Organizations representing urban interests, broadly defined, were invigorated by these programs. On March 14–18, 2009, the National League of Cities convened its Annual Congressional City Conference, a gathering of local officials from across the country. By contrast to previous years, the conference revolved around a wide-ranging agenda featuring discussions of new federal initiatives in many areas, including infrastructure investment, jobs programs, green energy, and transportation. Local officials needed to share information because they found themselves involved in administering a broader variety of new federal programs than they have since the 1960s.

However, all of these programs taken together do not add up to an urban policy, or even a collection of policies with similar aims. Even in the heyday of urban and social welfare programs, when federal administrators of the Great Society showered the cities with money, a coherent urban policy never existed. Programs were created for different reasons and for different purposes, and to satisfy a variety of political needs and influential constituencies. There are still a large number of programs that influence cities, suburbs, and the people that live within them, but hardly any of these actually have "urban" aims. The stimulus package illustrates this fact perfectly: although local governments were deeply affected, the main policy objective was to stimulate the national economy. For a long time "urban" has not been a category that the federal government cares very much about, and that is unlikely to change.

Endnotes

1. Reported in the *New York Times* (December 1, 1959), p. 27, quoted in Mark I. Gelfand, *A Nation of Cities: The Federal Government and Urban America,* Urban Life in America Series (New York: Oxford University Press, 1975), p. 295. See also John F. Kennedy, "The Great Unspoken Issue," in *Proceedings, American Municipal Congress 1959* (Washington, DC: American Municipal League, n.d.), pp. 23–28; and John F. Kennedy, "The Shame of the States," *New York Times Magazine* (May 18, 1958).

2. Quoted in Theodore H. White, *The Making of the President, 1960* (New York: Atheneum, 1961), p. 206. Nixon's strategy, which White contends was no strategy at all, was a "national" one, in which he committed himself to visit all 50 states; Kennedy, in contrast, used an urban strategy centered on the industrial states with large blocs of electoral votes (see pp. 267–352).

3. John C. Donovan, *The Politics of Poverty,* 2nd ed. (New York: Bobbs-Merrill, Pegasus, 1973), p. 19.

4. Quoted in White, *The Making of the President,* p. 165.

5. Donovan, *The Politics of Poverty,* p. 225.

6. Ibid., p. 104.

7. Nelson W. Polsby and Aaron Wildavsky, *Presidential Elections: Contemporary Strategies of American Electoral Politics,* 7th ed. (New York: Free Press, 1988). The statistics given are for "nonwhite" voters.

8. White, *The Making of the President,* p. 354.

9. For good recent summary accounts, see ibid.; also James A. Morone, *The Democratic Wish: Popular Participation and the Limits of American Government* (New York: Basic Books, 1990), Chapter 6.

10. Quoted in Richard Blumenthal, "The Bureaucracy: Antipoverty and the Community Action Programs," in *American Political Institutions and Public Policy,* ed. Allan P. Sindler (Boston: Little, Brown, 1969), p. 149.

11. *Message of the President to Congress,* reprinted in *Congressional Quarterly Weekly Report* 32, no. 2 (January 11, 1964).

12. *Congress and the Nation, 1945–1964* (Washington, DC: Congressional Quarterly Service, 1965), p. 1379.

13. Refer to Daniel J. Elazar, *The American Partnership: Intergovernmental Cooperation in the Nineteenth Century United States* (Chicago: University of Chicago Press, 1962).

14. Manpower Development and Training Act of 1962, Public Law 87–415, 87th Cong. (1962); emphasis added.

15. Economic Opportunity Act of 1964, Public Law 88–452, 88th Cong. (1964); emphasis added.

16. Demonstration Cities and Metropolitan Development Act of 1966, Public Law 89–754, 89th Cong. (1966); emphasis added.

17. See James L. Sundquist and David W. Davis, *Making Federalism Work: A Study of Program Coordination at the Community Level* (Washington, DC: Brookings Institution Press, 1969), pp. 3–5.

18. Lyndon B. Johnson, "Total Victory over Poverty," Message to Congress, March 15, 1964, reprinted in *The Failure of American Liberalism: After the Great Society,* ed. Marvin E. Gettleman and David Mermelstein (New York: Vintage Books, 1970), p. 181.

19. U.S. Office of Economic Opportunity, *Community Action Program Guide* (Washington, DC: U.S. Government Printing Office, 1965).

20. Frances Fox Piven and Richard A. Cloward, *Regulating the Poor: The Functions of Public Welfare* (New York: Pantheon, 1971).
21. Ibid., p. 295.
22. U.S. Advisory Commission on Intergovernmental Relations, *Fiscal Balance in the American Federal System,* vol. 1 (Washington, DC: U.S. Government Printing Office, 1967), p. 169.
23. U.S. Office of Management and Budget, *Special Analyses: Budget of the United States Government: Fiscal Year 1981* (Washington, DC: U.S. Government Printing Office, 1982), p. 254.
24. Michael D. Reagan, *The New Federalism* (New York: Oxford University Press, 1972), p. 97.
25. U.S. Department of the Treasury, Office of Revenue Sharing, *Reported Uses of General Revenue Sharing Funds, 1974–1975: A Tabulation and Analysis of Data from Actual Use,* Report 5 (Washington, DC: U.S. Government Printing Office, 1966), p. 5.
26. Ibid., p. 25.
27. "New Directions Cited in First Annual Block Grant Reports," *Housing and Development Reporter* (January 12, 1976), p. 761.
28. Housing and Community Development Act of 1974, sec. 104(a).
29. Reported in *Housing and Development Reporter* (January 10, 1977), p. 684.
30. Interview by Sharon Cribbs (investigator for the Southern Governmental Monitoring Project) with Nathaniel Hill, Director, Department of Human Resources, Little Rock, Arkansas (Summer 1975), quoted in Southern Governmental Monitoring Project, *A Time for Accounting: The Housing and Community Development Act in the South: A Monitoring Report,* ed. Raymond Brown with Ann Coil and Carol Rose (Atlanta: Southern Regional Council, 1976), p. 53.
31. Ann R. Markusen and David Wilmoth, "The Political Economy of National Urban Policy in the U.S.A.: 1976–81," *Canadian Journal of Regional Science* (Summer 1982): 145–163.
32. Rochelle L. Stansfield, "Federalism Report: Government Seeks the Right Formula for Community Development Funds," *National Journal* (February 12, 1977), p. 242.
33. Ann R. Markusen, "The Urban Impact Analysis: A Critical Forecast," in *The Urban Impact of Federal Policies,* ed. Norman Glickman (Baltimore: Johns Hopkins University Press, 1979); see also discussion by Ann R. Markusen, Annalee Saxenian, and Marc A. Weiss, "Who Benefits from Intergovernmental Transfers?" in *Cities Under Stress: The Fiscal Crises of Urban America,* ed. Robert W. Burchell and David Listokin (New Brunswick, NJ: Center for Urban Research, 1981), p. 656; and Stansfield, "Federalism Report."
34. Quoted in Robert Reihold, "President Proposes a Broad New Policy for Urban Recovery," *New York Times* (March 28, 1978).
35. "Excerpts from the President's Message to Congress Outlining His Urban Policy," *New York Times* (March 28, 1978).
36. F. J. James, "President Carter's Comprehensive National Urban Policy: Achievements and Lessons Learned," *Environment and Planning C: Government and Policy* 8 (1990): 34.
37. Markusen and Wilmoth, "The Political Economy of National Urban Policy," p. 15.
38. "Washington Update: Administration Officials, Mayors Have Love Fest," *National Journal* (January 29, 1977), p. 189.
39. Quoted in Theodore H. White, *America in Search of Itself: The Making of the President, 1956–1980* (New York: Harper & Row, 1982), p. 381.

40. D. Lee Bawden and John L. Palmer, "Social Policy: Challenging the Welfare State," in *The Reagan Record,* ed. John L. Palmer and Isabel V. Sawhill (Cambridge, MA: Ballinger, 1992), p. 200.
41. *New York Times* (October 23, 1981), p. 1.
42. President's Commission for a National Agenda for the Eighties, *A National Agenda for the Eighties* (Washington, DC: U.S. Government Printing Office, 1980), p. 66.
43. Ibid., p. 4.
44. Ibid., p. 66.
45. Timothy K. Barnekov, Daniel Rich, and Robert Warren, "The New Privatism, Federalism, and the Future of Urban Governance: National Urban Policy in the 1980s," *Journal of Urban Affairs* 3, no. 4 (Fall 1981): 3.
46. U.S. Department of Housing and Urban Development, *The President's National Urban Policy Report* (Washington, DC: U.S. Government Printing Office, 1982), pp. 2, 23.
47. Ibid., p. 14.
48. Ibid., p. 135.
49. Ibid., p. 138.
50. Robertson and Judd, *The Development of American Public Policy,* p. 233.
51. U.S. Office of Management and Budget, *Budget of the United States Government, Fiscal Year 1996, Historical Tables* (Washington, DC: U.S. Government Printing Office, 1996), Table 12.3.
52. Henry J. Aaron and Associates, "Nondefense Programs," in *Setting National Priorities: The 1983 Budget,* ed. Joseph A. Pechman (Washington, DC: Brookings Institution Press, 1982), p. 119.
53. White House press release, March 7, 1983.
54. Quoted in Robert Pear, "Quayle Criticizes New York as Proof of Welfare's Ills," *New York Times* (February 28, 1992), p. 1.
55. *New York Post* (April 28, 1992), p. 1.
56. "The Willie Horton of 1992," *New York Times* (March 3, 1992), p. 3.
57. James H. Johnson Jr., Cloyzelle K. Jones, Walter C. Farrell Jr., and Melvin L. Oliver, "The Los Angeles Rebellion: A Retrospective View," *Economic Development Quarterly* 6, no. 4 (November 1992): 356–372.
58. Robert Pear, "Clinton, in Attack on President, Ties Riots to 'Neglect,' " *New York Times* (May 6, 1992), p. 1.
59. Clifford Krauss, "Congress Passes Aid to Cities," *New York Times* (June 9, 1992), p. A20.
60. U.S. Office of Management and Budget, *Budget of the United States Government, Fiscal Year 1996, Historical Tables,* Table 12.3.
61. U.S. Office of Management and Budget, *Budget of the United States Government, Fiscal Year 2003* (Washington, DC: U.S. Government Printing Office, 2003), Appendix, p. 485.
62. William Schneider, "The Suburban Century Begins," *Atlantic Monthly* (July 1992), pp. 33–44.
63. William Julius Wilson, *The Truly Disadvantaged: The Inner City, the Underclass, and Public Policy* (Chicago: University of Chicago Press, 1987), p. 155.
64. "A Visit with Bill Clinton," *Atlantic Monthly* (October 1992); and William Julius Wilson, "The Right Message," *New York Times* (March 17, 1992).
65. Bernard H. Ross and Myron A. Levine, *Urban Politics: Power in Metropolitan America,* 5th ed. (Itasca, IL: F. E. Peacock, 1996), p. 434.

66. Adam Clymer, "G.O.P. Senators Prevail, Sinking Clinton's Economic Stimulus Bill," *New York Times* (April 22, 1993), p. 1.
67. Quoted in Kenneth J. Cooper, "Gingrich Pledges a Major Package of Spending Cuts Early Next Year," *Washington Post* (December 13, 1994), p. 1.
68. U.S. Department of Housing and Urban Development, *Empowerment: A New Covenant with America's Communities* (Rockville, MD: HUD USER, July 1995).
69. Peter F. Nardulli, Jon K. Dalager, and Donald E. Greco, "Voter Turnout in U.S. Presidential Elections: An Historical View and Some Speculation," *PS: Political Science and Politics* (September 1996): 484.
70. Calculations are from Richard Sauerzopf and Todd Swanstrom, "The Urban Electorate in Presidential Elections, 1920–1992: Challenging the Conventional Wisdom," paper delivered at the annual meeting of the Urban Affairs Association (Indianapolis, April 22–25, 1993). Updated by authors.
71. Hal Wolman and Lisa Marckini, "Changes in Central City Representation and Influence in Congress," paper prepared for delivery at the annual meeting of the Urban Affairs Association, (Toronto, Canada, April 17, 1997). See also Demetrios Caraley, "Washington Abandons the Cities," *Political Science Quarterly* 107, no. 1 (1992): 20.
72. Margaret Weir, "Central Cities' Loss of Power in State Politics," *Cityscape: A Journal of Policy Development and Research* 2, no. 2 (May 1996): 23–40.
73. From CNN.com, http://www.cnn.com/ALLPOLITICS/1996/.
74. Nardulli, Dalager, and Greco, "Voter Turnout in U.S. Presidential Elections," p. 484.
75. "Stimulus Package Unveiled," *Wall Street Journal,* http://online.wsj.com/article/SB123202946622485595.html.
76. National League of Cities, "NLC Applauds Announcement of COPS Hiring Recovery Program," http://www.nlc.org/documents/Utility%20Navigation/News%20Center/NCW/2009/NCW032309.pdf.

CHAPTER 9

The Rise of the Sunbelt

Metropolitan south ↑ pop.
e.g Atlanta, Orlando...

A Historic Shift

Over the past half century, regional population shifts have brought radical changes to the nation's politics, economics, and culture. Historically, the center of gravity for the nation's politics had been located in the big industrial states and cities of the Northeast and the heartland. Because of its continued reliance on an agricultural economy, the South remained marginalized. Democratic politicians from the southern states could influence national politics only by voting as a bloc in the House and Senate and by maintaining a tenuous alliance with northern Democrats. Most Northerners regarded southern culture as a curious relic of a faded past. But at least its participation in the national party system allowed the South to maintain a presence in national politics. By contrast, until mid-century the Southwest was almost invisible. Its population, small and dispersed was, still defined largely by its frontier legacy. Except for Los Angeles, as late as the middle of the twentieth century there were no other cities of significant size in the vast region stretching from New Mexico to the southern California coast. Over 1.5 million people lived in Los Angeles in 1940, compared to San Diego, with its population of 203,000, Phoenix, at 65,000, and tiny Las Vegas, with just 8,500 residents. But over the next few decades, population growth would be so rapid in cities of the South and the Southwest that these two regions would become fused into a vast region that became known as the Sunbelt.

This historic redistribution of national population irreversibly changed the contours of national politics. The rise of the Sunbelt brought about a conservative shift in American politics. Beginning in the 1950s, business corporations began to move to southern and western states to escape higher labor costs in the industrial North and to take advantage of a vast pool of low-wage, non-unionized labor. Twelve of 15 Sunbelt states have right-to-work laws that allow employers to hire workers in a plant even if they refuse to join the plant's union. By contrast, two of the 14 states in the old industrial belt stretching from the Midwest and up through New England has a right-to-work law. These laws have discouraged unionization and kept wages lower than states where unions are stronger.[1] In the Sunbelt, these policies have reflected a political culture that is highly individualistic and generally hostile to governmental action, unless that action is geared toward helping business, supporting military bases, or financing water and other federal projects that promote economic development. Due in part to the rising influence of Sunbelt politicians in both parties who

OUTTAKE

The Electoral College Favors the Sunbelt

The term *Sunbelt* was popularized in the mid-1970s, and it quickly became almost indispensable in everyday discourse about national development and politics. Even though the geographic boundaries of the Sunbelt were rather vague in most people's minds, the term generally conveyed a positive image of a region of the country that was prosperous and growing: "When a person hears the term on radio or on television, or reads it in a magazine or book, or sees it in the telephone book or on a firm's letterhead, it is likely to conjure up an image of growing cities and booming economies in Southern or Southwestern cities with pleasant climates." It would be possible to regard the term as merely a "rhetorical ruse," as one scholar commented, or a "public relations coup," as the president of a corporation helping other companies move to the Sunbelt claimed, were it not for the fact that the long-term population growth in the region has resulted in a fundamental realignment of political power in the nation. Until Barack Obama, all the winning presidents since John F. Kennedy came from the Sunbelt. Over the past half century, the reapportionment that follows each decennial census has shifted the balance of power in Congress toward the congressional delegations that represent southern and western states. Without doubt, this realignment of power explains the shift toward conservative social policies in recent decades.

Over time, the Sunbelt was able to flex its muscles in Washington because population equals votes. Politicians could scarcely ignore this reality. The Republicans were strongest in the suburbs of urban regions in the West, and, after 1964, the South, all of which were booming. Each decennial census was followed by a reapportionment of seats in the House of Representatives, which, together with the two senators from each state, determines the number of Electoral College votes each state casts in a presidential election. The Sunbelt states increased the number of their votes in the Electoral College every time the country was reapportioned after 1928; over the same period, states in the Midwest and Northeast steadily lost Electoral College votes. In 1928, the 15 Sunbelt states were able to cast 146 votes in the Electoral College, compared to the 237 cast by electors representing 14 Midwestern and northeastern states. By the 2000 presidential election, the situation was reversed: The Sunbelt states held 222 votes, but by then the 14 northern states could cast only 180 votes in the Electoral College balloting. If Al Gore had won the same states but run for the presidency in 1960 instead of 2000, he would have carried the election by 275 to 262 Electoral College votes; likewise, John Kerry would have won the presidency in 2004. Barack Obama's victory in 2008 was achieved mainly because he added some border and western states, plus Florida, to the Democratic tally. By 2024, the Sunbelt states will have an estimated eight more electoral votes, making it all the more important to Democratic candidates that their party continues to make inroads there.

Sources: Bradley R. Rice, "Searching for the Sunbelt," in *Searching for the Sunbelt: Historical Perspectives on a Region*, ed. Raymond A. Mohl (Knoxville: University of Tennessee Press, 1990),

p. 217: David R. Goldfield, *Cotton Fields and Skyscrapers: Southern City and Region, 1706–1980* (Baton Rouge: Louisiana State University Press, 1982), p. 192, cited in Rice, "Searching for the Sunbelt," p. 218; Edward M. Burmila, "The Electoral College after Census 2010 and 2020: The Political Impact of Population Growth and Redistribution," *Perspectives on Politics* 7, no. 4 (December 2009): 839.

represented such values, the nation's political culture began to move rightward in the second half of the twentieth century, and in many respects the Sunbelt became the driving force in the nation's politics.

In the last couple of decades, however, the politics of the Sunbelt has been changing, so much so that the term is beginning to lose much of its meaning. Blacks have been moving back into the South from northern states, and millions of immigrants have been moving into southern and southwestern metropolitan regions and into smaller towns. The new demographic realities have created a shifting and unpredictable political landscape. Since the 1990s, Hispanics have accounted for almost 40 percent of the population growth in the United States, and Sunbelt cities and suburbs have attracted the largest numbers. In the first decade of this century, the Hispanic population accounted for more than half of the nation's growth. The 2010 census indicated that the U.S. Hispanic population grew 43 percent, from 35.5 million in 2000 to 50.5 million by 2010. This trend is expected to continue. The Census Bureau predicts that the non-Hispanic white population will drop to 50.8 percent of the total population by 2040, and even lower, to 46.3 percent, by 2050.[2]

Twelve of the 18 U.S. cities whose populations changed from a majority of non-Hispanic whites to a majority of minority residents during the 1990s were located in the South and Southwest.[3] In addition, the fast-growing suburbs of Sunbelt cities have attracted large numbers of highly educated professionals, and this group is not as reliably conservative as Sunbelt voters have been in the past.[4] The 2000, 2004, and 2008 presidential elections revealed that Democratic and independent-leaning voters have turned Florida and Arizona from solidly Republican into swing states, and California from a Republican to a solidly Democratic state. With Florida and Virginia peeling away in the presidential vote of 2008, it became apparent that parts of the South may have tipped into the Democratic-leaning column. The Sunbelt appears to be is breaking apart as a regional political force, but the volatile political climate that has prevailed since the 2008 election makes everything uncertain.

If the on-going sea change in national electoral alignments ultimately favors the Democratic Party, there is likely to be increasing support for an active national presence in health care, urban transportation and infrastructure, and other initiatives that people think of as "liberal." As in the past, changes in the regional balance of power will be of great consequence.

The Concept of the Sunbelt

Kevin Phillips, the chief political analyst for the 1968 Republican presidential campaign, is generally credited for coining the term *Sunbelt*. In his book *The Emerging Republican Majority*, published in 1969, Phillips asserted that the United States was going through a historic electoral realignment that was transforming the Republican Party into the nation's majority party. The basis of this national political realignment, he said, was the movement of millions of Americans out of the old industrial cities of the North to the suburbs and to the South and West. Phillips sometimes lumped the South and the West into an area he called the Sunbelt, although he never actually defined its boundaries; indeed, of the 47 maps in his book, none portrays such a region.[5]

Phillips's prediction that regionalism would increasingly influence the direction of national politics turned out to be correct. In 1973, an embargo on the sale of oil imposed by the Arab oil-producing nations drove the world price of oil sharply upward. The economies of oil-producing states such as Texas, Louisiana, Oklahoma, and Colorado boomed, and new jobs were created throughout the southern and western states. At the same time, energy-dependent industries and consumers in the northern states were hit hard. In 1974 and 1975, northern states went through an economic depression that saw hundreds of thousands of layoffs in industrial jobs. By the spring of 1975, New York City was facing bankruptcy and had to ask the federal government for loan guarantees. President Gerald Ford initially refused to help.[6] Congressional legislative battles began to divide along regional lines, pitting a prosperous South and West against an economically troubled North.

In this atmosphere, Kirkpatrick Sale's book *Power Shift*, published in 1975, quickly became a national best seller.[7] Sale wrote that the states of the South and West—a region he called the Southern Rim—were gaining national political power at the expense of the older industrial states. Trying to find a way to report on the political issues raised by the new regional antagonisms, the media revived Phillips's notion of the Sunbelt, and the term soon came into common use. In February 1976, the *New York Times* published a five-part series documenting the demographic and political trends favoring the Sunbelt. In May, *Business Week* devoted its feature article to "The Second War between the States."[8] The regional war became one of the hot topics helping sell newspapers and magazines in 1976 and 1977.

Although the concept of the Sunbelt quickly became part of the everyday language of Americans (the term has been included in dictionaries since the late 1970s), the precise boundaries of the region were hard to pin down. In a letter to a scholar researching the politics of the Sunbelt, Kevin Phillips defined it as the "territory stretching from the eastern Carolina lowlands down around (and excluding) Appalachia, picking up only the Greater Memphis area of Tennessee, omitting the Ozarks and moving west to Oklahoma, thence virtually due west," possibly also including Colorado.[9] It is understandable that Phillips would want to draw his boundaries to exclude pockets of poverty in the Border States, but his description was extremely imprecise. Sale's definition, displayed

FIGURE 9.1 The American Sunbelt and Frostbelt.

Source: Adapted from Richard M. Bernard and Bradley R. Rice, eds., *Sunbelt Cities: Politics and Growth Since World War II* (Austin: University of Texas Press, 1985), p. 7.

↑ $ in southern housing.

in Figure 9.1, encompassed the entire portion of the United States below the 37th parallel, extending across the country from North Carolina to the West Coast, including southern California and part of southern Nevada.[10] (For statistical purposes, we include all of California and Nevada in our discussion.) Thus, Sale's map put 15 states in the Sunbelt. The 14 states of the Northeast and the upper Midwest were lumped together into a region that for a time was called the *Frostbelt*, a term that has since pretty much disappeared from the national political discourse.

Right from the beginning, a significant number of scholars considered the concept of the Sunbelt to be suspect. For one thing, the vast region encompassed by Sale's definition was far from uniformly prosperous. The most rapid economic and population growth was occurring in Florida, parts of Texas, Arizona, southern Nevada, and southern California. Rural areas all across the Sunbelt and many urban areas of the South remained untouched by the prosperity that was proclaimed as the Sunbelt's principal defining feature, a fact that led two scholars to note that the Sunbelt had "collapsed into only a few 'sunspots.'"[11]

A second problem with the Sunbelt concept was that it assumed the South and the Southwest were similar enough to be lumped together under a single label. Until its image was burnished by its rhetorical association with the prosperous Sunbelt, the South was often thought of as a backward, poverty-ridden, violent region with a peculiar caste system. Most political studies of the South focused on issues of race, the enduring effects of the Civil War and Reconstruction, and the dominance of a single, authoritarian party (until the 1960s, the Republican Party rarely ran candidates in most southern states)—the elements making up a conservative political culture that had changed little since the Civil War. The main industries that had located in the South were those associated with low-wage labor. In the 1930s, Franklin Roosevelt and the New Deal administrators looked at federal programs as a way to bring economic development to this backward region.[12]

The image of the West, by contrast, tended to be "urban, opulent, energetic, mobile, and individualistic, a region of economic growth and openness to continual change which matched America's self-image."[13] If the image of perpetual sunshine gave the Sunbelt its name, then certainly this image fit the West better than the South. Because Los Angeles was the home of the movie and television industries, America's popular culture became increasingly identified with western images. Los Angeles served as a vision of America's future, with its sprawling suburbs, freeways, shopping centers, and even its smog.

Some observers argued thought that the idea of the Sunbelt was overplayed. Nicholas Lemann, who edited the *Texas Monthly* in the 1980s, observed that "millions of people were living in the Sunbelt without one of them realizing it. They thought of themselves as Southerners or Texans, or Los Angelenos."[14] The concept of the Sunbelt was regarded with suspicion not only because there were so many differences within it but also because all regions of the United States seemed to be becoming more alike. The industrial belt was becoming less industrial, urban populations were spreading out into suburbs in all parts of the country, and a media-based national culture was replacing regional cultural differences. "Just try to find a town anywhere in the United States without a McDonald's or a television happy-news format featuring an anchorperson with an unidentifiable accent."[15]

Despite the shortcomings of the Sunbelt/Frostbelt dichotomy, it remains useful as a starting point for understanding the regional demographic movements of the past half century, and how the these population shifts have contributed to the conservative turn in American national politics. The move away from urban and social welfare policies has occurred both because people moved out of the central cities and because large numbers of people left the old industrial heartland. For a variety of reasons, both the South and the Southwest have produced a political culture that is suspicious of government. For a brief time it seemed that the 2008 presidential election may have signaled a decisive change in direction, but the Republican gains in the congressional elections of 2010 made that very doubtful.

Regional Shifts

For the past half century, population and economic activities in the United States have been moving away from older urban areas. This population movement contrasts sharply with a long-standing pattern of national growth. Since the early years of the nineteenth century, the industrial cities had acted as magnets, drawing millions of immigrants from abroad and luring a steady stream of people from the countryside. The industrial cities were the engines of the nation's economy, and population movements reflected this fact. In 1950, 65 percent of the nation's metropolitan population lived in or near the industrial belt that reached from Boston and New York in the Northeast across to the Great Lakes and down to St. Louis.[16] More than two-thirds of the manufacturing jobs and 10 of the nation's 14 urban areas of more than a million people were stretched across this industrial zone. Over the next half century, however, a decisive shift in the regional distribution of population occurred.

In the five decades between 1940 and 1990, the population of the 15 Sunbelt states increased by 163 percent (to 103,868,000), compared to a population gain in the 14 Frostbelt states of 48 percent (to 92,818,000).[17] Over this half century, the fastest-growing states were Nevada (+50 percent), Arizona (+35 percent), Florida (+33 percent), and California (+26 percent). The only Frostbelt state to show a significant gain was New Hampshire (+20.5 percent), which grew because it was attracting commuters from elsewhere in the Northeast urban corridor.[18] As shown in Figure 9.2, these trends continued into the twenty-first century. Every state with a growth rate faster than 13.2 percent for the decade (the national average) was located in the West or in the Sunbelt, with the addition of Virginia. Three of the states that gained more than 25 percent in population—Colorado, Utah, and Idaho—were located in the West, as were two other rapidly growing states, Oregon and Washington.

Most metropolitan areas of the Sunbelt expanded so quickly after World War II that it was difficult to build infrastructure fast enough. Table 9.1 compares the growth rates for seven Sunbelt metropolitan areas with population

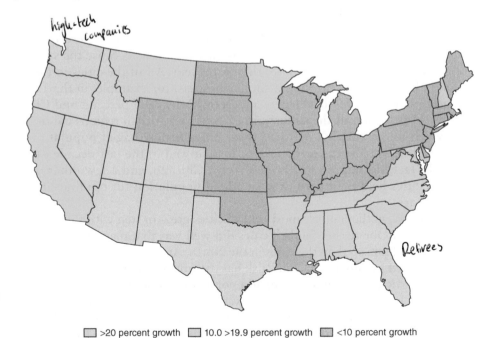

☐ >20 percent growth ☐ 10.0 >19.9 percent growth ☐ <10 percent growth

FIGURE 9.2 Population Growth in States, 1990–2000.

Source: U.S. Bureau of the Census, *Statistical Abstract of the United States, 2001* (Washington, DC: U.S. Government Printing Office, 2001), p. 7.

change in six Frostbelt urban regions from 1950 to 2000. All seven of the Sunbelt metropolitan areas boomed in the half century from 1950 to 2000, in many cases growing by more than 40 percent per decade. Phoenix had a population of 107,000 in 1950 but morphed into a metropolitan region of more than 3 million people in half a century. Las Vegas was transformed from a dusty, seedy gambling town of 24,000 in 1950 to a major metropolis (and entertainment city) of 1.4 million by 2000. Several smaller metropolitan areas in the Sunbelt grew even faster than the larger urban areas. For example, Fort Myers, Cape Coral, Ocala, Sarasota, and Naples (all in Florida) attracted large numbers of retirees. Other smaller cities in the Sunbelt and the West, such as Austin, Texas; San Diego and San Jose, California; Boise, Idaho; and Provo, Utah, thrived because of an influx of high-tech industries.

Meanwhile, the six Frostbelt metropolitan areas listed in Table 9.1 went in exactly the opposite direction. Until the late 1960s, the Chicago, Detroit, and St. Louis regions continued to prosper as industrial centers even though their central cities were losing populations. But the bottom fell out during the deindustrialization of the 1970s and 1980s. Modest gains in the 1950s and 1960s was followed by stagnation or population loss; indeed, five of the six Frostbelt metropolitan areas shown in Table 9.1 lost population in the 1970s. Manufacturing firms picked up and moved abroad or to cheaper sites in the South or Southwest, where labor unions were weak. Older metropolitan areas were able to reverse this trend in late century only by attracting the same kinds of service or high-tech firms that had already brought growth to the Sunbelt.

The old manufacturing cities fared much worse than their regions. In the 1970s, as deindustrialization reached its zenith, St. Louis lost 27 percent of its population but the St. Louis region shrunk just 2 percent because the suburbs were growing significantly, by more than 6 percent. All of the cities in the industrial belt were going through a similar process; for example, in the 1970s Chicago's population fell by 11 percent, Detroit's by 20.5 percent, and Cleveland's by 24 percent, but the suburbs in each of these urban regions continued to grow (although slowly). Most of these cities hemorrhaged population in the 1980s, but in most cases the rate of loss slowed in the last decade of the century. In fact, during the 1990s New York, Chicago, and a few other older industrial cities held their own or even added population for the first time in 20 or 30 years.

By contrast, in the Sunbelt most central cities grew in step with their metropolitan regions. One reason Sunbelt cities did well was that many of them were newer and less built-up than the cities in the North. Another is that they were not usually encircled by suburbs. David Rusk has categorized cities according to their degree of "elasticity"—their ability to add population either by filling in undeveloped land or by annexing new territory. Of the 52 metropolitan areas of more than 200,000 populations that Rusk rated as having "high" or "hyper" elasticity in 1990, 49 were located in the Sunbelt. No Frostbelt city made the list.[19]

Older cities have found it impossible to change their boundaries, mostly because they had long since become surrounded by independent suburban municipalities able to resist annexation or merger. Even in the Sunbelt, the older

TABLE 9.1 Population Growth of Selected Metropolitan Areas, 1950–2000

Metropolitan Area (Ranked by % Growth in 1970s)	Percentage Increase in Population				
	1950–1960	1960–1970	1970–1980	1980–1990	1990–2000
Sunbelt and West					
Denver–Boulder	52%	32%	31%	44%	32%
Houston	52	40	45	21	25
Las Vegas	123	115	69	61	85.5
Los Angeles–Long Beach	45.5	16	6	18.5	10
Phoenix	100	46	55	40	45
San Diego	85.5	32	37	34	12.6
Frostbelt					
Boston	7.5%	6%	−5%	6.5%	6%
Chicago	20	12	2	0.2	11
Detroit	28	12	−2	−2	5
New York City	12	8	−4.5	3	9
Pittsburgh	9	20	−5	−7	−1.5
St. Louis	20	12	−2	3	4.6

Factories moving out

Sources: U.S. Bureau of the Census, *1970 Census of Population*, vol. 1, *Characteristics of the Population*, pt. A (Washington, DC: U.S. Government Printing Office, 1973), p. 171, Table 32; U.S. Bureau of the Census, *1980 Census of Population, Supplementary Reports, Standard Metropolitan Statistical Areas and Standard Consolidated Statistical Areas* (Washington, D.C.: U.S. Government Printing Office, 1981), p. 3, Table 1; U.S. Bureau of the Census, *State and Metropolitan Area Data Book: 1991* (Washington, DC: U.S. Government Printing Office, 1991), Table A; U.S. Bureau of the Census, *Standard Metropolitan Area Data Book: 1997–98* (Washington, DC: U.S. Government Printing Office, 1999), pp. 60–65, Table B-1.

cities fit this profile; Atlanta, for instance, lost 14 percent of its population during the 1970s, but in the same decade its suburbs grew by 46 percent. Likewise, Denver's population fell (−4.5 percent) even while its suburbs were growing (by 60 percent). The newer Sunbelt cities were able to annex large tracts of land before they became land-locked. Oklahoma City, for example, spread out from about 51 square miles in 1950 to 636 square miles by 1970, and Phoenix expanded from just 17 square miles in 1950 to 469 square miles by 1996.[20] Sunbelt cities gobbled up a substantial amount of surrounding land in the 1950s and 1960s and at least some additional territory after that.[21] Because some of these Sunbelt cities were hit hard by the foreclosure crisis that began in 2008[22] any notion that the Sunbelt had fallen into decline turned out to be mistaken. Research supports the notion that the Sunbelt will maintain a faster rate of growth than the rest of the nation for some time.[23]

Why the Sunbelt Prospered

The movement of people to the Sunbelt has been matched by a redistribution of the nation's economic resources. In recent decades, job growth has heavily favored the South and West. Table 9.2 shows that in 1960, 58 percent of the nation's workforce was located in the Northeast and Midwest. The West still lagged behind, with only 15 percent of U.S. employment. By the 1980s, the share of jobs located in the Northeast and Midwest had slipped to 49 percent, and to 46 percent by 2000. Meanwhile, big gains were registered in the South and West, which together accounted for 56 percent of U.S. employment by 2000 (21 percent in the West).

The reasons for the Sunbelt's economic success are many and complex. Economic and technological factors played a major role.[24] The urban infrastructure of the older Frostbelt cities was geared to the high-density patterns of production of the industrial period. Sunbelt cities had an advantage because they could start afresh to build infrastructure suited to the postindustrial economy. The building of the interstate highways network provided the foundation for a national economy that favored the decentralization of economic activities.

TABLE 9.2 **Comparison of Regional[a] Shares of U.S. Employment and Shares of U.S. Job Growth 1960–2000 (in Percentages)**

	Share of U.S. Employment			Share of Job Growth	
	1960	1980	2000	1960–1980	1980–2000
Northeast	29%	23%	21%	13.5%	12%
Midwest	29	26	25	21.5	20
South	27	32	34	39.5	42
West	15	19	20	25.5	26

[a]Regions defined according to Bureau of the Census definition; North Central changed to Midwest in 1989.

Sources: Adapted from U.S. Bureau of the Census, *Statistical Abstract of the United States, 1973* (Washington, DC: U.S. Government Printing Office, 1973), using 1960 and 1970 census data, p. 227; U.S. Bureau of the Census, *U.S. Statistical Abstract of the United States, 2001* (Washington, DC: U.S. Government Printing Office, 2001), using 1990 and 2000 census data; U.S. Bureau of the Census, *Statistical Abstract of the United States, 1996* (Washington, DC: U.S. Government Printing Office, 1996), using 1980 census data.

The adoption of air conditioning made the Sunbelt more attractive both for living and for white-collar work.[25] The materials used in manufacturing shifted from heavy metals such as iron and steel to lighter materials such as aluminum and plastic, and the newer manufacturing plants could be located on relatively cheap, easily available land in Sunbelt metropolitan areas. Most important, the source of energy for industry and for homes shifted from Frostbelt coal to Sunbelt oil. Oil jumped from meeting less than half of the nation's energy needs in 1940 to almost 78 percent by 1975. By the mid-1970s, coal supplied no more than 17 percent of the nation's energy.[26]

Changing demographics and lifestyles favored the Sunbelt as well. More leisure time and a greater emphasis on recreation lured people to warmer climates. After World War II, tourism accounted for a larger share of the national economy. Major recreational and tourist facilities developed in Florida and California (homes of Disney theme parks) and in New Orleans and Las Vegas. Entire communities, such as Lake Havasu, Arizona, arose to serve the needs of an expanding class of retired people who preferred Sunbelt lifestyles and the lower cost of living found there.

However, demographic and economic trends do not explain why the Sunbelt prospered as much as it did. Federal spending exerted a powerful impact in stimulating local economies. In particular, the Pentagon budget induced military-dependent sectors to migrate to the Sunbelt. No other major industrialized nation used military spending so forcefully to relocate economic activity from one region to another.[27] The Great Depression ended in the United States when government spending for military procurement climbed steeply in 1940 in response to the stunning success of the Nazi blitzkrieg in Europe. As military contracting soared, the War Production Board made a policy decision to spread out defense installations and productive capacity to make bombing and a potential invasion more difficult. The South and West possessed the advantage of favorable weather for aircraft training facilities. Overall, an estimated 60 percent of the $74 billion wartime expenditures went into the 15 states of the Sunbelt at a time when those states contained less than 40 percent of the national population.[28]

The metropolitan areas of the South experienced the most rapid growth of any region. World War II jumpstarted the urbanization of the South and West by pulling thousands of workers into the cities in search of relatively well-paid industrial employment. In the three years between 1940 and 1943 the population of the metropolitan counties of the South grew by 4 percent and those of the West by 3 percent; by contrast, the metropolitan counties in the upper Midwest increased by only 2 percent and the northeastern metropolitan areas contracted by 0.6 percent.[29] Some cities, most of them located in the South and West, became overnight boomtowns. Between April 1940 and October 1941, 150,000 people poured into Los Angeles, which increased the city's population by a third. During the war years, San Diego's population shot up by 27 percent and Wichita, Kansas, by 20 percent.[30] The wartime boom taxed the housing stock, infrastructure, and public services in these cities to the breaking point.

Near the end of World War II, war production began to shift from heavy industry (tanks and guns) to high-tech weaponry such as missiles, jet airplanes, and sophisticated communications systems. All through the Cold War the nation's military spending remained high, and most of it went to the Sunbelt. One study showed a "definite regional shift" from the Northeast to the Sunbelt between 1950 and 1976 in the awarding of defense contracts.[31] During that period, the total number of defense employees in the nation increased by more than 35 percent; even so, their numbers fell by 3 percent in the 16 northeastern and upper Midwestern states.[32] By 1975, the defense budget contributed only 4 percent to personal incomes in the Northeast, compared to 9 percent in the states comprising the Sunbelt.[33]

Defense spending shifted to the Sunbelt not just because the region was an efficient location for some kinds of military production. For a long time, Democratic senators and representatives from the South had a lock on their seats because of uncontested one-party elections. Their long service in Congress gave them control of powerful committees because assignments were made on the basis of seniority. Congressional representatives from the South used their positions as committee chairs to steer defense spending and major infrastructure investments, such as dams and water projects, to their states and districts. Perhaps the best example is Mendell Rivers, who represented Charleston, South Carolina, for 40 years, from 1930 to 1970. As chair of the House Armed Services Committee, Rivers succeeded in getting the federal government to build in his hometown "an Army depot, a Marine Corps air base, a Marine boot camp, two Navy hospitals, a Navy shipyard, a Navy base, a Navy supply center, a Navy weapons center, a Navy submarine base, a Polaris missile base, two Air Force bases, and a federal housing development."[34] Because senators and representatives from more pluralistic and diverse Frostbelt districts usually served fewer terms in Congress before being defeated for reelection, they were not able to accumulate comparable seniority and congressional clout.[35]

Other federal spending programs also benefited the Sunbelt. Federal subsidies for highway building favored the Sunbelt because the long distances between cities and the larger size of metropolitan areas increased federal expenditures. Federal grants for the construction of sewer and water systems and for dams and water projects were also critically important to Sunbelt development. Some federal spending programs such as public employment programs and social welfare spending were biased toward the older industrial cities, but these did not tend to stimulate sustained economic development. By contrast, federal spending in the Sunbelt created permanent federal payrolls and infrastructure to support whole new industries, such as microelectronics. One of the most important ingredients of economic growth is a skilled labor force. The military actively recruited highly trained white-collar workers, engineers, and scientists to areas near Sunbelt military installations. Writing in the late 1980s, one scholar noted that "Every year the Department of Defense pays a number of companies a large sum of money to move college-educated (often at the public expense) engineers and scientists from the Midwest and other regions to the Southwest."[36]

In addition to direct spending, provisions in the federal tax code also favored the Sunbelt. In 1954, accelerated depreciation allowances deducted from corporate income taxes provided tax breaks for constructing new commercial and industrial structures but not for rehabilitating old buildings. Accelerated depreciation thus speeded up the flow of capital out of older industrial cities to suburban and Sunbelt locations.[37] Between 1954 and 1980, this subsidy was worth $30 billion in reduced taxes to corporations. The investment tax credit, which President Kennedy introduced in 1962, granted a dollar-for-dollar reduction in corporate taxes for investments in new plants and equipment. In this way the federal tax code encouraged companies to abandon older plants in the Frostbelt and build new plants in the Sunbelt. Between 1962 and 1981, this subsidy was worth $90 billion,[38] and in 1982 alone it was worth $20 billion.[39] A study conducted in the early 1980s of nine tax subsidies that promoted the mobility of investment (such as accelerated depreciation allowances on old plant and equipment and allowances for new equipment) found they were worth more than twice the total budget of the U.S. Department of Housing and Urban Development.[40]

Regional inequities in federal policy attracted the attention of public officials in the Midwest and Northeast. In June 1976, a group of governors formed the Coalition of Northeast Governors, and in September 1976 congressional representatives from 16 states formed the Northeast-Midwest Economic Advancement Coalition (today called the Northeast Midwest Institute). To counter the influence of the Frostbelt politicians, the Southern Growth Policy Board, which had been formed in 1971, stepped up its lobbying efforts.[41] Regional disparities in federal spending narrowed somewhat between 1975 and 1979,[42] but Ronald Reagan's election in 1980 decisively shifted the momentum the other way.[43] Once in office, Reagan sharply cut programs targeted to older central cities.[44] Between 1980 and 1987, grant programs of special importance to cities, such as mass transit, public housing, social welfare, and job training, were cut by 47 percent.[45] At the same time, his administration increased defense and highway programs that disproportionately benefited the Sunbelt.

The federal budget became a way to redistribute national resources from other regions of the country, in the process rewarding the constituencies that favored Republicans the most. Between 1983 and 1998, the citizens of just two states, New York and New Jersey, paid $500 billion more into the federal treasury than they received back in benefits.[46] In 1997, the citizens of nine southern and Border States paid $45 billion less in federal taxes than they paid into the federal treasury; in the same year, eight northern states paid an $82 billion surplus. Put simply, northern taxpayers subsidized much of the economic prosperity of the Sunbelt.

The Changing Politics of Sunbelt Cities

(Cleveland, Ohio rebranding downtown area)

Since the 1980s, the culture and the politics of Sunbelt cities have been undergoing a sea change. Only half a century ago, the South was an economically backward, generally poor region mired in a racist political tradition. The Southwest was an area of the country heavily dependent on military installations and agriculture, with a politics mainly devoted to securing more federal dollars for water projects and military bases. Today, from Florida to southern California, cities that have been growing rapidly since the 1950s are still on an upward trajectory. The population increases have been driven by the growth of services and high-tech industries, and the workers drawn to them; retirees; and a huge influx of immigrants, mainly from the Western Hemisphere. The politics of the Sunbelt have changed in step with these historic processes.

Before World War II, most Sunbelt cities were governed by caretaker governments presided over by politicians from long-established, sometimes prominent, families. The leadership structures looked a lot like party machines led by bosses or cliques that had been around for a long while, but in other respects they bore little resemblance to the turn-of-the-century machines of the northern cities. Working-class voters of the South were manipulated by scare-mongering about race and the alleged influence of outsiders. The political leadership of these cities wanted, above all, to protect local culture against change. Such organizations governed Tampa, Florida; San Antonio, Texas; and many other cities until well after World War II. New Orleans was run by a longtime machine, the Regular Democratic Organization, until de Lesseps S. Morrison was elected mayor in 1946.[47]

These tight-knit political machines were ill prepared for the changes set in motion by the defense buildup during World War II. After the war, a new generation of political activists came onto the scene. In city after city, "G.I. revolts" sprang up in which "bright young candidates marched against corrupt or inept city hall cliques under the banner of progress."[48] They appealed to middle-class voters who had few ties to the existing political establishment. Coalitions of white-collar professionals, business leaders, and growth-oriented city managers and bureaucrats came together to form business-dominated reform governments committed to modernization, new infrastructure, and growth.

This wave of reform transformed the political landscape throughout the Sunbelt, especially in cities of the Southwest. Between 1945 and 1955, San Antonio, Houston, Dallas, Oklahoma City, Albuquerque, Phoenix, and San Jose all adopted significant reforms, usually installing nonpartisan city-manager systems with at-large electoral arrangements.[49] These movements, instigated by such organizations as the Phoenix Charter Government Committee, the Albuquerque Citizens Committee, and San Antonio's Good Government League, were led by middle- and upper-class Anglo professionals and business leaders.

San Antonio produced a typical example of the Sunbelt version of municipal reform. In 1949, A. C. "Jack" White won the mayoralty with the support of good government reformers and the business community. It was not until 1951, however, that reformers put aside their disagreements and voted in a council-manager charter. Subsequently, the Good Government League began endorsing candidates. From 1955 to 1971, the league endorsed or recruited 77 out of San Antonio's 81 city council members. The Good Government League became the functional equivalent of a political party, a "sort of upper-middle-class political machine, officing not in Tammany Hall, but in a savings and loan association, whose electoral wonders are impressive to behold."[50]

The Good Government League succeeded in passing a series of bond referenda to finance infrastructure improvements to facilitate San Antonio's growth; for example, by 1986 the league had built a massive 98-mile freeway system within the city limits. It also sponsored urban renewal clearance and revitalization of the central business district and facilitated the construction of the HemisFair tourism and shopping project on 149 acres southeast of the Alamo. The HemisFair was a classic example of civic boosterism, with local government providing subsidies to a project that the private sector largely planned and operated.[51]

These postwar business-dominated coalitions campaigned for support from white middle-class voters, and minorities were as strictly excluded as they had been in the past. Over the years, whites had used various methods, both legal and extralegal, to discourage African Americans and Latinos from voting. The white primary, which kept blacks from casting ballots in Democratic primary elections, worked as an effective means of keeping blacks completely out of politics. In the southern states, the white primary was tantamount to disenfranchisement because where Democratic candidates always ran unopposed in general elections. In 1944, the U.S. Supreme Court struck down the white primary as a violation of the Fifteenth Amendment of the Constitution.[52]

Other methods continued to be used to dilute the electoral influence of blacks and Latinos. Many cities used at-large election districts to ensure that minority neighborhoods would be outvoted in the citywide totals. The 1965 Voting Rights Act, however, gave federal judges the power to strike down voting systems that systematically reduced minority representation. In 1975, the act was extended to Latinos. Both Houston and Dallas were forced to modify their at-large systems by adopting ward boundaries that would maximize representation for blacks and Latinos. Likewise, Los Angeles was forced to redraw its ward boundaries. Minority voters helped pass new city charters that provided for ward-based representation in San Antonio, Fort Worth, Albuquerque, San Francisco, Atlanta, Richmond, and several other cities.[53]

These measures began opening up political systems all across the Sunbelt, but even without reform the growing populations of African Americans and Latinos would have made political change impossible to resist. By 1990 blacks and Latinos made up a majority of the population in many cities in Florida and in a belt stretching from Texas to California, with Latinos outnumbering blacks about two to one. In Miami, more than 90 percent of the population was minority, compared to 60 percent in Los Angeles, Houston, and San Antonio. Minorities constituted more than 50 percent in most Sunbelt cities with populations of more than 500,000.

Minority populations in the suburbs of Sunbelt metropolitan areas shot upward in the 1990s—by more than 18 percent in the Fort Lauderdale area and by more than 11 percent in the Oakland, Las Vegas, Atlanta, San Jose, Houston, Orange County (California), Miami, and Dallas areas, among others.[54] Within Sunbelt areas, the biggest increases were in the suburbs. As a result of three decades of immigration, by the census of 2000 minorities made up at least 40 percent of the population of the suburbs in 20 metropolitan

TABLE 9.3 Suburban Minority Populations in Metro Areas with Population over 500,000 (Census of 2000)

Rank	Highest Suburban Minority Percentage		Lowest Suburban Minority Percentage	
	Metro Area[a]	Percentage	Metro Area[a]	Percentage
1	McAllen, TX	92%	Scranton, PA	3%
2	El Paso, TX	90	Fort Wayne, IN	4
3	Honolulu, HI	79	Knoxville, TN	5
4	Miami, FL	78.5	Syracuse, NY	5
5	Los Angeles, CA	69	Youngstown, OH	5.5
6	Jersey City, NJ	62.5	Indianapolis, IN	6
7	Albuquerque, NM	56	Akron, OH	6
8	Fresno, CA	55	Milwaukee, WI	6
9	Riverside, CA	53	Buffalo, NY	6
10	Bakersfield, CA	51.5	Albany, NY	6
11	Oakland, CA	48	Allentown, PA	6
12	Ventura, CA	45	Toledo, OH	7

[a]Several of the metropolitan areas list two or more central cities. In this table, they are identified only by the name of the first central city, as listed in alphabetical order by the Census Bureau.

Source: Adapted from William Frey, *Melting Pot Suburbs: A Census 2000 Study of Suburban Diversity* (Washington, DC: Center on Urban and Metropolitan Policy, Brookings Institution Press, June 2001), p. 5, Table 1.

areas in the Sunbelt. Table 9.3 shows that the urban areas with the highest proportions of minorities in the suburbs are located in the Sunbelt. Latinos accounted for 69 percent of the suburban population in the Los Angeles urban region by 2000, nearly 80 percent of the suburban population in the Miami and Honolulu areas, and 90 percent or more of the suburban populations of El Paso and McAllen, Texas.

By contrast, fewer minorities live in the suburbs of Frostbelt regions. In fact, in the middle-sized urban areas in the industrial belt—anchored by such cities as Scranton, Allentown, and Harrisburg, Pennsylvania; Youngstown, Akron, Toledo, and Columbus, Ohio; and Buffalo, Albany, and Rochester, New York—minority suburban populations are in the single digits. Clearly, the metropolitan areas of the Sunbelt owe much of their recent growth to a continuing stream of immigrants; by contrast, lower immigration rates partially explain the slow population increases of some of the urban regions in the North.

The number of African American and Latinos winning public office has kept pace with population change. Nationwide, the number of black elected officials increased from 1,469 in February 1970 to 9,040 in January 2000,[55] and to then 10,500 in 2011.[56] African Americans were elected mayors in some of the largest Sunbelt cities, including Los Angeles, New Orleans, Atlanta, and Birmingham, as well as in suburban and nonmetropolitan cities and counties. With about 20,000 Latino immigrants gaining citizenship and the right to vote each year, Hispanic gains have been especially dramatic, with the number of Hispanic public officials increasing from 3,147 in September 1985 to 5,205 in September 2000[57]; by 2008 the number was 5,240.[58] In the 1990s Hispanics were elected mayor in Miami, Denver, San Antonio, and many smaller cities.

The incorporation of minorities into the political systems of Sunbelt cities has brought significant policy change. Atlanta is a good example. African American mayors have governed Atlanta since 1973. The majority of the city council and of the school board is black, and blacks hold a majority of the key appointed and civil service positions in the city government. Under the city's first African American mayor, Maynard Jackson, the African American proportion of the police department rose from 19 to 35 percent in only four years, and complaints about police brutality fell.[59] The city established 24 neighborhood councils, each with professional staff, so that neighborhoods could influence city planning and development decisions. A preferential program begun under Jackson's first term raised the percentage of minority firms holding city contracts from one-tenth of 1 percent to 35 percent by 1988.[60]

Similar gains have been achieved in Birmingham, Alabama, and New Orleans, which have had African American mayors since 1979 and 1977, respectively. In both cities, political participation by minorities has increased significantly, and community organizations have become active in local politics. In both cities, police brutality, a major concern to blacks, has become less important as a policy issue.[61]

Hispanics have become incorporated into local political structures as well. In Miami, Hispanics have become the most important electoral constituency in the city because they are the largest population group and have become successful economically. In the 1990s, Hispanics succeeded in overturning at-large election systems that had disadvantaged them in Miami and surrounding counties. As a result, they have been able to win public offices at all levels, and Hispanics and African Americans have been well represented on boards and commissions and in public employment.[62] Similarly, African Americans and Hispanics have become powerful forces in the political system of Denver (a city with many Sunbelt characteristics). In 1983, with the election of Frederico Peña, Denver became the first American city without a Hispanic majority to elect a Hispanic mayor (at the time, 18 percent of Denver's population was Latino). After Peña's two terms, Wellington Webb was elected as the city's first black mayor at a time when blacks made up 11 percent of the city's population. Hispanics and blacks have become well represented on the city council and on city boards and commissions, in public employment, and on the civilian police board.[63]

Regional Convergence and National Politics

For a long time, scholars have predicted that the different regions of the nation would become increasingly similar.[64] At least to some degree their predictions have turned out to be accurate. Economic forces have diversified the economies as well as changed the demographic profiles of cities all over the nation. In the Frostbelt, corporate white-collar employment, services, and tourism have become critically important to urban regions and to downtown economies. Frostbelt metropolitan regions are less heavily blue collar and union than in the past, and central cities in the North have been attracting a significant proportion of affluent households. At the same time, many of the characteristics traditionally associated with older industrial cities—rapid immigration, concentrated poverty, and racial and ethnic conflict—have come to the cities of the Sunbelt. Cities all over the country are now multiracial and multiethnic.

Reflecting this convergence in demographics and politics, over time the public policies of cities have become more alike. Older industrial cities of all sizes have moved aggressively to become more "entrepreneurial" in their pursuit of business investment.[65] Accordingly, many of them have shifted resources away from social services and toward developmental programs that subsidize investment.[66] Large volumes of public money have been devoted to building facilities such as sports stadiums, convention centers, and redevelopment districts.[67] By investing in high-tech and corporate services and developing an infrastructure to support tourism and recreation, Frostbelt cities have become more like the cities of the Sunbelt.

Likewise, regional differences in voting behavior and party identification have become less extreme. In the past, the Sunbelt favored the Republican Party and pulled the country in a conservative direction. Recent research, however, shows that Democrats are gaining in metropolitan areas in both the North and the South, and in suburbs as well as central cities.[68] This trend is supported, in part, by immigration flows; African Americans, Latinos, and Asians, when combined, are about 75 percent Democratic. White-collar professionals, heavily concentrated in suburbs and in central cities with high-tech sectors, made up 21 percent of the electorate in 2000. They tend to be moderate on social issues and to support environmental protection, civil rights, and women's rights, and their numbers are rapidly growing throughout the Sunbelt. Notably, 54 percent of voters in the fastest-growing 50 counties in the nation—nearly all located in the Sunbelt—supported Al Gore in the 2000 election. In 2002 two scholars argued that these trends meant that an "emerging Democratic majority" was emerging in national politics.[69]

Their predictions seemed to come to fruition in the 2008 presidential election. A tier of southern states still went heavily Republican, but the electoral map showed big gains for the Democratic Party almost everywhere else. Four southern, four Midwestern, and three western states supported John McCain by more than 55 percent margins, while California, Nevada, Colorado, New Mexico, and Florida voted as blue states. Republicans made a big comeback in the congressional elections of 1910, but this happened in all regions of the country. Whatever utility the Sunbelt concept had in the past, in 2008 and 2010 it did not seem to explain the election result.

It would be tempting to interpret the Arizona anti-immigration law signed by Governor Jan Brewer on April 32, 2010, as a step backward to an earlier time in Sunbelt politics. Doubtlessly the law, which requires people to carry immigration papers and empowers police officers to determine immigration status, was motivated by deep resentments against not only illegal immigrants, but against all Hispanics in the state. Indeed, a June 2012 Huffington Post article asked: "Is Arizona the worst place in the country to be a Latina?"[70] Texas followed suit in June 2011, when the state Senate passed a bill giving police officers broad powers to ask those detained regarding their citizenship status. In fact, 2011 was a record year for anti-immigration legislation. Alabama, Georgia, Indiana, South Carolina and Utah all passed anti-immigration bills modeled after Arizona's 2010 law. Sunbelt states were no exception; from 2010 to 2011, all Sunbelt states passed at least one anti-immigration law, with the average number ranging between three and six laws.[71]

In other places, there was a strong reaction to these kinds of measures. On May 13, 2010, the Los Angeles city council passed a resolution banning the expenditure of any city funds for travel to Arizona. The debate over the resolution was highly emotional, with speakers mentioning the Holocaust and the World War II internment of Japanese Americans. From Miami to Los Angeles, cities with large Hispanic populations are sprinkled throughout the Sunbelt. Clearly, the Sunbelt—if there is any longer such a thing—does not speak with one voice, but with many.

The economic meltdown that began in the fall of 2008 put into question the vaunted economic advantages of the Sunbelt. More than anywhere else, much of the wealth of Sunbelt cities depends upon real estate and construction. These sectors were hit the hardest in the economic downturn, and as a result, the nation's highest home foreclosure rates and declines in housing values occurred in metropolitan areas of the South and Southwest: in the year from October 2007 to October 2008, housing values in Phoenix and Las Vegas fell by a third, compared to a decline in the New York region of 7.5 percent.[72] People in the Sunbelt must have been startled to see that after years of feeling sorry for those left behind in the frozen North, the shoe was on the other foot, at least for a time.

Endnotes

1. Robert Goodman, *The Last Entrepreneurs: America's Regional Wars for Jobs and Dollars* (New York: Simon & Schuster, 1979), p. 42.
2. Sudeep Reddy, "Latinos Fuel Growth in Decade," *The Wall Street Journal* (March 25, 2011), http://online.wsj.com/article/SB10001424052748704604704576220603247344790.html.
3. Alan Berube, "Racial and Ethnic Change in the Nation's Largest Cities," in *Redefining Urban & Suburban America: Evidence from Census 2000*, ed. Bruce Katz and Robert E. Lang (Washington, DC: Brookings Institution Press, 2003), p. 142.

4. John B. Judis and Ruy Teixeira, *The Emerging Democratic Majority* (New York: Scribner/A Lisa Drew Book, 2002).

5. Kevin P. Phillips, *The Emerging Republican Majority* (New Rochelle, NY: Arlington House, 1969).

6. Prompting the famous headline, "Ford to City: Drop Dead!" *New York Daily News* (October 29, 1975), p. 1.

7. Kirkpatrick Sale, *Power Shift: The Rise of the Southern Rim and Its Challenge to the Eastern Establishment* (New York: Random House, 1975).

8. "The Second War between the States," *Business Week* (May 17, 1976).

9. Quoted in Carl Abbott, *The New Urban America: Growth and Politics in Sunbelt Cities* (Chapel Hill: University of North Carolina Press, 1987), p. 6.

10. Sale, *Power Shift*, p. 11.

11. Bernard Weinstein and Harold Gross, interview quoted in Abbott, *The New Urban America* p. 4.

12. Bruce J. Schulman, *From Cotton Belt to Sunbelt: Federal Policy, Economic Development, and the Transformation of the South, 1938–1980* (New York: Oxford University Press, 1991), Chapter 2.

13. Abbott, *The New Urban America*, p. 22.

14. Quoted in David R. Goldfield and Howard N. Rabinowitz, "The Vanishing Sunbelt," in *Searching for the Sunbelt: Historical Perspectives on a Region*, ed. Raymond A. Mohl (Knoxville: University of Tennessee Press, 1990), p. 224.

15. Ibid., p. 231.

16. William H. Frey, "Metropolitan America: Beyond the Transition," *Population Bulletin* 45, no. 2 (July 1990): 14.

17. U.S. Bureau of the Census, *Statistical Abstract of the United States, 1980*, 101st ed. (Washington, DC: U.S. Government Printing Office, 1981), p. 10; U.S. Bureau of the Census, *Statistical Abstract of the United States, 1992*, 112th ed. (Washington, DC: U.S. Government Printing Office, 1992), p. 22.

18. U.S. Bureau of the Census, *Statistical Abstract of the United States, 1992*, p. 22.

19. David Rusk, *Cities without Suburbs* (Washington, DC: Woodrow Wilson Center Press, 1993).

20. Timothy Egan, "Urban Sprawl Strains Western States," *New York Times* (December 29, 1996), p. 6.

21. Rusk, *Cities without Suburbs*.

22. Haya El Nasser and Paul Overberg, "Slump Stunts Sun Belt Growth," *USA Today* (July 7, 2010), http://www.usatoday.com/news/nation/census/2010-06-22-census_N.htm.

23. Edward M. Burmila, "The Electoral College after Census 2010 and 2020: The Political Impact of Population Growth and Redistribution," *Perspectives on Politics* 7, no. 4 (December 2009): 839.

24. For a thorough analysis of the growth of the Sunbelt that emphasizes economic and technological factors, see John D. Kasarda, "The Implications of Contemporary Redistribution Trends for National Urban Policy," *Social Science Quarterly* 61, no. 3 (December 1980): 373–400.

25. Raymond Arsenault, "The End of the Long Hot Summer: The Air Conditioner and Southern Culture," in *Searching for the Sunbelt*, ed. Mohl, pp. 176–211.

26. Kirkpatrick Sale, "Six Pillars of the Southern Rim," in *The Fiscal Crisis of American Cities*, ed. Roger E. Alcaly and David Mermelstein (New York: Random House, Vintage Books, 1977), p. 174.

27. Ann R. Markusen, *Regions: The Economics and Politics of Territory* (Totowa, NJ: Rowman and Littlefield, 1987), p. 113.
28. Sale, "Six Pillars of the Southern Rim," p. 170.
29. Phillip J. Funigiello, *The Challenge to Urban Liberalism, Federal-City Relations during World War II* (Knoxville: University of Tennessee Press, 1978), pp. 12–13.
30. Abbott, *The New Urban America*, p. 103.
31. Maureen McBreen, "Regional Trends in Federal Defense Expenditures: 1950–76," in *Selected Essays on Patterns of Regional Change: The Changes, the Federal Role, and the Federal Response*, submitted by Senator Henry Bellmon to the Senate Committee on Appropriations (Washington, DC: U.S. Government Printing Office, 1977), p. 527.
32. A report issued by the Northeast-Midwest Economic Advancement Coalition, cited in Edward C. Burks, "16 Northeast and Midwest States Find Inequities in Defense Outlays," *New York Times* (September 22, 1977).
33. Richard S. Morris, *Bum Rap on America's Cities: The Real Causes of Urban Decline* (Upper Saddle River, NJ: Prentice Hall, 1978), pp. 148–149.
34. Sale, *Power Shift*, p. 149.
35. Since the early 1970s, both parties have permitted exceptions to the seniority rule, and the power of committee chairs has been reduced.
36. Ann R. Markusen, "Regional Planning and Policy: An Essay on the American Exception," Working Paper No. 9 (Brunswick, NJ: Center for Urban Policy Research, Rutgers University, July 1989).
37. See George Peterson, "Federal Tax Policy and Urban Development," in *Central City Economic Development*, ed. Benjamin Chinitz (Cambridge, MA: Abt Books, 1979), pp. 67–78.
38. Michael I. Luger, "Federal Tax Incentives as Industrial and Urban Policy," in *Sunbelt/Snowbelt: Urban Development and Regional Restructuring*, ed. Larry Sawers and William K. Tabb (New York: Oxford University Press, 1984), pp. 204–205.
39. John F. Witte, "The Growth and Distribution of Tax Expenditures," in *The Distributional Impacts of Public Policies*, ed. Sheldon H. Danziger and Kent E. Portney (New York: St. Martin's Press, 1988), p. 179.
40. Peter Marcuse, "The Targeted Crisis: On the Ideology of the Urban Fiscal Crisis and Its Causes," *International Journal of Urban and Regional Research* 5, no. 3 (1981): 339.
41. See Markusen, *Regions*, Chapter 8. The Southern Growth Policy Board relinquished its federal monitoring activities to the Congressional Sunbelt Council in January 1981.
42. "Neutral Federal Policies Are Reducing Frostbelt-Sunbelt Spending Imbalances," *National Journal* (February 7, 1981), pp. 233–236.
43. For evidence on the Sunbelt bias in direct federal military expenditures during the Reagan administration, see the data compiled in the *New York Times* (December 20, 1983), cited in Michael Peter Smith, *City, State, and Market: The Political Economy of Urban Society* (New York: Blackwell, 1988), p. 57.
44. Harold Wolman, "The Reagan Urban Policy and Its Impacts," *Urban Affairs Quarterly* 21, no. 3 (March 1986): 311–336.
45. Peggy L. Cuciti, "A Nonurban Policy: Recent Public Policy Shifts Affecting Cities," in *The Future of National Urban Policy*, ed. Marshall Kaplan and Franklin James (Durham, NC: Duke University Press, 1990), p. 243.
46. Thad Williamson, David Imbroscio, and Gar Alparovitz, *Making a Place for Community: Local Democracy in a Global Era* (New York: Routledge, 2002), p. 56.

47. See Gary Mormino, "Tampa: From Hell Hole to the Good Life," in *Sunbelt Cities: Politics and Growth Since World War II*, ed. Richard M. Bernard and Bradley R. Rice (Austin: University of Texas Press, 1983), pp. 138–161; and Abbott, *The New Urban America*.
48. Abbott, *The New Urban America*, p. 247.
49. Amy Bridges, "Politics and Growth in Sunbelt Cities," in *Searching for the Sunbelt*, ed. Mohl, p. 2.
50. Robert L. Lineberry, *Equality and Urban Policy: The Distribution of Municipal Public Services* (Beverly Hills, CA: Sage, 1977), pp. 55–56, quoting Abbott, *The New Urban America*, p. 139.
51. Our account of San Antonio's business-dominated reform movement relies on Abbott, *The New Urban America*.
52. *Smith v. Allwright*, 321 U.S. 649 (1944). See the discussion in V. O. Key, *Politics, Parties, and Pressure Groups*, 5th ed. (New York: Crowell, 1964), p. 607.
53. Abbott, *The New Urban America*, p. 217.
54. William Frey, *Melting Pot Suburbs: A Census 2000 Study of Suburban Diversity* (Washington, DC: Center for Urban and Metropolitan Policy, Brookings Institution Press, June 2001), p. 8.
55. Joint Center for Political and Economic Studies, *Black Elected Officials: A Statistical Summary, 2001* (April 2001), p. 250, www.jointcenter.org/databank/graphs/99beo.pdf.
56. *Roster of Latino Elected Officials* (Washington, DC: National Association of Hispanic Elected and Appointed Officials, annual).
57. Ibid., citing original source as *National Roster of Latino Elected Officials* (Washington, DC: National Association of Hispanic Elected and Appointed Officials, annual).
58. U.S. Bureau of the Census. *Hispanic Public Elected Officials by Office, 1985 to 2008, and State, 2008*. Table 421.
59. Michael Leo Owens and Michael J. Rich, "Is Strong Incorporation Enough? Black Empowerment and the Fate of Atlanta's Low-Income Blacks," in *Racial Politics in American Cities*, 3rd ed., ed. Rufus P. Browning, Dale Rogers Marshall, and David H. Tabb (New York: Longman, 2003), pp. 209–210.
60. Timothy Bates and Darrell Williams, "Preferential Procurement Programs and Minority-Owned Business," *Journal of Urban Affairs* 17, no. 1 (1995): 1.
61. Huey L. Perry, "The Evolution and Impact of Biracial Coalition and Black Mayors in Birmingham and New Orleans," in *Racial Politics*, ed. Browning, Marshall, and Tabb, pp. 228–254.
62. Christopher L. Warren and Dario V. Moreno, "Power without a Program: Hispanic Incorporation in Miami," in *Racial Politics*, ed. Browning, Marshall, and Tabb, pp. 281–306.
63. Rodney E. Hero and Susan E. Clarke, "Latinos, Blacks, and Multiethnic Politics in Denver: Realigning Power and Influence in the Struggle for Equality," in *Racial Politics*, ed. Browning, Marshall, and Tabb, pp. 309–330.
64. Theodore J. Lowi, "The State of Cities in the Second Republic," *Fiscal Retrenchment and Urban Policy*, ed. J. P. Blair and D. Nachmias (Beverly Hills, CA: Sage, 1979), pp. 43–54; John H. Mollenkopf, *The Contested City* (Princeton, NJ: Princeton University Press, 1983); Paul Kantor, *The Dependent City Revisited: The Political Economy of Urban Development and Social Policy* (Boulder, CO: Westview Press, 1995).
65. Peter K. Eisinger, *The Rise of the Entrepreneurial State: State and Local Economic Development Policy in the United States* (Madison: University of Wisconsin Press, 1988).

66. For evidence of this shift, see Kenneth K. Wong, *City Choices: Education and Housing* (Albany: State University of New York Press, 1990), p. 16.
67. Dennis R. Judd, ed., *The Infrastructure of Play: Building the Tourist City* (Armonk, NY: M. E. Sharpe, 2003).
68. Judis and Teixeira, *The Emerging Democratic Majority.*
69. Ibid.
70. Jessica Gonzales-Rojas, "Is Arizona the Worst Place in the Country to Be a Latina?" *Huffington Post* (June 20, 2010), http://www.huffingtonpost.com/jessica-gonzalezrojas/arizona-worst-for-latinas_b_1612776.html.
71. Ian Gordon and Tasneem Raja. "164 Anti-Immigration Laws Passed Since 2010? A MoJo Analysis," *Mother Jones* (March 1, 2010), http://m.motherjones.com/politics/2012/03/anti-immigration-law-database.
72. Richard Florida, "How the Crash Will Reshape America," *The Atlantic* (March 2009), p. 54.

PART III

The Fractured Metropolis

CHAPTER 10

The Rise of the Fragmented Metropolis

Metropolitan Turf Wars

A deeply ingrained distrust of cities has long been an important feature of American culture. Only a few years after the Constitution was ratified, Thomas Jefferson wrote, "I view great cities as pestilential to the morals, the health, and the liberties of man."[1] In the 1970s, John V. Lindsay, the former mayor of New York, observed that "in the American psychology, the city has been a basically suspect institution."[2] Although the harshest judgments have slowly melted away, a distrust of urban life has persisted despite the fact that, according to the 2000 census, 80 percent of Americans live in metropolitan areas.[3] But it is unclear what it means to observe that America is an urban nation. Residents of Phoenix or Dallas may feel they have little in common with residents of New York City or Boston, or even with the city just a few miles away. The feeling of separation is one of the important effects of the fragmented American metropolis.

Even before the suburban movements of the twentieth century, people living in the cities were sorting themselves out into different neighborhoods. Suburbanization accentuated this tendency in two respects: it increased the geographic distances between social and ethnic groups, and it gave the residents of the more privileged neighborhoods a set of tools for excluding racial and ethnic groups they considered undesirable. Suburban governments employed a variety of means to protect themselves from unwanted change. Early in the twentieth century, zoning laws emerged as the principle device for preserving land values and maintaining social class and racial segregation. A sharp separation among residential areas was also enforced by developers, who routinely imposed deed restrictions forbidding property owners from selling to blacks and other groups they deemed to be a threat to property values. It took decades, but eventually deed restrictions were overturned by the courts. Zoning laws, however, have continued largely unchanged, and suburban governments still use them as a means of determining patterns of development.

If they have the choice, suburban jurisdictions try to attract mainly affluent homeowners and the kinds of economic development that contribute positively to the local tax base. This calculus sets up an intensely competitive metropolitan game that often pits one local government against another. People living in suburbs with high property values and/or plenty of business investment are able to pay lower taxes even while they enjoy higher levels of public services than the residents of poorer municipalities. In the past, central cities were disadvantaged in this game, and as a consequence they became "the receptacle for all the functions the suburbs [did] not care to support."[4] Originally, the strategies used by suburbs to maintain residential segregation were aimed specifically at minorities, new immigrants, and the poor, most of whom remained clustered in decayed neighborhoods in central cities and, sometimes, in nearby older suburbs. But with the rise of multiethnic suburbs in the 1980s, the metropolitan turf wars have become more complicated. In many urban regions, higher-income residents have been moving to the historic central city even while some older suburbs have attracted poor people and waves of foreign immigrants. These movements have had the predictable consequence of keeping the metropolitan game, and the metropolitan fragmentation that it sustains, very much alive.

Recently, the strategies used by municipalities to attract affluent residents and "higher" land uses have been reinforced by the privatization and walling off of residential developments. By creating privately governed common interest developments (CIDs), homeowners are able to escape many of the burdens of the public realm altogether. Gated communities have become ubiquitous in all urban areas in all regions of the country. Surrounded, as they often are, by a perimeter of walls, fences, or other barriers, they have the effect of segmenting urban populations to a finer degree than was possible through the policies imposed by suburban governments. The effect they exert on metropolitan politics and geographic patterns is still evolving, but certainly they possess the potential to create an urban landscape that is, in key respects, even more fragmented than in the past.

OUTTAKE

There Is a Debate about Gated Communities

The proliferation of gated communities (perhaps more accurately called *common interest developments,* or *CIDs*) is fragmenting the urban landscape into a mosaic of publicly governed municipalities and privatized residential enclaves. A lively debate is being fought over the question: Is privatized government a good or a bad thing? Arguments on each side of the issue should be considered.

One of the points Evan McKenzie makes in his groundbreaking book,

Privatopia, is that gated communities constitute a strategy for segregating affluent urban residents from those who rely upon public services. He maintains that CIDs facilitate a "gradual secession" of the affluent from the political and social life of cities, potentially making them "financially untenable for the many and socially unnecessary for the few." He points out that the homogeneous populations that make up most CIDs also undermine any sense of shared social responsibility. Sheryll Cashin echoes this sentiment when she notes that residents of CIDs "tend to view themselves as taxpayers rather than citizens, and they often perceive local property taxes as a fee for services they should receive rather than their contribution to services local government must provide to the community as a whole." This change in perspective has consequences: private security guards replace police, and walled-off recreation areas replace community centers and swimming pools.

CIDs have defenders, too. Robert H. Nelson argues that they make it possible for residents to "protect their own neighborhood environment, and also provide a wider range of choice for new residents in search of a neighborhood physical and social environment corresponding to their own individual preferences." In his view, privately governed associations respect one of the most basic rights of human liberty, the right of free association. He maintains that homogeneity within individual neighborhoods is not necessarily a bad thing, since it is based upon the freedom to associate: "the special case of race aside, the right of a neighborhood association to discriminate among potential new unit owners should be

protected as a basic matter of defending the right of freedom of association under the U.S. Constitution."

Gated communities, common interest developments, or whatever we wish to call them, are becoming the norm in America's metropolitan regions. They are here to stay. As a result, in the next few years, the debate is likely to shift toward a middle ground, involving questions such as whether to compel neighborhood associations to respect constitutional rights and rules of procedural democracy. To this end, one scholar has proposed a bill of rights for private residential government. This might be an effective remedy for the rights of people living within CIDs, but it would not reduce the spatial fragmentation of metropolitan areas.

Sources: Evan McKenzie, *Privatopia: Home-owner Associations and the Rise of Residential Private Government* (New Haven, CT: Yale University Press, 1994), p. 186; Sheryll D. Cashin, "Privatized Communities and the 'Secession of the Successful': Democracy and Fairness beyond the Gate," *Fordham Urban Law Journal* 28 (2001): 1679; Robert H. Nelson, *Private Neighborhoods and the Transformation of Local Government* (Washington, DC: The Urban Institute Press, 2005), pp. 260–261, 400; Susan F. French, "The Constitution of a Private Residential Government Should Include a Bill of Rights," *Wake Forest Law Review* 27 (1992): 345–352.

How the Suburbs Became Segregated

Many narrative threads make up the story of how American suburbs became fragmented into a patchwork of segregated neighborhoods, subdivisions, and independent suburban jurisdictions. There is, to begin with, a cultural explanation: beginning in the early years of the Republic, Americans nurtured a negative attitude toward cities, and this antiurban bias was reinforced by the concentration of immigrants in cities during the nineteenth century and the massive demographic movements of the twentieth century. There is an economic interpretation, too, that stresses the material benefits that the residents of suburban jurisdictions realized by gaining control of local tax and spending policies. A third explanation, which we treat in this section, links the rise of the suburbs to the actions of developers who found residential segregation to be an effective marketing strategy for selling their product. Which came first: consumer preferences, or marketing? There may be no definitive answer to this question, but it is worth pondering nevertheless.

Clearly, there has been a popular preference for suburban living for a long time. The pent-up demand for housing coincided with new government policies to promote homeownership. Never before had it been so easy to secure a loan. In 1934, Congress created the Federal Housing Authority to ensure the home loans made by banks. The legislation was followed in 1944 by a law authorizing the Veterans Administration to make loans to returning veterans for no money down and for long amortization periods. These policies made it possible for millions of middle-class families to buy homes even if they had few savings—or none at all, in the case of returning veterans. The new homebuyers eagerly seized the opportunity to move out of overcrowded urban neighborhoods.

Federal policies and the real estate industry powerfully shaped the attitudes that favored suburban life. The policies of FHA (Federal Housing Administration) and VA (Veterans Administration) administrators and bank loan officers encouraged builders to promote construction almost exclusively outside the cities. In this sense, it may be said that the suburbs were created first by developers and the housing industry, and only later by the preferences of buyers. Developers influenced the character of the suburbs by selecting the clientele that could best supply profits, and by molding the tastes and preferences of potential buyers. Realtors, developers, and financial institutions aggressively marketed the suburbs because new housing construction maximized their profitability and it was easier to do than the rehabilitation of older neighborhoods.[5] Developers were quick to realize that an enormous market had been opened up, and they seized the opportunity. Within a few years, big development firms became the frontline agents that shaped the development of the suburban subdivisions that quickly spread across the urban landscape. As one scholar observed:

> The plain fact is that . . . the main force in our process of urban development is the private developer. The primacy of the bulldozer in transforming rural land to urban uses, the capacity of the private company to build thousands of homes on quiet rolling hills is a predominant fact of American urban life.[6]

What the developers put in place during the suburban boom of the postwar years became the foundation for the pattern of settlement that still exists in America's urban areas.

To market the houses they built, developers promised not only a home but also an entire way of life. They were not merely the builders of houses; they were "community builders" interested in shaping the character of entire neighborhoods.[7] In their attempt to market the new subdivisions, developers virtually invented an iconic image of the American dream—the suburban house. The suburbs were promoted as ways to achieve instant social status, escape the problems of the cities, and live in a closely regulated social environment. Thus, the suburbs became sharply differentiated from the cities, both in people's minds and in reality. Developers were careful to target the potential homeowners who could add to their bottom line. This strategy proved to be especially effective for the developers of exclusive subdivisions, who found that the bigger the house and the higher the income of buyers, the more money they could make.

One of the first and most influential of the community builders was Jesse Clyde Nichols, who pioneered the concept of planning entire communities decades before it became common practice. Born on a farm close to Kansas City, Kansas, Nichols attended the University of Kansas and later studied economics at Harvard. In 1900, Nichols took a trip to Europe, where he admired the beauty and grandeur of European cities. He saw no reason why cities in the United States could not be even more majestic than the cities of Europe. In 1905, Nichols began buying up land southwest of downtown Kansas City, where he intended to build and sell top-market residences.

Nichols was different from the typical small-time real estate operator, or "curbstoner," who bought a few small parcels of land on the edge of the city, divided them into lots, and hoped to make a speculative profit. Nichols believed in a scientific approach to land development. In a speech before a real estate convention in 1912, Nichols attracted national attention by criticizing those small-time land developers who went for the fast sale and the quick profit. Instead, he advocated a more comprehensive approach. He shocked his contemporaries by arguing that planning was not only compatible with private profit but could actually increase profits over the long run. As he later put it in a landmark article on suburban shopping centers, "good planning is good business."[8] Over the years, Nichols became a persuasive advocate for planned suburban development. He was a leader in the National Association of Real Estate Boards (NAREB), and in 1935 he founded the Urban Land Institute (ULI), which is influential in the housing industry to this day. In his lifetime, he saw the private planning he pioneered become public policy through local subdivision regulations, zoning laws, and federal loan guarantee programs.

Nichols put his principles into practice by developing the Country Club District on the edge of Kansas City, considered by many at the time to be the most beautiful suburb in the nation. Nichols appealed to his wealthy clientele with extraordinary aesthetics—he modeled the suburb's shopping center, the first in the nation, on the architecture of Seville, Spain. Nichols also applied the latest in household technology, such as piped gas and electric service, in a period when servants were becoming less common. Nichols's suburban houses promised to provide a secure haven far from the stresses and tensions of city life. Husbands could go off to work in the city secure in the knowledge that their wives and children were safe in the idyllic environment of the Country Club District.

Nichols's projects were strictly limited to affluent homeowners. To guarantee that his development would remain an exclusive preserve long after he completed his work, Nichols devised the self-perpetuating deed restriction, which required owners to follow requirements laid down by the developer.[9] The deed restrictions specified minimum lot sizes, minimum cost for houses, setbacks from the street, and even the color and style of houses. And the deeds specified that the houses could be bought by and sold to whites only.[10] These restrictions became an important marketing tool because they promised to protect exclusivity and secure property values.

Until the years after World War II, developments like those built by Nichols were available mainly to the upper middle class homebuyers. This began to change in the postwar years. In the late 1930s, Levitt & Sons succeeded as a medium-sized developer of plain tract housing for upper-middle-class families leaving New York City for Long Island, but the company's big break came during World War II, when it won contracts to build thousands of houses for the U.S. Navy around Norfolk, Virginia. It is here that the Levitts worked on the mass-production techniques that revolutionized home building throughout the United States. Within a few years after the war, the firm founded by William J. Levitt, his father Abraham, and his brother Alfred became the largest home builder in the United States.

Unlike Nichols, William Levitt drifted into building houses. Caring little for school, Levitt dropped out of New York University after his third year because, as he put it in a *Time* magazine cover story, "I got itchy. I wanted to make money. I wanted a big car and a lot of clothes."[11] In 1936, after he passed through several jobs, Levitt and his father decided to build a house on a Long Island lot they had been unable to sell. They made a profit. From this small beginning, Levitt launched his extraordinary career.

The Levitts quietly began buying up land from Long Island farmers and building inexpensive homes by using assembly-line methods. The basic process involved laying a concrete slab for a foundation, erecting preassembled walls, then tying the structure together with a roof trucked to the site. The Levitts broke down the complex process of building a house into 26 operations, and then assigned each step to a separate contractor. Because each contractor did the same job over and over again, it was possible to achieve incredible speed.[12] Levitt avoided unions and used piecework incentives to speed the process even more.[13] At the Levitt lumberyard, one man was able to cut parts for 10 houses in one day.[14] By 1950, the firm was producing one house every 16 minutes.[15] By preassembling as many components as possible, Levitt reduced the amount of skilled labor necessary on the job site, and by purchasing directly from the manufacturers, he eliminated middlemen's fees. Overall, Levitt was able to build a typical house for about $6,000, an affordable amount even for some working-class families.[16]

Between 1947 and 1951, the Levitts converted 4,000 acres of potato farms in Hempstead, Long Island, into the largest housing development in the nation's history.[17] Ultimately housing 82,000 residents, Levittown, as it came to be known, became a huge success. Because of the huge pent-up demand for inexpensive housing following World War II, in the first years people lined up and camped out for days waiting to purchase one of the homes. The basic Cape Cod model sold for $7,990. With federal guarantees for the loan and no down payment required for veterans, an ex-GI could buy a Levitt house for only $56 a month.[18]

Like Nichols, Levitt believed that tight controls over buyers and their behavior were the best way to guarantee rising real estate values. Restrictive covenants required the grass to be cut each week (if not done, one of Levitt's men would cut it and send a bill) and disallowed fences (but allowed hedges). Laundry could not be hung out on a clothesline. In addition, the covenants barred tenants or homeowners from selling to or even allowing their property to be used by blacks. The standard lease for the first homes in Levittown, in which the tenant had an option to buy, contained this language: "The tenant agrees not to permit the premises to be used or occupied by any person other than members of the Caucasian race. But the employment and maintenance of other than Caucasian domestic servants shall be permitted."[19] Levitt argued that economic realities required him to recognize that "most whites prefer not to live in mixed communities,"[20] but his determination to enforce his racial prejudices went beyond mere economics; he evicted two tenants who had allowed black children to play in their homes.[21] In 1960, not a single black family lived in Levittown,[22] and even 30 years later only about one-fourth of 1 percent of its residents were African American.[23]

In the mid-1950s, Levitt decided to build two more Levittowns, one in Pennsylvania and one in New Jersey. Opened in October 1958 and finished in 1965, Levittown, New Jersey, provided several new features. Fearing that an unfavorable image of sterile uniformity would damage sales, the company offered several house styles and floor plans. The idea of mixing styles was offered by William Levitt's wife and implemented by him over the objections of his executives.[24] Levitt did not offer changes from a standardized model to provide more aesthetically pleasing suburban residential areas. His motives were strictly economic; in order to sell houses, he needed to ensure that the houses would continue to appeal to the aspiring middle class.

Levitt attracted purchasers by other means as well. Long-term financing with low monthly payments was made possible through the firm. He also carefully selected the buyers by excluding applicants who did not conform to middle-class values in conduct and appearance. All homes were designed for families with young children. Advertisements stressed that it was a planned community with schools, churches, swimming pools, and parks. In all of these respects, the Levitt company constructed the kind of community that fit the developer's ideas about suburban life. If middle-class homebuyers wanted something different, they would have been hard put to find any other places to live, at least in the suburbs.

Levitt's fortunes began to change in 1968 when he sold his development company to the International Telephone and Telegraph Corporation (ITT) for $60 million in ITT stock. Soon after the sale, the stock, which he used as collateral for loans, plunged in value. Because of a clause in his sales contract, Levitt was forbidden to renew his building activities for 10 years, except in cities where ITT had no interest. Levitt invested $20 million in a project in Iran, but the new government took it over after the 1979 revolution. In 1987, at the age of 80, Levitt was forced to declare bankruptcy and was evicted from his New York City offices.[25]

The careers of Nichols and Levitt demonstrate the power of private developers to shape the suburbs to fit their own tastes and attitudes. Residential segregation on the basis of incomes and lifestyles was a natural result of the logic of profitability and marketing. These observations may be applied to contemporary suburbs as well. Whether a developer builds luxury single-family homes, townhouses for young middle-class homebuyers, condominiums for singles, or a gated community, the character of the community that results will reflect the developers' business plan. Buyers choose their environment before they move, but once they have decided where they are going to live, they "are very largely prisoners of that environment with but little opportunity of changing it."[26]

The Imperative of Racial Segregation

The rise of the twentieth-century American suburb went hand in hand with a cultural imperative of racial segregation. The precedents for segregation enforced by social custom, law, and the policies of the housing industry were established very early, and by the time these practices were abandoned in the late 1970s, a metropolitan land use landscape of racial segregation had become basically fixed.

Beginning in the early twentieth century, restrictive covenants became the main instrument used by the real estate industry to enforce racial segregation. When a buyer purchased a house, the deed often came with a printed covenant that restricted its subsequent sale. Typically, blacks were identified as a restricted group on the back of the deed, but sometimes Jews and "consumptives" (anyone with tuberculosis) were also be named. Restrictive covenants became, in effect, governmental policy when the supreme courts of 14 states upheld their legality and ruled they could be enforced in the courts.[27] It is estimated that restrictive covenants applied to homes sold in half of the subdivisions built in the United States before 1948, when the U.S. Supreme Court ruled they could not be enforced in courts of law.[28]

The National Association of Real Estate Boards (NAREB) was established in 1908 to represent the interests of builders and real estate agents. Everyone involved in the housing business accepted as a fundamental principle that the value of property was connected to the homogeneity of neighborhoods. Based on this premise, the NAREB "racialized" land use in urban areas by promoting the idea that whites and blacks must be strictly segregated.[29] From 1924 until 1950, Article 34 of the Realtors' national code (circulated to realtors everywhere by the NAREB) read, "A Realtor should never be instrumental in introducing into a neighborhood a character of property or occupancy, members of any race or nationality, or any individual whose presence will clearly be detrimental to property values in the neighborhood."[30]

To enforce this policy, local real estate boards issued written codes of ethics prohibiting members from introducing "detrimental" minorities into white neighborhoods. The textbooks and training materials used in real estate training courses took care to emphasize that real estate agents were ethically bound to promote homogeneous neighborhoods. The leading textbook used in such courses in the 1940s compared some ethnic groups to termites eating away at sound structures:

> The tendency of certain racial and cultural groups to stick together, making it almost impossible to assimilate them in the normal social organism, is too well known to need much comment. But in some cases the result is less detrimental than in others. The Germans, for example, are a clean and thrifty people. . . . Unfortunately this cannot be said of all the other nations which have sent their immigrants to our country. Some of them have brought standards and customs far below our own levels. . . . Like termites, they undermine the structure of any neighborhood into which they creep.[31]

Any real estate agent found breaking the code by selling to members of the wrong groups was subject to loss of license and expulsion from the local board. Even brokers who were not affiliated with the national association felt compelled to accept the Realtors' guidelines because most of their business depended upon referrals.

In 1948, in the case of *Shelly v. Kraemer*, the U.S. Supreme Court ruled that racially restrictive covenants violated the Fourteenth Amendment's guarantee of equal protection of the law, and that they could not therefore be enforced in the courts.[32] Despite the ruling covenants sometimes continued to be written, but now they were enforced not by the courts, but by pressure exerted by realtors, developers, homeowner associations, and neighbors. Banks refused to make loans to blacks trying to buy in white neighborhoods; in any case, realtors refused to show them the homes. The suburbs did not begin opening up to blacks until Congress passed the 1968 Housing Act, which barred racial discrimination in the sale and rental of housing.

By the time the housing act became law, patterns of racial segregation had already been firmly established, and they would have been hard to change even if racial discrimination, by some act of magic, had disappeared overnight. Change was also made more difficult because of the rise of common interest developments, which proved to be a remarkably efficient device for preserving the social-class uniformity of new housing developments. When homebuyers purchase a home in a CID, they automatically agree to abide by a list of restrictions on the use of their property. They also pay fees for their share in the cost and maintenance of services and amenities held "in common" (thus the term "common interest") with other residents. The "community" of homeowners is governed by a homeowner's association, which is responsible for enforcing the long list of covenants, contracts, and restrictions (CC&Rs). Such rules can be used to enforce the homogeneity of neighborhoods even more effectively than restrictive covenants, with one principal exception—they cannot be used explicitly to sort out buyers on the basis of race, ethnicity, or gender.

The number of CIDs, which includes cooperative apartments, condominiums, and single-family housing developments, exploded from fewer than 500 in 1964 to 10,000 by 1970 and to 150,000 by 1992, when 32 million Americans lived within them.[33] CIDs were concentrated especially in the Sunbelt, with California,

Florida, and Texas leading the way. All through the Sunbelt, large numbers of retired people moved into gated communities. By 2005, 54.6 million people lived in 274,000 developments governed by homeowner associations.[34] In many metropolitan areas, they have become so common that new homebuyers who do not want to live in one will find it hard to find a house anywhere else. Since 2000, 80 percent of all homes built in the United States are governed by homeowner associations that administer privately provided amenities.[35]

CIDs became the main device used by developers to become "community builders" in the tradition of Jesse Clyde Nichols. The CC&Rs that homebuyers agreed to were drawn up by the developer before the first resident moved in. Developers could point to the CC&Rs to reassure homebuyers that the future of their investment was secured against unwanted change. The CID mechanism also solved a pressing problem that immediately threatened developers' profits. By the late 1950s, suburbia had become synonymous with low-density tract housing, an equation that reflected the developers' success in marketing the suburbs as an escape from the cities. By the 1960s, however, this version of the suburban dream began to yield lower profits because the market for single houses constructed on individual lots was diminishing. Perceptive developers realized that there were huge demographic and income groups, such as retirees and young singles and married couples without children, which remained as vast untapped markets.

The problem for developers was that by the 1960s, the constantly rising price of suburban land meant that they could build homes affordable for the middle class only if they could achieve much higher densities than before. Accordingly, the housing industry initiated a campaign to market a revised version of the suburban dream that would include row houses and apartment buildings. Almost overnight, attached housing, which developers had always associated with inner-city neighborhoods, became desirable. By the late 1960s, the American Society of Planning Officials, the ULI, developers, and the Federal Housing Administration (FHA) became sudden critics of the "gridiron" housing tracts and large-lot, low-density development they had promoted for so long. The CID idea anchored a campaign to convince local governments and consumers that higher-density development was compatible with the maintenance of property values, exclusion, and status.[36]

In a report published in 1963, the Urban Land Institute pointed out that CIDs could exclude unwanted residents better than any alternative form of development: "Existing as private or semi-private areas they may exclude undesirable elements or trouble-makers drifting in."[37] The FHA agreed to insure loans for condominiums in multiunit buildings in 1961. Two years later, the FHA released its first manual explicitly encouraging developers to build planned units that would be governed by homeowner associations. In 1964, the FHA and the ULI copublished a 400-page volume describing the history of CIDs and setting forth detailed directions on how to establish CC&Rs and the homeowner associations to enforce them.[38] Since the early 1970s, the two biggest secondary mortgage purchasers, the Federal National Mortgage Association and the Federal Home Loan Corporation, have insisted on formulating and reviewing guidelines for residential associations before purchasing the loans on properties that will be governed by them. In only two decades, the institutional pressures applied by the housing industry and the federal government changed the face of the suburbs.

In popular parlance, CIDs are generally referred to as "gated communities," though this term is imprecise because many privatized developments are not actually physically gated. For developers, gates and walls are often used as a marketing tool; these features allow them to play upon themes of security, seclusion, and exclusivity.[39] Developers establish the rules and regulations and set up the homeowner association even before the first property is sold; in this way, they are able to promise to buyers that all residents who move in later will follow closely prescribed norms of behavior and decorum. The list of covenants and restrictions enforced by residents' associations is typically very long and detailed. They may dictate such things as the minimum and maximum ages of residents, hours and frequency of visitors, color of paint on a house, style and color of draperies hung in windows, size of pets and number of children (if either is allowed), parking rules, patios and landscaping, and even minute details like what vehicle a resident can park in the driveway. Many CID residents no doubt find such regulations comforting. For others, the restrictions become intolerable, as evidenced by the high number of lawsuits filed against community associations.

Gated communities are planned as remarkably homogeneous environments. Some of them are developed and marketed to appeal to people on the basis of particular shared interests or life conditions; for instance, communities have been built exclusively for retirees, golfers, singles, and even nudists. Green Valley, Nevada, a massive gated community just outside Las Vegas, is segmented not only by different architectural styles, but also by the cost and size of houses.[40] Each of these "villages" (as the developer calls them) carries the accoutrements of community: a name (Silver Springs or Valle Verde, for example), a community center, a school, a recreational center, and sometimes a park.[41] The separation between this private city and the outside world is, in effect, embellished by a finer-grained separation within.

The Housing Act of 1968 made it illegal to discriminate on the basis of race in the selling or rental of housing. To some degree, however, the intensified social-class segregation facilitated by CIDs acts as a partially effective substitute for earlier means of discrimination. In 2009, the median income for African Americans was 61 percent of the average earnings for non-Hispanic white families.[42] Because racial inequality is strongly reinforced by economic inequality, any effective remedy to residential segregation would require policies that directly interfere with the basic operations of the housing market. Since these would be politically and legally unacceptable, there is no practical way to fundamentally alter the patterns of segregation inherited from the past.

Walling Off the Suburbs: Incorporation

The many suburban jurisdictions that exist in a typical metropolitan region act as a powerful force preserving racial and socioeconomic segregation. In all older metropolitan areas, exclusive suburbs dating back to the late nineteenth century dot the landscape. When the automobile made it possible for more people to make the suburban move, a ring of middle-class suburbs grew up just beyond the city limits. The suburban boom following World War II created a true patchwork of white working-class, middle-class, and upper-class suburbs—for example, Levittown was a middle-class bastion on Long Island, but it remained worlds apart from the wealthier enclaves only a few miles away. Over time, this process fragmented urban areas into a multitude of jurisdictions, each eager to preserve its character and history.

For a variety of reasons the number of suburbs outside the big cities remained relatively small until the 1920s. Some of the people who moved beyond the city limits in the post–Civil War era sought annexation rather than separation because public services were otherwise too expensive or hard to get. At other times, suburban residents were coerced into joining the city. From the turn of the century to the 1920s, for example, Los Angeles used its monopoly over water supply to force neighboring communities, such as Hollywood, Venice, Lordsburg, Sawtelle, Watts, Eagle Rock, Hyde Park, Tujunga, and Barnes City, to become part of the city. This coercive behavior came to stop with the formation of the Metropolitan Water District in 1927, which ended Los Angeles's monopoly over water.[43] A subsequent agreement among local governments called the *Lakewood Plan* made it possible for suburbs to obtain municipal services by contracting with the county government.[44] Almost overnight, the number of suburbs outside Los Angeles began to multiply.

There are many reasons why suburbs proliferated so rapidly. On occasion, simple economic self-interest supplied a sufficient motive to incorporate. E. J. "Lucky" Baldwin was a notorious gambler and entrepreneur in California in the early twentieth century. He got his nickname by making a fortune gambling on mining stocks,[45] and he was the defendant in a number of seduction and paternity suits that culminated in spectacular trials. Baldwin wanted to build a racetrack, but he knew he would be opposed by southern California's foes of sin, led by the Anti-Saloon League. Accordingly, Baldwin decided to create his own suburb, called Arcadia. As the name implied, he intended the town to be his personal utopia. He imported his own employees as residents and handed out free watermelons on election day. Not surprisingly, they approved incorporation unanimously and elected a city council composed of Baldwin and his employees. Baldwin realized his dream when Santa Anita raceway opened on December 7, 1907.[46]

On other occasions, suburban governments came into being to protect businesses from taxes and regulation. Efforts to incorporate were almost always successful when they were led by powerful companies.[47] In 1907, meatpacking companies incorporated National City on the northern border of East St. Louis, Illinois, to escape being taxed by East St. Louis. A few years later, Monsanto Chemical Company created the city of Sauget on East St. Louis's border for the same purpose. In the 1950s, a group of industrialists tried to form a separate suburban jurisdiction in Los Angeles County as a means of avoiding having to pay for the services of a growing suburban population. When they found that the area did not include the 500 residents required for incorporation, they redrew the boundaries to include 169 patients of a mental sanitarium, which put them over the top. Appropriately, they named their new town "Industry."[48]

In most cases, though, the desire to incorporate was driven by more complicated motives. Put simply, the people who had left the city wanted to wash their hands of it. The only effective way to ensure they could never be annexed by the city they had fled was to draw legal boundaries around themselves. The formal incorporation of a new jurisdiction turned out to be a good strategy for gaining control over taxes and services, and in the bargain it provided a means of keeping out the riffraff of the city. At the turn of the century, residents of Oak Park on the border of Chicago feared that the Slavic population might spill over from neighboring Austin. Their motive for incorporating, according to one author, was that "Slavic persons with little aversion for alcohol were rapidly settling the Austin area, and the native American Protestant population of Oak Park feared the immoral influences that might accompany these foreigners."[49] Between 1899 and 1902, Austin joined the city of Chicago, but Oak Park formed a separate suburban government.

People began creating independent municipalities outside the boundaries of all the big cities. In 1890, Cook County, whose principal city is Chicago, had 55 governments; by 1920 it had 109. Similarly, the number of general-purpose governments in the New York City area grew from 127 in 1900 to 204 by 1920. There were 91 incorporated municipalities in the Pittsburgh area in 1890 but 107 in 1920.[50] During the 1920s, new suburbs were formed by the score.

Legal incorporation had not always been so easy to accomplish. Local governments are not mentioned in the U.S. Constitution; legally, they are creatures of the states. In the early part of the nineteenth century, the incorporation of a local government was viewed as a privilege bestowed by state legislatures. In their fights to persuade state legislators to allow them to form their own governments, the residents of place typically claimed that smaller governments were closer to the people and were therefore the best possible expressions of democracy.[51] Because legislators tended to view the cities with a measure of distrust anyway, their pleas got a favorable reception.

Gradually, state legislatures made it so much easier for groups of citizens to create new towns and cities that incorporation shifted from a privilege to a right.[52] Eventually, the legislatures of all of the states liberalized the rules by which citizens could come together to form a municipality. "By the early twentieth century suburbanites had begun carving up the metropolis, and the states had handed them the knife."[53] By 1930, every state legislature in the country had adopted liberalized incorporation laws that put the decision of whether suburban residents would or would not be annexed by the central city firmly into the hands of those who had already fled from it.

Suburban residents have pursued incorporation with great enthusiasm. According to the census of 2002, there were 19,431 municipalities in the United States.[54] The pace slowed somewhat late in the twentieth century, but by then it hardly made any difference. According to the 2002 census there were more than 35,000 municipalities in the United States. St. Louis County, Missouri, had 92; DuPage County, outside Chicago, had 38. As in the past, the proponents of incorporation are been motivated by a variety of concerns, but mainly they want to ensure that their communities will continue to develop in a way that fits with their own values. In June 2005, 94 percent of the affluent residents of Sandy Springs, Florida, voted to support incorporation to achieve smaller government so that "Sandy Springs can control its own destiny," or as another put it, "My major thing, let's make the decisions here rather than downtown."[55]

Mostly, the residents of Sandy Springs were upset that some of their tax money supported services supplied to less affluent people living in their home county. A simple desire for government closer to home combines with bare-knuckled economic self-interest in most incorporation proposals. The principle most often cited in these battles is the desire to gain control over tax revenues and land use decisions. In 2005, a resident supporting the incorporation of the Village of the Falls in Dade County, Florida (outside Miami), said, "We want to be able to have a say how our tax dollars are spent," and, he added, "we want to control zoning of our neighborhood to maintain and improve our quality of life."[56]

Control over land use decisions is important because these policies are directly connected to local economic growth. In the most affluent communities, residents may wish to keep out malls, big-box stores, and all other development they deem to be undesirable. The residents of less fortunate suburbs, however, are more likely to desire exactly the opposite. All but the richest suburban governments simply cannot raise revenues sufficient for providing adequate service levels unless they attract business; if they cannot do so, homeowners end up paying high property taxes. By the mid-1950s, local governments were fighting hard for the first generation of shopping centers, which later morphed into enclosed malls. Local officials encouraged development through direct subsidies to private firms, abatement of local taxes, and the provision of infrastructure such as access roads. In the process, local officials sometimes took money on the side, thus creating a culture of corruption that has cropped up in many places.[57]

The competition for growth is especially intense in the 28 states that have authorized local sales taxes. Receipts from sales taxes can generate 40 percent or more of local revenues. Accordingly, local officials go to great lengths to land a mall, big-box store, and smaller retailers. The competition is fierce; in the words of a vice president of the Utah Taxpayers Association, "It's kind of a Cold War mentality. Basically what you have is cities competing against each other for sales tax dollars."[58] Ventura, California, provides an apt example of what local officials are willing to do. To ensure the continued viability of the Buenaventura Mall, the city agreed to a $12.6 million subsidy package that obliged it to rebate 80 percent of the sales tax revenues that would be realized by an expansion and makeover of the mall. When a neighboring municipality, Oxnard, proposed a plan to share sales tax revenues among local governments, a Ventura city official summarily rejected the offer: "Now because their shopping center deteriorated . . . they want to share. I haven't seen any movement from them wanting to share Wal-Mart and all those stores along the . . . Freeway."[59] Battles motivated by attitudes exactly like this are constantly playing out in metropolitan areas all over the country.

Walling Off the Suburbs: Zoning

Zoning is the most powerful tool that municipalities can use to control land use. It may be used for many purposes, but without a doubt its origins are rooted in the desire to make it difficult or impossible for less affluent people to settle nearby. The nation's first zoning law was enacted in New York City on July 25, 1916. By the end of the 1920s, 768 municipalities with 60 percent of the nation's urban population had enacted zoning ordinances.[60] Quick adoption was made possible when real estate interests discovered what a useful tool zoning could be for protecting valuable land from uses deemed less desirable. As promoters of New York's ordinance explained it to audiences around the country, "The small homeowner and the little shopkeeper were now protected against destructive uses next door. Land in the lower Fifth Avenue section, which had been a drag on the market when zoning arrived, was now undergoing so successful a residential improvement that rents were on the rise. 'Blighted districts are no longer produced in New York City.' "[61] The principle claim made for zoning was that it kept land values high by segregating "better" from "inferior" land uses. In state after state, real estate groups and politicians lobbied for state laws enabling cities to zone their property.

New York City's zoning ordinance arose from the fear that fashionable sections of Fifth Avenue might be invaded by loft buildings from the garment district on the West Side. Their concerns were well founded. From 1850 to 1900, New York's population increased from 661,000 to 3,437,000. Such growth rewarded speculators and entrepreneurs who had been discerning enough to predict the path of the city's expansion. But there was a downside for the upper-class residents who kept establishing themselves at the city's edge, only to be pushed out again by encroaching waves of immigrants and businesses.

By the turn of the century, the upper class had established a mansion district and an exclusive shopping area on upper Fifth Avenue. The wealthy residents of the area felt threatened by the teeming masses only a few blocks away. The garment district, characterized by tall loft buildings in which thousands of poorly paid immigrant garment workers and carters worked, threatened to destroy the exclusive shopping district. A way—a legal way—had to be found to protect Fifth Avenue, which was often described (especially by the wealthy residents along the avenue) as the cultural fulcrum of New York, "a unique place" in "the traditions of this city and in the imagination of its citizens," "probably the most important thoroughfare in this city, perhaps any city in the New World," an area with a "history and associations rich in memories," "the common pride, of all citizens, rich and poor alike, their chief promenading avenue, and their principal shopping thoroughfare."[62] In 1916 the Fifth Avenue Association, which employed lawyers to invent this kind of lofty rhetoric, pleaded that Fifth Avenue was a special area that should be protected from encroachment. Fifty-four years later, the rationale behind zoning had changed little: "We moved out here . . . to escape the city. I don't want the city following me here," explained a Long Island resident.[63]

The Fifth Avenue Association looked for a way to keep loft buildings out. At first they tried to limit the building height, but soon hit upon a more ambitious scheme. In 1916, the Buildings Heights Commission, which had been appointed in 1913 to investigate the problems of tall buildings in New York City, proposed carving Manhattan into areas designated to ensure a "place for everything and everything in its place."[64] According to the commission, "the purpose of zoning was to stabilize and protect lawful investment and not to injure assessed valuations or existing uses."[65]

New York's law specified five zones, each defined by the uses and values of land. In the zoning pecking order, residential uses assumed first place even though commercial and industrial land was often more valuable. Next down the ladder were commercial business districts, differentiated on the basis of building height (the taller the buildings, the lower the place in the zoning hierarchy). Warehouses and industries were allotted last place.

New York City officials fanned out to other cities to publicize their law, in part to ensure it would be widely adopted before courts could challenge its constitutionality. "By the spring of 1918 New York had become a Mecca for pilgrimages of citizens and officials" who wanted to enact a similar ordinance. Within a year after passage of the legislation, more than 20 cities had initiated "one of the most remarkable legislative campaigns in American history."[66] Zoning was literally mass produced; most cities copied the New York ordinance and adopted it virtually verbatim. Zoning soon became the chief weapon used by urban real estate interests to protect land prices. By 1924, the federal government had given zoning its seal of approval. A committee of the Department of Commerce drafted the Standard State Zoning Enabling Act, which served as a model zoning law for all of the nation's cities.

In 1926, the U.S. Supreme Court reviewed a case from Ohio, *Village of Euclid v. Ambler Realty Co.*, and in a landmark decision it declared that zoning was a proper use of the police power of municipal authority.[67] One interesting facet of the case revealed how zoning would be used in the future. Ambler Realty had purchased property in the village of Euclid in hopes it would become valuable as commercial property. In 1922, the village zoned Ambler's property as residential, which had the effect of instantly lowering its market value. In bringing suit against the village, Ambler argued that Euclid's zoning law had lowered its property values without due process of law. In its decision, the Court set forth a classic statement in defense of restrictive zoning, arguing that the presence of apartment, commercial, and industrial buildings undermined residential neighborhoods. The justices took care to spell out the preferred hierarchy of uses:

> With particular reference to apartment houses, it is pointed out that the development of detached house sections is greatly retarded by the coming of apartment houses . . . the coming of one apartment house is followed by others, interfering by their height and bulk with the free circulation of air and monopolizing the rays of the sun which otherwise would fall upon the smaller homes, and bringing, as their necessary accompaniments, the disturbing noises incident to increased traffic and business, and the occupation, by means of moving and parked automobiles, of larger portions of the streets, thus detracting from their safety and depriving children of the quiet and open spaces and

play, enjoyed by those in more favored localities—until, finally the residential character of the neighborhood and its desirability as a place of detached residences is utterly destroyed.[68]

In its decision, the Court ruled that separating residential from other land uses was a legitimate use of the city's police power to promote the order, safety, and well-being of its citizens.

Zoning became popular at the very time that well-to-do suburbs began to ring the central cities—Beverly Hills, Glendale, and a multitude of other communities outside Los Angeles; Cleveland Heights, Shaker Heights, and Garfield Heights near Cleveland's city limits; and Oak Park, Elmwood Park, and Park Ridge outside Chicago. It is not difficult to understand why communities like this championed the concept of zoning. The possibility that the poor might disperse throughout metropolitan areas threatened people living in exclusive neighborhoods, both in central cities and in suburbs. From its inception, zoning became the legal means to ensure what informal social class barriers or the housing market might not have been able to achieve—the exclusion of the inner-city Great Unwashed.

To accomplish this separation, restrictive residential zoning attempted to exclude apartments, to set minimum lot sizes, or to stop new construction altogether. Apartments in the suburbs represented the possibility of class, lifestyle, or racial changes. The residential character of a tree-lined, curved-street subdivision with individual homes set well back seemed to be threatened by apartment buildings. "We don't want this kind of trash in our neighborhood" was an attitude applied even to luxury apartments. Apartments symbolized the coming to suburbia of city problems:

> The apartment in general, and the high-rise apartment in particular, are seen as harbingers of urbanization, and their visibly higher densities appear to undermine the rationale for the development of the suburbs, which includes a reaction against the city and everything for which its stands. This is particularly significant, since the association is strong in suburbia between the visual characteristics of the city and what are perceived to be its social characteristics.[69]

Any proposal to build an apartment complex invariably alarmed the residents of affluent suburban communities. An executive living in Westport, an exclusive suburb in Connecticut, exclaimed, "Thank god we still have a system that rewards accomplishment, and that we can live in places where we want to live, without having apartments and the scum of the city pushed on us."[70] Most suburbs banned the building of apartments entirely. In the 1970s, over 99 percent of undeveloped land zoned residential in the New York region excluded apartments.[71] Although this did not mean apartments could not be constructed, it did require apartment builders to secure zoning variances, a process that favored opponents.[72]

Subdivision regulations and building codes made developers go through a costly review process that artificially increased the cost of new houses and gave local residents an opportunity to oppose new developments. But the most common device for raising the minimum cost of new construction was (and is) large-lot zoning. Sometimes the regulations requiring large lots also specified minimum floor-space requirements, the use of particular building materials, and minimum street setbacks. These kinds of regulations raised the cost for the homebuyer and thus helped protect exclusive neighborhoods.

Large-lot zoning is an effective device to keep out people with lower incomes. In some upper-class communities, this means keeping out the middle class; in some middle-class communities, it means excluding the working class. A defender of 4-acre lot minimums in Greenwich, Connecticut, said that large-lot zoning is "just economics. It's like going into Tiffany and demanding a ring for $12.50. Tiffany doesn't have rings for $12.50. Well, Greenwich is like Tiffany." A New Jersey legislator defended large-lot zoning as a means of making sure "that you can't buy a Cadillac at Chevrolet prices." An official of St. Louis County, where 90,000 acres were zoned for 3-acre lots in 1965, indicated that his suburban county welcomed anyone "who had the economic capacity [to enjoy] the quality of life that we think our county represents . . . be they black or white."[73]

Exclusionary zoning often makes room for industrial and commercial investment that will provide more in taxes than it consumes in services. Of course, affluent communities want the kinds of industry that does not produce bothersome pollution and traffic or bring in the wrong kind of workers. Sy Schulman, a Westchester County (New York) planning commissioner, wryly noted that the ideal industry "is a new campus-type headquarters that smells like Chanel No. 5, sounds like a Stradivarius, has the visual attributes of Sophia Loren, employs only executives with no children and produces items that can be transported away in white station wagons once a month."[74] Because the demand for such clean industry exceeds the supply, there is a fierce competition for it.

The Challenge to Exclusionary Zoning

As a tool for perpetuating residential exclusion, zoning went largely uncontested in the federal and state courts for more than half a century.[75] But in the 1970s, it was challenged in the federal courts as a violation of the equal protection clause of the Fourteenth Amendment to the U.S. Constitution. Lawton, Oklahoma, just southwest of Oklahoma City, had attempted to use its zoning ordinance to keep out apartments, but in 1971 the federal appellate court for its circuit ruled that municipalities could not enact zoning ordinances that had the effect of excluding minorities unless they could show a nondiscriminatory intent concerning their land use objectives.[76] In April 1971, another case gave even more hope to proponents of residential integration. The U.S. Court of Appeals for the Second Circuit rejected an attempt by the city officials of Lackawanna, New York, to block the building of a black housing subdivision in a white neighborhood.[77] Clearly, suburban municipalities were under the gun to show that their zoning ordinances were not adopted simply to keep out blacks.

In a case from Black Jack, Missouri, the courts imposed a tougher standard yet, one that made it appear that exclusionary zoning might be in danger of collapsing altogether. In September 1974, a federal appeals court ruled that the city's new zoning ordinance forbidding the construction of multiunit housing had a discriminatory *effect* even if it did not have a discriminatory intent, and therefore it violated the U.S. Constitution. In June 1975, the U.S. Supreme Court refused to review the circuit court's decision, thereby upholding it. The Black Jack decision had an enormous potential to change suburban land practices in the United States: If the court's decision stood, local governments would lose their most effective weapon for keeping "undesirables" out.

It took only two years, however, for the Supreme Court to back away from their decision. The zoning ordinance of Arlington Heights, Illinois, barred a federally subsidized townhouse project from being built, a restriction identical to Black Jack's. After agreeing to hear a challenge to the law, the Court declared that the effect of zoning laws could not be used as the only argument against them; rather, they had to be shown to have been enacted with the intent to discriminate: "Disproportionate impact is not irrelevant, but it is not the sole touchstone of an invidious racial discrimination."[78] The Supreme Court had already made it much more difficult for litigants to challenge zoning ordinances by requiring them to show a "distinct and palpable injury."[79] By 1977, then, the courts had gotten out of the business of reviewing local zoning laws except in the rare case when it could be shown that they were adopted specifically to discriminate against minorities.

The courts have consistently held that discrimination on the basis of income or class is not prohibited by the U.S. Constitution. If suburbs can show that their zoning laws are designed to protect the tax base and the exclusive residential character of the local community, their laws will not be declared unconstitutional even if they happen to discriminate against poor people. In 1971, the Supreme Court upheld an amendment to the California constitution, passed in 1950, which required that low-rent housing could not be built without prior approval by a referendum of the voters of the city. Although clearly biased against those seeking low-income housing, the Court ruled that discrimination on the basis of income was not unconstitutional under the equal protection clause of the Fourteenth Amendment.[80] In the intervening years, that Court ruling has stood the test of time.

Since the federal courts have been unwilling to use the U.S. Constitution to break down the walls of suburban exclusion, state courts have become the main avenue of redress. But two well-publicized and highly controversial cases from Mount Laurel, New Jersey, reveal the formidable hurdles that stand in the way of meaningful change. In 1970, Mount Laurel, located not far from Camden and Philadelphia, was a mostly rural community. The area contained a small African American community that had been there since before the Civil War. Quakers had made Mount Laurel a sanctuary for runaway slaves on the Underground Railroad, and their descendants still resided in the area. Many of them lived in small shacks and converted chicken coops, and when these were condemned by the city of Mount Laurel, the residents realized they would be forced to move to the slums of Camden. They formed an action committee and applied for federal funds to build a subsidized housing project, but in 1970 the local planning and zoning board turned down the committee's proposal.

The residents then turned to the courts. They found three idealistic lawyers working for the Camden Region Legal Services who agreed to pursue a challenge to Mount Laurel's zoning laws, which allowed only single-family homes and specified big lots, large building sizes (a minimum of four bedrooms), and substantial setbacks from the street. In 1972 a trial court found that Mount Laurel's zoning laws violated language in the New Jersey constitution that guaranteed equal protection of the law for all persons. Further, the court ruled that not only Mount Laurel but all of New Jersey's 567 municipalities had an obligation to provide land uses that would meet regional housing needs. The U.S. Supreme Court subsequently refused to hear an appeal of this decision.

A few years later, in 1982, the chief justice of the New Jersey Supreme Court heard six cases showing that the city of Mount Laurel was ignoring the original trial court's decision. He combined the cases into one proceeding, and in 1983 the court issued a pathbreaking unanimous decision, widely known as *Mount Laurel II*. The court noted that the town of Mount Laurel had made no real attempt to comply with the original judicial directive; it had simply rezoned 33 of its 14,176 acres, and not one of the 515 low-income housing units required to meet the court's decision had been built.[81] To compel compliance with its original decision, *Mount Laurel II* required that New Jersey municipalities set aside land for low-income housing, if necessary, and make low-income housing attractive to developers through such devices as tax incentives and subsidies. Second, to encourage builders to pursue lawsuits against exclusionary zoning, the court established "builder's remedies," which allowed developers of low- and moderate-income housing to sue cities that tried to keep them out.

As a result of *Mount Laurel II*, New Jersey's suburban municipalities were besieged with lawsuits, and politicians were increasingly pressured to do something about the situation. Republican governor Thomas H. Kean, who won office in 1981, came out against what he called an "undesirable intrusion on the home rule principle." In a 1984 interview, Kean stated, "I don't believe that every municipality has got to be a carbon copy of another. That's a socialistic country, a Communistic country, a dictatorship."[82] Kean proposed an amendment to the New Jersey constitution that would place local zoning policy beyond review by state courts. Meanwhile, he signed legislation that moved exclusionary zoning cases out of the courts and into arbitration before a nine-member Council on Affordable Housing (COAH), to be appointed by the governor.[83] Cities and towns were given a grace period to achieve their "fair share" regional housing goals.

In actuality, most communities were let off the hook completely. Municipalities were allowed, for example, to allocate up to 25 percent of their "fair share" to elderly people, and any city was allowed to transfer up to half of its fair-share obligation to another city in the region (if the receiving city approved), along with the funds to help the receiving town pay to build the housing. Older central cities were put in the position of competing against one another for subsidies from wealthier suburbs so they could obtain funds to meet the pressing housing needs of their low-income residents. What had begun as an effort to open up the suburbs ended up doing exactly the opposite.

Despite the years of the political thunder and lightning, the payoff from the long, drawn-out Mount Laurel process was meager. Most New Jersey municipalities did nothing at all. In Mount Laurel, only 12 families had moved into low-cost mobile homes by the late 1980s, 12 more had put down deposits on similar units, and 20 low-cost subsidized condominiums had been completed. This was the grand total of low-income housing after 17 years and millions of dollars of litigation, and protracted political uproar.[84]

The New Jersey case illustrates the difficulty of changing local land use practices when a political consensus is lacking. Mount Laurel represents the clash between two deeply held American values: equal protection of the law, on the one hand, and local home rule, on the other. Americans are reluctant to support policies that force local governments to give up their autonomy. In an era when the federal government has cut housing subsidies drastically, even if local zoning laws could be successfully challenged, it is doubtful much low-income housing would be built in the suburbs. If the New Jersey experience offers a lesson, it is that exclusionary zoning, and the residential segregation that comes with it, is here to stay.

The New Face of Enclave Politics

Over time, the suburbs have changed. People of all racial and ethnic groups have become suburban. A lot of poor people, too, have finally made the move out of the central city. Middle- and working-class suburban homes built in the immediate postwar period tended to be small tract homes or bungalows that lacked the amenities and conveniences expected by a new generation of homeowners.[85] These older subdivisions were generally located in suburbs with depressed housing prices and a low level of public services, and some of them became a new kind of urban slum, but much more isolated from jobs and transportation networks than slums located in the urban core. Many of them are located in inner suburbs close to the central cities, but others are sprinkled in the spaces between more affluent suburbs located somewhat further out.[86]

Poor people and recent immigrants find it easier to find housing in older suburbs because there is less demand for housing in those areas, often because the homes are small and long out of fashion. In the 1990s, for example, Levittown and other 1950s-era suburbs of Long Island began to attract recently arrived immigrants from the Middle East, Central and Latin America, and Asia.[87] Some families crowded illegally into homes, and their children flooded into local schools. They remained hidden from the larger society in part because they were walled off into municipalities that had few resources—and therefore they were unable to make effective claims on the political system. A pair of writers asked, "Suburbs are now becoming—albeit not always willingly—multiclass, multiethnic, and multiracial. . . . Can older suburbs accommodate these new ethnic groups, or will outmoded, decentralized government structures and prejudice keep them hidden *baja del agua*—underwater?"[88]

The tendency to push marginalized groups "underwater" is reinforced by the rise of privatized enclaves of people trying to sever all connection to central cities and even with nearby neighborhoods.[89] Some gated communities built in the 1980s and 1990s seem like fortresses built to keep the menacing hordes at bay. The emphasis on security in some of these developments is akin to a state of war. Leisure World, a California retirement community, is surrounded by 6-foot walls topped with barbed wire. Quayside, a planned community in Florida, blends the atmosphere of a Norman Rockwell small town of the 1920s with the latest in high-tech security; laser beams sweep the perimeter, computers check the coded entry cards of the residents and store exits and entries from the property in a permanent data file, and television cameras continuously monitor the living and recreation areas. The many trappings of security constantly remind the inhabitants that the world beyond their walls is dangerous, so that "'being inside' becomes a powerful symbol for being protected, buttressed, coddled, while 'being outside' evokes exposure, isolation, and vulnerability."[90] In 2006, a Texas developer marketed a new subdivision as a "sex-offender free" development; prospective buyers would have to pass a criminal background check.[91]

By the 1990s, fortress enclaves had become a ubiquitous feature of suburban development all across southern California. In search of high-tech security, architects for the affluent were "borrowing design features from overseas embassies and military command posts," building hardened walls, improvising secret passages and doors, and installing a dazzling array of sophisticated electronic surveillance devices.[92] The demand for gated communities in the Los Angeles suburbs was so high that they quickly replaced all other kinds of development. This same process has occurred from coast to coast, and it has led the residents of some gated communities to try to withdraw support for services supplied by local governments, on the theory that paying for privatized as well as public services constitutes "double taxation." Political movements like this makes it clear that the urban crisis of the twentieth century may have come to an end only to be replaced by a different kind of politics, one that not only pits suburb against suburb, but also enclave against enclave and privatized privilege against public needs.

Endnotes

1. Quoted in James A. Clapp, *The City: A Dictionary of Quotable Thoughts on Cities and Urban Life* (New Brunswick, NJ: Center for Urban Policy Research, Rutgers University, 1984), pp. 128–129.
2. Quoted in ibid., p. 148.
3. U.S. Bureau of the Census, *Census 2000*, www.census.gov/cens2000.
4. Robert C. Wood, *Suburbia: Its People and Their Politics* (Boston: Houghton Mifflin, 1958), p. 106.
5. See Mark Gottdiener, *Planned Sprawl: Private and Public Interests in Suburbia* (Beverly Hills, CA: Sage, 1977).
6. Robert C. Wood, "Suburban Politics and Policies: Retrospect and Prospect," *Publius, The Journal of Federalism* 5 (Winter 1975): 51.
7. The term is taken from Mark Weiss, *The Rise of the Community Builders* (New York: Columbia University Press, 1987).
8. J. C. Nichols, "The Planning and Control of Outlying Shopping Centers," *Journal of Land and Public Utility Economics* 2 (January 1926): 22. By concentrating in one location and using leasing policy to determine store "mix," "Nichols created the idea of the planned regional shopping center," Kenneth T. Jackson, *Crabgrass Frontier: The Suburbanization of the United States* (New York: Oxford University Press, 1985), p. 258.

9. Gwendolyn Wright, *Building the Dream: A Social History of Housing in America* (Cambridge, MA: MIT Press, 1981), p. 202.

10. Mark H. Rose, "'There Is Less Smoke in the District,' J. C. Nichols, Urban Change and Technological Systems," *Journal of the West* 25 (January 1986): 48. Rose adds, "As late as 1917, no more than five Jewish families resided in the district, the result of resales."

11. "Up from the Potato Fields," *Time* (July 3, 1950), p. 70.

12. Ibid.

13. "The Most House for the Money," *Fortune* (October 1952): 156.

14. Jackson, *Crabgrass Frontier,* p. 234.

15. Wright, *Building the Dream,* p. 252.

16. "Up from the Potato Fields," p. 68.

17. Jackson, *Crabgrass Frontier,* p. 234.

18. "Up from the Potato Fields," p. 68.

19. Bruce Lambert, "Levittown Anniversary Stirs Memories of Bias," *New York Times* (December 28, 1997), p. 14.

20. Quoted in Herbert Gans, *The Levittowners: Ways of Life and Politics in a Suburban Community* (New York: Pantheon Books, 1967), p. 372.

21. Lambert, "Levittown Anniversary," p. 14.

22. Jackson, *Crabgrass Frontier,* p. 241.

23. Lambert, "Levittown Anniversary," p. 14.

24. Gans, *The Levittowners,* pp. 8–9.

25. Joe R. Feagin and Robert Parker, *Building American Cities: The Urban Real Estate Game,* 2nd ed. (Upper Saddle River, NJ: Prentice Hall, 1990), p. 211.

26. Robert Goldston, *Suburbia: Civic Denial* (New York: Macmillan, 1970), p. 68.

27. Kevin Fox Gotham, *Race, Real Estate, and Uneven Development: The Kansas City Experience, 1900–2000* (Albany: State University of New York Press, 2002), p. 38.

28. Ibid.

29. Ibid., pp. 34–37.

30. National Association of Real Estate Boards, *Code of Ethics* (1924), art. 34 (Washington, DC: Author).

31. Harry Grant Atkinson and L. E. Frailey, *Fundamentals of Real Estate Practice* (Upper Saddle River, NJ: Prentice Hall, 1946), p. 34, quoted in Evan McKenzie, *Privatopia: Homeowner Associations and the Rise of Residential Private Government* (New Haven, CT: Yale University Press, 1994), pp. 61–62.

32. *Shelly v. Kraemer,* 334 U.S. 1 (1948). The Court had struck down racial zoning some 30 years earlier in *Buchanan v. Warley,* 245 U.S. 60 (1917).

33. McKenzie, *Privatopia,* p. 11.

34. Community Associations Institute, Association Information Services, CtreeseAIS@aol.com (2006).

35. Ibid.

36. McKenzie, *Privatopia,* pp. 158–164.

37. Ibid., p. 158.

38. Ibid., pp. 163–164.

39. Dennis R. Judd, "The Rise of the New Walled Cities," in *Spatial Practices,* ed. Helen Liggett and David C. Perry (Thousand Oaks, CA: Sage, 1995), pp. 144–166.

40. David Guterson, "No Place Like Home: On the Manicured Streets of a Master-planned Community," *Harper's* (November 1992): 55–64.

41. Ibid., pp. 60–61.

42. U.S. Bureau of the Census, *The 2009 Statistical Abstract of the United States,* Table 669, www.census/gov/compendia/statab.

43. Gary J. Miller, *Cities by Contract: The Politics of Municipal Incorporation* (Cambridge, MA: MIT Press, 1981), p. 12.

44. Ibid.

45. C. B. Glasscock, *Lucky Baldwin: The Story of an Unconventional Success* (Indianapolis, IN: Bobbs-Merrill, 1933), p. 140.

46. Jon C. Teaford, *City and Suburb: The Political Fragmentation of Metropolitan America, 1850–1970* (Baltimore: Johns Hopkins University Press, 1979), pp. 18–19.

47. Charles Hoch, "City Limits: Municipal Boundary Formation and Class Segregation," in *Marxism and the Metropolis: New Perspectives in Urban Political Economy*, 2nd ed., ed. William K. Tabb and Larry Sawers (New York: Oxford University Press, 1984), pp. 101–119.

48. Miller, *Cities by Contract*, pp. 49–50. Another good example of an industrial suburb is Teterboro, New Jersey, which in 1977 had only 24 residents but employed 24,000 nonresidents. Michael N. Danielson and Jameson W. Doig, *New York: The Politics of Urban Regional Development* (Berkeley: University of California Press, 1982), p. 92.

49. Teaford, *City and Suburb*, p. 18.

50. Data cited in Wood, *Suburbia*, p. 69; and in National Municipal League, Committee on Metropolitan Government, *The Government of Metropolitan Areas in the United States*, prepared by Paul Studenski with the assistance of the Committee on Metropolitan Government (New York: National Municipal League, 1930), p. 26.

51. See Anwar Syed, *The Political Theory of American Local Government* (Clinton, MA: Random House, 1966).

52. Teaford, *City and Suburb*, p. 6.

53. Ibid., p. 31.

54. U.S. Bureau of the Census, *Census 2000*.

55. Jon C. Teaford, *The American Suburb: The Basics* (New York: Routledge, 2008).

56. Quoted in ibid., p. 132.

57. Dolores Hayden, *Building Suburbia: Green Fields and Urban Growth, 1820–2000* (New York: Pantheon Books), p. 168.

58. Quoted in Teaford, *City and Suburb*, p. 115.

59. Quoted in ibid., p. 112.

60. Seymour I. Toll, *Zoned America* (New York: Grossman, 1969), p. 193.

61. Ibid., p. 197.

62. Ibid., p. 159.

63. Quoted in Michael N. Danielson, *The Politics of Exclusion* (New York: Columbia University Press, 1976), p. 54.

64. Toll, *Zoned America*, p. 183.

65. Ibid., pp. 182–183.

66. Ibid., p. 187.

67. *Police power* refers to the implied powers of government to adopt and enforce laws necessary for preserving and protecting the immediate health and welfare of citizens. The meaning of this, of course, is subject to a wide variety of interpretations.

68. *Village of Euclid v. Ambler Realty Co.*, 272 U.S. 365, 47 S.Ct. 114, 71 L. Ed. 303 (1926).

69. Danielson, *The Politics of Exclusion*, pp. 53–54.

70. "The End of the Exurban Dream," *New York Times* (December 13, 1976).

71. Danielson, *The Politics of Exclusion*, p. 53.

72. Because of the fears concerning apartment developments, the planning process involving their construction was complicated, requiring petitions for zoning variances, public hearings, and lengthy review proceedings. For an excellent account of these

complexities, see Daniel R. Mandelker, *The Zoning Dilemma: A Legal Strategy for Urban Change* (Indianapolis, IN: Bobbs-Merrill, 1971).

73. Quoted in Danielson, *The Politics of Exclusion,* p. 60.

74. Quoted in Merrill Folson, "Westchester Finds Influx of Business a Worry," *New York Times* (April 18, 1967); cited in Danielson and Doig, *New York,* p. 90.

75. A detailed discussion of the legal status of zoning is not included in this section. For further information, the following sources are especially useful: Danielson, *The Politics of Exclusion*; Richard F. Babcock, *The Zoning Game* (Madison: University of Wisconsin Press, 1969); Richard F. Babcock and Fred P. Bosselman, *Exclusionary Zoning: Land Use Regulation and Housing in the 1970s* (New York: Praeger, 1973); Daniel R. Mandelker, *Managing Our Urban Environment* (Indianapolis, IN: Bobbs-Merrill, 1971); Randall W. Scott, ed., *Management and Control of Growth,* vol. 1 (New York: Urban Land Institute, 1975); and David Listokin, ed., *Land Use Controls Present Problems and Future Reform* (New Brunswick, NJ: Center for Urban Policy Research, Rutgers University, 1975).

76. *Dailey v. City of Lawton,* 425 F.2d 1037 (1970).

77. *Kennedy Park Homes v. City of Lackawanna,* 436 F.2d 108 (1971).

78. Quoted in *St. Louis Globe-Democrat* (January 11, 1977).

79. In 1975 the Supreme Court made it more difficult to challenge exclusionary zoning in federal courts by "refusing standing"—dismissing a case on the grounds that the plaintiffs had no right to sue. Those who want to challenge an exclusionary ordinance must prove "distinct and palpable injury"; a suit cannot be based on general injury to those who do not live in the town but want to live there; see *Warth v. Seldin,* 442 U.S. 490 (1975).

80. See *James v. Valtierra,* 91 S.Ct. 133 (1971), and *Shaffer v. Valtierra,* 402 U.S. 137 (1971).

81. Joseph F. Sullivan, "Restless Seeker for Justice," *New York Times* (January 22, 1983); Robert Hanley, "After 7 Years, Town Remains under Fire for Its Zoning Code," *New York Times* (January 22, 1983); Anthony DePalma, "N.J. Housing Woes Are All over the Map," *New York Times* (April 17, 1983).

82. Robert Hanley, "Some Jersey Towns, Yielding to Courts, Let in Modest Homes," *New York Times* (February 29, 1984).

83. 1985 J.J. Sess. Law Serv. 222 (West).

84. Anthony DePalma, "Subsidized Housing Hurt in Ailing Market," *New York Times* (May 15, 1990).

85. Ibid., pp. 42–43.

86. Ibid.

87. Rosalyn Baxandall and Elizabeth Ewen, *Picture Windows: How the Suburbs Happened* (New York: Perseus Books, 2000), p. 239.

88. Ibid., p. 250.

89. Peter O. Muller, *Contemporary Suburban America* (Upper Saddle River, NJ: Prentice Hall, 1981), p. 180.

90. Trevor Boddy, "Underground and Overhead: Building the Analogous City," in *Variations on a Theme Park: The New American City and the End of Public Space,* ed. Michael Sorkin (New York: Noonday Press, 1992), p. 139.

91. Betsy Blaney, "Texas Developers to Build Sex Offender-free Subdivision," *Chicago Tribune* (June 15, 2005), p. 34.

92. Mike Davis, "Fortress Los Angeles: The Militarization of Urban Space," in *Variations on a Theme Park,* ed. Sorkin, p. 173.

CHAPTER 11

Governing the Fragmented Metropolis

The Byzantine (Dis)Organization of Urban Regions

Population movement from the urban core is a feature of urban development all over the world. With transportation breakthroughs such as automated rail systems and the automobile, urban areas in the advanced Western countries have been spreading out for at least a century.[1] But what distinguishes the urban pattern in the United States most clearly from that of other Western nations is not the extent of sprawl, but the fracturing of metropolitan areas into a multitude of separate governments. In Europe and most other nations, there are fewer suburbs because cities tend to encompass a large part of their metropolitan areas. In addition, national and regional governments finance and administer crucial services that are, in the United States, provided by municipalities and special districts. American suburbs are different from the European model because they are autonomous entities that make taxation, spending, and land use decisions without any oversight from higher levels of government. There are a lot of them. The 2002 federal census of governments counted 87,849 local governments in the United States.[2] Statistics like these have led to a consensus that the "degree of governmental fragmentation in the United States is unique among the urban-industrial societies."[3]

The extreme fragmentation of urban regions makes it hard to find solutions to problems that are truly regional in scope. These difficulties have been overcome, to some degree, by the construction of a staggeringly complex maze of governmental responsibilities. Typically, urban counties do such things as administer building codes, run systems of parks and libraries, operate health clinics, offer police services, build roads and bridges, manage jails and courts, and sponsor 911 emergency services. Special-purpose districts also supply a variety of services that overlap municipal boundaries, and some of these, such as sewer and water and mass transit districts, are metropolitan-wide in scope. But most of the dozens of special districts within metropolitan areas are much smaller and virtually invisible. They raise taxes for and manage everything from hospitals to fire protection to mosquito abatement, plus a great number of other very specialized services. The jerry-rigged nature of these arrangements

OUTTAKE

The Costs of Sprawl are Hotly Debated

The urban specialist Neal Peirce has called Americans "the champion land hogs of history" because the country's urban areas are growing in land area at a rate four to eight times faster than the growth of the national population. The cost of sprawl, he said, is "frightening" because it brings "despair in the inner cities, environmental degradation, undermining of old neighborhoods and suburbs."

Peirce and other critics of urban sprawl have amassed convincing evidence to demonstrate its negative effects. They cite the many studies to show that it is more expensive to supply infrastructure—new highways, streets, and bridges; schools; sewer and water systems; street lighting; gas, electric, and telephone hookups; libraries and parks—to low-density areas than to high-density areas. They demonstrate that sprawl has contributed to the decline of the central cities and the abandonment of neighborhoods in the cities and older suburbs. And finally, they show that governmental fragmentation slows the economic growth of urban regions.

Critics of sprawl also argue that it creates serious environmental problems. Evidence to support their point of view is not difficult to find. Thousands of acres of farmland, wetlands, and open space disappear each year. Runoff from highways, parking lots, and lawns pollutes streams and rivers; auto and truck traffic spews ozone-depleting and greenhouse gases into the atmosphere. Excess energy consumption and air pollution are implicated in global environmental problems. Urban residents in the United States consumed about four times as much gasoline per capita as did urban residents in Europe in 1990. Urban sprawl was the basic reason for this difference. In the late 1980s, annual consumption in sprawled-out Houston was 567 gallons per person, compared to 335 gallons in New York City, where high population density facilitated the use of mass transit. (In Manhattan, gasoline consumption was only 90 gallons per person.)

Despite the accumulating weight of such facts, it should not be supposed that there is only one point of view about urban sprawl. In fact, it is a hotly contested issue. Fred Siegel, a prominent scholar and writer, has argued that sprawl is a logical outcome of prosperity and the pursuit of the American dream, "an expression of the upward mobility and growth in home-ownership generated by our past half-century of economic success." Expanding on this theme, he maintains that people on the lower end of the economic scale are able to find opportunities to escape from poor neighborhoods by moving into housing left behind by the middle class. In this way, he says, the construction of new housing at the metropolitan edge helps to expand opportunities for all residents of the metropolis. Siegel's logic is hard to refute. As their incomes go up, people usually move from high-density to low-density neighborhoods in a search for more space and better amenities. Low-density neighborhoods are usually located in newer communities located at some remove from the urban core. Until the Great Recession of 2008–2010, one in seven of newly constructed homes exceeded 3,000 square feet, a size reserved only for wealthy families in the past.

The two perspectives on urban sprawl suggest that there is a contradiction between freedom to choose, on the one hand, and regulation and planning, on the other. When forced to choose between these two values urban residents often seem to be of two minds. Americans have always been keenly sensitive about anything that intrudes on their individual property rights, but suburban residents have generally been willing to make an exception when it comes to land use controls such as zoning, growth control measures that impose a limit on housing permits, green belts to preserve open space, and ordinances restricting new infrastructure development. The problem is that local control over such policies comes at the cost of metropolitan-wide planning. The paradox is that even when people are disturbed about unplanned and runaway urban growth, their deep attachment to small-scale governance makes it hard to devise metropolitan-wide solutions to unplanned urban growth.

Sources: Neal Peirce, "The Senselessness of Urban Sprawl," *National Journal* (September 25, 1993), p. 2326; Burchell et al., *The Costs of Sprawl Revisited* (Washington, DC: National Academy Press, 1998); Arthur C. Nelson and Kathryn A. Foster, "Metropolitan Governance Structure and Income Growth," *Journal of Urban Affairs* 21, no. 3 (1999): 309–324; Peter G. Newman and Jeffrey R. Kenworthy, "Gasoline Consumption and Cities," *Journal of the American Planning Association* (Winter 1989): 26–27; Fred Siegel, "Is Regional Government the Answer?" *The Public Interest* (Fall 1999): 86.

makes a degree of regional service provision possible, but a coherent system of regional governance remains out of reach. It also makes many people wish for a system of regional governance that would be more democratic, efficient, and effective.

Over the years, there have been many attempts to bring some order to the task of governing metropolitan regions. The remedies that have been proposed may be grouped under four labels: Metro Gov, the New Regionalism, Smart Growth, and the New Urbanism. The Metro Gov movement, which began about a century ago, has been based on the ambitious idea that urban regions should be governed, as far as possible, by a single metropolitan-wide government or by a few consolidated governmental bodies. A drive through the many towns and suburban jurisdictions that make up a typical urban area makes it obvious to even the casual observer that metro reform has failed to achieve most of its aims. The *New Regionalism*, which dates back to the late 1980s, was founded on the premise that the flight from the cities to the suburbs has produced an unacceptable degree of inequality within urban areas. Rather than trying to reduce the number of governments, the advocates for a "new regionalism" have emphasized the importance of achieving cooperation among local governments to moderate the intense interjurisdiction competition for economic growth and reduce extreme differences in tax burdens and service quality. In the late 1990s, the *Smart Growth* movement came together around a collection of proposals designed to achieve "balanced" regional development by regulating land use and promoting community and environmental planning. At about the same time, the *New Urbanism* came onto the scene. This movement was energized by the idea that better urban design and architecture are the necessary ingredients for countering sprawl and achieving healthy neighborhoods and communities. Each of these movements confronts a formidable obstacle: the incredibly complicated governmental mosaic that already exists in America's urban regions.

The New Urban Form

The sprawled metropolis has spawned a set of chronic and sometimes vexing problems. Commuting is expensive, and is likely to become more so over the long run. In 2008, the cost of a gallon of gasoline rose to over $4 in the United States, although it was still cheap compared to the nearly $10 that people in the United Kingdom paid, or the $7 per-gallon price in France. Commuters experience traffic congestion and gridlock almost every day. The public has become concerned about such issues as air pollution, the loss of open space and farmland, and polluted water. Urban sprawl has blossomed as an important public policy issue. Growth control measures began to appear in the early 1970s, and the movement to regulate the pace and location of development continued to gain momentum over time. People want the freedom to move where they please, but they are not happy when their neighborhoods seem threatened by a steady stream of newcomers.

However serious the problems associated with sprawl may be, it is here to stay. One reason is that local governments jealously guard their powers. The other equally important reason is that the geographic structure of metropolitan areas has become basically fixed. The old urban form, which found a big city surrounded by rank on rank of spreading suburbs, has given way to a metropolis organized around many nodes of activity.[4] Once the suburbs were wholly dependent satellites of cities, where most of the jobs and businesses were located. Today, however, the center is only one of several clusters of activity. For a long time, suburban development was mainly a residential movement, but by the late 1940s jobs began to decentralize even faster than population.[5] Retailing followed in when regional shopping malls began to spring up to cater to the shopping and entertainment needs of suburban consumers.[6] Suburban residents no longer needed to go downtown, and thus a historic link between cities and suburbs was severed.

Manufacturing has been moving out of the old industrial cities for almost a century because of technical innovations that freed factories from a dependence on rail connections. Electrification made single-story plants more economical than multistory buildings that housed belt-driven machinery powered by water or steam. In the twentieth century, federal tax law allowed manufacturers to take tax deductions through "accelerated depreciation of assets" when they abandoned inner-city factories; at the same time, investment tax credits allowed manufacturing firms to write off the cost of new plant and equipment. In these ways the federal tax code subsidized the flight of industrial jobs to the suburbs and to the Sunbelt.[7] Manufacturing firms also left northern urban areas because they viewed them as hotbeds of union organizing and unrest.[8] By 1970, a majority of the manufacturing jobs in metropolitan areas were located outside the central cities, and many were moving out of older urban areas to the Sunbelt or abroad.

The service sector was the last to leave. Historically, professional and business activities were concentrated in or near central business districts, but the building of integrated urban highway systems fundamentally changed the urban landscape. As employees left the city and commuted greater distances to work, it made less sense for firms to stay downtown. Routine service employment, the so-called back-office functions such as copying and secretarial services, left expensive downtown office space. In 1975, for the first time, the volume of office construction in the suburbs exceeded the pace of construction in central cities. Higher-level and higher-paid corporate services, however, such as legal assistance, corporate consulting, accounting services, and investment services, continued to be located in the downtowns of large cities, partly for prestige reasons. Corporations, though, have many components, so that even if they kept their management and professional-service functions downtown they generally moved everything else either to suburbs or out of the country. Suburban office parks evolved as still another option. By moving their professional staff onto self-contained campuses, companies were able to recreate many of the characteristics of central business districts in the suburbs.

Within a few years, the suburbs became basically independent of their core cities. Cross-commuting became common; by 1980, twice as many people commuted from suburb to suburb as from the central city to suburb.[9] The historic urban form, in which a city is surrounded by dependent suburbs, was replaced by the "polynucleated metropolis" made up of several nodes of concentrated activity that combined residential, retail, recreational, light industry, and service firms. This geographic pattern has sometimes been called *exurbanization* or even *counterurbanization*,[10] plus a variety of odd and often confusing labels, such as "urban villages, technohubs, suburban downtowns, suburban activity centers, major diversified centers, urban cores, galactic city, pepperoni-pizza cities, a city of realms, superburbia, disurb, service cities, perimeter cities, and even peripheral centers."[11] What these entities have in common is that they keep springing up at the outer boundary of urban regions, often near freeway interchanges and airports.

Significant numbers of the new suburbs are large—in fact, some have grown bigger than their nearby central cities. Two researchers coined the term "boomburbs," which they define as suburbs that have grown by at least double-digit rates for every decade since 1970, and finally reaching a population of at least 100,000 by the census of 2000.[12] They discovered that 54 cities across the nation met this statistical standard, and that 12 of them contained more than 200,000 people. The total number of boomburbs in the nation might seem small, but they held one-quarter of all residents living in small- and medium-sized urban areas.[13] The census of 2000 showed that 15 boomburbs had joined the ranks of the 100 largest U.S. cities.

Despite their sudden appearance, boomburbs have attracted little attention, probably because they tend to lack the physical form and identity that might make them stand out. They generally do not have tall buildings and heavily favor the automobile over pedestrians, office workers tend to be clustered in office parks, and a large proportion of shopping is done in strip malls and mall clusters. Perhaps the most surprising fact about boomburbs is that they often defied the suburban stereotype. Forty-five of the 54 contained a larger percentage of Hispanic residents and 42 have a higher proportion of Asians than did the national population.[14]

Boomburbs are, in essence, fully developed cities, with a mixture of office, retail, residential, and sometimes light industry. They differ markedly from one another, but few, if any, fit the profile of the exclusive residential suburb or of the one-dimensional bedroom community. High-rise office and condominium towers are beginning to sprout in some of them and new housing construction often favors townhouse and condominium construction over free-standing homes. The growth of the boomburbs makes it clear that urban sprawl is tightly woven into the fabric of urban regions. The multi-nodal metropolis is here to stay.

The Concerns about Sprawl

The term *urban sprawl* generally refers to low-density residential development. Research published in 1974 defined it as residential density of two dwellings per acre, but a late 1980s study and another conducted by the Environmental Protection Agency in the early 1990s defined it as residential density of three dwellings per acre or less.[15] Even if we use the latter definition sprawl is rare in Europe and Asia, where land is scarcer than in the United States and land use controls are the norm. In such contexts, urban areas may be spreading outward, but not in such a way as to create the social and political dynamic that characterizes sprawl in the United States: low-density development at the edge of metropolitan regions that consumes huge tracts of land and entails the abandonment of older areas at the urban core.

When people move farther out, they generally are choosing lower-density suburbs as places to live. The result is that land is gobbled up at a rate all out of proportion to the population growth of urban regions—indeed, sprawl occurs even in metropolitan areas with steady-state or declining populations. For example, although the New York region's population grew by only 5 percent between 1964 and 1989, in the same years the amount of developed land increased by 61 percent.[16] Similarly, from 1950 to 1995, the population of the St. Louis region increased by just 35 percent, but the area of developed land exploded by more than 10 times that much, by 355 percent.[17] Even in slow-growth regions people have been drifting to the outer edges. From 1986 to 2001, 73,000 people moved from St. Louis County out to St. Charles County; in the same period St. Charles County attracted only 5,500 people from outside the metropolitan region. St. Charles County is now filling up, and its growth is now outpaced by Warren County, which lies still even farther out.[18] This restless movement to the urban edge is why almost all urban regions continued to sprawl in the 1990s, regardless of their population growth rates.[19]

Why does land disappear so fast even in slow-growth urban regions? First, families have become smaller in recent decades because of the increasing number of single-parent families, childless and unmarried couples, and singles. The smaller size of the typical suburban family requires more dwellings for a given population size and makes many of the single-family houses built only a couple of decades ago obsolete. Second, although average family sizes have been declining, the size of homes has steadily increased in step with a desire for more luxuries and amenities (although, it should be noted, the Great Recession arrested this trend for a time). And third, when people move within metropolitan areas, they tend to leave higher-density neighborhoods nearer the urban core for lower-density subdivisions farther out; only a small percentage move in the other direction. In a study conducted in the early 1990s, more than two-thirds of the survey respondents said that they preferred to live in low-density, single-family neighborhoods than in denser neighborhoods closer to the central city.[20]

Despite an overwhelming preference for low-density living, many suburban residents have discovered that there is a downside. Commuters experience some of the negative effects of sprawl every day, firsthand and close up. By the last decades of the twentieth century highway congestion had increased to the point that the daily commute has ceased to be merely annoying. In November 1999, *USA Today*, in a special report on national gridlock, offered up one horror story after another. The average commuter's daily experience seemed to be summed up by a Chicago driver's description of a bottleneck called "the Hillside Strangler": "It's not even a traffic jam. It's my enemy. It's my daytime bad dream."[21] In 2001, the knot of off-ramps that made up the Strangler was finally eliminated, but many other gridlocked spots remained. A study conducted in 2005 ranked Chicago second in the nation as the most congested (Los Angeles had the honor of first place). The report estimated that in 2003 Chicago-area commuters spent 58 hours in traffic jams each year, an increase of 55 hours from only three years earlier. The authors concluded that the term "rush hour" had become virtually meaningless.[22]

If commuters think that urban highways have become more crowded in the last few years, they are right. In the 1970s, there were 61 yards of roadway per vehicle in the United States, but by 1986 this space had shrunk by more than one-third, to 39 yards.[23] The number of vehicles on the roads has increased dramatically. Trucks by the dozen fill rearview mirrors because they have substantially eclipsed trains for the movement of goods. The number of licensed drivers jumped 65 percent between 1970 and 1997, but registered vehicles increased even more, by 87 percent. Demographic changes accounted for the higher traffic volumes. Although the U.S. population rose by only 32 percent between 1970 and 1997, the number of women in the workplace jumped by 240 percent.[24] As more women entered the workforce and recreational vehicles joined the family car in the garage, two- and three-car families became the norm. At the same time, cross-commuting gradually replaced trips to the metropolitan center. Even by 1980, years before sprawl reached its current dimensions, over 40 percent of all work trips were suburb to suburb, and only 20 percent were from suburb to the central city in the average metropolitan region.[25] Reverse commuting—travel by central-city residents to jobs in edge cities or elsewhere in the suburbs—also increased.[26] Longer commutes combined with high gas prices drove up the costs of getting to work. In 2000, some residents of sprawled-out metropolitan areas such as Houston and Atlanta spent more for transportation than for housing.[27]

A rising concern about sprawl became evident by the mid-1990s. In May 1995, *Newsweek* magazine devoted a cover story to the problems of urban sprawl in New York, Memphis, Miami, Los Angeles, San Francisco, and Washington, D.C. In all of these regions, said the *Newsweek* reporters, sprawl had created "blighted metropolitan landscapes" of strip malls, traffic, and monotonous sameness. In reference to California, they observed, "No wonder they're so sterile—sterility is designed into them!" They wrote about "the new American phenomenon, the suburban slum," with aging tract housing interspersed with strip development.[28]

Four years later, in its July 19, 1999, issue, *Newsweek* featured sprawl again, this time declaring it had become an urgent public issue, part of a "livability" agenda being promoted by affluent suburban residents, suburban politicians, and Vice President Al Gore. The key elements of this agenda, according to *Newsweek*, included "the triple evils of sprawl: air pollution, traffic congestion, and visual blight."[29] In the fall of 1999, as part of its continuing Challenge to Sprawl Campaign, the Sierra Club released its annual ratings of how effectively the states were regulating sprawl.[30] News stories about the report were carried in national and numerous local newspapers, often as feature stories.

Even the conservative *Wall Street Journal* chimed in with an article describing a battle between community groups and developers in the suburbs surrounding Colorado Springs, Colorado. According to the *Journal*, the conflicts in Colorado Springs were only one of the many skirmishes occurring in the rapidly growing metropolitan areas of the Rocky Mountain West. Always an advocate of an unfettered market, the *Journal* nevertheless noted the efforts of Boulder, Colorado, to slow growth through land-use regulation.[31] A couple of months later, in January 2000, the *Journal* reported that campaigns against sprawl had inspired a political revolution that was toppling pro-growth politicians.[32] Apparently trying to change public sentiment in its urban area, the *St. Louis Post-Dispatch* ran one of a series of articles on sprawl under the headline "Urban Sprawl Is a Hot Topic." The paper seemed puzzled by the attitude of its readers, observing, "But Missouri's attitude seems to be: 'What, us worry?' "[33]

Some politicians joined the media by turning sprawl into a political issue. In 1999, the editors of *Governing*, a magazine widely read by state and local public officials, devoted two issues and several other articles to the topic of urban sprawl.[34] In January 1997, Democratic governor Parris Glendening of Maryland promised to fight for an initiative to curb sprawl, and the next year the Republican governor of New Jersey, Christie Todd Whitman (appointed in 2001 to head the Environmental Protection Agency by President Bush), shepherded an even stronger bill through her legislature. In the latter half of the 1990s, more than half the nation's governors took on issues related to sprawl.

Years before it came onto the national scene the growth control movement was well underway. Leaders of local antigrowth crusades promoted caps on the pace of new construction, impact fees (imposed on developers as a way of paying some of the public costs of growth), linkage fees (which require developers to help pay for costs linked to development, such as affordable housing, schools, and day care), and a variety of other measures. Growth controls spread rapidly in the 1970s; by 1975, they were in effect in over 300 jurisdictions across the country.[35] Between 1971 and 1986, more than 150 growth control measures appeared on local ballots; 50 measures appeared on ballots in 1986 alone, with three-quarters of them winning.[36] More than a decade later, in 1998, voters passed 70 percent of the 240 local no-growth measures placed on ballots.[37]

Interestingly, regulations meant to curb growth were pushed hardest in politically conservative areas of southern California. In 1986, over the objections of Mayor Tom Bradley, Los Angeles voters passed Proposition U, which effectively ended most new office construction in residential neighborhoods on the West Side and in the San Fernando Valley.[38] In the same election, voters in Newport Beach in Orange County, a bastion of conservatism, defeated plans for a $400 million mixed-use complex overlooking the harbor. The no-growth forces won even though they were outspent in the campaign by $500,000 to $10,000.[39]

Growth control was especially popular in wealthier cities. Ventura County, California, provides an example of the kinds of regulations commonly adopted. In November 1998, voters passed several initiatives to create urban growth boundaries, which were designed to limit new development at the edges of the county's cities and towns. The new rules specified that areas of land located within designated growth boundaries could not be rezoned for development until 2020. To ensure their wishes could not be overridden by public officials, these laws even took the power to rezone land protected from development out of the hands of the county's board of supervisors.[40] In the same month, New Jersey voters approved $1 billion to protect about half of the state's undeveloped open land from urban development.[41] More than 2,000 miles away, in November 2002, Nevada voters approved a conservation bond issue to protect open lands from unplanned sprawl. The impetus for the measure came in response to a spurt of unbridled growth; in only 30 years the state's population had soared from less than a half million people to more than 2 million. By 2000, only 21 percent of Nevada residents were natives. The newcomers were trying to keep the Las Vegas and Reno urban areas from becoming as crowded as the places they had left.[42]

In the new century, antisprawl politics began to go well beyond measures designed to directly merely regulate the pace of growth. In 2004, a statewide initiative passed that sharply curbed Oregon's aggressive land use laws, but three years later voters reversed that decision when it got tagged as promoting sprawl and taxpayer-funded bailouts for greedy developers. Transportation projects that seemed to promote sprawl often went down in crushing defeat. For example, voters in the Virginia suburbs of Washington, D.C., fearful of a new stream of movement from the city, defeated Governor Mark Warner's 2002 proposal for a sales tax to finance new highway and transit construction.[43]

Despite voters' concerns, sprawl has remained a local rather than a national issue because there are so many other things on the nation's public policy agenda, such as the state of the economy, national security, health care reform, battles over social issues, and environmental regulation. In January 1999, Vice President Al Gore announced a proposal (never adopted) by the Clinton administration to spend $9.5 billion to preserve open space, build roads and public transit, and encourage local communities to plan new schools.[44] At one point, Gore promised to make urban sprawl an issue in the 2000 presidential campaign. Calling it his "livability agenda," Gore said the issue of urban sprawl would appeal to people caught in "tidal flows of traffic" who spent too much time trying to get to work and back, at the cost to their family lives. According to Gore, "There have been races for governor and mayor all over this country where the voters have made it very clear that this is an issue about which they feel passionately, and I plan in the next 13 months to take this issue to the voters of America."[45] When challenged on the question of whether such a complex topic could be turned into a hot political item, Gore answered, "Give me time."

In the end, the issue of sprawl played no role at all in the campaign. For his part, Republican presidential candidate George W. Bush refused to talk about it, saying it should be left to state and local governments.[46] In the 2004 presidential campaign, neither candidate mentioned urban sprawl at all, and neither did the candidates in the 2008 campaign for the White House. A very modest, though indirect, effort to address the problem appeared with the passage of the American Recovery and Reinvestment Act, signed into law by President Barack Obama on February 17, 2009. It reserved $12 billion for mass transit improvements, though not for the expansion of existing systems.[47]

It is clear that urban sprawl cannot be curbed without far-reaching changes in public policies and governance arrangements. There is an obvious tension, however, between governmental regulation and the deeply held cultural values of individualism and free enterprise that define American politics. Leaders of four movements—Metro Gov, the New Regionalism, Smart Growth, and the New Urbanism—have attempted to negotiate the treacherous terrain between personal autonomy and regional planning. Over the years, there have been numerous campaigns to reform the governance of metropolitan regions, but the successes have been relatively few. The New Regionalism has been directed mainly at more modest efforts to bring about interlocal agreements, share tax burdens, and achieve a level of cooperation in providing services as a way of reducing the extreme inequalities of local governments. The proponents of Smart Growth also shy away from large-scale solutions and believe that local governments must take the lead in reducing the environmental effects of unregulated urban growth and unplanned land use. For their part, the New Urbanists focus on land use and architectural regulations meant to facilitate development on a "human scale." We now will discuss these four movements, in turn.

A History of Metro Gov

The idea that governments should be guided by a singular ideal—the efficient provision of public services at the lowest possible cost—goes back a century, to the Progressive Era and the municipal reform tradition. The reformers who focused on municipal corruption and machine governance in the old industrial cities were cut from the same cloth as the reformers who pushed for metropolitan governance. The same principles of "good government" that applied to the cities were also relevant, they thought, to the governance of the metropolis. In both instances, efficiency and a clear distinction between politics and public administration were considered to be the main pillars of reform.[48] Reformers compared the proliferation of governments in urban regions to electoral wards in the cities—in their view, wards were nothing but hotbeds of parochial politics, with their representatives lacking the capacity or the perspective to attend to the overall problems of the city. Likewise, they said, too many governments at the regional level made it impossible to deliver urban services at the lowest cost. Thus, writing in 1912, one reformer said, "Here [in metropolitan Boston] are thirty-eight towns and cities as intimately related to everything that concerns daily life as the wards of an American city, but with no power or means . . . of constructing, or improving public works or of taking public action that is for the metropolitan district as a whole."[49] Obviously this analysis led to only one conclusion: metropolitan areas should be governed in the simplest and most cost-effective manner, that is, by a single governmental entity.

Almost 20 years later, an influential reformer picked up the same theme when he described what he saw as the parochialism and chaos arising from the fragmentation of local government: "They [the many governments] tend to divert attention of the inhabitants from the fact that they are members of one large community and lead them to act as members of separate units. They result in great variation in municipal regulations . . . and in standards of services, in sectional treatment of problems which are essentially metropolitan."[50] The "metro gov" reformers who promoted the idea that urban regions should be governed by a single governmental unit agreed to the principle, "Only a government with community-wide jurisdiction can plan and provide the services, physical facilities, guidance, and controls necessary to relate functional plans with real plans. None of the metropolitan areas has such a government today."[51]

The metro-gov reformers were fired by the conviction that truth and virtue were on their side. Such confidence fueled the bitter disappointment they felt when voters rejected their proposals. In metropolitan areas all across the country, campaign after campaign, decade after decade, the reformers put proposals before the voters, and they came up empty handed almost every time. Between 1921 and 1979, reformers went to voters 83 times in various metropolitan areas in an attempt to gain approval of city–county consolidations. They succeeded just 17 times, and only 2 of those successes came in metropolitan areas of 250,000 or more (Nashville–Davidson County, Tennessee, 1962, and

Jacksonville–Duval County, Florida, 1967). (The consolidation of Indianapolis with Marion County, Indiana, in 1969 was imposed by the state legislature and not by a popular referendum.)[52]

In other cases, reformers tried to consolidate governments by creating two-tier systems (a metropolitan district with specific service responsibilities, but with municipalities and counties continuing to possess important powers). The most notable success came with the creation of Metropolitan Dade County (Miami) in 1957. Under this reform, the county assumed many of the responsibilities (such as fire and police protection, traffic control, parks and recreation, health and welfare programs, air pollution control, and some other activities) formerly assumed by municipal governments.

Most of the ambitious schemes to impose metropolitan government went down in flames because both suburban and central-city voters wanted to preserve local control. The experience in the St. Louis metropolitan area was typical, except there the reformers tried, and failed, more times than anywhere else: in 1926, 1930, 1959, 1962, and 1989. In 1926, the voters in St. Louis County defeated a proposal to consolidate the city of St. Louis with the county. Four years later, the county's voters vetoed a somewhat less ambitious proposal that would have placed the city and county under a regional government, except for a few services and public functions.[53]

In 1959, local advocates for metropolitan reform gave it another try. This time they floated the idea of a Greater St. Louis City–County District that would have assumed responsibility for forging a regional plan and for promoting economic development; managing regional mass transit and traffic control on major streets and highways; administering all sewage facilities; and supervising all police training, communications, and civil defense. Municipalities would have been left with the responsibility of regulating local street traffic and providing police and fire protection and garbage pickup. Municipal officials reacted with a furious campaign of opposition, and voters soundly defeated the plan.[54] Tempers had not even completely cooled before reformers made another try. This time, in 1962, the "borough plan" would have placed the city and county under a single government and divided the county into 22 boroughs, each exercising some limited powers. This plan would have eliminated all existing municipalities. The plan was defeated by a 4-to-1 landslide, an even more lopsided margin than in 1959.

Despite the long string of ignominious defeats, the battle for reform in the St. Louis area was still not over. In 1989, an elected board of freeholders placed a consolidation plan before the voters of St. Louis County (language in the Missouri constitution empowered such a board of "freeholders"—property owners—to make such proposals). In addition to reducing the number of municipalities in the county from 90 to 37, the plan would have transferred most land use, zoning, and building inspections to the county and also created a county commission to oversee fire and emergency services. It quickly became obvious that opposition to reform was alive and well even though almost three decades had passed since the previous reform effort. An acrimonious campaign ensued, and both sides readied for the scheduled June 20, 1989, referendum.

CHAPTER 11 ▸ Governing the Fragmented Metropolis

Before election day, however, the U.S. Supreme Court declared the board of freeholders illegal because it denied equal protection of the law to non-property holders.[55]

The successive generations of reformers failed even though it was easy for them to demonstrate that tax burdens and service levels varied wildly among municipalities. It was also transparently obvious that the city of St. Louis was in economic decline and had been since the 1920s. A pattern of racial and so-cial-class segregation between the city and county, and between municipalities within the county, was a defining feature of the St. Louis region, and the zoning ordinances of the numerous suburban jurisdictions demonstrably helped establish and preserve such segregation. But St. Louis's citizens did not necessarily regard such facts in a negative light. Even if they had, it is doubtful that any reform cause could have overcome the deep attachment people felt to their local communities.

Some of the things that the metro gov reformers saw as problems—such as varying taxing levels and service provisions—others saw as solutions. Most suburban residents had long felt this way, and in the 1980s they began to find support for their point of view in academic quarters. In September 1988, just a few months before the vote on the freeholders' plan, the influential Advisory Commission on Intergovernmental Relations proclaimed that urban residents benefited when they were given the ability to shop around for different bundles of taxes, services, and amenities offered by municipalities.[56] This conclusion, which was also supported by several scholars, undermined the most sacred principle of the metropolitan reform movement. Finally, after several decades it became possible for the defenders of local autonomy to cite scholarly approval for the view that they were doing nothing but exercising their free choice to live wherever they wished rather than appearing to defend parochial self-interest.

The advocates for metro reform were given renewed hope in 2001, when the city of Louisville merged with Jefferson County, Tennessee. Reformers thought that this unusual event might break a long-standing logjam—a successful city–county consolidation had not been accomplished anywhere in the nation since a partial merger between Indianapolis and Marion County in 1969. Immediately, advocates for metropolitan reform in Albuquerque, Buffalo, Cleveland, Memphis, Milwaukee, and San Antonio picked up the cause.

The merger between Louisville and Jefferson County was made possible because an interlocal compact had already prepared the ground. In 1985, the city threatened to annex some economically attractive areas in the county. County officials found this proposal threatening because if the annexations were carried out the county would lose much of its revenue base. After three years of bickering, in 1988, the city and county agreed to divide occupational tax collections and to establish a centralized planning and development agency, which was charged with the task of reducing the competition among local governments for economic development. Even before the compact, voters had become accustomed to a cooperative agreement in which the city and county jointly ran a water and sewer authority, park, zoo, library system, and a consolidated metropolitan school district. Thus, by the time the vote for a merger was held in 1985, it did not seem threatening or even especially consequential to political elites, the business community, or to much of the electorate.

As a means of accomplishing a merger of taxes, services, and governmental administration, Louisville was officially absorbed into Jefferson County. Suburban voters gained a lot from the new arrangement. The fact that approximately two-thirds of the voters and metro council seats came from the former suburbs tilted political power in favor of affluent suburbanites at the expense of blue-collar inner-city residents, particularly African Americans. This realignment should have come as no surprise; in other metropolitan regions, inner-city voters have steadfastly opposed consolidation proposals precisely because it dilutes their influence.

As it turns out, the Louisville example did not become a rallying cry for reformers elsewhere because the political conditions that made reform possible there were hard to duplicate. An instructive example came in November 2004, when a proposal to merge Des Moines with its surrounding county, Polk (Public Measure Letter A), failed by margins of almost two to one in both the city and county.[57] If history is any guide, the Des Moines experience offers a more reliable glimpse into the future prospects for metro reform than the Louisville case. And for reformers there is another sour note. The main selling point for the Louisville merger—that services would become more efficient through streamlined administration—has not been realized to any measurable degree.[58] Neither has the merger resulted in a more equitable distribution of services than before.[59]

The successive generations of metro gov reformers have demonstrated a remarkable resolve even in the face of repeated failure. What accounts for this record of stubborn persistence? The explanation can probably be traced to the power of the ideal they promote. Almost everyone agrees that government should be efficient and that it should be able to solve the most pressing problems that citizens face. By these standards, the extreme fragmentation of America's urban regions is hard to defend, and thus the search for some alternative is impossible to resist. But it should be pointed out that despite a century of failure for metro gov, in many places more modest arrangements have been put in place to accomplish some of the reformers' goals. In this sense, perhaps reform has not been the abject failure that it sometimes appears to be.

Public officials who are close to the problems have shown a pragmatic willingness to reach across jurisdictional boundaries when the need arises. In some urban regions, an urban county has agreed to provide critical services that cannot be supplied by individual municipalities. Interlocal agreements among two or more governments have become a way of sharing and administering services. Sometimes tax collection and assessments, data processing, and other routine administrative tasks have also been pooled. Small steps of this kind may seem to be mundane and boring, but that is exactly the point: they sidestep the bitterly contested fights that inevitably break out when more ambitious schemes are proposed.

Some examples reveal both the promise and the limitations of piecemeal reform. In the 1940s, voters agreed to a new charter for St. Louis County (then the principal suburban county in the St. Louis region) that allowed the county to expand its service and administrative responsibilities. The county soon adopted a building code, and in the next few years it began to conduct electrical inspections of new construction in unincorporated areas; it also contracted with municipalities to provide this service. By 1964, the county was running 32 parks and an extensive library system. Following another charter revision in 1954, the county formed its own police force. Over the years, the county police department has contracted with numerous cities for police enforcement. In 1971, voters approved still another charter amendment, this one giving the county control over waste disposal and authorizing it to set minimum training and educational standards for firefighters. Today, the county also administers 911 emergency services, runs a system of health clinics, builds roads and coordinates transportation, and operates a system of jails and courts.[60]

Similarly, counties in other urban regions have expanded their responsibilities. By the mid-1980s, DuPage County, west of Chicago, ran an extensive parks system and coordinated municipal services for those cities that volunteered to participate. Through a regional planning commission, it provided planning expertise and advice to cities and applied for federal grants on behalf of municipalities and special districts.[61] Oakland County, Michigan, north of Detroit, has also, step-by-step, taken on more responsibilities, finally running an airport, providing contracted services to municipalities, and running a public library system and emergency services. Over time it has become, in effect, a regional government that coordinates public works projects.[62] By the early 1970s, Orange County, California, had evolved into an administrative structure sufficient to provoke repeated protests from local officials. Like other urban counties, it had grown less through big reform than by a gradual accumulation of responsibilities.

Urban areas have also been able to overcome many of the effects of governmental fragmentation by creating still more governments: special districts charged with providing a particular service. In 2002, there were 87,900 local governments in the United States; of these, fewer than one in four—19,431—were municipalities.[63] The fastest-growing form of local government is the special district—an authority granted taxing and spending powers so it can undertake designated responsibilities such as administering sewer systems, running toll tunnels and bridges, and providing mass transit services. Special districts are generally run more like private corporations than like governments, and most of them are virtually invisible.[64] Most of them come into existence to supply services to new developments (they are often organized, in fact, by developers for the purpose of providing public services to new subdivisions, malls, or other developments), but others are truly metropolitan in scope.

Urban counties, interlocal agreements, and special districts have facilitated improved service delivery even in the face of governmental fragmentation. It should be pointed out, however, that intergovernmental agreements and special districts constitute an interlocking web of incredible complexity. This is troubling because it undermines democratic accountability. Except for municipalities, almost everything local governments do generally occurs out of sight and mind. Special districts are run like private corporations that are not responsible to voters.[65] The Byzantine system of regional governance persists because each part solves a practical problem. It is hard to imagine that this system is efficient, but it is flexible enough to provide a level of public infrastructure and services that most people find satisfactory. It is a curious irony that local government officials and citizens have found a way to solve some of the most pressing problems posed by the crazy-quilt pattern of regional government by haphazardly stitching more pieces into the fabric.

Reform has taken this route because few people think of themselves as regional citizens; instead, they identify with a particular town or city.[66] Referring to the residents of the St. Louis area, E. Terrence Jones has observed, "They desire governments that are comfortable, like that old sweater in the closet [that] feels so snug when you put it on each winter."[67] The attachment to place and community is a powerful urge, and appeals based on the premise that people should be willing to give it up in exchange for the abstract and unknown benefits of regional governance have, in most cases, fallen on deaf ears. Resourceful people find practical ways around the problem of regional governance, and this is one of the reasons many of them do not consider it to be much of a problem at all.

The New Regionalism

In the late 1980s, the decades-long crusade for metropolitan reform took a turn when a new generation of reformers began to march under a banner calling for a New Regionalism. The New Regionalism brought together people who shared a conviction that "flight creates blight."[68] It is hard not to notice that governmental fragmentation divides metropolitan areas into a multitude of fiscal fiefdoms, with better-off cities able to provide superior services because they have access to good tax sources while poorer cities struggle. Several urban scholars have argued that such inequality undermines the economic health of metropolitan regions, and not just of the disadvantaged governments within them.[69] Of 13 studies conducted between 1989 and 1996, all but one showed that central-city economic performance was associated with the economic performance of suburbs and of metropolitan areas; in addition, studies revealed a negative relationship between greater interjurisdictional inequality and regional economic performance.[70] The lesson the New Regionalists draw from such evidence is that intergovernmental inequalities must be reduced if metropolitan regions are to prosper.

Probably more often than any other state, Minnesota legislature has entertained proposals for curbing the tendency toward polarization and competition among jurisdictions. Bills have been considered that would require all municipalities to accept a "fair share" of affordable housing, pool their tax bases, give up local land use decisions to a regional planning authority, and regionalize critical public services. The years of controversy in Minnesota reveal how hard it is to accomplish this kind of reform even in a state where the political reformers have had political clout.

In 1967, the state legislature approved the creation of a Metropolitan Council for the Minneapolis urban region. Four years later, in what advocates called the "Minnesota Miracle" because of the unlikely compromises that made it possible, the state legislature approved a plan to partially equalize local revenues by requiring cities and towns in some parts of the state to participate in tax-sharing plans.[71] Local governments surrounding Minneapolis participated in a regional tax-sharing arrangement that required each city to place the taxes gained from an increase in the value of commercial industrial growth into a common pool. The purpose of this tax-sharing scheme was to curb the tax abatements and direct subsidies used by municipalities to lure shopping centers and other businesses. The original legislation, amended in 1971, gave the Metropolitan Council the authority to review the master plans of local communities, but with no authority to penalize local governments that did not cooperate. As long as the legislature stuck to modest tax-sharing and cooperative planning arrangements the reforms provoked little controversy. This changed quickly in 1993 when Democratic majorities managed to push through a fair-share housing bill. The Republican governor, Arne Carlson, promptly vetoed it. In its original form, the legislation would have allowed the Metropolitan Council to penalize local communities that used their zoning and regulatory powers to stop affordable housing (these communities would lose funds from a local revenue-sharing pool and would be barred from using tax abatements or tax increment financing for development). Even after all the penalties were removed in an attempt to placate the governor and his allies, Carlson still exercised his veto. As it happens, the governor would not have had to take such action after the 1994 elections because Republicans gained seats in the state House and Senate, and this brought an end to fair-share housing legislation.

In 1994, a coalition of struggling suburbs joined representatives from Minneapolis and St. Paul to push a Metropolitan Reorganization Act through the legislature, which Governor Carlson agreed to sign. The Metropolitan Council for the Twin Cities suddenly became a $600 million regional government that operated sewer and transit services and supervised the regional airport.[72] In the same year, the legislature also took a step toward regional land use planning when it passed the Metropolitan Land Use Reform Act. The legislation did little—it only protected farmers from public assessments and tax increases that often forced them to sell to developers—but it provided a framework for a future that has never been realized, in large part because of the passionate opposition ignited by proposals that would curb the autonomy of local governments and the subsidy-seeking behavior of developers.

In 1995, a bill was introduced in the legislature that would have pooled all municipal taxes collected on homes valued above $150,000 and redistributed the money to local governments. The legislation was defeated. Another much weaker tax-sharing bill on residential property, this one completely voluntary, became the lightning rod for a vicious partisan battle. Jesse "The Body" Ventura, the pro wrestler who became Minnesota's governor in 1998, went on the offensive against Myron Orfield, the Democratic state representative who had introduced the legislation. Ventura's rhetoric harkened back to the communist-hunting days of the 1950s: "Representative Myron 'the Communist' Orfield, his latest wealth-sharing strategy, I mean this guy really needs to go to China. I mean I think he'd be most happy there. . . . Oh Myron, Myron, Myron. You never realized the communists folded for a reason. You didn't figure it out, did you Myron?"[73] The tax-sharing legislation went down in defeat.

Despite its limitations, New Regionalists still consider the tax-sharing plan of the Minneapolis region to be the best example of its kind in the nation, and they continue to hold out hope it will be emulated elsewhere. Likewise, they point to Portland, Oregon, as the "best practices" example of far-reaching land use reform as a way of achieving a metropolitan approach to growth and economic development. The Portland, Oregon, metropolitan region has the most rigidly enforced growth boundary in the United States. Because it is drawn around a rapidly growing city, the boundary is easy to see both from the air and from the ground—on one side townhouse developments and subdivisions crowd together; on the other, cows graze, grapevines leaf out, and wheat fields ripen. The growth boundary came about as a result of legislation passed by the Oregon state legislature in 1973 that required all local governments in the state to prepare a comprehensive land use plan and submit it to the State Land Conservation and Development Commission for approval. On the basis of the Commission's report, the legislature subsequently empowered an elected regional authority, the Metropolitan Service District, to establish and enforce a growth boundary in the Portland region. Portlanders began referring to the District as Metro, and in 1992 the name was made official when voters approved a referendum giving it expanded powers.[74]

In most states and metropolitan areas, an effective means of coordinating regional growth would be unthinkable because business organizations, developers, and local governments possess the power to stop the necessary state legislation. Oregon's unique political culture explains why it remains an exception. Environmental organizations and farmers supplied critical support for drawing a growth boundary around the state's largest city, Portland. A coalition supporting Portland's boundary worked hard to broaden its appeal with the argument that planned growth actually helps promote local prosperity.[75] After losing three attempts to overturn the growth boundary (in 1976, 1978, and 1982), businesses and developers seemed to become accustomed to the boundary because they "know what the rules are,"[76] but in 2004 a coalition led by developers managed to persuade the voters to approve Measure 37, a statewide initiative requiring local governments to compensate land owners if they could demonstrate that land-use restrictions had reduced their property values. It did not take long before voters began to understand that the law had given developers a way to tap into the public purse through a blizzard of lawsuits. In 2007, an overwhelming majority of voters approved Measure 49, which overturned the measure passed just three years before.[77]

Since the adoption of Measure 49, development that has leaped beyond the growth boundary has tended to occur in clusters sprinkled in and around the smaller cities and towns located within commuting distance of Portland. The subdivisions that normally sprawl across the landscape at the edges of urban areas are notably absent. The state government's willingness to override municipal governments is the key to preserving this unusual pattern. Historically, municipalities in all states have vigorously resisted attempts to control their land use decisions, and most state legislatures and administrative agencies have been reluctant to step into the fray. Oregon is exceptional in its attitude that "We've had some problems with them [municipalities] and had to whip them into line."[78]

The Minneapolis and Portland cases are bound to remain as exceptions because local governments guard their control over taxation and services, economic development, and land use with a special passion. But the problems of urban sprawl will not go away, and so suburbanites try to find ways of solving some of the problems of unplanned and uncontrolled growth without sacrificing the autonomy they so highly prize. *Smart Growth* has provided an answer.

Smart Growth

Smart Growth is a term coined in 1997 by Governor Parris Glendening of Maryland to describe policies he proposed that were aimed at building public infrastructure in designated growth areas while at the same time protecting other areas from development.[79] Because of its positive connotations, in the next few years Smart Growth became a label covering a diverse collection of land use policies and environment regulations meant to curb uncontrolled urban development. A wide range of groups, mostly notably the Sierra Club, the National Trust for Land Preservation, and the National Association of Home Builders, have embraced the principles of Smart Growth. The central message of the movement is that planned development is the answer to urban sprawl: Growth must occur, but it should be "quality development," that improves blighted areas. promotes environmental quality, lowers energy consumption through better transportation systems and improved urban design, assesses the cost and need for new public infrastructure, and protects open space.[80]

The environmental message of the Smart Growth movement has attracted support from across the political spectrum. To overcome the aversion to anything regarded as too radical, public officials have usually avoided the rhetoric of regional planning in favor of policies that promote the preservation of open space. In lieu of direct land use regulation, land trusts are commonly used to protect undeveloped areas. From 1988 to 1998, 4.7 million acres of open space were set aside in this way. In 1998, voters in New Jersey agreed to spend $98 million in state and local taxes and issue $1 billion in bonds to preserve open space. In the same year, the Florida legislature established a $3 billion bond program and Illinois committed $160 million for land acquisition. New York's governor launched a task force to study ways to favor redevelopment over new development, and Connecticut's governor set a goal of tripling the amount of open space within urban areas.[81]

Although the rhetoric of the Smart Growth movement generally stresses that urban development must be seen in metropolitan perspective, the phrase has often been used to promote more narrow objectives, namely to promote development that keeps poorer people or minorities from coming into a community. There is a rarely acknowledged contradiction at the heart of the movement. On the one hand, citizen and environmental groups may agree to the assertion, as stated in a study sponsored by the Bank of America, that "we continue to abandon people and investments in older communities as development leap-frogs out to fringe areas to accommodate another generation of low-density living."[82] In fact, however, the fate of older communities is rarely of any concern to affluent suburban residents; they care whether their new communities can avoid the problems associated with urban sprawl and new residential development.

The tensions within the Smart Growth movement were laid bare by a controversy that broke out in November 1999 in Loudoun County, Virginia, when developer John Andrews ran into furious opposition to his plans to subdivide a cornfield into 69 one-acre lots. He intended to build an upscale housing development so he anticipated no problems, especially in a county dominated by Republican voters. But in the November elections, a new group calling itself Voters to Stop Sprawl swept all eight seats on the county's board of supervisors. Reading the tea leaves, the planning commission of the tiny town of Hamilton, which held zoning jurisdiction over the new development, did the unthinkable. It voted against it.

This revolt of the affluent against the affluent grew its roots in the same fertile soil found on the margins of every metropolitan area in America. Located 16 miles from Washington, D.C., until the 1980s Loudoun County was dotted with farms and horse barns. By the turn of the twenty-first century its population had quadrupled, and even though the new residents were prosperous they brought with them traffic congestion, overcrowded schools, and new subdivisions. Explaining the sudden success of the revolt against sprawl, the newly elected Republican chair of the county board observed, "This wasn't a Republican or a Democrat thing. They [the new county board] did everything out there that the Republican Party should have done, but failed to do."[83]

Even in Loudoun County, Smart Growth carried a variety of meanings. In the part of the county that was already developing, the major issues included the costs of infrastructure and the quality and aesthetics of new development. In the sections of the county that were still mostly rural, the preservation of open space and the character of the landscape dominated the discussion.[84] Opposition to new growth in Loudoun County was also provoked by the spread of gated communities that had fragmented the county into a maze of protected enclaves. These developments came with a variety of names meant to signify affluence and high social standing: Brambleton, Forest Manor, Forest Run, Belle Terra. These developments left the people who had resided for a long time in the county isolated within "scraps of communities . . . where people live in the old-fashioned way: in a house, on a road open to other roads, forming a place that anyone might pass through on the way to somewhere else."[85]

The issues raised in Loudoun County highlight a desire by affluent suburbanites to regulate development so that the problems associated with metropolitan development can be kept from their front door. Smart Growth appeals so broadly across the political spectrum precisely because it means so many different things to so many people. Often it seemingly brings together an unlikely alliance of conservatives and environmentalists, but just as often it drives them apart. It all depends upon the particular issue at hand. As a result, the application of Smart Growth principles across the United States is uneven and it is likely to remain so.

A few communities have been aggressive in their attempts to regulate development and protect the environment. In May 2000, Congress authorized $42 billion to be spent over 15 years to protect open space from development, with the intention of encouraging the governments in urban regions to take action.[86] In Boulder, Colorado, the city and county have taken steps to reduce growth by designating a greenbelt around the city, establishing scenic areas, and refusing to supply public infrastructure or improvements except in areas approved for growth.[87] Montgomery County, Maryland, designated three corridors that distinguished between existing communities, fringe growth areas, and rural and agricultural areas, and adopted a timed growth plan intended to control the rate of development in each of these corridors.[88] Several metropolitan areas adopted the idea of corridors, or "tiers," and land use specialists of the American Bar Association got behind the idea.[89]

Despite this history it is clear that the proponents of Smart Growth still have a lot of work left to do. In many metropolitan areas there continues to be resistance to planning of any sort. In the St. Louis region, for instance, Republicans in suburban St. Charles County objected to the term *urban sprawl*, asserting they simply were exercising their "urban choice" when they moved to the suburbs. By this logic, sprawl is a positive good, simply a consequence of the freedom to live wherever one wants. This philosophy was reflected in a statement by a scholar, Fred Siegel, when he argued that sprawl "is not some malignancy to be summarily excised, but, rather, part and parcel of prosperity."[90] Siegel claims that fragmented government offers abundant advantages. It enables people who live in badly governed central cities to escape to other jurisdictions that provide an array of alternative places to live, shop, and conduct business. Most of all, he believes that fragmented government avoids the heavy hand of a single, powerful regional government that restricts choice.[91]

An even more biting critique has been leveled by Robert Bruegmann, who challenges the widely shared assumption that sprawl, if defined as low-density development, has even been occurring. His data show that much of suburban development of recent years has actually been of relatively high density. His description of Los Angeles's urban pattern makes it clear why this may be so: "From the air, virtually the entire Los Angeles basin appears as a dense carpet of buildings, with most houses packed together on lots that are considerably smaller than their counterparts in eastern cities. In addition, and in sharp contrast to many eastern cities, there are few vacant lots."[92] Bruegmann also presents evidence showing that the pace of decentralization is slowing down, having reached its peak in the 1960s and declining since. In the past, the suburban ideal was the freestanding house on a large lot. But row houses and small lots have now become the norm, and any empty spaces are being filled. Thus, in the Chicago region nearly one-fourth of recent new housing units are row houses, and similar practices have come to cities in the South and West as well.[93]

From such evidence Bruegmann draws the conclusion that antisprawl campaigns and the Smart Growth movement are misguided because they are aimed at fixing problems that are already being solved by the housing market and by consumer choice: "every individual has some role in determining how the city looks and functions. If I shop at a suburban Wal-Mart rather than a downtown department store or choose to live in an apartment near the old downtown rather than in a single-family house on five acres in exurbia, these choices have an urban form. If my choices are echoed by those of many other people, they can have a profound effect."[94] In other words, says Bruegmann, people's choices, not public policy, should mainly determine the shape of the metropolis.

Whatever the merits of the arguments made by the contenders in the sprawl debate, the outcome will be decided less by ideology than by practical politics. Smart Growth policies gain support to the degree that suburban residents are persuaded that land and environmental regulations are likely to improve the quality of their lives. Their judgments are more likely based on personal experience and immediate self-interest than on evidence marshaled by proponents of regional planning.

Several studies have demonstrated that the costs of public infrastructure are higher when urban development is left unregulated.[95] When infrastructure such as highways, sewers, water lines, and utilities are supplied in areas with low-density development, costs are much higher than in high-density areas. Infrastructure costs are also driven up when the existing public facilities in older areas are abandoned. A Smart Growth advocate has pointed out that in the 20 years between 1970 and 1990, a Maryland county spent $500 million to close 60 schools while opening 60 more, just to keep the schools located in areas where people had moved. He also cited a study estimating that by 2020 Maryland residents would spend $10 billion on new roads, sewers, and water systems in newly developed areas. From this evidence, he concluded that regional planning was necessary to stop the twin processes of abandonment and new investment.[96]

For most suburban residents, the argument that sprawl drives up the cost of infrastructure is not likely to carry much weight, especially because those costs are widely distributed, hard to measure, and paid, in large part, by the states and the federal government. It is even less likely that suburban residents will suddenly be struck with remorse by the thought that by moving out, they have contributed to the decay of older cities and neighborhoods. Possibly, however, suburban residents may pay some attention if an effective case can be made that decay at the urban center threatens the economic viability of their own communities. In an attempt to make the argument that everyone loses from unplanned development, some researchers have turned the familiar refrain that sprawl brings "despair to the inner cities"[97] on its head by claiming it may ultimately bring despair to the suburbs as well. Thirteen studies conducted between 1989 and 1996 found that the economic performance of metropolitan areas was associated with the economic performance of the nearby central cities. Such evidence makes it seem that it may be in the interest of even affluent suburban residents to pay some attention to larger issues facing their region.

Aside from the rather technical nature of such studies, it is hard to imagine that most suburban residents will buy into abstract arguments about how their own fate is linked to that of their poorer neighbors. Self-interest tends to be immediate—a lower tax bill, a better school, rising property values. These normally are regarded as purely local issues. Only with some reluctance do most urban residents support measures that focus on the larger region. Still, there is a widespread feeling among suburbanites that paradise is being sacrificed to the sheer ugliness of sprawl. For them, the New Urbanism may have special appeal because it offers benefits with practically no downside.

The New Urbanism

The New Urbanism was founded on the belief that a combination of land use changes, urban design, and architecture can revive a sense of community and make the urban environment more livable. The charter for the New Urbanism, as adopted in the first membership meeting in 2000, asserts that "individual architectural projects should be seamlessly linked to their surroundings," that "the economic health and harmonious evolution of neighborhoods, districts, and corridors can be improved through graphic design codes," and that "civic buildings and public gathering places require important sites to reinforce community identity and the culture of democracy."[98] In effect, the New Urbanists are making the case that cities and suburbs can be made more livable from the ground up as much as from the top down.

The New Urbanist movement is energized by a diagnosis of what they regard as a terrible disease—"blighted metropolitan landscapes," "banal places with the souls of shopping malls, affording nowhere to mingle except traffic jams, nowhere to walk except in the health club."[99] The proposed antidote is made up of transportation networks designed to reduce reliance on the automobile and carefully designed urban environments with harmonious streetscapes and pleasing design features (such as buildings with dormers, gables, and porticos) that integrate home, business, recreation, and community life. By fostering a sense of community in the suburbs, advocates of the New Urbanism hope to calm the restlessness that makes people constantly move on to the next subdivision in their search for a suburban Eden.

The alleged disease of the American suburb has long been the subject of commentary. The writer James Howard Kunstler begins his book *The Geography of Nowhere* with this vivid summary:

> Eighty percent of everything ever built in America has been built in the last fifty years, and most of it is depressing, brutal, ugly, unhealthy, and spiritually degrading—the jive-plastic commuter tract home wastelands, the Potemkin village shopping plazas with their vast parking lagoons, the Lego-block hotel complexes, the "gourmet mansardic" junk-food joints, the Orwellian office "parks" featuring buildings sheathed in the same reflective glass as the sunglasses worn by chain-gang guards, the particle-board garden apartments rising up in every little meadow and cornfield, the freeway loops around every big and little city with their clusters of discount merchandise marts, the whole destructive, wasteful, toxic, agoraphobia-inducing spectacle that politicians call "growth."[100]

In Kunstler's narrative, suburban residents have learned to live "in places where nothing relates to anything else," a landscape in which daily activities—home, work, shopping, recreation—are pulled apart into large-scale segregated developments accessible only by automobiles: "The houses are all in their respective income pods, the shopping is miles away from the houses," and schools, malls, and office parks are also set apart, together with their seas of cars glistening on massive parking lots.[101] Kunstler's storyline describes a dystopia in which human beings are forced to sit in their cars, gridlocked, or find themselves in the embrace of a gated community, school, or shopping mall—worst of all—a nameless suburban subdivision.

Like clear-cutting a forest, a parking lot, mall, or a housing subdivision can be most efficiently built by means of industrial methods; the first step is a bulldozer that removes everything in the way. Such methods link efficiency and wastefulness in an intimate dance. Urged on by advertising, constant changes in product lines and styles, and the proliferation of disposable packaging, "most consumer goods are destined for a one-night stand."[102] Applied to land and places, such a consumer habit has far-reaching social consequences—"cycling of people through places," a mobility and rootlessness that replaces community with the hope of renewal that comes from moving, "a kind of magic that keeps expectations high."[103] If the new place disappoints, the answer will be found in another move, and still another one after that.

Together with transportation systems that favor the automobile, the zoning regulations adopted by local governments keep in place the land use patterns that bother the followers of the New Urbanism. Virtually all suburban jurisdictions follow a standard zoning or planning regime that separates residential, commercial, and industrial development in big chunks. The effect is to make neighborhoods less walkable, because corner stores, strip malls, barber and beauty shops, and other things that people need are rigorously zoned out of large residential subdivisions, thereby forcing people to drive a long way for basic services. Can suburban environments be designed to discourage such practices? The founders of the New Urbanism think they can do it by designing neighborhoods that nurture community, transportation systems that get people out of their cars, and urban environments built to human scale. In its founding charter the Congress for the New Urbanism expressed the view that " divestment in central cities, the spread of placeless sprawl, increasing separation by race and income, environmental deterioration, loss of agricultural lands and wilderness, and the erosion of society's built heritage as one interrelated community-building challenge."[104] Although the Congress for the New Urbanism goes to some pains to point out that "we recognize that physical solutions by themselves will not solve social and economic problems," the New Urbanist approach is almost entirely oriented to the physical redesign of urban space. The 27 principles endorsed by the Congress emphasize "the neighborhood, the district, and the corridor as the essential elements of development." These principles stand in opposition to the style of urban development that has relied on the bulldozing of vast spaces for single uses such as subdivisions, shopping centers, and office parks. Such segmentation has created an urban pattern that favors cars over human beings, forcing people to spend time on the highway that might be spent at home or in a community setting.

In place of monotonous subdivisions of look-alike houses, "the goal of the New Urbanism is to promote diverse and livable communities with a greater variety of housing types, land uses, and building densities—in other words, to develop and maintain a melting pot of neighborhood homes serving a wide range of household family sizes, cultures, and incomes."[105] As an alternative to shopping centers, the New Urbanists urge the building of pedestrian-friendly shopping areas on streets and squares, within walking distance of nearby residences. Office parks are to be banned because they segregate work from home and shopping; like shopping centers, they entail the proliferation of huge parking lots and maximize reliance on the automobile.[106] The New Urbanists recognize "automobiles are a fact of modern life," but they urge that the grid of high-speed streets and highways intersecting urban areas be replaced by highway corridors clearly separated from neighborhoods. Within neighborhoods, they want to slow traffic by narrowing streets and creating traffic circles and other "traffic calming" devices. They also promote the idea that bicycle paths and sidewalks should be built along all streets and that mass transit must be made convenient.[107]

If fully realized, environments that incorporated all of these elements would not only constitute a revolution in urban planning and landscape and architectural design, they would also help cement bonds of community that have been severed by large-scale suburban development. Neighborhood residents would be walking and bicycling to a café, restaurant, or the drug store; stopping to visit with their neighbors; walking to work. Unfortunately, the New Urbanist developments do not fulfill that dream, and it is not likely they ever can.

For residents to be able to walk and bicycle to shop, work, and play, all while living in the same neighborhood, densities would have to be as high as those that exist in the downtowns of major cities. Density is a necessary condition for the clustering of diverse activities and services, and it can only be achieved through high-rise living. The problem is that most New Urbanist developments are composed of relatively low-density townhouses or single-family homes located within gated communities, which facilitate, rather than reduce, residential segregation. For this reason, the New Urbanism may actually contribute to urban sprawl.

The urban scholar Dolores Hayden describes her experience when she visited Celebration, the Disney Company's New Urbanism development near Orlando and Disney World: "After an hour and a half stuck on crowded freeways within Orlando, I spotted the white three-rail fence that wrapped the exterior of the development, an imitation of the rural fences used on the old horse farms and ranches of central Florida."[108] In one deft touch Hayden captured two issues arising from New Urbanist developments: residential projects by themselves do not (and cannot) change the geography of urban regions, and they are prone to nostalgic reconstructions that symbolize but do not create a sense of community. Both of these elements are apparent in New Town, a New Urbanist development in St. Charles, Missouri, a distant satellite suburb (or perhaps edge city) of St. Louis. The two-story antebellum porches and pillars of New Town are meant to echo a past—but is it Missouri's? A more consequential problem is that it is not located near any mass transit; clearly, it is built for commuters who drive cars. A critic observed, "You see these new developments and they look like something out of a magazine from the Urban Land Institute. They say they're sustainable development but they're in the middle of a friggin' desert. They're not connected to any public transportation. You still have to drive to get there."[109]

Urban residents may be tired of freeway congestion and gridlock, and they may sometimes revolt against the ugliness of large-scale development—especially when it is in their backyard—but unless it tackles such issues, the New Urbanism is likely to become little more than a recipe for design features that developers can use mainly for marketing purposes. In Celebration, all houses have front porches, a touch from the past that seems designed to encourage people to visit with their neighbors. As it happens, it is too hot in Florida for this to work. The houses also have other design features meant to signify a romanticized version of suburban life from another era—gables, neo-Victorian trim, picket fences. One suspects that Celebration is much like the Frontier Village or Main Street in Disneyland, California—"authentic reproductions" that evoke vague feelings of the real thing. If affluent homebuyers come to prefer the design features of the New Urbanism, developers will be happy to accommodate them. Many of the architectural touches of the New Urbanism—stone and copper facades, porches, elaborate door lintels and balconies—cost money, and thus they serve as markers more of social class than of community. They add to the real estate markup.

To serve as an effective remedy for urban sprawl, the New Urbanism must be able to realize a goal no other reform movement has been able to reach: persuade suburbanites that it is in their interest to support effective regional planning. This requires a long-term strategy for changing people's attitudes and building a political coalition sufficient for accomplishing the task. This is a tall order. Are suburban residents ready to give up their single-family homes, lawns, and multiple cars? Are they willing to tax themselves to support mass transit and rebuild highways? Are they willing to support sweeping land use reform? Do they really care about community? Judging from the history of suburban development, the answers to these questions are not likely to be reassuring.

Americans are deeply attached to their local governments. Racial and social class differences among jurisdictions continue to reinforce the tendency to separate, as does the fact that affluent residents benefit from fragmentation through lower taxes and higher service levels. State governments become involved in issues of local governance only reluctantly.[110] These facts of life have made the task of reform always difficult, whether the cause is Metro Gov, the New Regionalism, or Smart Growth. The New Urbanism escapes this constraint mainly because it focuses on small-scale and incremental steps that are only distantly related to urban sprawl.

The Prospect for Reform

Suburban residents are caught in a bind, and the way out is likely to be painful. They are fed up with gridlock and runaway development, especially when these threaten the quality of life they so highly value. In trying to solve the problems of the sprawling metropolis, there are three approaches available to them. One solution is to support reforms that will make it possible to achieve metropolitan planning and a high degree of cooperation among governments. A second solution directly contradicts the first: use the powers of municipal government as an instrument to forestall change. A third strategy they may exercise is to retreat as far as possible behind the walls of gated communities. In fact, suburban residents have used all three, but in the last few decades the last of these options has been enthusiastically embraced. Clearly, municipal autonomy and the proliferation of privatized gated communities make it much harder than ever to build support for metropolitan reform.

New Jersey's experience with land trusts suggests how difficult it will be to find ambitious solutions that go beyond parochial interests. In 1998, Governor Christie Todd Whitman announced that New Jersey's program—with its goal of acquiring more than a million acres of open space—could serve as a national model. But in the end, New Jersey was reluctant to place environmental concerns ahead of economic development. In 2000, when Merrill Lynch announced it would leave the state unless it was granted permission to build in a rural area, politicians quickly caved. An assistant in the governor's policy office explained, "They wanted a suburban-style campus, so it was either here or Pennsylvania."[111] Even in the unlikely event that politics elsewhere might be different, land trusts can do little more than preserve islands of open space in a moving stream of development.

As the urban historian Jon C. Teaford has observed, "change appears to be the ultimate enemy."[112] Local control of land use, economic development, and local taxes and services gives people a sense that they are masters of their own destiny. Governmental fragmentation will continue to be a fixture of the American metropolis, as will sprawl and its attendant problems. This is why the art of muddling through will continue to define the regional policy agenda.

Endnotes

1. For a comparative analysis of suburban development in advanced industrial countries, see Donald N. Rothblatt and Daniel J. Garr, *Suburbia: An International Assessment* (New York: St. Martin's Press, 1986), and Christopher M. Law, *The Uncertain Future of the Urban Core* (London: Routledge, 1988).
2. U.S. Bureau of the Census, *2002 Census of Governments, Preliminary Report No. 1* (Washington, DC: U.S. Government Printing Office, 2002), p. 5, Table A.
3. Kenneth Newton, "American Urban Politics: Social Class, Political Structure, and Public Goods," in *Readings in Urban Politics: Past, Present and Future,* 2nd ed., ed. Harlan Hahn and Charles H. Levine (New York: Longman, 1984).
4. Jon C. Teaford, *Post-Suburbia: Government and Politics in the Edge Cities* (Baltimore: Johns Hopkins University Press, 1997), p. 1.
5. James Heilbrun, *Urban Economics and Public Policy,* 2nd ed. (New York: St. Martin's Press, 1981), p. 48.
6. Peter O. Muller, *Contemporary Suburban America* (Upper Saddle River, NJ: Prentice Hall, 1981), p. 123.
7. George E. Peterson, "Federal Tax Policy and Urban Development," in *Central City Economic Development,* ed. Benjamin Chinitz (Cambridge, MA: Abt Books, 1979), pp. 67–78.
8. David M. Gordon, "Capitalist Development and the History of American Cities," in *Marxism and the Metropolis: New Perspectives in Urban Political Economy,* 2nd ed., ed. William K. Tabb and Larry Sawers (New York: Oxford University Press, 1984), p. 41.
9. Robert Cervero, "Unlocking Suburban Gridlock," *Journal of the American Planning Association* 52, no. 4 (Autumn 1986): 389.
10. Brian J. L. Berry, *The Open Housing Question: Race and Housing in Chicago, 1966–1976* (Cambridge, MA: Ballinger, 1979).
11. Joel Garreau, *Edge City: Life on the New Frontier* (Garden City, NY: Doubleday, 1991), p. 6.
12. Robert E. Lang and Jennifer B. LeFurgy, *Boomburbs: The Rise of America's Accidental Cities* (Washington, DC: Brookings Institution Press, 2007).
13. Ibid.
14. Ibid., pp. 56–57.
15. Office of Technology Assessment, Congress of the United States, *The Technological Reshaping of Metropolitan America,* OTA-ETI-643 (Washington, DC: U.S. Government Printing Office, 1995).
16. Anthony Downs, *The Costs of Sprawl: Environmental and Economic Costs of Alternative Development Patterns of Metropolitan America* (Washington, DC: Real Estate Research Corporation, 1974), p. 2.
17. Neal Peirce and Curtis Johnson, "St. Louis: Exploded Galaxy?" *St. Louis Post-Dispatch* (March 16, 1997), p. 6B.

18. Martha T. Moore, "Cool Climates, Hot Suburbs, Mixed Blessings," *USA Today* (November 11, 2003), p. 18A.

19. Russ Lopez and H. Patricia Hynes, "Sprawl in the 1990s: Measurement, Distribution, and Trends," *Urban Affairs Review* 38, no. 3 (January 2003): 325–352.

20. Office of Technology Assessment, *Technological Reshaping,* Chapter 8.

21. Scott Bowles, "National Gridlock," *USA Today* (November 23, 1999), p. 2A.

22. Texas Transportation Institute, Texas A&M University, *The Urban Mobility Annual Report* (Lubbock, TX, 2006).

23. Kenneth L. Wald, "How Dreams of Clean Air Get Stuck in Traffic," *New York Times* (March 11, 1990), p. 1.

24. Bowles, "National Gridlock," p. 2A.

25. Cervero, "Unlocking Suburban Gridlock," p. 389.

26. H. V. Savitch and Ronald K. Vogel, *Regional Politics: America in a Post-City Age* (Thousand Oaks, CA: Sage, 1996), p. 18.

27. Janet Frankston, "Suburban Sprawl's Sticker Shock," *Chicago Tribune* (January 5, 2003), Section 16, pp. 1–2.

28. Jerry Adler, "Bye, Bye Suburban Dream," *Newsweek* (May 15, 1995), pp. 40–45.

29. Daniel Pederson, Vern E. Smith, and Jerry Adler, "Sprawling, Sprawling . . .," *Newsweek* (July 19, 1999), pp. 23–27.

30. Ibid.

31. Vicki Lee Parker, "Western Cities Grapple with Rapid Growth," *Wall Street Journal* (September 22, 1999), p. B16.

32. John J. Fialka, "Campaign against Sprawl Overruns a County in Virginia, and Soon Perhaps Much of Nation," *Wall Street Journal* (January 4, 2000), p. A24.

33. Bill Lambrecht, "Urban Sprawl Is a Hot Topic," *St. Louis Post-Dispatch* (February 7, 1999), p. A6.

34. *Governing: The Magazine of States and Localities,* January 1999 and August 1999 issues.

35. D'vera Cohn, "Big Is No Longer Beautiful for Many U.S. Communities," *Santa Barbara News-Press* (March 4, 1979), cited in John R. Logan and Harvey L. Molotch, *Urban Fortunes: The Political Economy of Place* (Berkeley: University of California Press, 1987), p. 159.

36. Mark Baldassare, "Suburban Support for No-Growth Policies: Implications for the Growth Revolt," *Journal of Urban Affairs* 12, no. 2 (1990): 198.

37. Sierra Club, *Solving Sprawl: The Sierra Club Rates the States* (Washington, DC: Sierra Club, 1999), p. 2.

38. Robert Reinhold, "Growth in Los Angeles Poses Threat to Bradley," *New York Times* (September 22, 1987).

39. Charles Lockwood and Christopher B. Leinberger, "Los Angeles Comes of Age," *Atlantic Monthly* (January 1988): 48.

40. William Booth, "For Voters, the Target Is Sprawl," *Washington Post National* (December 7, 1998), pp. 30–31.

41. Ibid., p. 31.

42. Martin Griffith, "Alarmed by Growth, Nevadans Go 'Green,' " *Chicago Tribune* (December 19, 2002), p. 39.

43. See www.nosprawltax.org/.

44. Terence Samuel, "Gore Pushes a Plan to Help Curb Problems Related to Urban Sprawl," *St. Louis Post-Dispatch* (January 12, 1999), p. A8.

45. Terence Samuel, "Al Gore Makes Sprawl Central to His Campaign," *St. Louis Post-Dispatch* (October 12, 1999), www.postnet.com.

46. Fialka, "Campaign against Sprawl," p. A24.
47. Ibid.
48. G. Ross Stephens and Nelson Wikstrom, *Metropolitan Government and Governance: Theoretical Perspectives, Empirical Analysis, and the Future* (New York: Oxford University Press, 2000), pp. 31–32.
49. Quoted in ibid., p. 33.
50. Paul Studenski, *The Government of Metropolitan Areas in the United States* (New York: National Municipal League, 1930), p. 29.
51. Victor Jones, "Local Government Organization in Metropolitan Areas: Its Relation to Urban Redevelopment," in *The Future of Cities and Urban Redevelopment*, ed. Coleman Woodbury (Chicago: University of Chicago Press, 1953), pp. 604–605.
52. Vincent Marando, "City–County Consolidation: Reform, Regionalism, Referenda, and Requiem," *Western Political Quarterly* 32, no. 4 (December 1979): 409–422.
53. Teaford, *Post-Suburbia*, p. 110.
54. Ibid., pp. 110–112.
55. Ibid., p. 195.
56. Ibid., p. 194.
57. Hank V. Savitch, Ronald K. Vogel, and Lin Ye, "Beyond the Rhetoric: Lessons from Louisville's Consolidation," *American Review of Public Administration* 1 (2009).
58. The source for this discussion of the Louisville merger is H. V. Savitch and Ronald K. Vogel, "Suburbs without a City: Power and City–County Consolidation," *Urban Affairs Review* 39, no. 6 (July 2004): 758–790; also see Alan Greenblatt, "Anatomy of a Merger," *Governing* 16, no. 3 (December 2002): 2025.
59. Hank V. Savitch, Lin Ye, and Ron Vogel, "Promise versus Performance: The Louisville-Jefferson County Merger," paper delivered at the annual meeting of the Urban Affairs Association, (Seattle, Washington, April 2007).
60. Teaford, *Post-Suburbia*, pp. 136–138.
61. Ibid., pp. 145–146.
62. Ibid., p. 152.
63. U.S. Bureau of the Census, *2002 Census of Governments*, Report GC02-1P (Washington, DC: U.S. Government Printing Office, 2002).
64. Nancy Burns, *The Formation of American Local Governments: Private Values in Public Institutions* (New York: Oxford University Press, 1994).
65. Gerald E. Frug, "Beyond Regional Government," *Harvard Law Review* 115, no. 7 (May 2002): 1785.
66. E. Terrence Jones and Elaine Hays, "Metropolitan Citizens of St. Louis," paper prepared for a poster session at the annual meeting of the American Political Science Association (September 1, 2001); reprinted in Dick Simpson, *Inside Urban Politics: Voices from America's Cities and Suburbs* (New York: Longman, 2004), pp. 286–292.
67. E. Terrence Jones, *Fragmented by Design: Why St. Louis Has So Many Governments* (St. Louis: Palmerston and Reed Publishing, 2000), Foreword.
68. Fred Siegel, "Is Regional Government the Answer?" *The Public Interest* (Fall 1999): 88.
69. William R. Barnes and Larry C. Ledebur, *The New Regional Economies* (Thousand Oaks, CA: Sage, 1998).
70. Rosalind Greenstein and Wim Wiewel, eds., *Urban-Suburban Interdependencies* (Cambridge, MA: Lincoln Institute of Land Policy, 2000), pp. 25–28.

71. See the Minnesota Historical Society, "Public Education: The Minnesota Miracle," www.mnhs.org/library/tips/history_topics/18public.html.

72. Myron Orfield, *Metropolitics: A Regional Agenda for Community and Stability* (Washington, DC: Brookings Institution Press, and Cambridge, MA: Lincoln Institute of Land Policy, 1997), p. 13.

73. Quoted in ibid., p. 149.

74. Paul G. Lewis, *Shaping Suburbia: How Political Institutions Organize Urban Development* (Pittsburgh: University of Pittsburgh Press, 1996), pp. 105–107.

75. Christopher Leo, "Regional Growth Management Regime: The Case of Portland, Oregon," *Journal of Urban Affairs* 20, no. 4 (1998): 363–394.

76. Lewis, *Shaping Suburbia*, p. 115.

77. For a discussion on Measure 37 and 49, see www.oregon.gov/LCD/MEASURE49/index.shtml.

78. John DeGrove, *Land, Growth, and Politics* (Chicago: APA Planners' Press, 1984), pp. 249–250.

79. Elizabeth Gearing, "Smart Growth or Smart Growth Machine? The Smart Growth Movement and Its Implications," in *Up against the Sprawl*, ed. Jennifer Wolch, Manuel Pastor Jr., and Peter Dreier (Minneapolis: University of Minnesota Press, 2004), p. 280.

80. Robert H. Freilich, *From Sprawl to Smart Growth: Successful Legal, Planning, and Environmental Systems* (Washington, DC: American Bar Association, 1999), p. 323.

81. Terence Samuel, "Suburban Communities Grab Up Land to Keep Developers at Bay," *St. Louis Post-Dispatch* (May 14, 2000), p. A8.

82. Bank of America, "Beyond Sprawl: New Patterns of Growth to Fit the New California."

83. Fialka, "Campaign against Sprawl," p. A24.

84. Ibid.

85. Stephanie McCrummen, "Subdivisions Impose Social Divide," *Washington Post* (May 1, 2005), www.washingtonpost.com.

86. Ibid.

87. Ibid., pp. 195–196.

88. Ibid., pp. 131–132.

89. Ibid.

90. Siegel, "Is Regional Government the Answer?" p. 85.

91. Ibid., pp. 85–98.

92. Robert Bruegmann, *Sprawl: A Compact History* (Chicago: University of Chicago Press, 2005), p. 68.

93. Ibid., pp. 63–65.

94. Ibid., p. 225.

95. For a comprehensive review, see Office of Technology Assessment, *Technological Reshaping*, Chapter 8.

96. Edward T. McMahon, "Stopping Sprawl by Growing Smarter," *Planning Commissioners Journal* 26 (Spring 1997): 4–7.

97. Peirce and Johnson, "St. Louis: Exploded Galaxy?" p. 6B.

98. Congress for the New Urbanism, *Charter of the New Urbanism* (New York: McGraw-Hill, 2000).

99. Adler, "Bye, Bye Suburban Dream."

100. James Howard Kunstler, *The Geography of Nowhere* (New York: Touchstone, 1993), p. 10.

101. Ibid., p. 118.
102. John A. Jakle and David Wilson, *Derelict Landscapes: The Wasting of America's Built Environment* (Savage, MD: Rowman and Littlefield, 1992), p. 182.
103. Ibid., p. 40.
104. Congress for the New Urbanism, *Charter of the New Urbanism.*
105. Marc A. Weiss, in Congress for the New Urbanism, *Charter of the New Urbanism,* p. 91.
106. Elizabeth Moule, in ibid., pp. 105–108.
107. Douglas Farr, in ibid., pp. 141–146.
108. Dolores Hayden, *Building Suburbia: Green Fields and Urban Growth* (New York: Pantheon Books, 2003), p. 206.
109. Chad Garrison, "Brave New Town," *Riverfront Times* (June 1–7, 2006), p. 19.
110. For an excellent discussion of all these points, see Donald F. Norris, "Prospects for Regional Governance under the New Regionalism: Economic Imperatives versus Political Impediments," *Journal of Urban Affairs* 23, no. 5 (2001): 562–566.
111. Iver Peterson, "In New Jersey, Sprawl Keeps Outflanking Its Foes," *New York Times* (March 17, 2000), pp. A1, A19.
112. Jon C. Teaford, *The American Suburb: The Basics* (New York: Routledge, 2008).

CHAPTER 12

The Metropolitan Battleground

The Competition for Fiscal Resources

To the average citizen, local debates about taxes and spending may seem to be mostly routine and even boring. For urban officials, however, nothing could be more consequential. Without adequate resources, a city simply cannot offer the level of services and amenities that most people demand. This, basically, is the bottom line, and local officials may find themselves thrown out of office if they do not meet it. In finding revenues to finance these activities, though, municipal officials generally find that the choices available to them are extremely limited. One limitation is legal: state laws dictate the kinds of taxes fees that cities are allowed to impose. The other limitation is political: citizens and businesses do not like taxes. Local officials must be mindful that raising taxes past a certain point might tempt residents and businesses to other jurisdictions in search of a better deal. Because these considerations are always present, local fiscal policy is determined within a battleground in which cities are always trying to outbid one another, and there will be winners and losers.

Local officials devote a lot of attention to policies crafted to improve their competitive position. The stimulus package passed by Congress in 2009 revealed just how the competition among governmental jurisdictions works, whether for private or public dollars. When Congress authorized $144 billion for infrastructure projects, it set off a race that pitted states against states, states against cities, and cities against one another. Like every other public official in the country, Frank C. Ortis, the mayor of Pembroke Pines, Florida, declared, "We have a wish list."[1] In his case, the wish was to repair sewer lines. But it was clear that the federal money would not stretch far enough to fund all the wish lists across the country. States and cities scrambled to make the case that their projects were especially urgent, and that they fit the "shovel ready" criteria laid down by the Obama administration.

The stimulus package established a battleground among jurisdictions. The sudden availability of federal dollars made it newsworthy, but in fact this kind of interjurisdictional competition for sources of revenue goes on all the time. What cities compete for is virtually endless, ranging from federal and state dollars, to malls, big-box stores, office parks, sports stadiums, tourism facilities, and on and on. Depending upon one's point of view, this competition is a

OUTTAKE

Hundreds of Little Hoovers Make the Economic Crisis Worse

Many historians and economists have commented on the blunder by President Herbert Hoover and the Republican Congress in 1932, when they increased taxes and cut spending in an attempt to balance the federal budget. The nation had already slid into a serious economic downturn, and their actions took money out of the economy at a time when it was desperately needed. In a similar fashion, during the economic crisis that began in the late summer of 2008 states and cities took money out of the economy by raising taxes and cutting services. In this way, states and cities made the recession worse and, in effect, canceled out much of the economic stimulus provided by the federal government.

The American Recovery and Reinvestment Act, as passed by Congress on on February 13, 2009, sent $79 billion of fiscal assistance directly to the states and authorized $144 billion for infrastructure projects undertaken by state and local governments and $41 billion for school districts. The stimulus package provided a greater influx of federal money than at any time since the 1930s, but it did not do much to spare local governments from making deep cuts in their budgets. The federal dollars were designated for building and reparing infrastructure; cities were not allowed to use them to solve current budgetary problems. As a result, in 2010, cities slashed their budgets deeper in 2010 than they had the year before.

To make ends meet, states and local governments took increasingly desperate measures. By February 2009, 83 percent of cities had cut expenditures and services. By December, Philadelphia had closed 11 of its 54 libraries and announced that 67 of its 81 pools would not open in the summer. Beginning January 1, San Diego eliminated all six of the centers it had established to help citizens with city services, and cut the number of new police recruits by half. Seattle reduced spending on youth violence and homeless services. The hardest-hit cities began cutting even essential services; for example, Pontiac, Michigan, closed 8 public schools and reduced the number of police officers from 200 to only 73. Baltimore decided to consider allowing advertisements on their fire trucks to raise funds after closing several firehouses. Local governments even struggled to bury the indigent. The impact of such measures was magnified by budget cuts being imposed by state governments, which were feeling the same pressures. In March, 2009, 34 states were cutting a wide range of social-services programs.

A fundamental characteristic of the American intergovernmental system requires states and cities to balance their budgets despite the fact that they provide services that are essential to the immediate health and welfare of their citizens. The economist Paul Krugman wants to change the system so that it stops asking so much from the governments least equipped to adjust during times of economic hardship. He has proposed that the costs of most forms of medical care, education, and infrastructure be assumed by the federal government rather than by states and local governments. Most people, however, see strengths as well as weaknesses in America's intergovernmental system, and in any case the political mood of the last few years favors an even lesser federal role. For these reasons, fundamental changes like those suggested by Krugman are not likely to come any time soon, but he is right when he says that economic crises raise issues about the way that the United States finances its governmental activities.

Sources: Paul Krugman, "Fifty Herbert Hoovers," *New York Times* (December 28, 2008), http://www.nytimes.com/2008/12/29 /opinion/29krugman.html; also Mary Williams Walsh, "Under Strain, Cities Are Cutting Back Projects," *New York Times* (September 30, 2008), www.nytimes .com/2008/10/01business/01muni.html; Chris Hoene, "Fiscal Outlook for Cities Worsens in 2009," *Research Brief on America's Cities*, by National League of Cities, Issue 2009-1 (Washington, DC: National League of Cities, 2009), www.nlc.org; Legislative News, *Governing* (April 9, 2009); News, *Governing* (April 9, 2009).

positive and dynamic feature of the U.S. system, or it is a waste of public dollars when governments offer subsidies just to influence the location of activities that would occur anyway. The reality, though, is that the system is sustained by the fiscal needs of the governments that make it up, and this is one of the reasons why city budgets are intensely political, and why they matter.

Cities in the U.S. Federal System

Cities in the United States operate within a very peculiar system of governments, at least when compared with the practices in most of the world: "By not providing capital resources to subnational governments from the central government, the United States stands apart from almost every other advanced capitalist state, even other federal states."[2] In most Western nations, much of the basic infrastructure and many of the services provided to citizens are financed by the central governments even when they are administered by local governmental units. By contrast, cities in the United States derived only about 4 percent of their revenues from the national government in 2007, compared to 14 percent in Japan (in 2003) and one-half or much more in western European countries.[3] In addition, most cities outside the United States do not have to rely on private lenders to raise money for capital projects; those are generally financed by national governments. Such a system means that, unlike in the United States, local economic conditions only partly influence the ability of a city to find the revenues necessary to provide for critical services and build infrastructure.

Municipal governments in the United States are located at the bottom of a three-tiered federal system of governance. At the top, the federal government enjoys the greatest freedom to impose taxes and go into debt. At its discretion, it may make states and cities implement policies that are costly (such as drunk driving, education testing, and antipollution laws), but it does not necessarily provide the money for such "unfunded mandates." The federal government has access to the best, most flexible sources of revenue: the personal income tax, payroll taxes (for Social Security), and corporate income taxes. States are next in line, collecting personal income taxes (but at a lower rate), and impose sales and receipts taxes. The states are not allowed to run deficits year to year, and neither are their cities. Ninety-nine of the 100 largest cities in the nation are, by law, required to balance their budgets.[4] State and county governments spend money within cities for such things as education, pollution control, and infrastructure such as roads, bridges, water and sewer lines, health clinics, and the like, but the cities finance nearly all of the basic municipal services and a great many infrastructure projects with their own revenues. A consequence of being at the bottom of the federal system is that cities have fewer sources of revenue and operate under more stringent budget rules than governments at any other level.

Local governments may be at the bottom in powers, but not in responsibilities. As shown in Table 12.1, in 2007 local governments employed 13.2 million workers, with the largest employers being school districts, municipalities, and

TABLE 12.1　Federal, State, and Local Government Employment and Revenues, 2007

Employment (in Thousands)	
Federal civilian	2,730
Federal less U.S. Postal Service and Department of Defense	1,263
State	5,200
Local	14,186
Counties	2,928
Municipalities	3,001
Townships	510
School districts	6,925
Special districts	821
Revenues (Own Source; in Billions of Dollars)	
Federal	$2,540
State	1,024
Local	840

Note: The revenue figures do not include intergovernmental transfers or borrowing.

Sources: U.S. Bureau of the Census, *2007 Census of Governments, Government Employment and Payroll* (Washington, DC: U.S. Government Printing Office, 2002), Tables 1 and 3; state and local revenue data from U.S. Bureau of the Census, *2002 Census of Governments*, vol. 4, no. 5, *State and Local Finances by Level of Government,* Table 1, http://www2.census.gov/govs/estimate/07slsstab1a.xls; national revenue data from U.S. Bureau of the Census, *Statistical Abstract of the United States, 2008* (Washington, DC: U.S. Government Printing Office, 2008), Table 455.

counties. This was more than four times the 2.7 million people who worked for the federal government and more than six times as many federal workers when postal workers and civilian military personnel are excluded. Local governments also employed more than twice as many workers as the states.[5] Even so, the federal government collected $1.8 trillion in revenue in fiscal year 2002, three times as much as the $597 billion in own-source revenue collected by cities. One notable fact is that although local governments collect less revenue and spend less money, they hire far more workers than any other level of government because the services that local governments provide are extremely labor intensive, such as education, police, fire, and sanitation.

The budgetary policies of the federal or state government filter down to local governments. In December 2002, in the midst of a recession, state budget deficits reached levels not seen since World War II or, in some cases, since the Great Depression of the 1930s. Because the deficits had reached 13 to 18 percent of state expenditures, states took steps to slash spending. Because a substantial portion of state spending goes for functions that are extremely important to local residents, the impact of budgetary cuts made by the cities was magnified. When Congress passed the economic stimulus package in February 2009, it was the first time in many years that the national government provided substantial new resources to help cities, but the assistance was temporary.

Where the Money Goes

Only occasionally do the everyday operations of urban governments hit a nerve because most of what they do seems pretty routine. Because of this, it is difficult to appreciate the critical role that cities play in providing basic services. In a nation where nearly 40 percent of citizens lack health insurance, cities are front-line providers of health services provided through public hospitals and clinics, not only for the poor but also for families of the underinsured middle class. They provide essential housing services, even if most of this takes the form of contributing to or maintaining homeless shelters. During cold and heat emergencies, cities are expected to assist in providing immediate help.

Collectively, local governments in the United States spend huge sums of money. In fiscal 2005, for example, they spent $1.14 trillion; cities accounted for about one-third of this total. The leading municipal budget by far was New York City, with $52.9 billion in planned expenditures and appropriations for the 2007 fiscal year, compared to Chicago at $6.7 billion and Los Angeles at $5.7 billion.[6] These huge volumes of money finance everything from everyday services such as police and fire protection, maintenance of water and sewer pipes, and 911 emergency phone services. These tend to virtually hidden from view because they are ubiquitous and expected aspects of our daily lives.

City spending is driven by powerful forces that are largely beyond the control of local officials and voters. City governments are not sovereign entities. Higher levels of government (state and federal) allocate responsibilities—generally called *mandates*—to city governments within the intergovernmental system. Equally important, no matter how dire their budgetary situation may be, cities must provide a minimum level of services and infrastructure mainte-nance necessary for preserving the physical well-being of city residents and the viability of a city: public health, police and fire protection, education, water distribution, sewage collection, parks, highways, museums, and libraries.

The relative distribution of municipal expenditures among various ser-vices and responsibilities for 2002 is shown in Table 12.2. Most cities spend their money on a variety of services that most citizens take for granted, such as education, highways, parks and recreation, sewage and waste disposal, and police and fire protection. However, the biggest cities tend to devote a larger proportion of their budgets to social programs such as housing and commu-nity development, health and hospitals, and public welfare; indeed, the six cities with more than 1 million residents allocated a combined 14.5 percent for public welfare—more than twice the proportion spent by cities with populations of

TABLE 12.2 Direct Expenditures for Selected Services in the Largest U.S. Cities (Based on 2002 Population)

	Cities of 1,000,000 Population	Cities of 400,000 to 999,999 Population
Expenditures		
Education	22.4%	18.5%
Community development and housing	6.6	4.9
Public welfare	14.5	6.8
Health and hospitals	11.1	9.0
Police protection	11.9	12.7
Fire protection	4.7	6.5
Corrections	2.5	2.0
Highways	4.6	6.1
Parks and recreation	3.0	6.9
Sewerage	5.3	8.2
Waste management	2.7	3.1
Governmental administration	3.6	7.0
Interest on debt	7.0	8.2

Note: General expenditures only.

Source: Recalculated, using U.S. Bureau of the Census, *Statistical Abstract of the United States, 2006* (2006), Table 448 (online data book: www.census.gov/compendia/statab/).

400,000 to 1 million people. It should be noted that most cities, even most big cities, do not run the schools within their boundaries; normally, education is financed through independent school districts. The exceptions include some older cities, such as New York, Boston, San Francisco, and Baltimore, which built schools before it had become the usual practice to finance education through special districts, and Chicago, where the mayor took over the schools in 1995.

Except for education, many of the social services the cities provide would be considered by most people as redistributive in nature, in the sense that they disproportionately benefit less affluent residents. However, failure to treat the problems of the poor can reverberate through the urban community and affect everyone. Public hospitals and health clinics, for example, are used mostly by people without health insurance. In the absence of public health facilities, many families would quickly become reduced to desperation and penury in an attempt to find health services. Considered on its own merits, this would be a social disaster, but in addition, rates of communicable and contagious diseases such as tuberculosis and AIDS would spread more quickly.

Homelessness is another social problem that most big cities attempt to treat in a somewhat compassionate manner. Virtually all large cities have a population of homeless people wandering downtown streets. Law enforcement can manage but cannot solve the problem. In January 2003, Chicago's mayor, Richard M. Daley, announced an effort to end homelessness in the city by 2013 by closing homeless shelters and using the money to fund permanent housing and social services. The mayor's proposal, which was drafted by nonprofit organizations working with city administrators, was motivated, in part, by the expense and intractability of the problem. It cost $1,200 a month to provide temporary shelter for a family of three—money that could, instead, be devoted to rental of permanent housing and social services.[7]

Public health services account for a large chunk of the budgets of large cities, and they are too important to abandon. Cities and counties engage in restaurant inspections and move quickly when cases of food poisoning break out. Health clinics offer free flu shots and screening for diseases. There are constant reminders of the importance of such services. In the summer of 2002, an epidemic of the West Nile virus, which is carried by birds, spread throughout the Midwest, with a heavy outbreak in Illinois. The state of Illinois and city officials in Chicago moved fast in an attempt to track the disease. Local governments throughout the Chicago area sprayed ponds and rivers where mosquitoes might breed, and launched an aggressive campaign of eradication at the start of the mosquito-breeding season in the spring of 2003. But such measures do not reveal how critical public health services are to the urban population. A flu pandemic would overwhelm the public health systems of most cities.

Although smaller cities spend about the same proportion on health and hospitals, they spend less on other social services. Big cities take on more responsibilities for a variety of reasons: Their citizens demand more and better services (for example, well-trained police officers and firefighters), they pay higher salaries to their public employees, and they experience the high service costs made necessary by high-density populations, aging buildings and infrastructure, and high rates of poverty and unemployment. Because they do more, they spend more; on average, the cities with populations exceeding a million people spend about twice as much for each citizen as the average U.S. city and many times more than most small cities.

City expenditures rose sharply in the second half of the twentieth century, not only in total amount but also relative to the economy as a whole, increasing from 5 percent of the gross national product (GNP) in 1949–1950 to a high of 9 percent in 1975–1976. But after the recession of 1974–1975, the brakes were applied to municipal budgets. The six biggest cities experienced a 10 percent drop in their budgets from 1975 to 1980, when inflation is taken into account. After adjusting for inflation, cities of all sizes, on the average, did not increase spending at all over the same years. Since 1980, spending has declined slightly (after adjustment for inflation) for cities of all sizes.

Because they rely so much on their own sources of revenue, there is a close relationship between expenditure levels and local economic vitality. As shown in Table 12.3, some cities in the Frostbelt were forced to make deep cuts in their budgets in the 20-year period from 1975 to 1996. Measured in constant 1996 dollars (to account for inflation), Baltimore's budget shrank by 36 percent, Cleveland's by 16 percent, and St. Louis's by 27 percent. Of the Frostbelt cities shown in Table 12.3, only New York and Chicago were able to increase their budgets. The contrast with Sunbelt cities is striking. Of the five shown, four increased their budgets substantially; indeed, Phoenix more than doubled its spending. It is true that the populations of several Frostbelt cities fell during this period at the same time that Sunbelt cities grew rapidly. However, city expenditures are not related one to one with population; if anything, older cities bear a bigger burden because of old infrastructure and serious social problems.

The economic health of cities varies tremendously. Historically, central cities have been significantly disadvantaged compared to the suburbs in the capacity to generate revenue and in the ability to reduce the cost of services. A sample of 62 cities taken in 1962 revealed that central city residents earned, on average, $105 for every $100 earned by suburbanites. Clearly, more than a decade after the flight to suburbs had begun, a large number of affluent families had still not made the move. However, by 1989 the city–suburban ratio had reversed; now the average city resident made 84 percent as much. At the same time, in 1989 the poverty rate in central cities was 18 percent, which was more than double the metropolitan average of 8 percent.[8]

Almost all the older industrial cities experienced significant population losses due to the flight of the middle class to the suburbs. As the population of the central cities fell, the cost of providing infrastructure and basic services, such as police and fire, did not decline correspondingly.[9] Even if they have fewer people than in the past, cities still have the same sewer and water lines—often old and in need of frequent repair—and the same miles of streets to plow and patrol. Once the middle class has fled, there are fewer taxpayers to pay for these services, and the taxpayers who are left make less taxable income and own less valuable property than those in surrounding jurisdictions.

TABLE 12.3 Total Expenditures for Selected Frostbelt and Sunbelt Cities, 1975–1996 (in Millions of 1996 Dollars[a])

	Fiscal Year 1975 Expenditures	Fiscal Year 1996 Expenditures	Percentage Change 1975–1996	Percentage Change 1991–1996
Frostbelt Cities				
Baltimore	$2,811	$1,802	–36%	0%
Chicago	2,880	3,890	35	12
Cleveland	764	644	–16	2
New York	34,292	38,753	13	2
St. Louis	670	487	–27	–14
Sunbelt Cities				
Dallas	$614	$1,197	95%	32%
Denver	934	1,716	84	48
New Orleans	661	652	0	–15
Phoenix	567	1,221	115	6
San Jose	376	790	100	5

[a]Adjustments for inflation are calculated using the GNP Price Index for state and local government purchases, U.S. Bureau of Economic Analysis, *Survey of Current Business, Dec. 1999*, p. 141, Table 3.

Sources: U.S. Bureau of the Census, *City Government Finances: 1975–76*, GF 76, no. 4 (Washington, DC: U.S. Government Printing Office, 1977), Table 5; U.S. Bureau of the Census, *Statistical Abstract of the United States, 1995* (Washington, DC: U.S. Government Printing Office, 1995), Table 493; and U.S. Bureau of the Census, *Statistical Abstract of the United States, 1999* (Washington, DC: U.S. Government Printing Office, 1999), p. 335, Table 531.

Poverty boosts public spending not only for welfare and social services but also for a broad range of other services. Central-city governments spend money on lead paint poisoning prevention (a problem prevalent in older homes), rat control, and housing demolition. Courts have ordered cities to provide shelter for the homeless at a significant expense to local governments. In 1987, for example, a court order required New York City to provide emergency shelter to its homeless population, which cost the city $274 million.[10] Poverty also drives up the cost of everyday services. Fire protection, for instance, costs more in high-density areas where deteriorated and aging structures pose a high fire risk, and police protection is also more difficult in such environments.

Another factor that drives up the cost of city services is the panoply of expensive mandates forced on cities by higher levels of government. Cities are not mentioned in the U.S. Constitution; legally, city governments are the creatures of the states. Although many cities have home rule charters that allow them to govern themselves internally within broad guidelines, municipal corporations are not fully sovereign. The scope of a city's service responsibilities is beyond its control. State and federal governments can, and frequently do, order cities to provide particular services or meet minimum standards of service provision, and cities only rarely receive more money to cover the costs of the mandated standards and services.

Since the mid-1960s, the number of unfunded federal mandates imposed on cities have proliferated. In the case of concurrent powers shared by the federal and state governments, Congress has the power to preempt (override) state and local laws. According to the supremacy clause (Article VI) of the Constitution, when there is a conflict between a national law and a state (or local) law, the national law prevails. The Supreme Court upheld federal preemption in the 1985 *Garcia* decision.[11] In *Garcia*, the Court upheld the constitutionality of the 1974 amendments to the Fair Labor Standards Act, which applied minimum wage and overtime pay provisions to public transit workers in San Antonio. This decision made it clear that state and local governments are not protected from federal preemption statutes by the Tenth Amendment (which reserves powers not granted to the federal government to the states). Their only protection comes from political pressures they can put on Congress. In 1986, the U.S. Department of Labor estimated that the cost to state and local governments of complying with the new labor standards exceeded $1.1 billion.[12] The Clean Air Act of 1990, required 100 cities to install antipollution devices on their garbage incinerators at an estimated average cost of $20 million per incinerator.[13] The U.S. Environmental Protection Agency estimated that the total cost of environmental mandates for local governments increased from $7.7 billion in 1972 to $19.2 billion in 1987.

Responding to complaints from state and local officials, in March 1995 Congress passed, and President Clinton signed, the Unfunded Mandates Reform Act, which required Congress to weigh the costs and benefits of new rules and to help pay the costs if state and local governments were forced to implement them. This legislation came rather late in the day for most cities, and in any case, it has been ignored. In 2002, President Bush promised to defray the increased cost of security borne by cities because of the war on terrorism. As of April 2003, no aid was forthcoming, and the amount proposed was considered inadequate by local officials. During the Bush administration, mandates (though they are rarely called that) have become commonplace as a way of passing legislation without paying for the resulting programs. The No Child Left Behind Act, which took effect in 2002, makes federal aid of any kind to school districts dependent upon the ability of students in those districts to pass standardized tests. Though the federal government promised to pay for some of the costs of the testing, by 2005 it was $25 billion behind in reimbursements.[14]

Various economic and political forces beyond the control of local officials impact local government expenditures. Economic downturns, concentrated poverty, unfunded mandates, and terrorist threats impose unpredictable costs. As one fiscal expert observed,

> A city's fiscal health ... depends on economic, social, and institutional factors that are largely outside the city's control. Poor fiscal health is not caused by poor management, corruption, or profligate spending, and a city government's ability to alter the city's fiscal health is severely limited.[15]

Over the last half century, older cities became accustomed to dealing with chronic economic problems and a high level of poverty. Unfunded mandates added to the burden, and terrorist threats added still more responsibilities. The Great Recession dealt a blow to cities of all sorts, new and old, urban and suburban. For the first time in many years, they are all in the same boat.

Where the Money Comes From

The sources for the revenues that cities collect are dictated by two basic considerations: what state laws allow, and what the local officials feel they can impose without harming their ability to compete for investors and middle-class residents.[16] There are many different ways to solve the problem; the challenge is to find a way to raise revenue without inciting too much resentment and opposition. Over time, local officials have learned that property taxes are not popular, and as a result these have become less important to city budgets than in the past. A few states allow their cities to impose earnings or corporate income taxes, but these tend to be modest because they may drive away workers and their employers. In recent years, for obvious reasons, "stealth" taxes have become more and more common. These are charges imposed on citizens that amount to a tax, but go under some other name: a fee for entering a museum, for example, or higher parking charges, or fines. It is, in effect, a shell game that everyone agrees to play.

Almost all cities are allowed by their states to impose property taxes, probably because this tax has such a long history. Twenty-eight states allow their cities to impose taxes on retail sales, but only 8 percent of cities (most of them in Ohio and Pennsylvania) are able to impose income taxes.[17] Most of them are also allowed to charge user fees for such facilities as public parking, museums and zoos, ice rinks, and swimming pools, and in the same spirit, most cities are permitted to collect taxes that target visitors, such as hotel/motel and entertainment taxes. Cities also rely on a continuous flow of intergovernmental revenues, and a small amount from the federal government (e.g., for pollution control and law enforcement), but most of this is passed through the states or allocated by the states for particular functions; especially important are road construction and maintenance, corrections, and public safety. It is difficult to find a pattern that fits all cities.

The revenue source that saved the cities from the worst fiscal effects of the urban crisis in the years following World War II came in the form of federal aid in the 1960s and beyond. Between 1965 and 1974, intergovernmental transfers to all cities rose 370 percent, more than twice the 153 percent increase in

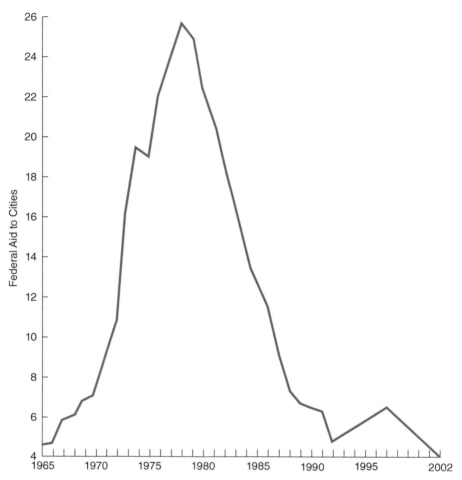

FIGURE 12.1 Direct Aid to Cities as a Percentage of Own-Source Revenue, 1965–2002.

Sources: Helen F. Ladd and John Yinger, *America's Ailing Cities: Fiscal Health and the Design of Urban Policy,* updated ed. (Baltimore: Johns Hopkins University Press, 1989), p. 270. Updated using U.S. Bureau of the Census, *2000 Census of Governments,* vol. 4, *Government Finances of Municipal and Townships Governments,* Report GC 97 (Washington, DC: U.S. Government Printing Office, September 2000); U.S. Bureau of the Census, *2002 Census of Governments,* vol. 4, no. 5, *Compendium of Government Finances* (2002), Table 2, www.census.gov/prod/2005pubs/gc024x5.pdf.

municipal expenditures.[18] Figure 12.1 shows that federal aid to cities increased sharply after the mid-1960s, peaked at 26 percent of cities' own-source revenue in 1978, and then dropped like a stone. President Reagan ended the special relationship that had been forged between the federal government and cities under previous Democratic administrations. By 1992, federal aid bottomed out at 4.5 percent of city revenues, climbed slightly to 6.4 percent by 1997, and fell to 4 percent by 2002.[19]

Since the era of significant federal aid ended, cities have been very resourceful in finding ways to raise revenue. The creativity of local officials has been checked mainly by two considerations. First, when taxes reach a high enough level, taxpayers are prone to rebel, as evidenced by the taxpayer revolts against property taxes that swept the nation in the 1970s. Second, local officials are always aware that an excessive level of taxation may chase businesses and middle-class taxpayers away. This checks and balances system does not work perfectly, of course, but it does impose some general rules of the game.

The property tax was once the principal source of revenue for local governments. The most important and widely used form of property tax is the ad valorem real property tax, a levy imposed as a percentage of the value of land and its improvements. From colonial times through the early years of the republic, real property was taken to be the best indicator of both wealth and the ability to pay taxes. At the time, this assumption was accurate. Most of the wealth of the era was tied to the land, and fortunes were made in land speculation. Therefore, a tax on real property seemed to be the fairest and most reliable way to finance state and local governmental services.[20]

Taxation of personal (or nonreal) property—that is, assets other than real estate and improvements—evolved as the cities became more complex. As trade and manufacturing grew in importance, more and more wealth became represented in bank accounts, merchandise, patent rights, machinery, capital stock, and corporate assets. Cities (and states) began to levy taxes on such sources of wealth in order to maintain a reliable relationship between individual tax burdens and personal wealth. Such assets were often hard to find and assess, however, and in any case wealthy people used their considerable influence to discourage this kind of taxation. For these reasons, although the numbers of people with significant personal assets mushroomed after the Civil War, the proportion of the property tax attributable to personal property actually fell.[21]

Because they stir resentment among residents and businesses, in recent years property taxes have steadily fallen as a proportion of the revenues collected by cities. In 1902, personal and real property taxes accounted for 73 percent of all municipal revenues, with license and franchise fees accounting for most of the rest. These taxes continued to provide approximately three-fourths of the tax receipts until the late 1930s and early 1940s, but after World War II the cities began finding new revenue sources.[22] By 1962, property taxes yielded barely 50 percent of municipal revenues in the 72 largest metropolitan areas (even though the property tax continued to generate almost all the revenue for school districts). Only a few years later, in fiscal year 1975, property taxes accounted for little more than a third (35 percent) of the revenues in the largest metropolitan areas, despite a 130 percent increase in the average per capita levy since the early 1960s.[23] Clearly, other tax sources had gone up much faster, and they have continued to do so. The hot new revenue sources have been sales taxes, user fees, and charges for such entertainment costs as hotels, motels, and rental cars. Because of this trend, by 1996 reliance on the property tax had dropped to 19 percent for cities over 400,000 in population to 15 percent by 2002, when in some big cities property taxes accounted for less than 10 percent of the budget.[24]

Over the past half-century, the property tax was an increasingly significant source of revenue growth only in the rapidly growing cities of the Sunbelt. This was possible because of rising property values. In Phoenix, the value of taxable property rose 251 percent from 1965 to 1973; by contrast, in Newark it increased only 2 percent and in Detroit 14 percent during the same period.[25] However, the decades-long march upward disappeared during the recession of 2008–2009, when property values fell even faster in the Sunbelt than elsewhere, with real estate values falling by more than 40 percent in Florida, Arizona, and California. Property tax revenues were predicted to fall by 10 percent in California over a three-year period, but it would be even worse if property tax assessments actually kept up with changes in the value of real estate. Santa Clara County, which had experienced a 7 percent increase in property tax revenues the year before, was bracing for a 2 percent reduction by June 2009, and the assessor expected to review almost half the properties in the county before the next year.[26] These delays buy cities time to reconcile shrinking budgets; however, some cities have faced five consecutive years of shrinking budgets due to property assessment delays. Across the nation, a tax revolt began brewing because homeowners who saw their property values fall expected their tax bills to fall as well, but this often did not happen. Tax assessors offices were inundated with appeals.[27]

Another disadvantage of the property tax is that a high proportion of property is tax exempt. According to one study, almost one-third of all real property in the United States is subject to some kind of exemption.[28] In 1982, in just 23 states and the District of Columbia, there was $15 billion in exempt property for religious institutions, $22 billion for educational institutions, $15 billion for charitable institutions, and $128 billion for government property.[29] In recent decades, the proportion of tax-exempt property has increased. Many cities have provided tax relief for the homes owned by elderly or poor people ("circuit breaker" laws). States and cities have tried to attract or retain businesses and investors by forgiving or reducing their property taxes. Many states have exempted various forms of business property, such as machines and inventory, from taxation without consulting local governments.[30]

The burden of tax-exempt property falls most heavily on those cities that are least able to afford it because central cities have twice as much exempt property located in them as their surrounding suburbs.[31] In 1985, more than 51 percent of the real property in Boston was tax exempt, up from 41 percent in 1972.[32] A 1983 article traced a 3.2-mile route through Boston where a walker would not set foot on a single parcel of taxable property.[33] Cities must provide services for these properties, including police and fire protection, but the owners pay no taxes. The situation in New York so incensed one taxpayer that he sued the city tax commission over the "subsidy of religion," going all the way to the U.S. Supreme Court before finally losing the case.[34]

Taxpayers' revolts that started in the 1970s forced governments to reduce their reliance on property taxes. During that period, at least 14 state legislatures enacted laws that limited property tax rates or spending by local governments.[35] Citizen initiatives went even further. The first widely publicized of these was

Proposition 13 in California, which was passed by popular referendum in June 1978. From March to November 1978, 16 states held initiatives or referenda to limit taxes or spending, although not all were binding on public officials.[36] Thirteen of the citizen initiatives passed. More such proposals were approved after 1978. Since that time, public officials have tended to regard any proposal to raise property taxes as the third rail of politics that they dare not touch. This, as much as any other consideration, explains why local officials have searched hard for alternatives.

More cities might use earnings taxes if their states allowed them to, but few do. Only about 8 percent of municipalities of 50,000 or more levy income taxes.[37] State law limits its use to Ohio, Pennsylvania, and Kentucky, although some of the larger cities in some other states, such as New York City, Kansas City, and St. Louis, but 90 percent of the cities that collect income taxes are in Pennsylvania and Ohio.[38] Figure 12.2 displays on what types of taxes cities rely by state. Cities in some states rely on property taxes, others on sales taxes, and even more on combinations of taxes.

Sales taxes, user fees, and fees for permits and special services have been the taxes of choice since the 1970s. As of 2002, 28 states allowed their cities to impose retail sales taxes, which added up to nearly 58 percent of cities with over 50,000 in population.[39] Sales taxes have been useful because they are highly flexible. Taxes on retail sales can yield big revenues even when they are adjusted by tiny increments, and a substantial portion of the tax is paid by

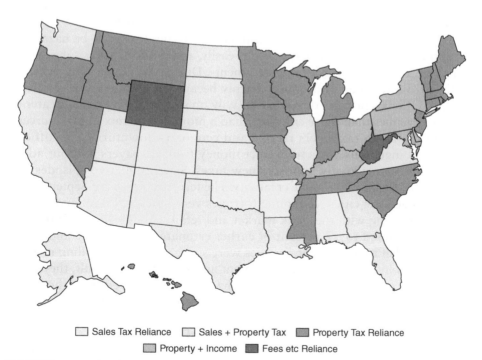

□ Sales Tax Reliance   □ Sales + Property Tax   ■ Property Tax Reliance
□ Property + Income   ■ Fees etc Reliance

FIGURE 12.2 Municipal Tax Reliance by State.

people not living within the city's boundaries. This is especially valuable for cities with large retailing centers serving a regional market, such as malls and big-box stores. Cities will go to great lengths to land big retailers, as revealed at the April 2009 meeting of the International Council of Shopping Centers held in Las Vegas. Economic development specialists and city officials from across the nation flocked to the convention to schmooze with developers and representatives of chain store retail outlets. For local officials, the stakes were both economic and symbolic: "Mom-and-pop stores may provide local flavor, but chain stores are societal benchmarks. Mayors hear it from their constituents all the time: 'Why don't we have a Trader Joe's? Why don't we have a Bass Pro Shops? What are we, some kind of backwater?' "[40] Changes in economic conditions question the long-term viability of sales taxes. While sales taxes cover the purchase of many goods, few cities extend their taxes to services. The expanding service sector promises an upside of economic growth and downtown renaissance but provides few added resources to the city's tax coffers.

With the fiscal bottom line and the reputation of local public officials riding on the outcome, the competition among jurisdictions for retail is extremely intense. Accordingly, governments try to outbid one another by offering subsidies to developers and retaining consultants to help them make deals. Businesses are skilled at shopping around, and they reap rewards for their efforts: in 1995 and 1996, state and local corporate subsidies added up to almost $49 billion.[41] To put such numbers in perspective, it may be helpful to consider a 1998 study, which reported that the combination of federal, state, and local incentives offered to influence the location of business cost "every working man and woman in America the equivalent of two weekly paychecks" a year.[42]

However attractive they may be, reliance on sales taxes can be hazardous. Stores that move in can move out just as easily, and if this happens subsidies appear to be a poor deal for local governments. During the 2008–2009 recession, the take from retail taxes dropped sharply because of declining sales and store closings. Officials in cities that relied heavily on sales taxes reported greater declines in revenues than those cities that had a more diverse mix of tax sources.[43]

In response to taxpayers revolts and economic downturns, city officials have found ingenious ways to extract money from taxpayers without admitting that they are actually imposing new taxes. Since 2000, two episodes have prompted bursts of remarkable creativity. The terrorist attacks of September 11, 2001, changed the cities' economic fortunes very quickly. Travel and tourism plummeted, along with the stock market and retail sales. By March 2002, sales taxes had declined to 97 percent of earlier estimates, and income and tourist taxes had fallen to 90 percent.[44] Cities were squeezed between falling revenues and increases in costs for law enforcement and security. As a result, they began making deep cuts in expenditures. They had barely recovered from those budgetary problems when the economy plunged into recession in 2008.

To create an illusion that they are not raising taxes at all, cities have imposed an astonishing variety of user and special-services fees. The trend began in earnest in the early 1990s. In 1991, 73 percent of cities increased user fees and 40 percent adopted new charges for at least one city service.[45] Fees for parking, museums, botanical gardens, zoos, aquariums, planetariums, ice rinks, and swimming pools were increased, and many of the institutions and programs supporting these services were expected to be self-supporting. In many cities, garbage collection became a private service for which each household pays instead of being a public service paid for out of general tax revenues.

In response to mounting budget deficits in 2003, states and cities all over the nation redoubled their efforts to raise revenues by imposing new fees or hiking those already on the books. New York's mayor, Michael Bloomberg, a Republican, increased fees by $139 million, while also proposing that the city's income tax rate be reduced. Literally dozens of fees were involved, including a 33 percent increase in subway and bus fares, a 7 percent jump in tuition for public colleges, increases in parking fines, and higher fees to obtain a marriage license and birth certificate or to place a cell phone call from within the city. Fees had already been hiked for the use of public tennis courts and baseball diamonds. In California, a long list of new fees increased the costs of college tuition, car licenses, hunting and fishing licenses, admission to museums and parks, and even tuberculosis (a proposed $50 charge for anyone testing negative and $400 for positive).

The Great Recession prompted city officials to become more inventive than ever. Winter Haven, Florida, now levies a fee to cover the services provided by police and firefighters when they respond to auto accidents. Londonderry, New Hampshire, decided to charge a $25 fine for any dog owner who failed to renew a dog license on time. Cities learned that they could reap a steady revenue stream by hiring private companies to install and monitor cameras at intersections to record traffic violations. One mayor floated the idea of a "streetlight user fee" of $4.25 to pay for the city's cost of operating streetlights. Honolulu, Hawaii, considered raising its fees for zoo parking by 500 percent.[46] The real problem that arises from raising money through fees rather than taxes is that it is extremely regressive in nature: the fee costs the same regardless of the income of the person paying it. Over the last few years, less regressive forms of taxation (which is what fees are, in reality) have remained steady or even dropped.[47]

However creative local officials may be, there are times when even the most extraordinary efforts may fall short. In 2013, Michigan Governor Rick Snyder put the city of Detroit into receivership and appointed an emergency manager, Kevyn Orr, to oversee its fiscal affairs. The task he inherited was challenging in the extreme. The city was within months of becoming the largest city in the United States history to go bankrupt; against a $15–$17 billion debt and pension obligation, its total revenues added up to only $14.7 billion. In June 2013, Orr announced that the city would have to sell off assets to meet its obligations to creditors. Everything might be on the auction block: Detroit's half of the Detroit–Windsor Tunnel (worth more than $65 million), Belle Isle Park, with its miles of waterfront; the contents of the Detroit Historical Museum (which has, for example, a collection of 60 classic cars), even artwork from the Detroit Institute of Art. It was possible that almost anything might be considered distressed property—even animals at the zoo.[48]

Detroit's situation is extreme; indeed, bizarre. The measures taken to save the city will affect the economy and quality of life for citizens of the region for years to come. Other questions arise: "the possibility of selling off city assets also leads directly to questions such as, how much does a giraffe cost? And how does a citizenry cope with no-win scenarios pitting one indispensable gem against another?"[49] The questions facing other cities may not rise to same level, but the issues are similar. When cities make normal services and amenities more expensive and its revenues sources more regressive, working-class families and poor are deeply affected. In this way, the fiscal policies of local governments go a long way toward canceling efforts by the federal government to erect a social safety net for people in need.

The Municipal Bond Market

If cities relied on taxation alone, they would never have been able to build the physical infrastructure on which all city life depends. Cities are authorized by state legislation to issue long-term bonds to pay for capital improvements, such as schools, highways, bridges, and hospitals, which will benefit city residents over a long period. To successfully compete in the market for municipal bonds, they must keep their credit rating as high as possible, and this requires them to please the rating services that advise investors about the soundness of the investment.[50] In the process, cities compete in a marketplace that is vastly larger than the metropolis. By competing for capital in this way, cities are subject to the same logic that drives the competition within urban regions: they must pursue policies that promote local economic growth. For private corporations, profits are a key indicator of health; for cities, it is the ability to generate enough revenues to provide adequate services and make the payments on long-term bonded debt.[51]

The continuing need to build and maintain public infrastructure makes access to the municipal bond market essential for the well-being of cities. Borrowing typically represents 20 to 25 percent of all state and local spending, making the municipal bond market a significant sector of the national economy. In 2007, the total long-term debt amortized by bond issues for all local governments amounted to $561 billion.[52] The reason municipal bonds are attractive to investors is that they are tax exempt, and for this reason investors are willing to buy municipal bonds at a lower interest rate than they would pay for corporate bonds. In effect, the federal government provides cities with a subsidy by exempting municipal bonds from taxation. Although the U.S. Supreme Court has ruled that state and local governments have no constitutional right to borrow at tax-exempt rates, it is very unlikely that Congress would ever take away this subsidy to state and local governments.[53]

Municipal bonds are purchased by commercial banks, casualty insurance companies, pension funds, and, increasingly, wealthy individual investors, who find the federal tax exemption especially attractive.[54] The federal subsidy to cities through the bond market is inefficient because only part of it, in the form of lower interest rates paid to investors, goes to cities. The rest of the federal subsidy is siphoned off to investors who avoid paying federal taxes by buying the tax-exempt municipal bonds. Legislation was proposed, but never passed, that would allow municipalities to float bonds at normal interest rates in exchange for a direct subsidy by the federal government.[55] In this way, the subsidy would go entirely to cities and not, indirectly, to investors.

Cities issue two types of long-term bonds: general obligation bonds and revenue bonds. General obligation bonds pledge the "full faith and credit" of the city's taxing powers to pay off the bonds, generally require approval by voters or a representative body, and are used to build public infrastructure such as bridges and parks. Revenue bonds are paid off by anticipated future revenues from the facilities that are constructed. They are usually issued by public authorities established by state-enabling legislation.[56] When revenues are not sufficient to pay bond premiums (and they sometimes are not), local governments generally must make up the difference. Convention centers typically fail to generate enough revenue to fully cover bond payments, and sports stadiums sometimes fail to do so as well. In such cases, a general-purpose government (such as a municipality) must step in to cover the difference. Even so, because the debt will, in theory, be paid entirely through revenues, revenue bonds do not require a public referendum. This feature makes them especially popular with local officials.

Almost any facility that can charge user fees—sports stadiums, convention centers, museums, aquariums—is financed through revenue bonds. Local government borrowing through revenue bonds has risen sharply since the 1970s. Until the 1970s, general obligation bonds represented about 60 percent of outstanding local long-term debt.[57] By 2002, however, nonguaranteed revenue-bond debt represented 60 percent of all outstanding debt issued by city governments and special authorities.[58]

Revenue bonds permit cities to use their tax-exempt borrowing privileges to support private programs and activities. In the late 1970s, cities began issuing mortgage revenue bonds to subsidize interest rates for middle-income homebuyers, although in 1980 Congress restricted this practice with the passage of the Mortgage Subsidy Act. In an attempt to stimulate economic growth, in the 1970s and 1980s cities increasingly issued industrial revenue bonds to subsidize a broad assortment of businesses, including big-box retailers such as Walmart or Kmart, fast-food franchises such as McDonald's, and a mix of other businesses ranging from liquor stores to law offices. Critics charged that the tax-exempt borrowing was being used for private purposes that did not serve any public interest. Examples of flagrant abuses abounded. Chester County, Pennsylvania, for example, issued revenue bonds for an adult bookstore and topless go-go bar in downtown Philadelphia. Congress, noting the hemorrhage of federal tax revenues, restricted the use of revenue bonds by passing the Tax Equity and Fiscal Responsibility Act of 1982 and the Deficit Reduction Act of 1984.[59] The Tax Reform Act of 1986 placed state-by-state limits on what it termed governmentally subsidized "private-activity bonds."[60]

Besides being used for questionable private purposes, municipal bonds have been subject to a number of other abuses. Even before the economic crisis of 2008–2009, some local governments got into trouble by borrowing money and putting it into high-risk investments, hoping to make substantial profits.

Unwilling to raise taxes, in 1993 Orange County, California, attempted to maintain services by putting the proceeds of bond sales into risky investments called *derivatives* that were essentially gambling on the direction of interest rates. When interest rates plunged, Orange County lost $1.6 billion. In April 1994, Orange County became the largest local government in history to file for federal bankruptcy protection under Chapter 9. More than 180 other governments lost money in similar high-risk investment pools in the same period.

Until the recent recession, however, such episodes were the exception rather than the rule. But the 2008–2009 downturn exposed serious deficiencies in the way the municipal bond market was run. In fact, the tip of the iceberg had been sighted years before. In the early 1990s, the municipal bond market had been rocked by charges that underwriters, in order to obtain lucrative government bond business, kicked back profits to public officials in the form of campaign contributions.[61] In April 1994, the Securities and Exchange Commission (SEC) enacted Rule G–37, which barred campaign contributions by municipal bond bankers. To get around this ban, municipal finance companies provided funding for lavish receptions at the 1996 Democratic and Republican conventions where bond underwriters could mingle with top state and local officials. At the Republican convention in San Diego, this included golf and tennis parties, a fishing expedition, and a luncheon honoring House Speaker Newt Gingrich.[62] A 1996 lawsuit alleged that underwriters overcharged municipalities for escrow accounts by as much as $1 billion.[63] Such abuses have led to repeated demands that the municipal bond industry be more closely regulated.[64]

As soon as the Great Recession began unfolding in the fall of 2008, hundreds of municipalities encountered problems with their bond investments. Like individuals, local government officials usually rely on experts in the financial industry to advise them on investments. One such advisor was David Rubin, who founded one of the leading consulting firms for municipal bonds, CDR Financial Products, in Beverly Hills, California. Beginning in the early 1990s, Rubin toured the country drumming up business, advising local government officials to refinance debt with risky interest-rate provisions (much like the adjustable-rate mortgages [ARMs] offered to homeowners) and invest in high-yielding but risky derivatives of the same kind that brought about the 2008 economic crisis. Rubin made campaign contributions even when these appeared to violate a ban imposed by the Securities and Exchange Commission. Some of his bonds ran up unusually high fees.[65] In Tennessee, Morgan Keegan was one of several firms invited by the state to run a seminar for local officials in 2008. By then the company had already cornered the market in municipal bonds within the state; since 2001 it had sold $2 billion in bonds to 38 towns and counties. Because Morgan Keegan, like other financial firms, made higher commissions on derivative bonds rather than fixed-rate bonds, it took care to steer the clients into them. Right at the time that cities and towns in Tennessee began to see their municipal revenues fall, the interest rates they paid on the bonds soared because they were now considered risky.[66]

News broke in January 2009 that three federal agencies and several state attorneys general had been gathering evidence on price-fixing and collusion among municipal bond brokers. The sums involved were vast: states and cities bought $400 billion in bonds each year. Brokers, banks, and other firms divided up the spoils by secretly parceling out the business by fixing bids, which allowed them to reap higher fees. A system of campaign contributions and suspicious payments to governmental officials helped keep the system in place. An antitrust lawyer representing state and local governments referred to it as "one of the longest-running, most economically pervasive antitrust conspiracies ever to be uncovered in the U.S."[67] Federal officials suggested that Congress adopt new regulations, but as late as February 2014 Congress had not taken up the matter. However, it is certain that federal and state agencies will continue their investigations, and more is bound to come to light.

Cities are at the mercy of the bond market because the cost of borrowing is basically determined by their bond ratings. A bond rating purports to represent the relative credit quality of the issuing municipality and thus determines the rate of interest a city must pay. A high rating means a lower interest rate, on the theory there is less risk for the investor. When a city's bond rating is lowered due to fiscal problems, a bond may be more difficult to sell, and the additional interest paid over the amortized life of the bond can amount to millions of dollars.

Bond ratings are published by several national rating firms, but the big three include Moody's Investors Service, Standard and Poor's Corporation, and Fitch's Investor Service. Cities pay to have their bonds rated, but they have no choice but to seek a rating if they want to be able to market their bonds. Although the purpose of the rating is to assess risk, in fact municipal bond ratings are totally unrelated to the likelihood of default. (Default may not mean the loan was not repaid; a payment may simply have missed a deadline.) The discrepancy in the interest rates between the highest and lowest investment grade bonds is inexplicable on the basis of relative risk.[68] From 1929 to 1933, when 77 percent of all municipal defaults of the twentieth century occurred, the highest rated bonds recorded the highest incidence of default.[69] These statistics seems to indicate that ratings are almost worthless as a guide to investment, even though they give the ratings agencies a powerful voice in municipal fiscal policies.

It would be more or less impossible for the ratings to accurately reflect risk because cities so rarely fail to pay their debts. True, from the first recorded default in 1838 (Mobile, Alabama) through 1969 more than 6,000 bond defaults were recorded by local governments. Less than a third of these, however, involved incorporated municipalities (cities); most of the rest were small special districts that provided particular services such as irrigation. Seventy-five percent of all such failures occurred between 1930 and 1939, and less than 10 percent after the Great Depression.[70] During the worst period for municipal bonds, 1929 through 1937, only 8 percent of all cities and 20 percent of their bonded debt were ever in default, and almost all of the debts were eventually paid.[71]

From World War II through early 1970, a total of 431 state and local units defaulted on their obligations. The total principal involved was $450 million, approximately 0.4 percent of the outstanding state and local debt. Three special authorities, the West Virginia Turnpike Commission, the Calumet Skyway Toll Bridge, and the Chesapeake Bay Bridge and Tunnel Commission, accounted for over 74 percent of this amount (virtually all local governments are considered municipal in the bond market). Only 2 of 24 major default situations ($1 million or more) were related to general obligation bonds.[72] Of 114 defaults of less than $1 million, almost all were temporary or technical defaults. Of these, only 34 involved general obligation bonds, and all of these involved cities with populations under 5,000 people.[73]

An analysis of cases filed in federal district courts between 1938 and 1971 reveals that nine cities took advantage of federal municipal bankruptcy legislation. With one exception (Saluda, North Carolina), all the cases came from rather obscure cities in Texas (Ranger, Talco, Benevides) or Florida (Manatee, Medley, Center Hill, Webster, Wanchula). Only in the case of Benevides (population 2,500) were general obligation bonds of post–World War II origin involved. In all other cases, the defaulted debt was of prewar origin, related to revenue bonds, or unrelated to bonds altogether.[74]

Before the state of Michigan put Detroit into receivership in 2013, no city had ever defaulted on its obligations, though in a very few cases there were brief delays in paying bondholders. On December 15, 1978, Cleveland became the first major city to default, even in a technical sense, since 1933. On that day, the city failed to make payments on $14 million in short-term notes; the city renewed payments a few months later and officially ended default in 1980.[75] For the first time in decades, several cities defaulted on their loan payments during the Great Recession. Stockton, California, Jefferson County (Birmingham), Alabama, and Detroit declared bankruptcy. In these notable cases investors may have to settle for less than full payment. Although we now know that in rare and extreme circumstances cities may default, it would be virtually unthinkable that a state ever would, no matter how dire its budgetary situation might be.

The overwhelming weight of evidence indicates that except in unusual circumstances when it is clear that city is in trouble (one does not a bond rater to determine such cases) there is little justification for the differential rating of city bonds except to make money for ratings services, brokers, and investors. Nevertheless, the market in municipal bonds exerts a powerful influence on public officials by imposing a tight fiscal discipline, and by reinforcing the dynamic of the metropolitan chase for business investment and affluent residents. The fact that local governments must finance nearly all their own activities without a regular source of aid from the national government forces them to place a high priority on promoting local economic development.

The Rise of Special Authorities

The terms "municipal debt" and the "municipal bond market" are convenient language devices used by just about everyone, but they are misleading in a very important respect: in fact, the biggest development and infrastructure projects are not financed directly by municipalities, but by independent special-purpose authorities that issue revenue bonds. If cities had been forced to rely on their own resources they could not possibly have sustained the incredible level of public investment that has been poured into new urban infrastructure in recent decades. More than $2 billion was spent annually in the first half of the 1990s on sports facilities and convention centers alone.[76] By 2007, there were more than 35,000 special authorities in the United States and they had issued $288 billion in new long-term debt.[77] In addition, billions of public dollars have been spent on urban entertainment and cultural districts, renovated waterfronts, aquariums, marketplaces, festival malls, and the other elements of urban lifestyle and the tourism/entertainment complex. Local officials have been resourceful in finding ways to finance public investment on this scale. The main instrument they have relied upon is the special-purpose authority.

Beginning in the 1980s, a generation of visionary mayors accepted the fact that they would have to find ways to regenerate their own economies. These "messiah mayors" preached a gospel of self-help for cities in desperate need of new ideas and directions. As noted by the historian Jon Teaford, "if nothing else the messiah mayors . . . boosted the spirits of many urban dwellers and made them proud of their cities."[78] But much more was involved than cheerleading. These mayors also pioneered in the creation of institutions capable of financing and administering projects considered important for promoting the economic viability of the city. Thus, sports authorities were created for the purpose of building sports stadiums, mall authorities were incorporated to build and administer mall and entertainment complexes, and development corporations came into being to implement local development projects. These special-purpose authorities—institutions created to accomplish a specific public purpose—were essentially public development institutions run like a private corporation, established specifically to receive a combination of public subsidies and private investment funds.[79] They were empowered to earmark taxes, charge user fees, issue bonds, establish trust funds, and use other mechanisms for bringing public and private money together to finance big undertakings.[80]

This institutional device gave municipal officials a way out of the straitjacket of debt limitations imposed on municipal governments because they were now able to offload the costs of development onto institutions that were capable of generating their own resources; in this way, general obligation bonds backed by the municipal government could be replaced by revenue bonds issued by a separate entity. These public/private institutions were generally established through enabling legislation passed by state legislatures, and they were run by boards appointed by a governor and mayor, the mayor alone, or some combination of public officials. They were not bound by the rules that frustrated public initiatives by general-purpose governments. They could make decisions without worrying about what voters thought. Because they were run much like private corporations, they were able to protect their information and books from public scrutiny, but at the same time, because they pursued public objectives, they could act just like governments and generate revenue, receive funds from other governments, and borrow money and sell tax-free bonds.

The sprawling McCormick Place convention center and the renovated Navy Pier entertainment complex in Chicago provide good examples of how this works. Both are administered by the Metropolitan Pier and Exposition Authority, which is governed by a board appointed by the mayor of Chicago and the governor of Illinois. The state of Illinois designates $98 million annually, derived from revenues from taxes (mainly a tax on cigarette sales) to pay off previous bonds for construction and remodeling.[81] In addition to this subsidy, in 2000 the Pier and Exposition Authority floated a $108 million tax-exempt bond issue to build and own the Hyatt Regency McCormick Place Hotel,[82] and completed a massive $750 million expansion in 2008. A combination of state subsidies and income from exhibitors and ticket sales for such events as the Chicago Auto Show, as well as rental fees for office space and other services, provide the center with the revenues to retire bonds and pay current operating expenses.

It is a mistake to describe special authorities as mere mechanisms for financing and administrating large undertakings. They are also political in nature, in the sense that they are always on the lookout for ways to promote their own projects and enhance their fiscal and administrative capacity. In the case of the professional football and baseball stadiums in Baltimore, for example, an agency of the state government, the Maryland Stadium Authority, financed the two stadiums through proceeds from a sports lottery offered through the Maryland State Lottery.[83] The campaign to build the sports stadium was guided by this new agency, which commissioned studies to show a powerfully positive impact on Baltimore's economy. However, another study by a state agency estimated that the economic impact would be much lower, and independent studies sharply contested even the lower estimate as unrealistic, concluding that stadium development brought virtually no measurable economic benefit.[84]

The political nature of special authorities is illustrated in the case of the Denver Metropolitan Stadium District, which the Colorado legislature created in 1990 as a means of pushing forward plans for a new baseball stadium. The bill establishing the district did not contain financing mechanisms, because any that would have been proposed would have ignited controversy. Instead, the task of lining up political support for a new stadium was left to the seven-member stadium district board. Securing financing was more a political than a fiscal exercise. In close collaboration with the city of Denver, the board ran an astute campaign that kept voters in the metropolitan counties outside Denver in the dark about whether the stadium might be built close to or within their own jurisdictions. The uncertainties about location carried the day. In August 1990, voters in the six-county district passed a sales tax levy to build the stadium; large majorities in the city and an adjacent county overcame a losing margin elsewhere.[85] Just as many voters had suspected, the fix had been in all along, and the stadium was built in downtown Denver.

Special-purpose authorities have sprung up to administer the many components that make up the tourism/entertainment complex in cities. In addition to the authorities established to finance and administer particular facilities such as convention centers, festival malls, and sports stadiums, redevelopment corporations have proliferated to refurbish business districts, revitalize neighborhoods, and provide amenities desired by local residents and visitors. In addition, since the 1980s, the number of tax increment finance (TIF) districts has multiplied. TIFs generate their revenues by marketing bonds to investors based on the taxes that are expected to be collected when a parcel of land is redeveloped. A TIF board, for example, might condemn homes in a residential neighborhood in order to take it for a new mall, which would be expected to generate sales tax revenue. These revenue projects would be used as the basis for a bond issue, which would provide the TIF district with the funds to make public improvements required by the mall developer. TIFs have become one of the main mechanisms for development in today's cities. For example, in 2002 there were more than 130 TIFs in the city of Chicago, and 217 in suburban Cook County.[86]

The proliferation of special-purpose authorities throughout metropolitan areas has removed more and more of the most important public policies from general-purpose municipalities. Although municipalities are run democratically—with mayors, city councils, and other elected officials—special-purpose authorities operate out of the public eye. Some of the most expensive and sometimes controversial undertakings have been assigned to special-purpose authorities. Convention centers and stadiums are built with public money, but with little or no public input. An absence of public accountability always raises troubling questions. In the 1950s urban renewal authorities regularly abused their powers. Transportation authorities rammed highways through urban neighborhoods. Then, as now, the application of governmental authority without adequate public accountability led to abuses. The fiscal politics of metropolitan competition tempts governments to build now, and ask questions later. In the competitive environment of today's metropolitan areas, it is a lesson worth remembering.

Fiscal Gamesmanship

Countless activities financed by cities are essential to the health and well-being of citizens. In a nation in which nearly 40 percent of citizens lack health insurance, they are frontline providers of health services provided through public hospitals and clinics, not only for the poor but also for families of the underinsured middle class. They provide essential housing services, even if most of this takes the form of contributing to or maintaining homeless shelters. These are only the normal, day-to-day activities. And in time of emergency, they are expected to do much more.

Between July 17 and 20, 1995, the city of Chicago was hit by a heat wave in which temperatures reached 106 degrees. City officials were not only unprepared, but they also did not feel it was in their purview to respond except through normal emergency services. By the time the heat wave had run its course, the number of excess deaths attributed to the heat wave reached 739. Realizing a repeat of such a disaster would become a public relations nightmare as well as a social catastrophe; the city subsequently (but quietly) put into place an emergency plan to mobilize its personnel and resources if a similar disaster struck.[87] The tragic events of that summer revealed a simple truth: cities simply cannot opt out of their responsibilities without endangering the welfare of their citizens.

The ability of city officials to respond when needed is determined by the resources at hand, and these are always subject to change. Economic downturns play havoc with local budgets, but there is little or nothing that cities can do to avoid them. They try to control what they can, and this leads them to a developmental politics that promotes growth, sometimes at the expense of other objectives. Paul Peterson, a leading scholar of urban politics, has taken the position that because economic or market standing is fundamentally important to cities and their citizens, they should do nothing that might compromise the possibility of achieving economic success.[88] This logic leads him to conclude that cities should avoid policies that redistribute resources from wealthier to poorer residents; obviously, health clinics and homeless shelters (for example) would fit into this category. This position may provoke disagreement, but urban leaders often act as if they believe it is true. This makes them play a delicate game in which they try to balance the needs of their citizens against the goal of preserving a climate that lures new investment, and keeps middle-class residents and businesses from moving elsewhere. It is a game made all the more dicey because most of the rules are set by other governments and by the institutions of the private economy.

Endnotes

1. Monica Davey, "States and Localities Angle for Stimulus Cash," *New York Times* (February 15, 2009), www.nytimes.com/2009/02/16/us/politics/16stimulus.html.
2. Thomas H. Boast, "A Political Economy of Urban Capital Finance in the United States" (Ph.D. dissertation, Cornell University, 1977), p. 114.
3. U.S. Bureau of the Census, *2007 Census of Governments* (2007), Table 2, http://www2.census.gov/govs/estimate/07slsstab2a.xls. For national government transfers as a proportion of local revenue in Japan, see Japanese Ministry of Internal Affairs and Communications, White Paper on Local Public Finance (2005), www.soumu.go.jp/iken/zaisei/17data/jyoukyou_e.pdf.
4. Carol W. Lewis, "Budgetary Balance: The Norm, Concept, and Practice in Large U.S. Cities," *Public Administration Review* 54 (November/December 1994): 517–518.
5. U.S. Bureau of the Census, *2002 Census of Governments,* vol. 3, *Public Employment* (2002), Tables 1 and 3, www.census.gov/prod/2004pubs/gc023x2.pdf; *2002 Census of Governments,* vol. 4, no. 5, *Compendium of Government Finances* (2002), Table 4; U.S. Bureau of the Census, *Statistical Abstract of the United States, 2003* (Washington, DC: U.S. Government Printing Office), p. 322, Table 475.
6. City of New York, "Adopted Budget Fiscal Year 2007: Expense Revenue Contract," http://www.nyc.gov/html/omb/downloads/pdf/erc7_06.pdf; City of Los Angeles, "Budget for the Fiscal Year 2006–2007," p. 26, www.lacity.org/cao/bud2006-07/Proposed_Budget_2006–07.pdf.
7. Gary Washburn, "City Maps Long-term Homeless Program," *Chicago Tribune* (January 22, 2003), p. 3.

8. Larry C. Ledebur and William R. Barnes, *City Distress: Metropolitan Disparities and Economic Growth* (Washington, DC: National League of Cities, 1991), pp. 2, 6. Figures based on the 85 largest metropolitan areas.

9. Roy Bahl, Jorge Martinez, and Loren Williams, "The Fiscal Conditions of U.S. Cities at the Beginning of the 1990s," Urban Institute Conference on Big City Governance and Fiscal Choices, Los Angeles (June 1991), pp. 5–6.

10. Jonathan Kozol, *Rachel and Her Children: Homeless Families in America* (New York: Crown, 1988), p. 14.

11. *Garcia v. San Antonio Metropolitan Transit Authority*, 469 U.S. 528 (1985).

12. Employment Standards Administration, *Minimum Wage and Maximum Hours Standards Under the Fair Labor Standards Act* (Washington, DC: U.S. Environmental Protection Agency, 1986), pp. 110–111; U.S. Congress, House Committee on Education and Labor, *Report to Accompany H.R. 3530*, 99th Cong., 1st sess., 1985. H. Rept. 99–331, p. 30; both cited in Joseph F. Zimmerman, "Federally Induced State and Local Governmental Costs," paper delivered at the annual meeting of the American Political Science Association (Washington, DC, August 29–September 1, 1991), p. 14.

13. Todd Sloane, "Clean Air Act Likely to Burn Many Municipalities," *City and State* (November 19, 1990), p. 2, cited in Zimmerman, "Federally Induced State and Local Government Costs," p. 12.

14. Alan Greenblatt, "The Washington Offensive," *Governing* 19, no. 1 (January 2005): 27.

15. Helen F. Ladd and John Yinger, *America's Ailing Cities: Fiscal Health and the Design of Urban Policy*, updated ed. (Baltimore: Johns Hopkins University Press, 1989), p. 291.

16. Any summary of revenue sources for all cities is misleading and therefore not presented in this chapter. Cities simply vary too much for such summaries to be meaningful; earnings taxes can be collected by a few cities, but not most, sales taxes are allowed by 28 states, and so forth.

17. Michael A. Pagano, *City Fiscal Conditions in 2002: A Research Report on America's Cities* (Washington, DC: National League of Cities, 2002), p. 3.

18. Eric A. Anderson, "Changing Municipal Finances," *Urban Data Services Reports* 7, no. 12 (Washington, DC: International City Manager Association, December 1975), p. 2.

19. U.S. Bureau of the Census, *2002 Census of Governments*, vol. 4, no. 5, *Compendium of Government Finances* (2002), Table 2.

20. Refer to Richard T. Ely, *Taxation in American States and Cities* (New York: Crowell, 1888), pp. 109–113; and Sumner Benson, "A History of the General Property Tax," in *The American Property Tax: Its History, Administration, and Economic Impact*, ed. C. G. Benson, S. Benson, H. McClelland, and P. Thompson (Claremont, CA: College Press, 1965), p. 24.

21. E. R. A. Seligman, *Essays in Taxation*, 9th ed. (New York: Macmillan, 1923), p. 24.

22. U.S. Bureau of the Census, *Historical Statistics of the United States: Colonial Times to 1970*, Bicentennial ed., pt. 2 (Washington, DC: U.S. Government Printing Office, 1975), p. 1133.

23. Calculated from the data in U.S. Bureau of the Census, *Local Government Finances in Selected Metropolitan Areas and Large Counties: 1969–70*, GF 70, no. 6 (Washington, DC: U.S. Government Printing Office, 1970), p. 7; U.S. Bureau of the Census, *Local Government Finances in Selected Metropolitan Areas and Large Counties: 1974–75*, GF 75, no. 6 (Washington, DC: U.S. Government Printing Office, 1976), p. 7.

24. U.S. Bureau of the Census, *2002 Census of Governments*, vol. 4, no. 4, *Finances of Municipal and Township Governments* (2002), Table 1, www.census.gov/prod/2005pubs/gc024x4.pdf.

25. George Peterson, "Finance," in *The Urban Predicament,* ed. William Gorham and Nathan Glazer (Washington, DC: The Urban Institute, 1976), p. 52.
26. Karen de Sa, "Santa Clara County Assessor Warns of Dramatic Plunge in Home Values, Lowered Taxes to Result," MercuryNews.com, www.mercurynews.com /ci_12068004?source.
27. Patrik Jonsson, "As Home Values Fall, Property Tax Revolt Brews," *The Christian Science Monitor* (April 2, 2009), features.csmonitor.com/economyrebuild/2009/04/02.
28. Alfred Balk, *The Free List—Property Without Taxes* (New York: Russell Sage Foundation, 1971), pp. 10–12.
29. J. Richard Aronson and John L. Hilley, *Financing State and Local Governments,* 4th ed. (Washington, DC: Brookings Institution Press, 1986), p. 136.
30. Ladd and Yinger, *America's Ailing Cities,* pp. 129–130, 180. See also Michael Wolkoff, "Municipal Tax Abatement: A Two-Edged Sword," *New York Case Studies in Public Management,* no. 4 (Albany, NY: Rockefeller Institute of Government, 1984).
31. Gregory H. Wassall, *Tax-Exempt Property: A Case Study of Hartford, Connecticut* (Hartford, CT: John C. Lincoln Institute, 1974), p. 27.
32. Todd Swanstrom, *Capital Cities: Challenges and Opportunities* (Albany, NY: Rockefeller Institute of Government), p. 17.
33. Michael J. Barrett, "The Out-of-Towners," *Boston Globe Magazine* (August 7, 1983).
34. *Walz v. Tax Commission of the City of New York,* 397 U.S. 664 (1970). See also Boris I. Bittker, "Churches, Taxes and the Constitution," *Yale Law Review* 78 (July 1969): 1285–1310.
35. John L. Mikesell, "The Season of Tax Revolt," in *Fiscal Retrenchment and Urban Policy,* ed. John P. Blair and David Nachmias (Beverly Hills, CA: Sage, 1979), p. 109.
36. Ibid.
37. Pagano, *City Fiscal Conditions in 2002,* p. 3.
38. Ibid.
39. Ibid., p. 3.
40. Christopher Swope, "The Retail Chase: Cities Will Do Almost Anything to Land the Store of Their Dreams," *Governing* (April 2007), p. 28.
41. Kenneth Thomas, *Competing for Capital: Europe and North America in a Global Era* (Washington, DC: Georgetown University Press, 2000), as cited in Rachel Weber, "What Makes a Good Economic Development Deal?" in *Retooling for Growth: Rebuilding a 21st Century Economy in America's Older Industrial Areas,* ed. Richard M. McGahey and Jennifer S. Vey (Washington, DC: Brookings Institution Press, 2008), p. 284.
42. Donald Bartlett and James Steele, "Corporate Welfare," *Time* (November 9, 1998), as quoted in ibid., p. 284.
43. Christiana McFarland, "State of America's Cities Survey: Local Retail Slowdown," Research Brief on America's Cities, by National League of Cities, Issue 2009-2, www.nlc.org.
44. Ibid., p. 20.
45. Pagano, *City Fiscal Conditions in 1991,* p. 24.
46. David Segal, "Cities Turn to Fees to Fill Budget Gaps," *New York Times* (April 10, 2009), www.nytimes.com/2009/04/11/busines/11fees.html.
47. Michael Powell and Christine Haughney, "Wary of Taxes, Officials Boost Fees; Tactic Hurts Poor and Working Class, Critics Say," *Washington Post* (April 7, 2003), p. A3.

48. Mark Stryker and John Gallagher, "Detroit Zoo giraffe? Belle Isle? Detroit's treasure trove could be vulnerable to sale to settle debt," *Detroit Free Press* (June 2, 2013), http://www.freep.com/article/20130602/NEWS01/306020080 /Detroit-bankruptcy-assets-sale-DIA.

49. Ibid.

50. Bonds issued not only by cities but also by states and all local governments are referred to as municipal bonds, a cause of endless confusion.

51. Cities in most states can also borrow short term, using tax anticipation notes (TANs) repaid in 30 to 120 days, to cover temporary budget shortages or to time their entry into the long-term bond market. Unlike the federal government, cities cannot use bond funds to cover long-term operating deficits.

52. U.S. Bureau of the Census, *2007 Census of Governments,* vol. 4, no. 5, *Local Government Finances by Type of Government and State* (2007), Table 2. http://www2 .census.gov/govs/estimate/07slsstab2a.xls.

53. *South Carolina v. Baker,* 108 S.Ct. 1935 (1988).

54. Alberta Sbragia, "Finance Capital and the City," in *Cities in Stress: A New Look at the Urban Crisis,* ed. Mark Gottdiener (Beverly Hills, CA: Sage, 1986), p. 210.

55. See Robert Huefner, *Taxable Alternatives to Municipal Bonds, Research Report No. 53* (Boston: Federal Reserve Bank of Boston, 1972); and *Building a Broader Market: Report of the Twentieth Century Fund Task Force on the Municipal Bond Market,* with a background paper by Ronald W. Forbes and John E. Peterson (New York: McGraw-Hill, 1976).

56. For insightful discussions of the powerful role of local authorities, see Ann Marie Hauck Walsh, *The Public's Business: The Politics and Practices of Government Corporations* (Cambridge, MA: MIT Press, 1978); and Alberta M. Sbragia, *Debt Wish: Entrepreneurial Cities, U.S. Federalism, and Economic Development* (Pittsburgh: University of Pittsburgh Press, 1996).

57. Elaine B. Sharp, "The Politics and Economics of the New City Debt," *American Political Science Review* 80, no. 4 (December 1986): 1271–1288.

58. U.S. Bureau of the Census, *Statistical Abstract of the United States* (Washington, DC: U.S. Government Printing Office, 1992), p. 285.

59. Thomas A. Pascarella and Richard D. Raymond, "Buying Bonds for Business: An Evaluation of the Industrial Revenue Bond Program," *Urban Affairs Quarterly* 18 (September 1982): 73–89.

60. Daphne A. Kenyon and Dennis Zimmerman, "Private-Activity Bonds and the Volume Cap in 1990," *Intergovernmental Perspective* 17, no. 3 (Summer 1991): 35–37.

61. For citations on municipal bond corruption, see Sbragia, *Debt Wish,* pp. 224–225.

62. Leslie Wayne, "Ban on Political Contributions Considered for Bond Lawyers," *New York Times* (August 5, 1996), p. D2.

63. Peter Truell, "Municipal Bond Dealers Face Scrutiny," *New York Times* (December 17, 1996), p. D1; Michael R. Lissack, "A Giant Shell Game Snares Taxpayers," *Albany Times Union* (August 1, 1996), p. A11.

64. "Shine the Light on Muni Deals," *BusinessWeek* (August 26, 1996).

65. Mary Williams, "Bond Advice Leaves Pain in Its Wake," *New York Times* (February 16, 2009), www.nytimes.com/2009/02/17/business/17muni.html.

66. Don Van Natta Jr., "Firm Acted as Tutor in Selling Towns Risky Deals," *New York Times* (April 7, 2009), www.nytimes.com/2009/04/08/us/08bond.html.

67. Mary Williams Walsh, "Nationwide Inquiry on Bids for Municipal Bonds," *New York Times* (January 8, 2009), www.nytimes.com/2009/01/09/business/09insure .html.

68. Thomas Geis, "Municipal Credit and Bond Rating System," paper delivered at the Municipal Officers Association Meeting (Denver, May 31, 1972), pp. 5–6.
69. Ibid.
70. U.S. Advisory Commission on Intergovernmental Relations, *City Financial Emergencies* (Washington, DC: U.S. Government Printing Office, 1971), p. 10.
71. Ibid., p. 12.
72. Ibid., p. 16.
73. Ibid., p. 17.
74. Ibid., pp. 81–82.
75. Todd Swanstrom, *The Crisis of Growth Politics: Cleveland, Kucinich, and the Challenge of Urban Populism* (Philadelphia: Temple University Press, 1985), Chapter 7.
76. Peter Eisenger, "The Politics of Bread and Circuses," *Urban Affairs Review* 35, no. 3 (January 2000): 316–333.
77. U.S. Bureau of the Census, *2007 Census of Governments, Local Government Finances by Type of Government* (2002), Table 2, http://www2.census.gov/govs /estimate/07slsstab2a.xls.
78. Jon Teaford, *The Rough Road to Renaissance: Urban Revitalization in America, 1940–1985* (Baltimore: Johns Hopkins University Press, 1990), p. 307.
79. These arrangements are described in Peter K. Eisenger, *The Rise of the Entrepreneurial State: State and Local Economic Development Policy in the United States* (Madison: University of Wisconsin Press, 1988).
80. James Leigland, "Public Infrastructure and Special Purposed Governments: Who Pays and How?" in *Building the Public City: The Politics, Governance, and Finance of Public Infrastructure,* ed. David C. Perry (Thousand Oaks, CA: Sage, 1995), p. 139.
81. State of Illinois, Compliance Audit Report (1998 and 1999), www.state.il.us/auditor.
82. William Fulton, "Paying the Bill," *Governing* 15, no. 11 (August 2002): 60.
83. Donald F. Norris, "If We Build It, They Will Come! Tourism-Based Economic Development in Baltimore," in *The Infrastructure of Play: Building the Tourist City,* ed. Dennis R. Judd (Armonk, NY: M. E. Sharpe, 2003), p. 162.
84. Ibid., p. 151.
85. Susan E. Clarke and Martin Saiz, "From Waterhole to World City: Place Luck and Public Agendas in Denver," in *The Infrastructure of Play,* ed. Dennis R. Judd (Armonk, NY: M. E. Sharpe, 2003), pp. 183–184.
86. Rachel Weber, "Equity and Entrepreneurialism: The Impact of Tax Increment Financing on School Finance," *Urban Affairs Review* 38, no. 5 (2003): 619–644.
87. Eric Klinenberg, *Heat Wave: A Social Autopsy of Disaster in Chicago* (Chicago: University of Chicago Press, 2002), p. 9.
88. Paul Peterson, *City Limits* (Chicago: University of Chicago Press, 1981), p. 22.

CHAPTER 13

The Renaissance of the Metropolitan Center

The Unexpected Recovery of the Central Cities

By the 1980s, it appeared to many observers that the historic city that anchored many metropolitan regions was pretty much slipping into its last death throes. The cities that had prospered in the industrial era struggled to regain their former glory, but for many of them there seemed to be little realistic chance for success. For decades, population, business, and jobs had been moving to the suburbs, and the rapid deindustrialization of the national economy that began in the early 1970s threatened to make the industrial cities utterly irrelevant to the nation's future. A report by the President's Commission on the National Agenda for the Eighties, issued at the end of President Jimmy Carter's term, reached the gloomy conclusion that that the nation's older cities were all but doomed:

> The economy of the United States, like that of many of the older industrial societies, has for years now been undergoing a critical transition from begin geographically-based to being deconcentrated, decentralized, and service-based. In the process, many cities of the old industrial heartland . . . are losing their status as thriving industrial capitals . . . [1]

The members of the commission agreed that "Ultimately, the federal government's concern for national economic vitality should take precedence over the competition for advantage among communities and regions."[2] It seemed obvious that unless they could find a way out of their predicament, the cities that had prospered in an earlier era were destined to whither on the vine.

Ironically, this bleak assessment was rendered right at the time when the first stirrings of a central-city revival were becoming apparent. By the 1990s it became clear that large numbers of central cities were on the rebound, and over the next decade the good news began to spread. Almost overnight, it seemed, downtown business districts and entertainment/tourist districts were becoming popular destinations for tourists and local residents alike. Nearby neighborhoods were also undergoing a revival. An informal *New York Times* survey of nine cities (Boston, Chicago, Houston, Los Angeles, Miami, New York, San Antonio, San Diego, and Washington, D.C.) conducted in 2000 found that businesses and new residents had begun pouring into residential areas previously considered off limits. The displacement of poorer residents was accompanied by dropping crime rates and a general improvement in the quality of life for the middle class.[3] Within a few years, it became apparent that the inner-city revitalization had reached a critical threshold, and that it was unlikely to be reversed. This optimistic prediction has held up for most cities. Even though the comeback has sometimes been slow and uncertain, even the economic downturn that began in 2008 seems not to have reversed the trend.[4]

Most American central cities have experienced at least some degree of downtown development and neighborhood gentrification. Affluent professionals and young people have been moving into areas previously occupied by the working class or poor. From 1990 to 2000, downtown populations increased in 18 of 24 cities studied by the Fannie Mae Foundation and the Brookings Institution.[5] Although the number of new residents was quite small in most cities, even modest growth represented a stunning turnaround. Some cities that had been losing population for a half century actually began to grow again in the 1990s, and even the few that continued to shrink did so at a reduced rate.[6] It is true that the recovery was uneven and some cities were still in fragile condition, but for most of them the signs were pointing in the right direction.

The revival of downtowns can be traced to two significant developments: globalization and economic transformation. Businesses connected to the new global economy, such as electronic trade and commerce, telecommunications, finance, marketing, and corporate services, are clustering in downtown areas. Cities that have attracted high-level services have done particularly well, especially in downtown areas, but many smaller places have also followed the trend.[7]

Tourism/entertainment, culture, and urban amenities are clustering in and near downtown areas as well. Affluent residents who live downtown want to commute less and also prefer to live in an environment with exciting street life, nightlife, culture, and entertainment. With their historic architecture, public monuments, redeveloped waterfronts, and older residential areas, cities are uniquely positioned to become settings for a robust urban culture. By the turn of the twenty-first century almost everyone could see that cities were entering a new urban era.

OUTTAKE

Baltimore's Revival Is Debated

Called the "Cinderella city of the 1980s," Baltimore is one of the nation's best-known examples of a downtown development strategy anchored by tourism and entertainment. Because of its size and proximity to New York City and Washington, D.C., Baltimore was not likely to attract a concentration of global corporations, so it focused singularly on tourism and entertainment.

In its heyday, Baltimore's Inner Harbor was a thriving center of commerce, but by the 1960s it was an eyesore, with its rotting, rat-infested piers, abandoned buildings, and desolate parking lots perched on a harbor that smelled, in the writer H. L. Mencken's words, "like a million polecats." The audacious idea was to transform this blighted mess into a national tourist attraction.

The linchpin of the plan to redevelop the Inner Harbor was Harborplace, anchored by two translucent pavilions enclosing a festival mall designed by the developer James Rouse. Rouse intended to create "a warm and human place, with diversity of choice, full of festival and delight." Completed in 1980, Harborplace succeeded beyond anyone's expectations, attracting 18 million visitors the first year, earning $42 million, and creating 2,300 jobs. In 1981, when the National Aquarium opened, it gave the Inner Harbor a dramatic tourist attraction. By 1992, more than 15 million visitors had toured the aquarium's exhibits, including a 64-foot glass pyramid housing a reproduction of a South American rain forest. Between 1980 and 1986, the number of visitors and the amount of money they spent in Baltimore tripled; to accommodate the increased demand, the number of hotel rooms also tripled. The success of the Inner Harbor development and other projects in the downtown unleashed a surge of private investment that spilled over into surrounding areas.

The energizing force behind Baltimore's redevelopment was William Donald Schaefer, who served four terms as the city's mayor from 1971 to 1987. The city's renaissance made him into a national political figure. In 1984, he was hailed as "The Best Mayor in America." In November 1986, Schaefer rode the wave of positive publicity about Baltimore's redevelopment into the Maryland governor's mansion. But the drumbeat of good news about the city's downtown revival overlooked the conditions in the city's deteriorating neighborhoods. Kurt Schmoke, who succeeded Schaefer as Baltimore's first black mayor in 1987, observed, "If you were revisiting Baltimore today after a 20-year absence, you would find us much prettier and much poorer."

In actuality there are two Baltimores, one inhabited by suburban workers and visitors, the other by poor people who live in the slums. Revitalization in the downtown and at the harbor did not stem the hemorrhaging of the city's population, which fell 2.1 percent between 2000 and 2009, having previously fallen by 135,000 people from 1980 to 2000, and by another 14,000 by 2007. Meanwhile, the suburbs continued to attract more people and better jobs. In 1950, the city's residents made slightly more than the residents of surrounding suburbs, but by 2000 they made half as much, a trend which continues—the median household income between 2006 and 2010 for Baltimore city was $39,386, less than half the average family income of $103,272 in Howard County.[8] Things would have been worse without the Harborplace development. The city's job development programs succeeded in placing 1,300 persons in jobs at Harborplace in just six years, and more than 40 percent of the Harborplace workforce was drawn from minorities. By 1990, the Inner Harbor and nearby projects had created an estimated 30,000 new jobs directly and indirectly; later, a study estimated that visitors to Baltimore spent $847 million in just one year, 1998, which supported a visitor-related payroll of $266 million and generated $81 million in state and local taxes. On the other side of the ledger, a lot of the jobs were near or at minimum wage, as indicated by the fact that in 2010, city residents made only half as much, on average, as the people living in surrounding suburbs.

This profile raises important questions about Baltimore's version of downtown revitalization: Have public dollars been wisely spent? Is development that focuses on tourism and entertainment misguided? There are opposing answers to these questions. According to one critic, the glitter of Inner Harbor merely hides the problems in the rest of the city:

> [T]he Inner Harbor functions as a sophisticated mask. It invites us to participate in a spectacle, to enjoy a festive circus that celebrates the coming together of people and commodities. Like any mask, it can beguile and distract in engaging ways, but at some point we want to know what lies behind it. If the mask cracks or is violently torn off, the terrible face of Baltimore's impoverishment may appear.

But there is an opposing view. Tangible benefits have accrued because of Baltimore's strategy, including the creation of jobs, an improving tax base (but not enough to offset losses in other parts of the city), and the physical reconstruction of an important part of the city. Without the revitalization of the downtown, nothing else would have been happening in the rest of Baltimore anyway.

Will the real Baltimore please stand up?

Sources: Neal R. Peirce, Robert Guskind, and John Gardner, "Politics Is Not the Only Thing That Is Changing America's Big Cities," *National Journal* 22 (November 26, 1983): 2480; Tony Hiss, "Annals of Place: Reinventing Baltimore," *New Yorker* (April 29, 1991), p. 62; Christopher Corbett, "What's Doing in Baltimore," *New York Times* (February 23, 1992); Bernard L. Berkowitz, "Rejoinder to Downtown Redevelopment as an Urban Growth Strategy: A Critical Appraisal of the Baltimore Renaissance," *Journal of Urban Affairs* 9, no. 2 (1987): 129; Donald F. Norris, "If We Build It, They Will Come! Tourism-Based Economic Development in Baltimore," in *The Infrastructure of Play*, ed. Dennis R. Judd (Armonk, NY: M. E. Sharpe, 2003), pp. 150–151; Richard C. Hula, "The Two Baltimores," in *Leadership and Urban Regeneration: Cities in North America and Europe*, ed. Dennis Judd and Michael Parkinson (Thousand Oaks, CA: Sage, 1990); David Harvey, *Spaces of Capital: Towards a Critical Geography* (New York: Routledge, 2001), pp. 143–144.

The Decline of Downtown

The distribution of economic activities in the United States has changed fundamentally over the past 100 years. Photographs of the period show that as late as the 1940s, downtown areas were a pandemonium of people, traffic, and frenetic energy. This urban form, with so much activity crowded into a few square blocks, was a defining feature of America's cities. In New York, the term *downtown* came into common usage in the nineteenth century to distinguish the commercial district at the southern tip of Manhattan from "uptown," the mostly residential areas a few blocks north. Through the years, "downtown" came to refer to the central commercial areas of cities everywhere. Downtown was where streetcars and passenger railways converged, where the buildings climbed to the sky, where retailing and professional businesses crowded together, and where throngs of people jostled one another on the streets. Downtown was busy and crowded; restaurants were packed at lunchtime. Writers in the popular press and in novels were fascinated by downtown because it seemed to be a microcosm representing the tremendous energy and anarchy of the American economic and social system.[9]

Almost all of the activities defining the downtown occurred in very small areas—one square mile in Chicago by the end of the 1920s, less than a square mile in St. Louis, Los Angeles, Boston, and Detroit, and an even smaller area in most other cities.[10] Almost all banks, public utilities, law firms, advertising agencies, accounting firms, and the head offices of large industrial corporations were clustered there, as were department stores and most other large retailing establishments.[11] Taller and taller buildings allowed the downtowns to grow up rather than out. The specialized nature of these buildings, devoted as they were strictly to commerce and professional activities, replaced the smaller buildings that had, at an earlier time, mixed together commercial, professional, and residential uses under one roof. The separation of business activities from everything else gave rise to a new term, the "central business district," although in practice the term tended to be used interchangeably with "downtown."[12]

By the twentieth century, downtown had become "an idealized public place and thus a powerful symbol" of American culture—a place where people of all backgrounds mingled, a "turf common to all."[13] But even in the 1920s, at a time when downtown areas were livelier than ever before, they began to lose their status as centers of goods production, wholesale trade, and retail sales. Chain retailers began opening stores closer to their customers in the outlying neighborhoods and in suburbs, a step signaling the gradual deconcentration of retailing. Small business districts began to sprout up that competed with downtown, a process aided by the automobile. Bigger troubles came with the Great Depression of the 1930s. Businesses closed their doors; older buildings fell into disrepair and decay.[14]

The Great Depression laid bare a truth that had mostly escaped notice in the prosperous decade of the 1920s. Within metropolitan areas, a spatial restructuring had been taking place for a long time. Manufacturing was beginning a slow exodus to the suburbs, a process speeded up by an emerging network of highways and truck transportation, and especially by the construction of the interstate highway system after World War II. Modern mass production techniques require large amounts of inexpensive land for one-story assembly-line production methods. With the range of commuting made possible by the automobile, it was possible to locate factories at some distance from residential areas and still be accessible to workers.

Shopping districts had also begun to compete with downtown. As late as the 1950s, the big downtown department stores still offered the best selection and prices, and middle-class shoppers had long ago developed the habit of saving a special day for shopping on the busy streets. It took a while, but by the 1960s suburban shopping centers were beginning to replace the downtown experience. With sprawling parking lots a few steps away and freeway interchanges nearby, the shopping centers and their later incarnation, the malls, were convenient for shoppers, who had, by now, completely abandoned mass transit for the automobile.

The civil rights protests, racial violence, and riots of the 1960s stigmatized downtowns as threatening and dangerous places, and as a result the white women shoppers who drove retail sales escaped to the quiet atmosphere of shopping centers located far away from the much-publicized turmoil.[15] Suburban developers seized the opportunity to create an ambience that contrasted sharply with city streets. In 1956, the first enclosed, climate-controlled mall, Southdale, opened in the Minneapolis suburb of Edina. By making shopping comfortable all year round, it was an instant success.[16] Mall owners created a leisurely environment conducive to consumption, including common hours for stores, directories and uniform signs, and benches and landscaping. By comparison, downtown shopping seemed chaotic and inconvenient, and sometimes even menacing. By 1974, 15,000 shopping centers had captured more than 44 percent of the nation's retail sales,[17] and before long downtown department stores began to close for good. Hudson's, a historic landmark in Detroit, finally shuttered its doors in 1981.[18]

Inner-city economies crashed in the 1970s. The events of the next two decades introduced a new tongue-twister into the English language, *deindustrialization*, a word invented to refer to the rapid restructuring of economies in all of the advanced nations. Technological advances in production processes, such as the use of robots for assembly, made it possible to produce goods with fewer workers than in the past. Although the volume of production increased between 1970 and 1988, the nation's manufacturing employment remained stable at 19 million jobs. At the same time, a lot of manufacturing firms were leaving the United States entirely, to such places as the Caribbean, Latin America, and Asia, where wages were lower and environmental regulations more lax.[19] Metropolitan regions that had prospered in the industrial age slid into a steep, abrupt decline, with unemployment rates rising, in some cases, to 20 percent of the workforce. The situation for inner cities seemed especially precarious. Having absorbed one blow after another, and now facing this final calamity, it was not clear that downtowns had any future whatsoever.

Globalization and the Downtown Renaissance

Though it was difficult to see at first, the dark clouds of deindustrialization had a silver lining. The loss of manufacturing was accompanied by a rapid rise in the number of service jobs. From 1975 to 1990, 30 million new jobs were created in service industries, so by the end of the 1980s, 84 million people were employed in services, as compared to 25 million in goods production.[20] Almost 80 percent of employment growth in the 1980s came in the form of service jobs.[21] At the same time that factory workers found their jobs disappearing, new opportunities opened up for educated white-collar workers. As shown in Table 13.1, in seven Northeastern and Midwestern metropolitan areas, the percentage of jobs in the manufacturing sector fell from 32 to 12 percent in the 40 years from 1960 to 2000. Over the same period, services grew from 15 to 36 percent of local employment. Wholesale/retail and finance, insurance, and real estate remained about the same, so it was clear that the increase in service jobs was driving economic growth. The new services economy pointed the way toward a strategy for reviving the inner cities and their downtowns.

TABLE 13.1 Change in Job Categories in Seven Northeastern and Midwestern Metropolitan Areas, 1960–2000

	Percentage Employed in Each Category				
	1960	1970	1980	1990	2000
Manufacturing	32%	26%	21%	14%	12%
Transportation, communications, and public utilities	8	7	6	5	5
Wholesale and retail trade	21	21	21	22	20
Finance, insurance, and real estate	7	7	8	9	8
Services	15	19	24	31	36
Government	13	16	17	16	14

Source: U.S. Department of Labor, Bureau of Labor Statistics, *Earnings and Employment* (Washington, DC: U.S. Government Printing Office, 1960, 1970, 1980, 1990, and 2000).

By the mid-1970s, civic leaders finally came to the conclusion that central cities were not likely to ever again compete head to head with suburbs for manufacturing, retailing, and wholesaling. Those sectors had already become highly decentralized within urban areas, and it was best to accept this reality. If central cities were going to find a way back, they would have to chart a new direction. Service-sector jobs in finance, corporate employment, and tourism pointed the way. A generation of "messiah mayors" who preached a gospel of self-help for their cities experimented with novel methods of promoting local economic development. They used public funds to leverage investment in office towers, malls, and tourist and entertainment facilities.[22] Cities offered property tax breaks, often over many years; and used eminent domain to take private property for glitzy projects. Tax increment finance districts (TIFs) and business improvement districts (BIDs) raised public funds to lure developers.

TIFs and BIDs were important because they were able to raise large amounts of capital by selling tax-free revenue bonds to investors. Investors get a tax break, and the TIF or BID public authority pays off the bonds (over 30 or 40 years) with the tax revenues generated by future development. Special authorities, such as convention and visitors' bureaus, mall authorities, sports authorities, museum districts, and many others, finance public improvements or new facilities by charging user fees (admission to events, for example), issuing bonds (to be paid by user fees), and gaining access to designated tax sources. Through such mechanisms, large amounts of money were raised for the remaking of downtown areas even though municipal governments were struggling just to pay their bills.

Public subsidies made the downtown renaissance possible. By the mid-1980s, most big cities were beginning to sport a "trophy collection," that typically included at least one luxury hotel (preferably one with a multistory atrium), a new sports stadium (usually domed), a downtown shopping mall, a redeveloped waterfront, and a new convention center.[23] These facilities and the activities they generated helped to support corporate white-collar employment, entertainment, culture, and a burgeoning tourism and convention trade.

The data in Table 13.2 show that downtown populations increased in cities in all regions of the nation. Some cities (such as Atlanta, Baltimore, Boston, Chicago, Los Angeles, and Philadelphia) built on a downtown population base that was already substantial in 1990 (ranging from 19,763 in Atlanta to 75,823 in Boston). Other cities (such as Cleveland, Denver, Detroit, Houston,

TABLE 13.2 Downtowns That Grew in the 1990s (18 Selected Cities)

City	1990 Downtown	2000 Downtown	Population Change	Percentage Change
Atlanta	19,763	24,731	4,968	25%
Baltimore	28,597	30,067	1,470	5
Boston	75,823	79,251	3,428	4.5
Chicago	27,760	42,039	14,279	51
Cleveland	7,261	9,599	2,338	32
Colorado Springs	13,412	14,377	965	7
Des Moines	4,190	4,204	14	0.03
Denver	2,794	4,230	1,436	51
Detroit	5,970	6,141	171	3
Houston	7,029	11,882	4,853	69
Los Angeles	34,655	36,630	1,975	6
Memphis	7,606	8,994	1,388	18
Milwaukee	10,973	11,243	270	2.5
Norfolk, VA	2,390	2,881	491	20.5
Philadelphia	74,655	78,349	3,694	5
Portland, OR	9,528	12,902	3,374	35
San Diego	15,417	17,894	2,477	16
Seattle	9,824	16,443	6,619	67

Sources: Adapted from Rebecca R. Sohmer and Robert E. Lang, *Downtown Rebound* (Washington, DC: Brookings Institution Press, Fannie Mae Foundation, 2001), pp. 2–3; also see Rebecca R. Sohmer and Robert E. Lang, "Downtown Rebound," in *Redefining Urban & Suburban America: Evidence from Census 2000*, ed. Bruce Katz and Robert E. Lang (Washington, DC: Brookings Institution Press, 2003), pp. 63–74.

Memphis, and Norfolk) attracted new residents to downtown populations that were small in 1990 (in all cases about 7,500 or less). The total number of people who moved into the downtown areas of these cities was not large, but the new residents nevertheless catalyzed a dramatic change. Condominium and apartment towers sprung up alongside historic buildings renovated into lofts and condos; restaurants, bars, and personal service businesses quickly followed. The decades-long flight from downtown and the neighborhoods around it seemed about to come to an end.

The economic sectors that led the revitalization of downtown constituted the components of a new globalized economy revolving around high-level corporate and professional services, telecommunications, and technology. Globalization has been facilitated by technologies that make information exchange nearly instantaneous and by the ability of corporations to manage operations in many places at once. Since the 1980s, corporations have been growing larger through mergers and buyouts. Large firms are able to coordinate activities on a global scale—the movement of capital investment, the location of factories, and the distribution and marketing of products. The innovations required by modern corporations in product design, advertising, the adoption of new technologies, and corporate organization are made possible by frequent coordination among highly specialized professionals, most of whom do not work within a single organization. In the global age, corporations prefer to locate in close proximity to the highly skilled and eclectic mix of professionals on whom they rely.

The skyscrapers that sprout from the downtowns of American cities are the physical manifestation of this clustering of economic activities. Although large numbers of corporations are located in edge cities and in office parks in the suburbs, downtown areas have continued to attract the firms that benefit from being close to one another. Especially (but not exclusively) in larger cities, high-level professional offices and information industries have become clustered into "strategic nodes with a hyperconcentration of activities"[24] supporting layer upon layer of highly educated, technologically sophisticated professionals offering specialized services—corporate managers, management consultants, legal experts, accountants, computer specialists, financial analysts, media and public relations consultants, and the like.

Corporate headquarters cluster more densely than anywhere else in a few global cities, such as New York, Paris, London, Chicago, Los Angeles, Miami, Hong Kong, Sydney, and Tokyo.[25] Sitting atop a new urban hierarchy created by globalization, these cities house corporations that manage production and distribution networks around the world. The largest firms, especially including international banks, stock and commodity exchanges, and media empires, are located in global cities. Second-tier cities, such as Montreal and Hamburg, normally host a few international companies, and further down the hierarchy, medium-sized cities such as Atlanta, Cleveland, and St. Louis serve as the hubs of regional corporate networks. Down the pyramid further still are cities that depend on quite specialized activities tied to the global economy, such as an auto plant (Smyrna, Tennessee), a cluster of electronics software firms

(San Jose, California), or a meatpacking plant (Beardstown, Illinois). The places that cannot find a way to tap into sectors of the global economy are destined to slip into irreversible decline.[26]

The professionals who locate near or in downtown areas demand an exceptional level of urban amenities, and the expectation that cities should provide a high quality of life has filtered down to include almost everyone. By the end of the 1990s, successful downtowns and gentrified neighborhoods offered a unique "urban culture" based on a varying mix of amenities that are best provided in dense urban environments: restaurants, blues and jazz clubs, art galleries, theaters and performance halls, bars, dance clubs, after-hours clubs, and coffee shops.[27] These cultural activities have great economic consequence for cities; they are a major source of jobs, and they help keep young professionals from moving to more interesting places. In this way, economics and culture have become inseparable in the twenty-first-century American city.

The New Urban Culture

The recent population growth in America's downtowns has been driven by empty-nest retirees and by affluent young professionals known by a number of slang terms, such as *yuppies* (young urban professionals), *dinks* (dual-income, no kids), and *jingles* (singles with joint living arrangements). In only a few years' time, this movement fundamentally changed the spatial geography of cities because affluent professionals tended to crowd into downtowns and nearby neighborhoods, and they have often done so by displacing people who had previously lived there. Affluent people live in downtown areas with high property values; outside of the downtown, there is a patchwork of gentrifying neighborhoods, some of them located near or even within poverty-stricken areas. What makes this patchwork pattern possible is the nature of the new development. Members of the affluent middle class often live within condominium towers or gated communities, well protected from nearby blight.[28]

The professionals who have flocked into downtown and gentrifying neighborhoods have driven up the cost of housing, sometimes to fantastic levels. New condominium towers and townhouse developments have become signifiers of urban regeneration, as has the renovation of old factory and warehouse buildings (some of them long abandoned) for retail and housing. Deteriorated neighborhoods have attracted an eclectic assortment of affluent yuppies, artists, and people with unconventional lifestyles who thrive on tolerance and diversity. Two characteristics have made these neighborhoods attractive—the presence of historic and architecturally significant buildings such as old Victorians and row houses, and their location near the central business district and amenities such as waterfronts, museums, parks, performing arts venues, and restaurants, bars, and nightlife.

The term *gentrification* is a shorthand way of referring to the process of displacement. The gentrification storyline goes something like this: affluent newcomers drive up demand, bringing sharp increases in land values; as a result, less affluent, minority, and older residents are forced to move. Property taxes escalate when land values rise; dilapidated property becomes subject to new standards of maintenance; and neighborhood institutions such as churches and schools close because families with children tend to be replaced by singles and childless couples. Some gentrified neighborhoods are mainly residential, but more frequently they are composed of a mixture of housing, retail, and services establishments (especially hair salons, health clubs, cleaners, and coffeehouses). Within these neighborhoods are restaurants, exclusive shopping districts, parks, and cultural facilities.

A leading urban scholar, Richard Florida, has argued that the rise of what he calls "the creative class," which is composed of highly educated professionals with rarified intellectual, analytic, artistic, and creative skills, places a higher value on the quality of life than almost anything else.[29] The members of this class demand social interaction, culture, nightlife, diversity, and a sense of authenticity, which have become to be defined by such things as "historic buildings, established neighborhoods, a unique music scene or specific cultural attributes. It comes from the mix—from urban grit alongside renovated buildings, from the comingling of young and old, colorful characters and yuppies, fashion models and 'bag ladies.' "[30] Florida claims that the creative class tends to reject the "canned experiences" associated with tourist enclaves, and is the main driver of the new generation of urban amenities that every city must have.[31]

Tourism and Entertainment

Tourism, entertainment, and culture are crucial to downtown revival. The reasons are not difficult to uncover. Travel and tourism is the world's largest industry (measured by value added to investment).[32] Travelers and tourists spend huge amounts of money on lodging, food, entertainment and culture, transportation, souvenirs, and other services and products. Worldwide, about one-tenth of all jobs are generated by travel and tourism.[33] To remake themselves into places that tourists want to visit, cities have invested heavily in tourism facilities and the reconstruction of downtown environments. Indeed, the rebuilding of downtown areas to make them friendly for visitors has been so massive that the current period of city building may be compared to the building of the industrial city a century ago, when cities invested in mass transit systems, paved streets, sewer and water systems, and parks. The only other city-building era that changed the urban landscape as dramatically occurred in the 1950s and 1960s, when federally funded urban renewal clearance leveled blocks of downtown real estate and entire neighborhoods.[34] The transformation that began in the late 1970s is still taking place, but already American cities have been changed almost beyond recognition.

In Chicago, as in many cities, the leading industry is now tourism and entertainment. The number of tourists increased from 32 million in 1993 to 43 million in 1997, a product of indefatigable promotion and a huge investment in the infrastructure of tourism.[35] Chicago has built the world's largest convention center, an entertainment district on a renovated pier (Navy Pier), and has one of the world's most extensive and beautiful park systems, which runs for miles along the Lake Michigan lakefront. The city is host to several extraordinary museums and other attractions (such as the John G. Shedd Aquarium and the Adler Planetarium), maintains elaborate floral and garden displays along Michigan Avenue and on many other streets, and hosts dozens of events each year in the parks. Grant Park, which stretches between the downtown Loop and Lake Michigan, is the most frequently visited park in the United States, attracting more visitors than even the Grand Canyon.[36] Chicago has a complex globalized economy, but it would be in trouble without tourism. Indeed, 2010 saw a decrease in tourism for Chicago, from 39.5 million visitors in 2009, to 38.11 million, a change which was felt as the local tourism industry battled the results of the struggling economy, high fuel prices, and competition from other cities. Chicago quickly unleashed a $1 million media campaign, aimed at both in and out of state residents, a campaign which has been said to have already boosted 2011 visitor statistics. Nevertheless, it is expected that regaining the peak numbers of 2007 will take several years.[37]

In older industrial cities, tourist and entertainment venues have often been constructed on sites that were once devoted to manufacturing, warehousing, retailing, or harbor activities. These developments often try to project a contrived, nostalgic, and idealized version of city life, and they do so by utilizing architectural features that call to mind an imagined city from the past. One example is South Street Seaport in New York, which strives to create an ambience evoked by "authentic reproductions" of a working harbor[38]—in effect, an urban mini-version of Disneyland (in Anaheim, California), with its Main Street U.S.A. and Frontier Village. Similar developments in other places include the Wharf and Ghirardelli Square in San Francisco and the several renovated Union Stations scattered from coast to coast (while the actual train stations are out of sight and sound).

Making older cities attractive to tourists was not an easy task. In the wake of the riots of the 1960s, downtowns became stigmatized as violent, dangerous places. Where crime, poverty, and urban decay made parts of a city inhospitable to visitors, specialized areas were built that were, in effect, tourist reservations. Such "tourist bubbles" made it possible for the tourist, who was unfamiliar with the local landscape, to move inside "secured, protected and normalized environments."[39] The aim was to create a secure and imaginary world within an otherwise alien or even hostile setting. Within a few years, falling crime rates allowed tourist venues to spill beyond the confines of these enclaves. Downtown office construction and neighborhood gentrification gained momentum, and street life and urban culture became the objects of fascination and consumption for locals and visitors alike. Where these processes have achieved critical mass, the central cities have once again become the true hubs of their metropolitan regions, the home of activities, culture, and a lifestyle not easily imitated in the suburbs.[40] In cities as different as Boston, San Francisco, Chicago, New York City, and Portland, Oregon, visitors wander and mingle freely with local residents. Indeed, except in and around convention centers, it is often hard to distinguish visitors from local residents. The "localization of leisure turned cities into entertainment destinations not only for out-of-town visitors but also for suburban commuters and the growing number of affluent downtown residents."[41] Increasingly, local residents have become "as if tourists," acting like tourists even when they stay home.[42]

The infrastructure that makes central-city tourism possible includes convention centers, sports stadiums, festival malls and urban entertainment districts, cultural venues such as performing arts centers and museums, and, in a few cities, gaming casinos.[43] Especially in the case of convention centers and sports stadiums, public funding has sometimes become a contentious issue, with proponents playing up the benefits associated with city marketing and economic growth, and opponents countering with the argument that public support for such facilities is both a bad investment and a case of misplaced priorities. However, for mayors and other public officials, the economic benefits of city image-making, whether it involves expanding a convention center, building a new sports stadium, or improving a museum, are beyond dispute.

Convention Centers

Until the 1960s, few cities had built the huge convention centers that are so prevalent in and near downtown areas today. Only a few decades ago, town halls doubled as assembly facilities, if any were needed. In the 1920s, some cities built the first generation of meetings and exhibition halls; St. Louis, for example, built the St. Louis Arena in 1929 to accommodate an agricultural exhibit. During the Great Depression, the federal government, through the Public Works Administration, financed large public assembly and exhibition facilities in a number of cities. This generation of halls often contained one or more auditoriums as well as exhibition space under one roof, and in many cases these structures were not replaced until the 1980s or 1990s. These facilities were expensive to operate and virtually always lost money, but they had the effect of attracting, and even helping to create, an array of travelling shows and exhibitions. The benefits to the local economy and to their own bottom line were soon comprehended by civic boosters, who then pushed for larger and better facilities.

In the 1950s, a few cities began constructing convention centers designed to attract professional meetings and trade shows. The proliferation of convention centers began in the 1960s and accelerated in the 1970s as air travel, growing affluence, and greater specialization in the job market gave rise to more meetings, exhibitions, and consumer shows (such as autos, boats, and electronics), and conventions. In the 1980s, cities began a virtual arms race for the convention trade, with even small towns joining the competition. More than 70 percent of the convention centers existing in 1998 had opened since 1970.[44] Actually, however, the race had just begun. In the ten years from 1993 to 2003, capital spending for convention centers doubled, to $2.3 billion annually, and in the 13 years from 1990 to 2003 convention-center space increased by 51 percent. In the latter year at least 40 cities were planning to build new facilities or expand the old ones. All of this activity meant that the size and cost of each facility escalated, but the available business had to be divided among an increasing number of contenders.[45]

All convention centers require annual subsidies for the payment of construction bonds and for operating costs, but rising construction, maintenance, and promotion costs have not deterred cities from investing in bigger and more elaborate facilities. Much is at stake. In 2002, there were nearly 23,000 associations and 6.5 million total private business establishments in the United States.[46] The 23,000-plus associations in the nation spent $32 billion for meetings in 1992, and corporations spent an additional $29 billion on off-premises meetings and conventions.[47] Tourism-related organizations alone had 1.4 million members in 1998, and the meetings industry produced $81 billion in economic output.[48] The average attendance at new exhibitions nearly quadrupled from 1990 to 1997.[49] Although only from 4 to 5 percent of meetings are held in convention centers (the rest are held in hotels, resorts, and other venues),[50] the size of the meetings and convention business has been large enough to prompt hundreds of cities to build or expand their existing facilities. Forty-one convention centers were being built or renovated in 2000, and 66 were slated for expansion or renovation.[51]

Indeed, as of January 2005, public capital spending on convention centers since the beginning of the decade had doubled to $2.4 billion annually, increasing convention space by over 50 percent since 1990. Nationwide, 44 new or expanded convention centers were in planning in 2005 alone. The economic downturn that began in the fall of 2008 prompted a sharp decline in both tourism and convention attendance, but in less than three years, attendance and construction had moved back to its pre-2008 vigor. Michigan's major convention venues reported a growth in bookings for 2011—the DeVos Palace in Grand Rapids, for example, forecast about 20 more event days in 2011 than 2010, and projected a revenue increase of about $150,000 from the previous year. The nearby Kalamazoo County Expo Center and Fairground, deemed "self-sufficient" by its operator, was in the midst of a $3.75 million expansion and planned to add 35,000 square feet to the facility.[52]

As more and more cities increased the size of their convention venues, the competition among cities became extraordinarily intense. In 2000, the top 15 cities in North America accounted for almost half of all conventions with exhibitions, but even the city that attracted the largest number of exhibitions—Orlando, Florida—accounted for only about 5 percent share of the nation's total convention business. As the number of cities competing for conventions increased, it became difficult for any one place to improve its share of the business no matter how much it invested. Additionally, from year to year there is a great deal of volatility because meeting planners are skilled at playing cities off against one another for the best deal.

Construction of a convention facility is necessary for a city to enter the race, but obviously a lot of other factors determine a city's ability to compete. In Orlando's case, obviously, Disney World is the big draw, but most cities cannot offer such a singularly powerful attraction. Cities that can offer an interesting mix of entertainment, culture, nightlife, and urban amenities have a built-in advantage. Las Vegas is a uniquely attractive place for visitors and conventioneers because it offers an inimitable blend of gambling, sin, luxury, and entertainment.

The publisher of Tradeshow Week, Adam Schaffer, commented that "Las Vegas is almost a nation unto itself. Everybody wants to go to Vegas—they want to go to a show, shop, etc., be entertained."[53] Of course visitors want to find a special experience in every city, so it is not sufficient to build a convention center and hotel and leave it at that. Cities must also provide the urban amenities and ambience that meetings planners and their clients will find attractive.

Virtually every major city in the United States had formed a convention and visitors bureau by the end of the 1980s, and over the years these have increased rapidly in personnel and budgets. The professional staff employed by convention bureaus construct lists of international, national, regional, and local associations that regularly sponsor or organize conventions and send out a blizzard of promotional literature. They man booths at the meetings of the organizations that might give them business, and often stage rather elaborate and costly promotional presentations and exhibits. And finally, cities make it a regular practice to invite representatives of the tourist industry and of important business and professional groups for a complimentary visit. In May 2003, for instance, the St. Louis Convention and Visitors Bureau hosted 4,000 professionals who were attending a meeting of the Travel Industry Association of America's Press Tour and Pow-Wow. The booths in the center were filled with representatives of rental and RV companies, hotels and hotel chains, airlines, and bus and cruise lines. States and cities set up booths as well.[54]

Despite such efforts, the St. Louis center failed to increase attendance significantly from 2000 to 2004. Meanwhile, the Renaissance Hotel, which had been built using funds from the city's empowerment zone, lost an estimated $2.4 million in only one year. Its low occupancy rate of 50 percent had already prompted Moody's Investment Service to put its bonds on a watch list.[55] St. Louis's experience was not unique; instead, it is replicated in many cities: in 2003 Seattle's center lost $5.3 million and the San Jose convention facility had a shortfall of $5 million. In a bid to get more business, convention center managers began offering special deals, but these bargains virtually guaranteed that operating losses would be locked in. The Hawaii, Seattle, Columbus, Indianapolis, and Nashville centers have offered free rent for specified periods (through 2010 for Hawaii's). Dallas has offered a half-rent bargain, plus rebates for hotel use and discounts on airfare, shuttle service, and exhibit setup costs.[56]

Sports Stadiums

Civic boosters believe that professional sports franchises are pivotal to the economic revitalization of central cities and often have used sports facilities as an anchor for development.[57] Cities compete vigorously for sports teams by helping to finance the construction of stadiums and by allowing owners to keep parking and concession fees and other revenues. Because teams sometimes threaten to move and occasionally do, sports cartels and team owners have been very successful in persuading cities to meet their demands. In the decade of the 1990s alone approximately $10 billion in public funds were devoted to the building of sports facilities in urban areas for major league professional teams.[58]

Although earlier studies seemed to make a convincing case that sports stadiums did not bring measurable benefits to local economies, recent research shows that in many contexts they do.[59] One study indicated that stadiums located in the downtown areas of six cities made a positive contribution to the regional economy, a study of the Gund Arena and Jacobs Field in Cleveland found that these facilities contributed to the economic redevelopment of downtown.[60]

It is important to add that economic impact is only one part of a complex picture. Sports teams have long been central to the civic and cultural life of American cities. Oddly, the assumption that a team expresses a city's essence, spirit, and sense of community has not been much eroded since teams and their players became highly mobile. Part of the reason for this is that local boosters regard professional sports teams as a signifier of "big league" status for a city. Sports teams carry a substantial emotional charge, so their worth is rarely, if ever, calculated in simple economic terms. Through the national and international publicity accompanying network broadcasts of games and playoffs, professional sports teams are a powerful vehicle for conveying a city's image and fostering a sense of identity and community. When a team wins a World's Series or the Super Bowl, a jolt of ecstatic happiness sweeps through the local population. For a moment everyone is a fan.

Professional sports is a big business. Between 2010 and 2011, the value of Major League Baseball teams increased 7 percent and reached an all-time high of $523 million. The New York Yankees topped the list at $1.7 billion, while the Mets lost 13 percent of their worth for a total value of $747 million.[61] The National Basketball Association (NBA) and professional hockey franchises could be bought for smaller sums, making it possible, in some cases, for someone with $100 to $200 million laying around to bid for a team.[62] Despite the claims of owners and the leagues, sports teams are profitable. In 2002, baseball commissioner Bud Selig testified to Congress that major league baseball generated an operating loss of $200 million that year, but *Forbes* magazine produced figures showing a $75 million profit.[63] The escalation of team values all through the previous decade made it a dubious claim that baseball owners lost money. The lucrative media contracts for most baseball teams made it even more suspect.[64]

For decades, professional sports teams were so closely identified with their cities of origin that moving would have been unthinkable. In baseball, this link was first broken in 1953, when the Boston Braves relocated to Milwaukee. The baseball franchise relocation game began in earnest in 1957, when owner Walter O'Malley moved the Brooklyn Dodgers to Los Angeles. O'Malley fought for years to find the land for a new stadium in Brooklyn to replace the decrepit Ebbets Field, which had opened in 1913. But he was repeatedly thwarted by Robert Moses, who, as head of New York's Bridge and Tunnel Authority, Park Commission, Construction Commission, and Slum Clearance Committee, controlled the land needed for a new park.[65] To lure the Dodgers out of New York, Los Angeles agreed to renovate its minor league stadium at Chavez Ravine and give the stadium to O'Malley. As the clincher, they offered him 300 acres of downtown Los Angeles real estate.[66] Considering the obstacles put in his way in Brooklyn, it would have been difficult for O'Malley to refuse the deal.

It did not take long for other owners to follow O'Malley's lead. Threats to move became potent weapons for prying more subsidies out of cities. Between 1953 and 1982, there were 78 franchise relocations in the four major professional sports: 11 in baseball, 40 in basketball, 14 in hockey, and 13 in football.[67] In only six years, from 1980 to 1986, more than half the cities with major league sports franchises were confronted with demands for increased subsidies, with relocation an implied if not always explicit threat hanging over negotiations.[68]

From 1980 to June 1992, an incredible amount of activity involved baseball and football teams. During this period, 20 cities sought baseball teams and 24 cities tried to attract football teams, an interesting statistic considering that there were, at that time, a total of 28 major league baseball and 28 professional football franchises (two new expansion football franchises were added in 1993, with several cities competing for them). Eleven cities had completed or were building stadiums, and 28 more considered building or had plans to build stadiums. New sports facilities were completed in the downtowns of 30 North American cities from 1990 to 2002. These were often the high-profile flagship projects of more comprehensive efforts at downtown development.[69] This impressive list includes cities from coast to coast and three cities in Canada. Approximately 50 minor league and collegiate sports facilities also were completed in the 1990s.[70]

Local boosters and investors are willing to bet that if they build it, they will come, and the eagerness to get in on the action may provoke local skirmishes. For example, since February 2011 there has been an ongoing dispute regarding the construction of a sports complex in Las Vegas. Plans have been drawn up by a development group in Las Vegas for a 40,000-seat domed stadium at UNLV. At the same time, a separate group has laid plans to construct a three-venue sport complex downtown (the Las Vegas National Sports Center), and it is lobbying the Board of Regents to vote against approving an exclusivity agreement with the UNLV venture. The $1.58 billion downtown project would include separate facilities for football, baseball, and basketball and is not projected to require public financing; consequently, significant private investment will be necessary.[71] If things go as planned, the Las Vegas National Sports Center will open as early as October 2014, and talks with multiple franchises have already begun in an effort to attract major sports teams to relocate.[72]

Except for baseball, where teams move less frequently, moves have become an ever-present possibility for many cities, in part because they pay off for the owners. In the 1990s, for example, the Quebec Nordiques (a hockey team) moved from a small market to Denver, Colorado, and renamed themselves the Avalanche. In 1995, in their first season, they won the Stanley Cup. In 1996, when the NFL Cleveland Browns became the Baltimore Ravens, the owner and the city signed a stadium deal that increased revenues substantially enough to allow the team to pay big signing bonuses to key players. In 2001, the Ravens won the Super Bowl. Perhaps even more dramatically, the perennially losing Rams left Los Angeles (actually Anaheim) for St. Louis in 1995. An extraordinary stadium deal was the lure, and after four more losing seasons, the team won Super Bowl XXXIV in 2000.[73]

Because cities are desperate to get and keep a professional sports team, owners realize that public subsidies are theirs for the asking. From 1953 to 1986, 67 of the 94 stadiums used by professional sports teams were publicly owned.[74] Beginning in the early 1980s, the two most important new revenue sources for sports teams came from network broadcasting and local and state subsidies.[75] By the end of the 1980s, it had become a rare exception when an owner agreed to build a stadium with private dollars. Owners came to expect other subsidies as well, in the form of guaranteed attendance minimums, the construction of luxury boxes, and control of stadium merchandising.

As teams became more and more footloose, cities found themselves at a disadvantage. In an attempt to improve their poor bargaining positions, some cities built stadiums even when they did not have teams. In the 1980s, Indianapolis built a football stadium, and then set about persuading the owner of the Baltimore Colts, Robert Irsay, to move. After the Maryland legislature passed an eminent domain law to make it possible for Baltimore to seize the Colts for public use, Irsay packed up the team's equipment in moving vans and left in the middle of the night. But probably the most famous case is the $139 million domed stadium built by St. Petersburg, Florida, in 1988 in the hopes of attracting a major league baseball team. Called "heaven's waiting room," boosters justified the Florida Suncoast Dome as a way of changing the city's image as a conservative retirement community.[76] For years, the stadium remained the site of tractor pulls and concerts. In the 1990s, St. Petersburg tried to lure several major league baseball teams, including the Seattle Mariners, the San Francisco Giants, and a National League expansion team. When Florida won a baseball team in 1991, it was awarded to Miami. In October 1993, an expansion team of the NFL was awarded to Jacksonville; St. Petersburg's stadium was built expressly for baseball and would not have been suitable for football. St. Louis, which also put in a bid for one of the NFL expansion teams, lost out. St. Louis undertook the construction of a domed stadium anyway, many months before the negotiations that eventually brought the Los Angeles Rams to the city in 1995.

Stadiums require generous land, infrastructure, and direct public subsidies because almost all of them (but not usually the teams playing in them) lose money. Annual operating deficits are generally considerable; the New Orleans Superdome lost about $3 million a year during the 1980s, for example, compared to the annual $1 million loss for the Silverdome in Pontiac, Michigan. In its first year, the Florida Suncoast Dome lost $1.3 million, plus $7.7 million in debt payments.[77] Modern domed stadiums cost so much to build that they can rarely schedule enough events or charge enough for them to avoid operating deficits; the only one in the country without deficits in 2004 was the Metrodome in Minneapolis, which did not require a tax subsidy.[78] Toronto ended up paying $400 million for its domed stadium; St. Louis's domed stadium, completed in 1995, cost $301 million.[79] The costs have only escalated since. In September 2008, the Indianapolis Colts played their first football game in the Lucas Oil Stadium, built at the cost of $720 million. In the New York area, three teams were looking forward to playing in new stadiums. The New

York Yankees opened their season in 2009 in a stadium built for $1.5 billion, while just a few miles away, the Jets and the Giants moved into one costing $1.6 billion.[80]

It is undoubtedly true, as civic boosters argue, that the most important benefits of a major sports franchise are intangible and therefore impossible to measure solely in economic terms. However, as teams became more mobile and owners asked for more, such arguments sometimes wear thin. In December 1996, the owners of the Seattle Mariners baseball team put the team up for sale, even though the city had earlier bought land and made plans to construct a new ballpark. Just a few months earlier, Seattle's football team, the Seahawks, had threatened to leave town, and it too demanded a new stadium. Together, the two stadiums were estimated to cost $760 million. A group called Citizens for More Important Things initiated a campaign opposing public subsidies behind this slogan: "Just say no to welfare for the wealthy."

From 2000 to 2006, public funds supplied 54 percent of the construction cost for new major league baseball stadiums and 55 percent of the costs for football stadiums.[81] These subsidies often provoked opposition, but there are other sources of dissatisfaction, too. Fans of the Mets, the Yankees, the Giants, and the Jets expressed outrage at the escalating price of tickets in the stadiums. At the three stadiums in New York, ticket prices in the new stadiums went up by two times or more. Season tickets for the best seats that had cost $1,000 each in the old Yankee stadium jumped to $2,500 when it opened in 2009.[82] In August 2008, the Giants announced that they would charge from $1,000 to $20,000 for personal seat licenses, which only entitled the holders to buy season tickets. "Here I am, buying a stadium for John Mara," a Giants ticket holder complained; "This is a greedy ploy with the only benefits going to them."[83]

St. Louis provides an example of the difficulties sometimes encountered by team owners who are seeking public funds. In 2000, the Cardinals baseball team launched an effort to persuade the state legislature and the city to build a new stadium to replace Busch Stadium, which had been constructed in 1965 with private funds (though public money was used to build an adjacent parking facility and to make public improvements). After going to the legislature three times and coming back empty handed, the Cardinals began an effort to piece together a package combining private funding and public subsidies from the city and other sources. Already the city's voters had passed a referendum requiring a vote on any public funding proposal of more than $1 million for stadiums. One day before the new law was to take effect, the Land Clearance and Redevelopment Authority, whose board members and chief administrator are appointed by the mayor of St. Louis, approved the elimination of a 5 percent tax that had always been assessed on the team's ticket sales. St. Louis County was also expected to commit $45 million and the state of Missouri $40 million in public infrastructure, such as highway and street improvements.[84]

In recent years, ticket prices have increased sharply to help pay for new stadiums, and as a consequence, professional sports attendance has become more stratified by income and class. For example, the new Cardinals stadium in St. Louis that opened in 2008 has twice the number of club seats as in the old

Busch Stadium, and prices for them are twice as high. There are fewer luxury boxes, but they cost more. All other ticket prices went up as well. Virtually all new stadiums have incorporated a larger number of premium and luxury seats as a means of increasing revenues.[85]

Malls, Entertainment, and Lifestyle Complexes

Malls have become a weapon that cities use in the regional competition for recreational shopping and tourism. To ensure that they are in the game, cities typically have heavily subsidized the construction of downtown malls by allocating Community Development Block Grant and Urban Development Action Grant funds, floated bonds to finance site acquisition and loans to developers, offered property tax abatements, created tax increment districts, built utilities tunnels, constructed sewer lines and water mains, rerouted and repaved streets; the list goes on. Civic leaders are eager to support mall development because it promises to bring a special form of "entertainment" retailing downtown. Boston's early success set the tone for such expectations.

On August 26, 1976, Boston's mayor, Kevin White, presided over opening-day ceremonies for Quincy Market in downtown Boston. The brainchild of developer James Rouse, who made a fortune developing suburban shopping malls, Quincy Market was housed in three 150-year-old market buildings that were renovated, at a cost of more than $40 million, into a collection of boutiques, gourmet food shops, and restaurants.[86] Few expected Quincy Market—located as it was in the center of a declining central city with inadequate parking and no big-ticket items to sell—to succeed. Indeed, six weeks before the opening day, the retail complex was less than 50 percent leased. To hide the empty stores, Rouse came up with the idea of leasing pushcarts to artists and craftspeople for $50 a day, plus a percentage of the sales.

By 11 o'clock in the morning on the opening day, only a modest crowd had gathered for the ceremonies. When the speeches were over Mayor White cut the ribbon, and developer Rouse and a company of kilted highland bagpipers led the crowd inside for a champagne reception. At lunchtime, the milling throng swelled as curious workers poured out of nearby office buildings, and by mid-afternoon, it was clear that opening day would be a huge success, with police estimating the crowd at 100,000.

People never stopped coming to Quincy Market. In its second year of operation, the market drew 12 million visitors—more than Disneyland that year. Newspapers reported the market's "instant acceptance" by the public, which delighted in the colorful sights, sounds, and smells of the food and imaginatively displayed merchandise and the festival air created by a liberal sprinkling of pushcarts, magicians, acrobats, and puppeteers. The banks that financed the project were originally skeptical; they calculated that Quincy Market would have to produce retail sales comparable to the most successful suburban shopping malls ($150 per square foot) to justify its unusually high development costs. Quincy Market shocked the experts by producing sales of $233 per square foot in its first year, with the pushcarts doing best of all. The opening of Quincy Market was hailed by the media as a sign of an urban renaissance in the making. It seemed to disprove the conventional wisdom that the downtowns of American cities were doomed to obsolescence and decline.

The first-generation downtown malls were important not only because they helped reverse the long-term decline of inner-city retailing but also because they provided a means of creating defended space in the midst of urban crime and decay. Malls built by the developers John Portman and James Rouse and their imitators became such common features of American downtowns that it was hard to recall how recently they had been constructed. The malls increasingly engulfed and centralized activities that were formerly spread through the urban community at large. Such complexes were easily criticized as "fortified cells of affluence,"[87] but there can be little doubt that as locations for tourism and entertainment, these spaces were extremely successful.

In the years after his Boston success, Rouse was invited to design festival malls for cities all across the country. What made Rouse's developments so distinctive and newsworthy was the artful combining of play and shopping. His formula was to create a carnival atmosphere, accomplished through a mixture of specialty shops, clothing stores, restaurants, and food stands, and with a changeable mix of musicians, jugglers, acrobats, and mimes to entertain shoppers. Rouse malls soon began to pop up all over the place: at the Gallery of Market Street East in Philadelphia, Grand Avenue in Milwaukee, Pike Street Market in Seattle, Horton Plaza in San Diego, Trolley Square in Salt Lake City, Union Station in St. Louis, Harborplace in Baltimore, South Street Seaport in New York, and on and on. Noticing the success of the formula, imitators began to appear, too. By the turn of the century, virtually every major city in the country had a Rouse mall or the equivalent.

Enclosed malls began opening in cities large and small, some modeled on Rouse's formula, some not. Many of them started modestly enough, but over time they accreted block by block, reaching over streets with a system of tubes and skyways. In Minneapolis, a sprawling mall complex grew almost invisibly by eating away the interiors of the downtown buildings, but leaving their historic facades intact. In Kansas City, the Crown Center inexorably spread from its beginnings as a luxury hotel; by the mid-1990s, it occupied several city blocks. In Montreal and Dallas, sprawling underground malls were connected through a network of tunnels. The mall's assault on Atlanta has been much more direct; the huge Peachtree complex has been built on the rubble of the historic downtown.

Because they are an aspect of leisure and tourism, the kinds of malls built in downtown areas do not necessarily compete head-to-head with suburban malls. Rather, they rely on a style of shopping that combines entertainment with consumption. The malls' mix of gift and souvenir shops, specialty food stores, bars, and franchised fast-food restaurants sometimes calls to mind tourist villages such as Jackson Hole, Wyoming, and Estes Park, Colorado. In the West Edmonton Mall in Alberta, Canada, for example, leisure facilities take up about 10 percent of the total floor space, but their presence is essential to an ambience of leisure that permeates the entire mall.[88] The West Edmonton Mall copies

Disney World in the theming of particular areas, such as an imitation Parisian street, Bourbon Street in New Orleans, Hollywood, and Polynesia. The combination of shopping and leisure in this way nurtures a "shop 'til you drop" consumer culture.

In these environments, consumers are prompted to act as if they are, in effect, moving in a dreamscape far removed from the outside world. The similarity between Disney theme parks and these mall environments is not accidental. Thirteen years before James Rouse opened Quincy Market in Boston, he asserted that Walt Disney was the most influential urban planner ever. And so he was. Malls and entertainment complexes establish the atmosphere and the context that potentially make every city, whatever its past function or present condition, a playground.

Sprawling indoor complexes connected by pedestrian bridges and tubes have proliferated in American cities.[89] For example, sprawling complexes have been built in Atlanta and Detroit, where large numbers of downtown office workers commute to the sealed realms of the Peachtree Center in Atlanta and the Renaissance Center in Detroit. In both of these structures, workers drive into parking garages and then enter a city-within-a-city where they can work, shop, eat lunch, and find a variety of diversions after work. They never have to set foot in the rest of the city or deal with its problems.

Architect John Portman pioneered the first "bubble city" when he opened the Peachtree Plaza in downtown Atlanta in 1967. The Peachtree complex was built outward from the cylindrical aluminum towers that distinguished Portman's first atrium hotel, which opened in downtown Atlanta in 1967. It was an instant hit with architectural critics, the media, and the public. The hotel lobbies and vaulted atriums that made up the complex were dazzling, filled with flowing water and pools, ascending ranks of balconies vanishing toward a skylight, corridors rigged with lights and mirrors, and glass elevators rising on the outside of the towers. Nobody had seen anything quite like it.

By the late 1980s, Peachtree Plaza had swallowed up Atlanta's historic downtown. Sixteen buildings clustered around the aluminum cylinder, which housed the Marriott Hotel. Shops, hotels and their lobbies, offices, food courts, and atriums were connected by a maze of escalators, skytubes, and arcades that isolated inhabitants from the streets below. The downtown streets of Atlanta were left almost deserted, especially at night. Pedestrians were able to gain access to the complex through a few grand porticos, usually the entrance to a hotel lobby. The effect was to create a separate city-within-a-city strictly segregated from the public streets on the outside.

Portman took his show on the road and built a series of stunning atriums, towers, and bubble environments. Although none of them approached the scale of Atlanta's, they were designed to provoke a sense of wonder and grandeur—the Renaissance Center in Detroit, the Hyatt at Embarcadero Center in San Francisco, the Bonaventure Hotel in Los Angeles, and the Marriott Marquis in Times Square, New York City. Unlike Atlanta, however, these indoor playgrounds do not swallow up an entire downtown, although they do enclose a large amount of space and house several related activities. Imitations of

Portman's creations quickly spread. There were several advantages to building indoors: the developer is able to create a total experience of sights, sounds, and movement, and also guarantee almost complete security. In this way a space attractive to affluent people could rise even in the midst of a seemingly hostile environment, thus providing even the most dilapidated cities with a strategy for revitalizing the urban core.

New York City's Times Square and San Francisco's Yerba Buena Center both anchor urban entertainment centers, but such complexes have sprung up elsewhere as well, usually in historic areas and often in connection with revitalized waterfronts. Over time, a remarkably eclectic variety of activities has been brought together into a single venue. Contained within these districts are restaurants, coffeehouses, sports bars, jazz clubs, dinner theaters, and arcades, plus an array of corporate retail tenants offering an assortment of clothes, shoes, electronic goods, jewelry, and an endless array of other items.[90]

The degree to which space is segmented in cities varies significantly. In general, the activities in spaces fortified by walls and bubbles have spilled out into public streets and neighborhoods, a process that has brought a sense of street life and excitement that had long been absent. In recent years, Boston, San Francisco, Seattle, Portland (Oregon), and Chicago—in fact, most cities—have opened up and become more accessible to visitors and local residents. Cities have invested heavily in amenities such as street plantings, pedestrian malls, parks, and riverfronts. Local residents and visitors fill busy streets that only a couple of decades ago were quiet and forbidding. Tourists visit enclaves such as South Street Seaport in New York and Ghirardelli Square in San Francisco, but they also stream into nearby streets and neighborhoods. This trend will continue as long as crime rates remain relatively low.

Casino Gaming

Until the 1980s, few casinos existed in any major city in the world, but in the last two decades of the century they spread like wildfire. Since the mid-1980s, gaming casinos have become established as a component of tourism promotion in a great number of places—notably, in Adelaide, Perth, Sydney, and Brisbane; in Montreal, Winnipeg, and Windsor; in Christchurch and Auckland; in Amsterdam and Rotterdam; and in several cities on the Mediterranean, such as Athens, Istanbul, and Cairo.[91] In the United States, casinos are often a major revenue source for Indian tribes, but few cities have joined in. There are many reasons why gaming has run into opposition, but religious opposition and ties to organized crime lead the list.

When Atlantic City, New Jersey, opened its first casinos in 1978, it became the first U.S. city to break Nevada's monopoly over gaming. In 1992, New Orleans did the same, but already it was clear that gaming was likely to pop up in other places, at least in some form. In 1990, Iowa became the first state to approve riverboat gaming. After the opening of the first boat in Iowa in April 1991, six riverboats generated $12 million in state income taxes within eight months, prompting neighboring states to begin steps to join the competition.[92]

In 1992, riverboats began operating in Illinois, two near St. Louis (one in East St. Louis, Illinois, directly across from St. Louis and the Gateway Arch). Mississippi began operating boats in 1993. Missouri, Louisiana, and Indiana all approved riverboat gaming soon after, with operations beginning in 1994.[93] Within a year, Kansas City and St. Louis, Missouri, joined in.

Since then, however, the spread of casino gaming in U.S. cities has nearly come to a full stop. This may seem surprising because of the obvious fact that gaming can make a significant contribution to the local economy, and because at the state level and in nonurban areas it has established a strong presence. As a means of promoting economic development on Indian reservations, in 1988 Congress passed the Indian Gaming Regulatory Act. The legislation permitted tribes to negotiate with states to run gaming operations and required the states to negotiate with the tribes that wanted to open casinos. In the years since, casinos have been opened on Indian lands in 22 states. In addition, all through the 1970s and 1980s, states adopted lotteries either through legislative action or referenda; by 1994, some 38 states ran lotteries. Following the spread of state lotteries, gambling became legitimated as a source of tax revenues. By 1996, 26 states allowed or had approved casino gaming in some form, but most gaming occurred on Indian-owned land.[94]

There are three major reasons why casino gaming has continued to encounter resistance. A national movement organized by the religious right to oppose gaming has enjoyed success because it taps into a widespread concern about the social and moral effects of gambling. Although most Americans have come to accept gambling as a legitimate activity over the past 30 years,[95] a Harris Poll conducted in 1992 still found that 51 percent of the public opposed casino gaming in their own state, and 56 percent opposed it in their own communities.[96] The media finds gambling to be a convenient topic for "controversy" and "analysis." For example, in its April 1, 1996, issue, *Time* magazine carried a feature story that documented a national backlash against gaming. Proposals to allow gaming typically are accompanied by controversy. In 1992, Colorado voters soundly defeated a constitutional amendment that would have allowed gaming to spread past the three small mountain communities named in an earlier referendum. In Missouri, three contentious voter referendums were required before the industry, with strong support from public officials, was able to secure approval for full casino operations. Even in this case, voters were eventually persuaded, in part, because of the fiction that the casinos were different because they operated on riverboats, which called forth nostalgic images of a time long past.

The gaming industry claims that gaming will constitute a magic elixir for urban economies. Surprisingly, even this appeal has fallen short. In 1996, ten state legislatures refused to pass laws to legalize casinos or slot machines,[97] and Congress passed legislation to initiate a two-year study of gaming. When completed in 1999, the study urged states and localities to be cautious about pursuing gaming. Local officials appear to have taken this advice, but the idea that gaming may help solve budgetary problems is hard to resist. In 2002, the mayor of Chicago, Richard M. Daley, mentioned the possibility that Chicago might seek approval for a casino license. This trial balloon was quickly shot down. However, in an attempt to solve the state and local fiscal problems created by the Great Recession, in May 2009 the Illinois legislature approved an expansion of video poker games throughout the state. Soon thereafter, and amidst much controversy, the Rivers Casino opened in July 2011, in Des Plains, which is strategically located next door to Chicago and in close proximity to the Rosemont convention center and O'Hare airport. Since its opening, Rivers Casino has proven to be beneficial to the Illinois economy, halting a statewide slide in profits. A report by the Commission on Government Forecasting and Accountability found that the Rivers Casino helped boost adjusted gross receipts by more than 20 percent in the first three quarters of the fiscal year, and has contributed to a more than 22 percent increase in casino goers throughout Illinois as a whole.

The Casino's success, however, has come with a price—while the number of casino goers statewide has increased, many of the riverboats near the Chicago metropolitan area have experienced a steep decline in profits. The Grand Victoria Casino in Elgin, for example, witnessed a total revenue drop of 21.4 percent in one fiscal year. Nevertheless, the relative success of Rivers has spurred an otherwise dormant industry.[98] In May 2012, the Illinois House passed a major expansion of gambling that was expected to put five new casinos in Chicago, Rockford, Danville, Lake County, and the south suburbs of Cook County, as well as placing slot machines at the state's racetracks, which have suffered as a result of riverboat expansion. As in Illinois, other states have also taken steps, though significantly smaller, to expand gaming, and it is only a matter of time before casinos break through the wall of resistance that has slowed their growth.

The Politics of Tourism

Critics often note that many of the facilities of tourism and entertainment do not pay for themselves. Public officials and civic boosters do not, on the whole, much care if they do. This apparently cavalier attitude toward taxpayers' money can be explained by noting the general irrelevance—to city officials and civic boosters—of cost–benefit analyses of tourism infrastructure. The attitudes of public officials toward development projects have "little [to] do with the . . . profitability . . . of a project" and far more to do with the vision officials share about the overall direction a city is taking.[99] The intense interurban competition dictates that cities must compete; to do so they must be as generous as their competitors in providing subsidies, and they must try to adopt every new variation that comes along. The competition imposes a logic of its own that is hard to resist.

Public officials may be proceeding on the basis of blind faith, but they feel they have little choice. It is true that abject, even humiliating failure is possible, as the attempt by Flint, Michigan, to become a tourist city makes clear. In the 1970s, after the closing of its General Motors plant devastated the local economy, public officials in Flint launched an effort at regeneration behind the motto "Our New Spark Will Surprise You." The city committed $13 million in subsidies to the construction of a luxury hotel, the Hyatt Regency. Within a year, it closed its doors. Approximately $100 million in public money was used to build AutoWorld, a museum that contained, among other items, the "world's largest car engine" and a scale model that portrayed downtown Flint in its more prosperous days. AutoWorld closed within six months. Still more public subsidies were committed to the construction of the doomed Water Street Pavilion, a theme park/festival market built by the renowned mall developer James Rouse. But few, if any, mayors would be deterred by Flint's fiasco, which was wryly portrayed in Michael Moore's popular movie *Roger & Me*.[100]

Virtually all cities of consequential size must take steps to promote tourism, recreation, and culture. Now that the basic infrastructure is in place in so many cities, public support for the arts and culture has become common. Every one of the nation's 50 largest cities allocates public dollars to support the arts, and a lot of small cities do so as well. From the big cities (New York, with the Kennedy and Lincoln Centers and, more recently, the Ford Center on 42nd Street) to villages (Riverhead, a hamlet outside New York City on Long Island, which is building an arts and historic district), from the downtowns in need of a boost (Newark, with its $180 million New Jersey Center, opened in October 1997) to the already prosperous (San Francisco, with a newly renovated opera house and several other performance halls), the development of local culture has become a leading formula for urban revival.[101] The text for a major exhibit in 1998 sponsored by the National Building Museum in Washington, D.C., noted that culture has replaced both the urban renewal bulldozer and the preservation movements that followed in its destructive wake as the main focus for downtown revitalization.

Collectively, cities of all sizes support an almost unimaginable variety of events that carry the signature of local culture and community. Jazz and blues festivals, strawberry and garlic festivals, jumping frogs and gold rush days, rodeos and fireworks—such activities help define and sometimes knit together local communities.[102] These activities usually take place in or near the new tourism/entertainment infrastructure (in smaller towns, this may mean at local parks, bandstands, waterfronts, or baseball diamonds). Every city must go through debates about how much of the public purse should be devoted to these activities, but few can afford to forgo public support altogether.

Old and New Downtowns

A host of writers have mourned the disappearance of the historic landscapes that once gave cities their identities and distinctive character. In 1961, when Jane Jacobs published her classic work *The Death and Life of Great American Cities*, she instantly became the best-known and most influential voice for preserving the everyday life of city streets. Writing in defense of her beloved Greenwich Village in the Lower East Side of New York, Jacobs attacked the master planning and large-scale development characteristic of the urban renewal era. Jacobs contrasted the virtues of small blocks, crowded streets, mixed uses, and what she called the "heart-of-the-day ballet" of street life with the "monotony and repetition of sameness" of planned environments.[103]

To Jacobs, a "marvelous order" was hidden beneath the surface of disorder on busy city streets, and both were necessary "for maintaining the safety of the streets and the freedom of the city."[104] Through their constant presence, people running the businesses fronting the sidewalk—storekeepers, barkeepers, shoe repairers, the owners of cleaners and barbershops, and their regular customers as well—kept their eyes on the comings and goings just outside the window. In this way the sidewalk ballet made room for everyone, but at the same time public safety and order was attended to, without anyone planning it or even thinking about it. Here is a description of the scene in front of her home on Hudson Street:

> When I get home from work, the ballet is reaching its crescendo. This is the time of roller skates and stilts and tricycles, and games in the lee of the stoop with bottletops and plastic cowboys; this is the time of bundles and packages, zigzagging from the drug store to the fruit stand back over to the butchers.[105]

More recently, Douglas Rae has decried the "end of urbanism," which he defines as the "patterns of private conduct and decision-making that by and large make the successful governance of cities possible."[106] Based on his study of New Haven, Connecticut, Rae concluded that in the past the life of the city was focused on downtown streets and the densely settled residential areas surrounding them. Echoing Jacobs, Rae writes of the "dense fabric of tiny stores" that were "only partly in the business of selling groceries: they were also governing sidewalks and the people who walked them."[107] This "sidewalk republic" made it unnecessary for formal government to intervene in people's lives because informal social networks were adequate for preserving public order and supplying people's basic needs.

What brought about the demise of urbanism? In Rae's account, the main suspects include the automobile, suburbanization and the policies that encouraged it, the decline of industrial employment, racial strife, and globalization, which replaced locally oriented businesses with national corporations.[108] Taken together, these factors (and others) led to the decentering of residential and economic activities. Federally sponsored urban renewal and highway projects, though intended to save the core, only made things worse through the wholesale clearance of historic buildings, business streets, and residential areas.

The recent revival of downtowns and the gentrification of nearby neighborhoods should not be taken as evidence that the world that Jacobs, Rae, and others[109] write about is being resurrected. It is just as well to accept that the old downtowns have died for good, and that they have been replaced by something else. Metropolitan regions continue to flow inexorably outward. Other nodes of activity—suburban business districts, malls, corporate campuses, edge cities—continue to grow. The downtowns of central cities will never be the singular focus of activity for their metropolitan regions that they were in the past.

In important respects, the new downtowns are also less diverse than those of the past. In central business districts, the dense collection of small shops has long been replaced by big buildings and, in the larger cities, by skyscrapers. Chain stores and outlets, such as Starbucks, the Gap, and Victoria's Secret, are outlets for national and international corporations. Cineplexes have replaced small theaters; chain supermarkets have replaced many of the specialized shops that separately sold meat, vegetables, candy, and ice cream.[110] Many business establishments, such as large appliance stores and automobile dealerships, have moved out of the downtowns entirely. Shopkeepers no longer keep their eyes on the street, if they can see it at all, and corporate minimum-wage employees do not have an interest in doing so.

Residential use is what drives the revival of downtowns today. In Manhattan, old commercial space has been in demand because the buildings are being turned into condominiums. In Philadelphia, office space has stayed about the same since 1990, but new residential towers poked into the skyline all over the downtown.[111] In St. Louis, many old warehouse and office buildings might have been torn down if not for condominium conversions; indeed, a downtown retail mall built as recently as the 1980s has been converted into a luxury condominium complex. By building inside the shells of historic structures, developers are able to give the new downtowns an ambiance of authenticity. According to the urban scholar Richard Florida, it mimics the kind of environment that young professionals prefer—places with "real buildings, real people, real history."[112]

However, it is important to recognize that the gentrification of downtown is quite different from the areas that have always been residential. Most of the residents who live downtown are exceptionally affluent, especially in global cities. In other parts of the city, the gentrified neighborhoods come in several variations, from those made up of new condominium towers filled with affluent people to those composed of renovated, architecturally significant buildings populated by a mélange of artists, musicians, and students, as well as affluent professionals.[113] This mix describes Wicker Park in Chicago, but does not apply to the Magnificent Mile on Michigan Avenue, with its rows of high-end chain stores and nearby condominium towers. Any generalizations about the character of gentrified areas must, to some degree, gloss over the fantastic differences in the urban environment from one neighborhood to the next, or even from block to block.

Are the new downtowns and the gentrified neighborhoods merely impoverished versions of what cities once had? It is hard to say. A century ago, the residential areas of New Haven that Rae studied contained people of all social classes, incomes, and ethnic backgrounds.[114] Similarly, diverse assortments of people live in some of the trendiest of today's inner-city neighborhoods. Superficially, these may bear a striking resemblance to another time, except that their historic buildings are occupied by restaurants, bars and taverns, music venues, art galleries, and shops, plus some sprinkling of chain stores. But the people walking the streets and the businesses they patronize are, in fact, completely unique to the twenty-first century. Those who live in such environments can put aside any anxiety about whether the city streets they walk on are authentic. They surely are, but that is because whatever exists in the present is fully as authentic as the lost world that many people pine for.

Endnotes

1. President's Commission for a National Agenda for the Eighties, *A National Agenda for the Eighties* (Washington, DC: Government Printing Office, 1980, pp. 66–67.
2. Ibid., p. 4.
3. New York Times News Service, "City Neighborhoods Are Undergoing a Renaissance as Crime Rates Drop," *St. Louis Post-Dispatch* (May 29, 2000), pp. A–12.
4. Richard Florida, "How the Crash Will Reshape America," *The Atlantic* (March 2009), p. 52.
5. Rebecca R. Sohmer and Robert E. Lang, *Downtown Rebound* (Washington, DC: Brookings Institution Press and Fannie Mae Foundation), pp. 1–4.
6. Patrick A. Simmons and Robert E. Lang, "The Urban Turnaround," in *Redefining Urban & Suburban America: Evidence from Census 2000*, ed. Bruce Katz and Robert E. Lang (Washington, DC: Brookings Institution Press, 2004), pp. 56–58.
7. Mark Abrahamson, *Global Cities* (New York: Oxford University Press, 2004).
8. "U.S. Census Bureau QuickFacts: Maryland," *U.S. Census Bureau.*
9. Robert M. Fogelson, *Downtown: Its Rise and Fall, 1880–1950* (New Haven, CT: Yale University Press, 2001). My discussion of the history of downtown borrows heavily from Fogelson's excellent book, which should become a standard reference work on every urban scholar's bookshelf.
10. Ibid., pp. 186–187.
11. Ibid., pp. 197–198.
12. Ibid., pp. 183–185.
13. Alison Isenberg, *Downtown America: A History of the Place and the People Who Made It* (Chicago: University of Chicago Press, 2004), pp. 5–6.
14. Ibid., pp. 218–219.
15. Isenberg, *Downtown America*, p. 219.
16. Ibid., p. 65.
17. Ibid., p. 69.
18. Kenneth T. Jackson, *Crabgrass Frontier: The Suburbanization of the United States* (New York: Oxford University Press, 1985), p. 261.
19. Barry Bluestone and Bennett Harrison, *The Deindustrialization of America* (New York: Basic Books, 1982).
20. U.S. Bureau of the Census, *Statistical Abstract of the United States, 1992*, 112th ed. (Washington, DC: U.S. Government Printing Office, 1992), p. 397.
21. Robert B. Reich, *The Work of Nations* (New York: Random House, Vintage Books, 1991), p. 86.
22. Jon C. Teaford, *The Rough Road to Renaissance: Urban Revitalization in America, 1940–1985* (Baltimore: Johns Hopkins University Press, 1990), p. 307.
23. Bernard J. Frieden and Lynn B. Sagalyn, *Downtown, Inc.: How America Builds Cities* (Cambridge, MA: MIT Press, 1989), p. 43.
24. Saskia Sassen, *Cities in a World Economy* (Thousand Oaks, CA: Pine Forge Press, 2001).
25. The concept of the global city is somewhat imprecise. Some scholars would question whether Chicago, Miami, and Los Angeles are global cities in the same sense as New York, London, and Tokyo, which clearly contain a much denser concentration of financial and media firms and corporations with true international reach. The two books to consult regarding this debate are Saskia Sassen, *The Global City: New York, London, Tokyo*, 2nd ed. (Princeton, NJ: Princeton University Press, 2001), and Janet L. Abu-Lughod, *New York, Los Angeles, Chicago: America's Global Cities* (Minneapolis: University of Minnesota Press, 1999).

26. Norman J. Glickman, "Cities and the International Division of Labor," in *The Capitalist City*, ed. Michael Peter Smith and Joe R. Feagin (Cambridge, MA: Basil Blackwell, 1987), pp. 66–86.

27. Richard Florida, *The Rise of the Creative Class and How It's Transforming Work, Leisure, Community and Everyday Life* (New York: Basic Books, 2002), p. 225.

28. Abrahamson, *Global Cities*, p. 33.

29. Florida, *The Rise of the Creative Class*, p. 224.

30. Ibid., p. 228.

31. Terry Nichols Clark, Richard Lloyd, Kenneth K. Wong, and Pushpam Jain, "Amenities Drive Urban Growth," *Journal of Urban Affairs* 24, no. 5 (1993): 493–516.

32. World Travel & Tourism Council (WTTC) website, www.wttc.org.

33. Ibid.

34. Norman Fainstein, Susan S. Fainstein, Richard Child Hill, Dennis Judd, and Michael Peter Smith, *Restructuring the City: The Political Economy of Urban Redevelopment* (New York: Longman, 1983).

35. Clark, Lloyd, Wong, and Jain, "Amenities Drive Urban Growth," p. 504.

36. Ibid, p. 505.

37. Wangui Maina, "Chicago Visitor Numbers Down for 2010," *Chicago Tribune* (June 20, 2011).

38. Christine Boyer, "Cities for Sale: Merchandising History at South Street Seaport," in *Variations on a Theme Park: The New American City and the End of Public Space*, ed. Michael Sorkin (New York: Hill and Wang, 1992), pp. 189–190.

39. G. J. Ashworth and J. E. Tunbridge, *The Tourist-Historic City* (London and New York: Belhaven Press, 1990), p. 153.

40. For an expanded discussion, see Dennis R. Judd, "Visitors and the Spatial Ecology of the City," in *Cities and Visitors*, ed. Lily M. Hoffman, Susan S. Fainstein, and Dennis R. Judd (New York: Blackwell, 2003), pp. 22–38.

41. John Hannigan, *Fantasy City: Pleasure and Profit in the Postmodern Metropolis* (New York: Routledge, 1998).

42. Richard Lloyd, *Neo-Bohemia: Art and Commerce in the Postindustrial City* (New York: Routledge, 2006), p. 126; also "Neo-Bohemia: Art and Neighborhood Redevelopment in Chicago," *Journal of Urban Affairs* 24, no. 5 (2002): 517–532.

43. See also Dennis R. Judd, "Constructing the Tourist Bubble," *The Tourist City*, ed. Dennis R. Judd and Susan S. Fainstein (New Haven, CT: Yale University Press, 1999).

44. David H. Laslo, "Proliferating Convention Centers: The Political Economy of Regenerating Cities and the St. Louis Convention Center Expansion" (Ph.D. dissertation, University of Missouri–St. Louis, May 1999).

45. All data from Heywood Sanders, *Space Available: The Realities of Convention Centers as Economic Development Strategy* (Washington, DC: Brookings Institution Press, January 2005), p. 1.

46. *Encyclopedia of Associations*, 38th ed., *National Organizations of the United States*, vol. 1–3 (New York: Author, 2002).

47. George G. Fenich, "The Dollars and Sense of Convention Centers" (Ph.D. dissertation, Rutgers University, 1992), p. 34.

48. Laslo, "Proliferating Convention Centers," p. 67.

49. *Tradeshow Week Data Book, 1998* (New York: Bill Communications, 1998), p. 6.

50. "State of the Industry 1993," *Successful Meetings* (July 1993): 32–33.

51. *Convene Magazine* website, www.pcma.org/convene.

52. Melissa Preddy, "Convention Centers Expect Traffic Gains," *The Center for Michigan* (June 29, 2011).

53. Associated Press, "Las Vegas Still the King of Convention Cities" (April 26, 2006), www.msnbc.msn.com/id/12498996.

54. Joe Pollack, "Visitors Fly under Media Radar," *St. Louis Journalism Review* (June 2003): 5.

55. Sanders, *Space Available*, p. 25.

56. Ibid., p. 22.

57. Robyne S. Turner and Mark S. Rosentraub, "Tourism, Sports and the Centrality of Cities," *Journal of Urban Affairs* 24, no. 5 (2003): 489.

58. Charles Santo, "The Economic Impact of Sports Stadiums: Recasting the Analysis in Context," *Journal of Urban Affairs* 27, no. 2 (2005): 177.

59. Ibid., pp. 177–191. Some leading studies are Robert A. Baade, "Professional Sports as Catalysts for Metropolitan Economic Development," *Journal of Urban Affairs* 18 (1996): 1–17; Mark Rosentraub, David Swinderll, M. Przybylski, and D. R. Mullins, "Sports and Downtown Development Strategy: If You Build It, Will Jobs Come?" *Journal of Urban Affairs* 16 (1994): 211–239; John Zipp, "The Economic Impact of the Baseball Strike of 1994," *Urban Affairs Review* 32, no. 2 (November 1996): 157–185; Dan Coates and B. Humphries, "The Growth Effects of Sports Franchises, Stadia, and Arenas," *Journal of Policy Analysis and Management* 18, no. 4 (1999): 601–624; Robert Noll and A. Zimbalist, eds., *Sports, Jobs, and Taxes: The Economic Impact of Sports Teams and Stadiums* (Washington, DC: Brookings Institution Press, 1997); and Phillip A. Miller, "The Economic Impact of Sports Stadium Construction: The Case of the Construction Industry in St. Louis, MO," *Journal of Urban Affairs* 24, no. 2 (2002): 159–173. Some smaller teams have been able to turn minor league teams into profitable investments for the public by resorting to public ownership—see Joseph W. Meder and J. Wesley Leckrone, "Hardball; Local Government's Foray into Sports Franchise Ownership," *Journal of Urban Affairs* 24, no. 3 (2002): 353–368. This option is not open with the major sports because the sports cartels are able to exclude all teams that do not meet their regulations, which include private ownership.

60. Z. Austrian and Mark S. Rosentraub, "Cleveland's Gateway to the Future," in Noll and Zimbalist, *Sports, Jobs, and Taxes*, pp. 355–384.

61. "Forbes: Mets' Value Drops 13 Percent; Yankees Top List," *CBS New York* (March 24, 2011).

62. Kurt Badenhausen, Cecily Fluke, Lesley Kump, and Michael K. Ozanian, "Double Play," *Forbes* (April 15, 2002), www.forbes.com.

63. Michael Ozanian, "Is Baseball Really Broke?" *Forbes* (April 3, 2002), www.forbes.com.

64. Infoplease.com; keywords Sports—Business/Ballparks/Arenas. Comparisons among the professional sports are difficult to make. The National Football League has a fully nationalized media arrangement, with teams sharing in revenues (which has promoted equity among the teams). By contrast, major league baseball teams sign their own contracts with mostly local or regional media outlets, with limited revenue sharing among the teams. Thus, in 2002, major league baseball's four-year media contract was estimated at almost $1.8 million, but this figure is a tiny proportion of all media revenues collected by the individual teams.

65. For a closely textured and entertaining account of the battle between O'Malley and Moses, see Michael Shapiro, *The Last Good Season: Brooklyn, The Dodgers, and Their Final Pennant Race Together* (New York: Doubleday, 2003).

66. Neil J. Sullivan, *The Dodgers Move West* (New York: Oxford University Press, 1987).

67. Arthur T. Johnson, "The Sports Franchise Relocation Issue and Public Policy Responses," in *Government and Sport: The Public Policy Issues*, ed. Arthur T. Johnson and James H. Frey (Totowa, NJ: Rowman and Allanheld, 1985), p. 232.

68. Arthur T. Johnson, "Economic and Policy Implications of Hosting Sports Franchises: Some Lessons from Baltimore," *Urban Affairs Quarterly* 21, no. 3 (March 1986): 411.
69. Tim Chapin, "Beyond the Entrepreneurial City: Municipal Capitalism in San Diego," *Journal of Urban Affairs* 24, no. 5 (1993): 567–568.
70. F. Jossi, "Take Me Out to the Ballgame," *Planning* 64, no. 5 (1998): 4–9.
71. Mark Anderson, "Three-Facility Downtown Stadium Proposal Would Compete with UNLV Dome," *Las Vegas Review – Journal* (February 9, 2011).
72. Buford Davis, "Milam sets 2012 groundbreaking goal," *The Henderson Press* (May 3, 2012).
73. Jacob Luft, "Relocation Celebrations: NFL, NHL Franchises Find Success in New Cities," CNNSI.com-Statitudes (January 26, 2001); *CNNSI.com-Statitudes*: "NFL, NHL Teams Benefit from Moving On."
74. Robert A. Baade and Robert E. Dye, "Sports Stadiums and Area Development: A Critical Review," *Economic Development Quarterly* 2 (1988): 265–275; Robert A. Baade, "Professional Sports and Economic Development," *Journal of Urban Affairs* 18, no. 1 (1996): 1–18.
75. Charles C. Eichner, *Playing the Field: Why Sports Teams Move and Cities Fight to Keep Them* (Baltimore: Johns Hopkins University Press, 1993), pp. 12–13.
76. Ronald Smothers, "No Hits, No Runs, One Error: The Dome," *New York Times* (June 15, 1991).
77. Eichner, *Playing the Field*, p. 67.
78. See the websites www.gophersports.com and www.msfc.com.
79. Donald Phares and Mark S. Rosentraub, "Reviving the Glory of Days Past: St. Louis's Blitz to Save Its Image, Identity, and Teams," in *Major League Losers: The Real Cost of Sports and Who's Paying for It*, ed. Mark S. Rosentraub (New York: Basic Books, 1997).
80. Richard Sandomir, "New Stadiums: Prices, and Outrage, Escalate," *New York Times* (August 28, 2008), www.nytimes.com/2008/08/26/sports/26tickets.html.
81. Josh Goodman, "Skybox Skeptics," *Governing* 19, no. 6 (March 2006): 41–42.
82. Sandomir, "New Stadiums."
83. Ibid.
84. Heather Cole, "Cardinals, City Sing Stadium Deal," *St. Louis Business Journal* (November 8, 2002), p. 1.
85. Ibid., p. C7.
86. This account of Quincy Market is based on Frieden and Sagalyn, *Downtown, Inc.*, pp. 1–7, 175.
87. Mike Davis, "Fortress Los Angeles: The Militarization of Urban Space," in *Variations on a Theme Park*, ed. Michael Sorkin (New York: Noonday Press, 1992), p. 155.
88. Myriam Jansen-Verbeke, "Leisure + Shopping = Tourism Product Mix," in *Marketing Tourism Places*, ed. Gregory Ashworth and Brian Goodall (London and New York: Routledge, 1990), p. 132.
89. Sharon Zukin, *Landscapes of Power: From Detroit to Disney World* (Berkeley: University of California Press, 1991).
90. The Urban Land Institute, *Developing Urban Entertainment Centers* (Washington, DC: Urban Land Institute, 1998).
91. William R. Eadington, "The Emergence of Casino Gaming as a Major Factor in Tourism Markets: Policy Issues and Considerations," in *Change in Tourism: People, Places, Processes*, ed. Richard Butler and Douglas Pearce (London and New York: Routledge, 1995), pp. 159–186.

92. Fred Faust, "It Wasn't in the Cards," *St. Louis Post-Dispatch* (April 10, 1994), pp. 1–5E.
93. *Company Analysis* (New York: Donaldson, Lufkin and Jenrette Securities Corporation, June 23, 1993), p. 12.
94. Eadington, "The Emergence of Casino Gaming," p. 4.
95. *Company Analysis*, p. 6.
96. Robert Goodman, *Legalized Gambling as a Strategy for Economic Development* (Northampton, MA: United States Gambling Study), p. 34.
97. Ellen Perlman, "The Gambling Glut," *Governing: The Magazine of States and Localities* 9, no. 8 (May 1996): 49–56.
98. "New Des Plaines Casino Helps Halt Dip in State Gambling Profits," *Associated Press* (May 5, 2012).
99. Michael A. Pagano and Ann Bowman, *Cityscapes and Capital: The Politics of Urban Development* (Baltimore: Johns Hopkins University Press, 1995), p. 74.
100. Michael Moore, *Roger and Me*, A Dog Eat Dog Films Production (Warner Bros. Pictures, 1989).
101. Bruce Weber, "Cities Are Fostering the Arts as a Way to Save Downtown," *New York Times* (November 18, 1997), p. A1.
102. Dennis R. Judd, William Winter, William Barnes, and Emily Stern, *Tourism and Entertainment as a Local Economic Development Strategy: The Report of a NLC Survey* (Washington, DC: National League of Cities: A Research Report, 2000), p. 8.
103. Jane Jacobs, *The Death and Life of Great American Cities* (New York: Vintage, 1961), pp. 51, 223.
104. Ibid., p. 50.
105. Ibid., p. 52.
106. Douglas Rae, *City: Urbanism and Its End* (New Haven, CT: Yale University Press, 2003), p. xiii.
107. Ibid.
108. Ibid., p. xiv.
109. Two other excellent books dealing with these themes are Ray Suarez, *The Old Neighborhood: What We Lost in the Great Suburban Migration: 1966–1999* (New York: Free Press, 1999); and Shapiro, *The Last Good Season.*
110. For details on New Haven's experience, see Rae, *City: Urbanism and Its End*, pp. 234–243.
111. Alan Ehrenhalt, "Extreme Makeover," *Governing* 20, no. 7 (July 2006): 29.
112. Florida, *The Rise of the Creative Class*, pp. 227–229.
113. Lloyd, *Neo-Bohemia.*
114. Rae, *City: Urbanism and Its End.*

CHAPTER 14

Governing the Divided City

A Delicate Balancing Act

City governments are, in effect, mechanisms for managing the social and political differences among the contending groups that make up the city. The legitimacy of democratic governance rests on popular perceptions that the governmental institutions that represent them are responsive to their preferences and needs. When enough people feel aggrieved, they often demonstrate their disaffection by withholding their vote, refusing to participate in organizational or political life, and resorting to protest. Sometimes, if they are angry enough, they turn to violence. When conflict reaches this level, it becomes obvious that the governmental system has failed to mediate the social and political differences that divide people. Judged by this standard, urban governments in the United States have an uneven record.

The history of American cities is peppered with episodes of violent unrest and conflict. On many occasions in the nineteenth century, mobs attacked immigrants, sometimes in bloody riots that lasted for days, and in the twentieth century blacks became the frequent target of racial violence. White mobs attacked blacks in New York City in 1863, East St. Louis in 1917, Chicago in 1919, and Tulsa in 1920. The harassment of blacks became commonplace in the era of suburban white flight in the 1950s.

In the face of police harassment and racial discrimination, blacks sometimes vented their frustrations through violence. Blacks rioted in Detroit in 1944 and dozens of times over several hot summers in the 1960s. Incidents involving the police precipitated virtually all of the riots in that turbulent decade.[1] Riots erupted in African American areas in Cuban-dominated Miami four times in the 1980s, beginning with the Liberty City disorders in May 1980. Each of the riots was associated with the killing of a black man by Hispanic white police officers.[2] Police conduct still stokes frequent controversy, and from time to time these have erupted into civil disorders. A quite typical incident occurred in early August 2006, in the Cabrini-Green public housing projects in Chicago, when police shot a 14-year-old boy who was brandishing a BB gun. In the wake of the shooting, demonstrators turned out to march around city hall.

More recently, ethnic and racial groups across the social spectrum have been caught up in urban violence. In 1991, rioting broke out in Washington, D.C., when an African American female police officer attempted to arrest some Hispanic men, and a few days later it broke out again when police shot a Salvadoran immigrant. Ethnic tensions reached a boiling point in the Crown Heights area of Brooklyn in 1991 and 1992, culminating in a boycott by the African American community of a Korean greengrocer and violent street confrontations between African Americans and Hasidic Jews. The most serious riot of the twentieth century occurred in Los Angeles in 1992, with 53 people dead, 2,383 injuries, 16,291 arrests, more than 5,500 fires, and over $700 million in property damage. Unlike previous riots, it was multiethnic, involving blacks, Hispanics, and Asians.[3] In the course of the riots 30 percent of the approximately 4,000 businesses destroyed were owned by Hispanics,[4] but looters and arsonists especially singled out Korean-owned businesses.[5] For a time it seemed that racial and ethnic tensions had subsided, but in April 2000 fears of rioting ran rampant in Miami the day after federal agents seized Elian Gonzalez from relatives in Miami and returned him to his father in Cuba. Cuban American leaders called for calm, fearful that rioting might break out.

Continuing episodes of violence show that racial and ethnic tensions continue to lie just below the surface. In 2006, 500 students rioted at Fontana High School in Illinois after a Latino and black student got into a verbal dispute, and fighting escalated when some Samoan students joined the fight. Though police were hesitant to describe them as such, the riots were attributed by many people to a long-rivalry between blacks and Latinos.[6] In 2003, a group of residents of Benton Harbor, Michigan, rioted for two days when Terrance Shurn, a black motorcyclist being chased by a mixed-race police officer, crashed into a building and died. Five homes were set on fire, dozens of cars were vandalized, and several people were injured. More than 300 law enforcement officers from surrounding communities converged on Benton Harbor to stabilize the situation. In 2005, a four-hour riot began in Toledo, Ohio when a Neo-Nazi organization planned a march to protest African American gang activity in the north end of the city. Twelve police officers were injured, and police, media, and emergency vehicles as well as some businesses were vandalized. The brief riot came as the culmination of long-simmering resentments. The Toledo neighborhood had long been a Polish enclave, though African Americans had been moving into the area over the past few years without any apparent problems. This changed after organizers of the annual Polish Fest began to require that minors be accompanied by parents—though community members were quick to notice that the new rule was enforced strictly with black children and less so with their white counterparts.[7]

Incidents such as these continue to occur even though urban governments have become increasingly sensitive to racial and ethnic diversity in their communities. Local political systems began to open up in response to the civil rights movement of the 1960s, which produced a generation of activist African American leaders and a newly energized black electorate. As late as the mid-1960s, it seemed unthinkable that an African American might become the mayor of a major American city, but within a few years it had become commonplace. Before long, Latinos also entered the local political arena in increasing numbers. The presence of minorities in public office made it possible for African American and Latino communities to turn from strategies of protest to incorporation into the politics of the city.

Incorporation into democratic processes provided an opportunity for minorities to work for change from within. Despite the gains, however, urban governance continues to be a delicate balancing act because incorporation has not always brought the hoped-for rewards. Affirmative action programs changed the complexion of police forces, fire departments, school programs, and municipal offices. Nevertheless, racial and ethnic inequalities continue to fuel conflict and resentment because African Americans and Hispanics continue to lag in income, educational attainment, and participation in the workforce, and they have been disproportionately affected by increasing inequality and rising poverty levels. Since the turn of the twenty-first century, the number of people living in poverty has been steadily rising in the United States, from a low of 11.4 percent in 2000 to 12.5 percent in 2003. In November 2012, the U.S. Census Bureau reported that more than 16 percent of the U.S. population was living in poverty, including 20 percent of children.[8] Such widespread poverty has not been seen since the 1960s, when the War on Poverty was launched.[9] At the same time, federal tax cuts enacted in 2001 and 2002 increased tax burdens for middle-income taxpayers while reducing them for upper-income households.[10] Such inequalities can be observed on the urban landscape, in the juxtaposition of troubled neighborhoods and the privatized enclaves that fragment the contemporary metropolis. As long as such inequalities persist, racial and ethnic tensions will continue to be a fact of life in America's metropolitan regions.

OUTTAKE

Multiethnic Coalitions Are Hard to Keep Together

Since the civil rights struggles of the 1960s, a profound transformation has thoroughly altered the urban political landscape. Civil rights and community organizing activities helped mobilize the African American electorate, and within a few years, African American mayors and other public officials were taking the reins of city governments. Over time, the drive for representation in the political system embraced other groups as well. In addition to the symbolic benefits of incorporation, the material benefits were substantial; the gains in public employment contributed to economic gains for the middle-class, the integration of municipal workforces, the hiring of minority personnel in administrative posts in municipal governments and school systems, changes in police behavior, and improvements in the tone of racial and ethnic relations.

But the complex ethnic makeup of urban politics has revealed just how hard it is to build and maintain multiethnic coalitions. The expectation that blacks and Latinos would find a common cause because both groups are disadvantaged has rarely been realized because there are significant differences between and within each of these groups. Within the Latino community, for example, "there is little consensus on a Latino political agenda . . . much less one that would reflect the shared concerns of blacks and Latinos over poverty, affordable housing, safety, health care, and neighborhood well-being."[11] Minority is a problematic term that papers over significant differences; the challenge is to forge alliances over issues that attract support across ethnic groups.[12]

The problem of defining a singular "minority agenda" explains why it is hard to assemble interethnic coalitions, and also why it is difficult to assess the actual gains from political incorporation. A frequently expressed view is that the minority middle-class reaped most of the benefits from political representation, and that the disadvantaged and poor were left out.

Perhaps an expectation that it could be any other way was always unrealistic, for two reasons. First, it overestimated the ability of city governments to change the basic structures of the economy and society; "The painful truth is that many of the forces shaping the conditions under which the mass of low-income minority people live are not under the control of city governments." Second, such an expectation amounted to a naïve assumption that there were few political differences among the groups lumped together under the "minority" label.

Sources: Albert K. Karnig and Susan Welch, *Black Representatives and Urban Policy* (Chicago: University of Chicago Press, 1980); Rufus P. Browning, Dale Rogers Marshall, and David H. Tabb, *Racial Politics in American Cities*, 3rd ed. (New York: Longman, 2002), pp. 374–377.

The Recent Revolution in Urban Governance

The civil rights struggles of the 1960s and community organizing activities of the same era precipitated a revolution in governance at all levels of the American political system. Until 1967, not a single African American had ever been elected mayor of a major American city. In that year, Richard Hatcher was elected mayor of Gary, Indiana, and Carl Stokes became the mayor of Cleveland. In the years since these watershed elections, blacks and Latinos have been elected to office in cities of all sizes from coast to coast; by 1988, 28 African American mayors had been elected in cities of more than 50,000 in population, and the number reached 38 only five years later.[13] As shown in Figure 14.1, from 1970 to 2001, the number of African American elected officials in the United States increased from 1,469 to 9,101; 454 of them were mayors.[14] Many of these officials were elected to positions in local governments, with large numbers in education, the judicial system, and law enforcement.

With the election of Kurt Schmoke as the first African American mayor of Baltimore in 1987, every city of more than 100,000 people that had a majority black population had elected an African American mayor. At different points in the 1980s, African American candidates won the mayor's office in four of the five largest cities in the country, even though African American voters were in the minority in all of those cities (David Dinkins in New York, Tom Bradley in Los Angeles, Harold Washington in Chicago, and Wilson Goode in Philadelphia). Again in the 1990s, African Americans won in several cities where they

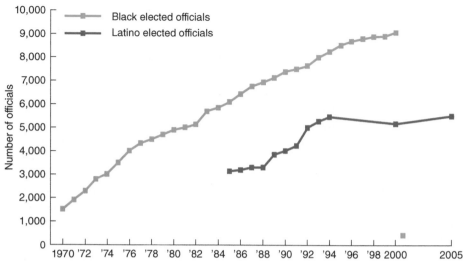

FIGURE 14.1 Black Elected Officials,[a] 1970–2001, and Latino Elected Officials,[b] 1985–2005.

[a]Includes Congress.
[b]Does not include Congress.

Sources: National Association of Latino Elected and Appointed Officials (Washington, DC: Author, *National Roster of Hispanic Elected Officials*, annual); National Association of Latino Elected and Appointed Officials, "NALEO At-A-Glance", http://www.naelo.org/ataglance.html; Joint Center for Political and Economic Studies, *Black Elected Officials: A Statistical Summary* (Washington, DC), p. 250, Table 399; Joint Center for Political and Economic Studies, *Black Elected Officials: A Statistical Summary, 2001* (Washington, DC: Author), p. 13.

constituted a minority of voters, including St. Louis, Denver, Kansas City, and Seattle.

City politics experienced another profound change in the 1980s, when Latinos began entering political office in large numbers. The data in Figure 14.1 reveal that the number of Latino elected officials at all government levels in the United States grew from 3,147 in 1985 to 5,459 in 1994 before dropping off slightly to 5,041 in 2005.[15] Latino mayors won office in Denver, Miami, San Antonio, and numerous smaller cities. Federico Peña's election in Denver in 1983 was considered a breakthrough because he was the first Latino to be elected mayor of a large American city without a Latino majority. At the time, Latinos constituted just 18 percent of the city's population, with blacks making up another 12 percent.[16] The gains realized in cities reverberated throughout the American political system. For instance, Peña and the former mayor of San Antonio, Henry Cisneros, were appointed to President Bill Clinton's cabinet in 1993.

African American and Latino mayors have faced a daunting challenge because in most cities where they have won, white voters have commanded a clear majority. Because of this political reality, minority candidates have been forced to walk a fine line: if they campaign on issues of great importance to their racial and ethnic constituents they risk alienating their white voters. Once in office, they have found that whatever the composition of their electoral coalition, they are unable to get much done unless they forge a good working relationship with the one group that can bring investment to the city—the business community. A politics of trade-offs and negotiation that fully satisfies no one at all is virtually guaranteed by this circumstance.

Political struggles in the nation's two largest cities, New York and Los Angeles, sheds light on the difficulties of governance when complex interracial and interethnic coalitions must be assembled. By 1990, non-Latino whites made up less than half—43 percent—of the population of New York City. Blacks accounted for 25 percent, Latinos 24 percent, and Asians 8 percent.[17] With a large Jewish population that was historically sensitive to discrimination and supportive of the civil rights movement, New York City seemed to be an ideal setting for within which a diverse racial and ethnic coalition might emerge. In fact, however, this context produced a fractious politics that resulted in the election of Ed Koch, a self-styled conservative white mayor. After serving three terms from 1977 to 1985 he was defeated in 1989 by an African American, David Dinkins, who was defeated after one term by a Republican conservative, Rudolph Giuliani, who served from 1993 to 1997.

By contrast, Los Angeles, which is also racially and ethnically diverse, elected an African American mayor, Tom Bradley, in 1973, and the voters kept him in office for five consecutive terms. Throughout this period, blacks accounted for no more than 14 percent of the population of Los Angeles. Much can be learned about the delicate nature of coalition politics by an examination of the Bradley years.

Tom Bradley, the son of Texas sharecroppers, moved to Los Angeles with his family at the age of seven. An exceptional student and athlete, he attended the University of California, Los Angeles, and then took a job with the Los Angeles Police Department. After putting down roots in a mostly white neighborhood on the West Side, he organized a community relations group, and through this activity he forged close personal contacts with Jewish merchants and civic leaders. By taking night courses he earned a law degree, quit the police force, and opened his own legal practice. His entry into the politics of the local Democratic Party came at a perfect time, just when an alliance of upwardly mobile African Americans, Jews, and liberals began to challenge the regular Democratic Party, which had previously excluded them.

In 1969, the reform coalition pushed Bradley forward as a challenger to the Democratic incumbent, Sam Yorty. Bradley's chances were hurt by the racial tensions that continued to linger in the wake of the devastating Watts riot that had shocked the city four years before. Yorty won the election by securing support from an overwhelming majority of white votes and received particularly strong support from upper-middle-class homeowners in the San Fernando Valley. When he ran against Yorty four years later, however, Bradley defused the issue of race by avoiding overt racial issues and emphasizing the importance of revitalizing the downtown and keeping taxes low. He defeated Yorty by assembling a diverse coalition composed of African Americans of all income levels, Latinos, and higher-income and especially Jewish white liberals. Bradley succeeded largely because he was able to symbolize different things to different people: "Whites saw Bradley as a symbol of racial harmony, while blacks saw him as a symbol of racial assertion."[18]

Bradley's success was predicated on a long history of collaboration between white liberals and the upwardly mobile black middle class. Both groups had been systematically excluded from local politics prior to Bradley's victory, and therefore they viewed each other as allies in the cause of ousting the Yorty regime. As soon as he entered City Hall, Bradley assembled a formidable coalition that would allow him not only to win elections but also to govern. To accumulate the resources necessary for realizing his aspiration to remake the downtown, he forged an alliance with downtown banks and business corporations. In this way he was always able to raise the massive amounts of money necessary for winning election in a city as diverse and sprawling as Los Angeles.

The conditions that allowed an African American to become the mayor of Los Angeles were absent in New York, despite the fact that blacks were already well entrenched in New York City's government by the mid-1960s.[19] By the time blacks entered New York City's political system, liberals and Jews had already established themselves by successfully electing a liberal Republican, John Lindsay, as mayor for two terms (1966–1973). Although New York's blacks, Jews, and white liberals could clearly cooperate, their leaders viewed one another with suspicion. These tensions came to a head in 1968, when the African American community launched an experiment in community control in the Ocean Hill–Brownsville schools in Brooklyn. The school board's plan to transfer 19 teachers, some of them Jewish, out of the district resulted in a bitter citywide strike by the teachers' union, which drove a wedge between blacks and Jews that endures in New York even to the present day. The same sorts of conflicts and suspicions have characterized the political relationships between African Americans and Latinos, who are themselves divided into many factions based of nationality and language.[20] Ed Koch was able to exploit these divisions, and he succeeded in assembling a coalition of Jews, Catholics, and ethnic whites. This alliance proved to be enduring enough to keep him in office through three elections.[21]

An African American, David Dinkins was able to beat him in 1989 because he had close ties to the regular Democratic Party and he possessed a dignified, non-confrontational style that did not seem threatening to white voters. In the early stages of the 1989 mayoral contest, Koch miscalculated by criticizing Jesse Jackson, who had made a run for the presidency the year before, for expressing support for the Palestine Liberation Organization (PLO). Koch commented that Jews "would have to be crazy" to vote for Jackson. An African American newspaper, *Amsterdam News*, replied bitterly by reminding Koch that "he is mayor of the city; not just of New York Jewry."[22] Dinkins secured enough support from voters who had tired of Koch's racial rhetoric to carry the election.

As it turned out, Dinkins' election did not bring an end to racially charged politics in New York City. After serving one term he was defeated by a self-styled political conservative, Rudolph Giuliani. Giuliani, a former prosecutor, broke the mold by winning as a Republican in a Democratic city. He quickly set out to terminate affirmative action programs, slash spending for welfare and housing, cut health services, and beef up the police forces.[23] Crime control became the central cause of his administration, and he became nationally known for championing the "broken windows" theory of crime control, which was based on the premise that a systematic punishment for small crimes would deter more serious ones (taken literally, this meant that if someone metaphorically "broke a window" by jaywalking or littering, he could be arrested). While in office, Giuliani went out of his way to snub African American leaders. In 2001, when he was forced to leave office because of term limits, he was succeeded by Republican Michael Bloomberg, who with his own money spent $99 per vote to narrowly defeat the Democratic candidate.[24]

New York's politics continued to be divisive only in part because of worries about crime and disorder. Conflict was built into the city's demographic makeup. The many groups that jostled for power resented it when benefits were conferred on any other group.[25] Ethnic whites and Latinos were convinced that blacks received a disproportionate share of municipal offices and perks. Latinos were divided among West Indians, Dominicans, Puerto Ricans, and Jamaicans. Asian voters also fought for a place at the table. Despite New York's example, coalitions that cut across racial and ethnic lines have been become more or less the norm in American cities. In Denver, for instance, Federico Peña became the city's first Mexican American mayor in 1983 when he was able to cobble together an electoral coalition of Latino and African American voters and educated white professionals connected to Denver's high-tech economy. Peña emphasized downtown and neighborhood development but also initiated affirmative action hiring in public agencies and appointed a large number of blacks and Latinos to boards and commissions. His African American successor in 1991, Wellington Webb, built upon Peña's programs by emphasizing infrastructure improvements throughout the city and by establishing a revolving fund for affordable housing.[26]

American cities contain a multitude of groups and interests, and urban officials have become skilled in the practical task of managing conflict within a complex political environment. They have learned how to do so because the politics of cities has become generally more accessible than in the past, making it hard to shut out anyone completely. A complex institutional structure provides numerous points of access into the political process. The result is a lively and often contentious struggle over the policy priorities of the city.

The Benefits of Incorporation

The incorporation of African Americans and Hispanics into local political structures has brought substantial benefits to both groups. The first generation of African American mayors successfully pushed for more spending for health, education, housing, and job training programs, and for increases in federal grants. Studies showed that cities with black mayors and council members had a higher proportion of social welfare expenditures than other cities. These findings seemed to apply to Latino officeholders as well. A study that measured the degree of incorporation of blacks and Latinos into the politics of 10 California cities in the early 1980s found that "political incorporation was responsible for dramatic changes in bureaucratic decision rules in many policy areas," such as local-government hiring and contracting procedures. The study also found that incorporation increased voter turnout and the mobilization of new leaders. Significant gains were achieved in integrating municipal labor forces, school administrators, and teachers, and neighborhood programs were initiated in many cities. Old racial barriers fell. Many observers interpreted these findings as a sign that more progress was yet to come.

Public employment provided an important avenue for minority employment. Research has consistently shown that when blacks became politically incorporated—that is, when they win the mayor's office and infiltrate the institutions of local government—minority employment in city government increased.[27] From 1973 to 1991, Mayor Bradley managed to increase the jobs held by blacks, Latinos, and Asians in municipal government from 36 to 50 percent. Minorities are often concentrated in lower-level jobs, but in Los Angeles during this period, minority representation in top-level city jobs increased as well.[28]

Minority mayors also initiated preferential procurement programs requiring that a minimum percentage of city contracts be given to minority business enterprises (MBEs). In 1973, blacks accounted for a majority of Atlanta's population, but firms owned by African Americans received only one-tenth of 1 percent of the city's contracts. By 1988, the preferential procurement program had raised the proportion to 35 percent. There were, though, two drawbacks. First, some MBEs acted as mere fronts for nonminority firms doing most of the work.[29] Secondly, preferential procurement generally benefited higher-income and better educated people within the minority community. Atlanta's first black mayor, Maynard Jackson, boasted that the minority set-asides for Atlanta's airport expansion created 21 African American millionaires; however, benefits to the low-income community were more difficult to identify.[30]

Beginning in 1989, the U.S. Supreme Court made it harder for cities and states to use preferential procurement programs to increase minority employment. In *City of Richmond v. J. A. Croson Co.* (1989), the Court ruled that Richmond's program requiring that 30 percent of contracts be set aside for MBEs violated the equal protection clause of the Fourteenth Amendment.[31] To withstand the "strict scrutiny" standard of constitutionality, cities must document past discrimination by city government and demonstrate that race-neutral alternatives will not solve the problem. This ruling makes preferential procurement difficult but not impossible to implement.[32]

Police reform was one of the most important policy benefits that flowed from political incorporation. Police brutality and inadequate police protection have long been two of the most frequently expressed grievances in minority communities around the country. For many years, the police department of Los Angeles was loathed in minority communities. Under the city's governmental structure, the LAPD operated well beyond the influence of elected officials. Appointed by an independent police commission, the chief of police had a free hand in running the department. The LAPD had always prided itself on its tough, law-and-order approach to law enforcement, and the chief liked to brag about the department's state-of-the-art, high-tech weaponry. In Los Angeles, policing relied on helicopters equipped with infrared cameras for night vision and 30-million-candlepower spotlights, called Nightsuns, that could turn night into day. Street numbers painted on rooftops gave police helicopters a navigable street grid from the air (now replaced by satellite navigation). Synchronization with patrol cars was facilitated by a communications system conceptualized by Hughes Aircraft and refined by NASA's Jet Propulsion Laboratory.[33] In low-income areas, this strategy meant the LAPD acted more like an occupying army than as an instrument for preserving public safety.

From 1978 to 1992, Chief Daryl Gates ran the LAPD as his personal fiefdom. Under operation HAMMER, patrol officers and elite tactical squads descended on South Central Los Angeles, arresting thousands of minority youths in each sweep. Young men were brought in for a wide range of infractions, from selling drugs to suspected gang activity to charges of loitering and jaywalking. In the absence of other charges, resisting arrest became a favorite police option. By 1990 as many as 50,000 suspects had been arrested in these sweeps, which is astounding considering only about 100,000 African American youths lived in all of Los Angeles.[34] The LAPD had a practice of using a dangerous chokehold to control people in custody. In 1982, after frequent use of the chokehold resulted in a rash of deaths among young black men, Chief Gates made the inflammatory statement that the problem could be traced to the anatomy of blacks rather than to police practices: "We may be finding that in some Blacks when [the carotid chokehold] is applied the veins or arteries do not open up as fast as they do on normal people."[35] The beating of Rodney King, which set off the 1992 riots, came as no surprise to blacks in Los Angeles.

Mayor Bradley, who had the advantage of being a former cop, succeeded in bringing the LAPD under some degree of civilian control, but only after 20 years of fierce political battles. The LAPD's share of the city's budget fell from 23 percent in 1972–1973 to 18 percent in 1987–1988. Between 1980 and 1988, minority representation in the LAPD increased from 20 to 32 percent, but the numbers of minorities in leadership positions still lagged. Most important, in June 1992, shortly after the riots, the voters approved Proposition F. Strongly supported by Bradley, Proposition F limited the terms of police chiefs and removed their civil service protection. Having campaigned vigorously against Proposition F, Chief Gates resigned and was succeeded by an African American, Willie Williams, who pledged to implement community-based policing.[36]

What the Los Angeles case shows is that even under adverse conditions, when minorities are incorporated into the political system they are able to bring about important changes. In Los Angeles, the black community considered it essential that more African American police officers be hired and the police department be brought under greater civilian control.[37] Racism and police brutality still occur within integrated police forces, but changing the composition of the force was a big step toward reform.

An assortment of racial and ethnic groups has recently sought incorporation into city politics. When these groups must cooperate to gain access to the political system, they are often able to put aside their differences and support a candidate. But these alliances are hard to keep together. A study of 41 cities that were at least 10 percent African American and 10 percent Latino found that, generally, black and Latino municipal employment was associated with the incorporation of both groups into local political systems. The same research demonstrated, however, that as the African American population increased, the Latino share of municipal employment fell.[38] Tensions arise because it is difficult to satisfy both groups with the limited jobs and other resources available. In New York City, the failure of blacks and Latinos to forge a stable electoral coalition facilitated the election of conservative mayors Ed Koch and Rudolph Giuliani. Similarly, after Bradley retired in Los Angeles, his black and Latino coalition fell apart, which paved the road to the mayor's office for Republican conservative Richard Riordan.

It may be difficult to forge political coalitions across racial and ethnic groups, but the biggest problem facing these alliances has not been their fragility but their lack of success in persuading state legislatures and the federal government to increase funding for social programs. In the 1960s and 1970s, when federal grants were flowing into cities, the first generation of minority mayors successfully lobbied for programs that benefited the poor. Since the withdrawal of federal funds, mayors have found it difficult to generate the revenues necessary to fund housing, health, jobs, recreation, and other initiatives. Minority mayors emphasize economic development as much as they do, not because they have given up on the goal of providing benefits to their constituents, but because they see no other way to raise the resources necessary to deliver on their promises. In short, they pursue trickle-down policies based on the logic that "private economic development in the city produces jobs in the private sector and tax money that may be used for jobs and purchases in the public sector. Through the various affirmative action devices . . . a certain proportion of these jobs and purchases may be channeled to the black community."[39]

The problem is that public-sector jobs have been marginal to the goal of advancing the economic well-being of blacks and Latinos.[40] At most, the public sector can supply employment to no more than 6 to 8 percent of the African American population of central cities—even assuming no jobs would go to other groups.[41] In any case, large proportions of public jobs, minority business contracts, and other benefits have gone to middle- and upper-income people and even to suburban residents.[42]

It is unrealistic to expect political participation to deliver a fundamental redistribution of economic resources. The political incorporation of a group cannot overturn of the economic arrangements that preserve inequality. As noted by one scholar, "There is no precedent for expecting political participation to produce revolutionary outcomes for any group in American urban politics specifically or American politics in general."[43] Still, considerable progress has been made. Minority regimes have been quite successful in altering hiring policies and curbing abuses by the police. These are important accomplishments.

Studies provide little evidence that the incorporation of blacks and Latinos into local political systems has led to significantly different taxing, spending, and service delivery policies. For the most part, African American mayors have been enthusiastic advocates for policies that favor business investment and the downtown development. Even so, the incorporation of African Americans and Latinos has had the effect of making people feel better about local politics. Survey research shows that blacks living in cities with an African American mayor expressed more trust in and paid more attention to political affairs, and more of them participated in politics.[44] Participation by Latinos has increased when they have been brought into local power structures.[45] Regardless of its limitations, minority incorporation has enhanced the legitimacy of city governments among a substantial portion of the urban population.

Striking a Balance

Over the years, community organizations have been key players in the process of opening up local political systems, and the gains have been realized regardless of whether a minority mayor happened to be in City Hall. In 1967 a white candidate, Kevin White, was elected mayor of Boston with the support from neighborhood groups that opposed urban renewal. Once in office, he supported rent control and set up "Little City Halls" in neighborhoods around the city to satisfy demands for more community control. Later, White lost his base of support in the neighborhoods when he reversed himself and came out against rent control and in favor of aggressive policies to promote downtown growth.

In 1972, a white candidate, Neil Goldschmidt, won the mayor's office in Portland, Oregon, with backing from neighborhood activists. A veteran of the civil rights movement before being elected to the Portland City Council, Goldschmidt had worked for Legal Services, which provided legal assistance to antipoverty and community groups. In 1971 and 1972, Goldschmidt cast the only dissenting votes on the city council on major urban renewal projects. As mayor, he granted neighborhood groups some authority over land use decisions, and the city even provided professional staff to neighborhood associations so they could review planning proposals. Between 1974 and 1979, the number of neighborhood groups in Portland doubled to 60.[46]

Another early success for the neighborhood movement came in Cincinnati. This was notable because the city's reform-style governmental structure—with a city manager and at-large nonpartisan elections—seemed to discourage the decentralization of decision making. But in 1971, several neighborhood groups came together to propose a slate of council candidates in the city council election. Enough members of the slate were elected to reorient the policies of the new council away from downtown development to neighborhood revitalization. Soon Cincinnati instituted neighborhood planning and began providing direct assistance to neighborhood associations.[47] Likewise, from 1969 to 1979, Hartford, Connecticut, operated under a city council whose members had strong roots in the neighborhoods. During these years, the city negotiated an equity partnership for neighborhood groups in major downtown developments, thus providing these organizations with a steady source of income and a stake in the downtown's success.[48] In 1981, Santa Monicans for Renters' Rights

(SMRR) swept the city council elections in Santa Monica, California, and the council then implemented a rent control ordinance that reportedly saved renters $1.1 billion between 1987 and 1997.[49]

The degree to which neighborhood organizations become influential varies greatly from one city to the next, but they play some role virtually everywhere. A political dynamic exists in which leaders close to neighborhoods tend to articulate issues of equity and social justice. Neighborhood organizations also receive a combination of public, foundation, and private funds to provide social services not always provided through municipal government. This activity tends to take place in the day-to-day operations of numerous organizations, large and small. Although they generally go about their business without much notice, this rich mixture of institutions is a crucial component of the political life of cities.

These institutions have become, for instance, an important means of delivering urban services, and they often do so for city governments. A 1990 survey of 161 cities with populations of over 100,000 people found that 60 percent of them had active systems of neighborhood councils, and 70 percent of these were officially recognized by city government.[50] By the early 1990s, New York City had instituted a system of partial decentralization wherein 59 community planning boards exercised advisory powers over land use and city services.[51] St. Paul has one of the most extensive systems of neighborhood control in the nation. In the early 1990s, 17 district councils, each elected by district residents, possessed substantial powers over zoning, the distribution of goods and services, and capital expenditures.[52] A 1991 survey of 133 cities with populations over 100,000 found that 64 percent had formed housing advocacy coalitions,[53] which worked with governments, nonprofit organizations, and developers to build housing for low- and moderate-income families. In most cities, a substantial proportion of the federal government's block grant funds flows through neighborhood and nonprofit organizations.

The institutional fabric that guarantees that neighborhoods and their residents will be able to exert some degree of influence in City Hall does not mean that they have become the most important powerbrokers in local political systems. This is not even the case in cities where they are relatively powerful. A mayor cannot afford to be captured in this way. Once a mayor takes office it becomes obvious that there are always more claimants than resources, and that it is impossible to satisfy everyone. In American cities, authority is fragmented and dispersed.[54] The mayor has political authority, but many other centers of power also exist. Mayors need cooperation from institutions well beyond the neighborhoods. Typically this may include the city council, labor unions, the media, independent authorities (such as school boards), the courts, state and federal officials, and, perhaps most of all, the business community.

In most cities there is a constant struggle that seems to pit downtown and economic development advocates against neighborhoods and their residents. Neighborhood groups are often viewed as antibusiness, indifferent to the need to promote economic development. Big downtown projects pushed by mayors and business elites—convention centers, sports stadiums, subsidized mall and entertainment districts—are questioned, if at all, mostly by neighborhood organizations and community activists. But no mayor can ignore the fact that little can be accomplished without the support of business. A few mayors manage to strike a balance, but the logic of economic development is so overwhelmingly strong that more often they end up pursuing a pro-growth agenda. This seems to happen regardless of the racial or ethnic background of the incumbent. African American mayors, for example, have invariably ended up advocating pro-growth downtown development policies even if their electoral base might suggest they would not.[55]

Atlanta's experience shows why. In 1973, Maynard Jackson was elected the first African American mayor of Atlanta. Jackson came into office with promises to reject what he termed "slavish, unquestioning adherence to downtown dicta."[56] What set Jackson apart from previous mayors was that he insisted that business elites "come to city hall to meet in his office and to ask for his support, rather than simply to inform him of their needs and assume his compliance."[57]

Jackson soon learned that to undertake expensive projects that he could take credit for when seeking reelection, he needed the support of the business community, and, over time, he was pulled toward accommodation with the downtown business elite. He supported all of the major redevelopment projects favored by downtown business, including construction of the Metro Atlanta Rapid Transit Authority (MARTA) system, which mainly connected downtown to the Atlanta airport. Jackson's successor, civil rights activist Andrew Young, continued Jackson's unqualified support of downtown development. Commenting on his partnership with business, Young said, "Politics doesn't control the world. Money does."[58]

The downtown and regional projects made it possible for Jackson and Young to increase African American public employment, government contracts for minority-owned firms, and African American representation on the police force. Their middle-class supporters gained from these programs, but the booming downtown and suburbs did even more for the white middle-class, and provided little to help blacks trapped in inner-city low-income neighborhoods. They were left behind.[59] From 1980 to 1985, predominantly white areas in the Atlanta region experienced job growth 14 times greater than predominantly black areas. Between 1970 and 1982, the percentage of central-city households living in poverty doubled. Atlanta's housing and job markets remained highly segregated. After 1980, applications to higher education, especially among Atlanta's black males, fell rapidly. A 1989 study by the *Atlanta Constitution* found that one black man in six had been imprisoned.[60]

The administration of Mayor Tom Bradley, who was elected the mayor of Los Angeles in 1973, also illustrates the importance that mayors attach to economic growth. Early on, Bradley stressed the need to make Los Angeles a "world class" city. He courted Japanese investors, who poured more than $3 billion into Los Angeles real estate in 1988 alone. Before Bradley, there was almost no downtown in Los Angeles; in 1975 only five buildings were above 13 stories. By 1990, there were over 50 such buildings—many of them visible in the dramatic footage that opened the television series *L.A. Law*.[61]

To subsidize downtown development, Los Angeles created a huge 255-block tax increment finance (TIF) district. The TIF district allowed the city to float bonds to provide public improvements and services to stimulate private investment. But because the city was required to use all of the additional taxes from the downtown redevelopment to retire the bonds or to support further development, the new taxes could not be used for projects or services elsewhere in the city.[62] The downtown office complex experienced a boom, but the high-level professional jobs generated by corporate investment were taken either by suburban residents or by professionals who moved into gentrified neighborhoods close to the downtown. The overall effect was to displace lower-income residents, drive up the cost of housing, and segment urban space into enclaves. Finally recognizing the depth of the housing crisis, in 1991 Mayor Bradley began to push for "linkage" fees that would require developers to allocate funds for low-income housing in exchange for approval of downtown building projects. But it was too little, too late.

The 1992 riots showed how difficult it was for Bradley to satisfy all of the contending interests in the city's politics. His policies had mainly aided real estate developers and expanded opportunities for white-collar professionals, including some who were black and Latino. Redevelopment did not benefit the poor. According to the 1990 census, the poverty rate in South Central Los Angeles, where the riots started, was 33 percent. The area was seething with tensions between newly arrived Central American immigrants and longtime African American residents. The riots exposed the depth of the racial and ethnic tensions in the city.

Bradley did not even succeed in satisfying affluent white voters. When development spread from downtown to the affluent West Side, Bradley began to encounter stiff opposition from environmentalists who objected to increased air pollution and traffic congestion. Unable to keep up with new development, the sewage system broke down in 1987, dumping millions of gallons of raw sewage into Santa Monica Bay. Bradley proposed a cap on new sewer construction to slow the pace of new development. The next year, however, Bradley infuriated environmentalists by reversing his long-standing opposition to oil drilling in the Pacific Palisades, an area on the ocean floor extending several miles out from Los Angeles. Under siege from residents in low- as well as high-income neighborhoods, Bradley chose not to run for a sixth term in 1993.

Despite the risks that such a strategy sometimes poses, the fact remains that the policy priorities of most cities continues to be focused on downtown development. In a large number of cities, especially in Sunbelt cities such as Phoenix, Las Vegas, and Houston, neighborhood groups have had little influence at all. Commenting on politics in Houston, one study called its neighborhood groups "largely invisible." During the 1970s and 1980s, Houston had only one organization representing poor neighborhoods, The Metropolitan Organization (TMO).[63] Although TMO won infrastructure improvements for high-poverty areas, it failed to stop the Hardy Toll Road that, for the convenience of white suburban commuters, destroyed many units of moderate-income housing.[64] Denounced as radical, TMO has been excluded from the governing regime.

Compared with cities like Boston and San Francisco, which have hundreds of community-based nonprofit housing developers, Houston had only five in the early 1990s. In 1988, Houston spent only 10 percent of its Community Development Block Grant (CDBG) on housing, compared to 75 percent in Boston and Santa Monica.

In cities with strong neighborhood organizations, mayors must somehow strike a balance between a downtown growth agenda and a program for neighborhood development. Ray Flynn of Boston was one of the nation's most successful mayors in bridging this gap. First elected in 1983, Flynn left office nine years later to become ambassador to the Vatican. Growing up in South Boston, Flynn's father was an immigrant longshore worker, and his mother cleaned downtown office buildings. After serving 15 years on the city council, Flynn mounted a surprisingly vigorous campaign in the 1983 mayoral race by building on his support from tenants' groups and neighborhood organizations. He stirred up his poor, largely Roman Catholic followers by pitting them against the Yankee blue-bloods and downtown Republicans and promised to implement linkage policies to force developers to help the neighborhoods.

Once in office, Flynn recognized the importance of forging a governing coalition. Abandoning the confrontational rhetoric that had gotten him elected, he forged an alliance with business based on a program that would pursue downtown development and residential revitalization at the same time. Boston's booming downtown office market allowed developers to make profits even while paying linkage fees, which required them to help pay for public improvements in exchange for development permits. He strengthened the city's rent control laws and enacted regulations to limit the conversion of rental units into condominiums. Flynn persuaded the city council to enact a housing policy that required developers of projects with 10 or more units to set aside 10 percent of the units for low- and moderate-income families, and a "linked deposit" policy in which the city would deposit its funds only with banks that demonstrated a commitment to their surrounding areas. The city contributed funds to Boston's nonprofit housing developers and also gave crucial support to one of the most successful comprehensive neighborhood revitalization projects in the country, the so-called Dudley Street Neighborhood Initiative (DSNI). With one-third of the land vacant, DSNI was blocked from assembling desirable parcels by an impossibly complex jigsaw puzzle of private ownership. In an unprecedented move, the city gave DSNI, a community-based organization, the power of eminent domain so that it could force owners to sell their properties.[65]

How successful was Flynn in improving the lives of neighborhood residents? By 1993, linkage fees had raised about $70 million and helped build 10,000 affordable housing units, and by the end of Flynn's second term, community-based housing corporations had built or rehabilitated another 5,000 units. The banks agreed to commit $400 million to a community reinvestment plan for low- and moderate-income areas. The Flynn administration even gave a few neighborhood councils authority over land use decisions. But only so much could be accomplished purely through local efforts.[66] Innovative local housing policies could not compensate for cuts in federal housing assistance imposed by the Reagan administration. And there was relatively little the Flynn administration could do about the income inequality arising in Boston from the combination of a booming corporate services sector and a rapidly declining industrial base.

The Decisive Turning Point

For as long as most people can remember, the central cities had been the special preserve for Democratic, liberal politicians. But beginning in the 1980s, white working-class and middle-class voters began supporting a new generation of mayors who promised to cut taxes by holding down spending, and in the 1990s the national conservative movement began to put down roots in local politics, energized in considerable measure by racial, ethnic, and class divisions within the cities. To bring order to the streets, the new breed of urban leaders promised to get tough with criminals, panhandlers, and homeless people. Within a few years, self-styled conservative white mayors replaced prominent African American mayors in several cities. In 1993 Rudolph Giuliani, a former district attorney, defeated New York's first black mayor, David Dinkins; that same year in Los Angeles, millionaire financier Richard Riordan defeated Mike Woo, an Asian American who tried unsuccessfully to reconstruct Tom Bradley's coalition. A year earlier, Bret Schundler had become the first Republican in 75 years to be elected mayor of Jersey City, New Jersey, and Republican Stephen Goldsmith became mayor of Indianapolis. Elsewhere, African American mayors were defeated by Democrats who advocated distinctly downtown-oriented agendas. Richard M. Daley, the son of Democratic machine boss Richard J. Daley, twice defeated African American opponents, and Edward Rendell replaced Philadelphia's first black mayor, Wilson Goode. Although it would not be accurate to call all of these mayors conservative if we are using the ideological yardstick employed in national political discourse, their rise to power signaled a distinct turn towards new policy priorities.

The change in direction was provoked by resentments about minority political demands, especially in the areas of affirmative action and busing; opposition by downtown business elites to higher taxes and programs with a social welfare dimension; and widespread anxiety about crime and disorder. The first generation of conservative mayors came into office during a period of high tension. In the wake of the Los Angeles riots of 1992, issues connected to social disorder, drugs, and crime reverberated all through the American political system. By playing on such themes, Republican Rudolph Giuliani was able to overcome a six-to-one Democratic advantage in party registration in the 1993 mayoral race in New York City. Giuliani received 78 percent of the white vote; by contrast, the African American incumbent, David Dinkins, carried 95 percent of the African American vote. Giuliani's campaign slogan, "Taking Back the City," played on a law-and-order theme and racial antagonisms. Latinos played a crucial role in the election. Giuliani had lost by a narrow margin in 1989, when he received 34 percent of the Latino vote. In the 1993 election, Giuliani put a prominent Latino politician, Herman Badillo, on his ticket for the office of city comptroller. This time, Giuliani got 39 percent of the Latino vote. He also benefited from an unusually high voter turnout in the borough of Staten Island, a turnout stimulated by a ballot initiative calling for secession from New York City. Racial tensions provided the main motivation for the controversial proposal to secede.[67]

Latino voters also supplied the swing vote in the 1993 Los Angeles mayoral race. A Republican, Richard Riordan, carried only 14 percent of the African American vote that year, but he defeated a Democratic candidate, Mike Woo. Riordan won the election by persuading 67 percent of white voters and 43 percent of Latino voters to support him. To achieve name recognition, Riordan poured $6 million of his own money into the campaign. Riordan had acquired his fortune by financing leveraged buyouts through junk bonds and by speculating in downtown Los Angeles real estate. He had been a frequent contributor to Tom Bradley's campaigns, and by portraying himself as a pragmatic manager "tough enough to turn L.A. around," he was able to win 31 percent of the votes cast by previous Bradley supporters.[68] In April 1997, Riordan won reelection with 61 percent of the vote; he improved his support among Latino voters but lost the African American vote by a three-to-one ratio.

The conservative mayors fought hard to reverse policies perceived as unfairly benefiting blacks. At the time Giuliani was elected, 38 percent of New York City's municipal jobs went to African Americans, even though they constituted only 29 percent of the city's population.[69] On taking office, Giuliani repealed the city's affirmative action policies in hiring and contracting, and he began to reduce city payrolls. Within two years, the city's workforce had been trimmed by 17,000 workers.

Concerns about law and order also contributed to the new turn in city politics. Crime became a highly charged symbolic issue, "a shorthand signal, to crucial numbers of white voters, of broader issues of social disorder, tapping powerful ideas about authority, status, morality, self-control, and race."[70] Some voters perceived black mayors as being soft on crime because they tended to advocate more spending on social services and supported civilian review boards to monitor police conduct.[71] Conservatives vowed to "get tough" with criminals. As a former federal prosecutor, Giuliani was ideally situated to portray himself as a law-and-order candidate.

Giuliani delivered on his promises by cutting budgets for almost every city agency except the police and fire departments. He hired William Bratton as his police commissioner. Bratton instituted three controversial policing strategies. First, officers were allocated to hotspots identified from daily computer mappings of shootings and drug sales. Second, police began to crack down on minor offenses such as drinking in public, urinating on the street, and hassling motorists by demanding money for cleaning their windshields. This strategy was derived from the so-called broken windows theory of urban decline. Stated broadly, the theory suggested that small signs of decay, such as broken windows and trash on empty lots, serve as signs that an area is dangerous and in decline. As applied to crime control, it meant that even small offenses would be punished. Third, officers were encouraged to frisk people who were stopped for minor violations, such as playing loud music or drinking in public, in order to get guns off the street.

The new policing strategies appeared to work when New York's crime rate dropped dramatically. The number of murders fell nearly 60 percent, from a high of 2,262 in 1990 to 983 by 1996. Formerly regarded as one of the most dangerous cities in the nation, for the first six months of 1996 New York City ranked 144th out of the largest 189 cities in per capita total crime.[72] Although the media attributed the decline to the new policing strategies, in fact the crime rate had begun to drop in the last year of the Dinkins administration, and the fall in the city's crime rate followed a national trend that has continued to unfold. Nevertheless, Giuliani made the improved crime statistics a major plank in his successful 1997 reelection campaign. In Giuliani's second term, crime continued to fall (again, in parallel with a national trend). There were 672 murders committed in the city in 2000.[73]

In addition to exploiting racially charged issues, the new generation of mayors also claimed to possess the magic formula for bringing prosperity to the local economy. The formula was made up of a combination of cuts in spending and aggressive policies to stimulate investment. Conservatives had initially developed their analysis of the urban condition in response to New York City's fiscal crisis of 1975. When the banks refused to underwrite any more of its loans in April of that year, the city suddenly found it impossible to borrow the money it needed to meet payroll obligations and redeem outstanding notes. Conservatives blamed the crisis on a habit of profligate spending. The writer Ken Auletta said the prominent conservative William F. Buckley had been right when he ran for mayor in 1965. As Auletta put it: "We [in New York City] have conducted a noble experiment in local socialism and income redistribution, one clear result of which has been to redistribute much of our tax base and many jobs right out of the city."[74]

Ed Koch won the mayoral race in 1977 by emphasizing just such an analysis of the causes of New York's fiscal crisis. Soon after entering city hall, Koch asserted that "the main job of municipal government is to create a climate in which private business can expand in the city to provide jobs and profit. It's not the function of government to create jobs on the public payroll."[75] As mayor Koch provided billions of dollars of incentives for businesses at the same time that he laid off 60,000 city workers. His policies appealed to homeowners in Brooklyn and Queens, who were sick of high taxes, and to real estate developers and to Wall Street firms, who expressed their gratitude in the form of generous campaign contributions.

In the 1990s conservatives continued to attack their opponents as representatives of special interests whose free-spending policies would bankrupt cities. At the same time, they argued that all the problems their cities faced could be solved if the private sector were unleashed. The rhetoric of fiscal crisis became a useful way of withdrawing the city from a variety of programs and services with a social content.[76] Mayor Giuliani cut city payrolls and services, reduced income taxes and property taxes on condominiums and co-ops, and slashed the commercial rent tax and the hotel tax on the grounds that reduced taxes would stimulate private investment. His counterpart across the country, Los Angeles mayor Richard Riordan, took a similar approach. "Economic development is the whole future of the city," Riordan said during his first year in office.[77] Working to reduce the regulatory burden on developers, Riordan pushed generous business subsidies. In one case, he put together a $70 million subsidy package to convince Dreamworks SKG to build its new studio in Los Angeles.[78]

Privatization, which was often identified as part of the conservative agenda of the 1980s, quickly became popular with mayors across the political spectrum. The term meant that to reduce costs, city governments should contract out such services as garbage collection and even education (in the form of charter schools). As a way of cutting costs and improving quality, privatization is long standing and noncontroversial. In the city-building era at the beginning of the twentieth century, cities contracted for streetcar, telephone, and utilities services, and many also contracted with private firms for water supply. The city of San Francisco contracted out garbage collection to private companies as early as 1932.[79] Partial privatization, which involves contracting out publicly funded services, often saves city governments money. One of the earliest scholarly evaluations concluded that Scottsdale, Arizona, by contracting for fire protection from a private firm, paid about half of what it would have had to pay if it had provided the service itself.[80] A 1982 survey of 1,780 cities found that the average city contracts approximately 26 percent of its services, in whole or part, to private firms.[81]

In the 1980s, however, privatization had become a strategy not only to make government more efficient but also to reduce its size and scope. E. S. Savas, called the "the godfather of privatization," served as assistant secretary of Housing and Urban Development (HUD) during the Reagan administration. In his several books, Savas stressed that privatization was a tool not only to make a better government but to make a more limited government—"limited in its size, scope, and power relative to society's other institutions."[82] Savas later became an adviser to the Giuliani administration, which used privatization mainly as a threat to squeeze concessions out of municipal unions.

Among mayors, Indianapolis mayor Stephen Goldsmith, who did not fit any ideological label, became one of the most ardent proponents of privatization. Elected in 1992, during his first 18 months in office Goldsmith privatized 14 services, sold off the municipal golf course, and slashed the city payroll from 5,700 to 4,200, giving Indianapolis the lowest number of employees per capita of any of the nation's 50 largest cities.[83] When Goldsmith attempted to contract with neighborhood groups and churches to maintain local parks, however, he found little interest, and his proposal to privatize two troubled public housing projects was vehemently opposed by the residents.[84] Called a "populist Republican," Goldsmith won support by allocating city resources to neighborhood organizations in distressed inner-city areas, but critics argued that this only crippled the ability of the city to regulate some of its key services.[85]

It is difficult to assess the political significance of the conservative mayors and their peers, in part because policies at the urban level rarely can be neatly put into an ideological box. Mayors respond to the constituencies that elect them, and to the overall demographic profiles of their cities. All mayors realize that they must appeal to a diverse array of racial and ethnic groups. For this reason, conservative mayors have not tended to toe the line in observing the national Republican platform. For example, in the 1990s and beyond both Giuliani and Riordan bucked the national Republican agenda and opposed legislation that would deny government benefits to immigrants who had not yet become citizens. Giuliani's stance cost him dearly in his bid for the presidency in 2008.

The Racial and Ethnic Future

The nature of a city's economy and its political culture powerfully shapes a mayor's municipal agenda. Urban leaders, even when they identify as conservatives, reflecting the complex makeup of their constituencies. They generally take moderate positions on such explosive social issues as affirmative action hiring and multicultural curriculums in the schools. Likewise, self-styled progressive mayors who emphasize issues of social justice tend to move to the political center and join their more conservative counterparts in pursuing policies that promote economic growth and downtown development. At the local level, partisan and ideological differences break down, and often do not matter at all.

Nevertheless, it is important to emphasize that racial and ethnic conflict remains as a powerful force shaping city politics. Examples are not hard to find. In 2012, for instance, the District of Columbia's District Ward 5 faced an election after its former councilman was forced from office by a criminal conviction. A crowded ballot, with 10 Democrats, an Independent and a Republican, assured that the campaign would be hotly contested, and the makeup of the district virtually guaranteed that it would have a racial dimension. An Advisory Neighborhood commissioner stated that the election's outcome could well be determined along racial lines: "I am very concerned that rigor mortis will set in and white folks will get mad and vote, and black folks will get mad and stay home."[86] The African American population is predominantly black but their numbers are decreasing, from 90 percent in 2000 to 77 percent in 2010.[87] Despite the commissioner's worries, Harry Thomas, Jr., an African American Democrat, won the election.

In an April 2013 column, *Washington Post* columnist Colber I. King, in a column about the April 23rd council elections, wrote that "race doesn't belong in D.C. Council election."[88] It was a forlorn hope. When one of the candidates pulled out of the race, Anita Bonds, a Democrat, remained the only African-American candidate in the race, and she quickly sought to garner the support of black voters on the basis of a shared racial identity. Candidate Patrick Mara, the only Republican candidate, responded in kind by appealing to the white residents of Chevy Chase, urging them to vote as a "bloc" and keep the only possible black candidate out of office.

In February 2013, civil rights activists in Antelope Valley, California, filed a complaint in Los Angeles County Superior Court alleging racial bias in the city's elections, arguing that Palmdale, California's system of at-large council seats unconstitutionally diminished the influence of minority voters. This conflict was merely the most recent in a series of high-profile conflicts over housing programs and police practices. For some time, blacks and Latinos had been moving into predominantly white neighborhoods, which kept the pot boiling.

Racial and ethnic issues are certain to remain as a pivotal feature of politics at all levels of governance into the foreseeable future. It has been estimated that around the year 2050, the United States will become a "majority minority," but such a statistic does not mean that "minorities," as a group, will be able to wield decisive power. The relationship between African Americans and Latinos is complex, and it is constantly evolving. A 2008 survey by Pew Research found that "overwhelming majorities of both blacks and Hispanics have favorable views of each other,"[89] and a majority from both "sides" agrees that the two groups get along well or fairly well. Hispanics and blacks living in counties with high concentrations of African Americans are more likely to say that the two groups get along well than Hispanics and blacks living in low-density black counties, indicating perhaps that proximity is associated with an increased tolerance or acceptance.

But the harmony that is sometimes achieved between different minority groups is a fragile thing. Recently, disagreements on issues of immigration threaten to increase, rather than bridge, the divide between the two groups. The growing Hispanic population, which is projected to surpass the African American population by 2050, is causing concern among some blacks, with many hoping that ". . . Latinos understand they're not White and that they will stay connected to African Americans . . . Black folks hear Latinos say 'We get it, and we're also discriminated against' . . . and have a hard time accepting that Latinos face any kind of discrimination that is similar or as extreme as what they experience."[90] The possibility for both cooperation and conflict is an ever-present reality in American urban politics, and it will not soon go away.

Endnotes

1. *Report of the National Advisory Commission on Civil Disorders* (New York: Bantam Books, 1968).
2. Christopher L. Warren, John G. Corbett, and John F. Stack Jr., "Hispanic Ascendancy and Tripartite Politics in Miami," in *Racial Politics in American Cities*, ed. Rufus P. Browning, Dale Rogers Marshall, and David H. Tabb (New York: Longman, 1990), p. 166.
3. James H. Johnson Jr., Cloyzelle K. Jones, Walter C. Farrell Jr., and Melvin L. Oliver, "The Los Angeles Rebellion: A Retrospective View," *Economic Development Quarterly* 6, no. 4 (November 1992): 356–372.
4. Jack Miles, "Blacks vs. Brown," *Atlantic* (October 1992): 41–68; see also Mike Davis, "In L.A., Burning All Illusions," *Nation* (June 1, 1992), pp. 743–746.
5. Tim Rutten, "A New Kind of Riot," *New York Review of Books* (June 11, 1992), pp. 52–54.
6. Wes Woods II, "Fontana Students Blame Riot on Simmering Racial Tension," *Inland Valley Daily Bulletin* (October 20, 2006).

7. Chris Maag, "What Triggered the Toledo Riots?" *Time Magazine* (October 16, 2005).
8. U.S. Census, The 2012 Statistical Abstract, www.census.gov.
9. Ibid..
10. Ibid.
11. Rodney E. Hero and Susan E. Clarke, "Latinos, Blacks, and Multiethnic Politics in Denver: Realigning Power and Influence in the Struggle for Democracy," in *Racial Politics in American Cities,* 3rd ed., ed. Browning, Marshall, and Tabb, p. 327.
12. Raphael Sonenshein, "The Prospects for Multiracial Coalitions: Lessons from America's Three Largest Cities," in *Racial Politics in American Cities,* 3rd ed., Browning, Marshall, and Tabb, pp. 333–356.
13. U.S. Bureau of the Census, *Statistical Abstract of the United States: 1995* (Washington, DC: U.S. Government Printing Office, 1995), p. 287.
14. Joint Center for Political and Economic Studies, *Black Elected Officials: A Statistical Summary, 2001* (Washington, DC: Author, 2001), p. 8.
15. National Association of Latino Elected and Appointed Officials (Washington, DC: Author, *National Roster of Hispanic Elected Officials,* annual).
16. Hero and Clarke, "Latinos, Blacks, and Multiethnic Politics in Denver," p. 316.
17. John Mollenkopf, *A Phoenix in the Ashes: The Rise and the Fall of the Koch Coalition in New York City Politics* (Princeton, NJ: Princeton University Press, 1992), p. 12.
18. Raphael J. Sonenshein, *Politics in Black and White: Race and Power in Los Angeles* (Princeton, NJ: Princeton University Press, 1993), p. 63.
19. Patrick D. Joyce, "A Reversal of Fortunes: Black Empowerment, Political Machines, and City Jobs in New York City and Chicago," *Urban Affairs Review* 32, no. 3 (1997): 291–318.
20. Charles P. Henry, "Urban Politics and Incorporation: The Case of Blacks, Latinos, and Asians in Three Cities," in *Blacks, Latinos, and Asians in Urban America: Status and Prospects for Politics and Activism,* ed. James Jennings (Westport, CT: Praeger, 1994), p. 18.
21. Our account of Koch is based on Mollenkopf, *A Phoenix in the Ashes.*
22. Quotes in ibid., pp. 171–172.
23. John Mollenkopf, "New York: Still the Great Anomaly," in *Racial Politics in American Cities,* ed. Browning, Marshall, and Tabb, p. 120.
24. Ibid.
25. Ibid.
26. Hero and Clarke, "Latinos, Blacks and Multiethnic Politics in Denver," p. 317.
27. Rufus P. Browning, Dale Rogers Marshall, and David H. Tabb, *Protest Is Not Enough: The Struggle of Blacks and Hispanics for Equality in Urban Politics* (Berkeley: University of California Press, 1984), pp. 171–174; Peter K. Eisinger, "Black Mayors and the Politics of Racial Economic Advancement," in *Urban Politics: Past, Present, and Future,* 2nd ed., ed. Harlan Hahn and Charles H. Levine (New York: Longman, 1984), pp. 249–260; Kenneth R. Mladenka, "Blacks and Hispanics in Urban Politics," *American Political Science Review* 83, no. 1 (March 1989): 165–191. Mladenka concludes that minority mayors have little impact on policy outcomes, but minority council majorities do.
28. Sonenshein, *Politics in Black and White,* p. 152.
29. Timothy Bates and Darrell Williams, "Preferential Procurement Programs and Minority-Owned Businesses," *Journal of Urban Affairs* 17, no. 1 (1995): 1.
30. Clarence N. Stone, *Regime Politics: Governing Atlanta 1946–1988* (Lawrence: University Press of Kansas, 1989), p. 145, Chapter 1.

31. *City of Richmond v. J. A. Croson Co.*, 109 S.Ct. 706 (1989).
32. Mitchell F. Rice, "State and Local Government Set-Aside Programs, Disparity Studies, and Minority Business Development in the Post-*Croson* Era," *Journal of Urban Affairs* 15, no. 6 (1993): 529–553.
33. Mike Davis, *City of Quartz: Excavating the Future in Los Angeles* (London: Verso, 1990), pp. 251–253.
34. Ibid., p. 277.
35. Ibid., p. 272.
36. Sonenshein, *Politics in Black and White*, pp. 155–161.
37. Albert Karnig and Susan Welch, *Black Representation and Urban Policy* (Chicago: University of Chicago Press, 1980); Eisinger, "Black Mayors"; Browning, Marshall, and Tabb, *Protest Is Not Enough;* Mladenka, "Blacks and Hispanics in Urban Politics"; Grace Hall Saltzstein, "Black Mayors and Police Policies," *Journal of Politics* 51, no. 3 (August 1989): 525–544.
38. Paula D. McClain and Albert Karnig, "Black and Hispanic Socioeconomic and Political Competition," *American Political Science Review* 84, no. 2 (June 1990): 535–545; Paula D. McClain, "The Changing Dynamics of Urban Politics: Black and Hispanic Municipal Employment—Is There Competition?" *Journal of Politics* 55, no. 2 (May 1993): 399–414.
39. Eisinger, "Black Mayors," p. 257.
40. See the detailed case studies of 12 cities in Browning, Marshall, and Tabb, *Racial Politics in American Cities*, 3rd ed.
41. Eisinger, "Black Mayors," p. 258.
42. William Julius Wilson, *The Truly Disadvantaged: The Inner City, the Underclass, and Public Policy* (Chicago: University of Chicago Press, 1987), p. 115.
43. Perry, in Browning, Marshall, and Tabb, *Racial Politics in America*, 3rd ed., p. 251.
44. Lawrence Bobo and Franklin D. Gilliam Jr., "Race, Sociopolitical Participation, and Black Empowerment," *American Political Science Review* 84, no. 2 (June 1990): 377–393.
45. See Browning, Marshall, and Tabb, *Racial Politics in American Cities*, 3rd ed.
46. Carl Abbott, *Portland: Planning, Politics, and Growth in a Twentieth-Century City* (Lincoln: University of Nebraska Press, 1983), Chapters 8 and 9.
47. John Clayton Thomas, *Between Citizen and City: Neighborhood Organizations and Urban Politics in Cincinnati (Lawrence: University Press of Kansas, 1986),* Chapter 6.
48. Pierre Clavel, *The Progressive City: Planning and Participation, 1969–1984* (New Brunswick, NJ: Rutgers University Press, 1986), Chapter 2.
49. Stella M. Capek and John I. Gilderbloom, *Community versus Commodity: Tenants and the American City* (Albany: State University of New York Press, 1992), p. 182.
50. Carmine Scavo, "The Use of Regulative Mechanisms by Large U.S. Cities," *Journal of Urban Affairs* 15, no. 1 (1993): 100.
51. Robert F. Pecorella, *Community Power in a Postreform City* (Armonk, NY: M. E. Sharpe, 1994).
52. Jeffrey M. Berry, Kent E. Portney, and Ken Thomson, *The Rebirth of Urban Democracy* (Washington, DC: Brookings Institution Press, 1993), p. 13.
53. Edward G. Goetz, *Shelter Burden: Local Politics and Progressive Housing Policy* (Philadelphia: Temple University Press, 1993), p. 52.
54. Barbara Ferman, *Governing the Ungovernable City: Political Skill, Leadership, and the Modern Mayor* (Philadelphia: Temple University Press, 1985), Chapter 1; Stone, *Regime Politics*, Chapter 1. Urban regime theory stresses that cities are not governed by elected officials but by "informal arrangements by which public bodies and

private interests function together in order to be able to make and carry out governing decisions." Ibid., p. 6.

55. See Adolph Reed, "The Black Urban Regime: Structural Origins and Constraints," *Comparative Urban and Community Research* 1, no. 1 (1987): 138–189; and "Demobilization in the New Black Political Regime: Ideological Capitulation and Radical Failure in the Postsegregation Era," in *The Bubbling Cauldron: Race, Ethnicity, and the Urban Crisis,* ed. Michael Peter Smith and Joe R. Feagin (Minneapolis: University of Minnesota Press, 1995), pp. 182–208.

56. Maynard Jackson, quoted in Stone, *Regime Politics,* p. 87.

57. Adolph Reed Jr., "A Critique of Neo-Progressivism in Theorizing About Local Development Policy: A Case from Atlanta," in *The Politics of Urban Development,* ed. Clarence N. Stone and Heywood T. Sanders (Lawrence: University Press of Kansas, 1987), p. 206.

58. Quoted in Stone, *Regime Politics,* p. 136.

59. The evaluation of black progress in Atlanta that follows is based on Gary Orfield and Carole Ashkinaze, *The Closing Door: Conservative Policy and Black Opportunity* (Chicago: University of Chicago Press, 1991).

60. Cited in ibid., p. 151.

61. Wilson, *The Truly Disadvantaged,* p. 135.

62. Sonenshein, *Politics in Black and White,* p. 168.

63. Ibid., p. 212.

64. Joe R. Feagin, *Free Enterprise City: Houston in Political and Economic Perspective* (New Brunswick, NJ: Rutgers University Press, 1988), pp. 279–280.

65. Peter Medoff and Holly Sklar, *Streets of Hope: The Fall and Rise of an Urban Neighborhood* (Boston: South End Press, 1994).

66. Peter Dreier and W. Dennis Keating, "The Limits of Localism: Progressive Housing Policies in Boston, 1984–1989," *Urban Affairs Quarterly* 26, no. 2 (December 1990): 191–216.

67. Karen M. Kaufmann, "A Tale of Two Cities: The Impact of Intergroup Conflict on Mayoral Voting Behavior in Los Angeles and New York," paper delivered at the American Political Science Association Meeting (San Francisco, August 29–September 1, 1996), p. 18. Giuliani was reelected by a wide margin in 1997.

68. Ibid., p. 22.

69. Institute for Puerto Rican Policy, *The Giuliani Budget Cuts and People of Color: Disproportionate Employment Impact* (New York: Institute for Puerto Rican Policy, 1994), p. 1; as reported in Michael Leo Owens, "Race, Place, and Government Employment," paper delivered at the New York State Political Science Association Meeting (Ithaca, NY, March 29–30, 1996), p. 12.

70. Thomas Byrne Edsall and Mary D. Edsall, *Chain Reaction: The Impact of Race, Rights, and Taxes on American Politics* (New York: Norton, 1991), p. 224. Emphasis on the word *signal* removed from the original.

71. Saltzstein, "Black Mayors and Police Policies," pp. 525–544.

72. Randy Kennedy, "FBI Reports New York Safer Than Most Cities," *New York Times* (January 6, 1997), p. B5.

73. University of Virginia Library, Geospatial and Statistical Data Center, http://cba.unomaha.edu/faculty/cdecker/WEB/Geospatial%20and%20Statistical%20Data%20Center.htm.

74. Quoted in William E. Simon, *A Time for Truth* (New York: Berkeley Books, 1978), p. 155.

75. Quoted in Martin Shefter, *Political Crisis/Fiscal Crisis: The Collapse and Revival of New York City* (New York: Basic Books, 1985), p. 175.

76. Ester R. Fuchs, *Mayors and Money: Fiscal Policy in New York and Chicago* (Chicago: University of Chicago Press, 1992).

77. Quoted in Laura Mecoy, "Ain't Too Proud to Beg: Is L.A.'s Businessman Mayor Good for L.A. Business?" *Los Angeles* (July 1996).

78. Ibid.

79. David F. Linowes, *Privatization: Toward More Effective Government. Report of the President's Commission on Privatization* (Urbana: University of Illinois Press, 1988), p. 2.

80. Roger S. Ahlbrandt Jr., *Municipal Fire Protection Services: Comparison of Alternative Organizational Forms* (Beverly Hills, CA: Sage, 1973).

81. Derived from *Rethinking Local Services: Examining Alternative Service Delivery Approaches* (Washington, DC: International City Management Association, 1984), Table B; as reported in E. S. Savas, *Privatization: The Key to Better Government* (Chatham, NJ: Chatham House, 1987), p. 72.

82. Ibid., p. 288.

83. Nancy Hass, "Philadelphia Freedom: How Privatization Has Worked Wonders in the City of Brotherly Love and Beyond," *Financial World* 162, no. 16 (1993): 37.

84. William D. Eggers, "Righting City Hall," *National Review* 46, no. 16 (1994): 40.

85. Rob Gurwitt, "Indianapolis and the Republican Future," *Governing* 7, no. 5 (February 1994): 24–28.

86. Liz Farmer, "Anti-Thomas Sentiment Expected to be Factor in Ward 5 Election," *The Examiner* (May 7, 2012).

87. Ibid.

88. John V. LaBaume, "Op-Ed: No Room for 'Race' in D.C. Council Election but There is Lots for 'Reform'," *The Examiner: Opinion* (April 16, 2013).

89. "Do Blacks and Hispanics Get Along?" *Pew Research: Social and Demographic* (January 31, 2008).

90. Wendy Conklin, "Latinos and Blacks: What Unites and Divides Us?" *The Diversity Factor* 16, no.1 (Winter 2008).

CHAPTER 15

City and Metropolis in the Global Era

Urban Politics in a Time of Change

Cities and urban regions have been utterly transformed by the globalization processes that have defined the twenty-first century. The rapid movement of capital around the globe has forced to cities into an intense inter-urban competition for investment. For many cities, the outcome was very much in doubt. Those that had prospered during the industrial era went through a painful period of economic restructuring when manufacturing jobs moved elsewhere and service employment became the new engine of growth. Those that have made the transition have experienced a stunning revival. Downtown skylines and old neighborhoods have been transformed, and as a visitor to one of these cities can observe, an exciting streetlife and urban culture has emerged. Bicycle and walking paths snake by sparkling waterfront developments and urban parks. All of these amenities are part of a new economy that makes the modern city into "a dreamscape of visual consumption."[1]

Most people would regard these changes as positive developments, but there is also another side to the story. Even while cities were becoming more prosperous, they were also becoming more divided. Two streams of movement have transformed large and small cities alike in the space of a remarkably few years. One stream has been made up of highly educated white-collar professionals: corporate managers, management consultants, legal experts, accountants, computer specialists, financial analysts, media and public relations specialists, and more. Another stream has been composed of service workers who fill jobs at the other end of pyramid. The maintenance, clerical, and personal services jobs required in high-rise office buildings and the low-wage, often seasonal work available in restaurants, entertainment venues, tourism, and associated businesses have drawn large numbers of immigrants and ethnic minorities. These twin migrations have created an easily recognized patchwork geography. While affluent professionals have moved into downtown condominium towers, gentrified neighborhoods, and suburban gated communities, newer immigrants, ethnic minorities, and the poor live in poorer neighborhoods sprinkled throughout the metropolitan region.

The latest version of the revitalized city and of the fragmented metropolis is different from what came before. Urban regions are no longer divided between troubled inner cities and affluent, white suburbs. The demographic movements

398

associated with the global economy have made the suburbs racially and ethnically diverse. But it is not easy to interpret what this means. Some observers find evidence of progress and improvement wherever they look; others believe it is the same old politics in a new guise. Convincing arguments can be offered for both points of view.

The New (but Actually Old) Growth Politics

In recent decades, cities (as well as nations) have joined in a fierce competition for a share of the global economy. Local efforts have had some effect, as evidenced by the groves of skyscrapers and clusters of entertainment facilities that have sprouted in recent years in the larger cities that house the new economic activities driving downtown development: finance, telecommunications, corporate and professional offices, tourism and leisure. Cities of all sizes and circumstances try to get their share. Just two months before Hurricane Katrina hit the city, the state of Louisiana agreed to give the New Orleans Saints $12.4 million to keep the team from leaving,[2] and in 2010 the Saints won the Super Bowl. Meanwhile, devastated neighborhoods still lied in ruins and levees were still in bad repair. For some people, this policy trade-off might be interpreted as a metaphor for the policy priorities that exist almost everywhere.

Who reaps the benefits of the global economy? The advantages for a cosmopolitan class that holds the best jobs can be observed in the images conveyed in the urban lifestyle magazines. These colorful, advertisement-filled publications are similar from city to city because the target audience is unvarying: an affluent middle class made up disproportionately of empty nesters and younger singles or childless couples. Each month, columns written by lifestyle writers and critics promote restaurants and entertainment spots, wine and cigar bars, shopping opportunities, and the other amenities and entertainments of an urbane lifestyle. One could get the impression that every downtown in America is unique and exciting, although they also seem to be little more than copies of one another.

It may be useful to consider whether affluent urban residents live, work, and play in "Potemkin cities,"[3] where a thriving downtown and a tourist bubble mask serious urban problems, or in "boutique cities" such as Seattle and Denver, where highly paid professionals are able to sustain a critical mass of expensive restaurants, international boutique and clothing stores, and neighborhoods with stratospheric housing prices.[4] In the 1950s and 1960s, African Americans in poor neighborhoods were often threatened by the urban renewal bulldozer. In the new century, ethnic minorities and new immigrants sometimes face a bulldozer with a friendlier face; after all, homeowners living in gentrifying neighborhoods can reap benefits from rising property values. But there is no use glossing over the fact that there are many losers: working-class residents and the poor are regularly shoved out by the gentrifying professional class. The politics of economic inequality plays out a little differently in the suburbs, but with equal force. The residents of older inner-ring suburbs often are displaced by gentrification, like their city cousins, and end up living in suburbs where the tax base is too low to support adequate services.

What remedies are there for these problems? Judging by the policies they favor, local political leaders seem to believe that the most effective thing they can do is more of the same. Other issues may seem pressing, but none receive more care and feeding than businesses, investors, affluent homeowners, and others (such as tourists) who might help bring prosperity to the local economy. At the same time, urban leaders go to great pains to persuade the citizenry that everyone benefits from these policies. Such public relations work often enough, but sometimes wear thin when ugly social problems become hard to ignore.

The Delicate Art of Urban Governance

Despite its manifest importance, the economic imperative sometimes must give way, or is balanced by, another imperative: the need to attend to the competing claims made by the complex mixture of groups making up the local polity. The flood tide of immigration set off by globalization makes guarantees that urban governance will remain a delicate art. Though issues of race and ethnicity are constantly present and sometimes contentious, it must be emphasized that the various "minority" groups are rarely brought together around a single cause. "Rainbow" coalitions that bring together African Americans with new immigrant groups have been rare, but tensions among the groups have been common.[5] If broad alliances within the central cities are uncommon, they are even rarer in the suburbs, where urban governance is complicated become it is divided up into a multitude of separate jurisdictions. A racial or ethnic group may exert influence in one community, but in the next suburb over the same group may be absent from the political scene altogether.

The gentrification of neighborhoods is a chronic source of change and dislocation. For more than 40 years, the Humboldt Park neighborhood in Chicago has been home to the largest Puerto Rican population in the city, and one of the largest in the United States. Two steel sculptures of the Puerto Rican flag serve as a reminder that the neighborhood has a distinctive culture. In the years before the housing boom went bust, white professionals and artists flooded into the neighborhood and housing prices rose, which drove out a longtime residents. In 2006, one store window displayed a "No Yuppies" sign, and verbal confrontations sometimes occurred. As if to pour gasoline onto the flame, one of the newcomers naively said, "I try to tell them before Puerto Ricans were there, there were European Jews. And before the Jews, the Polish community was here. Neighborhoods change."[6] Perhaps so, but not without resentment, resistance, and the myriad problems that displacement brings in its path.

Economic inequality is an issue shared in common by African Americans, Latinos, and new immigrants. Since the turn of the twenty-first century, the number of people living in poverty has been steadily rising in the United States, from a low of 11.4 percent in 2000 to 12.5 percent in 2003. The poverty figures were much higher for children; by 2003, 17.6 percent of the population under the age of 18 was living in poverty households. The numbers of the medically uninsured also rose during this period to 15.6 percent of the population.[7] Tax cuts enacted in 2001 and 2002 increased tax burdens for middle-income taxpayers while reducing them for upper-income households.[8] These tax policies were just the latest round in a series of policies that have been sharply redistributing incomes and wealth upward in the United States since the 1980s, a trend reinforced by the effects of the Great Recession of 2008–2009.

Poverty and inequality have always been closely associated with social disorder, expressed in the form of crime, riots, family disorganization, and community breakdown. High levels of family and community pathology still exist in poverty communities, but this does not matter much to the members of the middle class as long as it does not touch them directly. The expressions of social disorder that matter to them or that carry great symbolic weight—crime and urban rioting—have abated in the last decade. But this social peace may be fragile. In a survey conducted on the tenth anniversary of the Los Angeles riots of 1992, 50 percent of Los Angeles residents expressed the belief that riots were likely to break out in the next five years. This appraisal turned out to be overly pessimistic, but the relative quiet does not mean it will last forever.[9]

The disorganized response to the devastation visited upon New Orleans by Hurricane Katrina in September 2005 cast a national spotlight on the racial inequalities still present in America's cities. Because they lived in the least desirable areas of the city—the lowest elevation—blacks were disproportionately affected by the flooding. The political vulnerability of African American residents was also revealed. When disaster struck, the Bush administration's response was built on the assumption that everyone in New Orleans had ample personal resources. It "assumed that people would evacuate New Orleans on their own, without giving much thought to who these people were, what resources they had, or where they would go. They acted as if everyone had an SUV full of gas and family or friends (or a second home) waiting to take them in somewhere else."[10] For some people, this gaffe might be interpreted as a metaphor for the great divide that continues to haunt American society, and for the failure of government to effectively respond to it.

The Politics of the Patchwork Metropolis

The falling crime rates of the 1990s were directly related to the revival of street life and nightlife in central cities. In most American cities, people representing all income, ethnic, and racial groups mingle freely on streets and in tourist and entertainment venues. But at the same time, the new downtowns and gentrified neighborhoods are as segregated as the suburbs, though on a smaller scale. Many affluent urban residents commute from subdivisions, gated communities, townhouse developments, or condominium complexes (or at the other end of the social scale, from ghettos and rundown neighborhoods) to high-rise downtown office buildings or suburban office parks, and they drive to enclosed malls or mall complexes for shopping and commute to tourist bubbles to enjoy themselves.[11] This lifestyle creates a situation in which some urban residents experience the urban environment as little more than a series of enclosures, each connected by a transportation corridor that is itself cut off from the rest of the city.

Evidence indicates that the construction of enclaves and some degree of residential integration are happening at the same time. In the 1990s, Asians and Latinos settled in the suburbs in large numbers, but large proportions of both groups now live in ethnic enclaves that are more separated from whites than before.[12] Residential segregation levels for Latinos and Asians increased slightly in the 1990s,[13] but these groups were less segregated in the suburbs than in the central cities.[14] Some suburbs are highly segregated, whereas others provide housing opportunities for minorities and immigrants, especially if they earn middle-class incomes. Clearly, contradictory messages can be read in these trends.

It is difficult to predict the spatial future of the suburbs from present patterns. There can be no doubt that suburbs have opened to minorities and to the poor. The immigration of Asians, Latinos, and other groups has made most metropolitan areas, including their suburbs, multiethnic rather than biracial. During the 1990s, for example, two parallel streams moved to Orange County, California, just outside Los Angeles: highly educated professionals and foreign-born immigrants. The two streams could hardly have been more different; high-income families making more than $150,000 per year jumped by 184 percent in the county, but at the same time the number of foreign-born immigrants increased by 48 percent.[15] Commenting on these trends, a noted demographer said the county could go into two directions, either a "mostly gated-community-type mentality" or "immigrants start integrating into middle-class areas, so you have a blended suburbia."[16]

To some degree, residential patterns may be a consequence of how recently minorities and immigrants have moved into the suburbs. Over time, they may become incorporated into the politics of suburbs in the same way they long ago became part of the political process in central cities. Suburbs are highly variable. The adjoining suburbs of Oak Park and Cicero, both on the border of Chicago, have changed quickly in the last few years. Oak Park is a middle-class to upper-income suburb that also has a stock of affordable housing. Cicero is much different: Long a white working-class bastion known for rough-and-tumble, often corrupt politics, in only a decade it has become a majority-Latino city. Suburbs of all types are similarly changing in metropolitan areas across the United States. As these examples illustrate, cities and urban regions are more open than they were in the troubled period of urban riots, intense racial animosity, and rising crime; at the same time, the privatization and enclosure of urban space pulls in the opposite direction. These opposing tendencies will define the contours of American urban politics for many years to come.

Endnotes

1. Sharon Zukin, *Landscapes of Power: From Detroit to Disney World* (Berkeley: University of California Press, 1991), p. 221.
2. "Louisiana Forks over $12.4M to Saints," *USA Today* (July 6, 2005), p. 15C.
3. According to historical accounts, General Potemkin constructed fake villages in preparation for a tour by Catherine II of the Crimea in 1787. The purpose was to fool her into thinking his conquests were of great value to the Russian empire.

4. Neal R. Peirce, "Business Basic: Rx for All Cities," *Washington Post* (March 5, 1999).

5. Reuel R. Rogers, "Minority Groups and Coalitional Politics," *Urban Affairs Review* 39, no. 3 (January 2004): 283–317.

6. Antonio Olivo, "Edge about 'Yuppies'," *Chicago Tribune* (June 12, 2006), pp. 1, 20.

7. CNN.com, "Census: More Americans Living in Poverty" (August 31, 2004), www.cnn.com.

8. Ibid.

9. Mara A. Marks, Matt A. Barreto, and Nathan D. Woods, "Race and Racial Attitudes a Decade after the 1992 Los Angeles Riots," *Urban Affairs Review* 40, no. 1 (2004): 3–18.

10. Peter Dreier, "Katrina and Power in America," *Urban Affairs Review* 41, no. 4 (March 2006), p. 535.

11. Dennis R. Judd, "Enclosure, Community, and Public Life," in *Research in Community Sociology: New Communities in a Changing World,* ed. Dan A. Chekki (Greenwich, CT and London: JAI Press, 1996), pp. 217–238.

12. John R. Logan, "The New Ethnic Enclaves in America's Suburbs," a report by the Lewis Mumford Center for Comparative Urban and Regional Research (Albany, NY, 2002), pp. 1–2.

13. Ibid., p. 253.

14. William A. V. Clark and Sarah A. Blue, "Race, Class, and Segregation Patterns in U.S. Immigrant Gateway Cities," *Urban Affairs Review* 39, no. 6 (2004): 667–688.

15. Jim Hinch and Ronald Campbell, "Gated Enclaves One Future for Orange County," *Orange County Register* (May 15, 2002), www.ocregister.com.

16. Ibid., quoting William Frey, a demographer in the Milken Institute of Los Angeles.

INDEX

Lightning Source UK Ltd.
Milton Keynes UK
UKOW06f0558171215

264901UK00011B/60/P